D1312412

THE CANONGATE BURNS

Robert Burns (1759–96) entered the world on 25 January as the first of William Burnes and Agnes Brown's seven children (four boys and three girls). Originally from Kincardineshire, Burnes worked as a gardener in Ayrshire where he also leased land as a tenant farmer and built a two-roomed cottage at Alloway. Burnes was not a successful farmer and had to struggle with harsh land and demanding factors first at Mount Oliphant and then at Lochlie farm at Tarbolton. Nevertheless, he aimed to give Robert and his brother Gilbert a decent education, sending them to village schools and making arrangements for Robert to spend some of the summer months studying French and Mathematics with his former teacher as tutor. By the age of fifteen Burns was widely read in English literature and considered something of a 'prodigy' in French, but it seems likely that hard labour on the farm weakened his heart and eventually contributed to an early death.

Forming a bachelors' club and debating society at Tarbolton, young Robert became a Freemason, worked as a flax dresser in Irvine and enjoyed an active social and sexual life. He began to write poems, inspired to use Scots by the work of Robert Fergusson. His father's illness, his debts, and a court case over his rent arrears brought the poet back to Lochlie and when William Burnes died in 1784, Robert and Gilbert took up a farm at nearby Mossgiel and found themselves supporting the family. By this time Burns was involved with Betty Paton, by whom he had a daughter, and Jean Armour was also pregnant. (She was to bear him two pairs of twins before he eventually married her in 1788.) During these years (1784–6) Burns wrote some his most famous poems, including many epistles to various friends, his attacks on religious hypocrisy in 'Holy Willie's Prayer', his celebration of Rabelaisian energy in 'The Holy Fair' and 'The Jolly Beggars' and his subtle but scathing satire on social injustice 'The Twa Dogs'. Creative or not, these were difficult and exhausting years and, faced with local scandal, nervous strain, unrewarding hard labour and rising debt, Burns considered emigrating to Jamaica. The success of his first collection, *Poems, Chiefly in the Scottish Dialect* (1786) did much to change his mind. This first 'Kilmarnock edition' sold out, it was praised by Henry Mackenzie, the most influential author and critic in Edinburgh, and a revised 'Edinburgh Edition' followed in 1787 to even greater acclaim, with an American edition published the following year.

Burns spent the winters of 1786–7 and 1787–8 in Edinburgh, lionised by society and the literary establishment, if largely misunderstood and sentimentalised by them as a 'heaven-taught ploughman'. The winter of 1788 saw the start of a sentimental correspondence with Mrs Agnes McLehose in Edinburgh, remembered as 'Clarinda' in his letters from 'Sylvander'. Despite his literary success, Burns found it difficult to get any money from his Edinburgh publisher, William Creech, and was still in need of a patron or a job. Having spent the summer months of these years touring the Borders and the Highlands, he took an interest in old Scots songs and this led to his writing, collecting and re-writing songs for Johnson's *Scots Musical Museum* (1787–1803) and *Thomson's Select Scotish Airs* (1793–1818), a major task to which he devoted himself for the rest of his life. The poet took up farming again at Ellisland in the summer of 1788, and set about training to be an Excise Officer. In the early 1790s, like Wordsworth, Coleridge and Mary Wollstonecraft, Burns supported the libertarian ideals of the French revolution. Such opinions were dangerous, however, when government informers were on the look-out for sedition and his verses to the radical press were often published either anonymously or under various pseudonyms. The farm at Ellisland was not a success, and in 1791 Burns moved to Dumfries where he took up the post of Excise Officer. These last years were times of considerable political and social unrest throughout Britain and in 1795 severe shortages and food riots broke out in Dumfries. Burns's health was as uncertain as his finances. The poet's weak heart was exacerbated by the medicines of the day and, fevered and fearing for the future of his family, he died at home on 21 July at the age of 37.

ANDREW NOBLE is Senior Lecturer in the Department of English Studies at the University of Strathclyde. His books include *The Art of Robert Burns* edited and introduced with R.D.S. Jack (1982) and the uncollected Scottish criticism of Edwin Muir (1982). He has also edited and introduced critical studies of Robert Louis Stevenson (1983), as well as Stevenson's account of his emigrant journey, *From the Clyde to California* (1985). An authority on Scottish cinema, he has written particuarly on Bill Douglas, *A Lanternist's Account*, 1922.

PATRICK SCOTT HOGG is a native of rural Galloway and comes from a fishing family. After graduating in History (Stirling University) he took a postgraduate Diploma in Information Systems (University of Portsmouth). He returned to Scotland after a successful career in London publishing and lectured at Dumfries and Galloway College of Technology for three years. He is the author of *Robert Burns: The Lost Poems* (1997); has published essays in *The Edinburgh Review*, *The Herald* newspaper, *The Burns Chronicle* and most recently, in the American volume, *Critical Essays on Robert Burns*, edited by Prof Carol McGuirk (1998).

The Canongate Burns

Introduced by Andrew Noble

★

Edited by Andrew Noble
and Patrick Scott Hogg

★

CANONGATE
CLASSICS
104

This edition first published as a Canongate Classic in
2001 by Canongate Books Limited, 14 High Street,
Edinburgh EH1 1TE.

10 9 8 7 6 5 4 3 2 1

The editors wish to acknowledge research grants from
The Carnegie and Leverhulme Trusts which helped
make this book possible. Andrw Noble would also like
to thank the Institute for Advanced Studies in The
Humanities, University of Edinburgh for a Visiting Re-
search Fellowship in 1990.

The publishers gratefully acknowledge general subsidy
from the Scottish Arts Council towards the Canongate
Classics series and a specific grant towards the publica-
tion of this volume.

Typeset in Monotype Plantin by Hewer Text Ltd, Edin-
burgh. Printed and bound by WS Bookwell, Finland

British Library Cataloguing-in-Publication Data
A catalogue record for this volume
is available on request from the
British Library.

ISBN 0 86241 994 8

www.canongate.net

Contents

Acknowledgements

Patrick Scott Hogg would like to thank Dumfries and Galloway Council's Burns Bicentenary Committee, especially Shirley Bell and John Dowson, for its grant in 1995 to initiate the archival research programme. Two subsequent grants from The Carnegie Trust were also of invaluable assistance. Scott Hogg would like to repeat his gratitude expressed in *Robert Burns: The Lost Poems* (1997) to everybody who helped him. Particular thanks are due to Bobby Dalziel, John Manson and Peter Westwood and many other members of The Burns Federation. Outwith the Federation, Albert Calder and Norry Paton were sources of encouragement.

Andrew Noble would like to thank The Leverhulme Trust for a major grant, which allowed him to employ his co-editor in 1998–9 as a Research Assistant at Strathclyde University. He would also like to record his gratitude to The Institute for Advanced Studies at Edinburgh University, whose award of a Visiting Research Fellowship in 2000 gave him invaluable time and space to complete this project.

We would also record our thanks to librarians all over Britain; the most harassed were Donald Nelson and Harzara Singh of Glasgow's Mitchell Library's world-famous Burns Collection. For keying in various parts of the manuscript we received sterling help from Jordana Brown, John MacLeish, Martin Ogg and David Exley.

From the academic community Carol McGuirk, Tom Crawford, and David Daiches were consistently supportive in their sympathetic and objective scholarship. Thanks are also due to Rory Watson for his assistance and, with Cairns Craig, his editorial acceptance of the project. Of signal help was Liam McIlvanney's scholarship. His forthcoming book from Tuckwell (*The Radical Burns: Poetry and Politics in the Late Eighteenth Century*) complements and compliments this edition.

Last, but by no means least, Andrew Noble would like to thank his wife Jennifer, and Patrick Scott Hogg and his partner Helen for the patience shown in the face of this mammoth task. The last words, as always, should be the Bard's:

> Ah, gentle dames! it gars me greet,
> To think how many counsels sweet,
> How mony lengthen'd sage advices,
> The husband frae the wife despises!

'To select and arrange what ought to be published of Burns's will be no easy task, when you consider the variety of taste and opinions which obtain among men and the necessity there is for the strictest delicacy being ever kept in view. His poetry and letters were so often blended with Religion, Politics, Love, and Bawdry that the greatest care must be taken to render his thoughts and opinions consistent.'

Alexander Cunningham: The Syme-Cunningham Correspondence, *The Burns Chronicle*, 1938, XIII, p. 43.

'. . . the editing of his works was, for a full century after his death, in the hands of men temperamentally unfitted to sympathise with certain phases of his character, and incapable of frank and objective presentation of facts of which they disapproved.'

Professor J. De Lancey Ferguson, *The Letters of Robert Burns*, p. xxxix, Oxford, Clarendon Press, 1931.

Introduction

'The very ink with which all history is written is merely
fluid prejudice.'
Mark Twain, *Pudd'nhead Wilson's New Calendar*.

'I think this enlightened age, as it is called, is as much
given to persecution as the most barbarous. The trans-
portation of the Deputies and Directors is not perhaps
quite so bad as that of Muir, Palmer, etc., . . . Men
persecute because they love persecution and so far as I
am from believing fear to be the true cause of persecution
that I begin to think that fear is the only motive that ever
can persuade men to suffer those who differ in opinion
from them to breathe the same atmosphere with them.
This is not pleasant philosophy but I am afraid it is true.'
Charles James Fox to Charles Grey, 1801.

For the first time in over two centuries we have in this single volume
all Burns's *surviving* poems glossed and annotated. To do such
editorial work has been for us a salutary and revealing task. What
has fundamentally impressed us has been the tenacity of Burns's
creative drive which, despite all obstacles, sustained a flow of over
six hundred poems and songs over a period of twenty-two years.
Such productivity also entailed that he constantly metamorphosed
his day to day experiences into poetry. Thus, as we annotated the
poems, making as much use of that other source of parallel com-
mentary, his quite extraordinary and, arguably, still under valued
letters, not only his biographical shape but an encompassing picture
of the peculiarly fraught late eighteenth century emerged. As
admirable, and even more surprising, is the sustained quality of
his poetic achievement. If we compare him to Wordsworth or, even
more pertinently, Coleridge, briefly his creative contemporaries and
consistent admirers of his genius, Burns achieves a higher ratio of
poetry of the first order than either of them.

All this was achieved in opposition to a series of diverse and
formidable obstacles. With some few significant exceptions, Burns's

biographers and editors have been, as we shall see, either anodyne or, worse, in some early instances, deliberately mendacious about the harsh physical, social and political environment in which he had to survive as a creative writer. Consequently this edition lays stress on his capacity not only to endure but poetically to overcome the multiple constraints he experienced. Textually and contextually, this edition, therefore, lays unique emphasis, partly by bringing some recently retrieved archival material to bear, on Burns's necessarily ironic and often oblique political life and poems. Consequent on such a new explication of Burns's political values and poetry, will be an exploration into the calculated and deeply successful manner in which, from the moment of his death, his achievement as a radically dissenting democratic poet was denied and suppressed. Indeed, what is revealed is the degree to which a whole segment of late-enlightenment liberal, Scottish culture of which Burns was an integral part was, as far as possible, obliterated from the national memory by reactionary forces which were quick to build on their total victory in the 1790s. Burns's corpse, as we shall see, was not the only thing consigned to the grave in 1796. It is, indeed, a signal example of the fact that the victors *do* write history.

EARLY LIFE AND LABOUR
The primary and conditioning factor of Burns's life was his experience of the often harshly brutal and almost always near impoverished nature of late-eighteenth century farm labour. We should first contemplate the physical conditions under which he had to write as a prelude to understanding the psychological and political consequences for his poetry. This has been obscured from us by the mass of sentimental, mainly nineteenth-century writing on Burns which sees him as the spokesman for a pietistic, hence politically quiescent, peasant culture.

In his quite wonderful opening stanzas to *The Vision* Burns describes himself 'half-mad, half-fed, half-sarket', portraying the fierce restrictions of work, domestic squalor and poverty in which he mainly lived. Or as he wrote from Mauchline in 1788 to Robert Cleghorn:

I am so harassed [sic] with Care and Anxiety about this farming project of mine, that my Muse has degenerated into the veriest prose-wrench that ever picked cinders or followed a Tinker. — When I am fairly got into the routine of business, I shall trouble you with a longer epistle; perhaps with some queries respecting farming: at present the world sits such a load on my mind that it has effaced almost every trace of the image of God in me.

Routine, initiated by the harsh demands of the marginal farm, so prematurely imposed on his childhood, Burns loathed.[1] He described his early life as having 'the cheerless gloom of a hermit with the unceasing moil of a galley slave'. Or, as in this letter to Mrs Dunlop of 1788 where, so characteristic of his letters, wit and despair blend:

> . . . the heart of the man, and the fancy of the poet, are the two grand considerations for which I live: if miry ridges and dirty dunghills are to engross the best part of the functions of my soul immortal, I had better been a rook or a magpie all at once & then I would not have been plagued with any ideas superior to breaking of clods & picking up grubs: not to mention Barn-door Cocks or Mallards, creatures with which I could almost exchange lives at any time.

Some sort of acute nervous disorder was the result of his attempt to become disciplined to the mechanistic demands of becoming a flax worker in Irvine, 1784. After moving to Ellisland farm near Dumfries most of his new found wealth from the Edinburgh edition went to save the family farm at Mossgiel. The dwelling at Ellisland is described by the young lawyer, Robert Ainslie, as 'ill contrived – and pretty Dirty'. Mrs Jean Burns is 'Vulgar & Common-place in a high degree – and pretty round & fat . . . a kind Body in her own way, and the husband Tolerably Attentive to her.' The poet's local associates are 'a Vulgar looking Tavern keeper from Dumfries; and his wife, more Vulgar — Mr Millar of Dalswinton's Gardiner and his Wife — and said Wife's sister — and a little fellow from Dumfries, [probably John Drummond] who had been a Clerk.'[2] Hence, the poverty and hardship of his early years, described so eloquently and bluntly to Dr John Moore, 'the clouterly appearance of my ploughboy carcase, the two extremes of which were often exposed to all the inclements of all the seasons', was still with Burns after his temporary fame and even more temporary riches beyond his Edinburgh edition of 1787.

Nor, leaving aside the problem of his vowed fidelity to a Pittite regime he loathed, were his Excise duties any escape from devouring physical drudgery: 'I am jaded to death with fatigue. For these two months or three months, on an average, I have not ridden less than two hundred miles per week.' The paper work of the Excise also ate into not only his time but his spirit:[3]

> Sunday closes the period of our cursed revenue business, & may probably keep me employed with my pen until noon. —Fine

employment for a poet's pen! There is a species of the Human genius that I call, the Ginhorse Class: what enviable dogs they are! —round, & round, & round they go— Mundell's ox that drives his cotton mill, their exact prototype— without an idea or wish beyond their circle; fat sleek, stupid, patient, quiet & contented:— while here I sit, altogether Novemberish, a damned melange of Fretfulness & melancholy; not enough of the one to rouse me to passion; nor of the other to repose me in torpor; my soul flouncing & fluttering round her tenement, like a wild Finch caught amid the horrors of winter & newly thrust into a cage.

Burns's case as medical study, symptomatically discernible in the letters and, indeed, in much of the poetry, is a grim one. If he was atypical in the extreme mood swings that seem integral to his creativity (it was specifically with Burns in mind that Wordsworth wrote in *Resolution and Independence*: 'We poets in our youth begin in gladness:/ But thereof come in the end despondency and madness.'), he was wholly typical of the age, its life expectancy and its exposure to poverty related illness.

His life, as read in his letters, is a catalogue of fractures and worsening fevers: in temporary lodgings while the farmhouse at Ellisland by Dumfries was under construction, he complained

. . . but for some nights preceding I had slept in an apartment where the force of the wind and the rains was only mitigated by being sifted thro' numberless apertures in the windows, walls, &c. In consequence I was on Sunday, Monday, & part of Tuesday unable to stir out of bed with all the miserable effects of a violent cold.

Since medicine had so little ability to intervene, 'suffering', as Roy Porter has pertinently remarked, 'was *everyone's* lot sooner or later, low or high born'. Yet it was worse for the poor. As so often in Burns's poetry, *Death and Dr Hornbook* is a comic caricature with a savage edge to it: cholera in the clachan is not an oxymoron and crude, often lethal abortion is part of the women's lot. Further, as Porter has again remarked, the physical discrepancy between the rich and poor had deep political implications:

The wealthier were healthier and lived longer; sexually they probably matured earlier; being taller, they literally looked down on the poor. Their lives were lived by a different clock

—for example, the poor rose, ate and slept early (lighting was costly), the rich late. The show of superiority and deference was emphasised by the encrusted rituals of bowing and scraping, head-baring, standing, curtseying, and knuckling foreheads.[4]

In Burns's poetry, then, the repressed resentment of the common people towards their propertied masters becomes articulate. His letters are also obsessively, often more overtly, preoccupied with the multiple slights he feels inflicted on his assertively independent spirit as a consequence of the social gulf between rich and poor.

This is made deeply ambivalent by the fact that as a poet it was the people of property who formed his audience and to whom he not infrequently looked for creative support. His letters, consequently, are saturated with a sort of baffled rage. This over-wrought letter to Robert Graham, Commissioner of the Scottish Board of Excise, to whom Burns's looked in vain to be a replacement patron for the deceased Earl of Glencairn, is typical of the agonies he endured concerning the imposed, impoverished inferiority of his rank:

As I had an eye to getting on in the examiners list, if attainable by me, I was going to ask you if it would be of any service to try the service of some Great, and some *very* Great folks to whom I have the honour to be known; I mean in the way of a Treasury Warrant. —But much as early impressions have [impression (*deleted*)] given me the honour of Spectres, &c. still, I would [rather (*deleted*)] face the Arch-fiend, in Miltonic pomp, at the head of all his legions; and hear that infernal shout which blind John says: 'Tore hell's concave;' rather than crawl in, a dust-licking petitioner, before the presence of a Mighty Man, & bear [the(*deleted*)], amid all the mortifying pangs of Self-annihilation, the swelling consequence of his d-mn'd State, & the cold monosyllables of his hollow heart!

Worse, if he was to be the spokesman for the common people he had, certainly after his Ayrshire days, diminished faith that they had any sympathetic understandings of what he was writing. As he wrote in *Epistle to Hugh Parker*:

In this strange land, this uncouth clime,
A land unknown to prose or rhyme:
Where words ne'er cros't the Muse's heckles,
Nor limpit in poetic shackles:
A land that Prose did never view it,

Except when drunk he stacher't thro' it:
Here, ambushed by the chimla cheek,
Hid in an atmosphere of reek,
I hear a wheel thrum i' the neuk,
I hear it— for in vain I leuk:
The red peat gleams, a fiery kernel
Enhusked by a fog infernal.
Here, for my wonted rhyming raptures,
I sit and count my sins by chapters;
For life and spunk like other Christians,
I'm dwindled down to mere existence:
Wi' nae converse but Gallowa' bodies,
Wi' nae kind face but Jenny Geddes.

Such absence of stimulation and response increasingly led to severe
depression. Little wonder that Coleridge was so sensitive to this
dark side of Burns. This Burns letter of 1789 to David Blair could be
confused with the prose of the English poet:

Know you of anything worse than Gallery Bondage, a slavery
where the soul with all her powers is laden with weary fetters of
ever increasing weight: a Slavery which involves the mind in
dreary darkness and almost total eclipse of every ray of God's
image: and all this the work, the baneful doings of the arch-
fiend known among worlds by the name of Indolence.

His initial childhood experience had led him to hope for better; like
his English Romantic peers, Burns, anti-Calvinistically, profoundly
believed that the child entered the world as uncorrupted spirit. His
own childhood anticipations of an unrestricted, public social life
were, however, soon to be disabused. The Romantic poets, of
course, long pre-date Freud in grounding the nature of the adult
self on childhood experience. Burns's self-analysis, while hardly
Wordsworthian in its outcome, is extraordinarily keen in its aware-
ness of the forces that shaped him as man and poet:

My vicinity to Ayr was of great advantage to me.—My social
disposition, when not checked by some modification of spited
pride, like our catechism definition of Infinitude, was 'without
bounds or limits'. —I formed many connections with other
Youngkers who possessed superiour advantages; the youngling
actors who were busy with the rehearsal of PARTS in which
they were shortly to appear on that STAGE where, Alas! I was

destined to drudge behind the SCENES. — It is not commonly at these green years that the young Noblesse and Gentry have a just sense of the immense distance between them and their ragged Playfellows. —It takes a few dashes into the world to give the young Great man that proper, decent, unnoticing disregard for the poor, insignificant, stupid devils, the mechanics and the peasantry around him; who were perhaps born in the same village. —My young superiours never insulted the clouterly appearance of my ploughboy carcase, the two extremes of which were often exposed to all the inclemencies of all the seasons.— They would give me stray volumes of books; among them, even then, I could pick up some observations; and ONE, whose heart I am sure not even the MUNNY BEGUM'S scenes have tainted, helped me to a little French. — Parting with these, my young friend and benefactors, as they dropped off for the east or the West Indies, was often to me a sore affliction; but I was soon called to more serious evils.— My father's generous master died; the farm proved a ruinous bargain; and, to clench the curse, we fell into the hands of a Factor who sat for the picture I have drawn of one in my tale of two dogs.—My father was advanced in life when he married; I was the eldest of seven children; and he, worn out by early hardship, was unfit for labour.—My father's spirit was soon irritated, but not easily broken.— There was a freedom in his lease in two years more, and to weather these two years we retrenched expenses.— We lived very poorly; I was a dextrous ploughman for my years; and the next eldest to me was a brother, who could drive the plough very well and help me to thrash.— A Novel-Writer might perhaps have viewed these scenes with some satisfaction, but so did not I: my indignation yet boils at the recollection of the scoundrel tyrants insolent, threatening epistles, which used to set us all in tears.

This notion of it being an essential part of democracy that one be, so to speak, 'on stage', that all men have a right to be visible in the public domain of history, a visibility the schoolboy Burns believed he had, is a concept to which we will return. If there was no economic base for this, such freedom was impossible. Burns's experience was one of the intensification of power of the land-holding class fired by the energies and methods of agrarian capitalism which were making life for many economically worse. That, in fact, the Enlightenment pressures towards democratic reform expressed through the new Freemasonry and, for him, present in the

American Revolution were being undermined by a re-energised, even more avaricious propertied class. The childhood threat of being thrown off their farm stayed with Burns. Always, for diverse reasons, a keen Bible reader no book was more pertinent to him than that of the Book of Job where he clearly discerned both his father's ill-fate and his own in that nothing they turned their hands to would prosper. His father's death saved him from debtor's prison. The trauma stayed with the son:

> I am curst with a melancholy prescience, which makes me the veriest coward, in life. There is not any exertion which I would not attempt, rather than be in a horrid situation —to be ready to call on the mountains to fall on me, & the hills to cover me from the presence of a haughty Landlord, or his still more haughty underling, to whom I owed —what I could not pay.

The creative compensation was that this fear and rage drove some of his best poetry whether, as in the cunning irony of *The Twa Dogs* or the biting, black anger of his demonic monologue about the initial stages of the Highland Clearances, *The Address of Beelzebub*. Though Burns himself was never ejected, the fear of dispossession either through debt or due to his radical beliefs, haunted him to the end. As he wrote in that marvellously reworked late song of ancestral suffering, the primal agony of not being able to feed one's children, *O That I Had Ne'er Been Married*:

> Waefu' Want and Hunger fley me
>   Glowerin by the hallan en'
> Sair I fecht them at th' door
>   But ay I'm eerie they come ben.

And come ben they did. The physical agony of his death bed, as terrible as that of his great admirer Keats, was horrendously intensified by his sense that all he would leave his wife and children were the terrible consequences of his debts. Further, that the spectre of famine, as a consequence of the war with France, was loose in the Dumfries streets:

> Many days my family, & hundreds of other families, are absolutely without one grain of meal; as money cannot purchase it. —How long the *Swinish Multitude* will be quiet, I cannot tell: they threaten daily.

That Burns should so allude to Burke's remark of the pig-sty quality of the cultural life of the French common people, a remark unforgivably burnt into the consciousness of all the British radicals of that age, implies he did not die purged of his revolutionary aspirations.

Indeed, none of his contemporaries thought he had. Ironically, it was that singular English Romantic Tory, Thomas De Quincey, who most penetratingly and passionately revealed the social vision at the heart of so much of Burns's poetry. De Quincey had no doubt that Burns was a compendium of the radical vices of the Jacobin type, the quintessence of the revolutionary personality.[5] He feared and disliked, given his disposition to traditional order, Burns's 'peculiarly wild and almost ferocious spirit of independence'. As much as his friend Charles Lamb adored the poetry, De Quincey loathed the letters which he found self-declamatory, irascible, resentful, provocative manifestations of personal and public unrest. Yet of all the English Romantics, it was De Quincey, who had himself for a time lived among the dispossessed and, indeed, had come to Scotland to take ecclesiastical refuge from his creditors, who best defined, probably because of the very contradiction between his personal experience and his political ideology, Burns's social vision:

Jacobinism —although the seminal principle of all political evil in all ages alike of advanced civilisation— is natural to the heart of man, and, in a qualified sense, may be meritorious. A good man, a high minded man, in certain circumstances, *must* be a Jacobin in a certain sense. The aspect under which Burns's Jacobinism appears is striking; there is a thought which an observing reader will find often recurring, which expresses its particular bitterness. It is this: the necessity which in old countries exists for the labourer humbly to beg *permission* that he may labour. To eat in the sweat of a man's brow, —that is bad; and that is a curse, and pronounced such by God. But when *that* is all, the labourer is by comparison happy. The second curse makes that a jest: he must sue, he must sneak, he must fawn like an oriental slave, in order to win his fellow man, in Burns's indignant words 'to give him leave to toil'. That was the scorpion thought that was forever shooting its sting into Burns's meditations, whether forward looking or backward looking; and, that considered, there arises a world of allowance for that vulgar bluster of independence which Lord Jeffrey, with so much apparent reason, charges upon his prose writings.[6]

If De Quincey finds Burns's political position paradoxical, his own is no less so. Burns's compassion, according to De Quincey, touches the nerve of the greatest evil, not work but its denial from which stems starvation and dispossession. De Quincey supports an established order which not only turns its face from such suffering but also economically promotes it. Little wonder that *King Lear* haunted the writers of the 1790s for when the hierarchical King is made destitute, he finds a form of being hitherto unimaginable to him. Thus Burns, in that early bi-lingual cry of rage against social oppression and exploitation, *A Winter's Night*, invokes Shakespeare's earlier cry of outrage:

> Poor naked wretches, whereso'er you are,
> That bide the pelting and the pityless storm!
> How shall your houseless heads, and unfed sides,
> Your looped and window'd raggedness, defend you
> From seasons such as these.

As we have seen, Burns as a farmer led a near subsistence existence which his subsequent Excise work did not financially transform. Nor did the business of poetry ease his fear of debt and the abyss into which he might fall. Only the Edinburgh edition sold in great numbers. Even here, he significantly under-earned due to the contractual conditions then prevailing between book publisher and author, which was added by William Creech's, at best, dilatory behaviour. Even then, the bulk of his earnings from the Edinburgh edition went to save the family farm at Mauchline, propping up Gilbert Burns with money he never returned. Subsequent editions made money for Creech who purchased the copyright of the Edinburgh poems and laid claim to everything Burns wrote thereafter with a merciless callousness, which saw the poet receive only a few presentation copies of the 1793 edition. The later songs he wrote for the nation and not the cash. The covert political poetry was sent to newspapers to support the radical cause and not for personal gain. He was, in any case, characteristically both reckless and generous with money.

Burns's constant stress on his own personal, political and enforced fiscal independence found everywhere in his writings, partly stems from his constant sense of rejection by his social superiors. Hence, for example, his witty, wry, characteristic account of having to make it on his own:

> 'Twas noble, Sir; 'twas like yoursel,
>   To grant your high protection;

A great man's smile ye ken fu'well
  Is ay a blest infection.—

Tho' by his banes wha in a tub
  Match'd Macedonian Sandy!
On my ain legs thro' dirt and dub,
  I independent stand ay.—

And when those legs to gude, warm kail
  Wi' welcome canna bear me;
A lee dyke-syde, a sybow tail,
  And barley-scone shall chear me.—

This brilliant comic reduction of the world of Diogenes and Alexander the Great to his own terminal fate in the Scottish countryside ironises the desperation of his own financial situation. Great men smiled seldom; one can also smile and be a villain and, thus, spread infection. When he did occasionally think that he had encountered a relationship not polluted by social condescension, as with Lord Daer or Dugald Stewart, such men shone for him in an idealised glow. He craves that such a figure should enter his life so that, ironically, the democratic poet should return to a traditional, even feudal, situation where the patron provides both imaginative and financial succour. Hence, this account of the Earl of Glencairn, whose premature death struck him to the very core of his being:

The noble Earl of Glencairn took me by the hand today, and interested himself in my concerns, with a goodness like the benevolent BEING whose image he so richly bears.—'Oubliez moi, grand Dieu, si jamais je l'oublie!' He is a stronger proof of the immortality of the Soul than any that Philosophy has ever produced.— A mind like his can never die.— Let the Squire Hugh Logan, or Mass James Mckindlay, go into their primitive nothing.— At best they are but ill-digested lumps of Chaos, only one of them strongly tinged with bituminous particles, and sulphureous effluvia.— But my noble Patron, eternal as the heroic swell of Magnanimity and the generous throb of Benevolence shall look on with princely eye —

'Unhurt amid the war of elements,
The wrecks of matter, and the crush of Worlds.'

Glencairn being so defined in terms of that key Real Whig text, Addison's *Cato* is, as we shall see, politically important. For De

Quincey, however, even the notion that Glencairn was the true patron who tested the rule of Scottish aristocratic indifference to Burns was nonsense. He saw nothing in Glencairn's activities beyond the gestural:

> Lord Glencairn is the 'patron' to whom Burns appears to have felt the most sincere respect. Yet even he —did he give him more than a seat at his dinner table? Lord Buchan again, whose liberalities are by this time pretty well appreciated in Scotland, exhorts Burns, in a tone of one preaching upon a primary duty of life, to exemplary gratitude towards a person who has given him absolutely nothing at all. The man has not yet lived to whose happiness it was more essential that he should live unencumbered by the sense of obligation; and on the other hand, the man has not lived upon whose independence as professing benefactors so many people practised, or who found so many others ready to give value to their pretences.[7]

Though Burns often reached similar depths of despairing self-prognosis about his life and career, he did make extensive and misguided attempts to replace Glencairn in his life with Robert Graham of Fintry, a Commissioner of the Scottish Board of Excise. How misguided these attempts were we have recently discovered; Graham was not only looking with increased scepticism on reports of Burns's Dumfries activities but was himself on the payroll of that vast network of paid informers reporting back to Robert Dundas about the activities of radical dissidents. The only thing Fintry is to be thanked for was that he inspired two major English language poems, *To Robt. Graham of Fintry, Esq., with a request for an Excise Division* and *To Robert Graham of Fintry, Esq.* which are masterful, creative reworking of themes initially found in Swift's perhaps greatest poem, *On Poetry: A Rhapsody*. The latter Burns poem was of such quality, in fact, that only now has it become known that for years, a fragment of it, slightly bowdlerised, has been attributed to Coleridge. As well as learning from Swift, Burns's thinking on poetry and patronage was influenced by Dr Johnson. As he wrote:

> It is often a reverie of mine, when I am disposed to be melancholy, the characters & fates of the Rhyming tribe — there is not among all the Martyrologies that ever were penned, so rueful a narrative as Johnson's *Lives of the Poets*.— In the comparative view of the Wretches, the criterion is not what they are doomed to suffer, but how they are formed to bear.

Nor does Burns's analysis of the desperate life of the late-eighteenth century poet, an age replete in prematurely terminated and self-destructive careers, yield, especially in the two Fintry poems, to the quality of Johnson's psychological and sociological grasp of what was taking place. His rhetorical style may not be ours but there is actually little self-indulgence in what he sees as his own fate and that of his immediate predecessors. This is particularly so with regard to his beloved Edinburgh predecessor, Robert Fergusson, as mentioned in *To William Simson*:

> (O *Fergusson*! thy glorious parts
> Ill suited law's dry, musty arts!
> My curse upon your whunstane hearts,
>   Ye Enbrugh Gentry!
> The tythe o' what ye waste at *cartes*
>   Wad stow'd his pantry!)

He was not to know that not only was he to share Fergusson's pains in his life but, like Fergusson he was also to be pursued beyond the grave by the vilification of genteel Edinburgh and by its master spirit, Henry Mackenzie, who never forgave Fergusson's fine parody of *The Man of Feeling* in his poem, *The Sow of Feeling*. Underneath Mackenzie's simpering mask was a malice easily provoked by slights to his vanity or, in Burns's case, if he felt the reactionary power base, which propped up his doubtful talent and his monstrous ego, endangered.

THE RADICAL BURNS

It is not inevitable that out of a background of constantly threatening poverty, a profound sense of communal economic and political dissolution, bloody international warfare on land and sea, failure to make a living after being, initially, declared a poetic genius, a revolutionary spirit will emerge. Oliver Goldsmith, a poet Burns loved, came to the political conclusion that what the age needed to restrain the greedy, fractious aristocracy was an increase in the authority of the King. Burns, however, manifestly belongs to the temporarily dominant radical British literary culture which emerged with the loss of America. Hence all his actual and epistolary connections with the English radicals: Mary Wollstonecraft, Helen Maria Williams, William Roscoe, Dr Wolcot (pen name, Peter Pindar). Hence his persistent seeking to publish in not only Edinburgh and Glasgow radical newspapers but, from the very beginning of his career, in London ones. Hence the resemblance in his poetry's theme in image, if rarely in quality, to the outpouring of Scottish and English radical protest poetry accompanied by his signal influence on the dissenting Ulster radical poets. Hence the manifest parallels, albeit they were quite unaware of each other, with William Blake. De Quincey's definition of Burns as a Jacobin was anything but singular among the English radicals. John Thelwall, Wordsworth and Coleridge's political mentor, greatly admired Burns. James Perry, editor of the anti-government *Morning Chronicle* not only published his poetry but, simultaneously, sought to hire him and Coleridge to work in London for his newspaper. Indeed, this was a conversational paradise lost. Politically, of course, not only Coleridge but Wordsworth knew Burns for the revolutionary spirit which, at that early stage of their lives, they themselves were. In burying their own past, they were important influences in allowing subsequent reactionary critics to deny Burns. This denial of Burns is not the least of the offences Shelley holds against Wordsworth in his parody of him, *Peter Bell the Third*.

Further, if we look at the pattern of Burns's career, we can quite clearly discern his membership of politically active groups of an increasingly radical tendency. Freemasonry at Kilwinning led to his connections with Edinburgh's Crochallan Fencibles which, as well as being a bawdy drinking club, was an extraordinary hot-house for not only brilliantly rhetorical and theoretical, but practical radical political activity. His Dumfries years led not only to his attempt to send carronades to the French Revolutionaries but, as we now know, to his membership of the Dumfries cell of The Friends of the People. By this time he was not only under scrutiny by his masters in The Excise but by Robert Dundas's extensive security apparatus centred in Edinburgh and reporting to London. Little wonder that after the 1793–4 Sedition Trials Burns should write:

> The shrinking Bard adown an alley sculks
> And dreads a meeting worse than Woolwich hulks
> Tho' there his heresies in Church and State
> Might well award him Muir and Palmer's fate . . .

Given the poetry and the letters with this mass of corroborative contextual historical evidence from within and without Scotland, it is hard to understand why not only in current Scottish popular culture but, indeed, in significant elements of Scottish academic culture, there is still a persistent compulsion to downplay, even deny, the revolutionary Burns. One cannot imagine kindred spirits like Blake or Shelley being so treated. One tangible reason for the denial is due to the fact that we will never be able to retrieve the full volume of radical writing in the 1790s. Key newspapers, such as *The Glasgow Advertiser* 1795–7, are irretrievably lost. Governmental scrutiny was intensive against radicals and the postal system monitored to such a degree that communication was furtive and restricted. To corroborate Burns's radicalism further, he himself was wholly aware of this factor. As he wrote to Patrick Millar in March 1794:

> —Nay, if Mr Perry, whose honor, after your character of him I cannot doubt, if he will give me an Adress & channel by which anything will come safe from these spies with which he may be certain that his correspondence is beset, I will now & then send him any bagatelle that I may write.— . . . but against the days of Peace, which Heaven send soon, my little assistance may perhaps fill up an idle column of a Newspaper.— I have long had it in my head to try my hand in the way of Prose Essays, which I propose sending into the World through the medium of some Newspaper; and should these be worth his while, to these Mr Perry shall be welcome; & my reward shall be, his treating me with his paper, which, by the bye, to anybody who has the least relish for Wit, is a high treat indeed.

In the general implosion of British radical writing culture under governmental pressure, the loss of Burns's political writings was particularly severe due, as we shall see, to the panic surrounding his premature death at the darkest point of the 1790s.

While significant, however, the denial of Burns's radicalism is not essentially based on missing texts. The denial of Burns's actual politics is much more multiform and historically protracted than that. As we shall see, the after-shock of the revolutionary, even insurrectionary, activities of the 1790s was so colossal that it extended deep into the nineteenth century. It was particularly severely felt in Scotland. What we see, then, in Victorian Scotland is Burns, with oceans of whisky and mountains of haggis, being converted into an iconic national figure by a nation in almost complete denial of the political values he stood for. Editorial and critical work inevitably reflected this absurdity with activities which included sanitising, suppressing and trivialising any evidence, textual and otherwise, contrary to the travesty they were creating. Edward Dowden in his seminal *The French Revolution and English Literature*, written at the end of the nineteenth century, included Burns among writers so affected. If for English radical writers, this book marked the beginning of mature, objective scholarship regarding the reality of their engagement with the political issues of the 1790s, this was ignored by Scottish Burns scholars. Hugh Blair's remark that 'Burns's politics always smell of the smithy' held sway with almost all subsequent commentators. Indeed, in the early twentieth century W.P. Ker designated Burns as a Tory Unionist. Heroic efforts in the 1930s by that greatest of Burns scholars and critics, tellingly American, Professor De Lancey Ferguson, ended in bitter comments such as his attempt properly to locate Burns in history had been met in Scotland with 'passionate apathy'. Insofar as Burns was permitted to express political values, the critical strategy was either to claim that his political poems either did not meet their tests of aesthetic quality or that such poetry expressed confusion. These tactics persist. Dr James Mackay has recently noted that 'Burns's politics were . . . never less than moderately confused . . .'[8] Dr Mackay's opinion is hardly one to cause surprise since essentially his biography presents no advance on the nineteenth-century criticism of Burns but, in fact, is extensively based on and partly plagiarised from nineteenth-century published biographical sources.

Such assertions of confusion are grounded on ignorance of the radical tradition within which Burns was operating. A coherent tradition dating from the Civil War, British radical thought in the latter stages of the eighteenth century combined Scottish and English elements in alternating proportions. Burns is not to be understood as some sort of barely rational political oddity. With Blake, he is a central poet of a long established revolutionary vision. Consciously or otherwise, the vast bulk of Burns criticism has detached him from his proper intellectual, cultural and political context so that, an isolated figure, his politics can be seen as subjective, whimsical, even eccentric. In proper context, he is wholly different. Much of this, of course, smacks of a bourgeois condescension to not only Burns's class status but also the actual power of poetry itself. Poetry is not, for such minds, 'hard' knowledge. Burns himself constantly stresses the 'bedlamite' tendencies of the poetic personality but he never confused the turmoil and travails of the process of poetic productivity with the absolute perfection of the formal and linguistic nature of the poetic product. Also what we see constantly in his letters is a polemical and dialectical skill based on a wholly coherent grasp of the key intellectual issues of his age. Maria Riddell was not alone in thinking him an even greater conversationalist than poet. Never granted a public stage, his extraordinary prose suggests he would have been among the greatest in that arguably greatest of rhetorical ages.

Painful reality taught Burns economics, but he was not only aware of Adam Smith's sentimental theories but his economic ones. As he wrote of his current reading to Robert Graham in 1789:

> By and by the excise-instructions you mentioned were not in the bundle.— But 'tis no matter; Marshall in his Yorkshire, & particularly that extraordinary man, Smith, in his Wealth of Nations, find my leisure employment enough.— I could not have given any mere *man* credit for half the intelligence Mr Smith discovers in the book. I would covet much to have his ideas respecting the present state of some quarters of the world that are or have been the scenes of considerable revolutions since his book was written.

Central to the 'considerable revolutions' that had taken place was Burns's chastened experience that the manifest increase in wealth in the latter part of the century was not accompanied by any growth in equitable distribution. All boats were certainly not rising on this flood tide of new wealth. As David Cannadine has cogently pointed out there was throughout Burns's adult life an intense massification of wealth among the aristocracy both by carefully calculated pan-British marriages and their capacity to insert themselves in the burgeoning civil and military offices of a state expanding to meet its ultimate conflict with France.[9] Nor did the initially reformist middle-class, the 'stately stupidity of self-sufficient Squires or the luxuriant insolence of upstart "Nabobs"', offer the people political and financial hope. Thus in *The Heron Ballads*, Burns lifts a stone on Scottish provincial life to reveal a bourgeois world replete with sexual but mainly fiscal chicanery. His vision of the entrepreneurial personality is significantly close to John Galt. Indeed, his vision of crime and Edinburgh makes him a precursor of R.L. Stevenson. Indeed, even Stevenson never wrote anything quite of this order about his loved and loathed Edinburgh —the letter is to Peter Hill, the Edinburgh bookseller, a correspondent who always evoked his most extraordinary rhetorical salvoes:

> I will make no excuses my dear Bibliopolus, (God forgive me for murdering language) that I have sat down to write to you on this vile paper, stained with the sanguinary scores of 'thae curst horse leeches o' th' Excise'. —It is economy, Sir; it is that cardinal virtue, Prudence; so I beg you will sit down & either compose or borrow a panegyric (if you are going to borrow, apply to our friend, Ramsay, for the assistance of the author of

those pretty little buttering paragraphs of eulogiums on your thrice-honored & never-enough-to-be-praised MAGIS-TRACY —how they hunt down a [Shop (*deleted*)] house-breaker with the sanguinary perseverance of a bloodhound —how they outdo a terrier in a badger-hole, in unearthing a resettor of stolen goods —how they steal on a thoughtless troop of Night-nymphs as a spaniel winds the unsuspecting Covey — or how they riot o'er a ravaged B—dy house as a cat does o'er a plundered Mouse-nest —how they new-vamp old Churches, aiming at appearances of Piety —plan Squares and Colledges, to pass for men of taste and learning, &c. &c. &c. —while old Edinburgh, like [a (*deleted*)] the doting Mother of a parcel a rakehelly Prodigals, may sing 'Hooly & fairly,' or cry, 'Wae's me that e'er I saw ye,' but still must put her hand in her pocket & pay whatever scores the young dogs think proper to contract) —I was going to say, but this damn'd Parenthesis has put me out of breath, that you should get the manufacturer of the tinselled crockery of magistratial reputations, who makes so distinguished & distinguishing a figure in the Ev: Courant, to compose or rather to compound something very clever on my remarkable frugality; that I write to one of my most esteemed friends on this wretched paper, which was originally intended for the venal fist of some drunken Exciseman, to take dirty notes in a miserable vault of an Ale-cellar.

Burns's political thought, then, is created by his perception of political, institutional degeneration driven by individual economic rapacity and how this might be countered by alternative forms of justice-creating communality. The immediate question arising from this is, of course, the question of Burns's fidelity to the British State of which he was not only a subject but a paid civil-servant who, as Tom Paine had also been, was bound to it by an all-encompassing oath, which cast a shadow over the rest of his life. The Excise oath is deeply revealing of the pressure the British State exerted:

I, ..., do swear that I do, from my Heart, Abhor, Detest, and Abjure, as impious and heretical, that damnable Doctrine and Position, that Princes excommunicated or de-prived by the Pope, or any Authority of the See of Rome, may be deposed or murdered by their Subjects, or any other whatsoever. And I do declare, that no foreign Prince, Person, Prelate, State or Potentate hath, or ought to have, any Jurisdiction, Power, Superiority, Pre-eminence or Authority,

Ecclesiastical or Spiritual, within the Realm: so help me God.[10]

In part, Burns's protestations of fidelity to that state were wrung out of him as his masters in the Excise grew ever more worried about his revolutionary tendencies. In protesting fidelity, however, to the Glorious Revolution of 1688, Burns was not simply being hypocritically skin saving. That revolution had been acceptable, certainly as a stage to further democratic progress. What he and his fellow radicals believed, however, was that the trajectory of the British State with its Hanoverian monarchy was degenerately downwards. As he wrote to Mrs Dunlop in 1788:

> What you mention of the thanksgiving day is inspirational from above. —Is it not remarkable, odiously remarkable, that tho' manners are more civilised & the rights of mankind better understood, by an Augustan Century's improvement, yet in this very reign of heavenly Hanoverianism, & almost in this very year, an empire beyond the Atlantic has had its REVO-LUTION too, & for the same maladministration & legislative misdemeanours in the illustrious & sapientipetent Family of H[anover] as was complained in the tyrannical & bloody house of STUART.—

The 'Empire beyond the Atlantic' was for Burns, as Blake, a benchmark for his ideal of Republican, democratic virtue. It was the revolution that presaged the desired revolutions to come. As he wrote in *The Tree of Liberty*:

> My blessings ay attend the chiel,
>   Wha pitied Gallia's slaves, man
> And staw a branch, spite o' the Deil
>   Frae 'yont the western waves, man!

The demonic forces of reaction were for Burns, however, usually more successful in hindering and, indeed, destroying the transmission of the forces of liberty. Worse, Britain which had been because of its history the initiator and prime mover in the cause of liberty was now become the chief oppressor. In poetic terms this dialectic between a self-betraying England and a self-creating democratic America achieves its most complete expression in his *Ode for General Washington's Birthday*. This is a poem of extraordinary importance in terms of Burns's political ideas but one which his conservative commentators have almost wholly ignored by conveniently drawing attention to their sense of its linguistic and formal inadequacies caused by the poet's use of the Pindaric Ode. For Burns himself, however, the subject of the poem was 'Liberty: you know my honoured friend, how dear the theme is to me.' For Burns and his fellow radicals the cause of liberty was a pan-European phenomenon, nations were tested by the degree by which they had gone beyond absolutism towards democracy. Most of them, as he testifies in that brilliantly satiric tour de force and tour of Europe, *To a Gentleman who had sent a Newspaper*, failed the test miserably. It was, however, particularly painful to see England fallen from her pre-eminent position. As he wrote in the 'Washington' poem:

> Alfred, on thy starry throne,
> Surrounded by the tuneful choir,
> The Bards that erst have struck the patriot lyre,
> And roused the freeborn Briton's soul of fire,
> No more thy England own.—
> Dare injured nations form the great design,
> To make detested tyrants bleed?
> Thy England execrates the glorious deed!
> Beneath her hostile banners waving,
> Every pang of honor braving,
> England in thunder calls— 'The Tyrant's cause is mine!'
> That hour accurst, how did the fiends rejoice,
> And hell thro' all her confines raise the exulting voice,
> That hour which saw the generous the English name
> Linkt with such damned deeds of everlasting shame!

For Burns an England so fallen, inevitably dragged Scotland down with her. On occasion he could be defiantly nationalistic:

> You know my national prejudices. —I have often read & admired the *Spectator, Adventurer, Rambler, & World*, but still with certain regret that they were so thoroughly and entirely English.— Alas! Have I often said to myself, what are all the boasted advantages which my country reaps from a certain Union, that can counterbalance the annihilation of her independence, & even her very Name! . . .

Unlike many of his educated compatriots, the Anglo-British empire did not look to Burns a good deal for Scotland. He saw Scots sucked into the deadly wars of empire. He also saw the degeneration of Scottish leadership with Scots as sycophantic Westminster politi-

cians and bullies back home among their countrymen with Henry
Dundas, the quintessence of these vices, as his enemy incarnate. At
his bleakest, as in *Ode on General Washington's Birthday*, Burns's
perceived Scotland, despite her heroic history of asserting her
freedom, lost beyond resurrection:

> Thee, Caledonia, thy wild heaths among,
> Famed for the martial deed, the heaven-taught song,
>> To thee, I turn with swimming eyes.—
>> Where is that soul of Freedom fled?
>> Immingled with the mighty Dead!
> Beneath the hallowed turf where WALLACE lies!
> Hear it not, Wallace, in thy bed of death!
>> Ye babbling winds in silence sweep;
>> Disturb not ye the hero's sleep,
>> Nor give the coward secret breath.—
> Is this the ancient Caledonian form,
> Firm as her rock, resistless as her storm?
> Shew me that eye which shot immortal hate,
>> Blasting the Despot's proudest bearing:
> Shew me that arm which, nerved with thundering fate,
>> Braved Usurpation's boldest daring!
>> Dark-quenched as yonder sinking star,
>> No more that glance lightens afar;
> That palsied arm no more whirls on the waste of war.

Opposed to such national pessimism, he also perceived a resurrected
not morbid Scotland with himself as National Bard writing, a sort of
Yeatsian precursor, a historically derived national mytho-poetry. As
he wrote to Alex Cunningham in March 1791: '—When political
combustion ceases to be the object of Princes & Patriots, it then, you
know becomes the lawful prey of Historians and Poets.—' He knew
the explosively, for him, liberating forces locked up in Scottish
history. Sir Walter Scott knew them, too, and was terrified of them.
Burns, however, proceeded to create poetic time-bombs as in *Scots
Wha Hae*, where the subtext is an attack on the Pittite policies of
oppression against Scottish radicals in the Scots vernacular and the
words of the French Revolutionaries, making the Tennis Court
Oath to do or die, come from the mouths of fourteenth-century
Scottish soldiers. It may be questionable history but its purpose is to
detect semi-mythical antecedents in the Scottish past as precursors
for the reintegrated, resurrected nation. William Wallace and, to a
lesser extent, Robert Bruce were the obvious candidates:

What a poor, blighted, rickety breed and the virtues & charities when they take their birth from geometrical hypothesis & mathematical demonstration? And what a vigorous Offspring are they when they owe their origin to, and are nursed with the vital blood of a heart glowing with the noble enthusiasm of generosity, benevolence and Greatness of soul? The first may do very well for those philosophers who look on the world of man as one vast ocean and each individual as a little vortex in it whose sole business and merit is to absorb as much as it can in its own center (*sic*); but the last is absolutely and essentially necessary when you would make a Leonidas, a Hannibal, an Alfred, or a WALLACE.—

What Burns was attempting was a Scottish variant of the manner in which his English radical contemporaries were retrieving the English past. As Stephen C. Behrendt has remarked, 'Oppositional Radical rhetoric frequently sought to politicise the masses by linking their interests with ancient British (Saxon) traditions of individual and collective liberty ostensibly preserved in the House of Commons but increasingly imperilled by self-serving initiatives of the aristocracy and the monarchy.'[11] In an age whose rapacious entrepreneurial activities increasingly atomised society, Wallace, then, was the heroic selfless embodiment of the spirit of Scottish community. This looking to the past for virtuous political models and heroic embodiment of these models is, of course, characteristic of the seventeenth and eighteenth-century republican imagination with, of course, the virtuous pantheon to be derived from the classic republics of Greece and Rome. Like Shakespeare, with little Latin and less Greek, Burns certainly knew that central Real Whig text, Addison's *Cato* and he did also draw witty parallels between the reformist Scots of his own era and their classical predecessors:

> Erskine, a spunkie Norland billie;
> True Campbells, Frederick and Illay;
> An' Livinstone, the bauld Sir Willie;
>   An' monie ithers,
> Whom auld Demosthenes or Tully
>   Might own for brithers.

In this discussion of republican tendencies, an immediate difficulty presents itself regarding Burns's Jacobinism. As Hugh Miller remarked in the nineteenth century: 'The *Jacobite* of one year who addressed verses to the reverend defenders of the beauteous Stuart and composed *the Chevalier's Lament* had become in the next the uncompromising Jacobin who wrote *A Man's a Man for a' That.*' In actual fact there is no chronological transition in Burns from Jacobite to Jacobin; these themes intermingle throughout. Nor are they essentially contradictory. Miller's problem arises, as so many misunderstandings of Burns, from his belief that what he is dealing with is confusion unique to Burns. While Burns's personal life pursued a self-aware, sometimes chaotic, zigzag course, his political ideation was not similarly eccentric. Miller, however, does not understand how radical culture as a whole integrated the apparently opposing element of Jacobitism into itself. As Fintan O'Toole has cogently remarked in dealing with a similar apparent self-contradiction in the Irish dramatist and Whig politician, R.B. Sheridan:

> At first sight, there may seem to be a contradiction between the Jacobite tinge of Sheridan's political ancestry and the radical Whiggism to which he was now attaching himself. But by the time Sheridan became conscious of public life, the vestiges of Jacobitism had become, paradoxically, a few stray threads in the banners of the radical Whigs. Rather paradoxically, Tory blue became the colour of Wilkes's supporters. *The Public Advertiser* which published the Junius Letters also published Jacobite propaganda. Later, a number of prominent former Jacobites, including Sir Thomas Gasgoigne, Frances Plowden and Joseph Ritson, became adherents of the radical Whig, Charles James Fox. Sir Frances Burndett's family had come out for Bonnie Prince Charlie in the '45. The apparent conservatism of Jacobitism, its hankering after an increasingly mythic utopia in the past, was not really out of tune with the language and sentiments of the radicals. As Paul Kleber Monod puts it 'the illusion that a "golden age" might have existed at some time in the past fascinated radicals . . .' The old promises of unity and moral regeneration continued to appeal to the imagination of the English radicals even after the Stuart cause collapsed.[12]

Against Hanoverian triumphalism, misfortune, then, made strange political bedfellows. Also, like Sheridan, Burns's sense of Jacobitism was familial. His family were not rooted in Ayrshire; his father had come from the North-East Jacobite redoubt. Indeed, Burns claimed that in 1715 they had been 'out'. As he wrote in 1789 to Lady Winifred Maxwell Constable:

. . . with your ladyship I have the honor to be connected by one
of the strongest and most endearing ties in the whole Moral
world —Common Sufferers in a cause where even to be un-
fortunate is glorious, the cause of Heroic Loyalty! Though my
Fathers had not illustrious Honours and vast properties to
hazard in the contest; though they left their humble cottages
only to add so many units to the unnoted croud that followed
their leaders; yet what they could they did, and what they had
they lost; with unshaken firmness and unconcealed Political
Attachments, they shook hands with Ruin for what they es-
teemed the cause of their King and their Country.—

This language, and the inclosed verses, are for your Lady-
ship's eyes alone.— Poets are not very famous for their pru-
dence; but as I can do nothing for a Cause which is nearly no
more, I do not wish to hurt myself.

Excise officers, as part of their routine duty post-1745, were ex-
pected to compile and deliver to Edinburgh, a list of all known
Jacobite sympathisers in their area. This remained true until the
death of Charles Edward Stuart in Rome the year after Burns wrote
his dedicatory *Birthday Ode* to the exiled Stuart. Though he
thought Jacobitism in practical terms a spent force, Burns knew
it still had enough vitality to get him into trouble with his Hano-
verian masters, thus he did not sign his Jacobite songs. Also it
provided for him an image of Scottish self-loyalty which he in-
creasingly believed was lacking in the contemporary nation replete
with individuals variedly on the make at home and abroad. Nor did
he perceive authoritarian kingship and consequent petrified social
hierarchy as a solution to the nation's ills. What he did fear, and this
in his last years brought him ever closer to the views of Charles
James Fox and the Scottish Foxite Whigs, was that a massification
under Pitt of Hanoverian monarchical power was taking place. Thus
as early as 1787, at the very moment he was seeking to enter The
Excise, he did not only diamond cut these lines on a Stirling window
but subsequently published them in an Edinburgh newspaper thinly
disguised with the initials R.B.

HERE Stewarts once in triumph reign'd,
And laws for Scotland's weal ordain'd;
But now unroof'd their Palace stands,
Their sceptre's fall'n to other hands;
Fallen indeed, and to the earth,
Whence grovelling reptiles take their birth.—

The injur'd STEWART-line are gone,
A Race outlandish fill their throne;
An idiot race, to honor lost;
Who knows them best despise them most.

Indeed, the appeal of the Stewarts to his imagination was a mixture
of empathy for their suffering and displacement, as contrast gainers
against the loathed Hanoverians and, not least, the aesthetic tradi-
tion they represented. They may have had something of the knight
about them but, like the devil, they also had all the best tunes:

By the bye, it is singular enough that the Scottish Muses were
all Jacobites. I have paid more attention to every description of
Scots songs than perhaps any body living has done, I do not
recollect one single stanza, or even the title of the most trifling
Scots air, which has the least panegyrical reference to the
families of Nassau or Brunswick; while there are hundreds
satirizing them. This may be thought no panegyric on the Scots
Poets, but I mean it as such. For myself, I would always take it
as a compliment to have it said, that my heart ran before my
head. And surely the gallant but unfortunate house of Stewart,
the kings of our fathers for so many heroic ages, is a theme
much more interesting than an obscure beef-witted insolent
race of foreigners whom a conjuncture of circumstances kickt
up into power and consequence.

If the unmerited rise of the Hanoverians excited his rage, the fall of
the executed or exiled Stewarts caught his sympathy. Tudor Eng-
land's conduct towards Scotland proved as inflammatory to him as
that of the contemporary Hanoverians; 'What a rock-hearted, per-
fidious Succubus was that Queen Elizabeth! —Judas Iscariot was a
sad dog to be sure, but still his demerits sink into insignificance,
compared with the doings of infernal Bess Tudor.' This vision of
Mary Queen of Scots or Bonnie Prince Charlie is not, however, an
inversion of Burns's democratic principles. He viewed them, espe-
cially the Prince, as Shakespeare viewed Lear. As he wrote: 'A poor,
friendless wand'rer may claim a sigh,/ Still more if that Wand'rer
were royal.' If experience of Jacobite defeat and its 'Heroic Loyalty'
created social parity between himself and Lady Winifred, it made
brothers of a kind between himself and the fallen Prince who was not
only an outcast but also the father of an illegitimate child. People so
fallen from their proper station into obscurity and poverty con-
stantly preoccupied his imagination and filled his poetry. In con-

templating Pitt's fall from power in 1789, he compared his plight
with that of Nebuchadnezzar. Had he known what was to transpire,
he might well have wished that Pitt had indeed gone out to grass. He
also saw in the fate of the common supporters of the Jacobite cause a
grievous expulsion not simply from their ancestral home but into
Miltonic hyperspace:

> . . . the brave but unfortunate Jacobite Clans who, as John
> Milton tells us, after their unhappy Culloden in Heaven, lay
> 'nine times the space that measures day and night,' in oblivious
> astonishment, prone-weltering on the fiery surge.

This inspired casting of the Highlanders as the fallen angels of
Paradise Lost is not only a general expression of Burns's conceited
genius for creatively amalgamating diverse elements but a particular
example of his constant, synergic ability to fuse not only Scottish
and English poetic elements but also, with regard to radical political
philosophy, to be indebted to both English and Scottish sources as
means of energising his political poetry and thought. Consider, for
example, this little known poem, *On Johnson's Opinion of Hampden*;

> FOR shame!
> Let Folly and Knavery
> Freedom oppose:
> 'Tis suicide, Genius,
> To mix with her foes.

Greatly admiring of and influenced by Dr Johnson's *Lives of the Poets*,
wherein he saw so many of his own pains, Burns was provoked into this
remark by Johnson's acerbic Tory aside that John Hampden was 'a
zealot of rebellion'. Hampden, due to his struggles with Charles I, was
an exemplary, indeed iconic figure for Scottish as well as English
radicals. Indeed, not only did Burns but all radical thought, as it
developed throughout the eighteenth century, was an amalgam of
intermingling Scottish and English traditions. As is demonstrated in
Caroline Robbins's seminal work, *The Eighteenth-Century Common-
wealthmen* (1957), eighteenth-century radical political philosophy
was a functional construction made from diverse elements. As John
Dinwiddy has cogently remarked:

> The traditions or discourses on which they drew, and to some
> of which their conceptions of revolution were related, were
> numerous and diverse. They included 'Commonwealth' or

'Country' ideology, the myth of the ancient constitution, millennial religion, natural-rights theory, American republicanism, French Jacobinism, Irish insurrectionalism. Some of them
were quite closely linked to one another both historically and
conceptually, as American republicanism was to Country ideology. Others, such as historic rights and natural rights were
theoretically more distinct; but none the less they were often
treated in practise as mutually reinforcing rather than competing modes of argument, and radicals moved to and fro between
them without any great regard for logical consistency.[13]

From what has already been said and from our consequent textual
analyses of individual political poems, this description fits Burns
like a glove. His ideas are absolutely in the mainstream of eighteenth-century radicalism; it is not his beliefs but, like John Milton
or William Blake, the quality of his poetic genius that makes him
exceptional.

Should there still be any doubt about Burns's debt to eighteenth-
century radical thought, consider, for example, these extracts from
Cato's Letters published through the early 1720s and, tellingly,
jointly English and Scottish authored:

> There is nothing moral in Blood or in Title, or in Place; Actions
> only, and the Causes that produce them are moral. He therefore
> is best that does best. Noble blood prevents neither Folly, nor
> Lunacy, nor Crimes, but frequently begets or promotes them:
> And Noblemen, who act infamously, derive no honour from
> virtuous Ancestors whom they dishonour. A Man who does
> base Things, is not noble or great, if he do little Things: A sober
> Villager is a better Man than a debauched Lord; an honest
> Mechanick than a Knavish Courtier.[14]

It is of course no accident that the poet's closest friend during his
period at Ellisland, Robert Riddell, a highly respected Whig polemicist, wrote under the pen name *Cato*, Or, again from *Cato's
Letters*, on the rapacious cupidity and the political consequences of
the aristocratic and propertied classes at home and abroad:

> They will be ever contriving and forming wicked and danger
> ous Projects, to make the People poor, and themselves rich; well
> knowing the Dominion follows Property; that where there are
> Wealth and Power, there will always be crowds of servile
> Dependents; and that, on the contrary, Poverty dejects the

Mind, fashions it to Slavery, and renders it unequal to any generous Undertaking, and incapable of opposing any bold Usurpation. They will squander away the Publick Money in wanton Presents to Minions, and their Creatures of Pleasure or of Burthern, or in Pensions to mercenary and worthless Men and Women, for vile Ends and traiterous Purposes.

They will engage their Country in ridiculous, expensive, fantastical Wars, to keep the Minds of Men in continual Hurry and Agitation, and under constant Fears and Alarms, and, by such means, deprive them both of Leisure and Inclination to look into publick Miscarriages. Men, on the contrary, will, instead of such Inspection, be disposed to fall into all Measures offered, seemingly, for their Defence, and will agree to every wild Demand made by those who are betraying them.[15]

If this, as it should, sounds familiar so to is the stress that, with Lockean contractuality, power should reside not with a corrupt elite but with the people:

The first principles of Power are in the People; and all the Projects of Men in Power ought to refer to the People, to aim solely at their good, and end in it: And who will ever pretend to govern them without regarding them, will soon repent it. Such Feats of Errantry may do perhaps in *Asia*: but in the countries where the people are free, it is Madness to hope to rule them against their Wills. They will know, that Government is appointed for their Sakes, and will be saucy enough to expect some Regard and some from their own Delegates.[16]

While there is some doubt about Aberdonian Thomas Gordon's commitment to the Right Whig cause after his joint-authorship of *The Independent Whig* and *Cato's Letters*, he is certainly the forefather of a stream of Scots who went south to fill prominent and powerful positions in English radical circles. We need to modify the notion that Scottish writers going south, from giants like Smollett to minnows like Mallett (Malloch), were simply on the make by being hyper-patriotic propagandists in the forging of the Anglo-British Empire. Thus, for example we have the expatriate radical careers of Gilbert and Peter Stuart, Thomas Hardy, Secretary of the London Corresponding Society, James Perry (Pirie), editor of *The Morning Chronicle*, Dr Alexander Geddes, radical Catholic priest, poet and religious contributor to *The Analytical Review* and James Oswald, who not only, like a significant number of Scots, went to France, but died in the Vendée fighting for the revolutionary army. Certainly, if they were to emerge from historical darkness, their political values and consequent rhetoric would also help to return Burns to his appropriate cultural, political context. We need also to understand the headlong flight of poets and writers such as James Thomson Callander, James Kennedy and James 'Balloon' Tytler, mainly westward to America in the wake of the 1793/4 Treason trials, to see parallels between their lesser political poetry to that of Burns.[17] The absence of these radicals voices serves to diminish appreciation of the iron grip Dundas had in suffocating dissent by means not only of the prostitution of the Scottish legal system but because that system was inadequate in terms of defining treasonable behaviour. As John Thelwall, the great English radical and intimate friend of Coleridge and Wordsworth, in the 1790s, wrote:

> It is a protest against an alarming threat held out —not by the sovereign —not by the legislature but by Mr Secretary Dundas. —He alone it was who had the audacity to threaten the violation and subversion of those yet remaining laws that guarantee Englishmen an impartial trial by Jury of their country, and to substitute in their place, the arbitrary tyrannical practices of the Court of Justiciary in Scotland.[18]

Perhaps the single greatest source of reformative change affecting Burns, was, however, within Scotland itself and had its origin in that charismatic Ulsterman, Francis Hutcheson and his professorial tenure at Glasgow University. His tradition ended in the 1790s with Professor John Millar whose cosmopolitan scholarship, integrity and passionate commitment to democratic reformation was lost in the vortex of repression. His 1796 *Letter of Crito: On the Causes, Objects and Consequences of the Present War*, dedicated to his friend Charles James Fox, published along with John McLaurin's (Lord Dreghorn) anti-war poetry in Edinburgh's *The Scots Chronicle*, both confirm Burns's rhetoric and experiences in the same decade. They also signal the tragic death of Hutcheson's aspirations for not only Scotland but the still festering sore of the Irish problem. While we do not know if Burns read Hutcheson, there can be no doubt of his teaching's proximity to the poet's own values:

> In every form of government the people has this right of defending themselves against the abuse of power . . . the people's right of resistance is unquestionable.

But when there's no other way of preserving a people; and when their governors by their perfidious frauds have plainly forfeited their right; they may justly be divested of their power, and others put into their places, or a new plan of power established.

Nor does this doctrine of the right of resistance in defence of the rights of a people, naturally tend to excite seditions and civil wars. Nay they have been more frequently occasioned by the contrary tenets. In all ages there has been too much patience in the body of the people, and too stupid a veneration for their princes or rulers; which for each one free kingdom or state has produced many monstrous herds of miserable abject slaves or beasts of burden, rather than civil polities of rational creatures, under the most inhuman and worthless masters, trampling upon all things human and divine with the uttmost effrontery.[19]

Such Hutchesonian values would, in any case, have percolated down to Burns through his connection to Glasgow-trained New Licht clergy in Ayrshire. This entails that the wonderful anti-Auld Licht satires of the early Ayrshire period are not provincial storms in a tea cup but a variant on the intense British struggle by reforming religion to shake off the theocratic control of both the Trinitarian Anglican and, in Scotland, the reactionary Presbyterian churches whose vision of the innately sinful, fallen nature of man renders impossible a reformative, never mind utopian, politics. At the heart of the poetry of Burns and Blake is this preoccupation with removing the absolute political power given to the reactionary state by the teaching of what they saw as a perverted institutional Christianity. Burns's *Address to the Deil* is profoundly different in language and tone from Blake but not in essential purpose and meaning. Had he been aware of his true English peer he would have been transfixed by such Blakean lines:

> . . . & the purpose of the Priests & Churches
> Is to impress on men the fear of death; to teach
> Trembling & fear, terror, constriction; abject selfishness.
> Mine is to teach Men to despise death & to go on
> In fearless majesty annihilating Self . . .   (*Milton*, 11. 37–41)

As Richard Rorty has written,

The Romantics were inspired by the successes of antimonarchist and anticlericalist revolutions to think that the desire for something to obey is a symptom of immaturity. These successes made it possible to envisage building a new Jerusalem without divine assistance, thereby creating a society in which men and women would lead the perfected lives which had previously seemed possible only in an invisible, immaterial, post-mortem paradise. The image of progress towards such a society —horizontal progress, so to speak— began to take the place of Platonic or Dantean images of vertical ascent. History began to replace God, Reason and Nature as the source of human hope.[20]

This accounts, too, for the religio-mythical compatibility of Burns and Blake in that both are obsessed with those transgressive figures who destroy the institutional, regressive corruption of the established world in the name of a new earthly heaven. Blake is the more extreme and mythopoetic. Burns never similarly defines Blake's transgressive Christ as discovered in *The Everlasting Gospel*. But both are preoccupied with not only the heroic, vitalising figure of 'Blind John's' Satan but with the problematic figure of Job. Cynthia Ozick[21] has commented on Job:

> Like the noblest of prophets he assails injustice; and still he is unlike them. They accuse the men and women who do evil; their targets are made of flesh and blood. It is human transgression they hope to mend. Job seeks to rectify God. His is an ambition higher, deeper, vaster, grander than theirs; he is possessed by a righteousness more frenzied than theirs; the scale of his justice-hunger exceeds all that precedes him . . . he can be said to be the consummate prophet. And at the same time he is the consummate violator. If we are to understand him at all, if we are rightly to enter into his passions at the pinnacle, then we ought to name him prophet; but we may not. Call him, instead, antiprophet —his teaching, after all, verges on atheism: the rejection of God's power. His thesis is revolution.

Both Burns's poetry and prose are saturated with the deeply varied ways he employed his early exposure to the sermon and his life-long, intense reading of the Bible. No story affected him more deeply than that of Job's.

Liam McIlvanney, one of a tiny minority of the legion of Burns commentators to have sympathetic knowledge of Burns's true politics, traces in a particularly fine article, 'Presbyterian Radicalism and the Politics of Robert Burns', a similarly long tradition of radical political gestation from a more distinctively Scottish point of view. He highlights the ambivalence at the heart of Burns's relationship to Presbyterianism thus:

> . . . it remains unfortunate that Burns's run-ins with the kirk have obscured the extent to which his own political philosophy is grounded in his religious inheritance. His politics are shaped by two complimentary strands of Presbyterian thought: on the one hand, the New Light, with its subjection of all forms of authority to the tribunal of individual reason: on the other, the traditional contractarian political theory long associated with Presbyterianism. These influences are evident in Burns's repeated avowal of 'revolution' principles in his support for the American Revolution and, above all, in his satirical attacks on political corruption. The whole framework of assumption on which Burns's political satires rest recalls the contractarian principles of Presbyterian thought: that authority ascends from below; that government is a contract, and political power a trust; and that even the humblest members of society are competent to censure their governors. That Burns deplored certain aspects of Calvinism —its harsh soteriology, its emphasis on faith over works— should not blind us to his sincere identification with the Presbyterian political inheritance:

> The Solemn league and Covenant
>   Now brings a smile, now brings a tear.
> But sacred Freedom, too, was theirs;
>   If thou'rt a slave, indulge thy sneer.[22]

Burns, of course, was not the only Scotsman to embrace such radical ideals. We cannot properly understand his life and much of his poetry if we do not understand the degree to which his personal relationships and affiliations were directed towards and driven by seeking out similarly politically sympathetic groups and individuals. It was the Lodge friends and patrons who eased his path towards Edinburgh; that so politically riven city which was to prove so disastrous to him in both life and death. Without, as all his generation, fully understanding the political causes of what happened in the capital, the ever astute Edwin Muir put his finger on the events of his sensational first extended visit to the capital as the cause of Burns's subsequent accelerating decline:

> It was after his first trip to Edinburgh that his nature, strongly built and normal, disintegrated. He had hoped, in meeting the

first shock of his astonishing triumph in the capital, that an escape was at last possible from the life of hardly maintained poverty which as a boy he had foreseen and feared. He left Edinburgh recognising that there was no reprieve, that hardship must sit at his elbow to the end of his days. Fame had lifted him on the point of an immediate pinnacle; now the structure had melted away and, astonished, he found himself once more in his native county, an Ayrshire peasant. Some fairy had set him for a little in the centre of a rich and foreign society; then calmly and finally, she had taken it from under his feet. There is hardly another incident in literary history to parallel this brief rise and setting of social favour, and hardly one showing the remorselessness of fortune in the world. The shock told deeply on Burns, working more for evil than the taste for dissipation which he was said to have acquired from the Edinburgh aristocracy.[23]

Given Muir's lack of knowledge of the covert political forces operating on Burns, this is well said. It does, however, underestimate the extraordinary degree to which Burns, in the midst of his Edinburgh triumph, was conscious not only of its transience but the darkness to follow. As he wrote to Robert Ainslie on 16th December 1786:

You will very probably think, my honoured friend, that a hint about the mischievous nature of intoxicated vanity may not be unreasonable, but, alas! You are wide of the mark. Various concurring circumstances have raised my fame as a poet to a height which I am absolutely certain I have not merits to support; and I look down on the future as I would into the bottomless pit.

He realised that his Edinburgh fame was largely based on the temporary social novelty of a ploughman writing poetry. He also probably realised that his Preface to the Kilmarnock Poems was, as we shall see, a brilliant confidence trick on a willingly gullible genteel Scottish audience, for which a price had to be paid. In the same month he wrote, even more particularly and precisely, to Rev William Greenfield about the consequences of Edinburgh:

Never did Saul's armour sit so heavily on David when going to encounter Goliath, as does the encumbering robe of public notice with which the friendship and patronage of some 'names dear to fame' have invested me. I do not say this in the ridiculous idea of seeming self-abasement, and affected modesty. I have long studied myself and I think I know pretty exactly what ground I occupy, both as a man, & a poet; and however the world or a friend may sometimes differ from me in that particular, I stand for it, in silent resolve with all the tenaciousness of Property. I am willing to believe that my abilities deserved a better fate than the veriest shades of life; but to be dragged forth, with all my imperfections on my head, to the full glare of learned and polite observation, is what, I am afraid, I shall have bitter reason to repent I mention this to you, once for all, merely, in the Confessor style, to disburthen my conscience, and that 'When proud Fortune's ebbing tide recedes' you may hear me witness, when my bubble of fame was at its highest, I stood unintoxicated, with the inebriating cup in my hand. Looking forward, with rueful resolve, to the hastening time when the stroke of envious Calumny, with all the eagerness of vengeful triumph, should dash it to the ground.

Mozarts seem inevitably to have their Salieris. The treachery that Burns so accurately predicted for himself was also to be understood as not only psychologically motivated resentment of genuine creativity, but also essentially driven by political ideology. As the 1793–4 Sedition Trials revealed, Edinburgh was a politically schismatic society. This was not so apparent in 1789 and Burns's contacts with two utterly contrasting groups has never been fully understood in terms of the consequent conflicting politics or the terrible personal consequences for the poet of this division.

Initially, Burns was lauded by two utterly contrasting groups. He was a member of the boozy, boisterous, in many instances brilliant, radical, reformist club, The Crochallan Fencibles. He was also taken up, mildly patronised, by the aesthetically, politically and religiously conformist pro-Hanoverian group led by Henry Mackenzie and Hugh Blair. What has never been understood is not only how partisan to their own causes both groups were but, indeed, the degree to which, as the political scene darkened in the 1790s, they were sucked into active participation either towards not simply reform but insurrection on the radical side and covert anti-revolutionary activity on the government side. Of such undeclared civil war, Burns was among the chief victims.

Despite some excellent work by John Brims and Elaine MacFarland we still fall considerably short of understanding the fraught complexity of the extent and intensity of radical protest in Scotland in the 1790s. One consequence of this, of course, has been the contextually impoverished state of Burns criticism. Most of it has been written with the political dimension quite absent. Nor does space here allow anything like the necessary explication of the complex nature of that political culture. What can be said, however, is that most Scottish history seriously underestimates certainly the quantity and, arguably, the quality of radical opposition prevalent in Scotland which became genuinely divisive due to the American War of Independence.

It was that war which created that group so essential to understanding both Burns's political affiliations and what happened to him, The Crochallan Fencibles. The name was a deliberate parody of the loyalist militia groups springing up in opposition to the American cause. What the American war engendered in the radical, reformist side of Edinburgh can be gauged by the invited open letter of Dr Richard Price in 1784, 'To the Secretary of the Committee of Citizens of Edinburgh':

> God grant that this spirit might increase till it has abolished all despotic governments and exterminated the slavery which debased mankind. This spirit first rose in America (it soon reached Ireland) it has diffused itself in some foreign countries, and your letter informs me that it is now animating Scotland.[24]

Ingenuously, late eighteenth-century radicals had a kind of millennial vision of history as an American initiated domino game of collapsing crowns. For a time the reform of a particularly undemocratic Scotland seemed a distinct possibility. The bumpers, bawdy songs and personal badinage which Burns enlisted for with the Fencibles in their howff in Anchor Close was part of what must have seemed the initial stages of an ill-disguised victory celebration. The Fencibles were of course typically a heavy drinking culture. It was not, however, the most erotically inflamed of Scotland's men's clubs. Public masturbation was not on the agenda. Certainly, as camouflage, it was this side of the club's activities to which Burns confessed. He did not always publicly make the connection between libidinal energy and radical politics. Thus he wrote to Mrs Dunlop:

> You may guess that the convivial hours of men have their mysteries of wit and mirth, and I hold it a piece of contemptible baseness to detail the sallies of thoughtless merriment, or the orgies of accidental intoxication to the ear of cool sobriety or female delicacy.

Or, as he wrote in conclusion to a brilliant extended parody of *The Revelation of St John the Divine* in a letter to William Chalmers in December, 1786, that he had never seen 'as many wild beasts as I have seen since I came to Edinburgh.' Burns's own stressing of the social wildness of the Fencibles may have been a deliberate camouflage for the actual reality of their political beliefs and activities. Intellectually, they were an astonishing bunch. William Smellie, commissioned as 'Hangman', not only edited the first *Encyclopaedia Britannica* but had written much of it. Of all Burns's lost letters, those to Smellie would possibly have been of the most profound political importance. They were destroyed by Smellie's biographer, Robert Kerr, with an insouciance that we chillingly recognise as seminal for the manner in which Burns's texts were to be treated not only in the hyper-respectable nineteenth century: 'Many letters of Burns to Mr. Smellie which remained being totally unfit for publication, and several of them containing severe reflections on many respectable people still in life, have been burnt.' Smellie was also the author of a *Philosophy of Natural History* which postulated that the most highly refined, developed human consciousness was incompatible with the world. James 'Balloon' Tytler was an even more extraordinary polymath. As Burns wrote in November 1788 to Mrs Dunlop:

> Those marked T, are the work of an obscure, tippling but extraordinary body of the name of Tytler: a mortal, who though he drudges about Edinburgh as a common printer, with leaky shoes, a sky-lighted hat, & knee buckles as unlike as George-by-the-grace-of-God, & Solomon-the-son-of-David, yet that same unknown drunken Mortal is author and compiler of three-fourths of Elliot's pompous Encyclopaedia Brittanica.

Poet, song-writer, polymath, Scotland's first balloonist and eventually so politically active that he fled Scotland in 1793 to Belfast and then volunteered to return to Scotland to promote insurrection:

> . . . he was to traverse Scotland as a *Highland Piper*. He learned the tongue and was to have gone from town to town to organise a General Insurrection, from there to the South of Ireland (Cork), hence to Paris to enlist the French.[25]

To Tytler's extreme irritation, this mission did not take place. Like many others of his creed and generation, his journey was to be westwards to American safety. An almost equally irascible, restless

spirit was Dr Gilbert Stuart who had so upset genteel Edinburgh
with his writings in Smellie's *Edinburgh Magazine and Review* that
he had to seek employment in London thus initiating the long
tradition of Scots radicals forced South. Obviously extremely im-
portant in the Fencibles was the legal profession. Of a considerable
number of lawyers, the most prominent was Henry Erskine, Dean of
the Faculty of Advocates and brother of the even greater radical
lawyer Thomas. It was Henry Erskine's fall at the hands of the
Robert Dundas faction in the election for Dean of Faculty in 1795
that Burns turned into, in January 1796, a bitterly witty song about
the loss of the men of merit and worth to the reactionary loyalists.

> In your heretic sins may live and die,
>   Ye heretic Eight and thirty
> But accept, ye Sublime Majority,
>   My congratulations hearty.
> With your Honors and a certain King,
>   In your servants this is striking—
> The more incapacity they bring,
>   The more they're to your liking.

This, then, was the intimate company Burns was keeping. Nor did
he only wholly share their politics but was an active participant not
only in terms of his contributions to the radical press, but in actually
attempting to send carronades, captured from the smuggling brig
Rosamund as part of his excise duties, to the French revolutionaries.
It is little wonder that even during his first Edinburgh visit his
relationships with genteel, conformist, pro-Hanoverian society were
strained. How strained we can see, for example, in the fury of his
riposte to Mrs McLehose when a Mrs Stewart had checked him
over his seditious anti-Hanoverian lines on the Stirling window:

> I have almost given up the excise idea —I have just been now to
> wait on a great person, Miss N—'s friend, Mrs. Stewart. —
> Why will great people not only deafen us with the din of their
> equipage, and dazzle us with their fastidious pomp, but they
> must also be so very dictatorially wise? I have been questioned
> like a child about my matters, and blamed and schooled for my
> Inscription on Stirling window. Come, Clarinda—'Come,
> curse me Jacob; come, defy me Israel!'

Yet he needed his enemy's patronage. He did join the Excise. Blair
and Mackenzie, with their mixture of lachrymose and evangelical

values, expressed a faith not so much of a suffering Christ as a quiescently accepting Christ as exemplar to a politically similarly quiescent, hence an apolitical, common people. As Blake wrote: 'Pity would be no more, if we did not make someone poor.' They were, however, able to open doors to publishing connections and offer mainly ill-received poetic advice. In the name of rules and decency, they were always trying to get Burns to tidy up his, to them, unruly act. This had almost no effect other than to irritate the Bard. As he wrote to Greenfield:

> . . . I stumbled on two Songs which I here enclose you as a kind of curiosity to a Professor of the Belle lettres de la Nature: which allow me to say, I look upon as an additional merit of yours: a kind of bye Professorship, not always to be found among the systematic Fathers and Brothers of scientific Criticism.

These tensions were also not confined to matters aesthetic and linguistic. Unlike Heathcliff, Burns was not the brute, sub-literate, threat, that dark erotic stranger, which haunted the bourgeois imagination of the period. They were faced with someone hyper-literate, fecundly allusive to a degree far beyond their powers in canonical literary and biblical tradition, who could not only talk their pants off but, it was feared, those of their wives and daughters too. Command of language was directly related to a fixed hierarchical social order; Burns threatened social anarchy by the very nature of his poetic, rhetorical potency. It offered them some security to classify him as a class-bound 'heaven-taught ploughman' rather than great poet.

REPUTATION: CRITICS, BIOGRAPHERS AND BOWDLERISERS
Even more than Henry Dundas, Henry Mackenzie was probably the most sustained, malign influence on Burns's reputation. He may initially have genuinely wanted to help the poet. He also almost certainly sensed a bandwagon that his self-importance would not allow him *not* to join. As Donald Low has remarked, however, the nature of Mackenzie's praise was to be in the long term confining and destructive:

> . . . his was a disastrously inaccurate essay in criticism which gave rise to endless distortion of Burns's poetry. The whole tendency of Mackenzie's encomium was to emasculate *Poems*. He paid lip-service to humour and satire, but found them too

embarrassing to discuss: introduced a comparison with Sha-
kespeare, only to withdraw it at once: repeatedly shrank from
Burns's characteristic self-expression and fell back on general-
isations. He apologised for the language in which the poet did
his best work, and concentrated on the poems of sentiment in
English. This was to sacrifice truth, and therefore also Burns's
long-term interests as a poet, for instant acclaim.[26]

From the beginning Mackenzie's deeply influential aesthetic stric-
tures were socially and politically motivated. Hence Burns is turned
into a safe sentimentalist rather than, like Pope or Swift, a turbulent,
dissenting satirist of the established, corrupt order. He is a naïve
exception rather than, in terms of both poetry and politics, the most
knowing of men. Burns was as formally naïve in poetic tradition as
Mozart was in musical tradition. They were both examples of
creative pieces of ground, as Blake suggests, born spaded and
seeded. It was socially unacceptable for Mackenzie to grant Burns
such potency. As an extension of this, he had to define Burns as a
naïve innocent, coming from peasant origins. Mackenzie also down-
grades the actual vernacular language of that world with its elements
which bespoke the raw pleasures, pains and, indeed, turbulent
discontents of the common people. If there was genuine ambiva-
lence in Mackenzie's attitude to Burns at the beginning of their
relationship, it did not survive the poet's death. In his résumé of the
careers of Scotland three great eighteenth-century poets, Ramsay,
Fergusson and Burns, the first is praised for his achievement of
prudent respectability. The latter two are not:

Fergusson, dissipated and drunken, died in early life, after
having produced poems faithfully and humorously describing
scenes of Edinburgh and somewhat of blackguardism. Burns
originally virtuous, was seduced by dissipated companions, and
after he got into the Excise addicted himself to drunkenness,
tho' the rays of his genius sometimes broke through the mist of
his dissipation: but the habit had got too much power over him
to be overcome and it brought him, with a few lucid intervals, to
an early grave. He unfortunately during the greatest part of his
life had called and thought dissipation *spirit,* sobriety and
discretion a *want of it,* virtues too shabby for a man of genius.
His great admiration of Fergusson showed his propensity to
coarse dissipation.
. . . How different was the fate of *Burns* compared with that of a
Poet in birth, in Education, and many other circumstances like

him, tho' I do not arrogate to him so much creative genius, *Allan Ramsay*. He came into notice in a Station as mean as Burns, had no advantage over him in Birth, Connections, or any other circumstances independent of his own genius alas: it was the Patronage and Companionship which Burns obtained, that changed the colour of his later life: the patronage of dissipated men of high rank, and the Companionship of clever, witty, but dissipated men of lower rank. The notice of the former flattered his vanity, and in some degree unsettled his from an anecdote to be immediately mentioned he seemed to mingle with the most amiable feelings —but the levity of his Patrons and his associates Dwelt on the Surface of his Mind and prompted some of his Poetry which offended the serious, and lost him better friends than those which that poetry had acquired —Dugald Stewart who first introduced him to me, told me latterly, that his Conduct and Manners had become so degraded that decent persons could hardly take any notice of him.[27]

Given Fergusson's sweet, convivial personality and the terrible nature of his incarcerated death, Mackenzie's vicious pursuit of him beyond the grave beggars belief. In the history of poetic biographies, Ian Hamilton has remarked that Burns was the first poet to be character assassinated. Given Mackenzie's treatment of Fergusson, however, we would have to grant Fergusson unhappy precedence. Mackenzie tainted, wrongly, both their reputations with, at best, alcoholic tendencies. This alleged addiction was then implied to lead to other forms of licence where, certainly in Burns's case, sexual promiscuity was on the charge sheet.

This demonisation of Burns is not to be understood, however, without it being placed in its proper political context. The Mackenzie who penned these personal attacks was the same man who was writing fervid anti-revolutionary polemics in *The Edinburgh Herald* during 1790–1 under the pen name 'An Old Tradesman' and again in 1793, in *The Caledonian Mercury*, under the pen name 'Brutus' to prove that all was for the best in the best of all worn torn, economically distressed Hanoverian worlds. As spokesperson for the old regime he believed that strong government would 'save the people from that worst enemy of purely democratic states – the people themselves'.[28] The pinnacle of his loyalty is the 1792 *A Review of the Principal Proceedings of the Parliament of 1784*, a defense of William Pitt, when Pitt's pro-reformist views of 1784 were being thrown back in his face by radicals. Retrospectively referring to that pamphlet Mackenzie described the ideological clash of the 1790's as an 'epidemic insanity . . . which set up certain idols, under the names of Liberty, Equality and The Rights of Man'.[29] Pitt personally thanked Mackenzie for his loyal defence, and basking in such praise, he replied 'My Opinion, Sir, of you as a Minister I hold only in common with the Millions around me.'[30] (Letter 93, To William Pitt, March 1792). These 'millions' were not so loyal, as Mackenzie informed George Home on 26th March 1792:

> There is a Spirit of Sedition gone forth, of which it is very difficult to tell the Extent, but even if not so considerable as some timid people fear, so restless, so busy, so zealous, as to be truly alarming to every considerate Man. I forget the Calcula-tion made of the numbers of Manufactures in England, but we all know it is very great. Of these I believe I may say a Majority, but assuredly a great part, are determined enemies to the present Order of things[31] . . .

Theatre goers, as Mackenzie records, were among this swelling radical 'enemy' and in one incident he tells Home, open conflict erupted between radicals and loyalists at London's Haymarket theatre when the revolutionary song 'Ca Ira' was demanded by reformers, but chanted down by loyalist calls for 'God Save the King'. Similar tensions spread to the provincial theatres, includ-ing Dumfries and an unidentified informer reported to the Excise that Burns was in the reformist mob. Mackenzie goes on in the same letter to condemn Scottish academics: 'From my Communication with Men of Letters here, I can perceive that they are generally on the side of the Malcontents'.[32] Fanatically partisan, status obsessed, politically scared, Mackenzie so hated his reforming and radical political enemies that he could not speak their names. To do so would give them a credibility he utterly sought to deny. For Mackenzie the radical was equivalent to the bestial. This is why in Mackenzie and the subsequent Tory criticism he inspired always described Burns as surrounded by destructive groups of unnamed degenerates in Edinburgh and, even worse, Dumfries.

It should further be understood that Burns was not a unique case for such treatment. The heavily subsidised, reactionary literary, magazine and newspaper culture put together by Pitt and Dundas specialised in trashing the radical literary enemy by varied forms of abuse based on the relationship of personal licentiousness to consequent political anarchy if these people were to succeed. For example, Mary Wollstonecraft with whom Burns corresponded received treatment even worse than his, as a promiscuous woman she was even more reprehensible than a randy ploughman. Engrossed in destroying the careers of any radical sympathisers, Mackenzie boasted to the ultra-loyalist George Chalmers, in March 1793:

> One thing Mr Young suggests as never yet thought of, which however was thought of here, and enforced in two short Articles in the Newspapers by myself, at the very opening of this Business, namely the resolution of not employing Jacobin Tradesmen, which had a very excellent Effect in this Town. . . . contrary to my Expectations, the War has I think done good in this Country, given a Sort of Impulse to the good Part of the Community . . .[33]

An ever-willing anti-reform propagandist, Mackenzie helped organise the Scottish distribution of a vicious attack, printed by the same George Chalmers, on Tom Paine as a degenerate, dangerous individual. The black art of character assassination, well established before the death of Burns, won rich patronage for the loyal Mackenzie, appointed Comptroller of Taxes in Scotland in 1799.

The degree of Mackenzie's vindictiveness and his stress of the later Dumfries years, also alert us to one of the most pervasive and politically wilfully misconceived of myths surrounding Burns. Indeed, so pervasive that it has even penetrated the normally sceptical consciousness of Professor T.M. Devine who has recently written of 'the public recantation of such celebrated supporters of the radical cause as Robert Burns'.[34] This alleged recantation stems from one misinterpreted, truncated song, *The Dumfries Volunteers*. It avoids all the substantial poetic evidence of the Dumfries years to the contrary; not least *Extempore* [on the Loyal Natives' *Verses*]:

> Ye true 'Loyal Natives', attend to my song,
> In uproar and riot rejoice the night long:
> From envy and hatred your corps is exempt:
> But where is your shield from the *darts of contempt*?

The poem catches perfectly both Burns's contempt for the British cause under the war-mongering Pitt and the political company he was keeping in the bitterly politically factionalised little town from which he kept sending out not only radical poems to politically sympathetic London, Edinburgh and Glasgow newspapers, but, as his doctor William Maxwell had, weapons to the French. All this, of course, at ferocious risk to, at best, his Excise position as he was scrutinised by his rightly suspicious masters. This, too, accounts for his attempts in the last years to get free of the claustrophobic cockpit of Dumfries to the relatively safer, because larger Glasgow area where, even more than Edinburgh, Scottish history has still chronically underestimated the depth of a radical opposition to Pitt's war policy so great that Burke brought it up in the House.

If Burns had made any public recantation, Mackenzie and his ilk would have shouted it from the house-tops. That there was none accounts not only for the intensity of Mackenzie's malice but also for what we now know about his activities not only as literary propagandist but practically on behalf of the government. The nature of Mackenzie's key role in the government's scrutiny of Burns and the subsequent creation of a literary, psychological context by which to sanitise the poetry we now know from the archives of Edinburgh University. Here we have discovered letters from Robert Heron requesting payments from Robert Dundas via Henry Mackenzie for espionage services rendered:

My Lord . . . Five or six years since, I, too boldly introduced myself to your Lordship, by suggesting that it was requisite to counteract from the Press, the effects of those seditious associations and seditious writings which were then busily corrupting the political sentiments of the people of this country . . . you were pleased not to disapprove the ingenuiness and honesty of my wishes and intentions. I was, in consequence of this condescending goodness of your Lordship, noticed by the Committee of the Association for the Defence of the Constitution, which was soon after formed. Under the direction —particularly of Mr Mackenzie, Lord Glenlee and Mr Campbell, I was employed to write several little articles for the newspapers, and for other occasions, in order to oppose the malignant efforts of sedition . . .

. . . The Committee had, with sufficient liberality, already paid my petty services with the sum of thirty pounds . . . Your Lordship, within a short time, munificently sent me no less than fifty pounds.[35]

The core of these services involved his exploitation of a relationship built up with Burns in Edinburgh. Worse, on the poet's death he rushed to print with a memoir of the poet which was to prove ruinously influential for both Burns and his poetry.

Heron was too talented to be a mere hack. When he was the Rev. Hugh Blair's assistant he had met Burns in Edinburgh. Heron maintained the relationship and en route to his native Galloway made a point of visiting the poet. The often prescient Bard recorded a visit from Heron to Ellisand thus:

> The ill-thief blaw the Heron south!
> And never drink be near his drouth!
> He tald myself, by work o' mouth,
>   He'd take my letter;
> I lippened to the chief in trough,
>   And bade nae better.—

> But aiblins honest Master Heron
> Had at the time some dainty *Fair One*,
> To ware his theologic care on,
>   And holy study:
> And tired o' Sauls to waste his lear on,
>   E'en tried the *Body*.—

Burns got the scale of the betrayal wrong; it was infinitely in excess of a non-delivered letter to Dr Blacklock. The devil of his political enemies really had blown Heron south. Behind Heron's black-gowned clerical front, Burns also keenly observed his capacity for chronic alcoholic and sexual dissipation. A familiar of the debtor's prison, Heron was to die prematurely, again imprisoned for debt, in Newgate in 1807.

Along with the new factual evidence of the Mackenzie/Heron connection, it might have been deduced both from Heron's slavish taking of Mackenzie tactics against Burns to a biographical extreme and his equally slavish eulogy to his patron's critical prowess. This is Heron's account of Mackenzie's contribution, via his *Lounger* magazine article, to Burns's initial Edinburgh success:

> That criticism is now known to have been composed by HENRY MACKENZIE Esq, whose writings are universally admired for an *Addisonian* delicacy and felicity of wit and humour, by which the CLIO of the *Spectator* is more than rivalled; for a wildly tender pathos that excites the most exquisite vibrations of the finest chords of sympathy in the human heart, for a lofty, vehement, persuasive eloquence, by which the immortal *Junius* has sometimes perhaps been excelled and often almost equalled![36]

Heron's biographical memoir was not the occasion of his first writing about Burns. In 1793 he published a travel book where he created a contrast on the poet's not so much varied talents as antipathetic ones as expressed in the difference between *The Cotter's Saturday Night* and *Tam o' Shanter*. The latter is initially admitted as a masterpiece but this is then significantly qualified: 'Burns seems to have thought, with Boccacce and Prior, that some share of indelicacy was a necessary ingredient in a Tale. Pity that he should have debased so fine a piece, by any things, — having even the remotest relation to obscenity'. This kind of Mackenzie-initiated sentimentalism was the seminal language of nineteenth-century political pietism which would become, mainly though *Blackwood's*, the dominant mode of Scottish Toryism. Burns had to be converted into the pietistic poet of a quiescent common people. Whether they were properly reading its concluding stanzas, *The Cotter's Saturday Night* became the Ark of the Covenant for the Scottish upper and middle-classes as, increasingly anxious about the fetid, brutal potentially insurrectionary common life of the new emergent industry-based (coal, iron, tobacco, weaving) towns, they sought the politically calming notion of pastoral, god-fearing peace reigning in the Scottish countryside. Heron is a seminal figure in the concoction of this fantasy:

> The whole books of the sacred scriptures are continually in the hands of almost every peasant. And it is impossible, that there should not be some souls among them, awakened to the divine emotions of genius, by that rich assemblage which these books present, of almost all that is interesting in incidents, or picturesque in imagery, or affectingly sublime or tender in sentiments and character. It is impossible that those rude rhymes, and the simple artless music with which they are accompanied, should not excite some ear to fond perception of the melody of verse. That Burns had felt these impulses will appear undeniably certain to whoever shall carefully peruse his 'Cotter's Saturday Night'; or shall remark with nice observation, the various fragments of *scripture* sentiment, of *scripture* imagery, of *scripture* language, which are scattered throughout his works.[37]

Of course, Heron knew as well as anyone that the bulk of Burns poetry neither sociologically confirmed this view and expressed anything but personal or popular quiescence in the face of the established order. To deal with this what he did was sycophantically flesh out the bones of Mackenzie's account of the dead poet. Apparently more in sorrow than anger, Heron constructed the myth of Burns as betrayer of his own earliest spiritual impulses because he lacked 'that steady VIRTUE , without which even genius in all its omnipotence is soon reduced to paralytic imbecility, or to manic mischievousness'. Thus Burns's life becomes a melodrama where he always surrendered to those elements in himself which inevitably took him into increasingly bad company.

> The *bucks* of Edinburgh accomplished, in regard to BURNS, that in which the *boors* of Ayrshire had failed. After residing some months in Edinburgh, he began to estrange himself . . . from the society of his graver friends. Too many of his hours were now spent at the tables of persons who delighted to urge conviviality to drunkenness, in the tavern, in the brothel, on the lap of the woman of pleasure. He *suffered* himself to be surrounded by a race of miserable beings who were proud to tell that they had been in company with BURNS, and had seen Burns as loose and as foolish as themselves. He was not yet irrecoverably lost to temperance and moderation, but he was already almost too much captivated with their wanton rivals, to be ever more won back to a faithful attachment to *their* more sober charms. He now began to contract something of new arrogance in conversation. Accustomed to be among his favourite associates . . . *the cock of the company*, he could scarcely refrain from indulging in similar freedom and dictatorial decision of talk, even in presence of persons who could less patiently endure his presumption.[38]

Here the suppressed rage of sentimental, genteel Edinburgh wells up. The people's poet had no right to his creative superiority of language. Hence is evolved the fiction of the unstable genius who falls away from his prudent, real friends and into evil company and, by his sinful depravity, betrays not only his better self but the sanctified common people whom he represents. In Burke's great shadow, a Scottish conservatism is forged which converts the dialectic of opposing secular political systems to one which, on the conservative side, has divine sanction as embodying the inherent nature of reality. By definition, opposition to this is implicitly evil. Burns is a sinner (he *suffers* but for the wrong things), with even a hint of anti-Christ. As with Mackenzie's account, the speed of Burns's descent accelerates in Dumfries. He has crosses to bear, admittedly, but they are not properly borne:

In the neighbourhood were other gentlemen occasionally ad-
dicted, like Burns, to convivial excess, who, while they admired
the poet's talents, and were charmed with his licentious wit,
forgot the care of his real interests in the pleasure in which they
found in his company, and in the gratification which the plenty
and festivity of their tables appeared evidently to afford him.
With these gentlemen, while disappointments and disgusts
continued to multiply upon him in his present situation, he
persisted to associate every day more and more eagerly. His
crosses and disappointments drove him every day more into
dissipation, and his dissipation tended to enhance whatever was
disagreeable and by degrees, into the boon companion of mere
excisemen, spend his money lavishly in the ale house, could
easily command the company of BURNS. The care of his farm
was thus neglected, Waste and losses wholly consumed his little
capital.[39]

As with Edinburgh and The Crochallan Fencibles, the political
nature of Burns's affiliations in Dumfries, is not identified. What
Heron is mainly referring to here is that Real Whig bibulous bear of
a man, Robert Riddell. As we now know, Burns was the middle-man
responsible for Riddell's political essays being published under the
pen-name Cato. What, of course, Heron does not narrate is the story
of the collapse of Burns's political hopes under ferocious govern-
mental pressure but a moral fable whereby, in its terminal stage, the
sinner is driven to misanthropic blackness. The peculiar fevered
tearing apart of Burns's body, the agony of night sweats and pain
wracked joints, is seen as both a consequence of his heavy drinking
where, in fact, his rapidly deteriorating health made his tolerance to
alcohol ever less. Or, psychosomatically, his bodily agony is seen as a
punishing consequence of his sins. In actual fact, a convincing case
has been made that medically what was tearing Burns's body apart
in these last terrible months was brucellosis caught from infected
milk, although it is generally thought he died of rheumatic heart
disorder.[40] That alcoholic fornicator Heron, has a quite different
'spiritual' diagnosis:

Nor, amidst these agonising reflections, did he fail to look, with
an indignation half invidious, half contemptuous, on those, who,
with moral habits not more excellent than his, with powers of
intellect far inferior, yet basked in the sunshine of fortune, and
were loaded in the wealth and honours of the world, while *his*
follies could not obtain pardon, nor his wants an honourable

supply. His wit became, from this time, more gloomy sarcastic; and his conversation and writings began to assume something of a tone misanthropical malignity, by which they had not been before, in any eminent degree, distinguished. But, with all these failings; he was still that exalted mind which had raised above the depression of its original condition, with all the energy of *the lion, pawing to set free his hinder limbs from the yet encumbering earth*: he still appeared *not less than an archangel ruined!*[41]

Whether this 'archangel' image is knowingly derived from the genuine addict, S.T. Coleridge, the heroic but defeated lion fits perfectly Heron's sentimentally disguised assassination. Scottish sentimentalists have a penchant for weeping at the gravesides of their victims. Burns's long-term friend, William Nicol, had other thoughts concerning the death of his once rampantly *alive* friend. As he wrote almost immediately after Burns's death to John Lewars:

. . . it gives me great pain to see the encomiums passed upon him, both in the Scottish and English news-papers are mingled with the reproaches of the most indelicate and cruel nature. But stupidity and idiocy delight when a great and immortal genius falls; and they pour forth their invidious reflections, without mercy, well knowing that the dead Lion, from whose presence they formerly scudded away with terror, and at whose voice they trembled through every nerve, can devour no more.

The fanatics have now got it into their heads, that dreadful bursts of penitential sorrow issued from the breast of our friend, before he expired. But if I am not much mistaken in relation to his firmness, he would disdain to have his dying moments disturbed with sacerdotal gloom, like sacerdotal howls. I knew he would negotiate with God alone, concerning his immortal interests.[42]

Without the leonine Bard there to protect his manuscripts, the nature of his precipitous, premature death left his papers in disorder. Given that his death coincided exactly with the peak of the scrutiny, censorship and penal repression of the understandably Francophobic Pitt/Dundas security-state such disorder was heavily amplified by his literary executors, mainly anxiety-driven radicals, hiding, dispersing or, at worst, destroying his dissident writings. Some alleged friends, minor Judases like Robert Ainslie, also wished to retrieve their letters or mangle and censor those of the poet's that they had in their possession.

In his magisterial editorial work of the 1930s, De Lancey Fergu-
son calculated that 25% of Burns's epistolary output was irretrie-
vably lost. The poetry undoubtedly suffered similar depredations.
There was the difficulty of identifying texts pseudonymously and
anonymously published in radical London, Edinburgh and Glasgow
newspapers. It seems certain that a key notebook of late, unpub-
lished poems did go to William Roscoe but vanished without trace in
1816. Further, many of the central political poems (e.g. *Address of
Beelzebub* and the *Ode on General Washington's Birthday*) appeared
erratically and fortuitously in the course of the nineteenth century.
A burning of political and erotic material in the 1850s at Lesma-
hagow by Mr Greenshields (of the stamps fame) may not have been
the last instance of genteel Scotland deciding to save the poet's
reputation from himself.

The two men immediately involved in dealing with the manu-
scripts were the poet's Dumfries friend John Syme who enlisted a
mutual friend, Alexander Cunningham, to help in dealing with the
papers and to make an appeal for funds to aid the truly impoverished
family. In Edinburgh, enthusiasm had 'cooled with the corpse' and
Ayrshire proved equally miserly. For such virulent Scotophobes as
Hazlitt and Coleridge, this treatment of the nation's bard gave
further evidence, if evidence were needed, of the treacherous,
mean-spiritedness of the Scots. As Coleridge wrote in 1796:

> Is thy Burns dead?
> And shall he die unwept, and sink to earth
> 'Without the meed of one melodious tear'?
> Thy Burns, and Nature's own beloved bard,
> Who to the 'Illustrious of his native Land
> So properly did look for patronage'
> Ghost of Macenas! Hide thy blushing face!
> They snatched him from the sickle and the plough—
> To gauge ale-firkins.

To be fair to the committee of executors set up in Dumfries, the
situation was not only complex but carried real danger with it. Also
given the political spirit of the age, much of the material could not be
made public far less profitably so. As Ian Hamilton has written:

> The Dumfries executors' committee had already done some
> preliminary sifting and, fearing piracies, had advertised for any
> Burns material that was in private hands. The mass of the
> papers they found at the poet's house was in 'utter confusion'

but it took no more than a glance to determine that much of the collection ought probably to be destroyed: 'viz. Such as may touch on the most private and delicate matters relative to female individuals'. When, in August, a bonfire was arranged, Syme was more hesitant: 'Avaunt the sacrilege of destroying them and shutting them forever from the light: But on the other hand, can we bring them into the light?' On this occasion, only a few 'unimportant' notes and cards were burnt.[43]

As well as sexually intimate indiscretions, went political ones. Such were safer out of Scotland given that, comparatively, it was a more politically controlled environment than England.

Establishment Scots were even more zealous than their English masters in hunting down treason in a more demographically controlled environment. The radical English connection that Burns most prided himself on, indeed his intention had been to visit him, was William Roscoe of Liverpool. Roscoe, the centre of a vast web of radical connections was poet, historian and financier. His friend was a Scottish doctor and part-time scholar, Dr James Currie. Currie's initial response to receiving the papers is replete with the personal and textual terrible harm of which he was to be both initiator and chief agent:

My dear Syme: Your letter of the 6th January reached me on the 12th, and along with it came the remains of poor Burns. I viewed the large and shapeless mass with astonishment! Instead of finding . . . a selection of his papers, with such annotations as might clear up any obscurities . . . I received the complete sweepings of his drawers and of his desk . . . even to the copy book on which his little boy had been practising writing. No one had given these papers a perusal, or even an inspection . . . the manuscripts of a man of genius . . . were sent, with all their sins on their head, to meet the eye of an entire stranger.[44]

Why Currie, a man of allegedly radical political persuasion quite at odds with Heron's toadying Toryism was, indeed, complicit with Heron's account of Burns will probably remain not fully explicable. The most generous explanation is that Currie, given the spirit of the times, produced a work designed to sell to a conformist, bourgeois public in order to gain as much money as possible for the bereft family. The good doctor, however, went well beyond cosmetic surgery. Himself plagued by alcoholic tendencies, he was working in 1797 on a pseudo scientific paper 'Observations on the Nature of

Fever and on the Effects of Opium, Alcohol and Inanition'. Burns's later letters, replete with confessions of savagely black depressions and not a few severe hangovers were grist to Currie's diagnostic mill. Worse, one addiction led to another:

> His temper now became more irritable and gloomy, he fled from himself into society, often of the lowest kind. And in such company that part of the convivial scene, in which wine increases sensibly and excites benevolence, was hurried over, to reach the succeeding part, over which uncontrolled passion generally presided. He who suffers from pollution of inebriation, how shall he escape other pollution? But let us refrain from the mention of errors over which delicacy and humanity draw the veil.[45]

As Ian Hamilton has remarked: 'This then was the autopsy report: alcoholic poisoning plus maybe a touch of venereal disease had killed off Scotland's greatest poet'. Nor was Currie finished with delivering his patient into the hands of his enemies. Currie enunciated the notion that the poet, of his very nature, was susceptible to addiction. Too sensitive, the poet would always find the world on the margin of the tolerable. Again Burns's letters supplied Currie with significant evidence for this point of view. For example, this brilliant letter of August 1790 on the essential incompatibility of the poet and the world:

> It is often a reverie of mine, when I am disposed to be melancholy, the characters and fates of the Rhyming tribe. There is not among all the Martyrologies that were ever penned, so rueful a narrative as Johnson's Lives of the Poets. In the comparative view of Wretches, the criterion is not what they are doomed to suffer, but how they are formed to bear. Take a being of our kind: give him a stronger imagination and more delicate sensibility, which will ever between them engender a more ungovernable set of Passions, than the usual lot of man: implant in him an irresistible impulse to some idle vagary, such as, arranging wild flowers in fantastical nosegays, tracing the grasshopper (sic) to his haunt by the chirping song, watching the frisks of little minnows in the sunny pool, or haunting after the intrigues of wanton butterflies —in short, send him adrift after some wayward pursuit which shall eternally mislead him from the paths of Lucre; yet curse him with a keener relish than any man living for the pleasures that only

Lucre can bestow; lastly, fill up the measure of his woes, by bestowing on him a spurning sense of his own dignity; and you have created a wight nearly as miserable as a Poet.

Since Currie edited this letter, there is little wonder about from where his principal biographical evidence comes. Further, he had used for his template that most indulgent of defences of the libertine poet, Dr Johnson's *Life of Savage*. Steeped in Burns's confessional letters, it was not difficult for Currie to articulate the poet's frequent despairing self-diagnosis of his own tumultuous mood swings and lack of volition. Certainly from Ellisland onwards, the poet became increasingly prone to depression. As he wrote to Mrs Dunlop in June 1789:

Will you take the effusions, the miserable effusions, of low spirits, just as they flow from their bitter spring? I know not of any particular cause for this worst of all my foes besetting me; but for some time my soul has been beclouded with a thickening atmosphere of evil imaginations and gloomy presages.

All trouble, therefore, is located by Currie within Burns; he is an endogenous depressive rather than a reactive one. Yet, he had so much to react against. Ellisland was the last in an unbroken line of fiscal farm traps. After Edinburgh he felt profoundly deprived of creative company. His body was signalling premature dissolution accelerated by the physical and mental grind of his Excise duties. Also to someone so politically attuned he must have had an overbearing awareness of the darkening political scene as a wheel on which his personal and public hopes were to be brutally broken. Currie, setting the programme for all of nineteenth-century biographers and, indeed, most twentieth-century ones, paid no real attention to these grim external forces. Burns was for Currie destructively committed to his irrational, even fallen, self:

His understanding was equal to the other powers of his mind, and his deliberate opinions were singularly candid and just; but like other men of great and irregular genius, the opinions which he delivered in conversation were often the offspring of temporary feelings, and widely different from the calm decisions of his judgement. This was not merely true respecting the character of others, but in regard to some of the most important points of human speculation.[46]

From this Currie deduced a Burnsian dialectic 'in which virtue and passion had been at perpetual variance'. Fuelled by alcohol, passion had achieved overwhelming, self-destructive victory. Inevitably, intentionally this diagnosis destroys the poetry as much as the poet. Currie creates a situation in which, from now on, any conformist critical hack can and, indeed, did have the prescriptive power to censor any of Burns's poetry not conforming to that respectability which was the first line of defence of conservative political correctness. The political poet becomes a malcontented unstable neurotic, not an incisive diagnostician of manifest ills in the body politic.

There is some evidence, both contextual and textual, that Currie politically knew very well what he was up to. De Quincey had always loathed the Liverpool coterie to which Currie belonged to as a group of narcissistic radicals who were, particularly in the case of Burns, deeply condescending, at best, to the alleged object of their shallow affections. He particularly hated Currie as the physician who was 'unable to heal himself'. His 1801 account of this group is charged with shocked outrage at the gross indifference of these mendacious friends of the people who were deaf to the pain that he, as a Tory, could feel all too clearly:

I had for ever ringing in my ears, during that summer of 1801, those groans that ascended to heaven from his [Burns's] over-burthened heart those harrowing words, 'To give him leave to toil', which record almost as a reproach to the ordinances of God and I felt that upon him, amongst all the children of labour, the primal curse had fallen heaviest and sunk deepest. Feelings such as these I had the courage to express; a personal compliment, or so, I might now and then hear; but all were against me on the *matter*. Dr Currie said 'Poor Burns! Such notions had been his ruin'; Mr Sheperd continued to draw on the subject some scoff or groan at Mr Pitt and the Excise . . . Mr Clarke proposed that I should write a Greek inscription for a cenotaph which he was to erect in his garden to the memory of Burns; and so passed away the solitary protestation on behalf of Burns's jacobinism, together with the wine and the roses, and the sea-breezes of that same Verton, in that same summer of 1801 . . . three men who remain at the most of all who in these convivial meetings held it right to look down upon Burns as one whose spirit was rebellious overmuch against the institutions of man, and jacobinal in a sense which 'men of property' and master manufacturers will never brook, albeit democrats by profession.[47]

With friends like these, Burns's reputation hardly needed the legion of newspaper and magazine owning enemies whose overt Toryism gave them reason to destroy it. How deep Currie's radicalism had ever been is impossible to judge. Better men than he had become apostates to the radical cause.[48] It is hard not to believe that he knew what he was doing as he linked, albeit obliquely, Burns's alleged degeneration with political turpitude. He also had that classic bad doctor's ability to confuse mental or moral symptoms with physical ones:

> As the strength of the body decays, the volition fails; in proportion as the sensations are soothing and gratified, the sensibility increases; and morbid sensibility is the parent of indolence, because, while it impairs the regulating power of the mind, it exaggerates all the obstacles to exertion. Activity, perseverance, and self-command, and the great purposes of utility, patriotism, or of honourable ambition, which had occupied the imagination, die away in fruitless resolutions, or in feeble efforts.[49]

It is little wonder that Coleridge, irretrievably addicted to laudanum, called Currie's book 'a masterly specimen of philosophical biography'. He was so symptomatic of Currie's account that he must have felt as if struck by a cross-bow bolt from the blue. It is, however, most certainly *not* Burns. Further, the allusion to patriotism gives Currie's game away. It is an unequivocal linking of Burns with insurrectionary, hence definably degenerate, forces.

Not content, however, with rendering Burns's personality a suitable case for mistreatment, Currie followed exactly Heron's critical criteria for sifting the acceptable, sentimental chaff from the troublesome, satirical wheat. The literary analysis is an attack on the poetry as effective as the wholly related attacks on the Bard's character. Behind both psychological and aesthetic repudiation lie, of course, the real but unnamed political reasons. Burns's employment of the vernacular was the primary, obvious place of attack:

> The greater part of his earlier poems are written in the dialect of his country, which is obscure, if not unintelligible to Englishmen, and which though adheres more or less to the speech of almost every Scotsman, all the polite and ambitious are now endeavouring to banish from their tongues as well as their writings. The use of it in composition naturally therefore calls up ideas of vulgarity to the mind. These singularities are

increased by the character of the poet, who delights to express himself with a simplicity that approaches to nakedness, and with an unmeasured energy that often alarms delicacy, and sometimes offends taste. Hence in approaching him, the first impression is perhaps repulsive: there is an air of coarseness about him which is with difficulty reconciled with our established notions of poetical excellence.[50]

Along with such fundamental creative castration went covert politically motivated readings of these two satirical masterpieces with which Burns deliberately opened the Kilmarnock edition. That wickedly irreverent dialogue, *The Twa Dogs*, is defined, absurdly, as Burns's plan 'to inculcate a lesson of contentment on the lower classes of society by showing that their superiors are neither much better nor happier than themselves.' The quite extraordinary postscript to *The Author's Earnest Cry and Prayer* with its terrible national images of the Highland soldier slaughtered in the service of an alien Hanoverian cause and 'Mother Scotland' as an incontinent crone, are described as purely humorous. Currie, in fact, set a tactical fashion for conservative criticism of Burns to laugh, damagingly, in the wrong places. Needless to say, one poem floats free of the clarty waters occupied by the bulk of the achievement:

. . . the representation of these humble cottagers forming a wider circle round their hearth and uniting in the worship of God, is a picture most affecting of any which the rural muse has ever presented to the view. Burns was admirably adapted to this delineation. . . . The Cotter's Saturday Night is tender and moral, it is solemn and devotional, and rises at length into a strain of grandeur and sublimity which modern poetry has not surpassed. The noble sentiments of patriotism with which it concludes correspond with the rest of the poem. In no age or country have the pastoral muses breathed such elevated accents, if the 'Messiah' of Pope be excepted, which is indeed a pastoral in form only. It is to be regretted that Burns did not employ his genius on other subjects of the same nature which the manners and customs of Scottish peasantry would have amply supplied.[51]

Praise, indeed, but praise granted at the price of near complete distortion. Currie's misreading of the last two stanzas of the poem apart, this post-Burkean account of a peasant world of piety, humility and hence, hierarchical loyalty is used as the criterion by which the rest of Burns's poetry is not only judged but condemned.

In his 1808 review of Cromek's *Reliques* in *The Edinburgh Review* Jeffrey also expresses inordinate enthusiasm for this, indeed, exceptional poem: 'The exquisite description of *The Cotter's Saturday Night* affords, perhaps, the finest example of this sort of pathetic. Its whole beauty cannot indeed be discerned but by those whom experience has enabled to judge of the admirable fidelity and completeness of the picture.' This review of Jeffrey's is absolutely seminal to an understanding of the image of Burns and his poetry which was to dominate the nineteenth century and, indeed, elements of it still persist into the twenty-first. As well as Jeffrey's legally fine-honed intellect he was from 1802 to 1829 the editor of *The Edinburgh Review*. This magazine having freed itself from reviewing as a mere vehicle for the book trade was not only independent but, in terms of payment to contributors, unprecedently wealthy. Ironically, it was a Whig magazine, which was on political issues almost uniformly reformative. Hence its support of Catholic emancipation and its attacks on the sale of army commissions, flogging in the British Navy and Army and the Test and Corporations Act. So exceptional were its fiscal and intellectual powers that, with the subsequent Tory *Blackwood's*, it unprecedently, if temporarily, moved the locus of British critical intelligence from London to Edinburgh. It was from such a position of unparalleled authority that Jeffrey, with near total success, decided to contain, if necessary by emasculation and vilification, what he perceived to be the threat of the revolutionary impetus of Burns as man and poet. Jeffrey's arguments derived from Currie but even, in some instances, exceeding the latter's account are not to be understood in literary terms without understanding the politics that underlay the aesthetics.[52] Like all men of his class, the French terror had bitten into his soul. Evidence real or invented of a common people diligently, culturally, passively loyal was everywhere sought. Burns had consequently to be fitted to the procrustean bed of their political anxieties and phobias. Hence this account of the degree to which Burns and the Scottish peasantry exceed all others in educated, hence, conformist virtue:

> We shall conclude with two general remarks — the one national, the other critical. The first is, that it is impossible to read the productions of Burns, along with his history, without forming a higher idea of the intelligence, taste, and accomplishments of the peasantry, than most of those in the higher ranks

are disposed to entertain . . . it is evident . . . that the whole family, and many of their associates, who have never emerged from the native obscurity of their condition, possessed talents, and taste, and intelligence, which are little suspected to lurk in those humble retreats. His epistles to brother poets, in the rank of farmers and shopkeepers in the adjoining villages, — the existence of a book-society and debating club among persons of that description, and many other incidental traits in his sketches of his youthful companions, — all contribute to show, that not only good sense, and enlightened morality, but literature and talents for speculation, are far more generally diffused in society than is generally imagined; and that the delights and the benefits of these generous and humanizing pursuits, are by no means confined to those whom leisure and affluence have courted to their enjoyment. That much of this is peculiar to Scotland, and may be properly referred to our excellent institutions for parochial education, and to the natural sobriety and prudence of our nation, may certainly be allowed . . . It is pleasing to know, that the sources of rational enjoyment are so widely disseminated; and, in a free country, it is comfortable to think, that so great a proportion of the people is able to appreciate the advantages of its condition, and fit to be relied on in all emergencies where steadiness and intelligence is required.[53]

As analysis, this is, of course, an inversion of the cultural and political truth. The common readers of the Scottish late eighteenth century, especially key groups like the weavers, were more likely to be reading Tom Paine than anything else. Also, given that Burns's 'carnivalesque' poetry is the quintessence of dissidence against the prevailing church and state, it is not easy to see how it can be squared with the pacific vision of the lower orders. What Jeffrey did was to use his enormous authority to impose a crude binary division on Burns's poetry so that we have the 'good' acceptable poet as opposed to the 'bad' rejected one. Among other things this involved him in reinventing the Scottish vernacular tradition with that 'bletherin' bitch's' unique capacity for reductive, derisory satire, acute psychological insight, and often bitter realism, transformed into a mode suitable for historical and psychological regressive nostalgia. The Kailyard begins here:

We beg leave too, in passing, to observe, that this Scotch is not to be considered as a provincial dialect, the vehicle only of rustic vulgarity and rude local humour. It is the language of a whole country, — long an independent kingdom, and still separate in laws, character and manners. It is by no means peculiar to the vulgar; but is the common speech of the whole nation in early life, — and with many of its most exalted and accomplished individuals throughout their whole existence; and, if it be true that, in later times, it has been, in some measure, laid aside by the more ambitious and aspiring of the present generation, it is still recollected, even by them, as the familiar language of their childhood, and of those who were the earliest objects of their love and veneration. It is connected, in their imagination, not only with the olden times which is uniformly conceived as more pure, lofty and simple than the present, but also with all the soft and bright colours of re-membered childhood and domestic affection. All its phrases conjure up images of childhood innocence and sports, and friendships which have no pattern in succeeding years. Add to all this, that it is the language of a great body of poetry, with which almost all Scotchmen are familiar; and, in particular, of a great multitude of songs, written with more tenderness, nature and feeling, than any other lyric compositions that are extant, and we may perhaps be allowed to say, that the Scotch is, in reality, a highly poetical language; and that it is an ignorant, as well as an illiberal prejudice, which would seek to confound it with the barbarous dialects of Yorkshire or Devon.[54]

Opposed to this, was the dissident Burns who had, as man and poet, to be condemned to outer darkness as quickly as possible. While Currie could grant Burns's satirical poetry some virtue, Jeffrey could conceive of nothing in it but the malign manifestations of the poet's personality:

The first is, the undisciplined harshness and acrimony of his invective. The great boast of polished life is the delicacy, and even the generosity of its hostility, —that quality which is still the characteristic as it is that denomination of a gentleman, — that principle which forbids us to attack the defenceless, to strike the fallen, or malign the slain, —and enjoins us, in forging the shafts of satire, to increase the polish exactly as we add to their keenness or their weight . . . His ingenious and amiable biographer has spoken repeatedly in praise of his talents for satire, —we think, with a most unhappy partiality. His epigrams and lampoons appear to us, one and all, unworthy of him; —offensive from their extreme coarseness and violence, —and contemptible from their want of wit or brilliancy. They seem to have been written, not out of playful malice or virtuous indignation, but out of fierce and ungovernable anger. His whole raillery consists in railing; and his satirical vein displays itself chiefly in calling names and in swearing.[55]

In fact Jeffrey's criticism of Burns is overwhelmingly *ad hominem*. The poet is seen as the great transgressor in terms of his multiple morbid and impolite discontents. He is a threat, not least a sexual threat ('his complimentary effusions to ladies of the higher rank, is forever straining them to the bosom of her impetuous votary') to the desired, indeed, necessary order of things. Burns, in fact, is corrupted by the Romantic, revolutionary spirit of the age with its absolute moral dispensation for the self-anointed man of genius:

But the leading vice in Burns's character, and the cardinal deformity of all his productions, was his contempt or affectation of contempt for prudence, decency and regularity; and his admiration of thoughtlessness, oddity and vehement sensibility; his belief, in short, in the dispensing power of genius and social feeling, in all matters of morality and common sense. This is the very slang of the worst German plays, and the lowest of our out of town-made novels; nor can anything be more lamentable, than that it should have found a patron in such a man as Burns, and communicated to a great part of his productions a character of immortality, at once contemptible and hateful.[56]

Granted the applicability of contempt and hate for his poetry, Jeffrey returns to the fallible, fallacious nature of a man who, having forgotten the ordinary duties of life, loses himself in various forms of self-absorbed licentiousness:

It requires no habit of deep thinking, nor anything more, indeed, than the information of an honest heart, to perceive that it is cruel and base to spend in vain superfluities, that money which belongs of right to the pale industrious tradesman and his famishing infants; or that it is a vile prostitution of language, to talk of that man's generosity or goodness of heart, who sits raving about friendship and philanthropy in a tavern, while his wife's heart is breaking at her cheerless fireside, and his children pining in solitary poverty.[57]

This, of course, is derived from the language of *The Anti-Jacobin* of the previous decade with its insistent connection of exaggerated moral fallibility, especially sexual, with political anarchy. (*The Anti-Jacobin* of 1797 looked forward to an emergent generation of loyalist Tory poets to emulate and surpass the 'bards of Freedom' of the 1790s, with their 'wood-notes wild'. This latter description was, of course, on Burns's waxen seal.) Character assassination was and, indeed, is an essential establishment weapon. Jeffrey's intemperate indulgence in it gave open season to varied lesser talents as that for the first two decades of the nineteenth century memoir writers and biographers of Burns outdid each other in denigrating him. Such personal denigration always carried within it the connection between his varied irresponsible, dissolute behaviour and his revolutionary politics. Here again, Jeffrey provides the model:

> This pitiful cant of careless feeling and eccentric genius, accordingly, has never found much favour in the eyes of English sense and morality. The most signal effect which it ever produced, was on the muddy brains of some German youth, who left college in a body to rob on the highway, because Schiller had represented the captain of a gang as so very noble a creature. But in this country, we believe, a predilection for that honourable profession must have proceeded this admiration of the character. The style we have been speaking of, accordingly, is now the heroics only of the hulks and the house of correction; and has no chance, we suppose, of being greatly admired, except in the farewell speech of a young gentleman preparing for Botany Bay.[58]

This brutal allusion to the horrendous events of 1793–4 which manifested the criminal breakdown of the Scottish legal system with Braxfield as front-man for the Dundas clan demonstrates the depths of vindictive fear in Jeffrey's heart for radicalism. Hence Burns himself is to be spared nothing:

> It is humiliating to think how deeply Burns has fallen into this debasing error. He is perpetually making a parade of his thoughtlessness, inflammability and imprudence, and talking with much complacency and exultation of the offence he has occasioned to the sober and correct part of mankind. The odious slang infects almost all his prose, and a very great proportion of his poetry; and is, we are persuaded, the chief if not only the source of the disgust with which, in spite of his

genius, we know that he is regarded by many very competent and liberal judges.[59]

Jeffrey then, condescendingly, lets Burns wriggle, if not escape from, the hook on which he has impaled him:

> His apology, too, we are willing to believe, is to be found in the original lowness of his situation, and the slightness of his acquaintance with the world. With his talents and powers of observation, he could not have seen much of the beings who echoed this raving, without feeling for them that distrust and contempt which would have made him blush to think he had ever stretched over them the protecting shield of genius.[60]

The alleged naïvety inherent in inferior social status has forever haunted Burns criticism and commentary. Jeffrey's attempt to detach Burns from radical, Romantic connections was as successful as it was erroneous. Wordsworth's *Lyrical Ballads* and *The Edinburgh Review* appeared simultaneously and it was Jeffrey's intention, from the magazine's inception, to do as much harm to Wordsworth's poetic reputation as possible because he saw inherent in it a perverse democratic tendency which really was a manifestation of culturally and politically regressive tendencies. In Jeffrey there is, in fact, contempt and fear of the lower classes as not only threatening political disruption but of dragging civilised achievement backwards. Jeffrey feared that the adult condition which he believed his society had attained might be lost in the childish state inherent in socially inferior persons. One of his most repeated protests against the Romantics, Wordsworth in particular, was that their poetic diction was both an expression of and invitation to such regression. Infantilism was its essential mode of speech and society was thereby threatened. Wordsworth, linguistically, offended the law of literary progress:

> But what we do maintain is, that much of the most popular poetry in the world owes its celebrity chiefly to the beauty of its diction; and no poetry can be long or generally acceptable, the language of which is coarse, inelegant, or infantine.
> . . . the new poets are just as great borrowers as the old; only that, instead of borrowing from the more popular passages of their illustrious predecessors, they have preferred furnishing themselves from vulgar ballads and plebian nurseries.[61]

Given this principle, it was absolutely necessary for Jeffrey to detach Burns from any possibility of his poetry being infected by Wordsworth. It was not really his Europhobic attitude to Schiller's *The Robbers* but his attitude to Wordsworth in whom he discerned the dangerous source of aesthetic, psychological and political contagion. Thus he wrote:

> . . . the followers and patrons of that new school of poetry, against which we have thought it our duty to neglect no opportunity of testifying. Those gentlemen are outrageous for simplicity; and we beg leave to recommend to them the simplicity of Burns. He has copied the spoken language of passion and affection, with infinitely more fidelity than they have ever done . . . but he has not rejected the help of elevated language and habitual associations, nor debased his composition by an affectation of babyish interjections, and all the puling expletives of an old nursery maid's vocabulary. They may look long enough among his nervous and manly lines, before they find . . . any stuff about dancing daffodils and sister Emmelines . . . with what infinite contempt the powerful mind of Burns would have perused the story of Alice Fell and her duffle coat . . . Let them contrast their own fantastical personages of hysterical schoolmasters and sententious leech-gatherers, with the authentic rustics of Burns's 'The Cotter's Saturday Night', and his inimitable songs . . . Though they will not be reclaimed from their puny affectations by the example of their learned predecessors, they may, perhaps, submit to be admonished by a self-taught and illiterate poet, who drew from Nature far more directly than they can do, and produced something so much like the admired copies of the masters whom they have abjured.[62]

Not the least of the consequences of Jeffrey's obsessive fear and contempt and what he, initially and derogatorily, named as the Lake School, was a blindness, which this edition supplementing recent modern scholarship seeks to rectify, about the actual relationship of Wordsworth to Burns. As Wordsworth wrote in *At the Grave of Burns,* 1803: *Seven Years After His Death*:

> I mourned with thousands, but as one
> More deeply grieved, for He was gone
> Whose light I hailed when first it shone,
>   And showed my youth
> How Verse may build a princely throne
>   On humble truth.

What enraged Jeffrey was not simply the belief that the aesthetically highest art should engage with the socially lowest class, it was the radical political commitment behind that poetry. Aesthetically, linguistically to deny any possible connection between the English Wordsworth and the Scottish Burns was to deny a radical Scottish political poetry. In the 1790s Burns (especially in the Kilmarnock Edition) and Wordsworth were creatively preoccupied with precisely the same economic and political issues. Hence Wordsworth's retrospective account of *Guilt And Sorrow, or Incidents Upon Salisbury Plain*, is not only, as we shall see, related to Burns's *A Winter's Night*, but could be read as a summary of the Scottish poet's political sympathies and preoccupations at exactly the same period:

> During the latter part of the summer of 1793, having passed a month in the Isle of Wight, in view of the fleet which was then preparing for sea off Portsmouth at the commencement of the war, I left the place with melancholy forebodings. The American war was still fresh in memory. The struggle which was beginning, and which many thought would be brought to a speedy close by the irresistible arms of Great Britain being added to those of the Allies, I was assured in my own mind would be of a long continuance, and productive of distress and misery beyond all possible calculation. This conviction was pressed upon me by having been a witness during a long residence in revolutionary France, of the spirit which prevailed in that country. After leaving the Isle of Wight, I spent two days in wandering on foot over Salisbury Plain . . .
>
> The monuments and traces of antiquity, scattered in abundance over that region, led me unavoidably to compare what we know or guess of those remote times with certain aspects of modern society, and with calamities, principally those consequent upon war, to which, more than other classes of men, the poor are subject.[63]

Jeffrey's example opened the floodgates to a tide of abuse, denigration, innuendo which constantly made the connection between licentious character flaws and radical politics. In a gallantly unsuccessful attempt to stop this, an Edinburgh lawyer, Alexander Peterkin, brought out in 1815 *A Review of the Life of Robert Burns, and of Various Criticisms of his Character and Writings*. As well as mounting a lucid empirical case for the defence, he enlisted Gilbert Burns, James Gray of the Edinburgh High School, Alexander Findlater of the Excise and George Thomson, song publisher, to testify to Burns's actual practices as family man and gauger. In a controlled rage against what he considered a simian caricature of the poet, derived from 'the drivelling fanaticism' of right-wing politics, Peterkin wrote:

> We hold the adversaries of Burns to be aggressors; misguided, we are inclined to think, and ready, we trust, in charity, to renounce their errors on satisfactory proof, that they have been misinformed, or have misconstrued the conduct and writing of Burns. But by their public and voluntary assertions and reflections of an injurious tendency, they have, successively, thrown down the gauntlet to every Scotchman who takes an interest in the honour of his country, of its literature, and of human nature . . . from the system of reitered critical preaching, which has become fashionable in all the recent publications about Burns . . . remaining uncontradicted and unexposed, we are afraid that future biographers, might be misled by longer silence, and adopt declamatory ravings as genuine admitted facts. The most celebrated literary journal of which Britain can boast, and of which, as Scotchmen, we are proud, began the cry; all the would-be moralists in newspapers, magazines, and reviews, have taken it up, and have repeated unauthenticated stories as grave truths: at length these have found a resting-place in large and lasting volumes.[64]

Given the quantity and quality of the vilification of Burns as documented in Peterkin (not least Walter Scott's anonymous, execrable account in *The Quarterly Review*), Burns might have vanished from view perhaps beyond resurrection. What his critics also offered him, moreover, was celebrity on their terms. The bibulous, gustatory junketings which became ritualised in the Burns Supper began in the first decade of the nineteenth century with Jeffrey presiding. Burns was thus both for a period simultaneously radical scapegoat and sentimental national icon. To misquote Edwin Muir, he was the real Bard of a false nation. As the political anxieties calmed, the sentimental Burns of corrupt national imagining could occupy centre stage. He was a multi-purpose deity. The amnesia purging of Burns's radical politics, meant the nation could forget the actual events of the 1790s when not only Burns, but a generation of enlightened Scottish writers, political idealists and academics were driven into internal psychological exile or exile in England, France, Australia and America.

The subsequent Victorian Burns cult was bizarrely multicausal.[65] The anglophobic Professor John Wilson (Christopher North) harangued a crowd of 40,000 at the opening of the Burns mausoleum. The body was exhumed three times in the nineteenth century partly to seek phrenological confirmation of his genius. As with 'Ossian' MacPherson and John Home, Burns was seen as a titanic national poet fit to face down Shakespeare. This compensatory cultural account, partly derived from Scotland's lack of real political power, quite missed the point that Burns had much more of a creative relationship with Wordsworth, Blake, Shelley and the still disgraced Byron, quite absent from his relationship to his bourgeois Scottish apostles. Carlyle, that anti-democratic antithesis of everything the reforming humanism of the Enlightenment stood for, discovered in Burns a Scottish peasant who, like himself, had made good. Indeed, forgetting the bitter marginalised reality of Burns's premature death, Scotland saw in him the archetype of the 'lad o' pairts', the man whose sheer talent brings him to the top. Also, a society locked into the squalid suffering and mortality of the horrors of urban industrialization read Burns as a pseudo-pastoral antidote to everyday reality. As Richard J. Finlay has cogently put it:

The important point to emphasise here is that . . . for most of the nineteenth century his work was used to give credence to *laissez-faire* liberalism. Burnsian notions of freedom and liberty and the dignity of mankind were ideally suited to Scottish middle-class self-perception and the erection of statues in his honour throughout the country reinforced the belief that talent was God-given and not the preserve of noble birth. The achievement of Burns's rise from lowly birth was something that all Scots could aspire to emulate . . . Burns could be used to promote notions that the dignity of hard work, the perseverance of toil and calm stoicism in the face of adversity were values that were intrinsic to Scottish society.

Burns was praised for inculcating family values. According to Rosebery, Burns 'dwells repeatedly on the primary sacredness of the home and the family, the responsibility of fatherhood and marriage'. The vision of family life in 'The Cotter's Saturday Night' was an antidote to the widespread unease about moral degeneracy in the sprawling slums of urban Scotland. He was likewise praised for making respectable the old Scottish songs which contained language that was crude and vulgar and unfit for genteel company. Burns transformed the baseness of Scottish society into something sublime.[66]

Or as Lord Rosebery put it in his conception of an entirely apolitical poet:

> *A Man's A Man for A' That* is not politics — it is the assertion of the rights of humanity in a sense far wider than politics. It erects all mankind; it is the character of self-respect . . . it cannot be narrowed into politics. Burns's politics are indeed nothing but the occasional overflow of his human sympathy into past history and current events.

Hollow rhetorical misrepresentation disguised as eulogy, Rosebery's straw man cum icon is hoisted free of the contextual political events and ideals that helped forge the democratic anthem. Distortion and abuse of the dead artist's memory is the theme of Patrick Kavanagh's marvellous poem *A Wreath for Tom Moore's Statue*, dealing with the small minded betrayals and corruptions of Irish society to its artists. It catches better than anything what was done to Burns during the nineteenth century:

> They put a wreath upon the dead
> For the dead will wear the cap of any racket,
> The corpse will not put his elbows through his jacket
> Or contradict the words some liar has said.
> The corpse can be fitted out to deceive—
> Fake thoughts, fake love, fake ideal,
> And rogues can sell its guaranteed appeal,
> Guaranteed to work and never come alive.
> The poet would not stay poetical
> And his humility was far from being pliable,
> Voluptuary tomorrow, today ascetical,
> His morning gentleness was the evening's rage.
> But here we give you death, the old reliable
> Whose white blood cannot blot the respectable page.[67]

As well as the particularly Scottish virulent, conformist forces controlling the response to both Burns's reputation and writings, Burns was also a victim, as most eighteenth-century writers of substance, of a pronounced shift of the boundary of sexual acceptability in nineteenth-century Anglo-American culture. *Gulliver's Travels* is expurgated and on such as Smollett and Sterne the library key is firmly turned. Writing about Mozart, in several respects Burns's kindred spirit, Saul Bellow noted that:

The nineteenth century gave us an interregnum of puritanism.
I have often thought that 'repression' and 'inhibition' as de-
scribed by Freud refer to a temporary shift of 'moral' emphasis.
Students of English literature are familiar with this move from
the open sensuality of Fielding and Laurence Sterne to Victor-
ian prudery ('propriety') in Dickens or Trollope. Rousseau's
Confessions or Diderot's *Les Bijoux Indiscrets* confirm this . . .
Seventy years ago, my Russian immigrant uncles, aunts, and
cousins were still speaking freely and colourfully about bodily
functions and things sexual —'country matters', as Shakespeare
called them in *Hamlet*. (Such lewd double entendres are com-
mon in his plays, specialists in Tudor and Stuart literature have
collected them.) Bawdry has a long pedigree. Conversation in
the courts of Elizabeth and James I was not what we came later
to call 'respectable'.[68]

Of course, Eros may have been driven underground in the Victorian
world. He could not be obliterated. Prostitution and pornography
flourished and Burns himself became a set text for the elbow-
nudging male smoking room.

It is, however, this sort of respectability that, in part, conditions
Matthew Arnold's influential view of Burns. Despite his virtuous
courage in opposing the crass, material philistine Victorian world,
Arnold's ethnic prescriptions for literature were not happy ones.
Having designated, indeed invented, Celtic literature as fey and
ethereal, he saw in Burns's Scottish writing, the very opposite of
this, as often nauseatingly tangible. Thus he wrote in November,
1879:

> I have been reading Chaucer a great deal, the early French
> poets a great deal, and Burns a great deal. Burns is a beast with
> splendid gleams, and the medium in which he lived, Scotch
> peasants, Scotch Presbyterianism, and Scotch drink, is repul-
> sive. Chaucer on the other hand pleases me more and more, and
> his medium is infinitely superior.[69]

This epistolary remark, he fleshed out in *The Study of Poetry*:

> We English turn naturally, in Burns, to the poems in our own
> language, because we can read them easily; but in real poems we
> have not the real Burns.
>   The real Burns is of course in his Scotch poems. Let us say
> that much of his poetry, a poetry dealing perpetually with

Scotch drink, Scotch religion, and Scotch manners, a Scotch-
man's estimate is apt to be personal. A Scotchman is used to
this world of Scotch drink, Scotch religion, and Scotch man-
ners; he has a tenderness for it; he meets its poet half way. In
this tender mood he reads pieces like the 'Holy Fair' or
'Halloween'. But this world of Scotch drink, Scotch religion,
and Scotch manners is against a poet and not for him, when it is
not a partial countryman who reads him; for in itself it is not a
beautiful world, and no one can deny that it is of advantage to a
poet to deal with a beautiful world. Burns's world of Scotch
drink, Scotch religion, and Scotch manners, is often a harsh,
a sordid, a repulsive world; even the world of his 'The Cotter's
Saturday Night' is not a beautiful world. No doubt a poet's
criticism of life may have such truth or power that it triumphs
over its world and delights us.[70]

In one respect Arnold simply represents the consequences of the
insistent Scottish claims for exclusive possession of Burns. Arnold,
with a vengeance, locates him in a brutally circumscribed ethnic
world. In another respect, Arnold is quite wildly wrong. He assumes
Burns as a naïve realist, almost a poetic pig in clover in a Scottish
sty, whereas Burns was a political satirist of the very elements,
especially Hebraic spiritual and material hypocrisy, which Arnold
himself attacks. Worse, he disconnects Burns, partly linguistically,
from the radical *British* fraternity of the 1790s to which he belongs.
Burns's accent and examples are Scottish; his themes and insights
are comparable to Blake. Despite Edward Dowden's *The French
Revolution and English Literature* (1897) which reintegrates Burns
with his English peers, Arnold's authority caused damage so severe
that elements of it still exist. It may indeed have influenced the even
more authoritative figure of T.S. Eliot, that provincial American
who so yearned for Arnoldian metropolitan status, so that he saw in
Burns the last flare-up of a subsequently redundant Scottish tradi-
tion, rather than a poet who used that tradition to write some of the
greatest radical poetry of the late eighteenth century. Given of
course, Eliot's monarchical, High Anglican tendencies, it was not
in his interest to see in the Scottish literary tradition such virile,
dissident flexibility.[71]

By the latter part of the nineteenth century and with the em-
bryonic stirring of Modernism, the roots of the later self-defined
Scottish Renaissance Movement, a crucial problem for Scottish
creative writers was whether Burns could be exhumed as a creative
force from under the growing mountains of verbiage, false history

and commercial artefacts. The initial movement in this direction
came from R.L. Stevenson with his acutely attuned antennae both
to contemporary world literature and to the Scottish tradition.
Along with that went a peculiar, even psychic, identification with
Robert Fergusson and associated fellow-feeling with Burns. He also
grasped the degree to which Burns was indebted to Fergusson.
Hence his haunted, near death retrospective of Edinburgh's 'three
Robins':

> Burns alone has been just to his promise: follow Burns, he knew
> best, he knew whence he drew fire — from the poor, white-
> faced, drunken, vicious boy that raved himself to death in the
> Edinburgh madhouse. Surely there is more to be gleaned about
> Fergusson, and surely it is high time the task was set about . . .
> We are three Robins who have touched the Scots lyre this last
> century. Well the one is the world's, he did it, he came off, he is
> for ever: but I and the other — ah! What bonds we have — born
> in the same city: both sickly, both pestered one nearly to
> madness, one to the madhouse with a damnatory creed . . .
> and the old Robin, who was before Burns and the flood, died in
> his acute, painful youth and left the models of the great things
> that were to come . . . you will never know, nor will any man,
> how deep this feeling is; I believe Fergusson lives in me.[72]

Despite the genuine intensity of this feeling, Stevenson felt the task
of resurrection of Fergusson and Burns beyond him. The Calvinist
and genteel claustrophobia of Edinburgh which he believed had
destroyed his namesake was something, with Joycean acumen, from
which he fled into ever geographically further exile. Before doing so,
however, he diagnosed in his earliest journalistic writings the
remarkably over-inflated literary culture that infected Victorian
Scotland in general and Burns's false reputation in particular.
Rather than Arnold's vision of the Scots retreating north of the
Tweed, clutching to their bosoms their shibboleth poet, Stevenson,
with much more literary sociological realism, saw the Scots as
enormously successful commercial exporters and exploiters of a
pseudo-national literary tradition. While the more mature Steven-
son would not have adhered to these disparaging remarks about
Burns's vernacular poetry, his sense of national literary narcissism
did not abate:

> It is somewhat too much the fashion to pat Scotch literature on
> the back. Inhabitants of South Britain are pleased to commend

verses, which, short of a miraculous gift of tongues, it is morally impossible they should comprehend. It may interest these persons to learn that Burns wrote a most difficult and crude patois . . . there are not so very many people alive in Scotland who could read his works without a furtive reference to the margin . . . any Englishman need not be ashamed to confess he can make nothing out of the vernacular poems except a raucous gibberish — which is the honest belief of the present reviewer, is about the measure of his achievement. It is partly to this that we must attribute the exaggerated favour of 'The Cotter's Saturday Night', by no means one of his best poems, but one of the most easily understood . . .

But even the least intelligent condescension of the South Briton is better than the hysterical praise with which Mr Grant Wilson bedaubs his native literature . . . Wilson thinks that Burns spoke 'with too much extravagance' when he called *The Gentle Shepherd* 'the most glorious poem ever written'. . . this barbarous gallimaufry or hotch-potch of indiscriminate lauda-tion does not come fairly to the boil, until we hear that Falconer's 'Shipwreck' placed its author 'in the front rank of Scottish poets' . . . Was there ever such an irreverent hurly-burly of names, such a profane morris-dance of great men and little poetasters? Whaur's Wullie Shakespeare noo?[73]

At the end of this assault on the unfortunate James Grant Wilson, we also find this remark on Burns:

A point of curiosity is the rest of Burns's *Ode* about *Washington*, some lines of which appear already in his Correspondence. It is a very poor performance, but interesting as another testimony to the profound sympathy of Burns for all democratic move-ments. Why does Mr. Wilson tell us no more about the history of the piece.[74]

Or, indeed, why did Stevenson, given his brilliantly innovative essay on Walt Whitman in *Familiar Studies of Men and Books*, not himself write about the democratic Burns. Partly perhaps because when talking about Scottish subjects he was infected by a sort of internalized Calvinism so that the empathy he could extend to Villon and Baudelaire (he was preoccupied with both these anarchic French spirits) could not be replicated for Burns who, like Hazlitt, he declared a sexually out-of-bounds bounder.[75]

A second wave was to follow Stevenson in the wake of the First

World War. The British imperial economic and political project was damaged beyond repair, as correctly interpreted by the tiny Scottish avant garde, and it was felt that Scotland needed to be reconnected to its roots. Obstacles to this were the travesty of Celticism present in the sentimental tartanisation of the nation. 'Out of the Celtic twilight', as MacDiarmid wrote, 'and into the Gaelic sun'. Another cultural, political phenomenon as destructive to what the avant garde considered vital to a resurrected Scotland was the Burns phenomenon now incorporated into The Burns Federation. Between the avant garde and the established Burnsians there was no co-operation and, indeed, relations were soon to turn to active hostility. Catherine Carswell's honest, passionate biography of Burns was met with a bullet sent through the post to her. Written from her Lawrentian influenced position of a reintegrative instinctual and erotic vision, such open discussion of the poet's sexual nature was unacceptable. By far the greatest of all Burns's scholars the American John De Lancey Ferguson, as his correspondence with Mrs Carswell shows, was met not with open hostility but a marked lack of co-operation from the Federation regarding his magisterial edition of the poet's letters. His subsequent biography, the fine *The Pride and the Passion*, was met with, as he ruefully put it, 'passionate apathy'. Presbyterian Tory-Unionism would not release its death grip on a poet to whom, unlike Sir Walter Scott, it had absolutely no claim. Edwin Muir, while not personally empathetic to Burns as a poet, concisely summed up what he perceived as an end-game for Burns and Scotland. The occasion for Muir's observations was the unveiling of a new statue to Burns with that bastion of 'socialism', Ramsay McDonald, making the oration:

> The symbolism implicit in this scene is quite casual and involuntary. The churchyard could hold only a certain number of people; the 'platform party' (in Scotland one is always hitting against platform parties) was naturally chosen from the more well-to-do admirers of the poet: landlords, baronets, and officers in the British army. Objectively one can see that, Scotland being what it is, a ceremony in honour of its greatest poet should just take this form and no other. But at the same time one is driven to ask what can have happened to Burns since his death to make him now the implicit property of the middle and upper classes, when he was the property of the poor man at the beginning. This change may be briefly described by saying that Holy Willie, after being the poet's butt, has now become the keeper of his memory . . .

Burns set the world in a roar of laughing at the people who now unveil statuary in his honour. Why is it that they are so kind to his kail and potatoes?

One reason for this is that the figure of Burns has become quite vague, and that the vaguer he becomes the more universally he pleases his countrymen. His words no longer mean anything.[76]

Muir then turns to an exemplary example of this vagueness by dealing with MacDonald's eulogy to Burns. At this time Scottish society was in a state of political unrest, although somewhat different from the 1790s. There existed, however, a similar pattern of economic breakdown, profiteering and war weariness though the revolutionary cloud on the horizon was Russia, not France. Muir quotes MacDonald's maunderings on Burns as revolutionary whereby 'Burns's revolution, was a revolution in soul, a revolution in being, a revolution in manliness, a revolution in humanity'. That is, of course, a revolution whereby everything except economic power and social justice are effectively changed. With his customary lucidity, Muir pointed out how the events of the darkening 1930s cast their shadow on the then contemporary interpretations of the 1790s:

I think I have said enough to show that Burns has been ostentatiously but securely swallowed and digested by Holy Willie during the century and a bit since his death. Burns was not the revolutionist who Mr. MacDonald makes him out to be, but he was an honest writer. And though he was a revolutionist, he showed his sympathy with the French Revolution in a quite practical way, without stopping to consider whether it was a mere revolution in circumstance or a revolution in soul. We cannot imagine the Burns whose statue Mr. MacDonald unveiled sending arms even to the constitutional government of Spain against the expressed wishes of the established order, as the living Burns did to the leaders of the French revolution against a similar prohibition. Something has happened to him since his death, and it is what happens to all writers after their death, no matter what they have written. It may not be true that all writers reflect the economic ideology of the society in which they live — I do not think it is — but it does seem to be true that their writings are finally and in the long run made to reflect that ideology, by a process of elimination and transformation, until the most influential classes in society can finally put their seal

on the result. This necessity for social elimination and trans-
formation probably accounts for Mr. MacDonald's sharply
condemnatory but vague references to Burns's recent biogra-
phers (he could only have meant Mrs. Catherine Carswell's
plain-spoken and entirely sympathetic *Life*). For an honest
biography helps to destroy the imposed image and to undo
careful work of social transformation.[77]

Muir, of course, was not to know that in 1993, Tony Blair, then
Shadow Home Secretary, toasted the 'Immortal Memory' in the
Edinburgh Central constituency (we are reliably informed by a still
enraged Old Labour source) without mentioning Burns at all.

One would have anticipated that Hugh MacDiarmid, bourgeois
Scotland's worst nightmare, with his celebration of John Maclean,
Lenin and his intended book on Red Clydeside would have been
prolix on the parallels between the 1790s and 1930s. With his early
involvement in the Independent Labour Party (I.L.P.), he was,
overtly and expansively, a far more politically committed writer
than Muir. Even so, he rarely mentions Scottish culture's constant,
mendacious denial of Burns as a democratic revolutionary. He was,
however, constantly caustic about the literary implications of the
Burns cult and how it had diverted attention not only from Burns's
poetry but poetry *per se* into a morass of biographical, antiquarian
trivia. As he wrote:

> Those who love poetry best today, and understand best its
> nature and function, have least to say of Burns as poet. To the
> quest for increased facilities of human self-expression —to the
> evolution of the art of poetry— Burns contributes nothing. It is
> almost exclusively in non-literary circles, amongst people who
> seldom read poetry of any kind, that Burns is still enthusias-
> tically acclaimed as a great poet. . . . Burns the satirist is
> another matter. And the Burns of the verses that are not to
> be found in the expurgated editions —those little lewd revela-
> tions which enable us to discern in him (sed longe intervallo) a
> forerunner of James Joyce.[78]

Burns, for MacDiarmid, had a Janus-face. He saw him, by analogy
with Joyce, as a proto-modernist capable of literary innovation and
the changing of human consciousness. But he also saw him as a
redundant poet not entirely irresponsible for the sterile cult created
in his name. As MacDiarmid grew older, culminating in his dreadful
polemic, *Burns Today and Tomorrow* (1958), the latter view pre-

vailed. Initially, however, he thought that he could not only co-opt Burns but the Burns Federation into his programme for his version of radical, revolutionary change. Hence the sestet of this appalling sonnet *To Duncan McNaught, LLD., J.P., President of the Burns Federation*, written in 1923:

> Burns International! The mighty cry
> Prophetic of eventual brotherhood
> Rings still, imperative to be fulfilled.
> M'Naught, who follows you must surely try
> To take his stand, where living, Burns had stood
> Nor save on this foundation can he build.[79]

This grimly bad version of third-rate post-Miltonic Wordsworth was addressed to Dr McNaught who had distinguished himself by declaring that, 'After Burns became a Government official he was a shorn Samson whose duty was to be "silent and obey"; and his daily realisation of his dependant position dampened his energies and restrained the free action of his powers'. This was not propitious and led MacDiarmid to remark that, 'The same type of mind that quite unjustly vilified Burns is now most busily engaged in quite unnecessarily white-washing him'. By 1934, however, he had lost hope of the Burns Federation as a revolutionary agent for change, and indeed increasingly saw it as the antithesis of everything Burns stood for and what Scotland had been and should become:

> What an organization the World Federation of Burns Clubs could have been — could even yet become — if it were animated with the true spirit of Burns and fulfilling a programme based on his essential motives applied to crucial contemporary issues as he applied them while he was living to the crucial issues of his own time and generation! What a true Scottish Internationale that would be —what a culmination and crown of Scotland's role in history, the role that has carried Scotsmen to every country in the world and given them radical leadership every-where they went![80]

What obsessed MacDiarmid was not simply the need to galvanise his retarded nation but to put it at the very vanguard of what he perceived as a quantum, science-driven evolution in human con-sciousness. What he was faced with was an actual situation where the global network of Burns Clubs provided locations for the transmission, not of innovative consciousness, but of the worst aspects of sentimental banality. Within Scotland, things were even worse:

> It is an organisation designed to prevent any further renaissance of the Scottish spirit such as he himself encompassed, and in his name it treats all who would attempt to renew his spirit and carry on his work on the magnificent basis he provided as he himself was treated in his own day — with obloquy and financial hardship and all the dastardly wiles of suave Anglicized time servers . . .
>
> It has produced mountains of rubbish about him — to effectively bury the dynamic spirit — but not a single good critical study . . .
>
> It has failed . . . to get Burns or Scottish literature or the Scottish language to which Burns courageously and rightly and triumphantly reverted from English, taught in Scottish schools.
>
> Its gross betrayal of the Scots language — its role as a lying agent of the Anglicizing process Burns repudiated — was well seen in its failure to support the great new Scots dictionaries.
>
> . . . the need to follow his lead at long last is today a thousand times greater than when he gave it.
>
> We can — if we will . . . We can still affirm the fearless radical spirit of the true Scotland. We can even yet throw off the yoke of all the canting humbug in our midst. We can rise and quit ourselves like men and make Scotland worthy to have had a Burns — and conscious of it; and we can communicate that consciousness powerfully to the ends of the earth.
>
> . . . if we don't, if we won't, the Burns cult will remain a monstrous monument to the triumph of his enemies.[81]

What appears about this time in MacDiarmid's poetry is the image of Burns as a latter day Christ crucified by his cultish followers. This is best known from *A Drunk Man Looks at the Thistle*. Less well known is this disturbing English sonnet, *They Know Not What They Do*:

> Burns in Elysium once every year
> Ceases from intercourse and turns aside
> Shorn for a day of all his rightful pride,
> Wounded by those whom yet he holds most dear.
> Chaucer he leaves, and Marlowe, and Shakespeare,
> Milton and Wordsworth —and he turns to hide
> His privy shame that will not be denied,

And pay his annual penalty of fear.
But Christ comes to him there and takes his arm.
'My followers too,' He says, 'are false as thine,
True to themselves and ignorant of Me,
Grieve not thy fame seems so compact of harm;
Star of the Sot, Staff of the Philistine
—Truth goes from Calvary to Calvary!'[82]

MacDiarmid saw Burns as an incomplete revolutionary when compared to Byron, Baudelaire and (by implication) MacDiarmid himself:

He was intimidated in the most insidious fashion by the existing order of things . . . The pity about Burns is that he never got beyond good and evil. If he had been able to kick the traces over completely his potential genius might have been liberated —as was Gaugin's for instance, when he ceased to be a stockbroker and reverted to savagery. Burns went in the opposite direction —from genius to 'gauger'.[83]

This concept of an early Modernist, definably post-Nietzschean Burns, MacDiarmid may have derived from a little known poem by Swinburne (a poet he admired), *Burns: An Ode* (1896):

And Calvin, night's prophetic bird,
Out of his home in hell was heard
Shrieking; and all the fens were stirred
    Whence plague is bred;
Can God endure the scoffer's word?
    But God was dead.[84]

Not only does the poem personify Burns within terms of late nineteenth-century atheism and, perhaps expectedly, finds him inferior to Chaucer, but also, quite unexpectedly, it sees him as inferior to Dunbar:

But Chaucer's daisy shines a star
Above his ploughshare's reach to mar,
And mightier vision gave Dunbar
    More strenuous wing
To hear around all sins that are
    Hell dance and sing.

Ironically, MacDiarmid's slogan 'Not Burns, but Dunbar' may have been derived from an English source. What is certain, however, is that it was not Burns but Byron whom he saw as the quintessence of Scottish literary and associated virtues:

> Byron will come to his own yet in his own country, however. Scotland is shedding its super-imposed and unnatural religiosity. Unlike English literature Scottish literature remains amoral — full of illimitable potentialities, unexplored, let alone unexhausted, in the Spenglerian sense. And Byron was beyond all else a Scottish poet — the most nationally typical of Scottish poets, not excluding Burns. He answers — not to the stock conceptions, the grotesque Anglo-Scottish Kailyard travesty, of Scottish psychology — but to all the realities of our dark, difficult, unequal and inconsistent national temper.[85]

Implicit in MacDiarmid's concept of Byron as the essential Scottish writer, is the notion that he is also definably the pure, uncompromised revolutionary spirit. This is hardly borne out by either history or biography. Was the mine-owning self-dramatising aristocrat ever under the cosh in the way Burns was? Is individual nihilism of the Byron, Baudelaire variety the necessary prelude to utopian change? MacDiarmid seems not to have read Dostoevsky deeply enough to have understood that Russian's genius in tracing the demonically possessed connection between such nihilism and social catastrophe. In fact, MacDiarmid, as hierarchically preoccupied as Ezra Pound, was, at best, antipathetic to the universal democratic revolution of the late eighteenth century.[86] His revolution was predicated on a quantum leap in human consciousness to be made by a scientifically attuned, necessarily tiny *avant garde*. Iain Crichton Smith thought that this position destroyed him as a poet, committing his later poetry to versified, programmatic propaganda for his science-manual saturated version of beyond the human.[87] That is why he loathed Burns's *A Man's A Man*, seeing in it not a profound statement of fraternity but only crassly self-indulgent sentimentality. According to MacDiarmid, the real Scottish tradition, manifest in Byron, would return Scots to their hard, pristine selves, purged of the cloying psychological excesses and political corruptions of an imposed, Anglicised identity.

The failure to claim Byron for Scottish literature — the deference paid to English standards of taste in that and other 'Scottish' anthologies — is a characteristic of the Anglicisation

of Scotland. All the natural perspectives of Scottish literature
are arbitrarily manipulated in the light of entirely false inter-
pretations of Scottish character. The type of people who are
constrained to whitewash Burns are naturally anxious to dis-
avow Byron — whom it would be impossible to 'puritanise' . . .
He stands outwith the English literary tradition altogether. He
is alien to it and not to be assimilated. English literature . . . has
developed moral limitations — a quality of censorship which
renders it impossible to naturalise certain attitudes of life,
certain tendencies in expression . . .[88]

MacDiarmid's capacity for intellectual absolutism, albeit frequently
self-contradictory, has the ideological danger inherent in literary
criticism of thesis-driven misreading. There is no little irony in the
fact that it is an Englishman, W.H. Auden, who made a much more
convincing distinction between Burns and Byron and, in so doing,
makes one of the most acute critical remarks about the essence of
Burns's genius:

> At the beginning of the Romantic age stand two writers of
> Light Verse who were also major poets, Burns and Byron, one a
> peasant the other an aristocrat. The former came from a
> Scottish parish which, whatever its faults of hypocrisy and
> petty religious tyranny, was a genuine community where the
> popular tradition in poetry had never been lost. In consequence
> Burns was able to write directly and easily about all aspects of
> life, the most serious as well as the most trivial. He is the last
> poet of whom this can be said. Byron, on the other hand, is the
> first writer of Light Verse in the modern sense. His success lasts
> as long as he takes nothing very serious; the moment he tried to
> be profound and 'poetic' he fails. However much they tried to
> reject each other, he was a member of 'Society', and his poetry
> is the result of his membership. If he cannot be poetic, it is
> because smart society is not poetic.[89]

MacDiarmid's nationalist essentialism offers a heady, narcissistic
appeal. If, however, history should be written about relationships
between states not about mythically essential nations, literary his-
tory has constantly to concern itself with the inherent, ongoing
dialogue between literatures. This is why Burns and the 1790s have
been so misunderstood. Jeffrey wanted all relationships between
Burns and the English Romantics, especially Wordsworth, termi-
nated because the Scots were naturally loyal. MacDiarmid inverts

the terms of the equation, the Scots are innate radicals and the English inherent constitutionalists, but he too achieves the same end in divorcing Scottish and English writing. This, particularly, in the 1790s is nonsense. Albeit in differently accented voices, Blake and Burns are deeply compatible, just as Cowper and Burns are. That savagely funny, neglected English satirist and friend of James Perry of *The Morning Chronicle*, Professor Richard Porson, produced polemics in a Scots-styled stanza that could, to the untrained eye, be easily mistaken for Burns. Wordsworth in particular, but almost all English radical writers of that decade, knew exactly what politics were inherent in Burns's poetry. Indeed they were influenced by his example as man and poet. Equally, Burns along with the innate strengths of his native vernacular and the profound influence of Fergusson in particular, creatively plundered Shakespeare, Milton, the Tory Augustans, the Eighteenth-century Novel, and his sentimental English and Irish (Goldsmith) contemporaries to create a unique synthesis. As Thomas Preston has notably remarked in viewing Burns through the highly rewarding perspective of Bakhtin:

> Burns's poetry offers a gold mine of contestation among Scottish, English, classic, European, and non-European matters —
> a wondrous intertextuality of quotations, traditions, dictions, idioms, dialects, languages, meanings. His texts do not produce, I suggest, the agonistic of conflicted tongues heard by Thomas Crawford nor the Smollettian dialect of synthesized literary traditions sought by Carol McGuirk. Instead they orchestrate a polyphony of voices contesting languages, literary traditions, and cultures. Burns's poetic project is dialogical through and through, internally within and between poems and externally within and between Scottish and other cultures. It scripts a future Scottish national culture that is inherently diverse — an imagined community whose lack of uniformity would appal Tobias Smollett, whose last and dying years, despite his anglicizing in aid of a sublated British culture, nevertheless were spent, perhaps fittingly, outside of Britain. Kenneth Simpson has written the most persuasively, I think, of Burns's varying roles and poses, a poetic strategy he considers a reflection of the protean eighteenth-century Scot undergoing the dissociation of sensibility caused by the Union. Burns, he thinks, 'became trapped behind the roles he so readily created'. I would suggest instead that these roles register the rich profusion of personal and cultural possibilities, opportunities,

and identities made available to both individuals and Scottish society by the dialogic — indeed postmodern — world Burns's poetic project scripts. This paper serves merely to suggest the many possibilities for exploration that Burns's dialogism offers. Alan Bold misleadingly argues that Burns 'looked back in ecstasy and did not take the future of Scotland into account'. It can be argued that dominant Scottish discourse since the Union has instead looked back in ecstasy while enacting the literati's rather than Burns's implied national script, and this possibility may cause some subconscious guilt that the 'great tartan monster' and the annual Burns Supper orgies seek to absolve. If this is so, tartanry and toasts to the 'Immortal Memory' yet also serve to keep alive the possibility of attending to Burns's script.[90]

Preston's essay is a deeply perceptive and provocative argument in favour of Burns creating a sort of healthily open, dialogically en- ergised Scottish literature which was in opposition to the integration of Scottish writing into the standardised language, envisaged by such as the Irishman Thomas Sheridan and advocated by Edmund Burke and James Boswell, of the Anglo-British empire. Burns knew and loathed the power and accent of the Scots who served that imperium: 'Thou Eunuch of language — Thou Englishman who was never south of the Tweed — Thou servile echo of fashionable barbarisms'. Henry Dundas would be the prime example of that category though he, according to a jealous Boswell, had hardly the capacity to put pen to paper. Preston's account requires only the modification that the relationship with English literature in the 1790s was not only dia- logical but collusive in that these writers were seeking a republican reorientation of the British state through the resurrected democratic nationalism of its English, Scottish, Irish parts. The failure of this ambition is, as we shall see, tragically embodied in *Ode for General Washington's Birthday*. Though, as Preston notes, two hundred years later we seem to be entering similar territory. It is the primary impulse behind this edition, then, to make Burns available to a contemporary Scottish consciousness that is hopefully more openly responsive to the man, his values and, above all, his poetry than has largely been the case over the last two centuries.

NOTES

1 See John Strawhorn, 'Farming in 18th-century Ayrshire', in *Collections of the Ayrshire Archeological and Natural History Society*, 2nd Series, III (1955), pp. 136–73.

2 See J. De Lancey Ferguson *The Pride and the Passion* (New York: Oxford University Press, 1939), p. 114.

3 See John Brewer, *The Sinews of Power: War, Money and the English State 1688–1783* (London: Routledge, 1989), pp. 101–14.

4 Roy Porter, *The Pelican Social History of Britain: English Society in the Eighteenth Century* (London: Penguin, 1982), p. 30.

5 Robert Morrison, 'Red De Quincey', *The Wordsworth Circle*, Vol. 28, 1998, pp. 131–6.

6 Donald Low, *Robert Burns: The Critical Heritage* (London: Routledge, 1974), pp. 421–30.

7 *Ibid.*, p. 429.

8 James Mackay, *RB: A Biography of Robert Burns* (Edinburgh Mainstream, 1992), p. 519.

9 David Cannadine, 'The Making of the British Upper Class' in *Aspects of Aristocracy* (London: Penguin, 1994), pp. 9–36.

10 John Keane, *Tom Paine: A Political Life* (London: Bloomsbury, 1995), p. 54.

11 See Stephen C. Behrendt, *Romanticism, Radicalism and the Press* (University of Nebraska, 1997), p. 14.

12 Fintan O'Toole, *A Traitor's Kiss: The Life of Richard Brinsley Sheridan* (London: Granta, 1997), pp. 31–2.

13 J.R. Dinwiddy, 'Conceptions of Revolution in the English Radicalism of the 1790s' in *Radicalism and Reform in Britain, 1780–1850*, ed. H.T. Dickinson, (London: The Hambledon Press, 1992,) p. 169.

14 John Trenchard and Thomas Gordon, 'Cato's Letters' in *The English Libertarian Heritage*, ed. David L. Jacobson (San Francisco: Fox & Wilkes, 1994), p. 42.

15 *Ibid.* pp. 53–4.

16 *Ibid.* p. 63.

17 Michael Durey, *Transatlantic Radicals and the Early American Republic* (University of Kansas, 1997), pp. 50–79. *The Life and Letters of Alexander Wilson*, ed. Clark Hunter (Philadelphia, American Philosophical Society, 1983).

18 John Thelwall, *The Politics of English Jacobinism*, ed. Gregory Claeys (Pennsylvania State U.P., 1995), p. 40.

19 See Francis Hutcheson, *Short Introduction*, 5th edn (Philadelphia, 1799), pp. 289–92.

20 Richard Rorty, 'Afterword: Pragmatism, Pluralism and Postmodernism' in *Philosophy and Social Hope* (London: Penguin, 1999), p. 265.

21 Cynthia Ozick, 'From the *Book of Job*', (New York: Vintage Spiritual Classics, 1998), pp. xx–xxi.

22 *Love and Liberty*, ed. K.G. Simpson (Edinburgh: Tuckwell Press, 1997), p. 179.

23 Edwin Muir, 'Robert Burns' in *Edwin Muir: Uncollected Scottish Criticism*, ed. Andrew Noble (London/New York, 1982), p. 183.

24 Roger Fechner, 'Burns and American Liberty' in *Love and Liberty*, p. 278.

25 E.W. McFarlane, *Ireland and Scotland in the Age of Revolution* (Edinburgh University Press, 1994), p. 136.

26 *The Critical Heritage*, p. 16.

27 Henry Mackenzie, 'Three Scottish Poets' in *The Anecdotes and Egotisms of Henry Mackenzie*, ed. H.W. Thompson (Oxford University Press, 1927), pp. 150–2.

28 *Literature and Literati: The Literary Correspondence and Notebooks of Henry Mackenzie*, Vol. 2, 'Letters 1766–1827', ed. Horst W. Drescher, (Frankfurt, 1989), p. 358.

29 *Ibid.*, p. 358.

30 *Ibid.*, p. 172.

31 *Ibid.*, p. 74.

32 *Ibid.*, p. 175.

33 *Ibid.*, p. 178.

34 T.M. Devine, *The Scottish Nation 1700–2000* (London: The Penguin Press, 1999), p. 215.

35 Edinburgh University Library, Laing Collection, II, folio 269. Two other Heron letters in folio 500–501.

36 Robert Heron, *A Memoir of the Life of the Late Robert Burns* (Edinburgh, 1797). Reprinted in Hans Hecht, *Robert Burns: The Man and His Work* (London: William Hodge & Co., 1936), pp. 335–6.

37 *Ibid.*, p. 326.

38 *Ibid.*, pp. 338–9.

39 *Ibid.*, pp. 344–5.

40 Ian Hamilton, 'The Frailties of Robert Burns' in *Keepers of the Flame: Literary Estates and the Rise of Biography* (Boston/London: Faber & Faber, 1992), p. 101.

41 *A Memoir of the Life of Robert Burns*, p. 346.

42 Edinburgh University Library, Laing Collection, III, folio 586.

43 'The Frailties of Robert Burns', p. 93.

44 Quoted in R.D. Thornton, *James Currie: The Entire Stranger & Robert Burns* (Edinburgh: Oliver & Boyd, 1963), p. 358.

45 'The Frailties of Robert Burns', p. 98.

46 'The Frailties of Robert Burns', p. 101.

47 Low, *The Critical Heritage*, p. 431.

48 In 1793, Currie had written a Francophile, abrasively anti-Pitt pamphlet under the pseudonym, 'Jasper Wilson'. In consequence he considered American exile and lived in terror of disclosure. See Chapter 9, 'Dissenter' in Thornton's *The Entire Stranger*.

49 'The Frailties of Robert Burns', p. 97.

50 Low, *The Critical Heritage*, p. 152.

51 *Ibid.*, p. 144.

52 Andrew Noble, 'Versions of Scottish Pastoral' in *Order in Space and Society: Architectural Form and Its Context in the Scottish Englightenment*, ed. Thomas Marcus (Edinburgh: Mainstream, 1982), pp. 288–91.

53 Low, *Critical Heritage*, p. 194.

54 *Ibid.*, pp. 186–7.

55 *Ibid.*, p. 181.

56 *Ibid.*, p. 182.

57 *Ibid.*, p. 183.

58 *Ibid.*, p. 183.

59 *Ibid.*, pp. 183–4.

60 *Ibid.*, p. 181.

61 *Ibid.*, p. 180.

62 *Ibid.*, p. 195.

63 While this, revealingly, was not published till 1842 it was written between 1793 and 1794. This is the Advertisement to *Guilt and Sorrow or Incidents Upon Salisbury Plain. Poetical Works of Wordsworth* (Oxford University Press, 1956), pp. 18–19.

64 *The life and Works of Robert Burns*, as originally ed. by James Currie, to which is prefixed a review of its life of Burns and of various criticisms of his character and writings (Edinburgh: Macredie, Skelly and Muckersy, 1815), p. vii.

65 Andrew Noble, 'Burns and Scottish Nationalism', in *Burns Now* (Edinburgh: Canongate Academic, 1994), pp. 167–92.

66 'The Burns Cult and Scottish Identity in the Nineteenth and Twentieth Centuries' in *Love and Liberty*, p. 72.

67 *Patrick Kavanagh: Selected Poems* (London: Penguin, 1996) pp. 70–1. While Moore was not of Burns's militant spirit we are now also realising the degree to which his songs are coded expressions of the bloodier Irish political turmoil of the 1790s and arguably, an embryonic assertion of new national forces. See Matthew Campbell 'Thomas Moore's Wild Song: The 1821 Irish Melodies'. *Bullán*, Vol. v. No. 2, pp. 83–104.

68 Saul Bellow, 'Mozart: An Overture' in *It All Adds Up* (London, Secker and Warburg, 1994), pp. 9–10.

69 Matthew Arnold, Letter of November 1879, quoted in *Selected Poems and Prose*, ed. Miriam Allott (London: Everyman, 1991), p. 295.

70 *Ibid.*, 262–3.

71 T.S. Eliot, 'Was there a Scottish Literature?', *The Athenaeum*, No. 4657, 1st Aug. 1919, pp. 680–1.

72 Letter 2315, *The Letters of Robert Louis Stevenson*, Vol. 7, ed. Booth and Mehew (Yale University Press, 1995). p. 110.

73 R.L. Stevenson 'Review of *The Poets and Poetry of Scotland*', ed. James Grant Wilson, *The Academy*, 12 Feb., 1876, p. 30.

74 *Ibid.*, p. 31.

75 For Stevenson's profound ambivalence to Burns see Letter 635, Vol. 1, *The Letters of Robert Louis Stevenson*. In the same volume (Letter 424) there is a project for not only a book about Ramsay, Fergusson and Burns, but a book that would use Villon as context. He never really synthesised his Scottish roots with his Francophilia.

76 Edwin Muir, 'Burns and Holy Willie' in *Edwin Muir: Uncollected Scottish Criticism* (London/New York: Vision, 1982), pp. 189–90.

77 *Ibid.*, pp. 191–2.

78 'Burns and Baudelaire' in *Hugh MacDiarmid: The Raucle Tongue*, ed. Calder, Murray, Riach (Manchester: Carcanet, 1996), p. 69.

79 *The Complete Poems of Hugh MacDiarmid*, Vol. 2, ed. Grieve and Aitken (London: Penguin, 1985), p. 1224.

80 'The Burns Cult', in *Hugh MacDiarmid: Selected Prose*, ed. Riach (Manchester: Carcanet, 1992), p. 82.

81 *Ibid.*, p. 84. MacDiarmid's most sustained polemic against the Burns Federation and Cult can be found in *Burns Today and Tomorrow* (Edinburgh: Castle Wynd Printers Ltd, 1959).

82 *The Complete Poems of Hugh MacDiarmid*, Vol. 1, pp. 693–4. This can be

compared to the much more in your face 'Your Immortal Memory, Burns!',
pp. 77–9.
83 'Burns and Baudelaire', pp. 70–1.
84 'Robert Burns' in *A Channel Passage, and Other Poems* (London, 1904).
85 'The Neglect of Byron' in *The Raucle Tongue*, Vol. 1, p. 77.
86 Some qualification for this is to be found in *Burns Today and Tomorrow*
where MacDiarmid does address the politics of the 1790s and compares the
French and Russian Revolutions, pp. 105–10.
87 Iain Crichton Smith, 'The Golden Lyric' in *Towards the Human* (Edin-
burgh: Macdonald, 1986), pp. 176–91.
88 'The Neglect of Byron', p. 76.
89 W.H. Auden, 'Light Verse' in *The English Auden: Poems, Essays and
Dramatic Writings 1927–1939* (London: Faber & Faber, 1977), p. 367.
90 'Contrary Scriptings: Implied National Narratives in Burns and Smol-
lett' in *Love and Liberty*, p. 213.

Editorial Policy and Practice

As we have seen in our Introduction, nineteenth-century editors were seriously remiss, with varied degrees of ignorance and prejudice, in providing a proper context for the poems and the politically fractious culture out of which they emerged. One could simply not expect any knowledgeable enthusiasm for a revolutionary, democratic Burns given the victory of the British Old Regime during the ideological war of the 1790s, so complete was it that it virtually wiped the radical struggle from national memory. Towards the end of the century, the Henley–Henderson edition of 1896 brought Burns editorship to a nadir by combining Henley's rampant right-wing jingoism with a deliberate policy of 'correcting' the poet's spelling, punctuation and stresses according to modern standards. Burns's distinctive habit of spelling place and proper names in capitals, italicising idioms and ironies and his use of long dashes are virtually all purged from their edition. This constant, careless editorial meddling seriously disrupts the intelligible rhythm of the poems by an accelerated 'streamlining' of the reading process so that the poet's voice is significantly diminished.

In the twentieth century we had the heroic scholarship of the American, Professor J. De Lancey Ferguson, with his edition of the letters. This, as his correspondence with Catherine Carswell shows,[1] was achieved with, at best, the non-cooperation of the then Scottish Burns establishment. Despite his great scholarly virtues, De Lancey Ferguson was not sufficiently equipped in either the political history of ideas or comparative Romantic scholarship to provide the letters and their recipients with the literary and political context needed to bring Burns into fuller focus, although he did begin down this road with his last essay, the largely unknown but brilliant critique on previous editorship, *They Censored Burns*.[2] Sadly, Oxford's expensive re-edition of the letters in 1985 arguably achieved its most significant addition by appending Professor G. Ross Roy's name as editor.

The three-volume Oxford edition of *Burns: Songs and Poems* (1968) by James Kinsley, is by far the most important edition of the poems. He lists a formal number of 605 poems and songs within the canon. However, several works are counted by him under a number with sub-categories, 100A, 100B, and so on. This means he accepts 621 poems, songs and fragments to the canon. This is increased further by the poems within Kinsley's *Dubia* section – those works he could not properly date in terms of composition. Hence, the overall Kinsley total is around 630, with a few marked as 'probably' authentic.

There is, however, among his extensive, indeed, apparently exhaustive quarrying of Burns's poetry for the poet's quite enormous range of allusion to English, Scottish, Folk and, not least, Biblical sources, a degree of exhibitonist erudition. One really doubts that even so much a poet's poet as Burns (the very reverse of the limited ploughman) had access to such esoteric texts. Given that qualification, this new edition is everywhere marked by Kinsley's scholarly presence. As with Carol McGuirk's excellent *Robert Burns: Selected Poems* (Penguin, 1993), we have everywhere tried to acknowledge our specific debts. While Kinsley is almost Olympian in erudition, the same cannot be said of his degree of detachment. Though less obviously so, his edition carries many of the omissions and prejudices of nineteenth-century scholars. Kinsley, essentially, was a conservative eighteenth-century scholar with neither patience for nor understanding of Romantic radical poetics. It may be that such wilful obscuritanism in Kinsley is part of a much larger pattern prevailing in British literary criticism. David Norbrook, in a recent study of seventeenth-century English poetry[3] argues that there is an in-built, repressive prejudice in our national literary criticism to prefer a royalist over a republican poetics. He comments that the memory of republican poetry had been 'kept at bay by a *cordon sanitaire* of defensive ridicule'. The parallel between the bloody crucible of the mid-seventeenth century and the political tumult of the 1790s should be obvious from our introduction with relevance to Burns and Scotland and what was subsequently done to him.

In his Warton lecture to the British Academy on 23 January 1974, Kinsley summarised what he had learned from his work on Burns. Thus he wrote:

Indeed, the deep spring of his finest poetry was not literary at all – not even the vernacular tradition – but what he called his 'social disposition'; a heart 'completely tinder and . . . eternally lighted up by some Goddess or other' and a 'strong appetite for sociability' . . . This appetite led him often into 'scenes of swaggering riot and roaring dissipation' . . . It also gave him

the chance and capacity to see the rustic society about him with
the sympathy and critical clarity of a Breughel; to write some of
the most natural and generous verse letters in the language; and
give to the world some of its best songs.[4]

The implications of his bizarre conclusions are not those to induce
confidence in his editorial vision or practices, coming from an editor
whose perhaps over-laden commentary annotates the extraordinary
degree of Burns's allusiveness to other poetry. From the evidence of
his poetry and letters he is about as unliterary as James Joyce.
Indeed, from further remarks, it would seem Kinsley's intention
was to keep Burns's poetry marginalised on the rural farm, isolated
from his English contemporaries and de-politicised.

Dr James Mackay's 1993 edition, endorsed by the Burns Federa-
tion, parasitically plunders Kinsley's volume 3 annotations (often
presenting them as his own, without acknowledgement) and, to
make matters worse, reproduces the worst Burns text available, that
of the corrupted Henley–Henderson edition. Mackay enlarges the
Burns canon to around 650 works, without explanation. He does not
number each poem, so the increase is not noticeable. He includes
works *omitted* by Kinsley and *excludes* work Kinsley accepted. In the
appendix he asserts that Kinsley 'attempted to define the canon for
all time, listing 632 poems and songs which were incontrovertibly
the work of Burns'. He then states that all of the poems in Kinsley's
Dubia section are shown *not to be* from Burns, although most of these
are printed by Mackay as genuine. The net effect is to leave the
Burns canon confused.

The essential purpose of this edition, therefore, has been to
update Burns, by recontextualising him into the 1790s where he
was a central creative Scottish figure. As our commentaries try to
show, he was also a central figure in British radical consciousness
and widely admired in that circle. His poetry and rhetoric is only
properly understood as an inspired Scottish variant amid the crea-
tive language of that period for he shared the sense that generation
had of being in a sort of historical cyclotron where, accelerating to
breaking point, their initial Utopian hopes were eventually reduced
to 'dark despair' by the tyranny and fear inspired by Pitt's govern-
ment. In a recent article 'Beware of Reverence: Writing and Ra-
dicalism in the 1790s', Paul O'Flinn refers to the:

. . . extraordinary explosion of radical writing from the early
1790s, a period probably unmatched in British history for its
intellectual daring and its moral courage. The conventional and

surely correct explanation for this phenomenon is that it re-
presents the cultural articulation of a unique conjuncture in
Western history, the years that saw the American Revolution of
1776, the French Revolution of 1789 and, in Britain, the
onslaught of the Industrial Revolution.[5]

The real 'onslaught' was more the British elite's hysterical reaction
to the effects of the French Revolution. This was a war between
democratic reformist forces and conservatism which the latter over-
whelmingly won. The effect was to pervert the development of the
Industrial Revolution, displace and effectively destroy the Scottish
Enlightenment, silence and crush the voice of dissent, for at least a
generation.

This was largely achieved through the tyrannical spy network
overseen in Scotland by Robert Dundas and in London by Henry
Dundas and key Home Office personnel, including a Mr John
Spottiswood, a London based Scottish lawyer. Spottiswood dis-
pensed the Secret Service funds from London to John Pringle,
Sheriff Depute of Edinburgh on a regular basis from December
1792 onwards. A bill for £1000 was paid on 8 February, 1793 and
during the first quarter of the year £975 had been spent on secrect
service 'spying' activities. Out of this total the poet's apparent *loyal*
patron, Robert Graham of Fintry, as we commented in the Intro-
duction, was paid £26.6s.0d.[6] Burns's fear of persecution at the
close of 1792 is no isolated case. The cases of Tytler and Muir are
already mentioned, but less known is the case of Professor Richard-
son of Glasgow University, who had a personal letter intercepted by
the government. He wrote, 'I tread on dangerous ground. Many
things may be said which cannot be written . . . there is not a literary
man in Glasgow with whom I can speak freely on the topic of the
times'[7] Even the poet's friend William Dunbar, the 'Colonel' of the
Crochallan Fencibles, was suspected of being a radical Jacobin. In a
letter to a friend, Alexander Brodie, Dunbar pleaded for his job and
pledged his allegiance to the crown, constitution and personal
loyalty to the Lord Advocate, Robert Dundas.[8] We have tried to
integrate as much as possible of this political material into our poetic
commentary.

Thus, the structure of this edition, rather than chronological,
represents not simply the sequence in which Burns's poetry came
into the public domain, but, initially, the way he chose creatively to
reveal himself in the work published in his lifetime under his own
name. Hence, the Kilmarnock is followed by the two Edinburgh
editions. The first Edinburgh edition added 15 new poems and 8

new songs to the canon. The 1793 edition added several more, including *Tam o'Shanter* which, given that William Creech had purchased the poet's copyright, earned Burns merely a few 'presentation copies' of his own works. The 1793 edition was re-printed in 1794 without addition.

Our next section, the songs published in the poet's lifetime, mostly in James Johnson's *Scots Musical Museum*, include many Jacobite songs that were printed anonymously. For the benefit of the reader, we have included many of the tunes to the better known songs. The importance of Scottish traditional music, particularly fiddle-based slow airs, to Burns's lyrics, cannot be overestimated, given his extraordinary debt to musicians and music collectors of the period. However, Burns's debt to traditional song is also extensive as our notes reveal and it is in this section, particularly songs merely improved by Burns, where the genre of traditional song and the Burns canon tend to blur and overlap. Like a grand mural tapestry, traditional Scottish folk song from the eighteenth century was effectively rewoven by Burns with a mixture of his own and older lyrics.

We then move to the Anonymous and Pseudonymous section, where, like almost all the radical writers of that darkening decade, he had deliberately to disguise his identity. We hope we have shown, with painstaking archival research and detailed textual analyses, the way in which poems, especially those recovered from *The Edinburgh Gazetteer*, stylistically, linguistically and thematically match his other known ones. Ten of the poems printed here derive from Patrick Scott Hogg's *Robert Burns: The Lost Poems* (1997). Despite the over-heated, largely media-driven debate on the appearance of that book, it has stood up extremely well to proper academic scrutiny. Only two of Scott Hogg's discoveries have been found to be certainly not by Burns. These poems we now know came from the pen of the extraordinary Dr Alexander Geddes, a radical Roman Catholic priest (Burns knew and adored his uncle, John Geddes, Roman Catholic Bishop of Dunkeld). Geddes is at the top of the list of radical Scots to be retrieved from the abyss of the 1790s into which they vanished from the national memory. Geddes was a polymath. He was at the cutting edge of the new German inspired Higher Biblical Criticism. He was an intimate of Coleridge and, arguably, an influence on Blake's Biblical views. He was co-editor of the radical house-journal of the period, *The Analytical Review*. He not only went to France but read a celebratory ode written in Latin to the National Assembly.

The two Geddes poems identified by our then colleague at

the University of Strathclyde, Gerald Carruthers, are *Exhortatory Ode to the Prince of Wales on Entering his 34th Year* and *Ode for the Birthday of C.J. Fox*. The Burns/Geddes connection will be dealt with in detail with regard to particular, relevant poems in the following commentary. What should be stressed is that the retrieval of Geddes will be an enormously strong element in supporting this edition's argument for a pervasive literary and radical Scottish political culture at the end of the eighteenth century.

Scott Hogg's initial case and that of this edition has also been enormously strengthened by the discovery of Professor Lucyle Werkmeister's magisterial work on the radical press in the 1790s and, in particular, her two articles on the politically necessary complex but extensive relations between Burns and the London press. Why her work was ignored is problematic. Certainly it stems in part from a sort of Scottish psychological and political conservatism that has led to Burns being detached from his radical peers. We have tried in our poetic commentary to renew these connections with Burns and the English Romantics. He is not understandable without an awareness of advanced Romantic scholarship as is recently discoverable in such books as E.P. Thompson's *The Romantics: England in Revolutionary Age* (London: Merlin Press, 1998) or Kenneth Johnston's *The Hidden Wordsworth* (London: Norton, 1998).

In the Posthumous section, virtually half of this volume, we have tried to pinpoint the incalculable degree to which, after his death, Burns's work was hidden away, destroyed or even burned. The fact that such an enormous number of poems, many of the highest quality and importance, only surfaced after his death and that destruction of texts carried on for such a long period of time, is overwhelming proof of the enormous censorship he had, in life and death, to endure. For example the page torn from volume three of the *Interleaved Scots Musical Museum* with the song title *The Lucubrations of Henry Dundass, May* 1792, probably revealed Burns's satirical treatment of Dundas's clumsy and authoritarian action to cripple Borough reform, which resulted in street riots in Edinburgh and burning effigies of Dundas being paraded around the city. That such censorship has carried over into the twenty-first century is clear from a recent discovery of a private collection of transcripts to Burns's letters to Robert Ainslie which remain unpublished.

The final section *The Merry Muses of Caledonia* presents those bawdy songs known to have been written or improved by Burns, which, for so long, were the private amusement of smoking-room 'gentlemen' who sought to protect the general public from this earthy trait of the vital Burns. The volume closes with an appendix of as-yet undetermined and rejected works.

Andrew Noble

Patrick Scott Hogg

NOTES

1 Catherine Carswell, Letters, Mitchell Library, Glasgow, MS 53.

2 Prof. J. De Lancey Ferguson, 'They Censored Burns', in *Scotland's Magazine*, Vol. 51, January 1955, pp. 29–30.

3 David Norbrook, *Writing The English Republic: Poetry, Rhetoric and Politics 1627–1660*, Cambridge, 1999.

4 James Kinsley, Warton Lecture to the British Academy, 23 January 1974, printed by the British Academy, 1985.

5 Paul O'Flinn, in *Writing and Radicalism*, ed. Lucas (London: Longman), 1996, pp. 84–101.

6 See Laing MS. 500, ff.404–5. Additional letters Fintry to Robert Dundas, exist in Laing II, 500/f.734, f.747, f.751, ff.753–7, f.1076, f.1084.

7 RH 2/4/65f.84–5.

8 Laing II, 500, f.544.

PART ONE

The Kilmarnock Edition
1786

APRIL 14th, 1786
PROPOSALS,
FOR PUBLISHING BY SUBSCRIPTION,

SCOTCH POEMS,

BY ROBERT BURNS.

The work to be elegantly Printed in One
Volume, Octavo, Price, stitched *Three*
Shillings.

As the Author has not the most distant
Mercenary view in Publishing, as soon as so
many Subscribers appear as will defray the
necessary Expense, the Work will be sent to
the Press.

'Set out the brunt side o' your shin,
For pride in *Poets* is nae sin;
Glory's the Prize for which *they* rin,
And *Fame's* their jo;
And wha blaws best the Horn shall win:
And wharefare no?'

RAMSAY.

The following trifles are not the production of the Poet, who, with
all the advantages of learned art, and perhaps amid the elegancies
and idleness of upper life, looks down for a rural theme, with an eye
to Theocrites or Virgil. To the Author of this, these and other
celebrated names their countrymen are, in their original languages,
'A fountain shut up' and, a 'book sealed'. Unacquainted with the
necessary requisites for commencing Poet by Rule, he sings the
sentiments and manners, he felt and saw in himself and his rustic
compeers around him, in his and their native language. Though a
Rhymer from his earliest years, at least from the earliest impulses of
the softer passions, it was not till very lately, that the applause,
perhaps the partiality, of Friendship, wakened his vanity so far as to
make him think any thing of his was worth showing; and none of the
following works were ever composed with a view to the press. To

answering about being seen it written

amuse himself with the little creations of his own fancy, amid the toils and fatigues of a laborious life; to transcribe the various feelings, the loves, the griefs, the hopes, the fears, in his own breast; to find some kind of counterpoise to the struggles of a world, always an alien scene, a task uncouth to the Poetical mind; these were his motives for courting the Muses, and in these he found Poetry to be its own reward.

Now that he appears in the public character of an Author, he does it with fear and trembling. So dear is fame to the Rhyming tribe, that even he, an obscure, nameless Bard, shrinks aghast, at the thought of being branded as 'an impertinent blockhead, obtruding his nonsense on the world; and because he can make a shift to jingle a few doggerel, Scotch rhymes together, looks upon himself as a Poet of no small consequence forsooth'.

It is an observation of that celebrated Poet [Shenstone], whose divine Elegies do honour to our language, our nation, and our species, that 'Humility has depressed many a genius to a hermit, but never raised one to fame'. If any Critic catches at the word genius, the Author tells him, once for all, that he certainly looks upon himself as possest of some poetic abilities, otherwise his publishing in the manner he has done, would be a manoeuvre below the worst character, which, he hopes, his worst enemy will ever give him: but to the genius of a Ramsay, or the glorious dawning of the poor, unfortunate Ferguson, he with equal unaffected sincerity, declares, that, even in his highest pulse of vanity, he has not the most distant pretensions. These two justly admired Scotch Poets he has often had in his eye in the following pieces; but rather with a view to kindle at their flame, than for servile imitation.

To his Subscribers, the Author returns his most sincere thanks. Not the mercenary bow over a counter, but the heart-throbbing gratitude of the Bard, conscious how much he is indebted to Benevolence and Friendship, for gratifying him, if he deserves it, in that dearest wish of every poetic bosom – to be distinguished. He begs his readers, particularly the Learned and the Polite, who may honour him with a perusal, that they will make every allowance for Education and Circumstances of Life: but, if after a fair, candid, and impartial criticism, he shall stand convicted of Dulness and Non-sense, let him be done by, as he would in that case do by others – let him be condemned, without mercy, to oblivion.

R.B.

emerging into print in a polite literary culture.

Nature's Bard

First published on the front page of the Kilmarnock edition, 1786.

The Simple Bard, unbroke by rules of Art,
He pours the wild effusions of the heart:
And if inspir'd, 'tis Nature's pow'rs inspire;
Her's all the melting thrill, and her's the kindling fire.
                                        Anonymous.

The Kilmarnock edition begins with four lines supposedly from an anonymous poet, wholly appropriate to the image Burns wished to project to his readers. They are, in all probability, his own composition. In his *Preface*, Burns coyly suggests that he does not have 'all the advantages of learned art' in poetry – when, in fact, he is a master craftsman in poetic form and metre. He goes on to explain that his poetry is the product of Nature's influence on him. This projected persona is captured perfectly in the quatrain. The possibility that Burns wrote these lines was first suggested by the highly distinguished American scholar, Professor Carol McGuirk, in her excellent *Robert Burns: Selected Poems* (Penguin, 1993). A search of known anonymous poetry for the 18th century did not trace a potential author other than Burns. The lines are a hand-in-glove portrayal of Burns's self-projection of himself as a poet.

Dramatic monologue. Social satire [handwritten annotation]

The Twa Dogs: A Tale

First printed in the Kilmarnock edition, 1786.

'Twas in that place o' *Scotland's* isle		
That bears the name of auld King COIL,	old, Kyle	
Upon a bonie day in June,	bonny	
When wearing thro' the afternoon,		
5 *Twa Dogs*, that were na thrang at hame,	two, not busy, home	
Forgather'd ance upon a time.	met by chance, once	

The first I'll name, they ca'd him *Caesar*,   called
Was keepet for his Honor's pleasure: kept
His hair, his size, his mouth, his lugs,   ears
10 Shew'd he was nane o' Scotland's dogs;   none
But whalpet some place far abroad,   pupped
Whare sailors gang to fish for Cod.   where, go

His locked, letter'd, braw brass-collar
Shew'd him the *gentleman* an' *scholar*;   10
15   But tho' he was o' high degree,
The fient a pride na pride had he;   fiend, no
But wad hae spent an hour caressan,   would have
Ev'n wi' a Tinkler-gipsey's *messan*;   mongrel
At *Kirk* or *Market*, *Mill* or *Smiddie*,   smithy
20   Nae tawtied *tyke*, tho' e'er sae duddie,   matted cur, so ragged
But he wad stan't, as glad to see him,   would have stood
An' stroan't on stanes an' hillocks wi' him.   pissed, stones

The tither was a *ploughman's collie*,
A rhyming, ranting, raving billie,   fellow/character
25   Wha for his friend an' comrade had him,   who
And in his freaks had *Luath* ca'd him,   6
After some dog in *Highland Sang*,[1]
Was made lang syne, Lord knows how lang.   long ago

He was a gash an' faithfu' *tyke*,   wise, dog
30   As ever lap a sheugh or dyke!   leapt, ditch, stone wall
His honest, sonsie, baws'nt face   friendly, white marks
Ay gat him friends in ilka place;   always got, every
His *breast* was white, his touzie *back*   shaggy
Weel clad wi' coat o' glossy black;   well covered   8
35   His gawsie tail, wi' upward curl,   fine/full
Hung owre his hurdies wi' a swirl.   over, buttocks

Nae doubt but they were fain o' ither,   no, fond of each other
And unco pack an' thick thegither;   kept secrets/confidential
Wi' social *nose* whyles snuff'd an' snowcket;   whiles, sniffed
40   Whyles mice an' moudiewurks they howcket;   whiles, moles, dug for
Whyles scour'd awa' in lang excursion,   whiles, long   10
An' worry'd ither in *diversion*;
Till tir'd at last wi' monie a farce,   many
They sat them down upon their arse,   After *[...]* mice + digging
45   An' there began a lang digression   long   for *[...]* they
About the *lords o' the creation*.   have d discussion about
                                                                                    creation!

CAESAR
I've aften wonder'd, honest *Luath*,   often
What sort o' life poor dogs like you have;

1 Cuchullin's dog in Ossian's *Fingal*, R.B.

An' when the *gentry's* life I saw,
50　What way poor bodies liv'd ava.　　　　　　at all

Our *Laird* gets in his racked rents,　　　　　extortionate
His coals, his kane, an' a' his stents:　　　payments in kind, dues
He rises when he likes himsel;
His flunkies answer at the bell;　　　　　　servants
55　He ca's his coach; he ca's his horse;　　　calls
He draws a bonie, silken purse,　　　　　　carries
As lang's my *tail*, whare thro' the steeks,　long as, where, stiches
The yellow, letter'd *Geordie* keeks.　　　guinea (King's head) peeps

Frae morn to een it's nought but toiling,　from, evening, nothing
60　At baking, roasting, frying, boiling;
An' tho' the gentry first are steghan,　　　cramming
Yet ev'n the *ha' folk* fill their peghan　hall (servants), stomach
Wi' sauce, ragouts, an sic like trashtrie,　such like rubbish
That's little short o' downright wastrie:　wastage
65　Our *Whipper-in*, wee, blastit wonner,　　small, blasted wonder
Poor, worthless elf, it eats a dinner,
Better than onie *Tenant-man*　　　　　　any
His Honor has in a' the lan':　　　　　　all the land
An' what poor *Cot-folk* pit their painch in,　put, paunch
70　I own it's past my comprehension.

LUATH
Trowth, *Caesar*, whyles they're fash'd eneugh: sometimes, bothered
A *Cotter* howckan in a sheugh,　　　　　farm labourer, digging, ditch
Wi' dirty stanes biggan a dyke,　　　　　stones, building, stone wall
Bairan a quarry, an' sic like,　　　　　　clearing, such
75　Himsel, a wife, he thus sustains,
A smytrie o' wee duddie weans,　　　　　number, small ragged children
An' nought but his han'-daurk, to keep　　hands' work
Them right an' tight in *thack an' raep*.　snug, thatch, rope

An' when they meet wi' sair disasters,　　sore
80　Like loss o' health or want o' masters,
Ye maist wad think, a wee touch langer,　most would, longer
An' they maun starve o' cauld and hunger:　should, cold
But how it comes, I never kend yet,　　　knew
They're maistly wonderfu' contented;　　mostly
85　An' buirdly chiels, an' clever hizzies,　　stout lads, girls
Are bred in sic a way as this is.　　　　such

CAESAR

But then to see how ye're neglecket,   neglected
How huff'd, an' cuff'd, an' disrespecket!   scolded, slapped, disrespected
Lord man, our gentry care as little
90   For *delvers*, *ditchers*, an' sic cattle;   labourers, diggers, such
They gang as saucy by poor folk,   go, smugly
As I wad by a stinkan brock.   would, badger

I've notic'd, on our Laird's *court-day*,[2]
(An' monie a time my heart's been wae),   many, sad
95   Poor tenant bodies, scant o' cash,   short of money
How they maun thole a *Factor's* snash:[3]   would suffer, abuse
He'll stamp an' threaten, curse an' swear
He'll *apprehend* them, *poind* their gear;   seize & sell their goods
While they maun staun', wi' aspect humble,   must stand
100 An' hear it a', an' fear an' tremble!   all

I see how folk live that hae riches;   have
But surely poor-folk maun be wretches!   must

LUATH

They're nae sae wretched's ane wad think: not so, as one would
Tho' constantly on poortith's brink,   poverty's
105 They're sae accustom'd wi' the sight,   so
The view o't gies them little fright.   gives

Then chance an' fortune are sae guided,   so
They're ay in less or mair provided;   always, more
An' tho' fatigu'd wi' close employment,
110 A blink o' rest's a sweet enjoyment.

The dearest comfort o' their lives,
Their grushie weans an' faithfu' wives;   thriving children
The *prattling things* are just their pride,
That sweetens a' their fire-side.

115 An' whyles twalpennie worth o' *nappy*   sometimes, ale
Can mak the bodies unco happy: folk, very

2 The quarterly Circuit Court that travelled around the towns and counties
of Scotland.
3 The title of Factor is that of an Estate manager, who, in the West of
Scotland, cleared many 'cottars' from large estates during the late 18th
century.

They lay aside their private cares,
To mind the Kirk an' State affairs;
They'll talk o' *patronage* an' *priests*,
120 Wi' kindling fury i' their breasts,
Or tell what new taxation's comin,
An' ferlie at the folk in LON'ON.   wonder

As bleak-fac'd Hallowmass returns,   festival of All-Saints
They get the jovial, rantan *Kirns*,   harvest homes
125 When *rural life*, of ev'ry station,
Unite in common recreation;
Love blinks, Wit slaps, an' social Mirth
Forgets there's *Care* upo' the earth.

That *merry day* the year begins,
130 They bar the door on frosty win's;   winds
The nappy reeks wi' mantling ream,   ale, foaming froth
An' sheds a heart-inspiring steam;
The luntan pipe, an' sneeshin mill,   smoking, snuff box
Are handed round wi' right guid will;   good
135 The cantie, auld folks, crackan crouse,   jolly old, chatting, cheerful
The young anes rantan thro' the house —   one, running
My heart has been sae fain to see them,   so content
That I for joy hae *barket* wi' them.   have barked

is reminder they are dogs.

Still it's owre true that ye hae said   over, have
140 Sic game is now owre aften play'd;   such a, over often
There's monie a creditable *stock*   many
O' decent, honest, fawsont folk,   respectable
Are riven out baith root an' branch,   thrown out by force, both
Some rascal's pridefu' greed to quench,
145 Wha thinks to knit himsel the faster   who
In favor wi' some *gentle Master*,
Wha, aiblins thrang a *parliamentin'*,   who, maybe crowd
For *Britain's guid* his saul indentin' —   good, soul engaged

Caesar believes the MPs are doing for the public + caesar sets him right

CAESAR
Haith, lad, ye little ken about it: an exclamation, know
150 *For Britain's guid*! guid faith! I doubt it.   good
Say rather, gaun as PREMIERS lead him,   go
An' saying *aye* or *no 's* they bid him:
At Operas an' Plays parading,
Mortgaging, gambling, masquerading:

155 Or maybe, in a frolic daft,
     To HAGUE or CALAIS takes a waft,
     To mak *a tour* an' tak a whirl,
     To learn *bon ton*, an' see the worl'.   Fr. good breeding

     There, at VIENNA or VERSAILLES,
160 He rives his father's auld entails;   splits, old
     Or by MADRID he taks the rout,   road
     To thrum guittarres an' fecht wi' *nowt*;   strum, guitars, fight with cattle
     Or down *Italian Vista* startles,   courses
     Whore-hunting amang groves o' myrtles: among
165 Then bowses drumlie *German-water*,   drinks muddy
     To mak himsel look fair an' fatter,
     An' clear the consequential sorrows,
     Love-gifts of Carnival Signioras.
     For Britain's guid! for her destruction!
170 Wi' dissipation, feud an' faction!

     LUATH
     Hech man! dear sirs! is that the gate   way
     They waste sae monie a braw estate!   so many
     Are we sae foughten an' harass'd   so troubled
     For gear ta gang that gate at last!   wealth to go

175 O would they stay aback frae courts,   away from
     An' please themsels wi' countra sports,   country
     It wad for ev'ry ane be better,   would, every one
     The *Laird*, the *Tenant*, an' the *Cotter*!
     For thae frank, rantan, ramblan billies,   those, lads
180 Fient haet o' them's ill-hearted fellows;   few of them are
     Except for breakin o' their timmer,   timber
     Or speakin lightly o' their *Limmer*,   mistress
     Or shootin of a hare or moor-cock,
     The ne'er-a-bit they're ill to poor folk.

185 But will ye tell me, master Caesar,
     Sure *great folk's* life's a life o' pleasure?
     Nae cauld nor hunger e'er can steer them,   no cold, touch
     The vera thought o't need na fear them.   very, not

     CAESAR
     Lord, man, were ye but whyles whare I am,   whiles where
190 The *Gentles*, ye wad ne'er envy them!   would

	It's true, they need na starve or sweat,	not
	Thro' Winter's cauld, or Simmer's heat;	cold, summer's
	They've nae sair-work to craze their banes,	no sore work, bones
	An' fill *auld-age* wi' grips an' granes:	old-age, gripes & groans
195	But *human bodies* are sic fools,	such
	For a' their Colledges an' Schools,	
	That when nae *real* ills perplex them,	no
	They *mak* enow themsels to vex them;	
	An' ay the less they hae to sturt them,	always, have, fret
200	In like proportion, less will hurt them.	

A countra fellow at the pleugh, — country, plough
His *acre's* till'd, he's right eneugh; — well enough
A countra girl at her wheel, — country
Her *dizzen's* done, she's unco weel; — dozens (yarn), very well
205 But Gentlemen, an' Ladies warst,
Wi' ev'n down *want o' wark* they're curst: — work
They loiter, lounging, lank an' lazy;
Tho' deil-haet ails them, yet uneasy: — nothing
Their days insipid, dull an' tasteless;
210 Their nights unquiet, lang an' restless. — long

An' ev'n their sports, their balls an' races,
Their galloping thro' public places,
There's sic parade, sic pomp an' art, — such
The joy can scarcely reach the heart.

215 The *Men* cast out in *party-matches*, — compete
Then sowther a' in deep debauches; — patch up
Ae night they're mad wi' drink an' whoring, — one
Niest day their life is past enduring. — next

The *Ladies* arm-in-arm in clusters,
220 As great an' gracious a' as sisters; — all
But hear their *absent thoughts* o' ither,
They're a' run deils an' jads thegither. — downright, together
Whyles, owre the wee bit cup an' platie, — whiles, over, plate
They sip the *scandal-potion* pretty;
225 Or lee-lang nights, wi' crabbet leuks — live-long, bad tempered looks
Pore owre the devil's *pictur'd beuks*; — over, books (playing cards)
Stake on a chance a farmer's stackyard,
An' cheat like onie *unhang'd blackguard*. — any, villain

There's some exceptions, man an' woman;
230 But this is Gentry's life in common.

By this, the sun was out o' sight,
An' darker gloamin brought the night;   fading twilight
The *bum-clock* humm'd wi' lazy drone;   beetle
The kye stood rowtin i' the loan;   cattle, lowing, field
235 When up they gat, an' shook their lugs,   got, ears
Rejoic'd they were na *men*, but *dogs*;   not
An' each took aff his several way,   went his different
Resolv'd to meet some ither day.   other

Burns lived with animals, wild and domestic, in conditions of intimacy which few of us in this twenty-first century can easily appreciate. This poem, as much of his poetry, is filled with an empathetic, hence, detailed knowledge of them. The collie and the Newfoundland are sportively present to us. Throughout his writing there are also frequent, often obliquely political analogies, made between the lots of animals and men.

The genesis of this poem was his own collie, Luath, who, his brother tells us, was 'killed by some wanton cruelty of some person the night before my father's death'. This extraordinary witty, seminal poem is the result of his original intention to write, for the sinisterly murdered Luath, *Stanzas to the Memory of a Quadruped Friend* (Currie, Vol. 3, p. 386).

His wholly deliberate choice of opening The Kilmarnock edition with this particular poem is mockingly ironic. In that volume, he had no sooner come on stage with his highly successful self-promoting prose remarks about his poetic ploughman's pastoral naïvety, than he immediately delivers a poetic performance of not only formidable linguistic and double-voiced dramatic subtlety but one which is eruditely allusive to earlier Scottish and English poetry. Indeed, it would be, as in ll. 26–28, an extremely odd ploughman who would not only name his dog from a character in Macpherson's *Ossian* but also allude to that simmering controversy. Also both the octosyllabic verse and the dialogue form are derived from his beloved predecessor, Robert Fergusson's *The Mutual Complaint of Plainstanes and Causey, in their Mother Tongue*.

While the poem formally and linguistically is not indebted to English poetry, the content certainly is. As William Empson (*Some Versions of Pastoral*, 1935) and Raymond Williams (*The City and Country*, 1975) have revealed, English poetry from the sixteenth century had been preoccupied with the nature and representation of country life as a reflection of the quarrel between largely conservative poets and their aristocratic patrons due to the disruptive evolution in the life of the common people caused by the accelerating participation by the

aristocratic master class in agrarian capitalism. The greatest state-
ment of this theme, as we shall see Burns demonstrably knew in his
own *A Winter's Night*, is Shakespeare's *King Lear*. The consistently
cogent McGuirk in discussing this poem locates its tap-roots in
Augustan convention, especially Pope's *Moral Epistles*. Burns also
had, of course, the endorsement of his views from contemporary
sources such as Goldsmith, particularly *The Deserted Village*.
Although they diverged totally about the role of the monarchy, Burns
and Goldsmith were also part of that rising late eighteenth-century
tide of patriotic feeling about the 'Frenchified' degeneration of the
British aristocracy as increasingly they squandered their ill-gotten
agrarian rents in European fleshpots. (See Gerald Newman, *The Rise
of English Nationalism*, London, 1987.) Hence that quite wonderfully
sophisticated section, comparable to anything in Augustan satire,
from ll. 149–170 where Caesar describes into what The Grand Tour
has degenerated. This brilliantly echoes Fergusson's pronouncedly
anti-aristocratic lines from *Hame Content*:

>   Some daft chiel reads, and takes advice
> The chaise is yokit in a trice;
> Awa drives he like huntit deil,
> And scarce tholes time to cool his wheel,
> Till he's Lord ken how far awa,
> At Italy, or Well o' Spaw,
> Or to Montpelier's safer air;
> For far off fowls hae feathers fair.
>   There rest him weel; for eith can we
> Spare mony glakit gouks like he;
> They'll tell whare Tibur's water's rise;
> What sea receives the drumly prize,
> That never wi' their feet hae mett
> The marches o' their ain estate.

Stimulated by Fergusson, then, this dramatic dialogue, domesti-
cates in the Scottish vernacular this great English poetic quarrel
with a rapacious land-owning class. What further intensified this in
Burns is that from childhood he had been exposed to both brutal-
ising toil and chronic economic anxiety. Ll. 95–100 do, in fact, seem
to refer to actual events on the family farm at Lochlea of which he
wrote: 'my indignation yet boils at the recollection of the scoundrel
tyrant's insolent threatening epistles which he used to set us all in
tears' (Letter 137). As Burns's subsequent poetry reveals, this early
trauma about debt, bankruptcy and possible homelessness was to be

a subject of inflammatory repetition. Also, as much of his later poetry, the poem is filled with telling detail about the harsh, exposed, exhausting nature of farm work in the late eighteenth century as opposed to the pampered sloth of the aristocracy. Indeed, as in ll. 89–90, such brutal work leads to a Swiftian vision of the bestialisation of the common people: 'Lord man, our gentry care as little/For *delvers, ditchers* and sic cattle'.

Burns's strategy in the poem of course is to create through the dogs a kind of comic brio, which, at a primary level, disguises the poem's incisive documentation and its anti-establishment values. Further, he does not do the ideologically obvious thing by creating an oppositional dialogue between the people's collie and the master's newly fashionable Newfoundland. Caesar is not so much a traitor to his class as a natural democrat who will put his nose anywhere as a possible prelude to even more intimate entanglements. It is he who really spills the beans about the condition of the working people and the lifestyle of their masters. In Luath's speeches, especially ll. 103–38, we find the roots of Burns's vision of the nobility of the common people which is to recur throughout his poetry though, at times, especially in 'The Cotter's Saturday Night', somewhat questionably.

Scotch Drink

First printed in the Kilmarnock edition, 1786.

> *Gie him strong drink until he wink,*
> *That's sinking in despair;*
> *An' liquor guid to fire his bluid,*
> *That's prest wi' grief an' care:*
> *There let him bowse, and deep carouse,*
> *Wi' bumpers flowing o'er,*
> *Till he forgets his loves or debts,*
> *An' minds his griefs no more.*

Solomon's Proverbs, xxxi. 6, 7.I.
A paraphrase from Hugh Blair's *The Grave*, p. 8.

Let other Poets raise a frácas
'Bout vines, an' wines, an' drucken *Bacchus*,   drunken
An' crabbed names an' stories wrack us,   torment
    An' grate our lug: vex, ears
5 I sing the juice *Scotch bear* can mak us,   drink, barley
    In glass or jug.

O thou, my MUSE! guid auld SCOTCH DRINK!   good old
Whether thro' wimplin worms thou jink,   winding, frisk
Or, richly brown, ream owre the brink,   froth over
10   In glorious faem,   foam
Inspire me, till I *lisp* an' *wink*,
        To sing thy name!

Let husky Wheat the haughs adorn,   hollows
An' Aits set up their awnie horn,   oats, bearded
15   An' Pease an' Beans, at een or morn,
        Perfume the plain:
Leeze me on thee, *John Barleycorn*,   blessing on thee
        Thou king o' grain!

On thee aft Scotland chows her cood,   often, chews, cud
20   In souple scones, the wale o' food!   soft, pick
Or tumbling in the boiling flood
        Wi' kail an' beef;   greens
But when thou pours thy strong *heart's blood*,
        There thou shines chief.

25   Food fills the wame, an' keeps us livin;   belly
Tho' life's a gift no worth receivin,
When heavy-dragg'd wi' pine an' grievin;
        But oil'd by thee,
The wheels o' life gae down-hill, scrievin,   go, careering
30   Wi' rattlin glee.   noisy joy

Thou clears the head o' doited Lear,   muddled knowledge
Thou cheers the heart o' drooping Care;
Thou strings the nerves o' Labor-sair,   sore
        At's weary toil;
35   Thou ev'n brightens dark Despair
        Wi' gloomy smile.

Aft, clad in massy, siller weed,   often clothed
Wi' Gentles thou erects thy head;
Yet, humbly kind, in time o' need,
40   The *poorman's* wine:
His wee drap parritch, or his bread,   drop, porridge
        Thou kitchens fine.

Thou art the life o' public haunts;
But thee, what were our fairs and rants?   without, merry-makings
45 Ev'n goodly meetings o' the saunts,   saints
        By thee inspir'd,
When, gaping, they besiege the *tents*,
        Are doubly fir'd.

That *merry night* we get the corn in,
50 O sweetly, then, thou reams the horn in!
Or reekin on a *New-Year-mornin*   steaming
        In cog or bicker,   bowl, jug
An' just a wee drap *sp'ritual burn* in,   small drop
        An' *gusty sucker*!   tasty sugar

55 When Vulcan gies his bellys breath,   gives, bellows
An' Ploughmen gather wi' their graith,   gear
O rare! to see thee fizz an' fraeth   bubble and froth
        I' the lugget caup!   two-handled jug
Then *Burnewin* comes on like Death   blacksmith
60   At ev'ry chap.   stroke

Nae mercy, then, for airn *or* steel: no, iron
The brawnie, bainie, Ploughman-chiel,   sturdy, boney, fellow
Brings hard owrehip, wi' sturdy wheel,   over hip
        The strong forehammer,
65 Till block an' studdie ring an' reel,   anvil
        Wi' dinsome clamour.

When skirlin weanies see the light,   squalling infants
Thou maks the gossips clatter bright.   makes, chatter, cheerfully
How fumbling coofs their dearies slight;   fools
70   Wae worth the name!   woe betide
Nae Howdie gets a social night,   no midwife
        Or plack frae them.   coin

When neebors anger at a plea,   neighbours
An' just as wud as wud can be,   mad/wild
75 How easy can the *barley-bree*   -brew
        Cement the quarrel!
It's ay the cheapest Lawyer's fee,
        To taste the barrel.

Alake! that e'er my *Muse* has reason,
80 To wyte her countrymen wi' treason!   blame/charge
But mony daily weet their weason   many, wet their throat
        Wi' liquors nice,
An' hardly, in a winter season,
        E'er spier her price.   ask

85 Wae worth that *Brandy*, burnin trash!   woe to
Fell source o' monie a pain an' brash!   sickness
Twins mony a poor, doylt, drucken hash,   (deprives many,
        O' half his days;   weary drunken fellow)
An' sends, beside, auld *Scotland's* cash   old
90   To her warst faes.   worst foes

Ye Scots, wha wish auld Scotland well,   who, old
Ye chief, to you my tale I tell,
Poor, plackless devils like *mysel*,   penniless
        It sets you ill,
95 Wi' bitter, dearthfu' *wines* to mell,   meddle
        Or *foreign gill*.

May *Gravels* round his blather wrench,   stones, bladder
An' *Gouts* torment him, inch by inch,
Wha twists his gruntle wi' a glunch   who, mouth, grumble
100   O' sour disdain,
Out owre a glass o' *Whisky-punch*   over
        Wi' honest men!

O *Whisky*! soul o' plays an' pranks!
Accept a *Bardie's* gratefu' thanks!
105 When wanting thee, what tuneless cranks
        Are my poor Verses!
Thou comes — they rattle i' their ranks
        At ither's arses!

Thee, *Ferintosh*! O sadly lost!
110 Scotland lament frae coast to coast!   from
Now colic-grips, an' barkin hoast   coughing hoarse
        May kill us a';
For loyal *Forbes' Chartered boast*
        Is taen awa!   taken away

115	Thae curst horse-leeches o' th' Excise,	those
	Wha mak the *Whisky stills* their prize!	who make, stills
	Haud up thy han', *Deil*! ance, twice, thrice!	hold, hand, once
	There, seize the blinkers!	rascals/spies
	An' bake them up in brunstane pies	brimstone
120	For poor damn'd *Drinkers*.	

	Fortune! if thou'll but gie me still	give
	Hale breeks, a scone, an' *Whisky gill*,	whole breeches
	An' rowth o' *rhyme* to rave at will,	abundance/store
	Tak a' the rest,	
125	An' deal't about as thy blind skill	
	Directs thee best.	

Though not quite in the manner of his contemporary, William Blake, Burns found *The Bible* a constant source of inspiration and allusion. This vernacularisation of *Proverbs* with which he introduces the poem is characteristic of his delight in the often excessively erotic, violent and, in this case, alcoholic tales he found in *The Old Testament*. Such use of *The Bible* was not the least of his anti-clerical weapons. Nor was it the least of his offences against Hugh Blair and the pietistic critical sensibilities of genteel Edinburgh.

A copy of *Scotch Drink* was sent to Robert Muir in March, 1786, having been apparently written sometime in the preceding winter. This celebratory 'hymn' to the virtues of the national drink again owes its genesis and tone to the bibulous gaiety which pulses through Robert Fergusson's poetry. In particular it is related to Fergusson's *Caller Water* and *A Drink Eclogue* with its disputation between Brandy and Whisky. As in Fergusson's poems, whisky is ever the vital, democratising, somewhat chauvinistic heart's blood of the nation, energising and socialising everybody with whom it comes into contact. The sad exception is the impotent, cuckolded husband of ll. 67–72.

In ll. 102–8 Burns also associates whisky with the power to energise his own poetic creativity so that the quality of his verses catches up with those of his poetic competitors. We cannot know to what degree alcohol was a creative stimulant for Burns, though certainly some of his most extraordinary letters are self-confessedly written with well-plied glass in hand. See, for example, Letter 506 to Alexander Cunningham.

The reference in l. 109 to Ferintosh as Kinsley tells us, is that this Cromarty Firth whisky had been exempted from duty after 1695 in reparation for damage to the estates of Forbes of Culloden, the owner of the distillery, by the Jacobites in 1689. Forbes' loss of this privilege in 1785 drove the price of whisky up.

The penultimate stanza's consignment of the Excise to the fires of hell for their still-breaking activities must have caused Burns subsequent guilty grief. The Excise was the most hated and efficient arm of a state that had nothing to do with welfare and everything to do with intrusive, punitive taxation. Had he known it, Burns would have wholeheartedly agreed with Blake that 'Lawful Bread, Bought with Lawful Money, & a Lawful Heaven, seen thro' a Lawful Telescope, by means of a Lawful Window Light! The Holy Ghost, & whatever cannot be Taxed, is Unlawful & Witchcraft'.

The Author's Earnest Cry and Prayer
To The Scotch Representatives In The House of Commons[1]

First printed in the Kilmarnock edition, 1786.

Dearest of distillation! last and best —
— How art thou lost! —
Parody on Milton.

Ye Irish lords, ye *knights* an' *squires,*
Wha represent our BRUGHS an' SHIRES,   who, burghs
An' doucely manage our affairs   prudently
          In *Parliament,*
5 To you a simple Bardie's pray'rs
          Are humbly sent.

Alas! my roupet *Muse* is haerse!   husky, hoarse
Your Honors' hearts wi' grief 'twad pierce,   it would
To see her sittan on her arse
10   Low i' the dust,
And scriechan out prosaic verse,   screeching
          An' like to brust!   burst

Tell them wha hae the chief direction,   who have
Scotland an' *me's* in great affliction,
15 E'er sin' they laid that curst restriction   ever since
          On AQUAVITAE   whisky/water-of-life
An' rouse them up to strong conviction,
          An' move their pity.

1 This was written before the Act anent the Scotch Distilleries of session 1786; for which Scotland and the Author return their most grateful thanks. R.B.

Stand forth, an' tell yon PREMIER YOUTH
20 The honest, open, naked truth:
Tell him o' mine an' Scotland's drouth,   thirst
          His servants humble:
The muckle devil blaw you south,   great, blow
          If ye dissemble!

25 Does onie *great man* glunch an' gloom?   any, growl, grumble
Speak out, an' never fash your thumb!   trouble yourself
Let *posts* an' *pensions* sink or soom   swim
          Wi' them wha grant 'em: who
If honestly they canna come,   cannot
30   Far better want 'em.   lack them

In gath'rin votes you were na slack;   not lazy
Now stand as tightly by your tack:
Ne'er claw your lug, an' fidge your back,   scratch your ear, shrug
          An' hum an haw;
35 But raise your arm, an' tell your crack   tale
          Before them a'.

Paint Scotland greetan owre her thrissle;   weeping, over, thistle
Her *mutchkin stowp* as toom's a whissle;   pint-pot, empty as a whistle
An' damn'd *Excise-men* in a bustle,
40   Seizin a *Stell*,   still
Triumphant, crushan't like a mussel,
          Or laimpet shell.   limpet

Then on the tither hand present her,   other
A blackguard *Smuggler* right behint her,
45 An' cheek-for-chow, a chuffie *Vintner*   cheek-by-jowl, fat faced
          Colleaguing join, —
Pickin her pouch as bare as Winter   pocket
          Of a' kind coin.

Is there, that bears the name o' SCOT,
50 But feels his heart's bluid rising hot,   blood
To see his poor auld Mither's *pot*   old mother's
          Thus dung in staves,   broken in pieces
An' plunder'd o' her hindmost groat,   last coin
          By gallows knaves?

55 Alas! I'm but a nameless wight,   *— unpublished.*
     Trode i' the mire out o' sight!
     But could I like MONTGOMERIES fight,
          Or gab like BOSWELL,   talk
     There's some *sark-necks* I wad *draw* tight,   shirt-necks, would
60   An' tye some *hose* well.   tie

     God bless your Honors! can ye see't,
     The kind, auld, cantie Carlin greet,   old, jolly, wife weep
     An' no get warmly to your feet,
          An' gar them hear it,   make
65   An' tell them wi' a patriot-heat,   Scottish passion
          Ye winna bear it?   will not

     Some o' you nicely ken the laws,   know
     To round the period an' pause,
     An' with rhetoric clause on clause
70   To mak harangues;   *→ used in the Holy Fair*
     Then echo thro' Saint Stephen's wa's   Parliament's walls
          Auld Scotland's wrangs.   old, wrongs

     Dempster,[1] a true blue Scot I'se warran;   I'll warrant
     Thee, aith-detesting, chaste *Kilkerran*;[2]   oath   *clothing*
75   An' that glib-gabbet Highland Baron,   quick-tongued *linguistic*
          The Laird o' *Graham*;[3]   *decorum.*
     An' ane, a chap that's damn'd auldfarran,   one, shrewd
          Dundass[4] his name:

     Erskine,[5] a spunkie Norland billie;   spirited Northern young man
80   True Campbells, *Frederick* an' *Ilay*;[6]
     An' Livistone, the bauld *Sir Willie*;[7]   bold
          An' mony ithers,   many others
     Whom auld Demosthenes or Tully[8]   old
          Might own for brithers.   brothers

1 George Dempster, mentioned in *The Vision*.
2 Sir Adam Ferguson.
3 James Graham, Son of the Duke of Montrose.
4 Henry Dundas, Viscount Melville.
5 Thomas Erskine, M.P., brother of Henry Erskine.
6 Frederick Campbell and Ilay Campbell.
7 Sir William Cunninghame of Livingston.
8 Classical rhetorical orators – colloquial for Cicero.

85   Thee sodger Hugh, my watchman stented,[9]   soldier, assigned (M.P.)
     If Bardies e'er are represented;
     I ken if that your sword were wanted,   know
          Ye'd lend your hand;
     But when there's ought to say anent it,   about
90   Ye're at a stand.

     Arouse my boys! exert your mettle,
     To get auld Scotland back her *kettle*!   old, whisky still
     Or faith! I'll wad my new pleugh-pettle,   wager, plough scraper
          Ye'll see't or lang,   before long
95   She'll teach you, wi' a reekan whittle,   smoking knife
          Anither sang.   another song

     This while she's been in crankous mood,   fretful
     Her *lost Militia* fir'd her bluid;   blood
     (Deil na they never mair do guid,   not, more, good
100   Play'd her that pliskie!)   trick
     An' now she's like to rin red-wud   run stark mad
          About her *Whisky*.

     An' Lord! if ance they pit her till't,   once, put her to it
     Her tartan petticoat she'll kilt,   tuck up
105 An' durk an' pistol at her belt,   blade
          She'll tak the streets,
     An' rin her whittle to the hilt,   run her knife, handle
          I' the first she meets!

     For God-sake, Sirs! then speak her fair,
110 An' straik her cannie wi' the hair,   stroke, carefully
     An' to the *Muckle House* repair,   great Parliament
          Wi' instant speed,
     An' strive, wi' a' your Wit an' Lear,   knowledge
          To get remead.

115 Yon ill-tongu'd tinkler, *Charlie Fox*,[10]   gypsy
     May taunt you wi' his jeers an' mocks;
     But gie him't het, my hearty cocks!   give him it hot
          E'en cowe the cadie!   subdue, rascal
     An' send him to his dicing box
120   An' sportin lady.

     9 Hugh Montgomerie, Earl of Eglinton.
     10 Leader of the Whig Opposition.

Tell yon guid bluid of auld *Boconnock's*,[11]   good blood, old
I'll be his debt twa mashlum bonnocks,   mixed meal bannocks
An' drink his health in auld *Nanse Tinnock's*[12]   old
    Nine times a-week,
125 If he some scheme, like tea an' winnocks,   windows
    Wad kindly seek.   would

Could he some *commutation* broach,
I'll pledge my aith in guid braid Scotch,   oath, good broad
He needna fear their foul reproach   need not
130   Nor erudition,
Yon mixtie-maxtie, queer hotch-potch,   mixed up
    The *Coalition*.

Auld Scotland has a raucle tongue;   old, rough
She's just a devil wi' a rung;   bludgeon
135 An' if she promise auld or young   old
    To tak their part,
Tho' by the neck she should be strung,
    She'll no desert.

And now, ye chosen FIVE AND FORTY,
140 May still your Mither's heart support ye;   mother's
Then, tho' a Minister grow dorty,   haughty
    An' kick your place,
Ye'll snap your fingers, poor an' hearty,
    Before his face.

145 God bless your Honors, a' your days,
Wi' sowps o' kail and brats o' claes,   sups of broth, coarse cloth
In spite o' a' the thievish kaes,   jackdaws
    That haunt St. *Jamie's*!   parliament
Your humble Bardie sings an' prays,
150   While *Rab* his name is. *3rd person.*

POSTSCRIPT
Let half-starv'd slaves in warmer skies,
See future wines, rich-clust'ring, rise;

11 An allusion to William Pitt's grandfather, Robert.
12 A worthy old Hostess of the Author's in *Mauchline*, where he sometimes
studies Politics over a glass of guid auld *Scotch Drink*. R.B.

Their lot auld Scotland ne'er envies,   old
          But, blythe and frisky,
155   She eyes her freeborn, martial boys
          Tak aff their Whisky.   drink down

What tho' their Phoebus kinder warms,   sun
While Fragrance blooms and Beauty charms!
When wretches range, in famish'd swarms,
160   The scented groves,
Or hounded forth, *dishonor* arms
          In hungry droves.

Their *gun's* a burden on their shouther;   shoulder
They downa bide the stink o' *powther*;   do not, gun powder
165   Their bauldest thought's a hank'ring swither   boldest, uncertain doubt
          To stan' or rin,
Till skelp – a shot – they're aff, a' throw'ther,   crack, off, pell-mell
          To save their skin.

But bring a SCOTCHMAN frae his hill,   *unthinking*   from *Scottish spirit –*
170   Clap in his cheek a *Highlan* gill,   *– drunk.*   gill (measure)
Say, such is royal GEORGE'S will,   *– become the tools*
          An' there's the foe!   *of the*
He has nae thought but how to kill   no   *English King.*
          Twa at a blow.   two

175   Nae cauld, faint-hearted doubtings tease him;   no cold
Death comes, wi' fearless eye he sees him;
Wi' bluidy han' a welcome gies him;   bloody hand, gives
          An' when he fa's,   falls
His latest draught o' breathin lea'es him   leaves
180   In faint huzzas.

Sages their solemn een may steek   eyes, close
An' raise a philosophic reek,   smoke
An' physically causes seek,
          In *clime* an' *season*;
185   But tell me *Whisky's* name in Greek:
          I'll tell the reason.

SCOTLAND, my auld, respected Mither!   old, mother
Tho' whyles ye moistify your leather,   moisten, vagina

whisky now il the tool for highland fighting.

Till whare ye sit on craps o' heather	crops
190 Ye tine your dam,	lose your water
Freedom and whisky gang thegither,	go together
Tak aff your dram!	raise up your glass

The extended title which conveys the notion of self-mocking very minor prophetic biblical lamentation and political tract is given, by the parodic use in Milton, an added impulse to see the poem, despite its manifest political content, as laughing and lightweight. Surely the poet, unlike Adam for Eve, is not grieving for a fallen Scotland (*Paradise Lost*, Book IX, ll. 896–901)? The political, economic occasion for the poem was the Wash Act brought in by English pressure in 1784 to prevent what they considered preferential treatment to the Scottish distilling industry. This had not only severe effects on the Scottish whisky industry but was in breach of the terms of the Union and, for Burns, another symptom of the London Parliament's, at best, indifference to Scottish needs. By the time the poem appeared the injustice seemed, as Burns's footnote suggests, to have been corrected: 'This was wrote before the Act anent the Scotch Distilleries of session 1786; for which Scotland and the Author return their most grateful thanks.'

In February, 1789, the matter flared up again. On this occasion Burns chose for the second time to send a pseudonymous letter to the *Edinburgh Evening Courant* on the 9th February. The occasion for his first letter had been his request for compassion for the fallen House of Stuart along with his risky defence of the American Revolution as akin to the British events of 1688. This second letter was signed John Barleycorn and purports, remarkably, to be written on behalf of the Scottish Distillers to William Pitt who, at the time of composition, appears to be about to fall from power due to the Regency Bill as an antidote to the King's madness. The letter is based on the Scottish Distillers' alleged mutual sense of falling with Pitt from power and prosperity to exclusion and poverty. There is also an extraordinary parallel made with King Nebuchadnezzar which is implicitly to be read as Burns's own sense of sharing Pitt's exile. The letter also repeats the poem's allegations of political injustice to Scotland:

But turn your eyes, Sir, to the tragic scenes of our fate. An ancient nation that for many ages had gallantly maintained the unequal struggle for independence with her much more powerful neighbour, at last agrees to a union which should ever after make them one people. In consideration of certain circumstances, it was solemnly covenanted that the Former should

always enjoy a stipulated alleviation of her share of the public
burdens, particularly in that branch of the revenue known by
the name of the Excise.

This just priviledge has of late given great umbrage to some
invidious powerful individuals of the more potent half of the
Empire, and they have spared no wicked pains, under insidious
pretexts to subvert, what they yet too much dreaded the spirit
of their ancient enemies openly to attack.

By this conspiracy we fell; nor did we alone suffer, our
Country was deeply wounded. A number of, we will say it,
respectable characters largely engaged in trade where we were
not only useful but absolutely necessary to our Country in her
dearest interest; we, with all that was near and dear to us, were
sacrificed without remorse, to the Infernal Deity of Political
Expediency (Letter, 311).

Burns's second intrusion into *The Courant* is as seriously meant in
national and political terms as his first. The poem, also invoking Pitt,
depends on laughter but the comic tone is one that both covertly
asserts Burns's satirising superiority to his subject and his ability to
give tangible witness to the economic distresses caused by the whisky
tax. As well as the machinations of the London Parliament and the
betrayals of Scotland therein by her forty-five Commons represen-
tatives , he also speculates on the degree to which available Scottish
talent could be employed to the Nation's benefit. Not least, running
through the poem, are insinuations of ancestral Scottish violence
resurrecting itself again to put right political injustice.

The poem begins with the ironic comment that, whilst Irish Lords
were allowed to represent Scotland in Parliament, the elder sons of
Scottish Peers were not. He then craftily invokes his coarse, arse-in-
the-dust muse. As well as the tactical self-denigration of his muse,
this allows the poet to distance himself in the wings, putting the muse
centre stage. But, at l. 55, this somewhat transparent mask drops and
he speaks, again, ironically, self-denigratorily, as himself.

Ll. 13–54 invoke the muse to have the courage to tell the truth
about establishment censure by revealing the social dereliction
caused by the related excesses of the Excisemen and the Smugglers.
He also looks to specifically Ayrshire heroes (See *The Vision*) such as
the military Montgomery and the writerly Boswell to save Mother
Scotland from dereliction. We get the first suggestion of reactive
violence (ll. 59–60), with a vengeful image of choking restriction
perpetrated by the poet on his nation's enemies.

The poem is, thus, both an analysis of post-Union Scottish

distress and a thesis about Scottish resurrection based on the available Scottish greatness. In a letter he wrote to Bruce Campbell on November 13th, 1788 he included the poem which he hoped would be passed to James Boswell, thus procuring him an introduction to the great writer:

> There are few pleasures my late will-o'-wisp character has given me, equal to that of having seen many of the extraordinary men, the heroes of Wit and Literature in my Country; and as I had the honour of drawing my first breath in almost the same Parish with Mr Boswell, my pride Plumes itself on the connection. To crouch in the train of meer, stupid Wealth & Greatness, except where the commercial interests of worldly Prudence find their account in it, I hold to be Prostitution in any one that is not born a Slave; but to have been acquainted with a man such as Mr Boswell, I would hand down to my Posterity, as one of the honours of their Ancestor (Letter 284).

Boswell received and endorsed the letter (13th Nov 1788, 'Mr Robert Burns the Poet expressing very high sentiments of me') but made no attempts to meet Burns. Burns's need for redemptive Scottish Heroes, ancestral and contemporary, certainly chose the wrong man in that sycophantic, anglophile prose genius. Also this poem's programme puts together a misalliance of talents who Burns then thought were the rhetorical equals of Demosthenes and Tully, whose eloquence would cause the triumph of Scotland at Saint Stephens, the then site of Parliament. Ll. 73–81 list the candidates allegedly worthy of this task.

That this élite legal, political corps would co-operate to save Scotland was to prove for Burns the wildest of hopes. By 1795, as his brilliant poem *The Dean of Faculty* reveals, Scotland was tearing itself apart with the brilliant radical Henry Erskine outvoted and ejected from office by Robert Dundas. Henry Dundas, as Pitt's ferociously repressive Home Secretary, was running a fatwah against his radical countrymen.

From ll. 85–100 we have images of Scottish outrage spilling into weapons bearing anarchy with echoes of recent Jacobite incursion. Pitt, auld Boconnocks, is praised for his new methods of taxation. 'Commutation' (l. 121) refers to his 1784 Commutation Act which diverted tax from tea to windows. Fox, at this time is still for Burns merely a licentious nuisance. After another invocation of Scottish capacity for violence, he ends by requesting the 45 MPs to support their Nation. His actual hopes of their doing so is summed up in a brilliantly ironic last stanza where he envisages these pursy placemen subsisting on the diet and in the rags of Scottish peasantry among the temptations of St James's in London.

This level of irony is sustained in the quite brilliantly subtle seven-stanza Postscript which Burns adds to the poem. Carol McGuirk suggests that this should be read as the Poet's first address to Parliament. On the face of it, derived from Enlightenment theories that national character is the product of climate and environment, the poem seems to be a celebration of Scottish machismo and militarism over the cowardice inherent to the wine drinking peasantry of warmer climes. This apparent celebration of Scottish militarism is, however, immediately, devastatingly undercut. Ll. 163–74 are an astonishingly compressed denunciation of the savage, self-destructive consequences to the *unaware* Highlanders of their post-Culloden integration into British Imperial armies. Equally dark for Scotland is the fact that the feminine part of the nation (ll. 181–3) has degenerated to an incontinent crone. Thus, the ultimate toast (ll. 185–6) is the blackest irony.

N.B. Stanza 15 here is not included in Kinsley. There is also a variation in the last stanza.

The Holy Fair

First printed in the Kilmarnock edition, 1786.

A robe of seeming truth and trust
   Hid crafty observation;
And secret hung, with poison'd crust,
   The dirk of defamation:
A mask that like the gorget show'd,
   Dye-varying on the pigeon;
And for a mantle large and broad,
   He wrapt him in Religion.

Tom Brown, *Hypocrisy A-La-Mode.*

Upon a simmer *Sunday morn*,	summer
When Nature's face is fair,	
I walked forth to view the corn,	
An' snuff the callor air:	fresh
5 The rising sun, owre GALSTON Muirs,	over, moors
Wi' glorious light was glintan;	
The hares were hirplan down the furs,	hobbling with uneven speed, furrows
The lav'rocks they were chantan	larks
Fu' sweet that day.	full

10 As lightsomely I glowr'd abroad,
    To see a scene sae gay,   *so*
Three *hizzies*, early at the road,   *young wenches*
    Cam skelpan up the way.   *came hurrying*
Twa had manteeles o' dolefu' black,   *two, mantles*
15   But ane wi' lyart lining;   *one, grey*
The *third*, that gaed a wee aback,   *went, behind*
    Was in the fashion shining
        Fu' gay that day.   *full*

The *twa* appear'd like sisters twin,   *two*
20   In feature, form, an' claes;   *clothes*
Their visage — wither'd, lang an' thin,   *long*
    An' sour as onie slaes: *any sloes*
The *third* cam up, hap-step-an'-lowp,   *hop-step-and-leap*
    As light as onie lambie, —   *any lamb*
25 An' wi' a curchie low did stoop,   *curtsey*
    As soon as e'er she saw me,
        Fu' kind that day.

Wi' bonnet aff, quoth I, 'Sweet lass,   *off*
    I think ye seem to ken me;   *know*
30 I'm sure I've seen that bonie face,   *pretty*
    But yet I canna name ye. — '   *cannot*
Quo' she, an' laughin as she spak,   *spoke*
    An' taks me by the hands,
'Ye, for my sake, hae gi'en the feck   *have given, bulk*
35 Of a' the *ten commands* - religion.
    A screed some day.   *rip*

'My name is FUN — your cronie dear,   *friend*
    The nearest friend ye hae;   *have*
An' this is SUPERSTITION here,
40   An' that's HYPOCRISY.
I'm gaun to Mauchline *Holy Fair*,   *going*
    To spend an hour in daffin: *larking/playing*
Gin ye'll go there, yon runkl'd pair,   *if, wrinkled*
    We will get famous laughin
45   At them this day.'

Quoth I, 'Wi' a' my heart, I'll do't;
    I'll get my Sunday's sark on,   *shirt*
An' meet you on the holy spot;
    Faith, we'se hae fine remarkin!'   *we'll have*

50 Then I gaed hame at crowdie-time,   *went, breakfast/gruel*
     An' soon I made me ready;
For roads were clad, frae side to side,   *filled*
     Wi' monie a wearie body,   *many*
       In droves that day.

55 Here farmers gash, in ridin graith,   *smart, gear*
     Gaed hoddan by their cotters;   *went jogging, farm workers*
There swankies young, in braw braid-claith,   *strapping fellows, fine broadcloth*
     Are springan owre the gutters.   *jumping over*
The lasses, skelpan barefit, thrang,   *hastening barefoot, crowded*
60   In silks an' scarlets glitter;
Wi' *sweet-milk cheese*, in monie a whang,   *many, large slice*
     An' *farls*, bak'd wi' butter,   *cakes*
       Fu' crump that day.   *hard or crisp*

When by the *plate* we set our nose,   *collection plate*
65   Weel heapèd up wi' ha'pence,
A greedy glowr *Black-bonnet* throws,   *stare, Church elder*
     An' we maun draw our tippence.   *must give*
Then in we go to see the show:
     On ev'ry side they're gath'ran;
70 Some carryin dails, some chairs an' stools,   *bench planks*
     An' some are busy bleth'ran   *talking gossip*
       Right loud that day.

Here, stands a shed to fend the show'rs,   *ward off*
     An' screen our countra Gentry;   *country*
75 There *Racer Jess*, an' twa-three whores,   *two or three*
     Are blinkan at the entry.
Here sits a raw o' tittlan jads,   *giggling girls*
     Wi' heavin breasts an' bare neck;
An' there a batch o' *Wabster lads*,   *group of weavers*
80   Blackguardin frae Kilmarnock,   *mischief making from*
       For fun this day.

Here some are thinkan on their sins, *A*
     An' some upo' their claes; *B*   *clothes*
Ane curses feet that fyl'd his shins, *A*   *one, soiled, shoes/feet*
85   Anither sighs an' prays: *B*   *another*
On this hand sits a Chosen swatch, *C*   *sample*
     Wi' screw'd-up, grace-proud faces; *P*
On that, a set o' chaps, at watch, *C*
     Thrang winkan on the lasses *D*   *busy*
90   To *chairs* that day. *E*

O happy is that man an' blest! — *allusion to a pslam. 31*

Nae wonder that it pride him! — no

Whase ain dear lass, that he likes best, — whose own

Comes clinkan down beside him! — sitting quickly

Wi' arm repos'd on the *chair back*,

He sweetly does compose him;

Which, by degrees, slips round her *neck*,

An's loof upon her *bosom*, — hand

Unkend that day. — unnoticed

100 Now a' the congregation o'er

Is silent expectation;

For Moodie speels the holy door, — reaches

Wi' tidings o' damnation:

Should *Hornie*, as in ancient days, — the Devil

105 'Mang sons o' God present him;

The vera sight o' Moodie's face, — very

To's ain *het hame* had sent him — to his own hot home

Wi' fright that day.

Hear how he clears the points o' Faith

110 Wi' rattlin and thumpin!

Now meekly calm, now wild in wrath,

He's stampan, an' he's jumpan! — stomping

His lengthen'd chin, his turn'd-up snout,

His eldritch squeel an' gestures, — unearthly squeal

115 O how they fire the heart devout,

Like cantharidian plaisters — blister-producing plasters

On sic a day! — such

But hark! the *tent* has chang'd its voice;

There's peace an' rest nae langer; — no longer

120 For a' the *real judges* rise,

They canna sit for anger: — cannot

Smith opens out his cauld harangues, — cold

On *practice* and on *morals*;

An' aff the godly pour in thrangs, — off, groups

125 To gie the jars an' barrels — give

A lift that day. — to drink

What signifies his barren shine,

Of *moral pow'rs* an' *reason;*

His English style, an' gesture fine

130 Are a' clean out o' season.

[handwritten left margin:] guy getting to feel up his girlfriend in the kirk

[handwritten:] He's on such good form if the Devil came in he would be scared off.

Like SOCRATES or ANTONINE,
    Or some auld pagan heathen,   *old*
The *moral man* he does define,
    But ne'er a word o' *faith* in
135   That's right that day.

In guid time comes an antidote   *good*
    Against sic poison'd nostrum;   *such, preaching*
For Peebles, frae the water-fit,   *from, mouth of the river*
    Ascends the *holy rostrum*:
140 See, up he's got the Word o' God,
    An' meek an' mim has view'd it,
While COMMON-SENSE has taen the road,
    An' aff, an' up the *Cowgate*[1]
        Fast, fast that day.

145 Wee Miller niest, the Guard relieves,   *next*
    An' Orthodoxy raibles,   *recites by rote*
Tho' in his heart he weel believes,   *well*
    An' thinks it auld wives' fables: *old*
But faith! the birkie wants a *Manse*:   *fellow*
150   So, cannilie he hums them;   *carefully he humbugs*
Altho' his *carnal* Wit an' Sense
    Like hafflins-wise o'ercomes him   *almost half-wise*
        At times that day.

Now butt an' ben the Change-house fills,   *every corner of the Ale House*
155   Wi' *yill-caup* Commentators: *ale cup*
Here's crying out for bakes an' gills,   *biscuits*
    An' there the pint-stowp clatters;   *pint-jug slams*
While thick an' thrang, an' loud an' lang,   *crowded, long*
    Wi' *Logic* an' wi' *Scripture*,
160 They raise a din, that, in the end   *noise*
    Is like to breed a rupture
        O' wrath that day.

Leeze me on Drink! it gies us mair   *my blessings, gives, more*
    Than either School or Colledge;
165 It kindles Wit, it waukens Lear,   *wakens learning*
    It pangs us fou o' Knowledge: *crams, full*

1 A street so called, which faces the *tent* in *Mauchline*. R.B.

Be't *whisky-gill* or *penny wheep*,   small beer costing a penny
    Or onie stronger potion,   any
It never fails, on drinkin deep,
170   To kittle up our *notion*,   enliven spirits
        By night or day.

The lads an' lasses, blythely bent
    To mind baith *saul* an' *body*,   both soul
Sit round the table, weel content,   well
175   An' steer about the *Toddy*:   stir
On this ane's dress, an' that ane's leuk,   one's, look
    They're makin observations;
While some are cozie i' the neuk,   cosy, corner
    An' formin *assignations*
180   To meet some day.

But now the Lord's ain trumpet touts,   own, sounds
    Till a' the hills are rairan,   roaring back the echo
And echoes back return the shouts;
    Black Russell is na spairan: not sparing
185 His piercin words, like Highlan' swords,
    Divide the joints an' marrow;
His talk o' Hell, whare devils dwell,   where
    Our vera 'Sauls does harrow'[2]   very souls
        Wi' fright that day.

190 A vast, unbottom'd, boundless *Pit*,
    Fill'd fou o' *lowan brunstane*,   full, flaming brimstone
Whase ragin flame, an' scorchin heat,   whose
    Wad melt the hardest whun-stane!   would, whinstone
The *half-asleep* start up wi' fear,
195   An' think they hear it roaran;   roaring
When presently it does appear,
    'Twas but some neebor *snoran*   neighbour, snoring
        Asleep that day.

'Twad be owre lang a tale to tell,   over long
200   How monie stories past;   many
An' how they crouded to the yill,   crowded, ale
    When they were a' dismist;

2 Shakespeare's *Hamlet*, R.B. [Act I, Sc. 5].

How drink gaed round, in cogs an' caups,   *went, wooden jugs, cups*
   Amang the furms an' benches;   *among, a row of seats*
205 An' *cheese* an' *bread*, frae women's laps,   *from*
   Was dealt about in lunches,
     An' dawds that day.   *large pieces*

In comes a gausie, gash *Guidwife*,   *jolly, smart, good-*
   An' sits down by the fire,
210 Syne draws her *kebbuck* an' her knife;   *then, cheese*
   The lasses they are shyer:
The auld *Guidmen*, about the *grace*,   *old, good-*
   Frae side to side they bother;   *from*
Till some ane by his bonnet lays,   *one, cap*
215   An' gies them't, like a *tether*,   *gives, rope*
     Fu' lang that day.   *long*

Waesucks! for him that gets nae lass,   *Alas!, no*
   Or lasses that hae naething!   *have nothing*
Sma' need has he to say a grace,
220   Or melvie his braw claithing!   *dirty with meal, fine clothes*
O *Wives*, be mindfu', ance yoursel,   *once*
   How bonie lads ye wanted;   *handsome*
An' dinna for a *kebbuck-heel*   *do not, hard cheeese rind*
   Let lasses be affronted
225   On sic a day!   *such*

Now *Clinkumbell*,[3] wi' rattlan tow,   *noisy pull*
   Begins to jow an' croon;   *swing, toll*
Some swagger hame the best they dow,   *home, can*
   Some wait the afternoon.
230 At slaps the billies halt a blink,   *a dyke gap, young lads*
   Till lasses strip their shoon: *take off, shoes*
Wi' *faith* an' *hope*, an' *love* an' *drink*,
   They're a' in famous tune
     For crack that day.   *talk*

235 How monie hearts this day converts   *many*
   O' Sinners and o' Lasses!
Their hearts o' stane, gin night, are gane   *stone, come, gone*
   As saft as onie flesh is: *soft, any*

3 The Bell Ringer.

	There's some are fou o' *love divine*;	full
240	There's some are fou o' *brandy*;	full
	An' monie jobs that day begin,	many
	May end in *Houghmagandie*	sexual intercourse
	Some ither day.	other

This celebration of the sensual capacity of the Scottish people to resist the worst rhetorical excesses of their clerical masters was written in 1785 and revised in early 1786 for the Kilmarnock edition. As McGuirk notes it is a direct descendent of Fergusson's *Leith Races* which itself descends from Milton's *L'Allegro* and the nine-line Scottish medieval 'brawl' poem:

> I dwall amang the caller springs
> > That weet the Land o' Cakes,
> And aften tune my canty strings
> > At bridals and late-wakes.
> They ca' me Mirth; I ne'er was kend
> > To grumble or look sour,
> But blyth was be to lift a lend,
> > Gif ye was sey my pow'r
> > > An' pith this day.

[handwritten annotation: stanza form is christ/ork. (15th)]

Fergusson's poem is, of course, the celebration of a purely secular occasion; Burns is writing a more complex religious satire. Crawford (*Burns, A Study of the Poems and Songs*, p. 69) places the occasional poem accurately in the long Covenanter-originated Scottish tradition of open-air preaching. This specific event held in Mauchline in 1785 gathered together an audience of 2000 (four times the Mauchline population) of whom 1200 were communicants. Gilbert recorded that his brother was witness to this and had personal knowledge of the preachers he so incisively satirises.

Burns takes his epigraph from *Hypocrisy A-La-Mode*, a play written in 1704 by Tom Brown. That gale of liberal, satirical, enlightened laughter that runs through eighteenth-century English literature, especially Henry Fielding, as it attempts to sweep away institutionalised religious hypocrisy also blows powerfully through Burns's writings. He is the major Scottish variant on this anti-clerical Enlightenment project. His Scotland, however, was a darker, more theocratically-controlled state than almost anywhere else in Europe. In his early writing, as here, he senses victory over the savage forces of religious repression. Later, his mood was to darken as he despaired of the unbreakable grip Calvin's damnation had on the Scottish psyche and, hence, body politic.

This early poem has, however, the comic optimism of Fielding's *Tom Jones* rather than the demonic repression of Blake's *The Songs of Experience*. The roaring flames of hell here (ll. 190–8) are merely the snores of a fellow pew-member. Unlike Macbeth, who tragically meets three witches on the moor, our comic narrator meets only two, Superstition and Hypocrisy, but their gorgeous sister Fun is an immediately victorious Cinderella and her spirit drives the whole poem. If not promiscuous, Fun is a decidedly erotic young lady as are the young women running barefoot, to save their shoes, towards the thronging excitement and carrying gifts which might be for the satisfaction of appetites other than those of the stomach. Indeed, the whole poem is infused with the way in which the people convert the 'Occasion', so clerically defined, into an opportunity for their multiple, but especially sexual, appetites:

> O happy is that man an' blest!
> Nae wonder that it pride him!
> Whase ain dear lass, that he likes best,
> Comes clinkan down beside him!

This echo of *Psalm 46* also alerts us to the fact that the rhetorical world of these preachers breeds sexual ills. For example, in 1.116, 'cantharidian plaisters' were poultices made from the aphrodisiac Spanish fly.

Burns's assault on the various masters of pulpit oratory names names in a way that ensured there would be a severe backlash against him. 'Sawney' Moodie, with his old-time, 'Auld-Licht' undiluted gospel of damnation, is first on stage (ll. 100–17). Moodie (1728–99) was minister of Riccarton near Kilmarnock. He is followed by the 'New Licht' George Smith (d. 1823), minister of Galston. McGuirk subtly argues that while Burns is criticising Smith's rhetorical banality, he is more intent on satirising the congregation whose appetite for hell-fire preaching excludes the life of actual good-works. Smith's position is then assaulted by William Peebles of Newton-upon-Ayr (1753–1826) who, further inflaming the malign passions of the congregation, drives Common Sense, a central value of the new, more liberal Christianity, from the field. He is succeeded by Alexander Miller (d. 1804) whose professional self-seeking rebounded against him when the parishioners of Kilmaurs subsequently attempted to stop him getting that charge due, he claimed, to the effects of ll. 145–54. The worst is saved to the last. 'Black' John Russel (c. 1740–1817) was then minister at Kilmarnock. Subsequently minister at Cromarty, Hugh Miller (*My Schools and*

Schoolmasters) testified to his capacity to terrify, indeed, traumatise his congregation.

Along with such manifestations of theocratic control Burns adds some more overt political commentary. 'Racer Jess' is Janet Gibson (d. 1813), who is the daughter of Poosie Nansie, mine hostess of *Love and Liberty*, is with her like-inclined companions strategically placed beside the laird's tent. In the same stanza, the '*Wabster* lads/ Blackguarding from Kilmarnock' probably belong to the weaving community which was deeply and dissidently radical.

The poem moves from a celebration of alcohol (ll. 163–71) and the triumph of this earthy spirit over the one of false sanctimony to a triumphant assertion, implicit throughout the poem, of spontaneous eroticism. The experienced women may already be dealing out more than bread and cheese but, assignations made, loss of virginity happily looms at the poem's end. As Edwin Muir wrote, regarding the 'sordid and general tyranny' of the kirk session: 'it is only necessary to say that the time-honoured Scottish tradition of fornication triumphantly survived all its terrors' (*John Knox*, 1930, pp. 306–7).

Address to the Deil

First printed in the Kilmarnock edition, 1786.

> O Prince! O Chief of many thronèd pow'rs!
> That led th' embattl'd seraphim to war —
> > > Milton.

O Thou! whatever title suit thee —
Auld Hornie, Satan, Nick, or Clootie —   old, cloven-hoofed
Wha in yon cavern grim an' sootie,   who, filled with soot
    Clos'd under hatches,
5   Spairges about the brunstane cootie,   splashes, brimstone dish
    To scaud poor wretches!   scald

Hear me, *auld Hangie*, for a wee,   old hangman, while
An' let poor *damnèd bodies* be;
I'm sure sma' pleasure it can gie,   give
10   Ev'n to a *deil*,   devil
To skelp an' scaud poor dogs like me   hit/slap, scald
    An' hear us squeel!

what is his name?

Great is thy pow'r an' great thy fame;
Far kend, an' noted is thy name;   known
15 An' tho' yon *lowan heugh's* thy hame,   moaning, hollow, home
        Thou travels far;
    An' faith! thou's neither lag, nor lame,   backward
        Nor blate nor scaur.   bashful, afraid

    Whyles, ranging like a roarin lion,   sometimes
20 For prey, a' holes an' corners tryin;
    Whyles, on the strong-wing'd Tempest flyin,
        Tirlan the *Kirks*;   stripping – attacking
    Whyles, in the human bosom pryin,
        Unseen thou lurks.

25 I've heard my rev'rend *Graunie* say,   grannie
    In lanely glens ye like to stray;   lonely
    Or, where auld ruin'd castles grey   old
        Nod to the moon,
    Ye fright the nightly wand'rer's way
30   Wi' eldritch croon.   unearthly eerie moan

    When twilight did my *Graunie* summon,   grannie
    To say her pray'rs, douce, honest woman!   sober/prudent
    Aft yont the dyke she's heard you bumman,   away beyond
        Wi' eerie drone;
35 Or, rustlin, thro' the boortries coman,   alder trees coming
        Wi' heavy groan.

    Ae dreary, windy, winter night,   one
    The stars shot down wi' sklentan light,   slanting
    Wi' you mysel, I gat a fright: got
40   Ayont the lough,   beyond, loch
    Ye, like a *rash-buss*, stood in sight,   bunch of rushes
        Wi' waving sugh: moan

    The cudgel in my nieve did shake,   fist
    Each bristl'd hair stood like a stake;
45 When wi' an eldritch, stoor *quaick, quaick*,   unearthly harsh, duck quack
        Amang the springs,   among
    Awa ye squatter'd like a *drake*,   away, a noisy take-off
        On whistling wings.

Let *Warlocks* grim, an' wither'd *Hags*,
50 Tell how wi' you, on ragweed nags,   ragwort
They skim the muirs an' dizzy crags,   moors, high peaks
    Wi' wicked speed;
And in kirk-yards renew their leagues,
    Owre howket dead.   over those raised from the grave

55 Thence, countra wives, wi' toil an' pain,   country
May plunge an' plunge the *kirn* in vain;   churn
For Och! the yellow treasure's taen   taken
    By witching skill;
An' dawtit, twal-pint *Hawkie's* gaen   petted, 12-pint cow has gone
60   As yell's the Bill.   dry, bull

Thence, mystic knots mak great abuse
On *Young-Guidmen*, fond, keen an' croose   husbands, over confident
When the best *warklum* i' the house,   work-tool, penis
    By cantraip wit,   magic/evil
65 Is instant made no worth a louse,
    Just at the bit.   stopped before ejaculation

↑ controversial sexual content.

When thowes dissolve the snawy hoord,   thawes, snowy hoard
An' float the jinglin icy boord,   water's surface
Then, *Water-kelpies* haunt the foord,   imaginary water-spirits, ford
70   By your direction,
An' nighted Trav'llers are allur'd
    To their destruction.

An' aft your moss-traversing *Spunkies*   often, bog-, demons
Decoy the wight that late an' drunk is: fellow
75 The bleezan, curst, mischievous monkies
    Delude his eyes,
Till in some miry slough he sunk is,   dirty hole
    Ne'er mair to rise.   more

When MASONS' mystic *word* an' *grip*
80 In storms an' tempests raise you up,
Some cock or cat your rage maun stop,   shall
    Or, strange to tell!
The *youngest Brother* ye wad whip   would
    Aff straught to *Hell*.   off straight

85 Lang syne in *Eden*'s bonie yard, — long ago
    When youthfu' lovers first were pair'd,
    An' all the Soul of Love they shar'd,
        The raptur'd hour,
    Sweet on the fragrant flow'ry swaird, — grassy edge
90   In shady bow'r:

    Then you, ye auld, snick-drawing dog! — old, sly door opener
    Ye cam to Paradise incog, — came, disguised
    An' play'd on man a cursed brogue — trick
       (Black be your fa'!), — fall
95   An' gied the infant warld a shog, — gave, world, shake
       'Maist ruin'd a'. — almost

    D'ye mind that day when in a bizz — flurry/bustle
    Wi' reeket duds, an' reestet gizz, — smoky clothes, scorched wig
    Ye did present your smoutie phiz — smutty face
100   'Mang better folk;
    An' sklented on the *man of Uzz* — squinted at Job
       Your spitefu' joke?

    An' how ye gat him i' your thrall, — got, spell
    An' brak him out o' house an' hal', — broke
105 While scabs an' blotches did him gall,
       Wi' bitter claw;
    An' lows'd his ill-tongu'd wicked *Scawl* — — slackened, scolding wife
       Was warst ava? — worst of all

    But a' your doings to rehearse,
110 Your wily snares an' fechtin fierce, — fighting
    Sin' that day MICHAEL did you pierce
       Down to this time,
    Wad ding a *Lallan* tongue, or *Erse*, — would, beat, Lowland Scots, Irish
       In Prose or Rhyme.

115 An' now, auld *Cloots*, I ken ye're thinkan, — old, know
    A certain Bardie's rantin, drinkin,
    Some luckless hour will send him linkan, — hurrying
       To your black pit; — Hell
    But, faith! he'll turn a corner jinkin, — dodging
120   An' cheat you yet.

not raised the thought in the poem.

But fare-you-weel, auld *Nickie-ben*!   old
O wad ye tak a thought an' men'!   would, mend
Ye aiblins might — I dinna ken —   perhaps, do not know
     Still hae a *stake*:   have
125 I'm wae to think upo' yon den,   sad
     Ev'n for your sake.

— tare d thought + change your ways.

Burns mentions to John Richmond on 17th February 1786 that he had recently completed this poem. It is normally dated to the winter of 1785–6. A poem of this length Burns might have turned out quickly, so it is probably one of the fruits of his intense writing campaign leading to publication of the Kilmarnock edition.

This poem is now generally accepted as a relatively light-weight piece of near comic knockabout as Burns mocks the allegedly fast-fading figure of the Devil from his hitherto central role in Scottish theology and folk-lore. In his essay 'Robert Burns, Master of Scottish Poetry' (*Uncollected Scottish Criticism*, ed. Noble (London), pp. 199–200), Edwin Muir analyses this poem as the centre-piece of his persuasive argument that during the eighteenth century enlightened, improving, secularising Scotland had lost both its theological passion and its sense of supernatural mystery integral to its older poetry:

> . . . two centuries of religious terrors had faded under the touch of reason and enlightenment, and the mysterious problems of election and damnation, had turned into amusing doggerel:

> > O Thou wha in the Heavens dost dwell,
> > Wha, as it pleases best thysel';
> > Sends ane to heaven and ten to hell,
> >   A' for thy glory,
> > And no for any guid or ill
> >   They've done afore thee!

Calvinism, once feared as a power or hated as a superstition, became absurd under the attack of common reason. The growing powers of the Enlightenment encouraged the change in the universities, the churches, in popular debate, and among the people. The ideas of liberty and equality did their part; Scotland became a place where a man was a man for a' that; the new humanistic attitude to religion led people to believe that 'The hert's aye the pairt aye that mak's us richt or wrang.' The story of the Fall became a simple story of human misfortune to two

young people whose intentions had been so good, 'Lang syne in
Eden's bonnie yard'.

> Then you, ye auld sneck-drawing dog!
> Ye cam to Paradise incog.
> And played on a man a curse brogue
>   (Black be your fa!)
> An' gled the infant world a shog
>   Maist ruined a'.

Muir further thinks that this new enlightened poetry is, with
'something of Voltaire's contes and Bernard Shaw's plays', witty
but lightweight, even, relative to the old poetry, superficial. There
are two related fundamental miscomprehensions in Muir's account.
First, the power of folklore is present in the poem though not, say, as
we find its direct intrusion as in the great Scottish Ballad tradition,
so beloved by Muir, but in Burns's ambivalent treatment of it. As he
wrote to Dr Moore:

> I sometimes keep a sharp look-out in suspicious places; and
> though nobody can be more sceptical in these matters than I,
> yet it often takes an effort of Philosophy to shake of these idle
> terrors (Letter 125).

What we see in this particular poem from ll. 5–84 is no simple send-
up of foolishly atavistic folk-superstition. Not only is Burns intent
on anthropologically recording, as in *Halloween*, the customs and
beliefs of his rural community but, as in *Tam o' Shanter*, conveying
the still 'eerie' potency of that world. (See Edward J. Cowan, 'Burns
and Superstition', *Love and Liberty*, pp. 229–37.) He is also, as
usual, making salacious jokes inspired by the bottomless well of
sexual metaphor supplied to him by folk-tradition. Hugh Blair
wanted ll. 61–6 deleted as 'indecent' because they depend on the
identification of lume/loom with the penis. (See *BC*, 1932, p. 95.)

Muir, however, is absolutely wrong in thinking that it is the
diminished power of Calvinism on the Scottish psyche that leads to
the poem's, to him, lightweight tone. This is a particularly weird
error in Muir, who more than any other figure in a profoundly anti-
Calvinist, Scottish Renaissance group believed that Knox (of whom
he actually wrote a biography) had not lost his sadistic, disintegrat-
ing grip on the Scottish soul. Further, that Scottish reintegration
meant a return to catholic, European humanism.

Burns is certainly partly laughing at the Devil in the poem's
opening sequences (ll. 1–24) by the reductive ridicule of reducing

the devil's energies to being devoted to the poet's petty transgressions. The Devil, however, is not for his own sake being laughed out of court. Burns's poetic wit is in direct proportion to his most potent enemies. The enemy here is not the devil but those who seek demonically to control mankind in his name. For their power structure to remain intact the Devil could not be allowed to become a laughing matter. This is why, even more than the more personally abusive clerical satires, this poem caused such an outcry. As Carol McGuirk finely writes:

A ringing blow in Burns's quarrel with the Auld Licht, this satire caused a major local scandal. Several of the anonymous contributors to *Animadversions*, James Maxwell's compilation of evangelical attacks on Burns (Paisley, 1788), saw this poem as final proof of Burns's evil values. Alexander ('Saunders') Tait of Tarbolton, a mantua-maker and tailor who considered himself Burns's equal as a satirist, also seized upon this as Burns's most shocking poem, publishing his attack in 1790.

Burns intended it to shock, and so structures the poem round what any Auld Licht partisan would see as a heretical statement of Arminianism: the deil's long-ago invasion of Eden only 'almost' 'ruined all' for Adam and Eve (l. 96): the stain of sin is not ineradicable and even Satan (if he wished) could 'tak a thought' and mend = change and receive forgiveness. Burns's 'deil' is neither the sadistic demon of Auld Licht sermons nor the tragic hero Milton's Satan considered himself to be. A rather forlorn and unsuccessful mischief-maker, his smudged ('smoutie') face ashy from brimstone and his plots against humanity invariably thwarted, the deil is addressed more or less as just another 'poor, damned body'. The poet is dramatising his rejection of predestination. The Arminians had challenged Calvinist 'election' (salvation through grace alone, not human effort) but Burns focuses on its corollary—repudiation, a doctrine that insisted that the reprobated are eternally cast away from grace, whatever their benighted individual efforts to be (and do) good. Burns, by contrast, announces that he considers himself salvageable (ll. 119–20)–and if 'a certain Bardie' can be saved, then there must be hope for a mere devil. The poet is paying a backhanded compliment to his own sinfulness as he mocks the Auld Licht. No one – not even the deil – is all bad and forever incapable of change, the poem argues with a cheerful perversity that enraged the Auld Licht. A more orthodox point is also made: hope of heaven is more likely to convert sinners than fear of damnation. (pp. 233–4)

The Death and Dying Words of Poor Mailie,
The Author's Only Pet Yowe: An Unco Mournfu' Tale
First printed in the Kilmarnock edition, 1786.

As MAILIE, an' her lambs thegither,   *together*
Was ae day nibblin on the tether,   *one day, chewing*
Upon her cloot she coost a hitch,   *hoof, looped*
An' owre she warsl'd in the ditch: *over, floundered*
5 There, groanin, dying, she did ly,
When *Hughoc* he cam doytan by.   *walking/staggering*

Wi' glowrin een, an' lifted han's   *staring eyes*
Poor *Hughoc* like a statue stan's;
He saw her days were near hand ended,
10 But, wae's my heart! he could na mend it!   *woe, not*
He gaped wide, but naething spak.   *nothing spoke*
At length poor *Mailie* silence brak: —   *broke*

'O thou, whase lamentable face   *whose*
Appears to mourn my woefu' case!
15 My *dying words* attentive hear,
An' bear them to my *Master* dear.

'Tell him, if e'er again he keep
As muckle gear as buy a *sheep*,   *much money*
O, bid him never tie them mair,   *more*
20 Wi' wicked strings o' hemp or hair!
But ca' them out to park or hill,   *call/drive*
An' let them wander at their will:
So may his flock increase, an' grow
To *scores* o' lambs, an' *packs* o' woo'!

25 'Tell him, he was a Master kin',   *kind*
An' ay was guid to me an' mine;   *good*
An' now my *dying* charge I gie him,   *give*
My helpless *lambs*, I trust them wi' him.   *with*

'O, bid him save their harmless lives,
30 Frae dogs, an' tods, an' butchers' knives!   *from, foxes*
But gie them guid cow-milk their fill,   *give, good*
Till they be fit to fend themsel;   *themselves*
An' tent them duely, e'en an' morn,   *tend*
Wi' taets o' *hay* an' ripps o' *corn*.   *small amounts, handfuls*

35   'An' may they never learn the gaets,   ways
       Of ither vile, wanrestfu' *Pets* —   other, restless
       To slink thro' slaps, an' reave an' steal,   gaps in dykes
       At stacks o' pease, or stocks o' kail.   plants
       So may they, like their great *forbears*,
40   For monie a year come thro' the sheers: many
       So *wives* will gie them bits o' bread,   give
       An' *bairns* greet for them when they're dead.   children cry

       'My poor *toop-lamb*, my son an' heir,   tup/male
       O, bid him breed him up wi' care!   with
45   An' if he live to be a beast,
       To pit some havins in his breast!   conduct
       An' warn him, what I winna name,   would not
       To stay content wi' *yowes* at hame;   ewes
       An' no to rin an' wear his cloots,   run, hooves
50   Like other menseless, graceless brutes.   unmannerly

       'An' niest, my *yowie*, silly thing;   next, ewekin/female baby
       Gude keep thee frae a *tether string*!   from
       O, may thou ne'er forgather up,   make friends
       Wi' onie blastet, moorland *toop*;   any, blasted/damned
55   But ay keep mind to moop an' mell,   always, nibble & mix
       Wi' sheep o' credit like thysel!

       'And now, *my bairns*, wi' my last breath,
       I lea'e my blessin wi' you baith: leave, with, both
       An' when you think upo' your Mither,   mother
60   Mind to be kind to ane anither.   one another

       'Now, honest *Hughoc*, dinna fail,   do not
       To tell my Master a' my tale;
       An' bid him burn this cursed *tether*,
       An' for thy pains thou'se get my blather.'   thou will, bladder

65   This said, poor *Mailie* turn'd her head,
       An' clos'd her een amang the dead!   eyes, among

This poem fuses an actual experience at Lochlea, subsequently recorded by Gilbert Burns, with Burns's awareness of the tradition of comic animal monologue as integral to the eighteenth-century Scottish vernacular revival. As Burns noted, Hughoc was an actual neighbouring herdsman though, in reality, the sheep was freed from

the strangling tether and survived. Its 'poetic' death is necessary to
the comic pathos of the poem. The literary tradition of burlesquing
animal poetry commenced with William Hamilton of Gilbertfield
(c. 1665–1751) whose rhetorical greyhound's death-speech parodies
Blind Harry's *Wallace*. Burns would also be aware of the so-
influential Robert Fergusson's very funny parody of Henry Mac-
kenzie's *The Man of Feeling* (1771) with his Milton-burlesquing
The Sow of Feeling (1773). As we saw in the Introduction, Mac-
kenzie never forgave Fergusson's lachrymose porcine parody. The
tone of Burns's poem is more subtle since the mother's dying
warnings to her children, particularly against keeping the wrong
sexual company, are a mixture of his satirising snobbery and
prudery with genuine sympathy towards a mother's natural, pro-
tective love. Burns, indeed (see *Address to a Young Friend*), often
displayed a genuine paternal care, which revealed a desire to pre-
serve his varied dependants from the dangers inherent in his own
licentious excesses.

Poor Mailie's Elegy

First printed in the Kilmarnock edition, 1786.

Lament in rhyme, lament in prose,
Wi' saut tears tricklin down your nose;   salt
Our *Bardie's* fate is at a close,
    Past a' remead!   remedy
5 The last, sad cape-stane of his woes;   coping stone(final weight)
    Poor Mailie's dead!

It's no the loss of warl's gear,   worldly goods
That could sae bitter draw the tear,   so
Or mak our *Bardie*, dowie, wear   drooping/gloomy
10   The mourning weed:
He's lost a friend an' neebor dear   neighbour
    In *Mailie* dead.

Thro' a' the toun she trotted by him;   town
A lang half-mile she could descry him;   long
15 Wi' kindly bleat, when she did spy him,
    She ran wi' speed:
A friend mair faithfu' ne'er cam nigh him,   more, came near
    Than *Mailie* dead.

I wat she was a *sheep* o' sense,   wot
20 An' could behave hersel wi' mense: tact/grace
    I'll say't, she never brak a fence,   broke
        Thro' thievish greed.
    Our *Bardie*, lanely, keeps the spence   parlour
        Sin' *Mailie's* dead.

25 Or, if he wanders up the howe,   glen
    Her livin image in *her yowe*   ewe
    Comes bleatin till him, owre the knowe,   over the hill edge
        For bits o' bread;
    An' down the briny pearls rowe   roll
30   For *Mailie* dead.

    She was nae get o' moorlan tips,   not born from
    Wi' tawted ket, an' hairy hips;   matted fleece
    For her forbears were brought in ships,
        Frae 'yont the TWEED: from beyond
35 A bonier *fleesh* ne'er cross'd the clips   fleece, sheep shears
        Than *Mailie* dead.

    Wae worth the man wha first did shape   woe befall
    That vile, wanchancie thing — a *raep*!   dangerous, rope
    It maks guid fellows girn an' gape,   makes good, facial contortion
40   Wi' chokin dread;
    An' *Robin's* bonnet wave wi' crape   mourning
        For *Mailie* dead.

    O a' ye *Bards* on bonie DOON!
    An' wha on AIRE your chanters tune!   who, Ayr, bagpipes
45 Come, join the melancholious croon
        O' *Robin's* reed!
    His heart will never get aboon!   above/over
        His *Mailie's* dead!

This was probably written in 1785–6 as a companion piece for publication with the preceding Mailie monologue. Again the tone of the poem is mixed. Burns employs the six-line Standard Habbie used in vernacular eighteenth-century elegy while partly parodying the content of these poems. His most specified source is probably Fergusson's *Elegy on the Death of Mr David Gregory* with its repetitive end-line 'Sin Gregory's dead'. He is also partly sending up his own emotions. This is emphasised by the recent discovery

from a London saleroom catalogue for May 1962 of an hitherto
unknown last stanza:

> She was nae get o' runted rams,
> Wi' woo' like goat's an' legs like trams;
> She was the flower o' Fairlee lambs,
>   A famous breed:
> Now Robin, greetin', chows the hams
>   O' Mailie dead.

This peasant practicality would have been too much for his genteel
audience. On the other hand, there is real affection for its pedigree
beauty. This was the man who was still surrounding himself with
pet sheep at Ellisland. Further, as in his mouse poem, the lives of
men and beasts are both brutally intruded upon not only by lethal
elemental forces but by human-inspired, cruel economic and poli-
tical forces. The accidentally throttled beast has its more sinister
legally garrotted human counterpart:

> Wae worth the man wha first did shape
> That vile chancie thing – a rape!
> It maks guid fellows girn an' gape,
>   Wi' chokin dread . . .

Epistle to James Smith

First printed in the Kilmarnock edition, 1786.

Friendship, mysterious cement of the soul!
Sweet'ner of Life, and solder of Society!
I owe thee much.

> – BLAIR

Dear Smith, the sleest, pawkie thief,	slyest, cunning
That e'er attempted stealth or rief!	robbery/plunder
Ye surely hae some warlock-breef	have, wizard-spell
Owre human hearts;	over
5 For ne'er a bosom yet was prief	proof
Against your arts.	
For me, I swear by sun an' moon,	
And ev'ry star that blinks aboon,	above
Ye've cost me twenty pair o' shoon,	shoes
10 Just gaun to see you;	going
And ev'ry ither pair that's done,	other
Mair taen I'm wi' you.	more taken

That auld, capricious carlin, *Nature*,   hag
To mak amends for scrimpit stature,   make, stunted
15 She's turn'd you off, a human-creature
        On her *first* plan;
And in her freaks, on ev'ry feature
        She's wrote *the Man*.

Just now I've taen the fit o' rhyme,   taken
20 My barmie noddle's working prime,   excited head/brain
My fancy yerket up sublime,   pulled together
        Wi' hasty summon:
Hae ye a leisure-moment's time   have
        To hear what's comin?

25 Some rhyme a neebor's name to lash;   neighbour
Some rhyme (vain thought!) for needfu' cash;
Some rhyme to court the countra clash,   country gossip
        An' raise a din;
For me, an *aim* I never fash;   think of
30   I rhyme for *fun*.   — *spontaneous*.

The star that rules my luckless lot,
Has fated me the russet coat,   poor man's coat
An' damn'd my fortune to the groat;   smallest coin
        But, in requit,   as compensation
35 Has blest me with a *random-shot*
        O' countra wit.   country

This while my notion's taen a sklent,   taken a turn/bend
To try my fate in guid, black *prent*; — *being*   good, print
But still the mair I'm that way bent, *published*   more
40   Something cries, 'Hoolie!   halt
I red you, honest man, tak tent!   warn, heed
        Ye'll shaw your folly: show

'There's ither Poets, much your betters,   other
Far seen in *Greek*, deep men o' *letters*,   well versed
45 Hae thought they had ensur'd their debtors,   have
        A' future ages;
Now moths deform, in shapeless tatters,
        Their unknown pages.'

Then farewell hopes o' Laurel-boughs
50 To garland my poetic brows!
Henceforth, I'll rove where busy ploughs
        Are whistling thrang;   busily/at work
An' teach the lanely heights an' howes   lonely hills and dales
        My rustic sang.   song

55 I'll wander on, wi' tentless heed   carefree
How never-halting moments speed,
Till Fate shall snap the brittle thread;
        Then, all unknown,
I'll lay me with th' _inglorious dead_, – allude to Gray's
60   Forgot and gone!   elogy.

But why o' Death, begin a tale?
Just now we're living sound an' hale;   strong
Then top and maintop croud the sail,   crowd
        Heave _Care_ o'er-side!
65 And large, before Enjoyment's gale,
        Let's tak the tide.

This life, sae far's I understand,   so
Is a' enchanted fairy-land,
Where Pleasure is the Magic-wand,
70   That, wielded right,
Maks Hours like Minutes, hand in hand,   makes
        Dance by fu' light.

The _magic-wand_ then let us wield;
For, ance that five-an'-forty's speel'd,   once, climbed/reached
75 See, crazy, weary, joyless, Eild,   old age
        Wi' wrinkl'd face,
Comes hostin, hirplan owre the field,   coughing, limping over
        Wi' creepin pace.

When ance _life's day_ draws near the gloamin, once, twilight
80 Then fareweel vacant, careless roamin;   farewell
An' fareweel chearfu' tankards foamin,
        An' social noise:
An' fareweel dear, deluding Woman,
        The joy of joys!

85   O *Life*! how pleasant, in thy morning,
     Young Fancy's rays the hills adorning!
     Cold-pausing Caution's lesson scorning,
          We frisk away,
     Like school-boys, at th' expected warning,
90   To joy an' play.

     We wander there, we wander here,
     We eye the *rose* upon the brier,
     Unmindful that the *thorn* is near,
          Among the leaves;
95   And tho' the puny wound appear,
           Short while it grieves.

     Some, lucky, find a flow'ry spot,
     For which they never toil'd nor swat;   sweated
     They drink the *sweet* and eat the *fat*,
100   But care or pain;   without
     And haply eye the barren hut
           With high disdain.

     With steady aim, some Fortune chase;
     Keen Hope does ev'ry sinew brace;
105   Thro' fair, thro' foul, they urge the race,
          And seize the prey:
     Then cannie, in some cozie place,   quietly, snug
           They close the *day*.

     And others, like your humble servan',
110   *Poor wights*! nae rules nor roads observin,   no
     To right or left eternal swervin,
          They zig-zag on;
     Till, curst with Age, obscure an' starvin,
          They aften groan.   often

115   Alas! what bitter toil an' straining —
     But truce with peevish, poor complaining!
     Is Fortune's fickle *Luna* waning?
          E'en let her gang!   go
     Beneath what light she has remaining,
120   Let's sing our Sang.   song

My pen I here fling to the door,
And kneel, ye *Pow'rs*, and warm implore,
'Tho' I should wander *Terra* o'er,   world
    In all her climes,
125 Grant me but this, I ask no more,
    Ay rowth o' rhymes.   abundant

'Gie dreeping roasts to *countra Lairds*,   give dripping, country
Till icicles hing frae their beards;   hang from
Gie fine braw claes to fine *Life-guards*   give, handsome clothes
130   And *Maids of Honor*;
And yill an' whisky gie to *Cairds*,   ale, give, tinkers
    Until they sconner.   are sick of it

'A *Title*, DEMPSTER merits it;
A Garter gie to WILLIE PIT;   symbol of Knighthood, give
135 Gie Wealth to some be-ledger'd Cit,   give, accounting citizen
    In cent per cent;
But give me real, sterling Wit,
    And I'm content

'While ye are pleas'd to keep me hale,   healthy
140 I'll sit down o'er my scanty meal,
Be't *water-brose* or *muslin-kail*,   gruel, meatless broth
    Wi' cheerfu' face,
As lang's the Muses dinna fail   long, do not
    To say the grace.'

145 An anxious e'e I never throws   eye
Behint my lug, or by my nose;   behind, ear
I jouk beneath Misfortune's blows   dodge/duck
    As weel's I may;   well as
Sworn foe to *sorrow*, *care*, and *prose*,
150   I rhyme away.

O ye douce folk that live by rule,
Grave, tideless-blooded, calm an' cool,   serious/sober
Compar'd wi' you — O fool! fool! fool!   no rise & fall of passions
    How much unlike!
155 Your hearts are just a standing pool,
    Your lives, a dyke!   stone wall

Nae hair-brained, sentimental traces   no
In your unletter'd, nameless faces!
In *arioso* trills and graces
160   Ye never stray;
But *gravissimo*, solemn basses
          Ye hum away.

Ye are sae *grave*, nae doubt ye're *wise*;   so, no
Nae ferly tho' ye do despise   no wonder
165 The hairum-scairum, ram-stam boys,   wild, headlong
          The rattling squad:
I see ye upward cast your eyes —
          Ye ken the road!   know

Whilst I — but I shall haud me there,   hold
170 Wi' you I'll scarce gang *ony where* —   go any
Then, *Jamie*, I shall say nae mair,   no more
          But quat my sang,   quit, song
Content wi' YOU to mak a *pair*,   make
          Whare'er I gang.   go

James Smith (1765–1823) was initially a linen-draper in Mauchline who eventually emigrated to Jamaica after his business partnership in printing near Linlithgow collapsed. He was younger brother to one of the 'Mauchline Belles'. Smith is the recipient of several letters from Burns.

This is the first of a series of epistles written by Burns to either Ayrshire intimates or intended intimates. This phase of his life, energised by Masonic membership, is intensely social and, as we will see in *The Vision*, a central aspiration, despite so many influences to the contrary, was to put creative tap-roots into Ayrshire soil and anoint himself the Bard of its fertile but, as yet, poetically fallow terrain. Historically this meant, beginning with Wallace, a resurrection of Ayrshire heroes. In terms of his own life he looked to surround himself with fraternal like-minded spirits. Hence this sequence of significant poetic epistles to James Smith, David Sillar, Gavin Hamilton, John Lapraik, William Simpson and John Rankin.

The epistolary form derives, of course, from classical poetry and was heavily used in Augustan verse, most happily by Pope. The genre had been domesticated, however, by an exchange of epistles between Alan Ramsay and William Hamilton of Gilbertfield which were instrumental in reactivating Scottish vernacular poetry in the eighteenth century. As McGuirk has noted, these epistles were 'a

means of interchange between patriotic Scots poets' which 'also
incorporated Horatian themes: country pleasure, disdain of 'great-
ness', praise of friendship, discussion of current issues and (espe-
cially) the state of Scottish poetry'. The proper use of the genre
entails a degree of creative, technical parity between the correspon-
dents. This was denied Burns, but his desire for the comforts of a
poetic coterie was so strong that he often seriously overemphasised
the talents of his correspondents. Sillars, for example, was a fine
fiddler but a less than mediocre poet. Lapraik very likely plagiarised
the song for which he achieved local fame. Later in life Burns was to
show absolutely no patience with poetic inferiors who clung to his
coat-tail in terms of social identity but not creative ability. He was as
creatively hierarchical as Swift or Pope.

While the surface and formal, linguistic energy of these early
Ayrshire epistles is cheerful and, even, boisterous, almost all of them
are marked with a degree of black anxiety about not only the external
social, economic and political forces acting on his achieving identity
and recognition as a true poet but the often anarchic, even chaotic,
internal forces which, while creatively necessary, were incompatible
with the prudence and self-restraint necessary for a secure existence.
Or, as he brilliantly defined it, in *The Vision*:

> Had I to guid advice but harket,
> I might, by this, hae led a market,
> Or strutted in a Bank and clarket
>   My Cash-Account;
> While here, half-mad, half-fed, half-sarket,
>   Is a' th' amount.

This epistle was written in the winter of 1785–6. Smith was
(ll. 163–74) a key member of the 'ram-stam boys'. This testosterone
charged group, especially Gavin Hamilton, were in constant con-
flict with the ministry. Burns's comment on Smith being small but
perfectly formed (ll. 13–18) may be partly a response to clerical
condemnation of his friend. The extent of Smith's friendship also
extended to Jean Armour. Burns was to order from Smith, then a
partner in a Calico works, his first present for Jean: ''tis my first
present to her since I have irrevocably called her mine, and I have a
kind of whimsical wish to get it from an old and much valued
friend of hers and mine, a Trusty Trojan, on whose friendship I
count myself possessed on a life-rent lease' (Letter 237). The
'Trusty Trojan' was his sole Mauchline friend as the dispute with
the Armour family deepened.

McGuirk ('Loose Canons: Milton and Burns, Artsong and Folk-song', *Love and Liberty*, pp. 317–20) has drawn attention to parallels between this poem and Milton's *Lycidas* as a poem which not only 'addresses issues of friendship and bereavement, fame and obscurity, poetic immortality and premature death' but also includes a harsher satire on corrupt religiosity (ll. 151–68) and on the capricious, lethal intrusions of blind fate into human life.

The central dialectic of the poem is based on Burns's chronic anxiety, equally pervasive in his letters, about the problematic nature of forging a poetic identity for himself. At this particular point in his life he was considering trying 'fate in guid, black prent' and the poem charts his disbelief that even the printed page will grant him the laurel bow of poetic immortality so that the poem celebrates the compensatory, rural, russet-coated anonymous rhyming funster (ll. 31–6). The black star of ill-luck, his sense of being under a Job-like curse, is, however, not so easily dismissed. The pervasive melancholy of Gray's *Elegy Written in a Country Churchyard* alluded to in ll. 59–60, 'I'll lay me with th' inglorious dead,/Forgot and gone!' suggests also Gray's line 'Some mute inglorious Milton here may rest' as his own fate. Also, as in contemporary English sentimental poetry, Burns makes the equation between the inability of the poet to become socially visible with the similar fate of the mass of the common people not to appear as individually identifiable in the stream of history. Thus the poem links Burns the invisible poet, with not only Burns the impoverished, unknown farmer but the mass of the people who are neither to be identified nor rewarded by history. Life is appallingly ill-divided between the poor and the over-rewarded rich (ll. 127–38). Dempster (l. 133) known as 'Honest George' Dempster was a Whig M.P. for Forfar Burghs 1761–90 and an agricultural improver. Pitt, at this stage in his prime-ministerial career, was the object of Burns's approval; it was he in the darkening 1790s, not Burns, who was to change political identity. As well as this fatalistic sense in the poem of political and economic forces too strong to be resisted, Burns in ll. 109–14 mentions his own Shandean proclivities for eccentric forward motion wholly unconducive to making a prosperous, if not a poetic, life.

Political satire.

A Dream

First printed in the Kilmarnock edition, 1786.

Thoughts, words, and deeds, the Statute blames with reason;
But surely Dreams *were ne'er indicted Treason.*

On reading, in the public papers, the Laureate's Ode with the other
parade of June 4th, 1786, the Author was no sooner dropt asleep,
than he imagined himself transported to the Birth-day Levee; and,
in his dreaming fancy, made the following Address: —

GUID-MORNIN to your MAJESTY!
    May Heaven augment your blisses,
On ev'ry new *Birth-day* ye see,
    A humble Poet wishes!   (changed from *Bardie* in 1793)
5 My Bardship here, at your Levee,
    On sic a day as this is,   such
Is sure an uncouth sight to see,
    Amang thae Birth-day dresses   among they
        Sae fine this day.   so

10 I see ye're complimented thrang,   busily
    By monie a *lord* an' *lady*;   many
'God Save the King' 's a cuckoo sang   song
    That's unco easy said ay: mighty
The *Poets*, too, a venal gang,
15   Wi' rhymes weel-turn'd an' ready,   well-
Wad gar you trow ye ne'er do wrang,   would make, think,wrong
    But ay unerring steady,
        On sic a day.   such

For me! before a Monarch's face,
20   Ev'n *there* I winna flatter;   will not
For neither Pension, Post, nor Place,
    Am I your humble debtor:
So, nae reflection on YOUR GRACE,   no
    Your Kingship to bespatter;
25 There's monie *waur* been o' the Race,   many worse
    And aiblins *ane* been better   maybe one
        Than You this day.

'Tis very true, my sovereign King,
   My skill may weel be doubted;   *well*
30 But *Facts* are chiels that winna ding, *fellows, will not be upset*
   And downa be disputed: *cannot*
Your *royal nest*, beneath *Your* wing,
   Is e'en right reft and clouted,   *torn & patched*
And now the third part o' the string,
35   An' less, will gang about it   *go*
       Than did ae day.   *one*

Far be't frae me that I aspire   *from*
   To blame your Legislation,
Or say, ye wisdom want, or fire
40   To rule this mighty nation:
But faith! I muckle doubt, my SIRE,   *much*
   Ye've trusted 'Ministration
To chaps wha in a *barn* or *byre*   *who*
   Wad better fill'd their station,
45   Than *courts* yon day.

And now Ye've gien auld *Britain* peace, *given old*
   Her broken shins to plaister;   *plaster*
Your sair taxation does her fleece,   *sore*
   Till she has scarce a tester: *sixpence*
50 For me, thank God, my life's a *lease*, *a tenant farm lease*
   Nae *bargain* wearin faster,   *no*
Or faith! I fear, that, wi' the geese,
   I shortly boost to pasture   *must*
      I' the craft some day.

55 I'm no mistrusting *Willie Pit*,
   When taxes he enlarges,
(An' *Will's* a true guid fallow's get,   *good, breed*
   A Name not Envy spairges),   *bespatters*
That he intends to pay your *debt*,
60   An' lessen a' your *charges*;
But, God sake! let nae *saving fit*   *no*
   Abridge your bonie *Barges*   *handsome*
      An' *Boats* this day.

Adieu, my LIEGE! may Freedom geck   *sport*
65   Beneath your high protection;
An' may Ye rax Corruption's neck,
   And gie her for dissection!   *give*

But since I'm here I'll no neglect,
    In loyal, true affection,
70 To pay your QUEEN, wi' due respect,
    My fealty an' subjection
        This great Birth-day.

Hail, *Majesty most Excellent!*
    While Nobles strive to please Ye,
75 Will Ye accept a Compliment,
    A simple Bardie gies Ye?   *gives*
Thae bonie Bairntime, Heav'n has lent,   *that pretty brood*
    Still higher may they heeze Ye   *hoist*
In bliss, till Fate some day is sent,
80   For ever to release Ye
        Frae Care that day.   *from*

For you, young Potentate o' Wales,
    I tell your *Highness* fairly,
Down Pleasure's stream, wi' swelling sails,
85   I'm tauld ye're driving rarely;   *told, unusually well*
But some day ye may gnaw your nails,
    An' curse your folly sairly,   *sorely*
That e'er ye brak *Diana's pales*,   *break*
    Or rattl'd dice wi' *Charlie*
90   By night or day.

Yet aft a ragged *Cowte's* been known,   *colt*
    To mak a noble *Aiver*;   *make, old horse*
So, ye may doucely fill a Throne,   *soberly*
    For a' their clish-ma-claver: *gossip*
95 There, Him at *Agincourt* wha shone,   *who*
    Few better were or braver;
And yet, wi' funny, queer Sir John,[1]
    He was an unco shaver   *a great madcap*
        For monie a day.   *many*

100 For you, right rev'rend Osnaburg,
    Nane sets the *lawn-sleeve* sweeter,   *none, becomes*
Altho' a ribban at your lug   *ribbon, ear*
    Wad been a dress compleater: *would*

---

1 Sir John Falstaff, Vide Shakespeare. R.B.

As ye disown yon paughty dog,   proud
105   That *bears* the Keys of Peter,
Then swith! an' get a *wife* to hug,
    Or trowth, ye'll stain the *Mitre*   in truth
        Some luckless day.

Young, royal TARRY-BREEKS, I learn,
110   Ye've lately come athwart her;
A glorious *Galley*, stem an' stern
    Weel rigg'd for *Venus barter*;[2]   well
But first hang out that she'll discern
    Your *hymeneal Charter*;
115 Then heave aboard your *grapple-airn*,   grappling iron
    An', large upon her *quarter*,
        Come full that day.

Ye, lastly, bonie blossoms a',
    Ye *royal Lasses* dainty,
120 Heav'n mak you guid as weel as braw,   good, well, fair
    An' gie you *lads* a-plenty: give
But sneer na *British-boys* awa!   not, away
    For Kings are unco scant ay,   greatly scarce
An' German-gentles are but *sma'*,   small
125   They're better just than *want ay*
        On onie day.   any

God bless you a'! consider now,
    Ye're unco muckle dautet;   greatly fussed over
But ere the *course* o' life be through,
130   It may be bitter sautet: salted
An' I hae seen their *coggie* fou,   have, plate full
    That yet hae tarrow't at it;   shown reluctance
But or the *day* was done, I trow,   believe
    The laggen they hae clautet   bottom, have scraped
135   Fu' clean that day.

Byron must have read this with admiration; he himself never wrote anything funnier or, amidst the laughter, landed on the Hanoverians, he also so loathed, so many palpable hits. Describing it as a 'dream' allows Burns, as in the headquote, to claim its non-serious nature and intent. It also, of course, allows him direct, deadly access as 'humble poet' into the royal birthday levee.

2 Alluding to the Newspaper account of a certain royal Sailor's Amour. R.B.

George's birthday on 4th June 1786 had been celebrated by the laureate, Thomas Warton with a Pindaric ode. Burns's almost immediate response to this sycophantic work enabled him to insert the poem into the Kilmarnock edition. These were not the sentiments of a complicit 'heaven taught ploughman' and Mrs Dunlop was quick to warn him as to the commercial consequences of such satire. On 26th February 1787 she wrote to him urging that *A Dream* should be excluded from the second edition:

> I ought to have told you that numbers at London are learning Scots to read your book, but they don't like your address to the King, and say it will hurt the sale of the rest. Of this I am no judge. I can only say there is no piece . . . I would vote to leave out, tho' several where I would draw my pen over the lines, or spill the ink glass over a verse. (*Robert Burns and Mrs Dunlop*, ed. William Wallace (London: 1898), p. 11)

Burns's response was peremptory and unyielding:

> Your criticisms, Madam I understand very well, and could have wished to have pleased you better. You are right in your guesses that I am not very amenable. Poets, much my superiors, have so flattered those who possessed the adventitious qualities of wealth and power that I am determined to flatter no created being, either in prose or verse, so help me God. I set as little by kings, lords, clergy, critics, &c as all these respectable Gentry do by my Bardship. I know what I may expect from the world, by and by, illiberal abuse and contemptuous neglect: but I am resolved to study the sentiments of a very respectable Personage, Milton's Satan – Hail horrors! Hail infernal world!

> I am happy, Madam, that some of my favourite pieces are distinguished by you're particular approbation. For my DREAM which has unfortunately incurred your loyal displeasure, I hope in four weeks time or less to have the honour of appearing, at Dunlop, in it's defence in person (Letter 98).

It is hard to see what sort of convincing defence Burns could have mounted concerning the danger to his incipient poetic career with regard to the flagrantly disloyal, anti-Hanoverian elements of this poem. Beginning with the general weakened fiscal state of the nation resulting from the disastrously lost American war and

Pitt's subsequent punitive taxation policies and naval cuts (ll. 60–2) with an inverted political order where the lowest types are at the top of the government, Burns launches into a highly specific assault on the varied cupidities and promiscuities of what he consistently perceived as an irretrievably dysfunctional family of German upstarts. L. 26 contrasts the virtues of Charles Edward Stuart.

The treatment of the King and Queen is mild compared to that doled out to their children. Driven by infantile, Oedipal rage, the Prince of Wales, had flung himself into the grossly licentious world of whoring and gambling of 'Charlie' Fox's opposing Whigs. Brilliantly, ironically, Burns (ll. 91–9) compresses an allusion to post-Falstaffian redemption to *this* Prince of Wales. The ploughman poet, tellingly, feels he needs to explain this reference to *Henry IV* to his cultivated audience. The 'right rev'rend Osnaburg' is Frederick Augustus (1763–1827) who was 'elected' to the bishopric of Asnaburg in Westphalia by his father, George III, in 1764. He added to this clerical distinction by taking up with Letita Derby, the ex-mistress of Rann the highwayman. The 'Royal TARRY-BREEKS' (l. 109) is another prodigally gifted son, Prince William (1765–1837), who became William IV in 1830. He had become naughtily, nautically involved with Sarah Martin, daughter of the commissioner of the Portsmouth dockyard. This naval encounter may have been derived from what Kinsley describes as the 'ingenious model' in Robert Sempill's *Ballat Maid Upoun Margaret Fleming, callit the Fleming Bark in Edinburgh*, which was modernised in Ramsay's *The Ever Green* (1724). Similar metaphors of dropped tackle and predatory boarding parties can also be found in Donne, followed by Pope.

Burns claims that his knowledge of this particular incident came from a newspaper. It is probable that most of this kind of information so came to him. Unlike Wordsworth, who was wholly averse to what he saw as such vulgar contemporary contaminants, Burns belongs to an earlier satirical tradition. He not only throve on journalistic gossip, but could transmute it, like Byron, into great poetry. He also refers warmly to Hogarth and the whole world of eighteenth-century political caricature had undoubtedly a strong influence on him, perhaps not yet fully appreciated. The King also had five daughters (ll. 118–126) who were, needless to say, not noted for their beauty, unlike their chronic constipation.

The Vision
Duan First[1]

First printed in the Kilmarnock edition, 1786.

The Sun had clos'd the *winter-day*,
The Curlers quat their roaring play,   quit
And hunger'd Maukin taen her way,   hare, taken
    To kail-yards green,   kitchen-gardens
5 While faithless snaws ilk step betray   snows each
    Whare she has been.   where

The Thresher's weary *flingin-tree*,   flailing
The lee-lang day had tired me;   live-long
And when the Day had clos'd his e'e   eye
10   Far i' the West,
Ben i' the *Spence*, right pensivelie,   back, parlour
    I gaed to rest.   went

There, lanely by the ingle-cheek,   lonely, fire side
I sat and ey'd the spewing reek,   smoke
15 That fill'd, wi' hoast-provoking smeek,   cough, smoke
    The auld clay biggin;   old, building
An' heard the restless rattons squeak   rats
    About the riggin.   roof

All in this mottie, misty clime,   dusty specks
20 I backward mus'd on wasted time:
How I had spent my *youthfu' prime*,
    An' done naething,   nothing
But stringing blethers up in rhyme,   nonesense stories
    For fools to sing.

25 Had I to guid advice but harket,   good, listened
I might, by this, hae led a market,   have
Or strutted in a bank and clarket   clarked
    My *Cash-Account*:
While here, half-mad, half-fed, half-sarket,   half-clothed
30   Is a' th' amount.

1 Duan, a term of Ossian's for the different divisions of a digressive Poem.
See his *Cath-Loda*, Vol. 2. of M'Pherson's Translation. R.B.

I started, mutt'ring blockhead! coof!   fool
An' heav'd on high my wauket loof,   horny palm/hand
To swear by a' yon starry roof,
      Or some rash aith,   oath
35 That I, henceforth, would be *rhyme-proof*
          Till my last breath —

When click! the *string* the *snick* did draw;   door latch
And jee! the door gaed to the wa';   went, wall
And by my ingle-lowe I saw,   fire-flame
40   Now bleezan bright,
A tight, outlandish *Hizzie*, braw,   girl
      Come full in sight.

Ye need na doubt, I held my whisht;   not doubt, said nothing
The infant aith, half-form'd, was crusht;   oath/pledge
45 I glowr'd as eerie's I'd been dusht,   stared, touched
      In some wild glen;
When sweet, like *modest Worth*, she blusht,
      And stepped ben.   inside

Green, slender, leaf-clad *Holly-boughs*   leaf-clothed/covered
50 Were twisted, gracefu', round her brows;
I took her for some SCOTTISH MUSE,
      By that same token;
And come to stop those reckless vows,
      Would soon been broken.

55 A 'hair-brain'd, sentimental trace'
Was strongly marked in her face;
A wildly-witty, rustic grace
      Shone full upon her;
Her *eye*, ev'n turn'd on empty space,
60   Beam'd keen with *Honor*.

Down flow'd her robe, a *tartan* sheen,   bright
Till half a leg was scrimply seen;   barely
And such a *leg*! my bonie JEAN
      Could only peer it;   equal
65 Sae straught, sae taper, tight an' clean   so, straight, so
      Nane else came near it.   no-one

Her *Mantle* large, of greenish hue,
My gazing wonder chiefly drew;
Deep *lights* and *shades*, bold-mingling, threw
70   A lustre grand;
And seem'd, to my astonish'd view,
        A *well-known* Land.

Here, rivers in the sea were lost;
There, mountains to the skies were tosst;
75 Here, tumbling billows mark'd the coast,
        With surging foam;
There, distant shone *Art's* lofty boast,
        The lordly dome.

Here, DOON pour'd down his far-fetch'd floods;
80 There, well-fed IRWINE stately thuds: beats/churns
Auld hermit AIRE staw thro' his woods,   Ayr, stole/steals
        On to the shore;
And many a lesser torrent scuds   races along
        With seeming roar.

85 Low, in a sandy valley spread,
An ancient BOROUGH rear'd her head;
Still, as in *Scottish Story* read,
        She boasts a *Race*
To ev'ry nobler virtue bred,
90   And polish'd grace.

[By stately tow'r, or palace fair,
Or ruins pendent in the air,
Bold stems of Heroes, here and there,
        I could discern;
95 Some seem'd to muse, some seem'd to dare,
        With feature stern.

My heart did glowing transport feel,
To see a Race[2] heroic wheel,
And brandish round the deep-dy'd steel
100   In sturdy blows;
While, back-recoiling, seem'd to reel
        Their Suthron foes.   English

2 The Wallaces. R.B.

His COUNTRY'S SAVIOUR,[3] mark him well!
Bold RICHARDTON'S[4] heroic swell;
105 The Chief on Sark[5] who glorious fell
          In high command;
And *He* whom ruthless Fates expel
          His native land.

There, where a sceptr'd *Pictish*[6] shade
110 Stalk'd round his ashes lowly laid,
I mark'd a martial Race, pourtray'd
          In colours strong:
Bold, soldier-featur'd, undismay'd,
          They strode along.

115 Thro' many a wild, romantic grove,[7]
Near many a hermit-fancy'd cove
(Fit haunts for Friendship or for Love
          In musing mood),
An *aged Judge*, I saw him rove,
120   Dispensing good.

With deep-struck, reverential awe,[8]
The learned *Sire* and *Son* I saw:
To Nature's God, and Nature's law,
          They gave their lore;
125 This, all its source and end to draw,
          That, to adore.

3 William Wallace.
4 Adam Wallace of Richardton, cousin to the immortal Preserver of Scottish Independence.
5 Wallace Laird of Craigie, who was second in Command, under Douglas Earl of Ormond, at the famous battle on the banks of Sark, fought anno 1448. That glorious victory was principally owing to the judicious conduct and intrepid valour of the gallant Laird of Craigie, who died of his wounds after the action. R.B.
6 Coilus King of the Picts, from whom the district of Kyle is said to take its name, lies buried, as tradition says, near the family-seat of the Montgomeries of Coilsfield, where his burial place is still shown. R.B.
7 Barskimming, the seat of the Lord Justice Clerk. R.B.
8 Catrine, the seat of the late Doctor, and present Professor [Dugald] Stewart. R.B. His father was Matthew Stewart, also Professor of Moral Philosophy at Edinburgh.

BRYDON'S brave Ward I well could spy,[9]
Beneath old SCOTIA'S smiling eye;
Who call'd on Fame, low standing by,
130   To hand him on,
Where many a Patriot-name on high,
      And Hero shone].

The final seven stanzas, enclosed above in square brackets, were
added in the Edinburgh edition, 1787.

Duan Second

With musing-deep, astonish'd stare,
I view'd the heavenly-seeming *Fair*;
A whisp'ring *throb* did witness bear
      Of kindred sweet,
5 When with an elder Sister's air
      She did me greet.

'All hail! *my own* inspired Bard!
In me thy native Muse regard!
Nor longer mourn thy fate is hard,
10   Thus poorly low!
I come to give thee such reward,
      As we bestow.'

'Know, the great *Genius* of this land
Has many a light, aerial band,
15 Who, all beneath his high command,
      Harmoniously,
As *Arts* or *Arms* they understand,
      Their labors ply.

'They SCOTIA'S Race among them share:
20 Some fire the *Sodger* on to dare;
Some rouse the *Patriot* up to bare
      Corruption's heart;
Some teach the *Bard*, a darling care,
      The tuneful Art.

9 Colonel Fullerton. R.B.

25   'Mong swelling floods of reeking gore,   smoking
     They, ardent, kindling spirits pour;
     Or, 'mid the venal Senate's roar,
               They, sightless, stand,
     To mend the honest *Patriot-lore*,
30   And grace the hand.

     'And when the Bard, or hoary Sage,
     Charm or instruct the future age,
     They bind the wild Poetic rage
               In energy;
35   Or point the inconclusive page
               Full on the eye.

     'Hence, FULLARTON, the brave and young;[10]
     Hence, DEMPSTER'S zeal-inspirèd tongue;[11]
     Hence, sweet, harmonious BEATTIE sung[12]
40   His "Minstrel lays";
     Or tore, with noble ardour stung,
               The *Sceptic's* bays'.

     'To lower Orders are assign'd
     The humbler ranks of Human-kind,
45   The rustic Bard, the lab'ring Hind,
               The Artisan;
     All chuse, as various they're inclin'd,
               The various man.

     'When yellow waves the heavy grain,
50   The threat'ning *Storm* some strongly rein,
     Some teach to meliorate the plain,
               With *tillage-skill*;
     And some instruct the Shepherd-train,
               Blythe o'er the hill.

55   'Some hint the Lover's harmless wile;
     Some grace the Maiden's artless smile;
     Some soothe the Lab'rer's weary toil
               For humble gains,
     And make his *cottage-scenes* beguile
60   His cares and pains.

10 William Fullerton.
11 George Dempster, M.P. (1732–1818)
12 Dr James Beattie (1735–1803).

'Some, bounded to a district-space,
Explore at large Man's *infant race*,
To mark the embryotic trace
        Of *rustic Bard*;
65 And careful note each op'ning grace,
        A guide and guard.

'*Of these am I* — COILA my name;
And this district as mine I claim,
Where once the *Campbells*, chiefs of fame,
70   Held ruling pow'r:
I mark'd thy embryo-tuneful flame,
        Thy natal hour.

'With future hope I oft would gaze,
Fond, on thy little early ways;
75 Thy rudely caroll'd, chiming phrase,
        In uncouth rhymes;
Fir'd at the simple, artless lays
        Of other times.

'I saw thee seek the sounding shore,
80 Delighted with the dashing roar;
Or when the *North* his fleecy store
        Drove thro' the sky,
I saw grim Nature's visage hoar,
        Struck thy young eye.

85 'Or when the deep green-mantled Earth
Warm-cherish'd ev'ry floweret's birth,
And joy and music pouring forth
        In ev'ry grove;
I saw thee eye the gen'ral mirth
90   With boundless love.

'When ripen'd fields and azure skies
Call'd forth the *Reaper's* rustling noise,
I saw thee leave their ev'ning joys,
        And lonely stalk,
95 To vent thy bosom's swelling rise,
        In pensive walk.

'When *youthful Love*, warm-blushing, strong,
Keen-shivering, shot thy nerves along,
Those accents grateful to thy tongue,
100   Th' adored *Name*,
I taught thee how to pour in song
         To soothe thy flame.

'I saw thy pulse's maddening play,
Wild-send thee Pleasure's devious way,
105 Misled by Fancy's *meteor-ray*,
         By Passion driven;
But yet the *light* that led astray
         Was *light* from Heaven.

'I taught thy manners-painting strains
110 The *loves*, the *ways* of simple swains,
Till now, o'er all my wide domains
         Thy fame extends;
And some, the pride of *Coila's* plains,
         Become thy friends.

115 'Thou canst not learn, nor can I show,
To paint with *Thomson's* landscape glow;
Or wake the bosom-melting throe
         With *Shenstone's* art;
Or pour, with *Gray*, the moving flow
120   Warm on the heart.

'Yet, all beneath th'unrivall'd Rose,
The lowly Daisy sweetly blows;
Tho' large the forest's Monarch throws
         His army shade,
125 Yet green the juicy Hawthorn grows
         Adown the glade.

'Then never murmur nor repine;
Strive in thy *humble sphere* to shine;
And trust me, not *Potosi's* [13] *mine*,
130   Nor *King's* regard,
Can give a bliss o'ermatching thine,
         A *rustic Bard*.

13 Commenting on 'Potosi's mine' (in Bolivia, South America) to Peter Hill,
Burns wrote: 'these glittering cliffs of Potosi where the all-sufficient, all
powerful Deity, WEALTH, holds his immediate court of joys and pleasures'
(Letter 325).

'To give my counsels all in one:
Thy *tuneful flame* still careful fan;
135 Preserve *the dignity of Man*,
        With Soul erect;
And trust the UNIVERSAL PLAN
        Will all protect.

'*And wear thou this*' — She solemn said,
140 And bound the *Holly* round my head:
The polish'd leaves and berries red
        Did rustling play;
And, like a passing thought, she fled
        In light away.

The poem is structured in two 'Duans' which Burns tells us in his
footnote is a term derived from Macpherson's *Ossian* where it
signifies different sections within a digressive poem. This may have
been slightly exhibitionistic, given that contemporary Edinburgh's
enthusiasm for the 'Highland' poem was so great that it was even
subject to balletic theatrical performance. The games he played
with the local literati were, however, usually of a deeper kind. A
constant adopter, and adapter of a catholic range of earlier poetic
forms, what Burns may be doing here is taking a formal structural
device from Macpherson in order to deliver an *inverted* content. In
The Vision we have not a poet melancholically wandering in a
ghostly landscape littered with the Celtic-warrior dead, a culture
irretrievably lost, but a virile poet celebrating an Ayrshire land-
scape energised by the power and beauty of its rivers and its
organic, living connection with its heroic dead. The intrusion of
the supernatural in this poem is not elegiac but consoling and
celebratory. The Second Duan, indeed, not only reassures the poet
about the nature and success of his creative career but integrates
this individual success into an efflorescent Ayrshire, a land full of
land-owning local heroes whose varied talents are benevolently
directed to the nation's common good. Here the optimistic energies
and anticipations of the Scottish Enlightenment *seem* to be yielding
a rich harvest.

   This poem has always been deeply controversial. Daiches
(pp. 134–7) sees the poem as broken-backed with the anglicised,
literati-pleasing second Duan betraying the vernacular brilliance of
the first. Crawford in an extended treatment of the poem sees it as
one of Burns's most complete masterpieces with the stanzas xiv–xviii
of the second Duan achieving 'a unity of the personal and elemental

of the sort we associate with poets like Shakespeare and Yeats'. Nor does he think Burns was involved in any kind of sycophancy:

> To regard these stanzas as flattery of the local nobility and nothing more would be to misunderstand Burns's intention completely. *The Vision* is the work, above all others, in which Burns shows himself aware of the contemporary national renaissance: a movement which, in many spheres of life, from agricultural improvement to moral philosophy, was led by the most energetic and forward-looking of the landed gentry. (pp. 182–92)

The Vision, then, is an extraordinarily ambitious poem, which attempts to resolve, in a related fashion, the poet's personal crisis-ridden anxieties with those of the nation and perceives a happy-ending for both. That it has such national as well as personal aspirations is partly deducible from its main source which was a forgery also entitled *The Vision* which Ramsay alleged as being translated in 1524 from a fourteenth-century Latin text dealing with a warrior spirit appearing before the depressed narrator who is agonised by John Baliol's appeasement to England's King Edward. McGuirk writes (p. 209) that 'Ramsay's "sact" bears a thistle and a prophecy of Scottish history; "Coila" bears holly and a prophecy of Burns's poetic destiny.' Coila, however, also bears a prophecy of a revived Scotland and it is here that lies the poem's main difficulty and, indeed, final failure.

The largely successful, vernacular first Duan is one of the most beautiful and moving in all Burns's poetry. The varied movements of men and beasts through a winterscape lead to arguably the best, most compressed of all accounts by Burns of the toll of farm life on him with its exhausting labour and its rat infested restricted living space culminating in the chronic, constant pressure of poverty and his volatile inadequacy in making a prudent living in the face of it. This bitter introspection is tangibly present to us and it is typical of Burns that such detailed realism is always a prelude to the entry, usually partly comical, of the supernatural into his poetry. Hence the appearance of his holly-crowned, gorgeously-legged Muse. Initially, at least the legs, this may have been based on Bess Paton but she was replaced by another evidently leggy beauty, Jean Armour. Dazzlingly beautiful in herself, this divine woman, mystically, projects the beauty of Ayrshire (ll.62–72). This celebration of Ayrshire's spirit of place metamorphoses to celebration of the historical nation where, happily, Ayrshire's virtues converge with those of Scotland as a whole in Burns's archetypal Scottish hero,

William Wallace. Not the least of Mrs Dunlop's attractions for
Burns was as descendant of Wallace. This is one of several poems,
which confirm his early wish (Letter 55) 'to be able to make a Song
on his equal to his merits'. Hence Burns's own footnotes outlining
the unbroken lineage of Wallace to the present. Kinsley considers
that ll. 107–8 refer to Mrs Dunlop's eldest son Craigie, who became
bankrupt in 1783. He died in England in 1786. This, it should be
noted, is hardly the stuff of epic but the all too common experience
of the economically deeply unstable world of eighteenth-century
incipient capitalism.

Quite atypical of Burns, however, this poem is concerned not with
the destructive, often disruptive late eighteenth-century forces of
social and economic change but it is an optimistic, partly Utopian,
vision or, indeed, dream of a resurrected Ayrshire/Scotland by virtue
of the *top-down* activities of a liberal progressive land-owning and
professional élite. Thus we have not epic heroes drawn up for battle
but a list of new men of virtue who tangibly seem, in varied ways, to
be delivering the reformative Scottish Enlightenment project. Thus
ll. 109–14 celebrate the patriotic, military valour of the Montgom-
eries of Coylfield. This is no distant hero-worship, however, as
Burns was on fraternal terms with James Montgomerie in the
merged Tarbolton Masonic Lodge in 1781. L. 115 refers to Barskim-
ming, the home of the improving Sir Thomas Miller, Bt. (1717–89).
His steam-boat innovating brother Patrick Miller (1731–1815) of
Dalswinton let Ellisland to Burns in 1788. Thomas Miller had an
extremely successful legal career. As Lord Barskimming he became
Lord Justice Clerk in 1766 and, as Lord Glenlee, Lord President of
the Court of Session in 1788. He seems the antithesis of the terrible
Lord Braxfield who was to run amok in the political trials of the
1790s: 'Though well aware that offended justice required satisfac-
tion, he knew that the vilest criminal was entitled to a fair and
dispassionate trial. . . he never uttered a harsh or taunting word'
(Ramsay of Ochtertyre, *Scotland and Scotsmen in the Eighteenth
Century*, l. 343–50.) Ll. 121–6 deal with the noted Professor of
Mathematics at Edinburgh Matthew Stewart and his even more
celebrated son Dugald (1753–1828) who was a tangible friend to
Burns in Edinburgh. As Burns wrote to Mrs Dunlop (Letter 152A)
of this exceptional man: 'It requires no common exertion of good
sense and Philosophy in persons of elevated rank to keep a friendship
properly alive with one much their inferior.' The letter continues as
an act of homage to Stewart's innate democratic virtues. Ll. 127–32
refer to William Fullerton, diplomat, politician, soldier and agri-
cultural improver who accepted Burns's advice on the care of cattle

and to whom in 1791 the poet sent songs and poems (Letters, 472, 474). Unlike the absentee, Europhile, aristocratic degenerates of *The Twa Dogs* who, in Fergusson's lines, '. . . never wi' their feet hae mett/The marches o' their ain estate' these men are tangible assets to Ayrshire and Scotland. Further Burns enjoys support and degrees of intimacy with the best of them. There are, indeed, significant grounds for national optimism.

The second Duan is devoted to Coila's monologue in which she pours a cornucopia of promised gifts not only on the head of her chosen poet but over all Ayrshire by dint of the aid of her accompanying spirits (perhaps derived from *The Rape of the Lock*). In this very non-Burnsian happily hierarchical society, each is given according to his needs. Regarding the 'embryonic' Burns she gives a detailed account of the growth of the poet. Pre-Wordsworth, Burns believed that the child was father of the creative man. As a sort of angelic counsellor, she offers soothing solutions to the anxieties which, with varying intensity, preoccupied him concerning the nature of his poetic career. Ll. 235–40 are particularly memorable in dealing with the central, crucial problem in all Burns's poetry and thought concerning the rights of the instinctual self as opposed to imposed conformity. He knew libidinal energy was essential to his art; he was never certain whether it was not only a predatory force for others but, finally, also a self-destructive one. Coila also, in a poem concerned with Scotland's political independence, deals with his properly modest but worthy relationships to English poetry (ll. 247–8). Finally, l. 259 she reassures him that his true role as rustic poet more than compensates for the lack of money and fame. Crowning him with her holly she triumphantly asserts that:

> To give my counsels all in one,
> They tuneful-flame still careful fan;
> Preserve the *dignity of Man*,
> With Soul erect
> And trust the Universal Plan
> Will all protect.

Partly energised by his experience, social and intellectual, with Free Masonry this is a pre-Whitmanian dream of progressive, enlightened social and political virtue and not the thing itself. Ayrshire, of which Burns himself is the best witness, was a deeply frictive culture marked by severe economic instability even for the prosperous and much poverty for the rest. It was also subject to extreme clerical bigotry. The aesthetic stresses we feel in the second Duan derive

from the forced, if not false, historical vision Burns here unchar-
acteristically adopts. There is, of course, the problem, significantly
discussed in Issac Kramnick's *Republicanism and Bourgeois Radic-
alism: Political Ideology in Late Eighteenth-Century England and
America* (Cornell U.P.: 1990), as to whether such reformists could
deliver their partly practical, partly Utopian project. They were not
to be given the opportunity. By the mid 1790s these progressives
were, with their poet laureate, in the deepest of trouble as Burkean
derived hierarchy and economics brutally reinherited the world.
Dugald Stewart like his fellow Whig academics was suspiciously
confined. At least, unlike the octogenarian Thomas Reid, he was not
roughed up. The admired James Beattie (1735–1803), whose *The
Minstrel* influenced Wordsworth, and, as ll. 123–6 state, allegedly
defeated David Hume's atheism, relapsed, like James Boswell, into
a semi-hysterical Toryism to the degree of involving himself in
drinking bouts with the frequently besotted Henry Dundas.

Halloween

First published in the Kilmarnock edition, 1786

Yes! let the Rich deride, the Proud disdain,
The simple pleasures of the lowly train:
To me more dear, congenial to my heart,
One native charm, than all the gloss of art.
GOLDSMITH.

'The following poem will, by many readers, be well enough under-
stood; but for the sake of those unaquainted with the manners and
traditions of the country [region] where the scene is cast, notes are
added, to give some account of the principal charms and spells of
that night, so big with prophecy to the peasantry of the west of
Scotland. The passion of prying into futurity makes a striking part
of the history of human nature in its rude state, in all ages and
nations; and it may be some entertainment to a philosophic mind, if
any such honour the author with a perusal, to see the remains of it,
among the more unenlightened in our own.'
  To this headnote, Burns defines Halloween thus: 'Is thought to be
a night when Witches, Devils, and other mischief-making beings,
are all abroad on their baneful, midnight errands: particularly, those
aerial people, the fairies, are said, on that night, to hold a grand
anniversary.'
                                                              R.B.

Upon that *night*, when Fairies light
    On *Cassilis Downans*[1] dance,
Or owre the lays, in splendid blaze,   over, fields
    On sprightly coursers prance;
5 Or for *Colean* the rout is taen,   Culzean, taken
    Beneath the moon's pale beams;
There, up the *Cove*[2], to stray and rove,
    Amang the rocks and streams
        To sport that night:

10 Amang the bonie winding banks,
    Where Doon rins, wimplin, clear;   runs, winding
Where BRUCE[3] ance ruled the martial ranks,   once
    An' shook his *Carrick* spear;
Some merry, friendly, country-folks
15   Together did convene,
To *burn* their nits, an' *pou* their stocks,   nuts, pull
    An' haud their *Halloween*   hold
        Fu' blythe that night.

The lassies feat, an' cleanly neat,   trim
20   Mair braw than when they're fine;   more fair
Their faces blythe fu' sweetly kythe   show
    Hearts leal, an' warm, an' kin':   loyal, kind
The lads sae trig, wi' wooer-babs   so spruce, love-knots
    Weel-knotted on their garten;   well, garters
25 Some unco blate, an' some wi' gabs   very shy, chatting up
    Gar lasses' hearts gang startin   make, go beating
        Whyles fast at night.   sometimes

Then, first an' foremost, thro' the kail,   cabbage-plot
    Their *stocks*[4] maun a' be sought ance;   shall, once
30 They steek their een, an' grape an' wale   close, eyes, grope, choose
    For muckle anes, an' straught anes.   big ones, straight ones

---

1 Cassilis Downans – Certain little, romantic, rocky, green hills, in the
neighbourhood of the ancient seat of the Earls of Cassilis. R.B.
2 A noted cavern near Colean [Culzean] House, called the Cove of Colean;
which, as well as Cassilis Downans, is famed, in country story, for being a
favourite haunt of the fairies. R.B.
3 The famous family of that name, the ancestors of ROBERT, the great
Deliverer of his country, were Earls of Carrick. R. B.
4 The first ceremony of Halloween, is, pulling each a *Stock*, or plant of kail.
They must go out, hand in hand, with eyes shut, and pull the first they meet

Poor hav'rel *Will* fell aff the drift,   half-witted, lost the way
   An' wandered thro' the *Bow-kail*,   cabbage
An' pow't, for want o' better shift,   pulled
35   A *runt*, was like a sow-tail,   small cabbage stalk
         Sae bow't that night.   so bent

Then, straught or crooked, yird or nane,   straight, dirt, none
   They roar an' cry a' throu'ther;   pell-mell
The vera *wee-things*, toddlin, rin   very children, run
40   Wi' stocks out-owre their shouther: -over, shoulder
An' gif the *custock*'s sweet or sour,   if, pith
   Wi' joctelegs they taste them;   knives
Syne coziely, aboon the door,   then, comfortably, above
   Wi' cannie care, they've plac'd them   gentle
45   To lye that night.   lie

The lasses staw frae 'mang them a',   stole, from, among them all
   To pou their *stalks o' corn*;[5]   pull
But *Rab* slips out, an' jinks about,   dodges
   Behint the muckle thorn: large
50 He grippet *Nelly* hard an' fast;   gripped
   Loud skirl'd a' the lasses;   screamed
But her *tap-pickle* maist was lost,   top amount mostly
   Whan kiutlan in the *Fause-house*[6]   when cuddling, corn drier
        Wi' him that night.

with: its being big or little, straight or crooked, is prophetic of the size and shape of the grand object of all their Spells – the husband or wife. If any *yird*, or earth, stick to the root, that is *tocher*, or fortune; and the taste of the *custoc*, that is, the heart of the stem, is indicative of the natural temper and disposition. Lastly, the stems, or to give them their ordinary appellation, the *runts*, are placed somewhere above the head of the door; and the Christian names of the people whom chance brings into the house, are, according to the priority of placing the runts, the names in question. R.B.

5 They go to the barnyard, and pull each, at three several times, a stalk of oats. If the third stalk wants the 'top-pickle', that is, the grain at the top of the stalk, the party in question will come to the marriage bed anything but a Maid. R.B.

6 When the corn is in a doubtful state, by being too green or wet, the stack-builder, by means of old timber, &c., makes a large apartment in his stack, with an opening in the side which is fairest exposed to the wind: this he calls a 'Fause-house'. R.B.

superstition regarding love.

55 The auld Guidwife's weel-hoordet *nits*[7]   old, good-, well-hoarded nuts
       Are round an' round divided,
    An' monie lads' an' lasses' fates   many
       Are there that night decided:
    Some kindle couthie, side by side,   warm comfortably
60   An' *burn* thegither trimly;   together
    Some start awa wi' saucy pride,   away
       An' jump out-owre the chimlie   -over, fireplace
          Fu' high that night.

    Jean slips in twa, wi' tentie e'e;   two, watchful eye
65   Wha 'twas, she wadna tell;   who, would not
    But this is *Jock*, an' this is *me*,
       She says in to hersel:
    He bleez'd owre her, an' she owre him,   over
       As they wad never mair part;   would, more
70 Till fuff! he started up the lum,   chimney
       And *Jean* had e'en a sair heart   sore
          To see't that night.

    Poor *Willie*, wi' his *bow-kail runt*,   cabbage stalk
       Was *burnt* wi' primsie *Mallie*;   prudish
75 An' *Mary*, nae doubt, took the drunt,   no, huff
       To be compar'd to *Willie*:
    Mall's nit lap out, wi' pridefu' fling,   nut leaped
       An' her ain fit, it burnt it;   own foot
    While *Willie* lap, an' swoor by *jing*,   jumped, swore with conviction
80   'Twas just the way he wanted
          To be that night.

    Nell had the *Fause-house* in her min',   corn drying structure
       She pits hersel an' *Rob* in;   puts
    In loving bleeze they sweetly join,   heat/flame
85   Till white in ase they're sobbin: ashes
    Nell's heart was dancin at the view;
       She whisper'd *Rob* to leuk for't: tasted
    Rob, stownlins, prie'd her bonie mou,   stealthily, kissed, mouth
       Fu' cozie in the neuk for't,   snugly, corner
90   Unseen that night.

7 Burning the nuts is a favourite charm. They name the lad and lass to each
particular nut, as they lay them in the fire, and acccordingly as they burn
quietly together, or start from beside one another, the course and issue of the
Courtship will be. R.B.

But *Merran* sat behint their backs,   Marion
   Her thoughts on *Andrew Bell*;
She lea'es them gashan at their cracks,   gabbing, conversation
   An' slips out by hersel:
95 She thro' the yard the nearest taks,
   An' to the *kiln* she goes then,
An' darklins grapet for the *bauks*,   darkness, groped, cross-beam
   And in the *blue-clue*[8] throws them,   yarn
      Right fear't that night.

100 An' ay she *win't*, an' ay she swat,   winded, sweated
   I wat she made nae jaukin;   bet, no delay
Till something *held* within the *pat*,   pot/kiln
   Guid Lord! but she was quakin!   shaking
But whether 'twas the *Deil* himsel,
105   Or whether 'twas a *bauk-en'*,   end of a beam
Or whether it was *Andrew Bell*,
   She did na wait on talkin   not
      To spier that night.   inquire/find out

Wee Jenny to her Graunie says,   grandmother
110   'Will ye go wi' me, Graunie?
I'll *eat the apple*[9] at the *glass*,
   I gat frae uncle Johnie:'   got, from
She fuff't her pipe wi' sic a lunt,   puffed, such, smoke
   In wrath she was sae vap'rin,   so, agitated
115 She notic't na an aizle brunt   not, cinder, burnt
   Her braw, new, worset apron   good, worsted/twisted yarn
      Out thro' that night.

'Ye little Skelpie-limmer's-face!   hussy
   I daur ye try sic sportin,   dare, such
120 As seek the *Foul Thief* onie place,   any
   For him to spae your fortune: foretell

8 Whoever would, with success, try this spell must strictly observe these directions: Steal out all alone, to the kiln, and, darkling, throw into the *pot* a clew of blue yarn; wind it in a new clew off the old one; and, towards the latter end, something will hold the thread: demand *Wha hauds?*, i.e. Who holds? And answer will be returned from the kiln-pot, by naming the Christian and Sirname of your future Spouse. R.B.

9 Take a candle and go alone to a looking glass; eat an apple before it, and some traditions say, you should comb your hair all the time; the face of your conjugal companion, *to be*, will be seen in the glass, as if peeping over your shoulder. R.B.

Nae doubt but ye may get a *sight*!   no
  Great cause ye hae to fear it;   have
For monie a ane has gotten a fright,   many, one
125 An' liv'd an' died deleeret,   delerious/insane
    On sic a night.   such

'Ae Hairst afore the *Sherra-moor*,   one harvest before
  I mind't as weel's yestreen,   well as yesterday
I was a gilpey then, I'm sure   young girl
130 I was na past fyfteen: not
The Simmer had been cauld an' wat,   summer, cold, wet
  An' *Stuff* was unco green;   corn
An' ay a rantan Kirn we gat,   rollicking, harvest, got
  An' just on *Halloween*
135   It fell that night.

'Our *Stibble-rig* was *Rab M'Graen*,   leader of the reapers
  A clever, sturdy fallow;   fellow
His Sin gat *Eppie Sim* wi' wean,   son, got, child
  That lived in Achmachalla: got, well
140 He gat *hemp-seed*,[10] I mind it weel,   got, well
  An' he made unco light o't;
But monie a day was *by himsel*,   many
  He was sae sairly frighted   so sorely
    That vera night.'

145 Then up gat fechtan *Jamie Fleck*,   got fighting
  An' he swoor by his conscience,   swore
That he could *saw hemp-seed* a peck;   sow
  For it was a' but nonsense:
The auld guidman raught down the pock,   old good-, reached, bag
150 An' out a handfu' gied him;   gave
Syne bad him slip frae 'mang the folk,   then, bade, from
  Sometime when nae ane see'd him,   no one, sees
    An' try't that night.

10 Steal out unperceived and sow a handful of hemp-seed, harrowing it with anything you can conveniently draw after you. Repeat, now and then – 'Hemp-seed I saw [sow] thee, hemp-seed I saw thee; and him (or her) that is to be my true love, come after me and pou thee'. Look over your left shoulder, and you will see the appearance of the person invoked, in the attitude of pulling hemp. Some traditions say, 'Come after me, and shaw thee', that is, show thyself; in which case, it simply appears. Others omit the harrowing, and say, 'Come after me, and harrow thee.' R.B.

	He marches thro' amang the stacks,	among
155	Tho' he was something sturtan;	staggering
	The *graip* he for a *harrow* taks,	garden-fork
	And haurls at his curpan;	drags, rear
	And ev'ry now and then, he says,	
	'Hemp-seed I saw thee,	sow
160	An' her that is to be my lass	
	Come after me, an' draw thee	
	As fast this night.'	

	He whistl'd up *Lord Lenox' March*,	
	To keep his courage cheery;	
165	Altho' his hair began to arch,	stand with fear
	He was sae fley'd an' eerie;	so frightened
	Till presently he hears a squeak,	
	An' then a grane an' gruntle;	groan, grunt
	He by his shouther gae a keek,	shoulder gives, look
170	An' tumbl'd wi' a wintle	somersault
	Out-owre that night.	over

	He roar'd a horrid murder-shout,	
	In dreadfu' desperation!	
	An' young an' auld come rinnan out,	old, running
175	An' hear the sad narration:	
	He swoor 'twas hilchin *Jean M'Craw*,	halting
	Or crouchie *Merran Humphie* —	hunchback
	Till stop! she trotted thro' them a';	
	An' wha was it but *Grumphie*	who, the pig
180	Asteer that night?	moving about

	Meg fain wad to the *Barn* gaen,	content, would have gone
	To *winn three wechts o' naething*;[11]	dry corn, baskets, nothing
	But for to meet the Deil her lane,	all alone
	She pat but little faith in:	put

11 This charm must likewise be performed unperceived and alone. You go to the barn, and open both doors, taking them off the hinges if possible; for there is danger that the being that is about to appear may shut the doors, and do you some mischief. Then take that instrument used in winnowing the corn, which in our country-dialect we call a 'wecht', and go through all the attitudes of letting down corn against the wind. Repeat it three times, and the third time, an apparition will pass through the barn, in at the windy door, and out at the other, having both the figure in question, and the appearance or retinue, marking the employment or station in life. R.B.

185   She gies the herd a pickle nits,   gives, shepherd, few
            An' twa red-cheeket apples,   two, -cheeked
        To watch, while for the *Barn* she sets,   goes
            In hopes to see *Tam Kipples*
                    That vera night.   very

190   She turns the key wi' cannie thraw,   gentle, twist
            An' owre the threshold ventures;   over
        But first on *Sawnie* gies a ca',   Satan, gives, call
            Syne bauldly in she enters: once boldly
        A *ratton* rattl'd up the wa',   rat, wall
195   An' she cry'd, Lord preserve her!
        An' ran thro' midden-hole an' a',   dung-hole
            An' pray'd wi' zeal and fervour
                    Fu' fast that night.

        They hoy't out *Will*, wi' sair advice;   urged, sore
200   They hecht him some fine braw ane;   promised, fine one
        It chane'd the *Stack* he *faddom't thrice*,[12] fathomed
            Was timmer-propt for thrawin: wood stacked, support
        He taks a swirlie, auld *moss-oak*   twisted, old
            For some black gruesome Carlin;   old hag
205   An' loot a winze, an' drew a stroke,   cursed, swiped
            Till skin in blypes cam haurlin   shreds, peeling
                    Aff's nieves that night.   off his fists

        A wanton widow *Leezie* was,
            As cantie as a kittlen;   lively, kitten
210   But Och! that night, amang the shaws,   among, large leaves & branches
            She gat a fearfu' settlin!   got, severely unsettled
        She thro' the whins, an' by the cairn,   gorse bushes
            An' owre the hill gaed scrievin;   over, went careering
        Whare *three Lairds' lands met at a burn*,[13]   where
215   To dip her *left sark-sleeve* in   shirt-
                    Was bent that night.

12 Take an opportunity of going, unnoticed, to a 'bear-stack' [stack of bere or bigg, a kind of barley] and fathom it three times round. The last fathom of the last time, you will catch in your arms the appearance of your future conjugal yolk-fellow. R.B.

13 You go out, one or more, for this is a social spell, to a south-running spring, or rivulet, where 'three Lairds' lands' meet, and dip your left shirt-sleeve. Go to bed in sight of a fire, and hang your wet sleeve before it to dry. Ly awake, and sometime near midnight, an apparition, having the exact figure of the grand object in question, will come and turn the sleeve, as if to dry the other side of it. R.B.

Whyles owre a linn the burnie plays,   whiles over, waterfall, burns falls
 As thro' the glen it wimpl't;   meandered
Wyles round a rocky scaur it strays,   jutting rocky edge
220 Whyles in a wiel it dimpl't;   whiles eddy
Whyles glitter'd to the nightly rays,   reflected
 Wi' bickerin, dancin dazzle;   running fast
Whyles cookit underneath the braes,   whiles hid
 Below the spreading hazel
225   Unseen that night.

Amang the brachens, on the brae,   ferns, hillside
 Between her an' the moon,
The Deil, or else an outler Quey,   stray young cow
 Gat up an' gae a croon: got, gave, moan
230 Poor *Leezie's* heart maist lap the hool;   almost leaped, sheath
 Near lav'rock-height she jumpet,   lark-flying level, jumped
But mist a fit, an' in the *pool*   missed a foot
 Out-owre the lugs she plumpet   -over, ears, plummeted
   Wi' a plunge that night.

235 In order, on the clean hearth-stane,   -stone
 The *Luggies*[14] three are ranged;   dishes
And ev'ry time great care is taen   taken
 To see them duly changed:
Auld uncle *John*, wha *wedlock's joys*,   old, who
240 Sin *Mar's-year*[15] did desire,   since
Because he gat the toom dish thrice,   got, empty
 He heav'd them on the fire   — he would never marry.
   In wrath that night.

Wi' merry sangs, an' friendly cracks,   songs, conversation
245 I wat they did na weary;   know, not
And unco tales, an' funnie jokes,   wondrous
 Their sports were cheap an' cheary:

14 Take three dishes, put clean water in one, foul water in another, leave the
third empty; blindfold a person and lead him to the hearth where the dishes
are ranged; he (or she) dips the left hand: if by chance in the clean water, the
future husband (or wife) will come to the bar of Matrimony a Maid; if in the
foul, a widow; if in the empty dish, it foretells with equal certainty, no
marriage at all. It is repeated three times, and every time the arrangement of
the dishes is altered. R.B.
15 Mar's-year: This was the year 1715, when the 11th Earl of Mar, John
Erskine (1675–1732) spear-headed the Jacobite revolt to proclaim the Stuart
Pretender King.

Till *butter'd Sow'ns*,[16] wi' fragrant lunt,   sour oat pudding, steam
      Set a' their gabs a-steerin;   tongues, wagging
250 Syne, wi' a social glass o' strunt,   whisky
      They parted aff careerin   off/away
         Fu' blythe that night.

Mackay's edition omits the poet's detailed notes to this work. They
serve to assist the general reader in understanding the superstitious
rural beliefs associated with Halloween. Due to the broad Scots
language of the poem and its description of various superstitious
rituals associated with peasant belief, much of the poem is unin-
telligible without the poet's notes as in the Kilmarnock edition.
Kinsley (no. 73) gives the notes but without indicating that they are
Burns's. The prose explanations of Burns reveal another example of
his extraordinary talent for turning prose into poetry within the
body of *Halloween*.

The Auld Farmers New-year Morning Salutation to his Auld Mare, Maggie

on giving her the accustomed ripp of corn to hansel in the new-year

First printed in the Kilmarnock edition, 1786.

A *Guid New-Year* I wish thee, Maggie!
Hae, there's a ripp to thy auld baggie: handful, stomach
Tho' thou's howe-backit now, an' knaggie,   hollow-backed, knobbly
      I've seen the day
5 Thou could hae gaen like onie staggie,   have gone, any colt
      Out-owre the lay.   -over, lea

Tho' now thou's dowie, stiff, an' crazy,   drooping
An' thy auld hide as white's a daisie,   old
I've seen thee dappl't, sleek an' glaizie,   glossy
10   A bonie gray:
He should been tight that daur't to *raize* thee,   dared, excite
      Ance in a day.   once

16 Sowens, with butter instead of milk, to them, is always the Halloween
Supper. R.B.

Thou ance was i' the foremost rank,   once
A *filly* buirdly, steeve, an' swank;   strong, trim, stately
15   An' set weel down a shapely shank   well, leg
          As e'er tread yird;   earth
An' could hae flown out-owre a stank   have, -over, ditch
          Like onie bird.   any

It's now some nine-an'-twenty year
20   Sin' thou was my *Guidfather's Meere*;   good-, mare
He gied me thee, o' tocher clear,   gave, dowry
          An' fifty mark;   a coin worth 13s 4d
Tho' it was sma', 'twas *weel-won* gear,   small, well-won money
          An' thou was stark.   strong

25   When first I gaed to woo my *Jenny*,   went
Ye then was trottan wi' your Minnie: mother
Tho' ye was trickie, slee, an' funnie,   difficult, sly
          Ye ne'er was donsie;   mischievous
But hamely, tawie, quiet, an' cannie,   homely, placid, docile
30   An' unco sonsie.   very good-natured

That day, ye pranc'd wi' muckle pride,   great
When ye bure hame my bonie *Bride*:   bore/carried home
An' sweet an' gracefu' she did ride,
          Wi' maiden air!
35   KYLE-STEWART I could bragged wide,   boasted the district over
          For sic a *pair*.   such

Tho' now ye dow but hoyte and hobble,   can, limp, stumble
An' wintle like a saumont-coble,   twist, salmon-boat
That day, ye was a jinker noble,   runner
40   For heels an' win'!   wind
An' ran them till they a' did wauble,   wobble
          Far, far behin'!

When thou an' I were young and skiegh,   proud/fiery
An' *Stable-meals* at Fairs were driegh,   tedious
45   How thou wad prance, an' snore, an' scriegh,   would, snort, whinny
          An' tak the road!
Town's-bodies ran, an' stood abiegh,   out of the way
          An' ca't thee mad.   called

When thou was corn't, an' I was mellow,   fed
50 We took the road ay like a Swallow:
At *Brooses* thou had ne'er a fellow,   a horse race at a wedding
    For pith an' speed;
But ev'ry tail thou pay't them hollow,   beat
        Whare'er thou gaed.   went

55 The sma', droop-rumpl't, hunter cattle   small, short-rumped
Might aiblins waur't thee for a brattle;   perhaps beat, short race
But *sax Scotch mile* thou try't their mettle,   six
    An' gar't them whaizle: made, wheeze
Nae whip nor spur, but just a wattle   no, stick
60   O' saugh or hazle.   willow, hazel

Thou was a noble *Fittie-lan'*,   back left-hand plough horse
As e'er in tug or tow was drawn!
Aft thee an' I, in aught hours' gaun,   often, any, going
    On guid March-weather,   good
65 Hae turn'd *sax rood* beside our han'   have, six quarter acres
    For days thegither.   together

Thou never braing't, an' fetch't, an' flisket;   rushed, stalled, kicked
But thy *auld tail* thou wad hae whisket,   old, would have lashed
An' spread abreed thy weel-fill'd *brisket*,   across to, breast
70   Wi' pith an' pow'r;
Till sprittie knowes wad rair't, an' risket,   tough slopes were climbed
    An' slypet owre.   dreeled over

When frosts lay lang, an' snaws were deep,   long, snows
An' threaten'd *labour* back to keep,
75 I gied thy *cog* a wee bit heap   gave, feed bag
        Aboon the timmer: above the rim
I ken'd my *Maggie* wad na sleep   knew, would not
    For that, or Simmer.   summer

In *cart* or *car* thou never reestet;   rested
80 The steyest brae thou wad hae fac't it;   steepest hill, would have
Thou never lap, an' sten't, an' breastet,   leaped, reared
    Then stood to blaw;   puff for air
But just thy step a wee thing hastet,   a little shortened
    Thou snoov't awa.   pushed away

85 My Pleugh is now thy *bairn-time* a',   my plough-team is your offspring
    Four gallant brutes as e'er did draw;
    Forbye sax mae I've sell't awa,   six more, sold away
          That thou hast nurst: nursed
    They drew me thretteen pund an' twa,   thirteen pound, two
90   The vera warst.

    Monie a sair daurk we twa hae wrought,   many, sore day's work, two, have
    An' wi' the weary warl' fought!   world
    An' monie an *anxious day* I thought   many
          We wad be beat!   would
95 Yet here to *crazy Age* we're brought,
          Wi' something yet.

    An' think na, my auld trusty *Servan'*,   not, old
    That now perhaps thou's less deservin,
    An' thy *auld days* may end in starvin;   old
100   For my last fow,   bushel
    A heapet *Stimpart*, I'll reserve ane   heaped, 8th of a bushel
          Laid by for you.

    We've worn to crazy years thegither;   together
    We'll toyte about wi' ane anither;   totter, one another
105 Wi' tentie care I'll flit thy tether   heedful, change
          · To some hain'd rig,   reserved ground
    Whare ye may nobly rax your leather   stretch your body
          Wi' sma' fatigue.

Inevitably, in that now forever lost agrarian world, of all the deep bonds between man and beast, those with horses were the most intimate and profound. Burns's extraordinary empathy with his horses is everywhere present in his writing and is exemplified by his often naming them as expression of the current state of his own feelings. Thus, for example, the quixotic Rosinante or the disruptively comic, stool-throwing, anti-clerical Jenny Geddes. If Wordsworth needed the rhythmical stimulation of walking to write poetry, Burns discovered more varied, energised rhythms in the saddle. His Excise horse he named Pegasus, that mythical winged icon of poetical creativity. In a sense, however, all his horses had contained these magical energies as can be seen in those astonishing lines (ll. 17–44) of *The Epistle to Hugh Parker*.

    The horse honoured here is not a flyer of that kind, though her young power had allowed her eventually to outpace the lightweight hunters of the gentry in an actual and, hence, political victory. The poem is a deeply moving, heavily vernacularised, monologue by the old man as he parallels the life of his mare and himself. Not the least of Burns's intentions in the poem is to document the sheer, brutal harshness of the work conditions man and horse had to overcome in order to survive. McGuirk postulates that in part the poem is drawn from Burns's memories of his father. The poem was probably written in January 1786.

The Cotter's Saturday Night
Inscribed to R. Aiken, Esq.
First published in the Kilmarnock edition, 1786.

> *Let not Ambition mock their useful toil,*
> *Their homely joys, and destiny obscure;*
> *Nor Grandeur hear, with a disdainful smile,*
> *The short and simple annals of the Poor.*
> GRAY.

My lov'd, my honor'd, much respected friend!
    No mercenary Bard his homage pays;
With honest pride, I scorn each selfish end,
    My dearest meed, a friend's esteem and praise:
5 To you I sing, in simple Scottish lays,
    The *lowly train* in life's sequester'd scene;
The native feelings strong, the guileless ways,
    What Aiken in a *Cottage* would have been;
Ah! tho' his worth unknown, far happier there I ween!   trust

10 November chill blaws loud wi' angry sugh;   blows, whistling wind
    The short'ning winter-day is near a close;
The miry beasts retreating frae the pleugh;   dirty, from, plough
    The black'ning trains o' craws to their repose: crows
The toil-worn COTTER frae his labour goes,   from
15   *This night* his weekly moil is at an end,   toil/drudgery
Collects his *spades*, his *mattocks*, and his *hoes*,   a two-mouthed pick
    Hoping the *morn* in ease and rest to spend,
And weary, o'er the moor, his course does hameward bend.   homeward

At length his lonely *Cot* appears in view,   cottage
20   Beneath the shelter of an aged tree;
Th' expectant wee-things, toddlan, stacher through   children, totter
    To meet their *Dad*, wi' flichterin noise and glee.   fluttering

His wee bit ingle, blinkan bonilie,   fire, burning nicely
    His clean hearth-stane, his thrifty *Wifie's* smile,   fireside, wife's
25 The *lisping infant*, prattling on his knee,
    Does a' his weary kiaugh and care beguile,   anxiety
And makes him quite forget his labor and his toil.

Belyve, the *elder bairns* come drapping in,   by-and-by, kids, dropping
    At *Service* out, amang the Farmers roun';   among, round
30 Some ca' the pleugh, some herd, some tentie rin   work, shepherd,
                                                            attentively run
    A cannie errand to a neebor town: private, neighbour
Their eldest hope, their *Jenny*, woman-grown,
    In youthfu' bloom, Love sparkling in her e'e,   eye
Comes hame, perhaps, to shew a braw new gown,   home, show, fine
35   Or deposite her sair-won penny-fee,   sore-, wages
To help her *Parents* dear, if they in hardship be.

With joy unfeign'd, *brothers* and *sisters* meet,
    And each for other's weelfare kindly spiers: welfare, inquires
The social hours, swift-wing'd, unnotic'd fleet;
40   Each tells the uncos that he sees or hears.   news
The *Parents partial* eye their hopeful years;
    Anticipation forward points the view;
The *Mother*, wi' her needle and her sheers,   scissors
    Gars auld claes look amaist as weel's the new;   makes old clothes,
                                                            almost, well
45 The *Father* mixes a' wi' admonition due.

Their Master's and their Mistress's command
    The *youngkers* a' are warned to obey;   youngsters all
And mind their labors wi' an eydent hand,   diligent
    And ne'er, tho' out o' sight, to jauk or play: fool around
50 'And O! be sure to fear the LORD always!   always

    And mind your *duty*, duly, morn and night!
Lest in temptation's path ye gang astray,   go
    Implore His counsel and assisting might:
They never sought in vain that sought the LORD aright.'

55 But hark! a rap comes gently to the door;
    Jenny, wha kens the meaning o' the same.   who knows
Tells how a neebor lad came o'er the moor,   neighbour
    To do some errands, and convoy her hame.   home

no real sense of momentum.
slow stanzas speed, barely moves.
ponderous.

The wily Mother sees the *conscious flame*
60   Sparkle in *Jenny's* e'e, and flush her cheek;   *eye*
With heart-struck anxious care, enquires his name,
    While *Jenny* hafflins is afraid to speak;   *almost/partly*
Weel-pleas'd the mother hears, it's nae wild,   *no*
    worthless *Rake*.

is a syllable line slows down further.

With kindly welcome, *Jenny* brings him ben;   *inside*
65   A *strappan youth*, he takes the Mother's eye;   *boyfriend with.*
Blythe *Jenny* sees the *visit's* no ill taen;   *taken*
    The Father cracks of horses, pleughs, and kye.   *talks, ploughs, cattle*
The *youngster's* artless heart o'erflows wi' joy,
    But blate and laithfu', scarce can weel behave;   *shy, hesitating, well*
70 The Mother, wi' a woman's wiles, can spy   *cunning*
    What makes the *youth* sae bashfu' and sae grave;   *so*
Weel-pleas'd to think her *bairn's* respected like the   *well-, child's,*
    lave.   *the others*

O happy love! where love like this is found:
    O heart-felt raptures! bliss beyond compare!   *9 no regard for progression*
75 I've pacèd much this weary, *mortal round*,
    And sage EXPERIENCE bids me this declare —
'If Heaven a draught of heavenly pleasure spare,   *English idiom.*
    One *cordial* in this melancholy *Vale*,
'Tis when a youthful, loving, *modest* Pair,
80   In other's arms, breathe out the tender tale
Beneath the milk-white thorn that scents the ev'ning gale.'

Is there, in human form, that bears a heart —
    A wretch! a villain! lost to love and truth!   *10*
That can, with studied, sly, ensnaring art,
85   Betray sweet *Jenny's* unsuspecting youth?
Curse on his perjur'd arts! dissembling, smoothe!
    Are *Honor, Virtue, Conscience*, all exil'd?
Is there no Pity, no relenting Ruth,   *sorrow*
    Points to the Parents fondling o'er their Child?
90 Then paints the *ruin'd Maid*, and *their* distraction wild?

But now the Supper crowns their simple board,   *dinner*
    The halesome *Porritch*, chief o' SCOTIA'S food;   *wholesome porridge*
The soupe their *only Hawkie* does afford,   *drink/milk, cow*
    That, 'yont the hallan snugly chows her cood;   *beyond, partition, chews*

is reduced to eating porridge.
pointed again put upon it.

95   The *Dame* brings forth, in complimental mood,
      To grace the lad, her weel-hain'd kebbuck, fell;

                      well-matured cheese, tasty
   And aft he's prest, and aft he ca's it guid;   often, asked, calls, good
     The frugal *Wifie*, garrulous, will tell,   wife
   How 'twas a towmond auld, sin' Lint was i' the bell.

                     12 months old, flax, flower

100   The chearfu' Supper done, wi' serious face,
      They, round the ingle, form a circle wide;
   The sire turns o'er, wi' patriarchal grace,
      The big *ha'-Bible*, ance his *Father's* pride. hall Bible, once
   His bonnet rev'rently is laid aside,
105   His *lyart haffets* wearing thin and bare;   grey sidelocks
   Those strains that once did sweet in ZION glide,
      He wales a portion with judicious care,
   '*And let us worship GOD!*' he says, with solemn air.

   They chant their artless notes in simple guise,
110   They tune their hearts, by far the noblest aim;
   Perhaps *Dundee's* wild-warbling measures rise,
      Or plaintive *Martyrs*, worthy of the name;
   Or noble *Elgin* beets the heaven-ward flame,   fans
      The sweetest far of SCOTIA'S holy lays:
115   Compar'd with these, *Italian trills* are tame;
      The tickl'd ears no heart-felt raptures raise;
   Nae unison hae they, with our CREATOR'S praise.   no, have

   The priest-like Father reads the sacred page,
      How *Abram* was the Friend of God on high;
120   Or, *Moses* bade eternal warfare wage
      With *Amalek's* ungracious progeny;
   Or, how the *royal Bard* did groaning lye
      Beneath the stroke of Heaven's avenging ire;
   Or *Job's* pathetic plaint, and wailing cry;
125   Or rapt *Isaiah's* wild, seraphic fire;
   Or other *Holy Seers* that tune the *sacred lyre*.

   Perhaps the *Christian Volume* is the theme:
      How *guiltless blood* for *guilty* man was shed;
   How He, who bore in Heaven the second name,
130   Had not on Earth whereon to lay His head;

How His first *followers* and *servants* sped;
    The *Precepts sage* they wrote to many a land:
How *he*, who lone in *Patmos* banishèd,
    Saw in the sun a mighty angel stand,
135 And heard great *Bab'lon's* doom pronounc'd by Heaven's command.

Then kneeling down to HEAVEN'S ETERNAL KING,
    The *Saint*, the *Father*, and the *Husband* prays:
Hope 'springs exulting on triumphant wing,'[1] *— quoting in an*
    That *thus* they all shall meet in future days, *educated manner.*
140 There, ever bask in *uncreated rays*,
    No more to sigh or shed the bitter tear,
Together hymning their CREATOR'S praise,
    In *such society*, yet still more dear;
While circling Time moves round in an eternal sphere.

145 Compar'd with this, how poor Religion's pride,
    In all the pomp of *method*, and of *art*;
When men display to congregations wide
    Devotion's ev'ry grace, except the *heart*!
The POWER, incens'd, the Pageant will desert,
150   The pompous strain, the sacerdotal stole;
But haply, in some *Cottage* far apart,
    May hear, well-pleas'd, the language of the Soul,
And in His *Book of Life* the Inmates poor enroll.

Then homeward all take off their sev'ral way;
155   The youngling *Cottagers* retire to rest: youthful
The Parent-pair their *secret homage* pay,
    And proffer up to Heaven the warm request,
That 'He who stills the *raven's* clam'rous nest,
    'And decks the *lily* fair in flow'ry pride,
160 'Would, in the way His *Wisdom* sees the best,
    'For *them* and for their *little ones* provide;
'But, chiefly, in their hearts with *Grace Divine* preside'.

From Scenes like these, old SCOTIA'S grandeur springs,
    That makes her lov'd at home, rever'd abroad:

1 Pope's *Windsor Forest*, R.B.

165   Princes and lords are but the breath of kings,
         'An honest man's the noble work of GOD';[2] ~ *Pope again.*
      And *certes*, in fair Virtue's heavenly road,   verily
         The *Cottage* leaves the *Palace* far behind;
      What is a lordling's pomp? – a cumbrous load,
170   Disguising oft the *wretch* of human kind,
      Studied in arts of Hell, in wickedness refin'd!

      O SCOTIA! my dear, my native soil!
         For whom my warmest wish to Heaven is sent!
      Long may thy hardy sons of *rustic toil*
175   Be blest with health, and peace, and sweet content!
      And O! may Heaven their simple lives prevent
         From *Luxury's contagion*, weak and vile!
      Then, howe'er *crowns* and *coronets* be rent,
         A *virtuous Populace* may rise the while,
180   And stand a wall of fire around their much-lov'd ISLE.

      O THOU! who pour'd the *patriotic tide*,
         That stream'd thro' WALLACE'S undaunted heart,
      Who dar'd to, nobly, stem tyrannic pride,
         Or *nobly die*, the second glorious part:
185   (The Patriot's GOD, peculiarly Thou art,
         His *friend, inspirer, guardian,* and *reward*!)
      O never, never SCOTIA'S realm desert;
         But still the *Patriot*, and the *Patriot-bard*
      In bright succession raise, her *Ornament* and *Guard*!

As Kinsley noted (Vol. III, p. 112): 'What appealed to Burns
contemporaries . . . was the naturalism and the moral tone of *TC's
SN. The English Review* (Feb. 1787) thought it the best poem in the
Kilmarnock book, offering 'a domestic picture of rustic simplicity,
natural tenderness, and innocent passion that must please every
reader whose feelings are not perverted'. As Henry Mackenzie's and
Robert Heron's reviews show (See Low, *The Critical Heritage*),
conformist Scots were only too eager to build up such English
pieties.

   Unfazed that a 'heaven-taught' ploughman should be so canoni-
cally allusive, we find, embryonically in these Tory sentimentalists,
the enormous Victorian enthusiasm for a poem which seemed,

2 Pope's *Essay on Man*, R.B.

under the growing threat of the anarchic urban, industrial crowd, to offer the security and succour of a pietistically all-accepting rural folk. (See Andrew Noble, 'Some Versions of Scottish Pastoral: The Literati and the Tradition' in *Order in Space and Society*, ed. Markus (Edinburgh, 1982), pp. 263–310.

Twentieth-century critics have mainly been less easy with the poem. In his masterly reading Daiches compares it unfavourably to Fergusson's formally Spenserian precursor, *The Farmer's Ingle*. Compared to Fergusson's consistent vernacular, Daiches finds the language and voice uneven in the Burns poem. The problem Daiches believes is that, beginning with its initial homage to Robert Aitken: 'What Aitken in a Cottage would have been;/Ah! tho' his worth unknown, far happier there I ween', a most unlikely tale, the poem is muddled, in parts, especially the ruined maid sequence, by Burns too consciously looking over his shoulder to please genteel Edinburgh.' As he further notes:

> There is probably no poem of Burns in which the introduction of an artificial personality has spoiled a potentially fine work to the extent that it has in *The Cotter's Saturday Night*. The main trouble is that the poet has kept shifting his attitude, and with it his diction, between several incompatible positions. He is at one and the same time the sympathetic, realistic observer; at still another he is the sophisticated moralist acting as a guide showing off his rustic character for the benefit of a sentimental, genteel audience (p. 149).

Daiches is also rightly concerned with the semi, if not wholly, detached nature of the last two stanzas: 'But he overdoes the patriotic note, and in his final stanza seems to forget altogether the real theme of his poem.' Perhaps subconsciously, Burns did realise that some of the poem was complicit with values he detested and this invocation of a national, contractually governed common people was his attempt to deny some of the sentiments which preceded his inevitably inorganic conclusion. Certainly he is echoing the national spirit of Fergusson's *The Farmer's Ingle*:

> On sicken food has mony doughty deed
>   By Caledonia's ancestors been done;
> By this did mony wright fu' weirlike bleed
>   In brulzies frae the dawn to set o' sun:

> 'Twas this that brac'd their gardies stiff and strang
>   That bent the deidly yew in antient days,
> Laid Denmark's daring sons on yird alang,
>   Gar'd Scottish thristles bang the Roman bays;
> For near our crest their heads they doughtna raise.

It would be hard to overestimate Fergusson's influence in both national style and substance on Burns. From Fergusson, albeit often more elegiacally expressed, come the sense of the food, drink, music and personages that make up the Scottish spirit. Burns also understood that Fergusson was, if covertly, a profoundly political poet. Like himself, Fergusson was socially displaced because he also existed in a hierarchical world between masters and men. Their political poetry, then, had to be ironic, oblique, comically masked. In defining Fergusson as 'bauld and slee' (bold and sly) Burns, knowingly, defined himself. As we have already seen, Fergusson's brilliant *Hame Content: A Satire* with its denunciation of those Europhiliac, decadent aristocrats who will not remain responsibly at home was put, in *The Twa Dogs*, to equally brilliant use. These lines from the same Fergusson poem should remind us simultaneously of the relatively uneven failure of *The Cotter's Saturday Night* and the greatness in representing the harshness, beauty and injustice in the life of the common people found in so much of Burns's other poetry, significantly due to Fergusson's influence on him:

> Now whan the Dog-day heats begin
> To birsel and to peel the skin,
> May I lie streekit at my ease,
> Beneath the caller shady trees,
> (Far frae the din o' Borrowstown,)
> Whar water plays the haughs bedown,
> To jouk the simmer's rigor there,
> And breath a while the caller air
> 'Mang herds, an' honest cotter fock
> That till the farm and feed the flock;
> Careless o' mair, wha never fash
> To lade their kist wi' useless cash
> But thank the gods for what they've sent
> O' health eneugh, and blyth content,
> An' pith, that helps them to stravaig
> Owr ilka cleugh and ilka craig,
> Unkend to a' the weary granes
> That aft arise frae gentler banes,

On easy-chair that pamper'd lie,
Wi' banefu' viands gustit high,
And turn and fald their weary clay,
To rax and gaunt the live-lang day.

To a Mouse
On Turning Her Up in Her Nest with the Plough
November 1785

First printed in the Kilmarnock edition, 1786.

Wee, sleekit, cowrin, tim'rous *beastie*,   small, sleek
O, what a panic's in thy breastie!   breast
Thou need na start awa sae hasty,   away, so
    Wi' bickering brattle!   hasty, scurry
5 I wad be laith to rin an' chase thee,   would, loath, run
    Wi' murdering *pattle*!   a wooden plough-scraper

I'm truly sorry Man's dominion
Has broken Nature's social union,
An' justifies that ill opinion
10   Which makes thee startle
At me, thy poor, earth-born companion
    An' *fellow mortal*!

I doubt na, whyles, but thou may thieve;   not, sometimes
What then? poor beastie, thou maun live!   must
15 A *daimen icker* in a *thrave*   one ear of corn in 24 sheaves
    'S a sma' request;
I'll get a blessin wi' the lave,   remainder
    An' never miss't!

Thy wee-bit *housie*, too, in ruin!   small, house/nest
20 Its silly wa's the win's are strewin!   walls, winds
An' naething, now, to big a new ane,   nothing, build, new one
    O' foggage green!   thick winter grass
An' bleak *December's win's* ensuin,   winds
    Baith snell an' keen!   both bitter, biting cold

25 Thou saw the fields laid bare an' waste,
An' weary *Winter* comin fast,
An' cozie here, beneath the blast,   cosy
    Thou thought to dwell,
Till crash! the cruel *coulter* past   plough blade
30   Out thro' thy cell.

That wee bit heap o' leaves an' stibble,   small, stubble
Has cost thee monie a weary nibble!   many
Now thou's turned out, for a' thy trouble,
    But house or hald,   without, holding
35 To thole the Winter's *sleety dribble*,   endure, drizzle
    An' *cranreuch* cauld!   hoar-frost cold

But Mousie, thou art no thy lane,   not alone
In proving *foresight* may be vain:
The best-laid schemes o' *Mice* an' *Men*
40   Gang aft agley,   go often wrong
An' lea'e us nought but grief an' pain,   leave
    For promis'd joy!

Still thou art blest, compared wi' me!
The *present* only toucheth thee:
45 But Och! I backward cast my e'e,
    On prospects drear!
An' *forward*, tho' I canna *see*,   cannot
    I *guess* an' *fear*!

Formally, this is a companion to that other creaturely masterpiece, *To a Louse*. McGuirk defines them as both belonging to 'Horatian satire, linking an *exemplum* of observed experience with a final *sententia* or maxim' (p. 223). In terms of content, however, the two poems, presumably deliberately, could not be more different. The hypothermic mouse, houselessly unprotected, has the ice of winter penetrating its fast fading heart. The hyperactive louse, pulsing with grotesque energy and intentions, foresees a comfortable head-high residence.

This is truly one of the great animal poems of the Sentimental canon fit to stand with Fergusson's great goldfinch and butterfly poems and Smart's cat poem. The destructive ploughman poet's guilt and empathy for the creature are wholly realised as is the sense of the inherent relationship of all created things. It is, seriously, *The Ancient Mariner* in miniature.

Crawford, in a very fine reading of the poem, rescued it from its daisy-like sentimental reputation particularly by stressing the subtle political analogy in the poem between mice and peasant suffering similar, perhaps fatal, decanting in that age of agrarian revolution. As Crawford remarks:

The mouse becomes more than any animal; she is a symbol of the peasant, or rather of the 'poor peasant' condition. On a careful reading of the fifth stanza, the lines 'Till crash! the cruel coulter past/out thro' thy cell' affect us with all the terror of Blake's 'dark Satanic mills'. The coulter is in reality Burns's equivalent of the mills – part of the metaphorical plough of social change that breaks down the houses of both Lowland and Highland cotters. This is not to claim that the poem is allegorical in any crude or literal sense. The mouse does not 'stand for' the mother of 'The Cotter's Saturday Night' or the Highland 'hizzies' whom Beelzebub thought should be 'lessoned' in Drury Lane, but she belongs to the same world as these others and gains an extra dimension from those emotions whose intensity arises from the depth and power of Burns's own contemplation of human wretchedness and exploitation. (pp. 166–7)

It was written in the early winter of 1785.

Epistle to Davie, a Brother Poet

First printed in the Kilmarnock edition, 1786.

While winds frae aff BEN-LOMOND blaw,	from off, blow (north wind)
And bar the doors wi' drivin' snaw,	snow
And hing us owre the ingle,	*sit around*/over, fireplace
I set me down to pass the time,	
5 And spin a verse or twa o' rhyme,	two
In hamely, *westlin* jingle:	western
While frosty winds blaw in the drift,	blow
Ben to the chimla lug,	right, chimney bottom/fire
I grudge a wee the *Great-folk's* gift,	little
10 That live sae bien an' snug:	so comfortable
I tent less, and want less	care for
Their roomy fire-side;	
But hanker, and canker,	
To see their cursed pride.	
15 It's hardly in a body's pow'r,	
To keep, at times, frae being sour,	from
To see how things are shar'd;	
How *best o' chiels* are whyles in want,	people, often
While *Coofs* on countless thousands rant,	fools, make merry/riot
20 And ken na how to ware't;	know not, spend
But DAVIE, lad, ne'er fash your head,	trouble
Tho' we hae little gear;	have, wealth

We're fit to win our daily bread,
    As lang's we're hale and fier: *long as, whole, vigorous*
25   'Mair spier na, nor fear na,'[1]   *don't ask more, nor fear*
        Auld age ne'er mind a feg;   *old, fig*
    The last o't, the warst o't,   *worst*
        Is only but to beg.

To lie in kilns and barns at e'en,
30 When banes are craz'd, and bluid is thin,   *bones, blood*
        Is, doubtless, great distress!
    Yet then *content* could make us blest;
    Ev'n then, sometimes, we'd snatch a taste
        Of truest happiness.

35 The honest heart that's free frae a'   *from all*
        Intended fraud or guile,
    However Fortune kick the ba',   *ball – whatever misfortunes*
        Has ay some cause to smile;   *always*
    And mind still, you'll find still,
40   A comfort this nae sma';   *not small*
        Nae mair then, we'll care then,   *no more*
        Nae *farther* can we *fa'*.   *no, fall*

What tho', like Commoners of air,   *owners of air, not land*
We wander out, we know not where,
45   But either house or hal'?   *without house or hall*
    Yet *Nature's* charms, the hills and woods,
    The sweeping vales, and foaming floods,
        Are free alike to all.
In days when Daisies deck the ground,
50 And Blackbirds whistle clear,
With honest joy our hearts will bound,
        To see the *coming* year:
        On braes when we please then,   *hillsides*
            We'll sit an' *sowth* a tune;   *hum*
55   Syne *rhyme* till 't we'll time till 't,   *then*
            An' sing 't when we hae done.   *have*

It's no in titles nor in rank: *not*
It's no in wealth like *Lon'on Bank*,   *not, London*
        To purchase peace and rest.
60 It's no in makin muckle, *mair*:   *making much, more*
It's no in books, it's no in Lear,   *wisdom*
        To make us truly blest:

1 Ramsay, R.B.

If happiness hae not her seat   has
    An' centre in the breast,
65 We may be wise, or *rich*, or *great*,
    But never can be *blest*:
    Nae treasures nor pleasures   no
        Could make us happy lang;   long
    The *heart* ay 's the part ay   always is
70   That makes us right or wrang.   wrong

Think ye, that sic as *you* and *I*,   such
Wha drudge and drive thro' wet and dry,   who
    Wi' never ceasing toil;
Think ye, are we less blest than they,
75 Wha scarcely tent us in their way,   who, notice
    As hardly worth their while?
Alas! how oft, in haughty mood,
    GOD's creatures they oppress!
Or else, neglecting a' that's guid,   good
80   They riot in excess!
    Baith careless and fearless   both
        Of either Heaven or Hell;
    Esteeming and deeming
        It a' an idle tale!

85 Then let us chearfu' acquiesce,
Nor make our scanty Pleasures less
    By pining at our state:
And, even should Misfortunes come,
I here wha sit hae met wi' some,   who, have
90   An 's thankfu' for them yet,
They gie the wit of *Age to Youth*;   give
    They let us ken oursel;   know ourselves
They make us see the naked truth,
    The *real* guid and ill: good
95   Tho' losses and crosses
        Be lessons right severe,
    There's *Wit* there, ye'll get there,
        Ye'll find nae other where.   no

But tent me, DAVIE, *Ace o' Hearts*!   take heed
100 (To say aught less wad wrang the *cartes*,   anything, would wrong, cards
    And flatt'ry I detest)
This life has joys for you and I;

And joys that riches ne'er could buy,
    And joys the very best.
105 There's a' the *Pleasures o' the Heart*,
    The *Lover* an' the *Frien*';   friend
Ye hae your MEG, your dearest part,   have
    And I my darling JEAN!
    It warms me, it charms me
110   To mention but her *name*:
    It heats me, it beets me,   enraptures
        And sets me a' on flame!

O all ye *Pow'rs* who rule above!
O THOU whose very self art *love*!
115   THOU know'st my words sincere!
The *life blood* streaming thro' my heart,
Or my more dear *Immortal part*,
    Is not more fondly dear!
When heart-corroding care and grief
120   Deprive my soul of rest,
Her dear idea brings relief
    And solace to my breast.
    Thou BEING, All-seeing,
        O hear my fervent pray'r!
125   Still take her, and make her
        THY most peculiar care!

All hail! ye tender feelings dear!
The smile of love, the friendly tear,
    The sympathetic glow!
130 Long since, this world's thorny ways
Had number'd out my weary days,
    Had it not been for you!
Fate still has blest me with a friend
    In every care and ill;
135 And oft a more *endearing* band,
    A tye more tender still.   tie
    It lightens, it brightens
        The tenebrific scene,   darkening/depressive
    To meet with, and greet with
140   My DAVIE or my JEAN!

O, how that *Name* inspires my style!
The words come skelpin' rank an' file,   rattling/running
    Amaist before I ken!   almost, know

The ready measure rins as fine,   runs
145   As *Phoebus* and the famous *Nine*
          Were glowran owre my pen.   looking over
      My spavet *Pegasus* will limp,   lame, leg joint problems
          Till ance he's fairly het;   once, hot
      And then he'll hilch, an' stilt, an' jimp, hobble, limp, jump
150   And rin an unco fit;   run, rapid pace
          But least then, the beast then
              Should rue this hasty ride,
          I'll light now, and dight now   wipe clean
              His sweaty, wizen'd hide.   withered

David Sillar (1760–1830) was one of several recipients of Burns's Ayrshire epistolary poetry whom the Bard certainly overestimated poetically if not personally. Sillar had a mixed career as failed teacher then grocer but eventually inherited the family farm, Spittleside, Tarbolton and died a rich Irvine magistrate. This is the very reverse of the life of shared deprivation outlined for him and Burns himself in this poem. A good fiddler and composer (he composed the music to Burns's *The Rosebud*), he published his less than mediocre *Poems* at Kilmarnock in 1789. His proximity to Burns can be gauged by ll. 114–17 where, as in Sterne, rugged, biological reality constantly penetrates the surface of fine feeling. The poem is a technically formidable example of Burns's employment of Alexander Montgomerie's *The Cherry and the Slae* measure which James VI defined as one example of 'cuttit and broken verse, quhairof new formes daylie inuentit' (*Poems*, STS, l. 82). Burns is, however, hardly ever given to technique for its own sake. As Daiches has remarked (p. 163), the poem is remarkable for its ability to mould the process of thought to such complex form. However, the nature of this thought itself is more questionable. The exposed multiple, tangible distresses of penury are expressed with extraordinary power throughout the poem as is the sense of chronic injustice between rich and poor. The compensations of poverty are less credible. Edwin Muir was particularly unhappy with 'The heart ay's the part ay, /That makes us right or wrang.' Nor do the notions of compensatory and sexual harmony ring wholly true. Daiches in discussing stanza three, with its extraordinary initial delineation of the life of the beggars, defends the poem against such a sense of disparity between the desperate life it presents and the possible compensation for such a life thus:

Here the poet is not posturing for the benefit of the Edinburgh gentry, but letting the poem work itself easily into a lively

expression of careless, cheerful view of life. The theme is a
mood rather than a philosophy, a mood of defiance of the rich
and happy acceptance of easygoing poverty. To seek for pro-
fundity of ethical thought here would be to miss the point of the
poem, which seeks to capture a transitory state of mind rather
than to state general principles (p. 163).

Arguably, rather than refuting it, this repeats the poem's own
inadequacy. Daiches, however, also considers that, after stanza
seven, the poem falters badly. 'Tenebrific' (l. 138) is the poet's
neologism and not, certainly, the happiest of touches. The irresis-
tible, Pegasian flood of language in the last stanza is a quite
remarkable self-analysis of Burns in the grip of creativity.

The Lament
Occasioned by the Unfortunate Issue
of a Friend's Amour
First printed in the Kilmarnock edition, 1786.

Alas! how oft does Goodness wound itself,
And sweet Affection prove the spring of Woe!
HOME.

O thou pale Orb, that silent shines
    While care-untroubled mortals sleep!
Thou seest a *wretch* who inly pines,
    And wanders here to wail and weep!
5   With Woe I nightly vigils keep,
    Beneath thy wan, unwarming beam;
And mourn, in lamentation deep,
    How *life* and *love* are all a dream!

I joyless view thy rays adorn
10   The faintly-marked, distant hill;
I joyless view thy trembling horn
    Reflected in the gurgling rill.
My fondly-fluttering heart, be still!
    Thou busy pow'r, Remembrance, cease!
15 Ah! must the agonizing thrill
    For ever bar returning Peace?

No idly-feign'd, poetic pains
 My sad, lovelorn lamentings claim:
No shepherd's pipe — Arcadian strains;
20 No fabled tortures quaint and tame.
The *plighted faith*, the *mutual flame*,
 The *oft-attested Pow'rs above*,
The *promis'd Father's tender name*,
 These were the pledges of my love!

25 Encircled in her clasping arms,
 How have the raptur'd moments flown!
How have I wished for Fortune's charms,
 For her dear sake, and her's alone!
And, must I think it! is she gone,
30 My secret heart's exulting boast?
And does she heedless hear my groan?
 And is she ever, ever lost?

Oh! can she bear so base a heart,
 So lost to Honour, lost to Truth,
35 As from the *fondest lover* part,
 The *plighted husband* of her youth?
Alas! Life's path may be unsmooth!
 Her way may lie thro' rough distress!
Then, who her pangs and pains will soothe,
40 Her sorrows share, and make them less?

Ye winged Hours that o'er us past,
 Enraptur'd more the more enjoy'd,
Your dear remembrance in my breast
 My fondly treasur'd thoughts employ'd.
45 That breast, how dreary now, and void,
 For her too scanty once of room!
Ev'n ev'ry *ray* of *Hope* destroy'd,
 And not a *Wish* to gild the gloom!

The morn, that warns th' approaching day,
50 Awakes me up to toil and woe;
I see the hours in long array,
 That I must suffer, lingering slow:
Full many a pang, and many a throe,
 Keen Recollection's direful train,
55 Must wring my soul, ere Phoebus, low,
 Shall kiss the distant western main.

And when my nightly couch I try,
    Sore-harass'd out, with care and grief,
My toil-beat nerves and tear-worn eye
60   Keep watchings with the nightly thief:
Or, if I slumber, Fancy, chief,
    Reigns, haggard-wild, in sore affright:
Ev'n day, all-bitter, brings relief
    From such a horror-breathing night.

65 O! thou bright Queen, who, o'er th' expanse
    Now highest reign'st, with boundless sway!
Oft has thy silent-marking glance
    Observ'd us, fondly-wand'ring, stray!
The time, unheeded, sped away,
70   While Love's *luxurious pulse* beat high,
Beneath thy silver-gleaming ray,
    To mark the mutual-kindling eye.

Oh! scenes in strong remembrance set!
    Scenes, never, never to return!
75 Scenes if in stupor I forget,
    Again I feel, again I burn!
From ev'ry joy and pleasure torn,
    Life's weary vale I wander thro';
And hopeless, comfortless, I'll mourn
80   *A faithless woman's broken vow*!

Written in the rhyming format of Ramsay's *Ever-Green*, this expresses the poet's deep anguish at the forced break-up of his relationship with Jean Armour. He informed Dr Moore, after causing a stir among the Ayrshire clergy by circulating a copy of *Holy Willie's Prayer*, that:

> Unluckily for me, my idle wanderings led me, on another side, point-blank within the reach of their heaviest metal. – This is the unfortunate story alluded to in my printed poem, *The Lament*. 'Twas a shocking affair, which I cannot bear yet to recollect; and had very nearly given [me] one or two of the principal qualifications for a place among those who have lost the chart and mistake the reckoning of Rationality. – I gave up my part of the farm to my brother . . . (Letter 125)

Burns told Mrs Dunlop of his vexation at Jean being taken away by her family and their 'detestation of my guilt of being a poor devil, not only forbade me her company & their house, but on my rumoured West Indian voyage, got a warrant to incarcerate me in jail till I should find security in my about-to-be Paternal relation' (Letter 254). The closing line would suggest that Burns blamed Jean Armour as 'faithless' to him, although she was as much the victim of her parents' extreme action as Burns.

Kinsley notes two minor influences from Blair's poem *The Grave* and Goldsmith's popular *The Deserted Village* (Vol. III, no. 93, p. 1174). The poem could easily be mistaken for an early work of Samuel Taylor Coleridge, given lines such as '. . . I nightly vigils keep,/ Beneath thy wan, unwarming beam; /And mourn, in lamentation deep, /How life and love are all a dream!' It is an arguably underrated English poem.

Despondency: An Ode

First printed in the Kilmarnock edition, 1786.

Oppress'd with grief, oppress'd with care,
A burden more than I can bear,
    I set me down and sigh;
O Life! Thou art a galling load,
5   Along a rough, a weary road,
To wretches such as I!
Dim-backward, as I cast my view,
    What sick'ning Scenes appear!
What Sorrows *yet* may pierce me thro',
10   Too justly I may fear!
      Still caring, despairing,
          Must be my bitter doom;
    My woes here shall close ne'er
      But with the *closing tomb*!

15 Happy ye sons of Busy-life,
Who, equal to the bustling strife,
    No other view regard!
Ev'n when the wishèd *end*'s denied,
Yet while the busy *means* are plied,
20   They bring their own reward:
Whilst I, a hope-abandoned wight,
    Unfitted with an *aim*,
Meet ev'ry sad returning night
    And joyless morn the same.

25   You, bustling and justling,
               Forget each grief and pain;
       I, listless yet restless,
             Find ev'ry prospect vain.

   How blest the Solitary's lot,
30 Who, all-forgetting, all-forgot,
       Within his humble cell —
   The cavern, wild with tangling roots —
   Sits o'er his newly-gather'd fruits,
       Beside his crystal well!
35 Or haply to his ev'ning thought,
       By unfrequented stream,
   The *ways of men* are distant brought,
       A faint-collected dream:
          While praising, and raising
40   His thoughts to Heav'n on high,
       As wand'ring, meand'ring,
           He views the solemn sky.

   Than I, no *lonely Hermit* plac'd
   Where never human footstep trac'd,
45   Less fit to play the part;
   The *lucky moment* to improve,
   And just to stop, and just to move,
       With *self-respecting* art:
   But ah! those pleasures, Loves, and Joys,
50   Which I too keenly taste,
       The *Solitary* can despise,
       Can want and yet be blest!
       He needs not, he heeds not
          Or human love or hate;
55   Whilst I here, must cry here
          At perfidy ingrate!

   O enviable early days,
   When dancing thoughtless Pleasure's maze,
       To Care, to Guilt unknown!
60 How ill exchang'd for riper times,
   To feel the follies or the crimes
       Of others, or my own!
   Ye tiny elves that guiltless sport,
       Like linnets in the bush,

65   Ye little know the ills ye court,
        When Manhood is your wish!
           The losses, the crosses
                That *active man* engage;
           The fears all, the tears all
70   Of dim declining *Age*!

While this poem can be dated to the time of his estrangement from Jean Armour (see *The Lament*), it is also symptomatic of the bouts of depression, which, as their external causes increased, plagued his adult life. With masochistic logic he defines himself as a chronically displaced person with neither the opposing talents of the material man of business nor the spiritual hermit to locate himself appropriately in the world. The biographical letter of August 1787 to Dr Moore is another example of Burns turning prose, this time his marvellous own, into poetry:

> – The great misfortune of my life was never to have an aim –. I had felt early some stirrings of Ambition, but they were the blind gropins [*sic*] of Homer's Cyclops round the walls of his cave: I saw my father's situation entailed on me perpetual labor. – The only two doors by which I could enter the fields of fortune were, the most niggardly economy, or the little chicaning art of bargain-making: the first is so contracted an aperture, I never could squeeze myself into it; the last, I always hated the contamination of the threshold. – Thus, abandoned of [every (deleted)] aim or view in life; with a strong appetite for sociability, as well from native hilarity as from a pride of observation and remark; a constitutional hypochondriac taint which made me fly solitude; add to all these incentives to social life, my reputation for bookish knowledge, a certain wild, logical talent, and a strength of thought something like the rudiments of good sense, made me generally a welcome guest; so 'tis no great wonder that always "where two or three were met together, there was I in the midst of them" (Letter 125).

The semi-vacuous self of this poem is further pervaded by chronic guilt and, in the last stanza, a sense of childhood uncomprehending of the losses and crosses that await the adult. If this sounds more the agonised Coleridge than Burns, this is not accidental. An admirer of Burns's innovative prosody: 'Bowles, the most tender and, with the exception of Burns, *the only always-natural poet* in our Language' (Low, *Critical Heritage*, p. 108), Coleridge also identified profoundly with this dark side of the Scottish poet.

As George Dekker makes clear in *Coleridge and the Literature of Sensibility* (London, 1978), Burns's *Despondency: An Ode* was a seminal tonal and thematic influence on Coleridge's *Dejection: An Ode*. It is perhaps a case of it taking one to know one. Equally the manically protean self-mocking, self-making tone is a common factor in both poets' letters. Presumably it was not this quality which caused that inspired Scottish talent spotter, James Perry (Pirie) (1756 – 1821) to attempt to lure both men to come to London to work for his radically-inclined *Morning Chronicle*. If anything Coleridge's often also disguised contributions to the paper in the early 1790s are at least as dissidently radical as Burns's.

Man Was Made to Mourn: A Dirge

First printed in the Kilmarnock edition, 1786.
Tune: Peggy Bawn

When chill November's surly blast
    Made fields and forests bare,
One ev'ning, as I wand'red forth
    Along the banks of AIRE,   Ayr
5 I spy'd a man, whose aged step
    Seem'd weary, worn with care,
His face was furrow'd o'er with years,
    And hoary was his hair.

Young stranger, whither wand'rest thou?
10   Began the rev'rend Sage;
Does thirst of wealth thy step constrain,
    Or youthful Pleasure's rage?
Or haply, prest with cares and woes,
    Too soon thou hast began
15 To wander forth, with me to mourn
    The miseries of Man.

The Sun that overhangs yon moors,
    Out-spreading far and wide,
Where hundreds labour to support
20   A haughty lordling's pride:
I've seen yon weary winter-sun
    Twice forty times return;
And ev'ry time has added proofs,
    That Man was made to mourn.

25 O Man! while in thy early years,
   How prodigal of time!
 Mis-spending all thy precious hours,
   Thy glorious, youthful prime!
 Alternate Follies take the sway,
30   Licentious Passions burn;
 Which tenfold force gives Nature's law,
   That Man was made to mourn.

 Look not alone on youthful Prime,
   Or Manhood's active might;
35 Man then is useful to his kind,
   Supported is his right:
 But see him on the edge of life,
   With Cares and Sorrows worn;
 Then Age and Want, Oh! ill-match'd pair!
40   Shew Man was made to mourn!

 A few seem favourites of Fate,
   In Pleasure's lap carest;
 Yet think not all the Rich and Great
   Are likewise truly blest:
45 But Oh! what crouds in ev'ry land,
   All wretched and forlorn,
 Thro' weary life this lesson learn,
   That Man was made to mourn.

 Many and sharp the num'rous Ills
50   Inwoven with our frame!
 More pointed still we make ourselves
   Regret, Remorse, and Shame!
 And Man, whose heav'n-erected face,
   The smiles of love adorn,
55 Man's inhumanity to Man
   Makes countless thousands mourn!

 See yonder poor, o'erlabour'd wight,
   So abject, mean, and vile,
 Who begs a brother of the earth
60   To give him leave to toil;
 And see his lordly *fellow-worm*
   The poor petition spurn,
 Unmindful, tho' a weeping wife
   And helpless offspring mourn.

65 If I'm design'd yon lordling's slave,
        By Nature's law design'd,
    Why was an independent wish
        E'er planted in my mind?
    If not, why am I subject to
70   His cruelty, or scorn?
    Or why has Man the will and pow'r
        To make his fellow mourn?

    Yet let not this too much, my Son,
        Disturb thy youthful breast:
75 This partial view of human-kind
        Is surely not the *last*!
    The poor, oppressed, honest man
        Had never, sure, been born,
    Had there not been some recompence
80   To comfort those that mourn!

    O Death! the poor man's dearest friend,
        The kindest and the best!
    Welcome the hour my aged limbs
        Are laid with thee at rest!
85 The great, the wealthy fear thy blow,
        From pomp and pleasure torn;
    But, Oh! a blest relief to those
        That weary-laden mourn!

This was written sometime during the summer of 1785. It is entered in the *FCB* under August 1785. In his commentary on l. 5 of this poem Kinsley remarks that a 'meeting with a didactic sage is common in eighteenth-century poetry down to the time of Wordsworth. Burns's immediate model was apparently the white-haired "grateful form" encountered "on distant heaths beneath autumn skies" by Shenstone (*Elegies*, vii)'. It is characteristic of Kinsley that as a commentator on Burns's poems his eye is always fixed on the rear-view mirror hardly ever the road ahead. His commentary is eruditely, densely allusive to Burns's sources; he rarely has anything to say about Burns's seminal capacity to influence others, especially if the influence is of a political nature. Burns profoundly influenced Wordsworth. This poem, with its mixture of the elemental and political pains of existence, is probably the single best example of that influence. The depth of Burns's political passion in the poem can be gauged from Gilbert's account of its genesis when he noted that several of his brother's poems were written to 'bring forward some favourite sentiment of the author. He used to remark to me, that he could not well conceive a more mortifying picture of human life, than a man seeking work. In casting about in his mind how the sentiment might be brought forward, the elegy *Man was Made to Mourn* was composed' (Currie, iii. 384). Ll. 57–64 are this sentiment turned into poetry.

Mary Jacobus is particularly astute in her awareness of the degree to which Wordsworth creativity derived from the Scottish poet's sense of the terrible injustices of the rampant agrarian revolution. As she remarks:

> *The Last of the Flock* confronts, not death, but destitution – the plight of the labouring poor. Burns's *Man was Made to Mourn: A Dirge* was clearly in Wordsworth's mind during the spring of 1798, and its lament for the human condition shapes his poem (*Tradition and Experiment in Wordsworth's Lyrical Ballads 1798* (Oxford: 1976), p. 202).

Wordsworth's *Simon Lee, the Old Huntsman* is, if anything, even closer to Burns's dirge. Simon Lee, a tragic version of Tam Sampson, is faced with not only the increasingly severe symptoms of geriatric decline but the brutal redundancy of, no longer useful, being cast into helpless destitution. This combination of age and political injustice exactly follows Burns and his poem is deliberately echoed in the last lines of Wordsworth's:

> I've heard of hearts unkind, kind deeds
> With coldness still returning;
> Alas! The gratitude of men
> Hath oftener left me mourning.

The Dirge is also echoed in Wordsworth's *Lines Written in Early Spring*: 'Have I not reason to lament/ What man has made of man?', (ll. 23–4). The Leech Gatherer in *Resolution and Independence*, a poem in which Burns (ll. 45–9) makes an unnamed appearance, is also partly derived from the Dirge. Wordsworth's poem perhaps postulates a more spiritual consolation than Burns's Dirge with its vision of that ultimate and absolute democratic equaliser, Death itself.

Winter, a Dirge

Tune: MacPherson's Farewell
First printed in the Kilmarnock edition, 1786.

The Wintry West extends his blast,
    And hail and rain does blaw;
Or, the stormy North sends driving forth
    The blinding sleet and snaw: snow
5 While, tumbling brown, the Burn comes down,
    And roars frae bank to brae: from
While bird and beast in covert, rest,
    And pass the heartless day.

'The sweeping blast, the sky o'ercast,'[1]
10   The joyless *winter-day*,
Let others fear, to me more dear
    Than all the pride of May:
The Tempest's howl, it *soothes* my soul,
    My *griefs* it seems to join;
15 The leafless trees my fancy please,
    Their *fate* resembles mine!

Thou POW'R SUPREME, whose mighty Scheme
    These *woes* of mine fulfill,
Here, firm I rest, they *must* be best,
20   Because they are *Thy* Will!
Then all I want (Oh, do Thou grant
    This one request of mine!):
Since to *enjoy* Thou dost deny,
    Assist me to *resign*.

This song is 'The eldest of my printed pieces' Burns told Dr Moore
(Letter 125). In the *FCB* the poet records the influence upon him of
Nature during the most inclement of winter weather: 'There is
scarcely any earthly object gives me more – I don't know if I should
call it pleasure, but something which exalts me, something which
enraptures me – than to walk in the sheltered side of a wood or high
plantation, in a cloudy winter day, and to hear a stormy wind
howling among the trees & raving o'er the plain. – It is my best
season for devotion . . .' The imagery of winter desolation cast in a

1 Dr Young, R.B.

melancholy vein runs through the poetry of Burns as a motif for individual loss, or resignation to a person's fate.

A Prayer, in the Prospect of Death

First printed in the Kilmarnock edition, 1786.

O THOU unknown, Almighty Cause
    Of all my hope and fear!
In whose dread Presence, ere an hour,
    Perhaps I must appear!

5 If I have wander'd in those paths
    Of life I ought to shun;
As *Something*, loudly, in my breast,
    Remonstrates I have done.

Thou know'st that Thou hast formed me,
10   With Passions wild and strong;
And list'ning to their witching voice
    Has often led me wrong.

Where human *weakness* has come short,
    Or *frailty* stept aside,
15 Do Thou, ALL-GOOD, for such Thou art,
    In shades of darkness hide.

Where with *intention* I have err'd,
    No other plea I have,
But, *Thou art good*; and Goodness still
20   Delighteth to forgive.

This was almost certainly composed while the poet was at Irvine during the winter of 1781. The original title is, according to the copy in the *FCB*, 'A Prayer when fainting fits and other alarming symptoms of a pleurisy or some other dangerous disorder, which indeed still threatens me, first put Nature on the alarm'. Writing to his father, 27th December, 1781, Burns revealed his gloomy illness: 'The weakness of my nerves has so debilitated my mind that I dare not, either review past events, or look forward into futurity; for the least anxiety, or perturbation in my breast, produces most unhappy effects on my whole frame . . . I am quite transported at the thought

that ere long, perhaps very soon, I shall bid an eternal adieu to all the
pains, & uneasiness & disquietudes of this weary life; for I assure
you I am heartily tired of it' (Letter 4). The poem is partly derived
from the content of Pope's *Universal Prayer*, although the form is
that of the Scottish metrical psalms.

To a Mountain Daisy
On Turning One Down, with the Plough, in April, 1786
First printed in the Kilmarnock edition, 1786.

Wee, modest, crimson-tipped flow'r,		small
Thou's met me in an evil hour;		
For I maun crush amang the stoure		must, among, dust
Thy slender stem:		
5 To spare thee now is past my pow'r,		
Thou bonie gem.		pretty

Alas! it's no thy neebor sweet,   not, neighbour
The bonie *Lark*, companion meet!   handsome
Bending thee 'mang the dewy weet!   wet
10   Wi' spreckl'd breast,
When upward-springing, blythe, to greet
        The purpling East.

Cauld blew the bitter-biting *North*   cold
Upon thy early, humble birth;
15 Yet cheerfully thou glinted forth
        Amid the storm,
Scarce rear'd above the *Parent-earth*
        Thy tender form.

The flaunting *flow'rs* our Gardens yield,
20 High shelt'ring woods and wa's maun shield;   walls shall
But thou, beneath the random bield   shelter
        O' clod or stane,   turf, stone
Adorns the histie *stibble-field*,   dry, stubble
        Unseen, alane.   alone

25 There, in thy scanty mantle clad,
Thy snawie bosom sun-ward spread,   snow white
Thou lifts thy unassuming head
        In humble guise;
But now the *share* upteats thy bed,   ploughshare/blade
30   And low thou lies!

Such is the fate of artless Maid,   ✓
Sweet *flow'ret* of the rural shade!
By love's simplicity betray'd,
          And guileless trust;

[margin: ✓ lack of whereunce]

35   Till she, like thee, all soil'd, is laid
          Low i' the dust.

Such is the fate of simple Bard,   ✓
On Life's rough ocean luckless starr'd!
Unskilful he to note the card   *chart*
40   Of *prudent Lore*,   *wisdom*
Till billows rage, and gales blow hard,
          And whelm him o'er!

Such fate to *suffering Worth* is giv'n,
Who long with wants and woes has striv'n,
45   By human pride or cunning driv'n
          To Mis'ry's brink;
Till, wrench'd of ev'ry stay but HEAV'N,
          He, ruin'd, sink!

Ev'n thou who mourn'st the *Daisy's* fate,
50   *That fate is thine* — no distant date;
Stern Ruin's *plough-share* drives elate,
          Full on thy bloom,
Till crush'd beneath the *furrow's* weight
          Shall be thy doom!

Henry Mackenzie, a frequent kiss of death for twentieth-century
critical taste, waxed as eloquently about this poem as 'The Cotter's
Saturday Night':

> I have seldom met with an image more truly pastoral than that
> of the lark in the second stanza. Such strokes as these mark the
> pencil of the poet, which delineates Nature with the precision,
> yet with the delicate colouring of beauty and taste. (Low,
> *Critical Heritage*, p. 69).

Burns's own account of the poem in a letter to John Kennedy in
April 1786 seems to suggest that he had produced a mawkish poem
compatible with Mackenzie's cloying response:

> I have here . . . inclosed a small piece, the very latest of my
> productions. I am a good deal pleased with some sentiments in
> it myself, as they are just the native querulous feelings of a heart
> which, as the elegantly melting Gray says, "Melancholy has
> marked for her own" (Letter 27).

Certainly this is what Daiches (pp. 154–6) believes and he is also
correct in saying that the inherent danger of sentimentality in animal
poetry is even more extreme when dealing with plant life. Burns
(Letter 56) could certainly descend to terrible bathos in this branch
of his endeavours as he not infrequently set out his sentimentally-
baited traps for socially superior women: 'Even the hoary Hawthorn
twig that shot across the way, what heart at such a time, must have
been interested in its welfare, and wished it to be preserved from the
rudely browsing cattle, or the withering eastern Blast?'

This poem, however, is not self-promotingly narcissistic. Nor is it
a mere piece of lyric natural description as Mackenzie, probably
deliberately, certainly imperceptively, remarked. It is as political as
its 'Mouse' and 'Louse' companion pieces. Like the mass of men,
the daisy has to eke out its dangerously exposed existence outwith
the walled security of the aristocratic garden flowers. The specific
analogies of the daisy with the human world are all recurrent
archetypes of suffering in Burns's imagination: the sexually violated
women; the imprudently overwhelmed poet; the Job-like, ruined
but honest farmer. The poem has a dark, even apocalyptic tone
partly derived from Young's *Night Thoughts*, IX, ll. 167–8: 'Stars
rush; and final ruin fiercely drives/her ploughshare o'er creation!'
which Burns amends to 'Stern Ruin's *plough share* drives elate'. It is
definably sentimental but in the honourable sense that the senti-
mental poetry of the late eighteenth century, at its best, embodies a
tragically irreconcilable sense that the great Enlightenment impulse
towards the recognition of all human worth will not lead to a just,
fearless democratic society. In 1802, his radicalism diminished,
Wordsworth wrote his *To the Daisy*. It is, not least in metrical
form, significantly influenced by Burns's version:

> Methinks that there abides in thee
> Some concord with humanity,
> Given to no other flower I see
> The forest through.

To Ruin

First printed in the Kilmarnock edition, 1786.

All hail! inexorable lord!
At whose destruction-breathing word,
  The mightiest empires fall!
Thy cruel, woe-delighted train,
5 The ministers of Grief and Pain,
   A sullen welcome, all!
  With stern-resolv'd despairing eye,
I see each aimed dart;
For one has cut my *dearest tye*,
10   And quivers in my heart.
   Then low'ring and pouring,
    The *Storm* no more I dread;
   Tho' thick'ning and black'ning
    Round my devoted head.

15 And thou grim Pow'r, by Life abhorr'd,
While Life a *pleasure* can afford,
  Oh! hear a wretch's pray'r!
No more I shrink appall'd, afraid;
I court, I beg thy friendly aid,
20   To close this scene of care!
When shall my soul, in silent peace,
   Resign Life's *joyless day*?
My weary heart its throbbings cease,
   Cold-mould'ring in the clay?
25   No fear more, no tear more
    To stain my lifeless face,
   Enclasped and grasped
    Within thy cold embrace!

This was probably written in the winter of 1781–2. This melancholic work in the bob-wheel stanza of the old Scots poem *The Cherry and the Slae*, reveals the poet's holistic view that a God of Nature influences both the pleasure and the woes of life from the fall of historic Empires to individual experience. It is a distinctive brush-stroke of Burns to move from universal comment to a specific incident. The hardship of eighteenth-century rural existence on a leased farm, particularly during winter periods, energises the poem. The subtext is the poet's rejection by a lover who is believed to be Alison Begbie.

Epistle to a Young Friend May, 1786

First printed in the Kilmarnock edition, 1786.

I lang hae thought, my youthfu' friend,   long have
    A Something to have sent you,
Tho' it should serve nae ither end   no other
    Than just a kind memento;
5 But how the subject-theme may gang,   go
    Let time and chance determine;
Perhaps it may turn out a Sang;   song
    Perhaps, turn out a Sermon.

Ye'll try the world soon, my lad;
10   And, ANDREW dear believe me,
Ye'll find mankind an unco squad,   strange crowd
    And muckle they may grieve ye: much
For care and trouble set your thought,
    Ev'n when your end's attained;
15 And a' your views may come to nought,
    Where ev'ry nerve is strained.

I'll no say, men are villains a':
    The real, harden'd wicked,
Wha hae nae check but *human law*,   who have no
20   Are to a few restricked;   restricted
But, Och, mankind are unco weak   very
    An' little to be trusted;
If *Self* the wavering balance shake,
    It's rarely right adjusted!

25 Yet they wha fa' in Fortune's strife,   who fall
    Their fate we should na censure,   not
For still, th' *important end* of life
    They equally may answer:
A man may hae an *honest heart*,   have
30   Tho' Poortith hourly stare him;   poverty, look over him
A man may tak a neebor's part,   neighbour's
    Yet hae nae *cash* to spare him.   have no

Ay free, aff han', your story tell,   always, off hand/casual
    When wi' a bosom crony;   close friend
35 But still keep something to yoursel
    Ye scarcely tell to ony: any

Conceal yoursel as weel's ye can   well as
    Frae critical dissection: from
But keek thro' ev'ry other man   look
40   Wi' sharpen'd, sly inspection.

The *sacred lowe* o' weel-plac'd love,   flame, well-
    Luxuriantly indulge it;
But never tempt th' *illicit rove*,
    Tho' naething should divulge it: nothing
45 I waive the quantum o' the sin,
    The hazard of concealing;
But, Och! it hardens a' *within*,
    And petrifies the feeling!

To catch Dame Fortune's golden smile,
50   Assiduous wait upon her;
And gather gear by ev'ry wile   worldly goods, skill
    That's justify'd by Honor:
Not for to *hide* it in a *hedge*,   not to be a miser
    Nor for a *train-attendant*;   not for showy wealth
55 But for the glorious privilege
    Of being *independent*.

The *fear o' Hell's* a hangman's whip
    To haud the wretch in order;   hold
But where ye feel your *Honour* grip,
60   Let that ay be your border: always
Its slightest touches, instant pause —
    Debar a' side-pretences;   consider no distraction
And resolutely keep its laws,
    Uncaring consequences.

65 The great CREATOR to revere
    Must sure become the *Creature*;
But still the preaching cant forbear,
    And ev'n the rigid feature:
Yet ne'er with Wits prophane to range
70   Be complaisance extended;
An *atheist-laugh's* a poor exchange
    For *Deity offended*!

When ranting round in Pleasure's ring,   making merry/fun
      Religion may be blinded;
75 Or if she gie a *random-fling*,   give
      It may be little minded;
But when on Life we're tempest-driv'n,
      A Conscience but a canker —   peevishness
A correspondence fix'd wi' Heav'n
80   Is sure a noble *anchor*!

Adieu, dear, amiable youth!
      Your *heart* can ne'er be wanting!
May Prudence, Fortitude, and Truth,
      Erect your brow undaunting!
85 In *ploughman phrase*, 'GOD send you speed,'
      Still daily to grow wiser;
And may ye better reck the *rede*,   heed the advice
      Than ever did th' *Adviser*!

This was written for his friend Robert Aitken's son Andrew and was
finished in May, 1786. Robert Aitken is the legal hero of *Holy
Willie's Prayer*. Prudent counsellor is not the most probable of
Burns's multiple roles. The problems implicit in the poem are
highlighted by a deeply cautionary letter sent four years later to
his younger brother William who was moving from Newcastle to
London to pursue his career as a saddler:

> Now that you are setting out from that place, put on manly
> resolve, & determine to persevere; and in that case you will less
> or more be sure of success. – One or two things allow me to
> particularize to you. – London swarms with worthless wretches
> who prey on their fellow-creatures' thoughtlessness or inex-
> perience. – Be cautious in forming connections with comrades
> and companions. – You can be pretty good company to your-
> self, & you cannot be too shy of letting any body know you
> farther than to know you as a Sadler. – Another caution; I give
> you great credit for you [sic] sobriety with respect to that
> universal vice, Bad Women . . . – Whoring is a most ruinous
> expensive species of dissipation; is spending a poor fellow's
> money with which he ought clothe and support himself noth-
> ing? Whoring has ninety-nine chances in a hundred to bring on
> a man the most nauseous & excruciating diseases to which
> Human nature is liable; are disease & an impaired constitution
> trifling considerations? All this is independent of the crimin-
> ality of it (Letter 391).

This, from a man so addicted to women, should not be seen simply as massive hypocrisy. From as yet unpublished sources, Burns does seem to have suffered the venereal self-disgust of the so infected. More importantly, as in such Romantic libertine figures centrally present in the life and work of Mozart, Boswell, Byron and Pushkin, there exists, as a result of such serial fornication, a sense of self-punitive, guilty emptiness. Or, as it is brilliantly, vernacularly, put here:

> I wave the quantum o' the sin,
> The hazard of concealing;
> But Och! It hardens *a' within*,
> And petrifies the feeling.

R.L. Stevenson diagnosed this element in Burns and wrote him off because of it (*Familiar Studies of Men and Books*). G.K. Chesterton, more perceptively objective about the Scottish context, wrote in a brilliant foreword to A.A.Thomson's profoundly bad *The Burns We Love* (London: 1931):

> Nor is it true to say, as some have said, that this self-reproach was merely of the morbid or mawkish sort. So far from being mawkish and morbid, it could sometimes be both acrid and coarse. He really had a sense of something grotesque and even grovelling in his own orgies; of something of farce and bathos about the bad ending of so many of his love stories; a sense of being hooted from heaven with a sort of harsh laughter. In a word, he had a realistic as well as a romantic strain in him; and it is not altogether his fault that the national legend of his has become almost entirely romantic, to the extent of often forgetting how far his own view of himself was realistic (p. 5-6).

As well as the dangers, physical and moral, of sexual excess, Burns, in both the letter to William and in this poem, defines prudence as a necessary form of self- preservation in a world so variedly hostile. In a deeply perceptive essay, 'The Dialectics of Morality', Steven R. McKenna defines the question of necessary prudence as being a core problem in Burns's writings. In support of this thesis he identifies ll. 33–40 as a vernacular paraphrase of Polonius's cautionary speech to his son, Laertes in *Hamlet*, Act I, Scene iii. In extending these *Hamlet* parallels he finally reads the epistle as reaching for a kind of middle way of individual conscience, which avoids the one extreme of sadistically repressive conformity and the other of anarchic self-destruction. Burns himself appears to have understood how his repressed early life was partly responsible for his potentially self-destructive response to rigidly imposed order. As McKenna comments:

> Honour and self-protection are the issues here, and they form essential elements of this scene in the play, for Laertes in his long-winded, cautionary advice to his sister Ophelia regarding her relationship with Hamlet tells her she 'must fear' Hamlet, his greatness and his will. Says he, 'Fear it, Ophelia, fear it, my dear sister . . ./ Be wary then; best safety lies in fear' (I. 3.33, 42). A similar sentiment pervades Polonius's advice to her later in the scene: Hamlet's vows are to be held suspect that her honour is at stake. When taken together, these issues are a call to trust no one but oneself and to fear the power of others. And these are fundamental themes in Burns's 'Epistle to a Young Friend'. As in the case of Shakespeare's play, Burns's advice preaches an essential mistrust of the world, hence leads to a stultifying and isolating philosophy of life. Leaving aside the very possibility that Burns may be engaging in a bit of tongue-in-cheek irony with the epistle, the philosophy upon which it is premised is a matter of crime and punishment, and this takes two forms. First, insofar as religion and, broadly speaking, morality are concerned, fear particularly as something that can be manipulated by institutions and powers beyond the individual's control, is that which key 'To haud the wretch in order' as Burns says (l. 58). The second fear, and for Burns apparently the more important of the two, is the fear of self-punishment. In other words, one's sense of honour and integrity appears to be paramount, superseding potentially the 'fear o' hell' (l. 57). This is not to say Burns thumbs his nose at God, for stanzas nine and ten he sees the natural necessity of 'the Creature' revering the 'Creator'. Rather, this aspect of his epistle centres squarely on pitting the individual and conscience in opposition to formalised, institutionalised dogma. As he says, '. . . still the preaching cant forbear, / And ev'n the rigid feature' (67–8). Thus, in this case, organised religion is not the solution but rather the problem. Another case of churches built to please the priest, to bestow upon the ecclesiastical class the power to control people's lives. In the face of this, Burns posits the apparently radical notion that one's conscience should be one's guide (See *Love and Liberty*, p. 159).

On a Scotch Bard
Gone to the West Indies
First printed in the Kilmarnock edition, 1786.

	A' Ye wha live by sowps o' drink,	who, mouthfuls
	A' ye wha live by crambo-clink,	who, doggerel verse
	A' ye wha live and never think,	who
	Come, mourn wi' me	
5	Our *billie's* gien us a' a jink,	friend, given, the slip
	An' owre the Sea.	over
	Lament him a' ye rantan core,	merry crowd
	Wha dearly like a random-splore;	who, frolic
	Nae mair he'll join the *merry roar*,	no more
10	In social key;	
	For now he's taen anither shore,	taken another
	An' owre the Sea!	over
	The bonie lasses weel may wiss him,	handsome, well, wish
	And in their dear *petitions* place him:	
15	The widows, wives, an' a' may bless him	
	Wi' tearfu' e'e;	eye
	For weel I wat they'll sairly miss him	well I trust/know, sorely
	That's owre the Sea!	over
	O Fortune, they hae room to grumble!	have
20	Hadst thou taen aff some drowsy bummle,	taken off, bungler
	Wha can do nought but fyke an' fumble,	who, fuss
	'Twad been nae plea;	it would have, no
	But he was gleg as onie wumble,	keen-eyed, gimlet (phallus)
	That's owre the Sea!	over
25	Auld, cantie KYLE may weepers wear,	old, cheerful, mourning cuffs
	An' stain them wi' the saut, saut tear:	salt, salt
	'Twill mak her poor auld heart, I fear,	old
	In flinders flee:	splinters fly
	He was her *Laureat* monie a year,	poetic champion, many
30	That's owre the Sea!	over

He saw Misfortune's cauld *Nor-west*   cold, north-
Lang-mustering up a bitter blast;   long-
A Jillet brak his heart at last,   broke
    Ill may she be!
35 So, took a berth afore the mast,
    An' owre the Sea!   over

To tremble under Fortune's cummock,   rod
On scarce a bellyfu' o' *drummock*,   stomachful, meal & water
Wi' his proud, independent stomach,
40   Could ill agree;
So, row't his hurdies in a *hammock*,   rolled, hips/buttocks
    An' owre the Sea!   over

He ne'er was gien to great misguidin,   given
Yet coin his pouches wad na bide in;   pockets would not stay
45 Wi' him it ne'er was *under hidin*,
    He dealt it free: gave it away
The *Muse* was a' that he took pride in,
    That's owre the Sea!   over

Jamaica bodies, use him weel,   folk, well
50 An' hap him in a cozie biel: shelter, cosy place
Ye'll find him ay a dainty chiel,   friendly fellow
    An' fou o' glee: full of good nature
He wad na wrang'd the vera *Deil*,   would not wrong, very Devil
    That's owre the Sea!   over

55 Fareweel, my *rhyme-composing billie*!   farewell, friend
Your native soil was right ill-willie: ill-willed
But may ye flourish like a lily,
    Now bonilie!
I'll toast you in my hindmost *gillie*, last   gill (whisky)
60   Tho' owre the Sea!   over

There is unresolved critical contention about the reality of Burns's plan to immigrate to Jamaica. Kinsley writes (Vol. III, p. 1176):

> The spirit of *On a Scotch Bard*, though sturdily more cheerful than that of the letters, hardly justifies Daiches's view that Burns was never serious about emigrating (pp. 95, 189). He was volatile, and ready to shift to extremes; he was capable of representing his misfortunes as tragic or comic, as occasions for dependency or from a display of swaggering courage. 'I have

heard Wordsworth praise the ready flow of verse in this poem,'
says Cunningham (1834, II. 288), 'and recite with much emo-
tion the eighth and ninth stanza'.

Facts would seem to be on Kinsley's side. The poet's letters are
detailed about the voyage. The ship's delay seems to have prevented
the journey. What is not in doubt is the degree of tormented
uncertainty underlying the poetry of that period. He did want to
be the rooted, celebrated Bard of Kyle. The bitter fracas with Jean
Armour's family had, however, thrown him into the merciless path
of his Auld Licht enemies. He wrote to Dr Moore that:

> I had for some time been skulking from covert under all the
> terrors of a Jail; as some ill-advised, ungrateful people had
> uncoupled the merciless legal Pack at my heels (Letter 125).

The writ was taken out by Mr Armour, Jean's father (Letter 254).
Even in October 1786, after the Kilmarnock edition, he could still
write:

> . . . the consequences of my follies, which may perhaps make it
> impracticable to stay at home . . . I have some time been pining
> under secret wretchedness . . . the pang of disappointment, the
> sting of pride, with some wandering stabs of remorse, which
> never fail to settle on my vitals like vultures . . . My gaiety is the
> madness of an intoxicated criminal under the hands of the
> executioner (Letter 53).

Despite the moment of deeply ill-judged self-pity with the denigra-
tion of Jean (ll. 34–5) as mere jilt, the poem is fuelled, if not quite by
the 'madness of an intoxicated criminal' then certainly by the wild
energy of a partly comic revenge fantasy on his often betraying
fellow countrymen and women who, in his absence, will certainly
bitterly discover what they have lost. Exile and cunning but not
silence are part of *this* national poet's repertoire.

It should also be noted that this is, deliberately, not straight
biography. The poem's tone and content are wittily distanced by
being the monologue of an unnamed but sympathetic poet narrator.
This poet, addressing his impoverished fellow poets, turns Burns's
particular case into a general view, as in Goldsmith, of the penurious
state of the poetic career in the late eighteenth century. Words-
worth's perceptive admiration for its linguistic and metrical virtues
probably extended to a mutual sympathy for this theme.

A Dedication to Gavin Hamilton, Esq

First printed in the Kilmarnock edition, 1786.

	EXPECT na, Sir, in this narration,	not
	A fleechan, fleth'ran *Dedication*,	wheedling, flattering
	To roose you up, an' ca' you guid,	praise, call, good
	An' sprung o' great an' noble bluid,	blood
5	Because ye're surnam'd like *His Grace*,[1]	
	Perhaps related to the race:	
	Then, when I'm tired — and sae are ye,	so
	Wi' monie a fulsome, sinfu' lie,	many
	Set up a face, how I stop short,	
10	For fear your modesty be hurt.	
	This may do — maun do, Sir, wi' them wha	shall, who
	Maun please the Great-folk for a wamefou;	must, bellyful
	For me! sae laigh I need na bow,	so low, not
	For, LORD be thankit, *I can plough*;	
15	And when I downa yoke a naig,	do not/cannot, horse
	Then, LORD be thanket, *I can beg*;	
	Sae I shall say, an' that's nae flatt'rin,	so, not
	It's just *sic Poet* an' *sic Patron*.	such a
	The Poet, some guid Angel help him,	good
20	Or else, I fear, some *ill ane* skelp him!	one, beat
	He may do weel for a' he's done yet,	well
	But only — he's no just begun yet.	
	The Patron (Sir, ye maun forgie me,	must forgive
	I winna lie, come what will o' me)	will not
25	On ev'ry hand it will allow'd be,	
	He's just — nae better than he should be.	no
	I readily and freely grant,	
	He downa see a poor man want;	would not
	What's no his ain he winna tak it;	own, will not
30	What ance he says, he winna break it;	once, will not
	Ought he can lend he'll no refus't,	
	Till aft his guidness is abus'd;	often, goodness

1 The Duke of Hamilton.

And rascals whyles that do him wrang,   *sometimes, wrong*
Ev'n *that*, he does na mind it lang;   *not, long*
35   As Master, Landlord, Husband, Father,
He does na fail his part in either.   *not*

But then, nae thanks to him for a' that   *no*
Nae *godly symptom* ye can ca' that;   *no, call*
It's naething but a milder feature   *nothing*
40   Of our poor, sinfu', corrupt Nature:
Ye'll get the best o' moral works,
'Mang black *Gentoos*, and Pagan *Turks*,   *Indians, Hindus*
Or Hunters wild on *Ponotaxi*,   *Cotopaxi in Ecuador*
Wha never heard of Orthodoxy.   *who*
45   That he's the poor man's friend in need,
The GENTLEMAN in word and deed,
It's no thro' terror of Damnation:
It's just a carnal inclination,
[And Och! that's nae regeneration].[2]

50   Morality, thou deadly bane,   *poison*
Thy tens o' thousands thou hast slain!
Vain is his hope, whase stay an' trust is   *whose*
In *moral* Mercy, Truth, and Justice!

No — stretch a point to catch a plack;   *farthing/coin*
55   Abuse a Brother to his back;
Steal thro' the *winnock* frae a whore,   *window from*
But point the rake that taks the *door*;
Be to the Poor like onie whunstane,
And haud their noses to the grunstane;   *hold, grindstone*
60   Ply ev'ry art o' *legal* thieving;
No matter — stick to *sound believing*.

Learn three-mile pray'rs, an' half-mile graces,
Wi' weel-spread looves, an' lang, wry faces;   *well-, palms, long*
Grunt up a solemn, lengthen'd groan,
65   And damn a' Parties but your own;
I'll warrant then, ye're nae Deceiver,   *no*
A steady, sturdy, staunch *Believer*.

---

2 This line was omitted in the 1787 edition.

O ye wha leave the springs o' Calvin,
For *gumlie dubs* of your ain delvin!   muddy puddles, own digging
70 Ye sons of Heresy and Error,
Ye'll *some day* squeel in quaking terror,
When Vengeance draws the sword in wrath,
And in the fire throws the *sheath*;
When Ruin, with his sweeping *besom*,
75 Just frets till Heav'n commission gies him;   gives
While o'er the *Harp* pale Misery moans,
And strikes the ever-deep'ning tones,
Still louder shrieks, and heavier groans!

Your pardon, Sir, for this digression:
80 I maist forgat my *Dedication*;   almost forgot
But when Divinity comes 'cross me,
My readers still are sures me.

So, Sir, you see 'twas nae daft vapour;   no
But I maturely thought it proper,
85 When a' my works I did review,
To *dedicate* them, Sir, to YOU:
Because (ye need na tak' it ill)   not take it badly
I thought them something like *yoursel*.

Then patronize them wi' your favor,   howling
90 And your Petitioner shall ever —
I had amaist said, *ever pray*,   almost
But that's a word I need na say;   not
For prayin, I hae little skill o't,   have
I'm baith dead-sweer, an' wretched ill o't;   both loath, sick of it
95 But I'se repeat each poor man's *pray'r*,   I'll
That kens or hears about you, Sir —   knows

'May ne'er Misfortune's gowling bark   howling
Howl thro' the dwelling o' the CLERK!
May ne'er his gen'rous, honest heart,
100 For that same gen'rous spirit smart!
May Kennedy's far-honor'd name
Lang beet his hymeneal flame,   long fan
Till Hamiltons, at least a diz'n,   dozen
Are frae their nuptial labors risen: from
105 Five bonie Lasses round their table,
And sev'n braw fellows, stout an' able,   fine, sturdy

To serve their King an' Country weel,　　well
By word, or pen, or pointed steel!
May Health and Peace, with mutual rays,
110　Shine on the ev'ning o' his days;
Till his wee, curlie *John's* ier-oe,　　small, great-grandchild
When ebbing life nae mair shall flow,　　no more
The last, sad, mournful rites bestow!'

I will not wind a lang conclusion,　　long
115　With complimentary effusion;
But, whilst your wishes and endeavours
Are blest with Fortune's smiles and favours,
I am, Dear Sir, with zeal most fervent,
Your much indebted, humble servant.

120　But if, which Pow'rs above prevent,
That iron-hearted Carl, *Want*,　　fellow/old man
Attended, in his grim advances,
By *sad mistakes*, and *black mischances*,
While hopes, and joys, and pleasures fly him,
125　Make you as poor a dog as I am,
Your *humble servant* then no more;
For who would humbly serve the Poor?
But, by a poor man's hopes in Heav'n!
While recollection's pow'r is giv'n,
130　If, in the vale of humble life,
The victim sad of Fortune's strife,
I, thro' the tender-gushing tear,
Should recognise my *Master dear*,
If friendless, low, we meet together,
135　Then, sir, your hand — my FRIEND and BROTHER!

Gavin Hamilton (1751–1805) was a Mauchline writer (solicitor) who
was one of Burns's closest friends and one of the few professional
men to whom the poet was tangibly indebted. He, as landlord, sub-
leased Mossgiel to Robert and Gilbert to save them from their
father's bankruptcy and was also to the fore in supporting publica-
tion of the Kilmarnock edition. Like Burns he, too, fell foul of the
malign forces of local Calvinism and it was his dispute with William
Fisher over alleged breaches of Church discipline on Hamilton's
part which was the cause of the quite wonderful *Holy Willie's
Prayer*. We, as well as Burns, are, consequently deeply in his debt.
　　Thus the poem reflects these two principal issues: Burns's gra-

titude to an honest good-hearted man (a type he constantly evoked but rarely found) and the fanatical power of Calvinism to control through the creation of diabolic terror and its by-product of malignant hypocrisy. Ll. 53–66 are particularly eloquent on this subject. Hamilton not only provides in this poem the image of the appropriate patron but his singular example leads to a larger digression (ll. 37–48) on the global manifestations of The Enlightenment's belief of the good-hearted natural man as opposed to the vicious, rebarbative provincials who control Ayrshire. For Burns's knowledge of the Philosophes see Ian S. Ross's 'Burns and the 'Siècles des Lumières' (*Love and Liberty*, pp. 217–28).

Hugh Blair wished ll. 67–77 omitted on the grounds that: 'The poem will be much better without it, and it will give offence by the ludicrous views of punishments of Hell'. Kinsley remarks that 'for once he may have been right' but on the evidence Kinsley cites from Calvin's own statutes regarding the inherent, eternal corruption of the non-elect, it is hard to agree with him. There is also a pro-Byronic self-referential flippancy in the poem (ll. 78–81) as well as moments of darkness and how one might respond to the collapse of creative and social hopes.

For Gavin Hamilton, Esq.
First printed in the Kilmarnock edition, 1786.

The poor man weeps — here Gavin sleeps,
    Whom canting wretches blam'd;
But with *such as he*, where'er he be,
    May I be sav'd or damn'd.

For notes on Gavin Hamilton, see *A Dedication to Gavin Hamilton*.

To a Louse
On Seeing One on a Lady's Bonnet at Church
First printed in the Kilmarnock edition, 1786.

HA! whare ye gaun, ye crowlan ferlie!	where, going, crawling wonder
Your impudence protects you sairly:	very well
I canna say but ye strunt rarely	cannot, strut confidently
Owre *gauze* and *lace*,	over
5 Tho' faith, I fear ye dine but sparely	eat little
On sic a place.	such

[Handwritten annotations: "Burns stanza form.", "Social satire.", and the letters A A B C B C marking the rhyme scheme]

Ye ugly, creepan, blastet wonner,   blasted wonder
Detested, shunn'd by saunt an' sinner,   saint
How daur ye set your fit upon her —   dare, foot
10   Sae fine a *Lady*!   so
Gae somewhere else and seek your dinner   go
        On some poor body.

Swith, in some beggar's haffet squattle: away!, temples, squat
There ye may creep, and sprawl, and sprattle,   scramble
15   Wi' ither kindred, jumping cattle,   other
        In shoals and nations;
Whare *horn* nor *bane* ne'er daur unsettle   where, bone (comb), dare
        Your thick plantations.

Now haud you there, ye're out o' sight,   hold
20   Below the fatt'rels, snug an' tight,   ribbon-ends
Na, faith ye yet! ye'll no be right,   no, confound you
        Till ye've got on it,
The vera tapmost, tow'ring height   very topmost
        O' *Miss's* bonnet.   hat

25   My sooth! right bauld ye set your nose out,   bold
As plump an' grey as onie grozet: any gooseberry
O for some rank, mercurial rozet,   mercury pasted rosin
        Or fell, red smeddum,   deadly powder
I'd gie ye sic a hearty dose o't,   give
30   Wad dress your droddum!   would, backside

I wad na been surpris'd to spy   would not
You on an auld wife's *flainen toy*;   old flannel cap
Or aiblins some bit duddie boy,   perhaps, small ragged
        On 's *wylecoat*;   flannel vest
35   But Miss's fine *Lunardi*, fye!   balloon-shaped hat
        How daur ye do't?   dare

O *Jenny*, dinna toss your head,   do not
An' set your beauties a' abread!   abroad
Ye little ken what cursèd speed   know
40   The blastie's makin!   damned thing's
Thae *winks* an' *finger-ends*, I dread,
        Are notice takin!

O wad some Pow'r the giftie gie us   would, gift give
To *see oursels as ithers see us*!   others
45   It wad frae monie a blunder free us,   would from many
          An' foolish notion:
What airs in dress an' gait wad lea'e us,   would leave
          An' ev'n Devotion!

If perceptible animal motion in *To a Mouse* is reduced to a drift
towards cold death, the louse's world is charged with manic upward
mobility. Its achieved goal is the very top of the refined Jenny's
Lunardi bonnet. These height of fashion bonnets derived from the
shape of the Lunardi balloon flown over Edinburgh by Burns's
Crochallan Fencible comrade, James 'Balloon' Tytler in 1784. The
Italian aeronaut Vincenzo Lunardi made several flights in Scotland
in the following year. The church service which combines strict
social regimentation with, for the prosperous, fashionable display,
becomes the occasion for the louse to traverse the class barrier with a
vengeance leaving behind its accustomed world of greasy, dirty
flannel for that of gauze and lace. Burns's own ambivalent but
constant attraction for the world of women of a superior class
(cloyingly obvious with Mrs McLehose and frenzied with regard
to Maria Riddell) perhaps provides the poem with its dynamism and
profound sense of satirical social contrast. Kinsley calls the poem a
'minor triumph of whimsy' but David Craig surely comes nearer the
truth when he comments:

> *To a Louse* isn't radical in a usual or obvious sense. The point is
> that Burns's radicalism pervades his imagination through and
> through. The least domestic item reminds him of the hunger
> and shortages of poor folk, the unfeeling above-it-all stance of
> the well-to-do, the need to expose the shame of finery and what
> was then called rank. For Burns, the louse is an underdog and
> all his complicity is with it (ll. 9–16). Already the louse has come
> to stand for all the dispossessed and propertyless who one day
> will come and squat in the big houses when the upper class
> nightmare of a jacquerie comes to pass. The beauty of this poem
> is that it insinuates its radical challenge to the unequal nature of
> class society into a perfectly observed comic scene. The social
> point makes itself. It is the kind of piece we need when
> answering the usual conservative objection that radical litera-
> ture tends to blaze and tub-thump ('The Radical Literary
> Tradition', *The Red Paper on Scotland*, ed. Gordon Brown
> (Edinburgh University Publications Board: 1975), pp. 292–3).

Craig's is both a brilliant insight into this poem and a salutary reminder of the fact that Burns as poet is necessarily preoccupied with varied oblique strategies for his radical politics. As a writer he was a smuggler not an Excise man. It should also remind us not to read 'O wad some Pow'r the giftie gie us/*to see oursels as ithers see us*!' as a piece of sententious sentimentality but Burns's two line demolition of Adam Smith's concept of the creation of internalised spectator in his *Theory of Moral Sentiments* as a form of secular conscience adequate to controlling our materialism and social pretentiousness.

Epistle to J. Lapraik:
An Old Scotch Bard, April 1, 1785
First printed in the Kilmarnock edition, 1786.

WHILE briers an' woodbines budding green,
And Paitricks scraichin loud at e'en,   partridges screeching
An' morning Poossie whiddin seen,   hare scudding
    Inspire my Muse,
5 This freedom, in an *unknown* frien'   friend
    I pray excuse.

On Fasteneen we had a rockin,   Shrove Tuesday, meeting
To ca' the crack and weave our stockin;   call the conversation
And there was muckle fun and jokin,   much
10   Ye need na doubt;   not
At length we had a hearty yokin,   set-to
    At *sang about*.

There was *ae sang*, amang the rest,   one
Aboon them a' it pleas'd me best,   above
15 That some kind husband had addrest
    To some sweet wife:
It thirl'd the heart-strings thro' the breast,   thrilled
    A' to the life.

I've scarce heard ought describ'd sae weel,   anything, so well
20 What gen'rous, manly bosoms feel;
Thought I, 'Can this be *Pope* or *Steele*,
    Or *Beattie's* wark?'   work
They tald me 'twas an odd kind chiel   told, chap or person
    About *Muirkirk*.

25 It pat me fidgean-fain to hear't,   put, tingling/excited
    An' sae about him there I spier't;   so, asked
    Then a' that kent him round declar'd,   all, knew
        He had *ingine*;   genius
    That nane excell'd it, few cam near't,   none, came
30   It was sae fine: so

    That set him to a pint of ale,
    An' either douce or merry tale,   sober
    Or rhymes an' sangs he'd made himsel,   songs
        Or witty catches,
35 'Tween Inverness and Teviotdale,
        He had few matches.

    Then up I gat, an' swoor an aith,   got, swore an oath
    Tho' I should pawn my pleugh an' graith,   plough and harness
    Or die a cadger pownie's death,   hawker pony's
40   At some dyke-back,   beind a stone wall
    A *pint* an' *gill* I'd gie them *baith*,   give, both
        To hear your crack.   conversation

    But, first an' foremost, I should tell,
    Amaist as soon as I could spell,   almost
45 I to the *crambo-jingle* fell;   rhyming
        Tho' rude an' rough,
    Yet crooning to a body's sel,   humming, self
        Does weel eneugh.   well enough

    I am nae *Poet*, in a sense;   no
50 But just a *Rhymer* like by chance,
    An' hae to Learning nae pretence;   have, no
        Yet, what the matter?
    Whene'er my Muse does on me glance,
        I jingle at her.

55 Your Critic-folk may cock their nose,
    And say, 'How can you e'er propose,
    You wha ken hardly *verse* frae *prose*,   who know, from
        To mak a *sang*?'   make
    But by your leaves, my learned foes,
60   Ye're maybe wrang.

What's a' your jargon o' your Schools,
Your Latin names for horns an' stools?
If honest Nature made you *fools*,
      What sairs your Grammers?   *serves*
65 Ye'd better taen up *spades* and *shools*,   *shovels*
      Or *knappin-hammers*.   *stone-breaking*

A set o' dull, conceited Hashes,   *dunderheads/fools*
Confuse their brains in *Colledge-classes*!
They *gang in* Stirks, and *come out* Asses,   *go*
70   Plain truth to speak;
An' syne they think to climb Parnassus   *then*
      By dint o' Greek!

Gie me ae spark o' Nature's fire,   *one*
That's a' the learning I desire;
75 Then, tho' I drudge thro' dub an' mire   *puddle*
      At pleugh or cart,   *plough*
My Muse, tho' hamely in attire,
      May touch the heart.

O for a spunk o' ALLAN'S glee,   *spark*
80 Or FERGUSSON'S, the bauld an' slee,   *sly*
Or bright LAPRAIK'S, my friend to be,
      If I can hit it!
That would be *lear* eneugh for me,   *learning enough*
      If I could get it.

85 Now, sir, if ye hae friends enow,   *have, enough*
Tho' *real friends* I b'lieve are few;
Yet, if your catalogue be fow,   *full*
      I'se no insist;
But, gif ye want ae friend that's true,   *if, one*
90   I'm on your list.

I winna blaw about *mysel*,   *will not boast*
As ill I like my fauts to tell;   *faults*
But friends, an' folks that wish me well,
      They sometimes roose me;   *praise*
95 Tho', I maun own, as monie still   *shall, many*
      As far abuse me.

There's ae *wee faut* they whyles lay to me,   one small fault, whiles
I like the lasses — Gude forgie me!   God forgive
For monie a Plack they wheedle frae me   many a coin, get from
100   At dance or fair:
Maybe some *ither thing* they gie me,   other, give
          They weel can spare.   well

But MAUCHLINE Race or MAUCHLINE Fair,
I should be proud to meet you there;
105 We'se gie ae night's discharge to *care*,   we will give one
          If we forgather;   get together
And hae a swap o' *rhymin-ware*,   have
          Wi' ane anither.   one another

The *four-gill chap*, we'se gar him clatter,   four-gill cup, we will make
110 An' kirs'n him wi' reekin water;   christen
Syne we'll sit down an' tak our whitter,   then, draught
          To chear our heart;
An' faith, we'se be *acquainted* better
          Before we part.

115 Awa ye selfish, warly race,   worldly
Wha think that havins, sense, an' grace,   who, manners
Ev'n love an' friendship should give place
          To *catch-the-plack*!   hunt for coin/money
I dinna like to see your face,   do not
120   Nor hear your crack.   conversation

But ye whom social pleasure charms,
Whose hearts the *tide of kindness* warms,
Who hold your *being* on the terms,
          'Each aid the others,'
125 Come to my bowl, come to my arms,
          My friends, my brothers!

But to conclude my lang epistle,
As my auld pen's worn to the grissle,   old, stump of a quill
Twa lines frae you wad gar me fissle,   two, from, would make me tingle
130   Who am, most fervent,
While I can either sing, or whissle,   whistle
          Your friend and servant.

The recipient of this epistle was John Lapraik (1727–1807) who was
postmaster at Muirkirk when he received it after a life of fiscal

mischance which had involved him in the Ayrshire Bank failure of 1773, so losing his farm at Dalfarn, and concluded with his imprisonment for debt in Ayr in 1785. Diverting himself with poetry in prison and observing Burns's success, he published *Poems on Several Occasions* (1788). Inevitably sympathetic to a man whose fiscal record only slightly exceeded the misfortunes of his own family, Burns may have over-responded to the alleged Lapraik song, *When I Upon Thy Bosom Lean*, he heard sung at a rural gathering. It has been strongly suggested by J.L. Hempstead (*BC*, February, 1994, pp. 94–101) that this song, initially published in *The Weekly Magazine*, was plagiarised. Burns revised the song for inclusion in the S.M.M. and in his interleaved copy remarked that Lapraik was 'a worthy, facetious old fellow' who 'often told me that he composed (the song) one day when his wife had been fretting o'er their misfortunes'.

Certainly the associations in this epistle of the 'facetious' Lapraik as *creatively* comparable to Pope, Steele, Beattie, Ramsay and Fergusson are hyperbolic in the extreme. Perhaps unconsciously Burns is projecting his own influences onto the older man. It also adds irony, of course, the proto-Wordsworthian pastoral poet Burns here celebrates in the stanza beginning 'Gie me ae spark o' Nature's fire' does so in a line which McGuirk (p. 205) notes, contains deliberate associations with these two earlier well-known rural non-sophisticates, Sterne and Pope. Certainly it allows Burns to make merry with rule-constipated academic poets and, another old-enemy, those rigidly and successfully, quite unlike himself and Lapraik, making money. The celebration of social pleasures also involves, as so often the case, in ll. 97–101 witty sexual innuendo.

Second Epistle to J. Lapraik
April 21, 1785
First printed in the Kilmarnock edition, 1786.

While new-ca'd kye rowte at the stake	new driven cattle, low
An' pownies reek in pleugh or braik,	ponies, snort, plough, harrow
This hour on e'enin's edge I take,	
To own I'm debtor	
5 To honest-hearted, auld LAPRAIK,	old
For his kind *letter*.	

Forjesket sair, with weary legs,   jaded, sore
Rattlin the corn out-owre the rigs,   out-over, ridges
Or dealing thro' amang the naigs   dealing out food among ponies
10   Their ten-hours' bite,
My awkart Muse sair pleads and begs,   awkward, sore
          I would na write.   not

The tapetless, ramfeezl'd hizzie,   feckless, worn-out girl
She's saft at best an' something lazy: soft
15   Quo' she: 'Ye ken we've been sae busy   know, so
          This month an' mair,   more
That trowth, my head is grown right dizzie,
          An' something sair.'   sore/aching

Her dowf excuses pat me mad;   dull, put
20   'Conscience,' says I, 'ye thowless jad!   lazy
I'll write, an' that a hearty blaud,   screed
          This vera night;   very
So dinna ye affront your trade,   do not
          But rhyme it right.

25   'Shall bauld LAPRAIK, the *king o' hearts*,
Tho' mankind were a *pack o' cartes*,   cards
Roose you sae weel for your deserts,   praise, so well
          In terms sae friendly;   so
Yet ye'll neglect to shaw your parts   show
30   An' thank him kindly?'

Sae I gat paper in a blink,   so, got
An' down gaed *stumpie* in the ink: went
Quoth I, 'Before I sleep a wink,
          I vow I'll close it:
35   An' if ye winna mak it clink,   will not make
          By Jove I'll prose it!'

Sae I've begun to scrawl, but whether   so
In rhyme, or prose, or baith thegither,   both together
Or some hotch-potch that's rightly neither,
40   Let time mak proof;
But I shall scribble down some blether   chit-chat
          Just clean aff-loof.   off the cuff

My worthy friend, ne'er grudge an' carp,
Tho' Fortune use you hard an' sharp;
45   Come, kittle up your *moorland harp*   tickle
       Wi' gleesome touch!
Ne'er mind how Fortune *waft an' warp*;
       She's but a bitch.

She's gien me monie a jirt an' fleg,   given, many, jerk, scare
50   Sin' I could striddle owre a rig;   straddle over
But, by the Lord, tho' I should beg
       Wi' lyart pow,   grey head
I'll laugh an' sing, an' shake my leg,   dance
       As lang's I dow!   long as I can

55   Now comes the *sax an twentieth simmer*   six, summer
I've seen the bud upo' the timmer,   woods/trees
Still persecuted by the limmer   jade
       Frae year to year;   from
But yet, despite the kittle kimmer,   fickle gossip
60   *I, Rob, am here.*

Do ye envy the *city-gent*,
Behint a kist to lie an' sklent,   counter, cheat
Or purse-proud, big wi' cent per cent,   counting money
       An' muckle wame,   large belly
65   In some bit *Brugh* to represent   borough
       A *Bailie's* name?   town magistrate

Or is't the paughty feudal *Thane*,   haughty
Wi' ruffl'd sark an' glancing cane,   shirt, shining
Wha thinks himsel nae *sheep-shank bane*,   who, himself no, bone
70   But lordly stalks;
While caps an' bonnets aff are taen,   off, taken
       As by he walks?

'O Thou wha gies us each guid gift!   who gives, good
Gie me o' *wit* an' *sense* a lift,   give
75   Then turn me, if *Thou* please, *adrift*
       Thro' Scotland wide;
Wi' *cits* nor *lairds* I wadna shift,   citizens, would not
       In a' their pride!'

Were this the *charter* of our state,
80   'On pain o' *hell* be rich an' great,'
Damnation then would be our fate,
          Beyond remead;
But, thanks to *Heav'n*, that's no the gate
          We learn our *creed*.

85   For thus the royal *Mandate* ran,
When first the human race began:
'The social, friendly, honest man,
          Whate'er he be,
'Tis *he* fulfils *great Nature's plan*,
90   And none but *he*.'

O *Mandate* glorious and divine!
The followers o' the ragged Nine —   the Muses
Poor, thoughtless devils! yet may shine
          In glorious light;
95   While sordid sons o' Mammon's line
          Are dark as night!

Tho' here they scrape, an' squeeze, an' growl,
Their worthless neivefu' of a *soul*   fistful
May in some *future carcase* howl,
100   The forest's fright;
Or in some day-detesting *owl*
          May shun the light.

Then may LAPRAIK and BURNS arise,
To reach their native, kindred skies,
105   And *sing* their pleasures, hopes an' joys,
          In some mild sphere;
Still closer knit in friendship's ties,
          Each passing year!

As further proof of Wordsworth's passionate enthusiasm for Burns's poetry, Alan Cunningham recollects hearing him recite this epistle 'with commendations. . . pointing out as he went the all but inimitable ease and happiness of thought and language. He remarked, however, that Burns was either fond of out-of-the-way sort of words, or that he made them occasionally in his fits of feeling and fancy'. Other than Cowper, Burns's English peers rarely complained about vernacular difficulty though 'forjesket' and 'tapetless', not to mention 'ram-feezl'd' may have been a linguistic bridge too far. It is interesting that well into the nineteenth century the, by then, deeply reactionary Wordsworth should have so responded to so politically radical a poem. Not only (ll. 7–12) does Burns record the brutal cost of farm work to his creativity, but the bulk of the poem is a cry of defiant, satirical rage against the old land-owning classes and the newly emerging bourgeoisie. Those 'Cits' who are equally castigated by Oliver Goldsmith and Charles Churchill. Burns brilliantly inverts the prosperous's use of 'economic Calvinism' to control the poor by showing what the real political would be in an inversion worthy of Blake:

> Were this the *charter* of our state
> 'On pain o' hell to be rich an' great',
> *Damnation* then would be our fate,
>   Beyond remead;
> But, thanks to *Heav'n*, that's no the gate
>   We learn our creed.

Again, like Blake (ll. 85–90) he invoked the spirit of divinely natural democracy so that this poem becomes a splendid prelude to the later, more overtly political *A Man's a Man* and the American section of *Ode for General Washington's Birthday*. Thus Burns would enrol fully armed in Edinburgh's dissident Crochallan Fencibles.

The poem concludes with an extraordinary image of the poor but poetically creative inheriting Heaven, with Mammon's sordid sons suitably rewarded for their bestial conduct to their fellow human beings.

To William Simson, Ochiltree,
May 1785
First printed in the Kilmarnock edition, 1786.

I GAT your letter, winsome Willie;	got
Wi' gratefu' heart I thank you brawlie;	handsomely
Tho' I maun say't, I wad be silly	shall, would
And unco vain,	mighty
5 Should I believe, my coaxin billie,	fellow
Your flatterin strain.	

But I'se believe ye kindly meant it,   I'll
I sud be laith to think ye hinted   should be loath
Ironic satire, sidelins sklented,   squinted sideways
10   On my poor Musie;
Tho' in sic phraisin terms ye've penn'd it,   such wheedling
         I scarce excuse ye.

My senses wad be in a creel,   would
Should I but dare a *hope* to speel,   climb
15   Wi' *Allan*, or wi' *Gilbertfield*,
         The braes o' fame;   slopes
Or *Fergusson*, the writer-chiel,   fellow
         A deathless name.

(O *Fergusson*! thy glorious parts
20   Ill suited law's dry, musty arts!
My curse upon your whunstane hearts,   whinstone
         Ye Enbrugh Gentry!
The tythe o' what ye waste at *cartes*   tenth, cards
         Wad stow'd his pantry!)   would have stored

25   Yet when a tale comes i' my head,
Or lasses gie my heart a screed —   give
As whyles they're like to be my dead,   whiles, death
         (O sad disease!)
I kittle up my *rustic reed*;   tickle, pipe
30   It gies me ease.   gives

Auld COILA, now, may fidge fu' fain,   tingle with delight
She's gotten *Bardies* o' her ain,   own
Chiels wha their chanters winna hain,   fellows who, will not spare
         But tune their lays,
35   Till echoes a' resound again
         Her weel-sung praise.   well-sung

Nae *Poet* thought her worth his while,   no
To set her name in measur'd style;
She lay like some unkend-of isle   unknown
40   Beside *New Holland*,
Or whare wild-meeting oceans boil   where
         Besouth *Magellan*.   to the south of

Ramsay an' famous *Fergusson*
Gied *Forth* an' *Tay* a lift aboon;   gave, above
45   *Yarrow* an' *Tweed*, to monie a tune,   many
      Owre Scotland rings;   over
While *Irwin, Lugar, Aire*, an' *Doon*   old spelling of Ayr
      Naebody sings.   nobody

Th' *Illissus, Tiber, Thames*, an' *Seine*,
50   Glide sweet in monie a tunefu' line: many
But, *Willie*, set your fit to mine,   foot (in music timing)
      An' cock your crest!
We'll gar our streams and burnies shine   make, burns
      Up wi' the best.

55   We'll sing auld COILA'S plains an' fells,   Coila/Kyle, Ayrshire
      Her moors red-brown wi' heather bells,
Her banks an' braes, her dens an' dells,   slopes, hill sides, glens
      Whare glorious WALLACE   where
Aft bure the gree, as story tells,   often took victory
60   Frae Suthron billies.   from English people

At WALLACE' name, what Scottish blood
But boils up in a spring-tide flood?
Oft have our fearless fathers strode
      By WALLACE' side,
65   Still pressing onward, red-wat-shod,   shoes soaked in blood
      Or glorious dy'd!

O sweet are COILA's haughs an' woods,   hollows
When lintwhites chant amang the buds,   linnets, among
And jinkin hares, in amorous whids,   sporting, silent running
70   Their loves enjoy,
While thro' the braes the cushat croods   slopes, pidgeon coos
      With wailfu' cry!

Ev'n winter bleak has charms to me,
When winds rave thro' the naked tree;
75   Or frosts on hills of *Ochiltree*
      Are hoary gray;
Or blinding drifts wild-furious flee,
      Dark'ning the day!

O NATURE! a' thy shews an' forms
80 To feeling, pensive hearts hae charms!   have
Whether the summer kindly warms,
     Wi' life an' light;
Or winter howls, in gusty storms,
     The lang, dark night!   long

85 The *Muse*, nae *Poet* ever fand her,   no, found
Till by himsel he learn'd to wander,
Adown some trottin burn's meander,   running
     An' no think lang: long
O, sweet to stray, an' pensive ponder
90   A heart-felt sang!   song

The warly race may drudge an' drive,   worldly
Hog-shouther, jundie, stretch, an' strive;   shoulder push, jostle
Let me fair NATURE's face descrive,   describe
     And I, wi' pleasure,
95 Shall let the busy, grumbling hive
     Bum owre their treasure.   hum over

Fareweel, 'my rhyme-composing' brither!   farewell, brother
We've been owre lang unkenn'd to ither: too long unknown, other
Now let us lay our heads thegither,   together
100   In love fraternal:
May *Envy* wallop in a tether,   swing on a rope
     Black fiend, infernal!

While Highlandmen hate tolls an' taxes;
While moorlan' herds like guid, fat braxies;   good, sheep carcases
105 While Terra Firma, on her axis,
     Diurnal turns;
Count on a friend, in faith an' practice,
     In ROBERT BURNS.

POSTSCRIPT
My memory's no worth a preen: pin
I had amaist forgotten clean,   almost
Ye bade me write you what they mean   bid
     By this *new-light*,[1]
5 'Bout which our herds sae aft hae been   flocks so often
     Maist like to fight.   most

1 A cant-term for those religious opinions which Dr Taylor of Norwich has
defended so strenuously. –R.B.

In days when mankind were but callans;   striplings
At *Grammar, Logic*, an' sic talents,   such
They took nae pains their speech to balance,   no
10   Or rules to gie;   give
But spak their thoughts in plain, braid Lallans,   spoke, broad vernacular
    Like you or me.

In thae auld times, they thought the *Moon*,   those old
Just like a sark, or pair o' shoon,   shirt, shoes
15   Wore by degrees, till her last roon   round
    Gaed past their viewin;   went
An' shortly after she was done,
    They gat a new ane.   got, one

This past for certain, undisputed;
20   It ne'er cam i' their heads to doubt it,
Till chiels gat up an' wad confute it,   chaps got, would
    An' ca'd it wrang;   called, wrong
An' muckle din there was about it,   much
    Baith loud an' lang.   both, long

25   Some *herds*, weel learn'd upo' the beuk,   well, Book (Bible)
Wad threap auld folk the thing misteuk;   would, maintain old, mistook
For 'twas the *auld moon* turn'd a newk   old, corner
    An' out o' sight.
An' backlins-comin to the leuk,   backwards, look
30   She grew mair bright.   more

This was deny'd, it was affirm'd;
The *herds* and *hissels* were alarm'd;   shepherds, flocks
The rev'rend gray-beards rav'd an' storm'd,
    That beardless laddies   young men
35   Should think they better were inform'd
    Than their auld daddies.   old fathers

Frae less to mair, it gaed to sticks;   from, more, went
Frae words an' aiths, to clours an' nicks;   from, oaths, bumps, cuts
An' monie a fallow gat his licks,   many, fellow got, punishment
40   Wi' hearty crunt;   blow
An' some, to learn them for their tricks,
    Were hang'd an' brunt.   burned

This game was play'd in monie lands,   many
An' *auld-light caddies* bure sic hands,   lackeys bore such
45 That faith, the *youngsters* took the sands   fled
        Wi' nimble shanks,   legs
    Till *Lairds* forbade, by strict commands,
        Sic bluidy pranks.   such bloody

    But *new-light herds* gat sic a cowe,   got such a terror
50 Folk thought them ruin'd stick-an-stowe;   completely
    Till now, amaist on ev'ry *knowe*   almost, hill or hillock
        Ye'll find ane placed;   one
    An' some, their *New-Light* fair avow,
        Just quite barefac'd.

55 Nae doubt the *auld-light flocks* are bleatan;
    Their zealous herds are vex'd and sweatan;
    Mysel, I've even seen them greetan   crying
        Wi' girnan spite,   snarling
    To hear the *Moon* sae sadly lie'd on   so
60   By word an' write.

    But shortly they will cowe the louns!   terrify, rascals
    Some *auld-light herds* in neebor touns   neighbour towns
    Are mind't, in things they ca' *balloons*,   call
        To tak a flight,   take
65 An' stay ae month amang the *Moons*   one, among
        An' see them right.

    Guid observation they will gie them;   good, give
    An' when the *auld Moon's* gaun to lea'e them, old, going, leave
    The hindmost *shaird*, they'll fetch it wi' them, fragment
70   Just i' their pouch;
    An' when the *new-light* billies see them,   people
        I think they'll crouch!

    Sae, ye observe that a' this clatter   so, talk
    Is naething but a 'moonshine matter';   nothing
75 But tho' dull *prose-folk* Latin splatter   speak
        In logic tulzie,   quarrel
    I hope we, *Bardies*, ken some better   know
        Than mind sic brulzie.   such a brawl

William Simpson (1758–1815) was a Glasgow University graduate
who taught at Ochiltree and later at Cumnock. His relationship with
Burns was initiated by sending him a now lost verse epistle praising

Burns's anti-clerical satire, *The Holy Tulzie*. Burns was, of course, always looking for allies in his guerrilla warfare with the forces of Auld-Licht Calvinism. The attack, almost surreal, on crazed theology provides the poem's postscript. The bulk of the poem is, however, like its longer contemporary, *The Vision*, taken up with Burns's self-placing in the lineage of great Scottish poets and Ayrshire's topography and heroic dead. L. 9, 'Ironic satire, sidelins sklented' is of particular note because it is of the quintessence of Burns's own poetic strategy as a satirist since he was socially disempowered from full frontal assault on his enemies.

He celebrates his great eighteenth century vernacular predecessors, Ramsay, Hamilton of Gilbertfield but above all his wholly beloved Robert Fergusson to whom, as soon as he got to Edinburgh, he paid for a tombstone for his unmarked grave. Ironically Fergusson's fate at the hands of genteel Edinburgh (ll. 19–24) was to be a sorry prelude to his own.

Burns's genteel contemporaries thought his pastoral poetry imitatively conventional. John Logan wrote to Henry Mackenzie: 'Mr Burns is a clever fellow, a Man of Observation, and a Country Libertine, but I am much mistaken if he has anything of the Penseroso in his character' (Low, *Robert Burns: The Critical Heritage*, p. 79). Actually, Burns's intense intimate rural realism they shied away from; the harsh life of man and beast is not what they wished to countenance. Burns himself would not have disavowed the libertine. L. 29. 'I kittle up my *rustic reed*' arguably endorses his opinion that erotic and creative energy were always synergetic for him: in this case, ejaculatively so.

As in *The Vision* the poem looks forward to a Bardic celebration of Ayrshire, in this case as a poetic-newfoundland. Wordsworth when he came to pay pilgrimage to the poet to whom he owed so much was perturbed that Burns had not creatively, unlike himself, lifted his eyes unto the hills. The Arran Mountains were for the English poet disturbingly above Burns's line of vision. Burns is, however, like MacDiarmid a poet given to water music:

> The Muse nae Poet ever fand her,
> Till by himself he learn'd to wander,
> Adown some trottin burn's meander. . . .

Thus Coila's (Ayrshire's) rivers are to receive the poetic celebration given already to bardically celebrated Scottish and European streams. So, too, is Ayrshire's archetypal hero, William Wallace. Wallace haunts Burns's poetry and letters. A biography of Wallace was one of the first things he read: 'the story of Wallace poured a Scottish prejudice in my veins which will boil along there till the floodgates of life shut in eternal rest' (See Letters 55, 78, 125). Burns hoped that Wallace's example would energise the struggle for freedom of his own generation. More darkly, he perhaps came to associate Scotland's dismembered hero with his own fate. As in all these early Ayrshire epistles a compensatory natural freedom is celebrated in the face of the greedy (Mandevillism) of the prosperously secure (ll. 90–6).

The poem's Postscript is a deeply comic account of the controversy between Auld and New Licht Theology in terms of the analogy of a quarrel between the old and new thought about the nature of the moon. Ancestral thought believed that the moon, when it waned, was discarded and replaced by a completely new one in the sky. The Auld Lichts cling to this unscientific cosmology. The traditionalists then decide to set off into space in a balloon to prove their case empirically. There is controversy regarding how much Swift Burns knew. Certainly they were, for different reasons, both profoundly displaced persons which allowed them to view eccentrically worlds to which they never fully belonged and which they agonisingly saw as suffused with inequity and iniquity. Certainly also, as in this balloon fantasy, Burns is distinctively Swiftian in his send-up of the madness of scientific hyper-rationalism. Burns, as he footnotes, is also defending the theology of 'Dr Taylor of Norwich (1722)' whose tract *The Scripture Doctrine of Original Sin Proposed to Free and Candid Examination* (1740) provided the foundation for liberalising 'New Licht' doctrine.

Epistle to John Ranken,
Enclosing Some Poems
First printed in the Kilmarnock edition, 1786.

	O rough, rude, ready-witted RANKEN,	
	The wale o' cocks for fun an' drinkin!	pick/choice
	There's monie godly folks are thinkin'	many
	Your *dreams*[1] and tricks	
5	Will send you, Korah-like, a-sinkin	
	Straught to Auld Nick's.	straight, old, the Devil

1 A certain humorous dream of his was then making a noise in the world. R.B.

Ye hae sae monie cracks an' cants,   have so many stories & jokes
And in your wicked drucken rants,   drunken babble
Ye mak a devil o' the *Saunts*,   saints
10   An' fill them fou';   drunk
And then their failings, flaws, an' wants
        Are a' seen thro'.

Hypocrisy, in mercy spare it!
That *holy robe*, O dinna tear it!   do not
15   Spare 't for their sakes, wha aften wear it —   who often
        The lads in *black*;   robes
But your curst wit, when it comes near it,
        Rives 't aff their back.   rips, off

Think, wicked Sinner, wha ye're skaithing: who, slighting
20   It's just the *Blue-gown* badge an' claithing   clothing
O' Saunts; tak that, ye lea'e them naething   saints, take, leave, nothing
        To ken them by,   know
Frae ony unregenerate Heathen,   from any
        Like you or I.

25   I've sent you here some rhyming ware   items of poetry
A' that I bargain'd for, an' mair;   more
Sae, when ye hae an hour to spare,   so, have
        I will expect,
Yon *Sang*[2] ye'll sen 't, wi' cannie care,   song, send it, cautious
30   And no neglect.

Tho' faith, sma' heart hae I to sing: little, have
My Muse dow scarcely spread her wing: can
I've play'd mysel a bonie *spring*,   pleasant tune
        An' *danc'd* my fill!
35   I'd better gaen an' sair't the King   gone, served
        At Bunker's Hill.

'Twas ae night lately, in my fun,   one
I gaed a rovin wi' the gun,   went
An' brought a *Paitrick* to the *grun'*,   partridge, ground
40   A bonie *hen*;   pretty
And, as the twilight was begun,
        Thought nane wad ken.   none would know

2 A *Song* he had promised the author.

The poor, wee thing was *little hurt*;
I *straikit* it a wee for sport,   stroked, a little
45 Ne'er thinkan they wad fash me for't;   would, trouble
        But, Deil-ma-care!
Somebody tells the *Poacher-Court*   Kirk Session
        The hale affair.   whole

Some auld, us'd hands had taen a note,   old, taken
50 That *sic a hen* had got a *shot*;   such
I was suspected for the plot;
        I scorn'd to lie;
So gat the whissle o' my groat,   got, played a losing game
        An' pay't the *fee*.

55 But by my *gun*, o' guns the wale,   pick/choice
An' by my *pouther* an' my *hail*.   gunpowder
An' by my *hen*, an' by her *tail*,
        I vow an' swear!
The Game shall Pay, owre moor an' *dail*,   over
60   For this, niest year!   next

As soon's the *clockin-time* is by,   egg-hatching
An' the *wee pouts* begun to cry,   small chicks
Lord, I'se hae sportin by an' by   I'll have
For my *gowd guinea*;   gold
65 Tho' I should herd the *buckskin* kye   American cattle/slaves
        For 't, in Virginia!   in America

Trowth, they had muckle for to blame!   in truth, much
'Twas neither broken wing nor limb,
But twa-three *draps* about the *wame*,   two-, (sperm), belly
70   Scarce thro' the *feathers*;
An' baith a *yellow George* to claim   both, gold guinea
        An' *thole* their *blethers*!   suffer, gossip

It pits me ay as mad's a hare;   puts/makes, always
So I can rhyme nor write nae mair;   no more
75 But *pennyworths* again is fair,   a paid bargain
        When time's expedient:
Meanwhile I am, respected Sir,
        Your most obedient,
                Robt. Burns.

John Rankin (d. 1810) was a tenant farmer in Adamhill, Tarbolton. He was friendly with Burns in the Lochlea years. His sister Margaret was, appropriately, the first wife of John Lapraik since both Lapraik and Rankin belonged to that anarchic, anti-clerical 'ramstam' Ayrshire group. The specific occasion of the poem is Burns's 'allegorical' account of his impregnation of Betty Paton resulting in the birth of an illegitimate daughter represented in terms of the poacher and his gun. Hugh Blair was first uncomprehending and then horrified as understanding slowly dawned: 'The description of shooting the hen is understood, I find, to convey an indecent meaning tho' in reading the poem. . . I took it literally, and the indecency did not strike me. But. . . the whole poem ought undoubtedly to be left out of the new edition' (J. De Lancey Ferguson, 'Burns and Hugh Blair', *Modern Language Notes*, xlv (1930), 441–3). It was not in the least of Burns's resistances to Blair that he kept the poem in.

L. 5. is a direct reference to *Numbers* xvi, 29–33, again demonstrating the range of Burns's allusive grasp of the Bible. The initial part of the poem, especially ll. 13–18, is an attack on the clergy akin to Blake's *Songs of Experience*. These holy devils reassert themselves later in the poem as 'the Poacher-Court' kirk session which punished apprehended fornicators by putting them on black-gowned display.

While this Ayrshire epistle is much less concerned than the others with Burns's anxieties about his ability to create for himself a poetic career in such a hostile environment, American allusions betray doubts about both the worth of his creativity and its capacity to earn him a living. Thus ll. 35–6, 'I'd better gaen an' sair't the King/At Bunker's Hill' is, given both the fate of British arms and Burns's espousal of the American cause, a particularly self-denigrating remark. Troubling in a different way are ll. 65–66, 'Tho' I should herd the *buckskin* kye/For 't in Virginia!' which are arguably the least politically correct lines the Bard wrote. He is, of course, referring to his intended emigration as escape from Ayrshire's cloying fiscal and clerical restraints to become a 'poor Negro-driver' (Letter 125). On the other hand, he went on to write *The Slave's Lament*, praised by Maya Angelou because of its grasp not only of the substance but the very rhythm of Black American experience.

The Rigs o Barley
or It was upon a Lammas Night
First printed in the Kilmarnock edition, 1786.
Tune: Corn Rigs are Bonie

It was upon a Lammas night,   harvest festival
    When corn rigs are bonie,   ridges/rows
Beneath the moon's unclouded light,
    I held awa to Annie: away
5 The time flew by, wi' tentless heed;   carefree
    Till, 'tween the late and early,
Wi' sma' persuasion she agreed
    To see me thro' the barley.

Chorus
10 Corn rigs, an' barley rigs,
    An' corn rigs are bonie:
I'll ne'er forget that happy night,
    Amang the rigs wi' Annie.

The sky was blue, the wind was still,
15   The moon was shining clearly;
I set her down, wi' right good will,
    Amang the rigs o' barley:
I ken't her heart was a' my ain;   knew
    I lov'd her most sincerely;
20 I kiss'd her owre and owre again,   over
    Amang the rigs o' barley.
Corn rigs, &c.

I lock'd her in my fond embrace;
    Her heart was beating rarely:
25 My blessings on that happy place,
    Amang the rigs o' barley!
But by the moon and stars so bright,
    That shone that hour so clearly!
She ay shall bless that happy night   always
30   Amang the rigs o' barley.
Corn rigs, &c.

I hae been blythe wi' comrades dear;   have
  I hae been merry drinking;
I hae been joyfu' gath'rin gear;   making money
35 I hae been happy thinking:
But a' the pleasures e'er I saw,
  Tho' three times doubl'd fairly —
That happy night was worth them a',
    Amang the rigs o' barley.
40   Corn rigs, &c.

This joyful reminiscence of love has been one of the poet's most popular songs, perfectly matching his lyric to traditional music. The poem's Annie is supposed to be John Rankine's daughter. (See *Epistle to John Ranken*).

Composed in August –
Westlin Winds   *written at 16*
First printed in the Kilmarnock edition, 1786.
Tune: Port Gordon

Now westlin winds and slaught'ring guns   → *shooting season.*
  Bring Autumn's pleasant weather;   *from the west* *2 extremes*
The moorcock springs on whirring wings
  Amang the blooming heather:
5 Now waving grain, wide o'er the plain,
    Delights the weary Farmer;   → *snide comment.*
The moon shines bright, as I rove at night
  To muse upon my Charmer.

The Paitrick lo'es the fruitfu' fells,   partridge, loves
10 The Plover lo'es the mountains;
The Woodcock haunts the lanely dells,   lonely
  The soaring Hern the fountains;   heron
Thro' lofty groves the Cushat roves,   wood pigeon
  The path o' man to shun it;
15 The hazel bush o'erhangs the Thrush,
  The spreading thorn the Linnet.

Thus ev'ry kind their pleasure find,
  The savage and the tender;   – *2 worlds colliding.*
Some social join, and leagues combine,
20 Some solitary wander:
    → 2 extremes

[handwritten annotations: "To A mouse, man introducing the natural world."; "man destroying the world."; "hunting"; "sentimental incoherence"; "romantic element"; "every"; "he was obsessed with peggy"; "love"]

Avaunt, away! the cruel sway,
    Tyrannic man's dominion!
The Sportsman's joy, the murd'ring cry,
    The flutt'ring, gory pinion!

25   But, PEGGY dear, the ev'ning's clear,
    Thick flies the skimming swallow,
The sky is blue, the fields in view
    All fading-green and yellow:
Come let us stray our gladsome way,
30   And view the charms o' Nature;
The rustling corn, the fruited thorn,
    And ilka happy creature.

We'll gently walk, and sweetly talk,
    While the silent moon shines clearly;
35   I'll clasp thy waist, and, fondly prest,
    Swear how I lo'e thee dearly:
Not vernal show'rs to budding flow'rs,
    Not Autumn to the Farmer,
So dear can be as thou to me,
40   My fair, my lovely Charmer!

In August 1785, the first 8 lines were copied into the poet's *First Commonplace Book*. That version is not the final polished work. It reads:

Now breezy win's and slaughtering guns
    Bring Autumn's pleasant weather;
And the muir-cock springs on whirring wings
    Amang the blooming heather:
Now waving crops, with yellow tops.
    Delights the weary Farmer;
An' the moon shines bright, when I rove at night
    To muse on Jeanie Armour.

This early version is included in the printed Sales Catalogue of the London auction house, Puttock & Simpson, 1862, printed by R. Bigmore, Mitchell Library Collection.

It appears in SMM, no. 351, 1792 and later in SC, with a minor textual ammendment by Thomson, who characteristically softens the opening line from 'slaught'ring guns' to 'sportsmen's guns'. An early manuscript copy was sold in London, May, 1862, with different text from the final published song, suggesting that the poet improved the lyric considerably prior to the 1786 edition. Although begun around

1775, the song bears the mark of the mature poet during the winter of 1785–6. The Peggy referred to is Margaret Thompson of Kirkoswald. Burns told Dr Moore of his rapture with her, '. . . stepping out to the garden one charming noon, to take the sun's altitude, I met with my Angel "Like Prosperine gathering flowers, / Herself a fairer flower". [Milton's *Paradise Lost*, Book IV, line 269.] It was vain to think of doing any more good at school . . . I did nothing but craze the faculties of my soul about her, or steal out to meet her . . .' (Letter 125). The modern folk singer Dick Gaughan enhances the old music with a haunting re-tuned guitar (DAGDAD) pick style. Gaughan does not miss the dark, forceful condemnation, 'tyrannic man's dominion' whose 'murdering, gory pinion' claims to be sport being interwoven amid a song of love and nature.

From Thee Eliza

First printed in the Kilmarnock edition, 1786.
Tune: Gilderoy

From thee, ELIZA, I must go,
    And from my native shore:
The cruel fates between us throw
    A boundless ocean's roar;
5 But boundless oceans, roaring wide
    Between my Love and me,
They never, never can divide
    My heart and soul from thee.

Farewell, farewell, ELIZA dear,
10   The maid that I adore!
A boding voice is in mine ear,
    We part to meet no more!
But the latest throb that leaves my heart,
    While Death stands victor by,
15 That throb, ELIZA, is thy part,
    And thine that latest sigh!

This song appears to have been composed just prior to publication in 1786, when the poet considered a plan of emigration to Jamaica. However, possible exile may have occurred to Burns at an earlier stage in his life, given that he informs Dr Moore that the song was already written by the time he was twenty-three years old (Letter 125). The heroine, 'my quondam Eliza' (Letter 113) may be Elizabeth

Miller of Mauchline, although Mackay (1993) suggests an earlier acquaintance, Elizabeth Gebbie (1762–1823), as an alternative.

The Farewell to The Brethren of St James's Lodge, Tarbolton

Tune: Good-Night, and Joy be wi' You A'
First printed in the Kilmarnock edition, 1786.

Adieu! a heart-warm, fond adieu;
    Dear Brothers of the *mystic tye*!   fellow Masons
Ye favour'd, ye *enlighten'd* Few,
    Companions of my social joy!
5 Tho' I to foreign lands must hie,   speed
    Pursuing Fortune's slidd'ry ba',   slippery ball
With melting heart and brimful eye,
    I'll mind you still, tho' far awa.   away

Oft have I met your social Band,
10   And spent the cheerful, festive night;
Oft, honour'd with supreme command,
    Presided o'er the *Sons of light*:
And by that *Hieroglyphic* bright,
    Which none but *Craftsmen* ever saw!
15 Strong Mem'ry on my heart shall write
    Those happy scenes when far awa.   away

May Freedom, Harmony, and Love,
    Unite you in the *grand Design*,
Beneath th' Omniscient Eye above,
20   The glorious ARCHITECT Divine!
That you may keep th' *unerring line*,
    Still rising by the *plummet's law*,
Till *Order* bright completely shine,
    Shall be my Pray'r when far awa.   away

25 And *YOU* farewell! whose merits claim
    Justly that *highest badge* to wear:
Heav'n bless your honour'd, noble Name,
    To MASONRY and SCOTIA dear!   Muse of Scotland
A last request permit me here,
30   When yearly ye assemble a',
One *round*, I ask it with a *tear*,
    To him, *the Bard, that's far awa*.   away

The poet became an ordinary member of the Freemason movement in October 1781. He became Depute Master of the St James's lodge on 27th July 1784, where his oratorial skills in debate and discussion were clearly acknowledged. This song was written for his brother masons of the St James's lodge as the Kilmarnock edition was going to press. Burns used his influential contacts within the Ayrshire masonic movement to further his poetic career, particularly in selling the Kilmarnock and Edinburgh editions. Moreover, many of the leading Whigs and radicals of this period who were sympathetic to the poet's outspoken values, were brother masons.

Epitaph on a Henpecked Squire

First printed in the Kilmarnock edition, 1786.

As father Adam first was fool'd,
    A case that's still too common,
Here lies a man a woman rul'd:
    The Devil ruled the woman.

This was aimed at William Campbell and his wife, Lilias Campbell, of Netherplace who lived near Mauchline. This and the following two epigrams were dropped from the Edinburgh edition. Scott Douglas's comment on this is typical of reactionary conservativism, devoid of humour: 'Burns had a strong aptitude for producing these smart and often very biting things' (Vol. 1, p. 128).

Epigram on Said Occasion

First printed in the Kilmarnock edition, 1786.

O Death, had'st thou but spar'd his life,	
Whom we this day lament!	
We freely wad exchanged the *wife*,	would
An' a' been weel content.	well
Ev'n as he is, cauld in his graff,	cold, grave
The swap we yet will do't;	
Tak thou the carlin's carcase aff,	off/away
Thou'se get the *saul o' boot*.	soul, as well

This also relates to William Campbell of Netherplace.

Another

First printed in the Kilmarnock edition, 1786.

One Queen Artemisa, as old stories tell,
When depriv'd of her husband she lovèd so well,
In respect for the love and affection he'd show'd her,
She reduc'd him to dust and she drank up the Powder.

But Queen Netherplace, of a diff'rent complexion,
When call'd on to order the fun'ral direction,
Would have *eat* her dead lord, on a slender pretence,
Not to show her respect, but — *to save the expense.*

When first printed, it was not possible for general readers to identify
the satirical target of this epigram; the name 'Netherplace' was
merely a line of asterisks beginning with the letter 'N'. For notes on
William Campbell of Netherplace and his wife, see *Epitaph on a
Henpecked Squire*. This was omitted from the Edinburgh edition.

On a Celebrated Ruling Elder

First printed in the Kilmarnock edition, 1786.

Here Sowter Hood, in Death does sleep;   cobbler
   To Hell, if he's gane thither,   gone that way
Satan, gie him thy gear to keep;   give
   He'll haud it weel thegither.   hold, well together

Composed during the poet's Tarbolton period, on William Hood,
whose surname was marked by asterisks in the 1786 publication.
Dated in the *First Commonplace Book* for April, 1784, under the title
Epitaph for William Hood, senr., in Talbolton. Hood was a shoemaker.

On a Noisy Polemic

First printed in the Kilmarnock edition, 1786.

Below thir stanes lie Jamie's banes;   these stones, bones
   O Death, it's my opinion,
Thou ne'er took such a bleth'ran bitch,   talkative
   Into thy dark dominion.

It is believed this was written on James Humphrey (1755–1844)
who, in the Scots idiom, was a blether – he talked too much and with
little intelligence. It is alleged from folklore, perhaps garnished by
Cromek and later Cunningham, that Humphrey's claim to fame in
his old age was that Burns targeted him with these lines.

On Wee Johnie
Hic jacet *wee* Johnie
First printed in the Kilmarnock edition, 1786.

Whoe'er thou art, O reader, know,
   That Death has murder'd Johnie,
An' here his body lies fu' low —   full
   For saul he ne'er had onie.   soul, any

This is thought to be on John Wilson (d. 1839) who was a school-master and session clerk in Tarbolton, although Mackay asserts that the object was the Reverend John Kennedy of Ochiltree.

For the Author's Father
First printed in the Kilmarnock edition, 1786.

O ye whose cheek the tear of pity stains,
Draw near with pious rev'rence, and attend!
Here lie the loving Husband's dear remains,
The tender Father, and the gen'rous Friend.

The pitying Heart that felt for human Woe,
The dauntless heart that fear'd no human Pride;
The Friend of Man, to vice alone a foe;
For 'ev'n his failings lean'd to Virtue's side'.

William Burn[es]s died, 13th February, 1784, at Lochlie. He is clearly the role model of manly worth and virtue which permeates the poetry and letters of Burns, an honest, hard working, honour-able and noble provider who struggled against poverty, ill health and in his final year, the harshness of winter. In eight lines Burns describes his father as tender, generous, compassionate, dauntless – a man who did not cowe in deference to the 'pride' of the landed Gentry – a friend to manly virtue, a religious opponent to immoral behaviour and a person whose 'failings' were probably due to his religious beliefs. L. 8 is from Goldsmith's *The Deserted Village*, l. 164.

    It is remarkable that the extent of denigratory politically moti-vated malice expended on Burns for two decades after his death extended to examine even his father's misfortunes and consider them as symptomatic of a hidden moral flaw. Outraged by the character assassination of the poet 'under the dagger of literary patriots', Alexander Peterkin in his 1816 re-edition of Currie's edition (see Introduction) bitterly wrote of a particularly mendacious life by an alleged friend of the poet, Mr Walker of Perth:

> No better illustration can be given of this unsatisfactory style of biography, than the 'suspicion' which is excited against the unspotted worth of William Burn[es]s, the poet's father. We are instructed by a philosophical reverie, that the misfortunes of that worthy man *must probably* have arisen from some radical defect in his own character or conduct, since uniform mischance, it is assumed, always implies as much! How silly and cruel are such insinuations? God knows, there are many pressed down in adversity for life, without the slightest cause existing in their conduct or personal characters. We have known individuals possessing every quality that we can conceive of human worth, destined, like William Burn[es]s, to drink deeply in the cup of affliction—to struggle through life with poverty and disappointment and sorrow; and to descend, like him, into the grave with few other consolations than the prospects beyond it. The cause of·William Burn[es]s's uniform misfortune is very obvious to an ordinary observer: He had not money: that was his defect. And the want of capital alone fettered him to all the disasters which he experienced in his affectionate anxiety to keep his family around him in their tender years. There is no occasion for a refinement in speculation, when a fact stands manifestly in view sufficient to account for occurrences.

If Burns's father had Jacobite leanings, he gave his son through Murdoch an education in the key-texts, especially Addison, of the English Real Whigs which, though deliberately anti-Auld Licht Calvinism, stressed austere independence in thought and behaviour. In this sense, Gilbert, chaste and conformist, was much more his father's son than Robert. What this elegy does not, understandably, reveal is the tension and conflict between father and son. Thus in Letter 125, Burns records his attendance at a country dancing school against his father's wishes: 'from that instance of rebellion he took a kind of dislike to me, which I believe was one cause of that dissipation which marked my future years!' All Romantic literature, familial and political, pulses with oedipal conflict.

For an innovative study of Burns's father's educational influence on him, see Liam McIlvanney's *Burns the Radical: Poetry and Politics in Late Eighteenth-century Scotland* (Tuckwell Press, 2001).

For Robert Aiken, Esq.

First printed in the Kilmarnock edition, 1786.

Know thou, O stranger to the fame
Of this much lov'd, much honour'd name!
(For none that knew him need be told),
A warmer heart Death ne'er made cold

'The Cotter's Saturday Night' is dedicated to Robert Aitken (1739–1807), an intimate friend and correspondent of Burns who was a lawyer in Ayr. Only Aitken's initials were given in the publication to preserve anonymity.

A Bard's Epitaph

First printed in the Kilmarnock edition, 1786.

Is there a whim-inspired fool,
Owre fast for thought, owre hot for rule,   over/too
Owre blate to seek, owre proud to snool,   over, shy, tamely submit
  Let him draw near;
5 And owre this grassy heap sing dool,   over, sadly/lament
  And drap a tear.   drop

Is there a Bard of rustic song,
Who, noteless, steals the crowds among,
That weekly this area throng,
10   O, pass not by!
But with a frater-feeling strong,   brother-feeling
  Here, heave a sigh.

Is there a man, whose judgment clear
Can others teach the course to steer,
15 Yet runs, himself, life's mad career
  Wild as the wave,
Here pause — and, thro' the starting tear,
  Survey this grave.

The poor Inhabitant below
20 Was quick to learn and wise to know,
And keenly felt the friendly glow
  And *softer flame*;
But thoughtless follies laid him low,
  And stain'd his name!

25   Reader, attend — whether thy soul
        Soars Fancy's flights beyond the pole,
        Or darkling grubs this earthly hole,
                In low pursuit,
        Know, prudent, cautious, *self-controul*
30   Is Wisdom's root.

This is the final work of the Kilmarnock edition. It is a strangely
sombre ending to such a virile collection. After writing an actual
epitaph for his father and an apparent one for Robert Aitken, he
then writes his own. His sense of the symmetry of the Kilmarnock
edition may be partly responsible for this. Having begun by cele-
brating in *Nature's Bard* a formally unrestricted poet galvanised by
nature's energy, he ends by elegising the (self) image of a poet
brought to disaster by the promiscuity of both his creative mind and
randy body combined with a complete lack of prudence. One of the
sources for the poem is the Epitaph for the young country poet Gray
placed at the end of *Epitaph Written in a Country Churchyard*. That
poem, with its ineradicably melancholic sense that historical invi-
sibility is the common fate for people of worth, talent, even and
especially, poetic genius, 'some mute, inglorious Milton', was semi-
nal for Burns. It has also been suggested that Burns thought of
another deathly piece, *Elegy on the Death of Robert Ruisseaux*, to end
the volume. As we shall see, that poem is essentially an account of
the external pressures that brought 'Ruisseaux' (the French for
streams, i.e. burns) low. Here, however, he chooses to take upon
himself the alleged burden of his self-defined failure.

    While Victorian editors had no trouble with a concluding poem of
such self-denigratory didacticism, it has been either forgotten or
peremptorily dismissed by most modern commentators. Daiches
(pp. 150–1) sees the poem as manifesting the symptoms of *The
Cotter's Saturday Night* and thus spoiled by 'a combination of Scots
literary influences and an exhibitionism directed at the literati and
their tastes'. He further notes that it employs 'a Scots literary form'
but is 'otherwise English in inspiration and timidly genteel in
attitude'. In actual fact, the first stanza, puzzlingly, is wholly
vernacular. There was one near contemporaneous reader, however,
over whom the poem had an extraordinary, almost magnetic, attrac-
tion. Wordsworth must have felt that, in some psychic way, *he* was
the 'Bard of rustic song' summoned to the graveside. In his 1803
Scottish tour he and Dorothy went to Burns's graveside which
caused him to write three complex, fraught poems: *At the Grave of
Burns 1803; Thoughts Suggested the Day Following, on the Banks of*

the Nith, Near the Poet's Residence; To the Sons of Burns, After Visiting the Grave of their Father. The degree to which Wordsworth was troubled by these poems is partly manifested in their publishing history. The first two did not appear till 1842; only the third appeared close to the event in 1807. Stanzas two and eight of the first poem intensely catch the 'frater-feeling strong' that Wordsworth had for Burns:

> And have I then thy bones so near,
> And thou forbidden to appear?
> As if it were thyself that's here
>   I shrink with pain;
> And both my wishes and my fear
>   Alike are vain.

> . . . True friends though diversely inclined:
> But heart with heart and mind with mind,
> Where the main fibres are entwined,
>   Through Nature's skill,
> May even by contraries be joined
>   More closely still.

Describing this as a 'weird little Gothic lyric', Kenneth R. Johnston, *The Hidden Wordsworth* (N.Y./London: 1998), p. 799 asks 'where, exactly, is the "here" of line 3? Does it point to Burns's corpse under the sod or to Wordsworth's identification with it; or is he imagining that he himself is Burns standing on his own grave?' This, remember, is from the most self-composed of poets. George Dekker in *Coleridge and the Literature of Sensibility* (London: 1978), p. 67 gives this convincing answer to this complex identification:

> The career of Burns . . . offered a lesson that Wordsworth . . . could apply immediately to his own life. So different to Burns in most essentials, Wordsworth cannot have failed to notice a few striking parallels between his current experience and that of the Ayrshire peasant. He suffered from the same mysterious chest and headaches that presaged Burns's early dissolution; he too had been long prevented from marrying by untoward circumstances; and he was a man with 'Jacobin' sympathies to live down.

Burns, then, for Wordsworth is both the beloved creative brother and also the dark, dangerous stranger who embodied his own shadowy inner-self, a self passionate to the point of sexual and radical political violence, which after about 1800 he, conservatively, increasingly denied. For some understanding of the psychological, literary and creative ambivalence of Wordsworth towards Burns see Andrew Noble's 'Wordsworth and Burns: The Anxiety of Being Under the Influence', *Critical Essays on Robert Burns*, ed. McGurk (N.Y., 1998), pp. 49–62.

There is, literally, a final testimony to this deeply ambivalent relationship. In *A Bard's Epitaph* the poem is based on a series of interrogative requests as the poet appropriate to mourning his deceased brother-poet. Wordsworth was haunted by these questions because they seemed directed at his own poetic ambitions and hidden anxieties about his inner passions. Wordsworth's *A Poet's Epitaph* is also based on a series of questions as to the sort of person (statesman, lawyer, soldier, priest, merchant, scientist) appropriate to the act of mourning. As Kenneth Johnston has remarked (pp. 86–7): 'Both poems are indebted to the pastoral tradition of one shepherd piping a lament at the grave of another. But Burns invoked this tradition mainly to distinguish his poems from it: 'The following trifles are not the production of the Poet, who, with all the advantages of learned art, and perhaps amid the elegancies and idlenesses of upper life, look down for a rural theme, with an eye to Theocritus or Vergil.' This, the lead sentence of Burns's preface, helped prepare the way for Wordsworth's great preface of 1800.' This is undoubtedly part of the reason that the necessary mourner in Wordsworth's Epitaph is not simply the poet but *a russet-coated* poet who, not only in costume but in nature, is unmistakably, in his mixture of frailties and genius, Burns himself:

But who is He, with modest looks
And clad in homely russet brown?
He murmurs near the running brooks
A music sweeter than their own.

He is retired as noontide dew,
Or fountain in a noon-day grove;
And you must love him, ere to you
He will seem worthy of your love.

The outward shows of sky and earth,
Of hill and valley, he has viewed;
And impulses of deeper birth
Have come to him in solitude.

In common things that round us lie
Some random truths he can impart,—
The harvest of a quiet eye
That broods and sleeps on his own heart.

But he is weak; both Man and Boy,
Hath been an idler in the land;
Contented if he might enjoy
The things which others understand.

—Come hither in thy hour of strength;
Come, weak as is a breaking wave!
Here stretch thy body at full length;
Or build thy house upon this grave.

PART TWO

The Edinburgh Edition
1787

Dedication to the Noblemen and Gentlemen of the Caledonian Hunt

My Lords And Gentlemen,

A SCOTTISH BARD, proud of the name, and whose highest ambition is to sing in his Country's service, where shall he so properly look for patronage as to the illustrious Names of his native Land; those who bear the honours and inherit the virtues of their Ancestors? The Poetic Genius of my Country found me as the prophetic bard Elijah did Elisha – at the *plough*; and threw her inspiring *mantle* over me. She bade me sing the loves, the joys, the rural scenes and rural pleasures of my native Soil, in my native tongue: I tuned my wildness, artless notes, as she inspired. — She whispered me to come to this ancient metropolis of Caledonia, and lay my Songs under your honoured protection: I now obey her dictates.

Though much indebted to your goodness, I do not approach you, my Lords and Gentlemen, in the usual stile of dedication, to thank you for past favours; that path is so hackneyed by prostituted Learning, that honest Rusticity is ashamed of it. —Nor do I present this Address with the venal soul of a servile Author, looking for a continuation of those favours: I was bred to the Plough, and am independent. I come to claim the common Scottish name with you, my illustrious Countrymen; and to tell the world that I glory in the title. —I come to congratulate my Country, that the blood of her ancient heroes still runs uncontaminated; and that from your courage, knowledge, and public spirit, she may expect protection, wealth and liberty. —In the last place, I come to proffer my warmest wishes to the Great Fountain of Honour, the Monarch of the Universe, for your welfare and happiness.

When you go forth to waken the Echoes, in the ancient and favourite amusements of your Forefathers, may Pleasure ever be of your party; and may Social-joy await your return! When harassed in courts or camps with the justlings of bad men and bad measures, may the honest consciousness of injured Worth attend your return to your native Seats; and may Domestic Happiness, with a smiling welcome, meet you at your gates! May Corruption shrink at your kindling indignant glance; and may tyranny in the Ruler and licentiousness in the People equally find you an inexorable foe!

I have the honour to be,
    With the sincerest gratitude and highest respect,
        MY LORDS AND GENTLEMEN,
        Your most devoted humble servant,
            ROBERT BURNS.
                EDINBURGH *April* 4. 1787

Death and Doctor Hornbook:
A True Story
First printed in the Edinburgh edition, 1787.

SOME books are lies frae end to end, — from
And some great lies were never penn'd:
Ev'n Ministers, they hae been kenn'd, — have been known
    In holy rapture,
5 A rousing whid, at times, to vend, — lie
    And nail't wi' Scripture.

— idea that even the church lies.

But this that I am gaun to tell, — going
Which lately on a night befel, — occurred
Is just as true's the Deil's in hell
10   Or Dublin city:
That e'er he nearer comes oursel — ourselves
    'S a muckle pity. — it is, great

— the devil can be anywhere.

The Clachan yill had made me canty, — village ale, jolly
I was na fou, but just had plenty; — not drunk
15 I stacher'd whyles, but yet took tent ay — staggered whiles, was careful
    To free the ditches;
An' hillocks, stanes, an' bushes kend ay — stones, knew always
    Frae ghaists an' witches. — from ghosts

— he is blind drunk.

The rising Moon began to glowr — stare/glow
20 The distant *Cumnock* hills out-owre; — out-over
To count her horns, wi' a' my pow'r
    I set mysel,
But whether she had three or four,
    I cou'd na tell. — could not

25 I was come round about the hill,
And todlin down on *Willie's mill*, — walking sprightly
Setting my staff wi' a' my skill, — with all
    To keep me sicker; — steady
Tho' leeward whyles, against my will, — at tmes
30   I took a bicker. — unbalanced run

I there wi' *Something* does forgather, — meet
That pat me in an eerie swither; — put, ghostly dread
An awfu' scythe, out-owre ae shouther, — across one shoulder

Clear-dangling, hang;
35 A three-tae'd leister on the ither   three pronged spear, other
Lay, large an' lang.   long

Its stature seem'd lang Scotch ells twa;   long, 37 inches, two
The queerest shape that e'er I saw,
For fient a wame it had ava;   hardly a belly at all
40   And then its shanks,   legs
They were as thin, as sharp an' sma'   small
As cheeks o' branks.   parts of a horse bridle

'Guid-een,' quo' I; 'Friend! hae ye been mawin,   good evening, have you, mowing
When ither folk are busy sawin?'[1]   other, sowing
45 It seem'd to mak a kind o' stan',   make, stand
But naething spak;   nothing spoke
At length, says I: 'Friend! whare ye gaun?   where, going
Will ye go back?'

It spak right howe: 'My name is *Death*, — *introduces himself.*   spoke, hollow
50 But be na' fley'd.' — Quoth I, 'Guid faith,   not frightened
Ye're may be come to stap my breath;   stop
But tent me, billie;   heed, comrade
I red ye weel, tak care o' skaith,   counsel you well, injury
See, there's a gully!'   large knife

55 'Gudeman,' quo' he, 'put up your whittle,   blade/knife
I'm no design'd to try its mettle;
But if I did, I wad be kittle   would be inclined
To be mislear'd,   mischievous
I wad na mind it, no that spittle   would not
60   Out-owre my beard.   out-over

'Weel, weel!' says I, 'a bargain be't;
Come, gie's your hand, an' say we're gree't;   give me, agreed
We'll ease our shanks, an' tak a seat: legs, take
Come, gie's your news!   give me
65 This while ye hae been monie a gate,   many
At monie a house.[2]   many

1 This recounter happened in seed-time 1785. R.B.
2 An epidemical fever was then raging in that country. R.B.

'Ay, ay!' quo' he, an' shook his head,
'It's e'en a lang, lang time indeed   even a long, long
Sin' I began to nick the thread
70   An' choke the breath:
Folk maun do something for their bread,   must
          An' sae maun *Death*.   so must

'Sax thousand years are near hand fled   *she's been working u—*
Sin' I was to the butching bred,   since   *his job for*
75   An' monie a scheme in vain's been laid,   many   *6 two years.*
          To stap or scar me;   stop, scare
Till ane Hornbook's ta'en up the trade,[3]   one, taken up
          And faith! he'll waur me.   surpass me

'Ye ken *Jock Hornbook* i' the Clachan,   know, village
80   Deil mak his king's-hood in a spleuchan!   make his scrotum, tobacco-pouch
He's grown sae weel acquaint wi' *Buchan*,[4]   so well
          And ither chaps,   other
The weans haud out their fingers laughin,   children hold
          An' pouk my hips.   poke/prod

85   'See, here's a scythe, an' there's a dart,
They hae pierc'd monie a gallant heart;   have, many
But Doctor *Hornbook* wi' his art
          An' cursed skill,
Has made them baith no worth a fart,   both
90   Damn'd haet they'll kill!   damn all/nothing

''Twas but yestreen, nae farther gane,   no, gone
I threw a noble throw at ane;   one
Wi' less, I'm sure, I've hundreds slain;
          But Deil-ma-care!
95   It just played dirl on the bane,   went tinkle on the bone
          But did nae mair.   no more

'*Hornbook* was by wi' ready art,
An' had sae fortify'd the part,   so
That when I lookèd to my dart,
100   It was sae blunt,   so
Fient haet o't wad hae pierc'd the heart   little of it would have
          Of a kail-runt.   cabbage stalk

3 This Gentleman, Dr Hornbook, is, professionally, a brother of the
sovereign Order of the Ferula; but, by intuition and inspiration, is at once
an Apothecary, Surgeon, and Physician. R.B.
4 Buchan's Domestic Medicine. R.B.

'I drew my scythe in sic a fury,   such
I near-hand cowpit wi' my hurry,   almost, toppled
105 But yet the bauld *Apothecary*
              Withstood the shock;
I might as weel hae try'd a quarry   well have
              O' hard whin-rock

'Ev'n them he canna get attended,   cannot
110 Altho' their face he ne'er had kend it,   known
Just shit in a kail-blade an' send it,   cabbage leaf
              As soon's he smells't,
Baith their disease, and what will mend it,   both
              At once he tells't.

115 'And then a' doctor's saws and whittles,   all
Of a' dimensions, shapes, an' mettles,   all
A' kinds o' boxes, mugs, and bottles,
              He's sure to hae;   have
Their Latin names as fast he rattles   *[handwritten: and that if you don't know what you are talking about just say it in Latin.]*
120   As A B C.

'Calces o' fossils, earths, and trees;   *bone meal*
True Sal-marinum o' the seas;   salt-water
The Farina of beans an' pease,   vegetable meal
              He has't in plenty;
125 Aqua-fontis, what you please,   fresh water
              He can content ye.

'Forbye some new, uncommon weapons,
Urinus Spiritus of capons;   urine
Or Mite-horn shavings, filings, scrapings,
130   Distill'd *per se*;
Sal-alkali o' Midge-tail-clippings,   salt
              And monie mae.'   many more

'Waes me for *Johnie Ged's Hole* now,'[5]   woe is
Quoth I, 'if that thae news be true!   these
135 His braw calf-ward whare gowans grew   fine grazing plot, where daisies
              Sae white and bonie,   so
Nae doubt they'll rive it wi' the plew: no split, plough
              They'll ruin *Johnie*!'

5 The grave-digger. R.B.

The creature grain'd an eldritch laugh,   groaned, unearthly
140 And says: 'Ye needna yoke the pleugh,   need not, plough
       Kirkyards will soon be till'd eneugh,   enough
              Tak ye nae fear: no
       They'll a' be trench'd wi monie a sheugh   all, with many, ditch
              In twa-three year.

145 'Whare I kill'd ane, a fair strae-death   where, one, straw
       By loss o' blood, or want o' breath,
       This night I'm free to tak my aith,   take my oath
              That *Hornbook*'s skill
       Has clad a score i' their last claith,   clothed, clothes
150   By drap an' pill.   drop/potion

       'An honest Wabster to his trade,   weaver
       Whase wife's twa nieves were scarce weel-bred,   whose, two fists, well-bred
       Gat tippence-worth to mend her head,   got tuppence
              When it was sair;   sore
155 The wife slade cannie to her bed,   crept quietly
              But ne'er spak mair.   spoke more

       'A countra Laird had taen the batts,   country, taken colic
       Or some curmurring in his guts,   commotion
       His only son for *Hornbook* sets,
160   An' pays him well,
       The lad, for twa guid gimmer-pets,   two good pet-ewes
              Was Laird himsel.

       'A bonie lass, ye kend her name —   *self storing.* know
       Some ill-brewn drink had hov'd her wame,   swollen her stomach
165 She trusts hersel, to hide the shame,
              In *Hornbook*'s care;
       Horn sent her aff to her lang hame   off, long home/grave
              To hide it there.

       'That's just a swatch o' *Hornbook*'s way,   sample
170 Thus goes he on from day to day,
       Thus does he poison, kill, an' slay,
              An's weel paid for't;   and is well
       Yet stops me o' my lawfu' prey,
              Wi' his damn'd dirt!

175   'But, hark! I'll tell you of a plot,
      Tho' dinna ye be speakin o't;
      I'll nail the self-conceited Sot,
            As dead's a herrin:
      Niest time we meet, I'll wad a groat,   next, wager fourpence
180   He gets his fairin!'   reward

      But just as he began to tell,
      The auld kirk-hammer strak the bell   old, struck
      Some wee short hour ayont the *twal*,   beyond twelve
            Which raised us baith: both, made us stand up
185   I took the way that pleas'd mysel,
            And sae did *Death*.   so

Currie (iii. 32) reports Gilbert Burns as recording the origin of the
poem thus: 'written early in the year 1785. The Schoolmaster of
Tarbolton parish, to eke out its scanty subsistence allowed to that
useless class of men, had set up a shop of grocery goods. Having
accidentally fallen upon some medical books, and become almost
hobby-horsically attached to the study of medicine, he had added
the sale of few medicines to his little trade . . . and advertised that
'Advice would be given in common disorders at the shop gratis'.
This schoolmaster was John Wilson (c. 1751–1839) who com-
pounded his other errors by boasting at a Masonic meeting in
Burns's presence of his medical prowess. The poet's hatchet, un-
impaired, unlike Death's scythe, did the following job on him.
Extraordinarily, either because of innocence, or given the other
evidence, gross stupidity, Wilson bore the poet no ill will over this.
The poem did him no harm and when he was removed from
Tarbolton School, he wrote to the poet for help and Burns con-
siderately replied (Letter 420). He subsequently became a prosper-
ous session clerk in Govan. See J.C. Ewing *BC*, 1941, pp. 31–9 for
his biography.

   The poem involves two narratives. First that of the poet who on
meeting with Death surrenders the narrative to an even more thickly
vernacular voice, which, with splendid irony, laments the loss of a
six-thousand-year career of mayhem to Hornbook's more lethal
talents. With his ambivalence about folk-myth, Burns, jokingly,
inserts footnotes which give the appearance of tying the poem into
the mundane, everyday world. Hornbook's name is taken from the
hornbook used in Scottish schools whereby lettered pieces of
parchment were savingly inserted between a wooden back and a
transparent bone front. Hence, too, the joke (l. 120) of his rattling of

the A B C. As well as Wilson's illiterate incompetence derived from
a fragile knowledge of Buchan's *Domestic Medicine*, there is,
amongst the wit, a wider sense of how exposed these communities
were to illness and death, not least the child-aborting girl (ll. 163–8),
by a mixture of, at best, useless folk-remedies and sheer general lack
of adequate medical knowledge, professional or otherwise.

The Brigs o Ayr
Inscribed to John Ballantine, Esq., Ayr
First printed in the Edinburgh edition, 1787.

[Sir, Think not with a mercenary view
Some servile Sycophant approaches you.
To you my Muse would sing these simple lays
To you my heart its grateful homage pays,
5   I feel the weight of all your kindness past,
But thank you not as wishing it to last:
Scorn'd be the wretch whose earth-born grov'lling soul
Would in his *ledger-hopes* his Friends enroll.
Tho' I, a lowly, nameless, rustic Bard,
10 Who ne'er must hope your goodness to reward,
Yet man to man, Sir, let us fairly meet,
And like Masonic Level, equal greet.
How poor the balance! Ev'n what Monarch's plan,
Between two noble creatures such as Man.
15 That to your Friendship I am strongly tied
I still shall own it, Sir, with grateful pride,
When haply roaring seas between us tumble wide.

Or if among so many cent'ries waste,
Thro the long vista of dark ages past,
20 Some much-lov'd honor'd name a radiance cast,
Perhaps some Patriot of distinguish'd worth,
I'll match him if My Lord will please step forth.
Or Gentleman and Citizen combine,
And I shall shew his peer in Ballantine:
25 Tho' honest men were *parcell'd* out for sale,
He might be shown a sample for the hale.]   whole

The simple Bard, rough at the rustic plough,
Learning his tuneful trade from ev'ry bough;

The chanting linnet, or the mellow thrush,
30   Hailing the setting sun, sweet, in the green thorn bush,
The soaring lark, the perching red-breast shrill,
Or deep-ton'd plovers grey, wild-whistling o'er the hill;
Shall he, nurst in the Peasant's lowly shed,
To hardy Independence bravely bred,
35   By early Poverty to hardship steel'd,
And train'd to arms in stern Misfortune's field,
Shall he be guilty of their hireling crimes,
The servile, mercenary Swiss of rhymes?
Or labour hard the panegyric close,
40   With all the venal soul of dedicating Prose?
No! though his artless strains he rudely sings,
And throws his hand uncouthly o'er the strings,
He glows with all the spirit of the Bard,
Fame, honest fame, his great, his dear reward.
45   Still, if some Patron's gen'rous care he trace,
Skill'd in the secret to bestow with grace;
When Ballantine befriends his humble name,
And hands the rustic Stranger up to fame,
With heartfelt throes his grateful bosom swells,
50   The godlike bliss, to give, alone excels.

'Twas when the stacks get on their winter-hap,   *wrapping*
And thack and rape secure the toil-won crap;   *thatch & rope, crop*
Potatoe-bings are snuggèd up frae skaith   *-heaps, from damage*
O' coming Winter's biting, frosty breath;
55   The bees, rejoicing o'er their summer toils,
Unnumber'd buds' an' flowers' delicious spoils,
Seal'd up with frugal care in massive, waxen piles,
Are doom'd by Man, that tyrant o'er the weak,
The death o' devils, smoor'd wi' brimstone reek: *smothered, smoke*
60   The thund'ring guns are heard on ev'ry side,
The wounded coveys, reeling, scatter wide;
The feather'd field-mates, bound by Nature's tie,
Sires, mothers, children, in one carnage lie:
(What warm, poetic heart but inly bleeds,
65   And execrates man's savage, ruthless deeds!)
Nae mair the flower in field or meadow springs;   *no more*
Nae mair the grove with airy concert rings,   *no more*
Except perhaps the Robin's whistling glee,
Proud o' the height o' some bit half-lang tree;   *-long/half-sized tree*
70   The hoary morns precede the sunny days;

Mild, calm, serene, widespreads the noontide blaze,
While thick the gossamour waves wanton in the rays.

'Twas in that season, when a simple Bard,
Unknown and poor, simplicity's reward,
75 Ae night, within the ancient brugh of *Ayr*,   one, borough
By whim inspir'd, or haply prest wi' care,
He left his bed, and took his wayward rout,   route
And down by *Simpson's*[1] wheel'd the left about:
(Whether impell'd by all-directing Fate,
80 To witness what I after shall narrate;
Or whether, rapt in meditation high,
He wander'd forth, he knew not where nor why.)
The drowsy *Dungeon-Clock*[2] had number'd two,
And *Wallace Tower*[2] had sworn the fact was true:
85 The tide-swoln Firth, with sullen-sounding roar,   swollen
Through the still night dash'd hoarse along the shore:
All else was hush'd as Nature's closed e'e;
The silent moon shone high o'er tower and tree:
The chilly frost, beneath the silver beam,
90 Crept, gently-crusting, o'er the glittering stream.

When, lo! on either hand the list'ning Bard,
The clanging sugh of whistling wings is heard;   rustle
Two dusky forms dart thro' the midnight air,
Swift as the *Gos*[3] drives on the wheeling hare;
95 Ane on th' *Auld Brig* his airy shape uprears,   one, old
The ither flutters o'er the *rising piers*:   other

Our warlock Rhymer instantly descry'd   wizard
The Sprites that owre the *Brigs of Ayr* preside.   over
(That Bards are second-sighted is nae joke,   no
100 And ken the lingo of the sp'ritual folk;   know, language
Fays, spunkies, kelpies, a', they can explain them,   fairies, will-o-wisps,
                                                            water spirits
And ev'n the vera deils they brawly ken them).   very devils, well know
Auld Brig appear'd of ancient Pictish race,   old
The vera wrinkles Gothic in his face: very
105 He seem'd as he wi' Time had warstl'd lang,   wrestled long

1 A noted tavern at the Auld Brig end. R.B.
2 The two steeples. R.B. [plus the Wallace Tower]
3 The gos-hawk, or falcon. R.B.

Yet, teughly doure, he bade an unco bang.   stubborn, surprisingly robust
New Brig was buskit in a braw new coat,   dressed, fine
That he, at *Lon'on*, frae ane *Adams* got;   from one
In's hand five taper staves as smooth's a bead,   in his
110   Wi' virls an' whirlygigums at the head.   rings, flourishes
The Goth was stalking round with anxious search,
Spying the time-worn flaws in ev'ry arch;
It chanc'd his new-come neebor took his e'e,   neighbour, eye
And e'en a vex'd and angry heart had he!   even
115   Wi' thieveless sneer to see his modish mien,
He, down the water, gies him this guid-een —   gives, good evening

AULD BRIG

I doubt na, frien', ye'll think ye're nae
   sheep-shank,   person of little importance
Ance ye were streekit owre frae bank to bank!   once, stretched over from
But gin ye be a Brig as auld as me,   once/if, old
120   Tho' faith, that date, I doubt, ye'll never see;
There'll be, if that day come, I'll wad a boddle,   bet a half-farthing
Some fewer whigmeleeries in your noddle.   whims, head

NEW BRIG

Auld Vandal! ye but show your little mense,   old, decorum
Just much about it wi' your scanty sense;
125   Will your poor, narrow foot-path of a street,
Where twa wheel-barrows tremble when they   two
   meet,
Your ruin'd, formless bulk o' stane an' lime,   stone
Compare wi' bonie *Brigs* o' modern time?   handsome
There's men of taste would tak the *Ducat stream*,[4]   take
130   Tho' they should cast the vera sark and swim,   very shirt
E'er they would grate their feelings wi' the view
O' sic an ugly, Gothic hulk as you.   such

AULD BRIG

Conceited gowk! puff'd up wi' windy pride!   fool
This monie a year I've stood the flood an' tide;   many
135   And tho' wi' crazy eild I'm sair forfairn,   old age, sore, worn out
I'll be a *Brig* when ye're a shapeless cairn!   pile of stones
As yet ye little ken about the matter,   know
But twa-three winters will inform ye better.   two-

4 A noted ford, just above the old brig. R.B.

When heavy, dark, continued, a'-day rains   all-day
140   Wi' deepening deluges o'erflow the plains;
When from the hills where springs the brawling *Coil*,
Or stately *Lugar's* mossy fountains boil,
Or where the *Greenock* winds his moorland course,
Or haunted *Garpal*[5] draws his feeble source,
145   Arous'd by blustering winds an' spotting thowes,   thaws
In monie a torrent down the snaw-broo rowes;   many, snow-brew rolls
While crashing ice, borne on the roaring speat,   spate/flood
Sweeps dams, an' mills, an' brigs, a' to the gate;
And from *Glenbuck*[6] down to the *Ratton-Key*,[7]
150   Auld *Ayr* is just one lengthen'd, tumbling sea; old
Then down ye'll hurl, deil nor ye never rise!   devil
And dash the gumlie jaups up to the pouring skies.   muddy splashes
A lesson sadly teaching, to your cost,
That Architecture's noble art is lost!'

NEW BRIG

155   Fine *architecture*, trowth, I needs must say't o't!   in truth
The Lord be thankit that we've tint the gate o't!   lost, way/skill
Gaunt, ghastly, ghaist-alluring edifices,   ghost-
Hanging with threat'ning jut, like precipices;
O'er-arching, mouldy, gloom-inspiring coves,
160   Supporting roofs, fantastic, stony groves:
Windows and doors, in nameless sculptures drest,
With order, symmetry, or taste unblest;
Forms like some bedlam Statuary's dream,
The craz'd creations of misguided whim;
165   Forms might be worshipp'd on the bended knee,
And still the *second dread Command*[8] be free:
Their likeness is not found on earth, in air, or sea!
Mansions that would disgrace the building taste
Of any mason reptile, bird or beast,
170   Fit only for a doited Monkish race,   stupid/muddled
Or frosty maids forsworn the dear embrace,
Or Cuifs of later times, wha held the notion,   fools, who

5 The banks of *Garpal Water* is one of the few places in the West of
Scotland, where those fancy-scaring beings, known by the name of Ghaists,
still continue pertinaciously to inhabit. R.B.
6 The source of the river of Ayr. R.B.
7 A small landing-place above the large key. R.B.
8 This allusion is to the Second Commandment, that there should not be a
likeness of Heavenly things on earth.

That sullen gloom was sterling true devotion:
Fancies that our guid Brugh denies protection, good borough
175   And soon may they expire, unblest with resurrection!

AULD BRIG

O ye, my dear-remember'd, ancient yealings, contemporaries
Were ye but here to share my wounded feelings!
Ye worthy *Proveses*, an' mony a *Bailie*, Provosts, many
Wha in the paths o' righteousness did toil ay; who
180   Ye dainty *Deacons*, an' ye douce *Conveeners*,
To whom our moderns are but causey-cleaners; street-
Ye godly *Councils*, wha hae blest this town; who have
Ye godly brethren o' the sacred gown
Wha meekly gie your *hurdies* to the *smiters*; give, buttocks
185   And (what would now be strange), *ye godly Writers*;
A' ye douce folk I've borne aboon the broo, prudent, above, water
Were ye but here, what would ye say or do!
How would your spirits groan in deep vexation
To see each melancholy alteration;
190   And, agonising, curse the time and place
When ye begat the base, degen'rate race!
Nae langer Rev'rend Men, their country's glory, no longer
In plain, braid Scots hold forth a plain, braid story; broad
Nae langer thrifty Citizens, an' douce, no longer, prudent
195   Meet owre a pint, or in the Council-house; over
But staumrel, corky-headed, graceless Gentry, half-witted/silly
The herryment and ruin of the country; destruction
Men, three-parts made by Tailors and by Barbers,
Wha waste your weel-hain'd gear on damn'd who, well-saved wealth
     new Brigs and *Harbours*!

NEW BRIG

200   Now haud you there! for faith ye've said enough, hold
And muckle mair than ye can mak to through. much more, make good
As for your Priesthood, I shall say but little,
Corbies and *Clergy* are a shot right kittle: ravens, difficult to shoot
But, under favour o' your langer beard, longer/older age
205   Abuse o' Magistrates might weel be spar'd; well
To liken them to your auld-warld squad, old-world
I must needs say, comparisons are odd.
In Ayr, *Wag-wits* nae mair can hae a handle scandal-mongers, no more, have
To mouth 'A Citizen,' a term o' scandal:
210   Nae mair the Council waddles down the street, no more

In all the pomp of ignorant conceit;
Men wha grew wise priggin owre hops an'   who, haggling over
   raisins,
Or gather'd lib'ral views in Bonds and Seisins;
If haply Knowledge, on a random tramp,   walk
215 Had shor'd them with a glimmer of his lamp,   threatened
And would to Common-sense for once betray'd them,
Plain, dull Stupidity stept kindly in to aid them.

What farther clishmaclaver might been said,   nonsense
What bloody wars, if Sprites had blood to shed,
220 No man can tell; but, all before their sight,
A fairy train appear'd in order bright:
Adown the glittering stream they featly danc'd:
Bright to the moon their various dresses glanc'd:
They footed o'er the wat'ry glass so neat,
225 The infant ice scarce bent beneath their feet:
While arts of Minstrelsy among them rung,
And soul-ennobling Bards heroic ditties sung.

O, had *M'Lauchlan*,[9] thairm-inspiring Sage,   catgut-/musical
Been there to hear this heavenly band engage,
230 When thro' his dear *Strathspeys* they bore with Highland rage;
Or when they struck old Scotia's melting airs,
The lover's raptured joys or bleeding cares;
How would his Highland lug been nobler fir'd,   ear
And ev'n his matchless hand with finer touch inspir'd!
235 No guess could tell what instrument appear'd,
But all the soul of Music's self was heard;
Harmonious concert rung in every part,
While simple melody pour'd moving on the heart.

The Genius of the Stream in front appears,
240 A venerable Chief advanc'd in years;
His hoary head with water-lilies crown'd,
His manly leg with garter tangle bound.
Next came the loveliest pair in all the ring,
Sweet Female Beauty hand in hand with Spring;

9 A well-known performer of Scottish music on the violin. R.B. Wallace
(1896) records that James M'Lauchlan originated from the Highlands, was
once footman to a Laird at Inverary, then moved to Ayrshire as part of a
fencible regiment where he found a patron for his musical talent in Hugh
Montgomerie, Coilsfield, later Earl of Eglintoun.

245   Then, crown'd with flow'ry hay, came Rural Joy,
       And Summer, with his fervid-beaming eye:
       All-cheering Plenty, with her flowing horn,
       Led yellow Autumn wreath'd with nodding corn;
       Then Winter's time-bleach'd locks did hoary show,
250   By Hospitality, with cloudless brow.
       Next follow'd Courage, with his martial stride,
       From where the *Feal*[10] wild-woody coverts hide:
       Benevolence, with mild, benignant air,
       A female form, came from the towers of *Stair*:
255   Learning and Worth in equal measures trode,
       From simple *Catrine*, their long-lov'd abode:
       Last, white-rob'd Peace, crown'd with a hazel wreath,
       To Rustic Agriculture did bequeath
       The broken, iron instruments of Death,
260   At sight of whom our Sprites forgat their kindling wrath.

The opening passage (ll. 1–26) in brackets are generally not printed
as an integral part of this poem. However, given that they and the
body of the poem are dedicated to John Ballantine (1743–1812), they
are included. They first appeared in the *BC*, 1926, pp. 61–2 but the
original manuscript of ll. 1–26 is now lost.

    The poem was composed in late 1786 after the contruction of the
New Bridge of Ayr started in May 1786. John Ballantine, a friend of
Robert Aitken, was Dean of the Guild of Stone Masons and took
charge of construction with Alexander Steven. The architect was
Robert Adam (1728–92) of London. Ballantine was a banker and
merchant. He owned Castlehill estate near Kilmarnock and in 1787
was appointed Provost of Ayr. Through an initial introduction from
Robert Aitken, Ballantine became a keen patron of Burns and
promised to assist him with a financial guarantee for a proposed
second Kilmarnock edition, advising Burns to publish in Edinburgh.
Ballantine took delivery of 100 copies of the Edinburgh edition for
Ayrshire subscribers. There are 13 recorded letters by Burns to
Ballantine, two being no more than brief scribbled notes. As both
Daiches and Crawford have pointed out, the poem lacks both formal
and linguistic integration due to its being a 'mixtie, maxtie' amalgam
of Fergusson's vernacular dialogue and Thomson's socially celebra-
tory poetry. The dialectic between tradition and modernity was a
convention that never really energised Burns in this poem. Crawford
(1933–9) is both informative and perhaps too generous to it.

10 A tributary of the river Ayr, near Coilsfield.

The Ordination

For sense, they little owe to frugal Heav'n:
To please the mob they hide the little giv'n.

First printed in the Edinburgh edition, 1787.

	Kilmarnock Wabsters, fidge an' claw,	weavers, fidget/twitch, scratch

Kilmarnock Wabsters, fidge an' claw,   *weavers, fidget/twitch, scratch*
    An' pour your creeshie nations;   *greasy*
An' ye wha leather rax an' draw,   *who, stretch*
    Of a' denominations;
5 Swith! to the *Laigh Kirk*,[1] ane an' a',   *away!/haste!, one*
    An' there tak up your stations;
Then aff to *Begbie's*[2] in a raw,   *off/away, row*
    An' pour divine libations
      For joy this day.

10 Curst Common-sense, that imp o' hell,
    Cam in wi' *Maggie Lauder*;[3]
But Oliphant[4] aft made her yell,   *often*
    An' Russell[5] sair misca'd her: *sore*
This day M'Kinlay[6] taks the flail,   *for thrashing corn/whip*
15   An' he's the boy will blaud her!   *slap*
He'll clap a *shangan* on her tail,   *cleft stick*
    An' set the bairns to daud her   *children, hit*
      Wi' dirt this day.

Mak haste an' turn King David owre,   *metrical psalms, over*
20   An' lilt wi' holy clangor;   *sing*
O' double verse come gie us four,   *give*
    An' skirl up the *Bangor*:   *a popular church tune*
This day the Kirk kicks up a stoure,   *dust/noise*
    Nae mair the knaves shall wrang her,   *no more, wrong*
25 For Heresy is in her pow'r,
    And gloriously she'll whang her   *punish*
      Wi' pith this day.

1 The Leigh Kirk in Kilmarnock.
2 A tavern, later named the Angel Hotel, in Kilmarnock, across the bridge over the Marnock Water.
3 Alluding to a scoffing ballad which was made on the admission of the late Reverend and worthy Mr L—. to the Laigh Kirk. R.B.
4 Rev. James Oliphant, an 'Auld Licht' minister of Kilmarnock's High Church.
5 Rev. John Russell – took over from Oliphant in 1774.
6 Rev. James Mackinlay [spelt M'Kinlay by Burns in a letter, no. 21], whose ordination was opposed by 'New Licht' moderates.

Come, let a proper text be read,
 An' touch it aff wi' vigour,   off
30 How graceless *Ham*[7] leugh at his Dad, laughed
 Which made *Canaan* a nigger;
Or *Phineas*[8] drove the murdering blade
 Wi' whore-abhorring rigour;
Or *Zipporah*,[9] the scauldin jad,   scolding hussy
35 Was like a bluidy tiger   bloody
  I' th' inn that day.   in the

There, try his mettle on the Creed,
 And bind him down wi' caution,
That *Stipend* is a carnal weed
40 He taks but for the fashion;   takes
And gie him o'er the flock to feed, give
 And punish each transgression;
Especial, *rams* that cross the breed, the fornicators
 Gie them sufficient threshin, give, beating
45   Spare them nae day.   no

Now auld Kilmarnock, cock thy tail, old, stick up
 An' toss thy horns fu' canty;   merrily
Nae mair thou'lt rowte out-owre the dale, no more, roar, -over
 Because thy pasture's scanty;
50 For lapfu's large o' *gospel kail* armfuls, greens
 Shall fill thy crib in plenty,
An' *runts* o' *grace*, the pick an' wale, cabbage-stocks, choice
 No gien by way o' dainty,   not given
  But ilka day.   every

55 Nae mair by *Babel's streams* we'll weep no more
 To think upon our *Zion*;
And hing our fiddles up to sleep, hang
 Like baby-clouts a-dryin   cloth
Come, screw the pegs wi' tunefu' cheep, fiddle pegs, chirp/notes
60 And o'er the thairms be tryin; strings
Oh, rare! to see our elbucks wheep, elbows jerk/jig
 And a' like lamb-tails flyin
  Fu' fast this day!

7 Genesis, Ch. IX, verse 22. R.B.
8 Numbers, Ch. XXV, verse 8. R.B.
9 Exodus, Ch. IV, verse 25. R.B.

    Lang, *Patronage*, wi' rod o' airn,   iron
65   Has shor'd the Kirk's undoin;   threatened
    As lately *Fenwick*, sair forfairn,   sore distressed
      Has proven to its ruin:
    Our Patron, honest man! *Glencairn*,
      He saw mischief was brewin;
70   An' like a godly, elect bairn,   child/person
      He's waled us out a true ane,   picked, one
        And sound this day.

    Now Robertson[10] harangue nae mair,   no more
      But steek your gab for ever;   shut, mouth
75   Or try the wicked town of Ayr,
      For there they'll think you clever;
    Or, nae reflection on your lear,   no, wisdom/learning
      Ye may commence a Shaver;   barber
    Or to the *Netherton* repair,
80   An' turn a Carpet-weaver
        Aff-hand this day.   off-/at once

    Mutrie[11] and you were just a match,
      We never had sic twa drones: such two
    Auld *Hornie* did the *Laigh Kirk* watch, old Devil
85   Just like a winkin baudrons,   cat
    And ay he catch'd the tither wretch,   other
      To fry them in his caudrons;
    But now his Honor maun detach,   shall
      Wi' a' his brimstone squadrons,
90   Fast, fast this day.

    See, see auld Orthodoxy's faes   old, foes
      She's swingein thro' the city!   flogging/whipping
    Hark, how the nine-tail'd cat she plays! whip
      I vow it's unco pretty: mighty/very
95   There, Learning, with his Greekish face,
      Grunts out some Latin ditty;
    And Common-Sense is gaun, she says, going
      To mak to *Jamie Beattie*   make
        Her plaint this day.

10 Rev. John Robertson, a moderate colleague of Mackinlay.
11 Rev. John Mutrie, Minister of the Laigh Kirk prior to Mackinlay.

100 But there's Morality himsel,
        Embracing all opinions;
    Hear, how he gies the tither yell   gives, other
        Between his twa companions!   two
    See, how she peels the skin an' fell,   fleshy tissue under the skin
105   As ane were peelin onions!   one
    Now there, they're packèd aff to hell,   off/away
        An' banish'd our dominions,
            Henceforth this day.

    O happy day! rejoice, rejoice!
110   Come bouse about the porter!   drink/pass around
    Morality's demure decoys
        Shall here nae mair find quarter: no more
    Mackinlay, Russell, are the boys
        That Heresy can torture;
115 They'll gie her on a rape a hoyse,   give, rope, hoist
        And cowe her measure shorter   cut/crop
            By th' head some day.

    Come, bring the tither mutchkin in,   other, pint
        And here's — for a conclusion —
120 To ev'ry *New Light*[12] mother's son,
        From this time forth, Confusion:
    If mair they deave us wi' their din   more, deafen
        Or Patronage intrusion,
    We'll light a spunk, and, ev'ry skin   match
125   We'll run them aff in fusion   off
            Like oil, some day.

'I have been very busy with the Muses since I saw you,' Burns wrote
to Richmond on 17 February, 1786, 'and have composed among
several others, The Ordination, a poem on Mr M'Kinlay's being
called to Kilmarnock' (Letters, 21). Prior to its appearance in the
Edinburgh edition the poem was, in the form of Ayrshire samizdat,
locally available under the pen-names of 'Rob Rhymer' or 'Ruis-
seaux'. The latter being a play on Rousseau and the French word for
streams or (Scottish) burns. Thus Burns's pseudonymous, covert
satirical career, a rehearsal for the darker, more dangerous world of
the 1790s, was with him from the beginning. When it appeared in

12 New Light is a cant phrase in the West of Scotland for those religious
opinions which Dr Taylor of Norwich has defended so strenuously. R.B.

The Edinburgh, the names of his specific 'Auld Licht' targets were identified only by the first, capital letter of their surname. These men were tangible and powerful enemies. As Daiches has commented, the specific, proper named detail of the poem, as in the similarly undervalued *Holy Fair* and the other early ecclesiastical satires, creates difficulties of contextual retrieval for the modern reader. This poem is certainly worth the difficulty and Burns's own footnotes are of considerable help. While not achieving the manically, perhaps demonically, inspired level of *Holy Willie's Prayer* or *The Address of Beelzebub*, it shares with these poems Burns's savage, post-Swiftian power of destroying one's enemies by ironically assuming their voice, person and values and, hence, to the mad, destructive conclusions inherent in them. In many respects it is a darker version of *The Holy Fair*. It shares with that poem the same sense of the fanatical, 'Auld Licht' Calvinism on Scottish consciousness with its power of denigratory pulpit rhetoric. This poem, however, goes beyond tongue lashing into tangible sadism as a mode of clerical control. The image of the whip recurs through the poem. See, for example, ll. 43–5, partly autobiographical from his own kirk-punished fornication, and ll. 91–4. From the second stanza the poem is saturated in vengeful violence as the mode of 'Auld Licht' doctrinaire control. This pervasive, perverted violence extends to the hanging image of ll. 113–17 and the burning one of the poem's conclusion.

A note by Burns to the poem reveals his knowledge of the history of 'Auld Licht' fanaticism which surrounded this particular Kilmarnock charge. In it he refers to a 'scoffing ballad' written when the 'New Licht' Mr Lindsay had been inducted in 1764. Maggie Lauder of l. 11 was Lindsay's wife and had been the Earl of Glencairn's housekeeper. On this occasion, however, Glencairn had submitted to 'Auld Licht' pressure and appointed one of their own. Glencairn, whom Burns was to idealise as his patron, was not yet known to the poet. In his 1896 edition of the poems, William Wallace gives evidence of the reality of 'Auld Licht' violence in 1764: 'The violence of the people was so extreme at the attempted induction of Mr. Lindsay as to put an effectual stop to the proceedings. . . . The clergy dispersed in terror. . . Three young men. . . were whipped through the streets' (p. 153, fn.1).

As well as 'Auld Licht' violence Burns brilliantly ironises their self-congratulatory Biblically derived singing and pulpit rhetoric as their 'New Licht' moderate and 'commonsensical' enemies are everywhere put to flight. Both the cacophonous singing and choice of texts in ll. 19–36 are in form and content the reverse of Christian love. Kinsley, as uneasy perhaps with Burns as an ecclesiastical satirist as a political one, totally misreads this stanza when he remarks: 'But the texts proposed are all indecorous' (Vol. III, p. 1165). The image, both megalomaniac and self-pitying (ll. 55–6) of the 'Auld Lichts' having undergone a Babylonish captivity is quite marvellous. Also Burns points to the fact that while they hated Patronage, the power of the landowner to appoint the minister (see Galt's more muted, ironic treatment of this theme from a different point of view in *Annals of the Parish*), these creatures of pure spirit were not averse to the material prosperity the acquisition of a Manse would bring. Ll. 46–54 celebrate their new-found prosperity. Burns revelled in plucking from *The Old Testament* anecdotes suffused with sex and violence to expose and embarrass the hypothetically pious.

Ll. 39–40 provided an excuse for this acquisitiveness as accepted in the fashionable way that tobacco is accepted. Nor are they averse to (l. 118) alcohol. As in all ecclesiastical satires, as in Blake, varied, savage, devouring, punitive appetites are located behind hypocritical masks. L. 99 refers to James Beattie (1735–1803) who was in his day a major figure as the alleged proponent of Common Sense philosophy and, thereby, the antidote to Humean scepticism. He was also author of the influential 'Spenserian' poem *The Minstrel*; or, *The Progress of Genius* (1771–4) admired by the not easily impressed Wordsworth.

The Calf

First printed in the Edinburgh edition, 1787.

To the Rev. Mr James Stephen, on his text, Malachi, IV, Verse 2 –
'And ye shall go forth, and grow up, like CALVES of the stall.'

Right, Sir! your text I'll prove it true,
    Tho' Heretics may laugh;
For instance, there 's yoursel just now,   *yourself*
    God knows, an unco *Calf*!   *great*

5 And should some Patron be so kind,
    As bless you wi' a kirk,   *give his own church*
I doubt na, Sir, but then we'll find   *not*
    You're still as great a *Stirk*.   *young bullock*

But, if the Lover's raptur'd hour
10   Shall ever be your lot,
Forbid it, ev'ry heavenly Power,
     You e'er should be a *Stot*!   *young bullock*

Tho', when some kind, connubial Dear
     Your But-an-ben adorns,   *small house*
15 The like has been that you may wear
     A noble head of *horns*.

And, in your lug, most reverend James,   *ear*
     To hear you roar and rowte,   *rant/bellow*
Few men o' sense will doubt your claims
20   To rank among the *Nowte*.   *cattle*

And when ye're number'd wi' the dead,
     Below a grassy hillock,
With justice they may mark your head —
     'Here lies a famous *Bullock*!'

This *jeu d'esprit* was composed after a challenge by Gavin Hamilton that Burns could not produce a poem on the subject of the Rev. James Stephen's sermon at Mauchline on Sunday 3rd September 1786 'in a given time' (Letter 46). Hamilton was to miss the sermon and asked Burns for a poem on the visiting minister's sermon. Originally only four stanzas, as read to Hamilton by Burns and so winning his bet, a further two were added that evening.

The publication of this work in the Edinburgh edition obviously omitted the name of the kirk minister. A pamphlet publication of the poem had been circulated, presumably without the poet's knowledge, which included *The Calf*; *The Unco Calf's Answer*; *Virtue to a Mountain Bard*; and *The Deil's Answer to his Vera Worthy Frien Robert Burns*. Later in 1786 another anonymous work appeared called *Burns' Calf Turned a Bull;* Or *Some Remarks on His Mean and Unprecedented Attack on Mr S —*. Steven's identity did not remain anonymous, although unnamed by Burns. The poet was attacked as irreligious and associated with the Devil. Even by the late 19th century Scott Douglas attacks the poet for his verses: 'very clever, but recklessly severe; for the author could have no personal dislike to this victim of his satirical propensity' (Vol. I, p. 155). The Rev. Stephen, who later worked in London and ended up in Kilwinning, bore the nickname of 'the calf' thereafter. It is highly probable that if Burns had not been attacked in the doggerel pamphlet poems over this work, the minister's identity would not have been made public.

Address to the Unco Guid
or The Rigidly Righteous
First printed in the Edinburgh edition, 1787.

> *My Son, these maxims make a rule,*
> > *An' lump them ay thegither:*   together
> *The Rigid Righteous is a fool,*
> > *The Rigid Wise anither;*   another
> *The cleanest corn that e'er was dight*   sifted
> > *May hae some pyles o' caff in;*   have, piles, chaff
> *So ne'er a fellow-creature slight*
> > *For random fits o' daffin.*

> Burns's Paraphrase of Solomon
> (*Eccles.* vii. 16).

O YE wha are sae guid yoursel,   you who, so good
    Sae pious and sae holy,   so
Ye've nought to do but mark and tell   nothing
    Your Neebours' fauts and folly!   neighbours' faults
5 Whase life is like a weel-gaun mill,   whose, well going
    Supplied wi' store o' water,
The heapet happer's ebbing still,   heaped hopper
    An' still the clap plays clatter!   clapper of a Mill, moving grain.

Hear me, ye venerable Core,   group
10   As counsel for poor mortals,
That frequent pass douce Wisdom's door   sober
    For glaikit Folly's portals;   careless/stupid
I, for their thoughtless, careless sakes
    Would here propone defences,
15 Their donsie tricks, their black mistakes,   hapless/unlucky
    Their failings and mischances.

Ye see your state wi' theirs compared,
    And shudder at the niffer,   comparison
But cast a moment's fair regard,
20   What makes the mighty differ;
Discount what scant occasion gave,
    That purity ye pride in,
And (what's aft mair than a' the lave)   oft more, remainder
    Your better art o' hidin.

25   Think, when your castigated pulse
        Gies now and then a wallop,   *gives, violent beat*
    What ragings must his veins convulse,
        That still eternal gallop:
    Wi' wind and tide fair i' your tail,
30   Right on ye scud your sea-way   *move fast*
    But, in the teeth o' baith to sail,   *both*
        It maks an unco leeway.   *uncommon*

    See Social-life and Glee sit down,
        All joyous and unthinking,
35   Till, quite transmugrify'd, they're grown
        Debauchery and Drinking:
    O, would they stay to calculate
        Th' eternal consequences;
    Or your more dreaded hell to state,
40   Damnation of expenses!

    Ye high, exalted, virtuous Dames,
        Ty'd up in godly laces,
    Before ye gie poor *Frailty* names,   *give*
        Suppose a change o' cases;
45   A dear-lov'd lad, convenience snug,
        A treach'rous inclination —
    But, let me whisper i' your lug,   *ear*
        Ye're aiblins nae temptation.   *maybe no*

    Then gently scan your brother Man,
50   Still gentler sister Woman;
    Tho' they may gang a kennin wrang,   *go a little wrong*
        To step aside is human:
    One point must still be greatly dark,
        The moving *Why* they do it;
55   And just as lamely can ye mark,
        How far perhaps they rue it.

    Who made the heart, 'tis *He* alone
        Decidedly can try us,
    He knows each chord its various tone,
60   Each spring, its various bias:
    Then at the balance let's be mute,
        We never can adjust it;
    What's *done* we partly may compute,
        But know not what's *resisted*.

The date of the poem is uncertain. Prose sentiments very similar to those of the poem are to be found in the *FCB* for March 1784. It may also, with its emphasis on sexual transgression, in particular, female frailty, relate to Betsy Paton and Jean Armour in 1786. In the CB we find the following entry:

> I have often observed . . . that every man even the worst, have something good about them . . . Let any of the strictest char-acter for regularity of conduct among us, examine impartially how many of his virtues are owing to constitution and educa-tion; how many vices he has never been guilty of, not from any care or vigilance, but from want of opportunity . . . how much he is indebted to the World's good opinion, because the world does not know all; I say any man who can thus think, will scan the failings, nay the faults and crimes of mankind around him, with a brother's eye.

From this young man's somewhat sententious, self-conscious prose, this vivid, knowingly witty, anti-Pharisaical poem emerges. Burns invokes the true spirit of charitable religion against the hypocritical, repressed and repressive, 'unco guid'. Thus his own epigraph against the 'Rigid Righteous' and the 'Rigid Wise' is taken from *Ecclesiastes*, vii.16: 'Be not righteous over much; neither make thyself over wise: why shouldst thou destroy thyself.' Thus against the absolutist judgment inherent in Calvinism he propounds the compassion of a Christ who was implicitly opposed to those judge-mentally throwing stones at adulterous women (*John*: 3-7). The translation of *Ecclesiastes* into vernacular Scots constitutes, as The First Psalm, an original work in its own right.

While not as obsessed as William Blake with Christ not as lawmaker but lawbreaker (*The Marriage of Heaven and Hell* and *The Everlasting Gospel*), Burns does not see in him a spirit not only charitable and empathetic but insurrectionary against conventional social piety. Hence, like himself, a keeper of unconventional company.

Tam Samson's[1] Elegy

First printed in the Edinburgh edition, 1787.

'An honest man's the noblest work of God.'
Alexander Pope.

	Has auld Kilmarnock seen the Deil?	old, Devil
	Or great M'Kinlay[2] thrawn his heel?	hurt his ankle
	Or Robertson[3] again grown weel	well/healthy
	To preach an' read?	
5	'Na, waur than a'!' cries ilka chiel,	no, worse, every one
	'*Tam Samson's* dead!'	
	Kilmarnock lang may grunt an' grane,	long, groan
	An' sigh an' sab, an' greet her lane,	sob, cry alone
	An' cleed her bairns, man, wife an' wean,	clothe, children, child
10	In mourning weed;	
	To Death she's dearly pay'd the kane,	rent in kind
	Tam Samson's dead!	
	The Brethren o' the mystic *level*	masons
	May hing their head in woefu' bevel,	hang, down/slope
15	While by their nose the tears will revel,	
	Like ony bead;	any
	Death's gien the Lodge an unco devel,	given, terrible blow
	Tam Samson's dead!	
	When Winter muffles up his cloak,	
20	And binds the mire like a rock;	
	When to the loughs the Curlers flock,	lochs
	Wi' gleesome speed,	
	Wha will they station at the cock? —	who, mark
	Tam Samson's dead!	

1 When this worthy old Sportsman went out last muir-fowl season, he supposed it was to be, in Ossian's phrase, 'the last in his fields'; and expressed an ardent wish to die and be buried in the muirs. On this hint the author composed his Elegy and Epitaph. R.B.
2 A certain Preacher, a great favourite with the Million. *Vide The Ordination*, stanza 2. R.B.
3 Another Preacher, and equal favourite with the Few, who was at that time ailing. For him, see also *The Ordination*, stanza 9. R.B.

25   He was the king of a' the Core,   company of curlers
      To guard, or draw, or wick a bore,   curling terms
      Or up the rink like *Jehu* roar
          In time o' need;
      But now he lags on Death's *hog-score*,   a line across the curling ice
30   Tam Samson's dead!

      Now safe the stately Sawmont sail,   salmon
      And Trouts bedropp'd wi' crimson hail,   spots
      And Eels weel-kend for souple tail,   well-known, supple
          And Geds for greed,   pike (fish)
35   Since, dark in Death's *fish-creel* we wail fish-basket
          Tam Samson dead!

      Rejoice, ye birring Paitricks a';   whirring partridges
      Ye cootie Moorcocks, crousely craw;   leg-feathered, boldly crow
      Ye Maukins, cock your fud fu' braw,   hares, tail, fine well
40   Withoutten dread;   without
      Your mortal Fae is now awa',   foe, away
          Tam Samson's dead!

      That woefu' morn be ever mourn'd
      Saw him in shootin graith adorn'd,   gear/clothes
45   While pointers round impatient burn'd,
          Frae couples freed;   from
      But, Och! he gaed and ne'er return'd!   went
          Tam Samson's dead!

      In vain Auld-age his body batters;   old-
50   In vain the Gout his ankles fetters;   ankles
      In vain the burns cam down like waters,   came
          An acre-braid!   broad/wide
      Now ev'ry auld wife, greetin, clatters: old, crying, exclaims
          'Tam Samson's dead!'

55   Owre mony a weary hag he limpit,   over, many, moss, limped
      An ay the tither shot he thumpit,   always, other, he hit
      Till coward Death behind him jumpit,   jumped
          Wi' deadly feide;   feud/rage
      Now he proclaims, wi' tout o' trumpet,   blast
60   Tam Samson's dead!

When at his heart he felt the dagger,
He reel'd his wonted bottle-swagger,
But yet he drew the mortal trigger,
    Wi' weel-aim'd heed;   well-aimed
65 'Lord, five!' he cry'd, an owre did stagger;   over
    Tam Samson's dead!

Ilk hoary Hunter mourn'd a brither;   each, brother
Ilk Sportsman-youth bemoan'd a father;   each
Yon auld gray stane, amang the heather,   the old grey stone, among
70   Marks out his head;   where, nonsense
Whare *Burns* has wrote, in rhyming blether,
    Tam Samson's dead!

There, low he lies in lasting rest;
Perhaps upon his mould'ring breast
75 Some spitefu muirfowl bigs her nest,   builds
    To hatch an' breed:
Alas! nae mair he'll them molest!   no more
    Tam Samson's dead!

When August winds the heather wave,
80 And Sportsmen wander by yon grave,
Three volleys let his memory crave,
    O' pouther an' lead,   (gun) powder
Till Echo answer frae her cave,   from
    Tam Samson's dead!

85 Heav'n rest his saul, whare'er he be!   soul, where'er
Is th' wish o' mony mae than me: many more
He had twa fauts, or maybe three,   two faults
    Yet what remead?
Ae social, honest man want we: one
90   Tam Samson's dead!

THE EPITAPH
Tam Samson's weel-worn clay here lies,   well-
    Ye canting Zealots, spare him!
If Honest Worth in heaven rise,
    Ye'll mend or ye win near him.   before, get

PER CONTRA

95 Go, Fame, an' canter like a filly   *young horse*
    Thro a' the streets an' neuks o' *Killie*,[4]   *alleys/closes, Kilmarnock*
    Tell ev'ry social, honest billie   *person*
        To cease his grievin,
    For yet, unskaith'd by Death's gleg gullie,   *sharp knife*
100   *Tam Samson's leevin!*   *living*

If Mark Twain believed that reports of his death had been greatly exaggerated, Burns builds this boisterous poem on a similar joke. Beginning with a dig at the propensity for theatrical clamour in two of his 'Auld Licht' clerical enemies, also savaged in *The Ordination*, Burns runs a declamatory 'headline' through the poem with his multi-voiced proclamations of Tam Sampson's death whereby men, animals, birds, fish and Death itself join the chorus. Tam's enormous vigour for field sports is echoed in the vocal, mixed response to his alleged demise; hardly surprisingly the creaturely victims of his energetic skill are ecstatic. Thomas Sampson (1722–95) was a nurseryman, sportsman and Freemason (ll. 13–18) in Kilmarnock. His poetic immortalisation stems from a combination of his eccentric strength of character and Burns's access to the form and theme of the eighteenth-century Scots comic elegiac tradition with specific relation to Robert Semphill of Beltree's *Piper of Kilbarchan*. Burns's celebration of his aged hunter-killer is uncharacteristic of his general attitude to hunting where, so much of the poetry of the late eighteenth century is suffused with it, the suffering and destruction of creaturely life is dominant. Here this is controlled partly by the comic convention and also possibly by the fact that Tam is an honest man of the people and not a bloodsport-aristocrat. *The Epitaph* (ll. 91–4) is another attack on the sanctimoniously judgemental and the *Per Contra* (ll. 95–100) which undercuts the previous ebullient statements of grief may have resulted from Alan Cunningham's story (ii. 235) that Burns wrote it in response to Sampson's protest that 'I'm no dead yet. . . I'm worth ten dead fowk'. Kinsley pertinently refers here to Ramsay's *To my Friends in Ireland, who on a report of my death,. . . Elegies*, ll. 5–6 (*Works*, STS, ii, 203):

> Dight your Een, and cease your grieving,
> ALLAN's hale, and well, and living . . .

4 Killie is a phrase the country-folks sometimes use for the name of a certain town in the West. R.B.

A Winter Night

First printed in the Edinburgh edition, 1787.

Poor naked wretches, wheresoe'er you are,
That bide the pelting of this pityless storm!
How shall your houseless heads and unfed sides,
Your loop'd and window'd raggedness, defend you
From seasons such as these?

SHAKESPEARE.

When biting *Boreas*, fell and doure,   the North wind, keen, hard
Sharp shivers thro' the leafless bow'r;
When *Phoebus* gies a short-liv'd glow'r, the Sun, gives, stare
  Far south the lift,   horizon/sky
5 Dim-dark'ning thro' the flaky show'r,
  Or whirling drift.

Ae night the Storm the steeples rocked, one
Poor Labour sweet in sleep was locked,
While burns, wi' snawy wreeths up-choked, with snowy
10 Wild-eddying swirl,
Or, thro' the mining outlet bocked,   vomited
  Down headlong hurl.

List'ning the doors an' winnocks rattle, windows
I thought me on the ourie cattle,   shivering
15 Or silly sheep, wha bide this brattle who endure, noise
  O' winter war,
And thro the drift, deep-lairing, sprattle, scramble
  Beneath a scar.   jutting rock (for shelter)

Ilk happing bird, wee, helpless thing! each hopping
20 That, in the merry months o' spring,
Delighted me to hear thee sing,
  What comes o' thee?
Whare wilt thou cow'r thy chittering wing, where
  An' close thy e'e?   eye

25 Ev'n you, on murd'ring errands toil'd,
Lone from your savage homes exil'd,
The blood-stain'd roost and sheep-cote spoil'd,
  My heart forgets,
While pityless the tempest wild
30 Sore on you beats.

Now *Phoebe*, in her midnight reign,   the Moon
Dark-muffl'd, view'd the dreary plain;
Still crouding thoughts, a pensive train,   crowding
          Rose in my soul,
35 When on my ear this plaintive strain,
          Slow-solemn, stole —

'Blow, blow, ye Winds, with heavier gust!
'And freeze, thou bitter-biting Frost!
'Descend, ye chilly, smothering Snows!
40 'Not all your rage, as now, united shows
          'More hard unkindness unrelenting,
          'Vengeful malice, unrepenting,
'Than heaven-illumin'd Man on brother Man bestows!

'See stern Oppression's iron grip,
45   'Or mad Ambition's gory hand,
'Sending, like blood-hounds from the slip,
       'Woe, Want, and Murder o'er a land!
'Ev'n in the peaceful rural vale,
'Truth, weeping tells the mournful tale,
50 'How pamper'd Luxury, Flatt'ry by her side,
       'The parasite empoisoning her ear,
       'With all the servile wretches in the rear,
'Looks o'er proud Property, extended wide;
       'And eyes the simple, rustic Hind,
55 'Whose toil upholds the glitt'ring show,
       'A creature of another kind,
'Some coarser substance, unrefin'd,
'Plac'd for her lordly use, thus far, thus vile, below!'

'Where, where is Love's fond, tender throe,
60 'With lordly Honor's lofty brow,
       'The pow'rs you proudly own?
'Is there, beneath Love's noble name,
'Can harbour, dark, the selfish aim,
       'To bless himself alone!
65 'Mark Maiden-Innocence a prey
       'To love-pretending snares,
       'This boasted Honor turns away,
       'Shunning soft Pity's rising sway,

'Regardless of the tears and unavailing pray'rs!
70   'Perhaps this hour, in Mis'ry's squalid nest,
     'She strains your infant to her joyless breast,
'And with a mother's fears shrinks at the rocking blast!

     'Oh ye! who, sunk in beds of down,
     'Feel not a want but what yourselves create,
75   'Think, for a moment, on his wretched fate,
     'Whom friends and fortune quite disown!
'Ill-satisfy'd, keen nature's clam'rous call,
     'Stretch'd on his straw, he lays himself to sleep,
     'While through the ragged roof and chinky wall,
80   'Chill, o'er his slumbers piles the drifty heap!
'Think on the Dungeon's grim confine,
'Where Guilt and poor Misfortune pine!
'Guilt, erring Man, relenting view!
'But shall thy legal rage pursue
85   'The Wretch, already crushed low
'By cruel Fortune's undeservèd blow?
'Affliction's sons are brothers in distress;
'A Brother to relieve, how exquisite the bliss!'

I heard nae mair, for *Chanticleer*   no more
90   Shook off the pouthery snaw,   powdery snow
And hail'd the morning with a cheer,
     A cottage-rousing craw.   crow

But deep this truth impress'd my mind —
     Thro' all His works abroad,
95 The heart benevolent and kind
     The most resembles GOD.

Given that in successful poetry form and content are always mutually expressive, this poem has been seen as a puzzling failure
because of its apparently disparate elements. Beginning with an
epigraph from *King Lear*, the poem moves to five vernacular stanzas
in the 'Habbie Simpson' form brilliantly detailing the impact of a
stormy winter night on the exposed beasts and birds. We then, in
standard English, having another linking 'Habbie Simpson' stanza
which introduces an internal voice which, in the form of a Pindaric
Ode, presents a hellish vision of a society overwhelmed by corruption and predatory sexuality manifest in the relation of the aristocratic rich to the destitute poor. Finally, the poem switches back to

two 'Habbie Simpson' vernacular stanzas which reassuringly sug-
gest the whole thing should be viewed as a dream from which we
have wakened to find ourselves in the presence of a benevolent God.

On the face of it this seems a 'mixtie maxie' well beyond *The Brigs
of Ayr*. However, the thread of *King Lear* leads us through this
apparent maze. In the Kilmarnock edition Burns has already used
Shakespearean allusion with telling effect in, for example, *A Dream/
Henry IV* and *Epistle to a Young Friend/Hamlet*. Despite making no
comment on the *Lear* epigraph Kinsley picks up this and another
bitter Shakespearean echo in ll. 37–43 of *A Winter Night*:

> Blow, blow ye Winds, &c. Cf. King Lear, III.ii, 1–9, 'Blow
> windes . . . all germaines spill at one/That makes ingrateful
> Man; the song in *As You Like It*, II.vii:

> Blow, blow, thou winter winde,
> Thou art not so unkinde, as mans ingratitude . . .
> Freize, freize, thou bitter skie that does not
> Bight so night as benefitts forgot . . .

Unfortunately, however, Kinsley, despite his enormous erudition
expressed in the allusory density he brings to Burns's poetry,
consistently identifies Burns's relationship to other writers in an
apolitical way. In the 1790s, *King Lear* was the most politically
loaded and relevant of Shakespeare's plays. First, it was, given a
contemporarily, if transiently, mad king on the throne, another mad
one could not be provocatively put on stage. Second, what is
revealed in *King Lear* is the utter failure of an allegedly patriarchal
ruling class so demonically selfish that, in a hellish, a hallucinatory
night scene, the terrible condition of the common people is revealed
in their uprooted homelessness, naked hunger and alienated grief
bordering on madness.

King Lear, at the heart of Shakespeare's darkness, reveals what
happens when 'natural' man becomes a *creature* of unbridled pre-
datory, libidinous appetites. In Burns's 'night' poem the animals
are, as always, empathetically treated, and, unlike the wolfish
humanity of the Pindaric section, even the barn-robbing vernacular
fox is seen more as victim than villain.

It is further characteristic of Kinsley that having not explored this
sort of poetic terrain, he further denies such an obvious political
reading by means of arguments based on aesthetic deficiency. He
describes this particular instance of his sense of Burns's chronic
general incapacity to write in the Pindaric form thus:

> Burns's strophes have rhythmical strength—though that is not always sustained—rather than exalted energy; his images are too predictable, his diction too conventional. The success of the opening scene, in his familiar style . . . only emphasized his failure to rise above the commonplace in the Pindaric part.

Two things need to be said about this. First, if Burns failed with the Pindaric Ode he was not alone in this. As Geoffrey Hartman noted: 'The sublime or greater or Pindaric ode flourished in the eighteenth century like a turgid weed.' (*The Fate of Reading* (Chicago: 1975), p. 138.) The criticism levelled at Burns by Kinsley could be easily replicated dealing with Coleridge's dissident poetry of the 1790s with its terminal, apocalyptic sense of communal breakdown due to established economic, military violence unchecked by either the duty or compassion of the ruling class.

Kinsley has no patience with Burns's radically dissenting poetry because he is wilfully ignorant of its radical context. He makes little of Burns's multiple connections with other radical writers of the period or, as in the case of Dr Walcot (Peter Pindar), a still deeply underestimated political satirist, he dismisses him, quite ignoring Burns's own high evaluation of him (Letter 578) with a crass Boswellian put-down: 'a contemptible scribbler (who), having dis-graced and deserted the clerical character . . . picks up in London a scanty livelihood by scurrilous lampoons under a feigned name (Vol. III p. 1423)'. Missing the unjustly forgotten, if lesser, radical writers, Kinsley compounds his mistake by not perceiving how close the now canonical Romantic poets were in theme and form to Burns in the mid-1790s. As well as the now better-understood complexity of Wordsworth's relationship to Burns, we should contemplate the proximity of Coleridge to Burns as political satirist and commentator (Perry, as noted, wanted them both on the London staff of *The Morning Chronicle*) and poet of the mid-1790s' radical apocalypse. Consider, for example, Coleridge's *Fire, Famine, and Slaughter* with its ferocious, catastrophic sense of the consequences of the unnamed Pitt's policies in Ireland and against the French Revolution by supporting the monarchists in the terrible civil war raging in the Vendée. This poem, written the year after Burns's death, is not subjective hysteria but at the core of a national nightmare of unrewarded blood, toil and tears. Coleridge was horrified by the Scottish sedition trials of 1793–4 and hated and feared 'brazen-faced' Dundas, but it was Pitt ('Letters four do form his name') for whom, in this poem, he reserved his most savage assault:

Slau. Letters four do form his name—And who sent you?
Both. The same! the same!
Slau. He came by stealth, and unlocked my den,
And I have drunk the blood since then
Of thrice three hundred thousand men.
Both. Who bade you do't?
Slau. The same! the same!
Letters four do form his name.
He let me loose, and cried Halloo!
To him alone the praise is due.
Fam. Thanks, sister, thanks! the men have bled,
Their wives and their children faint for bread.
I stood in a swampy field of battle;
With bones and skulls I made a rattle,
To frighten the wolf and carrion-crow
And the homeless dog—but they would not go.
So off I flew: for how could I bear
To see them gorge their dainty fare?
I heard a groan and a peevish squall,
And through the chink of a cottage-wall—
Can you guess what I saw there?
Both. Whisper it, sister! in our ear.
Fam. A baby beat its dying mother:
I had starved the one and was starving the other!
Both. Who bade you do't?
Fam. The same! the same!
Letters four do form his name.
He let me loose, and cried, Halloo!
To him alone the praise is due.
Fire. Sisters! I from Ireland came!
Hedge and corn-fields all on flame,
I triumph'd o'er the setting sun!
And all the while the work was done,
On as I strode with my huge strides,
I flung back my head and I held my sides,
It was so rare a piece of fun
To see the sweltered cattle run
With uncouth gallop through the night,
Scared by the light of his own blazing cot
Was many a naked Rebel shot:
The house-stream met the flame and hissed,
While crash! fell in the roof, I wist,
On some of those old bed-rid nurses,

That deal in discontent and curses.
Both. Who bade you do't?
Fire. The same! the same!
Letters four do spell his name.
He let me loose, and cried Halloo!
To him alone the praise is due.
All. He let us loose, and cried Halloo!
How shall we yield him honour due?
Fam. Wisdom comes with lack of food.
I'll gnaw, I'll gnaw the multitude,
Till the cup of rage o'erbrim:
They shall seize him and his brood—
Slau. They shall tear him limb from limb!
Fire. O thankless beldames and untrue!
And this is all that you can do
For him, who did so much for you?
Ninety months he, by my troth!
Hath richly catered for you both;
And in an hour would you repay
An eight years' work?—Away! away!
I alone am faithful! I
Cling to him everlastingly.

As noted, the instigator of this barbarism ('Letters four do form his name') is William Pitt. As we shall see in the *Anonymous & Pseudonymous* section, the multiple consequences of Pitt's warmongering were to become also the objects of Burns's satire in the 1790s. Not even he was, however, prepared to speak so directly about Irish matters as Coleridge. Ireland was, in fact, the epicentre of the intended radical insurrection of the 1790s, trying and failing to provoke similar militant resistance in England and Scotland. In 1798 30,000 dissident Irish were to pay with their lives at Wicklow. (See Roger Wells, *Insurrection: The British Experience, 1795–1803* (Gloucester: 1983).)

Like Burns, Coleridge's poetry is impregnated with Biblical allusion; not least *Revelations*. Like Burns he also saw in *King Lear* another text which strengthened his sense of apocalypse now. As he wrote of III.iv., Lear's despair and growing madness in the storm:

What a world's convention of agonies! Surely never was such a scene conceived before or since. Take it but as a picture for the eye only, it is more terrific than any a Michelangelo inspired by a Dante could have conceived, and none but a Michelangelo could have executed. Or let it have been uttered to the blind, the howlings of convulsed nature would seem converted into the voice of conscious humanity.

The 'howlings of convulsed nature' is what *Fire, Famine and Slaughter, A Winter Night* and *Guilt and Sorrow*; or *Incidents upon Salisbury Plain* are about. Further, these convulsions are elemental *and* political. Writing to John Thelwall, one of the chief radicals of the day and a keen enthusiast for Burns's poetry, Coleridge remarked that he would send him *Guilt and Sorrow* from the as yet unknown Wordsworth who 'thinks that the lines from 364 to 375 & from 403 to 428 the best in the Volume—indeed worth all the rest—And this man is a Republican & at least a *Semi*-atheist.—' Indeed the poem is so radical that it was not published in full till 1842. Its dreadful nightscape is replete with the economically uprooted and militarily press-ganged, in Hazlitt's bitter term, the redundant part of the population. Mary Jacobus had found echoes of *King Lear* in it but it is surely a *Lear* partly mediated through Burns's *A Winter's Night*; a world where animals but not men have a place to lay their heads. Even more singular is Wordsworth's evolution of Burns's theme of guilt in the poem: 'Think on the dungeon's grim confine . . . By cruel Fortune's undeserved blow?'

A final fact about this interpretation of *A Winter's Night* is that Burns chose, as we shall see in the *Anonymous & Pseudonymous* section in *The Gentleman's Magazine* for August 1794, to update the poem and print it under a new title, *Humanity: An Ode*. It is partially identified by his initials and is stripped of its vernacular opening and its falsely consolatory vernacular ending with some other significant changes to the intervening Pindaric poem. Burns must have felt its scream of rage even more politically relevant to 1794 than to 1787. Thus, ironically, the poem which was arguably its partial genesis, reappears the year following *The Female Vagrant* section of *Guilt and Sorrow*.

Stanzas Written in Prospect of Death

First published in the Edinburgh edition, 1787.

Why am I loth to leave this earthly scene?
    Have I so found it full of pleasing charms?
Some drops of joy with draughts of ill between;
    Some gleams of sunshine mid renewing storms:

5 Is it departing pangs my soul alarms?
      Or Death's unlovely, dreary, dark abode?
   For guilt, for guilt, my terrors are in arms;
      I tremble to approach an angry GOD,
   And justly smart beneath his sin-avenging rod.

10 Fain would I say, 'Forgive my foul offence!'
      Fain promise never more to disobey;
   But, should my Author health again dispense,
      Again I might desert fair Virtue's way;
   Again in Folly's path might go astray;
15   Again exalt the brute and sink the man;
   Then how should I for Heavenly Mercy pray,
      Who act so counter Heavenly Mercy's plan?
   Who sin so oft have mourn'd, yet to temptation ran?

   O Thou, Great Governor of all below! —
20   If I may dare a lifted eye to Thee,
   Thy nod can make the tempest cease to blow,
      Or still the tumult of the raging sea:
   With that controuling pow'r assist ev'n me,
      Those headlong furious passions to confine;
25 For all unfit I feel my pow'rs to be,
      To rule their torrent in th' allowed line;
   O, aid me with Thy help, *Omnipotence Divine*!

The title is normally *Stanzas on the Same Occasion*, to follow *A Prayer, in the Prospect of Death*. Composition is thus during the same period, or as the poet was recuperating from illness. The Stair Ms. has the title 'Misgivings of Despondency on the Approach of the Monarch of the Grave'. It is clearly evident in these early illness-inspired works that Burns employed his introspective thoughts in trying to comprehend the tensions between his own impulsive character traits and what he deemed the proper religious behaviour expected in the wider society. It is hard to disagree with Daiches that this and the following four poems, 'show Burns writing in conventional neo-classic English with no spark of genius or originality' (p. 218). He may have retrieved these very early, orthodoxly pious poems simply to pad out the Edinburgh edition. Or, it may have been as cover against the persistent complaints of the Hugh Blairites against his, at best, deeply unorthodox sallies into *Old Testament* exegesis.

Prayer: O Thou Dread Power

Lying at a Reverend Friend's House one Night, the author left the following verses in the room where he slept: -

First printed in the Edinburgh edition, 1787.

O Thou dread Pow'r, who reign'st above!
    I know Thou wilt me hear;
When for this scene of peace and love,
    I make my pray'r sincere.

5 The hoary Sire — the mortal stroke,
    Long, long be pleas'd to spare:
To bless his little filial flock,
    And show what good men are.

She, who her lovely Offspring eyes
10   With tender hopes and fears,
O bless her with a Mother's joys,
    But spare a Mother's tears!

Their hope, their stay, their darling youth,
    In manhood's dawning blush;
15 Bless him, Thou God of love and truth,
    Up to a Parent's wish.

The beauteous, seraph Sister-band,
    With earnest tears I pray,
Thou know'st the snares on every hand,
20   Guide Thou their steps alway.

When soon or late they reach that coast,
    O'er Life's rough ocean driven,
May they rejoice, no wand'rer lost,
    A Family in Heaven!

As the subtitle records, the poet composed and left these verses in the home of the Rev. Dr George Lawrie (1722–99), who was minister at Loudon, near Galston (by Kilmarnock). Currie quotes confirmation of this (Vol. III, p. 386) from Gilbert Burns who states that his brother first heard the spinnet played at Dr Lawrie's home when he visited there a few months after the publication of the Kilmarnock edition in the Autumn of 1786. George Lawrie's son Archibald became a friend of Burns.

Paraphrase of the First Psalm

First printed in the Edinburgh edition, 1787.

The man, in life wherever plac'd,
    Hath happiness in store,
Who walks not in the wicked's way,
    Nor learns their guilty lore!

5 Nor from the seat of scornful Pride
    Casts forth his eyes abroad,
But with humility and awe
    Still walks before his GOD.

That Man shall flourish like the trees
10   Which by the streamlets grow;
The fruitful top is spread on high,
    And firm the root below.

But he whose blossom buds in guilt
    Shall to the ground be cast,
15 And like the rootless stubble tost
    Before the sweeping blast.

For why? that GOD the good adore
    Hath giv'n them peace and rest,
But hath decreed that wicked men
20   Shall ne'er be truly blest.

A summation of the sentiments in the First Psalm placed in rhyme, this work is generally dated from the 1781–2 period. While mainly employing Biblical language, Burns neatly employs some 18th century phraseology to give the verses a contemporary context. The terms 'guilty lore', 'scornful pride', 'stubble', 'sweeping blast' and 'truly blest' are not found in the original Psalm.

A Prayer,
Under the Pressure of Violent Anguish
First printed in the Edinburgh edition, 1787.

O Thou Great Being! what Thou art,
    Surpasses me to know:
Yet sure I am, that known to Thee
    Are all Thy works below.

5 Thy creature here before Thee stands,
    All wretched and distrest;
Yet sure those ills that wring my soul
    Obey Thy high behest.

Sure Thou, Almighty, canst not act
10   From cruelty or wrath!
O, free my weary eyes from tears,
    Or close them fast in death!

But if I must afflicted be,
    To suit some wise design;
15 Then, man my soul with firm resolves
    To bear and not repine!

In the *FCB*, dated March 1784, the poet introduces this poem: 'There was a certain period of my life that my spirit was broke by repeated losses and disasters, which threatened, and indeed effected the utter ruin of my fortune. My body too was attacked by that most dreadful distemper, a Hypochondria, or confirmed Melancholy: in this wretched state, the recollection of which makes me yet shudder, I hung my Harp on the Willow trees, except in some lucid intervals, in one of which I composed the following.'

The Ninetieth Psalm Paraphrased
First printed in the Edinburgh edition, 1787.

O Thou, the first, the greatest friend
    Of all the human race!
Whose strong right hand has ever been
    Their stay and dwelling-place!

5   Before the mountains heav'd their heads
        Beneath Thy forming hand,
    Before this ponderous globe itself
        Arose at Thy command:

    That Power which rais'd and still upholds
10   This universal frame,
    From countless, unbeginning time
        Was ever still the same.

    Those mighty periods of years,
        Which seem to us so vast,
15   Appear no more before Thy sight
        Than yesterday that's past.

    Thou giv'st the word; Thy creature, man,
        Is to existence brought;
    Again Thou say'st, 'Ye sons of men,
20   'Return ye into nought!'

    Thou layest them with all their cares
        In everlasting sleep;
    As with a flood Thou tak'st them off
        With overwhelming sweep.

25   They flourish like the morning flow'r,
        In beauty's pride array'd;
    But long ere night, cut down, it lies
        All wither'd and decay'd.

Yet another example of the poet's versified religious inculcation. For all the critical attacks on Burns in Ayrshire by some elements of the clergy prior to his successful poetic career, works like this reveal his in-depth knowledge of Biblical subjects and his keen ability to interpret and paraphrase Biblical text. In the strict social stratification of 18th century society, members of the peasantry were meant to follow religious dictates, not question or debate them as Burns did. As the poet wryly recorded, 'ambitious of shining in conversation parties on Sundays between sermons, funerals, &c. used in a few years more to puzzle Calvinism with so much heat and indiscretion that I raised a hue and cry of heresy against me which has not ceased to this hour' (Letter 125).

To Miss Logan
With Beattie's *Poems*
A New Year's Gift January 1, 1787
First printed in the Edinburgh edition, 1787.

Again the silent wheels of time
    Their annual round have driv'n,
And you, tho' scarce in maiden prime,
    Are so much nearer Heav'n.

5   No gifts have I from Indian coasts
        The infant year to hail;
I send you more than India boasts
        In *Edwin's* simple tale.

Our Sex with guile, and faithless love
10   Is charg'd, perhaps too true;
But may, dear Maid, each Lover prove
        An *Edwin* still to you.

Miss Susan Logan was the younger sister of Major William Logan
of Park, a friend of Mrs Dunlop and the recipient of a copy of
Beattie's *Poems* sent by Burns from Edinburgh.

Address to a Haggis
First printed in *The Caledonian Mercury*, 20th December 1786.

Fair fa' your honest, sonsie face,   *good luck to, cheerful*
Great Chieftain o' the Puddin-race!
Aboon them a' ye tak your place,   *above*
    Painch, tripe, or thairm: *paunch, guts*
5   Weel are ye wordy of a *grace*   *well*
    As lang 's my arm.   *long as*

The groaning trencher there ye fill,
Your hurdies like a distant hill,   *buttocks*
Your *pin* wad help to mend a mill   *skewer would*
10   In time o' need,
While thro' your pores the dews distil
    Like amber bead.

His knife see Rustic-labour dight,   wipe
An' cut ye up wi' ready slight,   skill
15 Trenching your gushing entrails bright,
     Like onie ditch;   any
And then, O what a glorious sight,
     Warm-reekin, rich!   -steaming

Then, horn for horn, they stretch an' strive: eating with a horn-spoon
20 Deil tak the hindmost, on they drive,   devil take the slowest
Till a' their weel-swall'd kytes belyve   well-swollen stomachs eventually
     Are bent like drums;
Then auld Guidman, maist like to rive,   old, goodman, most, burst
     Bethankit hums.

25 Is there that owre his French *ragout*,   over
Or *olio* that wad staw a sow,   would, fill up/bloat
Or *fricassee* wad mak her spew   would make, throw up
     Wi' perfect sconner,   disgust
Looks down wi' sneering, scornfu' view
30   On sic a dinner?   such

Poor devil! see him owre his trash,   over
As feckless as a wither'd rash,   feeble, rush
His spindle shank a guid whip-lash,   thin leg, good
     His nieve a nit;   fist, nut
35 Thro' bluidy flood or field to dash,   bloody
     O how unfit!

But mark the Rustic, *haggis-fed*,   country man
The trembling earth resounds his tread,
Clap in his walie nieve a blade,   place, firm fist
40   He'll make it whissle;   whistle/cutting through air
An' legs, an' arms, an' heads will sned   cut off
     Like taps o' thrissle.   tops of thistle

Ye Pow'rs wha mak mankind your care,   who make
And dish them out their bill o' fare,
45 Auld Scotland wants nae skinking ware,   old, no watery
     That jaups in luggies;   splashes in bowls
But, if ye wish her gratefu' prayer,
     Gie her a *Haggis*!   give

Subject to endless repetition as *the* indispensable Burns Supper party-piece, this poem has probably been heard far too often for its own good. It is, however, arguably more subtly knowing and

dissident than first appears. The poem as we have it was completed
in Edinburgh in December 1786. There is, however, evidence that
the last verse was composed first in the house of John Morrison, a
Mauchline cabinetmaker, and was used as a free-standing grace.
This is the first-recorded version of the last stanza:

> Ye Pow'rs wha gie us a' that's gude
> Still bless auld Caledonia's brood,
> Wi' great John Barleycorn's heart's bluid
>   In stoups or luggies;
> And on our boards, that King o' food
>   A gude Scotch Haggis.

A peasant dish compounded of meat left-overs, oatmeal, spices, offal,
all packed in a sheep's stomach, Burns portrays the haggis as cau-
sative of the virility of the Scottish common people. Literally virility
as in ll. 7–9 the haggis's vast buttock-like shape culminated in a
pronounced phallic-like pin. It did provoke in those who partook of it
Breughel-like orgiastic appetites. It also gave stomach for battle with
its echo from Fergusson's *The Farmer's Ingle*, ll. 37–45:

> On sicken food has mony a doughty deed
>   By Caledonia's ancestors been done;
> By this did mony wight fu' weirlike bleed
>   In brulzies, &c.

An enthusiast, albeit with certain well-defined parameters, for
Burns as poet-recorder of Scottish peasant life, this poem caused
Kinsley not a little unease: 'But the *Address* is not merely a
burlesque poem, or a piece of convivial genre-poetry like its ante-
cedent, Fergusson's *Caller Oysters*. Through it there runs an asser-
tion, more than half-serious, of peasant virtue and strength,
expressed in harsh, violent diction and in images of slaughter'.
The nearest analogy to what Burns is doing here are ll. 85–102 of
The Author's Earnest Cry and Prayer.

Address to Edinburgh
First printed in the Edinburgh edition, 1787.

Edina! *Scotia's* darling seat!
    All hail thy palaces and tow'rs,
Where once beneath a Monarch's feet,
    Sat Legislation's sov'reign pow'rs!

5   From marking wildly-scatt'red flow'rs,
         As on the banks of *Ayr* I stray'd,
    And singing, lone, the ling'ring hours,
         I shelter in thy honor'd shade.

    Here Wealth still swells the golden tide,
10   As busy Trade his labours plies;
    There Architecture's noble pride
         Bids elegance and splendour rise;
    Here Justice, from her native skies,
         High wields her balance and her rod;
15 There Learning, with his eagle eyes,
         Seeks Science in her coy abode.

    Thy Sons, *Edina*, social, kind,
         With open arms the Stranger hail;
    Their views enlarg'd, their lib'ral mind,
20   Above the narrow, rural vale:
    Attentive still to Sorrow's wail,
         Or modest Merit's silent claim;
    And never may their sources fail!
         And never Envy blot their name!

25 Thy Daughters bright thy walks adorn,
         Gay as the gilded summer sky,
    Sweet as the dewy, milk-white thorn,
         Dear as the raptur'd thrill of joy!
    Fair Burnet strikes th' adoring eye,
30   Heav'n's beauties on my fancy shine;
    I see the *Sire of Love* on high,
         And own His work indeed divine!

    There, watching high the least alarms,
         Thy rough, rude Fortress gleams afar;
35 Like some bold Vet'ran, grey in arms,
         And mark'd with many a seamy scar:
    The pond'rous wall and massy bar
         Grim-rising o'er the rugged rock,
    Have oft withstood assailing War,
40   And oft repell'd th' Invader's shock.

With awe-struck thought, and pitying tears,
    I view that noble, stately Dome,
Where *Scotia's* kings of other years,
    Fam'd heroes! had their royal home:
45 Alas, how chang'd the times to come!
    Their royal Name low in the dust!
Their hapless Race wild-wand'ring roam!
    Tho' rigid Law cries out, 'twas just!

Wild-beats my heart, to trace your steps,
50   Whose ancestors, in days of yore,
Thro' hostile ranks and ruin'd gaps
    Old *Scotia's* bloody lion bore:
Ev'n *I* who sing in rustic lore,
    Haply *my Sires* have left their shed,
55 And fac'd grim Danger's loudest roar,
    Bold-following where your Fathers led!

Edina! *Scotia's* darling seat!
    All hail thy palaces and tow'rs,
Where once, beneath a Monarch's feet,
60   Sat Legislation's sov'reign pow'rs!
From marking wildly-scatt'red flow'rs,
    As on the banks of *Ayr* I stray'd,
And singing, lone, the ling'ring hours,
    I shelter in thy honour'd shade.

The artificial English of this poem written not long after Burns's arrival in Edinburgh late in 1786 has achieved a degree of notoriety not least stemming from David Daiches' witty put-down:

> The 'Address to Edinburgh' was a 'duty' poem, written in December as a more or less official expression of gratitude to the city which had received him so hospitably; it too was published in the *Caledonian Mercury*, so that the Edinburgh public could see he had done his duty by the city. It is a frigid, artificial poem in stilted neoclassic English. Edinburgh is hailed as '*Edina! Scotia's* darling seat!' and the firm of Edinburgh plumbers and sanitary engineers who in a later generation adopted the name 'Edina' for their version of a necessary but hardly poetic kind of seat were demonstrating, if somewhat crudely, a real critical insight (p. 215).

Certainly the Thomsonian theme and style of the burgeoning vision of wealth, architecture and culture fails to convince. Nor does the specific praise of Lord Monboddo's daughter, Miss Burnett in l. 29 quite corroborate the epistolary fantasy version of this young lady, who actually bore a close resemblance to her physically unprepossessing father: 'the heavenly Miss Burnett, daughter of Lord Monboddo, at whose house I have had the honour to more than once. – There has not been anything nearly like her, in all the combinations of Beauty, Grace and Goodness the Great Creator has formed, since Milton's Eve on the first day of her existence' (Letter 68). The 'Sire of Love' (l. 31) is Coelus, begetter of Venus and, indeed, Burns was in thrall to that sky-god during his Edinburgh sojourn with a sexual voracity bordering on erotomania. Recent evidence indicates an involvement with another working-class woman and another illegitimate child as well as with Jenny Clow. Simultaneously he was besieging Mrs McLehose ('Clarinda') with a sentimental campaign of pious eroticism and in communication with Margaret (Peggy) Chalmers whom he had notions of marrying and who appears, even more than Maria Riddell, capable of sympathetic comprehension, if not reciprocation, of the Bard's deepest creative urges. The multiple, diverse, divisive nature of Burns's sexual desires at this period must surely also correspond to similar tensions in his social and cultural life. Edinburgh, as Daiches suggests, was hospitable to him, but in divided and temporary ways. The cosseted 'Stranger' pays his thanks but (ll. 21–4) at the very least, questions the longevity of this charitable celebration. His erstwhile sentimental supporters of genteel Edinburgh, especially Henry Mackenzie, were, of course, to indulge in posthumous, envious character assassination.

The poem's topographical reading of the city is also interesting. Before proceeding to a celebration of the splendours of the New Edinburgh, ll. 3–4 mark the physical disintegration of the Scottish court and parliament. While the Castle is seen (ll. 33–40) as a tangible bastion of self-defending, Scottish independence, the poem is much more concerned with the deserted Holyrood Palace as manifesting the fall of the Stuarts in whom Burns found both the public manifestation of a disintegrated Scotland and private expressions of his own sense of life as displaced, if not exiled, grief. Ll. 53–6 invoke his own family's coming-out in the 1715. Indeed, while it will be subsequently far better expressed, the essence of Burns's Jacobitism is to be found in this poem.

Thus a poem which apparently is a slight act of obeisance to Edinburgh actually obscures darker anxieties about the true state of the Scottish body politic. Indeed, utterly contradicting Walter Scott, it does not present a paradigm of burgeoning Scottish post-Union evolution but a sense of national loss at the heart of this city as symbol of the national spirit.

John Barleycorn: A Ballad [1]

Tune: Lull Me Beyond Thee
First printed in the Edinburgh edition, 1787.

There was three kings into the east,
    Three kings both great and high,
And they hae sworn a solemn oath   *have*
    John Barleycorn should die.

5   They took a plough and plough'd him down,
    Put clods upon his head,   *lumps of grassy soil/turf*
And they hae sworn a solemn oath   *have*
    John Barleycorn was dead.

But the cheerful Spring came kindly on,
10   And show'rs began to fall;
John Barleycorn got up again,
    And sore surpris'd them all.

The sultry suns of Summer came,
    And he grew thick and strong,
15   His head weel arm'd wi' pointed spears,   *with*
    That no one should him wrong.

The sober Autumn enter'd mild,
    When he grew wan and pale;
His bending joints and drooping head
20   Show'd he began to fail.

His colour sicken'd more and more,
    He faded into age;
And then his enemies began
    To show their deadly rage.

1 This is partly composed on the plan of an old song known by the same name. R.B.

25 They've taen a weapon long and sharp,   *taken*
        And cut him by the knee;
    Then ty'd him fast upon a cart,   *tied*
        Like a rogue for forgerie.

    They laid him down upon his back,
30   And cudgell'd him full sore;   *smashed*
    They hung him up before the storm,
        And turn'd him o'er and o'er.

    They filled up a darksome pit
        With water to the brim,
35 They heaved in John Barleycorn,
        There let him sink or swim.

    They laid him out upon the floor,
        To work him farther woe,
    And still, as signs of life appear'd,
40   They toss'd him to and fro.

    They wasted, o'er a scorching flame
        The marrow of his bones;
    But a Miller us'd him worst of all,
        For he crush'd him between two stones.

45 And they hae taen his very heart's blood,   *have taken*
        And drank it round and round;
    And still the more and more they drank,
        Their joy did more abound.

    John Barleycorn was a hero bold,
50   Of noble enterprise,
    For if you do but taste his blood,
        'Twill make your courage rise.

    'Twill make a man forget his woe;
        'Twill heighten all his joy;
55 'Twill make the widow's heart to sing,
        Tho' the tear were in her eye.

    Then let us toast John Barleycorn,
        Each man a glass in hand;
    And may his great posterity
60   Ne'er fail in old Scotland.

Composition is generally dated to around 1785, although Kinsley
believes it was written earlier. In the *FCB* Burns writes, 'John
Barleycorn. – A Song, to its own Tune. I once heard the old song
that goes by this name, sung; and being very fond of it, and
remembering only two or three verses of it viz the 1st, 2nd and
3rd, with some scraps which I have interwoven here and there in
the following piece', June 1785. Kinsley probably over-stresses the
importance of the myth of the Corn Spirit still prevalent in the
18th century as the 'kernel' theme of this song, the notion that
the 'old man of vegitation' is driven out of the corn at threshing
time to inhabit the fields, then returns to be the spirit of the
next crop (Vol. III, p. 1017). Low is probably right in assuming
Burns had read or heard the chapbook song of 1781, the allegory
of drink titled *The Whole Trial and Indictment of Sir John
Barleycorn, Knt., A Person of Noble Birth and Extraction . . .
Being Accused of Several Misdemeanours . . . killing some, wounding
others, and bringing thousands to Beggary* (p. 82). The song
celebrates both the positive social influence of whisky as a prompt
to friendship and waves the national flag of Scotland in the name
of John Barleycorn in the final stanzas. It is a record of events,
from seedtime to harvest, on till the brewing and consumption of
whisky. For Burns, John Barleycorn is a hero, not a villain.

When Guilford Good
or Ballad on the American War

Tune: Gillicrankie *or* The Earl of Glencairn's.
Printed in the Edinburgh edition, 1787.

	When *Guilford* good our Pilot stood,[1]	
	An' did our hellim thraw, man,	helm turn
	Ae night, at tea, began a plea,[2]	one
	Within *America*, man:	
5	Then up they gat the maskin-pat,	got, tea-pot
	And in the sea did jaw, man;	dash
	An' did nae less, in full Congress,	no
	Than quite refuse our law, man.	

1 Frederick, Lord North (1732–92).
2 The Boston tea party of 1773.

Then thro' the lakes *Montgomery* takes,[3]
10   I wat he was na slaw, man;   wot, not slow
Down *Lowrie's Burn* he took a turn,   St Lawrence river
And *Carleton* did ca', man:[4]   call
But yet, whatreck, he at *Quebec*   what matter
Montgomery-like did fa', man,   fall
15 Wi' sword in hand, before his band,
Amang his en'mies a', man.   among, all

Poor *Tammy Gage* within a cage[5]
Was kept at *Boston-ha'*, man;   hall
Till *Willie Howe* took o'er the knowe[6]   hill edge
20   For *Philadelphia*, man:
Wi' sword an' gun he thought a sin
Guid Christian bluid to draw, man;   good, blood
But at *New-York* wi' knife an' fork
Sir Loin he hacked sma', man.[7]   small

25 *Burgoyne* gaed up, like spur an' whip,[8]   went
Till *Fraser* brave did fa', man;[9]   fall
Then lost his way, ae misty day,   one
In *Saratoga* shaw, man.   wood
Cornwallis fought as lang's he dought,[10]   long as he could
30   An' did the Buckskins claw, man;   colonists
But *Clinton's* glaive frae rust to save,[11]   sword, from
He hung it to the wa' man.   wall

Then *Montague*, an' *Guilford* too,[12]
Began to fear a fa', man;   fall
35 And *Sackville* doure, wha stood the stoure[13] obstinate, who fought
The German Chief to thraw, man: thwart

3 Richard Montgomery.
4 Guy Carleton.
5 General Gage (1721–88), Governor of Massachusetts.
6 Sir William Howe (d. 1814).
7 This alludes to the seizure of rebel cattle by the Hudson, at Peekskill, 1776.
8 Sir John Burgoyne (1722–92).
9 Brigadier Simon Fraser.
10 Charles Conrnwallis (1738–1805).
11 Sir Henry Clinton (1738–95).
12 John Montague, Earl of Sandwich.
13 Lord George Sackville (1716–85) who was at Culloden with the Duke of Cumberland.

For Paddy *Burke*, like ony Turk,[14]   any
    Nae mercy had at a', man;   no, all
An' *Charlie Fox* threw by the box,[15]
40   An' lows'd his tinkler jaw, man.   let loose, gypsy mouth

Then *Rockingham* took up the game;[16]
    Till Death did on him ca', man;   call
When *Shelburne* meek held up his cheek,[17]
    Conform to Gospel law, man:
45 Saint Stephen's boys, wi' jarring noise,   M.P.'s, loud
    They did his measures thraw, man;   thwart/turn
For *North* an' *Fox* united stocks,
    An' bore him to the wa', man.   wall

Then Clubs an' Hearts were Charlie's cartes,   cards
50   He swept the stakes awa', man,   away
Till the Diamond's Ace, of *Indian* race,   Fox's East India Bill
    Led him a sair *faux pas*, man: sore
The Saxon lads, wi loud placads,   cheers
    On *Chatham's Boy* did ca', man;[18]   call
55 An' Scotland drew her pipe an' blew:
    'Up, Willie, waur them a', man!'   worst

Behind the throne then *Grenville's* gone,[19]
    A secret word or twa, man;   two
While slee *Dundas* arous'd the class[20]   sly
60   Be-north the Roman wa', man: wall
An' *Chatham's* wraith, in heav'nly graith,   ghost, garments
    (Inspired Bardies saw, man),
Wi' kindling eyes, cry'd, 'Willie, rise!
    Would I hae fear'd them a', man!'   have

65 But, word an' blow, *North, Fox, and Co.*
    Gowff'd *Willie* like a ba', man,   golfed, ball
Till *Suthron* raise an' coost their claise   rose, cast their clothes
    Behind him in a raw, man: naked

---

14 Edmund Burke (1727–97) ; alluding to his Irish origin.
15 Charles James Fox (1749–1806), Whig Leader.
16 The Marquis of Rockingham, Charles Watson Wentworth (1730–82).
17 The Earl of Shelbourne (1737–1805).
18 William Pitt, the Younger (1759–1806).
19 William Wyndham (1759–1834) Lord Grenville.
20 Henry Dundas (1742–1811), Secretary of State for Scotland.

An' *Caledon* threw by the drone,   bagpipe sound
70   An' did her whittle draw, man;   knife
An' swoor fu' rude, thro' dirt an' bluid,   swore full, blood
        To mak it guid in law, man.   good

Though he did not risk publishing it in the Kilmarnock edition, this is Burns's first political poem. It is, thus, seminal in several important ways. For the first time it brings not only the world of late eighteenth-century British but international politics before the wickedly reductive court of Burns's Scottish vernacular energies. Second, it demonstrates for the first time his astonishing powers of compressed narrative. Here he records in a mere nine stanzas not only the genesis of the American War of Independence and politically significant campaigns in that war but also the extreme disruption provoked in British politics by the loss of America. Third, it signals his acutely self-endangering ambition, from his marginal social position, to comment politically on the world of kings and counsellors. As he was soon to write:

> But Politics, truce! we're on dangerous ground;
>   Who knows how the fashions may alter:
> The doctrines today that are loyalty sound,
>   Tomorrow may bring us a halter.

Further, that this is a *song* with its thumping ('man') alternate line repetition entails that he desires maximum public exposure for it. This engenders a triple-headed problem that would increasingly preoccupy him. Would he be allowed to publish it? What final strategies might he employ to disguise the explosive nature of the material? If such strategies, most frequently that of the smiler with the knife, were impossible, how might he get such explosive political material into the political realm without disclosing his authorship?

This song emphasises the first of these problems. He had some thought of placing it in the Kilmarnock edition. He then consulted his Whig patron, the Earl of Glencairn, subsequently writing to his Masonic associate in the Canongate Lodge, Henry Erskine:

> I showed the enclosed political ballad to my Lord Glencairn, to have his opinion whether I should publish it; as I suspect my political tenets, such as they are, may be rather heretical in the opinion of some of my best friends. I have a few first principles in Religion and Politics which, I believe, I would not easily part with; but for the etiquette of, by whom, in what manners &c. I

would not have a dissocial word about it with any one of God's creatures, particularly an honoured Patron, or a respected Friend (Letter 70).

That he might upset Glencairn and Erskine, Whig sympathisers with the American cause, seems odd until we consider his treatment of the parliamentarian Rockingham Whigs, Fox and Burke, in the latter part of the poem. He did certainly, however, upset the Tory pro-Hanoverian Edinburgh establishment. It was of this poem that, according to Lockhart (Vol. I, p. 205), Hugh Blair remarked 'Burns's politics always smell of the smithy'. His card was thus marked from the outset.

This snooty disdain for the allegedly sooty is, embryonically, that pervasive state of mind which, consciously and otherwise, has so successfully sought to exclude Burns as socially inferior poet, no matter his political intelligence, from commenting on his alleged betters. With regard to American affairs, as we have seen in the Introduction, Burns was passionately pro-American. Further, by denying this political element in Burns, Blair was also disguising the strong pro-American republican culture in Edinburgh which Burns knew about both by his membership of the Crochallan Fencibles and his avaricious reading of the Edinburgh press. Alfred A. Kline in a stimulating Columbia University doctorate written as long ago as 1953, *The English Romantics and the American Republic: An Analysis of the Concept of America in the Work of Blake, Burns, Wordsworth, Coleridge, Byron and Shelley* is deeply salutary in two respects. In general terms, it reminds us of the political company which Burns's poetry keeps. Blake's *America*, for example, though mythopoetically distinct from Burns's, is profoundly similar in content. Central to Wordsworth's *Guilt and Sorrow* or *Incidents Upon Salisbury Plain* (See commentary on *A Winter Night*) is a hellish vision of the American war as recalled by the returned widowed vagrant of one of the dead British redcoats who, revealingly, became termed in that conflict, 'bloody-backs': 'dog-like wading at the heels of War . . . a cursed existence with the brood/ That lap, their very nourishment, their brother's blood'.

Kline also provides evidence of the degree to which radical elements in Edinburgh were attracted to the American cause. Thus Richard Price's *Letter to the Secretary of the Committee of Citizens in Edinburgh*, *The Scots Magazine* (April, 1784), comments:

God grant that this spirit may increase till it has abolished all despotic government and exterminated the slavery which debase mankind. This spirit first rose in America – it soon reached Ireland – it has diffused itself in some foreign countries, and your letter informs me that it is now animating Scotland (p. 179).

As we saw in the Introduction, Price was influential for Burns. In January 1791 we find (Letter 430) Burns ordering from Peter Hill Dr Price's *Dissertations on Providence, Prayer, Death & Miracles*. Whether Burns also read Price's subtle, balanced *Observations an the Importance of the American Revolution and the Means of Making It A Benefit to the World* is uncertain. What is certain is that he would have agreed with its provocative sentiments (See *Richard Price: Political Writings*, ed. D.O. Thomas, Cambridge: 1991). Kline also quotes Professor W.P. Ker, whose scholarship led him to define Burns as a Tory Unionist, saying 'Burns must have read the newspapers . . . and *The Scots Magazine* with extraordinary care', to which Kline adds that this included back issues. Thus the first part of this poem is again dependent on Burns transmuting newspaper prose into poetry, as, indeed, is the latter part dealing with the political shambles in Britain consequent to the American defeat.

The first stanza deals with the good Guilford, the Prime Minister, and Lord North, whose wrecking seamanship led to the loss of North America. After the inception of the war by the taxation policy leading to the Boston Tea Party, Burns narrates the campaign leading up to the Americans' ('Buckskins') culminating in victory with Cornwallis's surrender at Yorktown, 10th October 1781 with Clinton unable to break though from New York to relieve him.

The second stanza deals with a double pronged American attack in 1775 into Canada against Quebec and Montreal. What is of particular significance is that the second-in-command of the Montreal force was Richard Montgomery, one of the Montgomerys of Coylfield celebrated by Burns in his eulogy to the greatness sprung from Ayrshire soil in *The Vision*. Montreal surrendered to Montgomery who then set down 'Lowrie's Burn' to support Arnold at Quebec, where he was killed in the assault. What, of course, Burns is implying is the heroism of not just a Scottish but an Ayrshire martyr dying for the American cause.

The third stanza deals with the passive General Gage being replaced by Sir William Howe who, despite his victories over the Americans at Bunker Hill and near Philadelphia could not change the course of the war. Despite his deep reservations at spilling American blood, Howe's army 'butchered' three thousand colonists and captured many cattle at Peerskill Fort on the Hudson in November 1776.

The fourth stanza narrates the triumph of American arms. General Burgoyne advancing into Albany in the autumn of 1777 was forced to surrender to an American army three times his size at Saratoga on 17th October. Simon Frazer (another Scottish hero) was killed at the battle of Freeman's Farm.

The defeat in America was of such catastrophic proportions that it threw the British political system into extreme factionalism, especially given George III's hatred of the Whigs in general and Fox in particular. Added to this there was the problem of making peace with France, combined with the matter of India and the East India Company and the chronic Irish problem. This produced spasmodically rapid changes of administration based on the unlikeliest of alliances, in particular that between North and Fox. What is poetically astonishing about this, is that Burns, from a provincial viewpoint at the beginning of his poetic career, can compress the roller-coaster clamour of St Stephen's (then the site of Parliament) into a mere five stanzas. Undoubtedly he was aided by not only the newspapers but the cartoons. As for example, L.G. Mitchell (in *Charles James Fox*, London, 1992) notes:

> True, some cartoons appeared showing Fox as Cromwell or Carlo Khan, riding down Leadenhall St on the back of an Indian elephant but others portrayed him as the new Demosthenes or as the 'Champion of the People'. Against anti-Coalition songs must be set images showing Pitt, riding the white horse of Despotic Hanover, battling with Fox, sitting aside the British Lion . . . Hitherto, these two young men had jointly been the hope of the reformers. Now, they were opponents and shackled by alliances to non-reformers. Which of them would prove to be the long-term friend of reformers had to be debated at public meetings all over England, and the divisions set up at these assemblies fatally harmed the reform movement as a whole. Christopher Wyvill opted for Pitt, declaring that Fox wished to change our limited Monarchy into a mere Aristocratic Republic. William Mason thought that all politics would be corruption if 'Charles Fox had the Indies at his disposal' (pp. 68–9).

Mitchell's lucid remarks should also alert us to the fact that Burns's political responses to British party politics, often represented as eccentric and quixotic, were based on the national dilemma between the relative potential of Fox and Pitt to deliver reform. Fox, with his swarthy, 'tinkler jaw' remained, to a degree, oportunistic and licentious. Pitt, to many, including Burns, at this time looked the more reforming politician. Certainly Burns was not one of the 'inspired Bardies' when he wrote this. He was not to know how catastrophically his and Scotland's support for 'Willie' Pitt and, far worse, 'slee' Dundas was to rebound on them both. Compared to the political opportunism of the age, Burns is, however, a figure of profound stability. Who could, for example, switch positions more than 'Paddy' Burke? As we shall see this exclusive identification of Burke by his Irish forename diminutive is tellingly to reappear in the recently recovered poem *The Dagger* (see Anonymous and Pseudonymous Section).

My Nanie, O

Tune: My Nanie, O
First published, Edinburgh, 1787.

Behind yon hills where Stinchar flows[1]	those
'Mang moors an' mosses many, O,	
The wintry sun the day has clos'd,	
And I'll awa to Nanie, O.	

5	The westlin wind blaws loud an' shill,	shrill
	The night's baith mirk and rainy, O;	both, dark
	But I'll get my plaid an' out I'll steal,	cloth garment
	An' owre the hill to Nanie, O.	over

	My Nanie's charming, sweet, an' young;	
10	Nae artfu' wiles to win ye, O:	no
	May ill befa' the flattering tongue	befall
	That wad beguile my Nanie, O!	would

	Her face is fair, her heart is true,	
	As spotless as she's bonie, O;	
15	The op'ning gowan, wat wi' dew,	flower, wet
	Nae purer is than Nanie, O.	

	A country lad is my degree,	
	An' few there be that ken me, O;	know
	But what care I how few they be,	
20	I'm welcome ay to Nanie, O.	always

1 Burns, at the suggestion of George Thomson, allowed the name of the river to be changed from Stinchar to Lugar.

My riches a's my penny-fee,   paltry wages
    An' I maun guide it cannie, O;   will, careful
But warl's gear ne'er troubles me,   world's
    My thoughts are a', my Nanie, O.

25   Our auld Guidman delights to view   old, goodman
    His sheep an' kye thrive bonie, O;   cattle
But I'm as blythe that hauds his pleugh,   holds, plough
    An' has nae care but Nanie, O.

Come weel come woe, I care na by,
30   I'll tak what Heav'n will send me, O:
Nae ither care in life have I,   other
    But live, an' love my Nanie, O.

The date of composition is uncertain, although an early draft is
written in the *FCB*, April 1784. Mrs Begg claimed the poet's father
saw and liked the song. Given that he died in February 1784, that
would suggest composition sometime during the early 1780s. The
heroine of the song has been invariably named as Agnes Sherriff of
Kilmarnock, or Agnes Fleming, daughter of a Tarbolton tenant
farmer. Burns saw the song as 'pastoral simplicity' with a 'dash of
our native tongue' (Letter 511). The song was also printed in SC,
1793, then in S.M.M. (1803), no. 580.

Green Grow the Rashes, O
Tune: Green Grow the Rashes, O
First printed in the Edinburgh edition, 1787.

Chorus
Green grow the rashes, O;
    Green grow the rashes, O;
The sweetest hours that e'er I spend,
    Are spent among the lasses, O.

5   There's nought but care on ev'ry han',   nothing, hand
    In ev'ry hour that passes, O:
What signifies the life o' man,
    An' 'twere na for the lasses, O.   if it were not
    Green grow &c.

The war'ly race may riches chase,   worldly
10   An' riches still may fly them, O;
An' tho' at last they catch them fast,
        Their hearts can ne'er enjoy them, O.
                Green grow &c.

But gie me a cannie hour at e'en,   give, quiet, evening
        My arms about my Dearie, O;
15 An' war'ly cares, an' war'ly men,   worldly
        May a' gae tapsalteerie, O!   topsy-turvy
                Green grow &c.

For you sae douce, ye sneer at this,   so prudent
        Ye're nought but senseless asses, O: nothing
The wisest Man the warl' e'er saw,   world
20   He dearly lov'd the lasses, O.
                Green grow &c.

Auld Nature swears, the lovely dears
        Her noblest work she classes, O:
Her prentice han' she try'd on man,   hand
        An' then she made the lasses, O.

This song also featured in S.M.M. in 1787, number 77. It was
composed, bar the final verse, in 1784 and is recorded in the *FCB*,
dated August, where the song follows a lengthy prose commentary
on 'the two Grand Classes' of men, the 'Grave and the Merry'. The
song is a fine example of the poet's early skill, developed by his tutor
Murdoch, in writing out lines of poetry from his own prose. Having
written out his observations on the two main classifications of men,
the poet introduces the song: 'I shall set down the following
fragment which, as it is the genuine language of my heart, will
enable any body to determine which of the Classes I belong to'. A
further verse, developing this theme, but replacing the power of
Nature with God, is recorded by Low (p. 106) from the MSS, Lady
Stair's House, Edinburgh):

    Frae Man's ain side God made his wark
        That a' the lave surpasses O
    The Man but lo'es his ain heart's bluid
        Wha dearly lo'es the lasses O.

Again Rejoicing Nature Sees
Tune: Johnny's Grey Breeks
First printed in the Edinburgh edition, 1787.

Again rejoicing Nature sees
    Her robe assume its vernal hues,
Her leafy locks wave in the breeze
    All freshly steep'd in morning dews.

Chorus[1]
5 And maun I still on Menie[2] doat,   must, dote
    And bear the scorn that's in her e'e!   eye
For it's jet, jet-black, an' it's like a hawk,
    An' it winna let a body be!   will not

In vain to me the cowslips blaw,   blow
10   In vain to me the vi'lets spring;   violets
In vain to me in glen or shaw,   wood
    The mavis and the lintwhite sing.
        And maun I still &c.

The merry Ploughboy cheers his team,
    Wi' joy the tentie Seedsman stalks,   careful
15 But life to me 's a weary dream,
    A dream of ane that never wauks.   one, wakes
        And maun I still &c.

The wanton coot the water skims,
    Amang the reeds the ducklings cry,   among
The stately swan majestic swims,
20   And ev'ry thing is blest but I.
        And maun I still &c.

The Sheep-herd steeks his faulding slap,   shuts, sheep-fold gate
    And owre the moorlands whistles shill,   shrill
Wi' wild, unequal, wand'ring step
    I meet him on the dewy hill.
        And maun I still &c.

1 This chorus is part of a song composed by a gentleman in Edinburgh, a
particular friend of the Author's. R.B.
2 Menie is the common abbreviation of Marianne. R.B.

25   And when the lark, 'tween light and dark,
        Blythe waukens by the daisy's side,   wakens
     And mounts and sings on flittering wings,
        A woe-worn ghaist I hameward glide.   ghost, homeward
           And maun I still &c.

     Come Winter, with thine angry howl,
30   And raging bend the naked tree;
     Thy gloom will soothe my cheerless soul,
        When Nature all is sad like me!
           And maun I still &c.

The title of this is merely 'Song' in Kinsley (no. 138). In the Mackay
edition it is given as *And Maun I Still on Menie Doat*, being the first
line of the chorus (p. 266). The chorus, though, was written by a
friend of the poet's, as admitted by Burns in his notes when
published in 1787; the first line written by Burns is given here as
the title, 'Again rejoicing Nature sees'. In verse five, Mackay has
changed the original 'shill' to 'shrill', changing the older word for its
modern meaning, a word Burns did not employ. He further omits
the poet's note indicating he did not write the chorus.

The Gloomy Night is Gathering Fast

Tune: Roslin Castle
First printed in the Edinburgh edition, 1787.

     The gloomy night is gath'ring fast,
        Loud roars the wild inconstant blast,
     Yon murky cloud is filled with rain,
        I see it driving o'er the plain;
5   The Hunter now has left the moor,
        The scatt'red coveys meet secure,
     While here I wander, prest with care,
        Along the lonely banks of *Ayr*.

     The Autumn mourns her rip'ning corn
10   By early Winter's ravage torn;
     Across her placid, azure sky,
        She sees the scowling tempest fly:
     Chill runs my blood to hear it rave,
        I think upon the stormy wave,
15   Where many a danger I must dare,
        Far from the bonie banks of *Ayr*.   bonny

'Tis not the surging billows' roar,
　　'Tis not that fatal, deadly shore;
Tho' Death in ev'ry shape appear,
20　　　The Wretched have no more to fear:
But round my heart the ties are bound,
　　That heart transpierc'd with many a wound;
These bleed afresh, those ties I tear,
　　To leave the bonie banks of *Ayr*.

25 Farewell, old *Coila's* hills and dales,
　　Her heathy moors and winding vales;
The scenes where wretched Fancy roves,
　　Pursuing past unhappy loves!
Farewell my friends! farewell my foes!
30　　My peace with these, my love with those —
The bursting tears my heart declare,
　　Farewell, my bonie banks of *Ayr*.

This was composed in the late Autumn of 1786 when the problems of the poet's personal life still prompted him to think of emigrating from Scotland. To Dr Moore Burns explained that this was to be his final parting song to his friends and homeland (Letter 125). Personal vexations are evident in the final couplets, referring to a last farewell of 'friends!' and 'foes!' It is clearly the case that in the poet's thoughts of sailing to Jamaica he held concerns that a winter journey by sea could be perilous on 'the stormy wave, /Where many a danger I must dare'.

No Churchman am I

Tune: Prepare, my dear Brethren
The final song of the Edinburgh edition, 1787.

No Churchman am I for to rail and to write,
No Statesman nor Soldier to plot or to fight,
No sly man of business contriving a snare,
For a big-belly'd bottle's the whole of my care.

5 The Peer I don't envy, I give him his bow;
I scorn not the Peasant, tho' ever so low;
But a club of good fellows, like those that are here,
And a bottle like this, are my glory and care.

Here passes the Squire on his brother — his horse;
10   There Centum per Centum, the Cit with his purse,   citizen
But see you the Crown, how it waves in the air,   coins
There a big-belly'd bottle still eases my care.

The wife of my bosom, alas! she did die;
For sweet consolation to church I did fly;
15   I found that old Solomon proved it fair,
That a big-belly'd bottle's a cure for all care.

I once was persuaded a venture to make;
A letter inform'd me that all was to wreck;
But the pursy old landlord just waddled up stairs,   focused on money
20   With a glorious bottle that ended my cares.

'Life's cares they are comforts'[1]— a maxim laid down
By the Bard, what d'ye call him, that wore the black gown;
And faith I agree with th' old prig to a hair;
For a big-belly'd bottle's a heav'n of care.

A STANZA ADDED IN A MASON LODGE
Then fill up a bumper and make it o'erflow,
And honours Masonic prepare for to throw:
May ev'ry true Brother of the Compass and Square   Masonic instruments
Have a big-belly'd bottle, when harass'd with care!

The poet was entered an apprentice member of the Freemasons'
Lodge at Tarbolton in 1781 and composed this song, fully aware that
the tune formed part of Masonic culture, entitled *The Freemasons'
March* (Aird's collection of *Airs*, 1782). An earlier version of the
tune, 1730, was known as *Freemasons' Health* (Low, p. 84). Com-
position is assumed to be sometime in the winter of 1783–4, although
earlier editors place it in the 1781–2 period. Kinsley records that a
political stanza was suppressed in 1787 which alluded to William
Pitt and the governmental inquiry into Warren Hastings, which
would make the later date accurate. A song with the line 'And a big-
bellied bottle's a mighty good thing' was published in 1751, then
again in a collection owned by Burns in 1783, *A Select Collection of
English Songs*. The song was also printed in S.M.M. no. 587, 1803.
The quotation from Edward Young's *Night Thoughts*, 'Life's cares
they are comforts' is taken from Part II, l. 160.

1 Young's *Night Thoughts*. R.B.

PART THREE

The Edinburgh Edition

1793

Written in Friar's Carse Hermitage,

First printed in the Edinburgh edition, 1793.
On the Banks of Nith – Dec 1788.

Thou whom chance may hither lead,
Be thou clad in russet weed,
Be thou deckt in silken stole,
Grave these counsels on thy soul.

5   Life is but a day at most,
Sprung from night, in darkness lost:
Hope not sunshine ev'ry hour,
Fear not clouds will always lour.

As Youth and Love with sprightly dance
10   Beneath thy morning star advance,
Pleasure with her siren air
May delude the thoughtless pair;
Let Prudence bless Enjoyment's cup,
Then raptur'd sip and sip it up. –

15   As thy day grows warm and high,
Life's meridian flaming nigh,
Dost thou spurn the humble vale?
Life's proud summits would'st thou scale?
Check thy climbing step, elate,
20   Evils lurk in felon-wait:
Dangers, eagle-pinioned, bold,
Soar around each cliffy hold;
While cheerful Peace, with linnet song,
Chants the lowly dells among.

25   As the shades of ev'ning close,
Beck'ning thee to long repose;
As life itself becomes disease,
Seek the chimney-nook of Ease.
There ruminate with sober thought;

30   On all thou'st seen, and heard, and wrought;
     And teach the sportive Younkers round,
     Saws of experience, sage and sound:
     Say, man's true, genuine estimate,
     The grand criterion of his fate,
35   Is not, Art thou high or low?
     Did thy fortune ebb or flow?
     Did many talents gild thy span?
     Or frugal Nature grudge thee one?
     Tell them, and press it on their mind,
40   As thou thyself must shortly find,
     The smile or frown of awful Heav'n,
     To Virtue or to Vice is giv'n.
     Say, to be just, and kind, and wise,
     There solid self-enjoyment lies;
45   That foolish, selfish, faithless ways,
     Lead to be wretched, vile, and base.

          Thus, resign'd and quiet, creep
     To the bed of lasting sleep;
     Sleep, whence thou shall ne'er awake,
50   Night, where dawn shall never break,
     Till Future Life, future no more,
     To light and joy the good restore,
     To light and joy unknown before.

     Stranger, go! Heav'n be thy guide!
55   Quod the Beadsman of Nith-side.

This is generally described as the first poetical production to
flourish from the friendship of Burns and his nearest neighbour
at Ellisland, Captain Robert Riddell (1755–94). Riddell owned the
Friar's Carse estate and was well known as an antiquarian, musician
and outspoken Whig. Riddell contributed several radical polemical
essays to various newspapers of the period, one being the essay
signed Cato sent by Burns to *The Edinburgh Gazetteer* in December
1792 (Letter 530). Riddell built the small hermitage, situated almost
one mile from Ellisland, on the banks of the river Nith and provided
the poet with a key, allowing him to use it whenever he desired. The
hermitage is still extant, although it was re-built in the twentieth
century. Scott Douglas records that he visited the site and found it
in ruins in the latter part of the 19th century.
     Kinsley gives two versions of this poem. He presents the first
early draft as the main poem, then prints the final polished version

as a secondary work, titled 'Altered from the Foregoing – Dec – 1788', no. K223B. Although there are significant differences between the two versions, Burns only printed the final edition in 1793. He did not publish the early draft. It appeared as a separate poem in 1801 with Dr Currie's second edition of the poems of Burns. The version given here is the final draft, updated by Burns in December 1788 and published in 1793.

The earliest version found its way into print via an unauthorised source. Burns remarked to David Blair (a Birmingham Gunmaker) in August 1789, 'I know nothing how the Publishers could get it, but as I had given several copies to my friends, it has found its way, I suppose, thro' the well-meant, though blameable officiousness of some of them. – I have a little altered, and, I think, improved that poem . . .' (Letter 360). Kinsley mentions another unsanctioned publication in the *Glasgow Weekly Miscellany*, for 31st November 1791, which may have been forwarded by Robert Riddell. The final version is, as Burns comments, the superior work.

Elegy on Captain Matthew Henderson
A Gentleman who Held the Patent for his Honours Immediately from Almighty God!

First printed in the *Edinburgh Magazine*, August 1790, prior to publication in the Edinburgh edition, 1793.

> *But now his radiant course is run,*
> *For Matthew's course was bright:*
> *His soul was like the glorious sun*
> *A matchless, Heavenly light.*
> BURNS.

O DEATH! thou tyrant fell and bloody!
The meikle Devil wi' a woodie   great, halter
Haurl thee hame to his black smiddie,   trail, home, smithy
     O'er hurcheon hides,   hedgehog
5 And like stock-fish come o'er his studdie   strike, anvil
     Wi' thy auld sides!   old

He's gane! he's gane! he's frae us torn,   gone, gone, from
The ae best fellow e'er was born!   one
Thee, Matthew, Nature's sel' shall mourn   self
10   By wood and wild,
Where, haply, Pity strays forlorn,
     Frae man exil'd.   from

Ye hills, near neebors o' the starns,   neighbours, stars
That proudly cock your cresting cairns;   display
15   Ye cliffs, the haunts of sailing yearns,   eagles
            Where Echo slumbers,
Come join, ye Nature's sturdiest bairns,   children
            My wailing numbers.

Mourn, ilka grove the cushat kens;   every, wood-pigeon knows
20   Ye hazelly shaws and briery dens;   woods, hollows
Ye burnies, wimplin down your glens,   rivulets, winding
            Wi' toddlin din,   trickling noise
Or foaming, strang, wi' hasty stens,   strong, leaps/churns
            Frae lin to lin.   from, waterfall

25   Mourn little harebells o'er the lea;   hill edge
Ye stately foxgloves fair to see;
Ye woodbines hanging bonilie,
            In scented bowers;
Ye roses on your thorny tree,
30   The first o' flowers.

At dawn, when every grassy blade
Droops with a diamond at his head,
At even', when beans their fragrance shed,
            I' th' rustling gale,
35   Ye maukins whiddin through the glade,   hares, skipping
            Come join my wail.

Mourn, ye wee songsters o' the wood;
Ye grouse that crap the heather bud;   crop/eat
Ye curlews calling thro' a clud;   cloud
40   Ye whistling plover;
And mourn, ye whirring paitrick brood;   partridge
            He's gane for ever!   gone

Mourn, sooty coots, and speckled teals;   black
Ye fisher herons, watching eels;
45   Ye duck and drake, wi' airy wheels
            Circling the lake:
Ye bitterns, till the quagmire reels,
            Rair for his sake.   roar

Mourn, clam'ring craiks at close o' day,   corncrakes
50   'Mang fields o' flow'ring clover gay;
And when you wing your annual way
          Frae our cauld shore,   from, cold
Tell thae far warlds, wha lies in clay,   they, worlds, who
          Wham we deplore.   what

55   Ye houlets, frae your ivy bower,   from
In some auld tree, or eldritch tower,   old, haunted
What time the moon, wi' silent glowr,   glower/stare
          Sets up her horn,
Wail thro' the dreary midnight hour
60   Till waukrife morn.   wakeful

O rivers, forests, hills, and plains!
Oft have ye heard my canty strains: cheery/joyful
But now, what else for me remains
          But tales of woe?
65   And frae my een the drapping rains   eyes, dropping
          Maun ever flow.   must/shall

Mourn, Spring, thou darling of the year!
Ilk cowslip cup shall kep a tear: each, catch
Thou, Simmer, while each corny spear   summer
70   Shoots up its head,
Thy gay, green, flowery tresses shear,
          For him that's dead.

Thou, Autumn, wi' thy yellow hair,
In grief thy sallow mantle tear;
75   Thou, Winter, hurling thro' the air
          The roaring blast,
Wide o'er the naked world declare
          The worth we've lost.

Mourn him, thou Sun, great source of light!
80   Mourn, Empress of the silent night!
And you, ye twinkling starnies bright,   little stars
          My Matthew mourn;
For through your orbs he's taen his flight,   taken
          Ne'er to return.

85   O Henderson! the man! the brother!
     And art thou gone, and gone for ever?
     And hast thou crost that unknown river,   crossed
             Life's dreary bound?
     Like thee, where shall I find another,
90   The world around?

     Go to your sculptur'd tombs, ye Great,
     In a' the tinsel trash o' state!
     But by thy honest turf I'll wait,
             Thou man of worth!
95   And weep the ae best fellow's fate   one/very
             E'er lay in earth.

THE EPITAPH
     STOP, passenger! — my story's brief,
             And truth I shall relate, man;
     I tell nae common tale o' grief —   no
100   For Matthew was a great man.

     If thou uncommon merit hast,
             Yet spurn'd at Fortune's door, man,
     A look of pity hither cast —
             For Matthew was a poor man.

105 If thou a noble sodger art,   soldier
             That passest by this grave, man,
     There moulders here a gallant heart —
             For Matthew was a brave man.

     If thou on men, their works and ways,
110   Canst throw uncommon light, man,
     Here lies wha weel had won thy praise —   who well
             For Matthew was a bright man.

     If thou, at Friendship's sacred ca'   call
             Wad life itself resign, man,   would
115 Thy sympathetic tear maun fa' —   must fall
             For Matthew was a kind man.

     If thou art staunch without a stain,
             Like the unchanging blue, man,
120 This was a kinsman o' thy ain —   own
             For Matthew was a true man.

> If thou hast wit, and fun, and fire,
>   And ne'er guid wine did fear, man,   good
> This was thy billie, dam, and sire —   comrade
>   For Matthew was a queer man.   roguish

125 If onie whiggish, whingin' sot,   any, whining
>   To blame poor Matthew dare, man,
> May dool and sorrow be his lot!   woe/sadness
>   For Matthew was a rare man.

Kinsley gives the following biographical details: 'Matthew Henderson (1737–88) of Tannochside was a lieutenant in the Earl of Home's regiment, and later held a civil service post in Edinburgh. He was an acquaintance of Boswell's, one of a 'genteel, profligate society who live like a distinct nation in Edinburgh, having constant recruits coming and going' (*Boswell in Search of a Wife 1766–1769*, ed. Brady and Pottle, 1957, p. 125). Henderson was also a Mason and an antiquarian. He was forced by his convivial extravagance to sell his property, and when Burns met him in 1787 he was subsisting on a pension. He was buried in Greyfriars churchyard on 27 November 1788. What Kinsley fails to mention is that Henderson was a member of that dissident, reformist, pro-American, drouthy group, The Crochallan Fencibles. Thus in habits, interests and politics, this was a man after the Bard's own heart. In the copy of the letter he sent to Dugald Stewart he reported that Henderson:

> . . . was an intimate acquaintance of mine; and of all Mankind I ever knew, he was one of the first. . . for a nice sense of honour, a generous contempt for the adventitious distinctions of Men, and sterling tho' sometimes outré Wit. – The inclosed Elegy has pleased me beyond any of my late poetic efforts. – Perhaps 'tis 'the memory of the joys that are past,' and a friend who is no more that biases my criticism. – It is likewise, ever since I read your Aiken on the poetic uses of Natural history, a favourite study of mine, the characters of the Vegetable and the manners of the Animal kingdom. – I regret much that I cannot have your strictures on this Poem. – How I have succeeded on the whole – if there is any incongruity in the imagery – or whether I have not omitted some apt rural paintings altogether (Letter 410).

The poem has all the energy of Burns's elegy for Tam Sampson without, alas, the happy ending. The poet invokes landscape, fish, animals, the seasons, the sun and stars, the very grass itself into a hyperbolic chorus of pathetic fallacy which emerges from a synthesis of his readings in late eighteenth-century natural philosophy and his creative extension of the powerful elegiac poetry found in Ramsay and Fergusson, particularly in the latter's *Elegy On the Death of Scots Music*, ll. 13–18 (*Poems*, STS, ii, 38):

> Mourn ilka nymph and ilka swain,
> Ilk sunny hill and dowie glen;
> Let weeping streams and Naiads drain
>   Their fountain head;
> Let echo swell the dolefu' strain,
>   Since music's dead.

Crawford, in a fine reading of this poem (pp. 211–16), sees in it a synergetic fusion of earlier eighteenth-century Scottish and English elegiac elements and also recognises, appropriate to Henderson's character, the pronounced democratic politics of the piece:

> Since all of Burns is in the background of this elegy, it is not the least surprising that the last stanza should have political and moral undertones, drawing its main effect from the sharp dichotomy of the plebian's simple turf and the elaborate graves of the upper classes (ll. 91–6). The quiet rumination of Gray's *Elegy* has taken on a Scottish tinge and become imbued with the Honest Man's indignation against his aristocratic opponents. Even at his most traditional and writing an elegy, Burns could not avoid all trace of social criticism. It is only his very worst poems that are completely innocuous.
>
> *The Epitaph* which concludes the elegy proper is only superficially divided from the sixteen stanzas that precede it. In reality, it develops all the democratic implications of 'thy honest turf' and 'Thou man of worth' until it becomes like the second half of a diptych: taken together, the two parts constitute the complete poem.

Lament of Mary Queen of Scots on the Approach of Spring

First printed in the Edinburgh edition, 1793.

> Now Nature hangs her mantle green
>   On every blooming tree,
> And spreads her sheets o' daisies white
>   Out o'er the grassy lea:
> 5 Now Phoebus cheers the crystal streams,
>   And glads the azure skies;
> But nought can glad the weary wight
>   That fast in durance lies.

Now laverocks wake the merry morn,   larks
10   Aloft on dewy wing;
The merle, in his noontide bow'r,   blackbird
        Makes woodland echoes ring;
The mavis wild wi' monie a note,   thrush, many
        Sings drowsy day to rest:
15 In love and freedom they rejoice,
        Wi' care nor thrall opprest.

Now blooms the lily by the bank,
        The primrose down the brae;   hillside
The hawthorn's budding in the glen,
20   And milk-white is the slae: sloe
The meanest hind in fair Scotland
        May rove their sweets amang;   among
But I, the Queen of a' Scotland,   all
        Maun lie in prison strang!   must, strong

25 I was the Queen o' bonie France,   beautiful
        Where happy I hae been;   have
Fu' lightly rase I in the morn,   rose
        As blythe lay down at e'en: evening
And I'm the sovereign of Scotland,
30   And mony a traitor there;   many
Yet here I lie in foreign bands,
        And never-ending care.

But as for thee, thou false woman!
        My sister and my fae,   foe
35 Grim vengeance yet shall whet a sword   wet
        That thro' thy soul shall gae!   go
The weeping blood in woman's breast
        Was never known to thee;
Nor th' balm that draps on wounds of woe   drops
40   Frae woman's pitying e'e.   from, eye

My son! my son! my kinder stars
        Upon thy fortune shine!
And may those pleasures gild thy reign,
        That ne'er wad blink on mine!   would
45 God keep thee frae thy mother's faes,   from, foes
        Or turn their hearts to thee:
And where thou meet'st thy mother's friend,
        Remember him for me!

O soon, to me, may Summer suns
50　　　Nae mair light up the morn!　　　no more
Nae mair, to me, the Autumn winds　　　no more
　　　Wave o'er the yellow corn!
And in the narrow house o' death
　　　Let Winter round me rave;
55　And the next flowers, that deck the Spring,
　　　Bloom on my peaceful grave.

Composed in the early summer of 1790, the poem was sent to several correspondents of Burns, including Mrs Graham of Fintry, who was addressed as follows: 'Whether it is that the story of our Mary Queen of Scots has a peculiar effect on the feelings of a Poet, or whether in the enclosed ballad I have succeeded beyond my usual poetic success, I know not; but it has pleased me beyond any late effort of the Muse' (Letter 402). It is a ballad that mixes Scots and English with a dash of simple antiquated phraseology, particularly the use of 'glads', then 'glad' in the first stanza, and the rare description for a blackbird, a 'merle' in the second stanza. Set as spoken by Queen Mary, the highly descriptive narrative perfectly complements the mournful despair of Mary.

To Robert Graham of Fintry, Esq.

First printed in the Edinburgh edition, 1793.

Late crippled of an arm, and now a leg,
About to beg a *pass* for leave to beg;
Dull, listless, teas'd, dejected, and deprest,
(Nature is adverse to a cripple's rest);
5　Will generous Graham list to his Poet's wail?　listen
(It soothes poor Misery, hearkening to her tale),
And hear him curse the light he first surveyed,
And doubly curse the luckless rhyming trade?

Thou, Nature, partial Nature! I arraign;
10　Of thy caprice maternal I complain:
The lion and the bull thy care have found,
One shakes the forests, and one spurns the ground:
Thou giv'st the ass his hide, the snail his shell,
Th' envenomed wasp, victorious, guards his cell;
15　Thy minions, kings defend, control, devour,
In all th' omnipotence of rule and power;

Foxes and statesmen, subtile wiles ensure;
The cit and polecat stink, and are secure;
Toads with their poison, doctors with their drug,
20 The priest and hedgehog in their robes, are snug;
Ev'n silly woman has her warlike arts,
Her tongue and eyes, her dreaded spear and darts.

But, Oh! thou bitter step-mother and hard,[1]
To thy poor, fenceless, naked child — the Bard!
25 A thing unteachable in world's skill,
And half an idiot too, more helpless still;
No heels to bear him from the opening dun;
No claws to dig, his hated sight to shun;
No horns, but those by luckless Hymen worn,
30 And those, alas! not Amalthea's horn:
No nerves olfact'ry, Mammon's trusty cur,
Clad in rich Dulness' comfortable fur; —
In naked feeling, and in aching pride,
He bears th' unbroken blast from ev'ry side:
35 Vampyre booksellers drain him to the heart,
And scorpion critics cureless venom dart: —

Critics! — appalled, I venture on the name —
Those cut-throat bandits in the paths of fame:
Bloody dissectors, worse than ten Monroes!
40 He hacks to teach, they mangle to expose: —

His heart by causeless wanton malice wrung,
By blockheads' daring into madness stung;
His well-won bays, than life itself more dear,
By miscreants torn, who ne'er one sprig must wear;
45 Foiled, bleeding, tortur'd in th' unequal strife,
The hapless Poet flounders on thro' life;
Till fled each hope that once his bosom fired,
And fled each Muse that glorious once inspired,

1 In adapted form, lines 17–36 are found erroneously attributed to Samuel Taylor Coleridge in the Oxford edition of Coleridge, under the Latin title 'Habent Sua Fata – Poetae'. See p. 587, Appendix 1, 'First Drafts, Early Versions'. The lines were found in a Coleridge letter, dated January 1796. They were first ascribed to Coleridge in Cottle's *Early Recollections* (1839). Coleridge evidently identified strongly with Burns's view on critics and the fate of poets. It is surely a compliment to Burns's ability to write verse in English that this piece has been mistakenly attributed to one of England's finest poets.

Low-sunk in squalid, unprotected age,
50   Dead even resentment for his injured page,
He heeds or feels no more the ruthless Critic's rage!

So, by some hedge, the generous steed deceased,
For half-starv'd snarling curs a dainty feast;
By toil and famine wore to skin and bone,
55   Lies, senseless of each tugging bitch's son.

O Dulness! portion of the truly blest!
Calm sheltered haven of eternal rest!
Thy sons ne'er madden in the fierce extremes
Of Fortune's polar frost, or torrid beams.
60   If mantling high she fills the golden cup,
With sober selfish ease they sip it up:
Conscious the bounteous meed they well deserve,
They only wonder 'some folks' do not starve.
The grave sage hern thus easy picks his frog,
65   And thinks the mallard a sad worthless dog.
When Disappointment snaps the clue of hope,
And thro' disastrous night they darkling grope,
With deaf endurance sluggishly they bear,
And just conclude that 'fools are fortune's care.'
70   So, heavy, passive to the tempest's shocks,
Strong on the sign-post stands the stupid ox.

Not so the idle Muses' mad-cap train,
Nor such the workings of their moon-struck brain;
In equanimity they never dwell,
75   By turns in soaring heaven, or vaulted hell.

I dread thee, Fate, relentless and severe,
With all a Poet's, husband's, father's fear!
Already one strong hold of hope is lost,
Glencairn, the truly noble, lies in dust;
80   (Fled, like the sun eclips'd as noon appears,
And left us darkling in a world of tears:)
O hear my ardent, grateful, selfish pray'r! —
Fintry, my other stay, long bless and spare!
Thro' a long life his hopes and wishes crown,
85   And bright in cloudless skies his sun go down!
May *bliss domestic* smooth his private path;
Give energy to life; and soothe his latest breath,
With many a filial tear circling the bed of death!

Robert Graham (1749–1815) was the 12th Laird of Fintry, although he was forced to sell most of his estate in 1780. Burns met him during his Highland tour at Athole House, August 31st, 1787. In the same year, Fintry was made a Commissioner on the Board of Excise in Scotland. In terms of poetry, the consequence of this relationship was four poems over a three-year period: *To Robert Graham of Fintry Esq., with a request for an Excise Division* (1788); *To Mr Graham of Fintry, On being appointed to my Excise Division* (1789); *Epistle to Robert Graham of Fintry on the Election for the Dumfries string of Boroughs* (1790) and *To Robert Graham of Fintry, Esq.* (1791). The third poem, as we shall see, is a somewhat risky political satire. The other three all are preoccupied with patronage. The second is deeply sycophantic; a sort of inversion of all Burns's many assertions in his prose and poetry of creative independence at all costs. The other two are fragments of a bigger, incomplete project on the nature of the poet and poetry arising from a mixture of personal observation as found in his earlier vernacular epistles and his reading of, ironically, the dark *Tory* pessimistic prescriptions of the fate of the poet in society found in Dr Johnson's *Lives of the Poets*, Pope's *Moral Epistles* and, not least, Swift's great poem *On Poetry: A Rapsody*. The mixture is further leavened by his awareness, from the latter part of the eighteenth century, of the degree of psychological and economic incompatibility of the poetic personality (Fergusson, Gray, Cowper, Churchill, for example) with the world. Burns chose to publish only this, the last and best of the four 'Fintry' poems. Prior to the poetry, Burns wrote to Fintry within a few months of meeting him at Athole House regarding an entry to the Excise:

> When I had the honour of being introduced to you at Athole House, I did not think so soon of asking a favour from you. When Lear, in Shakespeare asked old Kent why he wished to be in his service, he answered 'Because you have that in your face that I would fain call master!' For, some such reason, sir, do I now solicit your patronage (Letter 172).

Given Burns's use of *King Lear* in *A Winter's Night*, this might seem the most sycophantic betrayal of his normal attitude to social dependency. On the other hand, Burns's soul did yearn, as with Glencairn and Lord Daer, for aristocrats of benevolent integrity. It is possible, too, traumatised by the loss of Glencairn that, on the rebound, he partly subconsciously projected onto Fintry's personality what he had experienced with the former patron. He was also in severe fiscal straits, with all the consequent anxieties of that situation.

As well as his direct approaches to Fintry regarding the limited security an Excise post would offer him, the first and fourth poems are a method of educating Fintry in the difficult, perhaps impossible, task of poetic existence. Obliquely, therefore, the poems insinuate the necessity of Fintry's support. Also, the money worries ran unstoppably on. This poem was written at a time of particular pecuniary stress. As well as his own family, he had another illegitimate child to provide for. The £400 for the Edinburgh edition had been swallowed up in a loan to Gilbert for Mossgiel where the older brother maintained their mother and sisters. The rest had gone into the bottomless pit of stocking Ellisland. His simultaneously injured leg must have been the last straw. Thus he wrote to Fintry on October 6th, 1791:

> — Along with two other Pieces, I inclose you a sheetful of groans, wrung from me in my elbow chair, with one unlucky leg on a stool before me.— I will make no apology for addressing it to *you*: I have no longer a *choice* of Patrons: the noble Glencairn is no more!
>   . . . I thought to have mentioned some Excise ideas that your late goodness has put in my head, but it so like the sorning impudence of a sturdy beggar, that I cannot do it.— It was something in the way of an Officiating job.—With the most ardent wish that you may be rewarded by HIM who can do it, for your generous patronage to a man, who, tho' feelingly sensible of it, is quite unable to repay it . . .

Victorian commentators tended to accept Fintry's benevolence at the value Burns here places on it. Thus Scott Douglas (p. 342) quoting Professor Wilson ('Christopher North'):

> Of all Burns's friends the most efficient was Graham of Fintry. To him he owed exciseman's diploma—settlement as a gauger in a district of ten parishes, when he was a gudeman at Ellisland—translation as a gauger to Dumfries—support against insidious foes, despicable, yet not to be despised, with rumour at their head—vindication at the Excise Board—a temporary supervisorship—and, though he knew not of it, security from dreaded degradation on his death bed.

Wilson, because he was so aware of the savage social discontents of the nineteenth century, was only too eager to represent the Burns/

Fintry relationship in the most positive light. Despite his fiscal needs and functional abilities as an Exciseman, Burns was never promoted. Nor, as Wilson suggests, was it unfounded political rumour that Fintry was benevolently dealing with. Fintry was no neutral. From our recent archival research Fintry did, in fact, receive payments from the government's secret service fund for activities against individuals in the radical movement from 1793 to 1796. (See Laing Ms. collection, II, folio 500, pp. 404–5, Edinburgh University Library.) For example, the payment of £26.6 shillings is dated April, 1793, itemised for Graham of Fintry and paid out of the 'account of Secret Service': payments were made initially to John Pringle, Sherriff Depute of the County of Edinburgh, from the administrator of spies in London, Mr John Spottiswood, a Scot with a Scottish estate, who worked directly for Henry Dundas. There are also in the archive several letters from Fintry, to inter-alia, Robert Dundas on curbing radical activity and placing these loyal to the government in public posts and sinecures. From this it is possible to speculate that, rather than looking after Burns, Fintry was keeping him dependent and cornered in Dumfries. Burns himself, of course, was desperate to have the Excise move him to the more radically sympathetic West of Scotland.

Nor does Wilson's meliorism begin to explain the known course of events. The general tenor of the fifteen extant letters of Burns to Fintry is friendly, sometimes even frank. However, the pattern is totally disrupted in December, 1792 in Burns's near hysterical response to reports that he was about to be investigated for alleged sedition/treason due to both his writing and public behaviour. On the very last day of that year, he wrote to Fintry thus:

I have been surprised, confounded & distracted by Mr Mitchel, the Collector, telling me just now, that he has received an order from your Honble Board to enquire into my political conduct, & blaming me as a person disaffected to Government.—Sir, you are a Husband—& a father—you know what you would feel, to see the much-loved wife of your bosom, & your helpless, prattling little ones, turned adrift into the word, degraded & disgraced from a situation in which they had been respectable and respected, & left [without (*deleted*)] almost without the necessary support of a miserable existence.—Alas, Sir! must I think that such, soon, will be my lot! And from the damned, dark insinuations of hellish, groundless Envy too!—I believe, Sir, I may aver it, & in the sight of Omnipotence, that I would not tell a deliberate Falsehood, no, not though even worse horrors, if worse can be, than those I have mentioned, hung over my head; & I say, that the allegation, whatever villain has made it, is a LIE! To the British Constitution, on Revolution principles, next after my God, I am most devoutly attached!—

You, Sir, have been much & generously my Friend—Heaven knows how warmly I have felt the obligation, how gratefully I have thanked you.—Fortune, Sir, has made you powerful, & me impotent; has given you patronage, & me dependance.—I would not for my *single Self* call on your Humanity; were such my insular, unconnected situation, I would despise the tear that now swells in my eye—I could brave Misfortune, I could face Ruin: for at the worst, 'Death's thousand doors stand open;' but, Good God! the tender concerns that I have mentioned, the claims & ties that I, at this moment, see & feel around me, how they ennerve Courage, & wither Resolution! To your patronage, as a man of some genius, you have allowed me a claim; & your esteem, as an honest Man, I know is my due: to these, Sir, permit me to appeal; & by these may I adjure you to save me from that misery which threatens to overwhelm me, & which, with my latest breath I will say it, I have not deserved.—

Pardon this confused scrawl.—Indeed I know not well what I have written.— (Letter 528)

This is not so out of control as it seems. As well as alluding 'death's thousand doors' from Blair's *The Grave*, his reference to 'the British Constitution, on Revolution principles next after my God', is an escape clause since the establishment Tories and Whig radicals interpreted the constitutional settlement of the Glorious Revolution wholly differently. The former group saw it as perfectly formed and finished. The latter saw it as the embryo for indefinite reformative change. This first letter to Fintry was followed on 5th January by a more considered point by point rebuttal of the charges against him. He repeats his defence of the British Constitution. He denies his involvement in a Dumfries theatrical disturbance where the singing of the national anthem was overwhelmed by the provocative French revolutionary song, *Ça ira*. He claims to have weaned himself of his French affiliations after an imperial France's annexation of Savoy and an invasion of Holland's rights. What is, however, most relevant to his subsequent anonymous radical poetry is his disclaimer of all knowledge of Captain Johnston, the publisher of the dissenting *Edinburgh Gazetteer*.

Of Johnston, the publisher of the Edinr. Gazetteer, I know nothing.—One evening in company with four or five friends, we met with his prospectus which we thought manly and independant; & I wrote to him, ordering his paper for us.—If you think that I act improperly in allowing his Paper to come addressed to me, I shall immediately countermand it.—I never so judge me, God wrote a line of prose for the Gazetteer in my life.

The key word here, of course, is *prose*. It is also a defence based on the letter not the spirit of his previous communication with Captain Johnston. As he wrote to Johnston on 13th November, 1792, describing the magazine as 'the first Composition of the kind in Europe':

> Go on, Sir! Lay bare, with undaunted heart & steady hand, that horrid mass of corruption called Politics & State-Craft. Dare to draw in their native colors these
> 'Calm, thinking VILLAINS who no faith can fix'
> whatever be the shiboleth (sic) of their pretended Party (Quotation from Pope's *The Temple of Fame*, l. 410).

As to the poem itself, its genesis can be dated from a letter to Mrs Dunlop written three years before the poem was sent to Fintry:

> I began a Work lately, but what that work may be, I am totally ignorant.—As Young says, ' 'Tis nonsense destined to be future sense.'—I sent you a fragment of it by my last: take the following rough Sketch of the intended beginning, & let me know your opinion of the lines— The Poet's Progress, An embryotic Poem in the womb of futurity (ll. 9–55, quoted).

> Thus far only have I proceeded, & perhaps I may never again resume the subject.—I must mention one caution to you, Madam, with respect to these verses; I have a remote idea that I may one day use them as instruments of vengeance, & consequently I will hide them like a Conspirator's dagger (Letter 281).

Burns, indeed, as political poet is the archetypal smiler with a knife. This poem, however, has no specific targets but is a general analysis of the multi-displaced poetic personality. Kinsley was innately hostile to Burns's incursions into such Augustan linguistically

and thematically derived terrain. The poem, then, has never had the
attention it deserves. This is literally true, as Hogg discovered that
ll. 17–36 of Burns's poem were compressed by Coleridge into a
twelve-line verse and sent in a letter to Josiah Wade at Bristol *circa*
February 10, 1796. These lines appear in the Oxford Coleridge
under the title *Habent Sunt Fata Poetae* and are wrongly defined as a
sonnet by Molly Lefebre in her *Samuel Taylor Coleridge: A Bondage
of Opium* (London: 1977), p. 175. Here is Coleridge's compressed
version:

> The Fox, and Statesman subtile wiles ensure,
> The Cit, and Polecat stink and are secure:
> Toads with their venom, Doctors with their drug,
> The Priest, the Hedgehog, in their robes are snug!
5 > Oh, Nature! cruel step-mother, and hard,
> To thy poor, naked, fenceless child the Bard!
> No Horns but those by luckless Hymen worn,
> And those, (alas! alas!) not Plenty's Horn!
> With naked feelings, and with aching pride,
10 > He bears th' unbroken blast on every side!
> Vampire Booksellers drain him to the heart,
> And Scorpion Critics cureless venom dart!

The problem of plagiarism in Coleridge is notorious though in this
case, a private letter, he was not obviously trying to pass the Burns
lines off as his own. What it does demonstrate, however, is not only
the relevance Coleridge felt Burns's perceptions had for his own
awareness of his situation as poet but the degree to which Burns was
self-consciously, creatively aware of the chronic social, political,
critical and economic dilemma of poetry since the early part of the
eighteenth century. Carol McGuirk, always eruditely atuned to the
resonances of canonical English poetry in Burns, notes with regard
to this poem that 'among the sources for ll. 56–71, with their imagery
of blissful folly and triumphant Dulness are Pope's *Dunciad* and
Swift's . . .*Tale of a Tub*.' It is problematic as to how much of Swift
Burns knew. Both were peculiarly displaced men: Burns by reason
of class and Swift more by ethnicity. The psychological traumas of
this were creatively compensated for in the terms of the manner in
which their consequent detached, disguised personas could, with
varied laughter, undermine the madness of institutionalised power
especially in both its monarchical and Presbyterian states. It also
seems from the textual evidence highly probable that this Burns
poem is partly based on a reading of what Swift himself considered

his greatest poem, *On Poetry: A Rapsody*. Here is the opening of
Swift:

   All Human Race wou'd fain be *Wits*
And Millions miss, for one that hits
Young's universal Passion, *Pride*,
Was never known to spread so wide.
5   Say *Britain*, cou'd you ever boast,—
Three *Poets* in an Age at most?
Our chilling Climate hardly bears
A *Sprig* of Bays in Fifty Years:
While ev'ry Fool his Claim alledges,
10   As if it grew in common Hedges.
What Reason can there be assign'd
For this Perverseness in the Mind?
Brutes find out where their Talents lie:
A *Bear* will not attempt to fly:
15   A founder'd *Horse* will oft debate,
Before he tries a five-barr'd Gate:
A Dog by Instinct turns aside,
Who sees the Ditch too deep and wide.
But *Man* we find the only Creature,
20   Who, led by *Folly*, fights with *Nature*;
Who, when *she* loudly cries, *Forbear*,
With Obstinacy fixes there;
And, where his *Genius* least inclines,
Absurdly bends his whole Designs.
25   Not *Empire* to the Rising-Sun
By Valour, Conduct, Fortune won;
Nor highest *Wisdom* in Debates
For framing Laws to govern States;
Nor Skill in Sciences profound,
30   So large to grasp the Circle round;
Such heavenly Influence require,
As how to strike the *Muses Lyre*.
      Not Beggar's Brat, on Bulk begot;
Nor Bastard of a Pedlar Scot;
35   Nor Boy brought up to cleaning Shoes,
The Spawn of *Bridewell*, or the Stews;
Nor Infants dropt, the spurious Pledges
Of *Gipsies* littering under Hedges,
Are so disqualified by Fate
40   To rise in *Church*, or *Law*, or *State*,

As he, whom *Phebus* in his Ire
Hath *blasted* with poetick Fire.
    What hope of Custom in the *Fair*,
While not a soul demands your Ware?
45   Where you have nothing to produce
For private Life, or publick Use?
Court, *City*, *Country* want you not;
You cannot bribe, betray, or plot.
For Poets, Law makes no Provision:
50   The Wealthy have you in Derision.
Of State-Affairs you cannot smatter,
Are awkward when you try to flatter.

Both poems are obsessed with the dysfunctional role of the poet in a world where everything else is functionally placed. While Burns is more inclined to place the problem in the innate character of the poet, he is wholly complicit with Swift's analysis of a creative environment warped by the decline of aristocratic patronage, the corrupting effects of the new commercial, book-selling world and the institutionalisation of a rule-bound, pretentious criticism. Burns was a political radical but he is also as hierarchical and élitist as Tory Swift or Pope in his notion that the waters of the Helicon were increasingly polluted by usurping pseudo-poets. As he wrote to Mrs Dunlop: 'Besides, my success has encouraged such a shoal of ill-spawned monsters to crawl into public notice under the title of Scots Poets, that the very term, Scots poetry, borders on the burlesque'. Nor does he, despite Kinsley, suffer in the depth of the quality of his analysis with Swift.

L.7 again echoes Burns's obsession with the sufferings and response of Job. 'Amalthea's horn' (l. 30) was the horn of Zeus's nurse-goat which became a cornucopia unlike the more probably worn cuckold horns of the married (Hymen is the goddess of marriage) poet. Ll. 39–40 brilliantly extend a medical joke probably triggered by Pope's reference in *Imitations of Horace*, Ep.II.ii, l. 70 where he refers to James Monro, the physician of Bedlam: 'Sure I should want Care of ten *Munroes*'. Burns's Monro is Alexander Munro (1733–1817) part of a great Edinburgh medical dynasty who took up that city's first chair in surgery in 1777 in a world of amputation without anaesthetics.

Lament for James, Earl of Glencairn

First printed in the Edinburgh edition, 1793.

The wind blew hollow frae the hills,   from
  By fits the sun's departing beam
Look'd on the fading yellow woods
  That wav'd o'er Lugar's winding stream;
5 Beneath a craigy steep, a Bard,   craggy precipice
  Laden with years, and meikle pain, much
In loud lament bewail'd his lord,
  Whom Death had all untimely ta'en. taken

He lean'd him to an ancient aik,   oak
10 Whose trunk was mould'ring down with years;
His locks were bleached white with time,
  His hoary cheek was wet wi' tears;
And as he touch'd his trembling harp,
  And as he tun'd his doleful sang,   song
15 The winds, lamenting thro' their caves,
  To echo bore the notes alang!   along

'Ye scatter'd birds that faintly sing
  The reliques of the vernal quire;
Ye woods that shed on a' the winds
20 The honours of the aged year!
A few short months, and glad and gay,
  Again ye'll charm the ear and e'e; eye
But nocht in all revolving time   nothing
  Can gladness bring again to me.

25 'I am a bending aged tree,
  That long has stood the wind and rain;
But now has come a cruel blast,
  And my last hold of earth is gane: gone
Nae leaf o' mine shall greet the spring, no
30 Nae simmer sun exalt my bloom;   no
But I maun lie before the storm,   must
  And ithers plant them in my room. others

'I've seen sae monie changefu' years, so many
  On earth I am a stranger grown:
35 I wander in the ways of men,
  Alike unknowing and unknown:

Unheard, unpitied, unreliev'd,
    I bear alane my lade o' care,   _alone, load_
For silent, low, on beds of dust,
40   Lie a' that would my sorrows share.   _all_

'And last (the sum of a' my griefs!)   _all_
    My noble master lies in clay;
The flower amang our barons bold,   _among_
    His country's pride, his country's stay:
45 In weary being now I pine,
    For a' the life of life is dead,
And hope has left my aged ken,   _orbit_
    On forward wing for ever fled.

'Awake thy last sad voice, my harp!
50   The voice of woe and wild despair!
Awake! resound thy latest lay —
    Then sleep in silence evermair!   _evermore_
And thou, my last, best, only friend,
    That fillest an untimely tomb,
55 Accept this tribute from the Bard
    Thou brought from Fortune's mirkest gloom.   _darkest_

'In Poverty's low barren vale,
    Thick mists, obscure, involv'd me round;
Though oft I turn'd the wistful eye,
60   Nae ray of fame was to be found: _no_
Thou found'st me, like the morning sun
    That melts the fogs in limpid air,
The friendless Bard and rustic song
    Became alike thy fostering care.

65 'O why has Worth so short a date?
    While villains ripen grey with time;
Must thou, the noble, gen'rous, great,
    Fall in bold manhood's hardy prime!
Why did I live to see that day?
70   A day to me so full of woe!
O had I met the mortal shaft
    Which laid my benefactor low!

'The bridegroom may forget the bride,
    Was made his wedded wife yestreen;   *yesterday evening*
75 The monarch may forget the crown
    That on his head an hour has been;
The mother may forget the child
    That smiles sae sweetly on her knee;   *so*
But I'll remember thee, Glencairn,
80   And a' that thou hast done for me!'

James Cunningham (1748–91), 14th Earl of Glencairn was Burns's most important actual and potential patron. His premature death, dying at Falmouth on 30th January, 1791, after, like Henry Fielding, an unsuccessful winter in the Portuguese sun to regain his health, was a blow from which Burns never recovered. Burns went into deep mourning and for the Kilmarnock funeral proposed to 'cross the country and steal among the croud, to pay a tear to the last sight of my ever-revered Benefactor' (Letters 438, 439 467).

Despite De Quincey's scepticism about all Burns's patrons, Glencairn does seem to have been of tangible support. The letter of introduction that Burns carried to Edinburgh from Dalrymple of Orangefield, his wife was the Earl's sister, was sufficient to persuade Glencairn, an enthusiast for the Kilmarnock edition, that his Ayrshire compatriot deserved his influential support. Due to Glencairn, the aristocratic Caledonian Hunt subscribed to a man, making the first Edinburgh edition a runaway success.

There is a particular warmth in the three extant letters from Burns to Glencairn. Like Lord Daer, Glencairn appears to have been one of those very few Whig Friends of the People, who, theoretically politically sympathetic, were not driven by condescending egotism and anti-Tory ambition and not real commitment to the common people. Unlike, say, the Riddells, there is little ambivalence in Burns towards Glencairn as the following anecdote from Kinsley reveals:

Glencairn was the only nobleman who offended the poet's social sensibilities without incurring irrational abuse. On one occasion in Edinburgh, says Burns, he showed 'engrossing attention . . . to the only blockhead at table, as there was none but his Lordship, the Dunderpate and myself, that I was within half a point of throwing down my gage of contemptuous defiance, but he shook my hand and looked so benevolently good at parting – God bless him! Though I should never see

him more, I shall love him until my dying day! I am pleased to
think I am so capable of throes of gratitude, as I am miserably
deficient in some other virtues' (2CPB, p. 5).

It is, of course, absolutely typical of Kinsley that satirical dissent
from Burns's socially inferior position always tends to the irrational.
Kinsley had neither adequate knowledge nor sympathy for the
radical politics of the late eighteenth century. Thus he does not
bring to our attention the fact that Glencairn was a Foxite, support-
ing the India Bill, or, more crucially, that he possibly belonged to
that still largely submerged radical network so that the spy-admin-
istrator, Home Office Under-Secretary Spottiswood, dared to 'send
Sheriffs against. . . such an august personage as the Earl of Glen-
cairn' (See Robert Thornton's *William Maxwell to Robert Burns*,
John Donald, Edinburgh: 1979, p. 65).

Like his *Lament for Mary, Queen of Scots*, the regular ballad-like
metre (two sets of long-line couplets broken into tetrameters) is
formally the reverse of MacPherson's Ossianic epic. The tone and
language of the poem, including Biblical echoes, as Kinsley notes, to
Ecclesiastes and *Job*, is, however, deliberately pervaded by the tone
and verbal imagery of that work. To some extent, though the poem
grows increasingly personal, this simultaneously distances Burns
from his pain and invokes enormous Ossianic power of a world
irretrievably lost and existing only in Bardic lament.

Lines, Sent to Sir John Whiteford
with the Foregoing Poem
First printed in the Edinburgh edition, 1793.

Thou, who thy honour as thy God rever'st,
Who, save thy *mind's reproach*, nought earthly fear'st,
To thee this votive off'ring I impart,
The tearful tribute of a broken heart.
The *Friend* thou valued'st, I the *Patron* lov'd;
His worth, his honour, all the world approv'd.
We'll mourn till we too go as he has gone,
And tread the shadowy path to that dark world unknown.

Sir John Whitefoord (1734–1803) was a friend of James Cunning-
ham, Earl of Glencairn. Burns composed these brief lines in October
1791. Whitefoord's reply, written from Maybole, 16th October
1791, in acknowledgement of the *Lament* and lines addressed to

himself, remarked 'Let us cherish this hope for our departed friend, and moderate our grief for that loss we have sustained, knowing he cannot come to us, but we may go to him'. (See Scott Douglas's edition, Vol. I, p. 348 headnote.)

Prose Introduction to Tam O' Shanter

Prompted by the antiquarian Francis Grose, a friend of Robert Riddell of Glenriddell, Burns was asked to provide any ghost stories concerning Alloway church that might be utilised in Francis Grose's forthcoming book on Scottish antiquities. The result was a prose recollection, eventually honed into the comic-epic masterpiece, *Tam O'Shanter*. The poet's remarkable ability to translate prose into poetry is apparent in examining his comments to Grose and because they provide the genesis of the poem, we give them here as introduction:

Among the many Witch Stories I have heard relating to Alloway Kirk, I distinctly remember two or three. Upon a stormy night, amid whirling squalls of wind and bitter blasts of hail, in short on such a night as the devil would chuse to take the air in, a farmer or farmer's servant was plodding and plashing homeward with his plough-iron on his shoulder, having been getting some repairs on them at a neighbouring smithy. His way lay by the Kirk of Aloway, and being on the anxious look-out in approaching a place so well known to be a favourite haunt of the devil and the devil's friends and emissaries, he was struck aghast by discovering through the horrors of the storm and stormy night, a light, which on his nearer approach, plainly shewed itself to proceed from the haunted edifice. Whether he had been fortified from above on his devout supplication, as is customary with people when they suspect the immediate presence of Satan; or whether, according to another custom, he had got courageously drunk at the smithy, I will not pretend to determine; but so it was that he ventured to go up to, nay into the very kirk. As good luck would have it, his temerity came off unpunished. The members of the infernal junto were all out on some midnight business or other, and he saw nothing but a kind of kettle or caldron, depending from the roof, over the fire, simmering some heads of unchristened children, limbs of executed malefactors, &c. for the business of the night. It was, in for a penny in for a pound, with the honest ploughman: so without ceremony he unhooked

the caldron from off the fire, and pouring out the damnable
ingredients, inverted it on his head, and carried it fairly home,
where it remained long in the family a living evidence of the truth
of the story.

Another story which I can prove to be equally authentic was as
follows. On a market day in the town of Ayr, a farmer from Carrick,
and consequently whose way lay by the very gate of Alloway Kirk-
yard in order to cross the river Doon at the old bridge, which is
about two or three hundred yards further on than the said gate, had
been detained by his business, till by the time he reached Alloway, it
was the wizard hour, between night and morning. Though he was
terrified, with a blaze streaming from the kirk, yet as it is a well-
known fact that to turn back on these occasions is running by far the
greatest risk of mischief, he prudently advanced on his road. When
he had reached the gate of the kirk-yard, he was surprised and
entertained, through the ribs and arches of an old gothic window
which still faces the highway, to see a dance of witches merrily
footing it round their old sooty blackguard master, who was keeping
them alive with the powers of his bag-pipe. The farmer stopping his
horse to observe them a little, could plainly descry the faces of many
old women of his acquaintance and neighbourhood. How the gentle-
man was dressed, tradition does not say; but the ladies were all in
their smocks: and one of them happening unluckily to have a smock
which was considerably too short to answer all the purpose of that
piece of dress, our farmer was so tickled that he involuntarily burst
out, with a loud laugh, 'Well luppen Maggy wi the short sark !' and
recollecting himself, instantly spurred his horse to the top of his
speed. I need not mention the universal known fact, that no
diabolical power can pursue you beyond the middle of a running
stream. Lucky it was for the poor farmer that the river Doon was so
near, for notwithstanding the speed of his horse, which was a good
one, against the odds he reached the middle of the arch of the bridge,
and consequently the middle of the stream, the pursuing, vengeful,
hags, were so close at his heels, that one of them actually sprung to
seize him; but it was too late, nothing was on her side of the stream
but the horse's tail, which immediately gave way to her infernal grip,
as if blasted by a stroke of lightning; but the farmer was beyond her
reach. However, the unsightly, tailless condition of the vigorous
steed was to the last hour of the noble creature's life, an awful
warning to the Carrick farmers, not to stay too late in Ayr mar-
kets. . . . (Letter 401).

Tam O' Shanter: A Tale

First printed in *The Edinburgh Herald*, 18th March, 1791; then *The Edin-
burgh Magazine*, March 1791; followed by publication in Francis Grose's
Antiquities of Scotland, Vol. II, April 1791 before inclusion in the Edinburgh
edition, 1793.

Of Brownyis and of Bogillis full is this Buke.
GAWIN DOUGLAS.

	When chapman billies leave the street,	pedlar friends
	And drouthy neebors, neebors meet,	thirsty neighbours
	As market-days are wearing late,	
	An' folk begin to tak the gate;	road/go home
5	While we sit bousing at the nappy,	drinking, ale
	And getting fou and unco happy,	full/drunk, mighty
	We think na on the lang Scots miles,	not, long
	The mosses, waters, slaps, and styles,	bogs, pools, stiles
	That lie between us and our hame,	home
10	Whare sits our sulky sullen dame,	where
	Gathering her brows like gathering storm,	
	Nursing her wrath to keep it warm.	
	This truth fand honest *Tam o' Shanter*,	found
	As he frae Ayr ae night did canter,	from, one
15	(Auld Ayr, wham ne'er a town surpasses	who/that
	For honest men and bonie lasses).	pretty
	O *Tam!* had'st thou but been sae wise,	so
	As taen thy ain wife *Kate's* advice!	taken, own
	She tauld thee weel thou was a skellum,	told, well, rogue
20	A blethering, blustering, drunken blellum;	chattering, babbling, idle talker
	That frae November till October,	from
	Ae market-day thou was nae sober;	one, not
	That ilka melder, wi' the miller,	every meal grinding
	Thou sat as lang as thou had siller;	long, money
25	That ev'ry naig was ca'd a shoe on,	horse, shod
	The smith and thee gat roaring fou on;	got, full/drunk
	That at the Lord's house, even on Sunday,	
	Thou drank wi' Kirkton Jean till Monday.	
	She prophesied that late or soon,	
30	Thou would be found deep drown'd in Doon;	
	Or catch'd wi' warlocks in the mirk,	wizards, dark
	By *Alloway's* auld, haunted kirk.	old

Ah, <u>gentle dames!</u> it gars me greet,   *makes, weep*
To think how mony counsels sweet,   *many*
35   How mony lengthen'd, sage advices,   *many*
The husband frae the wife despises!   *from*

But to our tale: — Ae market-night,   *one*
Tam had got planted unco right;   *mighty*
Fast by an ingle, bleezing finely,   *fire, blazing*
40   Wi' reaming swats, that drank divinely   *foaming ale*
And at his elbow, Souter *Johnny*,   *cobbler*
His ancient, trusty, drouthy crony;   *drinking pal*
Tam lo'ed him like a very brither —   *loved, brother*
They had been fou for weeks thegither!   *full/drunk, together*
45   The night drave on wi' sangs and clatter   *drove, songs, chat*
And ay the ale was growing better:
The landlady and *Tam* grew gracious,
Wi' favours, secret, sweet and precious:
The Souter tauld his queerest stories;   *cobbler told*
50   The landlord's laugh was ready chorus:
The storm without might rair and rustle,   *roar*
Tam did na mind the storm a whistle.   *not*

Care, mad to see a man sae happy,   *so*
E'en drown'd himsel amang the nappy: *among, ale*
55   As bees flee hame wi' lades o' treasure,   *fly home, loads*
The minutes wing'd their way wi' pleasure:
Kings may be blest, but *Tam* was glorious,
O'er a' the ills o' life victorious!

But pleasures are like poppies spread,
60   You seize the flower, its bloom is shed;
Or like the snow falls in the river,
A moment white — then melts for ever;
Or like the borealis race,
That flit ere you can point their place;
65   Or like the rainbow's lovely form
Evanishing amid the storm. —
Nae man can tether time or tide;   *no, hold/control*
The hour approaches *Tam* maun ride;   *must*
That hour, o' night's black arch the key-stane, *-stone*
70   That dreary hour he mounts his beast in;
And sic a night he taks the road in,   *such, takes*
As ne'er poor sinner was abroad in.

The wind blew as 'twad blawn its last;   it would have blown
The rattling showers rose on the blast;
75 The speedy gleams the darkness swallow'd;
Loud, deep, and lang, the thunder bellow'd: long
That night, a child might understand,
The Deil had business on his hand.   devil

Weel mounted on his gray mare, *Meg* —   well
80 A better never lifted leg —
Tam skelpit on thro' dub and mire,   rode fast, puddle
Despising wind, and rain, and fire;
Whyles holding fast his guid blue bonnet;   good
Whyles crooning o'er some auld Scots sonnet;   muttering, old
85 Whyles glow'ring round wi' prudent cares,   looking with fear
Lest bogles catch him unawares: bogies
Kirk-Alloway was drawing nigh,
Whare ghaists and houlets nightly cry. —   where ghosts, owls

By this time he was cross the ford,
90 Whare in the snaw the chapman smoor'd;   burn ▷ *The design of the churchyard.*
And past the birks and meikle stane,   where, snow, pedlar, smothered
Whare drunken *Charlie* brak's neck-bane;   birches, big stone
And thro' the whins, and by the cairn,   where, broke his, -bone
Whare hunters fand the murder'd bairn;   gorse bushes
95 And near the thorn, aboon the well,   where, found, child
Whare *Mungo's* mither hang'd hersel. —   above
Before him *Doon* pours all his floods;   where, mother
The doubling storm roars thro' the woods;
The lightnings flash from pole to pole;
100 Near and more near the thunders roll:
When, glimmering thro' the groaning trees,
Kirk-Alloway seem'd in a bleeze;   blaze/lit up
Thro' ilka bore the beams were glancing;   every chink in the wall
And loud resounded mirth and dancing.

105 Inspiring bold *John Barleycorn!*
What dangers thou canst make us scorn!   ▷ *with drink we can believe anything*
Wi' tippenny, we fear nae evil;
Wi' usquabae, we'll face the Devil! —   cheap two penny ale, no
The swats sae ream'd in *Tammie's* noddle,   whisky
110 Fair play, he car'd na deils a boddle.   small beers, so, mind
But *Maggie* stood, right sair astonish'd,   cared not a farthing
Till, by the heel and hand admonish'd,   sore
          spurred and slapped

She ventur'd forward on the light;
And, vow! *Tam* saw an unco sight!   strange/wondrous
115 Warlocks and witches in a dance;   wizards
Nae cotillion brent new frae *France*,   no, brand new from
But hornpipes, jigs, strathspeys, and reels,
Put life and mettle in their heels.
A winnock-bunker in the east,   window recess
120 There sat auld Nick, in shape o' beast;   old
A tousie tyke, black, grim, and large,   shaggy dog
To gie them music was his charge: give
He screw'd the pipes and gart them skirl,   made, blare
Till roof and rafters a' did dirl. —   ring/shake
125 Coffins stood round, like open presses,   cupboards
That shaw'd the dead in their last dresses;   showed
And by some devilish cantraip sleight,   magic trick
Each in its cauld hand held a light. —   cold
By which heroic *Tam* was able
130 To note upon the haly table,   holy
A murderer's banes, in gibbet-airns;   bones, -irons
Twa span-lang, wee, unchristen'd bairns;   two, -long, babies
A thief new-cutted frae a rape,   from, rope
Wi' his last gasp his gab did gape;   mouth, gasp
135 Five tomahawks wi' blude red-rusted;   axes, blood
Five scymitars wi' murder crusted;
A garter, which a babe had strangled;
A knife, a father's throat had mangled,
Whom his ain son o' life bereft,   own
140 The grey-hairs yet stack to the heft;[1]   stuck, handle
[Three Lawyers' tongues, turned inside out,
Wi' lies seamed like a beggar's clout;
Three Priests' hearts, rotten black as muck,
Lay stinking, vile, in every neuk].   corner

145   As *Tammie* glowr'd, amaz'd, and curious,   stared
The mirth and fun grew fast and furious:
The piper loud and louder blew;
The dancers quick and quicker flew;

---

1 After the word 'heft', most editors print 'Wi' mair of horrible and awefu', /
Which even to name wad be unlawfu'.' The original lines written by Burns
are placed in square brackets. They were effectively edited out of the 1793
Edinburgh edition on the advice of Alexander Fraser Tytler, who thought
them offensive to priests and lawyers.

They reel'd, they set, they cross'd, they cleekit,   *clasped one another*
150 Till ilka carlin swat and reekit,   *every witch, sweated, steamed*
And coost her duddies to the wark,   *cast off clothes, work*
And linket at it in her sark!   *set to it, shirt*

Now *Tam*, O *Tam*! had thae been queans   *they, girls*
A' plump and strapping in their teens,   *— lusting over the teens.*
155 Their sarks, instead o' creeshie flannen,   *shirts, greasy flannel*
Been snaw-white seventeen hunder linen!   *snow-, fine threaded linen*
Thir breeks o' mine, my only pair,   *these breeches*
That ance were plush, o' guid blue hair,   *once, good*
I wad hae gi'en them off my hurdies,   *would have given, backside*
160 For ae blink o' the bonie burdies!   *one, pretty lasses*

Burns voice.

But wither'd beldams, auld and droll,   *hags, old*
Rigwoodie hags wad spean a foal,   *tough, would, abort*
Louping and flinging on a crummock,   *jumping, cudgel*
I wonder did na turn thy stomach.   *not*

165 But *Tam* kend what was what fu' brawlie,   *knew, full well*
There was ae winsome wench and wawlie,   *one comely, choice*
That night enlisted in the core,
(Lang after kend on *Carrick* shore;   *long, known*
For mony a beast to dead she shot,   *many*
170 An' perish'd mony a bonie boat,   *many, handsome*
And shook baith meikle corn and bear,   *both much, barley*
And kept the country-side in fear).

Her cutty-sark, o' Paisley harn   *short shirt, coarse cloth*
That while a lassie she had worn,
175 In longitude tho' sorely scanty,   *revealing*
It was her best, and she was vauntie. —   *proud of it*
Ah! little kend thy reverend grannie,   *knew   moralising*
That sark she coft for her wee Nannie,   *shirt, bought*
Wi' twa pund Scots ('twas a' her riches),   *two pounds*
180 Wad ever grac'd a dance of witches!   *would*

But here my Muse her wing maun cour;   *must fold/curb*
Sic flights are far beyond her pow'r;   *such*
To sing how Nannie lap and flang,   *leaped, kicked*
(A souple jad she was, and strang),   *supple lass, strong*
185 And how *Tam* stood like ane bewitch'd,   *one*
And thought his very een enrich'd;   *eyes*

Even Satan glowr'd, and fidg'd fu' fain,   stared, fidgeted excitedly
And hotch'd and blew wi' might and main: jerked
Till first ae caper, syne anither,   one, then another
190   *Tam* tint his reason a' thegither,   lost, together
And roars out, 'Weel done, Cutty-sark!'   well
And in an instant all was dark:
And scarcely had he *Maggie* rallied,
When out the hellish legion sallied.

> They stop dancing as
> they become aware
> of Tam.

195   As bees bizz out wi' angry fyke,   buzz, fret
When plundering herds assail their byke;   hive
As open pussie's mortal foes,   a hare's
When, pop! she starts before their nose;
As eager runs the market-crowd,
200   When 'Catch the thief!' resounds aloud;
So *Maggie* runs, the witches follow,
Wi' mony an eldritch skriech and hollow.   many, unearthly screech

Ah, *Tam*! ah, *Tam*! thou'll get thy fairin'!   reward/due
In hell they'll roast thee like a herrin'!
205   In vain thy *Kate* awaits thy comin'!
Kate soon will be a woefu' woman!
Now, do thy speedy utmost, Meg,
And win the key-stane of the brig;[2]   key-stone, bridge
There, at them thou thy tail may toss,
210   A running stream they dare na cross.   not
But ere the key-stane she could make,   -stone
The fient a tail she had to shake!   little of
For Nannie, far before the rest,
Hard upon noble *Maggie* prest,   pressed
215   And flew at *Tam* wi' furious ettle;   aim
But little wist she Maggie's mettle —   was
Ae spring brought off her master hale,   one, whole
But left behind her ain grey tail: own
The carlin claught her by the rump,   old witch caught
220   And left poor *Maggie* scarce a stump.

2 It is a well-known fact that witches, or any evil spirits, have no power to follow a poor wight any farther than the middle of the next running stream. It may be proper likewise to mention to the benighted traveller, that when he falls in with bogles, whatever danger may be in his going forward, there is much more hazard in turning back. R.B.

Now, wha this tale o' truth shall read,] *who* ~~foth~~ *poky fun*
Ilk man and mother's son take heed: *each* *at the*
Whene'er to drink you are inclin'd, *narrator.*
Or cutty-sarks run in your mind, *short shirts/skirts*
225 Think! ye may buy the joys o'er dear —
Remember *Tam o' Shanter's* mare.   *I – mock moral*

Tam O' Shanter, 'Burns's most sustained single poetic effort', as Daiches rightly comments, was written as a result of Burns being prompted to write a superstitious story for the English antiquarian Francis Grose, to accompany a sketch of Alloway Kirk in his forthcoming *Antiquities of Scotland*. From the prose evolved the poem, not in a day's work, as has been foolishly suggested, but over several months of composition and correction. Between the edition printed by Grose and the 1793 edition there are 59 noticeable differences in words and punctuation. An example of reworking is evident in a letter Mrs Dunlop wrote to Burns quoting back to him some lines of what is clearly an early draft:

> Kings may be blest, but thou art glorious,
> O'er a' the ills of life victorious;
> As bees fly home laden with treasure,
> By thee the moment's winged with pleasure.
> But pleasure will not always last;
> They're like the rainbow in the blast:
> Awhile it shows its lovely form,
> Then vanishes amid the storm. . .

The narrative tale behind the poem, given above to introduce the poem and explain its origin, reveals the poet's astonishing skill in translating prose into poetry. As Daiches notes (p. 251):

> . . . showed him a master of verse narrative as no Scots poet had been since the fifteenth century. The speed and verve of the narration, the fine, flexible use of the octosyllabic couplet, the effective handling of the verse paragraph demonstrate a degree of craftmanship that few other users of this verse form have achieved.

Unlike Wordsworth, Burns was not given to narrative poetry of this kind – it is his only example. When, however, Wordsworth tried to get some of the story and comic feel of *Tam* into *The Waggoner* it was almost a complete flop. Edwin Muir commented aptly on the poem thus:

'It is the privilege of poetic genius' he [Wordsworth] said
writing about *Tam O'Shanter*, 'to catch, under certain restric-
tions of which perhaps at the time of its being executed it is but
dimly conscious, a spirit of pleasure wherever it can be found –
in the walks of nature, and in the business of men'. Burns
caught this 'spirit of pleasure', and in a poem in which there was
not a weak line, not an uncertain intonation, rendered it with a
vigour and pliancy which must have astonished himself. He
painted corruption in colours so festive and at the time so
objective, that his picture had not only a poetic, but a philo-
sophic value (Muir, *Uncollected Scottish Criticism*, p. 186).

Probably the earliest criticism of *Tam* is still the most accurate. As
early as March 1791, it was apparent to A.F. Tytler that in this tale
Burns had ored the purest poetic gold:

Had you never written another syllable, [this poem] would have
been sufficient to have tramsmitted your name down to poster-
ity with high reputation. In the introductory part, where you
paint the character of your hero, and exhibit him at the ale-
house ingle, with his tippling cronies, you have delineated
nature with an honour and naivete, that would do honour to
Matthew Prior; but when you describe the unfortunate orgies
of the witches' sabbath, and the hellish scenery in which they
are exhibited, you display a power of imagination, that Sha-
kespeare himself could not have exceeded (Currie, 1800, Letter
CVI, 12th March 1791).

McGuirk's contextual and textual remarks on the poem in her
Selected Poems and *Robert Burns and the Sentimental Era* are
particularly cogent and stimulating.

On Seeing a Wounded Hare
limp by me, which a Fellow had Just Shot
First printed in the Edinburgh edition, 1793.

Inhuman man! curse on thy barb'rous art,
    And blasted be thy murder-aiming eye!
    May never pity soothe thee with a sigh,
Nor never pleasure glad thy cruel heart!

5   Go live, poor wanderer of the wood and field,
          The bitter little that of life remains:
          No more the thickening brakes and verdant plains
     To thee shall home, or food, or pastime yield.

     Seek, mangled wretch, some place of wonted rest,
10   No more of rest, but now thy dying bed!
          The sheltering rushes whistling o'er thy head,
     The cold earth with thy bloody bosom prest.

     Oft as by winding Nith I, musing, wait
          The sober eve, or hail the cheerful dawn,
15   I'll miss thee sporting o'er the dewy lawn,
     And curse the ruffian's aim, and mourn thy hapless fate.

This work was written during April of 1789, at Ellisland, after the poet witnessed the shooting of a hare. He wrote to Alexander Cunningham on 4th May 1789:

> One morning lately as I was out pretty early in the fields sowing some grass-seeds, I heard the burst of a shot from a neighbouring Plantation, & presently a poor little wounded hare came crippling by me. – You will guess my indignation at the inhuman fellow, who could shoot a hare at this season when they all of them have young ones; & it gave me no little gloomy satisfaction to see the poor injured creature escape him. Indeed there is something in all that multiform business of destroying for our sport individuals in the animal creation that do not injure us materially, that I could never reconcile to my ideas of native Virtue and eternal Right (Letter 336).

Later in the same letter Burns remarks 'I am doubtful whether it would not be an improvement to keep out the last stanza but one, altogether'. The dropped stanza develops the idea of the hare's 'little nurslings' being left to fend for themselves alone, without 'That life a mother only can bestow' (H & H, Vol. I, Notes, p. 443). Indeed, the same early draft contains the line 'The cold earth with thy blood-stain'd bosom warm', evoking a more graphic image of the dying hare's blood, running warm into the earth. So, in a sense, the final work is the less graphic and personal.

     The sentiments expressed to Cunningham reveal again the importance of the poet's holistic world view on his poetry: he judges all

creatures of creation as 'individuals' or creatures of God. This is
seen in poems such as *To A Mouse*,

> I'm truly sorry Man's dominion
> Has broken Nature's social union,
> And justifies that ill opinion
>   Which makes thee startle
> At me, thy poor, earth-born companion
>   And fellow mortal!

The real spark of indignation, though, is not that the hare has been
shot *per se*, but that it has been shot *out of season*. This is mentioned
specifically by Burns in the comment 'the inhuman fellow, who
could shoot a hare *at this season* when they all of them have young
ones'. There has always been a rural, country code of those who
shoot, that animals are not shot during the period when they are
having or rearing young ones. Such behaviour is generally con-
demned as it is so eloquently here.

Burns partly moderates his outrage when commenting on the poem
to Mrs Dunlop, merely to placate the hare-shooting, Major Dunlop:
'this set my humanity in tears and my indignation in arms. . . . please
read [it] to the young ladies. I believe you may include the Major too,
as whatever I have said of shooting hares I have not spoken one
irreverent word against coursing them' (Letter 330). Despite this, it is
evident that Burns was opposed to killing 'game' for mere *sport*. The
'slaughtering guns' of *Westlin Winds* remains a telling image.

Address, to the Shade of Thomson,
On Crowning his Bust at Ednam,
Roxburgh-Shire with a Wreath of Bays

First published in *The European Magazine*, November 1791, prior to
inclusion in the 1793 Edinburgh edition.

> While virgin Spring, by Eden's flood
>   Unfolds her tender mantle green,
> Or pranks the sod in frolic mood,
>   Or tunes Eolian strains between:

5
> While Summer with a matron grace
>   Retreats to Dryburgh's cooling shade,
> Yet oft, delighted, stops to trace
>   The progress of the spikey blade:

While Autumn, benefactor kind,
10   By Tweed erects his aged head,
And sees, with self-approving mind,
    Each creature on his bounty fed:

While maniac Winter rages o'er
    The hills whence classic Yarrow flows,
15 Rousing the turbid torrent's roar,
    Or sweeping, wild, a waste of snows:

So long, sweet Poet of the Year!
    Shall bloom that wreath thou well has won;
While Scotia, with exulting tear,
20   Proclaims that *Thomson* was her son.

The occasion of this poem was to prove ill-fated. David Erskine, Earl of Buchan, was the elder brother of the more celebrated Henry and Thomas. He had the family egotism without perhaps the talent. His celebration of James Thomson was spoiled by the bust being shattered the night before the unveiling ceremony. Burns had been commissioned to write a poem but could not appear, allegedly because of harvest business. Burns had referred Buchan to Collins's *Ode on the Death of Mr. Thomson*, which he despaired of equalling. Burns's four seasonal stanzas neatly replicate the more prolix chronology of Thomson's best-known poem. The attempt in the last stanza to repatriate Thomson was foredoomed to failure. Complicit with the forces of agrarian capitalism and a propagandist for Anglo-British imperialism (he actually wrote *Rule Britannia* for his *Masque of Alfred*), Thomson had, a poetic pig in clover, absolutely no notion of returning to his austere native land. In political and social values he is almost Burns's antithesis which may in part account for Burns's creative hesitancy and non-appearance.

On the Late Captain Grose's Peregrinations
Thro' Scotland Collecting the Antiquities of that Kingdom

First printed in *The Edinburgh Evening Courant*, 11th August 1789, designated an *Address to the People of Scotland*, signed Thomas A Linn.

Hear, Land o' Cakes, and brither Scots,	oatcakes, brother
Frae Maidenkirk to Johnny Groat's! —	Kirkmaiden parish
If there's a hole in a' your coats,	
I rede you tent it:	warn, attend
5 A chield's amang you takin notes,	fellow's among
And, faith, he'll prent it:	print

If in your bounds ye chance to light
Upon a fine, fat, fodgel wight,   plump
O' stature short but genius bright,
10   That's he, mark weel —   well
And wow! he has an unco sleight   uncommon skill
          O' cauk and keel.   chalk, pencil

By some auld, houlet-haunted biggin,[1]   old, owl-, building
Or kirk deserted by its riggin,   roof
15   It's ten to ane ye'll find him snug in   one
          Some eldritch part,   eerie/haunted
Wi' deils, they say, Lord safe' s! colleaguin'   conferring
          At some black art. —

Ilk ghaist that haunts auld ha' or chamer,   each ghost, old hall, chamber
20   Ye gipsy-gang that deal in glamour,
And you, deep-read in hell's black grammar,   spells/magic
          Warlocks and witches;
Ye'll quake at his conjuring hammer,
          Ye midnight bitches.

25   It's tauld he was a sodger bred,   told, soldier
And ane wad rather fa'n than fled;   one who would, fallen
But now he's quat the spurtle-blade,   quit, sword
          And dog-skin wallet,
And taen the — *Antiquarian trade*,   taken
30   I think they call it.

He has a fouth o' auld nick-nackets: fund, old, nick-nacks
Rusty airn caps and jinglin jackets,[2]   iron, metal armour
Wad haud the Lothians three in tackets,   would hold, shoenails
          A towmont guid;   twelvemonth good
35   And parritch-pats, and auld saut-backets,   porridge-pots, old salt boxes
          Before the Flood.

Of Eve's first fire he has a cinder;
Auld Tubalcain's[3] fire-shool and fender;   old, -shovel
That which distinguishèd the gender
40   O' Balaam's[4] ass;
A broomstick o' the witch of Endor[5],
          Weel shod wi' brass.   well

1 Vide his Antiquities of Scotland. RB.
2 Vide his treatise on ancient armour and weapons. R.B.
3 Genesis, IV, 22.
4 Numbers, XXII, 21.
5 Samuel, I, XXVIII, 7.

Forbye, he'll shape you aff fu' gleg   besides, off full smartly
The cut of Adam's philibeg;   kilt
45   The knife that nicket Abel's craig   cut, throat
        He'll prove you fully,
It was a faulding jocteleg,   folding clasp-knife
        Or lang-kail gullie. —   long cabbage knife

But wad ye see him in his glee,   would
50   For meikle glee and fun has he,   much
Then set him down, and twa or three   two
        Gude fellows wi' him;   good
And *port, O port*! shine thou a wee,   for a little
        And THEN ye'll see him!

55   Now, by the Pow'rs o' Verse and Prose!
Thou art a dainty chield, O Grose! —   fellow
Whae'er o' thee shall ill suppose,   whoever
        They sair misca' thee;   sore miscall
I'd take the rascal by the nose,
60   Wad say, Shame fa' thee.   would, fall

Francis Grose (1731–1791) was born at Greenford, Middlesex, the son of a jeweller who emigrated from Switzerland to England. After obtaining the rank of Captain in service to the Surrey Militia, he used his inheritance to follow an interest in the arts and became a travelling antiquarian, publishing the well-received *The Antiquities of England and Wales* (1773–87).

Various publications of this poem appeared in newspapers and journals throughout Britain after it first featured in the *Edinburgh Evening Courant* in August 1789, under the pen-name Thomas A. Linn, including appearing in the radical Irish newspaper, *The Northern Star*, issue April 14th–18th 1792. Scott Douglas mentions that it appears also in *The Kelso Chronicle*, 4th September, 1789. (Vol. 1, p. 360). The initial title by Burns was an *Address to the People of Scotland*.

Although the comic tone of the poem is added to by the deliberate naïveté of its point of view (ll. 29–30), Burns himself was influenced by the antiquarian, collecting tendencies of the late eighteenth century. Arguably antiquarianism bears a hidden anxiety that the past is not only different but retreating from us so that we need to preserve its artefacts. Burns was also well aware of the absurdity inherent in some forms of supposed preservation as in the brilliant send-up of Biblical bric-a-brac in ll. 37–48. For Tubalcain (l. 37), see *Gen*.iv.22.; Balaam's Ass, *Num*. xxii. 21ff; The Witch of Endor, 1 *Sam*. xxviii.7ff. Burns's deeply affectionate caricature of Grose in a letter to Mrs Dunlop is a small comic gem in itself. It also reveals his intense, admiring reading of the English eighteenth-century novel and its fundamental contribution to his sensibility as well as his own deep interest in local history of place. '. . . if you discover a chearful-looking gig of an old, fat fellow, the precise figure of Dr Slop, wheeling about your avenue in his own carriage with a pencil & paper in his hand, you may conclude, "Thou art the man!" (II *Samuel* 12:7).' It has also been suggested that 'Tubalcain' was Burns deliberately identifying a key word of Masonic ritual employed by both Grose and himself.

To Miss Cruickshank, a Very Young Lady
Written on the Blank Leaf of a Book,
presented to her by the Author
First printed in the Edinburgh edition, 1793.

Beauteous rose-bud, young and gay,
Blooming on thy early May,
Never may'st thou, lovely Flower,
Chilly shrink in sleety shower!
5   Never Boreas' hoary path,
Never Eurus' pois'nous breath,
Never baleful stellar lights,
Taint thee with untimely blights!
Never, never reptile thief
10 Riot on thy virgin leaf!
Nor even Sol too fiercely view
Thy bosom blushing still with dew!

May'st thou long, sweet crimson gem,
Richly deck thy native stem;
15 Till some evening, sober, calm,
Dropping dews and breathing balm,
While all around the woodland rings,
And ev'ry bird thy requiem sings;
Thou, amid the dirgeful sound,
20 Shed thy dying honours round,
And resign to parent Earth
The loveliest form she e'er gave birth.

This was composed for Miss Jean Cruikshank, the only daughter of William, a classics teacher at the High School Edinburgh and colleague of William Nicol (see Letters 142, 214, and 292 for Burns's correspondence to W. Cruikshank). The poem was probably written late in 1788, although dating the letter containing the poem to William Cruikshank is problematic, estimated for sometime in December 1788 or January 1789. Burns first describes the young girl as 'the sweet little Rose-bud' in March, 1788 (Letter 214). David Sillar of Irvine composed the music for these verses.

Anna Thy Charms
First printed in the London *Star*, 18th April, 1789.

Anna, thy charms my bosom fire,
    And waste my soul with care;
But ah! how bootless to admire,
    When fated to despair!

Yet in thy presence, lovely Fair,
    To hope may be forgiven;
For sure 'twere impious to despair
    So much in sight of Heaven.

This song is generally thought to have appeared first in the Edinburgh edition, 1793. It first publication, was, however, in a London newspaper. It is featured the day after *Ode on the Departed Regency Bill* in Peter Stuart's spurious *Star* (so named because another newspaper *The London Star* existed, the spurious Star being formed after Stuart led a breakaway from the main paper). It was copied and printed by *The London Gazetteer* a few days later, 20th April, 1789.

On Reading in a Newspaper, the Death of John M'Leod, Esq.
Brother to a Young Lady,
A Particular Friend of the Author's
First printed in the Edinburgh edition, 1793.

Sad thy tale, thou idle page,
    And rueful thy alarms;
Death tears the brother of her love
    From Isabella's arms.

5   Sweetly deckt with pearly dew
         The morning rose may blow;
     But cold successive noontide blasts
         May lay its beauties low.

     Fair on Isabella's morn
10   The sun propitious smil'd;
     But, long ere noon, succeeding clouds
         Succeeding hopes beguil'd.

     Fate oft tears the bosom chords
         That Nature finest strung:
15   So Isabella's heart was form'd,
         And so that heart was wrung.

     Dread Omnipotence, alone,
         Can heal the wound He gave;
     Can point the brimful grief-worn eyes
20   To scenes beyond the grave.

     Virtue's blossoms there shall blow,
         And fear no withering blast;
     There Isabella's spotless worth
         Shall happy be at last.

This is a poem of condolence to Miss Isabella McLeod, described
by Burns as 'Aunt to the young Countess of Loudon' near Kilmar-
nock (Letter 139). A copy of the poem was included in a letter to
Patrick Miller on 28th September 1787. John McLeod, the younger
brother of Isabella, died on 20th July 1787 and the poem was
composed shortly after Burns read of his death in an Edinburgh
newspaper.

The Humble Petition of Bruar Water,[1]
to the Noble Duke of Athole
First printed in the Edinburgh edition, 1793.

     My Lord, I know, your noble ear
         Woe ne'er assails in vain;
     Embolden'd thus, I beg you'll hear
         Your humble slave complain,

1 Bruar Falls, in Athole, are exceedingly picturesque and beautiful; but their
effect is much impaired by the want of trees and shrubs. – R.B.

5   How saucy Phoebus' scorching beams,   the Sun
        In flaming summer-pride,
    Dry-withering, waste my foamy streams,
        And drink my crystal tide.

    The lightly-jumping, glowrin' trouts,   staring/keen-eyed
10   That thro' my waters play,
    If, in their random, wanton spouts,   darts
        They near the margin stray;
    If, hapless chance! they linger lang,   long
        I'm scorching up so shallow,
15 They're left the whitening stanes amang,   stones among
        In gasping death to wallow.

    Last day I grat wi' spite and teen,   wept, vexation
        As Poet Burns came by,
    That, to a Bard, I should be seen
20   Wi' half my channel dry:
    A panegyric rhyme, I ween,   trust
        Ev'n as I was he shor'd me;   threatened/offered
    But, had I in my glory been,
        He, kneeling, wad ador'd me.   would have

25 Here, foaming down the skelvy rocks,   shelved
        In twisting strength I rin;   run/flow
    There high my boiling torrent smokes,
        Wild-roaring o'er a linn: a waterfall
    Enjoying large each spring and well
30   As Nature gave them me,
    I am, altho' I say't mysel,
        Worth gaun a mile to see.   going

    Would, then my noble master please
        To grant my highest wishes,
35 He'll shade my banks wi' towering trees,
        And bonie spreading bushes.   bonny
    Delighted doubly then, my Lord,
        You'll wander on my banks,
    And listen mony a grateful bird   many
40   Return you tuneful thanks.

The sober laverock, warbling wild,   lark
    Shall to the skies aspire;
The gowdspink, Music's gayest child,   goldfinch
    Shall sweetly join the choir:
45 The blackbird strong, the lintwhite clear,   linnet
    The mavis mild and mellow;
The robin pensive Autumn cheer
    In all her locks of yellow.

This, too, a covert shall ensure,
50   To shield them from the storm;
And coward maukin sleep secure,   hare
    Low in her grassy form: bed
Here shall the shepherd make his seat,
    To weave his crown of flowers;
55 Or find a sheltering, safe retreat,
    From prone-descending showers.

And here, by sweet, endearing stealth,
    Shall meet the loving pair,
Despising worlds with all their wealth,
60   As empty idle care:
The flowers shall vie in all their charms
    The hour of heaven to grace,
And birks extend their fragrant arms   birch trees
    To screen the dear embrace.

65 Here haply too, at vernal dawn,
    Some musing Bard may stray,
And eye the smoking, dewy lawn,
    And misty mountain, grey;
Or, by the reaper's nightly beam,
70   Mild-chequering thro' the trees,
Rave to my darkly dashing stream,
    Hoarse-swelling on the breeze.

Let lofty firs, and ashes cool
    My lowly banks o'erspread,
75 And view, deep-bending in the pool,
    Their shadows' wat'ry bed:
Let fragrant birks, in woodbines drest,   birches, dressed
    My craggy cliffs adorn;
And, for the little songster's nest,
80   The close embowering thorn.

So may Old Scotia's darling hope,
  Your little angel band,
Spring, like their fathers, up to prop
  Their honour'd, native land!
85 So may, thro' Albion's farthest ken,
  To social-flowing glasses,
The grace be — 'Athole's honest men
  And Athole's bonie lasses!'

This was composed during the first week of September 1787, when the poet was touring the Highlands. Writing from Inverness on 5th September, Burns sent a copy of the poem to Josiah Walker, tutor to the Duke of Atholl's son. He told Walker, 'I have just time to write the foregoing, and to tell you that it was, at least most part of it, the effusion of the half hour that I spent at Bruar. – I don't mean that it was extempore, for I have endeavoured to brush it up as well as Mr Nicol's chat and the jogging of the chaise would allow' (Letter 135). Walker replied by telling Burns how well his poem was received at Blair Atholl and that the family wished to see it in print. He responded to this idea: 'I would not like it published in any other newspaper than a magazine, nor there, but as if by chance, and "said" to be done by such a Man: but it is to me a matter totally indifferent: you are at perfect liberty to do as you please' (Letter 140). This final comment reveals how Burns instructed Walker on the manner in which the poem was to be printed and 'said' to be by him, a move that would, during this period, add some mystique to the publication and Burns would not be seen as a self-publicist. Of course, it was not an indifferent matter to him; all his poetic compositions were the 'offspring' of his Muse or creative genius and he would have been quietly delighted if the poem appeared in print. Later, Walker, appointed Professor at the University of Glasgow, looked back on the poet's visit to the castle at Blair Atholl, recording that it was 'ability alone that gave him [Burns] a title to be there' (Scott Douglas, Vol. I, p. 367).

This work makes an interesting comparison to *On the Destruction of the Trees at Drumlanrig*, a poem presented to the world as a work of Burns, but then claimed by Henry Mackenzie, although he did not add it to *his* collected writings.

On Scaring Some Water-Fowl in Loch Turit,
A Wild Scene among the Hills of Oughtertyre
First printed in the Edinburgh edition, 1793.

Why, ye tenants of the lake,
For me your wat'ry haunt forsake?
Tell me, fellow-creatures, why
At my presence thus you fly?
5   Why disturb your social joys,
Parent, filial, kindred ties? —
Common friend to you and me,
Nature's gifts to all are free:
Peaceful keep your dimpling wave,
10   Busy feed, or wanton lave;
Or, beneath the sheltering rock,
Bide the surging billow's shock.

Conscious, blushing for our race,
Soon, too soon, your fears I trace:
15   Man, your proud usurping foe,
Would be lord of all below:
Plumes himself in Freedom's pride,
Tyrant stern to all beside.

The eagle, from the cliffy brow,
20   Marking you his prey below,
In his breast no pity dwells,
Strong Necessity compels.
But Man, to whom alone is given
A ray direct from pitying Heaven,
25   Glories in his heart humane —
And creatures for his pleasure slain.

In these savage, liquid plains,
Only known to wandering swains,
Where the mossy riv'let strays,
30   Far from human haunts and ways;
All on Nature you depend,
And life's poor season peaceful spend.

Or, if Man's superior might
Dare invade your native right,

35 On the lofty ether borne,
    Man with all his powers you scorn;
    Swiftly seek, on clanging wings,
    Other lakes and other springs;
    And the foe you cannot brave,
40 Scorn at least to be his slave.

A note by Burns in his Glenriddell Manuscript reads: 'This was a production of a solitary forenoon's walk from Ochtertyre-house. – I lived there, Sir William's guest, for two or three weeks, and was much flattered by my hospitable reception. – What a pity that the mere emotions of gratitude are so impotent in this world! 'Tis lucky that, as we are told, they will be of some avail in the world to come.' The poet met Sir William Murray of Ochtertyre (1705–1793), the Earl of Mansfield, when visiting Blair Atholl in the first week of September 1787 and later visited the old man at his home in Strathearn, where he composed this work in October 1787. Euphemia Murray, a young cousin of Sir William, and daughter of Mungo Murray of Lintrose, is the subject of the poet's song, *Blythe Was She*. Euphemia was known as the 'flower of Strathmore'. The poem is another example of Burns's preoccupation with man as bestial predator.

Verses Written with a Pencil
over the Chimney-Piece, in the Parlour of the Inn
at Kenmore, Taymouth

First printed in *The Edinburgh Evening Courant*, 6th September 1787.

Admiring Nature in her wildest grace,
These northern scenes with weary feet I trace;
O'er many a winding dale and painful steep,
Th' abodes of coveyed grouse and timid sheep,
5   My savage journey, curious, I pursue,
    Till fam'd Breadalbane opens to my view. —
    The meeting cliffs each deep-sunk glen divides,
    The woods, wild-scattered, clothe their ample sides;
    Th' outstretching lake, embosomed 'mong the hills,
10 The eye with wonder and amazement fills;
    The Tay, meandering sweet in infant pride,
    The palace, rising on his verdant side;
    The lawns, wood-fring'd in Nature's native taste;
    The hillocks, dropt in Nature's careless haste,
15 The arches, striding o'er the new-born stream;
    The village, glittering in the noontide beam —

Poetic ardors in my bosom swell,
Lone wand'ring by the hermit's mossy cell:
The sweeping theatre of hanging woods;
20   The incessant roar of headlong tumbling floods —

Here Poesy might wake her heaven-taught lyre,
And look through Nature with creative fire;
Here, to the wrongs of Fate half reconcil'd,
Misfortune's lightened steps might wander wild;
25   And Disappointment, in these lonely bounds,
Find balm to soothe her bitter rankling wounds:
Here heart-struck Grief might heavenward stretch her scan,
And injur'd Worth forget and pardon man.

When published in the *Edinburgh Evening Courant* these verses were
described as the work of the 'celebrated Ayrshire bard' and found by
an unknown person, who gives only their initials, 'O.B.', while on
visit to Taymouth, where the verses were found on a Hermitage
wall. Most editors guess that Burns himself sent the verses to the
newspaper. A further variant edition appears in *The Bee* magazine
on 9th May 1792, under the title *Verses Written on a Window in
Breadalbane*, by Mr Robert Burns. There are several textual
changes between the two versions. The copy in *The Bee* is probably
a textual improvement made by Burns taken from a manuscript sent
to a friend as there is no evidence that Burns visited Breadalbane on
a second tour. If this is the case, Burns appears to have reverted to
the earlier version when including the poem in his 1793 Edinburgh
edition.

Written with a Pencil Standing by the Fall of Fyers, near Loch Ness

First printed in the Edinburgh edition, 1793.

Among the heathy hills and ragged woods
The roaring Fyers pours his mossy floods;
Till full he dashes on the rocky mounds,
Where, thro' a shapeless breach, his stream resounds,
5   As high in air the bursting torrents flow,
As deep recoiling surges foam below,
Prone down the rock the whitening sheet descends,
And viewless Echo's ear, astonished, rends.

Dim-seen through rising mists and ceaseless showers,
10 The hoary cavern, wide-surrounding, lours.
Still thro' the gap the struggling river toils,
And still, below, the horrid caldron boils —

This was composed around 5th September 1787, when Burns travelled from Loch Ness to Foyers. In form and metre, this verse follows on from the pastoral sketch of the previous work, on the scenic view from Breadalbane.

On the Birth of a Posthumous Child,
Born in Peculiar Circumstances of Family-Distress
First printed in the Edinburgh edition, 1793.

Sweet flow'ret, pledge o' meikle love,	much
And ward o' mony a prayer,	many
What heart o' stane wad thou na move,	stone would, not
Sae helpless, sweet, and fair.	so
5 November hirples o'er the lea,	limps
Chill, on thy lovely form;	
And gane, alas! the shelt'ring tree,	gone
Should shield thee frae the storm	from
May He who gives the rain to pour,	
10 And wings the blast to blaw,	blow
Protect thee frae the driving show'r,	from
The bitter frost and snaw!	snow
May He, the friend of Woe and Want,	
Who heals life's various stounds,	pangs/pains
15 Protect and guard the mother plant,	
And heal her cruel wounds.	
But late she flourished, rooted fast,	
Fair on the summer morn:	
Now, feebly bends she, in the blast,	
20 Unsheltered and forlorn.	
Blest be thy bloom, thou lovely gem,	
Unscath'd by ruffian hand!	
And from thee many a parent stem	
Arise to deck our land.	

The head-note to this poem, in the Glenriddell Manuscripts, reads: 'Extempore nearly – On the Birth of Monsr. Henri, posthumous child to a Monsr. Henri, a Gentleman of family and fortune from Switzerland; who died after three days illness, leaving his lady, a sister of Sir Thos. Wallace, in her sixth month of this her first child. – The lady and her Family were particular friends of the Author. – The child was born in November 1790'. James Henri married Mrs Dunlop's daughter Susan, but died 22nd June, 1790. Burns wrote to Mrs Dunlop, on hearing of the birth, 'I literally, *jumped for joy* . . . out skipt I among the broomy banks of Nith to muse over my joy by retail. – To keep within the bounds of prose was impossible. Mrs Little's is a more elegant, but not a more sincere Compliment to the sweet little fellow, than I extempore almost poured out to him in the following verses' (Letter 427).

   N.B. The Whistle: A Ballad was the last work printed in the 1793 Edinburgh edition. It was first published in Johnson's fourth volume of the *Scots Musical Museum*, August 1792 and is therefore printed in the next section, songs published by Burns during his lifetime.

PART FOUR

The Songs of Burns
Published During His Lifetime

Young Peggy

Tune: The Last Time I came O'er the Moor
First printed in the S.M.M., Vol. I, 22nd May, 1787.

Young Peggy blooms our boniest lass,
    Her blush is like the morning,
The rosy dawn, the springing grass,
    With early gems adorning:
5 Her eyes outshine the radiant beams
    That gild the passing shower,
And glitter o'er the crystal streams,
    And cheer each fresh'ning flower.

Her lips, more than the cherries bright,
10   A richer dye has grac'd them,
They charm th' admiring gazer's sight
    And sweetly tempt to taste them:
Her smile is as the ev'ning mild,
    When feather'd pairs are courting,
15 And little lambkins wanton wild,
    In playful bands disporting.

Were Fortune lovely Peggy's foe,
    Such sweetness would relent her,
As blooming Spring unbends the brow
20   Of surly, savage Winter.
Detraction's eye no aim can gain
    Her winning pow'rs to lessen;
And fretful Envy grins in vain,
    The poison'd tooth to fasten.

25 Ye Pow'rs of Honour, Love, and Truth,
    From ev'ry ill defend her;
Inspire the highly-favour'd Youth
    The destinies intend her;
Still fan the sweet connubial flame
30   Responsive in each bosom;
And bless the dear parental name
    With many a filial blossom.

Young Peggy was Margaret Kennedy (1766–95), daughter of Robert Kennedy of Daljarrock, where he worked as the factor to the Earl of Cassilis. The poet met Margaret because her father was Gavin Hamilton's brother-in-law. Burns sent a copy of the song in a letter to Miss Kennedy in the Autumn of 1785:

> Permit me to present you with the enclosed SONG, as a small tho' grateful tribute for the honour of your acquaintance. I have, in these verses, attempted some faint sketches of your PORTRAIT in the unimbellished, simple manner of descriptive TRUTH. Flattery I leave to your LOVERS; whose exaggerating Fancies may make them imagine you still nearer, if possible, to Perfection than you really are.
>
> . . . even the sight of a fine flower, or the company of a fine Woman (by far the finest part of God's works below), have sensations for the poetic heart that the HERD of Man are strangers to. . . . I am, as in many other things, indebted to Mr Hamilton's kindness in introducing me to you (Letter 20).

The aspirations of the last stanza are tragically ironic, given what happened to Margaret Kennedy nine years later, when, in 1794, she had an affair with a Captain Andrew McDoul, whose child she bore, resulting in a paternity row in which McDoul denied being the child's father. Young Peggy died before the £3000 award was made for the child's maintenance.

Johnson appears to have selected his own tune, *Loch Eroch Side*, when he printed the song. The poet was advised not to print the song in his Edinburgh edition (Letters 90 and 88) and decided to send it to the S.M.M.

Bonie Dundee

First printed in the S.M.M., Vol. 1, 22nd May, 1787.

'O whar did ye get that hauver-meal bannock?'		where, oatmeal
O silly blind body, O dinna ye see;		do you not
I gat it frae a young, brisk Sodger Laddie,		got, from, soldier
Between Saint Johnston and bonie Dundee.		Perth
5 O gin I saw the laddie that gae me't!		if, gave
Aft has he doudl'd me up on his knee;		often, dandled
May Heaven protect my bonie Scots laddie,		
And send him hame to his babie and me.		home

'My blessin's upon thy sweet, wee lippie!   lips
10   My blessins upon thy bonie e'e brie!   eyebrow
Thy smiles are sae like my blythe Sodger   Laddie, so,
    Thou's ay the dearer and dearer to me!
But I'll big a bow'r on yon bonie banks,   build
    Whare Tay rins wimplin by sae clear;   where, runs, so
15 And I'll cleed thee in the tartan sae fine,   clothe, so
    And mak thee a man like thy daddie dear.'   make

This is an updated version of a traditional song. The first verse is improved, the second is from Burns. The description 'hauver-meal bannock' is a euphemistic reference to being pregnant and showing it.

To the Weaver's Gin Ye Go

Tune: To the Weaver's Gin ye Go
First printed in the S.M.M., Vol. 2, 14th February, 1788.

My heart was ance as blythe and free,
    As simmer days were lang,   summer, long
But a bonie, westlin weaver lad   from the West
    Had gart me change my sang.   made, song

Chorus
5 To the weaver's gin ye go, fair maids,   if
To the weaver's gin ye go,   if
I rede you right, gang ne'er at night,   warn, go
To the weaver's gin ye go.   if

My mither sent me to the town   mother
10   To warp a plaiden wab;
But the weary, weary warpin o't
    Has gart me sigh and sab.   made, sob
To the weaver's &c.

A bonie, westlin weaver lad
    Sat working at his loom;
15 He took my heart, as wi' a net
    In every knot and thrum.
      To the weaver's &c.

I sat beside my warpin-wheel,
    And ay I ca'd it roun';   *always, drove*
And every shot and every knock,
20   My heart it gae a stoun.   *gave, thump*
        To the weaver's &c.

The moon was sinking in the west
    Wi' visage pale and wan,
As my bonie, westlin weaver lad
    Convoy'd me thro' the glen.
        To the weaver's &c.

25 But what was said, or what was done,
    Shame fa' me gin I tell;   *fall on, if*
But Oh! I fear the kintra soon   *countryside*
    Will ken as weel's mysel!   *know, as well as*
        To the weaver's &c.

This is based on an old song but the lyrics, bar the chorus, are from
Burns. The poet comments:

> The chorus of this song is old, the rest of it is mine. Here, once
> for all, let me apologise for many silly compositions of mine in
> this work. Many beautiful airs wanted words; in the hurry of
> other avocations, if I could string a parcel of rhymes together
> anything near tolerable, I was fain to let them pass. He must be
> an excellent poet indeed, whose every performance is excellent.

This self-deprecatory remark should not be taken seriously. Burns
had a phenomenal capacity to evolve lyrics from traditional music.
Having brought him wool to weave, the girl finds herself caught not
only in the rhythm of the shuttle but of the penis. The garment is
made and she also finds herself pregnant.

I'm o'er Young to Marry Yet

Tune: I'm o'er Young to Marry Yet
First printed in the S.M.M., Vol. 2, 14th February, 1788.

I am my mammie's ae bairn,   *one child*
    Wi' unco folk I weary, Sir,   *strangers*
And lying in a man's bed,
    I'm fley'd it make me irie, Sir.   *frightened/melancholy*

Chorus
5 I'm owre young, I'm owre young,   too
    I'm owre young to marry yet;
I'm owre young, 'twad be a sin
    To tak me frae my mammie yet.   from

Hallowmass is come and gane,   All Saints' Day, gone
10   The nights are lang in winter, Sir;   long
And you an' I in ae bed,   one
    In trowth, I dare na venture, Sir.   truth, not
      I'm o'er young, &c.

Fu' loud and shrill the frosty wind   full
    Blaws thro' the leafless timmer, Sir;   blows, timber/trees
15 But if ye come this gate again,
    I'll aulder be gin simmer, Sir.   older, come, summer
      I'm o'er young, &c.

This is a traditional song re-written by Burns. He kept the original
chorus and added new verses. The lyric plays on the subject of
viginity with the promise that, come next summer, the young lass
will let her suitor have his way. The female voices of these songs are
constantly frank and honest about their sexual desires.

The Birks of Aberfeldey –

First printed in the S.M.M., Vol. 2, 14th February, 1788.

Now Simmer blinks on flow'ry braes,   summer, hillsides
And o'er the crystal streamlets plays;
Come let us spend the lightsome days
    In the birks of Aberfeldey. –

Chorus
5 Bonie lassie, will ye go,
Will ye go, will ye go,
Bonie lassie, will ye go
    To the birks of Aberfeldey?

The little birdies blythely sing   happily
10 While o'er their heads the hazels hing,   hang
Or lightly flit on wanton wing
    In the birks of Aberfeldey. –

The braes ascend like lofty wa's,   walls
The foaming stream, deep-roaring fa's   falls
15 O'er hung with fragrant-spreading shaws,   leaves
    The birks of Aberfeldey. –

The hoary cliffs are crown'd wi' flowers,
White o'er the linns the burnie pours,   waterfall, small burn/stream
And, rising, weets wi' misty showers   makes wet
20 The birks of Aberfeldey. –

Let Fortune's gifts at random flee,
They ne'er shall draw a wish frae me,   from
Supremely blest wi' love and thee
    In the birks of Aberfeldey. –

Composed during the poet's tour of the Highlands in 1787. Burns
has a predilection for rivers and streams as the essence of the spirit of
place.

McPherson's Farewell

Tune: McPherson's Farewell
First printed in the S.M.M., Vol. 2, 14th February, 1788.

Farewell, ye dungeons dark and strong,
    The wretch's destinie!
M'Pherson's time will not be long,
    On yonder gallows-tree.

Chorus
5 Sae rantingly, sae wantonly,   riotously
    Sae dauntingly gae'd he: went
He play'd a spring, and danc'd it round   tune
    Below the gallows-tree.

O what is death but parting breath?
10   On many a bloody plain
I've dar'd his face, and in this place
    I scorn him yet again!
        Sae rantingly, &c.

Untie these bands from off my hands,
    And bring to me my sword,
15 And there's no a man in all Scotland
    But I'll brave him at a word.
        Sae rantingly, &c.

I've liv'd a life of sturt and strife;   trouble
    I die by treacherie:
It burns my heart I must depart
20   And not avenged be.
        Sae rantingly, &c.

Now farewell, light, thou sunshine bright,
    And all beneath the sky!
May coward shame distain his name,
    The wretch that dares not die!
        Sae rantingly, &c.

This song immortalises James MacPherson (illegitimate son of a
gentleman to a gypsy woman), a cattle thief who robbed in Moray-
shire and was hanged on 7th November, 1700. While myth and
folklore enshrine Macpherson's memory, it does seem factually true
that he did play a fiddle tune of his own composition prior to his
execution and then, before the crowd, destroyed his fiddle. Burns, in
opposition to the original ballad of the early 1700s, which was a
'confessional and crudely moralistic' song (Low, *The Songs of
Robert Burns*, p. 232) warning others not to steal cattle, character-
istically presents Macpherson as a rebellious hero.

My Highland Lassie, O
Tune: McLauchlin's Scots-Measure
First printed in the S.M.M., Vol. 2, 14th February, 1788.

Nae gentle dames, tho' ne'er sae fair,   no, so
Shall ever be my Muse's care;
Their titles a' are empty show;
Gie me my Highland Lassie, O.   give

Chorus
5 Within the glen sae bushy, O,   so
Aboon the plain sae rashy, O,   above, so rushy
I set me down wi' right guid will,   good
To sing my Highland Lassie, O.

O were yon hills and valleys mine,
10   Yon palace and yon gardens fine!
The world then the love should know
I bear my Highland Lassie, O.
    Within the glen &c.

But fickle Fortune frowns on me,
And I maun cross the raging sea;   *must*
15   But while my crimson currents flow,   *blood*
I'll love my Highland Lassie, O.
    Within the glen &c.

Altho' thro' foreign climes I range,
I know her heart will never change,
For her bosom burns with honor's glow,
20   My faithful Highland Lassie, O.
    Within the glen &c.

For her I'll dare the billows' roar;
For her I'll trace a distant shore;
That Indian wealth may lustre throw
Around my Highland Lassie, O.
    Within the glen &c.

25   She has my heart, she has my hand,
My secret troth and honor's band!
'Till the mortal stroke shall lay me low,
I'm thine, my Highland Lassie, O.

Final Chorus

Farewell, the glen sae bushy, O!   *so*
30   Farewell, the plain sae rashy, O!   *so*
To other lands I now must go
To sing my Highland Lassie, O.

This is an early work of Burns referring to Mary Campbell, so-called 'Highland Mary', whose premature death has provoked a myriad of largely pointless speculation. To some extent Burns himself in later life was responsible for this mythification of Mary Campbell; see, for example, Cromek's *Reliques* (1808), p. 237.

Though Cruel Fate

Tune: She Raise and Loot Me In *or* The Northern Lass.
First printed in the S.M.M., Vol. 2, 14th February, 1788.

Though cruel Fate should bid us part,
    Far as the Pole and Line,
Her dear idea round my heart
    Should tenderly entwine:

Though mountains rise, and desarts howl,
    And oceans roar between;
Yet dearer than my deathless soul
    I still would love my Jean.

This is signed as a work from Burns in Johnson's S.M.M. and unlike the songs marked only with an X or Z, it is original. It is essentially the progenitor of *Of A' The Airts*, written for Jean Armour.

Stay, My Charmer, Can You Leave Me

Tune: An Gille dubh ciar dhubh
First printed in the S.M.M., Vol. 2, 14th February, 1788.

Stay, my charmer, can you leave me?
Cruel, cruel to deceive me!
Well you know how much you grieve me:
    Cruel charmer, can you go!
5   Cruel charmer, can you go!

By my love so ill-requited:
By the faith you fondly plighted;
By the pangs of lovers slighted;
    Do not, do not leave me so!
10   Do not, do not leave me so!

Burns adored fiddle music, particularly sad, evocative and melodic slow airs. Accordingly, he wrote this lyric for a Highland air he heard during his tour of the Highlands in 1787. Scotland was, particularly after the 1745, fertile in tragic slow airs and defiant fast ones. Burns himself was defined as a 'home fiddler'; that is an amateur not good enough for public performance.

Strathallan's Lament

Tune: As song title.
First printed in the S.M.M., Vol. 2, 14th February, 1788.

Thickest night, surround my dwelling!
    Howling tempests, o'er me rave!
Turbid torrents wintry-swelling,
    Roaring by my lonely cave.
5 Crystal streamlets gently flowing,
    Busy haunts of base mankind,
Western breezes softly blowing,
    Suit not my distracted mind.

In the cause of Right engaged,
10   Wrongs injurious to redress,
Honor's war we strongly waged,
    But the Heavens deny'd success:
Ruin's wheel has driven o'er us,
    Not a hope that dare attend,
15 The wide world is all before us —
    But a world without a friend!

A haunting, evocative, and powerful Jacobite lyric, this elegiac monologue gives voice to the mourning of James Drummond, whose father, William, Viscount Strathallan, died at the battle of Culloden, 1746. The son fled, taking refuge in a cave, the setting of this first person lament. Unlike earlier commentators, Donaldson interprets this mythically rather than historically, believing it sung from the mouth of William Drummond, the dead father (pp. 80–1). The first stanza sets the scene and mood in poignant juxtaposition, nature's raw beauty contrasted with human desolation. The ferocious winter nightscape is, for a Jacobite, an appropriate metaphor for the complete destruction of his world.

A peculiar mirror image of this poem was collected by Scott Hogg in 1996 from *The Morning Chronicle*, August 1795 and considered by him as possibly by Burns. *Exiles* is written not about a Jacobite exile, but the exile of Thomas Muir, Fysche Palmer and the other radical martyrs of this period. Metrically and musically *Exiles* exactly fits *Strathallan's Lament*. The iconic, 'arm'd' Wallace is also compatible with Burns's newly discovered Bruce poems. It is difficult to imagine any specifically Scottish poem appearing in the *Chronicle* from any other source. It is also wholly characteristic of Burns to take a Jacobite theme and recontextualise it in a Radical

context. It can also be read in its last two stanzas as an embryonic
version of *Ode for General Washington's Birthday*.

    Dark in misty horror glooming,
        Where the Southern Ocean roars
    And the hoary Billows booming,
        Ceaseless lash barbaric shores,
5   Round the beach in deep emotion,
        Sternly rov'd a mournful train,
    While along the expanse of Ocean
        Echoed far the Patriot strain.

        . . . Arm'd alone with Truth and Reason,
10   Mammon's venal slaves we dar'd;
        Short of triumph was the season: -
    Virtue, view the base reward.

    Doom'd among these wilds to languish,
        Exil'd from our native shore;
15   Friends bewail in bitter anguish,
        Victims they behold no more.
    What the cause of our destruction?
        Tell th' astonish'd world around;
    'Twas the combat with Corruption;
20   Britain feels her mortal wound!

    Scotland, once our boast, our wonder,
        Fann'd by Freedom's purer gale,
    When thy Wallace, arm'd with thunder,
        Bade the baffl'd TYRANT wail:
25   O, our Country! Vultures rend thee,
        Proudly riot on thy store;
    Who deluded, shall befreind thee?
        Ah! do we thy lot deplore.

What Will I Do Gin My Hoggie Die

Tune: Moss Platt
First printed in the S.M.M., Vol. 2, 14th February, 1788.

What will I do gin my Hoggie die,	if, lamb
My joy, my pride, my Hoggie;	lamb
My only beast, I had nae mae,	no more
And vow but I was vogie. —	vain

5   The lee-lang night we watch'd the fauld,   *live-long, fold*
      Me and my faithfu' doggie;
    We heard nocht but the roaring linn   *nothing, waterfall*
      Amang the braes sae scroggie. —   *hillsides, so, scrub-covered*

    But the houlet cry'd frae the Castle-wa',   *owl, from, wall*
10   The blitter frae the boggie,   *snipe, from*
      The tod reply'd upon the hill,   *fox*
      I trembled for my Hoggie.   *lamb*

    When day did daw and cocks did craw,   *dawn, crow*
      The morning it was foggie;
15   An unco tyke lap o'er the dyke   *strange dog, stone wall*
      And maist has kill'd my Hoggie.   *almost, lamb*

Given his life long intimacy with and empathy for domestic and wild animals, this traditional song was particularly attractive to Burns.

Jumpin John
First printed in the S.M.M., Vol. 2, 14th February, 1788.

Her Daddie forbad, her Minnie forbad;
    Forbidden she wadna be: *would not*
She wadna trow't, the browst she brew'd   *would not believe it*
    Wad taste sae bitterlie.   *would, so*

Chorus
5   The lang lad they ca' jumpin John   *long, call*
      Beguil'd the bonie lassie,
    The lang lad they ca' jumpin John
      Beguil'd the bonie lassie.

A cow and a cauf, a yowe and a hauf,   *calf, sheep & lamb*
10   And thretty guid shillins and three;   *thirty good*
A vera gude tocher, a cotter-man's dochter,   *very good dowry, daughter*
    The lass with the bonie black e'e.   *eye*
      The lang lad &c.

Kinsley remarks 'Stenhouse says that this is "a fragment of the old humorous ballad, with some verbal corrections"; but the "ballad" has not been identified' (Vol. III, no. 199, p. 1263). Stenhouse clearly did not know the old song adapted by Burns which is

certainly *My Daddie Forbade* in Herd's Collection, beginning
'Though my Daddie forbade, and my Minnie forbade, /Forbidden
I will not be'. It is likely there never was an 'old humorous ballad'.

Up in the Morning Early

First printed in the S.M.M., Vol. 2, 14th February, 1788.

Cauld blaws the wind frae east to west,	cold, blows, from
The drift is driving sairly;	sorely
Sae loud and shill's I hear the blast,	so, shrill
I'm sure it's winter fairly.	

Chorus
5 Up in the morning's no for me,
     Up in the morning early;

When a' the hills are covered wi' snaw,	snow
I'm sure it's winter fairly.	

The birds sit chittering in the thorn,	
10 A' day they fare but sparely;	
And lang's the night frae e'en to morn,	long is, from
I'm sure it's winter fairly.	
Up in the morning's &c.	

The chorus of this is traditional, but the verses are by Burns.

The Dusty Miller

First printed in the S.M.M., Vol. 2, 14th February, 1788.

Hey the dusty Miller,
    And his dusty coat;
He will spend a shilling
    Or he win a groat:
5 Dusty was the coat,
    Dusty was the colour;
Dusty was the kiss

That I gat frae the Miller. —	got from

Hey the dusty Miller,
10   And his dusty sack;
Leeze me on the calling
    Fills the dusty peck:

       Fills the dusty peck,
          Brings the dusty siller;   money/coins
15   I wad gie my coatie   would give
          For the dusty Miller.

A traditional song adapted slightly by Burns. See Kinsley's notes
(Vol. III, no. 201, p. 1264), where he quotes the earlier lines: 'O the
dusty miller, O the dusty miller, / Dusty was his coat, dusty was his
colour, / Dusty was the kiss I got frae the miller'.

The Young Highland Rover

Tune: Morag.

First printed in the S.M.M., Vol. 2, 14th February, 1788.

       Loud blaw the frosty breezes,   blow
          The snaws the mountains cover;   snows
       Like winter on me seizes,
          Since my young Highland rover
5   Far wanders nations over.

       Chorus
       Where'er he go, where'er he stray,
          May Heaven be his warden;
       Return him safe to fair Strathspey
          And bonie Castle-Gordon. —

10   The trees, now naked groaning,
          Shall soon wi' leaves be hinging,
       The birdies dowie moaning   dolefully
          Shall a' be blythely singing,
          And every flower be springing.

       Second Chorus
15   Sae I'll rejoice the lee-lang day,   live long
          When by his mighty Warden
       My Youth's return'd to fair Strathspey
          And bonie Castle-Gordon.

This was written as a result of the poet's tour of the Highlands and
his visit to Castle Gordon in September 1787 to see the Duchess of
Gordon. Burns, keenly aware of Jacobite history, knew that Prince
Charles Edward Stuart visited Castle Gordon sometime before the
battle of Culloden.

The Winter It is Past

First printed in the S.M.M., Vol. 2, 14th February, 1788.

The winter it is past, and the summer's comes at last,
    And the small birds sing on ev'ry tree;
The hearts of these are glad, but mine is very sad,
    For my Lover has parted from me.

5   The rose upon the brier, by the waters running clear,
    May have charms for the linnet or the bee;
Their little loves are blest and their little hearts at rest,
    But my Lover is parted from me.

My love is like the sun, in the firmament does run,
10   For ever is constant and true;
But his is like the moon that wanders up and down,
    And every month it is new.

All you that are in love and cannot it remove,
    I pity the pains you endure:
15 For experience makes me know that your hearts are full of woe,
    A woe that no mortal can cure.

This is adapted from a lyric *The Love Sick Maid* published in 1765. The original words tell the story of an Irish woman whose lover, a highway robber, was hanged at the Curragh of Kildare, leaving her to mourn. Mackay has dropped the final two stanzas, which appear in S.M.M and most major editions, including Henley and Henderson and Kinsley.

I Dream'd I Lay

Tune: I Dream'd I Lay
First printed in the S.M.M., Vol. 2, 14th February, 1788.

I dream'd I lay where flowers were springing
    Gaily in the sunny beam,
List'ning to the wild birds singing,
    By a falling, chrystal stream;
5   Streight the sky grew black and daring,
    Thro' the woods the whirlwinds rave;
Trees with aged arms were warring,
    O'er the swelling, drumlie wave.   turbid

Such was my life's deceitful morning,
10   Such the pleasures I enjoy'd;
But lang or noon, loud tempests storming—   ere
    A' my flowery bliss destroy'd.
Tho' fickle Fortune has deceiv'd me,
    She promis'd fair, and perform'd but ill;
15 Of mony a joy and hope bereav'd me,   many
    I bear a heart shall support me still.

Burns wrote 'These two stanzas I composed when I was seventeen'.
Composition is therefore sometime in 1776. This provides another
example of the degree to which he was early, presciently haunted by
an ill-fated life.

Duncan Davison

First printed in the S.M.M., Vol. 2, 14th February, 1788.

There was a lass, they ca'd her Meg,   called
    And she held o'er the moors to spin;
There was a lad that follow'd her,
    They ca'd him Duncan Davison.   called
5 The moor was dreigh, and Meg was skeigh,   dull, fiery
    Her favour Duncan could na win;   not
For wi' the rock she wad him knock,   would
    And ay she shook the temper-pin.   speed regulator pin

As o'er the moor they lightly foor,   went
10   A burn was clear, a glen was green,
Upon the banks they eas'd their shanks,   rested limbs/legs
    And ay she set the wheel between:
But Duncan swoor a haly aith   swore, holy oath
That Meg should be a bride the morn;
15   Then Meg took up her spinnin-graith,   equipment
And flang them a' out o'er the burn.   threw

We will big a wee, wee house,   build
    And we will live like king and queen;
Sae blythe and merry's we will be,   so
20   When ye set by the wheel at e'en.   evening
A man may drink and no be drunk,
    A man may fight and no be slain:
A man may kiss a bonie lass,
    And ay be welcome back again.

Burns signed this with a 'Z' when published by Johnson to indicate that he had either made 'corrections, or additions' to a traditional work. The final lines have a natural flow indicative of Burns, as found in his version of *Logan Braes*.

Theniel Menzies' Bonie Mary

Tune: The Ruffian's Rant, or Roy's Wife
First printed in the S.M.M., Vol. 2, 14th February, 1788.

In comin by the brig o' Dye,   bridge
    At Darlet we a blink did tarry;   short while, stopped
As day was dawin in the sky   dawning
    We drank a health to bonie Mary. —

Chorus
5 Theniel Menzies' bonie Mary,
    Theniel Menzies' bonie Mary,
Charlie Grigor tint his plaidie   lost his plaid
    Kissin Theniel's bonie Mary. —

Her een sae bright, her brow sae white,   eyes so, so
10   Her haffet locks as brown's a berry,   temple
And ay they dimpl't wi' a smile,
    The rosy cheeks o' bonie Mary. —
      Theniel Menzies' &c.

We lap an' danc'd the lee-lang day,   jumped, live long
    Till Piper lads were wae and weary;   worn out
15 But Charlie gat the spring to pay   got
    For kissin Theniel's bonie Mary. —
      Theniel Menzies' &c.

The river Dye is near Stonehaven. The poet visited the area (where some of his relatives lived) with William Nicol on 10th September, 1787 during his tour of the Highlands. The music for the lyric is a strathspey known under the two titles listed above. Kinsley is probably right that the words are adapted from an original bawdy song.

Lady Onlie, Honest Lucky,
or A' the Lads o' Thorniebank
Tune: The Ruffian's Rant
First printed in the S.M.M., Vol. 2, 14th February, 1788.

A' the lads o' Thornie-bank
    When they gae to the shore o' Bucky,   go
They'll step in an' tak a pint   take
    Wi' Lady Onlie, honest lucky. —

Chorus
5 Lady Onlie, honest lucky,
    Brews gude ale at shore o' Bucky;   good
I wish her sale for her guid ale,   good
    The best on a' the shore o' Bucky. —

Her house sae bien, her curch sae clean,   so snug, kerchief
10   I wat she is a dainty Chuckie!   know, old darling
And cheery blinks the ingle-gleede   hearth-ember
    O' Lady Onlie, honest lucky. —

This is a traditional drinking song collected and brushed up by
Burns during his Highland tour in September 1787. 'Bucky' refers
to the small fishing town of Buckie. Lady Onlie is the old landlady.

The Banks of the Devon
Tune: Bhannerach dhon na chri
First printed in the S.M.M., Vol. 2, 14th February, 1788.

How pleasant the banks of the clear-winding Devon,
    With green-spreading bushes, and flow'rs
    blooming fair!
But the boniest flower on the banks of the Devon
    Was once a sweet bud on the braes of the Ayr.   hill sides
5 Mild be the sun on this sweet-blushing Flower,
    In the gay, rosy morn as it bathes in the dew;
And gentle the fall of the soft, vernal shower,
    That steals on the evening each leaf to renew!

O spare the dear blossom, ye orient breezes,
10   With chill, hoary wing as ye usher the dawn!
And far be thou distant, thou reptile that seizes
    The verdure and pride of the garden or lawn!

Let Bourbon exult in his gay, gilded Lilies,
    And England triumphant display her proud Rose;
15 A fairer than either adorns the green vallies
    Where Devon, sweet Devon meandering flows. —

This exquisite lyric celebrates Charlotte Hamilton (1763–1806), younger sister of Gavin Hamilton, Mauchline. Burns wrote to Gavin on 28th August, 1787, commenting – 'Yesterday morning I rode from this town [Stirling] up the meandering Devon's banks, to pay my respects to some Ayrshire folks at Harvieston [Clackmannanshire]. . . . Of Charlotte I cannot speak in common terms of admiration: she is not only beautiful, but lovely . . .' (Letter 132).

Weary Fa' You, Duncan Gray

Tune: Duncan Gray
First printed in the S.M.M., Vol. 2, 14th February, 1788.

WEARY fa' you, Duncan Gray,	fall
Ha, ha the girdin o't,	horse girthing/ galloping
Wae gae by you, Duncan Gray,	woe go
Ha, ha the girdin o't;	
5 When a' the lave gae to their play,	remainder go
Then I maun sit the lee-lang day,	must, live-long
And jeeg the cradle wi' my tae	rock, toe
And a' for the bad girdin o't. —	girthing for galloping (copulation)
Bonie was the Lammas moon	
10 Ha, ha the girdin o't,	
Glowrin a' the hills aboon,	glowing, above
Ha, ha the girdin o't;	
The girdin brak, the beast cam down,	girthing broke, horse came
I tint my curch and baith my shoon,	lost, kerchief, both, shoes
15 And Duncan ye're an unco loun;	strange rascal
Wae on the bad girdin o't. —	woe
But Duncan gin ye'll keep your aith,	if, oath
Ha, ha the girdin o't,	
I'se bless you wi' my hindmost breath,	I'll
20 Ha, ha the girdin o't;	
Duncan gin ye'll keep your aith,	
The beast again can bear us baith	horse, both
And auld Mess John will mend the skaith	old, Minister, damage
And clout the bad girdin o't. —	patch

This is based on a traditional bawdy song somewhat cleaned up by Burns, but left with happy overtones of horsy, sexual pleasure. The original lyric changed by Burns is from the David Herd collection.

The Ploughman

First printed in the S.M.M., Vol. 2, 14th February, 1788.

The Ploughman he's a bony lad,	
His mind is ever true, jo,	sweetheart
His garters knit below his knee,	
His bonnet it is blue, jo.	

Chorus

5	Then up wi't a', my Ploughman lad,	with it
	And hey, my merry Ploughman;	
	Of a' the trades that I do ken,	know
	Commend me to the Ploughman.	

	My Ploughman he comes hame at e'en,	home, evening
10	He's aften wat and weary:	often wet
	Cast aff the wat, put on the dry,	off, wet
	And gae to bed, my Dearie.	go
	Then up wi't a', &c.	

	I will wash my Ploughman's hose,	
	And I will dress his o'erlay;	necktie
15	I will mak my Ploughman's bed,	make
	And chear him late and early.	
	Then up wi't a', &c.	

	I hae been east, I hae been west,	have
	I hae been at Saint Johnston,	Perth
	The boniest sight that e'er I saw	
20	Was the Ploughman laddie dancin.	
	Then up wi't a', &c.	

	Snaw-white stockings on his legs,	snow-
	And siller buckles glancin;	silver
	A guid blue bonnet on his head,	good
	And O but he was handsome!	
	Then up wi't a', &c.	

25 Commend me to the Barn yard,
    And the Corn-mou, man;   corn stook
 I never gat my Coggie fou   got, (cup) *womb* full
    Till I met wi' the Ploughman.
       Then up wi't a', &c.

This is another traditional song worked over by Burns from the song
collection by David Herd. The second and third stanzas are from the
old song. The chorus is also old, leaving Burns's input as the first,
fourth, fifth and sixth stanzas.

Landlady, Count the Lawin

Tune: Hey Tuti Tatey –
First printed in the S.M.M., Vol. 2, 14th February, 1788.

 Landlady count the lawin,   bill
 The day is near the dawin,   dawning
 Ye're a' blind drunk, boys,
    And I'm but jolly fou. —   full/drunk

 Chorus
5 Hey tuti, tatey, How tuti, taiti,
 Hey tuti taiti, wha's fou now. —

 Cog an ye were ay fou,   drinking jug, always drunk
 Cog an ye were ay fou;
 I wad sit and sing to you,   would
10   If ye were ay fou. —
       Hey tuti, tatey &c.

 Weel may we a' be,   well, all
 Ill may ye never see!
 God bless the king
    And the Companie!
       Hey tuti, tatey &c.

This is a reworking of a traditional lyric. Like *Willie Brew'd A Peck
O Maut*, it is a drinking song to be sung as by a drunk. Given the
traditional tune and lyrics, it is certain the reference is to a Stuart not
a Hanoverian king.

Raving Winds around Her Blowing

Tune: McGrigor of Rora's Lament
First printed in the S.M.M., Vol. 2, 14th February, 1788.

Raving winds around her blowing,
Yellow leaves the woodlands strowing,
By a river hoarsely roaring
Isabella stray'd deploring.
5   Farewell, hours that late did measure
Sunshine days of joy and pleasure;
Hail, thou gloomy night of sorrow,
Cheerless night that knows no morrow.

O'er the Past too fondly wandering,
10   On the hopeless Future pondering;
Chilly Grief my life-blood freezes,
Fell Despair my fancy seizes.
Life, thou soul of every blessing,
Load to Misery most distressing,
15   Gladly how would I resign thee,
And to dark Oblivion join thee!'

This work was written in 1787 by Burns out of sympathy with Miss Isabella McLeod, on the death of her sister, Flora McLeod, and her sister's husband, the Earl of Loudon, who killed himself due to financial debts.

Musing on the Roaring Ocean

Tune: Druimionn dubh
First printed in the S.M.M., Vol. 2, 14th February, 1788.

Musing on the roaring ocean
   Which divides my Love and me,
Wearying Heaven in warm devotion
   For his weal where'er he be;
5   Hope and Fear's alternate billow
   Yielding late to Nature's law,
Whispering spirits round my pillow,
   Talk of him that's far awa. —

Ye whom Sorrow never wounded,
10   Ye who never shed a tear,
Care-untroubled, joy-surrounded,
      Gaudy Day to you is dear:
Gentle Night do thou befriend me;
      Downy sleep the curtain draw;
15 Spirits kind again attend me,
      Talk of him that's far awa!

Burns records that he composed this song as a 'compliment to a Mrs McLachlan, whose husband is an officer in the East Indies' (See Low, no. 82, p. 257).

Blythe was She –

Composed at Auchtertyre on Miss Euphemia Murray of Lentrose

Tune: Andro and his Cuttie Gun.

First printed in the S.M.M., Vol. 2, 14th February, 1788.

By Oughtertyre grows the aik,   oak
      On Yarrow banks the birken shaw;   birch woods
But Phemie was a bonier lass   Miss Murray
      Than braes o' Yarrow ever saw. —   hillsides

Chorus
5 Blythe, blythe and merry was she,
      Blythe was she butt and ben: outside, inside
Blythe by the banks of Ern,   river Earn
      And blythe in Glenturit glen!

Her looks were like a flower in May,
10   Her smile was like a simmer morn,   summer
She tripped by the banks o' Ern
      As light's a bird upon a thorn. —
            Blythe, blythe &c.

Her bonie face it was as meek
      As ony lamb upon a lee;   any, pasture
15 The evening sun was ne'er sae sweet   never so
      As was the blink o' Phemie's e'e.   eye
            Blythe, blythe &c.

The Highland hills I've wander'd wide,
 As o'er the lawlands I hae been;   lowlands, have
But Phemie was the blythest lass
20 That ever trod the dewy green. —
   Blythe, blythe &c.

Written in the Autumn of 1787 at Auchtertyre on Miss Euphemia
Murray of Lentrose as Burns records in the extended title to this
song.

To Daunton Me –

Tune: To Daunton Me -
First printed in the S.M.M., Vol. 2, 14th February, 1788.

The blude-red rose at Yule may blaw,   blood-, blow
The simmer lilies bloom in snaw,   summer, snow
The frost may freeze the deepest sea,
But an auld man shall never daunton me. — old, subdue

Chorus
5 To daunton me, to daunton me,
For an auld man shall never daunton me. —

To daunton me, and me sae young,   rule/subdue, so
Wi' his fause heart and flatt'ring tongue, false
That is the thing you shall never see
10 For an auld man shall never daunton me. — old

For a' his meal and a' his maut,   oatmeal, malt
For a' his fresh beef and his saut, salt
For a' his gold and white moníe,   money
An auld man shall never daunton me. old
   To daunton me &c.

15 His gear may buy him kye and yowes, wealth, cattle, ewes
His gear may buy him glens and knowes, hillocks
But me he shall not buy nor fee,   hire
For an auld man shall never daunton me. — old
   To daunton me &c.

He hirples twa-fauld as he dow,   limps, two-fold, able
20 Wi' his teethless gab and his auld beld pow, mouth, old bald head
And the rain rins down frae his red-blear'd e'e, runs, from, eye
That auld man shall never daunton me. — old
   To daunton me &c.

This is a song written in late 1787, adapted from an old Jacobite song. It is rearranged by Burns to focus on the married mismatch of age and youth with all its concomitant problems. The feisty female voice records its triumph over both her husband's material possessions and his tangible physical decay.

O'er the Water to Charlie –
First printed in the S.M.M., Vol. 2, 14th February, 1788.

Come boat me o'er, come row me o'er,
 Come boat me o'er to Charlie;
I'll gie John Ross another bawbee   halfpenny
 To boat me o'er to Charlie. —

Chorus
5 We'll o'er the water, we'll o'er the sea,
 We'll o'er the water to Charlie;
Come weal, come woe, we'll gather and go,
 And live or die wi' Charlie. —

I lo'e weel my Charlie's name,   love, well
10 Tho' some there be abhor him:
But O, to see Auld Nick gaun hame, old Devil, going home
 And Charlie's faes before him! foes
   We'll o'er the water, &c.

I swear and vow by moon and stars,
 And sun that shines so early!
15 If I had twenty thousand lives,
 I'd die as aft for Charlie. —   often
   We'll o'er the water, &c.

An obvious Jacobite song, as Low remarks (see no. 85, p. 265), based on a traditional work in *The True Loyalist* (1779), where the chorus is adapted from another song in the same collection. Donaldson notes that:

Burns matches the rhythmical impetus of the superb original
tune with subtly varied repetition and an unobtrusive pattern of
alliteration and internal rhyme to produce a heady evocation of
Jacobite exile with a distictly millenarian flavour (p. 81).

A Rosebud, by My Early Walk

First printed in the S.M.M., Vol. 2, 14th February, 1788.

A Rose-bud by my early walk,
Adown a corn-inclosed bawk,   unploughed rig end
Sae gently bent its thorny stalk
    All on a dewy morning. —

5   Ere twice the shades o' dawn are fled,
In a' its crimson glory spread,
And drooping rich the dewy head,
    It scents the early morning. —

Within the bush her covert nest
10 A little linnet fondly prest,
The dew sat chilly on her breast
    Sae early in the morning. —   so

She soon shall see her tender brood
The pride, the pleasure o' the wood,
15 Amang the fresh green leaves bedew'd,   among
    Awauk the early morning. —   awake

So thou, dear bird, young Jeany fair,
On trembling string or vocal air,
Shall sweetly pay the tender care
20   That tents thy early morning. —   tends

So thou, sweet Rosebud, young and gay,
Shalt beauteous blaze upon the day,
And bless the Parent's evening ray
    That watch'd thy early morning. —

The 'rosebud' of this song was Miss Janet (Jeany) Cruickshank,
daughter to Mr William Cruickshank, classics teacher, Edinburgh
High School. There are three extant letters from Burns to Mr
Cruickshank. On 8th October, 1787 Burns describes her as his 'dear

little Jeany' (Letter 142). In March 1788 he refers to her as a 'sweet little Rose-bud' (Letter 214). He sent the poem to Dr John Moore, February 1791.

To a Blackbird
or Revision for Clarinda
Tune: Scots Queen
First printed in the S.M.M., Vol. 2, 14th February, 1788.

Go on, sweet bird, and soothe my care,
Thy tuneful notes will soothe Despair;
Thy plaintive warblings void of art
Thrill sweetly thro' my aching heart.
5   Now chuse thy mate, and fondly love,
And all the charming transport prove;
While I a lovelorn exile live,
Nor transport or receive or give.

For thee is laughing Nature gay;
10 For thee she pours the vernal day:
For me in vain is Nature drest,
While Joy's a stranger to my breast!
These sweet emotions all enjoy;
Let love and song thy hours employ!
15 Go on, sweet bird, and soothe my care;
Thy tuneful notes will hush Despair.

This work was written by Clarinda, Agnes McLehose, then revised by Burns before publication. Ll. 8–14 are the contribution of Burns. Burns did not claim the song as his. It was published as 'By a lady'.

And I'll Kiss Thee Yet
Tune: Braes o' Balquhidder
First printed in the S.M.M., Vol. 2, 14th February, 1788.

Chorus
An I'll kiss thee yet, yet,
   An I'll kiss thee o'er again;
An I'll kiss thee yet, yet,
   My bonie Peggy Alison.

5   Ilk Care and Fear, when thou are near,   each/every
      I ever mair defy them, O;   more
   Young Kings upon their hansel throne   newly obtained
      Are no sae blest as I am, O!   not so
         An I'll kiss &c.

   When in my arms, wi' a' thy charms,
10   I clasp my countless treasure, O!
   I seek nae mair o' Heav'n to share,   no more
      Than sic a moment's pleasure, O!   such
         An I'll kiss &c.

   And by thy een sae bonie blue,   eyes, so
      I swear I'm thine forever O!
15   And on thy lips I seal my vow,
      And break it shall I never O!
         An I'll kiss &c.

The first verse does not appear in the S.M.M. but was included in a later manuscript. Burns notes in the Hastie MS: 'The chorus is the first, or lowest part of the tune – Each verse must be repeated twice to go through the high, or 2nd part – .' Burns signed this 'Z' to indicate the chorus is old; the verses his. Gilbert Burns and his sister Isobel tell differing stories of the possible heroine. As they cannot both be right, it is likely the name employed comes from the old song, not a woman Burns met.

Rattlin, Roarin Willie

First printed in the S.M.M., Vol. 2, 14th February, 1788.

   O Rattlin, roarin Willie,
      O he held to the fair,
   An' for to sell his fiddle
      And buy some other ware;   goods
5   But parting wi' his fiddle,
      The saut tear blin't his e'e;   salt, blinded, eye
   And Rattlin, roarin Willie,
      Ye're welcome hame to me.   home

   O Willie, come sell your fiddle,
10   O sell your fiddle sae fine;   so
   O Willie, come sell your fiddle,
      And buy a pint o' wine;

If I should sell my fiddle,
 The warld would think I was mad,   world
15 For mony a rantin day   many, jovial
 My fiddle and I hae had.   have

As I cam by Crochallan   came, the Fencibles' Club
 I cannily keekit ben,   cautiously looked in
Rattlin, roarin Willie
20 Was sitting at yon boord-en',   board-end/top of the table
Sitting at yon boord-en',
 And amang guid companie;   among good
Rattlin, roarin Willie,
 Ye're welcome hame to me!   home

The poet records in the Interleaved S.M.M. that only the final stanza of this song is his, the remainder being a traditional song. He states 'it was composed out of compliment to one of the worthiest fellows in the world, William Dunbar, Esq., writer to the Signet, Edinburgh, and Colonel of the Crochallan corps – a club of wits who took that title at the time of raising the fencible regiments'. There are seven letters between Burns and William Dunbar. See notes to *Where Wit May Sparkle*, a quatrain newly added to the canon, written by Burns to Dunbar.

Where, Braving Angry Winter's Storms
Tune: Neil Gow's Lament for Abercairny
First printed in the S.M.M., Vol. 2, 14th February, 1788.

Where braving angry Winter's storms
 The lofty Ochels rise,   Ochil hills
Far in their shade, my Peggy's charms
 First blest my wondering eyes. —

5 As one who by some savage stream
 A lonely gem surveys,
Astonish'd doubly marks it beam
 With art's most polish'd blaze. —

Blest be the wild, sequester'd glade
10 And blest the day and hour,
Where Peggy's charms I first survey'd,
 When first I felt their pow'r. —

The tyrant Death with grim controul
    May seize my fleeting breath,
15 But tearing Peggy from my soul
    Must be a stronger death. —

This was one of two songs went to Gavin Hamilton's cousin, Margaret (Peggy) Chalmers (1763–1843) in the early winter of 1787. In a letter to her Burns gives considerable indication not only of the genesis of the song but the complex intensity of his attitude to Margaret Chalmers:

> I have just now read yours. The poetic compliments I pay cannot be misunderstood. They are neither of them so particular as to point *you* out to the world at large; and the circle of your acquaintances will allow all I have said. Besides, I have complimented you chiefly, almost solely, on your mental charms. Shall I be plain with you? I will; so look to it. Personal attractions, madam, you have much above par; wit, understanding and worth, you possess in the first class. This is a cursed flat way of telling you these truths, but let me hear no more of your sheepish timidity. I know the world a little. I know what they will say of my poems; by second sight I suppose; for I am seldom out in my conjectures; and you may believe me my dear madam, I would not run any risk of hurting you by an ill-judged compliment, I wish to show the world the odds between a poet's friends and those of simple prosemen. More for your information *both* the pieces go in' (Letter 150).

Margaret's resistance was partly successful. The more obviously identifiable *My Peggy's Face, My Peggy's Form* did not appear till 1803 (S.M.M., no. 501). Manifestly this is more than a quarrel about a private relationship being made artistically public. There is an insistent pressure in these letters to Margaret Chalmers, cultured, musical, that bespeak more intimate needs. Margaret Chalmers is alleged to have in later life told the poet Thomas Campbell that Burns had proposed marriage but that she was already engaged to a banker, Lewis Hay, whom she in fact married in December, 1788. Burns's letters to her exist only in transcript; the originals were deliberately destroyed. None of her letters to him survive. This correspondence was being carried on simultaneously with the inflammatory melodrama with Mrs McLehose who certainly did not like to hide the light of her creative intentions under a bushel.

O Tibby, I Hae Seen the Day

Tune: Invercauld's Reel

First printed in the S.M.M., Vol. 2, 14th February, 1788.

Yestreen I met you on the Moor	yesterday evening
Ye spak na, but gaed by like stoor	spoke not, went by, dust
Ye geck at me because I'm poor	scoff, or toss the head
But fient a hair care I. —	not

Chorus

5	Tibby I hae seen the day	have
	Ye wadna been sae shy	would not, so
	For laik o' gear ye lightly me	lack of possessions
	But trowth, I care na by —	truly, I care as little

	When comin hame on Sunday last	home
10	Upon the road as I cam past	
	Ye snufft an' gae your head a cast	sniffed
	But trowth, I caretna by. —	truly, I care as little
	O Tibbie &c.	

	I doubt na lass, but ye may think	not, you
	Because ye hae the name o' clink	you, have, money
15	That ye can please me at a wink	
	Whene'er ye like to try. —	
	O Tibbie &c.	

	But sorrow tak him that's sae mean	take, so
	Altho' his pouch o' coin were clean	
	Wha follows onie saucy Quean,	any, girl
20	That looks sae proud and high. —	
	O Tibbie &c.	

	Altho' a lad were e'er sae smart	ever so
	If that he want the yellow dirt	
	Ye'll cast your head anither airt	another direction
	And answer him fu' dry. —	full
	O Tibbie &c.	

25	But if he hae the name o' gear	has, wealth
	Ye'll fasten to him like a breer	wild thorny brier
	Tho' hardly he for sense or lear	learning
	Be better than the ky. —	cattle
	O Tibbie &c.	

But, Tibbie, lass, tak my advice   take
30   Your daddie's gear maks you sae nice   wealth, haughty
The de'il a ane wad spier your price   devil, one, would ask
  Were ye as poor as I. —   you
   O Tibbie &c.

There lives a lass beside yon park,
I'd rather hae her in her sark   have, shirt or dress
35   Than you wi' a' your thousand mark
  That gars you look sae high. —   makes
   O Tibbie &c.

An' Tibby I hae seen the day
Ye wadna been sae shy
An' for laik o' gear ye lightly me   scorn
40   But fien' a hair care I. —

In the *First Commonplace Book* an early draught of this song appears, dated September 1784, although the poet records that he began the song when about seventeen years old. 'Tibbie' is believed to be Isabella Steven, who lived near Lochlie, where the Burns family farmed from 1777. Scott Douglas mentions a Tibbie Steen, as the heroine (Vol. 2, p. 235). The song is autobiographical, revealing an early sign of Burns's chronic problem in relating to socially superior women. Signed X in the S.M.M. where there are only six verses printed, rather than the eight of the final song.

Clarinda

First printed in the S.M.M., Vol. 2, 14th February, 1788.

Clarinda, mistress of my soul,
  The measur'd time is run!
The wretch beneath the dreary pole,
  So marks his latest sun.

5   To what dark cave of frozen night
  Shall poor Sylvander hie,
Depriv'd of thee, his life and light,
  The Sun of all his joy.

We part — but by these precious drops,
10   That fill thy lovely eyes!
No other light shall guide my steps,
  Till thy bright beams arise.

She, the fair Sun of all her sex,
    Has blest my glorious day:
15 And shall a glimmering Planet fix
    My worship to its ray?

This was the poet's parting song to Mrs McLehose when he left
Edinburgh in early 1788. Sylvander was Burns's pen-name in his
epistlotary relationship with Clarinda (Mrs McLehose). Unlike *Ae
Fond Kiss*, this poem echoes the sentimental clichéd tone of their
letters.

Second Epistle to Davie

First printed in 1789 by David Sillar, in his own collection of poems.

AULD NIBOR,	old neighbour
I'm three times, doubly, o'er your debtor,	
For your auld-farrant, frien'ly letter;	old-fashioned
Tho' I maun say't, I doubt ye flatter,	shall/must
5 Ye speak sae fair;	so
For my puir, silly, rhymin' clatter	poor, noise
Some less maun sair.	must, serve
Hale be your heart, hale be your fiddle;	
Lang may your elbuck jink an' diddle,	elbow, move fast, jig
10 To cheer you thro' the weary widdle	struggle
O' war'ly cares,	worldly
Till bairns' bairns kindly cuddle	children's children
Your auld grey hairs.	old
But DAVIE, lad, I'm red ye're glaikit;	informed, careless/foolish
15 I'm tauld the MUSE ye hae negleckit;	told, have, neglected
An' gif it's sae, ye sud be lickit	if, so, should, beaten
Until ye fyke;	fidget
Sic hauns as you sud ne'er be faiket,	such hands, should, excused
Be hain't wha like.	spared
20 For me, I'm on Parnassus brink,	
Rivin the words to gar them clink;	tearing at, make, rhyme
Whyles daez't wi' love, whyles daez't wi' drink,	sometimes dazed
Wi' jads or masons;	lasses
An' whyles, but ay owre late, I think,	sometimes, always over
25 Braw sober lessons.	fine

Of a' the thoughtless sons o' man,
Commen' me to the Bardie clan;   commend
Except it be some idle plan
    O' rhymin clink,   noise
30 The devil-haet, that I sud ban,   -have it/should
    They never think.

Nae thought, nae view, nae scheme o' livin',   no,
Nae cares to gie us joy or grievin',   no, give
But just the pouchie put the nieve in,   pocket, hand/fist
35   An' while ought's there,
Then, hiltie, skiltie, we gae scrivin',   helter-skelter, go writing
    An' fash nae mair.   trouble/bother no more

Leeze me on rhyme! It's ay a treasure,   commend me to/give me
My chief, amaist my only pleasure,   almost
40 At hame, a-fiel', at wark or leisure,   home, in the field, work
    The Muse, poor hizzie!   hussy
Tho' rough an' raploch be her measure,   coarse
    She's seldom lazy.

Haud to the Muse, my dainty Davie: hold
45 The warl' may play you [monie] a shavie;   world, many, trick
But for the Muse, she'll never leave ye,
    Tho' e'er sae puir,   so poor
Na, even tho' limpan wi' the spavie   no, spavin/worn joints
    Frae door to door.   from

Although this first appeared courtesy of David Sillar it did not enter
the Burns canon until published by Dr James Currie in 1800.
Sillar's own volume appeared in 1789, but the poem by Burns is
generally dated to the 1785 period. It is a letter epistle in colloquial
language written to encourage a friend to keep writing poetry. See
the first *Epistle to Davie* for notes on David Sillar.

Grace Before Meat

First printed in *The Caledonian Mercury*, August 27th, 1789.

O Thou, who kindly dost provide
    For ev'ry creature's want!
We bless thee, God of Nature wide,
    For all Thy goodness lent:

And, if it please thee Heavenly guide,
    May never worse be sent;
But whether granted or denied,
    Lord, bless us with content!
        Amen!!!

Burns printed this and the following grace under his own name in
The Caledonian Mercury, August 27th, 1789 but they were not
included in the 1793 Edinburgh edition. They appear in Currie,
1800, then along with *Grace After Meat*, in Stewart, 1802.

Grace After Meat

First printed in *The Caledonian Mercury*, August 27th, 1789.

O Thou, in whom we live and move,
    Who mad'st the sea and shore,
Thy goodness constantly we prove,
    And grateful would adore.

And if it please Thee, Pow'r above,
    Still grant us with such store;
The *Friend* we *trust*, the *Fair* we *love*;
    And we desire no more.

Like the above grace, Burns printed this under his own name in *The
Caledonian Mercury*, August 27th, 1789, but they did not enter the
canon until 1800 (See notes above).

I Love My Love in Secret

First printed in the S.M.M., Vol. 3, 2nd February, 1790.

My Sandy gied to me a ring,	gave
Was a' beset wi' diamonds fine;	all
But I gied him a far better thing,	gave
I gied my heart in pledge o' his ring.	gave

Chorus
5 My Sandy O, my Sandy O,
    My bony, bony Sandy O!
Tho' the love that I owe to thee I dare na show,   not
    Yet I love my love in secret, my Sandy O.

My Sandy brak a piece o' gowd,   broke, gold
10   While down his cheeks the saut tears row'd;   salt, rolled
He took a hauf and gied it to me,   half, gave
        And I'll keep it till the hour I die.
            My Sandy O, &c.

The traditional text was a bawdy song cleaned up by Burns. In such
rural songs the name Sandy was a stock name of this period.

Tibbie Dunbar

Tune: Jonny McGill
First printed in the S.M.M., Vol. 3, 2nd February, 1790.

O wilt thou go wi' me, sweet Tibbie Dunbar;
O wilt thou go wi' me, sweet Tibbie Dunbar:
Wilt thou ride on a horse, or be drawn in a car,
Or walk by my side, O sweet Tibbie Dunbar. —

I care na thy daddie, his lands and his money;   not
I care na thy kin, sae high and sae lordly: not, family, so
But say that thou'lt hae me for better for waur,   have, worse
And come in thy coatie, sweet Tibbie
   Dunbar. —

A traditional song renovated by Burns in his desire to put words to
and preserve an old tune by a Girvan fiddler, John McGill. During
the 19th century Hector MacNeil's lyrics, *Come Under My Plaidie*,
made the tune popular – a rare occasion of another poet upstaging
Burns's work.

Highland Harry Back Again

Tune: The Highlander's Lament
First printed in the S.M.M., Vol. 3, 2nd February, 1790.

My Harry was a gallant gay,
        Fu' stately strade he on the plain;   full, strode/walked
But now he's banish'd far awa,   away
        I'll never see him back again.

Chorus
5   O for him back again,
        O for him back again,
    I wad gie a' Knockhaspie's land   would give all
        For Highland Harry back again.

When a' the lave gae to their bed,   all, rest, go
10   I wander dowie up the glen;   sad
I set me down, and greet my fill,   weep
        And ay I wish him back again.
        O, for him &c.

O were some villains hangit high,   hanged
        And ilka body had their ain!   every, own
15 Then I might see the joyfu' sight,
        My Highland Harry back again.
        O, for him &c.

The poet states in the Interleaved S.M.M. that he collected the
chorus of this song from a woman's singing in Dunblane, 'the rest of
the song is mine'. The Chambers–Wallace edition (p. 321) give two
additional stanzas with sharper Jacobite lyrics, apparently not in the
hand of the poet but in manuscript in the British Museum. Knock-
haspie, l.7, refers, according to Cunningham, to a part of the farm
land at Mossgiel. Kinsley accepts this (Vol. III, no. 164, p. 1241), but
the chorus is not from Burns. The land referred to is more likely to be
in Aberdeenshire where the original song and chorus come from.

The Taylor Fell thro' the Bed
Tune: Beware of the Ripells
First printed in the S.M.M., Vol. 3, 2nd February, 1790.

The Taylor fell thro' the bed, thimble an' a',   tailor
The Taylor fell thro' the bed thimble an' a';
The blankets were thin and the sheets they were sma',   small
The Taylor fell thro' the bed, thimble an' a'.

5   The sleepy bit lassie, she dreaded nae ill,   no
The sleepy bit lassie she dreaded nae ill;
The weather was cauld and the lassie lay still,   cold, still
She thought that a Taylor could do her nae ill.

Gie me the groat again, cannie young man,   give, fourpence
10   Gie me the groat again cannie young man;
The day it is short and the night it is lang,   long
The dearest siller that ever I wan.   money, won

There's somebody weary, wi' lying her lane,   alone
There's somebody weary wi' lying her lane;
15   There's some that are dowie, I trow wad be fain   sad, trust would
To see the bit Taylor come skippin again.

The second and fourth verses are claimed by Burns in his notes to
the Interleaved S.M.M., the remainder is traditional.

Ay Waukin O

First printed in the S.M.M., Vol. 3, 2nd February, 1790.

Simmer's a pleasant time,   summer's
    Flowers of every colour;
The water rins owre the heugh,   runs, cliff or crag
    And I long for my true lover!

Chorus
5 Ay waukin, O,   waking
    Waukin still and weary:
Sleep I can get nane,   none
    For thinking on my Dearie. —

When I sleep I dream,
10   When I wauk I'm eerie,   wake, restless
Sleep I can get nane,   none
    For thinkin on my Dearie. —
    Ay waukin, O, &c.

Lanely night comes on,   lonely
    A' the lave are sleepin: rest/remainder
15 I think on my bonie lad,
    And I bleer my een wi' greetin. —   blur, eyes, weeping
    Ay waukin, O, &c.

This deceptively simple, but profoundly moving song of tormented
loss, is transformed by Burns from an original song. Some modern
recordings regrettably omit the Scots word 'heugh' from the first
verse, for which there is no adequate *sounding* translation in English.

Beware O' Bonie Ann

First printed in the S.M.M., Vol. 3, 2nd February, 1790.

Ye gallants bright I red you right,   advise/warn
    Beware o' bonie Ann;
Her comely face sae fu' o' grace,   so full
    Your heart she will trepan.   ensnare/trap
5 Her een sae bright, like stars by night,   eyes so
    Her skin is like the swan;
Sae jimply lac'd her genty waist   so tightly, graceful
    That sweetly ye might span.

Youth, grace and love attendant move,
10   And Pleasure leads the van:
In a' their charms, and conquering arms,
    They wait on bonie Ann.

The captive bands may chain the hands,
   But Love enslaves the man:
15 Ye gallants braw, I rede you a',   *advise, all*
   Beware o' bonie Ann.

Composed in 1788 on Miss Ann Masterton, daughter to the poet's
Edinburgh friend, the school teacher Allan Masterton (composer of
musical airs, inter alia, *Strathallan's Lament*).

The Gardener Wi' His Paidle

Tune: The Gardener's March
First printed in the S.M.M., Vol. 3, 2nd February, 1790.

When rosy May comes in wi' flowers
To deck her gay, green, spreading bowers;
Then busy, busy are his hours,
   The Gardener wi' his paidle. —   *hoe/spade*

5 The chrystal waters gently fa';   *crystal, fall*
The merry birds are lovers a';   *all*
The scented breezes round him blaw,   *blow*
   The Gardener wi' his paidle. —   *hoe*

When purple morning starts the hare
10 To steal upon her early fare;   *food*
Then thro' the dew he maun repair,   *must*
   The Gardener wi' his paidle. —

When Day, expiring in the west,
The curtain draws o' Nature's rest,
15 He flies to her arms he lo'es best,   *loves*
   The Gardener wi' his paidle. —

This was unsigned by Burns on publication, but he states in the
Interleaved S.M.M. that the title is old and the song his. This is a
man who fertilises everything he and his 'paidle' touches.

On a Bank of Flowers

Tune: The Bashful Lover
First printed in the S.M.M., Vol. 3, 2nd February, 1790.

On a bank of flowers in a summer day,
   For summer lightly drest,
The youthful blooming Nelly lay,
   With love and sleep opprest.
5 When Willie wand'ring thro' the wood,
   Who for her favour oft had sued;

He gaz'd, he wish'd, he fear'd, he blush'd,
    And trembled where he stood.

Her closed eyes like weapons sheath'd
10   Were seal'd in soft repose;
Her lips, still as she fragrant breath'd
    It richer dyed the rose.
The springing lilies sweetly prest,
    Wild, wanton kiss'd her rival breast;
15 He gaz'd, he wish'd, he fear'd, he blush'd,
    His bosom ill at rest.

Her robes light waving in the breeze,
    Her tender limbs embrace;
Her lovely form, her native ease,
20   All harmony and grace:
Tumultuous tides his pulses roll,
    A faltering, ardent kiss he stole;
He gaz'd, he wish'd, he fear'd, he blush'd,
    And sigh'd his very soul.

25 As flies the partridge from the brake
    On fear-inspired wings,
So Nelly starting, half-awake,
    Away affrighted springs.
But Willie follow'd, — as he should,
30   He overtook her in the wood;
He vow'd, he pray'd, he found the maid
    Forgiving all, and good.

This song is based on one of the same title printed in the *Tea Table Miscellany*, Volume 3, 1727. It is signed as from Burns in the S.M.M., suggesting that it is mostly new lyrics by Burns. On this type of lyrical romance Kinsley remarks 'The situation is a common one in Restoration and eighteenth-century pastoral' (Vol. III, no. 292, p. 1331). It could also be remarked that it is deeply pre-Keatsian.

My Love, She's but a Lassie Yet –

Tune: Miss Farquarson's Reel
First printed in the S.M.M., Vol. 3, 2nd February, 1790.

Chorus
    My love, she's but a lassie yet,
    My love, she's but a lassie yet;
    We'll let her stand a year or twa,   two
    She'll no be half sae saucy yet. —   so

5   I rue the day I sought her O,
     I rue the day I sought her O,
   Wha gets her needs na say he's woo'd,   *who, not*
     But he may say he has bought her O. —
       My love, she's &c.

    Come draw a drap o' the best o't yet,   *pour, drop*
10   Come draw a drap o' the best o't yet:
   Gae seek for Pleasure whare ye will,   *go, where*
     But here I never misst it yet. —   *missed*
       My love, she's &c.

    We're a' dry wi' drinkin o't,
     We're a' dry wi' drinkin o't:
15   The minister kisst the fiddler's wife,
     He could na preach for thinkin o't. —   *not*
       My love, she's &c.

This is another example of a song where Burns took the title from an old song and re-wrote the lyric: the first, repetitive lines of the chorus and the final 'half stanza' are old (See Scott Douglas, Vol. 1, p. 244 and Low, no. 133, p. 378). The tune is known as both the above title and *My Love, She's but a Lassie Yet.*

Jamie, Come Try Me

Tune: Jamie, Come Try Me.
First printed in the S.M.M., Vol. 3, 2nd February, 1790.

If thou should ask my love,
  Could I deny thee?
If thou would win my love,
  Jamie come try me.

Chorus
5 Jamie come try me,
   Jamie come try me,
  If thou would win my love
   Jamie come try me.

If thou should kiss me, love,
10 Wha could espy thee?
If thou wad be my love,
  Jamie come try me.
    Jamie, come try &c.

Here Burns, as Low comments (no. 153), has composed lyrics for a tune printed in Oswald's 1742 collection of Scottish tunes, he wished to preserve.

My Bony Mary

Tune: The Secret Kiss
First printed in the S.M.M., Vol. 3, 2nd February, 1790.

Go fetch to me a pint o' wine,
 And fill it in a silver tassie;   cup/goblet
That I may drink, before I go,
 A service to my bonie lassie:
5 The boat rocks at the Pier o' Leith,
 Fu' loud the wind blaws frae the Ferry, full, blows, from
The ship rides by the Berwick-law,
 And I maun leave my bony Mary.   must

The trumpets sound, the banners fly,
10 The glittering spears are ranked ready,
The shouts o' war are heard afar,
 The battle closes deep and bloody.
It's not the roar o' sea or shore,
 Wad mak me langer wish to tarry,   would, longer
15 Nor shouts o' war that's heard afar —
 It's leaving thee, my bony Mary!

Burns affirms that other than the first four lines, this song is his (Letter 586). The title in some editions is *The Silver Tassie*. On publication it was called *My Bony Mary,* so that title is given here. The 'Ferry' referred to is Queensferry. The Berwick-law, according to Chambers edition, is a hill near the shore on the Firth of Forth visible from Edinburgh, near Berwick; but it may refer to the Bass Rock.

The Lazy Mist

First printed in the S.M.M., Vol. 3, 2nd February, 1790.

The lazy mist hangs from the brow of the hill,
Concealing the course of the dark winding rill;
How languid the scenes, late so sprightly, appear,
As Autumn to Winter resigns the pale year.

5   The forests are leafless, the meadows are brown,
And all the gay foppery of Summer is flown:
Apart let me wander, apart let me muse,
How quick Time is flying, how keen Fate pursues.

How long I have liv'd — but how much liv'd in vain;
10   How little of life's scanty span may remain:
What aspects, old Time, in his progress has worn;
What ties, cruel Fate, in my bosom has torn.
How foolish, or worse, till our summit is gain'd!
And downward, how weaken'd, how darken'd, how pain'd!
15   Life is not worth having with all it can give,
For something beyond it poor man sure must live.

This is an original work of Burns. A copy was sent to Dr Blacklock from Mauchline on 15th November 1788. The final couplet carries the same sentiment as 'And a' the comfort we're to get,/ Is that ayont the grave, man' from *The Tree of Liberty* (ll. 71–2), without that later poem's sense of revolutionary, redemptive freedom achievable in this life.

The Captain's Lady

Tune: Mount Your Baggage
First printed in the S.M.M., Vol. 3, 2nd February, 1790.

When the drums do beat,
    And the cannons rattle,
Thou shalt sit in state,
    And see thy love in battle.

Chorus
5 O mount and go,
    Mount and make you ready,
O mount and go,
    And be the Captain's Lady.

When the vanquish'd foe
10   Sues for peace and quiet,
To the shades we'll go,
    And in love enjoy it.
       O, mount and go, &c.

Henley and Henderson suggest that a broadside called *The Liggar Lady* is probably the basis of this song (Vol. 3, p. 344). Kinsley also accepts this (Vol. III, p. 1332). The finished work differs significantly from the traditional one.

Of a' the Airts

Tune: Miss Admiral Gordon's Strathspey
First printed in the S.M.M., Vol. 3, 2nd February, 1790.

Of a' the airts the wind can blaw,		directions, blow
I dearly like the West,		
For there the bonie Lassie lives,		
The Lassie I lo'e best:		love
There 's wild woods grow, and rivers row,		roll
And mony a hill between;		many
But day and night my fancy's flight		
Is ever wi' my Jean. —		

Of a' the airts the wind can blaw,   directions, blow
    I dearly like the West,
For there the bonie Lassie lives,
    The Lassie I lo'e best: love
5 There 's wild woods grow, and rivers row,   roll
    And mony a hill between;   many
But day and night my fancy's flight
    Is ever wi' my Jean. —

I see her in the dewy flowers,
10   I see her sweet and fair;
I hear her in the tunefu' birds,
    I hear her charm the air:
There's not a bonie flower, that springs
    By fountain, shaw, or green;   woodland
15 There's not a bony bird that sings
    But minds me o' my Jean. —

In the Interleaved S.M.M. Burns writes 'This song . . . I composed out of compliment to Mrs Burns'. The evocative strathspey was composed by William Marshall who worked for the Duke of Gordon. A music-seller in Edinburgh, John Hamilton, added two stanzas to this song, but they were never fully incorporated by Burnsians due to their mediocrity. Hamilton is probably responsible for some other fake lyrics attributed to Burns during the nineteenth century (See Chambers–Wallace, 1896, p. 270, footnote 1).

Carl and the King Come

First printed in the S.M.M., Vol. 3, 2nd February, 1790.

An somebodie were come again,
Then somebodie maun cross the main,   must
And every man shall hae his ain,   have, own
    Carl an the King come.   old man

Chorus
5   Carl an the King come,
     Carl an the King come;
     Thou shalt dance and I will sing,
          Carl an the King come.

     I trow we swapped for the warse: trust, worse
10   We gae the boot and better horse;   gave
     An that we'll tell them at the cross,
          Carl an the King come.

     Coggie an the King come,   drinking jug
     Coggie an the King come,
15   I'll be fou an thou'se be toom,   drunk, empty
          Coggie an the King come.

'Carl', meaning old man, is a reference to Prince Charles Edward
Stuart. A song of this title existed in Cromwellian times, but several
variants appear as Jacobite songs in the eighteenth century. It is
partly traditional, partly Burns.

Whistle o'er the Lave o't

Tune: Whistle o'er the Lave o't
First printed in the S.M.M., Vol. 3, 2nd February, 1790.

     First when Maggy was my care,
     Heaven, I thought, was in her air;
     Now we're married — spier nae mair —   inquire no more
          But whistle o'er the lave o't. —   rest

5   Meg was meek, and Meg was mild,
     Sweet and harmless as a child —
     Wiser men than me's beguiled;
          Whistle o'er the lave o't. —   rest

     How we live, my Meg and me,
10   How we love and how we gree;   agree
     I care na by how few may see,   not
          Whistle o'er the lave o't. —

     Wha I wish were maggots' meat,   who
     Dish'd up in her winding-sheet;
15   I could write — but Meg wad see't —   would
          Whistle o'er the lave o't. —

These are Burns's new lyrics adapted considerably from a bawdy song in the David Herd collection (1769). On the evidence of several of Burns's songs, feminine submission was not, to say the least, implicit in the eighteenth century matrimonial state.

O, Were I on Parnassus Hill

Tune: My Love is Lost to Me
First printed in the S.M.M., Vol. 3, 2nd February, 1790.

O were I on Parnassus hill;
    Or had o' Helicon my fill;
That I might catch poetic skill,
    To sing how dear I love thee.
5 But Nith maun be my Muses' well,   *must*
    My Muse maun be thy bonie sell,   *must, self*
On Corsincon I'll glowr and spell,   *glower*
    And write how dear I love thee.

Then come, sweet Muse, inspire my lay!
10   For a' the lee-lang simmer's day,   *live-long summer*
I couldna sing, I couldna say,   *could not,*
    How much, how dear, I love thee.
I see thee dancing o'er the green,
    Thy waist sae jimp, thy limbs sae clean, *so neat, so shapely*
15 Thy tempting lips, thy roguish een —   *eyes*
    By Heaven and Earth I love thee!

By night, by day, a-field, at hame,   *in a field*
    The thoughts o' thee my breast inflame;
And ay I muse and sing thy name,
20   I only live to love thee.
Tho' I were doom'd to wander on,
    Beyond the sea, beyond the sun,
Till my last, weary sand was run;
    Till then — and then I love thee.

This song, as *The Vision*, has its inspiring domestic Muse in Jean Armour. It is different, however, from that long poem and uncharacteristic of Burns, in that his native landscape is felt as inadequate compared to that of the classical world. Helicon, the Greek river of inspirational water, neatly plays off against Corsicon, a hill viewable from Ellisland.

There's a Youth in this City

Tune: Neil Gow's Lament for his Brother
First printed in the S.M.M., Vol. 3, 2nd February, 1790.

There's a youth in this city, it were a great pity
That he from our lasses should wander awa';
For he 's bony and braw, weel-favor'd witha',   handsome, well-
An' his hair has a natural buckle an' a'. —   curl
5   His coat is the hue o' his bonnet sae blue;   so
His fecket is white as the new-driven snaw;   woollen waistcoat
His hose they are blae, and his shoon like the slae;   blue, shoes, sloe
And his clear siller buckles they dazzle us a'.   silver

For beauty and fortune the laddie's been courtin;
10   Weel-featur'd, weel-tocher'd, weel-mounted, an' braw;   (see notes)
But chiefly the siller, that gars him gang till her;   money, makes, go
The Pennie 's the jewel that beautifies a'. —
There 's Meg wi' the mailen that fain wad a haen him;   farm, gladly would
And Susie whase daddie was laird of the Ha',   whose, Hall
15   There 's lang-tocher'd Nancy maist fetters his fancy —   long-, most
But th' laddie's dear sel he loes dearest of a'. —   self, loves

Burns indicates in the Interleaved S.M.M. that the first 'half-stanza' is traditional and the remainder his own. He also states that the tune is by the famous fiddler Neil Gow. The explanation of the Scots hyperbole in l. 10 is too lengthy to be set in the right margin and is translated as follows: our hero is well endowed, rides a good horse, has money and is handsome, but, for all his show, as the final line suggests, he loves himself a little too much.

My Heart's in the Highlands

Tune: Failte na miosg
First printed in the S.M.M., Vol. 3, 2nd February, 1790.

Farewell to the Highlands, farewell to the North;
The birthplace of Valour, the country of Worth:
Wherever I wander, wherever I rove,
The hills of the Highlands for ever I love. —

Chorus
5   My heart's in the Highlands, my heart is not here;
     My heart's in the Highlands a chasing the deer;
     Chasing the wild deer, and following the roe;
     My heart's in the Highlands, wherever I go. —

     Farewell to the mountains high cover'd with snow;
10   Farewell to the Straths and green valleys below:
     Farewell to the forests and wild-hanging woods;
     Farewell to the torrents and loud-pouring floods. —
     My heart's in the Highlands, &c.

The chorus of this song is taken from a broadside called *The Strong
Walls of Derry* which narrates the forlorn love of a Highlander
emigrating to Ireland to find his true love has married another. The
remainder of the lyric is by Burns.

John Anderson My Jo

First printed in the S.M.M., Vol. 3, 2nd February, 1790.

John Anderson my jo, John,	darling/love
When we were first acquent;	acquainted
Your locks were like the raven,	
Your bonie brow was brent;	unwrinkled
5 But now your brow is beld, John,	bald
Your locks are like the snaw;	snow/white
But blessings on your frosty pow,	white head
John Anderson my Jo.	darling
John Anderson my jo, John,	
10 We clamb the hill thegither;	climbed, together
And mony a cantie day, John,	happy
We've had wi' ane anither:	one another
Now we maun totter down, John,	shall
And hand in hand we'll go;	
15 And sleep thegither at the foot,	together
John Anderson my Jo.	

This is surely Burns's best example of cleaning up an old bawdy
song to create a soothing lyric about love in old age, sung in the
feminine voice. A version of the original bawdy work is in the poet's
M.M.C. collection.

Awa', Whigs, Awa'

First printed in the S.M.M., Vol. 3, 2nd February, 1790.

Our thrissles flourish'd fresh and fair,   thistles
    And bonie bloom'd our roses;
But Whigs cam like a frost in June,   came
    An' wither'd a' our posies.

Chorus
5 Awa' Whigs awa',
    Awa' Whigs awa',
Ye're but a pack o' traitor louns,   rogues
    Ye'll do nae guid at a'.   no good

Our ancient crown's fa'n in the dust;   fallen
10   Deil blin' them wi' the stoure o't,   devil, dust
An' write their names in his black beuk   book
    Wha gae the Whigs the power o't!   who gave
    Awa' Whigs awa', &c.

Our sad decay in church and state
    Surpasses my descriving:.   describing
15 The Whigs cam o'er us for a curse,   came
    And we hae done wi' thriving.   have
    Awa' Whigs awa', &c.

Grim Vengeance lang has taen a nap,   long, taken
    But we may see him waukin: awaken
Gude help the day when Royal heads   God
20   Are hunted like a maukin.   hare
    Awa', Whigs, awa', &c.

This is adapted from a song in Herd's collection (See Kinsley, no. 303, Vol. III, p. 1336) where Burns lifts the chorus. Wallace suggests that only verses two and four are from Burns, but three sounds like him also. It is a stereotypical Jacobite protest song which, as Donaldson remarks (p. 80), 'could have been written at almost any point in the eighteenth century'.

Ca' the Yowes to the Knowes

[First version]
First printed in the S.M.M., Vol. 3, 2nd February, 1790.

As I gaed down the water-side   went
There I met my Shepherd-lad,
He row'd me sweetly in his plaid,   wrapped
    And he ca'd me his Dearie. —   called

Chorus
5 Ca' the yowes to the knowes,   call, ewes, hillocks
Ca' them whare the heather grows,   call, where
Ca' them where the burnie rowes,   stream runs/flows
    My bonie Dearie. —

Will ye gang down the water-side   go
10 And see the waves sae sweetly glide   so
Beneath the hazels spreading wide,
    The moon it shines fu' clearly. —
      Ca' the yowes, &c.

I was bred up at nae sic school,   no such
My Shepherd-lad, to play the fool;
15 An' a' the day to sit in dool,   sorrow
An' naebody to see me. —   nobody
    Ca' the yowes, &c.

Ye sall get gowns and ribbons meet,   shall
Cauf-leather shoon upon your feet,   shoes
And in my arms ye'se lie and sleep,
20 An' ye sall be my Dearie. —   shall
    Ca' the yowes, &c.

If ye'll but stand to what ye've said,
I'se gang wi' you, my Shepherd-lad,   go
And ye may row me in your plaid,   wrap
And I sall be your Dearie.
    Ca' the yowes, &c.

25 While waters wimple to the sea;   meander
While Day blinks in the lift sae hie;   sky so high
Till clay-cauld Death sall blin' my e'e,   -cold, shall, eye
    Ye sall be my Dearie. —   shall
      Ca' the yowes, &c.

This is the poet's first version of this duet, adapted from a traditional work. He wrote to Thomson retrospectively in September 1794: 'When I gave it to Johnson, I added some stanzas to the song and mended others, but still it will not do for *you*' (Letter 636). Stanzas four and five are old. Stanza three is missing in the Mackay version (p. 299). The later version (printed in Posthumous Works), interweaves the local, Lincluden scenery.

Kissin My Kate

Tune: Lord Breadalbine's March
First printed in the S.M.M., Vol. 3, 2nd February, 1790.

O merry hae I been teethin a heckle, *have, flax-dresser's comb*
 An' merry hae I been shapin a spoon: *have*
O merry hae I been cloutin a kettle, *have, mending*
 An' kissin my Katie when a' was done.
5 O, a' the lang day I ca' at my hammer, *long, knock*
 An' a' the lang day I whistle an' sing; *long*
O, a' the lang night I cuddle my kimmer, *long, mistress*
 An' a' the lang night as happy's a king. *long*

Bitter in dool I lickit my winnins *sorrow, made the best*
10 O' marrying Bess, to gie her a slave: *give*
Blest be the hour she cool'd in her linens, *shroud*
 And blythe be the bird that sings on her
  grave!
Come to my arms, my Katie, my Katie,
 An' come to my arms, and kiss me again!
15 Drucken or sober, here's to thee, Katie! *drunken*
 And blest be the day I did it again.

This is another adaption by Burns from an old song with the man ecstatically re-energised by replacing the loathed, deceased Bess with the beloved Katy. The phrase 'teethin a heckle' refers to putting teeth into a flax-dresser's comb.

Mrs Ferguson of Craigdarroch's Lamentation for the Death of her Son,

or A Mother's Lament

Tune: Finlayston House –
First printed in the S.M.M., Vol. 3, 2nd February, 1790.

'Fate gave the word , the arrow sped,'
    And pierc'd my Darling's heart;
And with him all the joys are fled,
    Life can to me impart. —

5   By cruel hands the Sapling drops,
    In dust dishonor'd laid:
So fell the pride of all my hopes,
    My age's future shade. —

The mother-linnet in the brake
10   Bewails her ravish'd young;
So I, for my lost Darling's sake,
    Lament the live day long. —

Death! oft, I've fear'd thy fatal blow;
    Now, fond, I bare my breast;
15 O, do thou kindly lay me low,
    With him I love at rest!

The title given here is the title Burns himself adopted when informing Mrs Dunlop of the song he had just written (Letter 275) on 27th September 1788. The title generally used is *A Mother's Lament*.

The Braes o' Ballochmyle

First printed in S.M.M., Vol. 3, 2nd February, 1790.

The Catrine woods were yellow seen,
    The flowers decay'd on Catrine lee,
Nae lav'rock sang on hillock green,   no lark
    But Nature sicken'd on the e'e.   eye
5   Thro' faded groves Maria sang,
    Hersel in beauty's bloom the while,   herself
And ay the wild-wood echoes rang —
    Fareweel the braes o' Ballochmyle.   farewell, hill sides

Low in your wintry beds, ye flowers,
10   Again ye'll flourish fresh and fair;
Ye birdies dumb, in with'ring bowers,
      Again ye'll charm the vocal air.
But here alas! for me nae mair   *no more*
      Shall birdie charm, or floweret smile;   *bird*
15 Fareweel the bonnie banks of Ayr,
      Fareweel, fareweel! sweet Ballochmyle!   *farewell, hill sides*

This song, in the voice of 'Maria', Mary Anne Whitefoord, Sir John Whitefoord's oldest daughter, laments the family loss of their country estate in Ayrshire when its finances were almost ruined by the collapse of the Ayr Bank. It was composed in 1785. The poet's Edinburgh friend Allan Masterton composed the music.

The Rantin Dog, the Daddie o't

First published in S.M.M., Vol 3, 2nd February 1790.

O wha my babie-clouts will buy,   *who, -linen*
O wha will tent me when I cry;   *who, attend to*
Wha will kiss me where I lie,   *who*
      The rantin dog, the daddie o't.   *fun-loving, of it*

5 O wha will own he did the faut,   *who, fault*
O wha will buy the groanin maut,   *who, groaning/midwife's ale*
O wha will tell me how to ca't,   *name it*
      The rantin dog, the daddie o't.

When I mount the Creepie-chair,   *stool of repentance*
10 Wha will sit beside me there,   *who*
Gie me Rob, I'll seek nae mair,   *give, no more*
      The rantin dog, the daddie o't.

Wha will crack to me my lane;   *converse, alone*
Wha will mak me fidgin fain;   *who, sexually excited*
15 Wha will kiss me o'er again   *who*
      The rantin dog, the daddie o't.

Burns comments in the Interleaved S.M.M., 'I composed this song very early in life, and sent it to a young girl, a very particular friend of mine, who was at that time under a cloud'. The likely recipient was probably Elizabeth Paton, who bore a child to Burns, although

this is not certain. What is interesting is that this song, unlike several
other poems on the subject, gives voice not to the father but to the
unmarried mother.

Thou Lingering Star

Tune: Captain Cook's Death
First printed in the S.M.M., Vol. 3, 2nd February, 1790.

Thou ling'ring Star with less'ning ray,
 That lovest to greet the early morn,
Again thou usherest in the day
 My Mary from my Soul was torn.
5 O Mary! dear departed Shade!
 Where is thy place of blissful rest?
Seest thou thy Lover lowly laid?
 Hearest thou the groans that rend his breast?

That sacred hour can I forget,
10 Can I forget the hallow'd grove,
Where by the winding Ayr we met,
 To live one day of Parting Love?
Eternity cannot efface
 Those records dear of transports past;
15 Thy image at our last embrace,
 Ah, little thought we 'twas our last!

Ayr gurgling kiss'd his pebbled shore,
 O'erhung with wild-woods, thickening, green;
The fragrant birch, and hawthorn hoar,
20 'Twin'd, amorous, round the raptur'd scene:
The flowers sprang wanton to be prest,
 The birds sang love on every spray;
Till too, too soon the glowing west
 Proclaim'd the speed of winged day. —

25 Still o'er these scenes my mem'ry wakes,
 And fondly broods with miser-care;
Time but th' impression stronger makes,
 As streams their channels deeper wear:
My Mary, dear, departed Shade!
30 Where is thy place of blissful rest!
Seest thou thy Lover lowly laid!
 Hearest thou the groans that rend his breast!

On 13th December 1789 Burns expostulated to Mrs Dunlop, discussing who he might meet if there were an after-life: 'There should I, with speechless agony of rapture, again recognise my lost, my ever dear MARY, whose bosom was fraught with Truth, Honour, Constancy & LOVE' (Letter 374). He had already sent a copy of the song to Mrs Dunlop in November, but requotes his own lines in December. The identity of Mary or 'Margaret' Campbell has been an obsessive preoccupation with some Burnsians since the early nineteenth century, culminating in the recent macabre call to exhume a grave near Greenock and employ D.N.A. testing to answer the myth.

Eppie Adair

Tune: My Eppie
First printed in the S.M.M., Vol. 3, 2nd February, 1790.

By Love, and by Beauty;
By Law, and by Duty;
I swear to be true to
    My Eppie Adair!

Chorus
5 An O, my Eppie,
My Jewel, my Eppie!
Wha wadna be happy   who would not
    Wi' Eppie Adair!

A' Pleasure exile me;
10 Dishonour defile me,
If e'er I beguile thee,
    My Eppie Adair!
        An' O, my Eppie, &c.

This is another example of an old song reworked by Burns.

The Battle of Sherramuir

Tune: Cameronian Rant
First printed in the S.M.M., Vol. 3, 2nd February, 1790.

O cam ye here the fight to shun,   came
    Or herd the sheep wi' me, man,
Or were ye at the Sherra-moor,
    Or did the battle see, man.

5   I saw the battle sair and teugh,   sore, tough
    And reekin-red ran mony a sheugh,   bloody-red, ditch
    My heart for fear gae sough for sough,   gave, sigh, sigh
    To hear the thuds, and see the cluds   clouds
    O' Clans frae woods, in tartan duds,   from, clothes
10   Wha glaum'd at kingdoms three, man.   who grasped

    The red-coat lads wi' black cockauds   Hanoverian cockades
        To meet them were na slaw, man,   not slow
    They rush'd, and push'd, and blude outgush'd,   blood
        And mony a bouk did fa', man: carcase, fall
15 The great Argyle led on his files,
    I wat they glanc'd for twenty miles,   wot
    They hough'd the Clans like nine-pin kyles,   mowed, skittles
    They hack'd and hash'd while braid-swords clash'd,   broad-
    And thro' they dash'd, and hew'd and smash'd,
20   Till fey men dee'd awa, man.   doomed, died

    But had ye seen the philibegs   kilts
        And skyrin tartan trews, man,   showy tight trousers
    When in the teeth they daur'd our Whigs,   dared
        And Covenant Trueblues, man;   Covenanter flag
25 In lines extended lang and large,   long
    When baiginets o'erpower'd the targe,   bayonets, shield
    And thousands hasten'd to the charge;
    Wi' Highland wrath they frae the sheath   from
    Drew blades o' death, till out o' breath
30   They fled like frighted dows, man.   doves

    O how deil Tam can that be true,   devil
        The chase gaed frae the north, man;   went from
    I saw mysel, they did pursue
        The horse-men back to Forth, man;
35 And at Dunblane in my ain sight   own
    They took the brig wi' a' their might,   bridge
    And straught to Stirling wing'd their flight,   straight
    But, cursed lot! the gates were shut
    And monie a huntit, poor Red-coat   hunted
40   For fear amaist did swarf, man.   almost swoon

    My sister Kate cam up the gate   came
        Wi' crowdie unto me, man;   oatmeal and water
    She swoor she saw some rebels run   swore
        To Perth and to Dundee, man:

45	Their left-hand General had nae skill;	no
	The Angus lads had nae gude will	no, good
	That day their neebours' blude to spill;	neighbours' blood
	For fear by foes that they should lose	
	Their cogs o' brose, they scar'd at blows	wooden bowls of porridge
50	And hameward fast did flee, man.	homeward

	They've lost some gallant gentlemen	
	Amang the Highland clans, man;	among
	I fear my Lord Panmure is slain,	
	Or in his en'mies' hands, man:	
55	Now wad ye sing this double flight,	would
	Some fell for wrang, and some for right,	
	But mony bade the warld gudenight;	good-
	Say pell and mell, wi' muskets' knell	
	How Tories fell, and Whigs to Hell	
60	Flew off in frighted bands, man.	

This is adapted by Burns from the broadside written by Rev. John Barclay (1734–1798), founder of the Barclayites sect, which records an alleged conversation between two shepherds on the day of the battle of Sherriffmuir, *Dialogue Between Will Lick-Ladle and Tom Clean-Cogue*. The battle occurred on 13th November 1715, when the Duke of Argyll led the Hanoverian crown troops, the men in black cockades (l. 11) against the white-cockaded Jacobites led by the Earl of Mar in a quite indecisive encounter.

Low follows Kinsley in commenting on the poem being composed 'in the manner of traditional battle poetry' but this is profoundly to miss the tension between form and content because the poem's reductive vision is the implicit chaotic incoherence of both the perception and experience of battle. Stendhal remarked that 'L'un des plus grandes poètes selon moi, aient paru dans ces derniers temps, c'est Robert Burns'. He had probably not read this song, but Burns's burlesquing manner in this mini-masterpiece prefigures Stendhal's own brilliant analysis of the subjective experience of battle in *The Charterhouse of Parma*. William Donaldson, remarking on Burns's ability to sustain a 'narrative of breathless pace, a headlong torrent of alliteration, assonance and internal rhyme', finely adds:

This amazing verbal tour de force has many admirable quali-
ties: the effortlessly sustained illusion of eye-witness contem-
poraneity (we have to force ourselves to remember that the

events described happened more than thirty years before the poet was born); the concentration upon the common man and the human fallibility of the participants; the way in which the conventionally heroic is both indulged and debunked throughout.

This essentially reductive technique is seen at its clearest in the fifth verse, where the timely retreat of the Angus lads is attributed not only to the absence of military appetite, but to the presence of an appetite of a ridiculously different kind. Despite the dreadful strokes and rivers of blood, the overall effect is deeply comic.

Burns's power of characterisation produces a picture rooted in everyday realities, where the epic and mundane are ludicrously entangled and the proverbial cast of common speech is wielded with ruthlessly deflationary effect . . . a burlesque of the conventionally heroic, which, in its refusal to consider men in the mass, dehumanised by uniforms or warlike array is fundamentally humane (pp. 83–4).

Sandy and Jockie

Tune: Jenny's Lamentation
First printed in the S.M.M., Vol. 3, 2nd February, 1790.

TWA bony lads were Sandy and Jockie;	two
Jockie was lo'ed but Sandy unlucky;	loved
Jockie was laird baith of hills and of vallies,	both
But Sandy was nought but the King o' gude fellows.	good

Jockie lo'ed Madgie, for Madgie had money,	loved
And Sandy lo'ed Mary, for Mary was bony:	
Ane wedded for Love, ane wedded for treasure,	one
So Jockie has siller, and Sandy had pleasure.	money

The first two lines are traditional, the remainder is from Burns. It expresses the poet's belief that natural, spontaneous love more than compensated for wealth.

Young Jockie was the Blythest Lad

First printed in the S.M.M., Vol. 3, 2nd February, 1790.

Young Jockey was the blythest lad
    In a' our town or here awa;   *away/round about*
Fu' blythe he whistled at the gaud,   *while goading*
    Fu' lightly danc'd he in the ha'.
5 He roos'd my een sae bonie blue,   *praised, eyes, so*
    He roos'd my waist sae genty sma;   *praised, so, small*
An ay my heart cam to my mou,   *mouth*
    When ne'er a body heard or saw.

My Jockey toils upon the plain
10   Thro' wind and weet, thro' frost and snaw; *wet, snow*
And o'er the lee I leuk fu' fain   *look fondly*
    When Jockie's owsen hameward ca'.   *oxen homeward drive*
An ay the night comes round again,
    When in his arms he taks me a';   *takes, fully*
15 An ay he vows he'll be my ain   *own*
    As lang's he has a breath to draw.   *long as*

This is signed by Burns with a 'Z' in the S.M.M to indicate it is a traditional song he improved. Jockey (l. 3) was the leader of the plough-horses and carried a stick as a goad.

A Waukrife Minnie

First printed in the S.M.M., Vol. 3, 2nd February, 1790.

Whare are you gaun, my bony lass,   *where, going*
    Whare are you gaun, my hiney.   *where, going, darling*
She answer'd me right saucilie,
    An errand for my minnie.   *mother*

5 O whare live ye, my bony lass,   *where*
    O whare live ye, my hiney.   *darling*
By yon burnside, gin ye maun ken,   *if, shall know*
    In a wee house wi' my minnie.   *mother*

But I foor up the glen at e'en,   *went, evening*
10   To see my bony lassie;
And lang before the grey morn cam,   *long, came*
    She was na hauf sae saucey.   *not half so*

O weary fa' the waukrife cock,   woe befall, wakeful
    And the foumart lay his crawin!   polecat
15 He wauken'd the auld wife frae her sleep,   wakened, old, from
    A wee blink or the dawin.   just before, dawn

An angry wife I wat she raise,   know
    And o'er the bed she brought her;
And wi' a meikle hazel rung   big, stick
20   She made her a weel-pay'd dochter.   well-, daughter

O fare thee weel, my bonie lass!   -well
    O fare thee weel, my hinnie!   -well, darling
Thou art a gay and a bony lass,
    But thou has a waukrife minnie.   wakeful mother

Burns notes in the Interleaved S.M.M. that this song was sung to
him by a girl in Nithsdale. It is generally included among his songs
on the assumption that he, at least, improved the old song. Kinsley
gives two possible sources (Vol. III, no. 311, p. 1339).

Tho' Women's Minds

Tune: For A' that an' a' that.
First printed in the S.M.M., Vol. 3, 2nd February, 1790.

Tho' women's minds, like winter winds,
    May shift, and turn an' a' that,
The noblest breast adores them maist,   most
    A consequence I draw that.

Chorus
5 For a' that, an' a' that,
    And twice as meikle's a' that,   much as
My dearest bluid to do them guid,   blood, good
    They're welcome till't for a' that.

Great love I bear to all the Fair,
10   Their humble slave an' a' that;
But lordly WILL, I hold it still
    A mortal sin to thraw that.   question
        For a' that, an' a' that, &c.

In rapture sweet this hour we meet,
   Wi' mutual love an' a' that,
15 But for how lang the flie may stang,   *long, fly, sting*
   Let inclination law that.
      For a' that, an' a' that, &c.

Their tricks and craft hae put me daft,   *have, stupid*
   They've taen me in an' a' that,   *taken*
But clear your decks, and here's the SEX!
20   I like the jads for a' that!   *hussies*
      For a' that, an' a' that, &c.

This is signed as the work of Burns in the S.M.M. It is an adapted
extract from his cantata, *The Jolly Beggars*, namely *The Bard's Song*.

Killiecrankie
Tune: Killiecranckie
First printed in the S.M.M., Vol. 3, 2nd February, 1790.

Whare hae ye been sae braw, lad!   *where have, so fine*
   Whare hae ye been sae brankie O?   *strutting smartly*
Whare hae ye been sae braw, lad?
   Cam ye by Killiecrankie O?   *come*

Chorus
5 An ye had been whare I hae been,   *where, have*
   Ye wad na been sae cantie O;   *would not, so cheerful*
An ye had seen what I hae seen ,   *have*
   On the braes o' Killiecrankie O.   *hill slopes*

I faught at land, I faught at sea,
10   At hame I faught my Auntie, O;   *home*
But I met the Devil and Dundee
   On th' braes o' Killiecrankie, O.   *hill slopes*
     An ye had been, &c.

'The bauld Pitcur fell in a furr,   *bold, dep ditch*
   An' Clavers gat a clankie, O;   *blow*
15 Or I had fed an Athole Gled   *hawk*
   On th' braes o' Killiecrankie, O.   *hill slopes*
     An ye had been, &c.

Although Burns visited the scene of this battle in the Autumn of 1787, during his Highland tour, it is uncertain how much of this song is his. He left no commentary and the remarks in the Interleaved S.M.M. are by Robert Riddell, who noted that the battle occurred on 27th July 1689 between the Jacobite forces of Graham of Claverhouse (Bonnie Dundee) and the Hanoverian loyalists led by General Mackay. As Kinsley states, the song is written in the voice of 'one of Mackay's men saved only by the deaths, in pursuit, of Claverhouse and Haliburton of Pitcur' (Vol. III, no. 313, p. 1340).

Willie Brew'd a Peck o' Maut

First printed in the S.M.M., Vol. 3, 2nd February, 1790.

O, Willie brewed a peck o' maut,	malt
And Rob and Allan cam to see;	came
Three blyther hearts, that lee-lang night,	live-long
Ye wad na found in Christendie.	would not

Chorus

5	We are na fou, we're nae that fou,	not full/drunk, not drunk
	But just a drappie in our e'e;	droplet, eye
	The cock may craw, the day may daw,	crow, dawn
	And ay we'll taste the barley bree.	-brew

	Here are we met, three merry boys,	
10	Three merry boys I trow are we;	pledge
	And monie a night we've merry been,	
	And monie mae we hope to be!	more
	We are na fou, &c.	

	It is the moon, I ken her horn,	know
	That's blinkin in the lift sae hie;	glinting, sky, high
15	She shines sae bright to wyle us hame,	so, lure, home
	But, by my sooth she'll wait a wee!	word, while
	We are na fou, &c.	

	Wha first shall rise to gang awa,	who, go away
	A cuckold, coward loun is he!	fool
	Wha first beside his chair shall fa',	who, fall
20	He is the king amang us three!	among
	We are na fou, &c.	

The music to this drinking song is by Allan Masterton, one of the poet's Edinburgh friends, who, with the poet, is alluded to in the first stanza. The brewer of this Bacchanalian song, Willie, is William Nicol, the Latin teacher at Edinburgh High School. The song celebrates a convivial evening when the three friends met in Moffat where Nicol was on holiday.

The Day Returns –
For Robert Riddell's Wedding Anniversary
Tune: Seventh of November
First printed in the S.M.M., Vol. 3, 2nd February, 1790.

The day returns, my bosom burns,
    The blissful day we twa did meet;   two
Tho' Winter wild in tempest toil'd,
    Ne'er simmer-sun was half sae sweet: so
5 Than a' the pride that loads the tide,
    And crosses o'er the sultry Line;
Than kingly robes, than crowns and globes,
    Heav'n gave me more — it made thee mine.

While day and night can bring delight,
10   Or Nature aught of pleasure give;
While Joys Above, my mind can move,
    For Thee and Thee alone I live!
When that grim foe of Life below
    Comes in between to make us part;
15 The iron hand that breaks our Band,
    It breaks my bliss — it breaks my heart!

This lyric was written by Burns to accompany a melody composed by his friend Robert Riddell of Glenriddell on his wedding anniversary, which fell on 7th November – hence the name of the tune. Burns was an intimate friend of the Riddells: 'At their fire-side I have enjoyed more pleasant evenings than at all the houses of fashionable people in this country put together . . . many of the happiest hours of my life' (quoted by Cromek, p. 269, from Burns's notes in the *Interleaved Scots Musical Museum*). The song is sung as from the lips of Robert Riddell to his wife. Ll. 7–8 are also politically apposite to Burns's relationship to Robert Riddell.

The Blue-Eyed Lassie

Tune: The Blathrie O' 't
First printed in the S.M.M., Vol. 3, 2nd February, 1790.

I gaed a waefu' gate, yestreen,   went, doleful, way, last night
    A gate, I fear, I'll dearly rue;
I gat my death frae twa sweet een,   got, from two, eyes
    Twa lovely een o' bonie blue.   two, eyes
'Twas not her golden ringlets bright,
    Her lips like roses, wat wi' dew,   wet
Her heaving bosom, lily-white,
    It was her een sae bonie blue.   eyes so

She talk'd, she smil'd, my heart she wyl'd,
    She charm'd my soul I wist na how;   know not
And ay the stound, the deadly wound,   heart ache
    Cam frae her een sae bonie blue.   came from, eyes so
But spare to speak, and spare to speed; shy & inattentive
    She'll aiblins listen to my vow: maybe
Should she refuse, I'll lay my dead
    To her twa een sae bonie blue.   two eyes so

This was composed on Jean Jaffray (1773–1850), daughter of Rev. Andrew Jaffray, minister at Lochmaben, Dumfriesshire. The initial air by Robert Riddell was changed to *The Blathrie O' 't* in Thomson's version.

Tam Glen

Tune: Merry Beggars
First printed in the S.M.M., Vol. 3, 2nd February, 1790.

My heart is a breaking, dear Tittie,   sister
    Some counsel unto me come len';   lend
To anger them a' is a pity,
    But what will I do wi' Tam Glen? —

5 I'm thinking, wi' sic a braw fellow,   such, fine
    In poortith I might mak a fen':   poverty, shift
What care I in riches to wallow,
    If I mauna marry Tam Glen. —   may not

There's Lowrie the laird o' Dumeller,
10   'Guid day to you, brute' he comes ben: good, on
He brags and he blaws o' his siller,   boasts, money
    But when will he dance like Tam Glen. —

My minnie does constantly deave me,   mother, chide
    And bids me beware o' young men;
15 They flatter, she says, to deceive me,
    But wha can think sae o' Tam Glen. —   who, so

My Daddie says, gin I'll forsake him,   if
    He'd gie me gude hunder marks ten: give, good
But if it's ordain'd I maun take him,   must
20   O wha will I get but Tam Glen?   who

Yestreen at the Valentines' dealing,[1]   last night
    My heart to my mou gied a sten;   mouth gave, leap
For thrice I drew ane without failing,   one
    And thrice it was written, Tam Glen. —

25 The last Halloween I was waukin   waken/watching
    My droukit sark-sleeve, as ye ken;   drenched shirt-, know
His likeness came up the house staukin,   image, stalking
    And the very grey breeks o' Tam Glen!   trousers

Come, counsel, dear Tittie, don't tarry;   sister
30   I'll gie ye my bonie black hen,   give
Gif ye will advise me to Marry   if
    The lad I lo'e dearly, Tam Glen. —   love

Burns sent this original dramatic lyric to Johnson in November
1788. A characteristic theme of Burns's women's songs is the
matrimonial choice of love as opposed to wealth. Aided by the
psychic forces occassioned by the Valentine's lottery and the Hal-
loween rituals, the girl is not to be denied her materially poor lover.
'Brute' is restored in l. 10 as earlier editors suppressed this female
denunciation of a social superior.

1 An old custom of sweethearts being chosen by lot on St. Valentine's Day.
R.B.

The Banks of Nith

Tune: Robie donna gorach
First printed in the S.M.M., Vol. 3, 2nd February, 1790.

The Thames flows proudly to the sea,
    Where royal cities stately stand;
But sweeter flows the Nith, to me,
    Where Cummins ance had high command: once
5 When shall I see that honor'd Land,
    That winding Stream I love so dear!
Must wayward Fortune's adverse hand
    For ever, ever keep me here.

How lovely, Nith, thy fruitful vales,
10   Where bounding hawthorns gaily bloom;
And sweetly spread thy sloping dales
    Where lambkins wanton thro' the broom!
Tho' wandering now must be my doom,
    Far from thy bonie banks and braes,   hill slopes
15 May there my latest hours consume
Amang my friends of early days!   among

This was, as Burns told Mrs Dunlop, his first compliment to the
river Nith, written on 20th August 1788. Cummins (l. 4) is Bruce's
rival, The Red Comyn.

Prologue Spoken at the Theatre of Dumfries
On New Year's Day Evening, 1790

First printed in *The St. James's Chronicle & British Evening Post*,
14th January, 1790.

No song nor dance I bring from yon great city,
That queens it o'er our taste — the more's the pity:
Tho' by the bye, abroad why will you roam?
Good sense and taste are natives here at home.
5 But not for panegyric I appear,
I come to wish you all a good New Year!
Old Father Time deputes me here before ye,
Not for to preach, but tell his simple story:
The sage grave Ancient cough'd, and bade me say,
10 'You're one year older this important day,'
If *wiser* too — he hinted some suggestion,
But 'twould be rude, you know, to ask the question;
And with a would-be-roguish leer and wink,
He bade me on you press this one word — 'THINK!'

15 Ye sprightly youths, quite flush with hope and spirit,
    Who think to storm the world by dint of merit,
    To you the dotard has a deal to say,
    In his sly, dry, sententious, proverb way!
    He bids you mind, amid your thoughtless rattle
20 That the first blow is ever half the battle;
    That tho' some by the skirt may try to snatch him,
    Yet by the forelock is the hold to catch him;
    That whether doing, suffering, or forbearing,
    You may do miracles by persevering.

25 Last, tho' not least in love, ye youthful fair,
    Angelic forms, high Heaven's peculiar care!
    To you old Bald-Pate smoothes his wrinkled brow,
    And humbly begs you'll mind the important — Now!
    To crown your happiness he asks your leave,
30 And offers, bliss to give and to receive.

    For our sincere, tho' haply weak endeavours,
    With grateful pride we own your many favours;
    And howsoe'er our tongues may ill reveal it,
    Believe our glowing bosoms truly feel it.

George Sutherland was manager of the Dumfries Theatre (the old theatre referred to here no longer exists, but the new theatre subscribed for during 1790 still stands). Burns got in touch with Sutherland, knowing the theatre was playing on New Year's Day, 1790, and enclosed an early draft of the above. The poet appears to have been in the audience that evening and wrote to his brother Gilbert on 11th January, 1790, remarking 'On Newyearday evening I gave him the following Prologue which he spouted to his Audience with great applause' (Letter 381).

Johnie Cope

First printed in S.M.M., Vol. 3, 1790.

Sir John Cope trod the north right far
Yet ne'er a rebel he cam naur,   near
Until he landed at Dunbar
Right early in the morning.

Chorus
5   Hey Johnie Cope are ye waulking yet,   wakened
    Or are ye sleeping I would wit;
    O haste ye get up for the drums do beat,
    O fye Cope rise in the morning.

He wrote a challenge from Dunbar,
10 Come fight me Charlie an ye daur;   dare
If it be not by the chance of war
I'll give you a merry morning.
    Hey Johnie Cope &c.

When Charlie look'd the letter upon
He drew his sword the scabbard from —
15 'So Heaven restore me to my own,
I'll meet you, Cope, in the morning'.
    Hey Johnie Cope &c.

Cope swore with many a bloody word
That he would fight them gun and sword,
But he fled from his nest like an ill scar'd bird,
20 And Johnie he took wing in the morning.
    Hey Johnie Cope &c.

It was upon an afternoon,
Sir Johnie march'd to Preston town;
He says, my lads come lean you down,
And we'll fight the boys in the morning.
    Hey Johnie Cope &c.

25 But when he saw the Highland lads
Wi' tartan trews and white cokauds,   cockades/white rose
Wi swords and guns and rungs and gauds,   cudgels, goads
O Johnie he took wing in the morning.
    Hey Johnie Cope &c.

On the morrow when he did rise,
30 He look'd between him and the skies;
He saw them wi their naked thighs,
Which fear'd him in the morning.
    Hey Johnie Cope &c.

O then he flew into Dunbar,
Crying for a man of war;   ship
35 He thought to have pass'd for a rustic tar,   sailor
And gotten awa in the morning.   away
    Hey Johnie Cope &c.

Sir Johnie into Berwick rade,   rode
Just as the devil had been his guide;
Gien him the warld he would na stay'd   given, world, not
40 To foughten the boys in the morning.   fight
    Hey Johnie Cope &c.

Says the Berwickers unto Sir John,
O what's become of all your men,
In faith, says he, I dinna ken,   *do not know*
I left them a' this morning.
    Hey Johnie Cope &c.

45   Says Lord Mark Car, ye are na blate,   *not shy*
To bring us the news o' your ain defeat;   *own*
I think you deserve the back o' the gate,
Get out o' my sight this morning.
    Hey Johnie Cope &c.

This is the poet's reworked version of an old, popular Jacobite ballad, most of which is traditional. Johnie Cope was Sir John Cope, General of the Hanoverian army defeated at the battle of Preston-pans in 1745 by the Jacobites.

O Dear Minny, What Shall I Do?

First printed in S.M.M. Vol. 3, 1790.

O dear Minny, what shall I do?
O dear Minny, what shall I do?
O dear Minny, what shall I do?
Daft thing, doylt thing, do as I do. —   *stupid*

5   If I be black, I canna be lo'ed;   *cannot, loved*
If I be fair, I canna be gude;
If I be lordly, the lads will look by me:
O dear Minny, what shall I do. —
      O dear Minny, &c.

Burns adapted this woman's song from a lyric in Herd's 1769 collection.

I'll Make You be Fain to Follow Me

First printed in S.M.M. Vol. 3, 1790.
Tune: I'll Make You be Fain to Follow Me

As late by a sodger I chanced to pass,   *soldier*
I heard him a courtin a bony young lass;
My hinny, my life, my dearest, quo he,   *darling*

I'll mak you be fain to follow me.
Gin I should follow you, a poor sodger lad,   if
Ilk ane o my cummers wad think I was mad;   each, one, wenches, would
For battles I never shall lang to see,   long
I'll never be fain to follow thee.   glad

To follow me, I think ye may be glad,
A part o my supper, a part o my bed,
A part o my bed, wherever it be,
I'll mak you be fain to follow me.   glad
Come try my knapsack on your back,
Alang the king's high-gate we'll pack;   along
Between Saint Johnston and bony Dundee,   Perth
I'll mak you be fain to follow me.

This is a traditional ballad slightly improved by Burns. It was
unsigned in the S.M.M. It first appears as a work of Burns in
Barke, 1955.

The White Cockade

First printed in S.M.M., 1790.

My love was born in Aberdeen,
The boniest lad that e'er was seen,
But now he makes our hearts fu' sad,   full
He takes the field wi' his White Cockade.

Chorus
5   O, he's a ranting, roving lad,
He is a brisk an' a bonie lad;
Betide what may, I will be wed,
And follow the boy wi' the White Cockade.

I'll sell my rock, my reel, my tow,   flaxing gear, fibre
10   My guid gray mare and hawkit cow;   good, spotted
To buy mysel a tartan plaid,   full body kilt
To follow the boy wi' the White Cockade.
        O he's a ranting, &c.

This is Burns's reworked version of a song in Herd's collection (1769)
called *The Ranting Roving Lad*. It was unsigned in the S.M.M. The
white rose (cockade) is the flower and emblem of the Jacobites.

The Campbells are Comin

First printed in S.M.M., Vol. 3, 1790.

Upon the Lomonds I lay, I lay,
Upon the Lomonds I lay, I lay,
I looked down to bonie Lochleven,
  And saw three bonie perches play — fish

5 The Campbells are comin, Oho, Oho!
The Campbells are comin, Oho, Oho!
The Campbells are comin to Bonie Lochleven,
  The Campbells are comin, Oho, Oho!

Great Argyle he goes before,
10 He makes his cannons and guns to roar,
Wi sound o trumpet, pipe and drum
  The Campbells are comin, Oho, Oho!

The Campbells they are a' in arms
Their loyal faith and truth to show,
15 Wi banners rattling in the wind
  The Campbells are comin, Oho, Oho!

The poet remarks in the *Interleaved Scots Musical Museum* that the
original lyric was 'Said to be composed on the imprisonment of
Mary Queen of Scots in Lochleven Castle'.

Craigie-burn Wood

First printed in Johnson's S.M.M., Vol. 4, 13th August 1792.

Sweet closes the evening on Craigie-burn Wood,
  And blythely awaukens the morrow; awakens
But the pride o' the spring on the Craigie-
    burn Wood
  Can yield me naught but sorrow. —

Old Chorus
5 Beyond thee, Dearie, beyond thee, Dearie,
  And Oh to be lying beyond thee!
O sweetly, soundly, weel may he sleep, well
  That's laid in the bed beyond thee. —

I see the spreading leaves and flowers,
10 I hear the wild birds singing;
But pleasure they hae nane for me have none
  While care my heart is wringing.

I can na tell, I maun na tell,   *not, shall not*
    I daur na for your anger: *dare not*
15 But secret love will break my heart,
    If I conceal it langer.   *longer*

I see thee gracefu', straight and tall,
    I see thee sweet and bonie;
But Oh, what will my torment be,
20   If thou refuse thy Johnie!

To see thee in another's arms,
    In love to lie and languish:
'Twad be my dead, that will be seen,
    My heart wad burst wi' anguish!   *would*

25 But Jeanie, say thou wilt be mine,
    Say thou loes nane before me;   *loves none*
And a' my days o' life to come
    I'll gratefully adore thee.

This is the first of two versions of this song, the second, more dense in Scots, was sent to Thomson. The lyric is original but the chorus is old. The heroine is Jean Lorimer (1775–1831) who lived at Kemmishall a few miles south of Ellisland farm and is celebrated in several works of Burns as his 'Chloris'. Burns wrote to Thomson that 'you are indebted for many of your best songs of mine . . . whenever I want to be more than ordinary *in song*; to be in some degree equal to your diviner airs . . . I put myself on a regimen of admiring a fine woman; and in proportion to the admirability of her charms, in proportion you are delighted with my verses' (Letter 644). She was indeed Burns's Gravesian 'White Goddess': 'she is, in a manner, what Sterne's Elza was to him – a Mistress, or Friend, or what you will, in the guiltless simplicity of platonic love.'

Frae the Friends and Land I Love

Tune: Carron Side
First printed in Johnson's S.M.M., Vol. 4, 13th August 1792.

Frae the friends and Land I love,   *from*
    Driv'n by Fortune's felly spite,   *deadly*
Frae my best Belov'd I rove,   *from*
    Never mair to taste delight. —   *more*
5 Never mair maun hope to find   *more shall*
    Ease frae toil, relief frae care: *from, from*
When Remembrance wracks the mind,
    Pleasures but unveil Despair.

	Brightest climes shall mirk appear,	gloomy
10	Desart ilka blooming shore;	desert, every
	Till the Fates, nae mair severe,	no more
	Friendship, Love, and Peace restore. —	
	Till Revenge, wi' laurell'd head,	
	Bring our Banish'd hame again;	home
15	And ilk loyal, bonie lad	each
	Cross the seas, and win his ain. —	own

Burns claims only the last four lines of this Jacobite song, asserting
that the remainder is traditional. Most editors suspect the song is
entirely his given that no earlier version has been traced. Although it
is not of the same quality as *Strathallan's Lament*, it is probably
correct that most of the song is his.

O John, Come Kiss Me Now –
First printed in Johnson's S.M.M., Vol. 4, 13th August 1792.

	O some will court and compliment,	
	And ither some will kiss and daut;	other, caress
	But I will mak o' my gudeman,	goodman
	My ain gudeman, it is nae faute. —	own, no fault

Chorus

5	O John, come kiss me now, now, now;	
	O John, my luve, come kiss me now;	
	O John, come kiss me by and by,	
	For weel ye ken the way to woo. —	well, know

	O some will court and compliment,	
10	And ither some will prie their mou,	other, kiss, mouth
	And some will hause in ithers arms,	embrace, other's
	And that's the way I like to do. —	
	O John, come kiss &c.	

Here Burns has created a version of an old popular song which
Kinsley believes is anti-courtly and derived from a fragment pre-
served in Herd's collection. (Vol. III, p. 1358)

Cock Up Your Beaver

First printed in Johnson's S.M.M., Vol. 4, 13th August 1792.

When first my brave Johnie lad came to this town,
He had a blue bonnet that wanted the crown,
But now he has gotten a hat and a feather,   _{a hat}
Hey, brave Johnie lad, cock up your beaver.

Cock up your beaver, and cock it fu' sprush;   _{full spruce}
We'll over the border and gie them a brush;
There's somebody there we'll teach better
    behaviour,
Hey, brave Johnie lad, cock up your beaver.

Wallace believed this to be based on an old work 'ridiculing Scotsmen who settled in London after the accession of James VI to the throne of England' (1896, p. 523). Even if this were so, Burns has converted it into a triumphalist assertion of émigré Scotsmen on the make.

My Tocher's the Jewel

First printed in Johnson's S.M.M., Vol. 4, 13th August 1792.

O meikle thinks my Luve o' my beauty,   _{much}
    And meikle thinks my Luve o' my kin;   _{much}
But little thinks my Luve I ken brawlie,   _{know well}
    My tocher's the jewel has charms for him.   _{dowry}
5   It's a' for the apple he'll nourish the tree;
    It's a' for the hiney he'll cherish the bee;   _{honey}
My laddie's sae meikle in luve wi' the siller,   _{so much, money}
    He canna hae luve to spare for me.   _{cannot have}

Your proffer o' luve's an airle-penny,   _{bargain money}
10   My tocher's the bargain ye wad buy;   _{would}
But an ye be crafty, I am cunnin,
    Sae ye wi' anither your fortune maun try.   _{so, another}
Ye're like to the timmer o' yon rotten wood,   _{trees}
    Ye're like to the bark o' yon rotten tree,
15 Ye'll slip frae me like a knotless thread,   _{from}
    An' ye'll crack ye're credit wi' mair nor me.   _{more}

The second last couplet of the first stanza and the final two of the second are old, the remainder is from Burns. This is another example of the sceptical, tough-minded women's voices in these songs.

Then Guidwife, Count the Lawin

First printed in Johnson's S.M.M., Vol. 4, 13th August 1792.

Gane is the day and mirk's the night,	gone, gloomy
But we'll ne'er stray for faute o' light,	fault/lack
For ale and brandy's stars and moon,	
And blude-red wine's the rysin Sun.	blood-, rising

Chorus

5 Then, guidwife, count the lawin, the lawin, the lawin,	goodwife, bill
Then guidwife count the lawin, and bring a coggie mair.	jug more

There's wealth and ease for gentlemen,	
And semple-folk maun fecht and fen';	simple, must fight
But here we're a' in ae accord,	one
10 For ilka man that's drunk 's a lord.	each
Then, guidwife, count the lawin, &c.	

My coggie is a haly pool,	jug, holy
That heals the wounds o' care and dool;	sorrow
And pleasure is a wanton trout,	lurking/ waiting
An ye drink it a', ye'll find him out.	
Then, guidwife, count the lawin, &c.	

The chorus of this is old but the verses are from Burns. The 'lawin' refers to the reckoning, or bill, an account to be paid at the end of the night's drinking – in modern colloquial Scots, the 'damage'.

The Whistle:
A Ballad

First printed in the S.M.M., Vol. 4, 13th August 1792.

Burns wrote the following introduction:

As the authentic Prose history of the WHISTLE is curious, I shall here give it. – In the train of Anne of Denmark, when she came to Scotland with our James the Sixth, there came also a Danish gentleman of gigantic stature and great prowess, and a matchless champion of Bacchus. He had a little ebony Whistle, which, at the commencement of the orgies, he laid on the table; and whoever was last able to blow it, every body else being disabled by the potency of the bottle, was to carry off the Whistle as a trophy of victory. – The Dane produced credentials of his victories, without a single defeat, at the Courts of Copenhagen, Stockholm, Moscow, Warsaw, and several of the petty courts in Germany; and challenged the Scots Bacchanalians to the alternative of trying his prowess, or else of acknowledging their inferiority. – After many overthrows on the part of the Scots, the Dane was encountered by Sir Robert Lowrie of Maxwelton, ancestor to the present worthy baronet of that name; who, after three days and three nights' hard contest, left the Scandinavian under the table, 'And blew on the Whistle his requiem shrill'.

Sir Walter, son to Sir Robert before mentioned, afterwards lost the Whistle to Walter Riddell of Glenriddell, who had married a sister of Sir Walter's. – On Friday, the 16th October, 1789, at Friar's-Carse, the Whistle was once more contended for, as related in the Ballad, by the present Sir Robert Lowrie of Maxwelton; Robert Riddell, Esq. of Glenriddell, lineal descendant and representative of Walter Riddell, who won the Whistle, and in whose family it has continued; and Alexander Ferguson, Esq. of Craigdarroch, likewise descended of the great Sir Robert, which last gentleman carried off the hard-won honours of the field. R.B

I sing of a Whistle, a Whistle of worth,
I sing of a Whistle, the pride of the North,
Was brought to the court of our good Scottish King,
And long with this Whistle all Scotland shall ring.

5   Old Loda[1], still rueing the arm of Fingal,
The god of the bottle sends down from his hall —
'This Whistle's your challenge, to Scotland get o'er,
And drink them to hell, Sir! or ne'er see me more!'

Old poets have sung, and old chronicles tell,
10   What champions ventur'd, what champions fell;
The son of great Loda was conqueror still,   the gigantic Dane
And blew on the Whistle their requiem shrill.

Till Robert, the lord of the Cairn and the Scaur[2],
Unmatch'd at the bottle, unconquered in war,
15   He drank his poor god-ship as deep as the sea,
No tide of the Baltic e'er drunker than he.

1 See Ossian's *Caric-thura*. R.B.
2 Sir Robert Lawrie. The Cairn is a stream in Glencairn parish, where Maxwelton House is erected. The Skarr, likewise, runs into the Nith.

Thus Robert, victorious, the trophy has gain'd,
Which now in his house has for ages remain'd;
Till three noble chieftains, and all of his blood,
20   The jovial contest again have renew'd.

Three joyous good fellows with hearts clear of flaw;
Craigdarroch so famous for wit, worth, and law;
And trusty Glenriddel, so skilled in old coins;
And gallant Sir Robert, deep-read in old wines.

25   Craigdarroch began, with a tongue smooth as oil,
Desiring Glenriddel to yield up the spoil;
Or else he would muster the heads of the clan,
And once more, in claret, try which was the man.

'By the gods of the ancients!' Glenriddel replies,
30   'Before I surrender so glorious a prize,
I'll conjure the ghost of the great Rorie More[3],
And bumper his horn with him twenty times o'er.'

Sir Robert, a soldier, no speech would pretend.
But he ne'er turn'd his back on his foe — or his friend,
35   Said, Toss down the Whistle, the prize of the field,
And knee-deep in claret he'd die ere he'd yield.

To the board of Glenriddel our heroes repair,
So noted for drowning of sorrow and care;
But for wine and for welcome not more known to fame,
40   Than the sense, wit, and taste of a sweet lovely dame.

A Bard was selected to witness the fray,
And tell future ages the feats of the day;
A Bard who detested all sadness and spleen,
And wish'd that Parnassus a vineyard had been.

45   The dinner being over, the claret they ply,
And ev'ry new cork is a new spring of joy;
In the bands of old friendship and kindred so set,
And the bands grew the tighter the more they were wet.

3 See Johnson's *Tour to the Hebrides.* R.B.

Gay Pleasure ran riot as bumpers ran o'er;
50   Bright Phoebus ne'er witness'd so joyous a corps,   core
And vow'd that to leave them he was quite forlorn,
Till Cynthia hinted he'd see them next morn.

Six bottles a-piece had well wore out the night,
When gallant Sir Robert, to finish the fight,
55   Turn'd o'er in one bumper a bottle of red,
And swore 'twas the way that their ancestor did.

Then worthy Glenriddel, so cautious and sage,
No longer the warfare, ungodly, would wage;
A high ruling elder[4] to wallow in wine!
60   He left the foul business to folks less divine.

The gallant Sir Robert fought hard to the end;
But who can with Fate and Quart Bumpers contend?
Though Fate said, a hero should perish in light;
So uprose bright Phoebus — and down fell the knight.

65   Next uprose our Bard, like a prophet in drink: —
'Craigdarroch, thou'lt soar when creation shall sink!
But if thou would flourish immortal in rhyme,
Come — one bottle more — and have at the sublime!

'Thy line, that have struggled for freedom with Bruce,
70   Shall heroes and patriots ever produce:
So thine be the laurel, and mine be the bay;
The field thou hast won, by yon bright god of day!'

Before inclusion in the poet's Edinburgh edition of 1793, this
ballad was printed in James Johnson's *Scots Musical Museum*, in
August 1792. There has been some controversy over whether or
not Burns witnessed this drinking contest, but it appears
that he did attend, without taking part, despite his undeserved
reputation for being a drunkard. While the alcohol consumed
here is abnormal, even by the standards of eighteenth-century
upper-class and professional Scotland, Burns was a moderate
drinker compared to many of his social superiors. Boswell, who

4 Robert Riddell was a Kirk Elder, representing the presbytery of Dumfries
at the Scottish Assembly from 1789–93.

became a hysterical loyalist under the impact of the French revolution, was a far heavier drinker. The reference to 'old coins' (l. 23) alludes to the fact that Riddell was, amongst other things, an antiquarian.

There'll Never be Peace till Jamie Comes Hame

First printed in Johnson's S.M.M., Vol. 4, 13th August 1792.

By yon castle wa' at the close of the day,	wall
I heard a man sing tho' his head it was grey;	
And as he was singing the tears down came,	
There'll never be peace till Jamie comes hame. —	home
5 The Church is in ruins, the State is in jars,	
Delusions, oppressions, and murderous wars:	
We dare na weel say't, but we ken wha's to blame,	not well, know, who's
There'll never be peace till Jamie comes hame. —	home
My seven braw sons for Jamie drew sword,	fine
10 But now I greet round their green beds in the yerd;	weep, graves, field
It brak the sweet heart o' my faithfu' auld Dame,	broke, old
There'll never be peace till Jamie comes hame. —	
Now life is a burden that bows me down,	
Sin I tint my bairns, and he tint his crown;	since, lost, kids, lost
15 But till my last moments my words are the same,	
There'll never be peace till Jamie comes hame. —	

Introducing this Jacobite inspired song to Alexander Cunningham, the poet wrote, 'When Political combustion ceases to be the object of Princes & Patriots, it then, you know, becomes the lawful prey of Historians & Poets' (Letter 441). This is a deliberately ambivalent remark. It does not necessarily mean that either history or poetry is a mere record of things irretrievably past, but that both have a disturbing, resurrectionary potential as a prelude to political action. Yeats would perhaps be the most tangible example of this sort of poetic influence.

What Can a Young Lassie Do wi' an Auld Man

First printed in Johnson's S.M.M., Vol. 4, 13th August 1792.

What can a young lassie, what shall a young lassie,
    What can a young lassie do wi' an auld man?   old
Bad luck on the pennie, that tempted my Minnie   mother
    To sell her puir Jenny for siller and lan'!   poor, money & land

5 He's always compleenin, frae mornin to eenin,   complaining, from, evening
    He hoasts and he hirpis the weary day lang: coughs, limps
He's doylt and he's dozin; his blude it is frozen,   worn-out, dull, blood
    O, dreary's the night wi' a crazy auld man!   old

He hums and he hankers, he frets and he cankers,   fretful, peevish, crabbit
10   I never can please him, do a' that I can;
He's peevish, an' jealous of a' the young fallows,
    O, dool on the day I met wi' an auld man!   sorrow, old

My auld auntie Katie upon me taks pity,   old
    I'll do my endeavour to follow her plan;
15 I'll cross him, an' wrack him until I heartbreak him,
    And then his auld brass will buy me a new   old money
      pan.

This is an original work by Burns, which he describes in the British
Museum manuscript as having 'some merit' but 'miserably long'
(See Wallace 1896, p. 370). Economically enforced May/September
relationships in the world of eighteenth-century Scottish folk songs
begin, never mind end, badly.

The Bonie Lad that's Far Awa

First printed in Johnson's S.M.M., Vol. 4, 13th August 1792.

O how can I be blythe and glad,
    Or how can I gang brisk and braw,   go, fine
When the bonie lad that I lo'e best   love
    Is o'er the hills and far awa. —

5 It's no the frosty winter wind,
    It's no the driving drift and snaw;   snow
But ay the tear comes in my e'e ,   eye
    To think on him that's far awa. —

My father pat me frae his door,		put from
10	My friends they hae disown'd me a';	have
But I hae ane will tak my part,		have one
The bonie lad that's far awa. —		

A pair o' gloves he bought to me,		
And silken snoods he gae me twa,		hair-ribbons, gave, two
15	And I will wear them for his sake,	
The bonie lad that's far awa. —		

O weary Winter soon will pass,		
And Spring will cleed the birken shaw:		clothe, birch woods
And my sweet babie will be born,		
20	And he'll be hame that's far awa.	home

Burns informed Thomson in October 1794 that this song 'is mine'
(Letter 644). It is partly modelled on an old fragment preserved by
Herd which begins 'How can I be blythe or glad, / Or in my mind
contented be'. Burns's poetry, as his world, was filled with harsh,
punitive separation with people either fiscally driven out or sucked
into the vortex of the French war. The winter pain of this woman,
bearing her illegitimate child, is, at least, lightened by anticipation
of Spring and return.

I Do Confess Thou art sae Fair –

First printed in Johnson's S.M.M., Vol. 4, 13th August 1792.

I do confess thou art sae fair,		so
I wad been o'er the lugs in luve;		would, ears
Had I na found, the slightest prayer		not
That lips could speak, thy heart could muve. —		

5	I do confess thee sweet, but find,	
Thou art so thriftless o' thy sweets,		
Thy favours are the silly wind		
That kisses ilka thing it meets.		every

See yonder rose-bud rich in dew,		
10	Amang its native briers sae coy,	among, so
How sune it tines its scent and hue,		soon, loses
When pu'd and worn a common toy!		pulled

Sic fate ere lang shall thee betide;   such, long, become
    Tho' thou may gayly bloom awhile,
15 And sune thou shalt be thrown aside,   soon
    Like onie common weed and vile. —   any

In the Interleaved S.M.M. Burns writes, 'This song is altered from
a poem by Sir Robert Ayton . . . I have improved the simplicity of
the sentiments, by giving them a Scots dress.'

Sensibility How Charming

Tune: Cornwallis Lament for Coln. Moorhouse
First printed in Johnson's S.M.M., Vol. 4, 13th August 1792.

Sensibility how charming,
    Dearest Nancy, thou can'st tell;
But Distress with horrors arming,
    Thou hast also known too well. —

5 Fairest flower, behold the lily,
    Blooming in the sunny ray.
Let the blast sweep o'er the valley,
    See it prostrate on the clay. —

Hear the woodlark charm the forest,
10   Telling o'er his little joys:
Hapless bird! a prey the surest
    To each pirate of the skies. —

Dearly bought the hidden treasure,
    Finer Feelings can bestow:
15 Chords that vibrate sweetest pleasure,
    Thrill the deepest notes of woe. —

In two separate letters (Letters 411 and 462) Burns informs both
Mrs Dunlop and Agnes McLehose that this work was written for
them, first as a condolence to Mrs Dunlop on the death of her son-
in-law and then as a compliment to his 'Clarinda': hence the
reference to 'Nancy', l. 2. This is probably due to the poet's desire
to comfort two close friends on separate occasions. Burns's under-
standing of the fact that hypersensitivity to pleasure necessarily,
dreadfully, entails hypersensitivity to pain, evoked a passionate
response among the English Romantic poets. Wordsworth, in

particular, saw Burns as symptomatic of this dire, manic depressive alternation of extreme emotional states. See, for example, *Resolution and Independence* (ll. 44–9):

> Of Him who walked in glory and in joy
> Following his plough, along the mountain-side:
> By our own spirits are we deified:
> We Poets in our youth begin in gladness;
> But thereof come in the end despondency and madness.

Yon Wild Mossy Mountains

First printed in Johnson's S.M.M., Vol. 4, 13th August 1792.

Yon wild, mossy mountains sae lofty and wide,   so
That nurse in their bosom the youth o' the Clyde;
Where the grouse lead their coveys thro' the heather to feed,
And the sheepherd tents his flock as he pipes on his reed.

5 Not Gowrie's rich valley, nor Forth's sunny shores,
To me hae the charms o' yon wild, mossy moors: have
For there, by a lanely, sequestered stream,   lonely
Resides a sweet Lassie, my thought and my dream. —

Amang thae wild mountains shall still be my path, among those
10 Ilk stream foaming down its ain green, narrow strath; each, own
For there wi' my Lassie, thy lang-day I rove, long
While o'er us, unheeded, flee the swift hours fly
  o' Love. —

She is not the fairest, altho' she is fair;
O' nice education but sma' is her share;
15 Her parentage humble as humble can be;
But I lo'e the dear Lassie because she lo'es me. —

To Beauty what man but maun yield him a prize, must
In her armour of glances, and blushes, and sighs;
And when Wit and Refinement hae polish'd her darts, have
20 They dazzle our een, as they flie to our hearts. — eyes, fly

But Kindness, sweet Kindness, in the fond-sparkling e'e, eye
Has lustre outshining the diamond to me;
And the heart beating love as I'm clasp'd in her arms,
O, these are my Lassie's all-conquering charms!

Burns writes in the Interleaved S.M.M. 'This tune is by Oswald: the song alludes to a part of my private history which it is of no consequence to the world to know' (quoted in Wallace, 1896, p. 372). It is, therefore, an original work although the identity of the romance is not known.

It is Na, Jean, Thy Bonie Face

Tune: The Maid's Complaint
First printed in Johnson's S.M.M., Vol. 4, 13th August 1792.

It is na, Jean, thy bonie face, *not*
　　Nor shape that I admire,
Altho' thy beauty and thy grace
　　Might weel awauk desire. — *well, awaken*

5　Something in ilka part o' thee *each*
　　To praise, to love, I find,
But dear as is thy form to me,
　　Still dearer is thy mind. —

Nae mair ungen'rous wish I hae, *no more, have*
10　Nor stronger in my breast,
Than, if I canna mak thee sae, *cannot, so*
　　At least to see thee blest.

Content am I, if Heaven shall give
　　But happiness to thee:
15　And as wi' thee I wish to live,
　　For thee I'd bear to die.

Although allegedly based on an old English song, which editorially still remains unlocated, this was written for Jean Armour. The ultimate rhyme of 'thee' and 'die' requires the Scots pronunciation *dee*.

Eppie Macnab –

First printed in Johnson's S.M.M., Vol. 4, 13th August 1792.

O saw ye my dearie, my Eppie McNab?
O saw ye my dearie, my Eppie McNab?
'She's down in the yard, she's kissin the Laird,
She winna come hame to her ain Jock Rab. — *will not, home, own*

5 O come thy ways to me, my Eppie McNab;
 O come thy ways to me, my Eppie McNab;
 What-e'er thou has done, be it late, be it soon,
 Thou's welcome again to thy ain Jock Rab. — own

 What says she, my dearie, my Eppie McNab?
10 What says she, my dearie, my Eppie McNab?
 She lets thee to wit that she has thee forgot,
 And for ever disowns thee, her ain Jock Rab.

 O had I ne'er seen thee, my Eppie McNab!
 O had I ne'er seen thee, my Eppie McNab!
15 As light as the air and as fause as thou's fair, false
 Thou's broken the heart o' thy ain Jock Rab!

This is Burns's somewhat sanitised version of an old bawdy song
with its political as well as erotic implications.

Wha is That at My Bower Door?
First printed in Johnson's S.M.M., Vol. 4, 13th August 1792.

 Wha is that at my bower-door?   who, cottage
  O, wha is it but Findlay;
 Then gae your gate, ye 'se nae be here! go, way, not
  Indeed maun I! quo' Findlay. — must

5 What mak ye, sae like a thief?   so
  O, come and see, quo' Findlay,
 Before the morn ye'll work mischief;
  Indeed will I, quo' Findlay. —

 Gif I rise and let you in,   what if
10 Let me in, quo' Findlay;
 Ye'll keep me waukin wi' your din; waken
  Indeed will I, quo' Findlay. —

 In my bower if ye should stay,
  Let me stay, quo' Findlay;
15 I fear ye'll bide till break o' day;
  Indeed will I, quo' Findlay. —

Here this night if ye remain,
    I'll remain, quo' Findlay;
I dread ye'll learn the gate again;   come back
20   Indeed will I, quo' Findlay. —

What may pass within this bower,
    Let it pass, quo' Findlay;
Ye maun conceal till your last hour;   must
    Indeed will I, quo' Findlay. —

This question and answer dialogue ballad is modelled on an old broadside *Who's that at my chamber door?* (Kinsley, Vol. III, no. 356, p. 1392).

The Bonny Wee Thing

First printed in Johnson's S.M.M., Vol 4, 13th August 1792.

Wishfully I look and languish
    In that bonie face o' thine;
And my heart it stounds wi' anguish,   beats
    Lest my wee thing be na mine. —   not

Chorus
5 Bonie wee thing, cannie wee thing,
    Lovely wee thing, wert thou mine;
I wad wear thee in my bosom,   would
    Lest my Jewel it should tine.   be lost

Wit, and Grace and Love, and Beauty,
10   In ae constellation shine;   one
To adore thee is my duty,
    Goddess o' this soul o' mine!
      Bonie wee thing, &c.

Deborah Duff Davies was a petite young Welshwoman who, especially from his letters to her (Letters 472A, 556A, 564) made, even by his inflammatory standards, an extraordinary impact on Burns. His erotic enthusiasm was further intensified by political approval. He met her as a friend of the Riddells at Woodley Park and, from the evidence of Letter 556A she shared his reformative radical passions: 'They talk of REFORM – My God! What a reform would *I* make among the Sons, & even the Daughters, of Men!' She died an early consumptive death.

Ae Fond Kiss

Tune: Rory Dall's Port
First printed in Johnson's S.M.M., Vol. 4, 13th August 1792.

Ae fond kiss, and then we sever;   one
Ae fareweel, and then forever!
Deep in heart-wrung tears I'll pledge thee,
Warring sighs and groans I'll wage thee. —

5   Who shall say that Fortune grieves him,
While the star of hope she leaves him:
Me, nae cheerfu' twinkle lights me;   no
Dark despair around benights me. —

I'll ne'er blame my partial fancy:
10 Naething could resist my Nancy: nothing
But to see her, was to love her;
Love but her, and love for ever. —

Had we never lov'd sae kindly,   so
Had we never lov'd sae blindly!
15 Never met — or never parted,
We had ne'er been broken-hearted. —

Fare-thee-weel, thou first and fairest!   -well
Fare-thee-weel, thou best and dearest!
Thine be ilka joy and treasure,   each/every
20 Peace, Enjoyment, Love and Pleasure! —

Ae fond kiss, and then we sever!
Ae fareweel, Alas, for ever!
Deep in heart-wrung tears I'll pledge thee,
Warring sighs and groans I'll wage thee. —

Kinsley has traced the source of this song to Dodsley:

One fond kiss before we part,
   Drop a Tear and bid Adieu;
Tho' we sever, my fond Heart
   Till we meet shall pant for you' (Vol. III, p. 1379).

If this is the ore, Burns has transmuted it into one of his most golden lyrics though Kinsley himself thinks the song's success depends on ll. 13–16.

Despite the over-heated artificiality of much of the relation-
ship, Burns, because of his class, and Mrs MacLehose, because of
her separated status, were, to a degree, outsiders in polite Edin-
burgh society. Her decision to rejoin her husband who she,
against her Edinburgh surgeon father's advice, had married when
seventeen and, five years and three children later, had separated
from, led her to take ship, ironically, to Jamaica. The song, then,
is charged with a combination of sexual loss and foreign exile,
bringing together two of Burns's dominant themes. The journey,
too, led only to further humiliation for her. Her husband stayed
with his mistress, refused to meet her and so she took the same
ship home. She long outlived the poet and in 1831 recorded in her
Journal: 'This day (6 December) I can never forget. Parted with
Burns in the year 1791, never more to meet in this world. Oh, may
we meet in Heaven!'

As I Was a Wand'ring

Tune: Rinn m'eudial mo mhealladh – a Gaelic air
First printed in Johnson's S.M.M., Vol. 4, 13th August 1792.

As I was a wand'ring ae midsummer e'enin,	one, evening
The pipers and youngsters were makin their game,	having fun
Amang them I spyed my faithless fause luver,	among, false
Which bled a' the wounds o' my dolour again. —	

Chorus

5	Weel, since he has left me, may pleasure gae wi' him;	well, go
	I may be distress'd, but I winna complain:	will not
	I'll flatter my fancy I may get anither,	another
	My heart it shall never be broken for ane. —	one

	I could na get sleepin till dawin, for greetin;	not, dawn, weeping
10	The tears trickl'd down like the hail and the rain:	
	Had I na got greetin, my heart wad a broken,	not, crying, would
	For Oh, luve forsaken's a tormenting pain!	
	Weel, since he has left me &c.	

	Although he has left me for greed o' the siller,	money
	I dinna envy him the gains he can win:	do not
15	I rather wad bear a' the lade o' my sorrow,	would, load
	Than ever hae acted sae faithless to him. —	have, so
	Weel, since he has left me &c.	

This is omitted by Mackay but accepted by Kinsley. Two versions of this traditional song have been given as the work of Burns. On this version, Kinsley asserts that only the last verse is by Burns. Kinsley has repeated Scott Douglas's error. The latter printed Johnson's text and asserted that only the final stanza came from Burns. The original text from the S.M.M. should not be the one attributed to Burns. This can be clearly seen if we compare the original text with the revised Burns one above:

> As I was walking ae May morning,
> The fiddlers and youngsters were makin their game;
> And there I saw my faithless lover,
> And a' my sorrows returned again.
>
> Chorus
> 5 Weel, since he's gane – may joy gae wi' him!
> It's never be he that shall gar me complain:
> I'll cheer up my heart, and I *will* get another,
> I'll never lay a' my luve upon ane ane. –
>
> I could na get sleepin' yestreen, for weepin,
> 10 The tears trickl'd down like showers o' rain;
> And had I no got greetin, my heart wad ha' broken,
> And O! but love's a tormenting pain!
>   Weel, since he has gane &c.
>
> Although he has left me for greed o' the siller,
> I dinna envy him the gains he can win:
> 15 I rather wad bear a' the lade o' my sorrow,
> Than ever hae acted sae faithless to him. –
>   Weel, since he has gane &c.

Lovely Davies

Tune: Miss Muir
First printed in Johnson's S.M.M., Vol. 4, 13th August 1792.

O how shall I, unskilfu', try
    The Poet's occupation?
The tunefu' Powers, in happy hours,
    That whisper, inspiration,
5 Even they maun dare an effort mair   *may, more*
    Than aught they ever gave us,
Or they rehearse in equal verse
    The charms o' lovely DAVIES. —

Each eye it cheers, when she appears,
10   Like Phoebus in the morning,
When past the shower, and every flower
      The garden is adorning:
As the wretch looks o'er Siberia's shore,
      When winter-bound the wave is;
15 Sae droops our heart when we maun part   *so, must*
      Frae charming, lovely DAVIES. —   *from*

Her smile's a gift frae boon the lift,   *from above, sky*
      That maks us mair than princes;   *more*
A sceptred hand, a king's command,
20   Is in her darting glances:
The man in arms 'gainst female charms,
      Even he her willing slave is;
He hugs his chain, and owns the reign
      Of conquering lovely DAVIES. —

25 My Muse to dream of such a theme,
      Her feeble powers surrender;
The eagle's gaze alone surveys;
      The sun's meridian splendour:
I wad in vain essay the strain,   *would*
30   The deed too daring brave is;
I'll drap the lyre, and, mute, admire   *drop/cease*
      The charms o' lovely DAVIES. —

Letter 472A, which presumably accompanied this song, is a much
more astonishing piece of prose than his conventional song.

The Weary Pund o' Tow

First printed in Johnson's S.M.M., Vol. 4, 13th August 1792.

I bought my wife a stane o' lint,   *stone in weight, flax*
      As gude as e'er did grow;   *good*
And a' that she has made o' that
      Is ae poor pund o' tow.   *one, pound string*

Chorus
5 The weary pund, the weary pund,   *pound*
      The weary pund o' tow;   *flax string*
I think my wife will end her life,
      Before she spin her tow. —

	There sat a bottle in a bole,	hole in a wall
10	Beyont the ingle lowe;	near, fireside flame
	And ay she took the tither souk	another such
	To drouk the stourie tow. —	wet, dusty flax string
	The weary pund, &c.	

	Quoth I, for shame, ye dirty dame,	
	Gae spin your tap o' tow!	go
15	She took the rock, and wi' a knock,	distaff
	She brake it o'er my pow. —	head
	The weary pund, &c.	

	At last her feet, I sang to see't,	
	Gaed foremost o'er the knowe;	went, edge of hill
	And or I wad anither jad,	wed another hussy
20	I'll wallop in a tow. —	
	The weary pund, &c.	

As Kinsley has rightly remarked (Vol. III, no. 360, p. 1395), this is based on a traditional English song, published in a collection *The Charmer* in 1782, beginning 'I bought my woman and my wife half a pound of tow'. As with other English songs, Burns has given this what he termed a *Scots dress*.

I Hae a Wife o' My Ain

First printed in Johnson's S.M.M., Vol. 4, 13th August 1792.

	I hae a wife o' my ain,	have, own
	I'll partake wi' naebody;	nobody
	I'll tak Cuckold frae nane,	take, from none
	I'll gie Cuckold to naebody. —	give, nobody

5	I hae a penny to spend,	have
	There, thanks to naebody;	
	I hae naething to lend,	have nothing
	I'll borrow frae naebody. —	from nobody

	I am naebody's lord,	
10	I'll be slave to naebody;	
	I hae a gude braid sword,	have good broad
	I'll tak dunts frae naebody. —	blows from

I'll be merry and free,
 I'll be sad for naebody;
15 Naebody cares for me,
 I care for naebody. —

This is adapted from an old simple Scots ballad on defiant self-sufficiency against poverty and was not composed by Burns just after his marriage as some editors have erroneously believed. If it had been Burns's own work he would have signed it in the S.M.M.

When She Cam Ben, She Bobbed

First printed in Johnson's S.M.M., Vol. 4, 13th August 1792.

O when she cam ben she bobbed fu' law, came in, bowed
O when she cam ben she bobbed fu' law;
And when she cam' ben she kiss'd Cockpen,
 And syne she deny'd she did it at a'. — later, at all

5 And was na Cockpen right saucy witha', not, everyone
And was na Cockpen right saucy witha',
In leaving the dochter o' a lord, daughter
 And kissin a Collier-lassie an' a'. —

O never look down, my lassie at a',
10 O never look down, my lassie at a';
Thy lips are as sweet, and thy figure compleat, complete
 As the finest dame in castle or ha'. — hall

Tho' thou hast nae silk and holland sae sma, no, so small
Tho' thou hast nae silk and holland sae sma,
15 Thy coat and thy sark are thy ain handywark shirt, own work
 And Lady Jean was never sae braw. so fine

This is an improved version of a traditional song about a Laird who had an affair with a common girl, printed in Herd's collection (Vol. 2, p. 206). The first two stanzas are almost unaltered while the last two are from Burns.

O, for Ane and Twenty, Tam

Tune: The Moudiewart
First printed in Johnson's S.M.M., Vol. 4, 13th August 1792.

They snool me sair, and haud me down,	snub, sore, hold
And gar me look like bluntie, Tam;	make, fool
But three short years will soon wheel roun',	round
And then comes ane-and-twenty, Tam.	one-

Chorus

5	An O, for ane and twenty, Tam!	one-
	And hey, sweet ane and twenty, Tam!	
	I'll learn my kin a rattlin sang,	song
	An I saw ane and twenty, Tam.	

	A gleib o' lan', a claut o' gear,	piece, handful
10	Was left me by my Auntie, Tam;	
	At kith or kin I needna spier,	need not ask
	An I saw ane and twenty, Tam.	
	An' O, for ane and twenty, &c.	

	They'll hae me wed a wealthy coof,	have, fool
	Tho' I mysel hae plenty, Tam;	have
15	But hear'st thou, laddie, there's my loof,	hand
	I'm thine at ane and twenty, Tam!	one
	An' O, for ane and twenty, &c.	

Although published anonymously in the S.M.M., Burns acknowledges to George Thomson in October 1794 that this is his song, with the remark ' "In summer when the hay was mawn", "An O for ane and twenty Tam" are both mine' (Letter 644). Again, this is a song of significant female defiance regarding an 'unsuitable' marriage partner.

O Kenmure's on and Awa, Willie

First printed in Johnson's S.M.M., Vol. 4, 13th August 1792.

O Kenmure's on and awa, Willie,	
O, Kenmure's on and awa;	away
An' Kenmure's Lord's the bravest Lord	
That ever Galloway saw.	

5   Success to Kenmure's band, Willie!
    Success to Kenmure's band,
There's no a heart that fears a Whig
    That rides by Kenmure's hand.

    Here's Kenmure's health in wine, Willie,
10   Here's Kenmure's health in wine,
There ne'er was a coward o' Kenmure's blude,   blood
    Nor yet o' Gordon's Line.

O Kenmure's lads are men, Willie,
    O Kenmure's lads are men,
15   Their hearts and swords are metal true,
    And that their faes shall ken.   foes, know

They'll live, or die wi' fame, Willie,
    They'll live, or die wi' fame,
But soon wi' sounding victorie
20   May Kenmure's lord come hame.   home

Here's Him that's far awa, Willie,
    Here's Him that's far awa,
And here's the flower that I lo'e best,   love
    The rose that's like the snaw!   snow/white cockade

Previous editors have assumed this is based on an old Galloway song, but no evidence of such an earlier work exists. It is not impossible that Burns converted a Highland Jacobite song (akin to *Up an Warn A' Willie*) so that Galloway becomes the location and Viscount William Gordon of Kenmure Castle, who led the Jacobite troops in the South of Scotland in 1715, becomes the hero. The poet and John Syme spent three days at Kenmure Castle (sadly now in ruins), near New Galloway village at the end of July, into August, 1793, on the poet's first tour of Galloway. The snow white rose is the Jacobite emblem (the white cockade) which even the Marxist McDiarmid writes of with considerable pathos. The song is original and carries overtones of *Here's A Health Tae Them That's Awa'*, a later song where Jacobite dissidents meet and merge with the radicalism of the 1790s.

Bessy and her Spinning Wheel

Tune: The Sweet Lass that Loves Me
First printed in Johnson's S.M.M., Vol. 4, 13th August 1792.

O leeze me on my spinnin-wheel,   delight me with
And leeze me on my rock and reel;   distaff
Frae tap to tae that cleeds me bien,   from, head, toe, clothes, well
And haps me fiel and warm at e'en!   covers, well, evening
5 I'll set me down, and sing and spin,
While laigh descends the summer sun,   low
Blest wi' content, and milk and meal,
O leeze me on my spinnin-wheel. —

On ilka hand the burnies trot,   either, small burns run
10 And meet below my theekit cot;   thatched cottage
The scented birk and hawthorn white   birch
Across the pool their arms unite,
Alike to screen the birdie's nest,
And little fishes' callor rest: cool
15 The sun blinks kindly in the biel'   glimmers, shelter
Where blythe I turn my spinnin-wheel. —

On lofty aiks the cushats wail,   oaks, wood pigeons
And Echo cons the doolfu' tale;   woeful
The lintwhites in the hazel braes,   linnets, rows of
20 Delighted, rival ither's lays:
The craik amang the claver hay,   corncrake, clover
The paitrick whirrin o'er the ley,   partridge, grass land
The swallow jinkin round my shiel,   darting, sheiling
Amuse me at my spinnin-wheel. —

25 Wi' sma to sell, and less to buy,   little
Aboon distress, below envy,   above
O wha wad leave this humble state,   who would
For a' the pride of a' the Great?
Amid their flairing, idle toys,
30 Amid their cumbrous, dinsome joys,
Can they the peace and pleasure feel
Of Bessy at her spinnin-wheel!

This song derives its title, if not its form and content from Ramsay's *The Loving Lass and Spinning Wheel*. The song is a eulogy to Elizabeth Burgess of Watcarrick in Eskdalemuir.

The song is a celebration of what were to become Wordsworthian pastoral, sessile virtues of economic and environmental contentment, but with a personal, intimate, charming sense of specific character of which the English poet was arguably not capable.

My Collier Laddie

First printed in Johnson's S.M.M., Vol. 4, 13th August 1792.

Whare live ye, my bonie lass,	where
And tell me how they ca' ye?	what, call
My name, she says, is Mistress Jean,	
And I follow the Collier laddie.	
My name, she says, is Mistress Jean,	
And I follow the Collier laddie.	

5	See you not yon hills and dales	
	The sun shines on sae brawlie?	so finely
	They a' are mine and they shall be thine,	
	Gin ye'll leave your Collier laddie.	if
	They a' are mine &c.	

	Ye shall gang in gay attire,	go/dress
10	Weel buskit up sae gaudy;	well dressed so splendidly
	And ane to wait on every hand,	one/servants
	Gin ye'll leave your Collier laddie.	if
	And ane to wait &c.	

	Tho' ye had a' the sun shines on,	
	And the earth conceals sae lowly;	so
15	I wad turn my back on you and it a',	would
	And embrace my Collier laddie.	
	I wad turn my &c.	

	I can win my five pennies in a day	
	An' spen 't at night fu' brawlie;	full/well
	And make my bed in the Collier's neuk,	corner
20	And lie down wi' my Collier laddie.	
	And make my bed &c.	

Loove for loove is the bargain for me,   love
    Tho' the wee Cot-house should haud me;   hold
And the warld before me to win my bread,   world
    And fair fa' my collier laddie!   blessings on
And the warld before &c.

A responsive female song of celebratory love for her collier husband, combined with economic hope. There was an embryonic Ayrshire coalfield by the 1790s, the Fife field was much older, but it remains uncertain to what degree this was a traditional song.

Nithsdale's Welcome Hame

Tune: The Country Lass
First printed in Johnson's S.M.M., Vol. 4, 13th August 1792.

The noble Maxwels and their powers
    Are coming o'er the border,
And they'll gae big Terreagles' towers   go build
    And set them a' in order:
5   And they declare, Terreagles fair,
    For their abode they chuse it;
There's no a heart in a' the land   not
    But 's lighter at the news o't. —

Tho' stars in skies may disappear,
10   And angry tempests gather;
The happy hour may soon be near
    That brings us pleasant weather:
The weary night o' care and grief
    May hae a joyfu' morrow,   have
15   So dawning day has brought relief,
    Fareweel our night o' sorrow. —   farewell

This song celebrates the return of Lady Winifred Constable-Maxwell to rebuild Terreagles, the family seat, which had been forfeited by the participation of her grandfather, William Maxwell, 5th Earl of Nithsdale, in the 1715 rebellion. Discussed in the Introduction, Lady Winifred (Letter 377) was the passionate object of Burns's still contentious claim of the mutual Jacobite history of their respective families.

The Country Lassie
or In Simmer, when the Hay was Mawn
First printed in S.M.M., Vol. 4, 13th August 1792.

In simmer, when the hay was mawn,   summer, mown
    And corn wav'd green in ilka field,   every
While claver blooms white o'er the lea,   clover, grass lands
    And roses blaw in ilka bield;   blow, shelter
5 Blythe Bessie, in the milking shiel   hut
    Says, I'll be wed, come o't what will;
Out spake a dame in wrinkled eild,   age
    O' gude advisement comes nae ill.   good, no

Its ye hae wooers mony ane,   have, many a one
10 And lassie, ye're but young, ye ken;   know
Then wait a wee, and cannie wale,   while, cautious chose
    A routhie butt, a routhie ben: well-stocked kitchen, parlour
There Johnie o' the Buskieglen,
    Fu' is his barn, fu' is his byre;   full
15 Tak this frae me, my bonie hen,   take, from
    It 's plenty beets the luver's fire.   fans

For Johnie o' the Buskieglen,
    I dinna care a single flie;   do not
He lo'es sae weel his craps and kye,   so well, crops, cattle
20 He has nae loove to spare for me: no
But blythe's the blink o' Robie's e'e,   eye
    And weel I wat he lo'es me dear;   well, know
Ae blink o' him I wad na gie   one, would not give
    For Buskieglen and a' his gear.   possessions

25 O thoughtless lassie, life's a faught,   struggle
    The canniest gate, the strife is sair;   prudent way, sore/harsh
But ay fu'-han't is fechtin best,   full-handed, fighting
    A hungry care's an unco care: heavy
But some will spend, and some will spare,
30 An' wilfu' folk maun hae their will;   shall have
Syne as ye brew, my maiden fair,   while/thus
    Keep mind that ye maun drink the yill.   must, ale

O gear will buy me rigs o' land,   wealth
    And gear will buy me sheep and kye;   cattle
35 But the tender heart o' leesome loove,   gladsome
    The gowd and siller canna buy: gold, coins cannot
We may be poor, Robie and I,
    Light is the burden Loove lays on;
Content and Loove brings peace and joy,
40   What mair hae queens upon a throne.   more have

Burns acknowledges authorship of this work in a letter to George
Thomson in October 1794, mentioning the song along with *An O for
Ane and Twenty Tam*, remarking they 'are both mine' (Letter 644).
Youthful feminine passion is, characteristically, wholly victorious
over aged prudence.

Fair Eliza

First printed in Johnson's S.M.M., Vol. 4, 13th August 1792.

Turn again, thou fair Eliza,
    Ae kind blink before we part;   one, glance
Rew on thy despairing Lover,   have pity
    Canst thou break his faithfu' heart!
5 Turn again, thou fair Eliza,
    If to love thy heart denies,
For pity hide the cruel sentence
    Under friendship's kind disguise!

Thee, sweet maid, hae I offended?   have
10   The offence is loving thee:
Canst thou wreck his peace for ever,
    Wha for thine wad gladly die!   who
While the life beats in my bosom,
    Thou shalt mix in ilka throe: every
15 Turn again, thou lovely maiden,
    Ae sweet smile on me bestow. —   one

Not the bee upon the blossom,
    In the pride o' sinny noon;   sunny
Not the little sporting fairy,
20   All beneath the simmer moon;   summer
Not the Poet in the moment
    Fancy lightens in his e'e,   eye
Kens the pleasure, feels the rapture,   knows
    That thy presence gies to me.   gives

It is assumed this song was the result of a promise by Burns to James Johnson that he would compose a love song for him on a lady: 'Have you never a fair Godess that leads you a wild-goose-chase of amorous devotion? . . . and I shall task my Muse to celebrate her' (Letter 258).

Ye Jacobites By Name

First printed in Johnson's S.M.M., Vol. 4, 13th August 1792.

Ye Jacobites by name, give an ear, give an ear;
   Ye Jacobites by name, give an ear;
      Ye Jacobites by name
         Your fautes I will proclaim,   faults
5   Your doctrines I maun blame,   will
         You shall hear. —

What is Right, and what is Wrang, by the law, by the law?
   What is Right, and what is Wrang, by the law?
      What is Right, and what is Wrang?
10   A short Sword, and a lang,   long
         A weak arm, and a strang
         For to draw. —

What makes heroic strife, fam'd afar, fam'd afar?
   What makes heroic strife, fam' d afar?
15   What makes heroic strife?
         To whet th' Assassin's knife,
         Or hunt a Parent's life
         Wi' bludie war. —   bloody

Then let your schemes alone, in the State, in the State,
20   Then let your schemes alone in the State,
      Then let your schemes alone,
         Adore the rising sun,
         And leave a Man undone
         To his fate. —

This song has generally been seen as a traditional Whig anti-Jacobite polemic. This would be an unusual viewpoint for Burns. Donaldson (pp. 85–6) produces a subtle, complex reading which reveals it as a Jacobite's renunciatory perception of the terrible, ideological violence that pervades *all* political systems.

The Posie

First printed in Johnson's S.M.M., Vol. 4, 13th August 1792.

O luve will venture in where it daur na weel be seen,   *dare not well*
O luve will venture in where wisdom ance hath been;   *once*
But I will doun yon river rove, amang the woods sae green,   *down, so*
 And a' to pu' a posie to my ain dear May. —   *pull, own*

5 The primrose I will pu', the firstling o' the year;
And I will pu' the pink, the emblem o' my Dear,
For she's the pink o' womankind, and blooms without a peer;
 And a' to be a posie to my ain dear May. —

I'll pu' the budding rose when Phoebus peeps in view,   *the Sun*
10 For it's like a baumy kiss o' her sweet, bonie mou;   *mouth*
The hyacinth's for constancy, wi' its unchanging blue,
 And a' to be a posie to my ain dear May. —

The lily it is pure, and the lily it is fair,
And in her lovely bosom I'll place the lily there;
15 The daisy's for simplicity and unaffected air,
 And a' to be a posie to my ain dear May. —

The hawthorn I will pu', wi' its locks o' siller gray,   *silver*
Where, like an agèd man it stands at break o' day;
But the songster's nest within the bush I winna tak away;   *will not*
20 And a' to be a posie to my ain dear May. —

The woodbine I will pu' when the e'ening star is near,
And the diamond draps o' dew shall be her een sae clear;   *drops, eyes so*
The violet's for modesty which weel she fa's to wear,   *well has a right*
 And a' to be a posie to my ain dear May. —

25 I'll tie the posie round wi' the silken band o' luve,
And I'll place it in her breast, and I'll swear by a' abuve,   *above*
That to my latest draught o' life the band shall ne'er remuve,   *remove*
 And this will be a posie to my ain dear May.

This beautiful lyric originates with Mrs Jean Burns, who rarely receives credit for her role in singing old and new songs to the poet – a valuable service to any songwriter. Burns was delighted with the song *There was a Pretty May, and A-Milkin' She Went* as sung to him by Jean. He composed new lyrics for the song and wrote to Thomson several years later that it was 'My composition . . . the old words are trash' (Letter 644). *B.C.*, 1922, p. 9 gives the traditional lyric.

Ye Flowery Banks o' Bonie Doon

Tune: Cambdelmore

First printed in Johnson's S.M.M., Vol. 4, 13th August 1792.

Ye flowery banks o' bonie Doon,
    How can ye blume sae fair;   *bloom so*
How can ye chant, ye little birds,
    And I sae fu' o' care!   *so full*

5 Thou'll break my heart, thou bonie bird
    That sings upon the bough;
Thou minds me o' the happy days
    When my fause luve was true.   *false*

Thou'll break my heart, thou bonie bird
10   That sings beside thy mate;
For sae I sat, and sae I sang,   *so*
    And wist na o' my fate.   *knew nothing*

Aft hae I rov'd by bonie Doon,   *often have*
    To see the wood-bine twine,
15 And ilka bird sang o' its luve,   *each*
    And sae did I o' mine.   *so*

Wi' lightsome heart I pu'd a rose   *pulled*
    Frae aff its thorny tree,   *from off*
And my fause luver staw my rose,   *false, stole*
20   But left the thorn wi' me.

Wi' lightsome heart I pu'd a rose,   *pulled*
    Upon a morn in June:
And sae I flourish'd on the morn,   *so*
    And sae was pu'd or noon!   *so, pulled ere*

This is essentially the first version of *Ye Banks and Braes*, set to a different tune than the final version. The contrast between birds and singer is simple but emotionally profound.

Ye Banks and Braes o' Bonie Doon

Tune: The Caledonian Hunt's Delight
First printed in Johnson's S.M.M., Vol. 4, 13th August 1792.

Ye banks and braes o' bonie Doon,   hill slopes
    How can ye bloom sae fresh and fair;   so
How can ye chant, ye little birds,
    And I sae weary, fu' o' care!   so
5 Thou'll break my heart, thou warbling bird,
    That wantons thro' the flowering thorn:
Thou minds me o' departed joys,
    Departed never to return. —

Aft hae I rov'd by bonie Doon,   often have
10   To see the rose and woodbine twine;
And ilka bird sang o' its Luve,   each
    And fondly sae did I o' mine. —   so
Wi' lightsome heart I pu'd a rose,   pulled
    Fu' sweet upon its thorny tree;
15 And my fause Luver staw my rose,   stole
    But, ah! he left the thorn wi' me. —

Although a revision of the earlier lyric set to a different air, both
were printed in the same volume by Johnson. This version brings
the song to a perfect pitch.

Willie Wastle

Tune: The Eight Men of Moidart
First printed in Johnson's S.M.M., Vol. 4, 13th August 1792.

Willie Wastle dwalls on Tweed,   dwelt
    The spot they ca' it Linkumdoddie.   called
A creeshie wabster till his trade,   weaver good
    Can steal a clue wi' ony bodie: any
He has a wife that's dour and din,   sulky, pale
    Tinkler Madgie was her mither;   gypsy, mother
Sic a wife as Willie's wife,   such
    I wadna gie a button for her. —   would not give

She has an e'e, she has but ane,   eye, one
   The cat has twa, the very colour;   two
Five rusty teeth, forbye a stump,   also
   A clapper-tongue wad deave a miller: would deafen
5 A whiskin beard about her mou,   mouth
   Her nose and chin they threaten ither;   each other
Sic a wife as Willie's wife,   such
   I wadna gie a button for her. —   would not give

She's bow-hough'd, she's hem-shin'd,   bandy-legged, splayed feet
10 Ae limpin leg a hand-bread shorter;   one, hand-breadth/size
She's twisted right, she's twisted left,
   To balance fair in ilka quarter: each
She has a hump upon her breast,
   The twin o' that upon her shouther;   shoulder
15 Sic a wife as Willie's wife,
   I wadna gie a button for her. —

Auld baudrans by the ingle sits,   old cat, fireside
   An' wi' her loof her face a washin;   paw
But Willie's wife is nae sae trig,   not so dainty
20 She dights her grunzie wi' a hushian: wipes, mouth, arm stockings
Her waly nieves like midden-creels,   big fists, byre baskets
   Her face wad fyle the Logan-water;   would foul
Sic a wife as Willie's wife,
   I wadna gie a button for her. —

A splendid exercise in the comic grotesque derived from the Scottish flyting tradition and eighteenth-century cartoon caricature. The word 'clue' (l. 4) is from 'clew', thread. Part of the craft must have been a proficiency in stealing material. Linkumdoddie was apparently once a village or hamlet five miles from Broughton, near the Logan Water's confluence with the Tweed.

Lady Mary Ann

First printed in Johnson's S.M.M., Vol. 4, 13th August 1792.

O Lady Mary Ann looks o'er the castle-wa',   wall
She saw three bonie boys playing at the ba',   ball
The youngest he was the flower amang them a',
   My bonie laddie's young but he's growin yet. —

5   O Father, O Father, an ye think it fit,
We'll send him a year to the College yet,
We'll sew a green ribban round about his hat,   ribbon
    And that will let them ken he's to marry yet. —   know

Lady Mary Ann was a flower in the dew,
10   Sweet was its smell and bonie was its hue,
And the langer it blossom'd, the sweeter it grew,   longer
    For the lily in the bud will be bonier yet. —

Young Charlie Cochran was the sprout of an aik,   oak
Bonie, and bloomin and straucht was its make,   straight, like
15   The sun took delight to shine for its sake,
    And it will be the brag o' the forest yet. —   boast

The Simmer is gane when the leaves they were green,   summer, gone
And the days are awa that we hae seen,   away, have
But far better days I trust will come again,
20   For my bonie laddie's young but he's growin yet. —

This is adapted from an old song Burns may have heard sung. Hans
Hecht quotes the old words in *Songs From David Herd's Manu-
scripts* (1904, p. 145) – 'She looked o'er the castle wa', /She saw three
Lords play at the ba': /O the youngest is the flower of a', /But my
love is lang o' growing'. The difference in metre with the traditional
verse is due to Burns matching his revised lyric to a new tune.

Such a Parcel of Rogues in a Nation

First printed in Johnson's S.M.M., Vol. 4, 13th August 1792.

Fareweel to a' our Scottish fame,   farewell
    Fareweel our ancient glory;
Fareweel even to the Scottish name,
    Sae famed in martial story!   so
5   Now Sark rins o'er the Solway sands,   runs
    And Tweed rins to the ocean,   runs
To mark whare England's province stands,   where
    Such a parcel of rogues in a nation!

What force or guile could not subdue,
10   Thro' many warlike ages,
Is wrought now by a coward few,
      For hireling traitors' wages.
The English steel we could disdain,
      Secure in valour's station;
15 But English gold has been our bane,
      Such a parcel of rogues in a nation!

O would, or I had seen the day
      That Treason thus could sell us,
My auld grey head had lien in clay,   old, lain
20   Wi' BRUCE and loyal WALLACE!
But pith and power, till my last hour,
      I'll mak this declaration;
We're bought and sold for English gold,
      Such a parcel of rogues in a nation!

With his customary erudition, Kinsley has detected a group of popular anti-Union songs out of which this pristine national elegiac lyric has been distilled. Most of these are located in James Hogg's, *The Jacobite Relics of Scotland*, 1819, nos. xl-xlii and lxii. The most likely source found in Hogg, no xxxix, is *The Awkward Squad*, an attack on the 'Thirty-one Rogues', the Scottish Commissioners who allegedly sold the nation out in 1707:

      Shame fa' my een,
      If e'er I have seen
      Such a parcel of rogues in a nation.

From this memorable phrase, Burns creates a song which combines defiance and despair where his two great national heroes are entombed beyond resurrection. The song, thus, is the antithetical companion piece to *Scots Wha Hae*. Consciously or otherwise on the part of the modern poets, it prefigures poems like Muir's *Scotland's Winter* and MacDiarmid's *At Dunbar's Grave* which also enact burial rites for the Scottish spirit. The song was published unsigned partly because its political vision is the reverse of the soon to be wholly triumphal forces of pro-Union Scottish Toryism, most manifest in Walter Scott's writings.

Kellyburn Braes –

First printed in Johnson's S.M.M., Vol. 4, 13th August 1792.

There lived a carl in Kellyburnbraes,   old man
Hey and the rue grows bonie wi' thyme;
And he had a wife was the plague o' his days,
And the thyme it is wither'd and rue is in prime;
5 And he had a wife was the plague o' his days,
And the thyme it is wither'd and rue is in prime. —

Ae day as the carl gaed up the lang-glen,   one, went, long
Hey and the rue &c.
He met wi' the Devil, says how do you fen?   fend/how are you
10 And the thyme it is wither'd and rue is in prime;

I've got a bad Wife, sir, that's a' my complaint,
Hey and the rue &c.
For, saving your presence, to her ye're a saint,
And the thyme &c.

15 It's neither your stot nor your staig I shall crave,   bullock, colt
Hey and the rue &c.
But gie me your wife, man, for her I must have,   give
And the thyme &c.

O, welcome most kindly! the blythe carl said;   old man
20 Hey and the rue &c
But if ye can match her — ye're waur than ye're ca'd,   worse, called
And the thyme &c.

The Devil has got the auld wife on his back,   old
Hey and the rue &c.
25 And like a poor pedlar he's carried his pack,
And the thyme &c.

He's carried her hame to his ain hallan-door,   home, own, front-
Hey and the rue &c.
Syne bade her gae in for a bitch and a whore,   go
30 And the thyme &c.

Then straight he makes fifty, the pick o' his band,
Hey and the rue &c.
Turn out on her guard in the clap o' a hand,
And the thyme &c.

35 The carlin gaed thro' them like onie wud bear,   *went, any mad*
    Hey and the rue &c.
    Whae'er she gat hands on, cam ne'er her nae mair,   *got, no more*
    And the thyme &c.

    A reekit, wee devil looks over the wa',   *smoking devil, wall*
40 Hey and the rue &c.
    O help, Master, help!, or she'll ruin us a',   *master*
    And the thyme &c.

    The Devil he swore by the edge o' his knife,
    Hey and the rue &c.
45 He pitied the man that was ty'd to a wife,
    And the thyme &c.

    The Devil he swore by the kirk and the bell,
    Hey and the rue &c.
    He was not in wedlock, thank Heaven, but in Hell,
50 And the thyme &c.

    Then Satan has travell'd again wi' his pack,
    Hey and the rue &c.
    And to her auld husband he's carried her back,   *old*
    And the thyme &c.

55 I hae been a Devil the feck o' my life,   *have, most*
    Hey and the rue &c.
    But ne'er was in Hell till I met wi' a wife,
    And the thyme it is wither'd, and rue is in prime.
    But ne'er was in Hell till I met wi' a wife,
60 And the thyme it is wither'd, and rue is in prime.

This is signed by Burns in the S.M.M. It is partly based on an old
English song, *The Farmer's Old Wife*, but the body of the lyric is by
Burns. It has all the hallmarks of a traditional male drinking club
song combined with the wit of Burns, humorously lamenting the old
man's marriage to a wife who is so difficult to live with that even the
Devil returns her to him.

Jockey Fou and Jenny Fain
First printed in Johnson's S.M.M., Vol. 4, 13th August 1792.

[Ithers seek they kenna what,
Features, carriage, and a' that,
Gie me loove in her I court;
Loove to loove maks a' the sport.]

Let loove sparkle in her e'e;   love, eye
Let her loe nae man but me;   love, no
That 's the tocher gude I prize,   dowry, good
There the Luver's treasure lies. —

The second stanza is by Burns and was written to accompany an old
song he lifted from *The Tea-Table Miscellany* (1726) and printed by
Johnson with the poet's additional stanza.

The Slave's Lament
First printed in Johnson's S.M.M., Vol. 4, 13th August 1792.

It was in sweet Senegal that my foes did me enthrall
    For the lands of Virginia-ginia O;
Torn from that lovely shore, and must never see it more,
    And alas! I am weary, weary O!
        Torn from &c.

5   All on that charming coast is no bitter snow and frost,
        Like the lands of Virginia-ginia O;
    There streams for ever flow, and the flowers for ever blow,
        And alas! I am weary, weary, O!
            There streams &c.

    The burden I must bear, while the cruel scourge I fear,
10   In the lands of Virginia-ginia O;
    And I think on friends most dear with the bitter, bitter tear,
        And Alas! I am weary, weary O!
            And I think &c.

No less an authority than Maya Angelou has discovered in Burns,
most specifically in this song, an empathy with the enslaved, brutal-

ised quality of Black experience. Kinsley, however, would have absolutely no truck with such a relationship. Here is his dismissive treatment of the song:

> Burns's part in this song is uncertain. It is ascribed to him only on the evidence of the Hastie MS. There is nothing in the argument that it represents 29 [*The Ruined Farmer*] (Chambers–Wallace, IV, 355). It is related in form and theme, with some verbal correspondences, to the broadside *The Trapann'd Maid* (*Roxburghe Ballads*, ed. Ebsworth, vii 513). (Vol. III, p. 1405.)

Kinsley's peremptory rebutal of the Chambers-Wallace claim that the refrain from Burns's early song The Ruined Farmer , 'It's O fickle fortune O' has no resonance with 'And alas! I am weary, weary O!' is, at least, debatable. What is certain is that Kinsley had neither knowledge nor sympathy for the radical social context out of which this song emerged. Anti-slavery was the integrative factor in all the varied British radical and reform groupings in the latter eighteenth century. It was particularly strong in Scotland which had over sixty anti-slave societies. Further, the successful legal appeal by Joseph Knight, which particularly interested Dr Johnston, to repeal his slave status created a connection with the white Scottish colliers whose actual status was little better than that of plantation slaves. This enlightened Scottish impulse, of which Burns is the creative voice, to see history as an evolving process of the mass of humanity freeing itself from bondage is most cogently and powerfully dicovered in the writings of that great, now sadly submerged, figure of the Scottish radical Enlightenment, Glasgow University's Professor John Millar. Thus Millar on American slavery:

> It affords a curious spectacle to observe that the same people who talk in a high strain of political liberty, and who consider the privilege of imposing their own taxes as one of the unalienable rights of mankind, should make no scruple of reducing a great proportion of their fellow creatures into circumstances by which they are not only deprived of property, but of almost every species of right. Fortune perhaps never produced a situation more calculated to produce a liberal hypothesis, or to show how little the conduct of men is at the bottom directed by philosophical principles. (William C. Lehmann, *John Millar of Glasgow, 1735–1801*, C.U.P., 1960, p. 321).

The Song of Death
or Orananaoig – A Gaelic Air.

First printed in Johnson's S.M.M., Vol. 4, 13th August 1792.

Scene – A Field of Battle – Time of the day, evening – The wounded and dying of the victorious army are supposed to join in this song.

Farewell, thou fair day; thou green earth; and ye skies,
    Now gay with the broad setting sun!
Farewell, loves and friendships, ye dear tender ties!
    Our race of existence is run.
5 Thou grim king of terrors, thou life's gloomy foe,
    Go frighten the coward and slave!
Go teach them to tremble, fell tyrant! but know,
    No terrors hast thou to the Brave.

Thou strik'st the dull peasant, he sinks in the dark,
10   Nor saves e'en the wreck of a name:
Thou strik'st the young hero, a glorious mark!
    He falls in the blaze of his fame.
In the field of proud honour, our swords in our hands,
    Our King and our Country to save,
15 While victory shines on Life's last ebbing sands,
    O, who would not die with the Brave?

As we saw in the Introduction, this poem was seized on by Robert Nares, the governmental reviewer of *The British Critic*, as evidence that Burns, particularly with l. 14's apparent patriotism, had seen the gross error of his political ways. This poem was allegedly the antidote to the seditious *Scots Wha Hae* with its connection of the fourteenth-century Scottish Wars of Independence with the on-going French Revolution. Nares further claimed that:

> In 1795 when we were first threatened with invasion, he appeared in the ranks of the Dumfries Volunteers and con-tributed to rouse the martial genius of his countrymen, by the following animated and almost sublime war-song.

Unfortunately for this conservative argument the song was written as early as May 1791, a few years before Britain went to war with France and at a time when many people in Britain still supported the French experiment. Explaining the song to Mrs Dunlop he wrote:

I have just finished the following Song, which to a lady the descendant of Wallace, & many heroes of his truly Illustrious line: & herself the mother of several Soldiers, needs neither preface nor apology. . . . The circumstance that gave rise to these verses was – looking over with a musical friend, McDonald's collection of Highland airs, I was struck with one, an Isle of Skye tune, entitled 'Oran an Aoig' or 'The Song of Death', to the measure of which I have adapted my stanzas' (Letter 453).

This song is an elemental, post-Ossianic in mood, account of death in battle for both rich and poor. The peasant who dies, even his name is forgotten, but he who dies in battle, is through history, remembered as a hero. Sung from the lips of the dead and wounded soldiers of the victorious army, the 'king of terrors' (l. 5) and 'fell tyrant' (l. 7) not feared by the 'Brave' is Death itself.

Afton Water

First printed in Johnson's S.M.M., Vol. 4, 13th August 1792.

Flow gently, sweet Afton, among thy green braes,	hill slopes
Flow gently, I'll sing thee a song in thy praise;	
My Mary's asleep by thy murmuring stream,	
Flow gently, sweet Afton, disturb not her dream.	

5 Thou stock dove whose echo resounds thro' the glen,
   Ye wild whistling blackbirds in yon thorny den,
   Thou green-crested lapwing, thy screaming forbear,
   I charge you disturb not my slumbering Fair.

   How lofty, sweet Afton, thy neighbouring hills,
10 Far mark'd with the courses of clear, winding rills;
   There daily I wander as noon rises high,
   My flocks and my Mary's sweet Cot in my eye.   cottage

   How pleasant thy banks and green vallies below,
   Where wild in the woodlands the primroses blow;
15 There oft, as mild ev'ning weeps over the lea,
   The sweet-scented birk shades my Mary and me.   birch trees

   Thy chrystal stream, Afton, how lovely it glides,
   And winds by the cot where my Mary resides;
   How wanton thy waters her snowy feet lave,   clean
20 As, gathering sweet flowerets she stems thy clear wave.

Flow gently, sweet Afton, among thy green braes,
Flow gently, sweet River, the theme of my lays;
My Mary's asleep by thy murmuring stream,
Flow gently, sweet Afton, disturb not her dream.

This fine song appears first on 5th February, 1789, in a letter from Ellisland to Mrs Dunlop: 'There is a small river, Afton, that falls into the Nith, near New Cumnock, which has some charming, wild, romantic scenery on its banks. – I have a particular pleasure in those little pieces of poetry such as our Scots songs, &c. where the names and landskip-features of rivers, lakes or woodlands, that one knows are introduced. – I attempted a compliment of that kind, to Afton, as follows' (Letter 310). The quotation found in the letter begins 'Flow gently, clear Afton . . .', not 'sweet Afton', suggesting it was re-drafted before publication. The spot described by Burns would appear to be Glen Afton, near New Cumnock.

My Bonie Bell

First printed in Johnson's S.M.M., Vol. 4, 13th August 1792.

The smiling Spring comes in rejoicing,
    And surly Winter grimly flies;
Now crystal clear are the falling waters,
    And bonie blue are the sunny skies.
5 Fresh o'er the mountains breaks forth the morning,
    The ev'ning gilds the Ocean's swell;
All Creatures joy in the sun's returning,
    And I rejoice in my Bonie Bell.

The flowery Spring leads sunny Summer,
10   The yellow Autumn presses near,
Then in his turn comes gloomy Winter,
    Till smiling Spring again appear.
Thus seasons dancing, life advancing,
    Old Time and Nature their changes tell,
15 But never ranging, still unchanging,
    I adore my Bonie Bell.

The metre and flow of this song is irregular and does not have the expected natural ease of Burns's best songs. It was found in transcript, not in the poet's holograph. It is, however, signed as from Burns in the S.M.M. It is not known for certain if it is an original work or a substantially updated traditional work. If the words 'are' and 'forth' were taken from lines 4, 5, and 6 – with further minor textual changes – it would read more like Burns. Whether Johnson modified lyrics we do not know given that their correspondence is incomplete. As it is signed as from Burns in print during his lifetime, there is little to question its authenticity.

The Gallant Weaver

Tune: The Weaver's March
First printed in Johnson's S.M.M., Vol. 4, 13th August 1792.

Where Cart rins rowin to the sea,	runs
By mony a flower and spreading tree,	many
There lives a lad, the lad for me,	
He is a gallant Weaver. —	

5 Oh I had wooers aught or nine,	eight
They gied me rings and ribbans fine;	gave, ribbons
And I was fear'd my heart wad tine	would break
And I gied it to the Weaver. —	gave

My daddie sign'd my tocher-band	dowry agreement
10 To gie the lad that has the land,	give
But to my heart I'll add my hand	
And give it to the Weaver. —	

While birds rejoice in leafy bowers,	
While bees delight in opening flowers,	
15 While corn grows green in simmer showers	summer
I love my gallant Weaver. —	

Mackay affirms this is a 'reworking of a traditional ballad' (p. 464) but it is signed in the S.M.M. This suggests it is a substantial re-write of the old song. It is surprising that Burns allowed 'gied' in stanza 2 and 'give' in stanza 3 to stand, which, although incongruous, makes the ending of the song more English. The river Cart runs through Paisley, important to the weaving industry during the 1780s and '90s. The weaving community was definably politically radical.

Hey, Ca' Thro'
or The Carls of Dysart

First printed in Johnson's S.M.M., Vol. 4, 13th August 1792.

Up wi' the carls of Dysart,
    And the lads o' Buckhaven,
And the Kimmers o' Largo,
    And the lasses o' Leven.

Chorus

5	Hey ca' thro' ca' thro'	pull
	For we hae mickle ado,	have much to do
	Hey, ca' thro' ca' thro'	
	For we hae mickle ado.	have much to do

	We hae tales to tell,	have
10	And we hae sangs to sing;	have songs
	We hae pennies to spend,	
	And we hae pints to bring.	
	Hey ca' thro' &c.	

	We'll live a' our days,	
	And them that comes behin',	
15	Let them do the like,	
	And spend the gear they win.	wealth
	Hey ca' thro' &c.	

This is based on an old Fifeshire fishing song. It has been assumed that Burns collected this work when passing through Fife at the close of his Highland tour in the late Autumn of 1787. It is not certain that Burns improved the song but, on the assumption he did, it is placed in the canon. Given that many such old works are irregular in metre and uneven in quality, this song does appear to have been tightened up by Burns. The deceptively simple clarity of lyric would appear to be his handiwork.

Can Ye Labour Lea

First printed in Johnson's S.M.M., Vol. 4, 13th August 1792.

I fee'd a man at Martinmass,	hired
Wi' airle-pennies three;	bargain money
But a' the faute I had to him,	fault
He could na labour lea.	could not, till grass land

Chorus
5   O can ye labour lea, young man,
        O can ye labour lea;
    Gae back the gate ye came again,   go, way
        Ye'se never scorn me. —

    O clappin's gude in Febarwar,   caressing, February
10   An' kissin's sweet in May;
    But what signifies a young man's love,
        An't dinna last for ay.   does not, ever
            O can ye &c.

    O kissin is the key o' luve,
        An' clappin is the lock,   caressing
15 An' makin-of 's the best thing,
        That e'er a young Thing got. —
            O can ye &c.

This is based on an old song Burns heard his own mother sing. As
the original is unknown it is assumed Burns re-wrote the lyric. A
bawdy version collected by Burns is in the *Merry Muses*.

The Deuk's Dang o'er My Daddie

First printed in Johnson's S.M.M., Vol. 4, 13th August 1792.

    The bairns gat out wi' an unco shout,   child's got, great
    The deuk's dang o'er my daddie, O,   duck, beaten
    The fien-ma-care, quo' the feirrie auld wife,   devil-may-, lusty old
    He was but a paidlin body, O. —   wading/messsing about
5   He paidles out, an' he paidles in,   paddles
    An' he paidles late and early, O;
    This seven lang years I hae lien by his side,   seven, have lain
    An he is but a fusionless carlie, O. —   useless old man

    O haud your tongue, my feirrie auld wife,   hold, lustful old
10 O haud your tongue, now Nansie, O:
    I've seen the day, and sae hae ye,   so have
    Ye wad na been sae donsie, O. —   would not, so saucy
    I've seen the day ye butter'd my brose,   porridge/sexual connotations
    And cuddled me late and early, O;
15 But downa do's come o'er me now,   cannot perform, can't do has
    And, Oh, I find it sairly, O!

Although partly based on an old song this is signed in the S.M.M. indicating that it is substantially the work of Burns. This can be proven given the lines quoted by Charles Kirkpatrick Sharpe from the old song (see Wallace (1896), p. 382). This tragi-comic marriage dialogue is based on the old man's impotence.

She's Fair and Fause

Tune: The Lads of Leith.
First printed in Johnson's S.M.M., Vol. 4, 13th August 1792.

	She's fair and fause that causes my smart,	false
	I lo'ed her meikle and lang;	greatly, long
	She's broken her vow, she's broken my heart,	
	And I may e'en gae hang. —	go
5	A coof cam in wi' routh o' gear,	fool, plenty, money
	And I hae tint my dearest dear;	have lost
	But Woman is but warld's gear,	world's wealth
	Sae let the bonie lass gang. —	so, go
	Whae'er ye be that Woman love,	whoever
10	To this be never blind;	
	Nae ferlie 'tis tho' fickle she prove,	no wonder
	A Woman has't by kind:	
	O Woman lovely, Woman fair!	
	An angel form 's faun to thy share;	fallen
15	'Twad been o'er meikle to gien thee mair,	much, have given, more
	I mean an angel mind. —	

Editors prior to Kinsley have guessed this song was written about Alexander Cunningham's mistress Anna, who jilted him (See *Anna, Thy Charms*). There is no evidence to prove the claim. The song appears to be a traditional one improved by Burns. The tone of stanzas 1 and 2 is quite different: the first has a clumsy rhyme repitition on 'gear', indicative of an amateur poet. The second stanza flows naturally and is almost certainly, in sentiment, language and diction, from Burns. Since the original song cannot be traced this conclusion is conjectural. It is surprising that Burns did not also improve the first stanza.

The Deil's Awa wi' th' Exciseman

Tune: The Hemp-Dresser
First printed in Johnson's S.M.M., Vol. 4, 13th August 1792.

The Deil cam fiddlin thro' the town,   *devil, came*
    And danc'd awa wi' th' Exciseman;
And ilka wife cries, auld Mahoun,   *every, old*
    I wish you luck o' the prize, man.

Chorus
5 The deil's awa the deil's awa   *away*
    The deil's awa wi' th' Exciseman,
He's danc'd awa he's danc'd awa
    He's danc'd awa wi' th' Exciseman.

We'll mak our maut and we'll brew our drink,   *malt/whisky*
10   We'll laugh, sing, and rejoice, man;
And mony braw thanks to the meikle black deil,   *fine, great, devil*
    That danc'd awa wi' th' Exciseman.
        The deil's awa &c.

There's threesome reels, there's foursome reels,
    There's hornpipes and strathspeys, man,
15 But the ae best dance ere cam to the Land   *one, came*
    Was, the deil's awa wi' th' Exciseman.
        The deil's awa &c.

Despite being unsigned in the S.M.M. the evidence in Letter 500 (to John Leven) indicates this is an original work by Burns. The notion Burns wrote the work extempore while waiting for reinforcements before boarding and taking the smuggling ship *Rosamond* on the Solway is probably myth. Burns may have thought of the song at that time but there is no definite proof of this folk tale.

Wandering Willie

Tune: Here Awa, There Awa
First printed in Thomson's *Select Collection*, May 1793.

Here awa', there awa' wandering Willie,   *away*
    Here awa', there awa', haud awa' hame;   *hold, home*
Come to my bosom, my ae only deary,   *one, dearie*
    And tell me thou bring'st me my Willie the same.

5 Loud tho' the Winter blew cauld on our parting,   cold
   'Twas na the blast brought the tear in my e'e: not, eye
Welcome now Simmer, and welcome my Willie; summer
   The Simmer to Nature, my Willie to me.   summer

Rest, ye wild storms, in the cave o' your slumbers,
10   How your dread howling a lover alarms!
Wauken, ye breezes! row gently, ye billows! waken
   And waft my dear Laddie ance mair to my arms. once more

But oh, if he's faithless, and minds na his Nannie, not
   Flow still between us, thou wide roaring main:
15 May I never see it, may I never trow it, pledge
   But, dying, believe that my Willie's my ain! own

This is based on an old song called *Thro' the Lang Muir*, which
contains one stanza and a chorus, repeated with a variation (See
Scott Douglas, Vol. 1, p. 377). The original is a competent Scots
song – an additional stanza was added to the version printed in the
S.M.M. in 1787 – but the song is significantly improved by Burns. It
was written in early 1792, but redrafted for Thomson in March 1793
(Letter 543).

Braw Lads o' Galla Water

First printed in Thomson's *Select Collection*, May 1793.

Braw, braw lads on Yarrow braes,   fine, hill sides
   Rove amang the blooming heather; among
But Yarrow braes, nor Ettrick shaws, woods
   Can match the lads o' Galla water.

5 But there is ane, a secret ane,   one, one
   Aboon them a' I loe him better; above, love
And I'll be his, and he'll be mine,
   The bonie lad o' Galla water.

Altho' his daddie was nae laird,   no
10   And tho' I hae na meikle tocher, have no big dowry
Yet, rich in kindest, truest love,
   We'll tent our flocks by Galla water. tend

It ne'er was wealth, it ne'er was wealth,
 That coft contentment, peace, or pleasure; bought
15 The bands and bliss o' mutual love,
 O that's the chiefest warld's treasure! world's

The original of this song is found in Herd's collection, although a
version appears in S.M.M. in 1788, with slight variations in text,
which might have been minor improvements by Burns. However,
the above is merely modified on the old song and is significantly
changed to make a superior song.

Auld Rob Morris

First printed in Thomson's *Select Collection*, May 1793.

There's Auld Rob Morris that wons in yon glen, dwells
He's the king o' gude fellows and wale of auld men; good, pick
He has gowd in his coffers, he has owsen and kine, gold, oxen, cattle
And ae bonie lassie, his dawtie and mine. one, darling

5 She's fresh as the morning, the fairest in May,
She's sweet as the e'enin amang the new hay; among
As blythe and as artless as the lambs on the lea, pasture
And dear to my heart as the light to my e'e. eye

But oh, she's an Heiress, auld Robin's a laird; old
10 And my daddie has nocht but a cot-house and yard: nothing, cottage
A wooer like me maunna hope to come speed; must not, succeed
The wounds I must hide that will soon be my dead. death

The day comes to me, but delight brings me nane; none
The night comes to me, but my rest it is gane: gone
15 I wander my lane like a night-troubled ghaist, alone, ghost
And I sigh as my heart it wad burst in my breast. would

O had she but been of a lower degree,
I then might hae hop'd she wad smil'd upon me! would have
O, how past descriving had then been my bliss, describing
20 As now my distraction no words can express!

This is based on a traditional dialogue song between a mother and
daughter printed in the *Tea-Table Miscellany*, but only a couplet or
so of the original are kept by Burns. He struggled with the pedantic

Thomson to maintain an air of rustic simplicity in the song. He told Thomson, 'There is a naivete, a pastoral simplicity, in a slight intermixture of Scots words and phraseology, which is more in unison . . . than any English verses whatever. – For instance, in my Auld Rob Morris, you propose instead of the word 'descriving', to substitute the phrase 'all telling', which would spoil the rusticity, the pastoral, of the stanza' (Letter 535). The theme once again is the juxtaposition of love and wealth in a feudal social order. The rhyme at lines 15–16 of 'ghaist' and 'breast' relies on the west of Scotland Scots pronunciation of *breast* as *braist*. A version of this song appears in the *Scots Magazine*, July 1797, p. 479.

Open the Door to Me, Oh

Tune: Open the Door Softly
First printed in Thomson's *Select Collection*, May 1793.

Oh, open the door, some pity to shew,
  If love it may na be, Oh;   not
Tho' thou hast been false, I'll ever prove true,
  Oh, open the door to me, Oh.

5 Cauld is the blast upon my pale cheek,   cold
  But caulder thy love for me, Oh: colder
  The frost, that freezes the life at my heart,
  Is nought to my pains frae thee, Oh.   from

The wan moon sets behind the white wave,
10 And Time is setting with me, Oh:
False friends, false love, farewell! for mair
  I'll ne'er trouble them, nor thee, Oh.

She has open'd the door, she has open'd it wide,
  She sees his pale corse on the plain, Oh: corpse
15 My true love! she cried, and sank down by his side,
  Never to rise again, Oh.

The old song Burns has used here is Scottish, set to an Irish air. Thomson printed it with the headnote 'Altered by Robt. Burns' and placed rewritten lyrics for the same song by Dr John Wolcot (Peter Pindar) suggesting that Thomson thought Pindar's more English version as good as Burns's, which it is not. It was sent to Thomson in April 1793.

The Sodger's Return

Tune: The Mill, Mill O

First printed in Thomson's *Select Collection*, May 1793.

When wild War's deadly blast was blawn,   blowing
    And gentle Peace returning,
Wi' mony a sweet babe fatherless,   many
    And mony a widow mourning: many
5 I left the lines, and tented field,
    Where lang I'd been a lodger,   long
My humble knapsack a' my wealth,
    A poor and honest sodger.   soldier

A leal, light heart was in my breast,   loyal
10 My hand unstain'd wi' plunder;
And for fair Scotia, hame again   home
    I cheery on did wander.
I thought upon the banks o' Coil,
    I thought upon my Nancy,
15 And ay I mind't the witching smile   always, remembered
    That caught my youthful fancy.

At length I reach'd the bonny glen,
    Where early life I sported;
I pass'd the mill and trysting thorn,   meeting place
20 Where Nancy aft I courted: often
Wha spied I but my ain dear maid,   who, own
    Down by her mother's dwelling!
And turn'd me round to hide the flood
    That in my een was swelling.   eyes

25 Wi' alter'd voice, quoth I, sweet lass,
    Sweet as yon hawthorn's blossom,
O! happy, happy may he be,
    That's dearest to thy bosom:
My purse is light, I've far to gang,   go
30 And fain wad be thy lodger;   would
I've serv'd my king and country lang,   long
    Take pity on a sodger!   soldier

Sae wistfully she gaz'd on me,   so
    And lovelier was than ever;
35 Quo' she, a sodger ance I lo'ed,   loved
    Forget him shall I never:
Our humble cot, and hamely fare,   homely food
    Ye freely shall partake it,
That gallant badge, the dear cockade,   Jacobite white rose
40   Ye're welcome for the sake o't.

She gaz'd — she redden'd like a rose —
    Syne pale like ony lily,   then, any
She sank within my arms, and cried,
    Art thou my ain dear Willie? —   own
45 By Him who made yon sun and sky,
    By whom true love's regarded,
I am the man — and thus may still
    True lovers be rewarded!

The wars are o'er, and I'm come hame,   home
50   And find thee still true-hearted;
Tho' poor in gear, we're rich in love,
    And mair, — we'se ne'er be parted!   more
Quo' she, my grandsire left me gowd,   gold
    A mailen plenish'd fairly;   piece of arable land
55 And come, my faithfu' sodger lad,   soldier
    Thou 'rt welcome to it dearly!

For gold the merchant ploughs the main,   sea
    The farmer ploughs the manor;
But glory is the sodger's prize,   soldier
60   The sodger's wealth is honour;
The brave poor sodger ne'er despise,
    Nor count him as a stranger;
Remember, he's his country's stay
    In day and hour of danger.

This was the final song Burns sent to Thomson for inclusion in his Volume going to press in April for May 1793. Thomson's arrogance as an editor of song lyrics compelled him to change the lines 'Wi' monie a sweet babe fatherless /And monie a widow mourning' to the dull 'And eyes again with pleasure beam'd, /That had been blear'd wi' mourning'. According to Thomson, Burns's original lines did not suit the music. Characteristically this alleged aesthetic improve-

ment was, in reality, an act of political censorship. Thomson is
smoothing over the patently obvious anti-war connotations of the
song, resonant at that time since Britain was currently at war with
France (see notes to *Logan Braes* for a similar censorial act). It is
probably due to the editorial changes made by Thomson that Burns
printed his song in *The Glasgow Courier* in September 1793, in order
to see a corrected version in print. The theme of the poet's song is
found in one of Ramsay's works, *Beneath a Green Shade I Fand a
Fair Maid*, in the *Orpheus Caledonius*, 1733, where the soldier
returns from Flanders to find his true love. Given that the word
'sodger' is used through the song – soldier would not rhyme with
'lodger' – it seems incongruous to title the song *The Soldier's Return*.
The title given here is therefore the Scots *The Sodger's Return*.

A Red, Red Rose

Tune: Major Graham
First printed in Urbani's selection of Scots Songs, Edinburgh, 1794.

O my Luve 's like a red, red rose,
    That 's newly sprung in June;
O my Luve 's like the melodie
    That 's sweetly play'd in tune. —

5 As fair art thou, my bonie lass,
    So deep in luve am I;
And I will luve thee still, my Dear,
    Till a' the seas gang dry. —   go

Till a' the seas gang dry, my Dear,   go
10   And the rocks melt wi' the sun:
I will luve thee still, my dear,
    While the sands o' life shall run. —

And fare thee weel, my only Luve!   well
    And fare thee weel, a while!
15 And I will come again, my Luve,
    Tho' it were ten thousand mile!

This exquisite love song epitomises a central dilemma with the
poet's song output. Almost all of the phrases and images employed
here have been traced to various traditional songs. For example,
these old words are given in Kinsley:

Her cheeks are like the Roses
    That blossom fresh in June,
O, she's like a new-strung instrument
    That's newly put in tune;

/ . . . Altho' I go a thousand miles
    I vow thy face to see,
Altho' I go ten thousand miles
    I'll come again to thee, dear Love,
I'll come again to thee . . .
    The Day shall turn to Night, dear Love,
And the Rocks melt wi' the Sun,
    Before that I prove false to thee. (Vol. III, pp. 1454-5.)

Since frequently the seam cannot be detected between folk-song and Burns's verse, there exists an insoluble critical problem as to original compositon. With regard to this poem, Kinsley oddly remarks that: 'We may, however, be doing an injustice to oral tradition in regarding [this] even as a reconstruction by Burns.' Burns himself would be the last person to deny that, if his lyrics were golden, it was because of the quality of the traditional ore. On the other hand, he rightly feared the parochial, sentimental verse which would be written in his name.

Sonnet: On the Death of Robert Riddell Esq. of Glenriddell,
April 1794
This first appears in *The Dumfries Journal*, 22nd April, 1794.

No more, ye warblers of the wood, no more,
    Nor pour your descant grating on my soul!
    Thou young-eyed Spring, gay in thy verdant stole,
More welcome were to me grim Winter's wildest roar.

5   How can ye charm, ye flowers, with all your dyes?
    Ye blow upon the sod that wraps my friend:
    How can I to the tuneful strain attend?
That strain flows round th' untimely tomb where Riddell lies.

Yes, pour, ye warblers, pour the notes of woe,
10   And sooth *the Virtues* weeping o'er his bier.
        The *Man of Worth* — and 'as not left his peer —[1]
Is in his 'narrow house' for ever darkly low.[2]

Thee, Spring, again with joy shall others greet,
Me, mem'ry of my loss will only meet.

Robert Riddell (1755–94), died on 20th April, 1794, aged 39 years.
The sonnet which appeared under the poet's name in *The Dumfries
Journal* was also sent to the London *Star*, and printed on 30th April,
then subsequently copied by the *Morning Chronicle, 5th May*, and in
the May issue of *The Gentleman's Magazine*. The newspaper obit-
uary on Riddell is also thought to be by Burns, although it has never
been formally credited. Burns commented on Robert Riddell of
Glenriddell, who lived at Friars Carse, near Ellisland farm, that 'At
their fire-side I have enjoyed more pleasant evenings than at all the
houses of fashionable people in this country put together . . . many
of the happiest hours of my life' (Cromek, p. 269, from the
I.S.M.M). He is, therefore, a crucial, but still not fully-known
player in the Burns story.

Kinsley omits the most important factor about Riddell, that he
was a leading radical Whig, known throughout Britain (Vol. III,
p. 1274). As we have seen, he wrote the pro-reform essay printed
under the pen-name 'Cato' which Burns posted to *The Edinburgh
Gazetteer* (Letter 530). Several of his essays feature in *The Glasgow
Journal*; they fiercely debate with Edmund Burke the question of
imported manufactures and the India question relating to the trial of
Warren Hastings. Riddell was thus a key radical Whig of the period
(See our notes to *On Glenriddell's Fox Breaking its Chain*). Professor
Werkmeister cogently remarks that Burns's allowing his name to be
associated with Riddell was: '. . . a courageous resolve, for, since
Riddell was no friend of Government, a "tribute" to him had to be
regarded as political and hence publishable only in an Opposition
newspaper' (*Robert Burns and the London Daily Press, Modern
Philology*, LXIII, 1966, p. 326).

The sonnet sets a deliberate parallel between Burns and Riddell
and the profound loss felt by Milton when his friend Edward King
was drowned, as lamented in *Lycidas*, hence the quote (l. 11).

---

1 Adapted from Milton's *Lycidas*.
2 Gray's *Elegy*, '. . . in his narrow cell for ever laid'.

Wilt Thou Be My Dearie?

Tune: The Sutor's Dochter
First printed in *The Morning Chronicle*, 10th May, 1794.

Wilt thou be my dearie?
When Sorrow wrings thy gentle heart,
    O, wilt thou let me cheer thee?
By the treasure of my soul —
5   That's the love I bear thee —
I swear and vow that only thou
    Shall ever be my dearie!
Only thou, I swear and vow,
    Shall ever be my dearie!

10   Lassie, say thou lo'es me,   loves
Or, if thou wilt na be my ain,   will not, own
    Say na thou'lt refuse me!   not
If it winna, canna be,   will not, cannot
    Thou for thine may choose me,
15   Let me, lassie, quickly die,
    Trusting that thou lo'es me!
Lassie, let me quickly die,
    Trusting that thou lo'es me!

This appears first in the London Whig Opposition paper *The Morning Chronicle*, two days after the unsigned publication of *Scots Wha Hae*. It was signed as the work of Burns. It is not a controversial work, so there was no problem about his name being printed. Most editors assume the heroine of the song is Janet Miller, daughter of the poet's former landlord at Ellisland, Patrick Miller of Dalswinton. This is not known for certain. Both Kinsley and Mackay err in their notes to this work by going on to assert that Patrick Miller offered Burns a job with *The Morning Chronicle* in April 1794, when in fact it is known that the offer of removal for full time journalistic work in London was rejected by Burns in mid-March, 1794. Miller merely conveyed the offer from James Perry, the paper's editor.

O Wat Ye Wha's in Yon Town

Tune: We'll Gang Nae Mair to Yon Town
First printed in *The Glasgow Magazine*, September 1795.

NOW haply down yon gay green shaw   wood
     She wanders by yon spreading tree;
How blest ye flow'rs that round her blaw,   blow
     Ye catch the glances o' her ee.   eye

Chorus
5   O wat ye wha's in yon town,   know, who's
     Ye see the e'enin Sun upon,   evening
The dearest maid's in yon town,
     That e'enin Sun is shining on.

How blest ye birds that round her sing,
10   And welcome in the blooming year,
And doubly welcome be the Spring,
     The season to my Jeanie dear.
       O wat ye wha's &c.

The sun blinks blyth on yon town,
     Amang the broomy braes sae green;   among, hill slopes so
15   But my delight in yon town,
     And dearest pleasure, is my Jean.
       O wat ye wha's &c.

Without my Fair, not a' the charms
     O' Paradise could yield me joy;
But gie me Jeanie in my arms,   give
20   And welcome Lapland's dreary sky.
       O wat ye wha's &c.

My cave wad be a lover's bow'r,   would
     Tho' raging Winter rent the air;   rend
And she a lovely little flower,
     That I wad tent and shelter there.   would tend
       O wat ye wha's &c.

25   O sweet is she in yon town,
     The sinkin Sun's gane down upon: gone
A fairer than's in yon town
     His setting beam ne'er shone upon.
       O wat ye wha's &c.

If angry Fate is sworn my foe,
30   And suff'ring I am doom'd to bear;
I careless quit aught else below,   ought
      But spare me, spare me Jeanie dear.
            O wat ye wha's &c.

For while life's dearest blood runs warm,
      Ae thought frae her shall ne'er depart,   one, from
35 And she — as fairest is her form,
      She has the truest, kindest heart.
            O wat ye wha's &c.

Burns started this work when snow-bound in the village of Eccle-
fechan on the evening of 7th February, 1795. It was finished and
sent to Thomson in April (Letter 661). It is a modification of the
poet's own song *I'll Ay Ca' in by Yon Town* which had been sent to
Johnson.

The Dumfries Volunteers

Tune: Push About the Jorum
First published in *The Edinburgh Courant*, 4th May, 1795.

Does haughty Gaul invasion threat,
      Then let the loons beware, Sir!   fools
There's WOODEN WALLS upon our seas
      And VOLUNTEERS on shore, Sir:
5   The *Nith* shall run to *Corsincon*[1],
      And *Criffel* sink in *Solway*[2],
Ere we permit a Foreign Foe
      On British ground to rally!

O let us not, like snarling curs,   dogs
10   In wrangling be divided,
Till, slap! come in an *unco loun*,   strange fool
      And wi' a rung decide it!   cudgel
Be BRITAIN still to BRITAIN true,
      Amang oursels united: among ourselves
15 For never but by *British hands*
      Maun *British wrangs* be righted.   shall, wrongs

1 A high hill at the source of the Nith. R.B.
2 A high hill at the confluence of the Nith and the Solway Firth. R.B.

The *kettle* o' the Kirk and State,
    Perhaps a *clout* may fail in't;   patch
But Deil a *foreign* tinkler loon
20   Shall ever ca' a nail in't.   hammer
Our FATHERS' BLUDE the *kettle* bought,   blood
    And wha wad dare to spoil it,   who would
By Heav'ns! the sacrilegious dog
    Shall fuel be to boil it!

25   The wretch that would a *Tyrant* own,
    And the wretch, his true-sworn brother,
Who would set the Mob above the *Throne*,
    May they be damn'd together!
Who will not sing God Save The KING
30   Shall hang as high 's the steeple;
But while we sing God Save The KING,
    We'll ne'er forget THE PEOPLE!

After publication in *The Edinburgh Evening Courant* on 4th May
1795 this song appeared in *The Dumfries Journal* on 5th May, *The
Caledonian Mercury* on 7th May and was copied in *The Northern
Star*, Belfast, 29th October–2nd November 1795 issue. It was
printed by Currie in 1800 and features in S.M.M., no. 546, 1803.

A first draught, which has not survived and was probably de-
stroyed, contained a satirical attack on a 'ci-devant Commodore'
which the poet later omitted. The reason Burns dropped the satirical
lines is explained to Mrs Dunlop: 'Miss Keith will see that I have
omitted the four lines on the ci-devant Commodore which gave her
so much offence. Had I known that he stood in no less connection
than the Godfather of my lovely young Friend, I would have spared
him for her sake' (*Robert Burns and Mrs Dunlop*, edited by W.
Wallace, London, 1898, p. 419). The fact that this song originally
contained a satirical attack on a high ranking military officer is
missed by previous editors who distort the song into a statement of
the poet's loyalty to the Pitt government and hence, a cessation of his
radical values. This is far from the case. Indeed, the message of the
song is unequivocally in *support* of reform, that is, placing the
practice of politics back on a footing according to the principles
of the Constitution, a sentiment clearly echoed in the lines:

Be Britain still to Britain true,
    Amang oursels united!
For never but by British hands
    Maun British wrangs be righted!

A cleverly balanced criticism of the Pitt government hints that there are indeed problems that should be addressed and resolved. Extremes are exposed as no solution in themselves – the 'tyrant' and 'mob' – echoes his earlier line, 'Be Anarchy cursed and Tyranny damned'. It would be naïve to read the reference to singing 'God Save the King' as a statement of loyalism, given that it is Burns, as he does on many occasions, giving ironic assent to what he is actually attacking and preparing the song to end on a final and loudly emphasised phrase 'We'll ne'er forget THE PEOPLE!' The appearance of 'loyalty' is, in reality, a sleight of hand that refers more to an abstract loyalism to the higher ideal of reforming politics and placing into practice the ideals of the British constitution. By early 1795 the radical French leader Marat had been assassinated and the French Revolution had strayed far from its original ideals and was at this time in the hands of an oligarchy hell-bent on Empire building and the reactionary imperial cult of the young officer, Napoleon Bonaparte. It is therefore no contradiction and entirely consistent with the radical views of Burns that he would oppose a French invasion of Britain, given that their revolution had metamorphosed to being a tyrannical power. Hence, Burns could oppose a French invasion but at the same time still agree with the original principles of the French Revolution. Moreover, this song allowed him the breathing space of *appearing* to be a loyal subject, but one who actually opposed the political leadership of Pitt and Dundas. As he remarked to Mrs Dunlop in mid-January 1795, he looked forward to the day when a person might be able to criticise 'Billy Pitt' without being judged an enemy (all reformers were branded Jacobins at this time) of his country.

Given Burn's expurgation of the poem's specific satirical target combined with an understandably, fear-induced political tracks-disguising over-subtlety, Burns's legion of conservative enemies, from the outset, seized upon this poem as absolute, final evidence, despite the overwhelming mass of his politically contrary poetry, of his loyal, wholly anti-revolutionary, pro-Hanoverian stance. Fearfully living throughout the nineteenth century in the shadow of the French Revolution, almost all institutionalized, *published* Burns criticism followed this line. The radical Burns of the Chartist Movement and subsequent proto-socialism existed at a working class, oral level. (See William Power, 'The Song of Friendship', in *Robert Burns and Other Essays and Sketches* (London & Glasgow, 1926, p. 48). In the economically fraught, politically turbulent Scotland of the aftermath of the First World War, this political division became more extreme. Burns was, albeit simplistically, the poet-prophet of Red Clydeside and the ILP. The opposing bourgeois populism of the Burns Federation was of a decidedly reactionary, pro-Unionist order. Hence, for example, Duncan McNaught's account of Burns's politics as expressed in *The Dumfries Volunteers* in B.C. (No. 34, 1925), pp. 61–5:

> From the way in which Burns is quoted on political platforms and by the huge army of open-air preachers of social reform, one can only conclude that the intention of the orators is to represent Burns as the outstanding extremist of his generation. In some of his earlier poems, as, for instance 'Epistle to Davie', the case for Labour is put in the strongest of lights, and enforced with much the same arguments as the Socialist of today has rendered us so familiar with; but the whole volume of his poetry and prose will be searched in vain for a single line that expresses the slightest sympathy with the doctrines of the Bolshevism, Communism, and Socialism which are now so loudly proclaimed from the housetops. Burns's philosophy was on a higher plane; his opinions were founded on the axioms of political ethics which apply to all parties alike, and which have been subscribed to by all sensible men who have thought seriously on the subject. A short compendium of his political creed, written the year before his death, will be found in 'Does Haughty Gaul', a composition which effectually disposes of the mythical tradition that he was a disloyal subject and a Revolutionist.

Sadly, however, misinterpretation was not exlusively the prerogative of wilful reactionaries. The publication of *The Dumfries Volunteers* led to a back-lash against Burns by his erstwhile Ulster supporters who saw it as an act of apostasy akin, as Liam McIlvanney has pertinently pointed out ('Robert Burns and the Ulster-Scots Literary Revival of the 1790s', *Bullán: An Irish Studies Journal*, Vol. IV, No. 2, pp. 124–44), to the betrayal that the younger English radicals felt for Wordsworth. This led to the publication of this *Song* in the republican *Northern Star* (29 October–2 November, 1795):

> O Scotia's Bard! my muse alas!
> For you in private blushes!
>   You've dipt i' th' dish wi' slee D[unda]s
> An' prie'd the Loaves and Fishes!
>   When *bare-foot* owre the Ayr-shire hills,
> A rustic ye ran chanting,
>   Ye wadna took a score o' gills
> To hae deav'd us wi' sic ranting.

The *kettle* o' your *kirk* and *state*
For which your dads contended,
    Has been sae ding'd and spoil'd of late,
I fear it can't be mended!
    And if a British Tinkler dare
But shaw his bag and nails, man;
    O bid the meddling loun beware
O' shaving and South-Wales man.

There Muir and Palmer, tinklers good
As ever Scotia rear'd, man,
    Were banish'd owre the foaming flood,
For daring to repair man.
    Then sith ye canna mak' it staunch,
Swith fling it out of doors, man.
    Ye'll get a new ane frae the F——h
Ane worth a score o' yours, man.

But tent me, much revered Bob,
You err, and unco far man,
    For *those*, you Burke-like, call the *mob*,
The very PEOPLE are man.
    So now I sing, God Save the King,
And the Queen to keep him warm, sir;
    But may he high as Haman hing,
Who dares oppose – REFORM, sir.

That this specific charge was untrue has to be set against the general truth that Scotland did fail Ireland at its hour of need. See John Brims's very fine 'Scottish Radicalism and the United Irishman' in *The United Irishmen, Republicanism, Radicalism and Rebellion* (Dublin: 1993), pp. 151–66.

PART FIVE

Anonymous and Pseudonymous Works

Lines on Seeing the Royal Palace at Stirling in Ruins

First printed in *The Edinburgh Evening Courant*, 5th October, 1787.

> Here Stewarts once in triumph reign'd,
> And laws for Scotland's weal ordain'd;
> But now unroof'd their Palace stands,
> Their sceptre's fall'n to other hands;
> 5   Fallen indeed, and to the earth,
> Whence grovelling reptiles take their birth. —
> The injured STEWART-line are gone,
> A Race outlandish fill their throne;
> An idiot race, to honour lost;
> 10   Who know them best despise them most. —
>
>   R.B.

These anti-Hanoverian lines were inscribed anonymously on a window in Stirling by Burns during his first tour into the Highlands in August 1787. They reappeared in *The Edinburgh Evening Courant*, 5th October 1787, thinly disguised by the poet's initials 'R.B.' If the author's identity was not patently obvious at this point, it was made public knowledge by James Maxwell, an elderly mediocre Paisley poet, deeply envious of the young bard's success who published the lines and named Burns as the author. Maxwell used the opportunity to attack the poet in a pamphlet, *Animadversions on Some Poets and Poetasters* (Paisley, 1788). While accustomed to a degree of notoriety, at least in Ayrshire, this episode proved to be a mini-rehearsal of the graver trouble waiting ahead for Burns due to his bent for controversy. He wrote to Mrs McLehose on 27th January 1788: 'I have almost given up the Excise idea. I have been just now to wait on a great Person . . . Why will Great people not only deafen us with the din of their equipage, and dazzle us with their fastidious pomp, but they must also be so very dictatorially wise? I have been question'd like a child about my matters, and blamed and schooled for my Inscription on Stirling window' (Letter 189).

During the early nineteenth century Motherwell tried to omit these controversial lines from the canon by suggesting they were written by the bard's touring companion, William Nicol. The poet's somewhat vague title in the Glenriddell manuscript, *Written by Somebody in the Window of an Inn at Stirling* gave some credence to those who wished to deny his authorship. By 1834, as McGuirk remarks, Cunningham was too timid to publish the final anti-Hanoverian couplet. Acting as censor, Cunningham justifed his action thus: 'What was improper in the days of Burns is not proper now' (McGuirk, p. 245). Ll. 5–6 were added in the Glenriddell Manuscript and were probably not inscribed on the Stirling window.

Elegy on the Year 1788

First printed in *The Caledonian Mercury*, 10th January, 1789, under the pen name Thomas A. Linn.

	For Lords or kings I dinna mourn,	do not
	E'en let them die — for that they're born!	
	But oh! prodigious to reflect,	
	A *Towmont*, Sirs, is gane to wreck!	12 months, gone
5	O *Eighty-Eight*, in thy sma' space	small
	What dire events hae taken place!	have
	Of what enjoyments thou hast reft us!	taken from
	In what a pickle thou hast left us!	
	The Spanish empire's tint a head,	lost, leader
10	An' my auld teethless Bawtie's dead;	old, dog
	The toolzie's teugh 'tween Pitt and Fox,	struggle's tough
	An' our gudewife's wee birdie cocks;	goodwife's, small
	The tane is game, a bluidy devil,	one, bloody
	But to the *hen-birds* unco civil;	very
15	The tither's dour, has nae sic breedin',	other's is stubborn, no
	But better stuff ne'er claw'd a midden!	scratched, open dung heap
	Ye ministers, come mount the pupit,	pulpit
	An' cry till ye be haerse an' roupet;	hoarse, husky
	For *Eighty-Eight* he wished you weel,	well
20	An' gied ye a' baith gear an' meal;	gave, both, goods, food
	E'en mony a plack, an' mony a peck,	coin, sack of oats
	Ye ken yoursels, for little feck!	know, return

Ye bonie lasses, dight your een,   wipe, eyes
For some o' you hae tint a frien';   have lost, friend
25 In *Eighty-Eight*, ye ken, was taen   know, taken
What ye'll ne'er hae to gie again.   have, give

Observe the vera nowte an' sheep,   very, cattle
How dowff an' dowie they creep;   dull, weary
Nay, even the yirth itsel' does cry,   earth
30 For Embro' wells are grutten dry.   Edinburgh, wept

O *Eighty-Nine*, thou's but a bairn,   child
An' no owre auld, I hope to learn!   over old
Thou beardless boy, I pray tak care,
Thou now has got thy Daddy's chair,
35 Nae hand-cuff'd, mizzl'd, half-shackl'd *Regent*, no, muzzled
But, like himsel, a full free agent.
Be sure ye follow out the plan
Nae war than he did, honest man!   no worse
As muckle better as ye can.   much

This was written on 1st January, 1789 and published in *The Caledonian Mercury*, January 1789, under the pen-name, Thomas A. Linn (probably taken from the song *Tam Linn*). It was also printed anonymously in *Lloyd's Evening Post*, on 12th–14th January, 1789, where it may have been copied, as was common practice, by that paper.

This is politically a wickedly reductive little poem, salted with sexual slyness. A panorama of 1788, where 'great' events (the death of Charles III of Spain (l. 9) and the Regency Bill Crisis) are brought down to the vernacular earth of Burns's farmyard animals. Ll. 11–16 allude not only to the intensity of the quarrel between the still-favoured Pitt and Fox over the regency question but their utterly disparate sexuality. L. 30 alludes to the restriction of Edinburgh's water supply due to the severe frost of the winter of 1788–9. Even by the standards of Burns's anti-Hanoverianism, ll. 31–39 are stunning in that they brilliantly transpose the image of the metaphorically shackled Prince of Wales into the actual physical restraints now restraining his temporarily insane father.

Ode to the Departed Regency Bill

First printed in the London *Star*, 17th April, 1789, signed Agricola,
Edinburgh.

Daughter of Chaos' doting years,
Nurse of ten thousand hopes and fears;
Whether thy airy, unsubstantial Shade
(The rights of sepulture now duly paid)
5   Spread abroad its hideous form
       On the roaring Civil Storm,
       Deafening din and warring rage
       Factions wild with factions wage;
Or underground, deep-sunk, profound,
10   Among the demons of the earth,
With groans that make the mountains shake,
       Thou mourn thy ill-starred, blighted birth;
Or in the uncreated Void,
       Where seeds of future-being fight,
15   With lightened step thou wander wide,
       To greet thy Mother — Ancient Night,
And as each jarring, monster mass is past,
       Fond recollect what once thou wast:
In manner due, beneath this sacred oak,
20   Hear, Spirit hear! thy presence I invoke!
       By a Monarch's heaven-struck fate!
       By a disunited State!
       By a generous Prince's wrongs!
       By a Senate's strife of tongues!
25   By a Premier's sullen pride,
       Louring on the changing tide!
       By dread Thurlow's powers to awe,[1]
       Rhetoric, blasphemy and law!
       By the turbulent ocean,
30   A Nation's commotion!
       By the harlot-caresses
       Of borough-addresses!
       By days few and evil!
       Thy portion, poor devil!

1 Edward, Lord Thurlow (1731–1806). Lord Chancellor for the Fox–North
Coalition in 1778, who was asked to return to this post by Pitt.

35   By Power, Wealth, Show! the Gods by men adored!
       By Nameless Poverty! their Hell abhorred!
         By all they hope! by all they fear!
           Hear!!! And Appear!!!

     Stare not on me, thou ghastly Power;
40   Nor grim with chained defiance lour:
     No Babel-structure would *I* build
       Where, Order exil'd from his native sway,
     Confusion may the REGENT-sceptre wield,
       While all would rule and none obey:
45   Go, to the world of Man relate
       The story of thy sad, eventful fate;
       And call Presumptuous Hope to hear,
       And bid him check his blind career;
       And tell the sore-prest Sons of Care,
50   Never, never to despair. —

     Paint CHARLES'S speed on wings of fire,
       The object of his fond desire;
       Beyond his boldest hopes, at hand:
     Paint all the triumph of the Portland Band:[2]
55   Mark! how they lift the joy-exulting voice;
     And how their numerous Creditors rejoice:
     But just as hopes to warm enjoyment rise,
     Cry CONVALESCENCE! and the vision flies. —

     Then next pourtray a dark'ning twilight gloom
60   Eclipsing sad, a gay, rejoicing morn,
     While proud Ambition to th' untimely tomb
       By gnashing, grim, despairing fiends is borne:
     Paint Ruin, in the shape of high Dundas
       Gaping with giddy terror o'er the brow;
65   In vain he struggles, the Fates behind him press,
       And clamorous Hell yawns for her prey below:
     How fallen That, whose pride late scaled the skies!
     And This, like Lucifer, no more to rise!
       Again pronounce the powerful word;
70   See Day, triumphant from the night, restored. —

2 Whigs led by William Cavendish Bentick (1738–1809), the 3rd Duke of
Portland. He had been the First Lord of the Treasury under the Fox–North
Coalition.

Then know this truth, ye Sons of Men!
   (Thus ends thy moral tale)
Your darkest terrors may be vain,
   Your brightest hopes may fail. —

This parodic, pacey Pindaric ode satirises the clashing rhetoric of
manoeuvring politicians as they vied for position during the con-
stitutional Regency crisis of 1788–9. When he sent the first complete
version of the poem to Mrs Dunlop, Burns knew the risk he was
taking: 'I have this moment finished the following political Squib,
and I cannot resist the temptation of sending you a copy of it – the
only copy indeed that I will send to anybody except perhaps anon-
ymously to some London Newspaper. — Politics is dangerous
ground for me to tread on, and yet I cannot for the soul of me resist
an impulse of anything like Wit' (Letter 326). Thurlow (l. 27) refers
to Edward Lord Thurlow (1731–1806). Portland (l. 54) is the Duke of
Portland, who led an exodus of influencial Whigs to the Conserva-
tives when Britain went to war with France in 1793. Dundas (l. 63)
refers to Henry Dundas, Viscount Melville (1742–1811) whose power
over Scottish affairs during this period was near total. Burns here
displays his dislike of Dundas in a similar style to that which Shelley
later used so well to satirise Lord Castlereagh. Charles (l. 51) is
Charles James Fox, leader of the Whigs, who supported the Prince of
Wales taking the throne from his father after George III was declared
insane in late 1788. William Pitt favoured severe restrictions on the
monarchy, fearing that the Prince, who supported the Whigs, would
be placed on the throne. The King eventually recovered and con-
tinued his reign, bar certain aberrations, such as his speech about
unparalleled peace and tranquillity in December 1792 when in reality
the government tightened the sedition laws and declared Martial
Law in a panic at the rise of reform societies throughout Britain. In a
chaotic mixture of ambition and vanity, this episode provoked Burns
burlesques from the supposed loyal subjects of George III as they
clashed over who would benefit by the Prince's succession.

    The consequence of London publication is explained in Professor
Lucylle Werkmeister's *Robert Burns and the London Newspapers*, in
the *Bulletin of the New York Public Library* (Oct. 1961, Vol. 65,
no. 8). Werkmeister quotes the *Star*'s editor Stuart's introductory
note:

As the following fanciful verses contain the genuine energy and
commanding spirit of POETRY, the printer is happy in com-
municating them to the PUBLIC, and he assures his readers,

notwithstanding they appear under a fictitious signature, that they are the product of a GENIUS who ranks very highly in the REPUBLIC of LETTERS.

The same issue of Stuart's *Star* boasted in notes 'TO CORRESPON-DENTS' they would print a 'Love Sonnet by Mr. Burns, the Darling Poet of Caledonia, to-morrow'. Werkmeister goes on to quote Burns who was, at this juncture, unaware that Stuart had meddled with the poem to suit his own political views:

> I have had my usual luck in receiving your paper. – They have all come to hand except the two which I most wanted, the 17th and 18th, in which I understand my verses are. – So it has been with me always. – A damned Star has almost all my life usurped my zenith, and squinted out the cursed rays of its malign influences (Letter 339).

As Werkmeister remarks, the 'damned star' was the editor himself. Differing in politics from Burns, Stuart re-wrote some passages he did not agree with and deleted other passages. What Burns did not know was that the Portland Whigs were subsidising Stuart so that he amended the poem to serve their cause. Thus, for example, in ll. 51–4 Fox became Pitt and the Portland Band became the Tories. To hide his deceit, he stopped Burns from receiving a copy for 17th April. This was, as Werkmeister explains, the same newspaper that printed the ridiculous verse on the Duchess of Gordon's dancing and attrib-uted them to Burns, knowing full well they were not his composition. (Werkmeister totally discredits the notion that they were written by the semi-literate Henry Dundas and suggests that they were the work of someone on Stuart's staff in order to ridicule Dundas.) Stuart managed to stay on the right side of Burns by accident, since a friend of Burns misled him into believing that the guilty newspaper was the *London Gazetteer*, which innocently copied the nonsense from Stuart's *Star*. Burns eventually found out that the Ode had been considerably changed ('mangled', Letter 379) from the text he sent to London. While the image 'Daughter of Chaos' derives from Pope's *The Dunciad*, I, ll. 11–16, the language and sentiment is influenced more by Milton's *Paradise Lost*, II, ll. 894–7.

The pen-name 'Agricola', revealingly and perhaps deliberately so, means a farmer. Burns may have also picked this name given that the Roman general Agricola is supposed to have encamped a few miles to the north of Ellisland prior to the building of Hadrian's wall. The poem, on publication, was printed as a work sent from an Edinburgh poet, not a Dumfries one.

Ode, Sacred to the Memory of Mrs. Oswald Of Auchencruive

First printed in the London *Star*, 7th May, 1789, under the name Tim Nettle.

Dweller in yon dungeon dark,
Hangman of creation, mark!
Who in widow weeds appears,
Laden with unhonoured years,
5   Noosing with care a bursting purse,
Baited with many a deadly curse?

Strophe

View the wither'd beldam's face —
Can thy keen inspection trace
Aught of Humanity's sweet melting grace?
10   Note that eye, 'tis rheum o'erflows,
Pity's flood there never rose.
See those hands, ne'er stretch'd to save,
Hands that took — but never gave.
Keeper of Mammon's iron chest,
15   Lo, there she goes, unpitied and unblest,
She goes, but not to realms of everlasting rest!

Antistrophe

Plunderer of Armies! lift thine eyes,
(A while forbear, ye torturing fiends),
Seest thou whose step, unwilling, hither bends?
20   No fallen angel, hurl'd from upper skies;
'Tis thy trusty *quondam Mate*,
Doom'd to share thy fiery fate,
She, tardy, hell-ward plies.

Epode

And are they of no more avail,
25   Ten thousand glittering pounds a year?
In other worlds can Mammon fail,
Omnipotent as he is here?
O, bitter mockery of the *pompous bier*!
While down the wretched *vital part* is driven!
30   The cave-lodged beggar, with a conscience clear,
Expires in rags, unknown, and goes to Heaven.

The subject of this Ode, Mrs Oswald, was a Mary Ramsay who married Richard Oswald of London. He purchased Auchencruive estate, Ayrshire, in 1764, but died in 1784. The widow moved back to London thereafter. She died 6th December, 1788 and was brought to Ayrshire for burial. Burns explained the background in detail to Dr Moore:

> I spent my early days in her neighbourhood, and among her servants and tenants I know that she was detested with the most heart-felt cordiality . . . in the particular part of her conduct, which roused my Poetic wrath, she was much less blameable. In January last, on my road to Ayrshire, I had put up at Bailie Whigham's in Sanquar, the only tolerable Inn in the place. The frost was keen, and the grim evening and the howling wind were ushering in a night of snow and drift. My horse and I were both much fatigued with the labors of the day, and just as my friend the Bailie and I, were bidding defiance to the storm over a smoking bowl, in wheels the funeral pageantry of the late great Mrs Oswald, and poor I, am forced to brave all the horrors of the tempestuous night, and jade my horse, my young favourite horse whom I had just christened Pegasus, twelve miles further on, through the wildest moors & hills of Ayrshire, to New Cumnock, the next Inn. Suffice it to say that when a good fire at New Cumnock had so far recovered my frozen sinews, I sat down and wrote the enclosed Ode (Letter 322).

That an aristocrat could still be more important as a corpse than a living human being, thrown into the teeth of winter, is the spark that kindled Burns's poetic indignation.

Although first published under the name Tim Nettle in a London newspaper, this work was included in the 1793 Edinburgh edition. On both occasions, Mrs Oswald's identity was dashed out, to preserve anonymity. Burns's letter to Stuart, editor of the London *Star*, introduced the poem. Burns begins by pretending he does not know who the author of the poem is:

Mr Printer

> I know not who is the author of the following poem, but I think it contains some equally well-told and just compliments to the memory of a matron who, a few months ago, much against her private inclination, left this good world and twice five good thousands per annum behind her . . .
> . . . I dislike partial respect of persons, and am hurt to see the

public make such a fuss when a poor pennyless gipsey is
consigned over to Jack Ketch [the hangman], and yet scarce
take any notice when a purse-proud Priestess of Mammon is by
the inexorable hand of death prisoned in everlasting fetters of
ill-gotten gold . . .

          Tim Nettle (Letter 338).

Due to the chicanery of Peter Stuart, a personal letter Burns sent
him was, unknown to Burns, published beneath the Ode. This act of
betrayal, according to Lucylle Werkmeister, might have had appal-
ling consequences for Burns:

> It is therefore incredible that, immediately below the letter from
> Tim Nettle . . . Stuart should have printed the whole of Burns's
> personal letter to him, altering, it appears, only the salutation,
> which now read 'Mr PRINTER', and the name of the author,
> which was now in capital letters. Not only did this letter identify
> Mrs Oswald as subject of the 'Ode' and Burns as its author, but it
> reached back to identify him as the author of the 'Ode to the
> Departed Regency Bill' as well. A copy of this number of the
> newspaper, one can be certain, was also not sent to Burns
> (Werkmeister, *Robert Burns and the London Newspapers*, *Bulletin
> of the New York Public Library*, Vol. 65, 1961, p. 496).

It is surprising, therefore, that the poet's Excise employers did not
caution or discipline Burns at this juncture for his insurrectionary
social satire, although it is likely they would have been notified of his
publication.

It is not the least of Burns's many formal jokes that he borrows the
nomenclature and structure of this poem from Collins's *Ode to
Mercy*. Kinsley, always ready to agree with nineteenth century
denial of the poet's radical values, describes this as a 'savage satire
in the quite unsuitable Pindaric form' (Vol. III, p. 1292). On the
contrary, the Pindaric form succeeds, moving crisply from the
delivery of the deceased to the Devil (the hangman of Creation),
to the atmospheric cadence of the *Strophe*, examining the subject for
any trace of humanity, to the awakening of her dead husband, also in
hell, in the *Antistrophe*. In the final *Epode*, Burns reveals the art of
his dark painting, '. . . down the wretched vital part is driven',
meaning the loss of her soul (the vital part) in life and its transport to
Hell. It is excessive wealth and her oppressive nature that has, in
life, destroyed the woman's soul and condemned her to her fate. The
line 'Plunderer of Armies!' refers to Mrs Oswald's husband whose
'war-profiteering' had earned their fortune.

A New Psalm for the Chapel of Kilmarnock on the Thanksgiving-Day for His Majesty's Recovery –

First printed in the London *Morning Star*, 14th May, 1789, signed Duncan M'Leerie.

O, sing a new Song to the Lord!
  Make, all and every one,
A joyful noise, ev'n for the king
  His Restoration. —

5 The Sons of Belial in the land
    Did set their heads together;
  Come, let us sweep them off, said they,
    Like an o'erflowing river. —

  They set their heads together, I say,
10   They set their heads together:
  On right, and left, and every hand,
    We saw none to deliver. —

  Thou madest strong two chosen Ones,
    To quell the Wicked's pride:
15 That Young Man, great in Issachar
    The burden-bearing Tribe. —

  And him, among the Princes chief
    In our Jerusalem,
  The Judge that's mighty in thy law,
20   The Man that fears thy name. —

  Yet they, even they, with all their might,
    Began to faint and fail;
  Even as two howling, ravening wolves
    To dogs do turn their tail. —

25 Th' Ungodly o'er the Just prevail'd,
    For so thou hadst appointed,
  That thou might'st greater glory give
    Unto thine own Annointed. —

And now thou hast restored our State,
30   Pity our kirk also,
For she by tribulations
     Is now brought very low! —

Consume that High-Place, PATRONAGE,
     From off thine holy hill;
35 And in thy fury burn the book
     Even of that man M'GILL. —

Now hear our Prayer, accept our Song,
     And fight thy Chosen's battle:
We seek but little, Lord, from thee,
40   Thou kens we get as little.   knows

This was written to commemorate the day of public thanksgiving
declared when King George III recovered from his bout of insanity.
Burns describes his feelings on this occasion to Mrs Dunlop: 'As I
am not devoutly attached to a certain Monarch, I cannot say that my
heart run any risk of bursting . . . God forgive me for speaking evil
of dignities! But I must say that I look on the whole business as a
solemn farce of pageant mummery. The following are a few Stanzas
of new Psalmody for that 'Joyful Solemnity' which I sent to a
London Newspaper' (Letter 335). The poem appeared in the Lon-
don *Star* (not the *Edinburgh Star*, as Mackay suggests (p. 354), since
no such paper existed) with the indication that it was written at
Kilmarnock on the 25th April. It was signed under the pen name
Duncan M'Leerie. The note with the song suggested it had been
sung 'devoutly' in a chapel in Kilmarnock on the 23rd past. Burns
openly acknowledged to Mrs Dunlop in the same letter that Stuart,
the publisher of the London *Star* was 'an old acquaintance of mine,
and as I am a little tinctured with Buff & Blue myself, I now and
then help him to a Stanza' (Letter 335). This is another example of
how Burns protected his Excise career by employing a pen name and
printing the song as though it was written other than in Dumfries.
This was a procedure he was forced to extend in the darker political
years ahead.
     The 'Young Man' (l. 15) refers to William Pitt; while 'chief' (l.
17) alludes to Lord Thurlow (See footnote 1, *Ode to the Departed
Regency Bill*). Rev. McGill (l. 36) is Rev. Dr McGill (1732–1807) of
Ayrshire who was persecuted for his liberal views on religious
doctrine, published in his text *A Practical Essay on the Death of
Jesus Christ* (1786) and *The Benefits of the Revolution* (1789) in

which he defended his views against the illiberal attack by Dr Peebles, Kirk minister at Newton-upon-Ayr (See Vol. III, Kinsley, pp. 1306–7). Burns boasted to Mrs Dunlop that he would hunt down the persecutors of Dr McGill like wild prey (Letter 148). See also notes to *The Kirk's Alarm*.

The song is written in the style of the Presbyterian metrical psalms, paraphrasing in the first line from *Psalms*, CXLIV, line 9, 'I will sing a new song unto thee, O God'. Kinsley lists several biblical allusions from, inter alia, *Deuteronomy* and *Judges*. They are employed to mock the farcical new 'Jerusalem' of Pitt. Although printed during the poet's lifetime pseudonymously, this work did not feature in the canon until Hately Waddell's edition (1867), almost a century after its first appearance.

The Kirk's Alarm
or The Kirk of Scotland's Garland
Tune: Push about the Brisk Glass
First printed in 1789 as an anonymous broadside sheet.

Orthodox, Orthodox, wha believe in John Knox,   who
    Let me sound an alarm to your conscience;
A heretic blast has been blawn i' the West —   blown, West
    That what is not Sense must be Nonsense, Orthodox
5   That what is not Sense must be Nonsense. —

Doctor Mac,[1] Doctor Mac, ye should streek on a rack,   stretch
    To strike Evildoers wi' terror;
To join FAITH and SENSE upon ony pretence   any
    Was heretic, damnable error, &c.

10   Town of Ayr, Town of Ayr, it was rash, I declare,
    To meddle wi' mischief a brewing;
Provost John[2] is still deaf to the Church's relief,
    And Orator Bob[3] is its ruin, &c.

1 Rev. Doctor McGill, Ayr. R.B.
2 Provost John Ballantine. R.B.
3 Mr [Bob] Aitken. R.B.

D'rymple[4] mild, D'rymple mild, tho' your heart 's like a child,
15   And your life like the new-driven snaw;   snow
Yet that winna save ye, auld Satan maun have ye,   will not, shall
        For preaching that three 's ane and twa, &c.   one, two

Calvin's Sons, Calvin's Sons, seize your sp'ritual guns —
        Ammunition you never can need;
20   Your HEARTS are the stuff will be POWTHER enough,   powder
        And your SCULLS are store-houses o' LEAD, &c.

Rumble John,[5] Rumble John, mount the steps with a groan,
        Cry, the BOOK is wi' heresy cramm'd;
Then lug out your ladle, deal brimstone like aidle,   pull, cow's piss
25   And roar every note o' the DAMN'D, &c.

Simper James,[6] Simper James, leave the fair Killie dames,   Kilmarnock
        There 's a holier chase in your view:
I'll lay on your head that the PACK ye'll soon lead,
        For PUPPIES like you there 's but few, &c.

30   Singet Sawnie,[7] Singet Sawnie, are ye herding the PENNIE,   money
        Unconscious what danger await?
Wi' a jump, yell, and howl, alarm every soul,
        For the Foul Thief is just at your gate, &c.

Poet Willie,[8] Poet Willie, gie the Doctor a volley,   give
35   Wi' your 'Liberty's chain' and your wit:
O'er Pegasus' side ye ne'er laid a stride,
        Ye but smelt, man, the place where he shit, &c.

Andro' Gowk,[9] Andro Gowk, ye may slander the BOOK,
        And the Book not the waur, let me tell ye: worst
40   Ye are rich and look big, but lay by hat and wig —
        And ye'll hae a CALF'S-HEAD o' sma' value, &c.   have

4 Dr Dalrymple, Ayr. R.B.
5 John Russel, Kilmarnock. R.B.
6 James McKindlay, Kilmarnock. R.B.
7 A. Moodie, Riccartoun. R.B.
8 William Peebles in Newton upon Ayr, a Poetaster, who among many other
things, published an Ode on the Centenary of the Revolution in which was
this line – 'And bound in liberty's endearing chain'. R.B.
9 Dr Andrew Mitchel, Monkton. R.B.

Barr Steenie,[10] Barr Steenie, what mean ye, what mean ye?
 If ye'll meddle nae mair wi' the matter,   *no more*
Ye may hae some pretence, man, to havins and sense,
45 Wi' people wha ken ye nae better, &c.   *who know*

Jamie Goose,[11] Jamie Goose, ye hae made but toom roose *empty*
 In hunting the wicked Lieutenant;   *speculation*
But the Doctor's your mark, for the Lord's haly ark *holy*
 He has cooper'd and ca'd a wrang pin in, &c. *nailed, wrong*

50 Davie Rant,[12] Davie Rant, in a face like a saunt, *saint*
 And a heart that would poison a hog;
Raise an impudent roar, like a breaker lee-shore,
 Or the Kirk will be tint in a bog, &c.   *lost*

Cessnock-side,[13] Cessnock-side, wi' your turkey-cock pride,
55 O' manhood but sma' is your share;
Ye've the figure, it's true, even your faes maun allow, *foes must*
 And your friends daur na say ye hae mair, &c. *dare not, have more*

Muirland Jock,[14] Muirland Jock, whom the Lord made a rock
 To crush Common Sense for her sins,
60 If ill-manners were Wit, there 's no mortal so fit
 To confound the poor Doctor at ance, &c.   *once*

Daddie Auld,[15] Daddie Auld, there 's a tod i' the fauld, *fox*
 A tod meikle waur than the CLERK: *much worse*
Tho' ye do little skaith, ye'll be in at the death, *damage*
65 For if ye canna bite ye may bark, &c.   *can not*

Holy Will,[16] Holy Will, there was wit i' your skull,
 When ye pilfer'd the alms o' the poor;
The timmer is scant, when ye're taen for a saunt, *wood, taken, saint*
 Wha should swing in a rape for an hour, &c. *who, rope*

10 Stephen Young, [of] Barrr. R.B.
11 James Young in New Cumnock, who had lately been foiled in an ecclesiastic prosecution against a Lieutenant Mitchel. R.B.
12 David Grant, Ochiltree. R.B.
13 George Smith, Galston. R.B.
14 John Shepherd, Muirkirk. R.B.
15 Rev. William Auld, Mauchline. R.B.
16 An Elder in Mauchline. R.B. [See *Holy Willie's Prayer*.]

70   Poet Burns, Poet Burns, wi' your priest-skelping turns,
           Why desert ye your auld native shire?
       Tho' your Muse is a gipsey, yet were she ev'n tipsey,
           She could ca' us nae waur than we are, Poet Burns,   call, no worse
           She could ca' us nae waur than we are. —

POSTSCRIPTS

Afton's Laird,[17] Afton's Laird, when your pen can be spar'd,
     A copy of this I bequeath,
On the same sicker score as I mention'd before,   safe/confidential
     To that trusty auld Worthy, Clackleith,[18] Afton's Laird,
     To that trusty auld Worthy, Clackleith.

Factor John,[19] Factor John, whom the Lord made alone,
     And ne'er made another thy peer,
Thy poor servant, the Bard, in respectful regard,
     Presents thee this token sincere, Factor John,
     Presents thee this token sincere. —

The Kirk's Alarm first appears as an anonymous song under the title
*The Ayrshire Garland, an Excellent New Song; Tune – The Vicar and
Moses.* The first version contained only thirteen stanzas, compared
to the complete song's twenty. The song is a stalwart defence of the
Rev. Dr William McGill (1732–1807) against his persecution by the
Synod of Glasgow and Ayr (See our notes for *A New Psalm for the
Chapel of Kilmarnock*). This is made vividly clear by Burns as early
as November 1787: '. . . if the prosecution which I hear the Erebean
Fanatics are projecting against my learned and truly worthy friend,
Dr McGill, goes on, I shall keep no measure with the savages, but
fly at them with the faulcons of Ridicule, or run them down with the
bloodhounds of Satire, as lawful game, wherever I start them'
(Letter 124). On the opponents of McGill, listed in the poem,
Burns goes on, in July 1789, just after completing the ballad:
'Several of these reverend lads, his opponents, have come thro'
my hands before, but I have some thoughts of serving them up
again in a different dish. . . . I have just sketched the following
ballad . . . I am thinking to throw off two or three dozen copies at a
Press in Dumfries, & send them as from Edinburgh to some
Ayrshire folks on both sides of the question' (Letter 352). Mrs
Dunlop advised him not to do this but he disregarded her. The

17 John Logan. R.B.
18 James Johnson. R.B.
19 John Kennedy. R.B.

original broadside was probably paid for and circulated by Burns himself.

The work also appears in *Songs and Poems* by Alexander Tait (Paisley, 1790, pp. 170–3), under the bizzare and malicious pen-name 'Composed by Plotcock, the Foul Thief's Exciseman'. Tait's version matches the broadside text. He published the Burns poem as an occasional piece to set up his own reply, *The Answer to Plotcock*, an inferior work satirising Burns's work. He does not give away the poet's identity, although he knew Burns was the author. Sandy Tait was the author of three unpleasantly frivolous poems on Burns and his family, *Burns in His Infancy*, *Burns in Lochly* and *Burns's Hen Clockin in Mauchline*. The poem itself did not appear as a work by Burns until Stewart's edition, 1801.

Kinsley rightly remarks that the poetic form is common to drinking songs (the tune picked by Burns is that of a drinking song) and political squibs before Burns. Henderson and Henley point out that the immediate model may have been a pro-Pitt attack on Charles James Fox printed in *The Glasgow Mercury*, 23rd–30th December 1788 (See Kinsley, Vol. III, p. 1308). This is formally similar to *The Kirk's Alarm*:

Mr. Fox, Mr. Fox,
Thou'rt knock'd down like an Ox
By honest Will Pitt's argumentum:
'Twas a cruel mistake, &c.

Kinsley, who lifts his quote from H–H, misquotes the text of the newspaper poem, with 'argumentation' instead of 'argumentum'. Burns made several copies of the song; adding and modifying several verses; hence there are several variant readings. This is a rogues' gallery of ecclesiastics previously satirised by Burns, the 'auld lichts' whose interpretation of the 1688 revolutionary celebrations in 1788 differed markedly from the liberal McGill. The late eighteenth century did not differentiate theology and politics as we do.

Verses Written upon a Blank Leaf
in COWPER's POEMS Belonging to a Lady
First printed in *The Gentleman's Magazine*, April 1789.

Let dear Eliza pass the gliding hours,
By culling sweets from choice poetic flowers!
Of all those various beauties form'd to please,
There's none more choice, and none more sweet than these:

5   For truth with elegance is here display'd;
       Descriptive Nature beauteously array'd:
       Whether he trip, by Luna's silver sheen,
       Whether bright Pheobus gild with genial ray
       The blushing morning of the coming May;
10   Whether pourtray'd the shrub, or fragrant flower;
       His soft, his lively portraits, you'll admire.
       With gentle Thomson tracing wood and grove,
       He paints recesses, sweet for heaven-born love;
       Pope's softest numbers harmonize each line,
15   The fire of Dryden, Milton's thoughts sublime,
       The lash of Churchill, Waller's warbling lays,
       Sing loud their merit, loudly chant their praise.
       Describ'd the humble cot, proud city's tower
       The cloud-capt hill, the lovely vale or bower,
20   Still guided by the radiant son of Jove,
       In Nature's walks, behold his fav'rite rove!
                                              R.B.

Verses Written upon a Blank Leaf in COWPER's POEMS Belonging to a Lady was printed in the April 1789 issue of *The Gentleman's Magazine* (p. 353). It was recently brought to light after the discovery of a known Burns work in the same journal in 1794, *also* printed under his initials, 'R.B.' An abridged version of *A Winter Night* was printed under a new title, *Humanity: An Ode*. Given that the publication of this work had never before been recorded and no search of the journal for missing work by Burns ever documented, the magazine was consequently scanned for such a possibility. The above poem and an epigram on the death of Dr Adam Smith (signed under the known Burns pen name, Agricola) were the result.

The controversial *Lines on Seeing the Royal Palace at Stirling in Ruins* were first printed by Burns in a newspaper signed, 'R.B.' So, we know he employed his initials in this manner. The case for Burns being the author of *Humanity: An Ode* needs little argument because it is obviously a modified variant of *A Winter Night*, printed in the 1787 Edinburgh edition. Indeed, if *A Winter Night* had not already been in print, there could be no absolute certainty Burns wrote *Humanity: An Ode*; despite the fact that we could not trace another active poet employing these initials in that period.

During 1789 Burns, still farming Ellisland, was the neighbour of Robert Riddell. Riddell was a contributor to *The Gentleman's*

Magazine as an antiquarian long before he met Burns. It is quite probable that Riddell, a subscriber to the magazine, suggested Burns seek publication in it.

While not a poem of any great literary significance, the verse is reasonably competent in its limited task of impressing a lady that the author is familiar with the poetry of Cowper. In contrasting Cowper with so many other, well-known English poets and the Scottish Thomson, it is slightly exhibitionist. Burns was, by 1789, fond of Cowper verse, with a particular liking for the popular long poem, *The Task*, as glowingly mentioned to Mrs Dunlop (Letter 605). Indeed, the first literary comparison made in the poem (l. 12) is between Cowper and James Thomson, author of *The Seasons*. Burns compares these two poets in September 1788, in a letter to William Dunbar – '. . . Cowper's *Poems*, the best poet out of sight since Thomson' (Letter 274). Burns owned a copy of *The Lives of the English Poets* edited by Dr Johnson and was well acquainted with the poets listed (ll. 14–16). The poem rightly mentions the variegated literary influences of Thomson, Pope, Dryden, Churchill and Waller (ll. 12–16) in Cowper's verse. Having been so influenced himself, it is no surprise that Burns liked Cowper's somewhat evangelical-influenced poetry and in particular his stance against the slave trade which heavily permeated the popular radical press. Cowper, as Baird reveals, was an admirer of Burns. He told Samuel Rose, after poring over the Edinburgh edition:

> I think them on the whole a very extraordinary production. He is, I believe, the only poet these islands have produced in the lower rank of life since Shakespeare, (I should rather say since Prior,) who need not be indebted for any part of his praise to a charitable consideration of his origin, and the disadvantages under which he has laboured (John D. Baird, 'Two Poets of the 1780s: Burns and Cowper' in *Critical Essays on Robert Burns*, ed. Donald Low, (Routledge, London, 1975, p. 108).

It would be frivolous to speculate on the identity of the unknown young lady ('Eliza') but it suffices that Burns knew of several such ladies, one being Elizabeth Burnett mentioned in *Address to Edinburgh*. The missing line after l. 7 may be the result of a printer's error.

Epitaph: On Robert Fergusson
On the Tombstone in the Canongate Churchyard
Born Sept. 5th, 1750 Died Oct. 17th, 1774
First printed in *The Edinburgh Advertiser*, 7th–11th August, 1789.

By special Grant of the Managers to Robert Burns, who erected this
Stone, this Burial Place is to remain for ever sacred to the Memory
of ROBERT FERGUSSON.

No sculptur'd Marble here, nor pompous lay,
   'No storied Urn nor animated Bust;'
This simple stone directs pale SCOTIA'S way
   To pour her sorrow o'er the POET'S dust.

5 [She mourns, sweet tuneful youth, thy hapless fate:
   Tho' all the powers of song thy fancy fir'd,
Yet Luxury and Wealth lay by in State,
   And, thankless, starv'd what they so much admir'd.

This humble tribute with a tear he gives,
10   A brother Bard, he can no more bestow:
But dear to fame thy Song immortal lives,
   A nobler monument than Art can show.]

Only the first of these stanzas, written in early 1787, was printed in
The Edinburgh Advertiser of early August 1789; then subsequently
featured in Currie, 1800. The final stanzas were entered in the *SCB*.
They did not enter the canon until the notebook surfaced in the
1870s. Burns's headstone to Fergusson was not erected until August
1789. The newspaper printed the lines after the stone was erected. It
was inscribed on Burns's behalf by an Edinburgh architect named
Robert Burn. The dedicatory inscription on the stone is given as the
subtitle.

   The quote from Gray's *Elegy in a Country Churchyard* (l. 2) is
not always so identified by previous editors. Given that the poet
waited two years for the work to be finished, he deliberately took
two years to pay for the headstone, costing £5. 10 shillings (See
Letters 81 and 495). Fergusson died, apparently insane, in the
Edinburgh asylum.

On the Late Death of Dr Adam Smith

First printed in *The Gentleman's Magazine*, September 1790.

Death and *Hermes* of late in Elysium made boast,
That each would bring thither what earth valued most:
Smith's *Wealth of Nations Hermes* stole from his shelf;
DEATH just won his cause – he took off Smith himself.

Agricola.

This epigram which was recently found in *The Gentleman's Magazine*, September 1790, p. 843, is given here as a probable work of Burns for several reasons. The same pen-name (meaning a farmer) was employed by Burns the year previous in his *Ode on the Departed Regency Bill*. There is no other occurrence of this pen-name by any poet during the entire 1780–1800 period. Contextually the evidence points to Burns. As his letters show, he was well read not only in Smith's *The Theory of Moral Sentiments* but also *The Wealth of Nations*. The epigram reveals a mixture of respect and irony. Hermes, the God of commerce and communication thinks Smith's best-known book is the greatest thing on earth but Death goes one step further and whisks off Smith himself.

Epigram on Captain Francis Grose,
the Celebrated Antiquary

First printed in *The Belfast Newsletter*, 18th May 1792.

The Devil got notice that GROSE was a-dying,
So whip! at the summons, old Satan came flying;
But when he approach'd where poor FRANCIS lay moaning,
And saw each bed-post with its burthen a-groaning,
Astonish'd! confounded! cry'd Satan, by God,
I'll want 'im, ere take such a damnable load. —

This was written at Ellisland in 1789 when the pendulous Grose was alive not, as implied by Mackay, after the death of Grose in 1791 at Dublin. After appearing in *The Belfast Newsletter* it was subsequently printed by Stuart, Glasgow, 1801.

Extempore –
On Some Late Commemorations of the Poet Thomson
First published in *The Edinburgh Gazetteer*, 23rd November, 1792.

DOST thou not rise, indignant Shade,
 And smile wi' spurning scorn,
When they wha wad hae starved thy life,   who would have
 Thy senseless turf adorn? —

5 They, wha about thee mak sic fyke   make such fuss
 Now thou art but a name,
Wad seen thee damn'd ere they had spar'd would have
 Ae plack to fill thy wame. —   one farthing, belly

Helpless, alane, thou clamb the brae,   alone, climbed, hillside
10 Wi' meikle, honest toil,   much
And claucht th' unfading garland there, clutched
 Thy sair-won, rightful spoil. —   sore-

And wear it there! and call aloud,
 This axiom undoubted —
15 'Wouldst thou hae Nobles' Patronage?' have
 First learn to live without it!!!

'To wham hae routh, more shall be given' have plenty
 Is every Patron's faith;
But he, the friendless, needful wretch,
20 Shall lose the mite he hath. —

The above text is from *The Edinburgh Gazetteer* where it was printed under the pseudonym Thomas A. Rhymer. Despite appearing first in the Edinburgh newspaper in November 1792, it did not enter the canon until the 1820s.

 Kinsley suggests that the poem was written at the same time as the previous English tribute to Thomson. The only reference to the poem comes in a panic-stricken letter to Robert Graham of Fintry of 5th January, 1793, where Burns tried desperately to disassociate himself from the political implications of his relationship with the soon-to-be incarcerated Captain Johnston, editor of the dissident *Edinburgh Gazetteer*:

Of Johnston, the publisher of the *Edinburgh Gazetteer*, I know nothing. – One evening in company with four or five friends, we met with his prospectus which we thought manly and independent; & I wrote to him ordering his paper for us. If you think that I act improperly in allowing his Paper to come addressed to me, I shall immediately countermand it. – I never, so judge me, God! wrote a line of *prose* (our italics) for the Gazetteer in my life. – An occasional address, spoken by Miss Fontenelle on her benefit-night, here which I called, the Rights of Woman, I sent to the Gazetteer; as also some extempore stanzas on the Commemoration of Thomson: both of these I will subjoin for your perusal. – You will see that they have nothing whatever to do with Politics. – At the time I sent Johnson one of these poems, but which one I do not remember, I inclosed at the request of my warm & worthy friend, Robt. Riddell Esq: of Glendriddel, a prose Essay, signed Cato, written by him, & addressed to the delegates for the Country Reform, of which he was one for this Country. – With the merits or demerits, of that Essay I have nothing to do, farther than transmitting it in the same Frank, which Frank he had procured me (Letter 530).

In fact, on ordering *The Edinburgh Gazetteer*, Burns was driven by rampant enthusiasm for the edition he had acquired and, on behalf of four or five friends, suggests he will pay his subscription via Peter Hill, his Edinburgh bookseller friend. His enthusiasm for the newspaper is telling: 'Go on, Sir! Lay bare with undaunted heart & steady hand that horrid mass of corruption called Politics & State-Craft!' (*Letter*, 515). As we shall see, he did not stop contributing.

Nor is this bitter little poem devoid of political comment. It has little or nothing to do with Thomson, who, happily exiled, waxed fat in southern pastures. It is a compound of memories of Robert Fergusson's and his own grim Parnassian uphill struggle. The life of the true poet is seen as a particularly acute example of an aristocratic society gripped by injustice towards the poor. The last stanza pertinent to this theme echoes *Matthew* xiii.12; cf. *Mark* iv.25 and *Luke* viii.18. Further, the poem's retarded entry into the canon in the 1820s suggests a significant dissident content.

The Rights of Woman
An Occasional Address Spoken on her Benefit Night,
Nov. 26th, 1792, at Dumfries, by Miss Fontenelle

First published in *The Edinburh Gazetteer*, 30th Nov. 1792

WHILE Europe's eye is fix'd on mighty things,
The fate of Empires and the fall of Kings;
While quacks of State must each produce his plan,   doctors
And even children lisp, The Rights of Man;
5   Amid the mighty fuss, just let me mention,
THE RIGHTS OF WOMAN merit some attention. —

First, in the Sexes' intermix'd connexion,
One sacred Right of Woman is PROTECTION.
The tender flower, that lifts its head, elate,
10   Helpless, must fall before the blasts of Fate,
Sunk on the earth, defac'd its lovely form,
Unless *your Shelter* ward th' impending storm.

Our second Right — but needless here is caution —
To keep that Right inviolate's the fashion:
15   Each man of sense has it so full before him,
He'd die before he'd wrong it — 'tis DECORUM!
There was, indeed, in far less polish'd days,
A time, when rough, rude Man had naughty ways:
Would swagger, swear, get drunk, kick up a riot,
20   Nay, even thus invade a Lady's quiet. —
Now, thank our Stars! these Gothic times are fled;
Now, well-bred men — and you are all well-bred —
Most justly think (and we are much the gainers)
Such conduct neither spirit, wit, nor manners. —

25   For Right the third, our last, our best, our dearest:
That Right to fluttering Female hearts the nearest,
Which even the Rights of Kings, in low prostration,
Most humbly own — 'tis dear, dear ADMIRATION!
In that blest sphere alone we live and move;
30   There taste that life of life — Immortal Love!
Smiles, glances, tears, sighs, fits, flirtations, airs;
'Gainst such an host, what flinty savage dares —
When awful Beauty joins with all her charms,
Who is so rash as rise in rebel arms?

35   But truce with Kings, and truce with Constitutions,
With bloody armaments and Revolutions;
Let MAJESTY your first attention summon:
Ah! ça ira! THE MAJESTY OF WOMAN!!!   _{thus shall it go/let it go}

This was printed anonymously in *The Edinburgh Gazetteer*, 30th November, 1792 next to a political essay written by Robert Riddell. The text is from the Edinburgh newspaper. The original publication contains a minor spelling error, giving Miss Fontenelle's name as Foftenelle. Miss Louisa Fontenelle was a London actress who moved to the Theatre Royal, Edinburgh and played provincial theatres in Scotland. She was a favourite of Burns's (See *Occasional Address*, December 1794 and *On Seeing Miss Fontenelle in A Favourite Character*, same date). This, superficially, is an equally light-weight, even frivolous piece. Its implications are, however, of deeper political import and its performance and reception were to have far-reaching consequences for Burns.

Burns was fascinated by the actress as this belt and braces compliment suggests: 'To you Madam, on our humble Dumfries boards, I have been more indebted for entertainment, than ever I was in prouder Theatres.—Your charms as a woman would insure applause to the most indifferent Actress, and your theatrical talents would secure admiration to the plainest figure . . . Will the forgoing lines be of any service to you on your appearing benefit night? . . . They are nearly extempore . . .' (Letter 519). The poem was revised and sent to Mrs Graham of Fintry on 5 January, though Burns still describes it as 'this little poem, written in haste on the spur of the occasion, & therefore inaccurate; but a sincere Compliment to that Sex, the most amiable of the works of God . . .' Kinsley, while noting this, fails to remark that Mrs Graham received this a mere five days after Burns's semi-hysterical denial of revolutionary tendencies to her husband in which he had denoted *The Rights of Woman* as quite apolitical. This was evidently the frivolously anodyne evidence being offered to Fintry by way of his wife. Certainly the references in it to (1. 4) Paine's enormously popular *Rights of Man* (1792) and Mary Wollstonecraft's *The Rights of Woman* (1793) seem merely playful. There was correspondence between Wollstonecraft and Burns which, like so much else, has vanished forever. Certainly if Mary Wollstonecraft had read this poem she would have loathed it as it is replete with the kind of condescension to women that prevented them from occupying a creative, professional and intellectual level with men. Thus, for example, she could write: 'Taught from their infancy that beauty is woman's sceptre, the mind shapes itself to the body, and roaming around its gilt cage, only seeks to adore its prison (*Vindication of the Rights of Woman* (London, 1975), p. 197). The fact that the sexually predatory 'Gothic' age is passed would have been small consolation to her. Burns may also have been politically ironic in asserting this. Kinsley notes that 'Burns's lines are an ironical allusion to the annual saturnalia of the Caledonian Hunt at Dumfries' (Chambers–Wallace, iii.361). Cf Burns to Mrs Dunlop, 29 October 1794: 'We have had the Caledonians here for this bypast fortnight; and of course, we have the roar of Folly and Dissipation' (Letter 645).

The notion that the priapic Burns, the only rooster in the barn-yard, would have any affiliation to women's rights seems not credible. He was, however, more complex than that. His friendship with Maria Riddell was based on a common radicalism. Part of the extreme tension within that relationship derived from the fact that, because of her social position, she was able to articulate political ideas about which he had to keep his mouth shut. Through the Riddell connection, however, he met another young, apparently radically inclined Welshwoman, Deborah Duff Davies. Writing to her on April 6th, 1793, less than a year after the Dumfries perfor-mance we get this tormented letter written in the wake of the Sedition Trials as Burns rages at the impotence not only of his own radical values but the cost to this for even more depressed and suppressed women. Catherine Carswell, politically empathetic to Burns, believed that he was, because of his non-appearance in Edinburgh among The Scottish Friends of the People, guilt-driven as well as manifestly confined by his office and his alert enemies. Thus he writes:

Good God, why this disparity between our wishes & our powers!— . . . I know that your hearts have been wounded by the scorn of the Proud whom accident has placed above you, or worse still, in whose hands, perhaps, are placed many of the comforts of your life: but, there! ascend that rock of Indepen-dance, & look, justly, down on their littleness of soul.—Make the Worthless tremble under your indignation, & the Foolish sink before your contempt; & largely impart that happiness to others which I am certain will give yourselves so much pleasure to bestow!

. . . Why, amid my generous enthusiasm, must I find myself a poor, powerless devil, incapable of wiping one tear from the eye of Misery, or of adding one comfort to the Friend I love!— Out upon the world! say I; that its affairs are administered so ill!—They talk of REFORM—My God! what a reform would *I* make among the Sons, & even the Daughters of men!

Down, immediately, should go FOOLS from the high places where misbegotten CHANCE has perked them up, & through life should they sculk, ever haunted by their native insignificance, as the body marches accompanied by its shadow.—As for a much more formidable class, the knaves, I am at a loss what to do with them.—Had *I* a world, there should not be a knave in it: & on the other hand, Hell as our Theologians paint it, particularly an eternal Hell, is a deeper damnation than I could bear to see the veriest scoundrel in earth plunged into.— But the hand that could give, I would liberally fill: & I would pour delight on the heart that could kindly forgive, & generously love.—

Still, the inequalities of life are, among MEN, comparatively tolerable: but there is a DELICACY, a TENDERNESS, accompanying every view in which one can place lovely WOMAN, that are grated & shocked at the rude, capricious distinctions of Fortune.— Woman is the BLOOD-ROYAL of life: let there be slight degrees of precedency among them, but let them be all sacred.—

Whether this last sentiment be right, or wrong, I am not accountable: it is an original, component feature of my mind.— I remember, & 'tis almost the earliest thing I do remember, when I was quite a boy, one day at church, being enraged at seeing a young creature, one of the maids of his house, rise from the mouth of the pew to give way to a bloated son of Wealth & Dullness, who waddled surlily past her.— Indeed the girl was very pretty; & he was an ugly, stupid, purse-proud, money-loving, old monster, as you can imagine (Letter 556A).

This is marked by the trauma of failure of revolutionary anticipations, reiterated cries of despair found in the late Burns comparable in quality and intensity to those prevailing in William Hazlitt's prose. In 1792 all still seemed possible so that the actual performance of *The Rights of Woman* in the agitated Dumfries theatre, as reported by Scott Douglas, seems quite probable:

At the Dumfries Theatre, under the management of Mr. Sutherland, a pretty young actress—Miss Fontenelle—formed one of the company during the winter of 1792, and also of the year following. The local newspapers announced her benefit-night for 26th November, 1792, and that after the play—The Country Girl—she would 'deliver an occasional address, written by Mr. Robert Burns, called *The Rights of Woman*.' At that period the government of this country was in great alarm regarding the spread of what were termed liberal or revolutionary opinions. Paine had produced his 'Rights of Man,' and Mary Wollstoncroft was advocating the 'Rights of Woman,' and many thought that the line, 'Truce with kings, and truce with constitutions'— the fourth from the end in this Address, was by far too bold, and that the finishing-stroke, *ça ira!* was intolerable.

Chambers records, that a lady with whom he once conversed, 'remembered being present in the theatre of Dumfries, during the heat of the Revolution, when Burns entered the pit somewhat affected by liquor. On God save the King being struck up by the band, the audience rose as usual—all except the intemperate poet, who cried for *ça ira!* A tumult was the consequence, and Burns was compelled to leave the house.' (Vol. II, p. 156)

Burns's denial that the words of the great, inflammatory song of the Revolution ('Ça ira,/La liberté s'établira,/Malgré les tyrans tout réussira') ever exclusively left his lips in his letter to Fintry is a mini-masterpiece of self-defensive comic irony:

I was in the playhouse one night, when Ça ira was called for.—I was in the middle of the pit, & from the Pit the clamour arose.— One or two individuals with whom I occasionally associate were of the party, but I neither knew of the Plot, nor joined in the Plot; nor ever opened my lips to hiss, or huzza, that, or any other Political tune whatever.—I looked on myself as far too obscure a man to have any weight in quelling a Riot; at the same time, as a character of higher respectability, than to yell in the howlings of a rabble.—This was the conduct of all the first Characters in this place; & these Characters know, & will avow, that such was my conduct (Letter 530).

He repeats this denial to Mrs Dunlop with another variation of what happened in the theatre with the audience divided over the English national anthem and the French song of revolution but implies his poem was not that night's cause of disturbance:

We, in this country, here have many alarms of the reform, or rather the Republican spirit, of your part of the kingdom.— Indeed, we are a good deal in commotion ourselves, & in our Theatre here, 'God save the king' has met with some groans and hisses, while Ça ira has been repeatedly called for.—For me, I am a *Placeman*, you know; a very humble one indeed, Heaven knows, but still so much so as to gag me from joining in the cry.—What my private sentiments are, you will find out without an Interpreter.—In the mean time, I have taken up the subject in another view, and the other day, for a pretty Actress's benefit-night, I wrote an Address, which I will give on the other page, called *The Rights of Woman* (Letter 525).

Even if Burns believed that Mrs Dunlop lived in a 'republican' Ayrshire, it is extraordinary that he could, given she had sons fighting the French, have so misjudged her political sympathies as to believe she would continue to act as his political confidante. In fact, she broke off all connection with him till just before his death as a consequence of his revealed revolutionary sentiments to her. This reaches its climax in his extraordinary letter to her of December 31st of 1792 of which two three-quarter-page sections have been cut away as part of the largely unsystematic but catastrophic destruction of political evidence that has been such a curse for subsequent understanding, scholarly and otherwise. This is the real situation about both his beliefs and the tormentingly hostile environment in which he held them:

—I have corresponded with Commissr. Graham, for the Board had made me the subject of their animadversions; & now I have the pleasure of informing that all is set to rights in that quarter.—Now, as to these inquisitorial Informers, Spies, Persecutors, &c. may the d-vil & his angels be let loose to— but hold! I was praying most fervently in my last sheet, & I must not so soon fall accursing in this.—

Alas! how little do the wickedly, or wantonly, or idly, officious, think what mischief they do by their malicious insinuations, indiscreet impertinence, or thoughtless blabbings.— What a difference there is, in intrinsic worth; Candour, Benevolence, Generosity, Kindness—in all the Charities & all the Virtues; between one class of human beings & another!—[*three words deleted*] For instance, the amiable circle I so lately mixed with in the hospitable hall of Dunlop,—their gentle, generous hearts; their uncontaminated, dignified minds; their informed &

polished understandings what a contrast, when compared—if
such comparing were not downright sacrilege—with the pros-
tituted soul of the miscreant wretch, who can deliberately &
diabolically plot the destruction of an honest man who never
offended him; & with a hellish grin of satisfaction can see the
unfortunate man, his faithful wife, & prattling innocents, turned
over to Beggary & Ruin.—Can such things be? Oui! telles choses
se font! Je viens d'en faire une épreuve maudite.—(By the way, I
don't know whether this is French; & much would it go against
my soul, to mar anything belonging to that gallant people:
though my real sentiments of them shall be confined alone to
my [letters (*deleted*)] correspondence with you.) (Letter 529)

On the Commemoration
of Rodney's Victory
King's Arms, Dumfries, 12th April, 1793
First printed in *The Edinburgh Advertiser*, issue 16th–19th April, 1793.

Friday last, being the Anniversary of the late Admiral Rodney's
glorious victory, a party of gentlemen desirous to commemorate the
day, dined together in the King's Arms, Dumfries. Many loyal and
suitable toasts were drunk on the occasion, and several naval songs
were sung: the following EXTEMPORE by BURNS, when it was
his turn to sing, ought not to be omitted:

Instead of a song, boys! I'll give you a toast;
Here's the *Mem'ry of those on the twelfth that we lost*!
We lost! did I say? no, by Heav'n, that we found!
For their fame it shall live while the world goes round.
5   The next in succession I'll give you the KING.
And *who* would betray him, on high may *he* swing!
And here's the grand fabric, OUR FREE CONSTITUTION
As built on the base of THE GREAT REVOLUTION!
And, longer with Politics not to be cramm'd —
10   *Be Anarchy curs'd — and be Tyranny d[amn]'d;*
And *who* would to Liberty e'er prove disloyal,
May his son be a *hangman*, and *he* his first trial!!

Admiral George Brydges Rodney (1718–92) won a victory over the
French navy at Dominica on 12th April, 1782, securing British
control of the Atlantic. It was a major naval engagement, the 'Battle
of the Saints', where 36 British engaged 34 French ships.

The headnote is taken from *The Edinburgh Advertiser* where the verse was first printed. Given that there is no extant manuscript, this newspaper entry is the only evidence of the poet's authorship. Despite J.W. Egerer's dismissal of the poem as 'doggerel' Burns did not write (See Kinsley, Vol. III, p. 1425), it is obviously authentic. Kinsley accepts it into the canon, recording that it appears in the *Advertiser*, although he does not specify which *Advertiser* and clearly did not check the original source. The use of italics and capitals, not given in most editions, is vividly that of Burns in the newspaper copy, as printed above. The poem is not printed in the usual poetry section of the newspaper but presented as a news item.

Burns had a very good reason for seeing it printed in *The Edinburgh Advertiser*, Scotland's most loyal, governmental newspaper. He had been instructed formally by the Excise to keep out of radical politics. So, the introduction to the fragment suggests it was sent to the newspaper by someone *other* than Burns. The habitual stylistic stressing of the poem in the newspaper version could only have been copied from a manuscript. A manuscript could only have come from Burns himself, or someone to whom he gave a copy. If Burns acted with complicity in seeing the poem deliberately printed in a pro-government newspaper, then we are probably looking at a precursor to *The Dumfries Volunteers*, where Burns's verse appears in public to present him as a loyal subject of the King. If this is a correct assumption, it was intended to delight critics of the poet's radical politics who probably thought he had changed his views. While Burns might have set out deliberately to appease his Edinburgh Excise masters who would certainly have seen this song, it is apparent from his emphatic use of capitals that the Great Revolution, the Constitution and particularly Liberty (for radicals this meant reform) were still uppermost in his mind. The irony here is that most of the loyalist government supporters were avowed enemies of 'Liberty', seen at this time as the key principle of French Republicanism. Hence, in these few lines the politically chastened Burns disarms his critics by toasting the King, then drinks a toast to Liberty, declaring that those who would betray 'Liberty' should be hung by their own offspring. Admiral Rodney's victory was a convenient opportunity to do so. Indeed, it may have been sent to the loyalist newspaper to parry further accusations of being the author of works such as *The Dagger*. If questioned or accused of writing further radical work Burns could refer his employers to this 'loyal' song in *The Edinburgh Advertiser*. Werkmeister preceded us in identifying the 'decoy' strategy.

Kinsley's view that the lines were given in 1793 at a meeting of the Dumfries Volunteers is incorrect for the simple reason that the Volunteers were not yet established. Kinsley guesses that differences in printed texts suggest that a manuscript must have been seen by some editors, but he was unaware that Scott Douglas meddled with the text. The original was probably lost among the papers of *The Edinburgh Advertiser*.

The Dagger

First printed in *The Edinburgh Gazetteer*, 16th May, 1793.

	When a' the people thick an' thrang	crowded
	Disclose their minds sae fully,	so
	Permit me here to sing a sang	song
	Of Paddy and his gully;	knife/dagger
5	(For Paddy's e'en a dainty chiel;	fellow
	Glib gabbed an' auld farran;	smooth-tongued, old-fashioned
	An' can busk up a tale as weel	well
	As onie Lord or Baron)	any
	I trow this day.	pledge

10	Had ye but seen him in his glee,	
	When he drew out his gully,	dagger
	Ye maist wad swear that he should be,	most would
	The House o' Commons bully:	
	For when he's warmed in argument,	
15	An' wants to be a bragger,	
	He handles weel the instrument —	well
	The all-convincing DAGGER,	
	On onie day.	any

	The DAGGER mode that's been brought in	
20	By this Hibernian shaver,	Irish joker
	Has rais'd indeed an unco din,	lots of noise
	And muckle clishmaclaver,	great gossip
	An' been a topic o' discourse	
	To ilka lass and laddie;	every
25	While mony jokes are pass'd in course;	
	But fient a hair cares Paddy	not a
	For that this day.	

For tho' wi' aspect like a Turk,
   Demosthenes or Tully
30 Had tried an argument wi' Burke,
   An' gi'en him but his gully;   *given, dagger*
In spite o' a' their eloquence,
   Their rhetoric and logic,
Their Lettres Belle and Common Sense,
35   'Twad been a fruitless project.
      For them this day.

+ repetition reminds me of the format of a song.

For tho' a man can speak wi' grace,
   That matters na a spittle —   *not a drop*
Can onie man haud up his face,   *any, hold*
40   An' argue wi' a whittle?   *knife*
An' Paddy, should the DAGGER fail,
   Before he will knock under,
Can neist apply (to back his tale)   *next*
   A twa and forty pounder,   *two (cannon)*
45   Wi' birr some day.   *vigour*

But trouth I fear the Parliament
   Its ancient splendour fully,
When chiels man back an argument   *fellows must*
   By waving o' a gully: *dagger*
50 Yet some there are, wi' honest heart,
   (Whose courage never swaggers)
Will ne'er the public cause desert,
   For cannons or for daggers,
      By night or day.

55 Now Paddy be nae langer rude,   *no longer*
   But lay aside your storming;
And shew the 'Swinish Multitude'
   The folly o' reforming.
Convince them that their cause is wrang,   *wrong*
60   An' tell how sair they grieve ye;   *sore*
But swine are ay sae damned headstrang,   *always so, headstrong*
   They'll aiblins no believe ye   *maybe not*
      In that this day.

May peace and plenty bless our isle —
65   May placemen ne'er oppress us —
May Grey and Erskine's gracious smile
    O' grievances redress us.
May Fox and brave McLeod exert
    Their power with due attention;
70 And never from our cause depart
    For sake o' post or pension,
        Like some this day.

God bless our King, lang may he reign
    Owre subjects free and happy —
75 May ilka loyal British swain   every
    Toss off his health in nappy —   beer
May War be banish'd from our land,
    Wi' a' its dreadfu' thunder; —
And may our Constitution stand
80   The warld's pride and wonder   world's
        Ilk coming day.   each
                    Ane O' The Swine.   One of

This burlesque, in the eight-line stanza of *The Holy Fair*, targets Edmund Burke's speech in the House of Commons debate on the Alien Bill in late December 1792 when he brandished a dagger, declaring that the radicals in Britain would eventually rise in bloody rebellion. Burke is reported in *The Edinburgh Gazetteer*, 1st January 1793, saying 'every man in France has murder in his heart and in his face'. Even his colleagues laughed at these overwrought expostulations. The poem uses this incident to develop a brilliant satire on the wider campaign for parliamentary reform which dominated British politics during the winter of 1792–3.

    The person behind the campaign to raise a subscription for daggers to assist the French revolutionary troops was the poet's (future) doctor, William Maxwell. Burns boasted of his friend's radical past to Mrs Dunlop, 'the Doctor Maxwell whom Burke mentioned in the House of Commons about the affair of the daggers' (Letter 638). Mentioning Maxwell to George Thomson, he wrote 'the identical Maxwell whom Burke mentioned in the House of Commons' (Letter 637). The *Sun* of 8th October, 1792 included an article entitled 'English Jacobins. No. I. Doctor Maxwell.' Maxwell was reputed to have dipped a handkerchief in the blood of the guillotined French King. Not only does the poem mention Maxwell's daggers, but links daggers and cannons ('For cannons or for daggers', l. 53) to praise those who would help the French republicans. This is a startling reference, given Burns's own attempt covertly to send four carronade cannons captured in his semi-military customs duties from the smuggling ship *The Rosamond* which he subsequently purchased. Hence the full force of the line bringing his and Maxwell's treasonable activities together. It was not public knowledge at this time that Burns had tried to get the cannons to France. So, if a poet other than Burns were to write such a line, it would be a remarkable coincidence.

The target of ferocious radical satire and cartoon caricature for his derogatory description of the French masses as the 'swinish multitude', Burke's infamous remark was well known to Burns. To Mrs Dunlop, writing on food shortages in Dumfries, Burns ironically wrote 'How long the *Swinish Multitude* will be quiet, I cannot tell: they threaten daily' (Letter 688). Burns certainly detested Burke. This is clear in his epigram:

Oft have I wonder'd that on Irish ground
No poisonous reptile has ever been found:
Revealed the secret stands of great Nature's work:
She preserved her poison to create a Burke!

Further, the ex-Glasgow University rector, Burke, had previously disputed in the letter columns of *The Glasgow Journal* with the poet's intimate friend Robert Riddell, who wrote several pieces under the pen-name Cato.

Also revealing for the context of Burns's attitude to Burke in general and *The Dagger* in particular, is the fact that the Irishman had also been provoked by Dr William Maxwell's political print activities. Burns most probably had knowledge of the advertisement Maxwell had placed in *The Morning Chronicle* for 7th September, 1792 in which he referred to 'the present combination of Despots against the Rights of Human Nature'. In writing to no less than Henry Dundas on the urgent matter of charity for French loyalist refugees Burke ended thus:

But perhaps the temper of the common people may best be seen in the event of the late advertisement by Dr. Maxwell for the support of the Jacobins, and the maintenance of a war against the allies of this country, the Emperor and the King of Prussia; whom he had at the same time the insolence to revile in the coarsest language. (*The Correspondence of Edmund Burke, Vol. VII, 1792–4*, ed. Marshall and Woods (Cambridge University Press, 1968) p. 217).

Already inflamed against Maxwell, the matter of the dagger utterly enraged him. There is a quite fascinating letter reprinted again in Volume VII of Burke's correspondence for 16th January, 1793 from James Woolley of Birmingham, 'Manufacturer of all Kinds of Swords, Sword-hilts, Bayonets, Ram-rods, Matchets &c.', regarding both the volme (3,000) and nature of the weapons ordered. They were, in fact, to be fair to Burke, brutal foot-long blades designed for the sans culottes to eviscerate the horses of their mounted opponents. The editors conclude the letter with this fascinating footnote:

Burke read this letter to the House of Commons on 4 March [*Parliamentary History*, XXX, 554]. Two days later William Maxwell wrote to him complaining of 'Certain Slanders' which 'have been Countenanced by a Speech of your's in the house of Commons' [Ms at Sheffield]. Burke is reported to have given Maxwell an interview in which his behaviour was 'more temperate' than it had been in the House [*Morning Post*, 16 March]. Shortly afterwards Maxwell seems to have fled to France, where he had obtained an appointment in the French Army [*The Despatches of Earl Gower*, ed. Browning, p. 260].

Nor were Riddell and Maxwell the only intimates of Burns to lock horns with Burke; William Roscoe of Liverpool was also centrally involved. Roscoe wrote perhaps the most famous pro-French/radical song of that decade. It haunted Hazlitt for the rest of his life as a bitter elegy rather than a celebratory anthem. Roscoe wrote 'O'er the vinecover'd hills and gay regions of France' in 1791. On his death a copy of the song was found in Burns's hand among his papers. This copy was returned by Maria Riddell to Roscoe. These are the relevant lines:

Let Burke like a bat from the splendour retire,
    A splendour too strong for his eyes;
    Let pedants and fools his effusions admire,
Entrapt in his cobwebs like flies
Shall insolent Sophistry hope to prevail
    When Reason opposes her weight.

The 'cobweb' image of the great Irish spider was arguably to provoke Burns to one of his most complex political poems, *The Cobweb*, the penultimate poem in this section. (For the highly relevant conflict between Roscoe and Burke, see *The Writings and Speeches of Edmund Burke, Vol. IX*, ed. R.B. McDowell, Oxford, Clarendon Press, 1991, pp. 24–5).

Also highly important is the fact that Burns is the only poet of the period to describe Burke on the basis of his Irish origins, as 'Paddy Burke', in *When Guilford Good*. *The Dagger* also describes Burke as 'Paddy'. Also, the earlier poem rhymes 'Burke' with 'Turk' in the same fashion as *The Dagger* (ll. 27–9). Ll. 5–9 are echoed in Burns's *The Author's Earnest Cry and Prayer*:

> Dempster, a true blue Scot I'se warran
> Thee, aith detesting, chaste Kilkerran;
> An' that glib-gabbet Highland baron,
>   The Laird o Graham;
> An' ane, a chap that's damn'd auldfarran,
>   Dundas his name.

These old Scots words, 'glib-gabbet' and 'auldfarran' are uncommon among other Scottish radical poets of the period, a point emphasised by McGuirk in an American review of *Robert Burns: The Lost Poems* where she lists 'dainty chiel', 'fient a hair', 'Demosthenes or Tully', the rhyming of 'happy' with 'nappy', 'rhetoric and logic', 'clishma-claver', 'honest heart' and the repeated image of 'gullies' and 'whit-tles' – daggers' as stock-in-trade language of Burns (*Eighteenth Century Scottish Studies Newsletter*, 1997, *Books in Review*, pp. 14–15). In fact, *The Dagger* is without doubt the work of a poet steeped in the *œuvre* of Scots song, as Burns certainly was.

The burlesque of 'Now Paddy be nae langer rude,/ But lay aside your storming' (ll. 55–63) is echoed in Burns's *The Ordination*:

> Now Roberston, harangue nae mair
>   But steek your gab for ever;
> Or try the wicked town of Ayr,
>   For there they'll think you clever;
> Or, nae reflection on your lear,
>   You may commence a shaver.

The notion of Burke trying and failing to 'shew the Swinish Multitude' the 'folly o' reforming' politics is similar to a line of prose written by Burns to George Thomson. Burns wrote '& shew the swinish multitude that they are but beasts & like beasts must be led by the nose & goaded in the backside' (Letter 632). For this Burke too, the masses or 'swine are ay sae damned headstrang, /They'll aiblins no believe ye'.

The pantheon of contemporary radical icons, Colonel McLeod, Thomas Erskine, Charles James Fox and Charles Grey are praised in Burns's *Here's A Health tae Them That's Awa*. While any radical lyricists might applaud these Scottish and English politicians, close reading of the newspaper and printed songs of the period rarely, if ever, mention classical radical icons Demosthenes and Tully (Cicero), as mentioned in *The Author's Earnest Cry and Prayer*, 'Whom auld Demosthenes or Tully,/ Might own for brithers'. Burns, having previously and singularly grouped these radicals together, classical *and* modern, appears to have done so again.

The final burlesque on Burke is that no matter how loud the public laughs at his extremism, the more he rants, oblivious to 'Common Sense', which, in *The Holy Fair* was off and up the 'Cowgate', but here, is simply lost to Burke. Not only does the poem end with such Burns-like rhymes as 'nappy' and 'happy', but its closing sentiment dovetails with his known sentiments concerning the British constitution: he inscribed a copy of De Lolme's *The British Constitution*, 'Mr Burns presents this book to the Library, & begs they will take it as a creed of British Liberty – untill they find a better'. Ll. 83–5 of *The Dagger* reads 'And may our Constitution stand / The warld's pride and wonder, / Ilk coming day'. The final point which convinced McGuirk of the poem's provenance is Burns's peculiar skill, clear in the final stanza, of 'providing ironic assent to a position he really is attacking'. (See McGuirk, op cit, p. 15.) Daiches too, in conversation with the editors, emphasised this characteristic poetic device evident in *The Dagger*.

Robert Burns and Robert the Bruce

Of the following cluster of three 'Bruce' poems now presented, the middle and long-known one was anonymously published in *The Morning Chronicle* on 8th May, 1794 though from a letter of Burns to George Thomson of late August 1793 we know it was composed around that date. Burns's explanation of the creative impulse for that poem is also wholly relevant to the other two poems, published pseudonymously in *The Edinburgh Gazetteer*, despite the fact that their resonance is not that of Scottish vernacular poetry but of Miltonic blank verse:

> I do not know if the old Air, 'Hey, tuttie taitie', may rank among this number; but well I know that . . . it has often filled my eyes with tears. There is a tradition . . . that it was Robert Bruce's March at the Battle of Bannockburn. This thought in my yesternight's evening walk, warmed me to a pitch of enthusiasm on the theme of Liberty & Independence which I threw into a kind of Scots Ode . . . that one might suppose to be

the gallant ROYAL SCOT'S address to his heroic followers on
that eventful morning . . .

. . . I had no idea of giving myself any trouble on the Subject,
till the accidental recollection of that glorious struggle for
Freedom, associated with the glowing ideas of some other
struggles of the same nature, *not quite so ancient*, roused my
Rhyming Mania (Letter 582).

After quoting the poem, Burns adds: 'So may God ever defend the
cause of TRUTH and LIBERTY, as he did that day!—Amen!' The
other two blank verse poems are, literally, the answer to this prayer
as the solder/saint victor, rather than the martyred Wallace, returns
as visionary upholder of Scotland's endangered freedom. How
endangered it was can be gauged that these poems were written
at the nadir of reformist, radical fortunes with the terrible impact of
the Sedition Trials and Braxfield running fast and loose with a
Scottish legal system inherently inadequate in itself regarding the
definition of treason.

While Bruce never quite occupied the place of Wallace in Burns's
soul, the seeds of his devotion to him were early sown in this self-
dramatising account of an early visit to Bannockburn:

. . . two hours ago, I said a fervent prayer for old Caledonia
over the hole in a blue-whin-stone where Robert de Bruce
fixed his Royal Standard on the banks of Bannockburn
(Letter 131).

Further, the intrusion of spiritual aid at a moment of a dark night
for the *national* soul had also appeared in *The Vision*. As McGuirk
(p. 208) suggests, Burns derived this from a Ramsay forgery also
titled *The Vision* which deals with the national crisis caused by
John Balliol's appeasement of the English king. If Ramsay's lines
influenced *The Vision*, they resonate even more deeply in the two
Bruce poems:

Quhilk held a thistle in his paw,
And round his collar graift I saw
          This poesie pat and plain,
Nemo me impune lacess
–et: —In Scots Nane sall oppress
          Me, unpunist with pain.
Still schaking, I durst naithing say,
          Till he with kynd accent

Sayd, 'Fere let nocht thy hairt affray,
　　I cum to hier thy plaint;
　　　　　Thy graining and maining
　　　　　Hath laitlie reikd myne eir,
　　　　　Debar then affar then
　　　　　All eiryness or feir.'

(*Ever Green*, 1724; reprinted in *Longer Scottish Poems*, Vol. 2, ed.
Crawford, Hewitt, and Law, Edinburgh: Scottish Academic Press,
1987, p. 33.)

The Ghost of Bruce

First printed in *The Edinburgh Gazetteer*, 16th July, 1793.

As late I stroll'd through Bannockburn's proud field,
At midnight hour, close by the *Bore Stene* stood
A Form Divine illumin'd round with fire,
In ancient armour spendidly array'd:
5　'Stop passenger,' he said; 'art thou a Scot?
Does Caledonian blood flow in thy veins?
Art thou a friend or foe to Freedom's cause?'
A friend, aghast I said of Scottish blood.
'Then fear not,' he said; 'the Ghost of Bruce
10　Four hundred years and more, in quiet rest,
The shade of Bruce has silent kept the tomb,
But rest no longer can his Spirit have:
His country is in danger; chains anew
Are forging fast t' enslave his Native Land.
15　Go forth, my Son, for every Scot is mine
Whom brave unconquer'd Caledonia owns;
Go tell my Country that the Shade of Bruce
Is risen to protect her injur'd Rights; —
To reinstate in splendour, as before,
20　Her Liberty near lost — bid her not fear —
The time approaches fast when Brucian fire
Shall slash destruction on her perjur'd foes.
My Broad Egeant Shield shall guard my Sons,
My Arm shall bring them Victory and Peace,
25　And Happiness shall crown their honest toils.'
Thus spake the Ghost — and in a flame flew south:
Night seiz'd her mantle — and I heard no more.

Agrestis: April 16th 1793. Banks of Bannockburn.

Given that (see *To Robert Graham of Fintry*) Burns had under severe Excise scrutiny lied about his connection to Captain Johnston's *Edinburgh Gazetteer*, there is no reason to disbelieve that he would not subsequently pursue a course of pseudonymous publication in that newspaper. He continued such activity in *The Morning Chronicle*. See, for example, the following key 1794 poem *Bruce's Address to His Troops at Bannockburn*. The name 'Agrestis' is hardly a heavy disguise given its farming allusion and its obvious connection to the 'Agricola' pseudonym which he had used in *Ode on The Departed Regency Bill* and *Epitaph for Dr. Adam Smith*.

Burns's use of Miltonic resonant blank verse is ambivalent. On the one hand, it is a medium with which he would not be normally associated. His use of the medium was desultory and insignificant. Like his poetic generation, however, Burns was haunted by the shadow of the great republican poet. Leaving historical accuracy aside, if a Scottish King is to become manifest, it should be within a democratic, heightened tone and form. There is, given spiritual intrusion into the political realm, another distinctly Miltonic touch, to be echoed in the other poem, in the fact that the work is deliberately dated 16th April, 1793 which was Easter Sunday. The resurrected Christ/Bruce is to rise in an act of desperately needed national salvation. There are in the text several other Burnsian 'fingerprints'.

The question 'Art thou a Scot?' is taken from William Hamilton's *The Life and Heroic Actions of Sir William Wallace*, a work Burns not only knew but adapted two lines from for *Scots Wha Hae*. Abbreviating the world 'to' to merely the 't'' is common in the poetry of Burns but is exceptionally rare in the general poetry of this era, as in the above example, 'Are forging fast t' enslave his Native Land'. In Bruce's personal description of 'brave unconquer'd Caledonia' there is a remarkable echo of Burns's earlier song *Caledonia* which reads 'Bold, independent, *unconquer'd* and free'. The fact that Scotland was 'unconquered' under Bruce was evidently a key historical point for Burns and this point is stressed from the mouth of Bruce himself. If we add to this accumulative evidence the somewhat minor observation that the final 'e' from 'unconquer'd' is dropped by Burns in his song and is dropped from pronunciation in *The Ghost of Bruce*, this type of consistency is surely expected if Burns is the author. Such practice was not commonplace typography among newspaper printers. The powerful image of historical Scottish martial resistence to tyranny, evoked here by the return of Bruce's 'Shade' to address the poet, is reminiscent in tone and language of the lines Burns wrote in *Prologue Spoken by Mr. Woods*:

. . . to shield the honour'd land!
Strong may she glow with all her ancient fire;
May every son be worthy of his Sire;
Firm may she rise, with generous disdain
At Tyranny's, or dire Pleasure's chain;
Still self-dependent in her native shore,
Bold may she brave grim Danger's loudest roar,
Till Fate the curtain drops on worlds to be no more!

Robert Bruce's Address to His Troops at Bannockburn –
or Scots Wha Hae
Tune: Hey Tutti Taitie
First printed anonymously in *The Morning Chronicle*, 8th May, 1794.

Scots, wha hae wi' WALLACE bled,   who have
Scots, wham BRUCE has aften led,   whom, often
Welcome to your gory bed, —
 Or to victorie. —

5 Now's the day, and now's the hour;
See the front o' battle lour;
See approach proud EDWARD'S power,
Chains & Slaverie. —

Wha will be a traitor-knave?
10 Wha can fill a coward's grave?
Wha sae base as be a Slave? —   so
 Let him turn, & flie. —

Wha for SCOTLAND'S king & law,   who
Freedom's sword will strongly draw,
15 FREE-MAN stand, or FREE-MAN fa',   fall
 Let him follow me. —

By Oppression's woes & pains!
By your Sons in servile chains!
We will drain our dearest veins,
20 But they *shall* be free!

Lay the proud Usurpers low!
Tyrants fall in every foe!

LIBERTY 'S in every blow!
   Let US DO — or DIE!!!

The exact date and place of composition is unknown. There is, however, evidence to suggest that the lyric was radically reworked. A MS. of the song, sold by Puttock and Simpson in London in 1862, contains this early version:

Do you hear your children cry
'Were we born in chains to lie?'
No! come Death or Liberty!
Yes, they shall be free!

MacDiarmid's early insistence of the superiority of vernacular Scots to standard English is certainly, in this instance, borne out by the evolved, final song. As we have seen Burns's whole intention was to draw analogies with Scottish freedom past and Scottish freedom present. Even more riskily, he was alluding to contemporary French struggles. The last line of the poem, 'Let US DO—or DIE!!!' is, triple exclamatory, the tennis court oath of the French revolutionaries. Hence discussing his sending it to Perry's *Morning Chronicle*, he wrote to Patrick Miller Jnr. in mid-March 1794: 'they are most welcome to my Ode; only let them insert it as a thing they have met with by accident & unknown to me'. When Perry did publish it on 8th May, 1794, he did preserve the poet's anonymity:

If the following warm and animating Ode was not written near the time to which it applies, it is one of the most faithful imitations of the simple and beautiful style of the Scottish bards we ever read, and we know of but one living Poet to whom to ascribe it.

This complimentary but, surely for Burns, frighteningly transparent description, was followed by a weird printing error which read 'Scene-Lewis Garden' rather than 'Tune-Lewie Gordon'. This was corrected in the *Chronicle* of 10th May, 1794. Why there was a nine-month delay in the song's publication is unknown, but, as the least seditious of the three Bruce pieces, it is entirely possible that its publication in, for example *The Edinburgh Gazetteer* would have alerted authorities to link him with the other Bruce poems. The song did, however, reappear in *The Chronicle* with Burns's name attached a few months after he was safely dead.

As we saw in the Introduction, government critics were well able to discern the seditious nature of the song: 'So complete and deplorable was his delusion, that he thought he was doing honour to the ancient heroes of his native land, when he confounded them with the slaves of Robespierre, whom he thought the soldiers of liberty! and on whose arms he implored the benediction of God' (Low, p. 156). The song reappeared in Thomson's 1803 collection, not 1799 as Scott Douglas indicated. With Burns dead, Thomson had no compunction in impertinently perverting its political meaning into an *anti-French* song in a manner symptomatic of the whole nineteenth-century tendency in 'domesticating' the poet to Anglo-Scottish tribal pieties:

> By changing *wha* into who, *hae* into have, *aften* into often, and *sae* into so, the following song will be English; and by substituting *Gallia* for *Edward*, and Britain for *Scotland*, it will be adapted to the present time.

One could hardly think of a more direct linkage of linguistic and political emasculation. Not only of Burns himself, but of the Scottish tradition in that Burns had informed Thomson that he had adapted two lines from William Hamilton of Gilbertfield's epic poem on William Wallace to compose his own final stanza: 'A false usurper sinks in every foe/ And liberty returns with every blow' (Book VI, chapter 2, ll. 92–3). With his customary eclecticism, however, there is also a Scottish translation, noted by Hogg, from Shakespeare's *Julius Caesar* (Act III, scene ii) where Brutus asks the gathered crowds 'Who is here so base as would be a bondsman?' which turns into 'Wha sae base as be a slave?'

So powerful was the democratic impulse of the song that John Mayne, in his *A Patriotic Address to the Inhabitants of the United Kingdom* (1799), attempted by means of turgid verses to invert its meaning:

> English, Scots and Irishmen,
> All that are in Valour's ken! . . .
> . . . Now's the day, and now's the hour,
> Frenchmen wou'd the Land devour—
> Will ye wait till they come o'er
> To give ye Chains and Slavery?
> Who wou'd be a Frenchman's slave?
> Who wou'd truckle to the knave?
> Who wou'd shun a glorious grave?

The Ghost of Bruce

First printed in *The Edinburgh Gazetteer*, 24th September, 1793.

I WHO erewhile the Ghost of far fam'd Bruce
Bade aft the dread and eke the joy to see,
Alone went wandering through his laurel'd field
The other night, revolving all the ills,
5   Our Country has endur'd from P[it]t, D[unda]s,
And all their Pension'd Slaves – Curse of our Isle.
O'erwhelm'd with grief, and bursting into tears,
I cried, Indignant, 'Oh! dear Native land!'
'My country!' 'Is there not some chosen curse,
10   Some hidden thunder in the stores of Heaven,
Red with uncommon wrath to blast the men
Who owe their greatness to their Country's ruin!'
Scarce had I spoke, when, thick, involv'd in mist,
More awful and more grand than former fire,
15   The Chief of Men, great minded Bruce appear'd.
'Cheer up your heart, my Son; why grieve you so:
Your Country in her breast still carries Bruce,
And ne'er shall be enslav'd. Trust me (he said)
So far you've done your duty as I bade,
20   To warn my Country what she had to fear —
And what she had to hope for from my arm.
The time is now arriv'd, when all that's dear
To Briton's shall arouse them from their sleep —
To sleep no more, till each brave Briton's free:
25   But still it much imports each Patriot Scot
To act with prudence, keen and still reserve.
Their foes are wringing out their dying pangs
On Virtue; — but the strife will soon be o'er —
Bid all my Sons be firm; and when the storm
30   Shall gather thickest, boldly show their front,
United as in One. The work is done'.
He only added, When the clouds should burst,
That awful hover'd over Britain's Isle,
He would again appear to stay the hand
35   Of Vengeance, and bid Mercy take her place.

Agrestis – September 6th, 1793

This poem is a very close variation on the first 'Bruce' poem but is more dangerously outspoken in that (l. 5) Pitt and Dundas are named. It also opens with a specific echo of Milton in the first line of *Paradise Regained*: 'I who erewhile the happy garden sung'. Hence the concept of Bruce as risen, redemptive figure is re-emphasised in the first line. The Miltonic 'feel' of the two poems, a world penetrated by supernatural entities, is also as close to Blakean Milton influenced mytho-poetry as Burns ever came. 'When the clouds should burst/ That awful hover'd over Britain's Isle' could, indeed, come directly from Blake's *America*. Even more telling in identifying Burns as author is the fact that four lines from Addison's *Cato* are adapted and integrated into the poem. As Liam McIlvanney's forthcoming study shows, Addison, in particular, and eighteenth-century republican literature were the deliberate Murdoch selected texts in Masson's reader used in Burns's schooling. *Cato* is also mentioned four times in Burns's letters. The lines in question are those spoken by Marcus, Cato's son, to his brother Portious:

> Oh Portious! Is there not some chosen curse,
> Some hidden thunder in the store of Heav'n,
> Big with uncommon vengeance to blast the men
> Who owe their greatness to their country's ruin.

These lines are adapted and quoted by Burns/Agrestis. Addison was the first poet to inspire Burns to write poetry in his youth when he read his *Vision of Mirza*. Burns quotes Addison in his autobiographical letter to Dr Moore, stating that his lines 'for though in dreadful whirls we hung,/ High on the broken wave', were 'music to my boyish ears'. There are 22 references to Addison in the poet's letters, more than for Fergusson, Ramsay, Young or Milton. A further Burns–Addison–Robert the Bruce link occurs. Burns wrote to Captain Patrick Miller enclosing a copy of *Scots Wha Hae* and casually quotes Addison's poem *Letter from Italy to Lord Halifax*, 'O Liberty—, / Thou mak'st the gloomy face of Nature gay, / Giv'st beauty to the sun, & pleasure to the day' (Letter 613). Addison was not the most popular poet in Scotland at this time, so the notion that another poet *other than Burns* would link Addison's poetry with the story of Bruce in the context of a critique on contemporary politics in the way that Burns does in relation to *Scots Wha Hae*, *at this exact time* is, in the face of the textual evidence almost bizarre. The language of liberty might have been ubiquitous during the 1790s, but an association between Addison, Robert the Bruce and contemporary political problems in Scotland at this time is a triangle pointing one way, towards Burns.

In his explanatory letter to George Thomson, quoted earlier,

Burns refers to composing *Scots Wha Hae* during his yesternight's evening walk when he linked Bruce's fight for freedom and liberty with the modern struggle for the same ideals. This same experience, linking Bruce to contemporary political tumult, is woven into and narrated in this version of the second Bruce poem. How coincidental that Agrestis was, like Burns, wandering alone *the other night*, contemplating the 'ills' of contemporary Scotland, thinking of King Robert De Bruce. Agrestis, it would appear, was able not only to read the poet's mind, but his letters also.

Hogg also reveals in *The Lost Poems* that *The Ghost of Bruce* switches from the general use of 'Britons' to 'each patriot Scot' in ll. 22–5, a change of emphasis echoed by Burns in his earlier prose '. . . let every Briton, and particularly every Scotsman' (Letter 283). The phrase 'thick mists obscure involv'd me round', from *Lament for James, Earl of Glencairn*, is very akin to the image of Bruce appearing 'thick, involv'd in mist'. In such a tight description one would not expect three words to be repeated in this similar imagery, 'thick', 'involv'd' and 'mist'. The words 'thick' and 'mist' are commonplace and predictable, but 'involv'd' is the unexpected and quite improbable repetition in both examples, once again suggesting one author. Even the description of Bruce as the 'Chief o' Men' can be traced to the first version of *A Man's A Man*, where Burns wrote 'The honest man, tho' e'er sae poor, / Is chief o' men for a' that'. Not only is this exact phrase employed here, prior to the composition of the democratic anthem, but when Burns changed the phrase 'chief o' men' in *A Man's A Man*, he switched the word 'king' for 'chief': 'Is king o' men for a' that'. Having described King Robert the Bruce as a 'chief', the change in *A Man's A Man* from 'chief' to 'king' would appear to be almost a natural, subconscious word association. Furthermore, the image of the battle louring in *Scots Wha Hae* — 'See the front of battle lour' — that is, the enemy coming towards the Scottish troops like an ominous, dark and angry cloud, is one developed in more detail by Agrestis in *The Ghost of Bruce*, ll. 29–33.

Another trope in Burns, a powerful man given to the practice of explosive shot-putting (he left his shot-putt at Ellisland farm), is that of the sometimes vengeful, justice-giving arm. It is found, for example, in *A Birthday Ode* when in an analogous political situation, he envisages the return of the Stuarts and the overthrow of the present royal family:

So Vengeance's arm, ensanguined, strong
Shall with resistless might assail
   Usurping Brunswick's head shall lowly lay,
And Stewart's wrongs and yours with tenfold weight repay.

It is highly significant that this poem does not call for a similar act of restorative violence but rather for fortitude and patience till the nightmare political hurricane blows itself out. L. 31, with the phrase 'United as in One', may also be deeply relevant as not derived from history but contemporary radical rhetoric. Consider this passage from *Address from the Society of United Irishmen in Dublin, 1792* which was designed to provoke the Convention of Friends of the People in Scotland into action:

> We have told you what our Situation was, what it is, what it ought to be; our End, a National Legislature; our Means, an Union of the whole People. Let this Union extend throughout the Empire. Let all unite for all, or each Man suffer for all. In each country let the People assemble in peaceful and constitutional Convention. Let Delegates from each country digest a Plan of reform, best adapted to the Situation and Circumstances of their respective Nations, and let the Legislatures be petitioned at once by the urgent and unanimous Voice of England, Scotland and Ireland.

This radical vision of the enlightened end of history with each democratically united nation in a consequent equal, pacific union with nations similarly inclined, hence an end to both Anglo-British imperialism and Irish religious self-division, is to reappear in one of Burns's most important political poems, *Ode on General Washington's Birthday* in the posthumous section. This poem, however, is one that, with American exceptionalism, is of the British Isles as the scene of tri-national tragedy. The above quotation is taken from Appendix II of Elaine W. McFarland's indispensable *Ireland and Scotland in the Age of Revolution* (Edinburgh, 1994).

An Unpublished Letter on Robert the Bruce

As a natural appendix to these 'Bruce' poems, we add the following hitherto unpublished letter by Burns. This letter remained with its recipient Dr Hughes until his death in 1843 and was sold later in the century to a New York collector, Mr John Kennedy. In January 1928, the Hereford Burns Club published the letter with its history. A copy of this is available in the Mitchell Library, Glasgow and a facsimile of the letter is displayed in the Burns Room of the Murray Arms Hotel, Gatehouse of Fleet, in Galloway. Why the letter has not been included in the poet's collected letters is unknown. It is certainly genuine. It was written as an explanation to *Bruce's Address to His Troops at Bannockburn* and dated 1795:

> This battle was the decisive blow which put Robert the First, commonly called Robert de Bruce, in quiet possession of the Scottish throne. It was fought against Edward the Second, son to that Edward who shed so much blood in Scotland in consequence of the dispute between Bruce and Baliol.
>
> Apropos, when Bruce fled from London to claim the Scottish crown, he met with the Cummin, another claimant of the crown, at Dumfries. At the altar, in the Priory there they met, and it is said that Bruce offered to Cummin – 'Give me your lands and I'll give you my interest in the crown', or vice versa.
>
> What passed nobody knows, but Bruce came in a flurry to the door and called out to his followers – 'I am afraid that I have slain the Cummin'. 'Are you only afraid!' replied Sir Roger de Kilpatrick (ancestor to the present Sir James Kilpatrick of Closeburn), and ran into the Church and stabbed Cummin to the heart; and coming back said, showing a bloody dagger, 'I've sicker'd him!' – that is in English, I have secured him. Until lately this was the motto of the Closeburn family, but the late Sir Thomas changed it into 'I make sure' – the crest still is the bloody dagger. R.B.

The Scotian Muse:
An Elegy.

First printed in *The Edinburgh Gazetteer*, 1st October 1793.

The Muse unwilling leaves the sacred shore,
 Where every virtue held its peaceful reign —
Hangs with regret on scenes she lov'd before;
 The last sad wand'rer from the pensive plain.

5 She views where once the Sons of Freedom stray'd
 Whose hard misfortunes claim the sigh sincere:
She saw fair Genius fly his native shade,
 And pour'd the parting tribute of a tear.

But why, sweet maid, so fondly dost thou cling
10 To rugged rocks, where no soft verdure grows,
While climes more grateful court the tuneful string,
 And point to vales of pleasure and repose?

Haply thou lov'st to soothe th' afflicting smart
 That tears the breast, by misery doom'd to mourn;
15 To gild the gloom around the *victim's* heart;
 Or bend with *pity* o'er the *patriot's* urn.

Or haply, where beneath the iron hand
 Of stern *Oppression*, youth's fair flow'rets fade,
Kindly, with *Sympathy's* endearing band,
20 And bright-ey'd *Hope*, thou cheer'st the dungeon's shade.

For him, who warm'd by *Freedom's* genial fire,
 With soul unfetter'd, drags the *Despot's* chain,
Perhaps thy hand attunes the living lyre
 To soothe his woes by music's magic strain.

25 And thou, gay *Fancy*, bless his languid hours!
 Each flattering phantom let thy care bestow;
To strew his lonely path with fairy flowers,
 And pluck the noxious nettles as they grow.

Say (and, ye *Powers of Truth*, accordant join!)
30 'The time will come — that *Fate* has fix'd the doom —
'The *Friends of suffering virtue* shall combine,
 'And hurl each blood-stained Despot to the tomb!'

Lysander.

This appears in the *Edinburgh Gazetteer* a few weeks after the second *Ghost of Bruce*. The subject of the lament is the injustice of the transportation sentences to Botany Bay served upon the radical lawyer Thomas Muir and the Rev. Fysche Palmer on charges of sedition. The theme of the lament is the spirit of 'Freedom' departing Scotland in sorrow, but that the essential spirit of Scottish poetry, incarnated in Burns himself, gives them constant succour. This is in harmony with the bard's plaintive language, 'Where is the soul of freedom fled? / Immingled with the mighty dead' from the *Ode to General Washington on His Birthday*, written shortly after *The Scotian Muse*. The title is echoed in the first line of *To Miss Graham of Fintry* by Burns, 'Here, where the Scottish Muse immortal lives'. The language of this work is found in many verses by Burns, such as *Elegy on Captain Matthew Henderson*, 'Where haply, Pity strays forlorn'; and in *A Dedication to Gavin Hamilton*, 'The last, sad mournful rites bestow'. The lamentation is similar to *On the Death of Lord President Dundas*, 'Sad to your sympathetic glooms I fly' where the expression 'grim Oppression' is also found. There are other echoes in Burns's *Elegy on the Death of Sir*

James Hunter-Blair, 'I saw fair Freedom's blossoms richly blow', and 'Her form majestic droop'd in pensive woe', which compare to the *Scotian Muses*'s 'She saw fair Genius fly his native shade'. In *The Scotian Muse* the description an 'iron hand / Of stern Oppression' (ll. 17–18) is echoed in *A Winter Night,* 'See stern Oppression's iron grip'. L. 15's 'gild the gloom' is also found in Burns's *The Lament.* While it may be argued that these similarities are the result of contemporary standardised elegiac language, the high number of Miltonic lexical similarities point to Burns's hand. As in the *Gazetteer* 'Bruce' poems, this is absolutely the only Scottish published radical poetry derived from high Miltonic style.

There is, however, in this poem and the two rediscovered Bruce poems a similar pattern of a sense of the nightmare darkness of oppression before the final dawn of freedom. This is very similar to the patttern found in Shelley's response to the terrible events of 1819. Compare, for example, these stanzas from *The Revolt of Islam,* at the end of Canto ix:

> The seeds are sleeping in the soil: meanwhile
> The Tyrant peoples dungeons with his prey,
> Pale victims on the guarded scaffold smile
> Because they cannot speak; and, day by day,
> 5 The moon of wasting Science wanes away
> Among her stars, and in that darkness vast
> The sons of earth to their foul idols pray,
> And gray Priests triumph, and like blight or blast
> A shade of selfish care o'er human looks is cast.
>
> 10 This is the winter of the world; – and here
> We die, even as the winds of Autumn fade,
> Expiring in the frore and foggy air. —
> Behold! Spring comes, though we must pass, who made
> The promise of its birth, — even as the shade
> 15 Which from our death, as from a mountain, flings
> The future, a broad sunrise; thus arrayed
> As with the plumes of overshadowing wings,
> From its dark gulf of chains, Earth like an eagle springs.

The pen-name Lysander (echoing Sylvander?) may well be derived from Burns's early schooling. As Liam McIlvanney's forthcoming *The Radical Burns* will show, Burns's school-reader, an anthology of liberal sentiment, *Masson's Collection of Prose and Verse from the Best English Authors for the Use of School* had both a seminal and persistent influence on Burns. Lysander features in the book as an exemplary English gentleman of fine feeling and good works.

New Song

or A Wet Day at Walmer Castle

First published in *The Morning Chronicle*, 9th September, 1793.

O! Willy is a wanton wag,   *reckless joker*
   The blythest lad that ere I saw
And has so well the gift of *gab*,   *conversation*
   He makes *John Bull* his purse-strings draw. *the British public*
5 He can armies raise and navies,
   He can venture on a war;
Men and money how he levies —
   His like is neither near nor far.

For *Catskins* when he went to fight,
10   Of insults offer'd loud did bawl,
And honest John, who thought him right,   *John Bull*
   At last agreed to pay for all.
But Willy then was in a passion,
   Swore he'd give John, *Nootka Sound*;
15 Yet by his fam'd Negotiation
   John got ne'er an inch of ground.[1]

With *Russia* then he would be fighting,
   For *Oczakow*, to please the *Turks*;
But John not much in war delighting,
20   Fox soon *exposed his humbug works*.[2]
For Willy's *Plans* are always droll,
   Nor saw he *Poland* in his map;
All *Liberty* from Pole to Pole,
   He threw in Kate's *voracious lap*.[3]

---

1 'The Convention with Spain of October 28, 1790, which resolved the dispute over Nootka Sound and which the Opposition regarded as a great humiliation for Pitt. The dispute had begun in 1789, when Spain seized a British trading station on Nootka Sound and some English vessels. Pitt seemed determined to go to war over what the Opposition maintained was only a seizure of 'Catskins'.

2 Russia had seized Oczakow in 1788, but Pitt ignored the seizure until 1791, when he demanded that Catherine restore the town to Turkey. She refused, but there were so many petitions against the war that Pitt was compelled to forget the matter.

3 The second partition of Poland, which Pitt had not anticipated and which was an additional embarrassment to the government.

25   And now he's gone to war with France,[4]
          Where men and money he must send:
      In short he leads John such a dance,
          That God knows when his wars may end.
      From East to West, from South to North,
30   O'er all Europe the sword he'll draw,
      And not content, he'll still hold forth,
          And quarrel with *America*.[5]

      As he can *drink*, and not be *drunk*,
          As he can *fight*, and not be *slain*,
35   As he can *speak* and strike the *trunk*,
          That never dar'd to *strike again*;
      Then what cares he for thousands lost,
          Or what cares he for thousands slain?
      What cares he what wars may cost,
40   For *Widows tears*, or *Mother's pain*!

      And so for Sport he's gone to Dover,
          With D[undas], R[eeves], and L[ong],[6]
      Tho' bad at *dashing into cover*,
          They say he can do nothing wrong.
45   And they're a set of *wanton wags*,   reckless jokers
          The *blythest lads* that e'er we saw;
      While o'er their bottle Harry brags,
          That honest John must pay for a'.   all

These footnotes are derived from Professor Lucylle Werkmeister who first attributed the song to Burns in her seminal essay *Robert Burns and the London Daily Press*, published in *Modern Philology* (1966). Werkmeister explains the appearance of the poem:

> In September, 1793, Burns reminded George Thomson: 'For Willie was a wanton wag' – you have a song made on purpose,

4 The annoncement that Britain was now officialy at war with France was made on 1st February, 1793.
5 The new quarrels with America were just beginning. They were settled by 'Jay's Treaty' of 1794.
6 Dundas, who headed an army of spies and informers; John Reeves, organiser of the Association for Protecting Liberty and Property against Republicans and Levellers; and Charles Long (later Baron Farnborough), Secretary of the Treasury, who assisted in the subversion of the press. These three were regarded as the principal warmongers and conspirators against democratic liberties.

also by Hamilton, which you will find in Ramsay's [Tea-table] Miscellany, beginning 'Willy, ne'er enquire what end'. Supposedly Burns did not intend to write such a 'song' himself, and yet there is a political version of it in *The Morning Chronicle* of September 9 1793, which was certainly not provided by any of the Chronicle's usual contributors. The subject is sinecures and wars, and 'Willy' is the Prime Minister, William Pitt. In August 1792, Pitt had made himself Lord Warden and Admiral of the Cinque Ports and Governor of Dover Castle . . . on August 27 he and his intimate, Henry ('Harry') Dundas, Secretary of State for the Home Department, had gone to Dover to take possession of Walmer Castle. There they had remained for several 'wet' days, both of them being addicted to port wine. Since this was the choicest of the sinecures, assuring the holder of six country houses and an income of £4000 a year for life, Pitt's seizure of it was still a newspaper issue in 1793 and it had often enough been charged by Fox, Sheridan, and other Opposition leaders that Pitt had deliberately involved England in a war in order to safeguard this and other emoluments (p. 324).

Unaware of her work, it was recently re-attributed to Burns in Scott Hogg's *The Lost Poems*, where Werkmeister's research procedures and results were frequently replicated. The poem appears first in *The Morning Chronicle*, but a copy was also sent to *The Edinburgh Gazetteer* where it appears within a week of the London paper. Werkmeister goes on to argue:

Since by 1793 the *Morning Chronicle* was the principal Opposition newspaper, 'An Excellent New Song' would have attracted some attention. But there was no sequel, and three days later (12 September, 1793) the Ministerial *Public Advertiser* published 'LINES, On the BIRTH of a posthumous CHILD; Born in Peculiar Circumstances of Family Distress. By ROBERT BURNS'. The heading 'For the Public Advertiser' made it clear that Burns had submitted the poem himself, and he had evidently also authorized the use of his name. If there had been any suspicion that he was responsible for 'An Excellent New Song' these lines in the Ministerial *Public Advertiser* would have dispelled it . . . (p. 325).

She illustrates the fact that it was a customary tactic for Burns regularly to submit radical material to the Opposition press, while at the same time, sending non-radical verse under his own name to the pro-government Ministerial newspapers.

Not only do we see here Burns's unparalleled skill in turning old Scots lyrics into contemporary radical song, but his remarkable ability to compress a range of historical events into six condensed stanzas, always hitting the prime targets with satirical wit. *When Guilford Good Our Pilot Stood* is the perfect case in point, which meticulously chronicles the key events of the American-British war.

The chief satirical victims here are William Pitt and his deputy Henry Dundas (l. 42), who was in charge of the Home Office spy network which existed throughout Britain and successfully infiltrated many groups such as The Friends of the People in Scotland and monitored the London Corresponding Society, the leading intellectual and propaganda arm of British radicalism. John Reeves (l. 42) set up the Association for Protecting Liberty and Property against Republicans and Levellers, a propaganda arm of government supporters which rallied 'men of rank' to support the King and Constitution against the fear of invading Jacobins and their supporters at home. Charles Long (l. 42) was Secretary to the Treasury and through paying the pro-government press to speak the ministerial line, he was made a Baron. As Werkmeister comments, there is no evidence that these 'wanton wags' visited Walmer Castle at this time (1794) for a weekend's drinking session, so this visit may be poetic licence. It was, though, common knowledge that when announcing Britain's involvement in the war against Revolutionary France, both Pitt and Dundas were drunk; the latter falling and faltering at the despatch box. Burns would have been wholly aware of Dundas's public reputation for heavy drinking. Coleridge, accordingly, called him 'brazen faced' and Dr Walcot (Peter Pindar) and Professor Richard Porson also emphasised this issue in their satires on him.

Werkmeister did not feel the need to strengthen her case with textual comparison. A few examples, though, are persuasive. The echo of Burns's song *Duncan Davidson*, ll. 5–8 is apparent:

A man may drink, and no be drunk;
    A man may fight, and no be slain;
A man may kiss a bonie lass,
    And ay be welcome back again!

The *New Song* (ll. 33–36) has virtually the same text, suitably adapted. The similarity is striking. The same poetic sentiment, mourning the death caused by war; the 'widow's tears, the orphan's cry', is found in the final stanza of *Logan Braes*. A further description employing the Scots-derived 'Kate' for 'Catherine', referring to Catherine the Great, is also found in Burns's *Why Should Na Poor Folk Mowe*, 'Auld Kate laid her claws on poor Stanislaus,/ And Poland has bent like a bow'.

The textual similarities cannot, however, be explained by another poet's imitation of *Duncan Davison* and *Logan Braes*: the fomer was printed anonymously and the latter was yet to be published.

Moreover, the poem contains a stylistic peculiarity of Burns, evident in his Kilmarnock edition (where he acted as publisher): an excessive use of italics, compared to other contemporaneous poetry. It is probably no coincidence that a month after Burns mentioned *Willie is A Wanton Wag* to George Thomson that a political version of it appeared in *The Morning Chronicle*. Thomson had already poured scorn on Burns's anti-war *Logan Braes* and his squeamish, at best apolitical views would have warned Burns never to send him another overtly political piece.

In recent research on interactive British radical poetry of the 1790s, we are beginning to understand not simply English-Scottish interaction, but how Burns influenced the dissenting Ulster poets. This example, signed 'Paddy Burns', possibly written by John Orr, shows not simply radical Ulster's assimilation of Burns's poetic form (as in *The Holy Fair*) but also the Scottish poet's radical subject matter. Here, for example, are the first two stanzas of *An Address to Mr Pitt, In Guid Braid Scotch:*

Dear Billy, I'm right wae for you;
    Ye're in a hobble warse and warse:
Ye bred it a' your sell I trow,
    By pickin' quarrels like an Ass;
'Bout Nooska-Sound ye made a faird,
Ye wadna want the Spotet Cats;
    Trouth ye might your three millions spared,
    An' let them rin, and catch the Rats
        For mony a day.

'Bout Oszacow ye fine advis'd;
    Nane maun posses't but wha ye like:
But Kate your meddlin' gaits despis'd,
    An' sent you hame wi trailin' pike.
In sullen mood ye broodin' sat,
    Watchin' whar ye might hae a chance,
To breed a scrape: at last ye gat,
    A thick dust kicket up wi' France
        Ae luckless day.

We are not only indebted to Dr Liam McIlvanney's archival retrieval of this particular poem, but to his innovative awareness of the influence of Burns's political poetry in Ulster in the 1790s. As McIlvanney notes: 'The common vogue for Burns's poems is itself a symptom of this shared political culture. Burns's egalitarian and democratic sentiments, his outspoken pro-Americanism, and his depiction of the Westminster government as a 'system of corruption all endeared him to an Ulster Presbyterian audience, and to poets like Orr and Campbell, who were to participate in the 1798 Rising'. ('Robert Burns and the Ulster–Scots Literary Revival of the 1790s', *Bullán*, Vol. IV, No. 2, pp. 125–43).

Lines on Ambition

First published in *The Edinburgh Gazetteer*, 31st December, 1793.

As Caesar once perus'd the warlike page,
    Frought with the acts of Macedonia's Chief,
Discordant passions in his bosom rage,
    And sudden tears declare his inward grief.
5 And when his anxious friends, who round him stood,
    Ask'd, what disturb'd the quiet of his breast —
While yet his eyes distill'd a briny flood,
    The future tyrant thus his cares express'd —
'[. . . text unreadable . . .] my years attain'd,
10   His triumphs round the earth's wide orb were spread;
And [. . . text unreadable . . .] seat the hero gain'd,
    And Conquest twin'd her laurels round his head.
While I remain unnotic'd and unknown,
    A novice yet among the sons of Fame,
15 Where are the trophies I can call my own?
    What spoils of victory can Caesar claim?'
Thus Julius, burning with Ambition's fire,
    At length, thro' Roman blood, to empire rose —
But henceforth may that wretch accurs'd expire,
20   Whose glory on his country's ruin grows.
May fortune always their endeavours bless,
    Who struggle to defend their country's cause,
May victory crown their labours with success,
    Who fight for Freedom, and for Patriot Laws.
25 But those who dare a People's rights invade,
    Who millions, for dominion would enslave;
May all their toils with infamy be paid,
    Not *tears* – but *curses* visit them to the grave.
In deep oblivion may their acts be hid,
30   That none their despot victories may lead;
As Greece her sons, to sound *his name* forbid,
    Who, to be known, perform'd a villain's deed.[1]

                        A. Briton

1 The last two lines refer to Erestrates, who, to perpetuate his name, set fire to the temple of Diana, to Esphus. As well as this specific footnote, there is also an apparently unspecified footnote in the newspaper: '*See Plutarch's Life of Caesar*.'

This is attributed to Burns in Hogg's *The Lost Poems* (1997). The crucial pen-name 'A. Briton' was first used by Burns in his anti-Hanoverian letter in *The Edinburgh Evening Courant* of November 1788 (Letter 283). We know from his personal correspondence that he was the author of this seditious letter. We are now confronted in this section with two recently discovered poems and a political essay which use this pseudonymn. Checking of the *Dictionary of Anonymous and Pseudonymous Literature* showed no other usage of 'A. Briton' other than the Burns *Courant* letter during this period and mentions an obscure booklet of 1819 on bank coins, signed A. Briton. We then embarked on a sustained textual scansion of period newspapers and journals in order to discover this pen-name anywhere other than in *Lines on Ambition*, *The Cob-Web* and the political essay from Burns's main London radical outlet, *The Morning Chronicle*. No other usage was found. As we shall see, regarding the new essay, Burns was particularly keen to emphasise to *The Morning Chronicle* that he was, indeed 'a Briton'. Further, in the late eighteenth century, this pseudonym does not precede Burns's usage and also disappears after his death.

Textually, the new poem is strikingly similar to lines written by Burns during mid-1793 in John Syme's copy of *The British Album*, a volume of the Della Cruscan poets led by Robert Merry:

> PERISH their names, however great or brave,
> Who in the DESPOT's cursed errands bleed!
> But who for FREEDOM fill a hero's grave,
> Fame with a Seraph-pen, record the glorious deed!

These lines not only read as though they were embryonic of *Lines on Ambition* but could easily be inserted in the final part of the poem. Although the first part of the poem is rather cumbersome, Burns did compose very similar lines during mid-1793.

That the subject of 'Ambition' might be a topic for the poet's pen is evident if a letter to Thomson, written in June 1793, is considered:

> Have you ever, my dear Sir, felt your bosom ready to burst with indignation, on reading of, or seeing, how these mighty villains who divide kingdom against kingdom, desolate provinces & lay Nations waste out of the wantonness of Ambition, or often from still more ignoble passions? (Letter 566).

Moreover, the notion that Burns might curse the leaders of Britain for involving the country in a war against France (ll. 19–20, ll. 25–8), is clearly seen in a letter to Peter Hill in 1793: 'O! may the wrath & curse of all mankind, haunt and harass these turbulent, unprincipled misc[reants] who have involved a people in this ruinous business!!!' (Letter 553).

There is no evidence to suggest this poem was copied from an English newspaper or was the work of an English poet. It does not appear in English radical newspapers. It was almost certainly sent to *The Edinburgh Gazetteer* by Burns, who had previously employed the pen-name.

Indeed, the poet's primary educational text, under his influential tutor Murdoch, that is Arthus Masson's *A Collection of Prose and Verse from the Best English Authors*, carries a powerful essay 'The Twelve Caesars' which dwells on the corrupt abuse of power by the ambitious, beginning with the reign of Julius Caesar.

Remember the Poor

First printed in *The Glasgow Advertiser*, 27th January 1794.

	Frae Greenland's snawie mountain high,	snowy
	(Whare sleaks o' ice tumult'ous lye,	lie
	An' dismal scenes appear)	
	Bauld Boreas, wi' his surly train,	bold North Wind
5	Rides howling thro' the mirk domain,	dark
	An' leads and guides the weir: –	war of elements
	Nae mair the gowany field leuks gay,	no more, looks
	Nor flow'r-bespangled green,	
	To tempt our waunrin' feet to stray,	wandering
10	Or charm our rovin' een;	eyes
	Mair dowie they grow ay,	more woeful
	An' wither in the blast,	
	I'm vext now, perplext now,	
	To think their beauty's past.	
15	Happy are they, wha, without dread,	who
	Can hear the storm blaw owre their head,	blow over
	Nor danger needs to fear: –	
	Blest are ye, highly favour'd Great,	
	Wha coshly rest on beds o' state,	comfortably
20	Crown'd wi' ilk dainty chear; –	each
	Enrag'd ay whan I do compare	when
	Your blythsome lives wi' mine,	
	(For mine's a life opprest wi' care,	
	An' drudgery an' pine.)	
25	I snarl an' quarrell	
	Wi' Fortune, that blind wh – re,	whore
	That leuks down, an' does frown	looks
	On me, and hauds me poor:	holds, keeps

Reflect sae wretched's they maun be   so, must
30 That's doom'd tae pinchin' poverty   to
      And stern Misfortune's blows;
   An' O! thy pittance do thou grant –
   'Twill banish their ilk' care an' want,   every
      An' rid them o' their woes:
35 Wi' sauls quite liberal an' free   souls
      Your charity extend;
   Now is the time, – an' credit me
      Ye'll no' miss't in the end.
         Mak' haste then, nor waste then
40   Your siller on ought ill;   money
         Ease their need wi' a' speed
             Lest hunger does them kill.

   Hail ye wha ha'e wi' open heart   who have
   Come forth o' late, an' ta'en their part – taken
45   A noble gen'rous deed!
   Is there, whate blude rins in his viens,   what blood runs
   A wretch, wha's cash, an' yet refrains   who's
      Tae join ye wi' a speed –
   (Uwordy's he to see the light   not worthy
50   O' day, that e'er wad scan,   would
   An', for the sake o' riches, slight
      His fellow-creature, Man) –
         May his gear thro' ilk year   possessions, each
             Ay mair an' mair decrease,   always, more
55   Wha'll no join wi' his coin   who'll not
             To help fowks in distress.   folks

   Lang may ye live, Sirs, to defend   long
   An' stand the poor man's constant friend
      In ilka time o' need;   every
60 Syne, whan Death at your doors does ca',   then, when, call
   An' lays ye lifeless, ane an' a',   one and all
      Amang the silent dead,   among
   Fame on her trump your praise will soun',   sound
      An' mark ye in her pages,
65 That your deeds may be handed down
      Unto the latest ages; –
         An' may 't be your decree –
             'Throughout an' endless day,
         'T' inherit by merit
70   'The ever-sproutin' bay'.

      Jan 1794, JOB.

This poem was first ascribed to Burns in Hogg's *Robert Burns: The Lost Poems* (1997). It appears in *The Glasgow Advertiser* of 27th January, 1794. It was composed after a public plea for charity to feed the hungry in and around areas of Glasgow during the harsh winter of 1793–4. To launch the initial call for public charity Burns's poem *The Cottar's Saturday Night* was reprinted in Dr James Anderson's magazine *The Bee*, where the charity appeal originated in December 1793. Burns knew Anderson and added (Letter 426) a few friends' names to Anderson's subscriber list. By the time *Remember the Poor* was printed, over a month after the appeal went public, *The Bee* had been forcibly closed down in Edinburgh for its part in serialising the ferocious political critique on government by James Thomson Callender, *The Political Progress of Britain*. Hence perhaps, the poem's appearance in *The Glasgow Advertiser*.

There are several reasons to suggest this work is by Burns. He would have known *The Cottar's Saturday Night* was part of the charity appeal and his egalitarian sentiments were such that he would have surely wished to contribute. On several occasions Burns remarks that the only 'coin' a poet can pay with is *rhyme* (Letter 571). As we see in the Introduction, *The Book of Job* is compulsively present in Burns's poetry and letters (Letters 248, 362, 446). This identification of his own and his father's suffering with that of Job would make this an obvious choice of pen-name.

In addition, it is now known that Burns not only published prose in *The Glasgow Advertiser* but its subject was *poverty*. Here is the full text from the newspaper on 29th April–2nd May, 1791:

FRAGMENT – ON POVERTY

POVERTY! Thou half-sister of Death! Thou cousin-german of Hell! Where shall I find force of execration equal to thy demerits? – By thee, the venerable Ancient, though, in thy invidious obscurity, grown hoary in the practice of every virtue under Heaven, now laden with years and wretchedness, implores from a stony-hearted son of Mammon, whose sun of prosperity never knew a cloud, a little, little aid to support his very existence, and is by him, derided and insulted. – By thee, the man of sentiment, whose heart glows with Independence and melts with sensibility, [only – error] inly pines under the neglect, or wreathes [writhes] in bitterness of soul under the contumely, of arrogant, unfeeling Wealth. – By thee, the man of Genius, whose ill-starred ambition plants him at the tables of the Fashionable and Polite, must see, in suffering silence, his remark neglected and his person despised, while shallow greatness in his idiot attempts at wit, shall

meet with countenance and applause. – Nor is it only the family
of worth to have reason to complain of thee. – The children of
Folly and Vice, tho' in common with thee, the offspring of evil,
smart equal[ly] under thy rod. – Owing to thee, the man of
unfortunate disposition and neglected education, is condemned
as a fool for his dissipation; despised and shunned as a needy
wretch, when his follies, as usual, have brought him to want, and
when his unprincipled necessities drive him to dishonest prac-
tices, he is abhorred as a miscrent [miscreant], and perishes by
the justice of his country. – But far otherwise is the lot of the Man
of family and Fortune. – His early extravagance and folly are fire
and spirit; his consequent wants are the embarassments of an
Honest Fellow; and when, to remedy the matter, he sets out with
a legal commission to plunder distant provinces and massacre
peaceful nations, he returns laden with the spoils of rapine and
murder – lives wicked and respected – and dies a Villian and a
Lord. – Nay, worst of all, alas! For hapless Woman – the needy
creature who was shivering at the corner of the street, waiting to
earn the wages of casual prostitution, is ridden down by the
Chariot wheels of the CORONETED RAPE – hurrying out to
the adulterous assignation – She, who, without the same neces-
sities to plead, riots nightly in the same guilty trade!!!

Although anonymous, this flyting critique on poverty and social
oppression, bar a few minor textual and typographical differences, is
found in a letter by Burns to Peter Hill, Edinburgh, dated for 17th
January, 1791, some three months prior to appearing in the Glasgow
publication (see Letter 430). Given the poet's habit of making fair
copies of many of his letters and his tendency to repeat himself, it is
pretty certain he sent this material to the *Advertiser*. The only
known manuscript is without address and unsigned. Hence, here is
now definitive proof that Burns covertly published prose in *The
Glasgow Advertiser* during 1791.

The first stanza of the poem is its best. The winter scene is set
within a powerful image of the god of the North Wind riding,
'howling', through icy Greenland with an elemental power so wild
that they have decimated, as far away as Scotland, any flowers that
might have survived. This confidently flowing image is reminiscent
of Burns's characteristic painting of a winter scene to create a mood
fit for the human despair and loss in the ensuing verses. The
description of 'Bauld Boreas, wi' his surly train' is echoed in Burns's
'Cauld Boreas, wi' his boisterous crew' from *The Fête Champêtre*,
which was published posthumously. The phrase 'Bauld Boreas' is

found only in Ramsay's (1686–1758) *The Nipping Frost and Driving Sna'*. The description 'the mirk domain, / And leads and guides the weir' (ll. 5–6) is adapted from Fergusson's '. . . bleak domain / And guides the weir', *The Daft Days*, stanza 3. Also, the phrase (l. 10) 'Or charm our rovin' een' is partly adapted from Fergusson's *Leith Races*, 'To charm our rovin' een'. Such echoes of Ramsay and Fergusson are everywhere in Burns.

A further distinct feature of Burns in poetry and prose is his constant attack on the 'great folk' or 'highly favour'd Great', as seen here. Or in *Elegy on the Death of Captain Matthew Henderson*, 'Go to your sculptur'd tombs, ye Great, / In a' the tinsel trash o' state'. Ll. 15–20 read like a condensed version of the social and economic oppression suffered by the poor in *A Winter Night*, 'Oh ye! who, sunk in beds of down, / Feel not a want but what yourselves create, /Think, for a moment, on his wretched fate, / Whom friends and fortune quite disown!' This type of comment in Burns is found along with his motif of despair for the poor in general and himself in particular, his personal angst, suffering at the hands of 'Fortune' , as seen at ll. 21–8, a passage which is autobiographical as in Burns's: 'snarl an' quarrell / Wi' Fortune, that blind wh—ore'. The anonymously published prose by Burns, given above from *The Glasgow Advertiser* is a perfect example of Burns 'enrag'd' at the effects of poverty. (Further examples of this sentiment expressed in poetry and prose are found in *Lines Written on a Banknote*, *My Father Was A Farmer*, *The Creed of Poverty*, comments in the *FCB* and Letters 244, 335, 358, 347, 510 319, 605 and 638). As he wrote to Mrs Dunlop, 'Poverty, is to be my attendant to the grave' (Letter 638). Ll. 15–28 are a self-portrait of a poet unable to give cash to the charity plea who is deeply indignant at the semi-feudal economic structure which is implicitly blamed as the cause of poverty.

To Messrs Muir, Palmer, Skirving and Margarot

First printed in *The Edinburgh Gazetteer*, 15th January, 1794.

Among innumerable false – unmov'd,
Unshaken, unseduced, unterrify'd. – Milton.

Friends of the Slighted people – ye whose wrongs
From wounded FREEDOM many a tear shall draw
As once she mourn'd when mock'd by venal tongues
Her SYDNEY fell beneath the form of law.

5 O had this bosom known poetic fire
   Your names, your deeds, should grace my votive songs
   For Virtue taught the bard's far-sounding lyre
   To lift the PATRIOT from the servile throng.

   High o'er the wrecks of time *his* fame shall live
10 While proud Oppression wastes her idle rage.
   His name on history's column shall revive
   And wake the genius of a distant age.

   It shines – the dawn of that long promised day
   For eager Fancy bursts the midnight gloom
15 The patriot's praise, the grateful nations pay
   And tears the trophy from the oppressor's tomb.

   Yet what the praise far distant times shall sing
   To that calm solace Virtue *now* bestows.
   Round the dire bark She waves her guardian wing;
20 She guides her exiles o'er the trackless snows:
   With Joy's gay flowers She decks the sultry wild
   And sheds the beam of Hope where Nature never smil'd.

Whereas the most beautiful gem stones are the result of the raw
geological power in the vortex of Earth's volatile central core, the
genesis of this poetic gem is the intense crucible of political antagon-
ism that came to a head in December 1793 and January 1794 in
Edinburgh. Continuing the theme of *The Scotian Muse*, it laments
the oppression of radical activists and in particular, those convicted of
sedition and sentenced to transportation to the penal colony of
Botany Bay, namely Thomas Muir, the Rev. Fysche Palmer, William
Skirving and Maurice Margarot. It also accords Muir the honour
of being compared to the great hero-martyr of the Whig tradition
Algernon Sydney (1622–83), the English statesman, who was an icon
of the French as well as British radical movement at this period.

   Having tried and convicted Muir and Palmer for sedition and
served upon them sentences of 14 years' and 7 years' transportation
respectively, the Scottish Friends of the People branches – those
'Friends of the Slighted people' (l. 1) – were galvanised and grew,
despite the key Edinburgh branch, central to organisation of the
Scottish radicals, being infiltrated by the cousin of James Boswell,
Claude Irvine Boswell, Depute Sheriff of Fife. Another government
spy, P. Moir, described the Rev. Fysche Palmer bizarrely as a
bankrupt butcher from Birmingham paid by Joseph Priestley's

radical group (see RH 2/4/70/f.48, dated 8th March, 1793). The government moved to arrest William Skirving and Maurice Margarot when they were about to convene a meeting of the National Convention of the Friends of the People in Edinburgh near the end of 1793. The government feared the setting up of a Jacobin-derived government. Robert Dundas (nephew to Henry) wrote in early January 1794:

> You may believe that the present state of madness here, engrosses all our attention . . . if we take decided and strong measures against those Rebels, we shall be supported. . . . It is the only system that will have effect or, otherways, an Insurrection will be the consequence. (RH 2/4/74/f.76).

Political anxiety was running at such a pitch that at one point, it was thought Glasgow radicals were tunnelling from Glasgow to the Edinburgh Tolbooth to liberate Thomas Muir (such a crazy alarm is described in *The Edinburgh Gazetteer* October 1793). Prior to the arrests there were reports that 'Paisley & its neighbourhood' were in a 'state of tumult and unrest' (RH 2/4/74/f.76). Even worse, reports came in from a Charles Ogilvie of the Customs in Greenock that local people were supplying provisions to French naval ships at the town docks (RH 2/4/74/f.95). Edinburgh Supporters of the accused gathered at Calton Hill, Edinburgh as the trial went on. Scott, the Fiscal, ordered 'to have people on the watch' and list who was in attendance (Laing II, 500, f.533). In the following week, legal action against the editor of *The Edinburgh Gazetteer* was successful and it was forcibly closed. Being charged with sedition, James Thomson Callender (1758–1803), author of the savage critique on political corruption, *The Political Progress of Britain*, fled the country and was declared a fugitive. (See Michael Durey, *With the Hammer of Truth. James Thomson Callender*, University of Virginia, 1990.) Amid such tumult, upwards of '10,000' people helped take Maurice Margarot in a carriage to parliament square in Edinburgh on the opening of his trial: all 'well wishers . . . where we were received with such a universal shout . . . entered into the court & having taken my seat at the Bar between two soldiers with drawn bayonets' the court was adjourned due to a 'sudden illness of the Lord Advocate [Robert Dundas]' (TS 11/959/3505: Margarot to Thomas Hardy, LCS, London, January 1794). Despite their varied and eloquent defences, expressed in Enlightenment concepts and Biblical allusion, the accused were all found guilty of sedition. As a result, this and later political suppression of radicalism put back the cause of British democratic progress for over a generation. Burns, watching from Dumfries, was conscious of these events and wrote wryly in *From Esopus to Maria*, that 'his heresies in Church and State, / Might well award him Muir and Palmer's fate'.

The introductory quotation from Milton is an apt description of Burns's personal predicament in Dumfries, where his relationship with, inter alia, John Syme, was strained. He cast a keen glance at the London treason trials during early 1795, as he remarked to Mrs Dunlop:

> Thank God, these London trials have given us a little more breath, & I imagine that the time is not far distant when a man may freely blame Billy Pit[t], without being called an enemy to his Country (Letter 649).

It is evident from the extent of censorship outlined in our Introduction that Burns almost certainly had his say on these matters and that missing letters to Mary Wollstonecraft, William Roscoe, William Masterton, William Smellie and others, probably contained commentary and/or poetry on the Scottish sedition trials.

The language employed here is seen in the elegiac style of *Elegy on the Death of Sir James Hunter-Blair*, where the Muse of Caledonia loudly laments:

> I saw my sons resume their ancient fire,
>   I saw fair Freedom's blossoms richly blow;
> But ah! How hope is born but to expire,
>   Relentless fate has laid their guardian low.
>
> My patriot falls, but shall he die unsung,
>   While empty Greatness saves a worthless name?
> No: every Muse shall join her tuneful tongue,
>   And future ages hear his glowing fame.

Indeed, these stanzas might almost be placed within the new poem and read with natural continuity, despite the fact that the poems were written some four years apart.

What makes this a typical Burnsian political poem is that, despite his creative anxieties of being worthy of his theme, the poet's metaphorical darkness precedes a radical dawn. Thus, the poem ends with the beautiful image of poetry itself succouring the seaborne exiles. The feel is akin to Coleridge and, indeed, we might here recall the first lines of Coleridge's sonnet, *To the Honourable Mr [Thomas] Erskine* which also deals with the exiled Scots:

When British Freedom for an happier land
    Spread her broad wings, that flutter'd with affright,
    ERSKINE! thy voice she heard, and paus'd her flight
Sublime of hope, for dreadless thou didst stand

(Thy censer glowing with the hallow'd flame)
    A hireless Priest before the insulted shrine,
    And at her altar pour the stream divine
Of unmatch'd eloquence . . .

Coleridge's sonnet appeared in *The Morning Chronicle* at the end of the same year, 1794. As well as demonstrating poetic affinity between the two men, it records the enormous impact the Scottish Sedition Trials had on British radical consciousness.

The Ewe Bughts

First printed in *The Morning Chronicle*, 10th July, 1794.

'Will you go to the Ewe-bughts, Marian,	sheep pens
'And wear in the sheep wi' me?	bring
'The mavis sings sweetly, my Marian,	song thrush
'But not sae sweetly as thee'.	so
5 These aft were the words of my Sandy,	often
As we met in the how of the glen,	hollow
But nae mair shall I meet wi' my Sandy,	no more
For Sandy to Flanders is gane.	gone
How can the trumpets loud clarion	
10 Thus take a' the shepherds afar?	
Oh could na' the Ewe-bughts and Marian	not, sheep fold/pen
Please mair than the horrors of war?	more
But, oh, tis the fault o' them a', Sirs,	all
In search of gowd and of fame,	gold
15 The lads daily wander awa', Sirs,	away
And leave their poor lasses at hame.	home
Not a plough in the land has been ganging,	moving
The owsen hae stood in the sta',	oxen have, stall
Nae flails in our barns hae been banging,	no
20 For mair than this towmond or twa.	more, 12 months, two
Ilka Laird in the Highlands is rueing,	each
That he drove his poor tenants away,	
For naething is seen here but ruin,	nothing
As the haughs are a' lying in lay.	fertile lands, all

25	There's gowd in the garters of Sandy,	gold
	And silk in his blue-bonnet lug,	flap of a cap/bonnet
	And I'm not a kaerd nor a randy,	gypsy, rude person
	Nor a lass without blanket or rug;	
	Then why should he fight sae for riches,	so
30	Or seek for a sodger's degree,	soldier's commission
	Or fling by his kilt for the breeches,	throw, trousers
	And leave the dear Ewe-Bughts and me?	

This appears anonymously in *The Morning Chronicle*, 10th July, 1794. It was first ascribed to Burns by Professor Lucylle Werkmeister in her 1966 paper *Robert Burns and the London Daily Press* (*Modern Philology*, LXIII, p. 328). Werkmeister does not provide a textual argument for her case, but a formally contextual one as we shall see in notes to the immediately following 'A Cabinet Dinner'. It was subsequently ascribed to Burns in Scott Hogg's *The Lost Poems* (1997).

Textually, the song is based on an old song named *Will Ye Go to the Ewe Bughts, Marion* and its tune of the same name, which melody Burns had already set to *Will Ye Go to the Indies, My Mary*. This new version is significantly adapted from Allan Ramsay's earlier *Ewe Bughts, Marion*. Like Burns's treatment of *Logan Braes*, the new lyric has been transformed into a war-broken love song. The simple language and style is enhanced by the evocative use of the feminine voice; a characteristic trait of Burns's lyrics. Ramsay's version is written in the male voice. No poet of the eighteenth century possessed Burns's skill in employing the female voice in song.

L. 20 is almost straight from Burns's *The Ronnals of the Bennals*, which reads 'For mair than this towmond, or twa'. Burns employs the name 'Sandy' (l. 5) on many occasions; it was a stock-in-trade name within pastoral narrative or dialogue during the century (See Burns's *Sandy and Jockie*). Moreover, he sent a copy of *Ewe Bughts Marion* to James Johnson in 1795, commenting 'Another song – "Ewe Bughts Marion" – a quite different set from the one you have already published' (Letter 684). He also mentions it to Thomson (Letter 511) and in his reply to Burns, Thomson commented, 'What you say of The Ewe Bughts is just . . . All I requested was that you would try your hand on some of the inferior stanzas' (Currie, 1800, Correspondence, Letter VII, p. 191). Burns was aware that at least two older versions existed and wrote of the earliest text that he was 'not sure if this old and charming air be of the South, as it is commonly said, or of the North of Scotland. There is a song apparently as ancient as "Ewe Bughts Marion", which sings to the same time, and is evidently of the North' (Hogg, *The Lost Poems*, 1997, p. 158). The Ramsay collected version reads:

> Will ye go to the ewe-bught, Marion,
>   And wear in the sheep wi' me?
> The sun shines sweet, my Marion,
>   But nae half sae sweet as thee.
> 5 O Marion's a bonie lass,
>   And the blyth blinks in her e'e;
> And fain wad I marry Marion,
>   Gin Marion wad marry me.
>
> There's gowd in your garters, Marion,
> 10   And silk on your white hause-bane;
> Fu' fain wad I kiss my Marion,
>   At e'en when I come hame . . .
>
> /I'm young and stout, my Marion;
>   Nane dances like me on the green:
> 15 And gin ye forsake me, Marion,
>   I'll e'en gae draw up wi' Jean . . .

This is clearly the model for the new radical text. Such a radical revision would not have been sent to Thomson given his prudish slight on Burns's anti-war *Logan Braes*. The obvious outlet, given the demise of *The Edinburgh Gazetteer* in January 1794, was *The Morning Chronicle*. After all, as already shown, he did promise to send them such pieces. McGuirk describes *The Ewe Bughts* as a jewel among the recently recovered poems, stating it has 'the strongest claim' to be one of the 'previously unknown poems by Robert Burns' (*Books in Review, Eighteenth Century Scottish Studies Newsletter*, 1997, p. 15).

A Cabinet Dinner

Printed in *The Morning Chronicle* with *The Ewe Bughts*, 10th July, 1794.

> 'How shall we save the loaves and fishes;
>   Where safely shall we hide 'em?
> To keep them from the Gallic meshes,'
>   Says Loughb'rough, *'let's divide 'em'*.

'Ah! should they fail in savage hand,
  You know how they would treat 'em!
As friends, then, to our native land,
  'Tis better *we should eat 'em*'.

This was, as Professor Werkmeister comments in her 1966 paper, *Robert Burns and the London Daily Press*, printed next to *Ewe Bughts Marion*, 'paired but unsigned' (p. 328). On this basis she argues it is by the same author as *Ewe Bughts Marion* and ascribes it to Burns. It was the newspaper custom to pair poems or songs, set them out next to each other without a line across the page to indicate they are by the same author. In the second *Heron Ballad* (l. 76). Burns also refers to 'the fishes and loaves'. Loughborough (l. 4) was Alexander Wedderburn, the Lord Chancellor.

The 'loaves and fishes' reference is, of course, a brutally ironic inversion of Christ's miraculous feeding of the poor. This *anti-Christian governing class is predatorily grabbing everything for itself. It is a bitter double irony, and complete confirmation of Werkmeister's suggestion of Burns's authorship, that in 1795 an Ulster poet, believing, on the sole evidence of *The Dumfries Volunteers*, that Burns had betrayed the democratic cause, wrote these lines:

> O Scotia's Bard! my muse alas!
> For you in private blushes!
>   You've dipt i' th' dish wi' slee Dundas
> An prie'd the Loaves and Fishes.

For a full account of this Ulster context see Liam McIlvanney, 'Robert Burns and the Ulster-Scots Literary Revival of the 1790s', *Bullán*, Vol. IV, No. 2, pp. 125–43.

Humanity: An Ode

First printed in *The Gentleman's Magazine*, August 1794.

Blow, blow, ye winds! with heavier gust!
And freeze, thou bitter-biting frost!
Descend, ye chilly, smothering snows!
Not all your rage, united, shews
5   More hard unkindness, unrelenting,
Vengeful malice, unrepenting,
Than heav'n-illumin'd *Man* on brother *Man* bestows! —

See stern Oppressions iron lip,
    See mad Ambition's gory hand,
10   Sending like blood-hounds from the slip,
    Woe, Want and Murder, o'er a land![1]
Even in the peaceful, rural vale,
Truth, weeping, tells the mournful tale,
How Luxury, with Flattery by her side,
15   The parasite, empoisoning her ear,
With all the servile wretches in the rear,
Looks o'er proud Property extended wide;
And eyes the simple, lowly hind,
Whose toil upholds the glittering show,
20   A creature of another kind,
Some coarser substance, unrefin'd,
Plac'd for her Lordly use thus vile below!
Where, where, is Love's fond, tender throe,
With lordly Honour's lofty brow,
25   The powers you proudly own?
Is there, beneath Love's noble name,
Can harbour, dark, the selfish aim,
    To bless himself alone? —
Mark Maiden-Innocence, a prey
30   To love-pretending snares:
This boasted honour turns away,
Shunning soft Pity's rising sway,
Regardless all of tears, and unavailing prayers.
Perhaps this hour, in misery's squalid nest,
35   She strains your infant to her joyless breast,
And with a mother's fears shrinks at the rocking blast!

    O ye! who sunk in beds of down,[2]
Feel not a want but what *yourselves create*,

1 '– In our world, Death deputes
Intemperance to the work of age!
And, hanging up the quiver Nature gave him,
As flow of execution, for despatch
Sends forth imperial butchers; bids them slay
Their sheep [the silly sheep they fleec'd before]
And toss him twice ten thousand at a meal.' Young's *Consolation*. R.B.

'Cry havoc, and let slip the dogs of war.' Shakespeare. R.B.

2 'Ah, little think the gay, licentious proud,
Whom pleasure, power, affluence surround . . .' Thomson. R.B.

Think, for a moment, on his hapless fate,
Whom friends and fortune quite disown!
Ill-satisfy'd keen Hunger's clamorous call,
Stretched on his straw he lays himself to sleep,
While through the ragged roof, and chinky wall,
Chill, o'er his slumbers, falls the drifty heap!
Think on the dungeon's grim confine,
Think on the terrors of the mine,
Where Guilt and poor Misfortune pine!
Guilt, erring Man, relenting view!
Nor let thy legal rage pursue
The wretch, already beaten low
By dire *Misfortune's* undeserved blow!
Afflictions sons are brothers in distress;
A brother then relieve, and God the deed shall bless.

                                                  R.B.

Several major poems by Burns are recorded with variant stanzas or lines, depending on whether the poem was drafted on several occasions and modified significantly before publication, or changed after publication. The poem given here does not fall into the category of being merely a variant reading of *A Winter Night*, first published in 1787. It is an updated version, published by Burns himself in August 1794 also in *The Gentleman's Magazine,* some three months after *Sonnet on the Death of Robert Riddell*. Robert Riddell was a subscriber and contributor to the journal and would have made the poet familiar with its pages during their meetings at Friar's Carse. The poem *Humanity: An Ode* is not found in manuscript. It does not feature in any previous edition of Burns and lay undiscovered until Scott Hogg's 1997 research.

The main, obvious difference between the new version and *A Winter Night* is that the body of the poem is no longer presented as a *voice* heard at night by the poet. The opening stanzas of *A Winter Night* in Standard Habbie format are cut away and the consolatory ending is dropped. What remains is an exclusively dissident text expressing the humanitarian sentiment of the poem, hence the new title, *Humanity: An Ode*. There are, on close examination, several minor textual changes from the 1787 version to this final work, including new lines and a new ending to the poem. The differences are: 'as now' is dropped from the line 'Not all your rage, [as now] united, shews'; 'iron grip' is modified to 'iron lip'; 'Or mad Ambition's gory hand' becomes 'See mad Ambition's gory hand'; 'How pamper'd Luxury' is changed to 'How Luxury, with Flattery by her side'; 'rustic hind' becomes 'lowly hind'; 'thus far' is omitted from 'Plac'd for her Lordly use [thus far,] thus vile below!'; 'Regardless of the tears' is changed to 'Regardless all of tears . . .'; 'wretched fate' is changed to 'hapless fate'; 'piles the drifty heap!' becomes 'falls the drifty heap!' A new line, adding emphasis is given, 'Think on the terrors of the mine.' The question 'But shall thy legal rage pursue' is dropped for the more direct and forceful, 'Nor let thy legal rage pursue.' The phrase 'crushed low' is now 'beaten low'. The final section of the question ending with 'By cruel Fortune's undeserved blow?' is altered to the indignant expression 'By dire Misfortune's undeserved blow!' The poem concludes with a new, improved ending:

> Afflictions sons are brothers in distress;
> A brother then relieve, and God the deed shall bless.

The structural and stylistic changes made to the poem serve to sharpen the moral outrage of the values expressed. The rhythmical strophes of *A Winter Night,* lines supposedly heard by the narrator, are now presented as the unequivocal voice of the poet. While the original head quotation from *King Lear* has been left out, the new, additional footnotes add to the increased energy of the piece within the wholly new context of Britain's mendacious involvement in the European conflagration. Condemnation of war and its concomitant desolation of human affairs is given a new impetus in a 1794 context, where 'stern Oppression' and 'mad Ambition's gory hand' were responsible for unleashing 'Woe, Want and Murder, o'er a land!' Burns reinforces this by reference to Young's 'imperial butchers', implying criticism on contemporary warmongers, surrounded by indulgent 'pleasure' and 'power' from Thomson's ironic couplet. The Shakespearean debt of *Humanity: An Ode* (see notes to *A Winter Night*) is re-emphasised by the footnote 'Cry havoc, and let slip the dogs of war' (*Julius Caesar*, Act III. Sc. I, 1. 273) alluding to an earlier state overwhelmed with bloody civil strife. Battle had also been joined with France.

At Dumfries Theatre

First published in *The Morning Chronicle*, 7th February, 1795.

KEMBLE, thou cur'st my unbelief
> Of Moses and his rod: –
At YARICO's sweet Notes of Grief
> The rock with tears had flow'd.
> R.B.

This was not, as is generally accepted, first published by Stuart, Glasgow, 1801, but appears in *The Morning Chronicle* on 7th February, 1795, designated by the poet's initials. These lines are further proof Burns was, as promised, sending material to the Opposition press in London. Mrs Stephen Kemble (1763–1841), wife of Stephen Kemble the manager of the Edinburgh theatre, appeared at Dumfries theatre on 21st October, 1794, in the part of Yarico in the drama *Inkle and Yarico* by George Colman. With its potent anti-slave-trade sentiments, it was a popular drama among radicals of the period. Accordingly, these lines are an indirect political statement by Burns. They were written just after the performance. Kinsley, while drawing attention to the allusion to Exod. xviii, does not mention this political context.

The Heron Ballads
First Heron Ballad

Tune: For a' That and a' That
First printed as an anonymous broadside, 1795.

Wham will we send to London town,		who
To Parliament, and a' that,		
Wha maist in a' the country round,		who most, all
For worth and sense may fa' that. —		be up to/do
5	For a' that and a' that,	
Thro' Galloway and a' that,		
Where is the Laird, or belted Knight,		
That best deserves to fa' that?		do
Wha sees Kirrouchtree's open yett,		who, gate
10	And wha is 't never saw that,	who
Wha e'er wi' Kirrouchtree met,		who ever
That has a doubt of a' that?		
For a' that and a' that,		
Here's Heron yet for a' that;		
15	The independent Patriot,	
The Honest Man, and a' that.		
Tho' wit and worth, in either sex,		
Saint Mary's Isle[1] can shaw that;		show
Wi' Lords and Dukes let Selkirk mix,		
20	For weel does Selkirk fa' that.	well, do

1 The seat of the Earl of Selkirk, home of the poet's friend Lord Daer.

For a' that and a' that,
    Here's Heron yet for a' that;
An independent Commoner
    Maun bear the gree and a' that.   *shall win the day*

25 To paughty Lordlings shall we jeuk,   *insolent, bow*
    And it against the law, that:
For even a Lord may be a gowk,   *fool/cuckoo*
    Tho' sprung frae kings and a' that.   *from*
For a' that and a' that,
30   Here's Heron yet for a' that;
A Lord may be a lousy loon,   *idiot*
    Wi' ribban, star, and a' that. —   *ribbon*

Yon beardless boy comes o'er the hills,[2]
    Wi's uncle's gowd, and a' that: *with his, gold*
35 But we'll hae ane frae 'mang oursels   *have one from*
    A man we ken, and a' that. —   *know*
For a' that and a' that,
    Here's Heron yet for a' that;
We are na to the market come,   *not*
40   Like nowt and naigs and a' that. —   *cattle, horses*

If we are to be knaves and fools,
    And bought and sauld and a' that,   *sold*
A truant callan frae the schools   *lad, from*
    It 's ne'er be said did a' that.
45 For a' that and a' that,
    Here's Heron yet for a' that;
And Master Dicky, thou shalt get
    A gird and stick to ca' that.   *hoop, call*

Then let us drink, the *Stewartry*,
50   Kirrouchtree's Laird, and a' that,
Our Representative to be,
    For weel he's worthy a' that.   *well*
For a' that and a' that,
    Here's Heron yet for a' that;
55 A House of Commons such as he,
    They wad be blest that saw that.   *would*

2 Thomas Gordon of Balmagie, the Tory candidate. His wealthy 'uncle' was James Murray of Broughton.

The election for the Stewartry of Kirkcudbright, a significant part
of Galloway, took place in the Spring of 1795. Burns decided to give
unqualified support to his friend and new found patron Patrick
Heron (1736–1803), the Whig candidate, from Kirroughtree (this is
now the accepted spelling), near Newtown Stewart (then named
Newtown Douglas). Burns had probably met Heron prior to this
either at Edinburgh or the Caledonian Hunt races in Dumfries, but
in June 1794 he was Heron's guest at Kirroughtree. The song *The
Banks of Cree* was written for Lady Elizabeth Heron. The Tory
candidate opposing Heron was Thomas Gordon of Balmagie; he,
and almost all of his local aristocratic supporters are lampooned in
the four Heron ballads.

In a letter to Patrick Heron, Burns admits to circulating this and
the second ballad as printed broadsides: 'I have privately printed a
good many copies of both ballads, and have sent them among friends
all about the country' (Letter 660). They were written as ephemeral
verse, specific to one purpose; to assist the return of Heron to
Parliament. Burns boasted to Heron, his satire would:

> . . . pillory on Parnassus the rank reprobation of character, the
> utter dereliction of all principle, in a profligate junto which has
> not only outraged virtue, but violated common decency; which,
> spurning even hypocrisy as paltry iniquity below their daring; –
> to unmask their flagitiousness to the broadest day – to deliver
> such over to their merited fate, is surely not merely innocent
> but laudable; is not only propriety, but virtue. – You have
> already, as your auxiliary, the sober detestation of mankind on
> the heads of your opponents; and I swear by the lyre of Thalia
> to muster on your side all the votaries of honest laughter, and
> fair, candid ridicule (Letter 660).

More potent, more potentially treasonable anti-Pitt words, were not
spoken by the Botany Bay bound radicals Thomas Muir, Rev.
Fysche Palmer, William Skirving or Maurice Margarot. But Burns,
without the protection of the influential (deceased) Lord Glencairn,
saw in Heron a potential ally, a powerful friend who might be of
some use to him in the future. He spells this out to Heron, wishing
that one day he might gain promotion in the Excise to the level of
Collector, where richer, he would have free time to pursue literary
activities:

> I am on the supervisor's list, and as we come on there by
> precedency, in two or three years I shall be at the head of that

list, and be appointed, *of course*. Then, a FRIEND might be of service to me in getting me into a place in the kingdom which I would like. A supervisor's income varies from about a hundred and twenty, to two hundred per year; but the business is an incessant drudgery, and would be nearly a complete bar to every species of literary pursuit. The moment I am appointed supervisor, in the common routine, I may be nominated on the collector's list; and this is always a business purely of political patronage. A collectorship varies much, from better than two hundred a year to near a thousand. . . . besides a handsome income, a life of compleat leisure. A life of literary leisure with a decent competence, is the summit of my wishes (Letter 660).

However regrettable that this wish was never fulfilled, Burns may have won one partly influential friend with his Heron Ballads, but the Whigs were in Opposition and although Burns told Richarld Oswald of Auchincruive he had lately 'come forward with my services, as poet laureate' to the Whig Party (Letter 662), they were impotent to repay his services.

It mattered little that all of the individuals in the ballads had their names partly dashed out in the original publication, leaving only one or two letters as a hint of the satirical target. It was obvious who the individuals were, given the naming of places associated with the Tory candidate and his supporters. After the eulogy to Heron (ll. 1–24) as a somwhat idealised independent patriot, ll. 25–32 are a biting attack on Tory Landlordism, sharper in tone than the revolutionary *A Man's A Man*, particularly the treasonable 'For even a Lord may be a gowk, / Tho' sprung frae kings and a' that'. Giving voice to the voiceless peasant, ll. 39–42 hit on the brutal inequalities of the rural feudal system 'We are na to the market come,/ Like nowt and naigs and a' that. —/ If we are to be knaves and fools, / And bought and sauld and a' that'. It was probably evident to many readers that Burns was the author, despite his apparent loyalty to King and country in *The Dumfries Volunteers*. The Heron Ballads represent Burns's deliberate political intervention in an election, albeit cloaked in anonymity, which would have lost him both his liberty, his job as an Excise officer and his family income if he was discovered as the author and, accordingly, found guilty on a charge of sedition.

This ballad first entered the canon with Hogg and Motherwell, 1834, then the same year, in Cunningham.

SECOND HERON BALLAD:

The Election – A New Song

Tune: Fy, Let Us a' to the Bridal
First printed as an anonymous broadside, 1795.

Fy let us a' to Kirkcudbright,   now, go
    For there will be bickerin there;   a scrimmage
For Murray's *light horse* are to muster,[1]
    And O, how the heroes will swear!
5 And there will be Murray commander,
    An' Gordon the battle to win;[2]
Like brothers they'll stan' by each other,   stand
    Sae knit in alliance and kin.   so

And there'll be black-nebbit *Johnie*,[3]   -nosed
10   The tongue o' the trump to them a';   Jew's harp/spokesman
An he get na Hell for his haddin,   not, dwelling
    The Deil gets nae justice ava.   devil, no, at all
And there'll be *Kempleton's* birkie,[4]   lively fellow
    A boy no sae black at the bane;   not so, bone
15 But as to his fine *Nabob* fortune,
    We'll e'en let the subject alane.   even, alone

An' there'll be *Wigton's* new *Sheriff*,[5]
    Dame Justice fu' brawly has sped;   bravely
She's gotten the heart of a *Bushby*,
20   But Lord! what's become o' the head?
An' there'll be *Cardoness*, ESQUIRE,[6]
    Sae mighty in *Cardoness'* eyes;
A wight that will weather damnation,
    The Devil the prey will despise.

1 James Murray of Broughton.
2 Thomas Gordon of Balmagie, Tory candidate.
3 John Bushby, sheriff clerk, Dumfries.
4 William Bushby, John's brother.
5 Maitland Bushby, John's son.
6 David Maxwell of Cardoness, hit at in satire by Burns in the Galloway epigrams.

25   And there'll be *Douglasses* doughty,[7]
       New-christening towns far and near;
    Abjuring their democrat doings
       By kissing the arse of a *Peer*.
    An' there'll be *Kenmure* sae gen'rous,[8]   so
30   Whase honour is proof to the storm;   who's
    To save them from stark reprobation,
       He lent them his name to the *Firm*.

    But we winna mention *Redcastle*,[9]   will not
       The *body*, e'en let him escape:
35   He'd venture the gallows for siller,   money
       An' 'twere na the cost o' the rape.   rope
    An' whare is our King's *Lord Lieutenant*,[10]   where
       Sae famed for his *gratefu'* return?   so
    The billie is gettin his questions,   lad
40   To say in *St. Stephen's* the morn.   Westminster, tomorrow

    An' there will be Lads o' the gospel,
       Muirhead, wha's as *gude* as he's *true*:[11] who is, good
    An' there'll be *Buittle's Apostle*,[12]
       Wha's mair o' the *black* than the *blue*; who is more
45   An' there'll be Folk frae *Saint MARY's*,[13] from
       A *house* o' great merit and note;
    The deil ane but honours them highly,   devil a one/no-one
       The deil ane will gie them his vote.   give

    An' there'll be wealthy young *RICHARD*[14]—
50   Dame Fortune should hing by the neck   hang
    For prodigal thriftless bestowing —
       His merit had won him respect.
    An' there'll be rich brither *Nabobs*,[15]

7 Sir William Douglas & James Douglas. Newtown Douglas was later renamed Newton Stewart.
8 John Gordon, of Kenmure.
9 Walter Sloan Lawrie of Redcastle.
10 George Stewart, Lord Garlies.
11 Rev. James Muirhead, minister of Urr, near Castle Douglas.
12 Rev. George Maxwell, minister at Buittle.
13 The Earl of Selkirk's family home, St Mary's Isle, near Kirkcudbright.
14 Richard Oswald, Auchincruive.
15 Wallace's edition records this as a reference to the Hannay family of Sorbie tower. Mackay states 'D & J Anderson'. It was probably the Hannays, still an important Galloway family.

Tho' *Nabobs*, yet men o' the first:
55 An' there'll be *Collieston's* whiskers,[16]
An' Quinton — o' lads no the warst.[17]   not, worst

An' there'll be *Stamp-office Johnie*,[18]
Tak tent how ye purchase a dram;   be careful
An' there'll be gay *Cassencarry*,[19]
60 An' there'll be gleg *Colonel Tam*;[20]   quick-witted
An' there'll be trusty KIRROUCHTREE,[21]
Whase honour was ever his law;
If the VIRTUES were packt in a parcel
His WORTH might be sample for a'.   all

65 And can we forget the auld MAJOR,[22]
Wha'll ne'er be forgot in the *Greys*;
Our flatt'ry we'll keep for some other,
Him only it's justice to praise.
And there'll be maiden *Kilkerran*,[23]
70 And also *Barskimming's* gude Knight;[24]   good
And there'll be roaring *Birtwhistle*,[25]
Yet, luckily roars in the right.

And there frae the *Niddlisdale* border,   from
Will mingle the *Maxwells* in droves;
75 Teugh *Jockie*, Staunch *Geordie*, and *Walie*,[26]   tough
That girns for the fishes and loaves.   cries
An' there'll be *Logan M'Doual*,[27]
Sculdud'ry — an' he will be there;   skulduggery
An' also the *Wild Scot o' Galloway*,
80 Sogering, gunpowther *Blair*.[28]   soldiering, gunpowder

16 William Copeland of Colieston.
17 Quinton McAdam of Graigengillan.
18 John Syme, distributor of Stamps, Dumfries – the poet's friend.
19 Colonel McKenzie of Cassencarry.
20 Colonel Thomas Goldie of Goldielea.
21 Patrick Heron, the Whig candidate.
22 Major Basil Heron, brother of the Whig candidate.
23 Sir Adam Ferguson of Kilkerran.
24 Sir William Miller of Barskimming.
25 Alexander Birtwhistle, Provost of Kirkcudbright.
26 John Maxwell of Terraughty; George Maxwell of Carruchan; Wellwood Maxwell of the Grove.
27 Captain Andrew McDoul of Logan, Rhins of Galloway.
28 Major Blair of Dunskey near Portpatrick, Rhins of Galloway.

Then hey the *chaste Interest o Broughton*,
    And hey for the blessin 'twill bring;
It may send *Balmaghie* to the Commons,[29]
    In *Sodom* 'twould mak him a King.
And hey for the sanctified *Murray*,[30]
    Our land wha wi' Chapels has stor'd: who
He founder'd his horse among harlots,
    But gied the auld naig to the Lord!   gave old horse

For the original context of this ballad, see notes to the first Heron ballad. This, the second Heron ballad, is based on an old song *The Blythesome Wedding* which Burns probably saw in *The Orpheus Caledonius* (1733). Henderson and Henley record that a broadside copy of this ballad exists in the British Museum, marked 'Printed for private distribution by James Hill, Esq., W.S., 1795' (Vol. II, p. 402). This ballad first entered the canon in 1834, printed in Hogg and Motherwell, followed the same year by Cunningham's edition.

Unlike the oblique slight at the idle gentry's 'whoring' and squandering money playing cards, subtly interwoven in the dialogue of *The Twa Dogs*, these blatant acerbic verses probably had the effect of indiscriminate machine gun fire among Pittite Tory supporters throughout Galloway. The various personal failings, idiosyncrasies and hypocrisy of local Tory aristocrats are mocked in this broadside of biting polemical satire, which rings out not the titled but colloquial names for the landed families, thus reducing their importance to the level of local inn gossip. It exposes, then attacks the closed-shop alliance of political, economic and legal power controlled by landed families in the south west. That birth was the prerequisite to position and power in semi-feudal Scotland, profoundly irritated Burns, not primarily because he was envious of his so-called social superiors, but because it bred nepotism and corruption and allowed many people of rank into places of power their intellect or ability did not merit. This process, most radicals believed, acted as a barrier to social, economic and political progress. Political reform, though was not enough for Burns, as he commented to Deborah Duff Davies:

DOWN, immediately, should go FOOLS from the high places where misbegotten CHANCE has perked them up,

29 The Tory candidate.
30 Murray of Broughton.

> & through life should they sculk, ever haunted by their native insignificance, as the body marches accompanied by its shadow . . . But the hand that could give, I would liberally fill (Letter 556A).

While the underlying egalitarian values of Burns were often his impetus to satirical verse, an apologia for the Heron Ballads might argue that his hopes for a better, more enlightened society were destroyed by the disintegration of political freedom under Pitt's oppressive government.

There is, though, no substantive evidence that Burns was widely known to be the author of these verses during his lifetime, nor is it known how widely they penetrated the local peasant or aristocratic culture of Galloway during the election. What is known is that the Rev. James Muirhead (l. 42; footnote 11) replied in verse. His reply branded Burns a '. . . shabby son of a whore' and a '. . . rhymster, gauger, pimp'. Speaking as one of the dominant Tory hierarchy then ruling Galloway, Muirhead's libel became part of the black Tory gossip that marred Burns's character *before* and after his death. The lines which probably stung Muirhead, the minister at Urr near Castle Douglas, are in the fourth Heron Ballad (ll. 29–32), where Burns compares him unfavourably to a sour crab apple. The personal and political virulence of the backlash against Burns can be gauged from The Young Ms. in Edinburgh University. Alexander Young of Harben was a student friend of James Currie and Heron's Tory lawyer. His memoir in the form of a commentary on Currie's biography is reprinted in Professor Robert Fitzhugh's *Robert Burns, his Associates and Contemporaries* (Chapel Hill, N.C., 1943).

THIRD HERON BALLAD:

John Bushby's Lamentation

Tune: Babes o' the Wood

First printed in 1834 in Hogg and Motherwell, then Cunningham.

'Twas in the seventeen hunder year	hundred
O' Christ and ninety-five,	
That year I was the waest man	saddest
Of ony man alive. —	any

 5 On March, the three and twentieth morn,
        The sun raise clear and bright,   rose
     But Oh, I was a waefu' man   woeful
        Ere toofa' o' the night. —   nightfall

     Earl Galloway lang did rule this land   long
10   With *equal* right and fame,
     Fast knit in *chaste* and *haly* bands   holy
        With Broughton's noble name. —¹

     Earl Galloway's man o' men was I,
        And chief o' Broughton's host:
15   So twa blind beggars on a string,   two
        The faithfu' tyke will trust. —   dog

     But now Earl Galloway's sceptre's broke,
        And Broughton's wi' the slain;   with
     And I my ancient craft may try,
20   Sen honestie is gane. —   since, gone

     'Twas on the bonie banks o' Dee,
        Beside Kirkcudbright's towers,
     The Stewart and the Murray there
        Did muster a' their powers. —

25   The Murray on the auld grey yad,   old mare
        Wi' *wingèd spurs*, did ride;²
     That auld grey yad, a' Nidsdale rade,   old mare all, rode
        He lifted by Nidside.   alighted

     [An' there had na been the Earl himsel,   not
30   O there had been nae play;   no
     But Garlies was to London gane,³
        And sae the kye might stray. —]   so, cattle

     And there was Balmaghie, I ween,⁴   pledge
        I' th' front rank he wad shine;   would
35   But Balmaghie had better been
        Drinkin Madeira wine. —

---

1 The Earl's daughter, Lady Euphemia Stewart, wed Murray of Brought-
on's son Alexander.
2 An allusion to the winged spur crest of the Johnstone family, given that
Murray had eloped with a lady of that family.
3 George Stewart, Lord Garlies.
4 The Tory candidate.

And frae Glenkens cam to our aid[5]   from
    A Chief o' doughty deed:
In case that WORTH should wanted be,
40   O' Kenmure we had need. —

And by our banners march'd Muirhead,
    And Buittle was na slack,[6]   not
Whase haly Priest-hoods nane could stain,   whose holy, none
    For wha can dye the BLACK. —   who

45 And there, sae grave, Squire Cardoness,[7]   so
    Look'd on till a' was done:
Sae, in the tower o' Cardoness   so
    A howlet sits at noon. —   owl

And there led I the Bushby clan;
50   My *gamesome* billie WILL,[8]   friend
And my son Maitland, *wise* as *brave*,[9]
    My footsteps follow'd still. —

The DOUGLAS and the HERON'S name
    We set nought to their score:
55 The DOUGLAS and the HERON'S name
    Had felt our might before. —[10]

But DOUGLASSES o' weight had we,[11]
    The pair o' lusty lairds,
For building cot-houses sae fam'd,   so
60   And christening kail-yards. —   kitchen-gardens

And there Redcastle drew the sword[12]
    That ne'er was stain'd wi' gore;
Save on a wand'rer, lame and blind,
65   To drive him frae his door. —   from

5 Gordon of Kenmure Castle. Burns visited the Gordons during his first Galloway tour in 1793.
6 Rev. James Muirhead, of Urr, near Castle Douglas, and Rev. George Maxwell, of Buittle.
7 David Maxwell of Cardoness.
8 William Bushby, John's brother.
9 James Maitland, Earl of Lauderdale, was a Whig and friend of Burns.
10 This is a potent allusion to the failure of the Douglas and Heron Bank in 1773, placing the blame firmly at the door of the Galloway Tory families, particularly the Bushby clan.
11 Sir William Douglas and Sir James Douglas.
12 Walter Sloan Lawrie.

And last cam creepin Collieston,[13]   came
    Was mair in fear than wrath: more
Ae KNAVE was constant in his mind —   one
    To keep that KNAVE frae scathe. —   from harm

In this, the third Heron Ballad, Burns places the lament in the mouth of John Bushby, one of the leading supporters of the Tory candidate Thomas Gordon of Balmagie. Bushby was the former manager of the Dumfries branch of the defunct Douglas, Heron and Co. Bank. In the middle of this piece, Burns places the blame for the fall of the bank on the Bushby family and by implication, their family connections among Galloway's powerful aristocracy. He was Sheriff Clerk to the county of Dumfries when Burns knew him. We have included ll. 29–32, given in brackets above, missed by Kinsley but printed by Mackay. It was probably circulated as a broadside, like the other ballads.

FOURTH HERON BALLAD:

Buy Braw Troggin:
An Excellent New Song
Tune: Buy Broom Besoms
First printed as an anonymous broadside, 1796.

Wha will buy my Troggin,   who, misc. items sold by vagrants
    Fine ELECTION WARE;
Broken trade o' BROUGHTON,[1]
    A' in high repair.   all

Chorus
5   Buy braw Troggin,   fine
    Frae the banks o' DEE!   from
Wha want Troggin,   who
    Let them come to me.

Here's a noble Earl's
10   Fame and high renown,
For an auld sang —   old song
    It's thought the Gudes were stown.[2]   goods, stolen
      Buy braw Troggin &c.

13 William Copeland of Collieston.
1 James Murray of Broughton.
2 Earl of Galloway. An allusion to the loss of the Scottish parliament in 1707.

Here's the Worth o' BROUGHTON,
   In a *needle's e'e*:   eye
15 Here's a reputation
   Tint by BALMAGHIE.[3]   lost
      Buy braw Troggin &c.

Here's an HONEST CONSCIENCE,
   Might a Prince adorn,
Frae the *Downs o' Tinwald*,   from
20 — So was never worn.
      Buy braw Troggin &c.

Here's its Stuff and Lynin,
   Cardoness's Head;[4]
Fine for a Soger,   soldier
   A' the wale o' lead.   boast/choice
      Buy braw Troggin &c.

25 Here's a little Wadset —   mortgage
   Buittle's scrap o' TRUTH,[5]
Pawn'd in a gin-shop,
   Quenching haly drouth.   holy thirst
      Buy braw Troggin &c.

Here's Armorial Bearings,
30   Frae the Manse o' Urr: from
The crest, an auld *crab-apple*, old
   Rotten at the core.[6]
      Buy braw Troggin &c.

Here is Satan's Picture,
   Like a bizzard-gled,   buzzard kite
35 Pouncing *poor Redcastle*,[7]
   Sprawlin like a tade.   toad
      Buy braw Troggin &c.

---

3 The Tory candidate, Gordon of Balmaghie.
4 David Maxwell of Cardoness.
5 Rev. George Maxwell of Buittle.
6 Rev. James Muirhead of Urr, near Castle Douglas.
7 Walter Sloan Lawrie of Redcastle.

Here's the Font where *Douglas*
    Stane and mortar names;   stone
Lately used at *Caily*,[8]
40   Christening *Murray's* crimes.
        Buy braw Troggin &c.

Here's the Worth and Wisdom
    Collieston can boast;[9]
By a *thievish Midge*
    They had been nearly lost.
        Buy braw Troggin &c.

45 Here is *Murray's* Fragments
    O' the Ten Commands;
Gifted by BLACK JOCK[10]
    — To get them aff his hands.   off
        Buy braw Troggin &c.

Saw ye e'er sic Troggin?   such
50   If to buy ye're slack,   slow
HORNIE'S turnin Chapman,   the Devil
    He'll buy a' the *Pack*!   all
        Buy braw Troggin &c.

Buy braw Troggin,   fine
    Frae the banks o' DEE!   from
55 Wha want Troggin,   who
    Let them come to me.

For introduction, see notes to the first and second Heron ballads. During the 1796 election Patrick Heron's opponent was the son of the Earl of Galloway, Montgomery Stewart. This propaganda song was composed sometime in May or early June, 1796. One of Burns's last radical works, it is further evidence of his anonymous, underground support for the Opposition cause until his death. It displays remarkable brevity without losing its pointed satirical effect, employing the image of a trogger to reduce the Tory candidate to that of a travelling packman, or hawker, peddling election promises like worthless goods. One of its many satirical barbs alludes to the Earl

8 Cally House at Gatehouse of Fleet. This is an allusion to plunders of war.
9 William Copeland of Collieston.
10 John Bushby.

of Galloway's role (l. 12) in selling out the Scottish parliament in 1707, while the Laird of Cardoness, David Maxwell is the straw man of the Tory show. The Rev George Maxwell, of Buittle (l. 26) is castigated as a gin addict and the Rev. James Muirhead (l. 30) of Urr, near Castle Douglas, a sour faced crab-apple. These palpable hits were, probably developed from gossip circulating among radicals within Galloway. It was probably with an eye to the Heron Ballads that Burns told Maria Riddell in June 1796, '. . . if I must write, let it be Sedition, or Blasphemy' (Letter 697). A broadsheet was printed in 1796, probably by Burns himself. A copy of the broadsheet was sold in 1939 and now exists in the Spoor Library, Lot 107. It is further proof of his radical involvement on behalf of the Whig Opposition. This Heron Ballad was first included in the canon by Cunningham, 1834.

A Man's a Man for a' That
Published anonymously in *The Glasgow Magazine*, August, 1795.

Tune: – For a' That, and a' That.

	Is there, for honest Poverty	
	That hings his head, an' a' that;	hangs
	The coward-slave, we pass him by,	
	We dare be poor for a' that!	
5	For a' that, an' a' that,	
	Our toils obscure, an' a' that,	
	The rank is but the guinea's stamp,	
	The Man 's the gowd for a' that.	gold

	What though on hamely fare we dine,	homely foods
10	Wear hoddin grey, an' a' that?	coarse woollen cloth
	Gie fools their silks, and knaves their wine,	give
	A Man's a Man for a' that.	
	For a' that, an' a' that,	
	Their tinsel show, an' a' that;	
15	The honest man, tho' e'er sae poor,	so
	Is king o' men for a' that.	

	Ye see yon birkie ca'd a lord,	fellow called
	Wha struts, an' stares, an' a' that,	
	Tho' hundreds worship at his word,	
20	He's but a coof for a' that.	fool/lout
	For a' that, an' a' that,	

His ribband, star, an' a' that,
The man o' independent mind,
He looks an' laughs at a' that.

25   A Prince can mak a belted knight,
A marquis, duke, an' a' that!
But an honest man's aboon his might —   *above*
Guid faith, he mauna fa' that!   *good, must not be like*
For a' that, an' a' that,
30   Their dignities, an' a' that,
The pith o' Sense an' pride o' Worth
Are higher rank than a' that.

Then let us pray that come it may,
As come it will for a' that,
35   That Sense and Worth o'er a' the earth
Shall bear the gree an' a' that.   *win the day*
For a' that, an' a' that,
It's comin yet for a' that,
That Man to Man the warld o'er   *world*
40   Shall brithers be for a' that.   *brothers*

The first version of *A Man's a Man*, printed anonymously during
the poet's life, differs textually from the final version given above.
Rather than containing five, it has only four stanzas, beginning with
what became the second:

What tho' on hamely fare we dine,
Wear hodden grey, and a' that:
Gie fools their silk, and knaves their wine,
A man's a man for a' that.
For a' that, and a' that,
Their tinsel shew, and a' that;
An honest man, tho' ne'er sae poor,
Is Chief o' men for a' that.

It was this early version, printed in the *Glasgow Magazine*, August
1795 that was copied by the radical Belfast-based *The Northern
Star*, 19th–22nd October, 1795. A more sinister publication oc-
curred just prior to the poet's death, when the first Glasgow
version re-appeared in the pro-government London *Oracle*, 2nd
June 1796, but this time, disturbingly, with Burns's name as
author. Professor Werkmeister remarks on this: 'Considering the
character of the poem, one doubts even so that Burns had author-

ized it over his signature. The poem was copied by *The Star* on
June 3.' (*Robert Burns and the London Daily Press, Modern Philol-
ogy* 1966, p. 329). There can be little doubt that the governmental
spy network would have taken notice of the song and judged it as
seditious. While there is no mention that the song was published
under his name in surviving letters, it is certain to have caused
some considerable anxiety for Burns, given his Excise post. That
his employers took no action against him, or enquired formally into
the matter, is perplexing. With hindsight, it may be that the poet's
illness was well known to his Excise superiors and the Commis-
sioners in Edinburgh that they chose not to take action against him.
Either way, Burns not only feared imprisonment, being pursued
for the debt owed for his Dumfries Volunteers uniform, but must
have known about this named publication which could have had
him arrested at any moment from 2nd June, 1796 onward and
charged with sedition.

Another, hitherto undocumented version was printed in 1798 by
Professor Peter Urbani, Edinburgh. It too begins with what became
the second stanza. Its second stanza is the one Burns eventually
reworked to become the final version's first stanza:

> Wha wad for honest poverty,
> Hang down their heads an' a' that?
> The coward slave we pass him by
> And dare be poor for a' that.
>> For a' that and a' that,
>> Their purse-proud looks and a' that,
>> In ragged coats ye'll often find
>> The noblest hearts for a' that.

Kinsley mentions a 1793 songbook edited by Peter Urbani, but not
the more important 1798 publication containing version two of *A
Man's A Man*. Henley and Henderson are dismissive of variant lines
in another version they found, published by Brash and Reid (1801)
in Glasgow which is similar to the 1798 text, mentioning 'purse-
proud looks'. They refer to the 'absurd version of this half stanza,
apparently the invention of the ingenious Reid' (Vol. 3, p. 490)
unaware that it occurs in the 1798 Urbani version and they display
their ignorance of Burns's letters, where the phrase 'purse-proud'
occurs several times. Their commentary is mixed with obvious
political loathing and they appear unaware that the song had been
re-drafted several times by Burns. The second version has five
stanzas, not the four of the first edition.

Henley and Henderson were not perceptive enough to see the genesis of the final lyric, from the original publication, through Urbani's 1798 text to the intermediate Brash and Reid text, printed at Glasgow, *circa* 1801. The Brash and Reid print contains many of the peculair typographic stresses employed by Burns, evident among his manuscripts and it is the first publication to have the famous first verse in place as it is now known, although the text is rather more Scottish than the final version:

Wha wad for honest poverty,
    Hing down his head an' a' that?
The coward slave we pass him by
    And dare be poor for a' that.

For a' that, and a' that,
    Our toils obscure, and a' that,
The RANK is but the GUINEA stamp,
    The MAN's the GOWD for a' that.

In self-deprecatory mood Burns described the lyric to George Thomson as '. . . no Song; but will be allowed, I think, to be two or three pretty good *prose* thoughts, inverted into rhyme' (Letter 651). He did not hide his authorship to Thomson, but probably trusted the song collector implicitly not to pass copies around. When Thomson eventually printed the song in 1805, it had been in Currie's 1800 edition and was well known as a work of Burns, having surfaced in *The Morning Chronicle*, in late 1796 with the poet's name ascribed. Even then, Thomson felt compelled to make a few of his own meddling changes to the text. The many variant texts are ample proof that Burns considered this one of his best songs and the final draft was the result of considerable textual re-appraisal.

For Daiches, the merits of this song, dedicated to the worthiness of 'honest poverty' and democratic rights, is apparent:

It is a rhetorical poem, testifying to the effect on Burns of the French revolution and its ideological currents, and it owes its popularity to its effectiveness as a series of slogans . . . it represents a legitimate and in its way impressive use of the poetic medium . . . The poem has a well contrived structure, moving from the generalization about 'honest poverty' through specific illustrations of the difference between virtue and social rank to a final climactic generalization which is at once a prayer and a prophecy (pp. 302–3).

Crawford rightly refers to the 'revolutionary yearning for fraternity that underlies' the song, with its theme, 'a spontaneous and passionate democratic humanism'. Crawford quotes the introduction to Marshak's *Robert Burns in Translation*, Moscow, 1957: 'He was able to describe the finest and most truly human feelings and experiences of the simple people . . . not as a critic, but as a brother and friend' (Crawford, p. 337). Interestingly, Crawford shows specific influences on the song from Thomas Paine's *The Rights of Man* (Crawford, p. 365).

Due to the different texts of this marching revolutionary anthem it is certain that Burns produced the first text probably very late in 1794 and considering that the anonymous publication in August 1795 is of the first draft, he must have worked on the piece well into 1795 and possibly touched it up again early in 1796. Hence, the final draft would have been improved well *after* the composition of *The Dumfries Volunteers*.

A Prose Essay by Burns
To the Editor of The Morning Chronicle.
Printed 1st January, 1795.

It is a melancholy reflection, that in an age when the theory of Government and legislation has been so well developed by a long succession of celebrated writers, mankind still struggle with the imperfections experienced in more unenlightened days.

The People of France in endeavouring to unshackle themselves from the oppression of their Government, and trusting to the theories of philosophers, have fallen a prey to an oligarchy, who hold unbalanced every branch of government; this they have undergone, although theory has often said that the same persons must not be Legislators and Judges, and the dread occasioned by the misfortunes of that country, induced the people of this to fall into the opposite extreme – the adoration of Regal Power.

The Alarmists have cried down all Reform in Parliament as dangerous, and Parliament has given into the hand of the Crown our dearest rights. Nothing now remains, but to renew that act of Henry VIII by which the King's Proclamation may have the force of an Act of Parliament; for as the majority of our House of Commons is not elected by a majority of the People, nor by a majority of those, who, under the present system have a right to vote, we have no security for its speaking the sense of the People; and, like the Romans in the days of Augustus Caesar, are insulted, with the forms of a free Government, while, in some of the most important parts, the substance is lost.

To tell us that Reform is dangerous, is to say, my children, be good and don't complain, you will have all you desire granted you at a more convenient time. Will anyone who knows the history of mankind assert, that any liberty or privilege we shall have lost, will be ever spontaneously restored, even by the wisest and best of Kings? During the prosperous reigns of Nerva, Trajan, and the Antonines, the Roman world was governed with wisdom and equity; but those Emperors, although they knew the miseries which the People had suffered under their predecessors, never put one bar on the omnipotence of their own authority; and the succession of Commodus shews, that though a good Prince need not be shackled, those shackles ought to exist, as no Sovereign, let him be ever so good and just, can become immortal but in the page of history.

It therefore is proper, that every man who has a love for his King and country, should wish to see the Government brought back to the spirit of its institution: because every free man should hold his privileges dear; and because, when he sees ministers endeavouring, under insidious pretexts, to increase the power of the Crown at the expense of those privileges, he should forsee the most terrible consequences; for either the Government must become absolutely despotic, or the bulk of mankind, not properly sensible of the fine texture, and intrinsic value of our Constitution, may one day join in a general cry against Kings, and overturn the regal part of the Government.

The present time seems to be the crisis which is to determine whether England is to remain a free country or not. At this moment you and I are subject to be seized and confined without having a right to demand a trial; for when a Minister can send his *marechausée*[1] into your house, and take you in silence to a dungeon, what security can you have against a transportation to some distant region? This has not been the case as yet, but what does the annihilation of your dearest privileges tend to but this; will not our children, perhaps, be subject to such an iron sceptre?

---

1 French for *mounted policeman*. Burns knew French well and might have heard this phrase from Dr William Maxwell who spoke fluent French, or Maria Riddell.

This prospect of our future condition, whether we be over-whelmed by tyranny, or become the victims of anarchy, is alarming to men who value, and who understand the British Constitution. Ministers continually warn us to dread innovations, while we daily see the encroachments made on the free part of the Government, which, although they have not yet been called by that name, are not to be stopped by having the word innovation retaliated on them. I will briefly declare what reflection I have made on the subject of our Government, and if I am guilty of errors, shall hope to stand corrected through the medium of your paper.

The spirit of the British Constitution seems to consist in this: That the House of Commons are the deputies of the separate districts of this island, who meet to deliberate for the common good; while the House of Peers, forming the Aristocratical part of the Constitution, may be a check on the Tribune of the People, and, at the same time, constitute the highest Court of Judicature; from the Crown, we are insured in the quick execution of our laws, and we blend with the advantages of a Republic, all those of a Monarchy. But when the servants of the Crown are at the same time permitted to be Tribunes of the People; when the vassals of Nobles enjoy the same pre-eminence, on what do the bulk of this nation rest the bulwark of their liberty? The same parliament that has continued the suspension of the Habeus Corpus may establish a Committee of the House of Commons to take cognizance of cases of High Treason; the Tribunal of the Star Chamber may be renewed; and should that be the case, how are we to help ourselves, when so great a military force exists in these kingdoms.

Our present situation is critical: we are involved in a war without properly knowing why! Do we propose ourselves to re-establish the regal authority in France? That were a vain hope, all our Allies have nearly abandoned us. Do we wish to defend Holland? The Dutch are better disposed towards France than towards us. What object do we propose by the war? the Minister acquires great patronage, and he is thus enabled to keep his place, at the public expense, and by the lives of his fellow-subjects. How many have already been the victims of his ambition; and he tranquilly holds his place, though he knows that his countrymen daily bleed to keep him there? This might, one would think, better become a Rober-spierre; but before we feel abhorrence at the cruelty of the Con-vention, let us ask ourselves, Whether those who vote for the continuance of the war be not as unfeeling? What signifies it to the sufferers, whether they fall by the guillotine of Roberspierre, or by the massacres which the Great Catherine and the King of Prussia have committed for the sake of good order, Religion, &c. Will Poland feel any better effects from those, than France from the former? Does not the same hold good with regard to the subjects we daily lose on the Continent?

The true medium between anarchy and tyranny ought to be strictly kept in view, for extremities touch; and therefore, so far from its being dangerous to reform our Parliament, we ought to rouse from the present infatuation, and before it is too late, before every trace of our Constitution be effaced, bring it back to those principles on which it is established: that is, make the theory and practice tally better together.

A. Briton

Burns promised to send radical material to the London Whig newspaper *The Morning Chronicle* in a letter of mid-March 1794. Replying to an offer of full-time work on the literary staff of this, the main Whig Opposition newspaper, conveyed to him on behalf of James Perry, the editor, by Captain Patrick Miller Jnr., Burns promised to supply not only occasional poetry, but:

> . . . little Prose Essays, which I propose sending into the world through the medium of some Newspaper; & should these be worth his while, to these Mr. Perry shall be welcome; & all my reward shall be, his treating me with his Paper, which, by the bye, to any body who has the least relish for Wit, is a high treat indeed (Letter 620B).

A thorough search of *The Morning Chronicle* archives, looking specifically at anonymous and pseudonymous prose, has revealed this essay as being in all probability the result of his promise.

The essay appears in *The Morning Chronicle*, 1st January, 1795, printed over the pen-name 'A. Briton', a signature we know Burns exclusively employed in 1788 (See notes for *Lines on Ambition*). There are, also, contextual pointers which suggest this is his composition.

Wishing not to miss any issues of the paper, Burns, revealingly, wrote to the newspaper sometime in January 1795, to complain that specific copies of the newspaper had not been sent to him. The January 1795 letter begins:

> You will see by your subscribers' list, that I have now been about nine months one of that number. – I am sorry to inform

you, that in that time, seven or eight of your Papers either have
never been sent me, or else have never reached me. – To be
deprived of any one Number of the first Newspaper in Britain,
for information, ability & independence, is what I can ill brook
and bear; but to be deprived of that most admirable oration of
the Marquis of Landsdowne, when he made the great, though
ineffectual attempt, (in the language of the Poet, I fear too true)
'to save a SINKING STATE' – this was a loss, which I neither
can, nor will forgive you. That paper, Gentlemen, never
reached me; but I demand it of you. – I am a BRITON;
and must be interested in the cause of LIBERTY: I am a
MAN and the RIGHTS OF HUMAN NATURE cannot be
indifferent to me. . . . that humble domicile in which I shelter
my wife and children, is the CASTELLUM of a BRITON . . .
(Letter 654).

It was roughly nine months since Burns requested a free subscrip-
tion, in exchange for poetry or prose. Letter 620B is dated approxi-
mately for mid-March 1794 and Letter 654 is dated roughly for
January 1795. So, if Burns had kept his side of the bargain, it
appears he was disappointed to have missed several issues of the
newspaper. Yet, the letter is far more than merely a reader's request
for missed issues. Burns almost scolds the editor, demanding that he
receive a back copy of the newspaper. He does not tell the editor
which issue he wants, that is, the date or dates of the daily news-
paper(s) he missed. What jumps out of the page is the fact that Burns
tells the Editor quite categorically that he is 'a BRITON', a
description that occurs twice for emphasis and is spelt out in large,
bold letters. 'A. Briton' is, of course, the signature employed under
the new essay.

The newspaper demanded by Burns is one containing a speech by
the Marquis of Landsdowne. Landsdowne, a Whig, spoke in the
House of Lords on 30th December, 1794. The debate is covered on
31st December, 1794 and 1st January, 1795 in *The Morning Chronicle*.
The debate in the House of Lords and the House of Commons
centred on the King's speech. William Wilberforce added an
amendment to the debate, moving a motion to negotiate peace with
the French. The Marquis's speech is elaborate, powerful and anti-
war; it dwells on the increased losses of British troops on the
Continent and the fact that the allies arraigned against France were
in disarray. The final note on the debate refers to 'the abstract of the
operations of the French Armies, read by the Marquis of Lands-
downe'. Biographical studies have missed the fact that Burns

praised and aligned himself with the Marquis's passionate anti-war, anti-Pitt speech. Moreover, the political views outlined by Lands-downe are found in a more developed, elaborate and lucid essay under the psedonymn 'A. Briton' *in the same newspaper*. So, in Letter 654 Burns, declaring himself loudly to be 'a BRITON' demanded a copy of the newspaper in which the actual 'A. Briton' essay appeared, 1st January, 1795.

When Letter 654 appeared in Cromek in 1808, it was supposedly left unsigned. Finding the fair copy of the letter Cromek guessed it was not sent by Burns to London, neglecting the fact that Burns often made copies of his letters. Indeed, Cromek further estimated that the letter must have been written on behalf of a Dumfries friend, unaware that the poet had joined the free subsciption list nine months previous. There is no reason to doubt the recorded letter is both *by* Burns and *from* Burns. The original was probably forwarded to the London newspaper. It remains unknown if the issue for 1st January, 1795 was sent to Burns. Contextual evidence, therefore, before examining textually the new prose essay, suggests that Burns is probably the author.

A textual examination of the new prose essay finds many echoes in the letter Burns wrote in April 1793, to Erskine of Mar:

> Does any man tell me, that my feeble efforts can be of no service; & that it does not belong to my humble station to meddle with the concerns of a PEOPLE? – I tell him, that it is on such individuals as I, that for the hand of support and the eye of intelligence, a Nation has to rest . . . the titled, tinsel Courtly throng may be its feathered ornament, but the number of those who are elevated enough in life, to reason & reflect; yet low enough to keep clear of the venal contagion of a Court; these are a Nation's strength (Letter 558).

He goes on to pinpoint flaws in the British body politic:

> I would say that there existed a system of corruption between the Executive Power & the Representative part of the Legis-lature, which boded no good for our glorious Constitution; & which every patriotic Briton must wish to see amended (Letter 558).

The phrase 'every patriotic Briton' might be expected from an author who had already signed his name 'A. Briton', but such a description is also central to the radical legacy inherited by Burns

from Addison and other writers of the Commonwealth school. That
such were still his views in the Spring of 1793 is important in
considering the sentiments and the pen-name of the new 1795 essay.
To Erskine, Burns went on in a vein similar to the new prose:

> I have three sons, whom, I see already, have brought with them
> into the world souls ill qualified to inhabit the bodies of Slaves
> . . . the little independent Britons in whose veins runs my own
> blood? (Letter 558).

Here, even the poet's sons are 'independent *Britons*'. Burns's fear is
that if political oppression steadily increases or conversely, liberties
are further eroded, his children might eventually suffer. The new
essay comments on this topic 'will not our children, perhaps, be
subject to such an iron sceptre?' An early manuscript of *Scots Wha
Hae* expresses this very sentiment 'Do you hear your children cry |
Were we born in chains to lie?' The letter to Erskine thus displays
the poet's determination not to be silenced by his employers and
asserts his right to be independent in his views.

Further textual similarities occur. Having described the calcu-
lated manoeuvring of Pitt and his colleagues as '*invidious* powerful
individuals . . . *under insidious pretexts* to subvert' [our italics]
political opponents, in a letter of February 1789, signed John
Barleycorn (Letter 311), we find this same language blaming 'min-
isters endeavouring, *under insidious pretexts* [our italics], to increase
the power of the Crown' in the new prose. Also in setting out his
case in the first newspaper letter he signed 'A. Briton', Burns is
didactic and succinct, 'The simple state of the case, Mr. Printer,
seems to me to be this' (Letter 283) which is very like the language of
the new letter which reads 'The spirit of the British Constitution
seems to consist in this: That the House of Commons are . . .'.
While there were obviously various conventions expected in writing
a letter to the press during this period, it is quite evident that his
piece does contain many of the stylistic mannerisms and nuances of
Burns's prose.

The essay's concluding argument contrasts anarchy and tyranny,
'The true medium between anarchy and tyranny ought to be strictly
kept in view'. This is precisely the view expressed emphatically in
italics by Burns in his 1793 newspaper published poem, *On The
Commemoration Of Rodney's Victory*, '*Be Anarchy curs'd — and be
Tyranny d[amn]'d*'. A further similarity exists with the same poem,
where it is argued that reform is necessary before 'our Constitution
be effaced, bring it back to those principles on which it is estab-

lished: that is, make the theory and practice tally better together'. The poem records 'And here's the grand fabric, OUR FREE CONSTITUTION / As built on the base of THE GREAT REVOLUTION!' In both examples it is 'our constitution', not simply 'the consititution'. The poet's handwritten note within John Syme's copy of Jean Louis De Lolme's book on the British Consitution, indicating sarcastically that it would suffice until a better was created, is resonant in this last remark. That Burns was deeply read in Constitutional matters, as was Robert Riddell, his closest aristocratic friend during the Dumfries years, and acutely aware of political developments at this time, only makes it more plausible that he would compose such an essay.

It is now known after the appearance of *Ode for General Washington's Birthday*, that Burns wrote, in controlled rage, of England as a country in the grip of political tyranny. Most radical commentators saw the suspension of Habeas Corpus as a significant shift towards futher erosion of individual rights. The possibility seemed real that unaccountable and dictatorial rule by a 'Star Chamber' was to be the next step in Pitt's campaign of terror to crush radical dissent. The current essay asks the question whether or not England can remain a free country, answering in the negative, similar to the manner in which *The Tree of Liberty* deals with the same topic:

> But seek the forest round and round,
>> And soon 'twill be agreed, man,
> That sic a tree can not be found
>> 'Twixt London and the Tweed, man.

Between London and the river Tweed, is of course, England, not Britain. Burns does not condemn the political violence that occurred in revolutionary France in his song, nor is it condemned in the essay. Indeed, the massacres by Catherine the Great and the King of Prussia, in the name of law and order, are mentioned as greater crimes. What is seen as an equal crime to anything perpetuated by the French is the act of those British politicians who voted for the continuation of the war. They are blamed as being as unfeeling as a Roberspierre. Moreover, it would be expected that Burns would hit at Pitt's receipt of further patronage due to the war (See *A New Song, or A Wet Day at Walmer Castle*) and his increase in despotic powers, not only over the nation's purse by additional taxation, but, driven by ambition, the deeper urge to be remembered in the pages of history. (This of course, is the theme of *Lines on Ambition*, also signed 'A. Briton' and already ascribed to Burns in this edition.) If

The Tree of Liberty was written during early January 1795, its reformist sentiments – its concluding prayer that 'Auld England' may eventually plant the 'far-famed tree' of liberty, meaning reform, is consistent with the new political essay.

General acceptance of the new prose work is of essential importance to Burnsian studies. If, as we believe it to be Burns's last public commentary on wider British politics and the European scene, it not only maps out precisely what he thought of the Pitt government, and its involvement against France, but it answers emphatically the nineteenth- and twentieth-century notion that Burns was confused on political matters. Indeed, it not only reveals his passionate democratic reformism, his intellectual involvement with current affairs, his depth of knowledge in political theory and historical allusion, in particular Roman history, but a sharp ability to argue a case cogently, and logically, with a poet's eye to penetrate acidly that somewhat intangible, hidden aspect of a nation's history, the motive and ambition of its leading politicians. One can, from the vantage point of the twenty-first century, begin to see that in an unjust, socially and economically rigid hierarchical society, dominated by an oligarchy of aristocratical privilege, a critical thinking, democratic national poet, unable to accept his inferior social position, unable to keep 'silent and obedient', was, in a sense, the ruling élite's worst nightmare.

Without manuscript authority, the provenance of the new prose cannot be proven beyond doubt, but the evidence, contextual and textual, convincingly says Burns. That he would deliver on a promise should be no surprise. If correct, we finally have his last, emphatic political statement proving beyond doubt he was a committed democratic reformer.

The Cob Web – A Song

First printed in *The Morning Chronicle*, 22nd August, 1795.

The sweets of a blessing
Are had by possessing,
Hail! Britons! the cause is your own;
You are wonderful great,
5   You have Princes and State,
And the wisest and best on a Throne!

What a contrast is France,
Where is now the gay dance,
They are no way so happy as we;
10   We have flourishing Trade,
Plenty, beer, meat, and bread!
While madly they starve to be free!

It was once so for us,
Indeed it was thus,
15 Like them we once swore to maintain,
The blessing that God,
Sent to cheer man's abode,
And preserve free from blemish or stain.

Thus, they might suppose,
20   To be led by the nose,
Was not for a People, like them;
That we being free,
Should with freemen agree,
Nor those who sought freedom condemn.

25 But there they was wrong,
We have alter'd our song,
Resolv'd to have nothing to do —
With a good, full of evil,
Devis'd by the Devil,
30 That freedom for which the French rue.

Yet, lest it be thought,
We lov'd self to a fault,
We offer'd Court blessings to treat them;
Ah! could you expect
35   This they would reject,
And force us, unwilling, to beat them.

First a King, good as may be,
We made of a Baby,
Then demanded they'd fawn on the Child!
40 But, so wicked were they,
That they would not obey,
But beat us! for being so wild.

We brib'd to divide them,
Tried all arts to chide 'em,
45   To starve them, made a great fuss;
When, some Demon of Hell,
Inverting the spell,
Turn'd the picture of Famine on us!

So great is the blessing
50   We got by redressing
Each nation's faults but our own;
To destroy them, their Trade,
We, their country invade,
While our own is cut up to the bone.

55   But courage my Friends
We may yet gain our ends,
Perhaps in a circle they'll meet:
When, nine out of ten
They've kill'd of our men,
60   And the rest are left something to eat.

A. Briton

As an introduction to this song, the political prose essay signed 'A. Briton' is printed first, in chronological order. Both appear in *The Morning Chronicle* during 1795, and are signed under the same name. While it may not automatically follow that one author wrote both, evidence suggests that this is highly probable. The prose by 'A. Briton' employs the ironic description 'the wisest and best of Kings', while the song, written several months later, contains the lexically similar, ironic 'And the wisest and best on a Throne!' If, as already argued, Burns is the author of the prose, then, there is a strong case to argue that the song, too, is his.

This work was provisionally ascribed to Burns in Hogg's *The Lost Poems* (1997). There are several factors which suggest it may be from Burns. He, as we have seen, promised to send radical work to *The Morning Chronicle* (Letter 620B). For discussion of this crucial pen-name, see notes to *Lines on Ambition*. As also mentioned in the case for the new radical essay, Burns wrote to *The Morning Chronicle* in January 1795 and emphasised that he was 'a Briton' (Letter 654).

The song is almost certainly by a Scot, given the rhyme of 'trade' and 'bread' (ll. 10–11) where the latter is pronounced *braid*. More important, the song contains a peculiar, deliberate ungrammatical use of 'was' (rather than *were*) for colloquial effect, 'But there they was wrong' (l. 25). After an exhaustive check of period poetry scanning the eighteenth-century Poetry Database, and printed works, only one poet appears out of the crowd who employed this language quirk, Burns. His non-grammatical 'was' is found, inter alia, in *John Barleycorn*, 'There was three Kings unto the east'.

Textually, the song begins with ironic assent, setting up the target of attack by appearing to praise everything British, in contrast to the apparently monstrous French. In reality, the poem is a brilliantly ironic attack on the anti-French war policy of William Pitt. The notion that Britain has 'the wisest and best' on a 'throne' is absurd, given the madness of King George III and the public knowledge that Pitt and Dundas were behind almost every Royal Proclamation printed in the daily newspaper during the 1790s. In truth, King George remained a background puppet, in the shadow of Pitt's increasingly overt abuse of power.

The theme of the song is of Britons being caught in Pitt's political 'cob-web' of ambition and deceit. Burns's favourite contemporary radical song at this period, which he copied out in his own hand and quoted to Mrs Dunlop in January 1795, *The Vine Cover'd Hills and Gay Regions of France*, by William Roscoe, refers to the British people 'caught in his [Pitt's] cob-web like flies'. This song, the Burns-copied manuscript of which was presented to Roscoe by Maria Riddell after Burns's death, is probably the progenitor of the new song's title. Britain was being brought to its knees. Hunger and at times, famine, occurred in parts of England and Scotland, as reported in the press during the winter of 1794–5. Ll. 47–52 allude to this, suggesting that the Pitt government's early plan of starving the French into submission had backfired and was having such an effect at home. This point, far from being poetic fantasy, is eloquently put by the great Glasgow radical, Professor John Millar, a year later in *The Scots Chronicle*, September 2nd, 1796:

> We thought of no less than uniting all the states of Europe, whether great or small, against the French Republic; and we expected to employ successfully the two great engines of *force* and *famine* for affecting our purposes What a dreadful reverse of fortune we have sustained!

In these years destitution and famine are omnipresent in radical writing, culminating in Coleridge's Macbeth-derived incantational attack on Pitt, *Fire, Famine and Slaughter*.

While we know Burns personally experienced food shortages in the first three months of 1796, when he complained of his family going for days without food, his was not an isolated example. Dumfries witnessed food shortage problems in 1795 when this radical song was composed. David Staig wrote to Robert Dundas, Lord Advocate, on 4th February, 1795 requesting help due to extreme shortages of oatmeal in Dumfriesshire: 'The enclosed memorial was handed to me this morning by our Magistrates . . . under this alarm of scarcity . . . it is impossible for me as Collector of the Customs, to give the wished for relief.' (RH 2/4/ 78/f.25). A pamphlet by Dumfries bakers and grain dealers complains that grain from the area was being shipped out of Scotland and not enough was available to them to make a living or feed the local people (RH 2/4/78/f.27–28). Although there are no newspaper accounts of food riots in Dumfries during early 1795, there did exist a serious food problem, partly caused by exorbitant prices and exportation of grain and oatmeal from the area to London. (RH 2/ 4/79/f.3).

One critic has suggested *The Cob Web* might be the work of Dr Alexander Geddes, a radical Scot living in London. Granted Geddes was a prolific pro-Fox poet but he did not employ this pen-name. The entire canon of Geddes is extant in Chelmsford at the Essex County Record Office and the Scottish Catholic Archive in Edinburgh: both were examined. It is not among his papers. Not one of Geddes's radical works is known ever to have been destroyed. His complete poetic jottings and journals are extant, and they contain many of his favourite works copied out at least twice. Textually, there is no example among his poems where he employed the colloquial, common-language usage of 'was' in place of 'were'. Nor does he display the Burnsian skill of ironic assent to what he is actually attacking so evident here. Given this circumstantial and stylistic evidence, the song is attributed to Burns. Without definitive manuscript evidence, the attribution cannot be made with absolute certainty, but considering the evidence for the new political essay and its lexical similarity with *The Cob Web*, it appears that the same 'A. Briton' composed both prose and song.

Along with the poem's comic, sophisticated dramatic inversion, there are two other elements which strongly suggest Burns. First, as in *Ode on General Washington's Birthday*, the notion of a degenerate England betraying her libertarian heritage in order to destroy France. Second, his capacity for integrating on-going political events into his poetry. What ll. 37–9 refer to is the English support for solving the French crisis by returning the Dauphin to the throne as Child-King. This was mooted in 1791 when he was ten but the intended Louis XVII died on June 8, 1795 just prior to this poem's composition. Implicit in the poem (ll. 13–18) is the promise of freedom sent by God through the true child-king, Jesus Christ, as opposed to the false, worldly child-king. Burns did, indeed, belong to that category of writers defined by Herman Melville as those 'who breathe that unshackled democratic spirit of Christianity in all things'.

John Anderson My Joe

First printed in *The Morning Chronicle*, 5th December, 1795.

John Anderson my Joe, John,
    I wonder what you mean,
Approving of the Bills, John
    The Bills you ne'er had seen!
5 'Twas surely very foolish, John,
    And how could you do so?
Pray haud your tongue and say nae mair,   *hold, no more*
    John Anderson my Joe!

The story of the Phaeton, John,   *high carriage*
10   Was but an auld wife's saw,   *old, tale*
And like another Phaeton, John,
    You'll surely have a fa':   *fall*
This talking will undo you, John,
    And lack of truth much mo' —   *more*
15 You've neither brains nor gift o' Gab;   *conversation*
    John Anderson my Joe!

Hogg, *The Lost Poems*, pp. 189–90, attributed this poem to Burns. Burns had already adapted the traditional *John Anderson, My Jo* in a sexually expurgated, personal version. It is characteristic of him to use a traditional song for political purposes. John Anderson is the Scottish John Bull (see *New Song* or *A Wet Day at Walmer Castle*). Simplistic and sycophantic, he toes the Tory line by paying excessive war taxes and basking in a national glory not his own. The use of 'phaeton' is double-edged, being in Burns's usage, both mythological and contemporary. Ll. 9–12 allude to the fable of the son of Helios (the sun god), who rode his chariot too close to the earth, causing Zeus to strike him with a thunderbolt to prevent his incendiary danger to the planet. The contemporary meaning for 'phaeton', for Burns, as in his *To the Hon. Mr. Wm. R. Maule of Panmure on his High Phaeton*, is this sort of carriage as a sign of social vanity and fiscal iniquity.

By 1795, the vinegar on the sponge for heart-broken radicals was their inability to carry the common people with them in their programme of anti-establishment reform. Hazlitt bitterly summed it up thus.

> There is something in the human mind, which requires an object for it to repose on; and driven from all other sources of pride and pleasure, it falls in love with misery and grows enamoured of oppression. It gazes after the liberty, the happiness, the comfort, the knowledge, which have been torn from it by the unfeeling gripe of wealth and power, as the poor debtor gazes with envy and wonder at the Lord Mayor's show. Thus is the world by degrees reduced to a spital or lazar house, where the people waste away with want and disease, and are thankful if they are only suffered to crawl forgotten to their graves. ('*The Times Newspaper*. On the Connexion between Toad-Eaters and Tyrants', *The Selected Writings of William Hazlitt*, Vol. 4, Political Essays, ed. by Duncan Wu, Pickering & Chatto, 1998, p. 139).

PART SIX

Posthumous Works
Collected 1796 - 2000

O Once I Lov'd a Bonie Lass

Tune: I Am a Man Unmarried
First published in 1803 in S.M.M.

O once I lov'd a bonie lass,
  An' aye I love her still,
An' whilst that virtue warms my breast
  I'll love my handsome Nell.

5 As bonie lasses I hae seen,   have
     And mony full as braw   many, attractive
   But for a modest gracefu' mien
     The like I never saw.

   A bonny lass I will confess,
10   Is pleasant to the e'e,   eye
   But without some better qualities
     She's no a lass for me.   not

   But Nelly's looks are blythe and sweet,
     And, what is best of a',
15 Her reputation is compleat,
     And fair without a flaw;

   She dresses ay sae clean and neat,   always, so
     Both decent and genteel;
   And then there's something in her gait
20   Gars onie dress look weel.   makes, any, well

   A gaudy dress and gentle air
     May slightly touch the heart,
   But it's innocence and modesty
     That polishes the dart.

25 'Tis this in Nelly pleases me,
     'Tis this enchants my soul;
   For absolutely in my breast
     She reigns without controul.

The poet's autobiographical letter to Dr Moore, August 1787, tells
us this song was written sometime in 1774 (Letter 125). It was, in the
poet's own words, an early attempt at the 'sin of Rhyme'. The
heroine is generally believed to be Helen (Nelly) Kirkpatrick, who
worked in the harvest field alongside the young Burns. In the poet's
First Commonplace Book, this song is refered to as, ' . . .the first of
my performances, and done at an early period of life, when my heart
glowed with honest warm simplicity; unacquainted, and uncor-
rupted with the ways of a wicked world. The performance is,
indeed, very puerile and silly; but I am always pleased with it, as
it recalls to my mind those happy days when my heart was yet honest
and my tongue was sincere'.

Tragic Fragment
or A Penitential Thought in the Hour of Remorse – Intended for a Tragedy

First printed in *The Scots Magazine*, November, 1803.

All devil as I am, a damned wretch,
A harden'd, stubborn, unrepenting villain,
Still my heart melts at human wretchedness;
And with sincere tho' unavailing, sighs
5   I view the helpless children of Distress.
With tears indignant I behold th' Oppressor,
Rejoicing in the honest man's destruction,
Whose unsubmitting heart was all his crime.

Even you, ye hapless crew, I pity you;
10   Ye, whom the Seeming good think sin to pity;
Ye poor, despis'd, abandon'd vagabonds,
Whom Vice, as usual, has turn'd o'er to Ruin.
O, but for kind, tho' ill-requited friends,
I had been driven forth like you forlorn,
15   The most detested, worthless wretch among you!

O injur'd God! Thy goodness has endow'd me
With talents passing most of my compeers,
Which I in just proportion have abus'd;
As far surpassing other common villains
20   As Thou in natural parts has given me more.

The poet records that this fragment was written when in his late
teens (circa 1777–8) and formed part of a larger tragedy he had

sketched out, but did not complete. This is one of his earliest statements of his perhaps most compulsive theme of social expulsion and abandonment which was the common fate of mice and men in the 1790s.

One Night as I did Wander

Tune: John Anderson My Jo, John
This first appears in Cromek's *Reliques*, 1808.

One night as I did wander,
   When corn begins to shoot,
I sat me down to ponder
   Upon an auld tree root: old
Auld Aire ran by before me,   the river Ayr
   And bicker'd to the seas;
A cushat crouded o'er me,   pigeon
   That echoed thro' the braes.

This has all the hallmarks of a stanza written to set the scene for a much longer song. It may have formed part of a longer poem, possibly the lost satirical work *The Poet's Rambles by The Banks of Ayr*, which may have fallen victim to Currie's destruction, particularly if the poem denigrated aristocratic families around Ayr.

The Lass of Cessnock Banks

First printed by Cromek, 1808.
Tune: The Butcher Boy

On Cessnock banks a lassie dwells;
   Could I describe her shape and mien;
Our lasses a' she far excels,   all
   An' she has twa sparkling, rogueish een.   two, eyes

5 She's sweeter than the morning dawn
   When rising Phoebus first is seen,   the sun
And dew-drops twinkle o'er the lawn;
   An' she has twa sparkling, rogueish een.

She's stately, like yon youthful ash
10   That grows the cowslip braes between   hill ridges & slopes
And drinks the stream with vigour fresh;
   An' she has twa sparkling, rogueish een.   two, eyes

She's spotless, like the flow'ring thorn
    With flow'rs so white and leaves so green
15 When purest in the dewy morn;
    An' she has twa sparkling, rogueish een.   two, eyes

Her looks are like the vernal May
    When ev'ning Phoebus shines serene,
While birds rejoice on ev'ry spray;
20   An' she has twa sparkling, rogueish een.

Her hair is like the curling mist
    That climbs the mountain sides at e'en,
When flow'r-reviving rains are past;
    An' she has twa sparkling, rogueish een.

25 Her forehead's like the show'ry bow
    When gleaming sun-beams intervene
And gild the distant mountain's brow;
    An' she has twa sparkling, rogueish een.

Her cheeks are like yon crimson gem
30   The pride of all the flowery scene,
Just opening on its thorny stem;
    An' she has twa sparkling, rogueish een.

Her teeth are like the nightly snow
    When pale the morning rises keen
35 While hid the murmuring streamlets flow;
    An' she has twa sparkling, rogueish een.

Her lips are like yon cherries ripe
    Which sunny walls from Boreas screen;
They tempt the taste and charm the sight;
40   An' she has twa sparkling, rogueish een.

Her breath is like the fragrant breeze
    That gently stirs the blossom'd bean,
When Phoebus sinks behind the seas;
    An' she has twa sparkling, rogueish een.

45 Her voice is like the ev'ning thrush
    That sings on Cessnock banks unseen,
While his mate sits nestling in the bush;
    An' she has twa sparkling, rogueish een.

But it's not her air, her form, her face,
50   Though matching beauty's fabled Queen;
'Tis the mind that shines in ev'ry grace;
    An' chiefly in her rogueish een.

An additional stanza in Henley and Henderson (1896) is not normally printed in modern editions. It conveys a more authentic tone than the stanza on the simile of 'her teeth'. Given the natural flow of the song from simile to simile, it is improbable that Burns penned two stanzas on the one topic. Kinsley questions whether stanza 9 is by Burns or the 'importation from some artless popular song' (Vol. III, p. 1012).

[Her teeth are like a flock of sheep
    With fleeces newly washen clean,
That slowly mount the rising steep —
    An' she has twa sparkling, rogueish een!]

The song was originally collected by Cromek from 'the oral communication of a lady residing in Glasgow', believed to be Alison Begbie, who was once a servant girl to a country house, near Cessnock, close to Lochlie farm. That of course, is not a proper source to give the song's provenace. In 1839 the Pickering edition printed a version of this song supposed to be from 'the poet's own Manuscript' not seen by subsequent editors. Unlike *The Tree of Liberty*, seen in manuscript by Dr Robert Chambers, this apolitical song has never been questioned.

Fickle Fortune

First printed in Cromek, 1808.
Tune: I Dream'd I Lay

Tho' fickle Fortune has deceived me,
    She promis'd fair, and perform'd but ill;
Of mistress, friends, and wealth bereav'd me,
    Yet I bear a heart shall support me still. —

I'll act with prudence as far as I'm able,
    But if success I must never find,
Then come Misfortune, I bid thee welcome,
    I'll meet thee with an undaunted mind. —

This work is described in the *First Commonplace Book* as written 'extempore under the pressure of a heavy train of Misfortunes, which indeed, threatened to undo me altogether . . . at the close of that dreadful period'.

O Raging Fortune's Withering Blast
First printed in Cromek, 1808.

O Raging Fortune's withering blast
    Has laid my leaf full low! O
O raging Fortune's withering blast
    Has laid my leaf full low! O
5 My stem was fair my bud was green
    My blossom sweet did blow; O
The dew fell fresh, the sun rose mild,
    And made my branches grow; O
But luckless Fortune's northern storms
10   Laid a' my blossoms low, O
But luckless Fortune's northern storms
    Laid a' my blossoms low, O.

This dates from the period of the poet's perhaps psychosomatic illness, during the winter of 1781–2. The simile of Fortune as the raging winds of winter is simple and effective.

I'll Go and be a Sodger
First printed in Currie, 1800.

O why the deuce should I repine,
    And be an ill foreboder;
I'm twenty-three, and five feet nine,
    I'll go and be a sodger.   *soldier*

I gat some gear wi' meikle care,   *got, worldly goods, little*
    I held it weel thegither;   *well together*
But now it's gane, and something mair,   *gone, more*
    I'll go and be a sodger.   *soldier*

The song dates from April 1782, according to notes taken by Dr Currie from a farming memorandum notebook, which was last seen in the library of William Roscoe about 1815. There is no manuscript copy. Admittance to the canon has been on the word of Dr Currie. Perhaps ironically, out of economic necessity, certainly with a degree of self-dramatisation, Burns considered a military career: 'Hannibal gave my young ideas such a turn that I used to strut in raptures up and down after the recruiting drum and bagpipe, and wish myself tall enough to be a soldier' (Letter 125).

My Father was a Farmer

Tune: Jockie's Gray Breeks or The Weaver and his Shuttle, O
First printed by Cromek, 1808.

My father was a farmer upon the Carrick border O
And carefully he bred me, in decency and order O.
He bade me act a manly part, though I had ne'er a farthing O
For without an honest manly heart, no man was worth regarding O.

5   Chorus: Row de dow &c.

Then out into the world my course I did determine, O
Tho' to be rich was not my wish, yet to be great was charming O.
My talents they were not the worst, nor yet my education, O:
Resolv'd was I, at least to try, to mend my situation, O.

10   In many a way, and vain essay, I courted Fortune's favour; O
Some cause unseen, still stept between, to frustrate each endeavour; O
Sometimes by foes I was o'erpower'd, sometimes by friends forsaken, O
And when my hope was at the top, I still was worst mistaken, O.

Then sore harass'd, and tir'd at last, with Fortune's vain delusion, O,
15   I dropt my schemes, like idle dreams; and came to this conclusion; O
The past was bad, and the future hid; its good or ill untryed; O
But the present hour was in my pow'r, and so I would enjoy it, O.

No help, nor hope, nor view had I; nor person to befriend me; O
So I must toil, and sweat and broil, and labour to sustain me, O
20   To plough and sow, to reap and mow, my father bred me early, O
For one, he said, to labour bred, was a match for Fortune fairly, O.

Thus all obscure, unknown, and poor, thro' life I'm doom'd to wander, O
Till down my weary bones I lay in everlasting slumber; O

No view nor care, but shun whate'er might breed me pain or sorrow; O
25   I live to-day as well's I may, regardless of tomorrow, O.

But cheerful still, I am as well as a Monarch in a palace; O
Tho' Fortune's frown still hunts me down with all her wonted malice: O
I make indeed, my daily bread, but ne'er can make it farther; O
But as daily bread is all I need, I do not much regard her, O.

30   When sometimes by my labour I earn a little money, O
Some unforeseen misfortune comes gen'rally upon me; O
Mischance, mistake, or by neglect, or my good-natur'd folly; O
But come what will I've sworn it still, I'll ne'er be melancholy, O.

All you who follow wealth and power with unremitting ardour, O
35   The more in this you look for bliss, you leave your view the farther; O
Had you the wealth Potosi boasts, or nations to adore you, O
A cheerful, honest-hearted clown I will prefer before you, O.

Other than commentary on Burns's notes on the tune, that a North
of Ireland song, *The Weaver and his Shuttle, O*, was exactly the same
as the Scottish one, Kinsley says nothing about this song. Perhaps
he was prejudiced by Burns's own disparagement of it in his *First
Commonplace Book*, April, 1874: 'a wild rhapsody, miserably defi-
cient in versification; but as the sentiments are the genuine feelings
of my heart, for that reason, I have a particular pleasure in conning it
over'. This early, probably 1782 song, is indeed seminal in its
rehearsal of so many future themes: the constant frustration of
his worthy hopes; the harshness of farm toil and the compensatory
sense of independence despite all such difficulties. The first stanza is
of particular note. In Liam McIlvanney's forthcoming study, *Burns
the Radical: Poetry and Politics in Late Eighteenth-Century Scotland*,
we will have a revaluation of the influence on the child of his father's
passionate, liberal educational values. As McIlvanney writes: '. . . it
is crucial to appreciate that Burns's education was far more ex-
tensive than his formal schooling. It could hardly be otherwise,
given the fiercely intellectual presence of William Burnes, a man
who bought and borrowed books for his sons and remorselessly
engaged them in "improving" conversations.' McIlvanney also
notes the degree to which his father and his hired schoolmaster,
John Murdoch, combined forces to educate Robert and Gilbert with
a humane, often English Whig-inspired eighteenth-century liberal-
ism, against the prevalent Auld Licht Culture.

Montgomerie's Peggy

Tune: Galla Water
First printed by Cromek, 1808.

Altho' my bed were in yon muir,   that moor
  Amang the heather, in my plaidie,   among, old style kilt
Yet happy, happy would I be
  Had I my dear Montgomerie's Peggy. —

5 When o'er the hill beat surly storms,
  And winter nights were dark and rainy;
I'd seek some dell, and in my arms   wooden glen
  I'd shelter dear Montgomerie's Peggy. —

Were I a Baron proud and high,
10 And horse and servants waiting ready,
Then a' 'twad gie o' joy to me,   all it would give
  The sharin't with Montgomerie's Peggy. —   sharing it

Composition is dated for around 1782. In the *First Commonplace Book*
Burns writes this song is an 'imitation of the manner of a noble old
Scottish Piece called *MacMillan's Peggy*, and sings to the tune of
Galla Water. – My Montgomerie's Peggy was my Deity for six or
eight months'. After laying courtship 'siege' to her, he was mortified
to discover that she had already been pledged to another. Peggy is
believed to have been a house maid at Coylfield House, owned by the
Montgomerie family, according to the poet's sister, later Mrs Begg.

Remorse:
A Fragment
First printed by Currie, 1800.

Of all the numerous ills that hurt our peace;
That press the soul, or wring the mind with anguish;
Beyond comparison the worst are those
That to our Folly, or our Guilt we owe.
5 In ev'ry other circumstance the mind
Has this to say, it was no deed of mine:
But, when to all the evil of misfortune
This sting is added, blame thy foolish self;
Or worser far, the pangs of keen remorse:

10 The tort'ring, gnawing consciousness of guilt —   torturing
    Of guilt, perhaps, where we've involved others;
    The young, the innocent, who fondly lov'd us;
    Nay more, that very love their cause of ruin —
    O! burning Hell! in all thy store of torments
15 There's not a keener LASH —
    Lives there a man so firm who, while his heart
    Feels all the bitter horrors of his crime,
    Can reason down its agonizing throbs,
    And, after proper purpose of amendment,
20 Can firmly force his jarring thoughts to peace?
    O happy, happy, enviable man!
    O glorious magnanimity of soul!

This was composed after reading Adam Smith's *Theory of Moral Sentiments*, a book of philosophical inquiry (1759). In the *First Commonplace Book*, the lines are dated for September 1783. The poet paraphrases his own verse: 'I entirely agree with that judicious Philosopher Mr Smith in his excellent Theory of Moral Sentiments, that Remorse is the most painful sentiment that can embitter the human bosom . . . when our own follies or crimes, have made us miserable and wretched, to bear it up with manly firmness, and at the same time have a proper penitential sense of our misconduct, – is a glorious effort of Self-command'. It is clearly an experiment in Shakespearean blank verse, a poetic form the poet did not often employ and highly comparable, linguistically and formally, with the early, guilt-tormented Coleridge's use of that form.

On James Grieve, Laird of Boghead, Tarbolton
A Sanctimonious Rascal of the First Water
First printed with Chambers–Wallace, 1896.

Here lies Boghead amang the dead,   among
    In hopes to get salvation;
But if such as he, in Heav'n may be,
    Then welcome, hail! damnation. —

This was written on a Laird who lived near the Burns family at Lochlie. It is generally dated for 1783–4. In a 1787 edition of the poet's work a holograph copy of the epigram has the subtitle as above, 'A Sanctimonious Rascal of the First Water'.

On an Innkeeper in Tarbolton

First in Chambers–Wallace, 1896.

Here lies 'mang ither useless matters,   among other
A. Manson wi' his endless clatters. —   talk/chatter

In Chambers–Wallace this is titled *On Thomas Kirkpatrick, Late Blacksmith in Stoop*, with 'A. Manson' changed to 'Auld Thomas' in the last line. Kinsley has no remarks. Mackay records that a plaque marks the spot in Tarbolton where Andrew Manson had an Inn.

The Ruined Farmer

Tune: Go From My Window, Love, Do!
First printed with Chambers, 1838.

The sun he is sunk in the west;
All creatures retired to rest,
While here I sit, all sore beset,
    With sorrow, grief, and woe:
5   And it's O, fickle Fortune, O!

The prosperous man is asleep,
Nor hears how the whirlwinds sweep;
But Misery and I must watch
    The surly tempests blow:
10   And it's O, fickle Fortune, O!

There lies the dear Partner of my breast;
Her cares for a moment at rest:
Must I see thee, my youthful pride,
    Thus brought so very low!
15   And it's O, fickle Fortune, O!

There lie my sweet babies in her arms;
No anxious fear their little hearts alarms;
But for their sake my heart does ache,
    With many a bitter throe:
20   And it's O, fickle Fortune, O!

I once was by Fortune carest;
I once could relieve the distrest:
Now life's poor support, hardly earn'd,
    My fate will scarce bestow:
25   And it's O, fickle Fortune, O!

No comfort, no comfort I have!
How welcome to me were the grave!
But then my wife and children dear —
    O, whither would they go!
30   And it's O, fickle Fortune, O!

O whither, O whither shall I turn!
All friendless, forsaken, forlorn!
For in this world, Rest or Peace
    I never more shall know!
35   And it's O, fickle Fortune, O!

Unpublished during the poet's life, this song is written in the voice of a ruined farmer. There is a strong resonance of family biography relating to the poet's father during 1783–4 when he fell into rent arrears and was taken to court. Burns wrote about this episode in 1787: 'My indignation yet boils at the recollection of the scoundrel tyrant's insolent, threatening epistles, which used to set us in tears' (Letter 125). The song is included among the Stair manuscripts.

Lines on the Bachelor's Club, Tarbolton

First published here as verse by Burns.

Of birth or blood we do not boast,
    Nor gentry does our club afford;
But ploughmen and mechanics we
    In Nature's simple dress record.

This was written in the Autumn of 1782. Dr James Currie says of the Tarbolton Bachelor's Club – essentially a debating society – that in the Autumn of 1782, a book was purchased into which the rules and regulations were copied by the poet, as President. Introducing the annotations, Currie prints four lines of poetry, stating that the entire text inscribed is from Burns (See Currie, 1800, p. xliv). If so, it is almost certain the lines of poetry are by Burns, although they have never previously been included in the canon. The lines may have merely been quoted from another author, but Burns is generally open about attribution. Currie records in a footnote that actual topics debated at Tarbolton included the following, 'Whether do we derive more happiness from Love or Friendship? – Whether between friends who have no reason to doubt each other's friendship, there should be any reserve? – Whether is the savage man, or the peasant of a civilised country, in the most happy situation? – Whether is a young man of the lower ranks of life likeliest to be happy, who has got a good education, and his mind well informed, or he who has just the education and information of those around him?' (Currie, p. xlvii). Found in the hand of Burns, these lines are almost certainly his.

Mary Morison

Tune: Duncan Davison.
First published by Currie, 1800.

O Mary, at thy window be,	
It is the wish'd, the trysted hour;	
Those smiles and glances let me see,	
That make the miser's treasure poor:	
How blythely wad I bide the stoure,	would, abide, dust/struggle
A weary slave frae sun to sun;	from
Could I the rich reward secure,	
The lovely Mary Morison!	

Yestreen when to the trembling string	yesterday evening
The dance gaed thro' the lighted ha',	went, hall
To thee my fancy took its wing,	
I sat, but neither heard or saw:	
Though this was fair, and that was braw,	fine/good-looking
And yon the toast of a' the town,	an other, all
I sigh'd, and said amang them a',	among, all
'Ye are na Mary Morison.'	you are not

O Mary, canst thou wreck his peace,	
Wha for thy sake wad gladly die!	who, would
Or canst thou break that heart of his,	
Whase only faut is loving thee!	fault
If love for love thou wilt na gie,	will not give
At least be pity to me shown;	
A thought ungentle canna be	cannot be
The thought o' Mary Morison.	

This work was written somtime in the 1784–5 period. It is remarkable that Burns sent this song to George Thomson on 20th March, 1793 (Low has 1792) but he did not print it until 1818. Perhaps he was influenced by Burns's self-deprecatory comment that the song prefixed was 'one of my juvenile works. I leave it among your hands. I do not think it very remarkable, either for its merits, or demerits. It is impossible, at least I feel it in my stinted powers, to be always original, entertaining & witty' (Letter 540). Hugh MacDiarmid, on the other hand, rightly saw the song as a pure manifestation of the Scottish poetic spirit: 'The language of the Greeks is simple and concrete, without clichés and rhetoric. But what Greek epigram has a more magical simplicity than Burns's 'Ye are na Mary Morison!', or where shall a parallel be found for the terrific concision, the vertiginous speed of *Tam o' Shanter*' (See *Albyn* or *The Future of Scotland*).

Epitaph on My Own Friend, and My Father's Friend, Wm Muir in Tarbolton Miln
First published in Currie, 1800.

An honest man here lies at rest
As e'er God with His image blest.
The friend of man, the friend of truth;
The friend of Age, and guide of Youth:
Few hearts like his with virtue warm'd,
Few heads with knowledge so inform'd:
If there's another world, he lives in bliss;
If there is none, he made the best of this. —

A mock epitaph composed on a friend of the poet's family, William Muir (1745–93), and entered in the poet's *First Commonplace Book*, April 1784. Mackay errs by stating this epitaph was printed in the Kilmarnock edition (Mackay, p. 70).

The Ronalds of the Bennals
First printed by Robert Chambers 1851.

In Tarbolton, ye ken, there are proper young men,	know
And proper young lasses and a', man:	all
But ken ye the Ronalds that live in the Bennals,	know
They carry the gree frae them a', man.	come off best from
5 Their father's a laird, and weel he can spare't,	well
Braid money to tocher them a', man,	broad, dower

To proper young men, he'll clink in the hand — chink
    Gowd guineas a hunder or twa, man. — gold, a hundred or two

There's ane they ca' Jean, I'll warrant ye've seen — one, call
10   As bonie a lass or as braw, man; — well dressed
But for sense and guid taste she'll vie wi' the best, — good
    And a conduct that beautifies a', man.

The charms o' the min', the langer they shine, — mind
    The mair admiration they draw, man; — more
15 While peaches and cherries, and roses and lilies,
    They fade and they wither awa, man. — away

If ye be for Miss Jean, tak this frae a frien', — take, from a friend
    A hint o' a rival or twa, man, — two
The Laird o' Blackbyre wad gang through the fire, — would go
20   If that wad entice her awa, man. — would, away

The Laird o' Braehead has been on his speed — rushing about
    For mair than a towmond or twa, man; — more, twelve months, two
The Laird o' the Ford will straught on a board, — stretch
    If he canna get her at a', man. — cannot

25 Then Anna comes in, the pride o' her kin,
    The boast of our bachelors a', man:
Sae sonsy and sweet, sae fully complete, — so pleasant
    She steals our affections awa, man. — away

If I should detail the pick and the wale — choice, choicest
30   O' lasses that live here awa, man, — about
The faut wad be mine, if they didna shine — fault would
    The sweetest and best o' them a', man.

I lo'e her mysel, but darena weel tell, — love, dare not well
    My poverty keeps me in awe, man,
35 For making o' rhymes, and working at times,
    Does little or naething at a', man. — nothing

Yet I wadna choose to let her refuse, — would not
    Nor hae't in her power to say na, man, — have it, no
For though I be poor, unnoticed, obscure,
40   My stomach's as proud as them a', man.

Though I canna ride in well-booted pride,   cannot
    And flee o'er the hills like a craw, man.   fly, crow
I can haud up my head wi' the best o' the breed,   hold
    Though fluttering ever so braw, man.   fine

45   My coat and my vest, they are Scotch o' the best;
    O' pairs o' guid breeks I hae twa, man: good trousers, have two
And stockings and pumps to put on my stumps,
    And ne'er a wrang steek in them a', man.   wrong stitch

My sarks they are few, but five o' them new,   shirts
50   Twal'-hundred, as white as the snaw, man,   snow
A ten-shillings hat, a Holland cravat;   a linen neck-tie
    There are no monie Poets sae braw, man.   many, so well dressed

I never had frien's weel stockit in means,   friends well stocked, goods
    To leave me a hundred or twa, man,   two
55   Nae weel-tocher'd aunts, to wait on their drants   no well dowered, sulks
    And wish them in hell for it a', man.

I never was cannie for hoarding o' money,   careful
    Or claughtin't together at a', man,   grasping
I've little to spend and naething to lend,   nothing
60   But devil a shilling I awe, man.   owe

This is a light jocular poem on a theme which in his work and life was to become increasingly, obsessively darker; that is Burns's need for not so much the materialism as the culture of women of a higher class. Mrs McLehose, Margaret Chalmers and Maria Riddell are the most prominent examples. The Ronalds of the Bennals here mentioned were the prosperous William Ronald and his two daughters Jean and Anna. Burns sends up their suitors and ends on a note of personal defiance as to his own appearance and worth but the uncrossable line of class (ll. 33–4) hurts all the same. De Lancey Ferguson suggests that the prospective wife mentioned in Letter 18 is, in fact, Anna Ronald. Whether she is or not, that letter does present the earliest manifestation of desire in Burns for matrimonial security relevant to this particular poem:

We talk of air & manner, of beauty & wit, and lord knows what unmeaning nonsense; but – there – is solid charms for you. – Who would not be in raptures with a woman that will make him £300 richer. – And then to have a woman to lye with when one pleases, without running any risk of the cursed expence of bastards and all other concomitants of that species of Smuggling. —These are solid views of matrimony.— (Letter 18)

Kinsley and Low note that William Ronald went bankrupt in 1789. Burns mentions this in a letter: 'The only Ayrshire news that I remember, in which I think you will be interested is, that Mr Ronald is bankrupt. You will easily guess that from his insolent vanity in his sunshine of life, he will now feel a little retaliation from those who thought themselves eclipsed by him, for, poor fellow! I do not think he ever intentionally injured any one' (Letter 372).

The Tarbolton Lasses

First printed by Chambers in 1851.

If ye gae up to yon hill-tap,		yonder
Ye'll there see bonie Peggy:		pretty
She kens her father is a laird,		knows
And she forsooth's a leddy.		lady

5 There's Sophy tight, a lassie bright,
     Besides a handsome fortune:
Wha canna win her in a night   who cannot
     Has little art in courtin.

Gae down by Faile, and taste the ale,   go
10   And tak a look o' Mysie;   take
She's dour and din, a deil within,   stubborn; dirty complexion
     But aiblins she may please ye.   maybe/perhaps

If she be shy, her sister try,
     Ye'll may be fancy Jenny:
15 If ye'll dispense wi' want o' sense   with
     She kens hersel she's bonie.   knows herself

As ye gae up by yon hillside,   go
     Spier in for bonie Bessy: call
She'll gie ye a beck, and bid ye light,   give, curtsy
20   And handsomely address ye.

There's few sae bonie, nane sae guid   so, none so good
     In a' King George' dominion;
If ye should doubt the truth of this —
     It's Bessy's ain opinion.   own

Written about the same period as *The Ronalds of the Bennals*, in
1784. Faile, in Tarbolton parish, would have been little more than a
few houses at this time. This jovial song is like a young man's tourist
guide to the available young ladies of the area. For two main reasons
it was unpublished until the mid-19th century. First, it is a slight
work. Second, the young ladies were too easily identified at the time
of writing.

The Belles of Mauchline
Tune: Bonie Dundee
First printed by Currie in 1800.

In Mauchline there dwells six proper young Belles,
    The pride of the place and its neighbourhood a',
Their carriage and dress a stranger would guess,
    In Lon'on or Paris they'd gotten it a'.
Miss Millar is fine, Miss Murkland's divine,
    Miss Smith she has wit, and Miss Betty is braw;
There's beauty and fortune to get wi' Miss Morton,
    But ARMOUR'S the jewel for me o' them a'. —

This was composed probably just after the previous work, in late
1784 or early 1785. Robert Chambers furnished subsequent editors
with the names of all six Mauchline lassies: Helen and Betty Miller,
Jean Markland, Jean Smith, Christina Morton and the poet's
subsequent wife, Jean Armour.

O Leave Novels
Tune: Ye Mauchline Belles
First printed in Currie, 1800.

O leave novels, ye Mauchline belles,
    Ye're safer at your spinning wheel;
Such witching books, are baited hooks
    For rakish rooks like Rob Mossgiel.
Your fine *Tom Jones* and *Grandisons*
    They make your youthful fancies reel;
They heat your brains, and fire your veins,
    And then you're prey for Rob Mossgiel.

Beware a tongue that's smoothly hung;
 A heart that warmly seems to feel;
That feelin heart but acks a part,   acts
 'Tis rakish art in Rob Mossgiel.
The frank address, the soft caress,
 Are worse than poisoned darts of steel,
The frank address, and politesse,
 Are all finesse in Rob Mossgiel.

The explosion of print culture from the 1770s had obviously penetrated into provincial Ayrshire. Burns's reading of what we now perceive as the canonical eighteenth-century English novelists is a fundamental element of his creative awareness. He responded to the opposing versions of sexuality found in Fielding (*Tom Jones*) and Richardson (*Sir Charles Grandison*); from the picaresque Jack-the-laddish to the lachrymose, claustrophobic hot-house. Though unmentioned here, Sterne's labyrinthine form and psychological development as well as his obsessive preoccupation with *double entendres* were also avidly consumed and reactivated in Burns's work and life. There is, of course, a considerable degree of self-parody and self-irony present in the poem, playing on the poet's excessive reputation as a womaniser. For Burns's relationship to Sterne, see K.G. Simpson, 'The Impulse of Wit: Sterne and Burns's Letters' in *The Art of Robert Burns*, ed. Jack & Noble (London, 1982), pp. 151–90.

The Mauchline Lady

Tune: I Had a Horse, and I Had nae Mair
First printed in Cromek, 1808.

When first I came to Stewart Kyle
 My mind it was na steady,   not
Where'er I gaed, where'er I rade,   went, rode
 A mistress still I had ay:
But when I came roun' by Mauchline toun, round, town
 Not dreadin any body,
My heart was caught before I thought,
 And by a Mauchline lady —.

The first written record of this work is entered in the *First Commonplace Book*, dated August 1785, although the fragment was probably written before this date. The 'Mauchline lady' is assumed to be Jean Armour. Burns met Jean after he moved from Lochlie to Mossgiel.

The Twa Herds: An Unco Mournfu' Tale
or The Holy Tulzie   brawl

First printed by Stewart and Meikle in pamphlet form, 1796.

> *Blockheads with reason wicked wits abhor,*
> *But fool with fool is barbarous civil war.*
> Pope, *Dunciad*, Bk. III, ll. 175–6.

O a' ye pious, godly Flocks   all
Weel fed on pastures orthodox,   well
Wha now will keep you frae the fox   who, from
    Or worryin tykes?   dogs
5 Or wha will tent the waifs an' crocks   who, tend, stragglers, old ewes
    About the dykes?   stone walls

The twa best Herds in a' the wast,   two, west
That e'er gae gospel horn a blast   gave
These five an' twenty simmers past,   summers
10   O dool to tell!   sad
Hae had a bitter, black out cast   have, quarrel
    Atween themsel. —   between

O Moodie, man, and wordy Russel,
How could you raise so vile a bustle?
15 Ye'll see how New-Light herds will whistle,
    And think it fine!
The Lord's cause gat na sic a twistle   got not such a twist
    Sin' I hae min'. —   since, can recall

O Sirs! whae'er wad hae expeckit   whoever would have expected
20 Your duty ye wad sae negleckit?   would so neglect
Ye wha were no by lairds respeckit,   who, respected
    To wear the Plaid;
But by the very Brutes eleckit   elected
    To be their Guide. —

25 What Flock wi' Moodie's Flock could rank,
Sae hale an' hearty every shank?   so, leg
Nae poison'd soor Arminian stank   no, sour, stagnant pool
    He let them taste;
But Calvin's fountain-head they drank,
30   That was a feast!

The Fulmart, Wil-cat, Brock, an' Tod   *polecat, wildcat, badger, fox*
Weel kend his voice thro' a' the wood;   *well knew*
He knew their ilka hole an' road,   *every*
    Baith out and in: *both*
35 An' liked weel to shed their blood   *well*
    An' sell their skin. —

What herd like Russell tell'd his tale;
His voice was heard thro' muir and dale: *moor*
He kend the Lord's sheep ilka tail,   *knew, every*
40   O'er a' the height;
    An' tell'd gin they were sick or hale   *when/if, well*
    At the first sight. —

He fine a maingie sheep could scrub,   *dirty*
Or nobly swing the Gospel-club;
45 Or New-Light Herds could nicely drub
    And pay their skin;   *flog*
Or hing them o'er the burning dub,   *hang, pool*
    Or shute them in. —   *heave*

Sic twa — O, do I live to see't,   *such two*
50 Sic famous twa sud disagree't   *such, two, should*
An' names like 'Villain, Hypocrite,'
    Each other gi'en;   *giving*
While enemies wi' laughin spite
    Say, 'Neither's liein.' —   *lying*

55 O ye wha tent the Gospel-fauld,   *who pay heed to, fold*
Thee, Duncan deep, and Peebles, shaul,   *shallow*
But chiefly great Apostle Auld,
    We trust in thee,
That thou wilt work them hot an' cauld   *cold*
60   To gar them gree. —   *agree*

Consider, Sirs, how we're beset;
There 's scarce a new Herd that we get
But comes frae 'mang that cursed Set   *from among*
    I winna name: *will not*
65 I trust in Heaven to see them het   *hot*
    Yet in a flame. —

There's D'rymple has been lang our fae,   Dalrymple, long, foe
M'Gill has wrought us meikle wae;   great mischief
An' that curst rascal ca'd Mcquhey,   called
70   An' baith the Shaws,   both
Wha aft hae made us black an' blae   often have, blue
      Wi' vengefu' paws. —

Auld Wodrow lang has wrought mischief,   old, long
We trusted death wad bring relief;   would
75 But he has gotten, to our grief,
      Ane to succeed him;   one
A chap will soundly buff our beef   strike our flesh
      I meikle dread him. —   greatly

An' mony mae that I could tell   many more
80 Wha fair and openly rebel;   who
Forby Turn-coats amang oursel,   besides, among ourselves
      There 's Smith for ane;   one
I doubt he's but a Gray-neck still   a gambler
      An' that ye'll fin'. —   find

85 O a' ye flocks o'er a' the hills,
By mosses, meadows, moors, an' fells,
Come, join your counsel and your skills
      To cowe the Lairds,   humble
And get the Brutes the power themsels   themselves
90   To chuse their Herds. —   chose

Then Orthodoxy yet may prance,
And Learning in a woody dance;   hangman's noose
An' that curst cur ca'd Common Sense   called
      That bites sae sair,   so sore
95 Be banish'd o'er the sea to France
      Let him bark there. —

Then Shaw's an' Dairymple's eloquence,
M'Gill's close nervous excellence,
Mcquhey's pathetic manly sense,
100   An' guid M'Math,   good
Wi' Smith wha thro' the heart can glance,   who
      May a' pack aff. —   go packing

This work was written prior to *Holy Willie's Prayer*, probably late in 1784 or early in 1785. It first appeared with Stewart and Meikle in pamphlet form, probably just after the poet's death and again in 1799 and then in book format in their main 1801 collection.

It is a satire on a public row that erupted between two clerics, Mr Alexander Moodie of Riccarton and Mr John Russel of Kilmarnock. Their disagreement over parish boundaries led to a Church court hearing at Irvine in which both men, Auld Licht Calvinists, engaged in what Burns called a 'bitter and shameless quarrel . . . at the time when the hue and cry against patronage was at the worst' (British Museum, Egerton ms., no. 1656). He thought highly enough of it to write in some detail about it in his 'autobiographical' letter to Dr Moore:

—The first of my poetic offspring that saw the light was a burlesque lamentation on a quarrel between two revd. Calvinists, both of them dramatis personae in my Holy Fair.— I had an idea myself that the piece had some merit; but to prevent the worst, I gave a copy of it to a friend who was very fond of these things, and told him I could not guess who was the Author of it, but that I thought it pretty clever.— With a certain side of both clergy and laity it met a roar of applause.— Holy Willie's Prayer next made its appearance and alarmed the kirk-Session so much that they held three several meetings to look over their holy artillery, if any of it was pointed against profane Rhymers.— Unluckily for me, my idle wanderings led me, on another side, point blank within the reach of their heaviest metal (Letter 125).

His 'idle wanderings', of course, were sexual. The consequences of Jean Armour's pregnancy, the hostility of her family and the punitive engagement of the church in the business pushed him towards Jamaica for fear of something worse:

I had for some time been sculking from covert to covert under all the terrors of Jail; as some ill-advised ungrateful people had uncoupled the merciless legal Pack at my heels . . . (Letter 125).

There is always in Burns something of the hunted fox pursued by varied packs. The younger man always thought he was crafty enough to outrun them. What he gives witness to in this poem is the degree to which his specific, personal confrontation with provincial Ayrshire, 'Auld Licht' Calvinism led him to a wider understanding of the struggle for the soul of Presbyterian Scotland between 'Auld' and 'New' Licht Calvinism. Kinsley gives a cogent

account of this quarrel as, after the convulsions of the seventeenth
century, it raged unremittingly through the eighteenth century.

By the patronage Act of 1712 (10 Annae cap. 21) the right of
presenting ministers to vacant parishes was restored to the lay
patrons who were heirs of the original donors of ecclesiastical
properties. This violated the Act of Security (1707) which
protected the polity of the Presbyterian Kirk at the Union of
the Parliaments. Patronage was accepted by the 'Moderate'
core of the Kirk, which after the Revolution of 1688 had
acquiesced in the co-operation of the ecclesiastical and civil
powers; but the issue brought about a secession in 1732, when
an Act of Assembly gave the power of election to heritors and
elders whenever the patron did not exercise his right. A
further dispute took place in 1747 over the Burgher's Oath,
which required holders of public office to affirm the religion
'presently professed in this kingdom'. 'To a sober Presbyter-
ian no proposition seemed more self-evident. Yet by means of
perverse ingenuity in torturing words, did these wrong-headed
men insist that it was inconsistent with their principles and
professions' (Ramsay of Ochtertyre, ii. 12); and the 'Anti-
Burghers' seceded. The two parties formed 'distinct and
independent synods, which hated each other worse than the
Jesuits did the Jansenists' (ibid., ii. 13). The Burghers later
divided on the issue of civil compulsion in religious affairs.
The minority, holding to the obligations laid upon them by
the Solemn League and Covenant, seceded as 'Original Bur-
ghers' or 'Auld Lichts'; the majority, who wished to modify
Presbyterian commitment to the Covenant, were named 'New
Lichts.'
    Below differences in attitude to the establishment, these
terms represent a deeper distinction of theology and tempera-
ment. The 'Auld Lichts' were 'orthodox', Calvinist — with
traditional emphasis on the doctrines of original sin, election,
and predestination—stern in their discipline, evangelical and
rhetorical in their preaching. The 'New Lichts' were 'Armi-
nian' (see ll. 27–30 n.), 'Moderate', liberal in their theology and
moralistic in their preaching (Vol. III, pp. 1045–6).

At the core of the poem, however, is a deeply serious spiritual
problem. The image of the shepherd and his sheep, the nature of
pastoral care, runs through both Old and New Testaments. For
example Ezek. 34 which condemns shepherds who 'feed themselves'

but 'feed not the flock', the parable of the good shepherd (John 10) or Christ's final appearance when he commands him to 'feed my lambs' (John 21:15). Milton, of course, in *Lycidas* had raged against those priests who had inverted, perverted Christ's pastoral instruction. To McGuirk's seminal work on Miltonic resonance in Burns, including *Lycidas* ('Loose Canons: Milton and Burns, Artsong and Folksong', *Love and Liberty*, ed. K.G. Simpson, 1997), we should surely add this passage from that poem as relevant to Burns's assault on clerical corruption:

> He shook his mitred locks, and stern bespake,
> How well could I have spared for thee, young swain,
> Enow of such as for their bellies' sake,
> Creep and intrude, and climb into the fold?
> Of other care they little reckoning make,
> Than how to scramble at the shearers' feast,
> And shove away the worthy bidden guest.
> Blind mouths! that scarce themselves know how to hold
> A sheep-hook, or have learned aught else the least
> That to the faithful herdman's art belongs!
> What recks it them? What need they? They are sped;
> And when they list, their lean and flashy songs
> Grate on their scrannel pipes of wretched straw,
> The hungry sheep look up, and are not fed,
> But swoll'n with wind, and the rank mist they draw,
> Rot inwardly, and foul contagion spread:
> Besides what the grim wolf with privy paw
> Daily devours apace, and nothing said,
> But that two-handed engine at the door,
> Stands ready to smite once, and smite no more.

Holy Willie's Prayer

First printed by Stewart and Meikle, in pamphlet form, 1799.

And send the Godly in a pet to pray.
Alexander Pope.

O Thou that in the Heavens does dwell!	
Wha, as it pleases best Thysel,	who, thyself
Sends ane to Heaven an' ten to Hell,	one
A' for Thy glory!	all
5 And no for ony guid or ill	any good
They've done before Thee. —	

I bless and praise Thy matchless might,
When thousands Thou hast left in night,
That I am here before Thy sight,
10   For gifts an' grace,
A burning and a shining light
          To a' this place. —

What was I, or my generation,
That I should get sic exaltation?   such
15 I, wha deserv'd most just damnation,   who
          For broken laws
Sax thousand years ere my creation,   six
          Thro' Adam's cause!

When from my mither's womb I fell,   mother's
20 Thou might hae plung'd me deep in hell,   have
To gnash my gooms, and weep, and wail,   gums
          In burning lakes,
Whare damned devils roar and yell   where
          Chain'd to their stakes. —

25 Yet I am here, a chosen sample,
To show Thy grace is great and ample:
I'm here a pillar o' Thy temple
          Strong as a rock,
A guide, a ruler and example
30   To a' Thy flock. —

O Lord thou kens what zeal I bear,   knows
When drinkers drink, and swearers swear,
And singin' there, and dancin' here,
          Wi' great an' sma';   small
35 For I am keepet by Thy fear,   kept
          Free frae them a'. —   from, all

But yet — O Lord — confess I must —
At times I'm fash'd wi' fleshly lust;   troubled
And sometimes too, in warldly trust   worldly
40   Vile Self gets in;
But Thou remembers we are dust,
          Defiled wi' sin. —

O Lord — yestreen — Thou kens — wi' Meg —   last night, knows
Thy pardon I sincerely beg!
45 O may't ne'er be a living plague,
     To my dishonour!
An' I'll ne'er lift a lawless leg
     Again upon her. —

Besides, I farther maun avow,   must
50 Wi' Leezie's lass, three times — I trow —
But, Lord, that Friday I was fou   drunk
     When I cam near her;   came
Or else, Thou kens, Thy servant true   knows
     Wad never steer her. —   would, meddle with

55 Maybe Thou lets this fleshly thorn
Buffet Thy servant e'en and morn,   evening
Lest he owre proud and high should turn,   over
     That he's sae gifted;   so
If sae, Thy han' maun e'en be borne   so, hand must
60   Untill Thou lift it. —

Lord, bless Thy chosen in this place,
For here Thou has a chosen race:
But God, confound their stubborn face,
     An' blast their name,
65 Wha bring Thy elders to disgrace   who
     An' open shame. —

Lord mind Gaun Hamilton's deserts!   Gavin
He drinks, and swears, an' plays at cartes,   cards
Yet has sae monie takin arts   so many, popular
70   Wi' Great and Sma',   small
Frae God's ain priest the people's hearts   from, own
     He steals awa. —   away

And when we chasten'd him therefore,
Thou kens how he bred sic a splore,   knows, such, row
75 And set the warld in a roar   world
     O' laughin at us:
Curse Thou his basket and his store,
     Kail an' potatoes. —   cabbage/greens

Lord, hear my earnest cry and prayer
80 Against that Presbytry of Ayr!
Thy strong right hand, Lord, mak it bare
        Upon their heads!
Lord visit them, and dinna spare,   *do not*
        For their misdeeds!

85 O Lord my God, that glib-tongu'd Aiken!   *smooth-*
My very heart and flesh are quaking
To think how I sat, sweating, shaking,
        An' pish'd wi' dread, —*incongruing of*   *wet myself*
While Auld wi' hingin lip an' sneaking *idhem*   *hanging, sneering*
90   And hid his head!   *in dprayer.*

Lord, in Thy day o' vengeance try him!
Lord visit him wha did employ him!   *who*
And pass not in Thy mercy by them,
        Nor hear their prayer;   *don't listen to their*
95 But for Thy people's sake destroy them,   *prayers, listen*
        An' dinna spare!   *to me.*   *do not*

But Lord, remember me and mine
Wi' mercies temporal and divine!
That I for grace an' gear may shine,
100   Excell'd by nane!   *none*
And a' the glory shall be Thine!
        AMEN! AMEN!

Manuscript copies of this brilliant satire, probably a broadside
printing, were circulated among friends of the poet during his
lifetime. It first appeared in pamphlet form in 1799 from Stewart
and Meikle, Glasgow, who then included it in their 1801 volume.
Holy Willie, or Willie Fisher (1737–1809), is described by Burns in
the Glenriddell manuscript as an 'Elder in the parish of Mauchline,
and much and justly famed for that polemical chattering which ends
in tippling Orthodoxy, and for that Spiritualised Bawdry which
refines to Liquorish Devotion'. He further explains, 'In a Sessional
process with a gentleman in Mauchline, a Mr Gavin Hamilton, Holy
Willie, and his priest, father Auld, after full hearing in the Pres-
bytery of Ayr, came off but second best; owing partly to the
oratorical powers of Mr Robt Aitken, Mr Hamilton's Counsel;
but chiefly to Mr Hamilton's being one of the most irreproachable
and truly respectable characters in the country'. Gavin Hamilton

(1751–1805) and Robert Aitken (1739–1807) were intimate friends of Burns.

Again, like *To A Haggis*, this poem is over-used but it is, even by Burns's standards, a quite astonishing dramatic monologue as he gets under the alien skin of his subject. The idea of self-destructive monologue has medieval roots and the poem may have a specific origin in Ramsay's *Last Speech of a Wretched Miser* but Burns has a talent for the genre only equalled by Swift and Browning. Formally, as Kinsley notes, the poem is precisely a prayer which 'follows the traditional scheme of invocation (ll. 1–6) and praise (ll. 7–30); confession and penitence (ll. 37–60); intercession (ll. 61–2) and petition (ll. 63–102). As well as parodying form, Burns parodies language. Kinsley notes that: 'The poem is written in the "language of the saints" – that improbable amalgam of Biblical English and colloquial Scots which was characteristic of the Covenanter and the Presbyterian evangelical . . . and which, in Burns as in Galt, has an almost miraculous unction' (Vol. 3, p. 1048). The poem is saturated by the crazily inverted use of specific Biblical texts. Kinsley mentions one marvellous example from Deuteronomy, xxviii, 15–19: 'Ll. 77–8: "Curse Thou his basket and his store, /Kail an' potatoes".' A mean version of the magnificently comprehensive curse laid by Jehovah on the ungodly: 'Cursed shalt thou be in the city . . . Cursed be thy basket and thy store . . . and the flocks of thy sheep' (Vol. III, p. 1052).

In her detailed, perceptive treatment of the poem, McGuirk remarks:

Willie sees himself as marked by God for 'gifts an' grace'; readers experience him differently, however – as marked by Burns for ridicule. Yet this is not one of Burns's bitter or angry satires. Willie's spite comes to so little, after all. And he is so fluent in his self-love . . . Willie's prayer, for all its scriptural allusion, is notable mainly for its perverse projection of Willie's own spitefulness onto the deity . . . Burns was reared to scepticism about the Auld Licht . . .: William Burns taught all his children to reject the exclusive focus on divine election – salvation through grace alone – that has corrupted Willie. So Burns mocks Willie as any son of his father would. He also wrote as a grateful friend of Hamilton, who had generously provided shelter for the Burns family in its worst crisis – a kindness fresh in the poet's mind, as the bankruptcy trial and subsequent death of Burns's father had

occurred only a year before 'Holy Willie's Prayer' was
written (p. 202).

We are not so certain of how we laugh at Willie Fisher who died,
probably due to drink, frozen in a ditch in February 1809 and was
buried in Mauchline cemetery near Mary Morison.

Epitaph on Holy Willie

First published by Stewart, 1801.

Here Holy Willie's sair worn clay	sore
Taks up its last abode;	takes
His saul has taen some other way,	soul, taken
I fear, the left-hand road.	towards hell

5   Stop! there he is as sure's a gun,
        Poor, silly body, see him;
    Nae wonder he's as black's the grun,   *no, ground*
        Observe wha's standing wi' him!   *who is*

    Your brunstane devilship I see
10   Has got him there before ye:
    But haud your nine-tail cat a wee,   *hold, a while*
        Till ance you've heard my story.   *once*

    Your pity I will not implore,
        For pity ye have nane;   *none*
15   Justice, alas! has gi'en him o'er,   *given*
        And mercy's day is gaen.   *gone*

    But hear me, Sir, deil as ye are,   *devil*
        Look something to your credit;
    A coof like him wad stain your name,   *blockhead, would*
20   If it were kent ye did it. —   *known*

This was probably composed in 1785 after feedback from the private
circulation of *Holy Willie's Prayer*.

On Tam the Chapman

First printed by Willam Cobbett, circa 1820s.

As Tam the chapman on a day	pedlar
Wi' Death forgather'd by the way,	
Weel pleas'd, he greets a wight sae famous,	well, sturdy person
And Death was nae less pleas'd wi' Thomas,	no
Wha cheerfully lays down his pack,	who
And there blaws up a hearty crack:	starts up, conversation
His social, friendly, honest heart	
Sae tickled Death, they could na part;	so, not
Sae after viewing knives and garters,	so
Death taks him hame to gie him quarters.	home, give

In the Aldine edition (1839), noted for its retrieval of radical and bawdy works, this poem was allegedly printed by William Cobbett. Kinsley accepts this, though he could not locate it in *The Political Register* which, however, was not Cobbett's sole publication. Cobbett, like all English radicals, was certainly sympathetic to Burns. Thus in his 1832 *Tour in Scotland*, a travel journal which Burns would have appreciated, given its preoccupation with the degree to which he found both Highland and Lowland Scotland ravaged by agrarian capitalism, Cobbett reports his Dumfries visit thus:

We reached DUMFRIES about five o'clock in the evening of Tuesday, the 6. And I lectured at the Theatre at half-after seven; and, considering, that the people have been frightened half to death about the cholera morbus (of which disease great numbers have actually died here), the attendance was wonderfully good. Poor BURNS, the poet, died in this town, an *exciseman*, after having written so well against that species of taxation, and that particular sort of office. Oh! *Sobriety*! How manifold are thy blessings! How great thy enjoyments! How complete the protection which thou givest to talent; and how feeble is talent unless it has that protection! I was very happy to hear that his widow, who still lives in this town, is amply provided for; and my intention was to go to her, to tell her my name, and to say, that I came to offer my respects as a mark of my admiration of the talents of her late husband, one single page of whose writings is worth more than a cart load that has been written by WALTER SCOTT (p. 235).

Loving Burns, he loathed Scott as much as Coleridge did, seeing in his endless best-selling pages a sordid inflation of literature, analogous to the replacement of gold by paper currency.

A Poet's Welcome to his Love-Begotten Daughter
First printed in Stewart, 1801.

	Thou's welcome, Wean! Mishanter fa' me,	child, mishap, befall
	If thoughts o' thee, or yet thy Mamie,	mother
	Shall ever daunton me or awe me,	subdue
	My sweet, wee lady;	small
5	Or if I blush when thou shalt ca' me	call
	Tyta, or Daddie. —	pet-name for father
	Tho' now they ca' me Fornicator,	call
	An' tease my name in kintra clatter,	country gossip
	The mair they talk, I'm kend the better;	more, known
10	E'en let them clash!	tattle
	An auld wife's tongue's a feckless matter	old, feeble
	To gie ane fash. —	give one annoyance
	Welcome! My bonie, sweet, wee Dochter!	daughter
	Tho' ye come here a wee unsought for;	a trifle
15	And tho' your comin I hae fought for,	have
	Baith Kirk and Queir;	both Church and Court
	Yet by my faith, ye're no unwrought for,	
	That I shall swear!	
	Wee image o' my bonie Betty,	
20	As fatherly I kiss and daut thee,	pet
	As dear and near my heart I set thee,	
	Wi' as gude will,	good
	As a' the Priests had seen me get thee	
	That's out o' Hell. —	
25	Sweet fruit o' monie a merry dint,	occasion
	My funny toil is no a' tint;	not all lost
	Tho' thou cam to the warld asklent,	askew
	Which fools may scoff at,	
	In my last plack thy part's be in't,	coin
30	The better half o't.	

Tho' I should be the waur bestead,   worse provided
Thou's be as braw and bienly clad,   finely, comfortably
And thy young years as nicely bred
    Wi' education,
35 As onie brat o' Wedlock's bed   any
    In a' thy station.

Gude grant that thou may ay inherit
Thy Mither's looks an' gracefu' merit;   mother's
An' thy poor, worthless Daddie's spirit,
40   Without his failins!
'Twill please me mair to see thee heir it   more
    Than stocket mailins!   stocked farms

For if thou be, what I wad hae thee,   would have
An' tak the counsel I shall gie thee,   give
45 I'll never rue my trouble wi' thee,
    The cost nor shame o't,
But be a loving Father to thee,
    And brag the name o't.

Throughout his life Burn's attitude to his illegitimate off-spring was
the reverse of the sadistic stringency with which the 'Auld Lichts'
sought to discipline his fornication. The child in this poem is his first
illegitimate child, a daughter born to Elizabeth (Betsy) Paton who was
a servant at Lochlea during his father's terminal illness. Burns's
mother wanted her son to marry Betsy but his brother Gilbert and
his sisters thought her unsuitable: 'very plain looking . . . the faults of
her character would soon have disgusted (Burns). She was rude and
uncultivated to a great degree, a strong masculine understanding,
with a thorough (tho' unwomanly) contempt for every sort of refine-
ment' (Kinsley, Vol. III, p. 1068). The warmth of the poem com-
bined with the social defiance that his illegitimate daughter should
not be made to feel an inferior outcast is, happily, corroborated by
the remarkable course of the child's life as reported by McGuirk:

> The baby Elizabeth – first grandchild of the poet's mother –
> was reared by her grandmother at Mossgiel farm (Betsey Paton
> returning home to Lairgieside), though the poet offered to take
> the child when he settled down with Jean Armour in 1788. In
> 1786, Burns paid the elder Elizabeth £20 for the child's support
> out of the profits of the Kilmarnock edition (though at this time
> Betsey was not raising her). Ten years later – by then married to
> a farm servant – Elizabeth Paton did reclaim their daughter

when the poet died. Young Elizabeth received £200 of the profits from Currie's posthumous edition of her father's *Works* on her twenty-first birthday in 1806. She married John Bishop, land steward of the Baillie of Polkemmet; tradition reports that she died giving birth to her seventh child on 8 December 1816. Among her descendants is Viscount Weir of Cathcart, whose estate is near Mauchline (p. 211).

Epistle to John Goldie

of Kilmarnock, August 1785

First printed in Stewart, 1801.

[handwritten margin note: wine merchant. Author of religious essay]

O Gowdie, terror o' the Whigs,
Dread o' black coats and reverend wigs!
Sour Bigotry on her last legs
    Girns and looks back,   snarls
Wishing the ten Egyptian plagues
    May seize you quick. —

Poor gapin, glowrin Superstition!   wide-mouthed, staring
Wae's me, she's in a sad condition: woe is
Fye! bring Black Jock[1] her state-physician,   quick
    To see her water:
Alas! there's ground for great suspicion
    She'll ne'er get better. —

Enthusiasm's past redemption,
Gane in a gallopin consumption: gone
Not a' her quacks wi' a' their gumption   doctors, intelligence
    Can ever mend her;
Her feeble pulse gies strong presumption,   gives
    She'll soon surrender. —

Auld Orthodoxy lang did grapple   long
For every hole to get a stapple;   stopper
But now, she fetches at the thrapple,   gurgles, windpipe
    And fights for breath;
Haste, gie her name up in the Chapel,[2]   give
    Near unto death. —

[handwritten margin note: ad right minister.]

1 Black Jock refers to the Rev. John Russel of Kilmarnock, mentioned in *The Holy Fair* and *The Kirk's Alarm*.
2 Chapel – Mr Russel's kirk. R.B.

'Tis you an' Taylor[3] are the chief
To blame for a' this black mischief;
But could the Lord's ain folk gat leave, if, own, got
  A toom tar-barrel   empty
An' twa red peats wad bring relief,   two, would
  And end the quarrel. —

For me, my skill's but very sma',
An' skill in Prose I've nane ava';   none at all
But quietlenswise, between us twa, in confidence, two
  Weel may ye speed;   well, fare
And, tho' they sud you sair misca', should, sore mis-name
  Ne'er fash your head. —   bother

E'en swinge the dogs; and thresh them sicker! flog, sorely
The mair they squeel ay chap the thicker; more, strike
And still 'mang hands a hearty bicker drinking vessel
  O' something stout;
It gars an Owther's pulse beat quicker, makes, author's
  An' helps his wit. —

There's naething like the honest nappy; nothing, beer
Whare'll ye e'er see men sae happy,   where will, so
Or women sonsie, saft and sappy,   pleasant, soft, succulent
  'Tween morn and morn,
As them wha like to taste the drappie who, drop/alcohol
  In glass or horn. —

I've seen me daez't upon a time,   dazed
I scarce could wink or see a styme;   an outline
Just ae hauf-mutchkin does me prime, one half-pint
  (Ought less, is little)
Then back I rattle on the rhyme,
  As gleg's a whittle. —   keen as a knife

Even among the levels of virtuosity prevailing in the less specialised
Enlightenment, John Goldie (1717–1809), author of *The Gospel
Recovered*, is an extraordinary figure. Kinsley describes him:

  A Scottish example of the Augustan virtuoso and 'projector', he
  became a cabinet-maker and later a wine merchant in Kilmar-

3 Taylor – Dr Taylor of Norwich.

nock, speculating in coal-mining and canals; he was an amateur
mathematician, astronomer, and theologian; and one of Burns's
guarantors for the Kilmarnock edition. His *Essays on Various
Important Subjects Moral and Divine*, Goudie's 'Bible', ap-
peared in 1780 (Second edition 1785) (Vol. III, p. 1086).

Along with Dr Richard Taylor (see *To William Simpson, Ochiltree*)
Burns considered he had created the theological break with Calvi-
nism's concept of eternal sin and damnation necessary for the
creation of a liberal, humane, social and political life.

The whigs of l.1 are not, of course, the eighteenth-century
English constitutional reformers but the traditional seventeenth-
century Scottish covenanting group located in the South-West.
Burns makes wicked fun of them as terminally ill, especially with
the terrible Black Jock Russel as prophetic urine tester of his fallen
host. As always in these clerical satires, the poem is saturated with
violence. The Auld Lichts would impose fiery torture (ll. 28–30)
and Burns encourages the New Lichts to strike back. Ironically,
ll. 37–40 echo the brutal landlords' violence of ll. 31–43 in 'The
Address of Beelzebub'. The poem ends in anticipation of a bibulous
world freed from savage religious represssion. It was completed in
August 1785.

Third Epistle to J. Lapraik
Sept. 13, 1785
First published by Cromek, 1808.

Guid speed an' furder to you Johny,	good, progress/luck
Guid health, hale han's, an' weather bony;	good, whole hands, handsome
Now when ye're nickan down fu' cany	cutting, full well
The staff o' bread,	
5 May ye ne'er want a stoup o' bran'y	cup, brandy
To clear your head.	
May Boreas never thresh your rigs,	the North wind
Nor kick your rickles aff their legs,	corn rigs, off
Sendin' the stuff o'er muirs an' haggs	moors, bogs
10 Like drivin wrack;	storm-blown seaweed
But may the tapmast grain that wags	topmast, blows
Come to the sack.	cloth sack/bag

I'm bizzie too, an' skelpin at it,   *busy, striking*
But bitter, daudin showers hae wat it, *pelting, have wet*
15 Sae my auld stumpie-pen I gat it *so, old, short-, got*
   Wi' muckle wark,   *much work*
An' took my jocteleg an' whatt it   *knife, whittled*
   Like onie clark.   *any, clerk*

It's now twa month that I'm your debtor, *two*
20 For your braw, nameless, dateless letter, *fine*
Abusin me for harsh ill nature
   On holy men,
While deil a hair yoursel ye're better, *devil, yourself*
   But mair profane.   *more*

25 But let the kirk-folk ring their bells,
Let's sing about our noble sel's;   *selves*
We'll cry nae jads frae heathen hills *no, goddesses, from*
   To help, or roose us,   *rouse*
But browster wives an' whisky stills, *brewer*
30   *They* are the Muses.

Your friendship sir, I winna quat it, *will not quit*
An' if ye mak' objections at it,   *make*
Then hand in nieve some day we'll knot it, *fist, shake hands*
   An' witness take,
35 An' when wi' Usquabae we've wat it *whisky, wet*
   It winna break.   *will not*

But if the beast and branks be spar'd *bridles*
Till kye be gaun without the herd, *cattle, going*
And a' the vittel in the yard,   *victual/corn*
40   An' theeckit right,   *thatched*
I mean your ingle-side to guard   *fire-*
   Ae winter night.   *one*

Then Muse-inspirin' aqua-vitae   *water of life*
Shall mak us baith sae blythe an' witty, *both so*
45 Till ye forget ye're auld an' gutty, *old, fat*
   And be as canty   *jolly*
As ye were nine year less than thretty, *thirty*
   Sweet ane an' twenty!   *one*

But stooks are cowpet wi' the blast,　　　　corn bundles, knocked over
50 And now the sinn keeks in the west,　　　　sun, peeps, west
Then I maun rin amang the rest　　　　　　must run among
　　　　An' quat my chanter;　　　　　　quit, writing poetry
Sae I subscribe mysel in haste,　　　　　　so
　　　　Yours, RAB THE RANTER.

While this is a certainly briefer, perhaps slighter poem than the
two epistles to Lapraik which Burns chose to publish, it is a fine
poem in itself. Dealing with his second Mauchline harvest, the
poem, as always, is careful to detail farm life, not least its
difficulties. There is also, characteristically, a joking allusion to
what was certainly a shared antipathy to Auld Licht churchmen
(ll. 21–4) and a notion common to Burns (ll. 27–30) that his
energising muse is local not foreign. The poem ends abruptly as
the poet runs in the gathering dark to help save the wind-blown
stooks. Kinsley notes the source of this, one of many, pseudonyms
as derived from Frances Sempill's popular *Maggie Lauder*, ll. 13–16
(Ritson, ii. p. 325):

For I'm a piper to my trade,
　　　My name is Rob the Ranter,
The lasses loup as they were daft,
　　　When I blaw up my chanter.

The double-edged appeal of this image to Burns need not be
elucidated.

To The Rev. John M'math
Inclosing A Copy Of *Holy Willie's Prayer*
Sept. 17, 1785
First published by Cromek, 1808.

WHILE at the stook the shearers cow'r　　　corn sheaves, bend down
To shun the bitter blaudin' show'r,　　　　shelter, belting
Or in gulravage rinnin scow'r　　　　　　horseplay, running, rush about
　　　　To pass the time,
5 To you I dedicate the hour
　　　　In idle rhyme.

My musie, tir'd wi' mony a sonnet　　　　many
On gown, an' ban', an' douse black bonnet,　clerical robes, sombre

Is grown right eerie now she's done it, frightened
10 Lest they should blame her,
An' rouse their holy thunder on it
  And anathem her. curse

I own 'twas rash, an' rather hardy,
That I, a simple, countra Bardie, country
15 Should meddle wi' a pack sae sturdy, so
  Wha, if they ken me, who, know
Can easy, wi' a single wordie, word
  Louse Hell upon me. let loose

But I gae mad at their grimaces, go
20 Their sighan, cantan, grace-prood faces, hypocritical, -proud
Their three-mile prayers, an' hauf-mile graces, half-
  Their raxan conscience, stretching
Whase greed, revenge, an' pride disgraces whose
  Waur nor their nonsense. worse than

25 There's *Gau'n*,[1] miska't waur than a beast, miscalled, worse
Wha has mair honor in his breast who,
Than mony scores as guid's the priest many, good as
  Wha sae abus't him: who so, abused
And may a Bard no crack his jest
30 What way they've use't him?

See him, the poor man's friend in need,
The gentleman in word an' deed,
An' shall his fame an' honor bleed
  By worthless skellums, scoundrels
35 An' not a Muse erect her head
  To cowe the blellums? threaten, bullies

O Pope, had I thy satire's darts
To gie the rascals their deserts, give
I'd rip their rotten, hollow hearts,
40 An' tell aloud
Their jugglin hocus-pocus arts
  To cheat the crowd.

1 Gavin Hamilton.

God knows, I'm no the thing I should be,   not
Nor am I even the thing I cou'd be,
45 But twenty times, I rather would be
        An atheist clean,
Than under gospel colors hid be
        Just for a screen.

An honest man may like a glass,
50 An honest man may like a lass,
But mean revenge, an' malice fause   false
        He 'll still disdain,
An' then cry zeal for gospel laws,
        Like some we ken.   know

55 They take Religion in their mouth;
They talk o' Mercy, Grace, an' Truth,
For what? —To gie their malice skouth   give, play
        On some puir wight,   poor
An' hunt him down, o'er right an' ruth,   pity
60   To ruin streight.   straight

All hail, Religion! maid divine! *— endorsing religion.*
Pardon a Muse sae mean as mine,   so
Who in her rough imperfect line
        Thus daurs to name thee;   dares
65 To stigmatize false friends of thine
        Can ne'er defame thee.

Tho' blotch't and foul wi' mony a stain,   many
An' far unworthy of thy train,
With trembling voice I tune my strain
70   To join with those,
Who boldly dare thy cause maintain
        In spite of foes:

In spite o' crowds, in spite o' mobs,
In spite of undermining jobs,
75 In spite o' dark banditti stabs   bandit-like
        At worth an' merit,
By scoundrels, even wi' holy robes
        But hellish spirit.

O Ayr! my dear, my native ground,
80 Within thy presbytereal bound
A candid lib'ral band is found
    Of public teachers,
As men, as Christians too renown'd
    An' manly preachers.

85 Sir, in that circle you are nam'd;
Sir, in that circle you are fam'd;
An' some, by whom your doctrine's blam'd
    (Which gies ye honor)   gives
Even Sir, by them your heart's esteem'd,
90   An' winning manner.

Pardon this freedom I have ta'en,   taken
An' if impertinent I've been,
Impute it not, good Sir, in ane   one
    Whase heart ne'er wrang'd ye,   whose, wronged
95 But to his utmost would befriend
    Ought that belang'd ye.   anything, belonged to

Previous editors note that John McMath (d. 1825), a native of
Galston, graduated M.A. at Glasgow in 1772, and was ordained
assistant and successor (1782) to Patrick Wodrow, minister of
Tarbolton. He was, like Wodrow, a 'New Licht' moderate. He
'unhappily-fell into low spirits, in consequence of his dependent
situation, and he became dissipated' (Chambers–Wallace, i. 193). In
1791 he resigned and enlisted as a private soldier.

The poem was obviously written to accompany 'Holy Willie's
Prayer' combining as it does Burns's examination of his own
capacity to take on such a formidable enemy (ll. 13–18) with a
further defence (ll. 25–41) of Holy Willie's arch-enemy, Gavin
Hamilton. His wish for Pope's satirical power to assault the Auld
Lichts is not an empty one; this poem is as fine as anything Burns
wrote on their perverted, hypocritical Christianity. Also it resonates
(ll. 73–8) with images similar to those anti-clerical ones found in
Blake's *Songs of Experience* though he and his great English con-
temporary knew nothing of each other's work.

For the relationship of Burns to Blake, see Catherine Carswell,
'Robert Burns', in *From Anne to Victoria*, ed. Bonamy Dobree
(London, 1937), pp. 405–21; Leopold Damrosch, 'Burns, Blake
and the Recovery of the Lyric', *Studies in Romanticism*, 21 (Winter,
1982), pp. 637–60 and Andrew Noble, 'Burns, Blake and Romantic
Revolt', *The Art of Robert Burns*, ed. Jack & Noble (London, 1982),
pp. 191–204.

The Mauchline Wedding

First printed by Wallace, 1896.

When Eighty-five was seven months auld,	old
And wearing thro' the aught,	eighth
When rolling rains and Boreas bauld	north wind, bold/stormy
Gied farmer-folks a faught;	gave, fight
5 Ae morning quondam Mason Will,[1]	one
Now Merchant Master Miller,	
Gaed down to meet wi' Nansie Bell[2]	went
And her Jamaica siller,	money
To wed, that day. —	
10 The rising sun o'er Blacksideen[3]	
Was just appearing fairly,	
When Nell and Bess[4] get up to dress	
Seven lang half-hours o'er early!	long
Now presses clink and drawers jink,	
15 For linnens and for laces;	
But modest Muses only *think*	
What ladies' under dress is,	
On sic a day. —	such
But we'll suppose the stays are lac'd,	
20 And bony bosom steekit;	handsome, held firmly
Tho', thro' the lawn — but guess the rest —	
An Angel scarce durst keekit:	would look
Then stockins fine, o' silken twine,	
Wi' cannie care are drawn up;	prudent
25 An' gartened tight, whare mortal wight —	where
. . . .[5]	
But now the gown wi' rustling sound,	
Its silken[6] pomp displays;	
Sure there's nae sin in being vain	no
O' siccan bonie claes!	such pretty clothes

1 William Miller, a friend of Burns in Mauchline.
2 Nansie Bell, who inherited £500 from her brother who died in Jamaica, married Wm. Miller.
3 A hill. R.B.
4 Miller's two sisters. R.B. [Elizabeth and Helen].
5 As I never wrote it down, my recollection does not entirely serve me. – R.B. Ms.
6 The ladies' first silk gowns, got for the occasion. R.B.

Sae jimp the waist, the tail sae vast —   so narrow, behind so
    Trouth, they were bonie Birdies!
O Mither Eve, ye wad been grave   would have
    To see their ample hurdies   buttocks
        Sae large that day!!!   so

Then Sandy[7] wi's red jacket bra',   with his, fine
    Comes, whip-jee-whoa! about,   whipping to stop the horses
And in he gets the bonie twa —   two
    Lord, send them safely out!
And auld John Trot[8] wi' sober phiz   old, face
    As braid and bra's a Bailie,   broad, fine
His shouthers and his Sunday's giz   shoulders, wig
    Wi' powther and wi' ulzie   powder, oil
        Weel smear'd that day . . . .[9]   well

Burns sent this poem to Mrs Dunlop on 21st August, 1788 with this note: 'You would know an Ayr-shire lad, Sandy Bell who made a Jamaica fortune, & died some time ago. – A William Miller, formerly a Mason, now a Merchant in this place, married a sister german of Bell's for the sake of a £500 her brother had left her. – A Sister of Miller's who was then Tenant of my heart for the time being, huffed my Bardship in the pride of her new Connection; & I, in the heat of my resentment resolved to burlesque the whole business, & began as follows' (Letter 265). Implicit in the burlesque is the brilliant formal joke of situating these prosperous bourgeois in the context of the poetic, Breughelesque peasant brawl form used in *The Holy Fair*. As Galt's novels also testify, money from imperial enterprise was flooding into Scotland; these were the upwardly mobile, showy 'nabobs'. Dress, especially women's dress, reflected this excess consumption. Regarding the protuberances (ll. 30–4) Kinsley notes cf. Creech, who was later to be Burns's publisher: 'Spinal tenuity and mamillary exuberance, have for some time been the fashion with the fair, but a posterior rotundity, or a balance was wanting behind; and you may now tell the country lasses if they wish to be fashionable, they must resemble two blown bladders tied together at the necks' (S. Maxwell and R. Hutchison, *Scottish Costume 1550–1850*, 1958, pp. 89–90). Burns's apparent forgetfulness of that below-the-belt comment of l. 27 was undoubtedly devised to save Mrs Dunlop from further offence.

7 Driver of the post chaise. R.B.
8 Miller's father. R.B.
9 Against my Muse had come thus far, Miss Bess and I were more in Unison, so I thought no more of the Piece. R.B. Ms.

Poem on Pastoral Poetry

First published by Currie, 1800.

Hail, Poesie! thou Nymph reserv'd!
In chase o' thee, what crowds hae swerv'd   pursuit, have
Frae Common Sense, or sunk enerv'd   from
            'Mang heaps o' clavers;   nonsense
5   And och! o'er aft thy joes hae starv'd   often, lovers, have
            'Mid a' thy favours!

Say, Lassie, why thy train amang,   among
While loud the trumps heroic clang,   noise
And Sock and buskin skelp alang   drama symbols, move briskly
10   To death or marriage;
Scarce ane has tried the Shepherd-sang   one, -song
            But wi' miscarriage?

In Homer's craft Jock Milton thrives;
Eschylus' pen Will Shakespeare drives;
15 Wee Pope, the knurlin, till him rives   dwarf, clutches
            Horatian fame;
In thy sweet sang, Barbauld[1], survives
            Even Sappho's flame.

But thee, Theocritus, wha matches?   who
20 They're no Herd's[2] ballats, Maro's catches;
Squire Pope but busks his skinklin patches   smartens up, shining
            O' Heathen tatters: fragments
I pass by hunders, nameless wretches,   hundreds
            That ape their betters.   imitate

25 In this braw age o' wit and lear,   fine, knowledge
Will nane the Shepherd's whistle mair   none, more
Blaw sweetly in its native air   blow
            And rural grace,
And wi' the far-fam'd Grecian share
30   A rival place?

1 Anna L. Barbauld, English radical poet (1743–1825).
2 David Herd (d. 1810).

Yes! there is ane; a Scottish callan!   *one, fellow*
There's ane: come forrit, honest Allan!   *one, forward*
Thou need na jouk behint the hallan,   *not hide behind, partition*
    A chiel sae clever;   *chap so*
35 The teeth o' Time may gnaw Tamtallan,[3]   *chew/turn to rubble*
    But thou's for ever.

Thou paints auld Nature to the nines,   *old*
In thy sweet Caledonian lines;
Nae gowden stream thro' myrtles twines   *no golden, meanders*
40   Where Philomel,
While nightly breezes sweep the vines,
    Her griefs will tell!

Thy rural loves are Nature's sel';   *self*
Nae bombast spates o' nonsense swell;   *no, floods*
45 Nae snap conceits, but that sweet spell   *no*
    O' witchin loove,
That charm that can the strongest quell,
    The sternest move.

In gowany glens thy burnie strays,   *flowery, burn*
50 Where bonie lasses bleach their claes;   *pretty, clothes*
Or trots by hazelly shaws and braes   *bushes, hill sides*
    Wi' hawthorns gray,
Where blackbirds join the shepherd's lays
    At close o' day.

Ultimately, rightly authenticated by Kinsley, there had been doubt about this being by Burns. Despite a holograph, Gilbert Burns thought it not his brother's in the amended Currie edition of 1820. Scott–Douglas (1867) and Henley–Henderson (1896) repeated the old chestnut of Burns's classic knowledge being inadequate to the poem's range of allusion. The image of the restricted ploughman poet dies hard. In actual fact no Scottish vernacular voice in the late eighteenth century spoke with this degree and, indeed, intelligent ease of allusion. See, for example, the compressed comparisons (ll. 13–18) between classical and English literary achievement. Given as we now know that Burns not only avidly read about the classical world but transcribed parts of Gibbon's *Decline and Fall*, as surviving holograph notes in the Wisbech and Fenland Museum reveal.

3 A castle by North Berwick.

The poem's range of allusion is easily within his range. Characteristic of him, too, is the notion that post-Ramsay, there is a potential in the Scottish vernacular to achieve a quality of realistic pastoral poetry not achieved since the golden days of Greece. Certainly Wordsworth, trying himself to break through to a new plain rural speech, considered Burns had got there before him. See Andrew Noble 'Wordsworth and Burns: The Anxiety of Being under the Influence', in *Critical Essays on Robert Burns*, ed. McGuirk, GK. Hall (1998), pp. 49–62.

Love and Liberty:
A Cantata
or The Jolly Beggars

First printed by Stewart and Meikle, Glasgow, 1799.

RECITATIVO

When lyart leaves bestrow the yird,	withered, ground
Or, wavering like the Bauckie-bird,[1]	
Bedim cauld Boreas' blast;	cold, the North Wind
When hailstanes drive wi' bitter skyte,	-stones, lash
And infant Frosts begin to bite,	
In hoary cranreuch drest;	hoar frost
Ae night at e'en a merry core	one, evening, crowd
O' randie, gangrel bodies,	disorderly vagrants
In Poosie-Nansie's[2] held the splore,	merry meeting
To drink their orra duddies:	spare rags
Wi' quaffing, and laughing,	
They ranted an' they sang;	
Wi' jumping, an' thumping,	
The vera girdle rang.	very, iron baking plate
First, niest the fire, in auld red rags,	next, old
Ane sat; weel brac'd wi' mealy bags,	one, well – oat meal
And knapsack a' in order;	
His doxy lay within his arm;	lassie
Wi' USQUEBAE an' blankets warm,	whisky
She blinket on her Sodger:	leered

1 The old Scotch name for the Bat. R.B.
2 The Hostess of a noted Caravansary in M[auchline], well known to and much frequented by the lowest orders of Travellers and Pilgrims. R.B.

An' ay he gies the tozie drab   gives, tipsy
    The tither skelpan kiss,   smacking
While she held up her greedy gab   mouth
    Just like an aumous dish: wooden alms dish
25   Ilk smack still, did crack still,   each
        Just like a cadger's whup;   beggar's whip
      Then swaggering, an' staggering,
        He roar'd this ditty up —

Air – Tune: SOLDIER'S JOY *– military*

sense of march

I am a Son of Mars who have been in many wars,
    And show my cuts and scars wherever I come;
This here was for a wench, and that other in a trench,
    When welcoming the French at the sound of the drum.
5   Lal de daudle, etc.

My Prenticeship I past, where my LEADER breath'd his last,
    When the bloody die was cast on the heights of ABRAM;[1]
And I served out my TRADE when the gallant *game* was play'd,
    And the MORO[2] low was laid at the sound of the drum.

10 I lastly was with Curtis[3] among the *floating batt'ries*,
    And there I left for witness, an arm and a limb;
Yet let my Country need me, with ELLIOT[4] to head me
    I'd clatter on my stumps at the sound of the drum.

And now tho' I must beg with a wooden arm and leg,
15   And many a tatter'd rag hanging over my bum,
I'm as happy with my wallet, my bottle, and my Callet,
    As when I us'd in scarlet to follow a drum.

What tho,' with hoary locks, I must stand the winter shocks,
    Beneath the woods and rocks oftentimes for a home,
20 When the tother bag I sell and the tother bottle tell,
    I could meet a troop of HELL at the sound of a drum.

lass happy with life, but maybe just masking his pain.

---

1 A reference to Mount Maître Abraham, near Quebec, where Wolfe fought and died victorious in 1759.
2 El Moro, a castle near Santiago/St Jago, Cuba. British troops took Havana in 1762.
3 The siege of Gibraltar, 1782, when Captain Curtis destroyed the Spanish ships, 'floating batt'ries'.
4 George Elliot held Gibraltar after the siege and was made a Lord for his service to Britain.

RECITATIVO

He ended; and the kebars sheuk,	rafters shook
Aboon the chorus roar;	above
While frighted rattons backward leuk,	rats, look
An' seek the benmost bore:	innermost hole
5 A fairy FIDDLER frae the neuk,	corner
He skirl'd out, ENCORE.	
But up arose the martial CHUCK,	soldier's whore
An' laid the loud uproar —	

Air – Tune: SODGER LADDIE

I once was a Maid, tho' I cannot tell when,
And still my delight is in proper young men:
Some one of a troop of DRAGOONS was my dadie,
No wonder I'm fond of a SODGER LADDIE. soldier
5   Sing lal de dal, &c.

The first of my LOVES was a swaggering blade,
To rattle the thundering drum was his trade;
His leg was so tight, and his cheek was so ruddy,
Transported I was with my SODGER LADDIE.

10 But the godly old Chaplain left him in the lurch;
The sword I forsook for the sake of the church;
He ventur'd the SOUL, and I risked the BODY,
'Twas then I prov'd false to my SODGER LADDIE.

Full soon I grew sick of my sanctified *Sot*,
15 The Regiment AT LARGE for a HUSBAND I got;
From the gilded SPONTOON to the FIFE I was ready;
I asked no more but a SODGER LADDIE.

But the Peace it reduc'd me to beg in despair,
Till I met my old boy in a CUNNINGHAM Fair;
20 His RAGS REGIMENTAL they flutter'd so gaudy:
My heart it rejoic'd at a SODGER LADDIE.

And now I have lived — I know not how long,
But still I can join in a cup and a song;
And whilst with both hands I can hold the glass steady,
25 Here's to thee, MY HERO, MY SODGER LADDIE!

RECITATIVO

Poor Merry-Andrew in the neuk,   corner
    Sat guzzling wi' a Tinkler-hizzie;   -girl
They mind't na wha the chorus teuk,   not who
    Between themselves they were sae busy:
5 At length wi' drink an' courting dizzy,
    He stoiter'd up an' made a face;   staggered
Then turn'd an' laid a smack on Grizzie,   kiss
    Syne tun'd his pipes wi' grave grimace —   then

Air – Tune: AULD SIR SYMON

Sir Wisdom's a fool when he's fou;   drunk
    Sir Knave is a fool in a Session,
He 's there but a prentice, I trow,   trust/know
    But I am a fool by profession.

5 My Grannie she bought me a beuk,   book
    An' I held awa to the school;   away
I fear I my talent misteuk,   mistook
    But what will ye hae of a fool.   have

For drink I wad venture my neck;   would
10   A hizzie 's the half of my Craft: wench
But what could ye other expect
    Of ane that's avowedly daft.   one, half-witted

I ance was ty'd up like a stirk   once, tied, bullock
    For civilly swearing and quaffing;
15 I ance was abus'd i' the kirk,   once
    For towsing a lass i' my daffin.   touching up, fun

Poor Andrew that tumbles for sport,
    Let nae body name wi' a jeer;   nobody
There's even, I'm tauld, i' the Court   told
20   A Tumbler ca'd the Premier.   called

Observ'd ye yon reverend lad
    Mak faces to tickle the Mob;
He rails at our mountebank squad,
    It's rivalship just i' the job.

25 And now my conclusion I'll tell,
        For faith I'm confoundedly dry:
    The chiel that's a fool for himsel,   fellow
        Guid Lord, he's far dafter than I.

RECITATIVO

the theives to survive.

    Then niest outspak a raucle Carlin,   next, sturdy woman
    Wha kent fu' weel to cleek the Sterlin;   *the*   who knew well, steal money
    For mony a pursie she had hooked,   many
    An' had in mony a well been douked: *X*   many, ducked
5   Her LOVE had been a HIGHLAND
        LADDIE,
    But weary fa' the waefu' woodie!   fall, woeful gallows
    Wi' sighs an' sobs she thus began
    To wail her braw JOHN HIGHLANDMAN —

Air – Tune: O, AN' YE WERE DEAD, GUIDMAN

lowlands.

    A HIGHLAND lad my Love was born,
    The lalland laws he held in scorn;   lowland
    But he still was faithfu' to his clan,
    My gallant, braw JOHN HIGHLANDMAN.   fine

Chorus
5   Sing hey my braw John Highlandman!
        Sing ho my braw John Highlandman!
        There's not a lad in a' the lan'   *he's not as loyal*
        Was match for my John Highlandman.   ➤ *to her as she is*
                                                     to him.

    With his Philibeg, an' tartan Plaid,   kilt
10 An' guid Claymore down by his side,   good broadsword
    The ladies' hearts he did trepan,   ensnare
    My gallant, braw John Highlandman.
        Sing hey my braw &c.

    We ranged a' from Tweed to Spey,
    An' liv'd like lords an' ladies gay:
15 For a lalland face he feared none,   lowland
    My gallant, braw John Highlandman.
        Sing hey my braw &c.

They banish'd him beyond the sea,
But ere the bud was on the tree,
Adown my cheeks the pearls ran,
20   Embracing my John Highlandman.
     Sing hey my braw &c.

But Och! they catch'd him at the last,
And bound him in a dungeon fast,
My curse upon them every one,
They've hang'd my braw John Highlandman!
     Sing hey my braw &c.

25   And now a Widow I must mourn
The Pleasures that will ne'er return;
No comfort but a hearty can,
When I think on John Highlandman.
     Sing hey my braw &c.

RECITATIVO

A pigmy Scraper wi' his Fiddle,	
Wha us'd to trystes an' fairs to driddle,	cattle market, play
Her strappan limb an' gausy middle,	strong, buxom
(He reach'd nae higher)	no
5 Had hol'd his HEARTIE like a riddle,	sieve
An' blawn't on fire.	blown it
Wi' hand on hainch, and upward e'e,	haunch
He croon'd his gamut, ONE, TWO, THREE,	whispered
Then in an ARIOSO key,	melodious
10 The wee Apollo	
Set off wi' ALLEGRETTO glee	paced but graceful
His GIGA SOLO —	

Air Tune: WHISTLE OWRE THE LAVE O'T

Let me ryke up to dight that tear,	reach, wipe
An' go wi' me an' be my DEAR;	
An' then your every CARE an' FEAR	
May whistle owre the lave o't.	over, remainder

Chorus
5   I am a Fiddler to my trade,
      An' a' the tunes that e'er I play'd,
      The sweetest still to WIFE or MAID
      Was Whistle Owre the Lave O't.

      At KIRNS an' WEDDINS we'se be there,   harvest homes
10   An' O sae nicely's we will fare!   so
      We'll bowse about till Dadie Care   booze/drink
      Sing Whistle Owre the Lave O't.
          I am a &c.

      Sae merrily the banes we'll pyke,   so, bones, pick
      An' sun oursells about the dyke;   stone wall
15   An' at our leisure, when ye like
      We'll whistle owre the lave o't.
          I am a &c.

      But bless me wi' your heav'n o' charms,
      An' while I kittle hair on thairms,   move bow-hair, catgut
      HUNGER, CAULD, an' a' sic harms   cold, such
20   May whistle owre the lave o't.
          I am a &c.

RECITATIVO

      Her charms had struck a sturdy CAIRD,   gypsy
         As weel as poor GUTSCRAPER;   well, fiddler
      He taks the Fiddler by the beard,
         An' draws a roosty rapier —   rusty sword
5   He swoor by a' was swearing worth   swore
         To speet him like a Pliver,   spit, plover
      Unless he would from that time forth
         Relinquish her for ever:

      Wi' ghastly e'e poor TWEEDLEDEE   eye
10   Upon his hunkers bended,   knees
      An' pray'd for grace wi' ruefu' face,
         An' sae the quarrel ended;   so
      But tho' his little heart did grieve,
         When round the TINKLER prest her,
15   He feign'd to snirtle in his sleeve   snigger
         When thus the CAIRD address'd her —

Air – Tune: CLOUT THE CAULDRON

My bonie lass I work in brass,
    A TINKLER is my station;   *tinker*
I've travell'd round all Christian ground
    In this my occupation;
5 I've taen the gold an' been enroll'd   *taken*
    In many a noble squadron;
But vain they search'd when off I march'd
    To go an' clout the CAUDRON.   *mend, cauldron*
        I've taen the gold &c.

10 Despise that SHRIMP, that wither'd IMP,
    With a' his noise an' cap'rin;   *capering*
An' take a share, wi' those that bear
    The *budget* and the *apron*!
And *by* that STOWP! my faith an' houpe,   *cup, hope*
15   And *by* that dear KILBAIGIE[1]
If e'er ye want, or meet wi' scant,
    May I ne'er weet my CRAIGIE!   *wet, throat*
        And by that STOWP &c.   *cup*

RECITATIVO

The Caird prevail'd — th' unblushing fair   *gypsy*
    In his embraces sunk;
Partly wi' LOVE o'ercome sae sair,   *so sore*
    An' partly she was drunk:
5 Sir VIOLINO with an air,
    That show'd a man o' spunk,   *mettle/strength*
Wish'd UNISON between the PAIR,
    An' made the bottle clunk   *clink*
        To their health that night.

10 But hurchin Cupid shot a shaft,   *urchin*
    That play'd a DAME a shavie —   *trick*
The Fiddler RAK'D her FORE and AFT,   *had sex with*
    Behint the Chicken cavie: *hen-coop*

---

1 A peculiar sort of whisky so called, a great favourite with Poosie Nansie's clubs. R.B. It was distilled at a brewery of that name in Clackmannanshire.

15 Her lord, a wight of HOMER's craft,[2]
    Tho' limpan wi' the Spavie,   *spavin*
He hirpl'd up an' lap like daft,   *limped, leaped*
    An' shor'd them DAINTY DAVIE   *played*
        O' *boot* that night.   *for free*

[handwritten: → alters to this / class — inversion or / delusion? / blaming a nature of horses]

He was a care-defying blade,
20   As ever BACCHUS listed!
Tho' Fortune sair upon him laid,   *sore*
    His heart, she ever miss'd it.
He had no WISH but — to be glad,
    Nor WANT but — when he thristed;   *thirsted*
25 He hated nought but — to be sad,
    An' thus the Muse suggested
        His sang that night.

Tune: FOR A' THAT, AN' A' THAT *[handwritten: — exception, Scots idiom / in the song.]*

I AM a BARD of no regard,
    Wi' gentle folks an' a' that;
But HOMER LIKE the glowran byke,   *staring crowd*
    Frae town to town I draw that.   *from*

Chorus
5 For a' that an' a' that,
    An' twice as muckle's a' that,   *much as*
I've lost but ANE, I've TWA behin',   *one*
    I've WIFE ENEUGH for a' that.   *enough*

I never drank the MUSES' STANK,   *fountain*
10   Castalia's burn an' a' that,
But there it streams an' richly reams,   *froths*
    My HELICON I ca' that.

[handwritten: to his muse is she.]

Great love I bear to a' the FAIR,
    Their humble slave an' a' that;
15 But lordly WILL, I hold it still
    A mortal sin to thraw that.   *frustrate*

2 Homer is allowed to be the oldest ballad-singer on record. R.B.

In raptures sweet this hour we meet,
    Wi' mutual love an' a' that;
But for how lang the FLIE MAY STANG,   fly, sting
20   Let INCLINATION law that.

Their tricks an' craft hae put me daft,   have
    They've taen me in, an' a' that,   taken
But clear your decks, an' here's the SEX!
    I like the jads for a' that.   jades
25   For a' that an' a' that
        An' twice as muckle's a' that,   much as
My DEAREST BLUID to do them guid,   blood, good
    They're welcome till 't for a' that!

RECITATIVO

So sung the BARD — and Nansie's wa's   walls
Shook with a thunder of applause
    Re-echo'd from each mouth!
They toom'd their pocks, they pawn'd their   emptied pockets,
    duds,   clothes
5 They scarcely left to coor their fuds   cover, behinds
    To quench their lowan drouth:
Then owre again the jovial thrang   over, crowd
    The Poet did request
To lowse his PACK an' wale a sang,   untie, select
10   A BALLAD o' the best.
    He, rising, rejoicing
        Between his TWA DEBORAHS,   two
    Looks round him, an' found them
        Impatient for the Chorus.

[handwritten margin note: → pawned their clothes for drink.]

Air – Tune: JOLLY MORTALS, FILL YOUR GLASSES

See the smoking bowl before us,
    Mark our jovial, ragged ring!
Round and round take up the Chorus,
    And in raptures let us sing —

Chorus
5 A fig for those by law protected!
    LIBERTY'S a glorious feast
Courts for Cowards were erected,
    Churches built to please the PRIEST.

10
What is TITLE, what is TREASURE,
    What is REPUTATION'S care?
If we lead a life of pleasure,
      'Tis no matter HOW or WHERE.
        A fig for those &c.

_ *des hams back to Twa Rey*

With the ready trick and fable
    Round we wander all the day;
15 And at night, in barn or stable,
      Hug our doxies on the hay.   lassies
        A fig for those &c.

Does the train-attended CARRIAGE
    Thro' the country lighter rove?
Does the sober bed of MARRIAGE
20   Witness brighter scenes of love?
        A fig for those &c.

Life is all a VARIORUM,
    We regard not how it goes;
Let them cant about DECORUM,
25   Who have character to lose.
        A fig for those &c.

Here's to BUDGETS, BAGS, and WALLETS!
    Here's to all the wandering train!
Here's our ragged BRATS and CALLETS!   kids, wenches
30   One and all cry out, AMEN!
        A fig for those by LAW protected,
          LIBERTY'S a glorious feast!
        COURTS for Cowards were erected,
          CHURCHES built to please the Priest.

Love and Liberty was written in the winter of 1785. The alternative title *The Jolly Beggars* is not Burns's. It is unknown if Burns read Gay's *The Beggar's Opera* (1728), but various songs sprang from its influence and he would have met a few of them in Ramsay's *Tea Table Miscellany* (1724–37) such as *Jolly Beggars*, *Merry Beggars* and *Scots Cantata*. These works may have served as a literary framework after his experience of the rabble-rousing vagabonds in Poosie Nansie's tavern stirred him to write. There are, however, very few similarities between these texts and Burns's longer stage drama. The dark contrasts of the work are enhanced by the fact that the language of the narration or recitativo, is broad Scots, while the characters (all Scots) mainly speak or sing in neoclassical English.

Arnold's high praise.

Surprisingly, given his distaste for much of Burns's world and quite atypically of nineteenth-century criticism, Matthew Arnold in his 1880 *The Study of Poetry* wrote: 'In the world of *The Jolly Beggars* there is more than hideousness and squalor, there is bestiality; yet the piece is a superb poetic success. It has breadth, truth and power which make its famous scene in Auerbach's Cellar, of Goethe's *Faust*, seem artificial and tame beside it, and which are matched only by Shakespeare and Aristophanes.'

Kinsley, regrettably, sounding more like some nineteenth-century editors, denigrates the characters – 'The people of *Love and Liberty* are the vagrants who infested the Ayrshire roads; who "sorn and thieve, and pilfer and extort alms, from the weak and the timid, to the disgrace of the police, the terror of the inhabitants, and discredit of humanity" (Vol. III, no. 84, p. 1149). This, from W. Aiton's 1811 work on the agricultural life of Ayrshire and its poverty has little, if anything, to do with the personnel in *Love and Liberty*. Mackay repackages this commentary, 'The characters in this work are the vagabonds who then infested the highways "who sorn and thieve. . . ." (p. 182) without acknowledging either source. What we have in the *Cantata*, more than anything, is a window into a sort of pre-Dickensian underworld of Mauchline in 1785.

Kinsley also disagrees with Thomas Crawford's view that *Love and Liberty* embodies criticism of the eighteenth-century social order. In his British Academy Warton Lecture given in 1974, but printed only in 1985, he plays down the poem as anarchic criticism of the status quo and accuses Crawford of being:

. . . over-subtle, misleading us as to Burns's relation to his theme. Folk-poetry constantly mixes common speech and romance (and romantic) diction and it usually does this inno-cently . . . There is indeed much linguistic variety and paradox in *Love and Liberty*, and it is vastly amusing – a concomitant of the mock-heroic posturing of the beggars; but I do not read it as a deliberate social criticism. It seems to me only the kind of stylistic comedy Burns often indulged in just for fun; one way of looking at the beggars; and a means of taking part in the action by verbal proxy. The victims of his irony, indeed, are not his moral readers, but the beggars themselves.

. . . It is easy to draw parallels between sentiments and attitudes in *Love and Liberty* and passages in Burns's familiar epistles; but many of these are the common coin of eighteenth-century popular literature, and Burns's principles *were* 'abundantly motley'. He certainly did not think of *Love and Liberty* as a

significant personal manifesto; he wrote casually to George
Thomson in September 1793:

> I have forgotten the Cantata you allude to, as I kept no copy,
> and indeed did not know that it was in existence; however, I
> remember that none of the songs pleased myself, except the
> last – something about,

> Courts for cowards were erected,
> Churches built to please the priest.

↑playing down due to political intervention.

Characteristically, Kinsley pays no attention to the fact that Burns
was writing to George Thomson who is notoriously unresponsive to
such dissident sentiments against the established institutions. In-
deed, as Daiches has aptly commented, '. . . it is difficult to believe
that he [Burns] could have completely forgotten such a remarkable
work, and it is possible that the political atmosphere of 1793 sug-
gested caution in any reference to this wildly radical cantata' (p. 195).
In response to Kinsley's inadequate treatment we print here in its
entirety the views of that fine American critic, Professor John C.
Weston, who edited *The Jolly Beggars* in 1966. His *Afterword* reads:

> During the winter of 1785, one year before publishing his first
> book of poems, Burns wrote *The Jolly Beggars*. The final poem
> was a result of considerable revision: Burns' friend John Rich-
> mond reported that he had heard three other songs for it which
> are now lost, and Burns rejected another song and its introduc-
> tion which are traditionally included in the poem. But the
> poem, even in its most finished form, never received Burns'
> final polishing touch for publication. Professor Hugh Blair of
> Edinburgh University, one of Burns' many misadvised genteel
> advisers, was evidently so appalled by its bawdiness and fierce
> nihilism, and protested so strongly against letting it see the
> light, that Burns, probably with other such prudish admoni-
> tions echoing in his ears, resigned it to the relative oblivion of
> private circulation in manuscript. One of these manuscripts
> provided the text for a printing in a chapbook three years after
> his death, then a year and a half later in a collection of his
> posthumous pieces, and finally, at the urging of Sir Walter
> Scott, in his collected works, where it has since appeared in the
> many editions with its text in varying degrees of corruption.

> That Burns's best poem—perhaps among the four or five best in
> Britain during the century—should remain unpublished during
> the poet's lifetime seems remarkable and sad. But the explanation

is simple: the poet was unusually vulnerable by being poor, and the poem was and still is unusually heterodox. Burns's poverty, the insecurity of his various schemes of life, and the sometime pathetic eagerness of his efforts at public relations need no demonstration. But the bold theme requires some emphasis. Into this poem, more than into any of his others, Burns freely poured almost the full measure of his favorite ideas and attitudes. The eighteenth-century ideal of the Honest Man, the man whose worth is shown by inner not outward signs [*Second Epistle to J. Lapraik*, stanzas 11, 12, 15], appears here with an emphasis on contempt for the world of respectability [*Address to the Unco Guid*] in contrast to the vigorous 'hair-brained, sentimental . . . hairum-scairum, ram-stam' world of social deviation [*Epistle to James Smith*, stanzas 26–8]. Here also we find the favorite related theme that happiness comes from the heart alone, not from external rewards [*Epistle to Davie, a Brother Poet*, stanza 5]. Pushed further, since the duties necessary to external rewards are denied, this theme modifies into the hedonistic one that obeying inclination is, in a world that is all 'enchanted fairy-land,' the only real principle of life [*Epistle to James Smith*, stanza 12], and even into the complete moral nihilism that denies meaning to anything in the world [*Extempore to Gavin Hamilton*]. Liberty here is absolute and is contrasted to *any* kind of coercion, even that imposed by loyalty to a similar group. Thus independence is absolute too, and leads to an anti-social pride in self ['I Hae a Wife o' My Ain,' *To Mr. M'Adam*, stanzas 4–5]. Other attitudes enter: that those who are poor are more likely than those who are rich to be good lovers and poets [*Green Grow the Rushes, O; Second Epistle to J. Lapraik*, stanza 16] and the old theme, with its corollary of licensed irresponsibility, that those who are at the bottom can be comforted by knowing they cannot fall lower ['The last o't, the warst o't, / Is only but to beg'—*Epistle to Davie, a Brother Poet*, stanza 2].

These attitudes were not unique to Burns, of course, and were ready to his hand in the many seventeenth- and eighteenth-century songs, plays, and broadsides about beggars, gypsies, and other vagabonds. They still are not uncommon, although in different forms, in the literary and folk expressions of man's 'unofficial self,' to use George Orwell's phrase, which David Daiches has aptly borrowed to characterize what this poem appeals to in us. It appeals to our suppressed longing for freedom from the restraints of the official world. But Burns' poem is unique in that the themes are embodied in characters and actions of extraordinary energy. Even the little world surrounding Falstaff in the Boar's Head appears tired in comparison with the world in Poosie Nansie's. Goethe's carousers in Auerbach's cellar of *Faust* seem, as Matthew Arnold asserted, 'artificial and tame' in contrast to the 'breadth, truth, and power' of Burns' beggars. Blake's poems about individual freedom seem weak beside them. Dostoyevsky's Underground Man, with his legion of derivatives, is brooding and dim in contrast. What Burns has done is to write an 'immoral' poem which has a moral effect, because the life force of his outcasts makes us believe by extension in man's powers, endurance, and color. What is all the more remarkable, as the fine Scottish critic Thomas Crawford has noted, this poem, in contrast to other expressions of Rousseauistic and Shaftesburian primitivism in the century, does not arcadianize its subjects but brings them forward with a realism in which the occasional loathsomeness is balanced by the vivacity of their performances. These are the Noble Savages of the eighteenth century saved from the usual concomitant sentimentalism by Scots realism and abounding energy. The only weary, defeated, self-derisive singer, the Merry Andrew in the traditional text, Burns excised from an early draft.

The Jolly Beggars must be read as a miniature comic opera. It has three parts: an overture (the maimed veteran and the camp follower), and action (the rivalry between the fiddler and the tinker for the favors of the widowed pickpocket, with the resolution provided by the bard, who relinquishes one of his three women to the disappointed lover), and a finale (the bard's, second, climactic song). After the veteran begins the show, each character has a dramatic reason for coming forward to sing. The character's views of and positions in life are not exactly the same. The veteran is still loyal to the military establishment, but has been forced out of it by its own evils. His companion embodies total sexual permissiveness and contempt for respectability. Both have found a present substitute in vagabondage for a former better life during war times. The widowed pickpocket has found no satisfactory substitute for a life in which as a thief and a wife of an outlaw she was never accepted by society. She is the only dissatisfied one, whose unhappiness is mitigated by the obvious lusty pleasure she takes in singing of her lost love, and later, as part of the dramatic resolution, by her love match with the tinker. Her hatred of Lowland law and the camp follower's contempt for hypocritical sanctity are preludes to the bard's final devastating dismissal of the Establishment. The fiddler is more vulnerable than the rest, but his pluck and resilience save him from pathos; he just wants to be left alone to enjoy himself in his tiny way, and his ideal of the care free life is a dainty anticipation of the bard's more robust hedonism. The tinker presents another contrast: he is a hulking and bullying amoral materialist who vaunts the security his occupation and occasional bounty jumping give him. The bard, who rises to give his magnanimous approval to the fiddler's timely seduction of one of his three women, also has an occupation, but his is not to gain security but to celebrate the compensatory pleasures of a life of insecurity. After his first song, in which he divorces himself from the genteel world and declares himself for a life of indulgence in sex and art, he is then led by acclamation to sum up in his second song the common attitudes of all who have gone before him in the drama: their animal joy in the outcast's life, their jaunty and pugnacious *joie de vivre*, their belief in making the best of the moment. But in the excitement of the occasion he takes them along with him to a position more radical and explicit than their previous ones, by comparing the pale pleasures of the artificial world to the scarlet pleasures of the natural one. The artificial world, however, is only attacked by being contemned and not by charging that it is productive of involuntary miseries. These are voluntary beggars, whose attitudes are emotional, not intellectual. The beggars do not express any direct attack on the evils of society. The social criticism emerges indirectly, in the manner of burlesque, from the ironic language of gallantry and elegant sentiment put into their unconscious mouths and used to describe their actions. The criticism of life emerges as an exaltation of the freedom of the natural man, with all his real savagery and lust for life, in contrast to the slavery of the social man, with all his safe and tepid pleasures.

See Weston's *Robert Burns. The Jolly Beggars: A Cantata*, Northampton, MA: The Gehenna Press (1963) and Studies in Bibliography: Papers of the Biographical Society of the University of Virginia, ed. Fredson Bowers, Vol. XIII, 1960, pp. 239–47.

The Inventory

To Mr Robt Aiken in Ayr, in answer to his mandate requiring an account of servants, carriages, carriage-horses, riding horses, wives, children, &c.

This appears first with Stewart's collection in 1802.

Sir, as your mandate did request,
I send you here a faithfu' list,
O' gudes an' gear an' a' my graith,   commodities, wealth, clothes
To which I'm clear to gie my aith.   give, oath

5   *Imprimis*, then, for carriage cattle,
    I hae four brutes o' gallant mettle,   have
    As ever drew before a pettle.   plough stick
    My *Lan'-afore* 's[1] a guid auld *has been*,
    An' wight an' wilfu' a' his days been.

10 My *Lan'-ahin* 's[2] a weel-gaun fillie,   well-going horse
    That aft has borne me hame frae Killie,[3]   often, home from
    An' your auld burrough mony a time,   old, (town)
    In days when riding was nae crime —   no
    But ance whan in my wooing pride   once, when

15 I like a blockhead boost to ride,
    The wilfu' creature sae I pat to,   so
    (Lord pardon a' my sins an' that too!)
    I play'd my fillie sic a shavie,   horse such a trick
    She 's a' bedevil'd wi' the spavie.   spavin

20 My *Furr ahin* 's[4] a wordy beast,   rear furrow, worthy
    As e'er in tug or tow was traced. —
    The fourth's a Highland Donald hastie,   quick-tempered pony
    A damn'd red wud Kilburnie blastie;   stark mad, pest
    Foreby, a *Cowt*, o' *Cowtes* the wale,   colt, pick of

25 As ever ran afore a tail.
    If he be spar'd to be a beast,
    He'll draw me fifteen pun' at least. —   pound
    Wheel-carriages I hae but few,   have
    Three carts, an' twa are feckly new;   two, almost

30 An auld wheelbarrow, mair for token,   old, more
    Ae leg an' baith the trams are broken;   one, both, shafts
    I made a poker o' the spin'le,   spindle
    An' my auld mither brunt the trin'le. —   old mother, burned, wheel
    For men, I've three mischievous boys,

35 *Run-de'ils* for rantin an' for noise;   regular devils, frolic
    A gaudsman ane, a thrasher t'other,   plough driver
    Wee Davoc[5] hauds the nowte in fother.   holds, cattle, fodder
    I rule them as I ought, discreetly,
    An' aften labour them completely.   often

40 An' ay on Sundays duly nightly,

---

1 The fore-horse on the left hand, in the plough. R.B.
2 The hindmost horse on the lefthand, in the plough. R.B.
3 Kilmarnock. R.B.
4 The hindmost horse on the right hand, in the plough. R.B.
5 Wee Davoc was David Hutcheson, whom Burns took around with him on
Lochlea farm and according to tradition carried him on his shoulders and
taught him English.

I on the Questions *targe* them tightly; catechisms, question
Till faith, wee Davoc's turn'd sae gleg, so sharp
Tho' scarcely langer than your leg, longer
He'll screed you aff Effectual Calling,[6] repeat, off
45 As fast as ony in the dwalling. — any, dwelling
I've nane in female servan' station, none
(Lord keep me ay frae a' temptation!) always from
I hae nae wife; and that my bliss is, have no
An' ye hae laid nae tax on misses; have, no
50 An' then if kirk folks dinna clutch me, do not
I ken the devils darena touch me. know, dare not
Wi' weans I'm mair than weel contented, children, more, well
Heav'n sent me ane mair than I wanted. one more
My sonsie, smirking, dear-bought Bess, plump, Elizabeth Burns
55 She stares the daddy in her face,
Enough of ought ye like but grace;
But her, my bonny, sweet wee lady,
I've paid enough for her already,
An' gin ye tax her or her mither, if, mother
60 By the Lord! ye 'se get them a' thegither. together

And now, remember Mr. Aiken,
Nae kind of licence out I'm takin; no
Frae this time forth, I do declare, from
I'se ne'er ride horse nor hizzie mair; women more
65 Thro' dirt and dub for life I'll paidle, mire, wade
Ere I sae dear pay for a saddle; so
My travel a' on foot I'll shank it, walk
I've sturdy bearers, Gude be thankit. — legs, God, thanked
The Kirk and you may tak' you that,
70 It puts but little in your pat; pot
Sae dinna put me in your buke, so do not, book
Nor for my ten white shillings luke. look

This list, wi' my ain han' I wrote it, own
Day and date as under notit, noted
75 Then know all ye whom it concerns,
Subscripsi huic, I have endorsed this
Robert Burns.
Mossgiel, Feb. 22nd 1786.

6 This is one of the Shorter Catechisms to answer the question *What is Effectual Calling?*

This poem is a witty deviant form of Burns's standard satirical practice of reducing the great world of politics to the dimensions of his farmyard so that, for example, Pitt and Fox become midden-contending cockerels. The political event that intrudes on him here is Pitt's attempt in May 1785 to create a new tax system based on carriages, windows, married status, female servants and numbers of children. This was to pay for the growing debt initiated by the loss of America and a series of loans to foreign powers. This allows for a series of running jokes through the poem mainly based on the disparity between the poet's paucity of worldly goods and Pitt's fiscal intentions. He has no carriage horses but plough horses about which we are, characteristically, intimately informed as to their nature and function. The energy of the horse both for itself and as a metaphor for raw, randy male sexual energy also runs though the poem. First recorded in medieval texts, 'riding' has had extensive, ambivalent usage. See ll. 13–19 and ll. 63–4. Sexually, too, we are treated to the temptations for him of female servants (ll. 46–7) and, of course, his illegitimate daughter who is the beloved outcome of just such a previous encounter (ll. 52–60). Burns's near patriarchal appetite for surrounding himself with progeny derived in and out of wedlock also extends to wee Davoc the orphan son of a ploughman adopted by the family who, according to tradition, Burns carried on his shoulders round Lochlea while teaching him English. What he certainly would not be doing is imposing on Davoc and the older boys (ll. 40–5) the rote religious instruction of *The Shorter Catechism*. As Liam McIlvanney has noted, it was precisely against this kind of doctrinaire environment that their father hired Murdoch to give his sons an alternative, relatively liberal education. The intimate, wry, knowing tone of the poem is influenced, of course, by the addressee who is his true friend Robert Ai[t]ken (ironically governmentally appointed for this task), a powerful, practical supporter of the Kilmarnock edition and Gavin Hamilton's lawyer in their legal savaging of 'Holy Willie'.

To John Kennedy,
Dumfries House, Mossgiel, 3rd March, 1786.
First printed in 1834, by Cunningham.

	Now, Kennedy, if foot or horse	
	E'er bring you in by Mauchline Corss,	cross
	Lord, man, there's lasses there wad force	would
	A hermit's fancy,	
5	And down the gate in faith they're worse	road
	An' mair unchancy.	more dangerous

But as I'm sayin, please step to Dow's	Whitefoord Arms
An' taste sic gear as Johnnie brews,	such liquor
Till some bit callan bring me news	young lad
10 That ye are there,	
An' if we dinna hae a bouze,	do not, booze
I'se ne'er drink mair.	more

It's no I like to sit an' swallow	
Then like a swine to puke an' wallow,	
15 But gie me just a true guid fallow	give, good fellow
Wi' right ingine,	wit/inclination
And spunkie ance to mak us mellow,	whisky once
An' then we'll shine.	

Now if ye're ane o' warl's folk,	one, world's
20 Wha rate the wearer by the cloak	who
An' sklent on poverty their joke	look down on the poor
Wi' bitter sneer,	
Wi' you nae friendship I will troke,	no, exchange
Nor cheap nor dear.	

25 But if as I'm informed weel	well
Ye hate as ill's the vera deil	very Devil
The flinty heart that canna feel —	cannot
Come Sir, here's tae you:	to
Hae there's my han', I wiss you weel	have, hand, wish, well
30 An' Gude be wi' you.	good attend you

This occasional poem was sent to John Kennedy on 3rd March, 1786 in response to his request (Letter 22) for a copy of *The Cotter's Saturday Night*. Johnie Dow (l. 7) was the proprietor of the Whitefoord Arms, Mauchline. Kennedy was related to Gavin Hamilton's wife, Helen Kennedy and factor to the Earl of Dumfries. What the poem represents is clever sounding-out of the socially superior Kennedy as possible friend by a series of suggestions as to the degree of his liberalism on matters of drink, women and social sympathy.

Adam Armour's Prayer

First published in *The Edinburgh Magazine*, January 1808.

GUDE pity me, because I'm little,   God
For though I am an elf o' mettle,
And can, like ony wabster's shuttle,   any weaver's
    Jink there or here;   dodge
5 Yet, scarce as lang's a guid kail whittle,   long as, good cabbage knife
    I'm unco queer.   very odd

An' now Thou kens our woefu' case,   knows
For *Geordie's Jurr* we're in disgrace,   maid
Because we stang'd her through the place,   rode her on a stake
10   An' hurt her spleuchan,   purse/vagina
For which we daurna show our face   that reason, dare not
    Within the clachan.

An' now we're dern'd in dens and hollows,   hidden
And hunted as was William Wallace,
15 Wi' Constables, those blackguard fallows,   they, fellows
    An' Sodgers baith;   soldiers, both
But Gude preserve us frae the gallows,   God, from
    That shamefu' death!

Auld, grim, black-bearded Geordie's sell;   old
20 Oh, shake him owre the mouth o' Hell,   over
There let him hing, an' roar, an' yell,
    Wi' hideous din,
And if he offers to rebel,
    Then heave him in.

25 When Death comes in wi' glimmering blink,   glance
An' tips auld drucken Nanz the wink,   old drunken
May Satan gie her arse a clink,   give, smack
    Within his yet,   gate
An' fill her up wi' brimstone drink
30   Red, reeking, het.   smoking, hot

There's Jock an' the hav'rel Jenny,   half-witted
Some Devil seize them in a hurry,
An' waft them in th' infernal wherry
    Straught through the lake,
35 An' gie their hides a noble curry   give
    Wi' oil of aik.   a beating with oak

As for the *Jurr*, puir worthless body,   maid, poor
She's got mischief enough already,
Wi' stanget hips and buttocks bloody,   wounds from the stake
40   She's suffer'd sair;   sore
But may she wintle in a woodie,   swing from a noose
   If she whore mair.   more

This poem involves an explosive clash between two worlds: the licentious hostelry tribe of *The Jolly Beggars* and its would-be repressors, the lads of 'Auld Licht' conviction led by Jean Armour's brother, Adam. Sleeping with Jean, Burns was sleeping with a daughter of the enemy. Here, indeed, hatred for his wife's clan bursts forth in this vicious, strange account of her brother, Adam, and the state of mind he represents. The apparent biographical source of the story is that George Gibson, landlord of *Poosie Nancy's*, had hired a maid (Agnes Wilson) who was really a prostitute. Adam and his gang had responded by 'stanging' her; riding her out of town on a rail with all the bloody, bruising consequences to a drawerless woman of a rough wooden pole thrust between her legs. Gibson had sought legal reparation and the lads had made themselves scarce. Armour's identification of his cowardly brutality with Wallace's natural heroism is as crazily ironic as William Fisher's identification with God in that companion-piece prayer of total hypocrisy, *Holy Willie's Prayer*. Armour's rhetoric displays a similar level of hate-filled imaginings of eternal damnation being visited on his enemies. His apparent sympathy in the last stanza for the woman having suffered enough is undermined by the fact that any more whoring should lead to her lynching. Indeed, Auld Lichts' pathologically sadistic rhetoric becomes, in this poem, tangible sadism. Adam Armour was small but the first stanza seems to describe not as a human being but, surreally, a free-floating phallus. He is, indeed, 'unco queer'. The half-witted girl (l. 31) is Poosie Nansie's own daughter, known as 'Racer Jess'. The word 'arse' (l. 27) in often printed as 'doup'.

The Bonie Lass o' Ballochmyle

Tune: Etterick Banks.
First printed by Currie, 1800.

'Twas ev'n, the dewy fields were green,
    On ev'ry blade the pearls hang,
The Zephyr wanton'd round the bean,
    And bore its fragrant sweets alang;   *along*
5 In ev'ry glen the Mavis sang,   *thrush*
    All Nature list'ning seem'd the while;
Except where greenwood Echoes rang
    Amang the braes o' Ballochmyle.   *hill slopes*

With careless step I onward stray'd,
10   My heart rejoic'd in Nature's joy,
When, musing in a lonely glade,
    A Maiden fair I chanc'd to spy:
Her look was like the Morning's eye,
    Her air like Nature's vernal smile,
15 The lilies' hue and roses' dye
    Bespoke the Lass o Ballochmyle.

Fair is the morn in flow'ry May,
    And sweet an ev'n in Autumn mild;   *evening*
When roving through the garden gay,
20   Or wand'ring in the lonely wild;
But Woman, Nature's darling child,
    There all her charms she does compile,
And all her other works are foil'd
    By the bony Lass o' Ballochmyle.

25 O if she were a country Maid,
    And I the happy country Swain!
Though shelter'd in the lowest shed
    That ever rose on Scotia's plain:
Through weary Winter's wind and rain,
30   With joy, with rapture I would toil,
And nightly to my bosom strain
    The bony Lass o' Ballochmyle.

Then Pride might climb the slipp'ry steep
　　Where fame and honours lofty shine:
35 And Thirst of gold might tempt the deep
　　Or downward seek the Indian mine:
Give me the Cot below the pine,
　　To tend the flocks or till the soil,
And ev'ry day have joys divine
40 　　With the bony Lass o' Ballochmyle.

While this is, rightly, a much loved, much sung Burns song, the circumstances both surrounding its genesis and fate provide a kind of preliminary caricature of Burns's relationships with upper class women which, in the course of his life, evolve from this near farce to, with Maria Riddell, incipient tragedy. When actually briefly glimpsed on the autumnally wooded banks of Ayr, Miss Willhemina Alexander (1753–1843), sister of the new laird of Ballochmyle, Claud Alexander, was in her thirties, well beyond the usual marriageable age, and advancing towards permanent spinsterhood. Burns rushed home to write the song and on 18th November, 1786 wrote Miss Alexander an accompanying letter. The whole letter should be read as Burns at his excessively sentimental worst when, with the licence and identity of 'the poetic Reveur', he lays down his ill-disguised erotic credentials as 'hyperman' of feeling:

　. . . the favorite haunts of my Muse, the banks of Ayr . . . The sun was flaming o'er the distant western hills; not a breath stirred the crimson opening blossom, or the verdant spreading leaf. – 'Twas a golden moment for a Poetic heart. – I listened the feathered warblers, pouring their harmony on every hand, with a congenial, kindred regard; & frequently turned out of my path, lest I should disturb their little songs, or frighten them to another station. – 'Surely,' said I to myself, 'he must be a wretch indeed, who, regardless of your harmonious endeavours to please him, can eye your elusive flights, to discover your secret recesses, and rob you of all the property Nature gives you – your dearest comforts, your helpless little Nestlings' – Even the hoary Hawthorn twig that shot across the way, what heart at such a time, but must have been interested in its welfare, and wished it to be preserved from the rudely browsing cattle, or the withering eastern Blast? – Such was the scene, & such the hour, when in a corner of my prospect, I spied one of the fairest pieces of Nature's workmanship that has ever crowned a Poetic landscape; those visionary Bards excepted, who hold commerce with aerial beings (Letter 56).

Adam Smith

risingly shaken not stirred by this missive, Miss Alexander
ly enquired into the nature of her admirer. Again unsurpris-
ingly, reports of his character were such that she decided not to
reply. Symptomatic of the nineteenth-century Burns cult, she died
in 1843, aged ninety, with song and letter as her most treasured
possession. The smart of rejection stayed with Burns to the degree
that years later he recorded:

> Well, Mr Burns, and *did* the lady give you the desired permis-
> sion? No! She was too fine a Lady *to notice* so plain a compliment.
> As to her great brothers, whom I have since met in life on more
> equal terms of respectability – why should I quarrel their want of
> attention to me? When Fate swore their purses should be full,
> Nature was equally positive that their heads should be empty.
> 'Men of their fashion were surely incapable of being impolite?'
> Ye canna mak a silk-purse o' a sow's lug (Letter 217).

Ll. 15–16, read, in some texts, 'Perfection whisper'd, passing by — /
"Behold the lass o' Ballochmyle!" ' The improvement by Burns is
adopted above.

To James Tennant of Glenconner

First published by Stewart, 1802.

AULD com'rade dear and brither sinner,	old, brother
How 's a' the folk about Glenconner;	all
How do ye this blae eastlin win',	biting, wind
That's like to blaw a body blin':	blow, blind
For me my faculties are frozen,	
My dearest member nearly dozen'd:	penis, torpid
I've sent you here by Johnie Simson,[1]	
Twa sage Philosophers to glimpse on!	two
Smith, wi' his sympathetic feeling,	
10 An' *Reid*, to common sense appealing.	
Philosophers have fought and wrangled,	
An' meikle Greek an' Latin mangled,	much
Till, wi' their Logic-jargon tir'd,	
And in the depth of science mir'd,	
15 To common sense they now appeal,	
What wives and wabsters see an' feel;	weavers

arrest influence of Adam Smith

1 The dance teacher at Ochiltree.

But, hark ye, friend, I charge you strictly,
Peruse them, an' return them quickly;
For now I'm grown sae cursed douse,   so, serious
20   I pray and ponder *butt* the house,   within the
My shins, my lane, I there sit roastin,   alone
Perusing *Bunyan*, *Brown*, and *Boston*;
Till by an' by, if I haud on,   hold/wait
I'll grunt a real Gospel groan:
25   Already I begin to try it,
To cast my een up like a Pyet,   eyes, magpie
When by the gun she tumbles o'er,
Flutt'ring an' gasping in her gore:
Sae shortly you shall see me bright,   so
30   A burning an' a shining light.

My heart-warm love to guid auld Glen,[2]   good, old
The ace an' wale of honest men;   pick
When bending down wi' auld grey hairs,   old
Beneath the load of years and cares,
35   May He who made him still support him,
An' views beyond the grave comfort him.

His worthy fam'ly far and near,
God bless them a' wi' grace and gear.   wealth

My auld school-fellow, Preacher Willie,[3]   old
40   The manly tar, my mason billie,   comrade
An' Auchenbay,[4] I wish him joy;
If he's a parent, lass or boy,
May he be dad, and Meg[5] the mither,   mother
Just five and forty years thegither!   together
45   An' no forgetting wabster Charlie,[6]   weaver
I'm tauld he offers very fairly,   told
An' Lord, remember singing Sannock[7]
Wi' hale-breeks, saxpence, an' a bannock;   whole breeches, sixpence
And next, my auld acquaintance, Nancy,[8]

2 John Tennant, James's father.
3 Rev. William Tennant.
4 John Tennant Junior.
5 Margaret Colville.
6 This weaver is not identified by any editor.
7 Robert Tennant.
8 Agnes Tennant.

50 Since she is fitted to her fancy;
 An' her kind stars hae airted till her,   *have, given her*
 A guid chiel wi' a pickle siller: *good man, some money*
 My kindest, best respects I sen' it,
 To cousin Kate an' sister Janet,
55 Tell them frae me, wi' chiels be cautious; *from, men*
 For, faith they'll aiblins fin' them fashious: *maybe, trouble*
 To grant a heart is fairly civil,
 But to grant a maidenhead's the devil!
 An' lastly, Jamie, for yoursel,
60 May guardian angels tak a spell,
 An' steer you seven miles south o' Hell;
 But first, before you see Heaven's glory,
 May ye get mony a merry story,   *many*
 Mony a laugh and mony a drink,
65 And ay eneugh o' needfu' clink.   *enough, coins*

 Now fare ye weel, an' joy be wi' you,   *well*
 For my sake this I beg it o' you,
 Assist poor Simson a' ye can,
 Ye'll fin' him just an honest man: *find*
70 Sae I conclude and quat my chanter,   *so, end, song*
 Yours, saint or sinner,
 RAB THE RANTER.

This casual, colloquial rhyming epistle was written in 1786 to James Tennant (1755–1835) of Glenconner who was a miller in Ochiltree. It was his father, John, who advised Burns to take the Ellisland lease. Burns seems to have borne no grudge over this as the poem intimately recalls seemingly the whole Tennant clan. What is of most interest is the opposition Burns builds in the text between Smith and Reid's Enlightenment philosophical texts which he is sending to Tennant and the earlier religous tracts which, left with at home, he is endangering his soul by compulsively reading (ll. 19–30). Bunyan's *Pilgrim's Progress* was widely disseminated among the Scottish peasantry (David Craig, *Scottish Literature and the Scottish People 1680–1830*, p. 66). John Brown (1722–87) was author of *The Self-Interpreting Bible*. Thomas Boston (1676–1732) was the author of *The Four-fold State of Man*. If proof be further needed, this poems confirms Burns's easy grasp of theological and philosophical issues. Ll. 55–8 reveal Burns in his occasional mood of Polonian prudence.

Inscribed on a Work of Hannah More's
Presented to the Author by a Lady
First printed circa 1824.

Thou flattering mark of friendship kind
Still may thy pages call to mind
    The dear, the beauteous donor:
Tho' sweetly female every part
5 Yet such a head, and more the heart,
    Does both the sexes honor.
She showed her taste refined and just
    When she selected thee,
Yet deviating own I must,
10   For so approving me.
But kind still, I mind still,
    The giver in the gift;
I'll bless her and wiss her   wish
    A Friend aboon the Lift.   above, heavens

These lines were written by Burns in a letter to Robert Aitken, in April 1786 (Letter 24). The poet merely refers to the 'flattering' he obtained from 'Mrs C -'s notice'. The identity of Mrs C – who gave Burns a copy of Hannah More's poetry is still unknown. The original text in the book is missing. It would appear from the language of Burns, the lady was aristocratic. Previous editors speculatively list various names as possible candidates.

Ah, Woe is Me, My Mother Dear
Jeremiah, chap. 15, verse 10
First printed by James Hogg, 1835.

Ah, woe is me, my Mother dear!
    A man of strife ye've born me:
For sair contention I maun bear,   sore, must
    hey hate, revile, and scorn me. —

5 I ne'er could lend on bill or band,   bond
    That five per cent might blest me;
And borrowing, on the tither hand,
    The deil a ane wad trust me. —   devil, no one would

Yet I, a coin-denied wight,
10   By Fortune quite discarded,
Ye see how I am day and night,
        By lad and lass blackguarded. —   miscalled

This is a versification of Biblical prose and clearly alludes to the troubles suffered in 1786 by the poet while the wrangle ensued over his relationship with Jean Armour.

To Mr Gavin Hamilton, Esq., Mauchline
Recommending a Boy. Mossgaville, May 3, 1786
First printed in Cromek, 1808.

I hold it, Sir, my bounden duty
To warn you how that MASTER TOOTIE,
        Alías, Laird M'Gawn,
Was here to hire yon lad away
5   'Bout whom ye spak the tither day,   spoke, other
        An' wad hae don't aff han':   would have done it, off hand
But lest he learn the callan tricks,   boy
        As faith I muckle doubt him,   much
Like scrapin out auld Crummies' nicks,   old cows' horns
10   An' tellin lies about them;
            As lieve then I'd have then,   rather
                Your CLERKSHIP he should sair;   serve
            If sae be ye may be   so
                Not fitted otherwhere. —

15   Altho' I say't, he's gleg enough,   sharp
An' bout a HOUSE that's rude an' rough
        The boy might learn to SWEAR;
But then wi' you, he'll be sae taught,   so
An' get sic fair EXAMPLE straught,   such, straight
20   I hae na ony fear.   have not any
Ye'll catechise him, every quirk,
        An' shore him weel wi' HELL;   threaten, well
An' gar him follow to the kirk —   make
        — Ay when ye gang YOURSEL.   always, go
25   If ye, then, maun be then   must
            Frae hame, this comin Friday,   from home
        Then please Sir, to lea'e Sir,   leave
            The orders wi' your LADY.

My word of HONOR I hae gien,   have given
30   In PAISLEY JOHN'S, that night at e'en,
         To meet the WARLD'S WORM;   world's – a greedy person
     To try to get the twa to gree,   two to agree
     An' name the airles, an' the fee,   conditions/payment
         In legal mode an' form:
35   I ken, he weel a SNICK can draw,   know, well, play a trick
         When simple bodies let him;
     An' if a DEVIL be at a',
         In faith, he's sure to get him. —
     To phrase you, an' praise you,
40   Ye ken, your LAUREAT scorns: know, poet
     The PRAY'R still, you share still
         Of grateful MINSTREL BURNS.

This personal, genuinely occasional poem was not published till
Cromek's edition of 1808. It involves Burns's attempt to save a lad in
his service at the ironically Frenchified 'Mossgaville' from becom-
ing the servant of Master Tootie, known in Mauchline as 'Laird
McGaun'. One of McGaun's specialities was scraping the horns of
cattle to make them look younger. He wished instead to install the
lad in apprenticeship to Hamilton. The second stanza is, of course,
entirely ironic, given Hamilton's habits, as to the degree of religious
instruction and discipline the boy would receive. The last stanza
cautions Hamilton that, due to the poet himself, the proposed
apprenticeship of the boy to diabolic McGaun is far advanced.
What is also interesting is the degree to which Burns's immediate,
consummate technical virtuosity allowed him to dash off an occa-
sional piece in such elaborate metrical form.

Nature's Law
Humbly Inscribed to Gavin Hamilton, Esq.
First printed in the Aldine edition of 1830.

'Great Nature spoke, observant man obey'd'.
POPE

Let other heroes boast their scars,
    The marks o' sturt and strife;   violence/trouble
And other poets sing of wars,
    The plagues o' human life;
5   Shame fa' the fun; wi' sword and gun   fall
    To slap mankind like lumber!
I sing his name, and nobler fame,
    Wha multiplies our number.   who

Great Nature spoke, with air benign,
10   'Go on, ye human race;
This lower world I you resign;
      Be fruitful and increase.
The liquid fire of strong desire
      I've poured it in each bosom;
15 Here, on this hand, does Mankind stand,
      And there, is Beauty's blossom.'

The Hero of these artless strains,
      A lowly Bard was he,
Who sung his rhymes in Coila's plains,   Kyle's
20   With meikle mirth an' glee;   much
Kind Nature's care had given his share
      Large, of the flaming current;
And, all devout, he never sought
      To stem the sacred torrent.

25 He felt the powerful, high behest
      Thrill, vital, thro' and thro';
And sought a correspondent breast,
      To give obedience due:
Propitious Powers screen'd the young flow'rs,
30   From mildews of abortion;
And lo! the Bard — a great reward —
      Has got a double portion![1]

Auld cantie Coil may count the day,   old cheerful Kyle
      As annual it returns,
35 The third of Libra's equal sway,
      That gave another Burns,
With future rhymes, an' other times,
      To emulate his sire,
To sing auld Coil in nobler style,   old
40   With more poetic fire.

Ye Powers of peace, and peaceful song,
      Look down with gracious eyes;
And bless auld Coila, large and long,   old
      With multiplying joys;
45   Lang may she stand to prop the land,   long
The flow'r of ancient nations;
And Burnses spring, her fame to sing,
      To endless generations!

[1] A reference to the birth of the poet's twins.

It is not to be wondered at that this poem did not surface till the Aldine edition of 1830. While not seditious, it certainly provides a somewhat frisky and risky celebration (especially ll. 29–32) of the birth of Jean Armour's twins on 3rd September, 1786 ('The third of Libra's equal sway'). The poem begins with a general assertion, frequent in Burns, that procreation is everywhere and in every manner to be preferred to assassination. Like Blake, Burns was hypersensitive to the pervasive state and military violence of the late eighteenth century. Burns, indeed, could have been resurrected with Blake in the 1960s as an assertor against the bloody South-East Asian tide that it was better to make love than war.

Extempore – To Gavin Hamilton

First printed by Alexander Smith, 1868.

To you, Sir, this summons I've sent,
    Pray whip till the pownie is fraething;   pony, frothing
But if you demand what I want,
    I honestly answer you, naething. —   nothing

5 Ne'er scorn a poor Poet like me,
    For idly just living and breathing,
While people of every degree
    Are busy employed about — naething. —

Poor Centum per centum may fast,
10   And grumble his hurdies their claithing;   buttocks, clothing
He'll find, when the balance is cast,
    He's gane to the Devil for — naething. —

The Courtier cringes and bows,
    Ambition has likewise its plaything;
15 A Coronet beams in his brows,
    And what is a Coronet? naething. —

Some quarrel the presbyter gown,
    Some quarrel Episcopal graithing;   vestments
But every good fellow will own
20   The quarrel is all about — naething. —

The lover may sparkle and glow,
    Approaching his bonie bit gay thing;   handsome
But marriage will soon let him know,
    He's gotten a buskit up naething. —   dressed-up nothing

25   The Poet may jingle and rhyme,
    In hopes of a laureate wreathing,
And when he has wasted his time,
    He's kindly rewarded with naething. —

The thundering bully may rage,
30   And swagger and swear like a heathen;
But collar him fast, I'll engage
    You'll find that his courage is naething. —

Last night with a feminine Whig,
    A Poet she couldna put faith in,   could not
35   But soon we grew lovingly big,
    I taught her, her terrors were naething. —

Her Whigship was wonderful pleased,
    But charmingly tickled wi' ae thing;   one
Her fingers I lovingly squeezed,
40   And kissed her, and promised her —
        naething. —

The Priest anathemas may threat,
    Predicament, Sir, that we're baith in;   both
But when honor's reveillé is beat,
    The holy artillery's naething. —   clerical punishments

45   And now I must mount on the wave,
    My voyage perhaps there is death in;
But what of a watery grave!
    The drowning a Poet is naething. —

And now as grim Death's in my thought,
50   To you, Sir, I make this bequeathing:
My service as long as ye've ought,
    And my friendship, by God, when ye've naething. —

This poem was first printed by Alexander Smith in 1868. It was questioned first but later accepted when discovered in the Glenriddel Manuscript collection. Its retarded appearance is due to the fact that it is a disturbed and disturbing poem. The short jarring lines and the repetitive 'naething' at the end of the stanza gives the poem a Byronic or, indeed, modern feeling of nihilistic anxiety. It is not for nothing that John Berryman knew and admired Burns to the degree that the Scottish poet features in his extraordinary *Dream Songs*. The ascending catalogue of emptiness, including that of poetry itself, evolves to include the possibility of the poet's own death by drowning on the proposed Atlantic passage to Jamaica. Another reason for its non-publication is, of course, the allusion in ll. 33–40 of Jean Armour's Whig opposition's failure to withstand the Bard's (phallic) divine right. Ll. 41–0 again testify to his and Hamilton's mutual loathing of clerical intrusion. It is a bitter poem, quite without the consolations of the Ayrshire epistolary poetry contemporary with it.

Lines Written on a Bank-Note

First printed in *The Morning Chronicle*, 27th May, 1814.

WAE worth thy pow'r, thou cursed leaf!
Fell source of a' my woe and grief!
For lake o' thee I've lost my lass;   lack
For lake o' thee I scrimp my glass;
5   I see the children of Affliction
Unaided, thro' thy curs'd restriction;
I've seen th' Oppressor's cruel smile
Amid his hapless victims' spoil;
And for thy potence vainly wish'd
10   To crush the Villain in the dust:
For lake o' thee I leave this much-lov'd shore,
Never, perhaps to greet old Scotland more!
R. B. Kyle.

These lines were written by Burns on the back of a Bank of Scotland note for one guinea. The note is dated for 1780. They express the poet's despair at ever being able through farm labour to make ends meet. It is evident in the final couplet that composition occurred during 1786 when the poet felt he might be forced to leave Scotland. The modern folk band The McCluskey Brothers have put music to and recorded these biting, indignant lines.

Lines Addressed to Mr John Ranken

First published by Thomas Stewart, 1801.

Ae day, as Death, that grusome carl,	one, fellow
Was driving to the tither warl'	other world
A mixtie-maxtie motley squad,	hotch-potch
And mony a guilt-bespotted lad;	many
5 Black gowns of each denomination,	clerical robes
And thieves of every rank and station,	
From him that wears the star and garter	Knights
To him that wintles in a halter:	dangles, noose/rope
Asham'd himself to see the wretches,	
10 He mutters, glow'ring at the bitches,	
'By God I'll not be seen behint them,	behind
Nor 'mang the sp'ritual core present them,	
Without, at least, ae honest man,	one
To grace this damn'd infernal clan.'	
15 By Adamhill a glance he threw,	
'Lord God!' quoth he, 'I have it now,	
There's just the man I want, in faith,'	
And quickly stoppit Ranken's breath.	stopped

Kinsley allows this poem a single sentence noting that it was probably written in 1785. Extensively derivative of Kinsley, Mac-Kay inevitably provides no further help. While not of the order of *Death and Dr Hornbook*, the poem again presents Death in a quandary due, on this occasion, to the characteristically Burnsian image of criminality pertaining to all ranks of society. To save his self-respect, Death is forced to claim one honest man, John Rankine.

Addressed to Mr John Ranken
In Reply to an Announcement

First published by Thomas Stewart, Glasgow, 1801.

I am a keeper of the law	
In some sma' points, altho' not a';	small, all
Some people tell me, gin I fa',	if, fall
Ae way or ither,	one, other
5 The breaking of ae point, tho' sma',	one, small
Breaks a' thegither.	all together

I hae been in for 't ance or twice,	have, in trouble, once
And winna say o'er far for thrice,	would not
Yet never met wi' that surprise	
10 That broke my rest,	
But now a rumour's like to rise,	
A whaup's i' the nest.	curlew's

This was written after *Epistle to J. Ranken*, in either late 1784 or early 1785, in reply to Ranken's continued correspondence about Elizabeth Paton. The earlier work was provoked by news of the pregnancy, while this was written after news of the birth. The first stanza engages in expressing a Biblical notion that 'whosoever shall keep the whole law, and yet offend in one point, he is guilty of all' (*James*, ch. 2, verse x.) The final stanza is a confession of having been in front of the Church clergy once or twice for alleged fornication. This time, however, there is real danger as the woman is pregnant.

Lines to John Ranken –

First printed by Stewart in 1801.

He who of Ranken sang, lies stiff and dead,	song
And a green grassy hillock hides his head;	
Alas! Alas! a devilish change indeed.	

This is often described as lines written by Burns when on his death-bed and forwarded to Ranken in Ayrshire after the poet died. Given there is no evidence that Burns kept in touch with Ranken after leaving Ayrshire this story can be discarded as folklore.

Political satire.

Address of Beelzebub – *Dramatic monologue*

First printed in *The Scots Magazine*, February 1818.

To the Right Honorable the Earl of Breadalbane, President of the Right Honorable the HIGHLAND SOCIETY, which met on the 23rd of May last, at the Shakespeare, Covent Garden, to concert

ways and means to frustrate the designs of FIVE HUNDRED
HIGHLANDERS who, as the Society were informed by
Mr. M'Kenzie of Applecross, were so audacious as to attempt
an escape from their lawful lords and masters whose property they
were, by emigrating from the lands of Mr. Macdonald of Glengary
to the wilds of CANADA, in search of that fantastic thing —
LIBERTY.

LONG LIFE, My Lord, an' health be yours,
Unskaith'd by hunger'd HIGHLAN BOORS!
Lord grant, nae duddie, desp'rate beggar,   *no ragged*
Wi' dirk, claymore, or rusty trigger   *highland knife*
May twin auld SCOTLAND O' A LIFE,   *rob old*
She likes — as BUTCHERS like a KNIFE!

Faith! you and Applecross[1] were right
To keep the Highlan hounds in sight!
I doubt na! they wad bid nae better   *not, would, no*
10 Than let them ance out owre the water;   *once, over*
Then up amang thae lakes an' seas   *they*
They'll mak what rules and laws they please.

Some daring Hancocke,[2] or a Frankline,[3]
May set their HIGHLAN bluid a-ranklin;   *blood, boiling*
15 Some Washington[4] again may head them,
Or some MONTGOMERY,[5] fearless, lead them;
Till, God knows what may be effected,
When by such HEADS and HEARTS directed:
Poor, dunghill sons of dirt an' mire,
20 May to PATRICIAN RIGHTS ASPIRE;
Nae sage North,[6] now, nor sager Sackville,[7]   *no*
To watch an' premier owre the pack vile!
An' whare will ye get Howes[8] and Clintons[9]   *where*

1 Thomas McKenzie of Applecross.
2 John Hancock.
3 Benjamin Franklin.
4 George Washington, American President.
5 Richard Montgomery.
6 Lord Frederick North.
7 Lord George Sackville.

To bring them to a right repentance,
25 To cowe the rebel generation,
An' save the honor o' the NATION?
They! an' be damn'd! what right hae they   have
To Meat or Sleep or light o' day,
Far less to riches, pow'r, or freedom,
30 But what your lordships PLEASE TO GIE   give
    THEM?

But, hear me, my lord! Glengary,[10] hear!
Your HAND'S OWRE LIGHT ON   over
    THEM, I fear:
Your FACTORS, GRIEVES, TRUSTEES,
    AN' BAILIES,
I canna say but they do gailies;   cannot, gaily
35 They lay aside a' tender mercies
An' tirl the HALLIONS to the BIRSIES;   strip, sluts, bristle
Yet, while they're only poin'd, and herriet,   goods seized, harried
They'll keep their stubborn Highlan spirit.
But smash them! crush them a' to spails!   splinters
40 An' rot the DYVORS i' the JAILS!   rogues
The young dogs, swinge them to the labour,
Let WARK an' HUNGER mak them sober!   work
The HIZZIES, if they're oughtlins fausont,   girls, quite good looking
Let them in DRURY LANE be lesson'd!   turned to whores
45 An' if the wives, an' dirty brats,
Come thiggan at your doors an' yetts,   begging, gates
Flaffan wi' duds, an' grey wi' beese,   flogging rags, vermin
Frightan awa your deucks an' geese;   away, ducks
Get out a HORSE-WHIP, or a JOWLER,   hound
50 The langest thong, the fiercest growler,
An' gar the tatter'd gypseys *pack*   make
Wi' a' their bastarts on their back!

Go on, my Lord! I lang to meet you   long
An' in my HOUSE AT HAME to greet you;   home
55 Wi' COMMON LORDS ye shanna mingle,   shall not
The benmost newk, beside the ingle   nearest corner, fire
At my right hand, assign'd your seat

8 Viscount William Howe.
9 Sir Henry Clinton.
10 MacDonell of Glengarry.

'Tween HEROD'S hip an' POLYCRATE;[11]
Or, if you on your station tarrow,
60   Between ALMAGRO[12] and PIZARRO;[13]
A seat, I'm sure ye're weel deservin't;
An' till ye come — your humble servant,

BEELZEBUB. Hell, 1st June, Anno Mundi 5790

Reads if writing from hell.

That this poem did not appear till 1818 is evidence of the virulent intensity of its political dissent. Carol McGuirk has considered it Burns's perhaps most underrated dramatic monologue. It should, in fact, be seen as doing for reactionary, repressive political values what *Holy Willie's Prayer* does for the values of 'Auld Licht' Calvinism. If the devil is implicit in Willie's perverted, inverted values, here he is present in all his crazed, persuasive, sadistic rhetorical splendour. Unlike Pope, there is little direct evidence of Burns's knowledge of Swift but Swift, especially the monologue form and content of his demonic prose masterpiece, *A Modest Proposal*, is the obvious comparison. Like Swift, Burns demolishes his opponent's case by allowing him full reign for his social values. Like Swift he is making a persona who, out of his own eloquent mouth, destroys the case he is making. Again like Swift, Burns also concentrates his image of the most acute social deprivation on the Celtic part of their society; people – 'highland hounds' – treated literally as animals.

Some critics have misunderstood Burns's ferocious anger in this poem because they did not understand, unlike the subsequent Clearances, the desire in the Highland population to escape the breakdown of post-Culloden Highland society by emigrating to Canada and North America. For the actual context see 'British Diaspora: Emigration from Britain, 1680–1815', in *The Eighteenth Century, The Oxford History of the British Empire*, ed. P.J. Marshall (Oxford, 1998). At this point the feudal chieftains, unknowing of the commercial value of sheep, wish, while utterly careless of their needs, to keep their retainers at home. Consciously or not, this poem echoes another great poem of the late eighteenth-century diaspora, Goldsmith's *The Deserted Village*. Burns adored Goldsmith's poetry

11 Polycrates, 522 B.C. – tyrant of Samos.
12 Diego D'Almagro, chief officer in the Inca conquest of Peru, killed by Pizarro.
13 Francisco Pizarro, leader of the Incas who took Peru.

but his vision in this poem, as his general politics, is quite different. Goldsmith's exiles vanish into the jungle; Burns's Highlanders arrive in a landscape which mirrors their democratic ambitions. This also allows him to place in opposition his sense of an ideal America as opposed to extreme British distress and corruption. As in his first political poem 'When Guilford Good' he celebrates both American democratic values and American military success. Thus three leaders of the American revolution are eulogised: John Hancock (1737–93), Benjamin Franklin (1706–90) and George Washington (1732–99). Richard Montgomery, the Ayrshire American hero, we have already met with in 'When Guilford Good'. North, Sackville, Howe and Clinton also featured in that poem as British villains of the piece. Burns, in a sort of brilliant double irony, postulates that the very British politicians and soldiers who had lost America might bring the escaped Highlanders to order. This is to add satirical insult to the injury he had already delivered to the British imperial cause.

In a slightly later poem *A Winter Night*, Burns blows up a rhetorical storm to describe the sufferings of the common man at the hands of growing aristocratic, commercial power, partly by use of Augustan personification:

> See stern Oppression's iron grip,
>   Or mad Ambition's gory hand,
> Sending, like blood-hounds from the slip,
>   Woe, Want, and Murder o'er a land!

Here, however, his dense use of vernacular Scots makes extraordinarily tangible the sufferings of these Gaelic-speakers driven Southward in search for survival under the terms of varied sadistic punishments. Dispossession and exile were ever present in Burns's consciousness as central elements of his time's common experience. The Highland women in Drury Lane (l. 44) have resorted to prostitution. This ironically echoes the real prostitution of the absentee landlords who populate another but genuinely degenerate London.

The last lines of the poem list comparable *imperial* villains from the often genocidal régimes of Rome, Greece and Spain. Herod Antipas, Tetrarch of Galilee, executed John the Baptist and judged Jesus. Polycrates used his fleets in the fifth century B.C. to establish an Aegean empire. Diego D'Almargo (1475–1538) was put to death by his commander, Francisco Pizarro (1478–1541) during the conquest of Peru. It is with such monsters that our Highland Chiefs are to toast themselves in the after-life fireside of hell. Burns's apparently peculiar assortment of such historical figures is explained by his reading about their histories in an article in *The Annual Register*. Publication of this poem during the poet's life would have infuriated members of the Highland Society, so that it is somewhat ironic that one of the poet's first reviewers, Henry Mackenzie, later became President of the Highland Society.

Epitaph on John Dove, Innkeeper, Mauchline

First printed by Thomas Stewart, 1801.

	Here lies Johnie Pidgeon,	
	What was his religion,	
	Whae'er desires to ken,	know
	To some other warl'	world
5	Maun follow the carl,	must, old man
	For here Johnie Pigeon had nane.	none

	Strong ale was ablution,	
	Small beer persecution,	
	A dram was *memento mori*;	
10	But a full flowing bowl,	
	Was the saving his soul,	
	And Port was celestial glory.	

John Dove is reputed to have been a native of Paisley. He became landlord of the Whitefoord Arms where Burns held meetings of the Bachelors' Debating Club.

Epitaph on a Wag in Mauchline

First printed by the London *Telegraph*, August 16th, 1796.

The Schoolmaster of MACHLEN [sic], in Ayrshire, was an intimate companion of the lately deceased Caledonian bard, ROBERT BURNS. One Evening after a long, convivial Repast, the former observed that, it was most probable his Friend, the Poet, would survive him, and he was persuaded that his Muse would be invoked to celebrate his Virtues, and the endearing Society in which they had together passed so many festive Hours. 'Come BURNS (said he) let me *hear* what you will say upon that *melancholy* occasion'. Burns took up the Pen; and, alluding to the School-master's general character as an *Admirer* of the softer sex, wrote the following:

> Ye Machlen HUSBANDS, mourn him a',   Mauchline, all
>   The man who did assist ye;
> For, had ye been Seven Years awa',   away
>   Your Wives wad ne'er ha' mist ye!   would, have, missed

> Ye Machlen BAIRNS, as ye gae to   children, go
>   The School in Crouds together,
> Tread lightly on his green Grass-Turf:
>   *Perhaps* he was your Father!

This is the text printed in the London newspaper. It differs from the text normally printed, given below for comparison. Previous editors are wrong to record that it was first printed by Thomas Stewart, 1801. The version in the opposition London newspaper the *Telegraph*, a few weeks after the poet's death, reveal the poet's peculiar use of capitals and the italicisation of '*Perhaps*', pointing to an original manuscript. Hitherto the possible candidates for this randy Mauchline 'wag' were James Smith, the poet's friend, or 'Clockie Brown' as Kinsley's suggests. With the rediscovery of this first printed version it is evidently about Smith the schoolmaster. It may even have been sent to the newspaper by Smith.

The standard version is:

> Lament 'im Mauchline husbands a',
>   He aften did assist ye;   often
> For had ye staid whole weeks awa'   stayed, whole, away
>   Your wives they ne'er had missed ye.

> Ye Mauchline bairns as on ye pass,
>   To school in bands thegither,   together
> O tread ye lightly on his grass,
>   Perhaps he was your father!

This standard text may have been a version updated and improved by Burns.

To Willie Chalmers' Sweetheart

First printed in *The Edinburgh Literary Journal*, 21st November, 1829.

Madam,

	Wi' braw new branks in mickle pride,	fine, bridle, much
	And eke a braw new brechan,	also, fine, collar
	My Pegasus I'm got astride,	
	And up Parnassus pechin;	panting
5	Whyles owre a bush wi' downward crush,	sometimes over
	The doited beastie stammers;	half-stupid
	Then up he gets, and off he sets,	
	For sake o' *Willie Chalmers*.	
	I doubt na, lass, that weel kend name	not, well-known
10	May cost a pair o' blushes;	
	I am nae stranger to your fame,	no
	Nor his warm-urged wishes.	
	Your bonie face sae mild and sweet,	so
	His honest heart enamours,	
15	And faith ye'll no be lost a whit,	fragment
	Tho' wair'd on *Willie Chalmers*.	bestowed
	Auld Truth hersel might swear ye're fair,	old
	And Honour safely back her,	
	And Modesty assume your air,	
20	And ne'er a ane mistak her:	one
	And sic twa love-inspiring een,	such two, eyes
	Might fire even holy Palmers;	pilgrims
	Nae wonder then they've fatal been	no
	To honest *Willie Chalmers*.	
25	I doubt na Fortune may you shore	not
	Some mim-mou'd pouthered priestie,	prim-, powdered
	Fu' lifted up wi' Hebrew lore,	full
	And band upon his breastie;	breast
	But oh! what signifies to you	
30	His lexicons and grammars;	
	The feeling heart 's the royal blue,	
	And that's wi' *Willie Chalmers*.	

Some gapin' glowrin' countra laird,   big-mouthed, staring
   May warsle for your favour;   struggle
35 May claw his lug, and straik his beard,   scratch, ear, stroke
   And hoast up some palaver.   cough, story
My bonie maid, before ye wed
   Sic clumsy-witted hammers,   such, dunces
Seek Heaven for help, and barefit skelp   bare-foot, run
40   Awa wi' *Willie Chalmers*.

Forgive the Bard! my fond regard
   For ane that shares my bosom,   one
Inspires my Muse to gie'm his dues,   give him
   For deil a hair I roose him.   not, rouse
45 May Powers aboon unite you soon,   above
   And fructify your amours, —
And every year come in mair dear   more
   To you and *Willie Chalmers*.

This work was written sometime in 1786. In the Don manuscript
Burns wrote 'Mr Chalmers, a gentleman in Ayrshire, a particular
friend of mine, asked me to write a poetical epistle to a young lady,
his Dulcinea. I had seen her, but was scarcely acquainted with her,
and wrote as follows'.

To Dr. John Mackenzie
An Invitation to a Masonic Gathering
First printed by Motherwell and Hogg, 1834.

Friday first's the day appointed
By our Right Worshipful Anointed,
   To hold our grand Procession,
To get a blade o' Johnie's Morals,   screed
5 An' taste a swatch o' Manson's barrels,   drop
   I' th' way of our Profession:
Our Master and the Brotherhood
   Wad a' be glad to see you;   would all
For me, I wad be mair than proud   would, more
10   To share the MERCIES wi' you.
     If Death then wi' skaith then   harm
       Some mortal heart is hechtin,   menacing
     Inform him, an' storm him,
       That SATURDAY ye'll fecht him.   fight

Robert Burns. Mossgiel, 14th June, A.M. 5790.

This was composed on the date signed for the poet's friend, Dr John Mackenzie, a doctor in Mauchline. The St James Lodge in Tarbolton were to meet on 24th June, St John's Day.

The Farewell

First printed by Rev. Hamilton Paul, Ayr, 1819.

The valiant, in himself, what can he suffer?
Or what does he regard his single woes?
But when, alas! he multiplies himself,
To dearer selves, to the lov'd tender fair,
To those whose bliss, whose beings hang upon him,
To helpless children, — then, Oh then he feels
The point of misery festering in his heart,
And weakly weeps his fortunes like a coward:
Such, such am I! — undone!
                    THOMSON'S *Edward and Eleanora*

Farewell, old Scotia's bleak domains,
    Far dearer than the torrid plains,
Where rich ananas blow!   pineapples
    Farewell, a mother's blessing dear!
5   A brother's sigh! a sister's tear!
    My Jean's heart-rending throe!
Farewell, my Bess! tho' thou 'rt bereft
    Of my paternal care,
A faithful brother I have left,
10   My part in him thou'lt share!
        Adieu too, to you too,
            My Smith, my bosom frien';
        When kindly you mind me,
            O then befriend my Jean!

15   What bursting anguish tears my heart;
    From thee, my Jeany, must I part!
        Thou, weeping, answ'rest — 'No!'
    Alas! misfortune stares my face,
    And points to ruin and disgrace,
20   I for thy sake must go!
    Thee, Hamilton, and Aiken dear,
        A grateful, warm adieu:

I, with a much-indebted tear,
   Shall still remember you!
25   All-hail, then, the gale then,
         Wafts me from thee, dear shore!
   It rustles, and whistles,
      I'll never see thee more!

This is another less successful work from what is almost a separate sub-genre, Burns's songs and poems on departing Scotland for Jamaica in 1786.

To John Kennedy:
A Farewell
First printed by J. G. Lockhart, 1829.

Farewell Dear Friend! may Guid-luck hit you,
And 'mang her favorites admit you!
If e'er Detraction shore to smit you,   threaten, smite
   May nane believe him!   none
And onie deil that thinks to get you,   any devil
   Good Lord deceive him!!!

These lines are given in a letter (Letter 38) written by Burns to John Kennedy in August 1786, just after the Kilmarnock edition came out. The letter mentions the proposed Jamaica emigration.

Libel Summons
or The Court of Equity
First printed publicly in an appendix of Carswell's biography, 1951.

In Truth and Honour's name — AMEN —
Know all men by these Presents plain: —

This fourth o June, at Mauchline given,
The year 'tween eighty five and seven,
5 We, Fornicators by profession,
As per extractum from each Session,   extracted
In way and manner here narrated,
Pro bono Amor congregated;   for the sake of love
And by our brethren constituted,

10 A COURT OF EQUITY deputed. —
    WITH special authoris'd direction
    To take beneath our strict protection,
    The stays-out-bursting, quondam maiden,   pregnant, erstwhile
    With GROWING LIFE and anguish laden;
15 Who by the rascal is deny'd,
    That led her thoughtless steps aside. —
    He who disowns the ruin'd Fair-one,
    And for her wants and woes cares none;
    The wretch that can refuse subsistence,
20 To those whom he has given existence;
    He who when at lass's by-job,   vagina
    Defrauds her wi a frig or dry-bob;   mere play, no climax
    The coof that stands on clishmaclavers   fool, nonsense
    When women haflins offer favors: —   partly
25 All who in any way or manner
    Disdain the Fornicator's honor,
    We take cognisance thereanent,
    The proper Judges competent. —

    First, POET BURNS he takes the chair,
30 Allow'd by a', his title 's fair;
    And pass'd nem. con. without dissension,
    He has a DUPLICATE pretension. —
    Next, Merchant SMITH, our worthy FISCAL,
    To cow each pertinaceous rascal;
35 In this, as every other state,
    His merit is conspicuous great:
    RICHMOND the third, our trusty CLERK,
    The minutes regular to mark,
    And sit dispenser of the law,
40 In absence of the former twa;   two
    The fourth our MESSENGER AT ARMS,
    When failing all the milder terms,
    HUNTER, a hearty, willing brother,
    Weel skill'd in dead[1] and living leather. —   vagina
45 Without PREAMBLE less or more said,
    We, body politic aforesaid,
    With legal, due WHEREAS, and WHEREFORE,
    We are appointed here to care for
    The interests of our constituents,

1 A Tanner. R.B.

50 And punish contraveening truants,
Keeping a proper regulation
Within the lists of FORNICATION. —

WHEREAS, our FISCAL, by petition,
Informs us there is strong suspicion,
55 You, Coachman DOW[2], and Clockie BROWN,[3]
Baith residenters in this town;
In other words, you, JOCK, and SANDY,
Hae been at wark at HOUGHMAGANDIE;   sexual intercourse
And now when facts are come to light,
60 The matter ye deny outright. —

FIRST, YOU, JOHN BROWN, there's
witness borne,
And affidavit made and sworn,
That ye hae bred a hurly-burly   have
'Bout JEANY MITCHEL'S tirlie-whirlie,   vagina
65 And blooster'd at her regulator,
Till a' her wheels gang clitter-clatter. —   go
And farther still, ye cruel Vandal,
A tale might even in Hell be scandal!
That ye hae made repeated trials
70 Wi' drugs and draps in doctor's phials,
Mixt, as ye thought, wi' fell infusion,   deadly
Your ain begotten wean to poosion. —   own, child, poison
And yet ye are sae scant o' grace,   so
Ye daur to lift your brazen face,   dare
75 And offer for to take your aith,   oath
Ye never lifted JEANY'S claith. —   clothes
But tho' ye should yoursel manswear,
Laird Wilson's sclates can witness bear,   slates
Ae e'ening of a MAUCHLINE fair,   one
80 That JEANY'S masts they saw them bare;
For ye had furl'd up her sails,
And was at play — at heads and tails. —

NEXT, SANDY DOW, you're here indicted
To have, as publickly you're wyted,   accused
85 Been clandestinely upward whirlin
The petticoats o' MAGGY BORELAN,

2 A coachman. R. B.
3 A clockmaker. R.B.

And gien her canister a rattle,   given
That months to come it winna settle. —   would not
And yet, you offer your protest,
90 Ye never herried Maggy's nest;   harried
Tho, it 's weel ken'd that at her gyvel   well known, vagina
Ye hae gien mony a kytch and kyvel.   have given, thrust, bang

THEN BROWN AND DOW, before design'd,
For clags and clauses there subjoin'd,   claims
95 WE, Court aforesaid cite and summon,
That on the fifth o' July comin,
The hour o cause, in our Court-ha'.
At Whitfoord's Arms, ye answer LAW!

BUT, as reluctantly WE PUNISH,
100 An' rather, mildly would admonish:
Since BETTER PUNISHMENT prevented,
Than OBSTINACY sair repented. —   sore

Then, for that ANCIENT SECRET'S SAKE,
You have the honor to partake;
105 An for that NOBLE BADGE you wear,
YOU, SANDIE DOW, our BROTHER dear,
We give you as a MAN an' MASON,
This private, sober, friendly lesson. —

YOUR CRIME, a manly deed we view it,
110 AS MAN ALONE, can only do it;
But, in denial persevering,
Is to a SCOUNDREL'S NAME adhering.
THE BEST O MEN, hae been surpris'd;
THE BEST O WOMEN been advis'd:
115 NAY, CLEVEREST LADS hae haen a   have had
    TRICK O'T,
AN', BONNIEST LASSES taen a LICK O'T. —   taken

Then Brother Dow, if you're asham'd
In such a QUORUM to be nam'd,
Your conduct much is to be blam'd.
120 See, ev'n HIMSEL — there's GODLY BRYAN,
That auld WHATRECK he has been tryin;   old sexual intercourse
When such as he put to their han',
What man on CHARACTER need stan'?
Then Brother dear, lift up your brow,

125 And, like yoursel', the TRUTH avow;
Erect a dauntless face upon it,
An say, 'I am the man has done it;
'I SANDIE DOW GAT MEG WI' WEAN,   *got, child*
'An 's fit to do as much again.'

130 Ne'er mind their solemn rev'rend faces,
Had they — in proper times an' places,
But SEEN AN FUN' — I mukle dread it,   *greatly*
They just would done as you an' WE did. —
TO TELL THE TRUTH 's a manly lesson,

135 An doubly proper in a MASON. —

YOU MONSIEUR BROWN, as it is proven,
JEAN MITCHEL'S wame by you was hoven;   *belly, distended*
Without you by a quick repentance
Acknowledge Jean's an' your acquaintance,

140 Depend on 't, this shall be your sentence. —
Our beadles to the Cross shall take you,
And there shall mither naked make you;   *mother-*
Some canie grip near by your middle,   *careful*
They shall it bind as tight 's a fiddle;

145 The raep they round the PUMP shall tak   *rope*
An' tye your han's behint your back;   *tie, hands*
Wi' just an ell o' string allow'd
To jink an hide you frae the croud: *dodge, from*
There ye shall stan', a legal seizure,

150 In during Jeanie Mitchel's pleasure;
So be, her pleasure dinna pass   *do not*
Seven turnings of a half-hour glass:
Nor shall it in her pleasure be
To louse you out in less than THREE. —

155 This, our futurum esse DECREET,
We mean it not to keep a secret;
But in OUR SUMMONS here insert it,
And whoso dares, may controvert it. —
This, mark'd before that date and place is,

160 SIGILLUM EST, PER   *sealed by*
         BURNS THE PRESES.

This Summons and the signet mark,
EXTRACTUM EST, PER   *extracted by*
         RICHMOND, CLERK.

165 AT MAUCHLINE, idem date of June,
    'Tween six and seven, the afternoon,
    You twa, in propria personae,   two
    Within design'd, SANDY and JOHNY,
    This SUMMONS legally have got,
170 As vide witness underwrote:
    Within the house of JOHN DOW, vinter,
    NUNC FACIO HOC.   I now make this
        GULLELMUS HUNTER.

In this 1786 work, Burns sets up a fictional and mock-legal Court of
Equity in brilliant parody of the Ayrshire Kirk sessions on those
accused of fornication and condemned by clerics. The poem, never
intended as a publishable work, is partly a psychological release
valve for Burns and his close cronies, James Smith (1765–1823) and
John Richmond (1765–1846) who experienced the condemnation of
the Kirk over sexual matters. Smith is named as the Court's Fiscal
and Richmond, the Clerk. Satirically turning Church morality on its
head, the poet's Court does not condemn promiscuity, but lashes
those accused of fornication who are not manly enough to admit
their 'crime' and accept responsibility for the children they have
fathered. The 'crime' of dishonesty is made worse in Alex Dow's
case, the coachman, who is also a brother Mason – such honour is
'doubly proper in a Mason'. One of the so-called accused is threa-
tened with being tied to Mauchline Cross naked if he does not
confess and admit his responsibilities. The language employed both
parodies and levels the ritual seriousness of Kirk divines and the
legal establishment. Considering the three extant manuscripts in the
British Museum, it would appear that Burns never completed the
poem to his satisfaction. Standard editions of the poem combine text
from the earlier Egerton manuscript and append the closing cou-
plets from the Hastie manuscript, as above.

Answer to a Trimming Epistle Received from a Tailor

First printed by Stewart & Meikle, in pamphlet, 1799.

What ails ye now, ye lousie bitch,   bothers
To thresh my back at sic a pitch?   thrash, such
Losh man! hae mercy wi' your natch,   lord, notching-blade
    Your bodkin's bauld,   needle
5 I didna suffer ha'f sae much   did not, half so
    Frae Daddie Auld.   from

What tho' at times when I grow crouse,   cocksure
I gie their wames a random pouse,   give, bellies, thrust
Is that enough for you to souse   strike
10   Your servant sae!   so
Gae mind your seam, ye prick the louse,   go, nit-picker
    An' jag the flae.   flea

King David o' poetic brief,
Wrocht 'mang the lassies sic mischief   brought, such
15 As fill'd his after life with grief
    An' bloody rants,
An' yet he's rank'd amang the chief
    O' lang syne saunts.   old-time saints

And maybe, Tam, for a' my cants,   canters
20 My wicked rhymes, an' drucken rants,   drunken
I'll gie auld cloven Clootie's haunts   give old, devil
    An unco slip yet,   a good miss
An' snugly sit amang the saunts   among, saints
    At Davie's hip yet.   King David's

25 But, fegs, the Session says I maun   shall
Gae fa' upo' anither plan,   go fall
Than garren lasses coup the cran,   making, somersault
    Clean heels owre body,   over
An' sairly thole their mither's ban,   sorely endure
30   Afore the howdy.   midwife

This leads me on, to tell for sport,
How I did wi' the Session sort —
Auld Clinkum at the inner port   bell-ringer
    Cry'd three times, 'Robin!'
35 'Come hither lad, and answer for't,
    Ye're blam'd for jobbin'.'   fornication

Wi' pinch I put a Sunday's face on,
An' snoov'd awa' before the Session —   toddled off
I made an open, fair confession,
40   I scorn'd to lie;
An' syne Mess John, beyond expression,   Master
    Fell foul o' me.

A furnicator lown he call'd me,   *fool*
An' said my fau't frae bliss expell'd me;   *fault from*
45 I own'd the tale was true he tell'd me,
     'But, what the matter,'
Quo' I, 'I fear unless ye geld me,   *castrate*
     I'll ne'er be better.'

'Geld you!' quo' he, 'an' whatfore no,   *why not*
50 If that your right hand, leg, or toe,
Should ever prove your sp'ritual foe,
     You should remember
To cut it aff, an' whatfore no,
     Your dearest member.'

55 'Na, na,' quo' I, 'I'm no for that,
Gelding's nae better than 'tis ca't,   *no, it is called*
I'd rather suffer for my faut,   *fault*
     A hearty flewit,   *flogging*
As sair owre hip as ye can draw't!   *sore over*
60   Tho' I should rue it.

'Or gin ye like to end the bother,
To please us a', I've just ae ither,   *one other*
When next wi' yon lass I forgather,   *have sex*
     Whate'er betide it,
65 I'll frankly gie her 't a' thegither,   *give*
     An' let her guide it.'

But, Sir, this pleas'd them warst ava,   *worst, all*
An' therefore, Tam, when that I saw,
I said 'Gude night,' an' cam' awa,   *good-, came away*
70   An' left the Session;
I saw they were resolved a'
     On my oppression.

This was the poet's reply to an epistle by Thomas Walker, a friend
of William Simpson, school teacher at Ochiltree, who attacked the
bard's morals as a result of his rebuke by the Kirk session for
fornication. When it first appeared in 1799, Walker's letter and
poem to Burns were also printed (Kinsley prints Walker's Epistle as
no. 119A). It is believed Simpson had a hand in improving the
tailor's poem, given that a first attempt was ignored by Burns.
Locally, it was public knowledge that Burns had been rebuked by

the Kirk session for his sexual exploits outwith marriage and Walker took advantage of this gossip, along with Simpson, to poke fun at Burns. Walker's poem is partly written more in sorrow than in anger, but it does prophesy for the poet an after-life in the flames of Hell for his promiscuity. As earlier with his father, the austerely restraining hand simply led to greater excess. This was akin to pouring petrol on Burns's erotic bonfire. Invoking the example of King David's sexual excesses as a justified model for his own (Burns's avidly heterodox readings of *The Old Testament* drove his 'unco guid' critics to enraged despair), he waxes lyrical on the delights of the flesh and his consequent provocation of the Kirk session. The 'trimming' epistle denotes its author as both a despicable 'trimmer' and, perhaps, one who would use his shears in the self-proposed gelding of the Bard as the only way of stopping his activities.

To an Old Sweetheart
Wrote on the Blank Leaf of a copy of my First Edition, which I sent to an old Sweetheart, then married
First printed by Currie, 1800.

Once fondly lov'd, and still rememb'red dear,
    Sweet early Object of my youthful vows,
Accept this mark of friendship, warm, sincere,
    Friendship — 'tis all cold duty now allows.

And while you read the simple, artless rhymes,
    One friendly sigh for him — he asks no more,
Who, distant, burns in flaming torrid climes,
    Or haply lies beneath th' Atlantic roar.

Written in 1786 after the Kilmarnock volume appeared and sent to Peggy Thomson. A copy was written into the Glenriddel manuscript where it is recorded that Peggy Thomson was the person addressed. The last line may echo Henry King's death by drowning in Milton's *Lycidas*.

Extempore Verses on Dining with Lord Daer
Mossgiel, October 25th.

First printed in Stewart & Meikle's pamphlets, 1799.

	This wot all ye whom it concerns,	
	I, Rhymer Rab, alias BURNS,	
	October twenty-third,	
	A ne'er to be forgotten day!	
5	Sae far I sprachl'd up the brae,	so, clambered, hillside
	I dinner'd wi' a LORD.	
	I've been at drucken Writers' feasts;	drunken
	Nay, been bitch-fou 'mang godly Priests;	very drunk
	(Wi' rev'rence be it spoken!)	
10	I've even join'd the honor'd jorum,	
	When mighty Squireships o' the Quorum	
	Their hydra drouth did sloken.	thirst, satisfy
	But wi' a LORD! — stand out my shin!	shoes
	A LORD — a PEER — an EARL'S SON —	
15	Up higher yet, my bonnet!	
	An' sic a LORD — lang Scotch ells twa;	such, long, over six foot
	Our PEERAGE he looks o'er them a',	
	As I look o'er my sonnet.	
	But O! for Hogarth's magic pow'r,	
20	To show Sir Bardie's willyart glow'r,	awkward stare
	An' how he star'd an' stammer'd!	
	When goavan's he'd been led wi' branks,	staring stupidly, bridle
	An' stumpan on his ploughman shanks,	tramping, legs
	He in the parlour hammer'd.	
25	To meet good Stewart[1] little pain is	
	Or Scotia's sacred Demosthenes,[2]	
	Thinks I, they are but men!	
	But Burns, my Lord — Guid God! I doited,	stammered
	My knees on ane anither knoited,	one another, knotted
30	As faultering I gaed ben!	faltering, went in

1 Professor Dugald Stewart.
2 A reference probably to Dr Hugh Blair.

I sidling shelter'd in a neuk,   corner
An' at his Lordship staw a leuk,   stole a look
    Like some portentous omen;
Except GOOD SENSE, and SOCIAL GLEE,
35 An' (what surpris'd me) MODESTY,
    I marked nought uncommon.

I watch'd the symptoms o' the GREAT,
The GENTLE PRIDE, the LORDLY STATE,
    The arrogant assuming;
40 The fient a pride, nae pride had he,   not a jot of, no
Nor sauce, nor state, that I could see,
    Mair than an honest Ploughman.   more

Then from his Lordship I shall learn,
Henceforth to meet with unconcern,
45   One rank as well's another;
Nae honest, worthy man need care,   no
To meet with NOBLE youthfu' DAER,
    For he but meets a BROTHER.

Lord Daer, Basil William Hamilton-Douglas (1763–94), was a son
of The Earl of Selkirk whose family seat was in Galloway, near
Kircudbright. Burns met him at the family home of Professor
Dugald Stewart at Catrine near Mossgiel where he had been taken
by his friend and fellow-mason, Dr John MacKenzie of Mauchline.
(See Burns's note of thanks to Stewart, Letter 53A.) The italicised
stress on the personal Masonic connection in the poem's last line
cannot, like Burns's relationship to Freemasonry itself, be over-
estimated. He was a member of five Masonic Lodges and visited
many others. We still await the scholarly work on Freemasonry in
late-eighteenth century Scotland which fully reveals its propensity
for democratic reform. Indeed, the collapse of Freemasonry's for-
tunes almost exactly coincides with that of Burns himself. Professor
John Robison's paranoid book of 1797, *Proofs of Conspiracy against
All Religions and Governments of Europe* which specifically mentions
Burns as an individual who had sadly over-reached himself, signals
the end of the movement as a force for reform. Contemporary
Freemasonry has politically, of course, nothing to do with the values
of its eighteenth-century namesake. Mozart, as far as is known, did
not compose for the Lambeg Drum.

    Dugald Stewart had, as house guest, one of his brightest and best
students. We know this because when the poem appeared in 1799 in

a pamphlet with Burns's letter (52) to Dr MacKenzie marking the occasion, Currie printed Dugald Stewart's copy of the poem without ll. 20–5. Since these lines contain reference to Stewart himself and possibly Hugh Blair, this may have been because he did not want such luminaries associated with Daer who was by this time a deeply marked man by Dundas's security apparatus. Typically, Kinsley underplays Daer's political identity. He notes he was a successful agricultural 'improver' on the family estates and quotes Stewart's remark in the above pamphlet that: 'These lines will be read with no common interest by all who remember the unaffected simplicity of appearance, the sweetness of countenance and manners, and the unsuspecting benevolence of heart of Basil, Lord Daer.' Admittedly Kinsley also notes from the *Scots Peerage*, ii. 489 that Daer was a member of the society of 'The Friends of the People', and a zealous advocate for parliamentary reform. What he either omitted or did not know was that Daer, like Thomas Muir, was actually in France in 1792 with his brother-in-law Sir James Hall, the noted geologist and chemist, in attendance at the National Assembly.

Kinsley is even more remiss regarding the degree and intensity of Daer's radical activities in Scotland. He was a leading Scottish radical of the era and formed a branch of the Friends of the People in rural Wigtown, Galloway, during the early 1790s. When the Scottish Friends of the People set up in 1792 and met in National Convention, December 1792, Lord Daer was one of its leading figures and asked his fellow radicals to address him as Citizen Douglas, not Lord Daer, pointing out that such a title implied submission to feudal rank; that feudalism was itself at the very heart of political corruption in Britain and had to end before progress could be instituted. He is reported in the *Edinburgh Gazetteer* on 23rd January, 1793, commenting on the recent government onslaught on radical activity in Scotland:

> That the late proceedings respecting examinations of supposed seditious persons, have been in many cases, arbitrary, inquisatorial and unconstitutional; and that such proceedings have a direct tendency to inflame the minds of the People . . . to create sedition where it never before existed.

Daer himself is listed in the spy memorandum from Claude Irvine Boswell to William Scott, Procurator Fiscal, as the delegate from Wigtown at the Convention of the Friends of the People, Edinburgh, 19th November, 1793. (See RH 2/4/73/f.200.)

Daer's political importance and the quality of his intelligence can be perceived from his quite extraordinary letter to Charles Grey of 17th January, 1793. Part of the difficulties faced by the national radical groups (English, Irish, Scottish) was to synchronise and articulate their respective activities. As we know from Elaine McFarland's recent work (*Ireland and Scotland in the Age of Revolution*), the Irish in 1792 and 1793 made desperate attempts to strengthen the will of the Scottish radicals. What is less well known is that there developed at the end of 1792 a parallel crisis in Scottish and English relationships which caused Daer to write to Charles Grey in response to Grey's letter to William Skirving, the Scottish Secretary of the Friends of the People informing him of English withdrawal from the campaign for petitioning and parliamentary reform. This elicited this extraordinary response from Daer which is here quoted in full since it takes us, more than perhaps any other single document, to the heart of Scottish radicalism in the 1790s and to a retrospective analysis of Anglo-Scottish relationships of a kind we have learned not to anticipate in the late eighteenth century because of the biased pro-Union emphasis initiated by Walter Scott and still prevalent in the 'integrationist' thesis favoured by most contemporary Scottish historians. Burns certainly did not share the concept of such easy integration. In *Ode on General Washington's Birthday*, he saw an England self-betraying her inheritance of political liberty and, in so doing, dragging Scotland down with her. Daer's retrospective analysis of Anglo-Scottish relations has the added benefit of, after over two centuries, being the best possible commentary on and analysis of the complex political attitudes to England that run through Burns's writing. For once, as the poem suggests, Burns had found an aristocrat of the deepest integrity. Daer's savagely premature death, three years before Burns himself, must have been a terrible blow. He was, as we will see in *A Scots Prologue*, Burns's choice for the leader of a reformed, redeemed Scotland. This letter is taken from Edward Hughes's invaluable 'The Scottish Reform Movement and Charles Grey 1792–94: Some Fresh Correspondence', *Scottish Historical Review*, v.35, 1956, pp. 26–41.

Dear Sir

I write to you in some alarm from a passage in your letter of the 13th inst. to our Secretary Skirving. You there say 'In this part of the country I am afraid our supporters are not sufficiently numerous to render the attempt to procure petitions at present adviseable'. I am desired by several Gentlemen to ask an explanation. You must tell us explicitly whether you mean to petition or not, for if you don't in England, neither (say they) will we in Scotland. I deprecate the idea of your not petitioning. Were your petitioners as few in number as the members of your societies, you should petition. When you talk of not petitioning do you think likewise of not moving in Parliament for a Reform? If so, many will consider it almost treachery in you & your friends. Not that I or anyone who knows you can think so. Nor do I mention it to influence you personally, for I trust to God that in the great line you have taken up you have set your mind above being influenced even by the disapprobation of your personal friends. But I mention it because I look upon it as of great consequence to keep our leading men and societies in London high in the estimation of the supporters of freedom at a distance. If you begin to petition in England, I am convinced from my local knowledge of several parts that a great body of the common people are inclined to petition and that it may very probably take a run amongst them. At any rate the strength of the Cause both here and in England consists more in its goodness, in the vigour of the men who support it and in the numbers who we are sure hereafter must join it than the numbers who are already declared. It is curious to see the error which prevails amongst the supporters of freedom in every place in England & in Scotland where I have been, that the declared friends of Reform are more numerous everywhere else. Our folks here are astonished at your information that you are not innumerable about London as perhaps you may be surprised when I say that the declared friends of Reform in Scotland are most contemptible in the view of counting noses, what ever they may be in counting heads. This I aver to be the fact, tho' I believe immense numbers of non-declarants would sign a petition. Every reason you urge for petitioning to keep up the spirit etc. applies equally to England as to Scotland, but I ought perhaps to apologise for being carried away to speak of what should be done in England, instead of what is the likely consequences to result from it in Scotland. If the idea gets abroad that the friends of Reform in any place, or at least any leading place, are to lye by for any reason whatever, I believe it will in every place for the moment damp the ardor of their coming forward, if not extinguish it. You wish us in Scotland to come forward because we are more numerous. I believe that small as our numbers are, they are greater in proportion than in England, but far from enough to command protection from the

Executors of the forms of law. If we are more numerous I believe also we are much more oppressed. By every act implying favor to Reform the people here expose themselves either to the heavy hand of Government or to the unceasing weight of little aristocratical oppression. If set forward alone, the arbitrary attacks against them will be more pointed than if countenanced by their friends in England: at least, they may think so which is the same, and they will feel all the bitterness of desertion in distress. It may even have a national bad effect, if this should go so far, or anything else should take such a turn as to make the Tweed appear a boundary in political sentiment or action, it requires more confidence in the good sense of our countrymen than even I can reasonably have not to believe that it is possible (though I do not think probable) that a fatal national jealousy may arise. Scotland has long groaned under the chains of England and knows that its connection there has been the cause of its greatest misfortunes. Perhaps you may shrug your shoulders at this and call it Scot's prejudice, but it is time at moments like these when much may depend on suiting measures to the humour of the people, that you Englishmen should see this rather as it is or at least be aware of how we Scotsmen see it. We have existed a conquered province these two centuries. We trace our bondage from the Union of the Crown and find it little alleviated by the Union of the Kingdoms. What is it you say we have gained by the Union? Commerce, Manufactures, Agriculture. Without going deep into the principles of political economy or asking how our [sic] Government or any country can give these to any nation, it is evident in this case that the last Union gave us little assistance in these except removing a part of the obstacles which your greater power had posterior to the first union thrown around us. But if it did more what would that amount to, but to the common saying that we bartered our liberty and with it our morals for a little wealth? You say we have gained emancipation from feudal tyranny. I believe most deliberately that had no Union ever taken place we should in that respect have been more emancipated than we are. Left to ourselves we should probably have had a progression towards Liberty and not less than yours. Our grievances prior to the accession of the Stewarts to your throne were of a kind which even had that event not taken place, must before this time have been annihilated. Any share of human evil that might have awaited us we are ignorant of, whereas we feel what we have undergone. Even to the last of our separate parliaments they were always making laws for us and now and then one to remedy a grievance. And a people acquiring knowledge must have compelled a separate legislature to more of these. Since the parliaments were united scarcely four acts have been passed in as many score of years affecting Scots law or merely the incongruitities which must arise betwixt old laws and modern manners. As our courts of law found something of this to be necessary they instead of applying to the parliament at London have taken upon themselves with a degree of audacity which can hardly be made credible to a stranger, to make under pretence of regulating of court Little Laws (acts of parliament as they call them) materially affecting the liberty of the subject. Kept out of view by your greater mass so as never to make our concerns be the principal objects even to our own representatives, at a distance so as not to make our cries be heard in the capital which alone awes and arbitrary government; our laws and customs different so as to make our grievances unintelligible; our law establishment distinct so as to deprive us of the benefit of those constant circuits from the capital which by rendering the learned and spirited defender of the laws, dwelling at the source of actual power, acquainted with the lesser transactions of the remotest corner of the country, provides perhaps the greatest remedy to a half free state against some of the bad consequences of an extended territory. Our civil establishment distinct, so as to isolate the petty tyranny of office; even our greed and national vanity working to retain all these offices to natives so as still more to leave you (our then only protectors, although oppressors) ignorant of our internal situation. We have suffered the misery which is perhaps inevitable to lesser and remote country in a junction where the Governing powers are united but the Nations are not united. In short, thinking we have been the worse of every connection hitherto with you, the Friends of Liberty in Scotland have almost universally been enemies to Union with England. Such is the fact, whether the reasons be good or bad. I for one should still be of that opinion did I not look upon it that a thorough Parliamentary Reform would necessarily place us in a much better situation and higher in the political sphere whilst at the same time it would relieve you from that vermin[1] from this country who infect your court, your parliament and every establishment. I, therefore, wish a closer Union of the Nations,

1 An interesting anticipation of a later controversy.

but many here differ from me, some through principle, others through prejudice or pique, for these cannot at once be thrown off even by the rapid progress of philosophy and philanthropy amongst us. Perhaps we may require to be treated with delicacy and tenderness as a Nation whose temper is somewhat sour, who have sometimes met with insults & always felt the degradation of artificial inferiority. A steady watch ought to be kept and regard paid to every circumstance in our political progress which may be made a means further to cement or sever the two nations. Of these a possible one of the most important kind has long hung upon my mind and seems fast approaching. The keen Friends of Liberty here have commenced a plan of a Convention for Scotland of Delegates from all the Societies for Reform throughout this part of the Kingdom. It is this Convention who addressed our Society at Free Mason's tavern and with whom you correspond, and most properly, for their declarations are strong, explicit, and strictly constitutional and their conduct, under provoking circumstances, firm and temperate. But though weak in its infancy it may, especially by the folly of the measures of Government, grow to a great strength. I doubt that you in England will never make great progress till you adopt something similar. It is requisite for keeping up that degree of knowledge and concert amongst your scattered friends, which the acquaintance by letters is inadequate to. It may even be necessary to save them from temporary extinction. As to such assemblies I believe you and I differ and you dread the magnitude of power which might thereby be accumulated, a degree of power which I look upon as necessary to withstand and prevail over the immense power of the Opposers of Reform and which I think might more safely be entrusted to a delegated, renovating body even tho' sent from self-elected Societies, than to any self-elected body like the Jacobins in France, like the Society for Constitutional Information, or even like ourselves at Free Mason's tavern. But without pretending to convince, I will speak hypothetically. If in England any such Convention or Assembly should take place and not in separate delegated Meetings for different districts in England but in one meeting for all England, I look upon it as of the highest consequence (though perhaps very difficult in the management) to get Scotland to unite in the same Assembly without sending its Delegates thro' any intermediate Assembly for Scotland alone. In this and every view, I should wish the particular Societies to be encouraged to correspond directly with yours and others in London. One of the greatest bonds of union betwixt the two nations at present is that the Reformers here feel that they have need to lean upon you. If it be possible once to teach them that they can take the lead many may be for bidding you farewell. The very grievance of our present persecution may be thus turned to account. Were you to neglect us, it might excite the worst spirit of indignation and despair and even if contrary to our information, you are as much persecuted as us, but still show that you think of us and that you exert yourselves for us; tho' it should be in vain, it will help to rivet us to you. Whilst I speak thus you will readily believe how particularly pleased I was as well as with others most grateful for the reception your Society gave to Mr. Thomas Muir and the interest you took in his relation of the proceedings in Scotland. Should a case ever happen to occur when a man thus appears before you, whose manner even disgusts and whose conduct cannot be approved of as wise or prudent, yet I trust the good sense of your Society will recollect only that he is a Martyr or an Envoy from Brethren in distress.

Yours with the greatest regards, Daer.

Daer, was almost certainly, in the eyes of Burns, a potential leader of a reformed Scotland.

Ye Sons of Old Killie

Tune: Shawnboy
First printed in Cunningham, 1834.

Ye sons of old Killie, assembled by Willie,
    To follow the noble vocation;
Your thrifty old mother has scarce such another
    To sit in that honored station.
5 I've little to say, but only to pray,
    As praying's the ton of your fashion;
A prayer from the Muse you well may excuse,
    'Tis seldom her favourite passion.

Ye Powers who preside o'er the wind and the tide,
10   Who marked each element's border;
Who formed this frame with beneficent aim,
    Whose sovereign statute is order;

Within this dear mansion may wayward contention
    Or withered envy ne'er enter;
15 May secrecy round be the mystical bound,
    And brotherly love be the centre.

A note on the manuscript of this song reads: 'This song, wrote by
Mr Burns, was sung by him in the Kilmarnock Kilwinning Lodge,
in 1786, and given by him to Mr [William] Parker, who was Master
of the Lodge'. William Parker is referred to in l. 1.

Epistle to Captain William Logan at Park
30th October, 1786
First printed in Cunningham, 1834.

Hail, thairm-inspirin, rattlin Willie!	fiddle string
Tho' Fortune's road be rough an' hilly	
To every fiddling, rhyming billie,	fellow
We never heed;	
5 But take it like th' unback'd Fillie,	unbroken young horse
Proud o' her speed.	
When, idly goavin, whyles we saunter,	staring stupidly, wander
Yirr, Fancy barks, — awa we canter,	a growl, away
Up-hill, down-brae, till some mishanter,	hill-slope, mishap
10 Some black Bog-hole,	
Arreests us; then the scathe an' banter	harm
We're forced to thole.	
Hale be your HEART! Hale be your	healthy/sound
FIDDLE!	
Lang may your elbuck jink an' diddle,	long, elbow, play
15 To cheer you through the weary widdle	trouble
O this vile Warl:	world
Until you on a cummock dridle,	short stick, totter
A gray-hair'd Carl!	old man
Come WEALTH, come POORTITH, late	poverty
or soon,	
20 Heaven send your HEART-STRINGS ay	
IN TUNE!	
And screw your TEMPER-PINS aboon	fiddle-pegs, above
A FIFTH or mair,	more
The melancholious, sairie croon	sad notes
O' cankrie CARE!	ill-natured

25 May still your Life, from day to day
    Nae LENTE LARGO, in the play,   *no, slow/monotony*
    But ALLEGRETTO FORTE, gay,   *lively/graceful*
        Harmonious flow:
    A sweeping, kindling, bauld STRATHSPEY,   *bold, fiddle tune*
30   Encore! Bravo!

    A' blessings on the cheery *gang*   *folk*
    Wha dearly like a Jig or sang;   *who, song*
    An' never think o RIGHT an WRANG   *wrong*
        By square and rule,
35 But as the CLEGS O' FEELING stang,   *gadflies, sting*
        Are wise or fool!

    My hand-wal'd CURSE keep hard in chase   *-chosen*
    The harpy, hoodock, purse-proud RACE,   *crow-like/greedy*
    Wha count on POORTITH as disgrace!   *who, poverty*
40   Their tuneless hearts,
    May FIRE-SIDE DISCORDS jar a BASS
        To a' their PARTS!

    But come — your hand — my careless
        brither —
    I' th' tither WARLD, if there 's anither,   *other, another*
45 An' that there is, I've little swither   *doubt*
        About the matter;
    We, cheek for-chow, shall jog thegither,   *-jowl, together*
        I'se ne'er bid better.

    We've faults an' failins, — granted clearly:
50 We're frail, backsliding Mortals meerly:
    Eve's bonie SQUAD, Priests wyte them sheerly   *blame, entirely*
        For our grand fa':   *fall*
    But still — but still — I like them dearly;
        GOD bless them a'!

55 Ochon! for poor CASTALIAN DRINKERS,   *alas, inspiration/poets*
    When they fa' foul o' earthly Jinkers!   *sprightly women*
    The witching, curst, delicious blinkers   *alluring girls*
        Hae put me hyte;   *have, daft*
    An' gart me weet my waukrife winkers   *made, wet wakeful eyes*
60   Wi' girnan spite.   *snarling*

But by yon Moon! an' that's high swearin;
An' every Star within my hearin!
An' by her een! wha was a dear ane,   *eyes, who, one*
 I'll ne'er forget;
65 I hope to gie the JADS a clearin   *give, wenches*
 In fair play yet!

My loss I mourn, but not repent it:
I'll seek my pursie whare I tint it: *purse, lost*
Ance to the Indies I were wonted,   *once, destined*
70 Some cantraip hour,   *magic*
By some sweet Elf I'll yet be dinted,   *enchanted*
 Then, VIVE L'AMOUR!

Faites mes BAISSEMAINS respectueuse, *respectful greetings*
To sentimental Sister Susie,
75 And honest LUCKY; no to roose you,   *praise*
 Ye may be proud,
That sic a couple Fate allows ye   *such*
 To grace your blood.

Nae mair at present can I measure;
80 An' trowth my rhymin ware's nae treasure; *truth, no*
But when in Ayr, some half-hour's leisure,
 Be 't light, be 't dark,
Sir Bard will do himself the pleasure
 To call at PARK.

Robert Burns.

Burns met William Logan in 1786 when he was a Lieutenant on half pay who had served in the American war. From the epistle it is evident Logan's skill as a fiddler warmed Burns to him. Other editors have given the title as *Epistle to Major Logan*, not the title written by Burns, since it was in the service of the West Lowland Fencibles from 1794 that Logan was designated a Major. Burns celebrates a manifestly free fellow spirit with witty extended musical analogies in his customary praise of the spontaneous over the cautionary.

Extempore Reply to an Invitation

First printed in Cunningham, 1834.

Sir,
Yours this moment I unseal,
    And faith! I'm gay and hearty!
To tell the truth and shame the deil,   devil
    I am as fou as Bartie: drunk
But Foorsday, Sir, my promise leal,   Thursday, true
    Expect me o' your partie,
If on a beastie I can speel   horse, climb
    Or hurl in a cartie.   cart
        Yours, — Robert Burns.
Mauchlin, Monday Night, 10 o'clock

The composition date of this is estimated as somtime in 1785 or
1786. Who the invitation was from is not known, but it may have
been James Kennedy or John Richmond.

The Night was Still

First printed in Blackie's *Land of Burns*, 1840.

The night was still, and o'er the hill
    The moon shone on the castle wa';   wall
The mavis sang, while dew-drops hang
    Around her on the castle wa'.

Sae merrily they danc'd the ring,   so
    Frae e'enin till the cocks did craw,   from, evening, crow
And aye the owerword o' the spring
    Was Irvine's bairns are bonie a'.   children

This charming little lyric was written and given to a daughter of Dr
George Lawrie in 1786.

Rusticity's Ungainly Form

First printed in Lockart, 1827.

RUSTICITY'S ungainly form
  May cloud the highest mind;
But when the heart is nobly warm,
  The good excuse will find.

Propriety's cold cautious rules
  Warm Fervour may o'erlook;
But spare poor Sensibility
  The ungentle harsh rebuke.

This was included on a blank leaf of a book given by Burns to Dr
Lawrie's son Archibald. Hearsay recorded by Scott Douglas sug-
gests the words refer to a conversation between Mrs Lawrie and
Burns about Peggy Kennedy (see Scott Douglas, Kilmarnock edi-
tion, vol. II, p. 306, headnote).

Verses Intended to be Written Below a Noble Earl's Picture

First printed in Cunningham, 1834.

WHOSE is that noble, dauntless brow?
  And whose that eye of fire?
And whose that generous, Princely mien,
  Ev'n rooted Foes admire?

Stranger, to justly show that brow,
  And mark that eye of fire,
Would take HIS hand, whose vernal tints,
  His other Works admire.

Bright as a cloudless Summer-sun,
  With stately port he moves;
His guardian Seraph eyes with awe
  The noble Ward he loves.

Among th' illustrious Scottish Sons
  That Chief thou may'st discern,
Mark Scotia's fond-returning eye,
  It dwells upon GLENCAIRN.

This was written probably late in 1786. A copy was sent to Lord Glencairn on 13th January, 1787 asking permission to print the verses. Glencairn declined (see Letter 334). The verses first appear in Cunningham, although Kinsley (Vol. III, p. 1223), errs in stating that they appear first in Chalmers, 1851.

There was a Lad

Tune: Daintie Davie
First printed in Cromek, 1808.

THERE was a lad was born in Kyle,	the parish name
But what na day o' what na style,	
I doubt it 's hardly worth the while	
To be sae nice wi' *Robin*.	so

Chorus
5   *Robin* was a rovin' Boy,
     Rantin', rovin', rantin', rovin';
Robin was a rovin' Boy,
     Rantin' rovin' *Robin*.

Our monarch's hindmost year but ane	1759
10 Was five-and-twenty days begun,	
'Twas then a blast o' Janwar' Win'[1]	January winds
Blew hansel in on *Robin*.	A first gift
Robin was &c.	

The Gossip keekit in his loof,	glanced, face
Quo' scho wha lives will see the proof,	quoth she, who
15 This waly boy will be nae coof,	sturdy, no fool
I think we'll ca' him *Robin*.	call
Robin was &c.	

He'll hae misfortunes great an' sma',	have, small
But ay a heart aboon them a';	above
He'll be a credit 'till us a',	to
20 We'll a' be proud o' *Robin*.	
Robin was &c.	

1 January 25th 1759, the date of my Bardship's vital existence. R.B.

But sure as three times three mak nine,
 I see by ilka score and line,   *every*
This chap will dearly like our kin',   *kind*
  So leeze me on thee, *Robin*.   *commend*
   Robin was &c.

25 Guid faith quo' scho I doubt you Stir, *good, she*
  Ye'll gar the lasses lie aspar;   *make, legs apart*
 But twenty fauts ye may hae waur — *faults, have worse*
  So blessin's on thee, *Robin*.
   Robin was &c.

This features in the S. C. B. dated 9th April 1787. The chorus is
adapted from a traditional song but the versification is the poet's
own celebration of his birthday. The song may have been begun
earlier but the lyrics here are from 1787. It is an optimistic auto-
biographical piece, written with future fame in mind, given the
success of his Kilmarnock edition and his success in Edinburgh. It is
ironic that this work was probably never sung publicly during the
poet's life as it first appears in print in 1808. After the first Burns
Clubs were set up in the early 19th century, it gained a growing
popularity and is now one of the most sung Scots songs. The second
line of the last stanza still condemns that stanza to a degree of
discreet censorship in performance.

Elegy
On the Death of Robert Ruisseaux
First printed in Cromek, 1808.

Now Robin lies in his last lair,
He'll gabble rhyme, nor sing nae mair, *talk, no more*
Cauld Poverty, wi' hungry stare,   *cold*
  Nae mair shall fear him;   *no more*
5 Nor anxious Fear, nor cankert Care, *crabbed*
  E'er mair come near him.   *more*

To tell the truth, they seldom fash't him, *troubled*
Except the moment that they crush't him;
For sune as Chance or Fate had hush't 'em *soon*
10 Tho' e'er sae short,   *so*
Then wi' a rhyme or sang he lash't 'em, *song*
  And thought it sport.

Tho' he was bred to kintra wark,   country-work
And counted was baith wight and stark,   both, sturdy, strong
15 Yet that was never Robin's mark
          To mak a man;
But tell him, he was learn'd and clark,   well read, scholar
          Ye roos'd him then!   roused

This mock-elegy was written during 1787. The poet plays on the
French for 'brook' by employing 'Ruisseaux', meaning streams, i.e.
Scottish *burns*. The reference to Jean Jacques Rousseau (1712–78),
as a seminal influence on the French revolution was not noted by
Kinsley.

On Robert Fergusson – I

First printed in Cromek, 1808.

Curse on ungrateful man, that can be pleas'd,
And yet can starve the author of the pleasure!

O thou, my elder brother in Misfortune,
By far my elder Brother in the Muse,
With tears I pity thy unhappy fate!
Why is the Bard unfitted for the world,
Yet has so keen a relish of its Pleasures?

See notes to *Epitaph: On Robert Fergusson*. These lines were
inscribed by Burns in a copy of Fergusson's poetry he gifted to
Rebeccah Carmichael on 19th March 1787, when he was in Edin-
burgh.

On Robert Fergusson – II

First printed in *The Scots Magazine*, November 1803.

ILL-FATED Genius! Heaven-taught Fergusson,
          What heart that feels and will not yield a tear,
To think Life's sun did set e'er well begun
          To shed its influence on thy bright career.

O why should truest Worth and Genius pine
          Beneath the iron grasp of Want and Woe,
While titled knaves and idiot-greatness shine
          In all the splendour Fortune can bestow?

These lines were inscribed by Burns in a copy of the periodical *The World*. The enraged sentiments are heart felt and largely accurate in terms of Fergusson's untimely fate and prophetic with regard to his own.

To a Painter

First printed in Chambers, 1851.

DEAR – , I'll gie ye some advice,	give
You'll tak it no uncivil:	take
You shouldna paint at angels, man,	should not
But try and paint the Devil.	
To paint an angel's kittle wark,	tricky work
Wi' Nick there 's little danger;	the Devil
You'll easy draw a lang-kent face,	long-known
But no sae weel a stranger.	so well
R.B.	

There is no definitive manuscript proof that Burns wrote these lines. It is claimed the verses were written by Burns on the back of a sketch by an Edinburgh artist, whose identity is unknown. Kinsley merely refers to the Chambers-Wallace remarks (Vol. IV, p. 309) on the alleged origin of the lines. The verses are in the colloquial, impromptu style of Burns. Previous editors have probably been right to accept them.

On Elphinstone's Translation of Martial

First printed in Stewart, 1801.

O Thou, whom Poesy abhors,
Whom Prose has turnèd out of doors;
Heard'st thou yon groan? — proceed no further!
'Twas laurel'd Martial calling, Murther!

James Elphinstone (1721–1809) translated Martial's *Epigrams* and published them in 1782. Burns records in a letter of 14th January 1788 that 'somebody' presented him with the translations while he was in Edinburgh and 'asked my opinion of it' (see Letter 178). The poet viewed the book and after requesting permission to write his response on a blank leaf of the edition delivered the deadly evaluation.

To the Guidwife of Wauchope House
– Mrs. Scott
First printed (incomplete) by Currie, 1800.

Guidwife,   good

I mind it weel, in early date,   well
When I was beardless, young and blate,   bashful
   An' first cou'd thresh the barn,
5 Or haud a yokin at the pleugh,   hold, harnesses, plough
An' tho' fu' foughten sair eneugh,   exhausted, sore enough
   Yet unco proud to learn.   mighty
When first amang the yellow corn   among
   A man I reckon'd was;
10 An' wi' the lave ilk merry morn   others, each
   Could rank my rig and lass;   ridge
     Still shearing, and clearing
      The tither stooked raw;   other, row/sheaths
     Wi' clavers an' haivers   gossip, nonsense
15   Wearing the day awa: away

E'en then, a wish (I mind its power)
A wish, that to my latest hour
   Shall strongly heave my breast;
That I for poor auld Scotland's sake   old
20 Some useful plan, or book could make,
   Or sing a sang at least.   song
The rough burr-thistle spreading wide   Scots thistle
   Amang the bearded bear,   among, barley
I turn'd the weeding heuk aside,   hook/hoe
25 An' spar'd the symbol dear.
     No nation, no station
      My envy e'er could raise:
     A Scot still, but blot still,   without
     I knew nae higher praise.   no

30 But still the elements o' sang   song
In formless jumble, right an' wrang,   wrong
   Wild floated in my brain;
Till on that hairst I said before,   harvest
My partner in the merry core,   crowd
35   She rous'd the forming strain.

I see her yet, the sonsie quean,   buxom girl
    That lighted up my jingle;
Her pauky smile, her kittle een,   shrewd eyes
    That gart my heart-strings tingle.   made
40   So tiched, bewitched,
            I raved ay to mysel;   look
        But bashing and dashing,
            I kend na how to tell.   always

Hale to the sex, ilk guid chiel says,   each good man
45 Wi' merry dance in winter-days,
    An' we to share in common:
The gust o' joy, the balm of woe,
The saul o' life, the heav'n below,   soul
    Is rapture-giving woman.
50 Ye surly sumphs, who hate the name,   boors
    Be mindfu' o' your mither: mother
She, honest woman, may think shame
    That ye're connected with her.
        Ye're wae men, ye're nae men,   sad, no
55   That slight the lovely dears:
        To shame ye, disclaim ye,
            Ilk honest birkie swears.   each, fellow

For you, na bred to barn and byre,
Wha sweetly tune the Scottish lyre,   who
60   Thanks to you for your line.
The marl'd plaid ye kindly spare,   multi-coloured
By me should gratefully be ware;   worn
    'Twad please me to the Nine.   utmost
I'd be mair vauntie o' my hap,   more proud, clothes
65   Douce hingin owre my curple,   soberly, over, crupper
Than ony ermine ever lap,   any, folded
    Or proud imperial purple.
        Farewell then, lang hale then,   long health
            An' plenty be your fa':   lot
70   May losses and crosses
            Ne'er at your hallan ca'.   doorway/hall, call

R. Burns. March, 1787

Among the many verse epistles Burns received after the publication
of his Kilmarnock edition, one of the best was by Elizabeth Scott

(1729–89) of Wauchope House, by Jedburgh. The poet visited her
during his Border tour on 10th May 1787, describing her favourably
but castigating her 'hottentot' husband. Mrs Scott was married to a
Walter Scott and was a niece of the poetess, Alison Cockburn. Her
epistle to Burns appeared in the Scottish press during early 1796,
probably sent to the press by Burns himself. Lines 25–30 of her
work would have pleased the poet:

> An' then sae slee ye crack yer jokes
> O' Willie Pitt and Charlie Fox.
> Our Great men a' sae weel descrive,
> An' how to gar the nation thrive,
> Ane maist wad swear ye dwalt amang them,
> An' as ye saw them, sae ye sang them.

Indeed, Mrs Scott identifies exactly the unique vernacular quality
of the subtly undermining intimacy Burns achieves with the poli-
tical objects of his satire. It is this uniquely intimate tone that is one
of our major reasons for accepting *The Dagger* and *A New Song*, into
the canon.

Coleridge's enormous admiration for Burns's vernacular poetry
(only Cowper of his English contemporaries found him linguistically
opaque) achieved particular expression in stanza 3 in the thistle image:

> I cannot here refuse myself the pleasure of recording a speech of
> the Poet Burns, related to me by the lady to whom it was
> addressed (Letter 541). Having been asked by her, why in his
> more serious Poems he had not changed the two or three Scotch
> words which seemed only to disturb the purity of the style? the
> poet with great sweetness and his usual happiness in reply,
> answered why in truth it would have been better, but (quotes
> ll. 20–24). An author may be allowed to quote from his own
> poems, when he does it with as much modesty and felicity as
> Burns did in this instance (Low, *The Critical Heritage*, p. 109).

To Miss Isabella McLeod

First printed in Chambers-Wallace, 1896.

The crimson blossom charms the bee,
    The summer sun the swallow;
So dear this tuneful gift to me
    From lovely Isabella.

Her portrait fair upon my mind
    Revolving time shall mellow;
And Mem'ry's latest effort find
    The lovely Isabella.

No Bard nor lover's rapture this,
    In fancies vain and shallow;
She is, so come my soul to bliss!
    The lovely Isabella.

Edinburgh, March 16, 1787

Isabella McLeod was a sister of John McLeod (See *On the Death of John McLeod*), whose father was McLeod of Raasay. Her sister was the Countess of Loudon and it is probably this connection, through Mrs Dunlop, that led to her meeting the poet. Kinsley suggests that Gavin Hamilton may have introduced Burns to her.

Extempore in the Court of Session

Tune: Gilliecrankie
First printed by Cromek, 1808.

LORD ADVOCATE

	He clench'd his pamphlets in his fist,	
	He quoted and he hinted,	
	Till in a declamation-mist,	
5	His argument, he tint it:	lost it
	He gaped for 't, he graped for 't,	groped
	He fand it was awa, man;	found, away
	But what his common sense came short,	
	He eked out wi' law, man.	

10	MR. ERSKINE	
	Collected, HARRY stood awee,	a moment
	Then open'd out his arm, man;	
	His lordship sat wi' ruefu' e'e,	eye
	And ey'd the gathering storm, man:	
15	Like wind-driv'n hail it did assail,	
	Or torrents owre a linn, man;	over, waterfall
	The BENCH sae wise lift up their eyes,	so
	Hauf-wauken'd wi' the din, man.	half-wakened

In 1787 Burns attanded the Court of Session to witness the case of
Maxwell Campbell vrs. Captain James Montgomerie, who fathered
a child by the former's wife. Harry Erskine (1746–1817) was the
Dean of the Faculty and Ilay Campbell (1734–1823), Lord Advocate
(prior to Robert Dundas taking the position). Erskine became a
friend and patron of Burns, who, here catches perfectly the famous
torrent of his allusive legal rhetoric.

Extempore Epistle to Mr. M'adam of Craigengillan
In Answer to an Obliging Letter He Sent in the
Commencement of my Poetic Career. Written in Nanse
Tinnock's, Mauchline.

First printed by Cromek, 1808.

	Sir, o'er a gill I gat your card,	whisky, got
	I trow it made me proud;	pledge
	See wha taks notice o' the Bard!	who takes
	I lap and cry'd fu' loud. —	leapt, full
5	Now deil-ma-care about their jaw,	little may, talk
	The senseless, gawky million;	
	I'll cock my nose aboon them a',	above, all
	I'm roos'd by Craigengillan.—	praised
	'Twas noble, Sir; 'twas like yoursel,	
10	To grant your high protection:	
	A great man's smile ye ken fu' well,	you know full
	Is ay a blest infection. —	always
	Tho', by his banes wha in a tub	bones who
	Match'd Macedonian Sandy![1]	
15	On my ain legs thro' dirt and dub,	own
	I independent stand ay. —	always
	And when those legs to gude warm kail	good, broth
	Wi' welcome canna bear me;	cannot
	A lee dyke-side, a sybow-tail,	stone-wall, onion-
20	An' barley-scone shall cheer me. —	

1 Diogenes. R.B.

Heaven spare you lang to kiss the breath   long
    O' monie flowery simmers!   many
An' bless your bonie lasses baith,   girls both
    I'm tauld they're loosome kimmers!   told, lovable girls

25 An' God bless young Dunaskin's laird,[2]
    The blossom of our gentry!
An' may he wear an auld man's beard,   old
    A credit to his country!

John McAdam was an agricultural improver known to Burns (by repute) through his friend David Woodburn, factor of Craigengillan, an estate south of Mauchline. Editors prior to Kinsley suggest the poem was written in 1786, after the publication of the Kilmarnock edition; but Kinsley, on the basis that McAdam only appears in the addenda of the Edinburgh subscription list, takes this as indication that the poet's link with McAdam occurs only in 1787. This appears to be a case of switching one assumption for another, then having to argue that Burns must have misdated the poem in his Glenriddel Manuscript. It is probable Burns wrote it when and where he states, that McAdam's late subscription to the Edinburgh edition has no connection with the above poem, written as a response to a letter.

Prologue:
Spoken by Mr. Woods on his Benefit Night
Monday, 16th April, 1787.
First printed by Stewart, 1801.

WHEN by a generous Public's kind acclaim,
That dearest meed is granted — honest fame;
When *here* your favour is the *actor's* lot,
Nor even the *man* in *private life* forgot;
5 What breast so dead to heav'nly Virtue's glow,
But heaves impassion'd with the grateful throe.

Poor is the task to please a barb'rous throng,
It needs no Siddons's[1] powers in Southern's song;
But here an ancient nation fam'd afar,
10 For genius, learning high, as great in war —

2 Col. Quinton McAdam, son of John McAdam.
1 Sarah Siddons (1755–1831), an English actress who played at Edinburgh in the 1780s.

Hail, CALEDONIA, name for ever dear!
Before whose sons I'm honor'd to appear!
Where every science — every nobler art —
That can inform the mind, or mend the heart,
15   Is known; as grateful nations oft have found
Far as the rude barbarian marks the bound.
Philosophy, no idle pedant dream,
Here holds her search by heaven-taught Reason's beam;
Here History paints, with elegance and force,
20   The tide of Empire's fluctuating course;
Here *Douglas*[2] forms wild Shakspeare into plan,
And Harley[3] rouses all the God in man.
When well-form'd taste, and sparkling wit unite,
With manly lore, or female beauty bright,
25   (Beauty, where faultless symmetry and grace
Can only charm us in the second place,)
Witness my heart, how oft with panting fear,
As on this night, I've met these judges here!
But still the hope Experience taught to live,
30   Equal to judge — you're candid to forgive.
No hundred-headed Riot here we meet,
With Decency and Law beneath his feet;
Nor Insolence assumes fair Freedom's name;
Like CALEDONIANS, you applaud or blame.

35   O Thou, dread Power! Whose empire-giving hand
Has oft been stretch'd to shield the honor'd land!
Strong may she glow with all her ancient fire;
May every son be worthy of his sire;
Firm may she rise with generous disdain
40   At Tyranny's, or direr Pleasure's chain;
Still self-dependent in her native shore,
Bold may she brave grim Danger's loudest roar,
Till Fate the curtain drop on worlds to be no more!

William Woods (1751–1802), an English actor, moved to Edinburgh during the 1770s and pursued his dramatic career there. He was latterly a friend of the poet Robert Fergusson and is mentioned in Fergusson's *Last Will*. It was probably this connection that drew

2 John Home's tragedy *Douglas* (1756) was viewed by many Scots as an improvement to Shakespeare.
3 The Man of Feeling, wrote by Mr MacKenzie. R.B.

Burns to Woods, who played 'Ford' in *The Merry Wives of Windsor* during his benefit night on 16th April, 1787. Stewart (1801) took his text from a newspaper publication, while Henley and Henderson's version is from an early draft.

This poem is far more complicit than *Address to Edinburgh* with the genteel capital's deep but doubtful self-regard in aesthetics and social matters. Ironically, given Woods' friendship with Fergusson, it is the very antithesis of Fergusson's satirical vision of the middle class 'national' sentimentality of Edinburgh's propertied classes. Ll. 30–1 are also particularly unBurnsian. Consciously or otherwise, the *Scots Prologue* later written for the Dumfries theatre almost exactly reverses what is said here about Scotland and poetry.

Where Wit May Sparkle –
To William Dunbar of the Crochallan Fencibles
First published here as lines by Burns.

Where Wit may sparkle all its rays,
    Uncurst with Caution's fears;
And Pleasure, basking in the blaze,
    Rejoice for endless years.

These lines were written by Burns in a letter of 30th April, 1787 to William Dunbar, the *Rattlin Roarin Willie* of Burns's song and Colonel of the convivial, radical Enlightenment club, the Crochallan Fencibles. They are introduced '. . . I have a strong fancy that in some future excentric Planet, the Comet of a happier System than any which Astronomy is yet acquainted, you and I, among the harum-scarum Sons of Imagination and Whim, shall recognise OLD AQUAINTANCE –' (Letter 99). There are no quotation marks to indicate they are by another author. Burns normally marks the work of other authors with quotation marks, or applies the poet's name. No editor of the collected letters suggests an author, nor have the lines been identified as the work of Burns or another. The letter first appeared with Hogg and Motherwell's edition in 1835, but since, no one has commented on the lines. As they are in the poet's hand and without quotation marks, it is almost certain they are his.

Epistle to Wm. Tytler of Woodhouselee,
Author of a Defence of Mary Queen of Scots -
With an Impression of the Author's Portrait
First printed by Currie in 1800.

REVERED Defender of beauteous Stuart,
    Of Stuart! — a Name once respected,
A Name which to love was once mark of a true heart,
    But now 'tis despis'd and neglected.

5   Tho' something like moisture conglobes in my eye,
    Let no man misdeem me disloyal;
A poor, friendless wand'rer may well claim a sigh,
    Still more if that Wand'rer were royal.

My Fathers that *name* have rever'd on a throne,
10   My Fathers have fallen to right it;
Those Fathers would spurn their degenerate Son
    That NAME should he scoffingly slight it.

Still in pray'rs for King George I most cordially join,
    The Queen and the rest of the gentry:
15 Be they wise, be they foolish, 'tis nothing of mine,
    Their title 's avow'd in the Country.

But why of that Epocha make such a fuss,
    That gave us th' Electoral Stem?
If bringing them over was lucky for *us*,
20   I'm sure 'twas as lucky for *them*!

But Politics, truce! we're on dangerous ground;
    Who knows how the fashions may alter:
The doctrines today that are loyalty sound,
    Tomorrow may bring us a halter.

25 I send you a trifle, a head of a Bard,
    A trifle scarce worthy your care;
But accept it, good Sir, as a mark of regard,
    Sincere as a saint's dying prayer.

Now Life's chilly evening dim shades on your eye,
30   And ushers the long dreary night;
But you, like the star that athwart gilds the sky,
    Your course to the latest is bright.

May 1787

This work, where Jacobite sympathy is in inverse proportion to anti-Hanoverian antipathy, was addressed to William Tytler (1711–92), Laird of Woodhouselee, a writer to the Signet and author on various subjects, including a defence of Mary Queen of Scots, music and antiquities. It is notorious for, arguably, the worst line Burns ever wrote, 'Tho' something like moisture conglobes in my eye . . .' What is forgotten as opposed to such saccharine Jacobitism is the wicked anti-Hanoverian dig of ll. 17–20, edited out by Currie (1800), but restored in Pickering, 1839. It was Tytler, the musician who collected old songs for Johnson's Scots Musical Museum, who gravely upset David Hume with his *A Historical and Critical Enquiry into the Evidence . . . against Mary Queen of Scots*. With his examination of the Rev. Dr Robertson's *Dissertation* and Hume's *History* (1760), Hume felt that a 'sound beating or even a Rope too good for him' and that a 'Scots Jacobite, who maintains the innocence of Queen Mary must be considered as . . . beyond the reach of argument or reason, and must be left to his Prejudices' (E.C. Mossner, *David Hume*, 1954, pp. 413–14). The affair is discussed by L.L. Bongie, in 'The Eighteenth Century Marian Controversy', *Studies in Scottish Literature*, 1964, pp. 236–52). Hume does not emerge from this article as clear winner but, in places, irascible and unconvincing. It also reveals the depth of passion personal and political that Mary Queen of Scots could evoke in eighteenth-century Scotland. Hume would have found Burns at least as invidious as Tytler in this respect. This, for example, is Burns writing to Dr Moore whose novel *Zeluco* contains a duel fought over Mary's reputation:

> The Ballad on Queen Mary, was begun while I was busy with Percy's Reliques of English Poetry. By the way, how much is every honest heart which has a tincture of genuine Caledonian Prejudice, obliged to you for your glorious story of Buchanan & Targe . . . What a rocky-hearted, perfidious Succubus was that Queen Elizabeth! Judas Iscariot was a sad dog to be sure, but still his demerits shrink to insignificance, compared with the doings of the infernal Bess Tudor (Letter 437).

The poem was sent to Tytler on 4th May 1787, along with an engraving of Burns by Beugo, prior to the poet's departure on his Border tour with Robert Ainslie.

To Miss Ainslie in Church
First printed in Cromek, 1808.

Fair maid, you need not take the hint,
    Nor idle texts pursue;
'Twas guilty sinners that he meant,
    Not angels such as you.

This was composed during the poet's Border tour with Robert Ainslie in 1787. On 6th May, Burns attended church at Duns accompanied by Ainslie and his sister. The story has it that when the minister denounced all sinners, Miss Ainslie appeared agitated; on observing this, Burns used a blank leaf in his bible to write the epigram.

For William Creech
Selkirk, 13th May, 1787.
First printed by Cromek, 1808.

Auld chuckie REEKIE 's[1] sair distrest,	old, mother-hen, sore
Down droops her ance weel-burnish'd crest,	once, well-
Nae joy her bonie buskit nest	no, trimmed
Can yield ava;	at all
5 Her darling bird that she loes best,	loves
Willie's awa. —	away

O Willie was a witty wight,
And had o' things an unco sleight;   uncommon skill
Auld Reekie ay he keepit tight,   old, kept in order
10   And trig an' braw: trim, handsome
But now they'll busk her like a fright,   dress, freak
        Willie's awa. —

The stiffest o' them a' he bow'd,
The bauldest o' them a' he cow'd,   boldest

1 Old Reekie refers to Edinburgh.

15   They durst nae mair than he allow'd,   *did no more*
        That was a law:
     We've lost a birkie weel worth gowd,   *blade, well, gold*
        Willie's awa. —

     Now gawkies, tawpies, gowks, and fools,   *boobies, silly girls, dolts*
20   Frae colleges and boarding-schools ,   *from*
     May sprout like simmer puddock-stools   *summer, toadstools*
        In glen or shaw;   *wood*
     He wha could brush them down to mools   *who, dust*
        Willie's awa. —

25   The brethren o' the Commerce-Chaumer   *chamber*
     May mourn their loss wi' doolfu' clamour;   *doleful*
     He was a dictionar and grammar
        Amang them a':
     I fear they'll now mak mony a stammer,   *make many*
30   Willie's awa. —

     Nae mair we see his levee door   *no more*
     Philosophers and Poets pour,
     And toothy Critics by the score
        In bloody raw;   *row*
35   The Adjutant of a' the core   *band*
        Willie's awa. —

     Now worthy Greg'ry's[2] Latin face,
     Tytler's and Greenfield's[3] modest grace,
     McKenzie, Stuart,[4] such a brace
40   As Rome ne'er saw;
     They a' maun meet some ither place,   *must, other*
        Willie's awa. —

     Poor BURNS — even Scotch Drink canna   *cannot*
        quicken,
     He cheeps like some bewilder'd chicken,
45   Scar'd frae its minnie and the cleckin   *from, mother, brood*
        By hoodie-craw: *hooded carrion crow*
     Grief's gien his heart an unco kickin,   *given, uncommon beating*
        Willie's awa. —

2 Dr James Gregory (1753–1821).
3 Alexander Fraser Tytler (1747–1813) and Rev. William Greenfield (d. 1827).
4 Henry Mackenzie (1745–1831) and Professor Dugald Stewart (1753–1828).

Now ev'ry sour-mou'd, girnin blellum,   bad-mouthed, snarling nag
50 And Calvin's folk are fit to fell him;   kill
    Ilk self-conceited, critic-skellum   each, -scullion
        His quill may draw;
    He wha could brawlie ward their bellum   who, finely repel, attack
        Willie's awa. —

55 Up wimpling, stately Tweed I've sped,   meandering
    And Eden scenes on chrystal Jed,
    And Ettrick banks now roaring red
        While tempests blaw;
    But every joy and pleasure's fled,
60   Willie's awa. —

    May I be Slander's common speech;
    A text for Infamy to preach;
    And lastly, streekit out to bleach   stretched
        In winter snaw   snow
65 When I forget thee, WILLIE CREECH,
        Tho' far awa! —

    May never wicked Fortune touzle him,   ruffle
    May never wicked men bamboozle him,
    Until a pow as auld's Methusalem   head of hair, old as
70   He canty claw: cheery scratch
    Then to the blessed, new Jerusalem
        Fleet-wing awa. —

This was written on 13th May 1787 while Burns was on his tour of
the Borders. He wrote to William Creech (1745–1815), his Edin-
burgh printer, enclosing the poem 'wrote, nearly extempore, in a
solitary Inn at Selkirk, after a miserable wet day's riding' (Letter
106). This humorous, Ramsay-derived mock elegy was written prior
to the decline in their friendship.

To Symon Gray

First printed in Cunningham, 1834.

I
SYMON Gray,
You're dull to-day.

II
Dullness, with redoubled sway,
Has seized the wits of Symon Gray.

III
Dear Cimon Gray,
                    The other day,
        When you sent me some rhyme,
I could not then just ascertain
5   Its worth, for want of time.

But now today, good Mr. Gray,
        I've read it o'er and o'er,
Tried all my skill, but find I'm still
        Just where I was before.

10   We auld wives' minions gie our opinions,
        Solicited or no;
Then of its fauts my honest thoughts
        I'll give — and here they go.

Such damn'd bombast no time that's past
15   Will show, or time to come,
So, Cimon dear, your song I'll tear,
        And with it wipe my [bum].

These epigrams were penned by Burns during May 1787 on his
tour of the Borders. Simon Gray, who, according to oral tradition,
was a retired businessman, met Burns in Duns, on 6th May (See
Kinsley's note, Vol. 3, p. 1237) and pestered the bard with his
home-spun versification. Scott Douglas, in 1876, was too prudish
to print the last two lines, choosing to pretend that he had been
'told the piece concludes' with the line ending 'nor time to come'
(See Vol. II, p. 308).

To Mr. Renton of Lamerton

First printed in Chambers, 1851.

Your billet, Sir, I grant receipt;	letter
Wi' you I'll canter ony gate;	any road
Tho' 'twere a trip to yon blue warl	world
Where Birkies march on burning marl.[1]	fellows, stone
Then, Sir, God willing, I'll attend ye;	
And to His goodness I commend ye. —	

R. Burns.

1 A reference to Hell, alluding to Milton's *Paradise Lost*, Book I, l. 296.

Mr John Renton of Lamerton invited Burns to join him at Mordington House, by Berwick, during the poet's tour of the Borders in 1787. The above reply was written about 18th May, 1787. There is no evidence from the poet's journal or letters that he visited Renton, who was related to the poet's Dumfries friend Charles Sharpe, though this verse suggests he did.

Epigram at Inveraray

First printed by Stewart, 1801.

Whoe'er he be that sojourns here,
    I pity much his case,
Unless he come to wait upon
    The Lord their God, His Grace.

There 's naething here but Highland pride,   nothing
    And Highland scab and hunger;
If Providence has sent me here,
    'Twas surely in an anger.

This was composed on 24th June, 1787 when Burns was travelling through Argyllshire. Stewart (1801) remarks in his introduction to these verses, 'Burns, accompanied by a friend, having gone to Inverary at a time when some company were there on a visit to his Grace the Duke of Argyll, finding himself and his companion entirely neglected by the Inn-Keeper, whose whole attention seemed to be occupied with the visitors of his Grace, expressed his disapprobation of the uncivility with which they were treated in the following lines'.

Elegy on the Death of Sir James Hunter Blair

First printed by Currie, 1800.

The lamp of day, with ill-presaging glare,
    Dim, cloudy, sank beneath the western wave:
Th' inconstant blast howl'd thro' the darkening air,
    And hollow whistled in the rocky cave.

5   Lone as I wander'd by each cliff and dell,
        Once[1] the lov'd haunts of Scotia's royal train;
    Or mus'd where limpid streams, once hallow'd, well;[2]
        Or mouldering ruins mark the sacred Fane.[3]

Th' increasing blast roared round the beetling rocks;
10   The clouds, swift-wing'd, flew o'er the starry sky;
The groaning trees, untimely, shed their locks,
        And shooting meteors caught the startled eye. —

The paly moon rose in the livid east,
        And 'mong the cliffs disclos'd a stately Form,
15   In weeds of woe, that frantic beat her breast,
        And mix'd her wailings with the raving storm. —

Wild to my heart the filial pulses glow;
        'Twas CALEDONIA'S trophy'd shield I view'd;
Her form majestic droop'd in pensive woe,
20   The lightning of her eye in tears imbu'd. —

Revers'd that spear, redoubtable in war,
        Reclin'd that banner, erst in fields unfurl'd,
That like a deathful meteor gleam'd afar,
        And brav'd the mighty monarchs of the world. —

25   'My patriot-Son fills an untimely grave!'
        With accent wild and lifted arms she cry'd;
'Low lies the hand that oft was stretch'd to save,
        Low lies the heart that swell'd with honor's pride. —

'A weeping Country joins a Widow's tear,
30   The helpless Poor mix with the Orphan's cry;
The drooping Arts surround their Patron's bier,
        And grateful Science heaves the heart-felt sigh. —

'I saw my Sons resume their ancient fire;
        I saw fair Freedom's blossoms richly blow:
35   But ah, how hope is born but to expire!
        Relentless Fate has laid their Guardian low. —

1 The King's Park at Holyrood House. R.B.
2 St Anthony's Well. R. B.
3 St Anthony's chapel. R.B.

'My Patriot falls — but shall he lie unsung,
　　While empty Greatness saves a worthless name?
No: every Muse shall join her tuneful tongue,
40　　And future ages hear his growing fame. —

'And I will join a Mother's tender cares,
　　Thro' future times to make his virtues last,
That distant years may boast of other BLAIRS —'
　　She said, and vanish'd with the sweeping blast.

Sir James Hunter Blair (1741–87) was originally from Ayr, the son of a merchant. He was a Whig politician, M.P for Edinburgh 1780–4, became the city's Lord Provost in 1784 and a Baronet, 1786. In notes to the Glenriddell manuscript Burns wrote of Blair as a friend: '. . . my grief was sincere . . . a worthy, public-spirited man'. His death occurred on 1st July, 1787.

To Miss Ferrier
With a Copy of *Elegy on the Death of Sir James Hunter Blair*
First printed in Chambers, 1851.

Madam
Nae Heathen Name shall I prefix,
　　Frae Pindus or Parnassus;
AULD REEKIE dings them a' to sticks　　　Edinburgh, knocks down
　　For rhyme-inspiring Lasses. —

5　Jove's tunefu' Dochters three times three　　daughters
　　Made Homer deep their debtor;
But gien the body half an e'e,　　　given, eye
　　NINE FERRIERS wad done better. —　　would [have]

Last day my mind was in a bog,
10　　Down George's Street I stoited;　　staggered
A creeping, cauld, PROSAIC fog　　cold
　　My very senses doited. —　　dulled

Do what I dought to set her free,　　dared
　　My Muse lay in the mire;　　soul
15　Ye turned a neuk — I saw your e'e —　　corner
　　She took the wing like fire. —

The mournfu' Sang I here enclose,   song
   In GRATITUDE I send you;
And pray in rhyme, sincere as prose,
20   A' GUDE THINGS MAY ATTEND   good
   YOU.

Robt Burns. St James' Square, Saturday even:

This was sent to Miss Jane Ferrier (1767–1846), daughter of James
Ferrier, Writer to the Signet. Burns met her in Edinburgh, during
July 1787. The poem first appears in the Glasgow *College Album* in
1828, where it is recorded that Miss Ferrier asked Burns for a copy
of one of his poems. The 1828 text is inadequate. For commentary,
see J.C. Ewing, *Burns Chronicle*, 1939. Chambers is mentioned as
the first genuinely public version to obtain a wide readership. Jove's
daughters (l. 5) is a reference to the nine Muses.

Verses Written on a Window of the Inn at Carron
Printed first by Stewart, 1801.

We cam' na here to view your warks,   came not, works
   In hopes to be mair wise,   more
But only, lest we gang to Hell,   go
   It may be nae surprise: no
But whan we tirl'd at your door,   rattled
   Your porter dought na bear us;   did not, admit
Sae may, shou'd we to Hell's yetts come,   so, gates
   Your billie Satan sair us!   comrade, serve

These lines were written on 26th August 1787, when Burns left
Falkirk and travelled to Carron Ironworks, but was refused admit-
tance.

Reply to a Censorious Critic
First printed by Cunningham, 1834.

These imprudent lines were answered, very petulantly, by some-
body, I believe a Revd. Mr Hamilton. – In a M.S.S. where I met
with the answer I wrote below – R.B.

With Esop's lion, Burns says, sore I feel
Each other blow, but damn that ass's heel!

This couplet, based on the public reaction to the poet's *Lines on Seeing the Royal Palace at Stirling in Ruins*, is included in Kinsley (no. 166B) but omitted from the canon by Mackay (1993).

The Reproof
First printed by Cunningham, 1834.

RASH mortal, and slanderous Poet, thy name
Shall no longer appear in the records of fame;
Dost not know that old Mansfield, who writes like the Bible,
Says the more 'tis a truth, Sir, the more 'tis a libel?

This appears in Kinsley, but is missing from Mackay. This *seeming* self-reproof was written on the window of the same Stirling Inn where he had dangerously diamond-inscribed his pro-Stuart anti-Hanoverian lines. He is really, of course, re-asserting his anti-Hanoverian position. William Murray (1705–93), the Earl of Mansfield, was a friend of Graham of Fintry. Burns met the Earl and his sons sometime after writing these lines. Kinsley remarks that there is no manuscript authority for these lines. The current editors were allowed to view these lines and the associated anti-Hanoverian Stirling verses in a privately owned transcript collection and have no doubt of their provenance.

Epitaph for William Michie
A Schoolmaster of Cleish Parish, Fifeshire
First published by Cromek, 1808.

Here lie Willie Michie's banes,	bones
O Satan, when ye tak him,	take
Gie him the schulin o' your weans;	give, schooling, children
For clever Deils he'll mak 'em!	devils

Burns is supposed to have met William Michie, according to Chambers-Wallace, in Edinburgh. The story goes that Michie fell asleep drunk at a party in Burns's Edinburgh lodgings. Chambers gives Michie's first name as Ebenezer, not William and in line 1, his version reads 'Eben Michie' (Chambers-Wallace, Vol. IV, p. 304).

Amang the Trees

Tune, The King of France, he rade a race.
First printed by Cromek, 1808.

AMANG the trees, where humming bees
    At buds and flowers were hinging, O!   hanging
Auld Caledon drew out her drone,   old
    And to her pipe was singing, O!
5 'Twas Pibroch, Sang, Strathspey, or Reels,   bagpipes, songs
    She dirl'd them aff, fu' clearly, O!   rang, off full
When there cam a yell o' foreign squeels,   came
    That dang her tapsalteerie, O!   knocked upside down

Their capon craws an' queer ha, ha's,
10   They made our lugs grow eerie, O!   ears, strange
The hungry bike did scrape and pike[1]   swarm, pick [at strings]
    Till we were wae and weary; O!   sad
But a royal ghaist, wha ance was cas'd   ghost, who once
    A prisoner aughteen year awa,   eighteen
15 He fir'd a Fiddler in the North   inspired
    That dang them tapsalteerie, O!   knocked

This song is based on a traditional work (See Kinsley, Vol. III, p. 1245). The song is a robust defence of Scottish bagpipe and fiddle music, in contrast to 'foreign squeels' of Italian and German music, then popular among many aristocrats of Scotland. The 'royal ghaist' refers to King James I. Kinsley suggests that the song is a compliment to the brilliant Scots fiddler Neil Gow, 'fir'd' or inspired by King James I. Burns met the great musician at Dunkeld, 31st August, 1787. It was Neil's son, Nathaniel Gow, who met Burns in Dumfries in 1793. Burns was a competent fiddler of slow airs, as Mrs Burns has recollected, but unable to play reels, jigs or strathspeys with any skill. This association of music with the national spirit was partly derived from Fergusson and Burns's letters are replete with his keen awareness for the ethnic identity of national music.

---

1 Scott Douglas changed this original word to 'fyke', meaning to make a fuss or fidget. His so-called correction was carried by Henley and Henderson and repeated by Mackay. It is correct in Kinsley.

A Highland Welcome

First printed by Currie, 1800.

When Death's dark stream I ferry o'er,
    A time that surely *shall* come;
In Heaven itself, I'll ask no more,
    Than just a Highland welcome.

The poet's headnote reads 'A verse composed and repeated by *Burns*, to the Master of the House, on taking leave at a place in the Highlands, where he had been hospitably entertained'. It was written on 2nd September, 1787, during the poet's Highland tour, when, accompanied by William Nicol, they dined at Dalnacardoch or Dalwhinnie.

Castle Gordon

First printed in *The Morning Chronicle*, 25th September, 1800.

Streams that glide in Orient plains,
Never bound by Winter's chains;
Glowing here on golden sands,
There immixed with foulest stains
5 From Tyranny's empurpled hands:
These, their richly gleaming waves,
I leave to tyrants and their slaves,
Give me the stream that sweetly laves
    The banks by CASTLE GORDON. —

10 Torrid forests, ever gay,
Shading from the burning ray
Hapless wretches sold to toil;
Or the ruthless Native's way,
Bent on slaughter, blood and spoil:
15 Woods that ever verdant wave,
I leave the tyrant and the slave,
Give me the groves that lofty brave
    The storms, by CASTLE GORDON. —

Wildly here without control,
20 Nature reigns and rules the whole;
In that sober, pensive mood,
Dearest to the feeling soul,
She plants the forest, pours the flood:
Life's poor day I'll musing, rave,
25 And find at night a sheltering cave,
Where waters flow and wild woods wave
　　By bonny CASTLE GORDON. —

This song appeared in the London *Morning Chronicle* just prior to being printed in Currie's edition. The political content of the first two stanzas may have led the *Chronicle* to print it. During his time in Edinburgh, Burns was invited to Castle Gordon by Jane Maxwell, the Duchess of Gordon. His visit occurred on 7th September, 1787. William Nicol did not attend the meeting with Alexander, Duke of Gordon, but stayed at the Inn in Fochabers and later refused to accompany Burns back to the Duke's castle. Burns sent the Duke this song as an apology for their non-appearance.

My Peggy's Face

Tune: My Peggy's Face
First printed in Currie, 1800, then in the S.M.M., 1803.

My Peggy's face, my Peggy's form,
The frost of hermit Age might warm;
My Peggy's worth, my Peggy's mind,
Might charm the first of human kind.
5 I love my Peggy's angel air,
Her face so truly heav'nly fair,
Her native grace so void of art,
But I adore my Peggy's heart.

The lily's hue, the rose's die,　　　　　　　　dye
10 The kindling lustre of an eye;
Who but owns their magic sway,
Who but knows they all decay!
The tender thrill, the pitying tear,
The generous purpose nobly dear,
15 The gentle look that Rage disarms,
These are all Immortal charms. —

This work was supposed to have appeared with *Where, Braving Angry Winter Storms*, in the second Volume of Johnson's S.M.M.

Margaret (Peggy) Chalmers did not want either song published and in this case, was successful. Burns appears, in so far as he was able, to have had a Platonic devotion to Peggy Chalmers which she did not reciprocate. Alluding to the awe he felt towards her he wrote, 'I look on the sex [women in general] with something like the admiration with which I regard the starry sky in a frosty December night. I admire the beauty of the Creator's workmanship; I am charmed with the wild but graceful eccentricity of their motions, and – wish them, good night' (Letter 143). This was probably an apt metaphor for their relationship.

Epitaph for William Nicol

First printed by Motherwell and Hogg, 1826.

Ye maggots, feed on Willie's brains,
    For few sic feasts you've gotten;   such
And fix your claws into his heart,
    For fient a bit o't 's rotten.   not a bit of

William Nicol (1744–97) was the classics master of Edinburgh High School. Originally from Annan, Nicol was one of the versatile and able sons of the people who educated themselves into the new professional middling classes of Edinburgh, having studied theology and medicine. He toured the Highlands with Burns and, being one of the poet's intimate friends, was honoured that Burns named one of his sons after the wayward Latin teacher. Scott Douglas makes the error of stating that Nicol outlived Burns by 'some years' (Vol. 2, p. 332). Douglas meddled with the text and his amended text survives in Henley and Henderson (1896) and Mackay (1993).

On the Death of Lord President Dundas –

First printed in *The Edinburgh Magazine*, June 1818.

LONE on the bleaky hills, the straying flocks
Shun the fierce storms among the sheltering rocks;
Down foam the rivulets, red with dashing rains,
The gathering floods burst o'er the distant plains;
5 Beneath the blast the leafless forests groan,
The hollow caves return a sullen moan. —

Ye hills, ye plains, ye forests and ye caves,
Ye howling winds, and wintry-swelling waves,
Unheard, unseen, by human ear or eye,
10 Sad to your sympathetick glooms I fly;
Where to the whistling blast and water's roar,
Pale Scotia's recent wound I may deplore. —

O heavy loss thy Country ill could bear!
A loss these evil days can ne'er repair!
15 Justice, the high vicegerent of her God,
Her doubtful balance ey'd and sway'd her rod;
Hearing the tidings of the fatal blow,
She sunk abandon'd to the wildest woe. —

Wrongs, Injuries, from many a darksome den,
20 Now gay in hope explore the paths of men:
See from his cavern grim Oppression rise,
And throw on Poverty his cruel eyes;
Keen on the helpless victim let him fly,
And stifle, dark, the feebly-bursting cry. —
25 Mark ruffian Violence, distain'd with crimes,
Rousing elate in these degenerate times;
View unsuspecting Innocence a prey,
As guileful Fraud points out the erring way:
While subtle Litigation's pliant tongue
30 The life-blood equal sucks of Right and Wrong. —
Hark, injur'd Want recounts th' unlisten'd tale,
And much-wrong'd Mis'ry pours th' unpitied wail!

Ye dark, waste hills, ye brown, unsightly plains,
Congenial scenes! ye soothe my mournful strains:
35 Ye tempests, rage; ye turbid torrents, roll;
Ye suit the joyless tenor of my soul:
Life's social haunts and pleasures I resign,
Be nameless wilds and lonely wanderings mine,
To mourn the woes my Country must endure,
40 That wound degenerate ages cannot cure. —

Robert Dundas of Arniston (1713–87), Lord Advocate in 1754 and
Lord President from 1760, died on 13th December, 1787. He was a
brother of Henry Dundas, Lord Melville who ruled Scotland during
the political storm of the 1790s. It was Alexander Wood, an
Edinburgh surgeon who asked Burns to write an elegy on the death

of Dundas, not, as Scott Douglas suggests, Charles Hay, advocate. Aware that such an act might be seen to be a coded request for patronage from the Dundas dynasty, the poet felt considerable anxiety at the request but complied. He wrote, in retrospect to Alexander Cunningham, on 11th March, 1791:

> I have two or three times in my life composed from the wish, rather from the impulse, but I never succeeded to any purpose. One of these times I shall ever remember with gnashing of teeth. – 'Twas on the death of the late Lord President Dundas. . . . Mr Alexander Wood, Surgeon, urged me to pay a compliment in the way of my trade to his Lordship's memory. – Well, to work I went, & produced a copy of Elegiac verses, some of them I own rather commonplace, & others rather hide-bound, but on the whole though they were far from being in my best manner, they were tolerable; & had they been the production of a Lord or a Baronet, they would have been thought very clever. – I wrote a letter, which however was in my best manner, & enclosing my Poem, Mr Wood carried altogether to Mr Solicitor Dundas that then was, & not finding him at home, left the parcel for him. – His Solicitorship never took the smallest notice of the Letter, the Poem, or the Poet. From that time, highly as I respect the talents of their Family, I never see the name, Dundas, in the column of a newspaper, but my heart seems straightened for room in my bosom; & if I am obliged to read aloud a paragraph relating to one of them, I feel my forehead flush, & my nether lip quivers. – Had I been an obscure Scribbler . . . or had I been a dependant Hangeron for favour or pay . . . Mr Solicitor might have had some apology (Letter 441).

There is a terrible historical and personal irony present in Burns's ill-judged, sycophantic, if unpublished, poem. Dundas's death, Scotland's perhaps 'mortal wound', turns flood water into blood. In this stormy, apocalyptic landscape we see the degenerate breakdown of civil order due to political oppression, collapse of legality, criminality, and chronic poverty. It is perhaps, in theme and language, closest to *A Winter's Night*. For Burns and the radicals, this nightmare was to become, in the 1790s, not the consequence of this Dundas's death, but the very creation of his successors in the Dundas dynasty. Sadly the true Dundas poem of the 1790s, *The Lucubrations of Henry Dundass*, exists only in its asinine title as the page was torn from Riddell's copy of the Interleaved S.M.M.

Sylvander to Clarinda

First printed in *The Clarinda Correspondence*, 1834.

When dear Clarinda, matchless fair,
    First struck Sylvander's raptur'd view,
He gaz'd, he listen'd to despair,
    Alas! 'twas all he dared to do. —

5 Love, from Clarinda's heavenly eyes,
    Transfix'd his bosom thro' and thro';
But still in Friendship's guarded guise,
    For more the demon fear'd to do. —

That heart, already more than lost
10   The imp beleaguer'd all *perdue*;   lost
For frowning Honor kept his post,
    To meet that frown he shrunk to do. —

His pangs the Bard refus'd to own,
    Tho' half he wish'd Clarinda knew:
15 But Anguish wrung the unweeting groan —
    Who blames what frantic Pain must do?

That heart, where motley follies blend,
    Was sternly still to Honor true:
To prove Clarinda's fondest friend,
20   Was what a Lover sure might do. —

The Muse his ready quill employ'd,
    No nearer bliss he could pursue;
That bliss Clarinda cold deny'd —
    'Send word by Charles how you do!' —

25 The chill behest disarm'd his Muse,
    Till Passion all impatient grew:
He wrote, and hinted for excuse,
    ''Twas 'cause he'd nothing else to do.' —

But by those hopes I have above!
30   And by those faults I dearly rue!
The deed, the boldest mark of love,
    For thee that deed I dare to do! —

O, could the Fates but name the price,
    Would bless me with your charms and you!
35 With frantic joy I'd pay it thrice,
    If human art or power could do!

Then take, Clarinda, friendship's hand,
    (Friendship, at least, I may avow;)
And lay no more your chill command,
40   I'll write, whatever I've to do. —

Sylvander. Wednesday night

Although it traces the painful fluctuations of the sexually repressed
relationship, this poem has the artificial, sentimental tone of most of
the Burns/McLehose epistolary correspondence. It has none of the
austere power of *Ae Fond Kiss*.

To Clarinda
With a Pair of Wine-Glasses
First printed by Stewart, 1802.

Fair Empress of the Poet's soul,
    And Queen of Poetesses;
Clarinda, take this little boon,
    This humble pair of Glasses.

5 And fill them high with generous juice,
    As generous as your mind;
And pledge them to the generous toast —
    'The whole of Humankind!'

'To those who love us!' — second fill;
10   But not to those whom we love,
Lest we love those who love not us: —
    A third — 'to thee and me, Love!'

Long may we live! Long may we love!
    And long may we be happy!!!
15 And may we never want a Glass,
    Well charg'd with generous Nappy!!!!

This was written by Burns to Mrs McLehose before he left Edin-
burgh in March 1788. The verses and present of glasses were given

on 17th March, 1788. Mackay, surprisingly, has dropped the final
stanza (See p. 321), an error found in Henley and Henderson (1896).
The final stanza is included by most editors from 1834 onwards and
is found in Kinsley (no. 219, p. 327–8).

The Bonie Lass of Albanie

Tune: Mary weep no more for me, or Mary's Dream
First printed by Chambers, 1838.

MY heart is wae and unco wae,   sad, mighty sad
    To think upon the raging sea,
That roars between her gardens green,
    An' th' bonie lass of ALBANIE. —

5 This lovely maid's of noble blood,
    That ruled Albion's kingdoms three;
But Oh, Alas! for her bonie face!
    They hae wranged the lass of ALBANIE. —   have wronged

In the rolling tide of spreading Clyde
10   There sits an isle of high degree;[1]
And a town of fame[2] whose princely name
    Should grace the lass of ALBANIE. —

But there is a youth, a witless youth,[3]
    That fills the place where she should be,
15 We'll send him o'er to his native shore,
    And bring our ain sweet ALBANIE. —   own

Alas the day, and woe the day,
    A false Usurper wan the gree,   won the honours
Who now commands the towers and lands,
20   The royal right of ALBANIE. —

We'll daily pray, we'll nightly pray,
    On bended knees most ferventlie,
That the time may come, with pipe and drum,
    We'll welcome hame fair ALBANIE. —   home

1 Isle of Bute.
2 Rothesay.
3 Prince George, later King George IV.

Charlotte Stuart (1753–89) was the daughter of Charles Edward Stuart and his mistress Clementina Walkinshaw. On 6th December, 1787 she was officially titled Duchess of Albany. Charles Edward lived in exile from Scotland until his death on 31st January, 1788. Aware of the former Jacobite leader's daughter being given this title, Burns wrote the above in dedication to the forlorn cause of the Stuarts and their claim to the British throne. Evidence from an as yet unpublished manuscript collection of letters between Burns and Robert Ainslie reveal that the poet considered naming one of his illegitimate children, if a girl, Charlotte, after the Duchess of Albany.

A Birthday Ode. December 31st 1787

First printed as a censored fragment by Currie, 1800.

AFAR th' illustrious Exile roams,
    Whom kingdoms on this day should hail!
An Inmate in the casual shed;
    On transient Pity's bounty fed;
5 Haunted by busy Mem'ry's bitter tale!
Beasts of the forest have their savage homes,
    But He who should imperial purple wear
Owns not the lap of earth where rests his royal head:
    His wretched refuge, dark Despair,
10 While ravening Wrongs and Woes pursue,
    And distant far the faithful Few
      Who would his sorrows share!
      False flatterer, Hope, away!
Nor think to lure us as in days of yore:
15 We solemnize this sorrowing natal day,
To prove our loyal truth — we can no more;
    And, owning Heaven's mysterious sway,
      Submissive, low adore.

      Ye honor'd, mighty Dead
20 Who nobly perish'd in the glorious cause,
    Your King, your Country, and her Laws;
From great Dundee[1] who smiling Victory led,
    And fell a Martyr in her arms,
    (What breast of northern ice but warms)

1 'Bonnie' Dundee: John Grahman of Claverhouse, d. 1689.

25 To bold Balmerino's[2] undying name,
Whose soul of fire, lighted at Heaven's high flame,
Deserves the brightest wreath departed heroes claim;
    Not unreveng'd your fate shall lie;
    It only lags, the fatal hour:
30   Your blood shall with incessant cry
    Awake at last th' unsparing Power!
As from the cliff with thundering course
    The snowy ruin smokes along,
With doubling speed and gathering force,
35 Till deep it crashing whelms the cottage in the vale;
    So Vengeance' arm, ensanguin'd, strong,
    Shall with resistless might assail:
Usurping Brunswick's[3] head shall lowly lay,
And Stewart's wrongs and yours with tenfold weight repay.

40 Perdition, baleful child of Night,
Rise and revenge the injur'd right
    Of Stewart's ROYAL RACE!
Lead on th' unmuzzled hounds of Hell
Till all the frighted Echoes tell
45   The blood-notes of the chase!
Full on the quarry point their view,
Full on the base, usurping crew,
The tools of Faction, and the Nation's curse:
    Hark! how the cry grows on the wind;
50   They leave the lagging gale behind;
Their savage fury pitiless they pour,
With murdering eyes already they devour:
    See, Brunswick spent, a wretched prey;
    His life, one poor, despairing day
55 Where each avenging hour still ushers in a worse!
    Such Havock, howling all abroad,
        Their utter ruin bring;
    The base Apostates to their God,
        Or Rebels to their KING!

2 Lord Balmerino, Arthur Elphinstone (1688–1746) fought at Sheriffmuir
with the Earl of Mar. He was captured at Culloden and executed in London,
18th August, 1746.
3 The Duke of Brunswick (1735–1806) was brother-in-law to George III and
led the Prussian and Austrian armies against France in 1792, boasting he
would bring Paris to its knees through starvation.

Currie printed only a fragment of this work in 1800, leaving out ll. 1–12, and ll. 36–59 due to their violent, anti-Hanoverian imagery which would have been construed as treasonable. They contain a wished-for image in which King George III's brother-in-law, the Duke of Brunswick, has his head chopped off (l. 38). Henley and Henderson censored this image and doctored the poem with their own anodyne phrase to read that Brunswick's '*pride* shall lay' rather than his *head* 'shall lowly lay'. Kinsley rightly corrects this, but it is copied in the Mackay edition which so often employs the 1896 Henderson and Henley texts. The poem was printed in full by Chambers-Wallace, after the Glenriddell manuscripts appeared. Scott Douglas reverted back to the Currie fragment in 1876.

Jacobitism was still politically taboo in 1800 and criticism of the British monarchy and their relations was for most of the nineteenth century, not the proper thing for a poet to indulge in. When Currie printed the fragment he, quite pathetically, tried to add a Hanoverian gloss to the already censored piece by claiming that those who gathered with Burns in Edinburgh on 31st December, 1787 to celebrate the exiled Stuart King's birthday, were all 'perfectly loyal to the King [George] on the throne'. This is far from the case. As Donaldson comments, those who met to celebrate the birthday of Charles Edward Stuart (still living at this time, in France) were 'not sentimental dabblers but the hard core of the party in Scotland and the poet was clearly *persona grata* amongst them' (W. Donaldson, *The Jacobite Song*, p. 76). Aware he was among people related by blood to the Jacobites who died or lost lands after the 1745 rebellion, Burns wrote on his manuscript that was passed around that evening: 'Burn the above verses when you have read them, as any little sense that is in them is rather heretical, and do me the justice to believe me sincere in my grateful remembrances of the many civilities you have honoured me with since I came to Edinburgh' (Donaldson, p. 76).

Currie denigrates the poem's literary quality, describing it as a 'rant' that was 'deficient in the complicated rhythm and polished versification that such compositions require' (Currie, Vol. 1, pp. lxi–lxii). Kinsley, who was not under any political pressure to denigrate the politics of Burns, flogs the same horse in his disdainful: 'it is another of Burns's calamitous attempts at the Pindaric Ode' (Vol. III, p. 1256). For a contrary view of Burns and the Pindaric Ode, see notes to *A Winter's Night*.

The cataclysmic forces of the avalanche are here shown to deluge the Hanoverians in vengeance for their treatment of the Stuarts (ll. 33–9) by a masterly kinetic use of language. The image of Scotland deluged in blood at the degenerate anarchy described in *On the Death of Lord President Dundas* is surpassed in what is only partly a Pindaric Ode, given that an adapted form of the Scots stanza of *The Cherry and the Slae* is neatly employed to bring the poem to its climax. The image of 'Vengeance' arm' (l. 36) and the declamatory 'Nation's curse' are repeated in the new *The Ghost of Bruce*, second version.

Hunting Song
or The Bonie Moor-Hen
Tune: I Rede You Beware at the Hunting
First printed by Cromek, 1808.

The heather was blooming, the meadows were mawn, mown
Our lads gaed a-hunting, ae day at the dawn, gone, one
O'er moors and o'er mosses and mony a glen, many
At length they discovered a bonie moor-hen.

Chorus
5 I rede you beware at the hunting, young men;
I rede you beware at the hunting, young men;
Take some on the wing, and some as they spring,
But cannily steal on a bonie moor-hen. carefully

Sweet brushing the dew from the brown heather bells,
10 Her colours betray'd her on yon mossy fells;
Her plumage outlustred the pride o' the spring,
And O! as she wanton'd sae gay on the wing. so
   I rede you beware &c.

Auld Phoebus himsel, as he peep'd o'er the hill,
In spite at her plumage he tryed his skill;
15 He levell'd his rays where she bask'd on the brae — hillside
His rays were outshone, and but mark'd where she lay.
   I rede you beware &c.

They hunted the valley, they hunted the hill;
The best of our lads wi' the best o' their skill;
But still as the fairest she sat in their sight,
20 Then, whirr! she was over, a mile at a flight.
   I rede you beware &c.

Evidence suggests that Burns did not print it on the wishes of Agnes McLehose, who felt the sexual undertones of the hunting metaphor were indelicate (See headnote, Scott Douglas, Vol. II, p. 275). It has been suggested that other stanzas probably existed, as Cromek printed asterisks at the end to indicate suppressed verses. Kinsley records that Henley and Henderson saw a manuscript with no additional verses. Given Cromek's notoriety in doctoring texts, there is every likelihood that verses were cut away from the original by him.

On Johnson's Opinion of Hampden

First printed in *The Scotsman*, 22nd November 1882.

For shame!
Let Folly and Knavery
    Freedom oppose:
'Tis suicide, Genius,
    To mix with her foes.

Burns inscribed the above in a copy of Samuel Johnson's *The Lives of the Poets*, next to a comment by Johnson that the poet Edmund Waller's mother was a sister of John Hampden 'the zealot of rebellion'. The edition is supposed to have been gifted by Burns to Alexander Cunningham (1594–1643). The exact date of composition is unknown. Dr Johnson was profoundly problematic for Burns (See Letters 94, 223, 325 and 413). He was intimately touched by his *Lives of the Poets*. On the other hand, the high Tory advocate, hostile to the Civil War and its multiple, radical consequences, seemed to Burns a 'Genius' (l. 4) self-destructively allied with the reactionary enemies of freedom. John Hampden was an iconic figure of inspiration among the radicals of the 1790s. Many pro-reform letters of this era employed 'Hampden' as a pen-name. Coleridge initially intended to name his first son after him.

An Extemporaneous Effusion
On Being Appointed to the Excise

First printed by Cromek, 1808.

Searching auld wives' barrels,	old
Ochon, the day!	alas
That clarty barm should stain my laurels;	dirty yeast/blame
But — what'll ye say!	
These muvin' things ca'd wives an' weans	called, children
Wad muve the very hearts o' stanes!	would, stones

Burns obtained his commission to join the Excise on 14th July, 1788, but had considered the Excise as a possible future career two years earlier, in 1786. He received training in Edinburgh for six weeks and it was probably at this time that he wrote these lines. In a letter to Margaret Chalmers he records stoically, 'The question is not at what door of Fortune's palace shall we enter in; but what doors does she open for us? . . . I got this without any hanging on, or mortifying solicitation; it is immediate bread, and though poor in comparison of the last eighteen months of my existence, 'tis luxury in comparison of all my preceding life: besides the commissioners are some of them my acquaintances . . .' (Letter 207). Fiscal necessity forced Burns into the most loathed part of the government executive.

The degree of guilt and self-contempt evident in these lines can be gauged from l. 4 which exactly echoes Ramsay's monologue of an Edinburgh prostitute *Lucky Spence's Last Advice*. Hence Lucky's stanza on the punitively sadistic consequences of selling oneself:

> There's ae sair cross attends the craft,
> That curst Correction-house, where aft
> Vild Hangy's taz ye'r riggings saft
>   Makes black and blue,
> Enough to pit a body daft;
>   But what ye'll say.

Where Helen Lies

First printed in Thomson, 1805.

O That I were where Helen lies,
Night and day on me she cries;
O that I were where Helen lies
    In fair Kirconnel lee. —
5 O Helen fair beyond compare,
A ringlet of thy flowing hair,
I'll wear it still for ever mair
    Untill the day I die. —

Curs'd be the hand that shot the shot,
10 And curs'd the gun that gave the crack!
Into my arms bird Helen lap,
    And died for sake o' me!
O think na ye but my heart was sair;
My Love fell down and spake nae mair;
15 There did she swoon wi' meikle care
    On fair Kirconnel lee. —

I lighted down, my sword did draw,
I cutted him in pieces sma';
I cutted him in pieces sma'
20   On fair Kirconnel lee. —
O Helen chaste, thou were modest,
If I were with thee I were blest
Where thou lies low and takes thy rest
    On fair Kirconnel lee. —

25 I wish my grave was growing green,
A winding sheet put o'er my een,   *eyes*
And I in Helen's arms lying
    In fair Kirconnel lee!
I wish I were where Helen lies!
30 Night and day on me she cries:
O that I were where Helen lies
    On fair Kirconnel lee. —

This is largely a traditional song, reworked by Burns. It is based on
the story of Ellen Irvine of Kirkconnel House, who was pursued by
two male suitors. One, in an attempt to kill the other, accidentally
shot and killed Ellen as she sat with Adam Fleming on the banks of the
Kirtle water. Fleming rose and killed his rival but, fearing a jail
sentence or worse, fled to Spain in panic. He eventually returned to
Scotland and was interred with his lover. The story is printed in
Thomas Penant's *A Tour in Scotland*, published in 1774, pp. 88–9 – a
source quoted by Kinsley (no. 203). Burns informed Thomson in
1793 that the version of this song printed in S.M.M. was not much
better than the 'silly' traditional verses (Letter 569). The song has
been updated by several authors including Walter Scott.

Your Friendship
or Interpolation
Tune: The Banks of Spey
First printed in Barke, 1955.

Your friendship much can make me blest,
    Oh, why that bliss destroy!
Why urge the only, one request
    You know I will deny!

Your thought, if Love must harbour there,
    Conceal it in that thought;
Nor cause me from my bosom tear
    The very friend I sought.

These lines were written by Burns to Mrs McLehose to be added to some verses she had written. They were included in a letter of 4th January, 1788.

Up and Warn a' Willie

First printed in Barke, 1955.

Up and warn a' Willie,
    Warn, warn a';
To hear my cantie Highland sang,   *joyful, song*
    Relate the things I saw, Willie. —

5 When we gaed to the braes o' Mar,   *went*
    And to the wapon-shaw, Willie,   *show of weapons*
Wi true design to serve the king
    And banish whigs awa, Willie. —
Up and warn a', Willie,
10   Warn, warn a';
For Lords and lairds came there bedeen,   *early*
    And wow but they were braw, Willie. —   *handsome*

But when the standard was set up
    Right fierce the wind did blaw, Willie;   *blow*
15 The royal nit upon the tap   *nut, top*
    Down to the ground did fa', Willie. —
Up and warn a', Willie,
    Warn, warn a';
Then second-sighted Sandie said
20   We'd do nae gude at a', Willie. —   *no good*

But when the army join'd at Perth,
    The bravest ere ye saw, Willie,
We didna doubt the rogues to rout,
    Restore our king and a', Willie.
25 Up and warn a' Willie,
    Warn, warn a';
The pipers play'd frae left to right   *from*
    O whirry whigs awa, Willie. —   *harry*

But when we march'd to Sherramuir
30   And there the rebels saw, Willie;
Brave Argyll attack'd our right,
    Our flank and front and a' Willie. —

Up and warn a', Willie,
    Warn, warn a';
35 Traitor Huntly soon gave way
    Seaforth, St. Clair and a' Willie. —

But brave Glengarry on our right,
    The rebel's left did claw, Willie,
He there the greatest slaughter made
40   That ever Donald saw, Willie. —
Up and warn a', Willie,
    Warn, warn a';
And Whittam shat his breeks for fear   trousers
    And fast did run awa, Willie. —

45 For he ca'd us a Highland mob
    And soon he'd slay us a', Willie;
But we chas'd him back to Stirling brig
    Dragoons and foot and a', Willie. —
Up and warn a', Willie,
50   Warn, warn a';
At length we rallied on a hill
    And briskly up did draw, Willie. —

But when Argyle did view our line,
    And them in order saw, Willie,
55 He streight gaed to Dumblane again   straight went
    And back his left did draw, Willie. —
Up and warn a', Willie,
    Warn, warn a',
Then we to Auchterairder march'd
60   To wait a better fa' Willie. —   outcome

Now if ye spier wha wan the day,   ask, who won
    I've tell'd you what I saw, Willie,
We baith did fight and baith did beat   both
    And baith did rin awa, Willie. —   run
65 Up and warn a', Willie,
    Warn, warn a' Willie,
For second-sighted Sandie said
    We'd do nae gude at a', Willie. —   no good

This song is based on a traditional work which records an indecisive
battle at Sheriffmuir during the Jacobite rebellion of 1715, in which
both sides claimed that the other retreated in panic. In his notes to

Scottish songs Burns states he obtained a copy of this song from 'Tom Niel' who was well known in Edinburgh. The Neil text is expanded by Burns into a satirical lyric sung as a colloquial reminiscence, mocking the key players in the battle, namely the Earl of Huntly, the Earl of Seaforth, McDonnell of Glengarry and 'Whittam' (General Whetham), 'who *shat his breeks*'. The song does not have the same effect and success of *The Battle Of Sheriffmuir*.

Surprisingly, the song did not surface as a work of Burns until Barke in 1955. Mackay's version is missing the two final stanzas, leaving the narrative drama incomplete (pp. 317–18).

The Chevalier's Lament

Tune: Captain Okean
First printed in Thomson's *Select Collection*, 1799.

The small birds rejoice in the green leaves returning,
    The murmuring streamlet winds clear thro' the vale;
The primroses blow in the dews of the morning,
    And wild-scatter'd cowslips bedeck the green dale;
5 But what can give pleasure, or what can seem fair,
    When the lingering moments are number'd by Care?
No birds sweetly singing, nor flow'rs gaily springing,
    Can soothe the sad bosom of joyless Despair. —

The deed that I dared, could it merit their malice,
10   A KING and a FATHER to place on his throne;
His right are these hills, and his right are these valleys,
    Where the wild beasts find shelter but I can find none:
But 'tis not my suff'rings, thus wretched, forlorn,
    My brave, gallant friends, 'tis your ruin I mourn;
15 Your faith proved so loyal in hot, bloody trial,
    Alas, can I make it no sweeter return!

This is in the lamenting voice of Prince Charles Edward Stuart after the Jacobite defeat at Culloden. Thus, through the voice of its defeated leader this song displays the poet's skill in juxtaposing the simple beauties of nature, with the despair of the Jacobite cause. This is Burns writing what is in effect, a political version of *Ye Banks and Braes*, where the love is for a country and a people, both forever lost to the Young Pretender. The leading English radical John Thelwall remarked in marginalia on a copy of his friend Coleridge's *Biographia Literaria* that this song was by far the best example in the English language of simple language to convey emotion.

Epitaph on Robert Muir –

First printed in the Aldine edition, 1893.

What Man could esteem, or what woman could love,
    Was He who lies under this sod:
If Such Thou refusest admittance above,
    Then whom wilt Thou favour, Good God!

This was written for Robert Muir (1758–88) of Loanfoot, near
Kilmarnock, who died on 22nd April, 1788. He was a friend of
the poet and sold 72 copies of the Kilmarnock edition and 40 of the
first Edinburgh edition.

Epistle to Hugh Parker

First printed by Cunningham, 1834.

	In this strange land, this uncouth clime,	
	A land unknown to prose or rhyme;	
	Where words ne'er crost the Muse's heckles,	crossed, hackles
	Nor limpet in poetic shackles;	limped
5	A land that prose did never view it,	
	Except when drunk he stacher't thro' it;	staggered
	Here, ambush'd by the chimla cheek,	chimney side
	Hid in an atmosphere of reek,	smoke
	I hear a wheel thrum i' the neuk,	spin, corner
10	I hear it — for in vain I leuk. —	look
	The red peat gleams, a fiery kernel,	
	Enhusked by a fog infernal:	
	Here, for my wonted rhyming raptures,	
	I sit and count my sins by chapters;	
15	For life and spunk like ither Christians,	spirit, other
	I'm dwindled down to mere existence,	
	Wi' nae converse but Gallowa' bodies,	no, people
	Wi' nae kend face but Jenny Geddes.	no known
	Jenny, my Pegasean pride!	
20	Dowie she saunters down Nithside,	sad, wanders
	And ay a westlin leuk she throws,	westward look
	While tears hap o'er her auld brown nose!	cover, old
	Was it for this wi' canny care,	cautious
	Thou bure the Bard through many a shire?	bore
25	At howes or hillocks never stumbled,	hollows
	And late or early never grumbled? —	

O, had I power like inclination,
I'd heeze thee up a constellation,   lift
To canter with the Sagitarre,
30 Or loup the ecliptic like a bar;
Or turn the Pole like any arrow;
Or, when auld Phoebus bids good-morrow,   old
Down the zodiac urge the race,
And cast dirt on his godship's face;
35 For I could lay my bread and kail   bet, broth
He'd ne'er cast saut upo' thy tail. —   salt
Wi' a' this care and a' this grief,
And sma', sma' prospect of relief,   small
And nought but peat reek i' my head,   smoke
40 How can I write what ye can read? —
Tarbolton, twenty-fourth o' June,
Ye'll find me in a better tune;
But till we meet and weet our whistle,   wet, mouth
Tak this excuse for nae epistle.   no
Robert Burns.

This little-known poem is as bitter an account of his life in a bothy at Ellisland prior to his long delayed farm house being built there as the sense of physical privation in the early stanzas of *The Vision*. He felt almost completely cut off at Ellisland from compatible company with Jean and the children still in Ayrshire, hence his horse's tears for a lost western world. Almost all nineteenth-century critics, as we have seen, disguised the true nature of Burns's rural experience. A notable, formidable exception is the great American writer, Nathaniel Hawthorne, who, as a devotee of the poet, visited Mossgeil and Dumfries in the early 1850s and was astonished at the claustrophobic, squalid conditions he saw. Having utopianly attempted to be a farmer himself, Hawthorne had found the nature of the work akin to crucifying and could not understand the level of energy Burns required to engage simultaneously as poet and farmer.

The customary combination of horse-riding and creativity runs through the poem with, of course, the ironic joke that his beloved 'Jenny Geddes' (named after the stool-hurler of St Giles Cathedral, Edinburgh) is no Pegasus. The latter part of the poem changes gear, as so often in the letters, to a fantasy release in the zodiac from an all too tangibly, restricting reality. It was addressed and sent to Hugh Parker, a friend of the poet and brother of Major William Parker, the Kilmarnock banker. Mackay errs in his headnote, stating Hugh Parker was a banker.

The Fête Champetre

Tune: Gilliecrankie
First printed by Cunningham, 1834.

O wha will to Saint Stephen's House,   who, House of Commons
    To do our errands there, man;
O wha will to Saint Stephen's House   who
    O' th' merry lads of Ayr, man?
5 Or will ye send a Man-o'-law,
    Or will ye send a Sodger?   soldier
Or him wha led o'er Scotland a'   who
    The meikle URSA-MAJOR?   Great Bear

Come, will ye court a noble Lord,
10   Or buy a score o' Lairds, man?
For Worth and Honor pawn their word
    Their vote shall be Glencaird's, man?
Ane gies them coin, ane gies them wine,   one gives
    Anither gies them clatter;   another, talk
15 Annbank, wha guess'd the ladies' taste,   who
    He gies a Fête Champetre. —

When Love and Beauty heard the news,
    The gay green-woods amang, man,   among
Where gathering flowers and busking bowers   dressing
20   They heard the blackbird's sang, man;   song
A vow they seal'd it with a kiss
    Sir Politicks to fetter,
As theirs alone, the Patent-bliss,
    To hold a Fête Champetre. —

25 Then mounted Mirth, on gleesome wing,
    O'er hill and dale she flew, man;
Ilk wimpling burn, ilk chrystal spring,   each winding
    Ilk glen and shaw she knew, man: each, wood
She summon'd every SOCIAL SPRITE,
30   That sports by wood or water,
On th' bonie banks of Ayr to meet,
    And keep this Fête Champetre. —

Cauld Boreas, wi' his boisterous crew,   cold, North Wind
    Were bound to stakes like kye, man;   cattle

35 And Cynthia's car, o' silver fu',   full
    Clamb up the starry sky, man: climbed
Reflected beams dwell in the streams,
    Or down the current shatter;
The western breeze steals through the trees,
40   To view this Fête Champetre. —

How many a robe sae gaily floats!   so
    What sparkling jewels glance, man!
To HARMONY's enchanting notes
    As moves the mazy dance, man!
45 The echoing wood, the winding flood,
    Like Paradise did glitter,
When Angels met, at Adam's yett,   gate
    To hold their Fête Champetre. —

When Politics came there, to mix
50   And make his ether-stane, man,   amulet
He circl'd round the magic ground,
    But entrance found he nane, man: none
He blush'd for shame, he quat his name,   quit
    Forswore it every letter,
55 Wi' humble prayer to join and share
    This festive Fête Champetre. —

This semi-political song is a mock celebration of a 'fête' organised by William Cunninghame, when he came of age, on inheriting the estates of Annbank and Enterkin, near Tarbolton, from his grand-father. It was publicly assumed this event was his prelude to canvassing the wealthy landowners and aristocrats of Ayrshire – who were invited to the dinner and ball – to become a Member of Parliament, which was soon to be dissolved. The song records the way in which 'wine' and 'coin' were used to buy votes among the almost exclusively aristocratic voters of the period. Appearing to celebrate the event, Burns gives ironic assent to what he is target-ting, the sham of aristocratic 'politics' and burlesquely describes the hyper-importance of the event as such that not only does Love, Beauty and Mirth appear but even the forces of nature and every 'social Sprite' attend.

    The allusion to Dr Samuel Johnson as 'Ursa-Major' (l. 8) points to James Boswell of Auchinleck, who toured 'o'er Scotland' with Johnson. (Crawford, p. 210, comments in a footnote that Boswell's wife had said 'she had seen many a bear led by a man, but never . . . a man led by a bear' referring to seeing her husband going off with Johnson.) Boswell and Sir John Whitefoord (Glencaird's man) were seen as the two other contenders for parliament. Cunninghame's conspicuous, glittering ball came to nothing as he was not chosen as a candidate. The last two stanzas mockingly compare, from *Paradise Lost*, Politics to Satan attempting to penetrate Eden.

To Alexander Cunningham
Ellisland, July 27th, 1788.
First printed in Chambers, 1851.

My godlike Friend —nay do not stare,   no
    You think the praise is odd like;
But, 'God is Love,' the Saints declare,
    Then surely thou art Godlike.

5 And is thy Ardour still the same?
    And kindled still at Anna?
Others may boast a partial flame,
    But thou art a Volcano. —

Even Wedlock asks not love beyond
10   Death's tie-dissolving Portal;
But thou, omnipotently fond,
    May'st promise Love Immortal. —

Prudence, the Bottle and the Stew
    Are fam'd for Lovers' curing:
15 Thy Passion nothing can subdue,
    Nor Wisdom, Wine nor Whoring. —

Thy Wounds such healing powers defy;
    Such Symptoms dire attend them;
That last great Antihectic try,
20   Marriage, perhaps, may mend them. —

Sweet Anna has an air, a grace,
    Divine magnetic touching!
She takes, she charms — but who can trace
    The process of BEWITCHING?

Alexander Cunningham (circa 1763–1812) was an Edinburgh lawyer who eventually through marriage owned a share in Robertson's jewellers in the city. When Burns met him in Edinburgh he was a law student and engaged to Anne Stewart, who jilted him for an Edinburgh surgeon. The poet wrote *Anna, Thy Charms* for his jilted friend. Cunningham was a close friend to Burns until the bard's death and became a chief player in promoting the subscription for the Burns family after 1796. There are nineteen extant letters to Cunningham.

Stanza four is dropped in Henley and Henderson, probably because it mentions 'whoring'. It is also missing in Mackay.

O Mally's Meek, Mally's Sweet

Tune: Deil Flee o'er the Water
First printed in S.M.M., 1803.

As I was walking up the street,
 A barefit maid I chanc'd to meet,   barefoot
But O, the road was very hard
 For that fair maiden's tender feet.

Chorus
5 Mally's meek, Mally's sweet,
 Mally's modest and discreet,
Mally's rare, Mally's fair,
 Mally's ev'ry way compleat.

It were mair meet, that those fine feet   more
10 Were weel lac'd up in silken shoon,   well, shoes
An' 'twere more fit that she should sit
 Within yon chariot gilt aboon.   above
  Mally's meek, Mally's sweet, &c.

Her yellow hair, beyond compare,
 Comes trinkling down her swan white neck,
15 And her two eyes like stars in skies
 Would keep a sinking ship frae wreck.   from
  Mally's meek, Mally's sweet, &c.

Burns sent this song with others, including *O, Were I on Parnassus Hill*, to Johnson in August 1788, from Mauchline. It was not printed until 1803. The manuscript is now part of the Law Collection.

To Robert Graham of Fintry, Esq.,
With a request for an Excise Division.
Ellisland, September 8th 1788.
First printed by Currie, 1800.

WHEN Nature her great Masterpiece designed,
And framed her last, best Work, the Human Mind,
Her eye intent on all the mazy Plan,
She forms of various stuff the various Man. —
5   The USEFUL MANY first, she calls them forth,
Plain, plodding Industry, and sober Worth:
Thence Peasants, Farmers, native sons of earth,
And Merchandise' whole genus take their birth:
Each prudent Cit a warm existence finds,   citizen
10   And all Mechanics' many-apron'd kinds. —
Some other, rarer Sorts are wanted yet,
The lead and buoy are needful to the net. —
The *caput mortuum* of Gross Desires,
Makes a material for mere knights and squires:
15   The Martial Phosphorus is taught to flow;
She kneads the lumpish Philosophic dough;
Then marks th' unyielding mass with grave Designs,
Law, Physics, Politics, and deep Divines:
Last, she sublimes th' Aurora of the Poles,
20   The flashing elements of Female Souls. —

The order'd System fair before her stood,
Nature, well pleased, pronounced it very good;
Yet ere she gave creating labour o'er,
Half-jest, she tryed one curious labour more. —
25   Some spumy, fiery, *ignis fatuus* matter,
Such as the slightest breath of air might scatter,
With arch-alacrity and conscious glee,
(Nature may have her whim as well as we;
Her Hogarth-art perhaps she meant to show it)
30   She forms the Thing, and christens it — A POET. —
Creature, tho' oft the prey of Care and Sorrow,
When blest today, unmindful of tomorrow;
A being form'd t' amuse his graver friends,
Admir'd and praised — and there the wages ends;
35   A mortal quite unfit for Fortune's strife,
Yet oft the sport of all the ills of life;

Prone to enjoy each pleasure riches give,
Yet haply wanting wherewithal to live;
Longing to wipe each tear, to heal each groan,
40 Yet frequent all un-heeded in his own. —

But honest Nature is not quite a Turk;
She laught at first, then felt for her poor Work:
Viewing the propless Climber of mankind,
She cast about a Standard-tree to find;
45 In pity for his helpless wood-bine state,
She clasp'd his tendrils round THE TRULY GREAT:
A title, and the only one I claim,
To lay strong hold for help on generous GRAHAM. —

Pity the tuneful Muses' hapless train,
50 Weak, timid Landsmen on life's stormy main!
Their hearts no selfish, stern, absorbent stuff
That never gives — tho' humbly takes enough;
The little Fate allows they share as soon,
Unlike sage, proverbed Wisdom's hard-wrung boon:
55 The world were blest, did bliss on them depend,
Ah, that the FRIENDLY e'er should want a FRIEND!

Let Prudence number o'er each sturdy son
Who life and wisdom at one race begun,
Who feel by reason, and who give by rule,
60 (Instinct's a brute, and Sentiment a fool!)
Who make poor, 'Will do' wait upon, 'I should,'
We own they're prudent — but who owns they're good?
Ye Wise Ones, hence! ye hurt the social eye;
God's image rudely etch'd on base alloy!
65 But come, ye who the godlike pleasure know,
Heaven's attribute distinguish'd, — to bestow,
Whose arms of love would grasp all human-race;
Come, thou who givest with all a courtier's grace,
Friend of my life! (true Patron of my rhymes)
70 Prop of my dearest hopes for future times. —

Why shrinks my soul, half-blushing, half-afraid,
Backward, abashed, to ask thy friendly aid?
I know my need, I know thy giving hand,
I tax thy friendship at thy kind command:

75 But, there are such, who court the tuneful Nine,
    Heavens, should the branded character be mine!
    Whose verse in manhood's pride sublimely flows,
    Yet vilest reptiles in their begging prose.
    Mark, how their lofty, independant spirit
80 Soars on the spurning wing of injured Merit!
    Seek you the proofs in private life to find? —
    Pity, the best of words should be but wind!
    So to Heaven's gates the lark's shrill song ascends,
    But grovelling on the earth the carol ends. —
85 In all the clam'rous cry of starving Want
    They dun Benevolence with shameless front:
    Oblidge them, patronize their tinsel lays,
    They persecute you all your future days. —

    E'er my poor soul such deep damnation stain,
90 My horny fist, assume the Plough again;
    The pie-bald jacket, let me patch once more;
    On eighteenpence a week I've liv'd before. —
    Tho', thanks to Heaven! I dare even that last shift,
    I trust, meantime, my boon is in thy gift:
95 That, plac'd by thee upon the wished-for height,
    Where Man and Nature fairer in her sight,
    My Muse may imp her wing for some sublimer flight. —

Burns did not choose to publish this 1788 epistle to Robert Graham
of Fintry because it is certainly a lesser poem than the 1791 poem
printed in the second Edinburgh edition. He may also have con-
sidered the seeking of Fintry's favour too overt. Certainly it was, like
its successor, driven by deep economic need. In September of that
year he wrote to Graham that his Ellisland farm 'does by no means
promise to be such a Pennyworth as I was taught to expect. – It is in
the last stage of worn out poverty, and will take some time before it
pays the rent'. Kinsley is not sensitive to such matters and is wholly
condemnatory of the poem, seeing in it, particularly Mrs Dunlop's
specific enthusiasm for it, genteel Scotland's wrong-headed encour-
agement for Burns to write derivative, outmoded English verse:

> This kind of response did Burns no good; it encouraged him, as
> some of his criticism he had got in Edinburgh had done, in a
> vain attempt to write 'Augustan' poetry. The weakness of the
> epistle does not lie only in loose-strung couplets and conven-
> tional notions; the description of the poet (ll. 21–40) is a mask

unnatural to Burns (contrast *Epistle to J. Lapraik*, ll. 49–78); and the conjunction of flattery – to a patron he hardly knew and owed little as yet – with an equally insincere posture of independence (ll. 89–97) is absurd (Vol. III, p. 1279).

Burns certainly did not disguise his debt to Pope in this poem. On September 16th, 1788, he wrote to Margaret Chalmers that he had 'since harvest began, wrote a poem not in imitation, but in the manner of Pope's *Moral Epistles*. It is only a short essay, just to try the strength of my Muse's pinion in that way' (Letter 272). This is, of course, echoed in the last line: 'My Muse may imp her wing for some sublimer flight'. If the poem is a product of Burns's 'prentice hand' in this genre, it was also one to which he gave deep attention. Writing to Henry Erskine, the great radical lawyer and one of his heroes, he enclosed a copy, while also discussing the iniquitous agony of seeking favour from the great and the specific necessity for securing Graham's patronage:

> I have no great faith in the boasted pretensions to intuitive propriety and unlaboured elegance. – The rough material of Fine Writing is certainly the gift of Genius; but as I firmly believe that the workmanship is the united effort of Pains, Attention & Repeated – trial. – The piece addressed to Mr. Graham is my first essay in that didactic epistolary way; which circumstance I hope will bespeak your indulgence (Letter 299).

Kinsley's refusal to indulge him should certainly not be seen as mandatory. Burns was attempting to educate Graham in these two English language epistles as to his complex, educated vision of the role and fate of the poet in society in order to receive his understanding and patronage. The complexity of the vision is the necessary product of his synthesis of his knowledge of Robert Fergusson's fate with examples taken from Pope, Swift, Dr Johnson and, contemporaneously, Oliver Goldsmith, William Cowper and the peculiarly self-destructive Charles Churchill.

Ll. 1–20 denote a world more feudal than democratic whereby everything has its place. It is perhaps derived from his friend William Smellie's evolutionary vision of life ascending by a law of refinement. Thus the female soul is the highest earthly form. Smellie further argued that the highest of human life forms, such as the creative poet, might attain to states which made earthly reality incompatible to his spirit. Indeed, Burns's vision here would arguably make him more compatible with Ezra Pound than Pablo

Neruda. Burns, partly jokingly, sees Nature as a Hogarth-like power which (ll. 21–40) creates the poet as a sort of incompatible freak. Burns's letters are filled with self-analysis of his eccentric, agonised creative relationship with the world: 'It is not easy to imagine a more helpless state than his whose poetic fancy unfits him for the world' (Letter 61). If this is seen as self-indulgent Romantic agony slightly before the event, it also went in Burns with a spiritually derived agony that he had not power to give succour to the pain of the world: ' – Oh, how often had my heart ached to agony, for the power, To wipe away all tears from all eyes!' (Letter 491). If he had a tendency to endorse the Devil, or at least Milton's version of him, he was also tempted to imitate Christ. This, too, is not without its spiritual perils. In terms of the worldly appetites, Burns also believed the poet to have a particularly keen sensuality which was never accompanied by the fiscal capacity to indulge: 'Take a being of our kind; give him a stronger imagination and more delicate sensibility, which will ever between them engender a more ungovernable set of Passions, than the usual lot of man. . . curse him with a keener relish than any man living for the pleasures that only Lucre can bestow. . . and you have created a wight nearly as miserable as a Poet' (Letter 413). If this sounds somewhat like Keats before the event, Keats thought so, too, as his Ayrshire letters recording Burns's victimage by the repressive forces of the Scottish church, contain a chilling premonition of his own sensual thwarting and premature death.

The poem then argues for a compensatory element in Nature (ll. 41–8) where the poet's lack of worldly strength is compared to a climbing plant moving upwards supported by the tree-trunk provided by the benevolent, if rare, great man. Burns then makes a characteristic comparison, often also found in his letters, between the altruistic, empathetic poetic personality, emotions on which a just world could be erected, and the prudential, self-absorbed, materialists who actually run the world.

Ll. 65–70 are, as Kinsley suggests, far beyond the reality, present or subsequent, with regard to Graham's patronage. Ll. 71–88 have, however, a quality worthy of the best Augustan verse in their analysis so common in eighteenth-century verse of the caninely sycophantic poet whose apparently divine song masks degenerate self-seeking. The poem ends with an assertion, again very common in the Ayrshire vernacular epistles, of retaining his independence by, if necessary, returning to the plough. Kinsley rather tartly remarks that l. 92 is an exaggeration as the *day* rate for an Ayrshire labourer was around eighteen pence.

On William Creech

First printed by Cromek, 1808.

A little upright, pert, tart, tripping wight,
And still his precious Self his dear delight;
Who loves his own smart shadow in the streets
Better than e'er the fairest She he meets.
5 Much specious lore, but little understood
(Fineering oft outshines the solid wood)
His solid sense by inches you must tell,
But mete his subtle cunning by the ell!
A man of fashion, too, he made his tour,
10 Learn'd 'Vive la bagatelle et vive l'amour';
So travell'd monkies their grimace improve,
Polish their grin — nay, sigh for ladies' love!
His meddling vanity, a busy fiend,
Still making work his Selfish-craft must mend.

William Creech was the publisher of the 1787 Edinburgh edition. He purchased the poet's copyright and brought out the 1793 and 1794 editions of Burns for his own profit allowing the poet a few complimentary copies. This means Creech obtained Scotland's most popular poem *Tam O'Shanter* and other poems at no cost. Creech, a one-time member of the Crochallan Fencibles, lost his early Enlightenment-influenced radical ideals as the tumult of the 1790s ensued. He published most of the loyalist government propaganda during this period and his business thrived while radical publications such as *The Edinburgh Gazetteer* and *The Bee* were either persecuted or driven out of business. Mackay omits this poetic fragment from the 1993 edition, but includes the next piece on Smellie. Both are belived to have formed part of an early, proposed work *The Poet's Progress* which eventually formed *To Robert Graham of Fintry*, published in 1793. Ll. 7–8 do not appear in Kinsley.

On William Smellie

First printed by Currie, 1800.

Crochallan came:
The old cock'd hat, the brown surtout the same;
His grisly beard just bristling in its might
('Twas four long nights and days to shaving-night);

His uncomb'd, hoary locks, wild-staring, thatch'd
A head for thought profound and clear unmatch'd;
Yet, tho' his caustic wit was biting rude,
His heart was warm, benevolent, and good. —

William Smellie (1746–95) was a leading Edinburgh intellectual and a
key member of the Crochallan Fencibles. He was the printer of the
Edinburgh edition. His reputation for humorous verbal flyting was
such that he is reputed to have verbally thrashed Burns on the poet's
inauguration to the Fencibles Club. He published work on medicine
and natural philosophy. He was more of a friend to Burns than
Creech. Maria Riddell befriended the old man via the poet's intro-
duction. His biographer mentions that most of the letters from Burns
to Smellie were unfit for publication because of the caustic remarks on
people still living. They were burned. As the above poetic fragment
on Creech, this fragment is viewed as an early piece intended for *The
Poet's Progress* which ended up as the 1793 poem to Graham of Fintry.

To the Beautiful Miss Eliza J—N,
On her Principles of Liberty and Equality –
First printed in Chambers-Wallace, 1896.

How Liberty, girl, can it be by thee nam'd?
Equality too! hussey, art not asham'd:
FREE and EQUAL indeed; while mankind thou enchainest,
And over their hearts a proud DESPOT so reignest. —

This is undated and the identity of Elizabeth is unknown. Kinsley
guesses that it may be Elizabeth Johnston, a friend of Dr Blacklock
in Edinburgh. Like much of *The Rights of Woman*, this is a poem to
set feminists' teeth on edge, with its apparent traditional view of
erotic power being greater than democratic rights.

Sketch for an Elegy
First printed in 1851 by Robert Chambers.

CRAIGDARROCH, fam'd for speaking art
And every virtue of the heart,
Stops short, nor can a word impart
    To end his sentence,
5 When mem'ry strikes him like a dart
    With auld acquaintance.   old

Black James — whase wit was never laith,   whose, reluctant
But, like a sword had tint the sheath,   lost
Ay ready for the work o' death —
10   He turns aside,
And strains wi' suffocating breath
          His grief to hide.

Even Philosophic Smellie tries
To choak the stream that floods his eyes:
15   So Moses wi' a hazel-rice
          Came o'er the stane;   stone
But, tho' it cost him speaking twice,
          It gush'd amain.

Go to your marble graffs, ye great,   graves
20   In a' the tinkler-trash of state!
But by thy honest turf I'll wait,
          Thou man of worth,
And weep the ae best fallow's fate   one, fellow's
          E'er lay in earth!

This was composed in 1788. The final stanza is more or less the same
as in *Elegy to Matthew Henderson*. Due to this, it is viewed by most
editors as a first draft for the Henderson poem. Craigdarroch was
Alexander Fergusson of Craigdarroch (d. 1796), an advocate and
justice given to bibulous disorder (see *The Whistle*). Black James
(l. 7) is almost certainly not James Boswell as has been suggested.

Auld Lang Syne

Tune: Can Ye Labour Lea
First published in S.M.M, December 1796.

Should auld acquaintance be forgot   old
          And never brought to mind?
Should auld acquaintance be forgot,
          And auld lang syne!   long ago

Chorus
5   For auld lang syne, my jo,   friend
          For auld lang syne,
We'll tak a cup o' kindness yet
          For auld lang syne.

And surely ye'll be your pint stowp!   pay for
10   And surely I'll be mine!
And we'll tak a cup o' kindness yet,
      For auld lang syne.
          For auld lang syne, &c.

We twa hae run about the braes,   two, hillsides
      And pou'd the gowans fine;   pulled, daisies
15 But we've wander'd mony a weary fitt,   many, foot
      Sin auld lang syne.
          For auld lang syne, &c.

We twa hae paidl'd in the burn,   two have paddled
      Frae morning sun till dine;   from, dinner
But seas between us braid hae roar'd,   broad have
20   Sin auld lang syne.
          For auld lang syne, &c.

And there's a hand, my trusty fiere!   companion
      And gie's a hand o' thine!   give me
And we'll tak a right gude-willie-waught, good-will drink
      For auld lang syne!
          For auld lang syne, &c.

When first printed after the poet's death, this was signed 'Z', a letter
previously employed by Burns to indicate a lyric he had altered
somewhat from the original text. Speculation has continued over
this world-famous lyric, prompted by Burns himself when he
informed Mrs Dunlop that he merely took it down from the singing
of an old man (Letter 290). Burns, however, often pretended that his
own songs were traditional works. If Kinsley is right to assert that
there is 'no good evidence on which to question Burns's story that he
got *Auld Lang Syne* from oral tradition' (Vol. III, p. 1291), then
Kinsley should probably have dropped it from the canon. There is,
though, some evidence that Burns was familiar with one or two
previous versions. Henley and Henderson quote a broadside ballad
which reads 'On old long syne, my jo, / That thou canst never once
reflect / On old long syne' (Vol. III, p. 408). A song of the same title,
but a significantly different text, is printed by Ramsay in his *Tea-
Table Miscellany*. They are considerably different from the final,
reworked Burns text, which, in his first draft ll. 3–4 (II) ran 'Let's
hae a waught o' Malaga, For old long syne'. Daiches comments:

That the song as we have it is essentially Burns's cannot be doubted, though he never claimed authorship, and there is undoubtedly something preserved from an earlier version. We have only to set it beside the earlier extant poems of the same title to see the vast difference between Burns's version . . .

Its greatness lies in the linking of the central emotion to the idea of time and change through precise contrasts between past and present (p. 319).

Cromek's (1808) claim that the poet told Johnson verses three and four were exclusively his own, is almost certainly true. Thus, it is comprehensively reworked from its original sources and contains what Burns called 'more of the fire of native genius in it, than in half a dozen of modern English Bacchanalians' (Letter 290). Ironically, as the poet's best known song, it was not published during his lifetime.

Epitaph for J. H., Writer in Ayr
First printed in Barke, 1955.

Here lies a Scots mile of a chiel,
If he's in heaven, Lord, fill him weel!

This was included in a letter sent to Mrs Dunlop, 7th December, 1788 (Letter 290). The poet only gives the initials 'J. H.' but most editors agree it is probably about John Hunter, Writer to the Signet, who later owned the estate of Doonholm, by Ayr.

Versicles on Sign-Posts
First printed by Alexander Smith, 1868.

(A)   He looked
Just as your sign-post Lions do,
With aspect fierce and quite as harmless too. —

(B)   Patient Stupidity
So heavy, passive to the tempest's shocks,
Dull on the Sign-post stands the stupid Ox. —

(C)
His face with smile eternal drest
Just like the Landlord to his guest,
High as they hang with creaking din
To index out the Country Inn. —

(D)
A head pure, sinless quite of brain and soul,
The very image of a Barber's Poll;
Just shews a human face, and wears a wig,
And looks when well friseur'd, amazing big. —

These fragments were found in the poet's *SCB* and appear to have
formed part of many such verses, given that pages 23–6 of the book
are ripped out. They were introduced as follows: 'The everlasting
surliness of a lion, Saracen's head, &c. or the unchanging blandness
of the Landlord welcoming a Traveller, on some Sign-Posts, would
be no bad similies of the constant affected fierceness of a Bully, or
the eternal simper of a Frenchman or a Fiddler.'

Pegasus at Wanlockhead,
or To Mr John Taylor
First printed by Cunningham, 1834.

With Pegasus upon a day
    Apollo, weary flying,
(Thro' frosty hills the journey lay)
    On foot the way was plying. —

Poor, slip-shod, giddy Pegasus
    Was but a sorry walker,
To Vulcan then Apollo goes
    To get a frosty calker. —

Obliging Vulcan fell to wark,   work
    Threw by his coat and bonnet;
And did Sol's business in a crack,
    Sol paid him with a sonnet. —

Ye Vulcan's sons of Wanlockhead,
    Pity my sad disaster,
My Pegasus is poorly shod,
    I'll pay you like my Master. —

Ramage's Inn, 3 o'clock   Robt. Burns.

This was written to thank Mr John Taylor of Wanlockhead who
used his influence with the local blacksmith to enable Burns and his

friend John Sloan to jump the blacksmith's queue and have their horses' shoes sharpened, to provide better grip on the icy roads. The travellers waited at Ramage's Inn. This event occurred in the winter of 1788–9. Burns had named his new horse, Pegasus.

A Sonnet upon Sonnets

First printed by Henley and Henderson, 1897.

Fourteen, a sonneteer thy praises sings;
What magic myst'ries in that number lie!
Your hen hath fourteen eggs beneath her wings
That fourteen chickens to the roost may fly.
Fourteen full pounds the jockey's stone must be;
His age fourteen — a horse's prime is past.
Fourteen long hours too oft the Bard must fast;
Fourteen bright bumpers — bliss he ne'er must see!
Before fourteen, a dozen yields the strife;
Before fourteen — e'en thirteen's strength is vain.
Fourteen good years — a woman gives us life;
Fourteen good men — we lose that life again.
What lucubrations can be more upon it?
Fourteen good measur'd verses make a sonnet.

This was sold in manuscript during May 1861, but did not appear until 1897 after the private owner from Newcastle allowed Henley and Henderson to copy the original. It is probably in imitation of Lopez de Vega's sonnet on sonnets, which was imitated by other writers, notably in Dodley's Collection (1758). (See Kinsley, Vol. III, p. 1294).

The Cares o' Love

First printed by Henley and Henderson, 1897.

HE
The cares o' Love are sweeter far
  Than onie other pleasure;   any
And if sae dear its sorrows are   so
  Enjoyment, what a treasure!

SHE

I fear to try, I dare na try	not
A passion sae ensnaring;	so
For light's her heart and blythe's her song	
That for nae man is caring.	no

This song fragment was sold in 1861 by Puttock and Simpson in London and purchased by the same Newcastle buyer who allowed the publication of the previous poem, *Sonnet upon Sonnets*.

Louis, What Reck I by Thee
First printed in *S.M.M*, December 1796.

Louis, what reck I by thee,
　　Or Geordie on his ocean:
Dyvor, beggar louns to me,
　　I reign in Jeanie's bosom.

Let her crown my love her law,
　　And in her breast enthrone me:
Kings and nations, swith awa!
　　Reif randies, I disown ye.

This is signed 'R' in the *Scots Musical Museum* in 1796, to indicate the lyrics are by Burns. It appears to be a fragment of a song he never fully completed, dedicated to Jean Armour when she became Mrs Burns. Henley and Henderson display an astounding historical ignorance by remarking on the reference to King Louis of France, that the song must have been written 'before the revolution of 1795' (Vol. III, p. 410). The revolution occurred in 1789 and in January 1793 the King and Queen of France were executed. It was probably written in early 1789 when Jean came to live at Ellisland farm, by Dumfries.

Sketch. New Year's Day:
To Mrs Dunlop.
First printed by Currie, 1800.

This day, Time winds th' exhausted chain,
To run the twelvemonth's length again: —
I see the old, bald-pated fellow,
With ardent eyes, complexion sallow,
5　Adjust the unimpair'd machine
To wheel the equal, dull routine.

The absent lover, minor heir,
In vain assail him with their prayer,
Deaf as my friend, he sees them press,
10   Nor makes the hour one moment less.
Will you (the Major 's with the hounds,
The happy tenants share his rounds;
Coila's fair Rachel's care to day,[1]
And blooming Keith's engaged with *Gray*;)
15   From housewife cares a minute borrow —
— That grandchild's cap will do to-morrow —
And join with me a moralizing,
This day 's propitious to be wise in.

First, what did yesternight deliver?
20   'Another year has gone for ever.'
And what is this day's strong suggestion?
'The passing moment 's all we rest on!'
Rest on — for what? what do we here?
Or why regard the passing year?
25   Will Time, amus'd with proverb'd lore,
Add to our date one minute more?
A few days may — a few years must —
Repose us in the silent dust:
Then is it wise to damp our bliss?
30   Yes — all such reasonings are amiss!
The voice of Nature loudly cries,
And many a message from the skies,
That something in us never dies:
That on this frail, uncertain state,
35   Hang matters of eternal weight:
That future life in worlds unknown
Must take its hue from this alone;
Whether as heavenly glory bright,
Or dark as Misery's woeful night —
40   Since then, my honor'd, first of friends,
On this poor being all depends;
Let us th' important *now* employ,
And live as those who never die.
Tho' you, with days and honours crown'd,
45   Witness that filial circle round,

1 This young lady was drawing a picture of Coila from *The Vision*. R.B. (See Letter 524).

(A sight life's sorrows to repulse,
A sight pale Envy to convulse)
Others now claim your chief regard;
Yourself, you wait your bright reward. —

This tender, intimate little poem was composed on 1st January, 1789 and dedicated to Mrs Dunlop (Frances Anne Wallace by her own name, eldest daughter of Sir Thomas Wallace of Craigie, who claimed descent from Sir William). Propitious for New Year's Day, it dwells on time, death and immortality as it affected 'my honor's first of friends' Mrs Dunlop and her family circle. The obvious intimacy of tone is a reflection of their relationship up until Burns's political sentiments became vividly apparent when Britain went to war with France and the poet continued to hold radical sentiments, specifically expressed to Mrs Dunlop in a letter of 12th January, 1795 when he dismissed the execution of the King (a 'perjured Blockhead') and Queen of France ('an unprincipled Prostitute') as an unimporant event on a historical scale, when the future of Europe was at stake (Letter 649). Mother-Confessor and avid fan of Burns from when she first read the Kilmarnock edition, Mrs Dunlop thought herself Burns's first literary critic and guardian, but the social division between them opened to a chasm with his political outburst, particularly given the fact her sons were engaged in war against the French.

Mrs Dunlop died in May 1815. Her portrait in the family home at Lochryan House, Cairnryan, shows her as a youthful beauty. L. 9 refers to her partial, but temporary deafness. The old Major (l. 11) is Andrew Dunlop. Rachel and Miss Keith (ll. 15–16) refer to Mrs Dunlop's daughters. The copy of Thomas Gray's poetry (l. 14) was a present from Burns. The Burns–Dunlop correspondence was printed in 1896 by William Wallace, her descendant.

Robin Shure in Hairst

Tune: Rob Shear'd in Hairst
First printed in S.M.M., 1803.

I gaed up to Dunse,	went
To warp a wab o' plaiden;	weave, web, plaid
At his daddie's yett,	gate
Wha met me but Robin.	who

Chorus

5 Robin shure in hairst,   sheared, harvest
 I shure wi' him;
Fient a heuk had I,   not a sickle
 Yet I stack by him.   stuck

Was na Robin bauld,   not, bold
10 Tho' I was a cottar,
Play'd me sic a trick   such
 An' me the Eller's dochter!   Elder's daughter
  Robin shure &c.

Robin promis'd me
 A' my winter vittle;   food
15 Fient haet he had but three   not a thing
 Goos feathers and a whittle.   Quills, knife
  Robin shure &c.

This is a traditional song reworked by Burns. Commonly, he employs a woman's viewpoint. Ironically, however, it is the imagined voice of the lower-class woman (Letter 252) impregnated and betrayed by his then lawyer friend, Robert Ainslie. Even more ironically, Burns was simultaneously using Ainslie as a go-between to the similarly pregnant May Cameron: 'Please call at the Ja^s Hogg mentioned, and send for the wench and giver her ten or twelve shillings, but don't for Heaven's sake meddle with her as a *Piece*. – I insist on this, on your honor; and advise her out to some country friends. – You may not like the business, but I tax your friendship thus far. Call immediately, [for God (deleted)] or at least as soon as it is dark, for God's sake, lest the poor soul be starving.' (Letter 246) He sent the song to Robert Ainslie, stating 'I have brushed up the following favourite old Song a little, with a view to your worship. – I have only altered a word here and there; but if you like . . . we shall think of a Stanza or two to add to it' (Letter 295). Ainslie was born at Berrywell, near Duns (l. 1). The mention of 'goos feathers', meaning quills, and a 'whittle', meaning a knife, refers to the implements used by a lawyer. Ainslie was a law student when Burns met him.

Caledonia

Tune: Caledonian Hunt's Delight.
First printed in Currie, 1800.

There was on a time, but old Time was then young,
    That brave Caledonia, the chief of her line,
From some of your northern deities sprung,
    (Who knows not that brave Caledonia's divine)
5 From Tweed to the Orcades was her domain,   Orkney
    To hunt, or to pasture, or do what she would;
Her heav'nly relations there fixèd her reign,
    And pledged her their godheads to warrant it good. —

A lambkin in peace, but a lion in war,
10   The pride of her kindred the Heroine grew;
Her grandsire, old Odin, triumphantly swore,
    'Whoe'er shall provoke thee, th' encounter shall rue!'
With tillage or pasture at times she would sport,
    To feed her fair flocks by her green-rustling corn;
15 But chiefly the woods were her fav'rite resort,
    Her darling amusement the hounds and the horn. —

Long quiet she reign'd, till thitherward steers
    A flight of bold eagles from Adria's strand;
Repeated, successive, for many long years,
20   They darken'd the air and they plunder'd the land.
Their pounces were murder, and horror their cry,
    They'd ravag'd and ruin'd a world beside;
She took to her hills and her arrows let fly,
    The daring invaders they fled or they di'd. —

25 The Cameleon Savage disturb'd her repose
    With tumult, disquiet, rebellion, and strife;
Provok'd beyond bearing, at last she arose,
    And robbed him at once of his hopes and his life.
The Anglian Lion, the terror of France,
30   Oft prowling ensanguin'd the Tweed's silver flood;
But taught by the bright Caledonian lance,
    He learned to fear in his own native wood. —

The fell Harpy-Raven took wing from the North,
    The scourge of the seas and the dread of the shore;
35 The wild Scandinavian boar issued forth,
    To wanton in carnage and wallow in gore:

O'er countries and kingdoms their fury prevail'd,
    No arts could appease them, no arms could repel;
But brave Caledonia in vain they assail'd,
40   As Largs well can witness, and Loncartie tell. —

Thus bold, independent, unconquer'd and free,
    Her bright course of glory for ever shall run;
For brave Caledonia immortal must be,
    I'll prove it from Euclid as clear as the sun:
45 Rectangle-triangle, the figure we'll chuse,
    The upright is Chance, and old Time is the Base;
But brave Caledonia's the Hypothenuse,
    Then, Ergo, she'll match them, and match them always. —

This was sent to Johnson for the S.M.M. but was first printed by
Currie in 1800. It is a patriotic song which, set in a semi-mythical
past, conceives of Caledonia as descended from Pictish Odin.
Caledonia retains its integrity by repulsing a series of invaders.
The 'eagles from Adria's strand' (l. 18) refer to the Romans. The
'Camelon Savage' (l. 25) alludes to the area of Falkirk, the 'ancient
Metropolis of the Picts' as remarked by Burns in his tour of the
Highlands (*Journal of a Tour in the Highlands*, l. 12). The battle of
685 AD (ll. 30–2) refers to the Picts' victory over the Normans of
Northumbria. The 'Harpy-Raven' (l. 33) refers to the Danish and
the 'Scandinavian Boar' (l. 35), the Norwegians. The Scots victories
over Haakon's fleet at Largs (1263) and the defeat of Norsemen at
Loncartie (990) are mentioned (l. 40). Hence, the 'spirit' of Cale-
donia, first manifest as the martial warfaring strength of the Picts, is
eventually inherited by the Scots. This historical vision is unchar-
acteristic of Burns's customary pessimistic view of the degeneration
of Scottish nationhood by virtue of its relationship with the 'Anglian
Lion' (ll. 29–32). See, in particular, *Ode on General Washington's
Birthday*.

At Whigham's Inn, Sanquhar

First printed in *The Burns Chronicle*, 1896.

Envy, if thy jaundiced eye,
Through this window chance to spy,
To thy sorrow thou shalt find,
All that's generous, all that's kind,
Friendship, virtue, every grace,
Dwelling in this happy place.

These lines were written by Burns on a window-pane at the Queensberry Arms, Sanquhar. They were also found in a copy of the Kilmarnock edition, gifted to Edward Whigham (1750–1823), the innkeeper, who later became Provost of the Burgh. Burns probably visited the inn while travelling between Mauchline and Ellisland.

To William Stewart

First printed in *Notes and Queries*, Vol. IV, 1881.

Brownhill, Monday even:
Dear Sir,

In honest Bacon's ingle-neuk,   fireside corner
    Here maun I sit and think;   must
5 Sick o' the warld and warld's fock,   world, folk
    An' sick, damn'd sick, o' drink!

I see, I see there is nae help,
    But still down I maun sink;   must
Till some day, *laigh enough*, I yelp,   low
10   'Wae worth that cursed drink!'

Yestreen, alas! I was sae fu',   so full/drunk
    I could but yisk and wink;   burp
And now, this day, sair, sair I rue,   sore
    The weary, weary drink. —

15 Satan, I fear thy sooty claws,
    I hate thy brunstane stink,   brimstone
And ay I curse the luckless cause,
    The wicked soup o' drink. —

In vain I would forget my woes
20   In idle rhyming clink,
For past redemption damn'd in Prose,
    I can do nought but drink. —

For you, my trusty, well-try'd friend,
    May Heaven still on you blink;
25 And may your life flow to the end,
    Sweet as a dry man's drink!

Robt. Burns.

This was composed at Brownhill Inn, several miles from Ellisland on the road towards Sanquhar. William Stewart was brother-in-law of Bacon, the landlord at Brownhill. Stewart was a close friend of Burns and is mentioned in the song *Your Welcome, Willie Stewart* (See Letter 253). For comments on drink by Burns, see Letters 467, 482, 506 and 529.

Lines Written in Lamington Kirk

First printed in Lockhart, 1828.

As cauld a wind as ever blew;   cold
A caulder kirk, and in't but few;
As cauld a minister's ever spak;
Ye'se a' be het or I come back.   be hot [in Hell]

It has become customary for editors to accept this without manuscript evidence. It was first printed by Lockhart in 1828 from lines supposedly inscribed by Burns on a window pane of the Kirk at Lamington, which sits off the old Dumfries to Edinburgh road. It probably is by Burns.

Inscribed to the Right Hon. C. J. Fox

First printed in part by Currie, 1800; completed in Aldine, 1839.

How Wisdom and Folly meet, mix, and unite;
How Virtue and Vice blend their black and their white;
How Genius, th' illustrious father of fiction,
Confounds rule and law, reconciles contradiction,
5 I sing; if these mortals, the Critics, should bustle,
I care not, not I, let the Critics go whistle!

But now for a Patron, whose name and whose glory
At once may illustrate and honor my story: —

Thou, first of our orators, first of our wits,
10 Yet whose parts and acquirements seem mere lucky hits;
With knowledge so vast, and with judgment so strong,
No man, with the half of 'em, e'er could go wrong;
With passions so potent, and fancies so bright,
No man with the half of 'em e'er could go right;
15 A sorry, poor, misbegot son of the Muses,
For using thy name offers fifty excuses. —

Good Lord, what is Man! for as simple he looks,
Do but try to develope his hooks and his crooks,
With his depths and his shallows, his good and his evil,
20   All in all, he 's a problem must puzzle the Devil. —

On his one ruling Passion Sir Pope hugely labours,
That, like th' old Hebrew walking switch, eats up its neighbours;
Human Nature 's his show-box — your friend, would you know him?
Pull the string *Ruling Passion*, the picture will show him. —
25   What pity, in rearing so beauteous a system,
One trifling particular, Truth, should have miss'd him!
For spite of his fine theoretic positions,
Mankind is a science defies definitions. —

Some sort all our qualities each to its tribe,
30   And think Human Nature they truly describe.
Have you found this, or t'other! there's more in the wind,
As by one drunken fellow his comrades you'll find. —
But such is the flaw, or the depth of the plan
In the make of that wonderful creature called MAN,
35   No two virtues whatever relation they claim,
Nor even two different shades of the same,
Though like as was ever twin brother to brother,
Possessing the one must imply you've the other. —

But truce with abstraction, and truce with a Muse,
40   Whose rhymes you'll perhaps, Sir, ne'er deign to peruse:
Will you leave your justings, your jars and your quarrels,
Contending with Billy for proud-nodding laurels?
(My much-honor'd Patron, believe your poor Poet,
Your courage much more than your prudence you show it;
45   In vain with Squire Billy for laurels you struggle,
He'll have them by fair trade, if not, he will smuggle;
Nor cabinets even of kings would conceal 'em,
He'd up the back-stairs and by God he would steal 'em!
Then feats like Squire Billy's you ne'er can atchieve 'em,
50   It is not, outdo him, the task is, outthieve him.) —

This poetic sketch, inscribed to Charles James Fox (1749–1806),
was clearly intended as a current affairs newspaper poem in the
Spring of 1789. There is, however, no evidence that it was printed
during the poet's lifetime. Peter Stuart of the London *Star* would

never have printed it, given that it is not wholly laudatoty of Fox (See *Ode on the Departed Regency Bill*). An early draft was sent to Mrs Dunlop (Letter 335). The iambic-anapaestic metre, with its alliterative lines, is a form used by Prior, Swift and Goldsmith for satirical verse.

A partly comic mini-dissertation on human nature, Burns creates a light hearted, mock discussion of the struggle going on in the head of Charles James Fox, to debate whether knowledge will be overwhelmed by passion, or virtue will be victorious over vice, in the world of power and ambition. But, like the wooden show-box amusement cabinet (l. 23), found at country fairs, human nature cannot simply be shown by pulling a string. Unlike Pope's complex, lengthy *Essay on Man*, there is no panacea, 'one ruling Passion' (l. 21), for Burns. Ending rather like a Punch and Judy show, the joking advice to Fox is not to contend with Billy [William Pitt] for 'laurels' but copy his dishonest career through thieving. The 'Hebrew walking switch' (l. 22) alludes to Aaron's rod, from *Exodus*, vii. Fox, like John Thelwall and other leading radicals of the period, admired Burns's poetry, but this would have left him perplexed.

Burns wrote to Mrs Dunlop on 4th May, 1789: 'I have another Poetic whim in my head, which I at present dedicate or rather inscribe to . . . Fox . . . but how long the fancy may hold, I can't say.' This should not be again misdiagnosed as another example of Burns's political inconsistency. The difficulty was not in the poet but his subject. Fox, psychologically and politically, was and, indeed, remains an enigma. Was he a political idealist or a careerist trimmer? There was, as seen in Burns's earlier poetic treatment of him, the saturnine reckless gambler and inveterate womaniser who, until stopped by the mistress he later married, spat on the carpet till his mid-thirties (and did so in the House of Commons). There was the bibliophile and scholar who expressed the wish to withdraw from the world and write a study of Dryden. Indeed the aristocrat and ploughman shared, given Dryden's politics, a somewhat unlikely passion for his poetry. Fox, of course, had a classical training of a kind simply not available to Burns. Fox knew and admired Burns's poetry, believing him Cowper's superior, but he had no time for Wordsworth's poetry or his attempt to elicit patronage from him. As L.G. Mitchell noted in *Charles James Fox*:

With rare exceptions, English literature was a poor, grey thing, when compared to that of Europe. . . . Pope had written some useful lines, and, among his contemporaries, Burns and Campbell were worthy of some consideration. Even so, the list is a short one. Significantly, Fox saw no value whatever in the Lake School of poetry, and seemed indeed to be actively hostile to it . . .

. . . Poetry, in the 1790s, by its subject-matter and structure, could not avoid also being politics. Fox's rejection of Wordsworth and his friends was more than an aesthetic judgement. Foxite Whiggery felt altogether more at home in the classical world. Reading two ancient and three modern languages, Fox was not short of reading-matter that offered more pleasure and less risk than the foggy productions of the Lake District (Oxford, 1992, pp. 187–8).

Fox's response to Wordsworth takes us to the heart of his political enigma. To what degree was he a democrat or an ambitious factional leader of élite Whig power? This problem is cogently discussed by J.R. Dinwiddy in 'Charles James Fox and the People' in his *Radicalism and Reform in Britain 1780–1850* (London, 1992) where he cites this incisive comment from *The Edinburgh Review* in 1838:

Of Mr. Fox it must be said that while his political principles were formed upon the true model of the Whig School, and led him when combined with his position as opposing the Government's warlike and oppressive policy, to defend the liberty of America, and the cause of peace, both in that and the French war, yet he constantly modified these principles, according to his own situation and circumstances as a party chief;—making the ambition of the man and the interest of his followers the governing rule of his conduct (p. 17).

Burns is characteristic of other radicals who earlier were in varying degrees sceptical of Fox but who, in the darkening 1790s, coalesced around him as the anti-war leader and the opponent of the increasing royal power which Fox saw as akin to the struggle of the 17th century against monarchical divine right. There was a particularly strong Scottish Foxite faction which included figures of the intelligence and substance of Professor John Millar and Dr Alexander Geddes. Burns never was such a Foxite hyper-enthusiast. As in the marvellous *On Glenriddell's Fox Breaking Its Chain*, there was always in him a healthy degree of scepticism about the disparity between aristocratic Whig ideals, intentions and actual conduct. What this poem does show is, however, a degree of personal identification of Burns with Fox due, as with Charles James Stewart, to a recognition of mutual human failings. The poem also records Burns's break, by his criticism of Pope's concept of 'the one ruling Passion' (see Maynard Mack's 1950 introduction to *An Essay on Man*), with the eighteenth century's desire to uniform, abstract clarity. Burns was always aware of the conflicting bedlam within himself and many of his ideas mirror the turning of the Romantic mind to the subconscious springs of creativity and desire.

Scott Hogg was correct to note the similarities in *More Treason*, from *The Morning Chronicle* of 18th March, 1795, with the Burns poem on Fox:

To simple John Bull says imperious Pitt,
    'Don't you hear my Alarm Bell? – Pray listen to it:
Thieves! thieves! Look about you: these Jacobin dogs
Will steal your Roast Beef; – and they'll feed you with Frogs!
Of their Treasons and Plots should your faith have the staggers
Burke, will show you in proof, his invisible Daggers!'
John, apt to be frighten'd at rumours like those,
Star'd round, to discover his pilfering Foes:
But while he was dreaming of Peachums and Lockits
He found the fly Premier had rifled his pockets.

To John M'murdo
With a Pound of Loundiefoot Snuff –
First printed in Cunningham, 1834.

O could I give thee India's wealth
    As I this trifle send!
Because thy Joy in both would be —
    To share them with thy Friend.

But Golden Sands, Alas, ne'er grace
    The Heliconian stream:
Then take, what Gold could never buy —
    An honest Bard's esteem. —

John McMurdo (1743–1803), worked as chamberlain to the Duke of Queensberry at Drumlanrig, north of Ellisland, where the castle still stands. The poet let McMurdo borrow his collection of bawdy verses.

To Peter Stuart

First printed in Lockhart, 1828.

Dear Peter, dear Peter,
    We poor sons of metre
Are often negleckit, ye ken;   neglected, know
    For instance your sheet, man,
    (Tho' glad I'm to see't, man),
I get it no ae day in ten.   one

Peter Stuart set up the *London Star*, an evening newspaper, in 1788 with business partners. Later, after a quarrel about the Regency affair, he set up his own, short-lived *Morning Star*, to which Burns, pseudonymously, sent two radical poems. Peter was the older brother of Daniel Stuart, also a newspaper proprietor. It is assumed the poetic note from Burns was cut away from a letter Burns sent to Stuart. Seven letters from Burns to Stuart exist, although it has been commented that 'much of the correspondence between Peter Stuart and Robert Burns is missing' (L. Werkmeister's *Robert Burns and the London Newspapers, Bulletin of the New York Public Library*, Vol. 65, Oct. 1961, p. 492). As Werkmeister states, Daniel claimed his younger brother offered Burns £50 per year to send a weekly poem to his newspaper. When the spurious *Star* collapsed, Stuart purchased *The Oracle*, a pro-Pitt paper.

Sonnet to Robert Graham of Fintry
On Being Appointed to My Excise Division
19th August, 1789

First printed by James Currie, 1800.

I CALL no Goddess to inspire my strains,
A fabled Muse may suit a Bard that feigns:
'Friend of my life!' my ardent spirit burns,
And all the tribute of my heart returns,
5   For boons accorded, goodness ever new,
The Gift still dearer, as the Giver YOU. —

Thou Orb of Day! Thou Other Paler Light!
And all ye many-sparkling Stars of Night!
If aught that Giver from my mind efface;
10   If I that Giver's bounty e'er disgrace;

Then roll, to me, along your wand'ring spheres
Only to number out a VILLAIN'S YEARS!

I lay my hand upon my swelling breast,
And grateful would — but cannot speak the rest. —

This histrionic sonnet is the poet's reply of thanks to Graham of
Fintry at being given an Excise post which relieved him of farming
the stony land of Ellisland, that 'ruinous bargain'.

Election Ballad for Westerha'
or The Laddies by the Banks o' Nith
Tune: Up and Waur Them a', Willie
First printed in *The Spirit of British Song*, Glasgow, 1826.

The Laddies by the banks o' Nith	
Wad trust his Grace wi' a', Jamie;	would
But he'll sair them as he sair'd the King	serve
Turn tail and rin awa, Jamie.	run away

Chorus

5 Up and waur them a', Jamie,	overcome
Up and waur them a';	
The Johnstones hae the guidin o't,	have
Ye turncoat Whigs awa!	away

The day he stude his country's friend,	stood
10 Or gied her faes a claw, Jamie,	gave, foes
Or frae puir man a blessin wan,	from poor, won
That day the Duke ne'er saw, Jamie.	
Up and waur them a', &c.	

But wha is he, his country's boast?	who
Like him there is na twa, Jamie;	not two
15 There's no a callant tents the kye,	youth, tends, cattle
But kens o' Westerha', Jamie.	knows
Up and waur them a', &c.	

To end the wark, here's Whistlebirk,[1]	work
Lang may his whistle blaw, Jamie;	long, blow
And Maxwell[2] true, o' sterling blue;	
20 And we'll be Johnstones a', Jamie.	
Up and waur them a', &c.	

1 Alexander Birtwhistle, provost of Kirkcudbright.
2 Robert Maxwell, Provost of Lochmaben.

This was written during the Dumfriesshire election in the winter of 1789 to support Sir James Johnstone of Westerhall. Burns sent a copy to Graham of Fintry on 9th December, 1789, remarking with eloquent sarcasm on the Duke of Queensberry, who presented Patrick Miller Junior as his puppet Whig candidate —

> The Great Man here, like all Renegadoes, is a flaming Zealot . . . despised I suppose by the Party who took him in to be a mustering faggot at the mysterious orgies of their midnight iniquities, and a useful drudge in the dirty work of their Country Elections, he would fain persuade this part of the world that he is turned Patriot . . . has the impudence to aim away at the unmistrusting manner of a Man of Conscience and Principle. – Nay, to such an intemperate height has his zeal carried him, that, in convulsive violence to every feeling in his bosom, he has made some desperate attempts at the hopeless business of getting himself a character for benevolence and in one or two late terrible strides in pursuit of Party-interest, has actually stumbled on something like meaning the welfare of his fellow-creatures. . . his sins . . . of Omission . . . to this outraged Land . . . known . . . by the mischiefs he does . . . a character one cannot speak with patience (Letter 373).

The song, though, does not match the prose quality, blaming the Duke of Queensberry as a traitor to the Jacobite cause (l. 3). Although Patrick Miller senior was the poet's Ellisland landlord, his son was judged by Burns as a money-loving puppet for the Duke of Queensberry. The song reveals, not so much that Burns supported a Tory candidate but that he deeply despised the Duke of Queensberry and his chicanery.

The Laddies by the Banks o' Nith
An Early Variant of the above Election Ballad

As I cam doon the Banks o' Nith   *came down*
    And by Glenriddel's ha', man,   *hall*
There I heard a piper play
    Turn-coat Whigs awa, man.

5 Drumlanrig's towers hae tint the powers   *lost*
    That kept the lands in awe, man:
The eagle's dead, and in his stead
    We've gotten a hoodie-craw, man.   *carrion-crow*

The turn-coat Duke his King forsook,
10 When his back was at the wa', man:
The rattan ran wi' a' his clan   rat
  For fear the house should fa', man. fall

The lads about the Banks o' Nith,
  They trust his Grace for a', man:
15 But he'll sair them as he sair't his King, serve
  Turn tail and rin awa, man.   run

This early variant of the above ballad is substantially different from the completed song. It is therefore included here separately. The text is taken from the Rosebery MS sent to Graham of Fintry and is included as a footnote by Kinsley (K270, p. 382) but not by Mackay, who prints only the main ballad. Glenriddell was himself a leading Whig polemicist and it is clear that he, as well as the poet, disliked the choice of Whig candidate (see above notes).

The Five Carlins – A Ballad

Tune: Chevy Chase
First printed in Duncan, at Glasgow, 1800.

Written during the contested Election between Sir James Johnston and Captain Miller for the Dumfries district of Boroughs. R.B.

There was five Carlins in the South, old women (boroughs)
  They fell upon a scheme,
To send a lad to Lon'on town
  To bring them tidings hame. — home

5 Nor only bring them tidings hame,
  But do their errands there;
And aiblins gowd and honor baith maybe, both
  Might be that laddie's share. —

There was Maggy by the banks o' Nith,[1]
10 A dame wi' pride eneugh; enough
And Marjory o' the mony Lochs,[2] many
  A Carlin auld and teugh: woman/hag, tough

And Blinkin Bess of Annandale[3]
    That dwelt near Solway-side;
15 And Brandy Jean that took her gill[4]
    In Galloway sae wide: so

And Black Jöan frae Crichton-peel[5]   from
    O' gipsey kith an' kin:
Five wighter Carlins were na found   stronger, not
20   The South Coontrie within. —   Country

To send a lad to London town,
    They met upon a day;
And mony a knight and mony a laird   many
    That errand fain wad gae. —   would go

25 O mony a knight and mony a laird
    That errand fain wad gae;
But nae ane could their fancy please,   not one
    O ne'er a ane but tway. —   one, two

The first ane was a belted Knight,   one
30   Bred of a Border band,
And he wad gae to London town,
    Might nae man him withstand. —   no

And he wad do their errands weel,   would, well
    And meikle he wad say;   much, would
35 And ilka ane at London Court   each one
    Wad bid to him, Gude-day!   would

The neist cam in a Sodger-boy   next, soldier
    And spak wi' modest grace,   spoke
And he wad gang to London Town,   would go
40   If sae their pleasure was. —   so

1 Dumfries. R.B.
2 Lochmaben. R.B.
3 Annan. R.B.
4 Kirkcudbright. R.B.
5 Sanquar (Crichton old castle, or Peel). R.B.

He wad na hecht them courtly gifts,   would not promise
    Nor meikle speech pretend;   great
But he wad hecht an honest heart   would promise
    Wad ne'er desert his friend. —   would

45 Now wham to chuse, and wham refuse,   whom
    At strife thae Carlins fell;   they
For some had Gentle Folk to please,
    And some wad please themsel. —   would

Then out spak mim-mou'd Meg o' Nith,   prim-mouthed
50   And she spak up wi' pride,   spoke
And she wad send the Sodger-lad,   would
    Whatever might betide. —

For the Auld Guidman o' London Court,
    She didna care a pin;   did not
55 But she wad send the Sodger-lad,   would
    To greet his eldest son. —

Then started Bess of Annandale,
    A deadly aith she's taen,   oath, taken
That she wad vote the Border-knight,   would
60   Tho' she should vote her lane. —   alone

'For far-aff fowls hae feathers fair,   -off, have
    'And fools o' change are fain;
'But I hae try'd this Border Knight,
    I'll try him yet again.'—

65 Says Black Jöan frae Crichton-peel,   from
    A Carlin stoor and grim;   harsh
'The Auld Gudeman, or the young Gudeman,
    For me may sink or swim.

'For Fools will prate o' Right, or Wrang,   talk
70   While knaves laugh them to scorn;
But the Sodger's friends hae blawn the best,   have talked
    So he shall bear the horn'. —

Then Brandy Jean spak owre her drink,   *spoke over*
   'Ye weel ken, kimmers a',   *well know, gossips*
75 'The Auld Gudeman o' London Court,
   His back's been at the wa':

'And mony a friend that kiss'd his caup,   *cup*
   Is now a fremit wight;   *hostile*
But it's ne'er be sae wi' Brandy Jean,   *so*
80   We'll send the Border-Knight.' —

Then slaw rase Marjory o' the lochs,   *slow rose*
   And wrinkled was her brow;
Her ancient weed was russet-grey,
   Her auld Scots heart was true. —   *old*

85 'There 's some Great Folk set light by me,   *unrespected*
   I set as light by them;
But I will send to London town
   Wham I lo'e best at hame.' —   *whom, love, home*

Sae how this weighty plea may end,   *so*
90   Nae mortal wight can tell: *no*
God grant the King and ilka man,   *every*
   May look weel to themsel. —   *well*

In the same vein as *Election Ballad For Westerha'* this was written, as the headnote records, to support Sir James Johnstone in the election for the five boroughs of Dumfries in 1789. Each of the boroughs is represented in the song as an old woman or carlin. The reference to the 'Auld Guidman' and 'Young Guidman' of the London court, means King George III and the Prince of Wales, respectively. Captain Miller, the Whig candidate who won the election, was only 20 years old. He went on to represent the Dumfries Boroughs until 1796. As mentioned in notes to the *Election Ballad for Westerha'*, Burns thought him the puppet of the Duke of Queensberry. It was the young Miller who later, in 1794, relayed to Burns the invitation from James Perry, proprietor and editor of *The Morning Chronicle*, for Burns to join the literary staff of his Opposition newspaper.

Epistle to Dr. Blacklock

First printed in Currie, 1800.

Wow, but your letter made me vauntie!	proud
And are ye hale, and weel, and cantie?	well, cheerful
I kend it still, your wee bit jauntie	knew, small journey
Wad bring ye to:	would
5 Lord send you ay as weel's I want ye,	always, well as
And then ye'll do. —	

The *Ill-thief* blaw the *Heron* south![1]	devil
And never drink be near his drouth!	thirst
He tauld mysel, by word o' mouth,	told
10 He'd tak my letter;	
I lippen'd to the chiel in trouth,	trusted, man
And bade nae better. —	no

But aiblins honest Master Heron	maybe
Had at the time some dainty *Fair One*,	
15 To ware his theologic care on,	
And holy study:	
And, tired o' *Sauls* to waste his lear on,	souls, learning
E'en tried the *Body*. —	

But what d'ye think, my trusty Fier,	friend
20 I'm turned a Gauger — Peace be here!	exciseman
Parnassian *Quines*, I fear, I fear,	females [Muses]
Ye'll now disdain me,	
And then my fifty pounds a year	
Will little gain me. —	

25 Ye glaiket, gleesome, dainty Damies,	silly, giddy
Wha by Castalia's wimplin streamies	who, meandering
Lowp, sing, and lave your pretty limbies,	leap, bathe
Ye ken, ye ken,	know
That Strang necessity supreme is	strong
30 'Mang sons o' Men. —	

1 Robert Heron was born in 1764 at New Galloway, the son of a weaver. He attended the University of Edinburgh after working as an assistant to Hugh Blair and was a prolific literary hack.

I hae a wife and twa wee laddies,   have, two small
They maun hae brose and brats o' duddies;   must have food & clothes
Ye ken yoursels my heart right proud is,   know
    I need na vaunt;   not boast
35 But I'll sned besoms and thraw saugh woodies,   cut, twist willow withies
    Before they want. —

Lord help me thro' this warld o' care!
I'm weary sick o't late and air!   early
Not but I hae a richer share   have
40   Than mony ithers;   many others
But why should ae man better fare,   one
    And a' Men brithers!   brothers

Come, *Firm Resolve* take thou the van,
Thou stalk o' carl-hemp in man!   strength
45 And let us mind, faint heart ne'er wan   remember, won
    A lady fair:
Wha does the utmost that he can,   who
    Will whyles do mair. —   often, more

But to conclude my silly rhyme,
50 (I'm scant o' verse and scant o' time,)   short
To make a happy fireside clime
    To weans and wife,   children
That's the true *Pathos* and *Sublime*
    Of Human life. —

55 My Compliments to Sister Beckie;
And eke the same to honest Lucky,
I wat she is a daintie Chuckie   bet, hen
    As e'er tread clay!
And gratefully my gude auld Cockie,   good old cockerel
60   I'm yours for ay. —   always

Robert Burns, Ellisland, 21st Oct., 1789.

This was the poet's reply to a letter epistle from the Rev. Dr
Thomas Blacklock (1721–91), dated from Edinburgh, 24th August,
1789. Blacklock was born at Annan, the son of English parents. He
was blinded as a child by smallpox. He graduated as a divinity
student in Edinburgh. In practising religion in Kirkcudbright,
parishioners found his blindness a problem. He moved back to

Edinburgh in 1765 and set up a boarding school. He eventually printed his own volume of poetry, contributing songs to the Scots Musical Museum. Blacklock, by this time virtually a cult figure, contacted Burns after reading his Kilmarnock edition and suggested a larger edition to be printed in Edinburgh, which, according to the poet 'overthrew all my schemes by rousing my poetic ambition' (Letter 125). If Blacklock helped persuade Burns not to emigrate, he played a part in Scottish literature. Blacklock, who knew Dr Johnson, John Home and David Hume, was a minor Literati figure.

The second stanza was indeed prophetic, describing as it does, Robert Heron as 'The *Ill-thief*' or devil. The letter given by Burns to Robert Heron to pass on to Dr Blacklock never reached Blacklock (see Introduction).

Written under the Portrait of Miss Burns

First printed in Duncan, Glasgow, 1801.

Cease, ye *prudes*, your envious railing,
Lovely Burns has charms — *confess;*
True it is, she had one failing,
Had ae woman ever less?

Miss Margaret Burns was an Edinburgh prostitute who came originally from Durham, the daughter of a merchant. With a friend she set up a brothel in Rose Street, near to Lord Stonefield's home. It is reputed that the daughters of the Lord took action against her and she was banished from Edinburgh. An appeal at the Court of Session on 12th December, 1789 went in her favour and she was allowed to stay in Edinburgh. She died in 1792. Burns appears to have known her given his remarks to Peter Hill on 2nd February, 1790, '. . . how is the fate of my poor Namesake, Mademoiselle Burns, decided?' (Letter 387). He goes on in the letter to condemn the hypocrisy of judges who, as he asserts, have, for over 6000 years, taken advantage of such female frailty: 'shall the unfortunate sacrifice to thy pleasures have no claim on thy humanity!' Edinburgh prostitutes were 'advertised' in an annual pocketbook printed exclusively for 'gentlemen', which gave descriptions of each woman, not least their dental state, and where they were to be picked up.

Green Sleeves
or My Fiddle and I
First printed in Barke, 1955.

Green sleeves and tartan ties
Mark my truelove where she lies;
I'll be at her or she rise,
 My fiddle and I thegither. —   together

Be it by the chrystal burn,
Be it by the milk-white thorn,
I shall rouse her in the morn,
 My fiddle and I thegither. —

This is the poet's modification of the Elizabethan *Greensleeves*, the song of the inconstant female lover. The melody was still popular in the eighteenth century. Fiddling is employed as an obvious sexual metaphor in this erotic lyric. Professor De Lancey Ferguson believes this song is traditional and was merely copied by Burns. Kinsley disagrees (Vol. III, pp. 1324–5). Although there are two manuscript copies, there is no definite proof either way.

To a Gentleman
Who Had Sent a Newspaper and Offered to Continue it Free of Expense
First printed in Currie, 1800.

KIND SIR, I've read your paper through,
And faith, to me 'twas really new!
How guessed ye, Sir, what maist I wanted? most
This mony a day I've grain'd and gaunted, groaned, gaped
5 To ken what French mischief was brewin; know
Or what the drumlie Dutch were doin; muddled
That vile doup-skelper, Emperor Joseph,[1] bum-smacker
If Venus yet had got his nose off; given him v.d.

1 Emperor Joseph II, died 20th February, 1790.

Or how the collieshangie works   dogfight
10 Atween the Russians and the Turks;
Or if the Swede, before he halt,[2]
Would play anither Charles the twalt:[3] another, twelfth
If Denmark, any body spak o't; spoke of it
Or Poland, wha had now the tack o't; who, lease of it
15 How cut-throat Prussian blades were hingin;
How libbet Italy was singin; eunuch
If Spaniard, Portuguese, or Swiss,
Were sayin or takin aught amiss:
Or how our merry lads at hame, home
20 In Britain's court kept up the game:
How royal George, the Lord leuk o'er him! look
Was managing St. Stephen's quorum; parliament
If sleekit Chatham Will was livin,[4] sly
Or glaikit Charlie got his nieve in;[5] silly, fist
25 How Daddie Burke the plea was cookin,[6]
If Warren Hastings' neck was yeukin;[7] itching
How cesses, stents, and fees were rax'd, rates, taxes, raised
Or if bare arses yet were tax'd;
The news o' princes, dukes, and earls,
30 Pimps, sharpers, bawds, and opera-girls;
If that daft buckie, Geordie Wales,[8]
Was threshin still at hizzies' tails, hussies'
Or if he was grown oughtlins douser, any more sedate
And no a perfect kintra cooser, country stallion
35 A' this and mair I never heard of; more
And but for you I might despair'd of.
So gratefu', back your news I send you,
And pray a' guid things may attend you!

Ellisland, Monday Morning

---

2 Gustavus III, 1746–92.
3 Charles XII, 1697–1718.
4 William Pitt, Earl of Chatham.
5 Charles James Fox, Whig leader.
6 Edmund Burke, political theorist and Tory M.P.
7 Warren Hastings, whose trial for Impeachment ran from 1788–95.
8 The Prince of Wales, whose reputation as a womaniser was public knowledge.

By virtue of Professor Werkmeister's scholarship, this poem gives us entry not only into some of Burns's particular difficulties with Peter Stuart, but with the often ugly publishing world where creative writers interacted with the press. In 1838 an article in *The Gentleman's Magazine* attacked Peter Stuart for 'riding in his carriage' while 'Coleridge, who had made his fortune, was starving in Mr Gillman's garret'. Werkmeister goes on, 'Daniel undertook to defend his brother against attempting the charge of a similar exploitation of Burns'. Daniel wrote:

> My elder brother Peter, who started . . . *The Star* [in 1788] had written to Burns, offering him terms for communications to the paper, a small salary, quite as large as his Excise-office emoluments. I forget particulars, but I remember my brother shewing Burns's letters, and boasting of the correpondence with so great a genius. Burns refused an engagement. And if, as I believe, the 'Poem Written to a Gentleman who Had Sent Him a Newspaper, And Offered to Continue it Free of Expense' was written in reply to my brother, it was a sneering unhandsome return, though Dr Currie says fifty-two guineas per annum for a communication once a week was an offer 'for which the pride of genius disdained to accept'. We hear much of purse-proud insolence . . . In 1795, my brother Peter purchased the copyright of the Oracle newspaper . . . Then it was my brother again offered Burns an engagement, as appears by the account of Burns's Life, which was again declined . . . (Quoted in Werkmeister's *Robert Burns and the London Newspapers*, pp. 483–4, *Bulletin of the New York Public Library*, Vol. 65, 1961).

Given the irretrievably missing correspondence from Burns to Peter Stuart, we will never know the full truth about Daniel Stuart's claims. Given, however, the dangerously mendacious manner in which Peter Stuart distorted *Ode on the Departed Regency-Bill* and the way he publicly revealed Burns as the author of all of the pseudonymous verses he sent to Stuart (See *Ode, Sacred To The Memory of Mrs. Oswald Of Auchencruive*), one cannot count on either of the brothers' veracity.

The appearance of the popular newspaper and the accelerated hourly communication of events horrified Wordsworth as much as it energised Burns. This poem's newspaper flow of highly salacious European and British political gossip regarding 'sexually' degenerate power politics runs for a full stopless, breathless thirty-eight lines of

wonderfully reductive Scottish vernacular speech. This type of con-
centrated narrative also features in *A New Song*, *A Wet Day at Walmer
Castle*. It is possible that 'Daddie Burke' (l. 25) is a misprint for 'Paddy
Burke'. The latter nickname is used by Burns in *The Dagger*.

Elegy on Willie Nicol's Mare

Tune: Chevy Chase
First printed in Cromek, 1808.

Peg Nicholson was a good bay mare,
    As ever trod on airn;   *iron*
But now she's floating down the Nith,
    And past the Mouth o' Cairn.

5   Peg Nicholson was a good bay mare,
    An' rode thro' thick an' thin;
But now she's floating down the Nith,
    And wanting even the skin.

Peg Nicholson was a good bay mare,
10   And ance she bore a priest;   *once*
But now she's floating down the Nith,
    For Solway fish a feast.

Peg Nicholson was a good bay mare,
    An' the priest he rode her sair;   *sore*
15 And much oppress'd and bruis'd she was —
    As priest-rid cattle are.

William Nicol's mare was taken in by Burns at Ellisland to be
restored to health. Having tried treating the animal and obtaining
professional advice from a farrier, the beast died. Despite the tone of
the poem, the animal-loving Burns was predictably hurt to lose
Nicol's horse. His letter to Nicol on 9th February, 1790 catches
precisely this mixture of irritation and distress:

> That damned mare of yours is dead. I would freely have given
> her price to have saved her: she has vexed me beyond descrip-
> tion. . . . I took every care of her in my power . . . I drew her in
> the plough, one of three, for a poor week. I refused fifty-five
> shilling for her. I fed her up and had her in fine order for
> Dumfries fair; when four or five days before the fair, she was

seized with an unaccountable disorder in the sinews . . . in short the whole vertebrae of the spine seemed to be diseased and unhinged . . . every thing was done for her that could be done . . . (Letter 390).

Burns described the *Elegy* to Nicol's mare as 'barbarous stanzas'. The name Peg Nicholson is one given to the mare by Burns after Margaret Nicholson who attacked and tried to stab George III in August 1786. (He had previously named his own horse Jenny Geddes after a woman who had thrown a stool at a leading Edinburgh cleric.) The 'Mouth o' Cairn' (l. 4) is a tributary of the river Nith.

My Wife's a Wanton Wee Thing

First printed in Currie, 1800.

Mv wife's a wanton, wee thing,
My wife's a wanton, wee thing,
My wife's a wanton, wee thing,
　　She winna be guided by me.　　　　　　*will not*

5　She play'd the loon or she was married,　　*fool, before*
　 She play'd the loon or she was married,
　 She play'd the loon or she was married,
　　　She'll do it again or she die.

　 She sell'd her coat and she drank it,
10　She sell'd her coat and she drank it,
　 She row'd hersell in a blanket,　　　　　　*rolled*
　　　She winna be guided for me.

　 She mind't na when I forbade her,　　　　　*not*
　 She mind't na when I forbade her,
15　I took a rung and I claw'd her,　　　　　　*cudgel, beat*
　　　And a braw gude bairn was she.　　　　　*fine good child*

This is a traditional song reworked by Burns. He sent it to George Thomson in 1792 but he did not include it in his printed collection until 1818; even then Thomson printed a version where he had the audacity to correct the lyric.

Scots Prologue,
For Mrs. Sutherland's Benefit-Night,
Spoken at the Theatre, Dumfries, March 3rd, 1790
First printed in Oliver, Edinburgh; and in Stewart, Glasgow, 1800.

WHAT needs this din about the town o' Lon'on,
How this new Play an' that new Sang is comin?   song
Why is outlandish stuff sae meikle courted?   so much
Does Nonsense mend like Brandy — when imported —
5 Is there nae Poet, burning keen for Fame,   no
Will bauldly try to gie us Plays at hame?   boldly, give
For Comedy abroad he need na toil: not
A Knave and Fool are plants of ev'ry soil:
Nor need he hunt as far as Rome or Greece,
10 To gather matter for a serious piece;
There's themes enow in Caledonian story   enough
Wad shew the Tragic Muse in a' her glory.
Is there no daring Bard will rise and tell
How glorious Wallace stood, how hapless fell?
15 Where are the Muses fled, that could produce
A *drama* worthy o' the name of Bruce?
How on *this* spot he first unsheath'd the sword
'Gainst mighty England and her guilty Lord,
And after mony a bloody, deathless doing,
20 Wrench'd his dear country from the jaws of Ruin!
O! for a Shakespeare or an Otway scene
To paint the lovely hapless Scottish Queen!
Vain ev'n th' omnipotence of Female charms,
'Gainst headlong, ruthless, mad Rebellion's arms.
25 She fell — but fell with spirit truly Roman,
To glut that direst foe, a *vengeful woman*;
A *woman* — tho' the phrase may seem uncivil,
As able — and as wicked — as the Devil!
One Douglas lives in Home's immortal page,
30 But Douglasses were heroes every age:
And tho' your fathers, prodigal of life,
A Douglas followed to the martial strife,
Perhaps, if bowls row right, and Right succeeds,
Ye yet may follow where a Douglas leads!

35   As ye hae generous done, if a' the land
      Would take the Muses' servants by the hand,
      Not only hear — but patronise — defend them,
      And where ye justly can commend — commend them;
      And aiblins, when they winna stand the test,   maybe, will not
40   Wink hard and say, 'The folks hae done their best'.   have
      Would a' the land do this, then I'll be caition,   surety
      Ye'll soon hae Poets o' the Scottish nation,   have
      Will gar Fame blaw until her trumpet crack,   make, blow
      And warsle Time, an' lay him on his back.   thump

45   For us and for our Stage, should onie spier,   any ask
      'Whase aught thae chiels maks a' this bustle here?'   whose, they fellows
      My best leg foremost, I'll set up my brow,
      We have the honor to belong to you!
      We're your ain bairns, e'en guide us as ye like,   own children
50   But like guid mithers, shore before ye strike;   mothers, warn
      And gratefu' still, I trust, ye'll ever find us:
      For gen'rous patronage, and meikle kindness,   much
      We've got frae a' professions, sorts an' ranks: from
      God help us — we're but poor — ye'se get but thanks!   you'll

This work appears first in 1800 in both Edinburgh and Glasgow, by two different printers. Burns presented a copy to the Dumfries Provost, David Staig, prior to the evening it was to be recited at the theatre, in a letter of 1st March, 1790, to ask his advice on its degree of political controversy:

> . . . there is a dark stroke of Politics in the belly of the Piece, and like a faithful loyal Subject, I lay it before you, as the chief Magistrate of the country . . . that if the said Poem be found to contain any Treason, or words of treasonable construction, or any Fama clamosa or Scandulum magnatum, against our Sovereign lord the King, or any of his liege Subjects, the said Prologue may not see the light (Letter 394).

In commenting on this letter to Staig, Kinsley remarks that 'the anxiety over a merely patriotic poem was obviously Sutherland's, as Burns's tone suggests' (Vol. 3, p. 1341). Burns's tone suggests no such thing. The hyperbolically ironic terminology of the letter is a joke pointed at the ambigious, contemporary definition of treason. Kinsley rightly detects that ll. 29–34 are the 'dark stroke of Politics' but he seems not to understand that the second Douglas, after

Home's theatrical one, is 'Citizen Douglas', that is to say Lord Daer, who was the potential leader of a Scottish republican movement (See *Extempore Verses on Dining with Lord Daer*). Thus, Burns, albeit with a degree of subtle disguise which has lasted over two hundred years, was having declaimed in 1790 from the Dumfries stage a wholly treasonable political proposal. Were Douglas in the audience during the performance this poem would have had an even more powerful political resonance, particularly to those attuned to its contemporary, subtle nuances.

Daer, one of the leading figures in the Scottish Friends of the People movement, from Jacobite stock, is also in a lineage of Burns's favourite Scottish heroes and heroines, Wallace, Bruce and Mary Queen of Scots. The lines on Bruce (ll. 150–20) are a kind of prelude to the darker Bruce poems of 1793 retrieved from *The Edinburgh Gazetteer*. Some editors modify ll. 16–18 which tellingly emphasise that it was in Dumfries ('this spot') that Bruce killed his main rival for the Scottish throne and thus began his crusade to free Scotland from English domination. (See the hitherto unpublished letter on this subject printed as an appendix to *The Ghost of Bruce* and *Scots Wha Hae*.)

Election Ballad
or Epistle to Robert Graham of Fintry on the Election for the Dumfries Burghs, 1790

A fragment of this first appears in *The Edinburgh Magazine*, May 1811.

FINTRY, my stay in worldly strife,
Friend o' my Muse, Friend o' my Life,
    Are ye as idle 's I am?
Come then! wi' uncouth kintra fleg   country fling/kick
5   O'er Pegasus I'll fling my leg,
    And ye shall see me try him. —

But where shall I gae rin or ride,   go, run
That I may splatter nane beside,   none
    I wad na be uncivil: would not
10 In mankind's various paths and ways
There's ay some doytin body strays,   stupid person
    And I ride like the devil. —

Thus I break aff wi' a' my birr,   off, force
An' down yon dark, deep alley spur,
15   Where Theologies dander: stroll
Alas! curst wi' eternal fogs,
And damn'd in everlasting bogs,
           As sure's the Creed I'll blunder!

I'll stain a band, or jaup a gown,   splash, clerical dress
20 Or rin my reckless, guilty crown   run
           Against the haly door!   holy
Sair do I rue my luckless fate,   sore
When, as the Muse an' Deil wad hae't   would have it
           I rade that road before. —   rode

25 Suppose I take a spurt and mix
Amang the wilds o' Politics
           Electors and elected —
Where dogs at Court (sad sons o' bitches!)
Septennially a madness touches,
30   Till all the land's infected. —

All hail, Drumlanrig's haughty Grace,[1]
Discarded remnant of a race
           Once godlike — great in story!
Thy fathers' virtues all contrasted,
35 The very name of Douglas blasted,
           Thine that inverted glory!

Hate, envy, oft the Douglas bore
But thou hast superadded more,
           And sunk them in contempt;
40 Follies and crimes have stain'd the name;
But, Queensberry, thine the virgin claim,
           From aught that's good exempt. —

I'll sing the zeal Drumlanrig bears,
Wha left the all-important cares
45   Of fiddlers, whores, and hunters;
And, bent on buying Borough-towns,
Came shaking hands wi' wabster-loons,   weavers
           And kissing barefit bunters. —   barefoot harlots

1 The Duke of Queensberry, William Douglas.

Combustion thro' our Boroughs rode,
50   Whistling his roaring pack abroad
          Of mad, unmuzzled lions;
As Queensberry BUFF AND BLUE unfurl'd,   whig colours
And Westerha' and Hopeton hurl'd[2]
          To every Whig defiance. —

55   But cautious Queensberry left the war,
Th' unmanner'd dust might soil his star,
          Besides, he hated *Bleeding*:
But left behind him heroes bright,
Heroes in Cesarean fight
60   Or Ciceronian pleading. —

O, for a throat like huge Monsmeg,   a cannon at Edinburgh
To muster o'er each ardent Whig,
          Beneath Drumlanrig's banner!
Heroes and heroines commix,
65   All in the field of Politics
          To win immortal honor. —

McMurdo[3] and his lovely Spouse
(Th' enamour'd laurels kiss her brows)
          Led on the Loves and Graces:
70   She won each gaping Burgess' heart,
While he, sub rosa, play'd his part   in secret
          Among their wives and lasses.

Craigdarroch[4] led a light-arm'd Core,
Tropes, metaphors and figures pour,
75   Like Hecla streaming thunder: an Icelandic volcano
Glenriddell[5], skill'd in rusty coins,   antiquarian skills
Blew up each Tory's dark designs,
          And bar'd the treason under. —

In either wing two champions fought;
80   Redoubted STAIG[6], who set at nought
          The wildest savage Tory:

2 Sir James Johnstone of Westerhall and Earl of Hopetoun.
3 The Duke's Factor and Cousin. R.B. [John McMurdo & Jane Blair].
4 Alexander Ferguson.
5 Robert Riddell Esq. of Glenriddell. R.B.
6 Provost of Dumfries and Director of the Bank of Scotland. R.B. [David Staig].

While WELSH,[7] who ne'er yet flinch'd his ground,
High-wav'd his magnum-bonum round
          With Cyclopean fury. —

85 Miller[8] brought up th' artillery ranks,
The many-pounders of the banks,
          Resistless desolation!
While Maxwelton,[9] that baron bold,
'Mid LAWSON's[10] port entrench'd his hold,
90   And threaten'd worse damnation. —

To these what Tory hosts oppos'd,
With these what Tory warriors clos'd,
          Surpasses my descriving:
Squadrons, extended long and large,
95 With furious speed rush to the charge,
          Like furious devils driving. —

What Verse can sing, what Prose narrate,
The butcher deeds of bloody Fate
          Amid this mighty tulzie;   conflict
100 Grim Horror girn'd, pale Terror roar'd,   scowled
As Murder at his thrapple shor'd;   throat, threatened
          And Hell mix'd in the brulzie. —   brawl

As Highland craigs by thunder cleft,   crags
When lightnings fire the stormy lift,   sky
105   Hurl down with crashing rattle;
As flames among a hundred woods,
As headlong foam a hundred floods,
          Such is the rage of Battle. —

The stubborn Tories dare to die,
110 As soon the rooted oaks would fly
          Before th' approaching fellers:
The Whigs come on like ocean's roar,
When all his wintry billows pour
          Against the Buchan bullers. —[11]

---

7 Sheriff substitute. R.B. [John Welsh, Sheriff of Dumfriesshire].
8 Patrick Miller Esq. Of Dalswinton, the Candidate's father. R.B. [The poet's landlord at Ellisland].
9 Sir Robert Lowrie. R.B. [of Maxwelton, the Dumfriesshire M.P.].
10 A famous wine merchant. R.B. [John Lawson].
11 A rocky inlet on the coast near Peterhead notorious for crashing waves.

115 Lo, from the shades of Death's deep night
 Departed Whigs enjoy the fight,
    And think on former daring:
 The muffled Murtherer of CHARLES[12]
 The Magna Charta flag unfurls,
120   All deadly gules it's bearing. —   blazoned red

 Nor wanting ghosts of Tory fame;
 Bold SCRIMGEOUR[13] follows gallant
    GRAHAM,[14]
    Auld Covenanters shiver!
 (Forgive, forgive! Much wrong'd Montrose!
125 Now, Death and Hell engulph thy foes,
    Thou liv'st on high for ever).

 Still o'er the field the combat burns,
 The Tories, Whigs, give way by turns,
    But Fate the word has spoken:
130 For Woman's wit, and strength of Man,
 Alas! can do but what they can;
    The Tory ranks are broken. —

 O, that my een were flowing burns!   eyes
 My voice, a lioness that mourns
135   Her darling cub's undoing!
 That I might greet, that I might cry,   weep
 While Tories fall, while Tories fly
    From furious Whigs pursuing. —

 What Whig but melts for good SIR JAMES![15]
140 Dear to his Country by the names,
    Friend, Patron, Benefactor!
 Not Pulteney's wealth can Pulteney[16] save;
 And Hopeton falls, the generous, brave;
    And STEWART[17] bold as Hector!

12 Charles I was executed by a man in a mask. R.B.
13 Viscount Dundee. R.B.
14 Montrose. R.B. [John Graham, Marquis of Montrose].
15 Sir James Johnstone.
16 William Johnstone married into the wealth of the Pulteney family from Bath.
17 William Stuart of Hill-side. R.B.

145 Thou, Pitt,[18] shalt rue this overthrow,
And Thurlow[19] growl this curse of woe,
      And Melville[20] melt in wailing:
Now Fox and Sheridan[21] rejoice!
And Burke[22] shall shout, O Prince, arise!
150   Thy power is all-prevailing!

For your poor friend, the Bard, afar
He hears and sees the distant war,
      A cool Spectator purely:
So, when the storm the forest rends,
155 The Robin in the hedge descends,
      And, patient, chirps securely. —

Now, for my friends' and brethren's sakes,
And for my native LAND o' CAKES,
      I pray with holy fire;
160 Lord, send a rough-shod troop o' Hell
O'er a', wad Scotland buy, or sell,   would
      And grind them in the mire!!!

As is typical of so much of Burns's dissident political writings, this poem did not surface till 1811 in the pages of *The Edinburgh Magazine*, although it was missing a few stanzas. Kinsley prints it without stanzas 2–5. In this version stanzas 2–4 are a retrospective of his career as satirist, which mixes anxiety with self-mockery, especially with the results of his assaults of 'Auld Licht' Calvinism. Nor does his prospective political satire seem less likely to create problems for him as he surveys a world:

  . . . Where dogs at Court (sad sons o' bitches!)
 Septennially a madness touches,
     Till all the land's infected.

Such sentiments would seem extremely ill judged in a poem addressed to his new Excise master. Burns, however, develops in tone,

18 William Pitt, Prime Minister.
19 Edward, Baron Thurlow, the Lord Chancellor.
20 Henry Dundas, Lord Melville and Secretary of State for Scotland.
21 Charles James Fox, Opposition leader and the radical Whig M.P. and playwright, Richard Brinsley Sheridan.
22 Edmund Burke, political theorist and subsequently turncoat Whig M.P., who joined the Tories.

genre and content, strategies for by-passing superior condemnation for his intrusion into matters far above his lowly civil position. He turns the election for the Dumfries Burghs (held every seven years) into a mixture of mock-epic and Hogarth derived cartoon. While the Tories are beaten, Burns's sympathies are, on the whole, with them. Thus he cannot be seen as attacking the Pitt government. He is also assuring Graham that his position, a robin nestled safe from the storm, is 'A cool Spectator purely' (ll. 115–20). This, in fact, is partly true.

The occasion of the poem for Burns was one of happy convenience. At an earlier stage in the campaign, Burns had written to Provost Maxwell of Lochmaben that, 'If at any time you expect a Field-day in your town, a Day when Dukes, Earls and Knights pay their court to Weavers, Taylors and Coblers, I should like to know of it two or three days beforehand – It is not that I care three skips of a cur-dog for Politics, but I should like to see such an exhibition of Human Nature' (Letter 378). His creative wish was, indeed, granted. The Whig candidate was Captain Miller who was his landlord's son and the poet was summoned in support of Miller against the Tory candidate, Sir James Johnstone of Westerhall. He described the scene to Mrs Dunlop thus:

> I have just got a summons to attend with my men-servants armed as well as we can, on Monday at one o'clock in the *morning* to escort Captn Miller from Dalswinton in to Dumfries to be a Candidate for our Boroughs which Chuse their Member that day. – The Duke of Queensberry & the Nithsdale Gentlemen who are almost all friends to the Duke's Candidate, the said Captn, are to raise all Nithsdale on the same errand. – The Duke of Buccleugh's, Earl of Hopetoun's people, in short, the Johnstons, Jardines, and all the clans of Annandale are to attend Sir James Johnston who is the other Candidate, on the same account. – This is no exaggeration. – On Thursday last, at chusing the Delegate for the boro' of Lochmaben, the Duke & Captn Miller's friends led a strong party, among others, upwards of two hundred Colliers from Sanquar Coal-works & Miners from Wanlock-head; but when they appeared over a hill-top within half a mile of Lochmaben, they found such a superior host of Annandale warriors drawn out to dispute the Day, that without striking a stroke, they turned their backs and fled with all the precipitation the horrors of blood & murther could inspire. – What will be the event, I know not. – I shall go to please my Landlord, & see the Combustion . . . (Letter 403)

Whether or not the rival groups were on the verge of more tradi-
tional forms of violence to settle party disputes is hard to know.
Certainly, Burns uses it both to denigrate Queensberry for his
cowardice and turn the squalid seeking for votes into a glorious
mock-epic battle. While theoretically (see introduction) Burns al-
ways held Right Whig reformist, pro-democratic beliefs this is not
to say that he saw the Whig (aristocratic) establishment as manifest-
ing these beliefs in practice. He disliked Captain Miller. Burns had
met Queensberry and been on that occasion well treated by him
(Letter 471) and sent him a copy of *The Whistle*. Queensberry had,
however, the reputation of a selfish, even degenerate dilettante and
is here so presented. Though Glenriddel, his close political intimate
is mentioned, the poem is not sympathetic to the Whig cause nor,
indeed, as in ll. 79–84, to the bloody foundling act of that cause. For
a man undismayed by forthcoming French executions, these lines
have a dark, ironic ring:

> The muffled Murtherer of CHARLES
> The Magna Charta flag unfurls,
>   All deadly gules it's bearing. –

This is followed by a deeply sympathetic celebration of these
archetypal Jacobite heroes Dundee and Montrose (ll. 115–20).
Returning to the contemporary world, he hyperbolically laments
a Tory loss which cannot even be saved by the fact that its
candidate's brother is married into the family of William Pulteney,
Earl of Bath (d.1764) who was reputed to be one of the richest men
in the Empire.

Burns then analyses the impact on Westminster. First of Pitt and
his fellow Tories Thurlow and Melville. Edward, Baron Thurlow
(1731–1806) had been compelled to retire as Lord Chancellor by the
North–Fox coalition but had been brought back by Pitt. His was a
terrifying presence, able to instil apprehension and fear into char-
acters as disparate as Dr Johnson and Horne Tooke. Melville, of
course, is Henry Dundas (1742–1811), whom Pitt was to appoint
Home Secretary in 1791 and who was to cast such a terrible shadow
over the last years of Burns's life. Fox's Whig friends were the two
extraordinary Irishmen Richard Brinsley Sheridan (1751–1816) and
Edmund Burke (1729–97), who held such rhetorical sway over the
house; Burns, of course, being deeply ironic in that these reformist
Whigs were up to their ears in royal intrigue to gain governmental
power by way of the Prince of Wales during the King's madness. As
so often with Burns, the sting comes in the tail of the poem. It is

really an enraged cry of a plague on both Tory and Whig party politics carried out against Scottish national interests.

Yestreen I Had a Pint o' Wine

Tune: Banks of Banna
First printed in Oliver, Glasgow, 1801.

	Yestreen I had a pint o' wine,	last night
	A place where body saw na;	nobody saw
	Yestreen lay on this breast o' mine	
	The gowden locks of Anna. —	golden
5	The hungry Jew in wilderness	
	Rejoicing o'er his manna	
	Was naething to my hiney bliss	nothing, honey
	Upon the lips of Anna. —	
	Ye monarchs take the East and West,	
10	Frae Indus to Savannah!	from
	Gie me within my straining grasp	give
	The melting form of Anna. —	
	There I'll despise Imperial charms,	
	An Empress or Sultana,	
15	While dying raptures in her arms	
	I give and take wi' Anna!!!	
	Awa, thou flaunting god o' day;	away
	Awa, thou pale Diana;	
	Ilk star gae hide thy twinkling ray!	each, go
20	When I'm to meet my Anna. —	
	Come, in thy raven plumage, Night	
	Sun, moon, and stars, withdrawn a';	all
	And bring an Angel-pen to write	
	My transports wi' my Anna. —	
25	[The Kirk an' State may join, and tell	
	To do sic things I maunna;	such, must not
	The Kirk an' State may gae to Hell,	go
	And I'll gae to my Anna.	go
	She is the sunshine o' my e'e,	eye
30	To live but her I canna:	without, cannot
	Had I on earth but wishes three,	
	The first should be my Anna.]	

The subject here is the poet's affair with Anne Park, a relation of
William Hyslop, Globe Tavern, Dumfries. It is believed to have
occurred during a period when Jean Burns visited relatives in
Ayrshire. The result was a daughter born to Anne at Leith, Edin-
burgh, on 31st March, 1791, and eventually reared by Mrs Burns in
Dumfries. Anne Park went on to marry in Edinburgh but vanishes
from the Burns story after this incident. The final dissident stanza,
written as a postscript, is not included by Kinsley.

A Fragment –
On Glenriddell's Fox Breaking his Chain
Ellisland, 1791
First printed by H.A. Bright in 1874.

THOU, Liberty, thou art my theme;
Not such as idle Poets dream,
Who trick thee up a Heathen goddess
That a fantastic cap and rod has:
5   Such stale conceits are poor and silly;
I paint thee out, a Highland filly,
A sturdy, stubborn, handsome dapple,
As sleek's a mouse, as round's an apple,
That, when thou pleasest can do wonders;
10   But when thy luckless rider blunders,
Or if thy fancy should demur there,
Wilt break thy neck ere thou go further. —

These things premis'd, I sing a fox,
Was caught among his native rocks,
15   And to a dirty kennel chained,
How he his liberty regained. —

Glenriddell, a Whig without a stain,
A Whig in principle and grain,
Couldst thou enslave a free-born creature,
20   A native denizen of Nature?
How couldst thou with a heart so good,
(A better ne'er was sluic'd with blood)
Nail a poor devil to a tree,
That ne'er did harm to thine or thee?

25 The staunchest Whig Glenriddell was,
 Quite frantic in his Country's cause;
 And oft was Reynard's prison passing,   the fox
 And with his brother Whigs canvassing
 The Rights of Men, the Powers of Women,
30 With all the dignity of Freemen. —

 Sir Reynard daily heard debates
 Of Princes', Kings', and Nations' fates;
 With many rueful, bloody stories
 Of tyrants, Jacobites, and Tories:
35 From liberty how angels fell,
 That now are galley-slaves in Hell;
 How Nimrod first the trade began[1]
 Of binding Slavery's chains on man;
 How fell Semiramis — God damn her! —[2]
40 Did first, with sacrilegious hammer,
 (All ills till then were trivial matters)
 For Man dethron'd forge hen-peck fetters;
 How Xerxes, that abandoned Tory,[3]
 Thought cutting throats was reaping glory,
45 Untill the stubborn Whigs of Sparta
 Taught him great Nature's Magna Charta;
 How mighty Rome her fiat hurl'd
 Resistless o'er a bowing world,
 And kinder than they did desire,
50 Polish'd mankind with sword and fire:
 With much too tedious to relate
 Of Ancient and of Modern date,
 But ending still how Billy Pitt,
 (Unlucky boy!) with wicked wit
55 Has gagg'd old Britain, drain'd her coffer,
 As butchers bind and bleed a heifer. —

 Thus wily Reynard by degrees
 In kennel listening at his ease,
 Suck'd in a mighty stock of knowledge,
60 As much as some folks at a college. —
 Knew Britain's rights and constitution,

---

1 As mentioned in Genesis, x, verse 8–10.
2 She was the Queen of Assyria who had her husband killed.
3 A Persian king.

Her aggrandisement, diminution,
How Fortune wrought us good from evil;
Let no man, then, despise the Devil,
65   As who should say, I ne'er can need him,
Since we to scoundrels owe our Freedom. —

A manuscript copy of this was sold in May 1862 in London at the
Puttock and Simpson auction of almost 200 pages of Burns's
holograph (*Autograph Poems of Robert Burns*, a sales catalogue
printed by E.C. Bigmore, p. 18. Mitchell Library collection). It
did not appear in public until the book by H. Bright, based on the
Gledriddell manuscripts, was printed in 1874.

It is an important poem because it reveals further the friendship
between Burns and one of the age's leading radical Whig polemi-
cists, Robert Riddell. Recent research has revealed that in *The
Glasgow Journal* during 1790 and 1791 a feud erupted between
Riddell and Edmund Burke. Riddell, employing the pen-name
Cato, locked horns with Burke on the constitutional issue. In one
essay, quoted in *The Glasgow Advertiser* by Burke, it is clear the
Tory minister was struggling for credibility against an opponent he
praised as a learned expert on the constitution. One essay of January
1791, in *The Glasgow Advertiser*, titled 'To The Citizens of Glas-
gow', blasts Pitt's government for practising 'tyranny, by the
grossest abuse of power and the most shocking perversion of law
. . . [of] the most intolerable kind, under the guise of a free
government'. Riddell's forceful remarks in defence of Hastings
who was persecuted by Burke, help to explain the description,
'The staunchest Whig Glenriddel was, /Quite frantic in his coun-
try's cause'. Henry Mackenzie and others who tarred Burns as a
drunkard in his Dumfries years remarked that this was due to the
company Burns kept, implying that Riddell was one of the degen-
erate influences over Burns (See Introduction). The denial of
Riddell as a major Whig polemicist in the Burns story is merely
another part of the suppression of the counter-radical culture of the
period.

Riddell's radical prose, particularly the essay posted to *The
Edinburgh Gazetteer* by Burns in December 1792, signed under
the pen-name Cato is an important document. Due to the closeness
of their friendship (see notes to *The Whistle*) Burns may have had a
hand in its composition. If not, he probably agreed wholeheartedly
with its sentiments. If he did have a hand in writing it – although he
distanced himself from the essay when pleading with Graham of
Fintry not to lose his Excise job – then having Riddell's signature on

the letter was an ideal escape if anti-radical spies wanted to trace the author. How compatible Riddell's is with Burns's own political values can be seen from the following:

At a period when the Kingdoms of Europe are asserting their just rights and privelages, and are trampling under their feet religious and civil tyranny; – at a period when Kings are no longer considered as the 'chara deum soboles' by a herd of dastardly slaves, but are held in estimation by wise and enlightened people, in proportion as they exert themselves for the general good of the state; and at a period when a Reform of many abuses that have crept into our excellent Constitution, is loudly called for, – I would caution my fellow citizens from running into the other extreme; and beg leave to advise them to draw a line between liberty and licentiousness. The first a blessing that cannot be held in too great estimation – the second a curse that cannot be held in too great detestation. . . .

. . . A very great abuse has crept into our Constitution, which has long called for the pruning knife of Reform to lop off – I mean the very numerous unequal representation of the people in the British Parliament. Their intolerable grievances is much more felt than formerly. When the National Debt was comprised within the compass of a nut-shell, our taxes were of course very small and very little felt; but now the case is altered; the people are taxed to the teeth – higher than any nation in Europe is – which taxes are in great measure paid by a class of men, who have comparitively speaking, no more to say in the election of their representatives in Parliament, than an Indian – a Chinese or a Laplander! . . .

. . . The next abuse to be corrected is the abolition of the office of Lord Advocate; and substituting in its place, Grand Juries in every County. – How can the sacred fountains of justice ever flow pure and unadulterated, when so overgrown a power is vested in one person; and that person must be a ministerial tool, removeable from this important office at the breath of the favourite (of the monarch's) of the day. . . . And last of all – an abolition of that monstrous abuse of the holy symbols of our sacred religion; – I mean an abolition of the corporation and test acts.

Now, if the Landed Interest in Scotland will firmly unite in bringing forward a bill to Parliament, to correct these abuses, it will equally rebound to their honour in asking as it will to the glory and honour of the British legislative bodies, in granting redress to a brave people, who have at all times shown their zeal to support their king and Constitution.

This foresighted democratic statement sets goals far in advance of the reforms achieved by the so-called Great Reform Act of 1832. It appears, in light of the recovered writings of Riddell, that he was a far more important radical figure in the Burns equation than has hitherto been thought.

It is also, of course, a fact that the poem brilliantly keeps a sceptical detachment of the *Foxy* poet from his slightly pompous, Right Whig instructor. Burns was never absolutely certain that such ideological Whigs ever quite lived up to their own perhaps somewhat self-indulged ideals. This is particularly true of his complex relationship to the Riddells. Crawford's (p. 242) commendation of the quality of the English poetry in this satire, especially ll. 1–12, is absolutely correct.

To Captain Riddell on Returning a Newspaper
Ellisland, Monday Even:
First printed by Cromek, 1808.

Your News and Review, Sir,
    I've read through and through, Sir,
With little admiring or blaming:
    The Papers are barren
5   Of home-news or foreign
No murders or rapes worth the naming. —

    Our friends, the Reviewers,
    Those Chippers and Hewers,
Are judges of Mortar and Stone, Sir;
10   But of *meet* or *unmeet*,
    In a Fabrick complete
I'll boldly pronounce they are none, Sir.

    My Goose-quill too rude is
    To tell all your goodness
15 Bestow'd on your servant, The Poet;
    Would to God I had one
    Like a beam of the Sun,
And then all the World, should know it!
                    Robt. Burns.

The date of this anecdotal verse to Robert Riddell is not known, but it is certainly from the Ellisland period. Kinsley places this (K527) chronologically in the wrong place, assuming it was composed during the 1795–6 period.

Reply to Robert Riddell
Ellisland
First printed by Scott Douglas, 1876.

DEAR Sir, at onie time or tide   any
I'd rather sit wi' you than ride,
    Tho' 'twere wi' royal Geordie:
And trowth your kindness soon and late
Aft gars me to mysel look blate —   oft makes, backward
    THE LORD IN HEAVEN REWARD YE!

R. Burns.

Burns wrote this in response to a poetic invitation from Robert Riddell to visit Glenriddell house. In the invitation, Riddell advises Burns not to go on his Excise ride, due to the threatening inclement weather, but visit him and 'We'll twa or three leaves fill up with scraps . . . And spend the day in glee.' This, like the above, is misplaced chronologically by Kinsley (K529) who puts it in the 1795–6 period.

On Captain Grose
Written on an Envelope,
Enclosing a Letter to Him
Tune: Sir John Malcolm
First printed in Currie 1800.

Ken ye ought o' Captain Grose?   know
    Igo and ago —
If he's amang his friends or foes?
    Iram, coram, dago. —

5   Is he South, or is he North?
       Igo and ago —
   Or drowned in the river Forth?
       Iram, coram, dago. —

   Is he slain by Hieland bodies?   Highland
10   Igo and ago —
   And eaten like a wether haggis?   ram's stomach bag
       Iram, coram, dago. —

   Is he to Abram's bosom gane?   gone
       Igo and ago —
15   Or haudin Sarah by the wame?   holding, belly
       Iram, coram, dago. —

   Where'er he be, the Lord be near him!
       Igo and ago —
   As for the Deil, he daur na steer him,   dare not lead
20   Iram, coram, dago. —

   But please transmit th' enclosed letter,
       Igo and ago —
   Which will oblige your humble debtor
       Iram, coram, dago. —

25   So may ye hae auld Stanes in store,   have old stones
       Igo and ago —
   The very Stanes that Adam bore;   stones
       Iram, coram, dago. —

   So may ye get in glad possession,
30   Igo and ago —
   The coins o' Satan's Coronation!
       Iram, coram, dago. —

This song on Francis Grose, first printed by Currie 1800, is based on an oyster dredging song Burns knew about from The Firth of Forth, which reads: 'Ken ye ought o' Sir John Malcolm? Igo and ago; / If he's a wise man, I mistak' him! Iram, coram, dago' (See Scott Douglas, Vol. III, p. 149). The letter containing the verses was sent to a colleague of Grose in Edinburgh in the Autumn of 1789, written on the inside wrapper to be passed to the antiquarian then in the city on business.

Elegy on the Late Miss Burnet of Monboddo
First printed by Currie, 1800.

Life ne'er exulted in so rich a prize,
As Burnet, lovely from her native skies;
Nor envious Death so triumph'd in a blow,
As that which laid th' accomplish'd Burnet low. —

5 Thy form and mind, sweet Maid, can I forget,
In richest ore the brightest jewel set!
In thee high Heaven above was truest shown,
For by His noblest work the Godhead best is known. —

In vain ye flaunt in summer's pride, ye groves;
10 Thou crystal streamlet with thy flowery shore,
Ye woodland choir that chaunt your idle loves,
Ye cease to charm, Eliza is no more. —

Ye heathy wastes immix'd with reedy fens,
Ye mossy streams with sedge and rushes stor'd,
15 Ye rugged cliffs o'erhanging dreary glens,
To you I fly, ye with my soul accord. —

Princes whose cumbrous pride was all their worth,
Shall venal lays their pompous exit hail;
And thou, sweet Excellence! forsake our earth,
20 And not a Muse with honest grief bewail!

We saw thee shine in youth and beauty's pride
And Virtue's light, that beams beyond the spheres;
But like the sun eclips'd at morning tide,
Thou left us darkling in a world of tears. —

25 The Parent's heart that nestled fond in thee,
That heart how sunk a prey to grief and care!
So deckt the woodbine sweet yon aged tree;
So, rudely ravish'd, left it bleak and bare. —

The subject of this elegy is Elizabeth Burnet, the daughter of James
Burnet, Lord Monboddo. She died of tuberculosis on 17th June,
1790, twenty-five years old. The poet visited her home when he was

in Edinburgh and the elegy is not to be surprised at given his description of her in *Address to Edinburgh* (See our notes for the *Address*). The poet laboured to complete this work on 'the amiable and accomplished Miss Burnet' (Letter 433) and remarked to Mrs Dunlop, 'Elegy is so exhausted a subject that any new idea on the business is not to be expected' (Letter 435). Currie's version of the Elegy was the incomplete one as sent to Alexander Cunningham in Letter 433.

I Look to the North
or Out Over the Forth
First printed in S.M.M., 1796.

Out over the Forth, I look to the North
    But what is the North, and its Highlands to me;
The South nor the East, gie ease to my breast,   give
    The far foreign land, or the wide rolling sea:
But I look to the West, when I gae to rest,   go
    That happy my dreams and my slumbers may be;
For far in the West lives he I lo'e best,   love
    The man that is dear to my babie and me. —

This work, with Jacobite connotations, is mentioned by Burns as his own composition in a letter to Alexander Cunningham on 11th March, 1791.

On Mr. James Gracie
First printed in McDowall's *Burns in Dumfriesshire*, 1870.

Gracie, thou art a man of worth,
    O be thou Dean for ever!
May he be damn'd to Hell henceforth,
    Who fauts thy weight or measure!   faults

James Gracie (1756–1814) was a banker and Dean of Guild in Dumfries.

Thou Gloomy December

Tune: Thru the Lang Muir
First printed in S.M.M. 1796.

Ance mair I hail thee, thou gloomy December!   once more
    Ance mair I hail thee, wi' sorrow and care;
Sad was the parting thou makes me remember;
    Parting wi' Nancy, Oh ne'er to meet mair!   more
5 Fond lovers' parting is sweet, painful pleasure,
    Hope beaming mild on the soft parting hour,
But the dire feeling, 'O farewell for ever!'
    Anguish unmingl'd and agony pure. —

Wild as the winter now tearing the forest,
10   Till the last leaf o' the summer is flown,
Such is the tempest has shaken my bosom,
    Till my last hope and last comfort is gone:
Still as I hail thee, thou gloomy December,
    Still shall I hail thee wi' sorrow and care;
15 For sad was the parting thou makes me remember:
    Parting wi' Nancy, Oh ne'er to meet mair. —

This was signed 'R' in the S.M.M. It is written for Clarinda, Mrs
Agnes McLehose. The two stanzas were sent to her on 27th
December, 1791 before she left for Jamaica in late January 1792,
hoping to repair her marriage with her estranged husband.

Saw Ye Bonie Lesley

Tune: The Collier's Dochter
First printed in Thomson's *Select Collection*, 1798.

O saw ye bonie Lesley,   pretty
    As she gaed o'er the Border?   went
She's gane, like Alexander,   gone
    To spread her conquests farther.

5 To see her is to love her,
    And love but her for ever;
For Nature made her what she is,
    And never made anither.   another

Thou art a queen, fair Lesley,
10   Thy subjects, we before thee:
Thou art divine, fair Lesley,
     The hearts o' men adore thee.

The Deil he could na skaith thee,   *not harm*
     Or aught that wad belang thee: *would belong*
15 He'd look into thy bonie face,
     And say, 'I canna wrang thee!'   *cannot wrong*

The Powers aboon will tent thee,   *above*
     Misfortune sha' na steer thee;   *shall not trouble*
Thou 'rt like themsel sae lovely,   *so*
20   That ill they 'll ne'er let near thee.

Return again, fair Lesley,
     Return to Caledonie!   *Caledonia*
That we may brag we hae a lass   *have*
     There's nane again sae bonie. —   *none, so*

This was composed after the poet spent most of a day in the company of Miss Lesley Baillie, her father Robert, a sister and friend, who called to visit the poet in Dumfries as they travelled to England. The poet rode a few miles with them beyond Dumfries and composed this on his return, basing it on an old work beginning with 'My Bonie Lizie Baillie' (Letter 505).

Grim Grizzle

First printed in Hogg and Motherwell, 1834.

GRIM Grizzle was a mighty Dame
     Weel kend on Cluden-side: *well known*
Grim Grizzle was a mighty Dame
     O' meikle fame and pride.   *great*

5 When gentles met in gentle bowers
     And nobles in the ha',   *hall*
Grim Grizzle was a mighty Dame,
     The loudest o' them a'.

Where lawless Riot rag'd the night
10   And Beauty durst na gang,   dared not go
Grim Grizzle was a mighty Dame
        Wham nae man e'er wad wrang.   no, would wrong

Nor had Grim Grizzle skill alane   alone
        What bower and ha' require;
15 But she had skill, and meikle skill,   much
        In barn and eke in byre.   also/even

Ae day Grim Grizzle walked forth,   one
        As she was wont to do,
Alang the banks o' Clouden fair,   along
20   Her cattle for to view.

The cattle shit o'er hill and dale
        As cattle will incline,
And sair it grieved Grim Grizzle's heart   sore
        Sae muckle muck to tine.   so much, lose

25 And she has ca'd on John o' Clods   called
        Of her herdsmen the chief,
And she has ca'd on John o' Clods   called
        And tell'd him a' her grief: —

'Now wae betide thee, John o' Clods!   woe
30   I gie thee meal and fee,   give, work
And yet sae meikle muck ye tine   so much, lose
        Might a' be gear to me!

'Ye claut my byre, ye sweep my byre,   scrape/clean
        The like was never seen;
35 The very chamber I lie in
        Was never half sae clean.   so

'Ye ca' my kye adown the loan   call, cattle
        And there they a' discharge:
My Tammy's hat, wig, head and a'
40   Was never half sae large!   so

'But mind my word's now, John o' Clods
        And tent me what I say: take heed
My kye shall shite ere they gae out,   cattle, go
        That shall they ilka day.   every

45 'And mind my word's now, John o' Clods,
  And tent now wha ye serve;   mind, who
 Or back ye 'se to the Colonel gang,   going
  Either to steal or starve.'

 Then John o' Clods he looked up
50   And syne he looked down;   then
 He looked east, he looked west,
  He looked roun' and roun'.

 His bonnet and his rowantree club
  Frae either hand did fa';   from, fall
55 Wi' lifted een and open mouth   eyes
  He naething said at a'.   nothing

 At length he found his trembling tongue,
  Within his mouth was fauld: —   folded
 'Ae silly ward frae me, madam,   one, word from
60   Gin I daur be sae bauld.   If, dare, so bold

 'Your kye will at nae bidding shite, cattle, no
  Let me do what I can;
 Your kye will at nae bidding shite
  Of onie earthly man.   any

65 'Tho' ye are great Lady Glaur-hole,
  For a' your power and art
 Tho' ye are great Lady Glaur-hole,
  They winnie let a fart.'   will not

 'Now wae betide thee John o' Clods! woe
70   An ill death may ye die!
 My kye shall at my bidding shite,
  And that ye soon shall see.'

 Then she's ta'en Hawkie by the tail,
  And wrung wi' might and main,
75 Till Hawkie rowted through the woods ran
  Wi' agonising pain.

 'Shite, shite, ye bitch,' Grim Grizzle roar'd,
  Till hill and valley rang;
 'And shite, ye bitch,' the echoes roar'd
80   Lincluden wa's amang.   walls among

This was only partly printed by Hogg and Motherwell in 1834. Henderson and Henley give a fuller version in their notes, with some polite censorship (Vol. III, pp. 459–61). The tale is based on the widow, Mrs Grizzel Young of Lincluden. Burns wrote an explanatory note on the manuscript, 'Passing lately through Dunblane, while I stopped to refresh my horse, the following ludicrous epitaph, which I pickt up from an old tombstone among the ruins of the ancient Abbey, struck me particularly, being myself a native of Dumfriesshire'.

Hughie Graham

Tune: Druimionn Dudh
First printed in S.M.M., 1792.

Our lords are to the mountains gane,	gone
A hunting o' the fallow deer;	
And they hae gripet Hughie Graham	grasped
For stealing o' the Bishop's mare,	

5 And they hae tied him hand and foot,   have
    And led him up thro' Stirling town;
The lads and lasses met him there,
    Cried, Hughie Graham thou art a loun. —   fool

O lowse my right hand free, he says,   loosen
10   And put my braid sword in the same;   broad
He's no in Stirling town this day
    Daur tell the tale to Hughie Graham. —   dare

Up then bespake the brave Whitefoord,
    As he sat by the bishop's knee;
15 Five hundred white stots I'll gie you,   young bullocks, give
    If ye'll let Hughie Graham gae free. —   go

O haud your tongue the bishop says,   hold
    And wi' your pleadings let me be;
For tho' ten Grahams were in his coat,
20   Hughie Graham this day shall die. —

Up then bespake the fair Whitfoord,
    As she sat by the bishop's knee;
Five hundred white pence I'll gie you,   give
    If ye'll gie Hughie Graham to me. —

25 O haud your tongue now lady fair,   hold
        And wi' your pleading let me be;
    Altho' ten Grahams were in his coat,
        It's for my honor he maun die. —   shall

    They've taen him to the gallows knowe,   taken, hill
30   He looked to the gallows tree,
    Yet never colour left his cheek,
        Nor ever did he blin' his e'e. —   blink, eye

    At length he looked round about,
        To see what he could spy;
35 And there he saw his auld father,   old
        And he was weeping bitterly. —

    A haud your tongue, my father dear.   hold
        And wi' your weeping let it be;
    Thy weeping's sairer on my heart,   sorer
40   Than a' that they can do to me. —

    And ye may gie my brother John   give
        My sword that's bent in the middle clear,
    And let him come at twelve o'clock
        And see me pay the bishop's mare. —

45 And ye may gie my brother James   give
        My sword that's bent in the middle brown;
    And bid him come at four o'clock
        And see his brother Hugh cut down. —

    Remember me to Maggy my wife,
50   The niest time ye gang o'er the moor;   next, go
    Tell her, she staw the bishop's mare,   stole
        Tell her, she was the bishop's whore. —

    And ye may tell my kith and kin,
        I never did disgrace their blood;
55 And when they meet the bishop's cloak,
        To mak it shorter by the hood. —

Burns comments in the *Interleaved Scots Musical Museum* that he took this work from oral tradition and made minor improvements to the lyric. His verse is set in Stirling; a few older versions take place in Carlisle. Kinsley states there are 'marks of literary revision' (Vol. III, p. 1384). The reference to the Whitefoord family of Ayrshire was inserted by Burns. This ballad has all the stark, intransigent violence we associate with such great Scottish poetry.

Lord Ronald My Son
First printed in S.M.M 1796.

O where hae ye been, Lord Ronald, my son?   have
 O where hae ye been, Lord Ronald, my son?
I hae been wi' my sweetheart, mother, make
  my bed soon;   have
 For I'm weary wi' the hunting,
  and fain wad lay down. —   desire to lie down

What got ye frae your sweetheart, Lord Ronald, from
 my son?
 What got ye frae your sweetheart, Lord Ronald, my son?
I hae got deadly poison, mother, make my bed soon;
 For life is a burden that soon I'll lay down. —

Burns abbreviated a longer, traditional ballad *Lord Ronald*, to make this brief lyric.

Bonie Laddie, Highland Laddie
Tune: The Old Highland Laddie
First printed in S.M.M. 1796.

 I hae been at Crookieden,   have
  My bonie laddie, Highland laddie,
 Viewing Willie and his men,
  My bonie laddie, Highland laddie,
5 There our faes that burnt and slew,
  My bonie laddie, Highland laddie,
 There at last they gat their due,   got
  My bonie laddie, Highland laddie.

 Satan sits in his black neuk,   corner
10 My bonie laddie, Highland laddie,
 Breaking sticks to roast the Duke,
  My bonie laddie, Highland laddie. —
 The bloody monster gae a yell,   gave
  My bonie laddie, Highland laddie,
15 And loud the laugh gaed round a' Hell!
  My bonie laddie, Highland laddie. —

This is a song reworked by Burns, sent for inclusion in the 1796 edition of S.M.M. Willie (l. 3) and the Duke (l. 11) are both, in this Highland revenge fantasy, Cumberland, the Butcher of Culloden.

Geordie – An Old Ballad

First printed in S.M.M 1796.

There was a battle in the north,
 And nobles there was many,
And they hae kill'd Sir Charlie Hay,
 And they laid the wyte on Geordie.   blame

5 O he has written a lang letter,   long
 He sent it to his lady;
Ye maun come up to Enbrugh town   must, Edinburgh
 To see what words o Geordie.

When first she look'd the letter on,
10 She was baith red and rosy;   both
But she had na read a word but twa,   not, two
 Till she wallow't like a lily.   went pale

Gar get to me my gude grey steed,   go, good
 My menzie a' gae wi' me;   armed company all go
15 For I shall neither eat nor drink,
 Till Enbrugh town shall see me.

And she has mountit her gude grey steed,   mounted, good
 Her menzie gaed wi her;
And she did neither eat nor drink
20 Till Enbrugh town did see her.

And first appear'd the fatal block,
 And syne the aix to head him;   axe, behead
And Geordie cumin down the stair,   coming
 And bands o' airn upon him.   iron

25 But tho he was chain'd in fetters strang,   strong
 O' airn and steel sae heavy,   iron, so
There was na ane in a' the court,   not one
 Sae braw a man as Geordie.   so fine

O she's down on her bended knee,
30   I wat she's pale and weary,   *bet*
O pardon, pardon noble king,
     And gie me back my Dearie!   *give*

I hae born seven sons to my Geordie dear,   *have*
     The seventh ne'er saw his daddie;
35 O pardon, pardon noble king,
     Pity a waefu lady!   *woeful*

Gar bid the headin-man make haste!   *go, axeman*
     Our king reply'd fu' lordly:
O noble king, tak a' that's mine,
40   But gie me back my Geordie.   *give*

The Gordons cam and the Gordons ran,
     And they were stark and steady;   *strong*
And ay the word amang them a'   *among*
     Was, Gordons keep you ready.

45 An aged lord at the king's right hand
     Says, noble king but hear me;
Gar her tell down five thousand pound   *go*
     And gie her back her Dearie.   *give*

Some gae her marks, some gae her crowns,   *give*
50   Some gae her dollars many;
And she's tell'd down five thousand pound
     And she's gotten again her Dearie.

She blinkit blythe in her Geordie's face,   *glanced*
     Says, dear I've bought thee, Geordie;
55 But there sud been bluidy bouks on the green,   *should have, bloody corpses*
     Or I had tint my laddie.   *before, lost*

He claspit her by the middle sma,   *clasped, small*
     And kisst her lips sae rosy;   *so*
The fairest flower o woman-kind
60   Is my sweet, bonie Lady.

Various versions of this ballad existed during Burns's period. It is
generally agreed that this was improved by Burns. Geordie has been
identified as either George Gordon, Fourth Earl of Huntly who was

apparently imprisoned in Edinburgh castle in 1554, or the Fifth Earl
of Huntly who was convicted of treason in 1563. Sir Charles Hay
(l. 3) has never been adequately identified.

To John Maxwell, Esq. of Terraughtie
on his Birth-Day

First printed with Cromek, 1808.

HEALTH to the Maxwells' vet'ran Chief!
Health, ay unsour'd by care or grief:
Inspir'd, I turn'd Fate's sibyl leaf,
    This natal morn,
5   I see thy life is stuff o' prief,   substance
    Scarce quite half-worn. —

This day thou metes threescore eleven,   completes
And I can tell that bounteous Heaven
(The Second-sight, ye ken, is given   know
10   To ilka Poet)   every
On thee a tack o' seven times seven   lease
    Will yet bestow it. —

If envious buckies view wi' sorrow   young people
Thy lengthen'd days on thy blest morrow,
15 May DESOLATION'S lang-teeth'd harrow,   long-
    Nine miles an hour,
Rake them like Sodom and Gomorrah,
    In brunstane stoure. —   brimstone dust

But for thy friends, and they are monie,   many
20 Baith honest men and lasses bonie,   both, bonny
May couthie Fortune, kind and cannie   loving, careful
    In social glee,
Wi' mornings blythe and e'enings funny
    Bless them and thee: —

25 Fareweel, auld birkie! Lord be near ye,   old fellow
And then the Deil, he daur na steer ye: devil, dare not, afflict
Your friends ay love, your foes ay fear ye!   always
    For me, Shame fa' me,   befall
If neist my heart I dinna wear ye,   next, do not
    While BURNS they ca' me!   call

John Maxwell was born 7th February 1720 and died 25th January, 1814, 94 yrs old. Although the estate at Terraughty had been in the Maxwell family, it was sold due to financial problems. Maxwell managed to buy back the family estate and by the late 1780s and early 1790s, when Burns met him, he was among the notable landowners of the Dumfries area. One of the manuscripts of this work is dated 10th February, 1792, which indicates composition just after the old man's 72nd birthday, not the 71st as generally believed.

The Shepherd's Wife

First printed in S.M.M 1796.

The Shepherd's wife cries o'er the knowe,   *hill's ridge*
Will ye come hame, will ye come hame;   *home*
The Shepherd's wife cries o'er the knowe,
Will ye come hame again een, jo?   *evening, darling*

5 What will I get to my supper,
Gin I come hame, gin I come hame?   *if, home*
What will I get to my supper,
Gin I come hame again een, jo?

Ye'se get a panfu' o' plumpin parridge,   *porridge*
10 And butter in them, and butter in them,
Ye'se get a panfu' o' plumpin parridge,
Gin ye'll come hame again een, jo. —

Ha, ha, how! that 's naething that dow,   *nothing, of value*
I winna come hame, I canna come hame;   *will not, cannot*
15 Ha, ha how! that 's naething that dow,   *can*
I winna come hame gin een, jo. —   *at evening*

Ha, ha, how! &c. ?
The Shepherd's wife &c.
What will I get &c.

A reekin fat hen, weel fryth'd i' the pan,   *cooking, well fried*
Gin ye'll come hame, gin ye'll come hame,
A reekin fat hen weel fryth'd i' the pan,
20 Gin ye'll come hame again een, jo. —

Ha, ha, how! &c.
The Shepherd's wife &c.
What will I get &c.

A weel made bed and a pair o' clean sheets,   well
Gin ye'll come hame, gin ye'll come hame,
A weel made bed and a pair o' clean sheets,
Gin ye'll come hame again een, jo. —

Ha, ha, how! &c.
The Shepherd's wife &c.
What will I get &c.

25   A luving wife in lily-white linens,
Gin ye'll come hame, gin ye'll come hame,
A luving wife in lily-white linens.
Gin ye'll come hame again een, jo. —

Ha, ha, how! that's something that dow,   of value
30   I will come hame, I will come hame;
Ha, ha, how! that's something that dow,
I will come hame again e'en, jo. —

This was taken and reworked by Burns from a song in Herd's
collection (1769). It again reveals the complete erotic compatibility
between Burns and the folk tradition that nourished him, as it did
the shepherd of this matrimonial dialogue.

Johnie Blunt

First printed in S.M.M. 1796.

There liv'd a man in yonder glen,
     And John Blunt was his name, O;
He maks gude maut, and he brews gude ale,   good malt
     And bears a wondrous frame, O. —

5   The wind blew in the hallan ae night,   porch, one
     Fu snell out o'er the moor, O;   well bitter
'Rise up, rise up, auld Luckie,' he says,   old
     'Rise up and bar the door, O'.

They made a paction tween the twa,
10   They made it firm and sure, O,
Whae'er sud speak the foremost word,   should
     Should rise and bar the door, O.

Three travellers that had tint their gate,   lost their way
    As thro' the hills they foor, O,   went/fared
15 They airted by the line o light,   followed
    Fu' straight to Johnie Blunt's door, O. —   right

They haurl'd auld Luckie out o' her bed,   hurled old
    And laid her on the floor, O;
But never a word auld Luckie wad say,   would
20 For barrin o the door, O. —

Ye've eaten my bread, ye hae drunken my ale,   have
    And ye'll mak my auld wife a whore, O —   make, old
Aha, Johnie Blunt! ye hae spoke the first word,   has
    Get up and bar the door, O. —

This work is based on a song in the Herd collection (1769). Johnie
Blunt was a proverbial name extensively given to the equivalent of a
village idiot during the eighteenth century. However, Johnson
alleges, in notes to his index of songs, that Burns based Blunt on
a real character who lived in Crawford Muirs.

Will Ye Go to the Indies, My Mary

Tune: Ewe Bughts Marion
First printed in Currie, 1800.

Will ye go to the Indies, my Mary,
    And leave auld Scotia's shore;   old
Will ye go to the Indies, my Mary,
    Across th' Atlantic roar.

5   O sweet grows the lime and the orange
    And the apple on the pine;
But a' the charms o' the Indies
    Can never equal thine.

I hae sworn by the Heavens to my Mary,   have
10   I hae sworn by the Heavens to be true,
And sae may the Heavens forget me,   so
    When I forget my vow!

O plight me your faith, my Mary,
    And plight me your lily-white hand;
15 O plight me your faith, my Mary,
    Before I leave Scotia's strand.

We hae plighted our troth, my Mary,   have
    In mutual affection to join;
And curst be the cause that shall part us;
20   The hour and the moment o' time. —

This is based on the old song *Will Ye Go to the Ewe-Bughts, Marion* (see the anti-war song of this title written in 1794 and attributed to Burns in our Anonymous & Pseudonymous Works section). It was sent to Thomson on 27th October, 1792 and based on an earlier lyric by Burns. This song forms part of the Highland Mary myth.

Answer to an Invitation

First printed by Stewart, 1802.

The King's most humble servant, I
    Can scarcely spare a minute;
But I'll be wi' ye by and bye,
    Or else the deil 's be in it.

This was the poet's answer on being invited to the drinking contest outlined in *The Whistle*, written on a page torn from an Excise book. Mackay (1993) questions the authenticity of this rhyming scribble, written extempore, saying it has been 'long suspect as Burns had not yet begun his Excise career' (p. 370). Such a conclusion replicates the error made by Scott Douglas, who obviously misdates the poet's start to his Excise career in September 1789. The contest at Friar's Carse took place on 16th October, 1789, over a month after the poet commenced his Excise duties. The note was preserved at Craigdarroch. There is no evidence to doubt authenticity.

Highland Mary

Tune: Katherine Ogie
First printed in Thomson's *Select Collection*, 1799.

Ye banks, and braes, and streams around   *hill slopes*
    The castle o' Montgomery,
Green be your woods, and fair your flowers,
    Your waters never drumlie!   *muddied*
5 There Summer first unfald her robes,   *unfolded*
    And there the langest tarry: *longest stay*
For there I took the last Fareweel   *farewell*
    O' my sweet Highland Mary.

How sweetly bloom'd the gay, green birk,   *birch*
10   How rich the hawthorn's blossom;
As underneath their fragrant shade,
    I clasp'd her to my bosom!
The golden Hours, on angel wings
    Flew o'er me and my Dearie;
15 For dear to me as light and life
    Was my sweet Highland Mary.

Wi' monie a vow, and lock'd embrace,   *many*
    Our parting was fu' tender;   *so*
And, pledging aft to meet again,   *often*
20   We tore oursels asunder:
But Oh, fell Death's untimely frost,
    That nipt my Flower sae early!
Now green's the sod, and cauld's the clay,   *cold is*
    That wraps my Highland Mary!

25 O pale, pale now, those rosy lips
    I aft hae kiss'd sae fondly!   *oft, so*
And clos'd for ay, the sparkling glance,   *always*
    That dwalt on me sae kindly!   *dwelled, so*
And mouldering now in silent dust,
30   That heart that lo'ed me dearly!
But still within my bosom's core
    Shall live my Highland Mary.

Burns wrote 'The foregoing Song pleases myself; I think it is my happiest manner' (Letter 518). Thomson, a meddler with Burns's lyrics, wanted to change the words, but Burns stood his ground and refused. It is the song at the heart of the Mary (or Margaret) Campbell Highland Mary myth.

My Wife's a Winsome Wee Thing

Tune: As title.
First printed in Currie, 1800.

She is a winsome wee thing,
She is a handsome wee thing,
She is a lo'esome wee thing,   lovesome
    This sweet wee wife o' mine.

5   I never saw a fairer,
I never lo'ed a dearer;   loved
And neist my heart I'll wear her,   next to
    For fear my jewel tine.   lost

She is a winsome wee thing,
10   She is a handsome wee thing,
She is a lo'esome wee thing,
    This dear wee wife o' mine.

The warld's wrack, we share o't,   world's suffering
The warstle and the care o't;   struggle
15   Wi' her I'll blythely bear it,
    And think my lot divine.

This was written for Thomson's *Select Collection* but the editor meddled with the lyrics and eventually printed a version in 1824 with some lines from Burns, but containing some twenty lines of his own. There are many occasions where Thomson picked up on self-effacing remarks by Burns on his own songs and decided to improve the bard's lyrics. Burns told Thomson, 'The following I made extempore . . . I might give you something more profound, yet it might not suit the light-horse gallop of the air so well as this random clink' (l. 514).

Here's a Health to Them That's Awa

First printed in fragment by Cromek (1808) then in full in
The Scots Magazine, January 1818.

	Here's a health to them that's awa,	away
	Here's a health to them that's awa;	
	And wha winna wish gude luck to our cause,	who will not
	May never gude luck be their fa'!	lot
5	It 's gude to be merry and wise,	
	It 's gude to be honest and true,	
	It 's gude to support Caledonia's cause	
	And bide by the Buff and the Blue.	Whig colours
	Here 's a health to them that 's awa,	away
10	Here 's a health to them that 's awa;	
	Here 's a health to Charlie, the chief o' the clan,[1]	
	Altho' that his band be sma'.	small
	May Liberty meet wi' success!	
	May Prudence protect her frae evil!	from
15	May Tyrants and Tyranny tine i' the mist,	get lost in
	And wander their way to the Devil!	
	Here 's a health to them that 's awa,	
	Here 's a health to them that 's awa;	
	Here 's a health to Tammie, the Norland laddie,[2]	
20	That lives at the lug o' the Law!	ear (is intimate with)
	Here 's freedom to him that wad read,	would
	Here 's freedom to him that would write!	
	There's nane ever fear'd that the Truth should be heard,	none
	But they whom the Truth wad indite.	
25	Here 's a health to them that 's awa,	
	An' here 's to them that 's awa!	
	Here 's to Maitland and Wycombe! Let wha does na like 'em[3]	who, not
	Be built in a hole in the wa'!	wall

1 Charles James Fox, leader of the Whig Opposition.
2 Thomas Erskine, brother of Henry (Dean of the Faculty of Advocates in Scotland), was the great radical lawyer of this era. He defended Thomas Paine and spearheaded the association for Freedom of the Press while writing a few radical pamphlets of his own.
3 James Maitland, Earl of Lauderdale. Burns knew him personally. John Petty, Earl Wycombe was another aristocratic Whig.

Here 's timmer that 's red at the heart,   timber
30   Here 's fruit that is sound at the core;
And may he that wad turn the buff and blue coat   would
        Be turn'd to the back o' the door![4]

Here 's a health to them that 's awa,
        Here 's a health to them that 's awa;
35   Here 's Chieftain M'Leod, a chieftain worth gowd,[5]   gold
        Tho' bred amang mountains o' snaw!   among, snow
Here 's friends on baith sides o' the Forth,   both
        And friends on baith sides o' the Tweed,   both
And wha wad betray old Albion's right,   who would England's
40   May they never eat of her bread!

Kinsley suggest that the Egerton MS of this song is apparently a short early version of the song published in *The Edinburgh Gazetteer* in December 1792. This may be the case, but there is no trace of the song in the extant issues in the Mitchell Library, Glasgow, which contains almost the full run. (A handful of issues exist in Edinburgh and London.) Part of a page is missing from an issue of late December 1792 and the poetry column on page 4 is ripped out of the issue, 15th January, 1793. If the song was in that radical paper, it would certainly have heightened Burns's near hysterical denial to Graham of Fintry (Letter 530) of sending anything treasonable to the Edinburgh paper. In the growing mood of repression, the song is probably Burns's most overt and unambiguous commitment to the Whig 'Buff and Blue' cause (l. 8). In part Burns is making a joke of Charles James Fox (l. 11) as clan chief of the intensely loyal Scottish Foxites but he is also using the energy of a Jacobite song to boost the prospects of their one-time enemies.

Tammie, the Norland Laddie (l. 19) is Thomas Erskine (1750–1823), the almost equally celebrated brother of Henry Erskine (Dean of the Faculty of Advocates). An intimate of Fox and Sheridan he defended Thomas Paine in 1792 (in Paine's absence) and later other London radicals tried for treason. Not only a political pamphleteer, he spearheaded the association for Freedom of the Press. James Maitland (1759–1839), eighth Earl of Lauderdale, was known personally by Burns. Like Thomas Muir he was a student

4 This is probably a slight on Edmund Burke, who changed parties from the Whigs to the Tories.
5 Colonel Norman McLeod, Whig M.Mp. At this time McLeod made a lot of noise about how Scotland should have the right to raise its own army. His criticism of Henry Dundas and Pitt was vitriolic.

and friend of Glasgow's great Enlightenment radical, Profesor John Millar. He had to defend himself and his friends in the House of Lords in 1792 from the 'gross calumnies' levelled by royal procla- mation against them and on one occasion provocatively turned up dressed as a Republican Sans Culotte. He was a sympathiser with the French revolution and went to France with Dr Moore at the same time Lord Daer was there. John Henry Petty Fitzmaurice (1765–1809), Earl of Wycombe was also involved in the protests in the House of Lords in 1792. Chieftain McLeod is Colonel Norman McLeod of McLeod (1754–1801). He was extremely outspoken in Parliament and many of his speeches and political letters were recorded in *The Edinburgh Gazetteer*, to the extent that some letters of late 1792 were even re-printed in January 1793 due to public demand. Here is an extract of a letter to Charles Grey, dated Edinburgh, 30th November, 1792 which captures the heightened political consciousness of Scotland at that juncture:

Dear Sir

I sit down to perform my promise of keeping you apprised of the situation of Scotland . . . The Proclamation [against so-called 'wicked and seditious writings'] acted like an Electric shock! it set people of all ranks a-reading and as everybody in this Country can read, the people are already astonishingly informed. Farmers, ploughmen, peasants, manufacturers, artificers, shopkeepers, sailors, merchants are all employed in studying and reasoning with great deliberation on the nature of Society and Government . . . The present Ministry is extremely odious from three causes: the Proclamation; the resistance to the Borough reform; and the firing on the Mob on the King's Birthday here, for burning Dundas in effigy. The pension of £100 a year given immediately to Pringle the Sheriff who ordered the troops to fire and creating the Provost a Baronet, have greatly aggravated the insult to the people. The conduct of Government seems to be a mixture of timidity and cunning; they are really afraid of insurrections on the one hand and on the other they court and provoke them. On the slightest occasion the troops are put in motion. On the 4th June, before there was the slightest appearance of riot, the dragoons paraded thro' all the principal streets of Edinbr. with drawn swords, the Regiment in the Castle were furnished with ball cartridges, a signal by cannons and flags from the Castle was concerted to make the men of war in Leith roads land their Marines, and another for a regiment of Dragoons to gallop into the city: and all this to rescue the Secretary's effigy which had been threatened in anonymous letters. A few days ago some boys assembled at Dundee to plant the tree of liberty: one of the Magistrates immediately announced an insurrection and it was industriously given out here that the inhabitants of that town had risen, had seized the Custom House amd Excise officers and refused to pay taxes . . . In consequence however of this [false] alarm the 42nd Reg[iment] is ordered southward from Fort George and are to be quartered in Perth and Dundee. It is also said that the 57th Reg[iment] is to be sent down from England and to be quartered in the town and suburbs, a thing unknown since 1745. . . . Dundas's person was certainly in some degree of danger for their hatred and contempt of him is beyond all bounds . . . The people are everywhere associating, reading, deliberating and corresponding . . .the result of this steady calmness of consultation may be great and aweful. I have attended two of their meetings, one in Glasgow, the other here; both composed of delegates from various associations. . . . I addressed both meetings, strongly inculcating the excellence of our Constitution if restored to its purity by more equal representation and short Parliaments . . . I was . . . the first man of rank or fortune who had appeared among them . . .

It is readily apparent why Burns listed McLeod for praise among this pantheon of contemporary radicals. McLeod was, as Burns wrote in *The Author's Earnest Cry and Prayer* standing forth to tell 'The honest, open, naked truth' and despite his *guinea stamp* of rank, he is 'a chieftain worth *gowd*' (gold). The 'friends' on both sides of the Forth and Tweed are radicals in the various Friends of the People associations.

The Lea-Rig

Tune: My ain kind dearie, O.
First printed in Currie, 1800.

When o'er the hill the eastern star
    Tells bughtin-time is near, my jo,   ewe-milking, dear
And owsen frae the furrow'd field   oxen from, ploughed
    Return sae dowf and weary, O: weak/listless
5 Down by the burn where scented birks   birches
    Wi' dew are hangin clear, my jo,

I'll meet thee on the lea-rig,   sheltered ridge
   My ain kind Dearie, O.   own

At midnight hour, in mirkest glen,   darkest
10   I'd rove, and ne'er be eerie O,   afraid
If thro' that glen I gaed to thee,   go
   My ain kind Dearie, O: own
Altho' the night were ne'er sae wild,   so
   And I were ne'er sae weary O,   so
15 I'll meet thee on the lea-rig,
   My ain kind Dearie, O.   own

The hunter lo'es the morning sun,   loves
   To rouse the mountain deer, my jo,   dear/darling
At noon the fisher takes the glen,
20   Adown the burn to steer, my jo;   to wander
Gie me the hour o' gloamin grey,   give, almost nightfall
   It maks my heart sae cheery O,   so
To meet thee on the lea-rig
   My ain kind Dearie O.   own

Although based on an old song, this lyric has been considerably improved by Burns. Robert Fergusson's earlier version, *The Lee Rig*, is also commendable but lacks the darker erotic edge of the Burns poem.

Duncan Gray –
original
First printed in Thomson's *Select Collection*, 1798.

Duncan Gray cam here to woo,   find romance
   Ha, ha, the wooing o't,
On blythe Yule-night when we were fu ',   Christmas, drunk
   Ha, ha, the wooing o't.
5 Maggie coost her head fu' high,   tossed, full
   Look'd asklent and unco skeigh,   askance, very disdainful
Gart poor Duncan stand abeigh,   made, at a distance
   Ha, ha, the wooing o't.

Duncan fleech'd, and Duncan pray'd;   flattered
   Ha, ha, the wooing o't,
10 Meg was deaf as Ailsa craig   a stone (Island off Girvan)
   Ha, ha, the wooing o't.

Duncan sigh'd baith out and in,   both
    Grat his een baith bleer't an' blin',   cried, eyes both, bleary
15 Spak o' lowpin o'er a linn;   spoke, jumping, waterfall
    Ha, ha, the wooing o't.

Time and Chance are but a tide,
    Ha, ha, the wooing o't.
Slighted love is sair to bide,   sore, tolerate
20   Ha, ha, the wooing o't.
Shall I, like a fool, quoth he,
    For a haughty hizzie die?   stern hussy
She may gae to — France for me! —   go
    Ha, ha, the wooing o't.

25 How it comes, let Doctors tell,
    Ha, ha, the wooing o't,
Meg grew sick as he grew hale,   healthy
    Ha, ha, the wooing o't.
Something in her bosom wrings,
30   — For relief a sigh she brings;
And O her een they spak sic things!   eyes, spoke such
    Ha, ha, the wooing o't!

Duncan was a lad o' grace,
    Ha, ha, the wooing o't.
35 Maggie's was a piteous case,
    Ha, ha, the wooing o't.
Duncan could na be her death,   not
    — Swelling pity smoor'd his Wrath;   smothered
Now they're crouse and canty baith,   merry, cheerful both
40   Ha, ha, the wooing o't.

An earlier version by Burns was sent to Johnson for the S.M.M. but
this version sent to Thomson was his final draft. The traditional
song can be found in Herd's collection (1769) but here Burns has
adapted it considerably. Another version exists in *The Merry Muses
of Caledonia*, the poet's collection of bawdy verse. It is one of the
more popular, recorded songs by modern folk performers.

The Creed of Poverty

First printed in Stewart, 1802.

In politics if thou would'st mix,
    And mean thy fortunes be;
Bear this in mind, be deaf and blind,
    Let great folks hear and see.

This untitled epigram was written in pencil, according to Robert Ainslie, on the reverse of an envelope received by Burns from Excise Commissioner Robert Graham in early January 1793. This context would explain the epigram as a spontaneous response to the poet's chastisement to keep his nose out of politics. Ainslie's letter, dated 3rd September, 1834, states that the poet was a covert member of the radical Friends of the People and:

> The Commissioners of Excise, irritated at his opinions, wrote him a formal official letter, dealing with the large seal of office, informing him that a 'petty officer' had 'no business with politics'. The proud heart of Burns did not like this humbling; after a few wrathful words in secret to one of his friends, he took a pencil and wrote these lines on the envelope (See footnote, Cunningham's edition, 1834, p. 725).

This is probably an accurate account of the verse's origin. Kinsley (K536) misdates composition and guesses, wrongly, that the lines were inscribed on a window in The Globe Tavern, Dumfries.

O Poortith Cauld

Tune: Cauld Kail in Aberdeen
First printed in Thomson's *Select Collection*, 1798.

O Poortith cauld and restless love,	poverty cold
Ye wrack my peace between ye;	
Yet poortith a' I could forgive	poverty all
An 'twere na for my Jeanie.	not

Chorus

5	O why should Fate sic pleasure have,	such
	Life's dearest bands untwining?	
	Or why sae sweet a flower as love	so
	Depend on Fortune's shining?	

The warld's wealth when I think on,   world's
10   Its pride and a' the lave o't;   all, rest of it
My curse on silly coward man,
     That he should be the slave o't!
       O why should Fate, &c.

Her een sae bonie blue betray,   eyes so
     How she repays my passion;
15 But prudence is her o'erword ay,   refrain, always
     She talks o' rank and fashion.
       O why should Fate, &c.

O wha can prudence think upon,   who
     And sic a lassie by him: such
O wha can prudence think upon,   who
20   And sae in love as I am?   so
       O why should Fate, &c.

How blest the wild-wood Indian's fate,
     He woos his artless Dearie:
The silly bogles, Wealth and State,   demons
     Did never make them eerie.   agitated/concerned
       O why should Fate, &c.

This fine lyric of rejection due to wealth's enticements and not genuine love, is supposed to have been written by Burns for Jean Lorimer (1775–1831). Gilbert Burns, who arguably overplays the role of expert on his brother's works, despite their relationship being increasingly distant during the last years, told Thomson, the heroine was a Jane Blackstock. It is probably based on Jean Lorimer's rejection of the Exciseman John Gillespie, a colleague of Burns, in favour of a more showy Andrew Whelpdale, who eventually dropped Jean. Jean Lorimer was the poet's *Chloris* of many later verses.

Lord Gregory

First printed in Thomson's *Select Collection*, 1798.

O mirk, mirk is this midnight hour,   dark
     And loud the tempest's roar:
A waefu' wanderer seeks thy tower,   woeful
     Lord Gregory ope thy door.   open

5   An exile frae her father's ha',   *from, hall/house*
      And a' for sake o' thee;
   At least some pity on me shaw,   *show*
      If love it may na be.   *not*

   Lord Gregory mind'st thou not the grove
10   By bonie Irwine side,
   Where first I own'd that virgin-love
      I lang, lang had denied.   *long*

   How aften didst thou pledge and vow,   *often*
      Thou wad for ay be mine!   *would, always*
15   And my fond heart, itsel' sae true,   *so*
      It ne'er mistrusted thine.

   Hard is thy heart, Lord Gregory,
      And flinty is thy breast:
   Thou dart of Heaven that flashest by,
20   O wilt thou bring me rest!

   Ye mustering thunders from above
      Your willing victim see!
   But spare and pardon my fause Love,   *false*
      His wrangs to Heaven and me!   *wrongs*

This was written for Thomson and sent to him on 26th January, 1793. It is based on the old song *The Bonie Lass of Lochryan*. Dr John Walcot (Peter Pindar) wrote his own version of *Lord Gregory* and his appears next to Burns's in 1798. Burns, often self-effacing about his songs, praised Walcot's lyrics as 'beautiful' and denigrated his own, stating their chief merit was their 'ballad simplicity' (Letter 535). John Syme records that Burns recited *Lord Gregory* at the Earl of Selkirk's home, near Kirkcudbright, during their Galloway tour in 1793.

Sonnet –
On Hearing a Thrush Sing
on a Morning Walk in January
First printed by Currie, 1800.

Sing on, sweet thrush, upon the leafless bough,
Sing on, sweet bird, I'll listen to thy strain:
See aged Winter 'mid his surly reign
At thy blythe carol clears his furrowed brow. —

5   Thus in bleak Poverty's dominion drear
     Sits meek Content, with light, unanxious heart,
     Welcomes the rapid moments, bids them part,
     Nor asks if they bring ought to hope, or fear. —

     I thank thee, Author of this opening day,
10   Thou whose bright sun now gilds yon orient skies.
     Riches denied, thy boon was purer joys,
     What Wealth could never give, nor take away! —

     But come, thou child of Poverty and Care,
     The mite high Heaven bestowed, that mite with thee I'll share. —

This sonnet was, according to folklore, prompted by John Syme in
the wake of the poet's somewhat humiliating dictate by the Excise to
keep his nose out of politics. Syme wished Burns to turn his muse
to lighter topics than politics. This poem is not apolitical; it does
suggest the consolations of a simple, spiritual life lived on a plane
beyond material wealth. This consolation, manifest in the song of
the thrush, may have been an influence on that Burns admirer, Walt
Whitman. Whitman also employs the consolatory song of the thrush
in his great poem on Lincoln's death, *When Lilacs Last in the Door-*
yard Bloom'd.

On General Dumourier's Desertion
from the French Republican Army
First printed in Cromek's *Select Scottish Songs*, 1810.

     YOU'RE welcome to Despots, Dumourier;
     You're welcome to Despots, Dumourier. —
         How does Dampiere do?
         Aye, and Bournonville too?
5   Why did they not come along with you, Dumourier?

     I will fight France with you, Dumourier, —
     I will fight France with you, Dumourier: —
         I will fight France with you,
         I will take my chance with you;
10   By my soul, I'll dance with you, Dumourier. —

     Then let us fight about, Dumourier;
     Then let us fight about, Dumourier;

Then let us fight about,
'Till Freedom's spark is out,
15 Then we'll be damn'd — no doubt — Dumourier.

This parody of the Scots song *Robin Adair* castigates the French General Charles François Dumouriez (1739–1823) who deserted the French Republican army in late March 1793. The incident was reported in *The Edinburgh Advertiser* (and other newspapers) of 5th–19th April, 1793 under the news title 'A Counter Revolution in France'. Stories emerged from France that Dumouriez wanted to re-establish a French monarchy as the only way to European peace, a policy the Convention rejected on 30th March, denouncing Dumouriez as a traitor. Count Ajax de Beurnonville (l. 4), the minister at war, Camus, and four deputies from the Convention were sent to arrest Dumouriez, but he captured them and sent the threat to the Convention that his army would march on Paris and set up a new monarchy. Dampiere's (l. 3) forces attacked Dumouriez's troops (now bolstered by the Austrians who had defeated Dumouriez who made an armistice with them) and repelled them. Dampiere was killed several weeks after this work was written. Pro-government newspapers in Britain turned Dumouriez into a hero and he was eventually welcomed to Britain in June 1793 and toured London in a hackney carriage, to large crowds, before attending the House of Commons as a guest to hear a debate on the war. Burns, as an avid newspaper reader would have known all this. Dumouriez eventually died in 1823 at Turville Park, Buckinghamshire, England.

Given that Britain went to war with France on 1st February, 1793, the royalist 'Despots' attacked in this song are principally Britain and Austria. The second stanza gives ironic assent to those loyalists who would line up with Dumouriez to fight France, culminating in the final stanza where Freedom itself is eventually destroyed. This pro-French revolutionary song is written with obvious anti-war sentiments further exposing the myth that Burns ceased to write controversial work from early January 1793. A similar ironic ending is found in the recently discovered *The Cob Web*, where it is concluded that there would be food enough for everyone to eat when eventually most of the British soldiers in France had been killed. Burns and his contemporaries all employed the spelling 'Dumourier' for Dumouriez's surname, even Dumouriez himself did so in at least one letter addressed to British newspapers.

Young Jessie

Tune: Bonie Dundee
First printed in Thomson's *Select Collection*, 1798.

TRUE-HEARTED was he, the sad swain o' the Yarrow,
    And fair are the maids on the banks of the Ayr;
But by the sweet side o' the Nith's winding river,
    Are lovers as faithful, and maidens as fair:
5 To equal young Jessie, seek Scotia all over;
    To equal young Jessie, you seek it in vain:
Grace, Beauty, and Elegance fetter her lover,
    And maidenly modesty fixes the chain. —

Fresh is the rose in the gay, dewy morning,
10   And sweet is the lily at evening close;
But in the fair presence o' lovely, young Jessie,
    Unseen is the lily, unheeded the rose.
Love sits in her smile, a wizard ensnaring;
    Enthron'd in her een he delivers his law: eyes
15 And still to her charms she alone is a stranger,
    Her modest demeanor's the jewel of a'.

This was written on Miss Jenny Staig, daughter of David Staig, Provost of Dumfries. It was sent to Thomson in early 1793 but remained unpublished until 1798. Kinsley (p. 542) misprints l. 13 as 'Love tits in her smile'.

Farewell, Thou Stream

Tune: Nancy's to the Green-Wood Gane
First printed in Thomson's edition of 1799.

FAREWELL, thou stream that winding flows
    Around Eliza's dwelling;
O mem'ry, spare the cruel throes
    Within my bosom swelling:
5 Condemn'd to drag a hopeless chain,
    And yet in secret languish;
To feel a fire in every vein,
    Nor dare disclose my anguish. —

Love's veriest wretch, unseen, unknown
10   I fain my griefs would cover;

The bursting sigh, th' unweeting groan,   tearless
    Betray the hapless lover:
I know thou doom'st me to despair,
    Nor wilt, nor canst relieve me;
15 But, Oh Eliza, hear one prayer,
    For pity's sake forgive me!

The music of thy voice I heard,
    Nor wist while it enslav'd me;
I saw thine eyes, yet nothing fear'd,
20   Till fears no more had sav'd me:
Th' unwary Sailor thus, aghast,
    The wheeling torrent viewing,
Mid circling horrors sinks at last
    In overwhelming ruin. —

This was written to the air employed by Allan Ramsay in his song *The Last Time I Came o'er the Moor*. Burns changed the name in the second line to Eliza from Maria after his quarrel with the Riddells.

Meg o' the Mill:

Tune: O Bonnie Lass, Will Ye Lie in a Barrack.
First printed in Currie, 1800.

O ken ye what Meg o' the mill has gotten,   know, got
An' ken ye what Meg o' the mill has gotten?
She's gotten a coof wi' a claute o' siller,   fool, lots, money
And broken the heart o' the barley Miller. —

5 The Miller was strappin, the Miller was ruddy,   strong, rugged
A heart like a lord, and a hue like a lady;
The Laird was a widdifu', bleerit knurl;   rascal, bleary dwarf
She's left the gude-fellow and taen the churl. —   good, taken

The Miller, he hecht her a heart leal and luving,   offered, loyal
10 The Laird did address her wi' matter more muving,
A fine pacing horse wi' a clear chain'd bridle,
A whip by her side, and a bony side-saddle. —

O wae on the siller, it is sae prevailing,   woe, money, so
And wae on the luve that is fixed on a mailen!   woe, farm
15 A tocher's nae word in a true lover's parle,   dowry no, pledge
But gie me my luve and a fig for the warl!   give, world

Here Burns has reworked an old song he sent to Johnson. For the old version, see our Appendix of rejected and doubtful works. This version was sent to Thomson in 1793, but was rejected by him.

Blythe Hae I Been on Yon Hill

Tune: Liggeram cosh, or My Bonnie Wee Lass
First printed by Thomson, 1799.

Blythe hae I been on yon hill,	have
As the lambs before me;	
Careless ilka thought and free,	every
As the breeze flew o'er me:	
5 Now nae langer sport and play,	no longer
Mirth or sang can please me;	song
Lesley is sae fair and coy,	so
Care and anguish seize me. —	
Heavy, heavy is the task,	
10 Hopeless love declaring:	
Trembling, I dow nocht but glow'r,	do nothing, stare
Sighing, dumb, despairing!	
If she winna ease the thraws,	will not, throes
In my bosom swelling;	
15 Underneath the grass-green sod	
Soon maun be my dwelling. —	must

Burns wrote this on Miss Lesley Baillie, the heroine of *Saw Ye Bonie Lesley*. The poet describes the song as one of 'the finest songs I ever made in my life . . . composed on a young lady, positively the most beautiful, lovely woman in the world' (Letter 586).

Logan Braes

Tune: Logan Water
First printed in Currie, 1800.

O Logan, sweetly didst thou glide	
The day I was my Willie's bride;	
And years sin syne hae o'er us run	since then
Like Logan to the simmer sun.	summer
5 But now thy flowery banks appear	
Like drumlie Winter, dark and drear,	gloomy
While my dear lad maun face his faes,	must, foes
Far, far frae me and Logan braes. —	from, hill slopes

Again the merry month o' May
10   Has made our hills and vallies gay;
The birds rejoice in leafy bowers,
    The bees hum round the breathing flowers:
Blythe Morning lifts his rosy eye,
    And Evening's tears are tears o' joy:
15 My soul delightless, a' surveys,   all
    While Willie's far frae Logan braes. —   from

Within yon milk white hawthorn bush,   that
    Amang her nestlings sits the thrush;   among
Her faithfu' Mate will share her toil,
20   Or wi' his song her cares beguile:
But I wi' my sweet nurslings here,
    Nae Mate to help, nae Mate to cheer,   no
Pass widowed nights and joyless days,
    While Willie's far frae Logan braes. —   from

25 O wae upon you, Men o' State,   woe
    That brethren rouse in deadly hate!
As ye make mony a fond heart mourn,   many
    Sae may it on your heads return!   so
How can your flinty hearts enjoy
30   The widow's tears, the orphan's cry:
But soon may Peace bring happy days,
    And Willie, hame to Logan braes!   home

Burns knew several old songs that mention Logan Braes, one by his
contemporary, John Mayne. Here the poet takes the original lyric
and turns it into an anti-war song, sung, characteristically, in the
feminine voice. He introduced it to Thomson, who did not like the
dissenting tone of the final lines, which Burns defends as the voice of
'plaintive indignation of some swelling, suffering heart, fired at the
tyrannic strides of some Public Destroyer; and overwhelmed with
private distresses, the consequence of a Country's Ruin' (Letter
566). Logan Water joins the river Nethan in Lanarkshire.

On Miss Davies

First printed by Stewart, 1801.

Ask why God made the GEM so small,
    And why so huge the granite?
Because God meant, mankind should set
    That higher value on it.

This was written about the diminutive Miss Deborah Duff Davies, the subject of *Bonnie Wee Thing*. Some editors mention a 'Mrs A' who is contrasted with Miss Davies. This unidentified woman is described in a manner only Burns could have written – 'a huge, bony, masculine, cowp-carl, horse-godmother, he-termagant of a six-feet figure, who might have been bride to Og, King of Bashan: a Goliath of Gath' (Letter 563).

Epigram on Maxwell of Cardoness
or On a Galloway Laird not Quite so Wise as Solomon
First printed in Morison, 1811.

Bless Jesus Christ, O Cardoness,
    With grateful lifted eyes;
Who taught that not the soul alone,
    But body too shall rise.

For had he said, the soul alone
    From death I will deliver:
Alas, alas, O Cardoness!
    Then hadst thou lain for ever!

David Maxwell of Cardoness, near Gatehouse of Fleet in Galloway, was made a Baronet in 1804 and died in 1825. Burns obviously met him at some point and described him as a 'stupid, money-loving dunderpate of a Galloway Laird' (Letter 563). Maxwell, a loyalist landowner, during 1792 and 1793 paid two of his workers to travel among the peasantry of Dumfriesshire to track down and report to him anyone active as a reformist radical (See RH 2/4/65/ff.54–57). Maxwell also wrote to the Duke of Buccleuch and mentioned Dumfries in horror due to the 'rapidity with which these mad ideas [reformist] had made sheer progress' (See RH 2/4/65/f.48).

On Being Shown a Beautiful Country Seat
Belonging to the Same
First printed in Scott Douglas, 1876.

We grant they're thine, those beauties all,
    So lovely in our eye:
Keep them, thou eunuch, Cardoness,
    For others to enjoy!

See above notes on David Maxwell of Cardoness. This was supposedly written during the poet's Galloway tour in the summer of 1793.

On Seeing the Beautiful Country Seat of Lord Galloway –

First printed in Cromek, 1808.

What dost thou in that mansion fair,
    Flit, Galloway! and find
Some narrow, dirty, dungeon cave,
    The picture of thy mind. —

John Stewart (1736–1805) was the 7th Earl of Galloway. When Burns toured with John Syme through Galloway during 1793, Burns is supposed to have composed this extempore on seeing Galloway house across the bay of Wigtown, after the two travellers left Gatehouse of Fleet on their way to Kirkcudbright. Many previous editions mention that Stewart was a pious and loyal public servant who served as a Tory M.P. for many years and never merited these angry epigrams by Burns. Local folklore, however, still tells of Stewart's habit of sending out a servant with a whip to clear the streets in Garlieston in order that he could ride through the small town without having to see any of the local peasantry. Burns never usually hit at anyone of high rank without justification. This grand house still stands.

On Lord Galloway 2

First printed in Cromek, 1808.

No Stewart art thou, Galloway,
    The Stewarts all were brave:
Besides, the Stewarts were but fools,
    Not one of them a knave. —

Burns, according to Syme, also wrote this on Lord Galloway during the Galloway tour. See above notes.

On Lord Galloway 3

First printed in Cromek, 1808.

Bright ran thy LINE, O Galloway,
    Thro' many a far-fam'd sire:
So ran the far-fam'd ROMAN WAY,
    And ended in a mire. —

See above notes.

To Lord Galloway
On The Author Being Threatened With Vengeance
First printed in Cromek, 1808.

Spare me thy vengeance, Galloway;
    In quiet let me live:
I ask no kindness at thy hand,
    For thou hast none to give.

It was supposedly reported to Burns that Stewart of Galloway had heard of his critical epigrams and would take action against him. Prompted by this story, Burns wrote the above.

Lines by Burns in The British Album.
Wisdom and Science –
First printed in *The Burns Chronicle*, 1940.

WISDOM and Science – honor'd Powers!
    Pardon the truth a sinner tells;
I owe my dearest, raptured hours
    To FOLLY with her cap and bells. —

Burns wrote four scraps of verse in John Syme's copy of a volume of radical poetry called *The British Album*, a collection mostly written by Robert Merry, who spearheaded the group known as the 'Della Cruscan' poets. Syme's recollection dates composition to around June 1793, although the second piece may have been penned earlier, given that it was also supposedly found in a lady's pocket book, hence the title. Syme's copy of *The British Album* is now in the Dumfries Museum. The first piece is written at the foot of Merry's Ode ending 'Then still for you my bosom swells, / O Folly, with your Cap and Bells!' The Mackay edition drops this epigram and two others, admitting only the second piece to the canon, stating in error, 'The second of these alone has been so far admitted to the canon' (Appendix B, *Burns: A-Z, The Complete Wordfinder*, p. 753). Kinsley rightly accepts all four. (See notes to no. 412A-D, Vol. III, p. 1432.)

Lines in a Lady's Pocket Book
First printed in Cunningham, 1834.

Grant me, indulgent Heaven, that I may live
To see the miscreants feel the pains they give:

Deal Freedom's sacred treasures free as air,
Till SLAVE and DESPOT be but *things which were*!

These lines were supposedly written extempore by Burns but feature in two separate places. They are not written *against* the French revolution as some nineteenth century editors presented them but are lines aimed directly at the 'terror' imposed by Pitt's government in Britain during the early to mid-1790s. They are very close in sentiment and expression to the poem *On the Year 1793*, printed in *The Edinburgh Gazetteer* on 8th January, 1793 and if inserted at the end of that poem, seamlessly complete it.

Perish their Names –

First printed in *The Burns Chronicle*, 1940.

PERISH their names, however great or brave,
Who in the DESPOT's cursed errands bleed!
But who for FREEDOM fill a hero's grave,
Fame with a Seraph-pen, record the glorious deed!

These lines are written after Mrs Cowley's *Stanzas to Della Crusca* in Syme's copy of *The British Album*. Kinsley accepts them (no. 412C) but Mackay rejects them. The lines are, in fact, very close in tone and language to the newly, discovered *Lines on Ambition* written in 1793.

Love's Records –

First printed in *The Burns Chronicle*, 1940.

LOVE's records, written on a heart like mine,
Not Time's last effort can efface a line.

There is no evidence in *The British Album* or elsewhere that these lines were copied by Burns from another poet, but appear to have been prompted by the poem *Henry Deceived* in the anthology.

O, Were My Love Yon Lilack Fair

First printed in Currie, 1800.
Tune: Hughie Green

O were my Love yon Lilack fair
    Wi' purple blossoms to the Spring,
And I, a bird to shelter there,
    When wearied on my little wing,

5   How I wad mourn, when it was torn   would
        By Autumn wild and Winter rude!
    But I wad sing on wanton wing,   would
        When youthfu' May its bloom renew'd.

    O, gin my love were yon red rose,   were/if
10   That grows upon the castle wa'!   wall
    And I mysel a drap o' dew,   drop
        Into her bonie breast to fa'!   fall
    Oh, there beyond expression blesst
        I'd feast on beauty a' the night;
15 Seal'd on her silk-saft faulds to rest,   -soft folds
        Till fley'd awa by Phoebus' light!   put to flight

The first stanza of this song is from Burns, the last is from the
traditional song in Herd's collection (1769).

Bonie Jean
or There was a Lass
First printed in Currie, 1800.

There was a lass, and she was fair,
    At kirk and market to be seen;
When a' our fairest maids were met,
    The fairest maid was bonie Jean.

5   And ay she wrought her country wark,   labour
        And ay she sang sae merrilie;   so
    The blythest bird upon the bush
        Had ne'er a lighter heart than she.

    But hawks will rob the tender joys
10   That bless the little lintwhite's nest; linnet's
    And frost will blight the fairest flowers,
        And love will break the soundest rest.

    Young Robie was the brawest lad,   finest
        The flower and pride of a' the glen;
15 And he had owsen, sheep, and kye,   oxen, cattle
        And wanton naigies nine or ten.   horses

    He gaed wi' Jeanie to the tryste,   went, cattle sale
        He danc'd wi' Jeanie on the down;
    And, lang ere witless Jeanie wist,   long, knew
20   Her heart was tint, her peace was stown. lost, stolen

As in the bosom of the stream
    The moon-beam dwells at dewy e'en;   <small>evening</small>
So, trembling, pure, was tender love
    Within the breast of bonie Jean.

25 And now she works her Mammie's wark,   <small>labour</small>
    And ay she sighs wi' care and pain;
Yet wist na what her ail might be,   <small>knew not, ailment</small>
    Or what wad make her weel again.   <small>would, well</small>

But did na Jeanie's heart lowp light,   <small>not, jump</small>
30   And did na joy blink in her e'e;   <small>not, eye</small>
As Robie tauld a tale o' love,   <small>told</small>
    Ae e'enin on the lily lea.   <small>one</small>

The sun was sinking in the west,
    The birds sang sweet in ilka grove: <small>each</small>
35 His cheek to hers he fondly laid,
    And whisper'd thus his tale of love.

O Jeanie fair, I loe thee dear;   <small>love</small>
    O canst thou think to fancy me!
Or wilt thou leave thy Mammie's cot,   <small>mother's cottage</small>
40   And learn to tent the farms wi' me.   <small>tend</small>

At barn or byre thou shalt na drudge,   <small>not</small>
    Or naething else to trouble thee;   <small>nothing</small>
But stray amang the heather-bells,   <small>among</small>
    And tent the waving corn wi' me.   <small>gather</small>

45 Now what could artless Jeanie do?
    She had nae will to say him na: <small>no, refuse</small>
At length she blush'd a sweet consent,
    And love was ay between them twa.   <small>two</small>

Bonie Jean is the most appropriate title for this work. The heroine is
Jean McMurdo, daughter of John McMurdo. Thomson eventually
printed the song in 1805.

On the Death of Echo, a Lap-Dog

First printed in Currie, 1800.

Ye warblers of the vocal grove,
    Your heavy loss deplore;
Now half your melody is lost,
    Sweet Echo is no more.

Each shrieking, screaming bird and beast,
 Exalt your tuneless voice;
Half your deformity is hid,
 Here Echo silent lies.

The authenticity of these verses relies somewhat on the reminis-
cence of John Syme that Burns composed lines at the Gordons of
Kenmure Castle, in late July 1793, on their pet dog, Echo, who had
recently died. Kinsley prints two versions, suggesting that the first
is probably lines remembered by Syme and gives the second, above,
as the authentic (See Vol. III, p. 1434). This, though, may be open
to question given that the holograph in the Rosenbach catalogue is
considered a hurried scrawl which might not be by Burns. The
version printed by Mackay is placed in our Appendix with other
works doubted or rejected.

On John Morine, Laird of Laggan

First printed in Cromek, 1808.

When Morine, deceas'd, to the Devil went down,
 'Twas nothing would serve him but Satan's own crown!
Thy fool's head, quoth Satan, that crown shall wear never;
 I grant thou'rt as wicked —but not quite so clever. —

This was found among the Glenriddell manuscript collection. John
Morine of Laggan, near Ellisland, purchased the poet's farm. He
and Burns supposedly quarrelled over the amount that should be
paid for a large heap of dung.

Phillis The Fair

Tune: Robin Adair
First printed in Currie, 1800.

While larks with little wing
 Fann'd the pure air,
Viewing the breathing Spring,
 Forth I did fare:
5 Gay, the sun's golden eye
Peep'd o'er the mountains high;
Such thy morn! did I cry,
 Phillis the fair.

In each bird's careless song,
10 Glad, I did share;
While yon wild flowers among
  Chance led me there:
Sweet to the opening day,
Rosebuds bent the dewy spray;
15 Such thy bloom, did I say,
  Phillis the fair.

Down in a shady walk,
  Doves cooing were;
I mark'd the cruel hawk,
20 Caught in a snare:
So kind may Fortune be,
Such make his destiny!
He who would injure thee,
  Phillis the fair.

This was written on Phillis McMurdo, younger sister of Jean and
daughter of John McMurdo of Drumlanrig. Burns picked up the
tune from a Highlander based in Dumfries with the Breadalbane
Fencibles.

Had I a Cave

Tune: Robin Adair.
First printed in Thomson, 1799.

Had I a cave on some wild, distant shore,
Where the winds howl to the waves' dashing roar:
  There would I weep my woes,
  There seek my lost repose,
5 Till grief my eyes should close,
    Ne'er to wake more.

Falsest of womankind, canst thou declare,
All thy fond, plighted vows — fleeting as air!
  To thy new lover hie,
10 Laugh o'er thy perjury —
  Then in thy bosom try,
    What peace is there!

Burns wrote this lyric in recollection of the unfortunate break-up of
Alexander Cunningham and his beloved Anna, as also expressed in

Anna, Thy Charms. Writing to Thomson in August 1793 Burns admitted he had not succeeded in matching the lyrics perfectly to the music of *Robin Adair* (Letter 576).

O, Whistle an' I'll Come to Ye, My Lad

First printed in Thomson, 1799.

But warily tent, when ye come to court me,		take care
And come nae unless the back-yett be a-jee;		not, -gate, ajar
Syne up the back-style and let naebody see,		then, -stile, nobody
And come as ye were na comin to me —		not
5 And come as ye were na comin to me. —		not

Chorus
O WHISTLE an' I'll come to ye, my lad,
O whistle an' I'll come to ye, my lad;
Tho' father, an' mother, an' a' should gae mad,   *go*
    Thy JEANIE will venture wi' ye, my lad.

10 At kirk, or at market whene'er ye meet me,		
Gang by me as tho' that ye car'd na a flie;		go, cared not, fly
But steal me a blink o' your bonie black e'e,		eye
Yet look as ye were na lookin to me —		not
Yet look as ye were na lookin to me. —		not
O whistle an' I'll, &c.		

15 Ay vow and protest that ye care na for me,		not
And whyles ye may lightly my beauty a wee;		at times, a little
But court na anither tho' jokin ye be,		not another
For fear that she wyle your fancy frae me —		lure, from
For fear that she wyle your fancy frae me. —		lure, from
20 O whistle an' I'll, &c.		

An earlier version of this song features in Johnson's S.M.M. Vol. II, 1788. The earlier version is omitted in favour of the later. The chorus is taken from a fragment in the Herd collection (1769).

Adown Winding Nith

Tune: The Muckin o Geordie's Byre
First printed in Thomson, 1799.

ADOWN winding Nith I did wander,
    To mark the sweet flowers as they spring;
Adown winding Nith I did wander,
    Of Phillis to muse and to sing. —

Chorus
5 Awa wi' your Belles and your Beauties;   *away*
    They never wi' her can compare:
Whaever hae met wi' my Phillis,   *whoever has*
    Has met wi' the Queen o' the Fair. —

The Daisy amus'd my fond fancy,
10   So artless, so simple, so wild:
Thou emblem, said I, o' my Phillis,
    For she is Simplicity's child. —[1]
        Awa wi' your Belles &c.

The Rose-bud's the blush o' my Charmer,
    Her sweet balmy lip when 'tis prest:
15 How fair and how pure is the lily,
    But fairer and purer her breast. —
        Awa wi' your Belles &c.

Yon knot of gay flowers in the arbour,
    They ne'er wi' my Phillis can vie:
Her breath is the breath o' the woodbine,
20   Its dew-drop o' diamond, her eye. —
        Awa wi' your Belles &c.

Her voice is the songs o' the morning,
    That wake thro' the green-spreading grove;
When Phebus peeps over the mountains
    On music, and pleasure, and love. —
        Awa wi' your Belles &c.

1 Here the *Poet* trusts that he shall also be found a *Prophet*; and this charming feature willl ever be a distinguishing trait in his Heroine. R.B.

25 But Beauty, how frail and how fleeting,
        The bloom of a fine summer's day;
    While Worth in the mind o' my Phillis
        Will flourish without a decay. —
            Awa wi' your Belles &c.

The heroine of this work is Phillis McMurdo, daughter of John, as
mentioned in notes to *Phillis the Fair*.

By Allan Stream

Tune: Allan Water.
First printed in Thomson, 1799.

    By Allan-side I chanc'd to rove,
        While Phebus sank beyond Benledi;[1]
    The winds were whispering thro' the grove,
        The yellow corn was waving ready:
5   I listen'd to a lover's sang,   song
        An' thought on youthfu' pleasures mony;   many
    And ay the wild-wood echoes rang —
        O dearly do I lo'e thee, Annie. —   love

    O happy be the woodbine bower,
10   Nae nightly bogle make it eerie;   no, demon, fearful
    Nor ever sorrow stain the hour,
        The place and time I met my Dearie!
    Her head upon my throbbing breast,
        She, sinking, said, 'I'm thine for ever!'
15 While mony a kiss the seal imprest,
        The sacred vow, we ne'er should sever. —

    The haunt o' Spring 's the primrose-brae.   hill slope
        The Simmer joys the flocks to follow;   summer
    How cheery thro' her shortening day,
20   Is Autumn in her weeds o' yellow:
    But can they melt the glowing heart,
        Or chain the soul in speechless pleasure,
    Or thro' each nerve the rapture dart,
        Like meeting HER, our bosom's treasure. —

1 A mountain, to the north of Stirling. R.B. [near Strathallan].

Burns wrote this work because he felt the lyrics to the tune *Allan Water* in the S.M.M were mediocre. Kinsley gives the title of the tune as the song title, *Allan Water*.

Come, Let Me Take Thee

Tune: Cauld Kail
First printed in Thomson, 1799.

COME, let me take thee to my breast,
    And pledge we ne'er shall sunder;
And I shall spurn, as vilest dust,
    The warld's wealth and grandeur: world's
5 And do I hear my Jeanie own,
    That equal transports move her?
I ask for dearest life alone
    That I may live to love her.

Thus in my arms, wi' a' thy charms,   with all
10   I clasp my countless treasure;
I'll seek nae mair o' Heav'n to share,   no more
    Than sic a moment's pleasure: such
And by thy een, sae bonie blue,   een, so
    I swear I'm thine for ever!
15 And on thy lips I seal my vow,
    And break it shall I never!

The final stanza of this song forms part of the earlier work *And I'll Kiss Thee Yet*. The heroine of the song, if one did exist, is not known. Mackay quotes Burns's remark 'the Muse that presides o'er the shores of Nith . . . whispered me the following' (p. 487). This is misleading, suggesting as it does, that it was not inspired by the poet's Ayrshire muse, 'Coila'. In the same letter, Burns makes it clear that he does mean Coila, 'or rather my old inspiring dearest nymph, Coila, whispered me the following' (Letter 580).

Dainty Davie

First printed in Thomson, 1799.

NOW rosy May comes in wi' flowers,   with
    To deck her gay, green-spreading bowers;
And now comes in the happy hours,
    To wander wi' my Davie. —

Chorus
5   Meet me on the warlock knowe,   _witching hill_
      Dainty Davie, Dainty Davie;
    There I'll spend the day wi' you,
      My ain dear Dainty Davie. —   _own_

    The crystal waters round us fa',   _fall_
10   The merry birds are lovers a',
    The scented breezes round us blaw,   _blow_
      A-wandering wi' my Davie. —
        Meet me on, &c.

    When purple morning starts the hare,
      To steal upon her early fare,
15   Then thro' the dews I will repair
      To meet my faithfu' Davie. —
        Meet me on, &c.

    When day, expiring in the west,
      The curtain draws o' Nature's rest,
    I flee to his arms I lo'e the best,   _love_
20   And that's my ain dear Davie. —   _own_
        Meet me on, &c.

Final Chorus
    Meet me on the warlock knowe,
Bonie Davie, Dainty Davie!
    There I'll spend the day wi' you,
      My ain dear Dainty Davie. —   _own_

This is another example by Burns of a fine lyric in the feminine voice. The arrangement of the song was the subject of an argument between Burns and that incessant meddler Thomson. Burns reacted with horror at the collector's suggested modification to the music:

> Dainty Davie, – I have heard sung, nineteen thousand, nine hundred & ninety nine times, & always with the chorus to the low part of the tune; & nothing, since a Highland wench in the Cowgate once bore me three bastards at a birth, has surprised me so much, as your opinion on this Subject' (Letter 586).

Thomson not only meddled with the lyrics of Burns but had the audacity to change Beethoven's music. This makes the poet's outburst of reiterated sexual hyperbole comprehensible. Kinsley comments on this episode that Thomson's 'dogmatism hardened against Burns's reitered self-assurance . . . unmoved by Burns's lurid (and fictitious) comparison' (Vol. III, p. 1438).

To Maria Riddell
Epigram – On My Lord Buchan's vociferating, in an argument, that 'Women must be always flattered grossly or not spoken to at all'.
First printed in Scott Douglas, 1876.

'Praise Woman still,' his Lordship roars,
    'Deserv'd, or not, no matter,'
But thee, Maria, while I praise,
    There Flattery cannot flatter. —

Maria, all my thought and dream,
    Inspires my vocal shell:
The more I praise my lovely Theme,
    The more the truth I tell. —

This was written on the reverse of a manuscript of *Scots Wha Hae*. Maria Banks Woodley Riddell (1772–1808), daughter of William Woodley, married Walter Riddell (brother of Robert) in 1790 and lived at Goldielea house. It was later renamed Woodley Park. She published some minor verse after Burns's death and through the poet became a friend of William Smellie who printed her travel book.

The 1862 manuscript sale by Puttock and Simpson in London contained a holograph copy of the above epigram titled 'On My Lord Buchan's vociferating, in an argument, that "Women must be always flattered grossly or not spoken to at all"' (*Autograph Poems of Robert Burns*, The Sales Catalogue of Puttock and Simpson, May 1862, London, p. 14, printed by E.C. Bigmore). We have changed the standard sub-title given by Scott Douglas (used by subsequent editors) to that given by Burns.

As Down the Burn Davie

First printed in Currie, 1800.

As down the burn they took their way,
    And thro' the flowery dale;
His cheek to hers he aft did lay,   oft
    And love was ay the tale. —   always

With, 'Mary, when shall we return,
    Sic pleasure to renew;'   such
Quoth Mary, 'Love, I like the burn,
    And ay shall follow you.'—

This is a modification of a traditional bawdy song *Down the Burn, Davie*, written at Thomson's request. The song collector later substituted his own lines to replace those of Burns (See Henley–Henderson, Vol. IV, p. 104).

Passion's Cry

First printed in part by Stewart, 1802, then completed
in Scott Douglas, 1876.

'*I cannot but remember such things were,*
And were most dear to me'.
Adapted from Shakespeare's *Macbeth*, Act 4, scene 3.

In vain would Prudence with decorous sneer,
Point out a cens'ring world, and bid me fear:
Above that world on wings of love I rise:
I know its worst, and can that worst despise. —
5   'Wrong'd, injur'd, shunn'd, unpitied, unredrest
The mock'd quotation of the scorner's jest.' —
Let Prudence' direst bodements on me fall,
Clarinda, rich reward! o'erpays them all. —
As low-borne mists before the sun remove,
10 So shines, so reigns unrivalled mighty LOVE. —
In vain the Laws their feeble force oppose;
Chain'd at his feet, they groan Love's vanquish'd foes;
In vain Religion meets my shrinking eye;
I dare not combat, but I turn and fly:
15 Conscience in vain upbraids th' unhallow'd fire;

Love grasps his scorpions, stifled they expire:
Reason drops headlong from his sacred throne,
Thy dear idea reigns, and reigns alone;
Each thought intoxicated homage yields,
20 And riots wanton in forbidden fields. —

By all on High, adoring mortals know!
By all the conscious villain fears below!
By what, Alas! much more my soul alarms,
My doubtful hopes once more to fill thy arms!
25 Ev'n shouldst thou, false, forswear the guilty tie,
Thine and thine only I must live and die!!!

This began as a poetic fragment in 1788. It was modified and expanded in 1789, but remained unfinished until 1793. The first stage written about Clarinda (Mrs McLehose) included the lines:

'I burn, I burn, as when thro' ripen'd corn
By driving winds the crackling flames are borne.'
Now, maddening-wild, I curse that fatal night,
Now bless the hour that charm'd my guilty sight.

The topic of the 1789 version changed from Clarinda to the affair of Mrs Maxwell Campbell of Cumnock who had given birth to a child by the then married Captain James Montgomery. Letter 307 reveals that this version was written in the voice of Mrs Maxwell Campbell, to her lover. The affair was public knowledge given that the dispute over the child went to the Court of Session. (See also Letter 310 to Mrs Dunlop.) Montgomerie went overseas: here are some of the lines written in her plaintive voice, later dropped,

Mild zephyrs waft thee to life's farthest shore,
Nor think of me and my distresses more!
Falsehood accurst! No! Still I beg a place,
Still near thy heart some little, little trace!
For that dear trace the world I would resign:
O, let me live, and die, and think it mine!

By all I lov'd, neglected, and forgot,
No friendly face e'er lights my squalid cot.
Shunn'd, hated, wrong'd, unpitied, unredrest
The mock'd quotation of the scorner's jest;

Ev'n the poor support of my wretched life,
Snatched by the violence of legal strife;
Oft grateful for my very daily bread,
To those my family's once large bounty fed;
A welcome inmate at their homely fare,
My griefs, my woes, my sighs, my tears they share:
Their vulgar souls unlike the souls refined,
The fashion'd marble of the polish'd mind.

The poem eventually reverted to its original plan, as a work dedicated to Clarinda, when Burns met her again in 1791. The title *Passion's Cry*, employed by all modern editors, is not by Burns.

The Primrose

First printed in Scott Douglas, 1876.
Tune: Todlin Hame –

Dost ask me, why I send thee here,
This firstling of the infant year?
Dost ask me, what this primrose shews,
Bepearled thus with morning dews? —

5   I must whisper to thy ears,
       The sweets of loves are wash'd with tears.

This lovely native of the dale,
Thou seest, how languid, pensive, pale:
Thou seest this bending stalk so weak,
10   That each way yielding doth not break?

       I must tell thee, these reveal,
       The doubts and fears that lovers feel.

This is based on an old English song by Robert Herrick, 1648. Another version of *The Primrose* is given by Henley and Henderson (1896), but this is the final lyric by Burns, with little change from the original.

Thou Hast Left Me Ever

Tune: Free Him Father
First printed in Thomson, 1799.

THOU hast left me ever, Jamie,
   Thou hast left me ever.
Thou hast left me ever, Jamie,
   Thou hast left me ever.
Aften hast thou vow'd that Death   *often*
   Only should us sever:
Now thou'st left thy lass for ay —   *always*
   I maun see thee never, Jamie,   *may*
     I'll see thee never. —

Thou hast me forsaken, Jamie,
   Thou hast me forsaken:
Thou hast me forsaken, Jamie,
   Thou hast me forsaken.
Thou canst love anither jo,   *darling*
   While my heart is breaking:
Soon my weary een I'll close —   *eyes*
   Never mair to waken, Jamie,   *more*
     Never mair to waken.

This was sent to Thomson in September 1793. It was composed, according to the bard, 'by the leaside of a bowl of punch' just after midnight (Letter 586).

Behold the Hour

Tune: Oran gaoil –
First printed in Currie, 1800.

BEHOLD the hour, the boat arrive;
   Thou goest, the darling of my heart:
Sever'd from thee, can I survive,
   But Fate has will'd — and we must part.
5 I'll often greet the surging swell,
   Yon distant Isle will often hail:
'E'en here I took the last farewell;
   There, latest mark'd her vanish'd sail.'

Along the solitary shore,
10   While flitting sea-fowl round me cry,
Across the rolling, dashing roar
     I'll westward turn my wistful eye:
Happy, thou Indian grove, I'll say,
     Where now my Nancy's path may be!
15 While through thy sweets she loves to stray,
     O, tell me, does she muse on me!

This was appropriately printed in *The Clarinda Correspondence* in 1834 given that it is written about Agnes McLehose's departure from Scotland for Jamaica in December 1791 on her quest to be reunited with her estranged husband. Kinsley rightly suggests there are similarities with a song printed in *The Edinburgh Magazine* of 1774. He underestimates Burns's originality by calling it a 'Scotticized revision' (Vol. III, p. 1444). Kinsley takes his information from *The Burns Chronicle*, 1962. Having examined the original text, the song by Burns possesses the tone of the earlier song, but it is significantly different. Mackay gives two versions. This is the latter.

Fair Jenny

Tune: The Grey Cock *or* Saw Ye My Father
First printed in Currie, 1800.

WHERE are the joys I hae met in the morning,   have
     That danc'd to the lark's early sang?   song
Where is the peace that awaited my wandering,
     At evening the wild-woods amang?   among

5 Nae mair a winding the course o' yon river,   no more
     And marking sweet flowerets sae fair,   so
Nae mair I trace the light footsteps o' Pleasure,   no more
     But Sorrow and sad-sighing Care. —

Is it that Summer's forsaken our vallies,
10   And grim, surly Winter is near?
No, no! the bees humming round the gay roses
     Proclaim it the pride o' the year. —

Fain wad I hide, what I fear to discover,   would
     Yet lang, lang, too well hae I known: long, have
15 A' that has caus'd the wreck in my bosom
     Is Jenny, fair Jenny alone. —

Time cannot aid me, my griefs are immortal,
    Not Hope dare a comfort bestow:
Come then, enamor'd and fond of my anguish,
20   Enjoyment I'll seek in my woe. —

As is often the case, Mackay remarks verbatim from Kinsley on this song: 'Probably the song sent to Janet Miller of Dalswinton, elder daughter of Burns's former landlord, on 9th September, 1793'. Burns wrote to her, 'I have formed in my fancy a little love story for you' (Letter 585).

On a Noted Coxcomb
Capt. Wm. Roddick Of Corbiston
First printed in *The Wanderer*, Glasgow, 1818.

Light lay the earth on Billie's breast,
    His chicken heart's so tender;
But build a castle on his head —
    His scull will prop it under. –

This was sent (Letter 590) to Marion Riddell. Kinsley (p. 1446) acutely points out it is a parody of Henry Mackenzie's *The Man of Feeling*, ch. xx. The reactionary Henderson and Henley typically denounce this piece: 'the rubbish is also inscribed in *The Glenriddell Book*' (Notes, Vol. II, p. 456).

Thine am I, My Chloris Fair
Tune: The Quaker's Wife.
First printed in Thomson, 1799.

Thine am I, my Chloris fair,
    Well thou may'st discover;
Every pulse along my veins,
    Tells the ardent Lover.

5   To thy bosom lay my heart,
    There to throb and languish;
Tho' Despair had wrung its core,
    That would heal its anguish.

Take away those rosy lips,
10   Rich with balmy treasure:
Turn away thine eyes of love,
    Lest I die with pleasure!

What is Life when wanting Love?
    Night without a morning:
15 Love's the cloudless summer sun,
    Nature gay adorning.

A variant of the above song exists referring to Nancy McLehose
rather than Chloris (Jean Lorimer). The heroine was changed in the
Autumn of 1794. Kinsley gives the final version as above but
Mackay opts for the earlier, ignoring the general editorial rule of
printing the last version (p. 505).

To Captain Gordon
On being Asked Why I was not to be of the Party
With him and his Brother Kenmure at Syme's
First printed in Barke, 1958.

DOST ask, dear Captain, why from *Syme*
    I have no invitation,
When well he knows he has with him
    My first friends in the nation?

5 Is it because I love to toast,
    And round the bottle hurl?
No! there conjecture wild is lost,
    For *Syme* by God's no churl! —

Is 't lest with bawdy jests I bore,
10   As oft the matter of fact is?
No! *Syme* the theory can't abhor —
    Who loves so well the practice. —

Is it a fear I should avow
    Some heresy seditious?
15 No! *Syme* (but this entre nous)
    Is quite an old Tiresias. —

In vain Conjecture would thus flit
    Thro mental clime and season:
In short, dear Captain, *Syme's* a Wit —
20   Who asks of Wits a reason? —

Yet must I still the sort deplore
    That to my griefs adds one more,
In baulking me the social hour
    With you and the noble Kenmure. —

Captain Adam Gordon, of Kenmure Castle near New Galloway (now in ruins), was the son of John Gordon, whom Burns visited during his tour of Galloway in July 1793. There is a mixture of friendly wit and some indignation with Syme brought out in the poem's clever question-and-answer pattern regarding Syme's drinking, bawdry and politics. Was he a prophet of the coming political catastrophe? Certainly there were tensions between him and Burns. In his 1815 introduction to the re-issue of Currie's edition, Peterkin was absolutely furious with Walter Scott's treatment of a row between Burns and Syme involving Burns gesturally drawing his Excise sword. Sadly, but predictably, the Carswell archive in the Mitchell Library, Glasgow, talks of seventy missing letters from Syme to Cunningham which would have shed invaluable light on the politics of the Dumfries years (Mitchell Library MS 53).

Impromptu, on Mrs. Walter Riddell's Birthday
4th Nov. 1793
This first appears in Currie, 1800.

OLD Winter, with his frosty beard,
Thus once to Jove his prayer preferred.
What have I done of all the year,
To bear this hated doom severe?
5   My chearless suns no pleasure know;
Night's horrid car drags dreary, slow:
My dismal months no joys are crowning,
But spleeny English hanging, drowning.

Now Jove, for once be mighty civil;
10   To counterbalance all this evil;
Give me, and I've no more to say,
Give me MARIA's natal day!
That brilliant gift shall so enrich me,
Spring, Summer, Autumn, cannot match me.

15 'Tis done!!! says Jove: so ends my story,
    And Winter once rejoiced in glory.

Mrs Walter Riddell was Maria Woodley to her own name, the
daughter of William Woodley, Governor of St Kitts. Burns wrote
several pieces on Maria, particularly *The Last Time I Came O'er the
Muir*.

Occasional Address, Spoken by Miss Fontenelle
On Her Benefit-Night, Dec. 4th, 1793,
At The Dumfries Theatre
First printed in Currie, 1800.

STILL anxious to secure your partial favor,
And not less anxious, sure, this night than ever,
A Prologue, Epilogue, or some such matter,
'Twould vamp my Bill, thought I, if nothing better;
5 So sought a Poet, roosted near the skies,
Told him, I came to feast my curious eyes;
Said, nothing like his works was ever printed,
And last, my Prologue-business, slily hinted.

    Ma'am, let me tell you, quoth my Man of RHYMES,
10 I know your bent — these are no laughing times;
Can you, but, Miss, I own I have my fears,
Dissolve in pause — and sentimental tears —
With laden sighs, and solemn-rounded sentence,
Rouse from his sluggish slumbers, fell Repentance;
15 Paint Vengeance, as he takes his horrid stand,
Waving on high the desolating brand,
Calling the storms to bear him o'er a guilty Land!

    I could no more — askance the creature eyeing,
D'ye think, said I, this face was made for crying?
20 I'll laugh, that's pos — nay more, the world shall know it;
And so, your servant, gloomy Master Poet.

Firm as my creed, Sirs, 'tis my fix'd belief,
That Misery's another word for Grief.
I also think — so may I be a Bride!
25 That so much laughter, so much life enjoy'd.

Thou man of crazy care, and ceaseless sigh,
Still under bleak Misfortune's blasting eye;
Doom'd to that sorest task of man alive —
To make three guineas do the work of five;
30 Laugh in Misfortune's face — the beldam witch!
Say, you 'll be merry — tho' you can't be rich.

Thou other man of care, the wretch in love,
Who long with jiltish arts and airs hast strove;
Who, as the boughs all temptingly project,
35 Measur'st in desperate thought — a rope — thy neck —
Or, where the beetling cliff o'erhang the deep
Peerest to meditate the healing leap:
[For shame! For shame! I tell thee, thou art no man:
This for a giddy, vain, capricious woman?
40 A creature, though I say't, you know, that should not;
Ridiculous with her idiot, 'Would and would not'.]
Would'st thou be cur'd, thou silly, moping elf?
Laugh at her follies, laugh e'en at thyself:
Learn to despise those frowns, now so terrific;
45 And love a kinder — that's your grand specific!

To sum up all — be merry! I advise;
And as we're merry, may we still be wise. —

The *Address*, in first draft, was sent to Miss Louisa Fontenelle on 1st December, 1793. Burns deleted ll. 38–41. They are now reinserted within brackets. Fascinated by Miss Fontenelle, this poem grants her near-magical female powers to laugh Burns out of his dark preoccupations with his two great recurrent enemies, reactionary politics and poverty. The last section, dealing with the suicidal lover is probably a jokey reference to his feelings for the actress. While mainly a witty piece, ll. 14–17 are charged with the dark political forces of 1793.

On Seeing Miss Fontenelle in a Favourite Character

First printed in Cunningham, 1834.

Sweet naiveté of feature,
    Simple, wild, enchanting elf,
Not to thee, but thanks to Nature
    Thou art acting but thyself.

Wert thou awkward, stiff, affected,
   Spurning Nature, torturing art,
Loves and Graces all rejected,
   Then indeed thou 'd'st act a part.

This was probably included in the letter Burns sent to Miss Fonte-
nelle in December 1793 (Letter 599). Dr Currie was guilty of
detaching, or tearing away fragments of poetry from Burns's letters.
The manuscript, which was in private hands in 1834, is now lost.

Husband, Husband, Cease Your Strife

Tune: My Joe Janet
First printed in Thomson, 1799.

HUSBAND, husband, cease your strife,
   Nor longer idly rave, Sir:
Tho' I am your wedded wife,
   Yet I am not your slave, Sir.

5   'One of two must still obey,
      Nancy, Nancy;
   Is it Man or Woman, say,
      My Spouse Nancy.'

If 'tis still the lordly word,
10   Service and obedience;
   I'll desert my Sov'reign lord,
      And so good bye, Allegiance!

'Sad will I be, so bereft,
      Nancy, Nancy;
15   Yet I'll try to make a shift,
      My Spouse Nancy.'

My poor heart then break it must,
      My last hour I am near it:
When you lay me in the dust,
20   Think, how will you bear it. —

'I will hope and trust in Heaven,
      Nancy, Nancy;
Strength to bear it will be given,
      My Spouse Nancy.'

25 Well, Sir, from the silent dead,
    Still I'll try to daunt you;
Ever round your midnight bed
    Horrid sprites shall haunt you. —

'I'll wed another, like my Dear,
30   Nancy, Nancy;
Then all Hell will fly for fear,
    My Spouse, Nancy.'—

This eloquent song in the alternate voice of husband and wife was sent to Thomson in December 1793. Henley and Henderson quote a further verse, probably from an early draft which reads:

If the word is still obey,
Always love and fear you,
I will take myself away
And never more come near you.

Burns, often now presented as exclusively a Jack-the-lad male chauvinist, gives the more dominant voice here to the female, who is robustly egalitarian.

To Miss Graham of Fintry

First printed in Currie, 1800.

Here, where the Scottish Muse immortal lives,
    In sacred strains and tuneful numbers join'd,
Accept the gift; though humble he who gives,
    Rich is the tribute of the grateful mind.

5 So may no ruffian feeling in thy breast,
    Discordant, jar thy bosom-chords among;
But Peace attune thy gentle soul to rest,
    Or Love ecstatic wake his seraph song.

Or Pity's notes, in luxury of tears,
10   As modest Want the tale of woe reveals;
While conscious Virtue all the strain endears,
    And heaven-born Piety her sanction seals.

Dumfries, 31st January, 1794

This was sent to Anne Graham, the elder daughter of Graham of Fintry, along with a copy of Thomson's *Select Collection* of Scots songs on 31st January, 1794. While apolitical, the poem in language and tone, strongly echoes the sombre, elegiac *The Scotian Muse* written in October 1793.

Monody on a Lady Famed for her Caprice

First printed in Currie, 1800.

HOW cold is that bosom which Folly once fired,
 How pale is that cheek where the rouge lately glisten'd;
How silent that tongue which the echoes oft tired,
 How dull is that ear which to flatt'ry so listen'd. —

5 If sorrow and anguish *their* exit await,
 From friendship and dearest affection remov'd;
How doubly severer, Maria, thy fate,
 Thou diedst unwept, as thou livedst unloved. —

Loves, Graces, and Virtues, I call not on you;
10 So shy, grave, and distant, ye shed not a tear:
But come, all ye offspring of Folly so true,
 And flowers let us cull for Maria's cold bier. —

We'll search through the garden for each silly flower,
 We'll range thro' the forest for each idle weed;
15 But chiefly the nettle, so typical, shower,
 For none e'er approach'd her but rued the rash deed. —

We'll sculpture the marble, we'll measure the lay;
 Here Vanity[1] strums on her idiot lyre;
There keen Indignation shall dart on his prey,
20 Which spurning Contempt shall redeem from his ire. —

The Epitaph

Here lies, now a prey to insulting Neglect,
 What once was a butterfly, gay in life's beam:
Want only of wisdom denied her respect,
 Want only of goodness denied her esteem. —

1 N.B. The lady affected to be a Poetess. R.B.

This was written on Maria Riddell when her friendship with the poet was temporarily suspended after an incident in December 1793 during discussion of the classic 'Rape of the Sabines' at Robert Riddell's home. The episode is normally cited as a prelude to condemning Burns out of court for drunken, shameful behaviour towards his host, Mrs Robert Riddell. Few actual facts are known. Most commentary is circumstantial, stressing the poet's over dramatic apology (Letter 608). The poet's personal acceptance of guilt is too often equated with complete responsibility for all that occurred. As a result, Burns was effectively ostracised by Maria Riddell, sister-in-law to Mrs Robert Riddell. It is now known that Mrs Robert Riddell had a reputation for spiteful behaviour and had rowed with Francis Grose. She also detested her brother-in-law Walter Riddell (See headnotes to Letter 608). The 'scene' may have been an aristocratic prank that embarrassed the poet and led to his being asked to leave. Whatever occurred, it led to a breakdown in cordiality between Burns and the Riddells.

Kinsley and Mackay damn Burns for writing what they both describe as a 'tasteless libel'. Burns tells the story as follows to Mrs McLehose:

> The subject of the foregoing is a woman of fashion in this country, with whom, at one period, I was well acquainted. By some scandalous conduct to me, & two or three other gentlemen here as well as me, she steered so far to the north of my good opinion, that I have made her the theme of several ill-natured things (Letter 629).

Mackay, always quick to condemn the poet's behaviour, castigates Burns: 'The scandalous conduct was her temerity in rebuking Burns' (p. 511). When Currie first printed this work he substituted 'Eliza' for Maria, to eliminate embarrassment to Maria Riddell. He was certainly not trying to protect the poet's reputation. Indeed by printing the apologetic letter to Mrs Robert Riddell, Currie was unfavourably representing Burns, loading him with the guilt of all, leaving everyone else stainless. By so doing Currie added to the mythology of Burns as an ill-mannered peasant drunkard. Maria Riddell obsessed Burns erotically, creatively and politically. The withdrawal of her favour led him to deadly, if transient, antagonism and in *From Esopus to Maria* to pathological jealousy. Burns is a perfect example of Blake's dictum that: 'Love & Hate are fed by the same nerve.'

Pinned to Mrs. Walter Riddell's Carriage –
First printed in Cunningham, 1834.

If you rattle along like your Mistress's tongue,
    Your speed will outrival the dart:
But, a fly for your load, you'll break down on the road,
    If your stuff be as rotten's her heart. —

This epigram was sent to Mrs McLehose with the *Monody* addressed to Maria in the letter Burns wrote from Castle Douglas around the end of June 1794 (Letter 629). It was also offered to Patrick Miller Jnr to be passed on to *The Morning Chronicle* signed under the pen-name 'Nith'.

On Robert Riddell
or At Friars Carse Hermitage
First printed in Cunningham, 1834.

To Riddell, much-lamented man,
    This ivied cot was dear;   cottage
Reader, dost value matchless worth?
    This ivied cot revere.

Cunningham records that he copied this from a window at Friar's Carse Hermitage, alleging that Burns wrote it on a visit after the death of Robert Riddell. Kinsley doubts this but without further substantiation accepts the epigram into the canon. One version replaces the word 'Reader' with 'Wand'rer'. It reads as authentic despite the lack of manuscript authority.

The Banks of Cree
or Here is the Glen
Tune: The Banks of Cree.
First printed in Thomson, 1798.

Here is the glen, and here the bower,
    All underneath the birchen shade;
The village-bell has told the hour,
    O what can stay my lovely maid.

5   'Tis not Maria's whispering call;
         'Tis but the balmy-breathing gale,
     Mixt with some warbler's dying fall
         The dewy star of eve to hail.

     It is Maria's voice I hear;
10   So calls the woodlark in the grove
     His little, faithful Mate to chear,
         At once 'tis music — and 'tis love.

     And art thou come! And art thou true!
         O welcome dear to love and me!
15   And let us all our vows renew
         Along the flowery banks of Cree.

Burns wrote these lyrics to match an air composed by Lady Eliza-
beth Heron (1745–1811) of Kirroughtree, wife to Patrick Heron.
The poet visited their country estate home during a second tour
across Galloway in 1795. After the poet's death Thomson printed
the lyrics to the tune of *The Flowers of Edinburgh*.

On Rev. Dr Babington
In answer to one who affirmed of a well-known Character
here, Dr Babington, that there was Falsehood in his very
looks

First printed in Cromek, 1808.

That there is a Falsehood in his looks
    I must and will deny;
They say, their Master is a Knave —
    — And sure they do not lie.

Dr William Babbington (1746–1818) was a priest of the Episcopal
Church in Dumfries. A copy of this exists in the Glenriddell
manuscript collection.

Ye True Loyal Natives
First printed in Cromek, 1808.

Ye true 'Loyal Natives', attend to my song,
In uproar and riot rejoice the night long;
From *envy* and *hatred* your corps is exempt;
But where is your shield from the *darts of contempt*?

The 'Loyal Natives' was an association set up in Dumfries in January 1794 to preserve the Constitution, and display loyalty to King and Country against French Jacobins and their radical supporters in Britain. It is known that there was friction between members of this group and Burns's circle of friends in the town. Burns is supposed to have written the above after being provoked by reading *The Loyal Native's Verses*:

> Ye Sons of Sedition, give ear to my song,
> Let Syme, Burns, and Maxwell pervade every throng,
> With Cracken the attorney, and Mundell the quack,
> Send Willie the monger to Hell with a smack.

The Dumfries loyal association was no exception during these times. In the intense political tumult of December 1792 up until early 1796 the loyalty of all Scots, particularly those of position and rank, was called upon to help maintain social stability against the threat of so-called 'Jacobins'. It is now known as fact that such a pro-French group existed in Dumfries and that its delegate to the National Convention of the Friends of the People in Edinburgh in 1794 was John Drummond, a friend of the poet's. This information was collated by a spy, Claude Irvine Boswell, the Depute Sheriff of Fife and passed to Robert Dundas in Edinburgh. So, from late 1794 onwards, the authorities in Edinburgh knew for certain there was a cell of the Friends of the People in Dumfries.

Ode for General Washington's Birthday
First published in *Notes and Queries*, March 1874.

> No Spartan tube, no Attic shell,
>   No lyre Æolian I awake;
> 'Tis Liberty's bold note I swell,
>   Thy harp, Columbia, let me take.
> 5   See gathering thousands, while I sing,
>   A broken chain, exulting, bring,
>   And dash it in a tyrant's face!
>   And dare him to his very beard,
>   And tell him he no more is fear'd,
> 10   No more the Despot of Columbia's race.
>   A tyrant's proudest insults brav'd,
> They shout, a People freed! They hail an Empire saved.

Where is Man's godlike form?
Where is that brow erect and bold,
That eye that can, unmov'd, behold
The wildest rage, the loudest storm,
That e'er created Fury dared to raise!
Avaunt! thou caitiff, servile, base,
That tremblest at a Despot's nod,
Yet, crouching under the iron rod,
Canst laud the arm that struck th' insulting blow!
Art thou of man's Imperial line?
Dost boast that countenance divine?
Each skulking feature answers, No!
But come, ye sons of Liberty,
Columbia's offspring, brave as free,
In danger's hour still flaming in the van,
Ye know, and dare maintain The Royalty of Man.

Alfred, on thy starry throne
Surrounded by the tuneful choir,
The Bards that erst have struck the patriot lyre,
And rous'd the freeborn Briton's soul of fire,
No more thy England own. —
Dare injured nations form the great design,
To make detested tyrants bleed?
Thy England execrates the glorious deed!
Beneath her hostile banners waving,
Every pang of honour braving,
England in thunder calls — 'The Tyrant's cause is mine!'
That hour accurst, how did the fiends rejoice,
And Hell thro' all her confines raise th' exulting voice,
That hour which saw the generous English name
Link't with such damnèd deeds of everlasting shame!

Thee, Caledonia, thy wild heaths among,
Fam'd for the martial deed, the heaven-taught song,
To thee, I turn with swimming eyes. —
Where is that soul of Freedom fled?
Immingled with the mighty Dead!
Beneath that hallow'd turf where WALLACE lies!
Hear it not, Wallace, in thy bed of death!
Ye babbling winds in silence sweep;
Disturb not ye the hero's sleep,
Nor give the coward secret breath. —

Is this the ancient Caledonian form,
55   Firm as her rock, resistless as her storm?
Shew me that eye which shot immortal hate,
        Blasting the Despot's proudest bearing:
Shew me that arm which, nerv'd with thundering fate,
        Braved Usurpation's boldest daring!
60   Dark-quench'd as yonder sinking star,
        No more that glance lightens afar;
That palsied arm no more whirls on the waste of war. —

General George Washington (1732–99) was born on 22nd February. Burns probably began writing this work *after* the American president's birthday, but dedicated the work to him because of his iconic position as a leading world figure of Liberty and Independence. During the 1793–4 period there are many letters by Washington printed in the British radical press.

On June 25, 1794 Burns wrote to Mrs Dunlop from Castle Douglas in a letter that travelled 'through many devious paths', in Galloway:

I am just going to trouble your critical patience with the first sketch of a stanza I have been framing as I passed along the road.—The Subject is, LIBERTY: you know, my honored Friend how dear the theme is to me. I design it as an irregular Ode for Genl. Washington's birth-day.—After having mentioned the degeneracy of other kingdoms I come to Scotland thus—

Burns then quotes the last stanza of the poem dealing with a disinherited, morbid Scotland. It is impossible to know his intentions regarding the poem. Nor, like his newly retrieved Bruce poems, was the poem suitable in 1794 for rallying the dispersing, ever more pressurized radicals. In this poem Washington, as hero, is tragically exclusive to America. The poem did not finally emerge in all its four stanzas till 1874 in *Notes and Queries*, then during the same year, in *The Glasgow Herald*. Kinsley, in an extreme example of his, at best, political evasiveness, deals with the poem in a few lines by citing its, to him, formal deficiencies. In fact, it is one of Burns's most important and darkest political poems. Its theme is, precisely as Burns defined it, the relationship between liberty and degeneracy. Liberty is expressed by the virile success of the American Revolution but the success of this child of British democratic ideals is not being replicated in the British Isles. American democratic values are being not simply dissipated but actively destroyed. Burns's initial response in his poetry to the American War was to celebrate republican American victory. Quite unknown to him, Blake, differently expressed, is writing similar political sentiments. This, for example from his *Plate 13* of *America*:

> . . . the flames cover's the land, they rouze, they cry;
> Shaking their mental chains, they rush in fury to the sea
> To quench their anguish; at the feet of Washington down fall'n
> They grovel on the sand and writhing lie, while all
> The British soldiers thro' the thirteen states sent up a howl
> Of anguish, threw their swords & muskets to the earth, & ran
> From their grim encampments and dark castles, seeking where
> to hide . . .

As Roger Fechner has written in 'Burns and American Liberty' in *Love and Liberty*:

> As one author has noted, 'A new lyrical note appears in Burns's treatment of America after 1793.' No longer was Burns simply empathising with the American Revolution, while ridiculing British military and political blunders. Rather, he was now universalizing the War of American Independence by making the outcome a victory for liberty the world over. His mature idea of America still represented freedom fighting oppression (p. 283).

While generally true, Fechner's comment is problematised by this particular poem. Each of the four stanzas of the poem is relevant to four different countries: America, Ireland, England and Scotland but the poem charts a course of democratic degeneration in the latter two.

As we now know from Hogg's research, the second, recently discovered two-stanza version of the poem, 'Columbia's offspring brave as free' refers to the Irish Radicals. This, of course, is before the bloody end of the Irish insurrection in 1798 with 30,000 supporters of 'The Royalty of Man' dead. Burns may have had knowledge of the *Address from the Society of United Irishmen in Dublin, 1792* to encourage their Scots counterparts. Stanza two certainly reflects such Irish values. First, the sense that rather than traditional hostility between nations their only competition should be in who first achieves democratic reform:

We will lay open to you our Hearts;—our cause is your cause. If there is to be a Struggle between us, let it be which Nation shall be foremost in the Race of Mind; let this be the noble Animosity kindled between us, who shall first attain that free Constitution, from which both are equidistant, who shall first be the Saviour of the Empire.

Further, in saving the British Empire by converting it into a federation of harmonious democratic nations, the Irish were responsive to the luminous American example:

A sudden light from America shone through our prison. Our volunteers arose, the chains fell from our hands. We followed Grattan, the angel of our deliverance, and in 1782 Ireland ceased to be a province, and became a nation. But, with reason, should we despise and renounce this revolution, as merely a transient burst through a bad habit; the sudden grasp of necessity in despair, from tyranny to distress, did we not believe that the revolution is still *in train*; that it is only the herald of liberty and glory, of Catholic emancipation, as well as Protestant independence; that, in short, this revolution indicates new principles, foreruns new practices, and lays a foundation for advancing the whole people higher in the scale of being, and diffusing equal and permanent happiness.

The roots of such Irish dissent, nourished by the sort of Hutchesonian-derived Protestantism combined with elements of Freemasonry (See A.T.Q. Stewart, *A Deeper Silence: The Hidden Origins of the United Irishmen*, London, 1993) were the same as those influencing Burns himself. He did not think, however, that by 1794 they were strong enough to defeat the evil empire of an increasingly reactionary England. Further, an England that was betraying its own founding democratic principles. As we saw in the introduction, Burns was well aware of the historiography of English radicalism. Hence his invocation in this poem of King Alfred, the English equivalent of William Wallace. In fact, ll. 39–43 are an attack on England's contemporary activities in putting together a reactionary European coalition to destroy the French Revolution. Professor John Millar's great cry of despair in his remarkable analysis of Pitt and Dundas's war policy, *Letters of Crito, On the Causes, Objects and Consequences of the Present War* (republished by the Faculty of Political Science, University of Rome in 1984 and discovered with its pages uncut on the library shelves of Millar's own university) can be read as a prose scansion of Burns's response to the matter. This is from Letter VIII: 'Does not this abundantly show, that the danger of conquest by the French was a mere bugbear, set up by those persons to terrify and delude the nation; and that, so far from wishing to force a peace, as they might easily have done, by offering to guarantee a reasonable treaty, and by threatening upon the refusal of either party, to throw the weight of Britain on the opposite scale, our ministers were in reality desirous of joining the framers of the league of Pilnitz and of entering the war of extermination against France, not for the reasons they assigned, but from motives best known to themselves.'

The last stanza presents a nation over which the Bard weeps real un-Ossianic tears. There is no redeeming Bruce as in *The Edinburgh Gazetteer* poems of the previous year. Wallace is a buried corpse whose spirit would be violated by what has happened in Dundas's Scotland. Perhaps this image of the incarcerated Scottish spirit was one repeated in Edwin Muir's image of Bruce under the permafrost in his poem, *Scotland's Winter*. This stanza is an inversion of his earlier, unconvincing *Caledonia* which portrayed a nation never conquered. Unlike Bruce's arm in the 1793 poems Scotland's arm is now palsied. Heroic Scotland is dead and gone and with Wallace in the grave.

Ode for Hibernia's Sons

This appears here for the first time.

No Spartan tube, no Attic shell,
    No lyre Æolian I awake;
'Tis Liberty's bold note I swell,
    Thy harp, Hibernia, let me take.
5   See gathering thousands, while I sing,
    A broken chain, exulting, bring,
        And dash it in a tyrant's face!
    And dare him to his very beard,
    And tell him he no more is fear'd,
10   No more the Despot of Hibernia's race.
    A tyrant's proudest insults brav'd,
They shout, a People freed! They hail an Empire saved.

      Where is Man's godlike form?
      Where is that brow erect and bold,
15   That eye that can, unmov'd, behold

The wildest rage, the loudest storm,
That e'er created Fury dared to raise!
Avaunt! thou caitiff, servile, base,
That tremblest at a Despot's nod,
20   Yet, crouching under the iron rod,
Canst laud the arm that struck th' insulting blow!
Art thou of man's Imperial line?
Dost boast that countenance divine?
Each skulking feature answers, No!
25   But come, ye sons of Liberty,
Hibernia's offspring, brave as free,
In danger's hour still flaming in the van,
Ye know, and dare maintain The Royalty of Man.

This early version of *Ode for General Washington's Birthday* refers
to Hibernia (Ireland), and was sold in holograph in London during
May 1862. It is recorded in manuscript along with many other
authentic pieces which surfaced from the original Currie archives in
Liverpool, as sold by auctioneers Puttock and Simpson. (A copy of
the sales catalogue is in the Mitchell Library.) It would appear that
the manuscript was later destroyed or is still in private hands. If the
auction sale's catalogue had not been printed, no-one would have
known that Burns crucially passed commentary on Irish political
affairs. This was probably written in early 1794 when the Dublin
offices of the Friends of the People were raided and their leaders
arrested for seditious pamphleteering. By the end of 1794 over
200,000 people across Ireland had taken the oath of the radical
and reformist group the United Irishmen, who had made links with
many such groups in Scotland and England, particularly the United
Scotsmen. Leading Irish radicals attended the National Convention
of Friends of the People in Edinburgh.

On Mr. Walter Riddell, Esq.

First printed in 1801 by Oliver (Edinburgh);
then by Duncan, 1801 (Glasgow).

So vile was poor Wat, such a miscreant slave,
That the worms ev'n damn'd him when laid in his grave.
'In his scull there is famine,' a starv'd reptile cries;
'And his heart it is poison,' another replies.

Walter Riddell (1764–1802) was Robert Riddell's younger brother.
He married Maria Woodely in 1790 and lived at Woodley Park.

On the Seas and Far Away

Tune: O'er the Hills
First printed in Currie, 1800.

How can my poor heart be glad,
When absent from my Sailor lad;
How can I the thought forego,
He's on the seas to meet the foe:
5   Let me wander, let me rove,
Still my heart is with my Love;
Nightly dreams and thoughts by day
Are with him that's far away.

Chorus
On the seas and far away,
10 On stormy seas and far away,
Nightly dreams and thoughts by day,
Are ay with him that 's far away.   always

When in summer noon I faint,
As weary flocks around me pant,
15 Haply in this scorching sun
My Sailor 's thund'ring at his gun:
Bullets spare my only joy!
Bullets spare my darling boy!
Fate do with me what you may,
20 Spare but him that 's far away.

Chorus
On the seas and far away,
On stormy seas and far away,
Fate, do with me what you may,
Spare but him that's far away.

25 At the starless midnight hour
When Winter rules with boundless power;
As the storms the forests tear,
And thunders rend the howling air:
Listening to the doubling roar,
30 Surging on the rocky shore,
All I can — I weep and pray
For his weal that 's far away.

Chorus
On the seas and far away,
On stormy seas and far away,
35 All I can — I weep and pray
For his weal that 's far away.

Peace, thy olive wand extend
And bid wild War his ravage end,
Man with brother Man to meet,
40 And as brother kindly greet:
Then may Heaven with prosperous gales
Fill my Sailor's welcome sails,
To my arms their charge convey,
My dear lad that 's far away.

Chorus
45 On the seas and far away,
On stormy seas and far away,
To my arms their charge convey,
My dear lad that 's far away.

This was sent to Thomson on 30th August, 1794. Picking up on the
poet's self-effacing remarks on the song (Letter 635), Thomson
rejected it claiming that the young lady referred to would not plead
that 'bullets' should spare her lover. It is more probable Thomson
rejected it on the grounds of its anti-war stance, given that he
disliked every anti-war lyric by Burns. The lyric, like the new
radical song *The Ewe Bughts*, is in the feminine voice.

To Dr. Maxwell,
On Miss Jessy Staig's Recovery
First printed in Currie, 1800.

Maxwell, if merit here you crave,
    That merit I deny:
You save fair Jessie from the grave!
    An ANGEL could not die.

Jessy Staig was the daughter of David Staig, the Provost of Dum-
fries. Dr William Maxwell, son of James Maxwell of Kirkconnell,
was born in 1760 and died in 1834. He studied medicine at Paris. He
was a member of the guard at the execution of the King and Queen

of France, before returning to Scotland to practise medicine. When he raised a subscription to manufacture daggers for the French Republican army he was dubbed by the London *Sun* newspaper as Britain's most dangerous Jacobin. Burns, obviously proud of his friend, describes him to Mrs Dunlop as 'the identical Dr Maxwell whom Burke mentioned in the House of Commons' (Letter 637). See commentary on *The Dagger*. Robert Thornton's *William Maxwell to Robert Burns* (Edinburgh, 1979) is informative but politically naïve.

Ca' the Yowes to the Knowes

Second Version
First printed in Currie, 1800.

Hark, the mavis' evening sang	thrush, song
Sounding Clouden's woods amang;	among
Then a faulding let us gang,	to sheep pens, go
My bonie Dearie.	

Chorus
5 Ca' the yowes to the knowes,   *call, ewes, hill slopes*
     Ca' them whare the heather grows,   *call/drive*
  Ca' them where the burnie rowes,   *stream flows*
    My bonie Dearie.

We'll gae down by Clouden side,   *go*
10 Thro' the hazels spreading wide
O'er the waves, that sweetly glide
    To the moon sae clearly.   *so*
    Ca' the yowes, &c.

Yonder Clouden's silent towers
Where, at moonshine's midnight hours,
15 O'er the dewy bending flowers
    Fairies dance sae cheary.
    Ca' the yowes, &c.

Ghaist nor bogle shalt thou fear;   *ghost, demon*
Thou'rt to Love and Heaven sae dear,
Nocht of Ill may come thee near,   *nothing*
20   My bonie Dearie.
    Ca' the yowes, &c.

Fair and lovely as thou art,
Thou hast stown my very heart;   stolen
I can die – but canna part,   cannot
    My bonie Dearie.
        Ca' the yowes, &c.

This improved version was sent to Thomson in September 1794
(See Letter 636). He eventually printed the song in 1805. The
Clouden is a small tributary of the river Nith and the 'silent towers'
refer to Lincluden Abbey, built on the same design as Paisley
Abbey. It is still a beautiful area to walk, especially in Autumn.

She Says She Lo'es me Best of a' –
Or Sae Flaxen were her Ringlets
Tune: Oonagh's Waterfall
First printed by Johnson in S.M.M., December 1796.

Sae flaxen were her ringlets,   so
    Her eyebrows of a darker hue,
Bewitchingly o'er arching
    Twa laughing een o' bonie blue.—   two, eyes
5 Her smiling, sae wyling,   so, beguiling
    Wad make a wretch forget his woe;   would
What pleasure, what treasure,
    Unto those rosy lips to grow:
Such was my Chloris' bonie face,
10   When first that bonie face I saw;
And ay my Chloris' dearest charm,   always
    She says, she lo'es me best of a'. —   loves, all

Like harmony her motion;
    Her pretty ankle is a spy,
15 Betraying fair proportion,
    Wad make a saint forget the sky. —
Sae warming, sae charming,   so
    Her fautless form and gracefu' air,   faultless
Ilk feature — auld Nature   each, old
20   Declar'd that she could dae nae mair: do no more
Hers are the willing chains o' love,
    By conquering Beauty's sovereign law;
And ay my Chloris' dearest charm,
    She says, she lo'es me best of a'. —

25 Let others love the city,
        And gaudy shew at sunny noon;   show
    Gie me the lonely valley,   give
        The dewy eve, and rising moon
    Fair beaming, and streaming
30   Her silver light the boughs amang;   among
    While falling, recalling,
        The amorous thrush concludes his sang;   song
    There, dearest Chloris, wilt thou rove
        By wimpling burn and leafy shaw,   wood
35 And hear my vows o' truth and love,
        And say, thou lo'es me best of a'. —

This fine lyric is based on an old song Burns collected for *The Merry
Muses*, to which he adapted 'decent' verses, dedicating them to his
'Chloris' (Jean Lorimer). It was sent to both Johnson and Thomson.
We have returned a few words spelt in English in previous editions
to the original Scots.

Why Should We Idly Waste Our Prime
Or a Revolutionary Lyric
First printed by Cunningham, 1834.

Why should we idly waste our prime
    Repeating our oppressions?
Come rouse to arms! 'Tis now the time
    To punish past transgressions.
5 'Tis said that Kings can do no wrong —
    Their murderous deeds deny it,
And since from us their power is sprung,
    We have a right to try it.
Now each true patriot's song shall be —
10   'Welcome Death or Libertie!'

Proud Priests and Bishops we'll translate
    And canonize as Martyrs;
The guillotine on Peers shall wait;
    And Knights shall hang in garters.
15 Those Despots long have trode us down,
    And Judges are their engines:
Such wretched minions of a Crown
    Demand the people's vengeance!
To-day 'tis theirs. To-morrow we
20   Shall don the Cap of Libertie!

The Golden Age we'll then revive:
        Each man will be a brother;
    In harmony we all shall live,
        And share the earth together;
25 In Virtue train'd, enlighten'd Youth
        Will love each fellow-creature;
    And future years shall prove the truth
        That Man is good by nature:
    Then let us toast with three times three
        The reign of Peace and Libertie!

This song is given, on the basis of recent research, as one *improved* by Burns. The song originally appears, according to Mackay, in Cunningham (1834), then in Chambers (1838). Neither question its authenticity, given that it was, as Scott Douglas comments in the 1870s, found in manuscript. Scott Douglas dismissed it with *The Tree of Liberty* on tenuous grounds:

> The present editor has little doubt that this production, and also *The Tree of Liberty*, if really taken from Burns's MS, [must] have been merely transcribed by him from the pages of some wild Magazine of the period (Vol. II, p. 392).

This anti-radical prejudice was endorsed by Henderson and Henley in 1896. Robert Hughes, though, accepted the song in the 1920s. James Barke also endorsed it. Kinsley (1968) ignored it. Mackay followed suit, placing it in Appendix B of his *Burns: A-Z, The Complete Wordfinder* (no. 51, p. 731). Ross Roy brushed it aside in *Poems and Songs Spuriously Attributed to Robert Burns* without any argument (See *Critical Essays on Robert Burns*, ed. Carol McGuirk, G. K. Hall, New York, 1998, pp. 225–37).

Recent research located the original song, supposedly in the hand of the Scots London based radical leader of the London Corresponding Society, Thomas Hardy, a Scot, born in Larbert. The song is located in the Treasurer's Solicitor's Papers, Public Record Office, Kew, London, bundled among papers seized from Thomas Hardy's house when he was arrested on a spurious charge of High Treason at the end of 1794 (See TS 11/959/3505). The manuscript indicates that the song was written to the tune *The Vicar of Bray*. It is not in the handwriting of Hardy. It has been transcribed by a government official after the seizure and indicates in a head-note that it was found in the handwriting of a person unknown. This, however, is contradicted at the close of the song where it states 'in

Hardy's hand'. It would be wrong to suppose Hardy as the original author, even if the latter note is correct. He was not known to write any songs or poetry. As the prime mover in the London Corresponding Society, which established links throughout Britain with leading radicals – including Burns's friend Lord Daer – it is almost certain that Hardy received the song from a reformist associate. Given that there is evidence a manuscript existed in Burns's hand, he must have received a copy from a radical friend, possibly even Hardy himself. Here is the original:

A Revolutionary Lyric

Why should we vainly waste our prime
    Repeating our oppressions?
Come rouse to arms 'tis now the time
    To punish past transgressions.
5   'Tis said that Kings can do no wrong -
    Their Murderous deeds deny it,
And since from us their power has sprung,
    We have the right to try it.
        Chorus: *Come rouse to arms &c.*

The starving wretch who steals for bread
10   But seldom meets compassion -
And shall a Crown preserve the head
    Of him who robs a Nation?
Such partial laws we all despise
    See Gallia's bright example
15   The glorious sight before our eyes
    We'll on every Tyrant Trample.
        Come rouse to arms &c.

Proud Bishops next we will translate
    Among Priest crafted Martyrs;
The guillotine on Peers shall wait;
20   *And Knights we'll hang in Garters.*
Those Despots long have trod us down,
    And judges are their Engines:
These Wretched Minions of a Crown
    Demand a people's Vengeance!
        Come rouse &c.

25   Our juries are a venal pack
          See Justice Topsy Turvy
      In Freedom's cause they've turn'd aback
          Of Englishmen unworthy.
      The Glorious work but once begun
30   We'll Cleanse the Augean stable
      A moment lost and we are undone.
          Come strike while we are able.
              Come rouse &c.

      The Golden Age will then revive
          Each Man shall be a Brother;
35   In peace and harmony will live,
          And share the World together.
      In Virtue train'd, Enlightened Youth
          Will love each fellow creature;
      And future years shall prove the truth
40   That man is good by nature.

This is evidently the work of a passionately radical poet. The two most likely authors of the original are Thomas Spence, author of *Pig's Meat, Address to the Swinish Multitude,* and Joseph Mather, the Sheffield poet whose best known polemical works are *True Reformers, Britons Awake* and *The File Hewer's Lamentation.* Despite finding the above text in manuscript, it is not possible, as yet, to establish for certain the original author. However, it seems pretty clear that for Burns to make his own manuscript version, he must first have seen the above, original text.

The difference between the two songs is that the original has two additional stanzas. Contextually, the song can be dated to late 1794 when the London treason trials began. The Burns-attributed version drops the chorus to a double-line refrain. The first of these appears to echo *Scots Wha Hae,* 'Now each new patriot's song shall be:- / 'Welcome Death or Libertie'. The second sounds less like Burns, 'To-day 'tis theirs. To-morrow we/ Shall don the Cap of Libertie'. The third refrain vividly echoes *There Was A Lad* 'as sure as three times three . . .': 'Then let us toast with three times three, / The reign of Peace and Libertie!' The final lines ring true to expected improvements from Burns and he, in so doing, would have cut away the weaker verses.

So, although the Burns manuscript is no longer extant, we can now compare and contrast the so-called Burns version and conclude with little doubt that the song is not his. It was written, almost certainly by an English radical poet. However, on the evidence that Burns appears to have seen the original and made improvements to it, the song can be added to the canon in the category of works he improved. Around thirty percent of the songs allowed to the canon are only partly his. The song, of course, gives further evidence of Burns's integral relationship to British radicalism.

O Saw Ye My Phely

Tune: When She Cam Ben She Bobbit –
First printed in Currie, 1800.

O, saw ye my Dearie, my Phely?
O, saw ye my Dearie, my Phely?
She's down i' the grove, she's wi' a new Love,
    She winna come hame to her Willy. —   will not

What says she, my Dearest, my Phely?
What says she, my Dearest, my Phely?
She lets thee to wit she has thee forgot,
    And for ever disowns thee her Willy. —

O had I ne'er seen thee, my Phely!
O had I ne'er seen thee, my Phely!
As light as the air, and fause as thou's fair,   false
    Thou 's broken the heart o' thy Willy. —

This was sent to Thomson on 19th October, 1794. It is a variation on his earlier song *My Eppie McNab*.

How Lang and Dreary is the Night

Tune: Cauld Kail.
First printed by Thomson, 1798.

How lang and dreary is the night,   long
    When I am frae my Dearie;   from
I restless lie frae e'en to morn,
    Tho' I were ne'er sae weary. —   so

Chorus
5   For Oh, her lanely nights are lang;   lonely, long
    And Oh, her dreams are eerie;   fearful
And Oh, her widow'd heart is sair,   sore
    That's absent frae her Dearie. —   from

When I think on the lightsome days
10   I spent wi' thee, my Dearie;
And now what seas between us roar,
     How can I be but eerie. —   *fearful*
        For Oh &c.

How slow ye move, ye heavy hours;
     The joyless day how dreary:
15   It was na sae ye glinted by,
       When I was wi' my Dearie. —
       For Oh &c.

This was adapted from an old song and sent to Thomson on 19th
October, 1794: 'I have taken a stride or two across my room and
arranged it anew' (Letter 644). Mackay quotes part of this same
letter by Burns, but confuses the issue by printing the earliest
version of the song by Burns as the 'second version', making the
earlier lyric seem like the final lyric. An earlier version appears in
Johnson's S.M.M in 1788. Only the final version as sent to
Thomson is given here.

Let Not Women E'er Complain

Tune: Duncan Gray
First printed by Thomson, 1798.

LET NOT Woman e'er complain
     Of inconstancy in love;
Let not Woman e'er complain
     Fickle Man is apt to rove:
5 Look abroad thro' Nature's range,
     Nature's mighty law is CHANGE;
Ladies would it not be strange
     Man should then a monster prove. —

Mark the winds, and mark the skies;
10   Ocean's ebb, and ocean's flow:
Sun and moon but set to rise;
     Round and round the seasons go:
Why then ask of silly Man,
     To oppose great Nature's plan?
15 We'll be constant while we can —
     You can be no more, you know. —

Thomson had for commercial reasons asked Burns to compose
English lyrics to match traditional airs. The relatively unhappy

verses above corroborate Burns's response (Letter 644): 'These English songs gravel me to death. – I have not that command of the language . . . that I have of my mother tongue. – In fact, I think that my ideas are more barren in English than in Scots.'

The Auld Man's Winter Thought
or The Winter of Life
Tune: The Death of the Linnet
First printed by Johnson, December 1796.

BUT lately seen in gladsome green
    The woods rejoiced the day,
Thro' gentle showers the laughing flowers
    In double pride were gay:
5 But now our joys are fled —
    On winter blasts awa!   away
Yet maiden May, in rich array
    Again shall bring them a'. —

But my white pow — nae kindly thowe   head, no, thaw
10 Shall melt the snaws of Age;   snows
My trunk of eild, but buss and bield,   old age, bush, shelter
    Sinks in Time's wintry rage. —
Oh, Age has weary days!
    And nights o' sleepless pain!
15 Thou golden time o' Youthfu' prime,
    Why comes thou not again!

This was sent to Thomson among the bundle of songs dated 19th October, 1794. Burns told Thomson that the original melody was an 'Eastern air, which you would swear was a Scottish one' (Letter 644). The tune given above is the one used by Thomson who printed the song a few years after Johnson.

The Lover's Morning Salute to his Mistress
or Sleep'st Thou or Wauk'st Thou
Tune: Deil Tak the Wars
First printed by Thomson, 1798.

SLEEP'ST thou, or wauk'st thou, fairest creature;   wakest
    Rosy morn now lifts his eye,
Numbering ilka bud which Nature   each
    Waters wi' the tears o' joy.

5   Now, to the streaming fountain
       Or up the heathy mountain,
The hart, hind, and roe, freely, wanton stray;
       In twining hazel bowers,
       His lay the linnet pours;
10   The lavrock to the sky   *lark*
       Ascends, wi' sangs o' joy: *songs*
While the sun and thou arise to bless the day.

Phoebus, gilding the brow of morning,
       Banishes ilk darksome shade,   *each*
15 Nature gladdening and adorning:
       Such, to me, my lovely maid.
       When frae my Chloris parted,   *from*
       Sad, cheerless, broken-hearted,
Then night's gloomy shades o'ercast my sky:
20   But when she charms my sight,
       In pride of Beauty's light;
       When thro' my very heart,
       Her beaming glories dart;
'Tis then — 'tis then I wake to life and joy!

This was among the packet sent to Thomson on 19th October, 1794.
The title adopted here is that suggested by Burns and given in
Kinsley. 'Chloris' refers to Jean Lorimer.

To the Hon. Mr. Wm. R. Maule of Panmure on his High Phaeton

First printed in Henley and Henderson, 1896.

Thou Fool, in thy Phaeton towering,
    Art proud when that Phaeton's prais'd?
'Tis the pride of a Thief's exhibition
    When higher his pillory's rais'd.

William Ramsay Maule (1771–1841), Earl of Panmure, was seen by
Burns riding away from the Caledonian Hunt races in a high open
carriage or phaeton at the race ground at Tinwald Downs. His
display of self-importance provoked this epigram which was sent to
Mrs Dunlop in November 1794. Burns describes the scene and its
'roar of Folly and Dissipation . . . One of the Corps provoked my ire

the other day which burst out as follows' (Letter 645). The reference to a 'Thief' is probably Burns's idea that the Earl's inherited wealth was ill gotten. The winning horse in the Caledonian Hunt race at Dumfries in late Autumn 1792, named 'Sans Culotte' never features again after January 1793 or was given a more *loyal* name. Panmure in 1817 settled an annuity of £60 on Burns's widow (*The Burns Chronicle*, 1964, p. 23).

The Charming Month of May

Tune: Daintie Davie
First printed in Thomson, 1799.

It was the charming month of May,
When all the flowers were fresh and gay,
One morning, by the break of day,
    The youthful, charming Chloe;
5 From peaceful slumber she arose,
Girt on her mantle and her hose,
And o'er the flowery mead she goes,
    The youthful, charming Chloe.

Chorus
Lovely was she by the dawn,
10   Youthful Chloe, charming Chloe,
Tripping o'er the pearly lawn,
    The youthful, charming Chloe.

The feather'd people you might see,
Perch'd all around on every tree,
15 In notes of sweetest melody
    They hail the charming Chloe;
Till, painting gay the eastern skies,
The glorious sun began to rise,
Out-rivall'd by the radiant eyes
20   Of youthful, charming Chloe.
        Lovely was she &c.

This was sent to Thomson in November 1794. Burns told Thomson he took the idea for the song from an old lyric in *The Tea-Table Miscellany* (Letter 646).

Lassie wi' the Lint-White Locks

Tune: Rothiemurchie's Rant
First printed in Currie, 1800.

Now Nature cleeds the flowery lea,   clothes, meadow
And a' is young and sweet like thee,
O, wilt thou share its joys wi' me,
    And say thou'lt be my Dearie O.

Chorus
5 Lassie wi' the lint-white locks,
    Bonie lassie, artless lassie,
Wilt thou wi' me tent the flocks —   tend
    Wilt thou be my Dearie O.

The primrose bank, the wimpling burn,   meandering
10 The cuckoo on the milkwhite thorn,
The wanton lambs at early morn
    Shall welcome thee, my Dearie O.
      Lassie wi' &c.

And when the welcome simmer shower   summer
Has cheer'd ilk drooping little flower,   each
15 We'll to the breathing woodbine bower
    At sultry noon, my Dearie O.
      Lassie wi' &c.

When Cynthia lights wi' silver ray
The weary shearer's hameward way,   homeward
Thro' yellow waving fields we'll stray,
20   And talk o' love, my Dearie O.
      Lassie wi' &c.

And when the howling wintry blast
Disturbs my lassie's midnight rest,
I'll fauld thee to my faithfu' breast,
    And comfort thee, my Dearie O. —
      Lassie wi' &c.

This was among the songs sent to Thomson in November 1794.
Most editors assert that the heroine of the song is again Jean
Lorimer, 'Chloris', despite the reference to Cynthia, l. 17, and
the fact that Jean Lorimer did not have 'lint-white locks'.

To Chloris

Tune: Major Graham
First printed in the Aldine edition, 1839.

AH, Chloris, since it may not be,
    That thou of love wilt hear;
If from the lover thou maun flee,
    Yet let the *friend* be dear.

5   Altho' I love my Chloris, mair
    Than ever tongue could tell;
My passion I will ne'er declare —
    I'll say, I wish thee well.

Tho' a' my daily care thou art,
10   And a' my nightly dream,
I'll hide the struggle in my heart,
    And say it is esteem.

This is another work adapted from an old song in *The Tea-Table Miscellany* and dedicated to Miss Jean Lorimer.

O Philly, Happy be that Day
or Phily and Willy

Tune: The Sow's Tail to Geordie
First printed in Currie, 1800.

He.
O PHILLY, happy be that day
When, roving thro' the gather'd hay,
My youthfu' heart was stown away,   stolen
    And by thy charms, my Philly. —

She.
5   O Willy, ay I bless the grove
Where first I own'd my maiden love,
Whilst thou did pledge the Powers above
    To be my ain dear Willy. —   own

He.
As songsters of the early year
10 Are ilka day mair sweet to hear,   every, more
So ilka day to me mair dear
    And charming is my Philly. —

She.
As on the brier the budding rose
Still richer breathes, and fairer blows,
15 So in my tender bosom grows
    The love I bear my Willy. —

He.
The milder sun and bluer sky
That crown my harvest cares wi' joy,
Were ne'er sae welcome to my eye   so
20   As is a sight o' Philly. —

She.
The little swallow's wanton wing,
Tho' wafting o'er the flowery Spring,
Did ne'er to me sic tydings bring,   such
    As meeting o' my Willy. —

He.
25 The bee, that thro' the sunny hour
Sips nectar in the op'ning flower,
Compar'd wi' my delight is poor
    Upon the lips o' Philly. —

She.
The woodbine in the dewy weet
30 When ev'ning shades in silence meet,
Is nocht sae fragrant or sae sweet   not so
    As is a kiss o' Willy. —

He.
Let Fortune's wheel at random rin;   run
And fools may tyne, and knaves may win;   lose/be lost
35 My thoughts are a' bound up on ane,
    And that's my ain dear Philly. —   own

She.
What's a' the joys that gowd can gie?   all, gold
I care na wealth a single flie;   not (for), fly
The lad I love 's the lad for me,
40   And that's my ain dear Willy. —   own

Burns started this song in September 1794 but did not finish it until November when he sent a copy to Thomson. The poet considered employing the names of George Thomson and his wife Katherine but accepted that their names were not poetical enough for the lyric. Mackay titles the song *Philly and Willy* but lays the song out in a manner where it is unclear that the song alternates between the male and female voice (p. 529).

Canst Thou Leave Me Thus My Katy

Tune: Roy's Wife
First printed in Thomson, 1799.

Is this thy plighted, fond regard,
    Thus cruelly to part, my Katy:
Is this thy faithful swain's reward —
    An aching broken heart, my Katy. —

Chorus
5 Canst thou leave me thus, my Katy,
    Canst thou leave me thus, my Katy;
Well thou know'st my aching heart,
    And canst thou leave me thus for pity. —

Farewell! and ne'er such sorrows tear
10   That fickle heart of thine, my Katy!
Thou mayest find those will love thee dear —
    But not a love like mine, my Katy. —
      Canst thou leave me &c.

This was written in November 1794 by Burns as some 'English stanzas' to the tune *Rory's Wife* (Letter 647).

How Green the Groves

Tune: My Lodging is on the cold ground
First printed in Thomson, 1805.

BEHOLD, my Love, how green the groves,
    The primrose banks how fair;
The balmy gales awake the flowers,
    And wave thy flaxen hair:
5 The lav'rock shuns the palace gay,   lark
    And o'er the cottage sings;
For Nature smiles as sweet, I ween,   trust
    To shepherds as to kings. —

Let minstrels sweep the skilfu' string,
10   In lordly, lighted ha';   hall
The shepherd stops his simple reed,
    Blythe, in the birken shaw: birch wood
The princely revel may survey
    Our rustic dance wi' scorn,
15 But are their hearts as light as ours
    Beneath the milkwhite thorn. —

The shepherd, in the flowery glen,
    In shepherd's phrase will woo;
The courtier tells a finer tale,
20   But is his heart as true:
Here wild-wood flowers I've pu'd, to deck   pulled
    That spotless breast o' thine;
The courtier's gems may witness love —
    But 'tis na love like mine. —   not

This was sent to Thomson in November 1794. That it was written
about Chloris (Jean Lorimer) does not disguise the political theme
of the song, that rural romance and love among the peasantry is
more natural and untainted than the 'courtly' facade of love among
the aristocracy. It is a love song underpinned with the sentiments
expressed in *A Man's a Man*.

Contented wi' Little

Tune: Lumps o' Puddins
First printed in Thomson, 1799.

CONTENTED wi' little, and cantie wi' mair,   *happy, more*
Whene'er I forgather wi' Sorrow and Care,
I gie them a skelp, as they're creeping alang,   *give, slap, along*
Wi' a cog o' gude swats and an auld   *cup, good ale, old,*
    Scottish sang.   *song*

5 I whyles claw the elbow o' troublesome Thought;   *sometimes clasp*
But Man is a soger, and Life is a faught: *soldier, fight*
My mirth and gude humour are coin in my pouch,
And my FREEDOM 's my Lairdship nae monarch
    daur touch.   *no, dare*

A towmond o' trouble, should that be my fa',   *a year, fall/lot*
10 A night o' gude fellowship sowthers it a';   *good, patches it up*
When at the blythe end o' our journey at last,
Wha the Deil ever thinks o' the road he has past.   *who, Devil*

Blind Chance, let her snapper and stoyte on her way;   *stumble, stagger*
Be 't to me, be 't frae me, e'en let the jade gae: *from, hag go*
15 Come Ease, or come Travail; come Pleasure or Pain;
My warst word is — 'Welcome, and welcome again!'   *worst*

This is, by Burns's own assessment, one of his quintessential autobiographical lyrics. It was composed around 18th November, 1794 and sent to Thomson. Burns said of the lyric that it should be set next to a portrait done of him by Alexander Reid in order that 'the portrait of my face and the picture of my mind may go down the Stream of Time together' (Letter 670). The affirmation 'my FREEDOM'S my Lairdship nae monarch daur touch' is a characteristically defiant statement from Burns, who boldly asserts that no monarch will touch him and describes himself as a fighter, clawing the elbow of troublesome thought. It would be no surprise if this was not a political allusion to writing seditious poetry.

My Nanie's Awa –

Tune: There'll never be Peace –
First printed in Thomson, 1799.

NOW in her green mantle blythe Nature arrays,
And listens the lambkins that bleat o'er the braes,   *lambs, hillslopes*
While birds warble welcomes in ilka green shaw;   *each, wood*
But to me it's delightless — my Nanie's awa. —   *away/dead*

5   The snawdrap and primrose our woodlands adorn,   *snowdrop*
And violets bathe in the weet o' the morn;   *wet/dew*
They pain my sad bosom, sae sweetly they blaw,   *so, blow*
They mind me o' Nanie — and Nanie's awa. —

Thou lavrock that springs frae the dews of the lawn   *lark   from*
10   The shepherd to warn o' the grey-breaking dawn,
And thou mellow mavis that hails the night-fa',   *thrush, -fall*
Give over for pity — my Nanie's awa. —

Come Autumn, sae pensive, in yellow and grey,   *so*
And soothe me wi' tydins o' Nature's decay: *tidings*
15   The dark, dreary Winter, and wild-driving snaw   *snow*
Alane can delight me — now Nanie's awa. —   *alone*

This beautiful lyric with its interaction of mood and season was sent to Thomson on 9th December, 1794. Kinsley shows some literary influence on the song from a work by Hook (1768), 'My Laddie is Gane' (Vol. III, p. 1463), but it is hardly noticeable.

Dumfries Epigrams

This Collection of epigrams is only known in the transcript of John Syme, the poet's Dumfries friend and Distributor of Stamps for the area. They give us some inkling of not only the intimacy of Burns and Syme but of their shared political dissent. They are in the Hornel Collection.

Untitled

First printed in *The Burns Chronicle*, 1932.

C[opelan]d faithful likeness, friend Painter, would'st seize?
Keep out Worth, Wit and Wisdom: Put in what you please.

The subject of this is unknown. Assuming it is on a portrait of a local aristocrat, Mackay guesses, probably correctly, that it is written about William Copeland of Collieston, whose 'whiskers' are mentioned in the *Second Heron Ballad*.

Extempore

On Miss E. I ——, A lady of a figure indicating Amazonian
strength.
First printed in *The Burns Chronicle*, 1932.

SHOULD he escape the slaughter of thine Eyes,
Within thy strong Embrace he struggling dies.

Again the subject is uncertain, although it may be written on Elizabeth Inglis, daughter of the Rev. William Inglis, Loreburn church, Dumfries.

To a Club in Dumfries
who styled themselves the Dumfries Loyal Natives and
exhibited violent party work and intemperate Loyalty –
10th June 1794
First printed in *The Burns Chronicle*, 1932.

PRAY, who are these *Natives* the Rabble so ven'rate?
They're our true ancient *Natives*, and they breed undegen'rate.
The ignorant savage that weather'd the storm
When the *man* and the Brute differed but in form.

For commentary on the loyalist group, the Dumfries Loyal Natives, see notes to the earlier work *Ye True Loyal Natives*. The poet's known radical sentiments made him prickly to comments or jibes from loyalists in Dumfries, who often tried to provoke him to comment on the political situation. On at least one recorded occasion this almost led to him being challenged to a pistol duel with a Captain Dods (Letter 631) for toasting, 'May our success in the present war be equal to the justice of our cause'. Other toasts have been recorded such as 'May the last King be hung in the guts of the last Priest'. Indeed, it appears that another complete song satirising the 'Dumfries Loyal Natives' was discovered and sold in manuscript in 1861, but has never been recovered. In his printed sales catalogue of the greatest auction of Burns manuscripts to occur, Edward C. Bigmore records the first line of a song 'Here are we Loyal Natives' and describes it as 'Song in 8 verses. 2 pages folio, written in pencil and inked over in another hand, with two other Songs, all believed to be UNPUBLISHED' (p. 8).

On an old Acquaintance who seemed to pass the Bard without notice

First printed in *The Burns Chronicle*, 1932.

DOST hang thy head, Billy, asham'd that thou knowest me?
'Tis paying in kind a just debt that thou owest me.

DOST blush, my dear Billy, asham'd of thyself,
    A Fool and a Cuckold together?
The fault is not thine, insignificant elf,
    Thou wast not consulted in either.

It is not known who 'Billy' refers to in these lines. Given the inevitably fragmentary knowledge about the poet's acquaintances during his years in Dumfries conjecture is futile. They reinforce the poet's own negative description of fragmented friendships in *From Esopus to Maria*: 'The shrinking bard adown the alley skulks', that he was being shunned by many people in Dumfries society.

Immediate Extempore
on Being Told by W.L. of the Customs Dublin that Commissar Goldie Did Not seem Disposed to Push the Bottle

First printed in *The Burns Chronicle*, 1932.

FRIEND Commissar, since we're met and are happy,
Pray why should we part without having more nappy!
Bring in t'other bottle, for faith I am dry —
Thy drink thou can't part with and neither can I. —

Commissar Goldie, a legal official, was president of the Dumfries Loyal Natives.

On Mr. Burke
By an Opponent and a Friend to Mr. Hastings

First printed in *The Burns Chronicle*, 1932.

OFT I have wonder'd that on Irish ground
No poisonous Reptile ever has been found:
Revealed the secret stands of great Nature's work:
She preserved her poison to create a Burke!

Edmund Burke (1729–97), author of the famed and notorious *Reflections on the French Revolution*, became a leading member of the Tories under William Pitt, having abandoned his original Whig politics. Characteristically, Kinsley makes no comment on by far the most important of the Dumfries epigrams. Overtly (in an assumed voice) it is about Burke's obsessive pursuit of Warren Hastings concerning his fiscal corruption of the East India Company. *Reflections* had, however, appeared in 1790 and it is hard not to believe that Burns was using the Hastings affair to assault the, for him, serpentine apostate. *The Dagger* is certainly the wittiest, perhaps the best, of the flood of anti-Burke poetry that *Reflections* provoked.

On John M'Murdo and Baillie Swan

First printed in *The Burns Chronicle*, 1932.

At the Election of Magistrates for Dumfries, 1794, John M'Murdo, Esq., was chosen Provost & a Mr Swan one of the Baillies; and at the entertainment usually given on the occasions, Burns, seeing the Provost's Supporters on the Bench, took his pencil & wrote the following:

> Baillie Swan, Baillie Swan,
> Let you do what you can,
> God ha' mercy on honest Dumfries:
> But e'er the year 's done,
> Good Lord! Provost John
> Will find that his *Swans* are but *Geese*.

The above introductory note is inscribed on the manuscript transcript, recording accurately that in September 1794 at the election of Magistrates for Dumfries, John M'Murdo was selected as Provost and James Swan, one of the Baillies. Witnessing their success, Burns wrote the above. Swan was elected a merchant councillor on 22nd September, 1794 and after his father's death was admitted a burgess and freeman of the town, then baillie on 29th September, 1794. He was re-elected to this post in September 1795, then 'retained on Council' in October 1796, but was voted off the council in 1797 (See *The Burns Chronicle*, 1932, 'Burns Epigrams', by Frederic Kent, pp. 19–23).

On Chloris
Requesting Me to Give Her a Sprig of a Sloe-Thorn in Full Blossom –

First printed in *The Edinburgh Advertiser*, 8th August, 1800.

From the white-blossom'd sloe, my dear Chloris requested
    A sprig, her fair breast to adorn:
No, by Heavens! I exclaim'd, let me perish for ever,
    Ere I plant in that bosom a *thorn*!

This is another anecdotal verse on Jean Lorimer (Chloris). The lines
were collected by Stewart in 1802 from the Edinburgh newspaper.
It has been rightly noted that these lines were erroneously attributed
to Charles Dibdin, an English contemporary of the poet who, after
the poet's death and the publication of these lines, took the original
and turned them into a longer lyric (See Kinsley Vol. III, p. 1464,
and Mackay, p. 534).

Craigieburn Wood
Tune: Craigieburn Wood
First printed in Thomson, 1799.

Sweet fa's the eve on Craigieburn,   falls
    And blythe awakes the morrow,
But a' the pride o' Spring's return
    Can yield me nocht but sorrow. —   nothing
5 I see the flowers and spreading trees,
    I hear the wild birds singing;
But what a weary wight can please,
    And Care his bosom is wringing. —

Fain, fain would I my griefs impart,
10   Yet dare na for your anger;   not
But secret love will break my heart,
    If I conceal it langer.   longer
If thou refuse to pity me;
    If thou shalt love anither;   another
15 When yon green leaves fade frae the tree, from
    Around my grave they'll wither. —

This was the poet's second attempt at writing this lyric, given that
the original composition of October 1794 was deemed by Thomson

to have sexual overtones in the chorus. Burns took the opportunity to rework his original and sent the above to Thomson on 15th January, 1795. The Henley and Henderson and Mackay editions spoil the final rhyme by substituting the English 'another' (rather than the Scots *anither*) which does not rhyme with 'wither'.

The Tree of Liberty

First printed in Chambers, 1838.

HEARD ye o' the Tree o' France,
 I watna, what 's the name o't;   don't know
Around it a' the patriots dance —
 Weel Europe kens the fame o't.   well, knows
5 It stands where ance the Bastile stood, once
 A prison built by kings, man,
When Superstition's hellish brood ─ΔΝΜΝ to R C clergy
 Kept France in leading-strings, man.

Upo' this tree there grows sic fruit,   upon, such
10 Its virtues a' can tell, man;   all
It raises man aboon the brute,   above
 It mak's him ken himsel, man.   know
Gif ance the peasant taste a bit,   if once
 He's greater than a lord, man,
15 And wi' the beggar shares a mite
 O' a' he can afford, man.

This fruit is worth a' Afric's wealth,
 To comfort us 'twas sent, man:
To gie the sweetest blush o' health,   give
20 And mak' us a' content, man.
It clears the een, it cheers the heart, eyes
 Mak's high and low guid friends, man; good
And he wha acts the traitor's part,   who
 It to perdition sends, man.

25 My blessings aye attend the chiel   always, fellow/man
 Wha pitied Gallia's slaves, man,   who, France's
And staw a branch, spite o' the Deil, stole
 Frae yont the western waves, man. from beyond
Fair Virtue water'd it wi' care,
30 And now she sees wi' pride, man,
How weel it buds and blossoms there, well
 Its branches spreading wide, man.

But vicious folk aye hate to see   always
    The works o' Virtue thrive, man;
35 The courtly vermin 's bann'd the tree,
    And grat to see it thrive, man;   wept
King Loui' thought to cut it down,
    When it was unco sma', man;   very small
For this the watchman crack'd his crown,
40   Cut aff his head and a', man.   off

A wicked crew syne, on a time,   once
    Did tak' a solemn aith, man,   take, oath
It ne'er should flourish to its prime,
    I wat they pledg'd their faith, man.   bet
45 Awa they gaed wi' mock parade,   away, went
    Like beagles hunting game, man,
But soon grew weary o' the trade,
    And wish'd they'd been at hame, man.   home

Fair Freedom, standing by the tree,
50   Her sons did loudly ca', man;   call
She sang a sang o' Liberty,   song
    Which pleas'd them ane and a', man.   one, all
By her inspir'd, the new-born race
    Soon drew the avenging steel, man;
55 The hirelings ran — her foes gied chase,   gave
    And bang'd the despot weel, man.   well

Let Britain boast her hardy oak,
    Her poplar, and her pine, man,
Auld Britain ance could crack her joke,   old, once
60   And o'er her neighbours shine, man.
But seek the forest round and round,
    And soon 'twill be agreed, man,
That sic a tree can not be found   such
    'Twixt London and the Tweed, man.

65 Without this tree, alake this life   alas
    Is but a vale o' woe, man;
A scene o' sorrow mix'd wi' strife,
    Nae real joys we know, man.   no
We labour soon, we labour late,
70   To feed the titled knave, man;
And a' the comfort we 're to get,
    Is that ayont the grave, man.   beyond

Wi' plenty o' sic trees, I trow,   such, pledge/trust
    The warld would live in peace, man;   world
75 The sword would help to mak' a plough,
    The din o' war wad cease, man.   would
Like brethren in a common cause,
    We'd on each other smile, man;
And equal rights and equal laws
80   Wad gladden every isle, man.   would

Wae worth the loon wha wadna eat   woe befall, fool who would not
    Sic halesome, dainty cheer, man;   such wholesome
I'd gie the shoon frae aff my feet,   give, shoes from off
    To taste sic fruit, I swear, man.   such
85 Syne let us pray, Auld England may   so, old
    Sure plant this far-famed tree, man;
And blythe we'll sing, and hail the day
    That gives us Liberty, man.

The Tree of Liberty appeared in 1838 with Dr Chambers' edition. In headnotes to the poem Chambers argues:

> It is far from likely that the whole democratic effusions of Burns have come down to us. For many years, that kind of authorship was attended with so much reproach, that men of humanity studied to conceal rather than to expose the evidence by which it could be proved against him [Burns]. And even after the poor bard's death, the interests of his young family demanded . . . that nothing should be brought forward which was calculated to excite a political jealousy regarding him. Hence, for many years there was a mystery observed on this subject. During that time, of course, many manuscripts might perish . . .

Dr Chambers was not likely to have been fooled by a forged manuscript, nor invent seeing one that did not exist. His work, still relied upon heavily by modern biographers, is generally robust, despite being top heavy with anecdotal reminiscence from anyone who knew Burns, a friend of Burns or the poet's family. There are no grounds to suspect that the manuscripts seen by Chambers was a forgery. It is thus peculiar that there should still be an ongoing debate over the authenticity of this political song, while many other songs without manuscript are readily accepted. The manuscript vanished or was destroyed during the nineteenth century.

Chambers estimated wrongly in 1838 when he remarked, 'As

things now stand . . . there can be no great objection to the pub-
lication of any piece of the kind which may have chanced to be
preserved' (p. 87). The grounds upon which the provenance of the
song have been questioned, at least originally, are not scholarly.
Scott Douglas blasted its sentiments, arguing that they:

> . . . are so crude and unreasonable, that we would *rejoice* to be
> informed, some of these days, that the *Mosesfield manuscript*, on
> being more closely examined, turns out to be not Burns'
> penmanship after all! (Vol. II, p. 404).

This comment proves the manuscript still extant in 1877. Almost
twenty years later, Henderson and Henley swept the poem aside by
stating it was 'trash' Burns did not write but gave no textually
analytic defence of their case.

It is quite probable that the hysterical reaction to this song stems
from the line about the King of France being exectuted, 'Cut aff his
heid an' a', man'. That Burns could be so casual about Louis' head
being chopped off is clear from his letter to Mrs Dunlop in January
1795:

> Entre nous, you know my Politics; & I cannot approve of the
> honest Doctor's whining over the deserved fate of a certain pair
> of Personages. – What is there in the delivering over a perjured
> Blockhead & an unprincipled Prostitute into the hands of the
> hangman, that it should arrest for a moment, attention, in an
> eventful hour, when, as my friend Roscoe in Liverpool glor-
> iously expresses it —
>
> > 'When the welfare of Millions is hung in the scale
> > And the balance yet trembles with fate'
>
> But our friend is already indebted to People in power . . . so I
> can apologise for him; for at bottom I am sure he is a staunch
> friend to Liberty' (Letter 649).

It is surprising that this letter, let alone the revolutionary song,
survived the censorial flames or scissors.

Influenced unduly by this nineteenth century legacy and appar-
ently mistaking politicial bias for literary expertise, Kinsley places
The Tree of Liberty in his Dubia section (K625). He, too, accepts
many works to the canon without extant mansuscript authority, but
not this revolutionary work. Kinsley, though, does not wholly reject
the song, but leaves its provenance open. On literary style he claims

the song does not truly sound like Burns: 'the manner here is less firmly and finally expressive and less richly vernacular than that of Burns when he is fully engaged' (Vol. III, p. 1528).

Is this valid? *Scots Wha Hae* is certainly Scottish in theme but it is far less so in language. In fact, taking up Kinsley's key point, it is a revealing contrast to discover that the final verse of *A Man's a Man* has only two Scots words. By such language criteria, readers should question the validity of many known works by Burns. The first verse of *The Dumfries Volunteers* contains one Scots word and the final verse contains no Scots words. If the number of Scots words occurring in *The Tree of Liberty* is compared to *The Dumfries Volunteers* and *A Man's a Man*, the result for the first four verses is:

	Tree of Liberty	A Man's a Man	The Dumfries Volunteers
Verse 1	5	2	1
Verse 2	8	4	6
Verse 3	8	5	7
Verse 4	10	6	0

The number of actual words per verse for these three songs is roughly the same. The score of Scots words for *A Man's a Man* is increased to a count of 8, 10, 11, and 10 for the first four verses if each occurrence of the repetitive 'a'' meaning *all*, as in 'a' that and a' that' is included. The highest scoring verse in all three songs is the final verse of *The Tree of Liberty* which contains thirteen Scots words. Kinsley's main objection to *The Tree of Liberty*, that it is not densely vernacular enough to be from Burns, is, therefore, invalid. Indeed, our comparison shows the opposite to be true.

The ratio of Scots-to-English words is, of course, varied throughout the canon and cannot be employed as criteria to determine provenance. A more important aspect of language which Kinsley might have examined is the appearance of parochial words and regional spellings employed during the 1790s among other Scots poets, in examining the question of whether another poet might have written this song. There is considerable evidence to show that contemporaries of Burns like Alexander Wilson of Paisley, generally employ parochial spellings and words never found in Burns. Wilson's works are peppered with such spellings. There is no trace of parochial spelling, or non-Burns dialect words within *The Tree of Liberty*. The poem displays a linguistic fluidity in changing from Scots to English and vice versa, precisely in the manner found in Burns.

There has been no investigation about the Mosesfield manuscript shown to Dr Chambers by Mr James Duncan. Who was the mysterious Mr Duncan who pops up in 1838 and then vanishes? Did Burns know anyone of that name? There is no James Duncan mentioned in the poet's letters, but a William Duncan comes out of the pages of the Burns story in a letter to Crawford Tait of Edinburgh, 15th October, 1790. Burns wrote of this young friend and courier of the letter to Tait:

> Allow me to introduce to your acquaintance the bearer, Mr Will[m] Duncan, a friend of mine whom I have long known & loved. – His father, whose only Son he is, has a decent little property in Ayrshire, & has bred the young man to the Law; in which department he comes up an adventurer to your Good Town (Letter 425).

There is another reference to William Duncan on 25th October, 1787 (Letter 146). It is, of course, purely speculative but it may be that the James Duncan who gave the manuscript to Dr Chambers was a relation, possibly the son of William Duncan.

Mackay accepts the poem into the canon but places its composition with chronological vagueness, declaring that it 'accords with Burns's Jacobin sympathies in 1792–3' (p. 478). This contradicts his public statements to national newspapers during early 1996 when he argued that Burns would not have written 'lost' radical poetry from the first week of January 1793 onwards, given his job in the Excise. But *The Tree of Liberty* refers specifically to the death of the French King in stanza 5, an event that did not occur until the end of January 1793, after the Excise enquiry into the poet's politics. So, Mackay should have argued that Burns did continue to write radical poetry after being chastised by his Excise employers.

Crawford suggests the possible date of composition for around the end of January 1795, when Burns writes of Dr John Moore's rather anti-Jacobin book on travelling through France. Crawford tellingly argues, 'it chimes in perfectly with his prose remarks about the execution of Louis XVI and Marie Antoinette, which so offended Mrs Dunlop' (Crawford, p. 246). The letter to Mrs Dunlop, quoted above, does mention the executions in a cold, matter-of-fact manner in the same way that the song almost shockingly, in a style of casual gossip tells of the King's death, 'Cut aff his head and a'', man'. *A Man's a Man*, written about this time, has many similarities with *The Tree of Liberty*. Both songs finish on a note of future optimism set in the form of a prayer: 'Then let us pray that come it may', and,

'Syne let us pray, auld England may /Sure plant this far-famed tree, man'. This lexical similarity in sentiment and style is surely no mere coincidence. Crawford is almost certainly correct that *The Tree of Liberty* was written around the same time as *A Man's a Man*. His view that the song is a far better work than some editors have suggested is surely right.

In fact, the poem is developed with considerable skill, in narrative and imagery. It is particularly expressive of the poet's developing views in mid-to-late 1794, that freedom in England was being crushed by the London government – trees of liberty are not to be found "twixt London and the Tweed'. This is put more forcibly in the *Ode for General Washington's Birthday*, where he condemns England for going to war against revolutionary France, then damns her for crushing the green shoots of liberty at home with a brutal tyrannical crackdown. Indeed, Crawford makes a very important point in discussing *The Tree of Liberty* when he writes, 'during the Scottish Reform Movement of the 1790s the Tree of Liberty became almost as much a Scottish symbol as the kilt, the lion, the thistle or the holly' (p. 246).

The current editors have completed a thorough investigation of late-eighteenth-century radical poetic voices in Scotland and have found no other appropriate candidate. It is a powerful reflective work looking back on the development of the French revolution and its influence from the American War of Independence (l. 28). It is written with a fluidity of language that moves from rich vernacular Scots to English passages with the ease so characteristic of Burns. Close linguistic scrutiny and contextual evidence suggests that the lack of an extant manuscript is not a bar to canonical acceptance. It is possible that, as some other political poems, *The Tree of Liberty* was published in the radical *Glasgow Advertiser*. Crucially, however, the copies of that newspaper for the years 1795–6 seem irretrievably lost.

Let Me in this ae Night –

Tune: Will Ye Lend Me Yer Loom Lass
First printed in Currie, 1800.

O lassie, are ye sleepin yet,	
Or art thou waukin, I wad wit,	waking, would bet
For Love has bound me hand and fit,	foot
And I would fain be in, jo. —	my dear

Chorus
5 O let me in this ae night,   one
      This ae, ae, ae night;
   For pity's sake this ae night,
      O rise and let me in, jo.   my dear

   Thou hear'st the winter wind an' weet,   wet
10 Nae star blinks thro' the driving sleet;   no
   Tak pity on my weary feet,
      And shield me frae the rain, jo. —   from
         O let me in &c.

   The bitter blast that round me blaws   · blows
   Unheeded howls, unheeded fa's;   falls
15 The cauldness o' thy heart's the cause   coldness
      Of a' my care and pine, jo. —   pining/distress
         O let me in &c.

HER ANSWER

   O tell na me o' wind an' rain,   not
   Upbraid na me wi' cauld disdain,   not, cold
20 Gae back the gate ye cam again,   go
      I winna let ye in, jo. —   will not

   Chorus
   I tell you now this ae night,   one
      This ae, ae, ae night,
   And ance for a' this ae night,   once, all
25   I winna let ye in, jo.   will not

   The snellest blast, at mirkest hours,   coldest, darkest
   That round the pathless wanderer pours,
   Is nocht to what poor She endures,   nothing
      That's trusted faithless Man, jo. —
         I tell you now &c.

30 The sweetest flower that deck'd the mead,
   Now trodden like the vilest weed —
   Let simple maid the lesson read,
      The weird may be her ain, jo. —   fate, own, my dear
         I tell you now &c.

The bird that charm'd his summer day,
35   And now the cruel Fowler's prey,
Let that to witless Woman say,
      The gratefu' heart of Man, jo. —
         I tell you now &c.

This lyric, based on a song in Herd's collection (1769), was sent to
Thomson in August 1793 but Burns was unhappy with the female
reply and tried his hand at improving it on two separate occasions,
eventually sending the final song in February 1795. Thomson
printed it in 1805.

From Esopus to Maria
or Fragment – Part Description of a Correction House
First printed, incomplete, by Cunningham, 1834.

From those drear solitudes and frowsy Cells,
Where Infamy with sad Repentance dwells;
Where Turnkeys make the jealous portal fast,
And deal from iron hands the spare repast;
5   Where truant 'prentices, yet young in sin,
Blush at the curious stranger peeping in;
Where strumpets, relics of the drunken roar,
Resolve to drink, nay half — to whore — no more;
Where tiny thieves, not destin'd yet to swing,
10 Beat hemp for others riper for the string:
From these dire scenes my wretched lines I date.
To tell Maria her Esopus' fate.

    'Alas! I feel I am no actor here!'
'Tis *real* Hangmen *real* scourges bear!
15 Prepare, Maria, for a horrid tale
Will turn thy very rouge to deadly pale;
Will make thy hair, tho' erst from gipsy poll'd,
By Barber woven and by Barber sold,
Though twisted smooth by Harry's nicest care,
20 Like hoary bristles to erect and stare!
The Hero of the mimic scene, no more
I start in Hamlet, in Othello roar;
Or, haughty Chieftain, 'mid the din of arms,
In Highland bonnet woo Malvina's charms;
25 While Sans Culottes stoop up the mountain high,
And steal me from Maria's prying eye.

Blest Highland bonnet! once my proudest dress,
Now, prouder still, Maria's temples press!
I see her wave thy towering plumes afar,
30 And call each coxcomb to the wordy war!
I see her face the first of Ireland's sons,
And even out-Irish his Hibernian bronze.
The crafty Colonel leaves the tartan'd lines
For other wars, where He a hero shines;
35 The hopeful youth, in Scottish Senate bred,
Who owns a Bushby's heart without the head,
Comes 'mid a string of coxcombs, to display
That Veni, vidi, vici, is his way — .

The shrinking Bard adown the alley skulks,
40 And dreads a meeting worse than Woolwich hulks,
Tho' there his heresies in Church and State
Might well award him Muir and Palmer's fate:
Still she, undaunted, reels and rattles on,
And dares the public like a noontide sun.

45 What scandal called Maria's janty stagger
The ricket reeling of a crooked swagger?
[What slander nam'd her seeming want of art
The flimsey wrapper of a rotten heart —].
Whose spleen (e'en worse than Burns's venom, when
50 He dips in gall unmix'd his eager pen,
And pours his vengeance in the burning line),
Who christen'd thus Maria's lyre-divine,
The idiot strum of Vanity bemus'd,
And even th' abuse of Poesy abus'd?
55 Who called her verse a Parish Workhouse, made
For motley foundling Fancies, stolen or strayed?

A Workhouse! ah, that sound awakes my woes,
And pillows on the thorn my rack'd repose!
In durance vile here must I wake and weep,
60 And all my frowzy Couch in sorrow steep:
That straw where many a rogue has lain of yore,
And vermin'd Gypseys litter'd heretofore.
Why, Lonsdale, thus thy wrath on vagrants pour?
Must Earth no Rascal save thyself endure?
65 Must thou alone in guilt immortal swell,
And make a vast Monopoly of Hell?

Thou know'st the Virtues cannot hate thee worse:
The Vices also, must *they* club their curse?
Or must no tiny sin to others fall,
70   Because thy guilt's supreme enough for all?

Maria, send me too thy griefs and cares,
In all of thee sure thy Esopus shares:
As thou at all mankind the flag unfurls,
Who on my fair one Satire's vengeance hurls!
75   Who calls thee, pert, affected, vain coquette,
A wit in folly, and a fool in wit!
Who says that Fool alone is not thy due,
And quotes thy treacheries to prove it true!
Our force united on thy foes we'll turn,
80   And dare the war with all of woman born:
For who can write and speak as thou and I?
My periods that decyphering defy,
And thy still matchless tongue that conquers all reply!

This partial parody of Pope's *Eloisa to Abelard* is written in the
voice of James Williamson (Esopus is a classic Roman actor)
who managed the Dumfries Theatre. Williamson and his crew
of players were acting in Whitehaven when a friend of the Earl
of Lonsdale (James Lowther, 1736–1802), after attending a play,
reported them to the Earl who summoned them and interrogated
each actor between 8 o'clock at night and 5 o'clock the next
morning. They were handcuffed and jailed in Penrith, supposedly
on a charge of vagrancy. From the newspaper clipping preserved
and apparently viewed by Henderson and Henley, it appears
to have been the content of the play that was reported to Lons-
dale and irritated him into taking legal action. (See Vol. II,
p. 353).
    Previous editors employ the text from a manuscript seen by
Cunningham in 1834 which has since vanished, presumed de-
stroyed. Henley and Henderson, who condemn the poem as 'inept
and unmanly', err in stating that the only authority for the poem
is the word of Cunningham (See Vol. II, p. 354). A much earlier
transcript in the hand of John Syme is preserved in the Hornel
Collection (See *The Burns Chronicle*, 1935, p. 33). The subtitle
now given is also new, taken from the Syme manuscript. Ll. 47–8
are not included by any previous editors, but they have been
restored to the poem from the transcript. They are a further slight
on Maria Riddell that may have been censored by Cunningham, if

he used an original manuscript (probably destroyed to conceal his censorship):

What slander nam'd her seeming want of art
The flimsy wrapper of a rotten heart —.

Textually, the Syme manuscript contains more words in capitals and in italics than the version of the poem normally printed in the bard's works, originating from Cunningham. This tends to reinforce the view that it represents a better and more accurate version of the poet's writing style, given his habit of employing capitals and italics throughout his verse. Cunningham was not a professional copyist and may have dropped the poet's emphasis on several occasions, so we have selected the text of the 1815 transcript made by Syme.

In one of his rare lapses of judgement, De Lancey Ferguson (*Modern Philology*, xxviii (1930), pp. 178–84) went to detailed lengths to prove this was not by Burns. Kinsley (p. 1471) very effectively denies this. One of the main points of Kinsley's case is that Ferguson did not know that, though there was no Burns holograph, there were three extant transcripts of which two denoted that the poem was by Burns.

In retrospect, it is hard to see how a case could be made against his authorship. There is not only the astonishing technical excellence of the opening (ll. 1–10); the pathologically jealous inner monologue he creates for James Williamson; the parody of Pope's poem of absolute sexual love, *Eloisa to Abelard* but in ll. 39–42 Burns's own appearance in the poem in the most *overt* lines he ever wrote about what his existence was like in Dumfries in the wake of the Sedition Trials. In these trials, it should be recalled, Braxfield had announced that since the constitution was perfect any proposals of change were, definably, made by enemies of the state.

The poem is not to be understood, however, without appreciation of the complex, passionate and tormented relationship between Burns and Maria Riddell. All his relationships with upper-class women were deeply problematic but Maria, creatively talented and radically inclined, was in a category of her own. She was Robert Riddell's sister-in-law. It is impossible to say whether her relationship to Burns was ever physical but, certainly on his side, it was profound. As he wrote to her in February 1792:

Yours by Mr Stoddart was the welcomest letter I ever received.
God grant that now when your health is reestablished, you may

take a little, little more care of a life so truly invaluable to your friends! As to your very very excellent epistle from a certain Capital of a certain Empire, I shall answer it in its own way sometime next week . . . Once more let me congratulate you on your returning health. God grant that you may live at least while I live, for were I to lose you it would leave a Vacuum in my enjoyments that nothing could fill up.

By April 1793, he is writing to her in terms of an intimacy which suggests not only a, at least, fantasised physical intimacy, but a political affinity. Sharing revolutionary sentiments, he promised, in a manner which exaggerates his own risk, to find her a pair of fashionable French gloves, despite such *enemy* products being prohibited. The mixture of the political and the erotic is obviously a heady brew for him as long as the only 'Satyr Man' familiar to Maria is himself. The fall out, which was eventually repaired between them, may have been the notorious 'Sabine incident' but the intensity of Burns's rage was not only thwarted sexuality but the difference between them in social class, which allowed Maria not sexual but political freedom. As ll. 43–4 suggest she has a freedom to speak politically quite denied to him.

How he deals with Maria's withdrawal of affection in this poem is, however, to locate his dislike for Maria not in himself but in the unfortunate James Williamson into whose pathologically inflamed consciousness we enter. His role as actor-director also allows Burns to play throughout with images of theatre versus reality. Thus we have not only Maria being made up by Harry, her servant (ll. 16–20) but the fact that Williamson cannot keep Maria focused on him on stage as her promiscuous eye is diverted from him as Highland hero to the kilted but breechless members of the cast. This nakedness they share with the *Sans Culottes* of the French Revolution so that implicit in Maria's politics is an element of rough trading. He also lists the alleged suitors besieging Maria at Woodley Park. The Irishman in ll. 31–2 is Captain Gillespie. Though the text gives 'bronze', 'brogue' makes much more sense because what Williamson is most jealous about is his loss of *verbal* intercourse with Maria. Even more than her appearance, her writing skills are attacked; she is a protean, derivative mimic who absorbs he language of her male admirers the better to plagiarise it. Colonel McDoual (l. 33–4) of Logan was a noted womaniser. Maitland Bushby (ll. 35–6) was sheriff of Wigtown.

In ll. 56–70 we return to the scene of Williamson's incarceration by James Lowther (1736–1802), Earl of Lonsdale who, Kinsley tells us, was 'more detested than any man alive, as a shameless political sharper, a domestic bashaw, and an intolerable tyrant over his tenants and dependents. . . . Robert Adam told me many stories of him, which made me conclude that he was truly a madman, though too rich to be confined' (Alexander Carlyle, *Autobiography*, 1910 edn, pp. 438–9). The kind of aristocrat Burns loved to hate, it was, ironically, the very man Boswell's sycophantic Anglophilia wretchedly got him into service with.

Prophetic of Burns's own relationship with Maria, the concluding (ll. 71–83) part of the poem calls for reconciliation and a return to their old linguistic alliance. Writing to Smellie (Letter 492) Burns described Maria Riddell as having 'one unlucky failing . . . where she dislikes, or despises, she is apt to make no more secret of it— than where she esteems or respects'. He might envy her freedom but, finally, he could not deny her talent nor withhold his admiration. Her own memoir of Burns (see Kinsley pp. 1545–7) confirms the rightness of, at least, his literary judgement.

On Miss Jean Scott

First printed in Stewart, Glasgow, 1801.

OH! had each SCOT of ancient times
    Been, JEANY SCOTT, as thou art,
The bravest heart on English ground
    Had yielded like a coward. —

The heroine here is still unknown. Kinsley picks up on the Chambers anecdote that it was based on Miss Jean Scott of Ecclefechan, daughter of the local postmaster (Chambers, Vol. IV, p. 193). Some editions print the title as *On Miss Jean Scott of Ayr*.

I'll Ay Ca' in by Yon Town

Tune: We'll Gang Nae Mair to Yon Town
First printed in Johnson, December 1796.

There's nane sall ken, there's nane sall guess,	none shall know
What brings me back the gate again,	journey
But she, my fairest faithfu' lass,	
And stownlins we sall meet again. —	secretly

Chorus:
5 I'll ay ca' in by yon town,   always call, that
   And by yon garden green, again;
 I'll ay ca' in by yon town,
   And see my bonie Jean again. —

 She'll wander by the aiken tree,   oak
10   When trystin time draws near again; meeting/cattle fair
 And when her lovely form I see,
   O haith, she's doubly dear again! a private oath

This is given as Burns's work because of the Hastie manuscript sent to Johnson, although it was printed without the poet's signature which usually indicates that it was either a traditional song or one he slightly updated.

On Chloris Being Ill

Tune: Ay Waukin O
First printed in Currie, 1800.

Can I cease to care,
  Can I cease to languish,
While my darling Fair
  Is on the couch of anguish. —

Chorus
5 Long, long the night,
  Heavy comes the morrow,
While my soul's delight
  Is on her bed of sorrow. —

 Ev'ry hope is fled;
10 Ev'ry fear is terror;
 Slumber even I dread,
  Ev'ry dream is horror. —
    Long, long the night, &c.

Hear me, Powers Divine!
  Oh, in pity, hear me!
15 Take aught else of mine,
  But my Chloris spare me!
    Long, long the night, &c.

Chloris (Jean Lorimer) is, once again, the heroine of this work.
Burns sent a copy to Thomson in April 1795, having already sent a
version to Maria Riddell in March when their friendship appears to
have been somewhat repaired. Thomson printed it in 1801.

Elegy on Mr. William Cruikshank, A.M.

First printed in Hogg and Motherwell, 1834.

Now honest William's gaen to Heaven,	gone
I wat na gin't can mend him:	don't know if it
The fauts he had in Latin lay,	faults
For nane in English kend them.	— none, knew

William Cruikshank died in early 1795. Burns met him through
either Robert Ainslie (both came from Duns) or William Nicol.
Cruikshank was a colleague of Nicol at the Edinburgh High School
where both men taught classics. Burns wrote *The Rosebud* for
Cruikshank's daughter.

Address to the Woodlark –

Tune: Loch Erroch side
First printed in Thomson, 1798.

O stay, sweet warbling wood lark stay,
Nor quit for me the trembling spray,
A hapless lover courts thy lay,
    Thy soothing, fond complaining. —

5 Again, again that tender part,	
That I may catch thy melting art;	
For surely that wad touch her heart	would
Wha kills me wi' disdaining.—	who

Say, was thy little mate unkind,	
10 And heard thee as the careless wind?	
Oh, nocht but love and sorrow join'd,	nothing
Sic notes o' woe could wauken!	such, waken

Thou tells o' never-ending care;
O' speechless grief, and dark despair:
15 For pity's sake, sweet bird, nae mair!   no more
Or my poor heart is broken!

On the Adam manuscript, a note states that the poet's son James Glencairn Burns claimed his father wrote this song at the request of Mrs John McMurdo. An early variant is recorded in Scott Douglas's Edinburgh edition, titled *Song Composed on Hearing a Bird Sing While Musing on Chloris*, allegedly taken from a pencil manuscript by Burns then in private hands.

Their Groves o' Sweet Myrtle

Tune: Humours of Glen
First printed in *The London Star*, 22nd December, 1796.

THEIR groves o' sweet myrtle let Foreign Lands reckon,
    Where bright-beaming summers exalt the perfume,
Far dearer to me yon lone glen o' green breckan   bracken
    Wi' th' burn stealing under the lang, yellow broom: long
5 Far dearer to me are yon humble broom bowers,
    Where the blue-bell and gowan lurk, lowly, unseen;
For there, lightly tripping among the wild flowers,
    A list'ning the linnet, aft wanders my JEAN.   oft

Tho' rich is the breeze in their gay, sunny vallies,
10   And cauld, CALEDONIA'S blast on the wave;   cold
Their sweet-scented woodlands that skirt the proud palace,
    What are they? The haunt o' the TYRANT and SLAVE.
The SLAVE'S spicy forests, and gold-bubbling fountains
    The brave CALEDONIAN views wi' disdain;
15 He wanders as free as the winds of his mountains,
    Save LOVE'S willing fetters, the chains o' his JEAN.

This twin eulogy of love and patriotism, to Mrs Jean Burns and to Caledonia was sent to Thomson in April 1795. It was published by him in 1799 to one of the poet's favourite melodies, *The Humours of Glen*. It was copied by *The Morning Chronicle* on 24th December, 1796, then *Edinburgh Magazine* in May, 1797, followed by the *Scots Magazine*, June 1797.

'Twas Na Her Bonie Blue E'e

Tune: Laddie Lie Near Me
First printed in Currie, 1800.

'Twas na her bonie blue e'e was my ruin;   <small>not, eye</small>
Fair tho' she be, that was ne'er my undoing:
'Twas the dear smile when naebody did mind us,   <small>nobody</small>
'Twas the bewitching, sweet, stown glance o' kindness.   <small>stolen</small>

5   Sair do I fear that to hope is denied me,   <small>sore</small>
Sair do I fear that despair maun abide me;   <small>sore, must stay</small>
But tho' fell Fortune should fate us to sever,
Queen shall she be in my bosom for ever.

Chloris I'm thine wi' a passion sincerest,
10 And thou hast plighted me love o' the dearest!
And thou 'rt the angel that never can alter,
Sooner the Sun in his motion would falter. —

This was sent to Thomson in April 1795 when the song collector requested that Burns provide lyrics to the tune *Laddie Lie Near Me*. Thomson never printed them.

How Cruel are the Parents

Tune: John Anderson My Jo
First printed in Thomson, 1799.

How cruel are the Parents
    Who riches only prize,
And to the wealthy booby
    Poor Woman sacrifice:
5   Meanwhile the hapless Daughter
    Has but a choice of strife;
To shun a tyrant Father's hate
    Become a wretched Wife. —

The ravening hawk pursuing,
10   The trembling dove thus flies,
To shun impending ruin
    Awhile her pinion tries;

Till of escape despairing,
  No shelter or retreat,
15 She trusts the ruthless Falconer
  And drops beneath his feet. —

This was, as the poet indicates in his first draft title: 'Altered from an Old English Song'. It was sent to Thomson on 9th May, 1795. It is only partly reworked from the traditional lyric.

Mark Yonder Pomp

Tune: Deil Tak the Wars
First printed in Currie, 1800.

MARK yonder pomp of costly fashion,
  Round the wealthy, titled bride:
But when compar'd with real passion,
  Poor is all that princely pride.
5   What are the showy treasures,
      What are the noisy pleasures,
The gay, gaudy glare of vanity and art:
      The polish'd jewel's blaze
      May draw the wond'ring gaze,
10   And courtly grandeur bright
      The fancy may delight,
But never, never can come near the heart. —

But did you see my dearest Chloris
  In simplicity's array;
15 Lovely as yonder sweet opening flower is,
  Shrinking from the gaze of day.
      O then, the heart alarming,
      And all resistless charming,
In Love's delightful fetters, she chains the willing soul!
20   Ambition would disown
      Th' world's imperial crown,
      Even Av'rice would deny
      His worshipp'd deity,
And feel thro' every vein love's raptures roll.

This was sent to Thomson in May 1795. Although Chloris (Jean Lorimer) is mentioned, her name is mere cover for the contrast of 'natural' feelings of love and passion, untainted by what Burns saw as the more artificial world of the aristocratic fiscally-arranged marriage, then increasingly in vogue.

Address to the Toothache
Written by the Author when he was grievously tormented by that Disorder.

First printed in *The Belfast Newsletter*, 11th September, 1797.

MY curse on your envenom'd stang,   sting
That shoots my tortur'd gooms alang,   gums along
An' thro' my lugs gies mony a bang   ears give, pain
  Wi' gnawin vengeance,
5 Tearing my nerves wi' bitter twang,   twinge
  Like racking engines.

A' down my beard the slavers trickle,   saliva
I cast the wee stools o'er the meikle,   small, largest
While round the fire the hav'rels keckle, idiots cackle
10 To see me loup;   jump
I curse an' ban, an' wish a heckle   flax-comb
  Were i' their doup.   backsides

Whan fevers burn, or ague freeze,   when
Rheumatics gnaw, or colic squeeze us,
15 Our neebors sympathise, to ease us,   neighbours
  Wi' pitying moan;
But thou — the hell o' a' diseases,
  They mock our groan.

O' a' the num'rous human dools,   woes
20 Ill-hairsts, daft bargains, *cutty-stools*, bad harvests, public shaming
Or worthy frien's laid i' the mools,   earth
  Sad sight to see!
The tricks o' knaves, or fash o' fools,   annoyance
  Thou bear'st the gree.   wins the prize

25 Whare'er that place be, priests ca' Hell,	*wherever*
Whare a' the tones o' misery yell,	*where*
An' plagues in ranked number tell	
In deadly raw,	*row*
Thou, *Tooth-ache*, surely bear'st the bell	
30 Aboon them a'!	*above*
O! thou grim, mischief-making chiel,	*chap/fellow*
That gars the notes o' discord squeel,	*makes*
Till human-kind aft dance a reel	*often*
In gore a shoe thick,	*blood*
35 Gie a' the faes o' Scotland's weal	*give all, foes*
A TOWMOND'S TOOTHACHE!	*year's*

This work is undated, but its composition probably coincides with the poet's letter of May 1795 where he describes suffering from an awful toothache in the following manner, that 'fifty troops of infernal Spirits are riding post from ear to ear along my jaw-bones' (Letter 671). This appeared first in the *Belfast Newsletter*, then a few days later, in *The Morning Chronicle*, 19th September, 1797. Burns had an avid, largely for political reasons, Ulster audience.

Forlorn My Love

Tune: Let Me in this ae Night
First printed in Currie, 1800.

FORLORN my Love, no comfort near,
Far, far from thee I wander here;
Far, far from thee, the fate severe
    At which I most repine, Love. —

Chorus
5 O wert thou, Love, but near me,
But near, near, near me;
How kindly thou wouldst chear me,
    And mingle sighs with mine, Love. —

Around me scowls a wintry sky,
10 Blasting each bud of hope and joy;
And shelter, shade, nor home have I,
    Save in these arms of thine, Love. —
        O wert thou, &c.

Cold, alter'd friends with cruel art
Poisoning fell Fortune's dart; —
15   Let me not break thy faithful heart,
           And say that fate is mine, Love. —
                O wert thou, &c.

But, dreary tho' the moments fleet,
O let me think we yet shall meet!
That only ray of solace sweet
20   Can on thy Chloris shine, Love. —
                O wert thou, &c.

This was first sent to Thomson in June 1795 (Letter 672) but
updated in early August that year (Letter 676). It was eventually
printed by Thomson in 1805. Chloris, again, refers to Jean Lorimer.

Now Spring has Clad the Grove in Green
Tune: Auld Lang Syne or The Hopeless Lover
First printed in Thomson, 1799.

Now Spring has clad the grove in green,   clothed
      And strew'd the lea wi' flowers: meadow
The furrow'd waving corn is seen
      Rejoice in fostering showers.
5   While ilka thing in Nature join   every
      Their sorrows to forego,
O why thus all alone are mine
      The weary steps o' woe. —

The trout within yon wimpling burn
10   That glides, a silver dart,
And, safe beneath the shady thorn
      Defies the angler's art:
My life was ance that careless stream,   once
      That wanton trout was I;
15   But Love wi' unrelenting beam
      Has scorch'd my fountains dry. —

The little floweret's peaceful lot
      In yonder cliff that grows,
Which save the linnet's flight, I wot,   thrush's, guess
20   Nae ruder visit knows,   no

Was mine; till Love has o'er me past,
    And blighted a' my bloom,   all
And now beneath the withering blast
    My youth and joy consume. —

25 The waken'd lav'rock warbling springs   lark
    And climbs the early sky,
Winnowing blythe his dewy wings
    In Morning's rosy eye;
As little reckt I sorrow's power,   heeded
30   Until the flowery snare
O' witching Love, in luckless hour,
    Made me the thrall o' care. —

O had my fate been Greenland snows,
    Or Afric's burning zone,
35 Wi' Man and Nature leagu'd my foes,
    So Peggy ne'er I'd known!
The wretch, whose doom is, hope nae mair,   no more
    What tongue his woes can tell;
Within whose bosom save Despair
40   Nae kinder spirits dwell. —   no

Burns sent the first sketch of this song to Maria Riddell, planning to 'interweave' the lines in the tale of a 'Shepherd, despairing beside a clear stream' (Letter 677). He sent it to Thomson in August 1795 (Letter 675).

The Braw Wooer

Tune: The Lothian Lassie
First printed in Thomson, 1799.

LAST May a braw wooer cam down the lang glen,   fine, came, long
And sair wi' his love he did deave me;   sore, deafen
I said there was naething I hated like men,   nothing
The deuce gae wi'm, to believe me, believe me,   go with him
5   The deuce gae wi'm, to believe me.

He spak o' the darts in my bonie black een,   spoke, eyes
And vow'd for my love he was dying;
I said, he might die when he liket for JEAN —
The Lord forgie me for lying, for lying,   forgive
10   The Lord forgie me for lying!

A weel-stocket mailen, himsel for the laird,   well-stocked farm
And marriage aff-hand, were his proffers: off-, proposals
I never loot on that I kenn'd it, or car'd,   let, knew
But thought I might hae waur offers, waur offers,   have worse
15   But thought I might hae waur offers.

But what wad ye think? In a fortnight or less,   would
The Deil tak his taste to gae near her!   go
He up the lang loan to my black cousin, Bess!   Long [Lowther hills]
Guess ye how, the jad! I could bear her, could bear her,   hussy
20   Guess ye how, the jad! I could bear her.

But a' the niest week as I fretted wi' care,   next
I gaed to the tryste o' Dalgarnock,   went, cattle fair
And wha but my fine, fickle lover was there,   who
I glowr'd as I'd seen a warlock, a warlock,   stared, wizard
25   I glowr'd as I'd seen a warlock.

But owre my left shouther I gae him a blink,   over, gave, look
Lest neebours might say I was saucy: neighbours
My wooer he caper'd as he'd been in drink,   drunk
And vow'd I was his dear lassie, dear lassie,
30   And vow'd I was his dear lassie.

I spier'd for my cousin fu' couthy and sweet,   asked after, friendly
Gin she had recover'd her hearin,   if
And how her new shoon fit her auld shackl't feet;   shoes, old shackled
But, heavens! how he fell a swearin, a swearin,
35   But, heavens! how he fell a swearin.

He begged, for Gudesake! I wad be his wife,   goodness, would
Or else I wad kill him wi' sorrow: would
So e'en to preserve the poor body in life,   even/just
I think I maun wed him tomorrow, tomorrow,   shall
40   I think I maun wed him tomorrow. —

This was sent to Thomson on 3rd July, 1795 (Letter 673). The poet
gave a copy to David Staig, Provost of Dumfries. Kinsley makes a
brief comment on the song, then quotes from Thomas Crawford
(p. 300), 'This is one of Burns's best genre-songs; expressing "the
interplay of character, motif and mask . . . with ruthless econo-
my"' (Vol. III, p. 1484). Mackay, characteristically, lifts both
Kinsley's remark and that of Crawford without indicating his

source, '. . . it is one of Burns's best genre song[s], expressing "the inter-play of character, motif and mask . . . with ruthless economy"' (p. 555).

Why, Tell Thy Lover
Tune: The Caledonian Hunt's Delight
First printed in Currie, 1800.

WHY, why tell thy lover,
    Bliss he never must enjoy;
Why, why undeceive him,
    And give all his hopes the lie?

O why, while Fancy, raptured, slumbers,
    Chloris, Chloris, all the theme,
Why, why would'st thou cruel
    Wake thy lover from his dream.

This song, again on Chloris (Jean Lorimer), was sent to Thomson on 3rd July, 1795. The poet admitted that he found it difficult to write additional verses to the music (Letter 673).

Poetical Inscription for an Altar of Independence
At Kerroughtrie, the Seat of Mr. Heron, Summer, 1795
First printed in Currie, 1800.

Thou, of an independent mind
With soul resolv'd, with soul resign'd;
Prepar'd Power's proudest frown to brave,
Who wilt not be, nor have a slave;
Virtue alone who dost revere,
Thy own reproach alone dost fear,
Approach this shrine, and worship here. —

On Patrick Heron, see notes to *The Heron Ballads*. Burns visited Heron's country house at Kirroughtrie in 1794, on his second tour of Galloway. The fact that these lines were written in the summer of 1795 suggests Burns may have visited Heron again that year, but there is no documented evidence to support this. Lines for an altar to 'Independence', dedicated to those who would face up to and confront 'Power's proudest frown to brave', are apt proof of the poet's continued radical commitment. Patrick Heron, more a career politician, erected no such altar.

To Chloris

First printed in Currie, 1800.

Written on the blank leaf of a copy of the last edition of my poems, presented to the lady whom, in so many fictitious reveries of passion, but with the most ardent sentiments of real friendship, I have so often sung under the name of – CHLORIS—.

'Tis Friendship's pledge, my young, fair FRIEND,
    Nor thou the gift refuse,
Nor with unwilling ear attend
    The moralising Muse.

5   Since thou, in all thy youth and charms,
    Must bid the world adieu,
(A world 'gainst Peace in constant arms)
    To join the Friendly Few:

Since, thy gay morn of life o'ercast,
10   Chill came the tempest's lour;
(And ne'er Misfortune's eastern blast
    Did nip a fairer flower:)

Since life's gay scenes must charm no more;
    Still much is left behind,
15 Still nobler wealth hast thou in store,
    THE COMFORTS OF THE MIND!

Thine is the self-approving glow,
    Of conscious Honor's part;
And (dearest gift of Heaven below)
20   Thine Friendship's truest heart.

The joys refin'd of Sense and Taste,
    With every Muse to rove:
And doubly were the Poet blest
    These joys could he improve. —

This was sent to Thomson on 3rd August, 1795. Chloris was, of course, the poetic name Burns employed for Jean Lorimer. The poet's own notes printed above explain the personal element of the song. L. 7, however, has a distinct political edge.

O This is No My Ain Lassie

Tune: This is no My Ain House.
First printed in Thomson, 1799.

I see a form, I see a face,
Ye weel may wi' the fairest place: well
It wants, to me, the witching grace,
　　The kind love that's in her e'e.   eye

Chorus
5　O this is no my ain lassie,   own
　　Fair tho' the lassie be:
Weel ken I my ain lassie,   well know
　　Kind love is in her e'e.

She's bonie, blooming, straight, and tall;
10　And lang has had my heart in thrall;   long
And ay it charms my very saul,   always, soul
　　The kind love that's in the e'e.
　　　O this is no &c.

A thief sae pawkie is my Jean   so sly
To steal a blink, by a' unseen;   glance
15　But gleg as light are lover's een,   bright, eyes
　　When kind love is in the e'e.
　　　O this is no &c.

It may escape the courtly sparks,
It may escape the learned clerks;
But well the watching lover marks
20　　The kind love that's in her e'e.
　　　O this is no &c.

This was sent to Thomson on 3rd August, 1795. Burns had known the melody for a few years and planned to write lyrics to it.

Yon Rosy Brier

Tune: I Wish My Love Was in A Mire
First printed in Currie, 1800.

O BONIE was yon rosy brier,
  That blooms sae far frae haunt o' man; <small>so, from</small>
And bonie she, and ah, how dear!
  It shaded frae the e'enin sun. — <small>from</small>

Yon rosebuds in the morning dew
  How pure among the leaves sae green; <small>so</small>
But purer was the lover's vow
  They witnessed in their shade yestreen. — <small>yesterday evening</small>

All in its rude and prickly bower
  That crimson rose how sweet and fair;
But love is far a sweeter flower
  Amid life's thorny path o' care. —

The pathless wild, and wimpling burn, <small>meandering</small>
  Wi' Chloris in my arms, be mine;
And I the warld nor wish nor scorn, <small>world</small>
  Its joys and griefs alike resign.—

This was sent to Thomson in August 1795 but he did not print it
until 1801.

Wat Ye Wha that Lo'es Me

Tune: Morag
First printed in Thomson, 1799.

O wat ye wha that lo'es me, <small>know, who, loves</small>
  And has my heart a keeping?
O sweet is she that lo'es me, <small>loves</small>
  As dews o' summer weeping,
5 In tears the rosebuds steeping. —

Chorus
O that's the lassie o' my heart,
  My lassie, ever dearer;
O that's the queen o' womankind,
  And ne'er a ane to peer her. — <small>one, equal</small>

10	If thou shalt meet a lassie	
	In grace and beauty charming,	
	That e'en thy chosen lassie,	even
	Erewhile thy breast sae warming,	so
	Had ne'er sic powers alarming. —	such
	O that's the lassie &c.	

15 If thou hadst heard her talking,
        And thy attention's plighted,
    That ilka body talking   every
        But her, by thee is slighted;
        And thou art all-delighted. —
            O that's the lassie &c.

20 If thou hast met this Fair One,
        When frae her thou hast parted,   from
    If every other Fair One,
        But her thou hast deserted,
        And thou art broken hearted. —
            O that's the lassie &c.

Burns sent a copy of this work to Robert Cleghorn in June 1796. He told Cleghorn he might have sent it 'long ago' had he not been the 'child of disaster' (Letter 687). The poet's health had suffered and, to make things worse, he lost his only living daughter Elizabeth Riddell Burns in September 1795.

To John Syme
On Refusing to Dine with Him, 17th Dec. 1795
First printed in Currie, 1800.

No more of your guests, be they titled or not,
And cook'ry the first in the nation:
Who is proof to thy personal converse and wit,
Is proof to all other temptation. —

John Syme (1755–1831) was a son of a Writer to the Signet and joined the army at 19 years. He lived at Barncailzie, near Kirkcudbright and became Distributor of Stamps for Dumfriesshire in 1791. After moving from Ellisland to Dumfries Burns lived above Syme's office before moving to a larger house at the Mill Hole Brae (now Burns Street). Syme largely shared and was sympathetic to the poet's radical views, but appears to have been more decorously circumspect of political radicalism during the oppressive mid-1790s than Burns.

To John Syme
With a Present of a Dozen of Porter
First printed in Currie, 1800.

O had the malt thy strength of mind,
    Or hops the flavour of thy wit;
'Twere drink for first of human kind —
    A gift that ev'n for Syme were fit.

Jerusalem Tavern, Dumfries

For notes on Syme, see *To John Syme, On Refusing to Dine with Him.*

On Mr. Pitt's Hair-Powder Tax
First printed in Barke, 1955.

PRAY Billy Pitt explain thy rigs,
    This new poll-tax of thine!
'I mean to mark the GUINEA PIGS
    From other common SWINE'.

Within four lines and by question and response of two couplets, Burns neatly yokes together two of the radicals most hated items, Pitt's increased taxation and Burke's remark about the 'Swinish multitude'. The 1795 hair-powder tax was charged at one Guinea. White corn flour was used, especially by the upper classes, to powder wigs. The tax was an attempt to raise money and curb the use of corn flour at a period when their were food shortages and regional famine there (See *The Cob-Web*). Dr John Walcot (Peter Pindar), of whom Kinsley is so dismissive, wrote a fine satirical piece on this same subject, called *Hair-Powder*:

'Lo, the poor Girl whom carrot-colour shocks,
Pines pennyless, and blushes for her Locks!'
Refused to fly to Powder's friendly aid,
She bids them seek in Caps the secret shade.
No ringlets now around her neck to wave,
Colleen must *hide* the reddening shame, or *shave*.
At thee she flings her curses, Pitt, and cries;
At thee she darts the Lightnings of her Eyes;
And thinks that Love ne'er warm'd *him* who could vex
With wanton strokes of cruelty, the Sex.

The Solemn League and Covenant

First printed in Cunningham, 1834.

The Solemn League and Covenant
   Now brings a smile, now brings a tear.
But sacred Freedom, too, was theirs:
   If thou'rt a slave, indulge thy sneer.

These lines were inscribed by Burns in a copy of Sir John Sinclair's *The Statistical Account for Scotland* 1794 [probably the Dumfries-shire volume], relating to the Covenanters killed in 1685. Cunningham's text is not the exact version. It was first printed verbatim in 1870 by McDowell in his excellent small book, *Burns in Dumfriesshire*. It perfectly catches Burns's ambivalence to his own Presbyterian inheritance.

The Bob o' Dumblane

First printed in Barke, 1955.

LASSIE, lend me your braw hemp-heckle,	fine flax comb
And I'll lend you my thripplin kame:	separating comb
My heckle is broken, it canna be gotten,	comb, cannot
And we'll gae dance the Bob o' Dumblane. —	go
Twa gaed to the wood, to the wood, to the wood,	two went
Twa gaed to the wood, three cam hame:	home
An 't be na weel bobbit, weel bobbit, weel bobbit,	if it were/not well
An 't be na weel bobbit, we'll bob it again. —	

This is a traditional song adapted by Burns. The first two lines are taken from Ramsay's version of *The Bob o' Dumblane*, which is a song about a dance of the same name. With Burns the song takes on a sexual dimension. Although he did not print it, it was sent to Johnson in the late Autumn of 1795.

To Collector Mitchell
Addressed to Mr Mitchell, Collector of Excise, Dumfries
First printed in Currie, 1800.

	FRIEND o' the Poet, tried and leal,	loyal
	Wha, wanting thee, might beg, or steal:	who, lacking
	Alake! Alake! the meikle Deil	alas, great Devil
	Wi' a' his witches	
5	Are at it, skelpin jig an' reel	slapping
	In my poor pouches.	pockets

	Fu' fain I, modestly wad hint it,	right well would
	That ONE POUND, ONE, I sairly want it;	sorely miss
	If wi' the hizzie down ye sent it,	maid, you
10	It would be kind;	
	And while my heart wi' life-blood dunted,	beat
	I'd bear't in mind.	

	So may the AULD YEAR gang out moanin,	old, go
	To see the NEW come, laden, groanin,	
15	Wi' double plenty, o'er the loanin,	pasture
	To THEE and THINE;	
	DOMESTIC PEACE and COMFORT crownin	
	The hale DESIGN.	whole

Hogmanai eve: 1795

POSTSCRIPT

	Ye've heard this while how I've been licket,	beaten
	And by fell Death 'maist nearly nicket;	taken
	Grim loon! he got me by the fecket,	fool, jacket
	And sair he sheuk;	sore, shook
5	But by gude luck, I lap a wicket,	good, leapt thro' a gap
	And turn'd a neuk.	corner

	But by that HEALTH, I've got a share o't!	
	And by that LIFE, I'm promis'd mair o't!	more
	My hale and weel, I'll tak a care o't	health, welfare
10	A tentier way:	more careful
	Then fareweel, Folly, hilt and hair o't,	every bit of it
	For ance and ay!	once, always

John Mitchell (1731–1806) was appointed Collector of Excise in
Dumfries in 1788, having worked in Kilmarnock and Fraserburgh.
Burns was introduced to him in 1789. He and Burns became close
friends and the poet often sent him first drafts of his songs.

A Lass wi' a Tocher

Tune: Balinamona Ora
First printed in Thomson, 1799.

Awa wi' your witchcraft o' Beauty's alarms,   away
The slender bit beauty you grasp in your arms:
O, gie me the lass that has acres o' charms,   give
O, gie me the lass wi' the weel-stockit farms.   well stocked

Chorus
5   Then hey, for a lass wi' a tocher,   dowry
Then hey, for a lass wi' a tocher,
Then hey, for a lass wi' a tocher;
The nice yellow guineas for me.

Your Beauty's a flower in the morning that blows,
10 And withers the faster the faster it grows;
But the rapturous charm o' the bonie green knowes,   hill ridges
Ilk spring they're new deckit wi' bonie white yowes.   each, decked, ewes
Then hey, for a lass &c.

And e'en when this Beauty your bosom has blest,   even
The brightest o' Beauty may cloy, when possesst;
15 But the sweet yellow darlings wi' Geordie imprest,   gold coins
The langer ye hae them,— the mair they're carest!   longer, have, more
Then hey, for a lass &c.

Burns wrote these lyrics, as he told Thomson 'to another Hibernian
melody I admire' (Letter 689). Uncharacteristic of Burns's songs,
this is an assertion of triumphant masculine materialism.

To Colonel De Peyster

Or Poem on Life – Dumfries, 1796
First printed in Currie, 1800.

MY honor'd colonel, deep I feel
Your interest in the Poet's weal;   welfare
Ah! now sma' heart hae I to speel   have, climb
The steep Parnassus,
5   Surrounded thus by bolus pill,   large pill
And potion glasses.

O what a canty warld were it,   jolly world
Would pain and care, and sickness spare it;

And Fortune favor worth and merit,
10 As they deserve:
 (And aye a rowth, roast beef and claret;   always plenty
  Syne, wha wad starve?)   then, who would

Dame Life, tho' fiction out may trick her,
And in paste gems and frippery deck her;
15 Oh! flickering, feeble, and unsicker   uncertain
  I've found her still,
 Ay wavering like the willow wicker,   branch
  'Tween good and ill.

Then that curst carmagnole, auld Satan, rascal, old
20 Watches, like bawdrons by a rattan,   pussy, rat
 Our sinfu' saul to get a claute on   soul, grip
  Wi' felon ire;
 Syne, whip! his tail ye'll ne'er cast saut on, salt
  He's aff like fire.   off/away

25 Ah! Nick, ah Nick it is na fair,   The Devil, not
 First shewing us the tempting ware,
 Bright wines and bonie lasses rare,
  To put us daft;
 Syne weave, unseen, thy spider snare then
30 O' Hell's damned waft.   web

Poor man the flie, aft bizzes bye,   often buzzes
And aft as chance he comes thee nigh,
Thy auld damned elbow yeuks wi' joy, old, itches
  And hellish pleasure;
35 Already in thy fancy's eye,
  Thy sicker treasure.   certain

Soon heels o'er gowdie! in he gangs, head over heels, goes
And, like a sheep-head on a tangs,   burning tongs
Thy girnin laugh enjoys his pangs   snarling
40 And murdering wrestle,
As dangling in the wind he hangs
  A gibbet's tassel.

But lest you think I am uncivil,
To plague you with this draunting drivel, droning
45 Abjuring a' intentions evil,
  I quat my pen: quit
 The Lord preserve us frae the Devil! from
  Amen! Amen!

Colonel Arentz Schuyler De Peyster was an American-born soldier serving in the British army until his retirement in 1794. Living at Mavis Grove near Dumfries, he was appointed Colonel of the Dumfries Volunteers. He was related, through marriage, to the poet's friend, John McMurdo. He was 68 years old when Burns wrote these stanzas. He died in 1822, aged 95 years. Ll. 9–12 carry a politically dissident load.

Here's a Health to Ane I Loe Dear

First printed in Thomson, 1799.

ALTHO' thou maun never be mine,   shall
    Altho' even hope is denied;
'Tis sweeter for thee despairing,
    Than ought in the warld beside — Jessy.

Chorus
5 Here's a health to ane I loe dear,   one, love
    Here's a health to ane I loe dear;
Thou art sweet as the smile when fond lovers meet,
    And soft as their parting tear — Jessy.

I mourn thro' the gay, gaudy day,
10   As hopeless I muse on thy charms;
But welcome the dream o' sweet slumber,
    For then I am lockt in thine arms — Jessy.
        Here's a health &c.

This was sent to Thomson in April 1796. It was written about Jessy Lewars (1778–1855), daughter of John Lewars, the poet's colleague in the Excise.

On Jessy Lewars

First printed in Cunningham, 1834.

Talk not to me of savages
    From Afric's burning sun,
No savage e'er can rend my heart
    As, Jessy, thou hast done.

But Jessy's lovely hand in mine,
    A mutual faith to plight,
Not even to view the heavenly choir
    Would be so blest a sight.

This was supposedly written on the reverse side of a sheet of paper
advertising a travelling show which was handed to Burns during his
last illness. On Jessie Lewars, see notes above to *Here's a Health to
Ane I Loe Dear*.

The Toast

First printed in Cunningham, 1834.

FILL me with the rosy wine;
Call a toast — a toast divine;
Give the Poet's darling flame,
Lovely Jessy be her name;
Then thou mayest freely boast,
Thou hast given a peerless toast.

This was, according to Cunningham, inscribed on a goblet pre-
sented to Miss Jessy Lewars.

Jessy's Illness

First printed in Cunningham, 1834.

Say, sages, what's the charm on earth
    Can turn Death's dart aside?
It is not purity and worth,
    Else Jessy had not died.

Jessie's Recovery

First printed in Cunningham, 1834.

But rarely seen since Nature's birth,
    The natives of the sky;
Yet still one seraph's left on earth,
    For Jessy did not die.

To Miss Jessy Lewars,
Dumfries, with Books which the Bard Presented Her
First printed in Currie, 1800.

THINE be the volumes, Jessy fair,
And with them take the Poet's prayer;
That Fate may in her fairest page,
With every kindliest, best presage,
5 Of future bliss, enrol thy name:
With native worth, and spotless fame,
And wakeful caution, still aware
Of ill — but chief, Man's felon snare;
All blameless joys on earth we find,
10 And all the treasures of the mind —
These be thy guardian and reward;
So prays thy faithful friend, *the Bard.*

Robert Burns.
June 26th, 1796

These lines were inscribed by Burns in a copy of James Johnson's *Scots Musical Museum* which Burns paid for as a present to Miss Jessy Lewars. Jessy lived almost opposite the Burns family house in the Mill Hole Brae (now Burns Street) and tended the poet during his final illness and assisted Jean during and after her pregnancy in July 1796.

O, Wert Thou in the Cauld Blast
Tune: Lennox Love to Blantyre
First printed in Currie, 1800.

Oh wert thou in the cauld blast,   *cold*
  On yonder lea, on yonder lea;   *pasture*
My plaidie to the angry airt,   *plaid, wind's direction*
  I'd shelter thee, I'd shelter thee:
5 Or did Misfortune's bitter storms
  Around thee blaw, around thee blaw,   *blow*
Thy bield should be my bosom,   *shelter*
  To share it a', to share it a'.   *all*

Or were I in the wildest waste,
10 Sae black and bare, sae black and bare,   *so*
The desart were a paradise,
  If thou wert there, if thou wert there.

Or were I monarch o' the globe,
    Wi' thee to reign, wi' thee to reign;
15 The brightest jewel in my crown,
    Wad be my queen, wad be my queen.   would

These beautiful lyrics, among the last Burns wrote, were dedicated to Jessy Lewars on her helping the poet (and Jean) during his illness.

Fairest Maid on Devon Banks
Tune: Rothiemurchie
First printed in Currie, 1800.

FULL well thou know'st I love thee dear,
Couldst thou to malice lend an ear!
O, did not Love exclaim, 'Forbear,
    Nor use a faithful lover so.'—

Chorus
5 Fairest maid on Devon banks,
Crystal Devon, winding Devon,
Wilt thou lay that frown aside,
    And smile as thou wert wont to do.

Then come, thou fairest of the fair,
10 Those wonted smiles O let me share;
And by thy beauteous self I swear,
    No love but thine my heart shall know. —
      Fairest maid &c.

This was sent to Thomson on 12th July, 1796 when Burns was at the Brow Well, on the Solway Firth, hoping its bitter iron-dark waters and sea-bathing would help alleviate his rapidly deteriorating health. Letter 706 is profoundly moving; Burns, uncharacteristically, pleads with Thomson, forced to swallow his pride and independent spirit so normally fixed against being paid for song-writing, promptly to despatch £5 to him. As he told Thomson, a 'cruel scoundrel of a Haberdasher' had started legal action against him for a minor debt that, at this moment, he could not afford to pay. For Burns, this was his father's nightmare come back to haunt the son. The 'horrors of a jail' he exclaimed exacerbated his illness and shook his nervous framework to the core. He had told Dr Moore that it was death that saved his father from the humiliation of being jailed for a debt. This was the last song and letter from Burns to Thomson. It was printed by Thomson in 1801.

Remorseful Apology

First printed in Currie, 1800.

THE friend whom, wild from Wisdom's way
    The fumes of wine infuriate send,
(Not moony madness more astray)
    Who but deplores that hapless friend?

Mine was th' insensate, frenzied part,
    (Ah! why did I those scenes outlive,
Scenes so abhorrent to my heart!)
    'Tis thine to pity and forgive. —

Currie printed this work as written to a 'gentleman' Burns had offended. Not in his commentary, but as a footnote to the poem in Vol. II, p. 642, Kinsley presents the following: '*To Mr. J. McKenzie. The recipient's note runs*: M^r. Robt. Burns with a pretended excuse for having used my character ill – 1796 – Delivered to me by Mr. Syme, – opposite the Inn possessed by Mrs. Riddick, in Bank Street.

Graces – at the Globe Tavern

BEFORE DINNER

First printed in Oliver, Edinburgh, 1801.

O Lord, when hunger pinches sore,
    Do Thou stand us in stead,
And send us from Thy bounteous store
    A tup- or wether-head!   ram or sheep-
        Amen.

AFTER DINNER – I

First printed in Chambers, 1851.

O Lord, since we have feasted thus,
    Which we so little merit,
Let Meg now take away the flesh,
    And Jock bring in the spirit!

AFTER DINNER – 2

First printed in *The Literary Magnet*, January 1826.

Lord we thank an' Thee adore,
    For temp'ral gifts we little merit;
At present we will ask no more,
    Let *William Hislop give the spirit.*

All of the above graces are meant to have been used by Burns at his favourite 'howff', the Globe Tavern, Dumfries, now known as the Burns Howff (it has a thriving Burns Club). The Selkirk Grace has been omitted given that it was not composed by Burns (see our Doubtful and Rejected section in Appendix).

Lines Written on a Window
at the Globe Tavern, Dumfries
First printed in Duncan, Glasgow, 1801.

The greybeard, old Wisdom, may boast of his treasures,
    Give me with gay Folly to live;
I grant him his calm-blooded, time-settled pleasures,
    But Folly has raptures to give.

This, and the following epigram, was written extempore by Burns on the windows of the Globe Tavern, Dumfries. The conjectural date is sometime in 1795. The glass panes were in the possession of a Mr J. P. Brunton of Galashiels during the 1890s.

ANOTHER –
First printed in Duncan, Glasgow, 1801.

My bottle is a holy pool,
    That heals the wounds o' care an' dool;   woe
And pleasure is a wanton trout,
    An ye drink it, ye'll find him out.   if you

Kinsley, then Mackay print as the last of these epigrams, the lines beginning 'If in Politics thou wouldst mix'. There is no evidence they were etched by Burns with his diamond stylus during 1795. They have been moved to their proper chronological place, the first week in 1793.

I Murder Hate
First printed in Duncan, Glasgow, 1801.

I murder hate by field or flood,
    Tho' Glory's name may screen us;
In wars at hame I'll spend my blood,
    Life-giving wars of Venus:
5 The deities that I adore
    Are social Peace and Plenty;
I'm better pleas'd to *make one more*,
    Than be the death of twenty. —

I would not die like Socrates,
10   For all the fuss of Plato;
Nor would I with Leonidas,
      Nor yet would I with Cato:
The zealots of the Church, or State,
      Shall ne'er my mortal foes be;
15 But let me have bold ZIMRI'S[1] fate
      Within the arms of COZBI! —

The first stanza of this song was etched by Burns on a window in the Globe Tavern, Dumfries. The song is an anti-war statement against Britain's war against America. This is certain due to the title on the Alloway mansucript, *On the Great Recruiting in the Year 17 – During the American War* (See Kinsley, Vol. III, no. 534, p. 1494). In 1795 the contemporary resonance of the lyric would have been judged as a criticism of Britain being at war with France.

Kirk and State Excisemen
Lines Written on a Window, at the King's Arms Tavern, Dumfries
First printed in Duncan, Glasgow, 1801.

Ye men of wit and wealth, why all this sneering
      'Gainst poor Excisemen? Give the cause a hearing:
What are your landlord's rent-rolls? taxing ledgers:
      What premiers, what? even monarchs' mighty gaugers:
Nay, what are priests? those seeming godly wisemen:
      What are they, pray? but spiritual Excisemen.

Kinsley prints this as part of the Burns canon without commentary. Mackay estimates the date of composition as 1789 when Burns joined the Excise. However, it is unlikely that the poet frequented the King's Arms Tavern while residing at Ellisland in 1789. They are probably from a later period, possibly 1793 or later when this hotel was the meeting place of the Dumfries cell of the Friends of the People. There are overtones here of the friction between Burns and the Pittite Loyal Natives faction in Dumfries.

---

1 See Numbers, ch. 25, vv. 8–15.

You're Welcome, Willie Stewart

First printed in Lockhart, 1829.

Come, bumpers high, express your joy,
　　The bowl we maun renew it;   must
The tappet-hen gae bring her ben,   big pewter jug, here
　　To welcome Willie Stewart.

Chorus
5   You're welcome, Willie Stewart,
　　You're welcome, Willie Stewart,
There's ne'er a flower that blooms in May,
　　That's half sae welcome's thou art.   so

May foes be strang, and friends be slack,
10 　　Ilk action, may he rue it;   each
May woman on him turn her back,
　　That wrangs thee, Willie Stewart.   wrongs
　　　　You're welcome &c.

William Stewart (1749–1812), the factor of Closeburn estate, was the father of Polly Stewart and son of the inn owner at Closeburn, near Dumfries. Mackay (p. 522) quotes an anecdotal story (from Lockhart's biography of Burns (1829)), regarding a glass goblet with these lines allegedly inscribed, but he does not record the source. He again appears to have lifted the quotation from Kinsley (Vol. III, p. 1495). It is difficult to believe the entire song could have been written on a goblet.

On Wm. Graham of Mossknowe

First printed in Cunningham, 1834.

'Stop thief!' dame Nature call'd to Death,
As Willie drew his latest breath:
How shall I make a fool again —
My choicest model thou hast taen. —   taken

William Graham (1756–1832) was laird at Mossknowe, near Annan. The lines are in the Glenriddell manuscripts.

On a Swearing Coxcomb
First printed in Cunningham, 1834.

Here, cursing swearing Burton lies,
A buck, a beau, or *Dem my eyes!*
Who in his life did little good,
And his last words were, *Dem my blood!*

The aristocratic target of this satirical epigram has not been identified.

On a Suicide
First printed in 1801 by both Oliver in Edinburgh and Duncan, Glasgow.

Here lies in earth a root of Hell,
    Set by the Deil's ain dibble;   own planting stick for holes
This worthless body damn'd himsel,
    To save the Lord the trouble.

This was printed on first publication about someone with the initials 'D.C.' There is no Burns manuscript, although a transcript exists in the Wisbech and Fenland Museum, Cambridgeshire. Cunningham's story that it was written about a person named Glendinning and that Burns was seen writing it and pushing the epitaph into the soil by the graveside is surely mere folklore.

Epitaph
On an Innkeeper Nicknamed 'The Marquis'
First printed in Duncan, Glasgow, 1801.

Here lies a mock Marquis whose titles were shamm'd,
If ever he rise, it will be to be damn'd.

This is written on a Dumfries innkeeper whose public house was demolished in the early nineteenth century, although, according to Cunningham, the place where it stood was known as the Marquess's Close till the 1830s (Cunningham, Vol. III, p. 310).

Epitaph on John Bushby
Tinwald Downs
First printed in Duncan, Glasgow, 1801.

Here lies John Bushby, *honest man!*
Cheat him devil — if you can. —

John Bushby was Sheriff Clerk to the county of Dumfriesshire and supported Gordon of Balmaghie in the parliamentary election of 1795. Burns wrote *John Bushby's Lamentation* as *The Third Heron Ballad*. Bushby owned the race course at Tinwald Downs.

On Capt. Lascelles

First printed in Scott Douglas, 1877.

When Lascelles thought fit from this world to depart,
Some friends warmly spoke of embalming his heart;
A bystander whispers — 'Pray don't make so much o't,
The subject is *poison*, no reptile will touch it.'—

Edward Lascelles (1740–1820), who eventually became an army Colonel, was an English M.P. in 1790. This is included in the Gledriddell manuscript collection.

On John M'murdo

First printed in Cunningham, 1834.

Blest be M'Murdo to his latest day!
No envious cloud o'ercast his evening ray;
No wrinkle furrowed by the hand of care,
Nor ever sorrow add one silver hair!
O, may no son the father's honor stain,
Nor ever daughter give the mother pain!

This is supposed to have been inscribed on a window at John McMurdo's house, on the Drumlanrig castle estate of the Duke of Queensberry, McMurdo's employer. See *To John McMurdo, With ' Pound of Lundiefoot Snuff* for additional notes. Mackay gives the above out of chronology of composition, with the earlier work (p. 356).

On Gabriel Richardson

First printed in Cunningham, 1834.

Here brewer Gabriel's fire's extinct,
    And empty all his barrels:
He's blest — if as he brew'd he drink —
    In upright, virtuous morals.

Gabriel Richardson (1759–1820) was a brewer in Dumfries. Cunningham took the lines from a goblet then in the Richardson family.

On Commissary Goldie's Brains

First printed in Cunningham, 1834.

Lord, to account who dares Thee call,
    Or e'er dispute Thy pleasure?
Else why within so thick a wall
    Enclose so poor a treasure?

Colonel Thomas Goldie was commissary to the Dumfries Sheriff court and President of the ultra-loyalist political group the Loyal Natives in Dumfries. Burns satirises him in *The Second Heron Ballad* as 'Colonel Tam'.

The Hue and Cry of John Lewars -

First printed in Barke, 1955.

A poor man ruined and undone by Robbery and Murder. Being an aweful WARNING to the young men of this age, how they look well to themselves in this dangerous, terrible WORLD.

A THIEF, AND A MURDERER! stop her who can!
    Look well to your lives and your goods!
Good people, ye know not the hazard you run,
    'Tis the far-famed and much-noted WOODS. —

5 While I looked at her eye, for the devil is in it,
    In a trice she whipt off my poor heart:
Her brow, cheek and lip — in another sad minute,
    My peace felt her murderous dart.—

Her features, I'll tell you them over — but hold!
10   She deals with your wizards and books;
And to peep in her face, if but once you're so bold,
    There's witchery kills in her looks.—

But softly — I have it — her haunts are well known,
    At midnight so slily I'll watch her;
15 And sleeping, undrest, in the dark, all alone —
    Good lord! the dear THIEF HOW I'LL CATCH HER!

The tone of the sub-title points to this being a jovial burlesque on the broken love affair between Burns's Excise colleague, John Lewars, and an Agnes Wood, the 'much-noted WOODS'.

The Keekin' Glass

First printed in Chambers, 1852.

HOW daur ye ca' me 'Howlet-face,' dare you call
    Ye blear-e'ed, wither'd spectre? -eyed
Ye only spied the keekin-glass, looking
    An' there ye saw your picture.

This was supposedly written at Dalswinton when Patrick Miller's daughter told the poet that a drunken judge visiting her father looked at her in their drawing room and, probably assuming she was a servant, asked, 'Wha's yon howlet-faced thing in the corner?' (See Henley–Henderson, Vol. II, p. 439).

Inscription on a Goblet

First printed in Cunningham, 1834.

THERE'S Death in the cup — sae beware!
    Nay, more — there is danger in touching;
But who can avoid the fell snare?
    The man and his wine's so bewitching!

These lines were written on a goblet owned by John Syme according to Cunningham. The text as Kinsley has remarked, is adapted from the Bible, the Second Book of Kings, iv, 40.

On Andrew Turner

First printed in Cunningham, 1834.

In Se'enteen Hunder 'n Forty-Nine
The Deil gat stuff to mak a swine, devil got
    An' coost it in a corner;; cast/threw
But wilily he chang'd his plan,
An' shap'd it something like a man,
    An' ca'd it Andrew Turner. — called

This was written about an English traveller Burns met in the King's Arms, Dumfries, who asked if the poet would write something for him. Having found out the traveller's name and age, the poet is supposed to have recited this extempore. Kinsley appears to have read this too seriously, missing the obvious humour, and calls it a 'tasteless epigram' (Vol. III, p. 1496). There is no manuscript.

The Toadeater -1
First printed in Lockhart, 1828.

OF Lordly acquaintance you boast,
    And the Dukes that you dined with yestreen,
Yet an insect's an insect at most,
    Tho' it crawl on the curl of a Queen!

The Toadeater -2

NO more of your titled acquaintances boast,
    Nor of the gay groups you have seen;
A crab louse is but a crab louse at last,
    Tho' stack to the c[unt] of a Queen.

Burns is supposed to have written several variations of this epigram, although the variants may be more a symptom of editorial and censorial squeamishness. There is no manuscript by Burns. A transcript by John Syme records 'Extempore on a young fellow W. I. who had made about £10,000 by a lucky speculation and who vaunted of keeping the highest company, &c. N.B. He was of low extraction' (See *The Burns Chronicle*, 1932, pp. 13–14). A crab louse is meant to attach itself to pubic hair.

The Lovely Lass o' Inverness –
First printed in Johnson, 1796.

THE luvely Lass o' Inverness,
    Nae joy nor pleasure can she see;   no
For e'en to morn she cries, Alas!
    And ay the saut tear blin's her e'e: salt, eye
5 Drumossie moor, Drumossie day,
    A waefu' day it was to me;   woeful
For there I lost my father dear,
    My father dear and brethren three!

Their winding-sheet the bludy clay,   bloody
10   Their graves are growing green to see;
And by them lies the dearest lad
    That ever blest a woman's e'e!   eye

Now wae to thee, thou cruel lord,   woe
    A bludy man I trow thou be;   bloody, know
15 For monie a heart thou has made sair   many, sore
    That ne'er did wrang to thine or thee!   wrong

Burns never claimed this Jacobite song as his own, although it is
signed 'B' in the S.M.M. It has been ascribed to him by most editors
as a song he improved. It is about the Scottish defeat at Culloden
(Drumossie) in 1746.

As I Stood by Yon Roofless Tower
Tune: Cumnock Plains
First printed by Johnson, 1796.

AS I stood by yon roofless tower,
    Where the wa'-flow'r scents the dewy air;
Where the houlet mourns in her ivy bower,   owl
    And tells the midnight moon her care:

Chorus
5 A lassie all alone was making her moan,
    Lamenting our lads beyond the sea;
In the bluidy wars they fa', and our honor's   bloody, fall
    gane an' a',   gone
    And broken-hearted we maun die.—   must

The winds were laid, the air was still,
10   The stars they shot along the sky;
The tod was howling on the hill,   fox
    And the distant-echoing glens reply.—
    A lassie all alone &c

The burn, adown its hazelly path,
    Was rushing by the ruin'd wa',   wall
15 Hasting to join the sweeping Nith
    Whase roarings seem'd to rise and fa'.—   whose, fall
    A lassie all alone &c

The cauld blae North was streaming forth   cold bitter
    Her lights, wi' hissing, eerie din;   fearful
Athort the lift they start and shift,   at the horizon
20   Like Fortune's favours, tint as win.—   lost
    A lassie all alone &c

Now, looking over firth and fauld,   (sea and land) fold
    Her horn the pale-fac'd Cynthia rear'd,   the moon
When, lo, in form of Minstrel auld,   old
    A stern and stalwart ghaist appear'd.—   ghost
      A lassie all alone &c

25 And frae his harp sic strains did flow,   from, such
    Might rous'd the slumbering Dead to hear;
But Oh, it was a tale of woe,
    As ever met a Briton's ear. —
      A lassie all alone &c

He sang wi' joy his former day,
30   He weeping wail'd his latter times:
But what he said it was nae play,   not
    I winna ventur't in my rhymes.—   will not
      A lassie all alone &c

This brilliant anti-war song was sent to Thomson in September, 1794 (Letter 637), but was first printed by Johnson in December 1796. It is an original work. It was signed 'B' in the S.M.M. The 'roofless tower' is Lincluden Abbey.

The 'lassie' lamenting the men who fall in 'bluidy wars' is not a reference to a Jacobite war, but to the war of Britain against revolutionary France. It could also be resonant of Britain's role against the American colonies, where 'our honor's gane an' a'' is an appropriate description. As Crawford has commented, the song 'reveals Liberty as emblematic, the "sacred posy" on the bonnet of the "stern and stalwart ghaist" of a minstrel of the olden time who bewails the political reaction which set in after the end of 1792' (p. 242). Within a similar eerie atmosphere to the appearance of Bruce in *The Ghost of Bruce*, the poet, conscious of printing the song in Johnson's collection, acts as self-censor, at the end of the song, declaring that what the minstrel said could not be printed: 'I winna ventur't in my rhymes'. Crawford also agrees with the American editor Gebbie that this was probably a prelude to *Ode on General Washington's Birthday* (pp. 242–3), or at the very least, written around the same time. What the penultimate stanza clearly suggests is another song of liberty possibly suppressed by Burns. It would, though, surely be difficult to consider the Washington 'Ode' as a *song*.

The reference to 'a Briton's ear' (l. 28) further emphasises Burns's dual or concentric Scottish/British identity.

The Wren's Nest

First printed by Johnson, 1796.

THE Robin cam to the wren's nest	
And keekit in and keekit in,	peeped
O weel 's me on your auld pow,	old head
Wad ye be in, wad ye be in.	would you
Ye 'se ne'er get leave to lie without,	
And I within, and I within,	
As lang 's I hae an auld clout	long as, have old cloth
To row you in, to row you in.	roll/wrap

Burns is supposed to have recorded this from his wife's singing and, on revising the lyric, sent it to Johnson. In the absence of a traditional text, it is impossible to know if the work was changed by him.

John Highlandman

First printed by Johnson, 1796.

There's sax eggs in the pan, gudeman,	six, goodman
There's sax eggs in the pan, gudeman;	
There's ane to you, and twa to me,	one, two
And three to our John Highlandman.—	

Chorus
5 O an ye were dead, gudeman,   *if*
    A green turf on your head, gudeman,
    I wad bestow my widowhood   *would*
    Upon a rantin Highlandman.—   *merry*

A sheep-head's in the pot, gudeman,	
10 A sheep-head's in the pot, gudeman;	
The flesh to him the broo to me,	broth
An' the horns become your brow, gudeman. —	

Chorus for the final verse
    Sing round about the fire wi' a rung she ran, *cudgel*
    An round about the fire wi' a rung she ran:
15 Your horns shall tie you to the staw, *stall*
    An I shall bang your hide, gudeman.—

This is the poet's revision of a song in the Herd Collection (1769). It is printed unsigned, which suggests that the changes by Burns were minimal to this song of violent female sexual aggression.

Tam Lin

First printed by Johnson, 1796.

	O I forbid you, maiden's a'	all
	That wear gowd on your hair,	gold
	To come, or gae by Carterhaugh,	go
	For young Tom-lin is there.	
5	There's nane that gaes by Carterhaugh	none, goes
	But they leave him in a wad;	pledge/bargain
	Either their rings, or green mantles,	
	Or else their maidenhead.	
	Janet has kilted her green kirtle,	petticoat
10	A little aboon her knee;	above
	And she has broded her yellow hair	braided
	A little aboon her bree;	above, brow
	And she's awa to Carterhaugh,	away
	As fast as she can hie.	run
15	When she cam to Carterhaugh	
	Tom-lin was at the well,	
	And there she fand his steed standing	found
	But away was himsel.	
	She had na pu'd a double rose,	not pulled
20	A rose but only tway,	two
	Till up then started young Tom-lin,	
	Says, Lady, thou's pu' nae me.	pull not
	Why pu's thou the rose, Janet,	pulls
	And why breaks thou the wand?	
25	Or why thou comes to Carterhaugh	
	Withoutten my command?	without
	Carterhaugh is my ain,	own
	Ma daddie gave it me;	my
	I'll come and gang by Carterhaugh	go
30	And ask nae leave at thee.	no

Janet has kilted her green kirtle   petticoat
    A little aboon her knee,   above
And she has snooded her yellow hair,   put in a band
    A little aboon her bree,   above, brow
35 And she is to her father's ha,   hall
    As fast as she can hie.   run

Four and twenty ladies fair
    Were playing at the ba,   ball
And out them cam the fair Janet,
40   Ance the flower amang them a'.   once, among, all

Four and twenty ladies fair
    Were playing at the chess,
And out then cam the fair Janet,
    As green as onie glass.   any

45 Out then spak an auld grey knight,   spoke, old
    Lay o'er the castle-wa,   -wall
And says, Alas, fair Janet for thee
    But we'll be blamed a'.

Haud your tongue ye auld-fac'd knight,   hold, old-
50   Some ill death may ye die,
Father my bairn on whom I will,   child
    I'll father nane on thee.   none

Out then spak her father dear,   spoke
    And he spak meek and mild,
55 And ever alas, sweet Janet, he says,
    I think thou gaes wi' child.   goes

If that I gae wi' child, father,   go
    Myself maun bear the blame;   shall
There's ne'er a laird about your ha,   hall
60   Shall get the bairn's name.   child's

If my Love were an earthly knight,
    As he's an elfin grey;
A wad na gie my ain true-love   would not give, own
    For nae lord that ye hae.   no, have

65 The steed that my true-love rides on,
        Is lighter than the wind;
    Wi' siller he is shod before,   silver
        Wi' burning gowd behind.   gold

    Janet has kilted her green kirtle   petticoat
70   A little aboon the knee;   above
    And has snooded her yellow hair   braided
        A little aboon her bree;   brow
    And she's awa to Carterhaugh   away
        As fast as she can hie.   go

75 When she cam to Carterhaugh
        Tom-lin was at the well;
    And there she fand his steed standing,   found
        But away was himsel.

    She had na pu'd a double rose   had not pulled
80   A rose but only tway,   two
    Till up then started young Tom-lin,
        Say's Lady thou pu's nae mae.   pulls not more

    Why pu's thou the rose Janet,
        Amang the groves sae green,   among, so
85 And a' to kill the bonie babe
        That we gat us between.   begot

    O tell me, tell me, Tom-lin she says,
        For 's sake that died on tree,
    If e'er ye was in holy chapel,
90   Or Christendom did see.

    Roxbrugh he was my grandfather,
        Took me with him to bide,
    And ance it fell upon a day   once
        That wae did me betide.   woe

95 Ance it fell upon a day,   once
        A cauld day and a snell,   cold, bitter
    When we were frae the hunting come   from
        That frae my horse I fell.   from

The queen o' Fairies she caught me,
100   In yon green hill to dwell,
And pleasant is the fairy-land;
    But, an eerie tale to tell!   *strange*

Ay at the end of seven years
    We pay a tiend to hell;   *tithe/fee*
105 I am sae fair and fu' o flesh   *so, full*
    I'm fear'd it be mysel.   *afraid*

But the night is Halloween, lady,
    The morn is Hallowday;
Then win me, win me, an ye will,
110   For weel I want ye may.   *well*

Just at the mirk and midnight hour   *darkest*
    The fairy folk will ride;
And they that wad their truelove win,   *would*
    At Milescross they maun bide.   *must stay*

115 But how shall I thee ken, Tom-lin,   *know*
    O how my truelove know,
Amang sae mony unco knights   *so, strange*
    The like I never saw.

O first let pass the black, Lady,
120   And syne let past the brown;   *then*
But quickly run to the milk-white steed,
    Pu' ye his rider down: *pull*

For I'll ride on the milk-white steed,
    And ay nearest the town;
125 Because I was an earthly knight
    They gie me that renown.   *give*

My right hand will be glov'd, Lady,
    My left hand will be bare;
Cockt up shall my bonnet be,
130   And kaim'd down shall my hair;   *combed*
And thae's the tokens I gie thee,   *these are, give*
    Nae doubt I will be there.   *no*

They'll turn me in your arms, Lady,
    Into an asp and adder,   viper
135 But hald me fast and fear me not,   hold
    I am your bairn's father.   child's

They'll turn me to a bear sae grim,   so
    And then a lion bold;
But hold me fast and fear me not,
140   As ye shall love your child.

Again they'll turn me in your arms
    To a red het gaud of airn;   hot bar of iron
But hold me fast and fear me not,
    I'll do to you nae harm.   no

145 And last they'll turn me, in your arms,
    Into the burning lead;
Then throw me into well-water,
    O throw me in wi' speed!

And then I'll be your ain truelove,   own
150   I'll turn a naked knight:
Then cover me wi' your green mantle,
    And cover me out o sight.

Gloomy, gloomy was the night,
    And eerie was the way,   strange
155 As fair Jenny in her green mantle
    To Milescross she did gae.   go

About the middle o' the night
    She heard the bridles ring;
This lady was as glad at that
160   As any earthly thing.

First she let the black pass by,
    And syne she let the brown;   then
But quickly she ran to the milk-white steed,
    And pu'd the rider down   pulled

165 Sae weel she minded what he did say   so well
    And young Tom-lin did win;
Syne cover'd him wi' her green mantle   then
    As blythe's a bird in spring.

Out then spak the queen o' Fairies,	spoke
170 Out of a bush o' broom;	
Them that has gotten young Tom-lin	
Has gotten a stately groom.	

Out then spak the queen o' Fairies,	
And an angry queen was she;	
175 Shame betide her ill-fard face,	-farrowed
And an ill death may she die,	
For she's ta'en awa the boniest knight	taken away
In a' my companie.	

But had I kend, Tom-lin, she says,	known
180 What now this night I see,	
I wad hae ta'en out thy twa grey een,	would have taken, two, eyes
And put in twa een o' tree.	two eyes, wood

This is based on a traditional ballad from the sixteenth century. Burns probably saw the short version of the original work in Herd's collection (1769), but it is more likely that he adapted and improved this from one of the longer versions known to have been collected by his close friend Robert Riddell of Glenriddell who was, *inter alia*, an antiquarian. Burns once used the pen-name Thomas A. Linn in a newspaper edition of his poem, *Elegy on the Year 1788*. Carterhaugh is near Selkirk.

Had I the Wyte

Tune: Come Kiss with me, Come Clap with me
First printed in Johnson, 1796.

Had I the wyte, had I the wyte,	were I to blame
Had I the wyte, she bade me;	
She watch'd me by the hie-gate-side,	high road
And up the loan she shaw'd me;	lane, showed
5 And when I wadna venture in,	would not
A coward loon she ca'd me:	fool
Had Kirk and State been in the gate,	way
I'd lighted when she bade me.—	

Sae craftilie she took me ben,	so, in
10 And bade me mak nae clatter;	make no noise
'For our ramgunshoch, glum Goodman	ill-tempered, surly
Is o'er ayont the water:'	beyond

Whae'er shall say I wanted grace,   *whoever, lacked*
    When I did kiss and dawte her,   *fondle*
15 Let him be planted in my place,
    Syne, say, I was the fautor.—   *then, one at fault*

Could I for shame, could I for shame,
    Could I for shame refus'd her;
And wadna Manhood been to blame,   *would not*
20   Had I unkindly used her:
He claw'd her wi' the ripplin-kame,   *wool-comb*
    And blae and bluidy bruis'd her;   *blue*
When sic a husband was frae hame,   *such, from*
    What wife but wad excus'd her?   *would*

25 I dighted ay her een sae blue,   *wiped, eyes so*
    An' bann'd the cruel randy;   *scoundrel*
And weel I wat her willin mou   *well, know, mouth*
    Was e'en like succarcandie.   *sugarcandy*
At gloamin-shote it was, I wot,   *early evening, know*
30   I lighted on the Monday;
But I cam thro' the Tiseday's dew   *Tuesday's*
    To wanton Willie's brandy.   *—*

This is adapted by Burns from an old song included in the Herd collection (1769). It was signed 'Z' in the S.M.M. A bawdy version was collected by Burns and included in the *Merry Muses of Caledonia*.

Comin Thro' the Rye

Tune: Miller's Wedding
First printed in Johnson, 1796.

COMIN thro' the rye, poor body,   *wheat-like grass*
    Comin thro' the rye,
She draigl't a' her petticoatie   *made a mess of*
    Comin thro' the rye.

Chorus
5 Oh Jenny's a' weet, poor body,   *wet*
    Jenny's seldom dry;
She draigl't a' her petticoatie,   *made a mess of*
    Comin thro' the rye.

Gin a body meet a body   if
10   Comin thro' the rye,
Gin a body kiss a body
    Need a body cry.
        Oh Jenny's &c

Gin a body meet a body
    Comin thro' the glen;
15   Gin a body kiss a body,
    Need the warld ken!   world know
        Oh Jenny's &c

On publication, Johnson's headnote reads: 'Written for this work by Robert Burns'. It is not, though, a wholly original work. It is partly taken from a folksong in Thomas Mansfield's collection begun in 1770. An English version, entered in Stationers Hall, London, for June 1796 reads, 'If a body meet a body, /Going to the Fair'. A further, more crude version exists in the *Merry Muses*.

The Rowin 't in Her Apron

First printed in Johnson, 1796.

OUR young lady's a huntin gane,   gone
Sheets nor blanket haes she ta'en,   has, taken
But she's born her auld son or she cam hame,   old, before, home
    And she's row'd him in her apron. —   rolled/wrapped

5   Her apron was o' the hollan fine,   linen from Holland
Laid about wi' laces nine;
She though it a pity her babe should tyne,   perish
    And she's row'd him in her apron. —

Her apron was o' the hollan sma,
10   Laid about wi' laces a',
She thought it a pity her babe to let fa,
    And she row'd him in her apron. —

Her father says within the ha'   hall
Amang the knights and nobles a'   among, all
15   I think I hear a babie ca,   call
In the chamber amang our young ladies. —   among

O father dear it is a bairn,   child
I hope it will do you nae harm.,   no
For the daddie I lo'ed, and he'll lo'e me again,   loved
20   For the rowin 't in my apron. —   rolling it

O is he a gentleman, or is he a clown,
That has brought thy fair body down,
I would not for a' this town
      The rowin 't in the apron. —

25 Young Terreagles he's nae clown,
He is the toss of Edinborrow town,   toast, Edinburgh
And he'll buy me a braw new gown,   fine
      For the rowin 't in my apron. —

Its I hae castles, I hae towers,   have
30 I hae barns, I hae bowers,
A' that is mine it shall be thine,
      For the rowin 't in thy apron. —

This song is about the problems of Jacobite families in the wake of the 1715 rebellion. Lord John Maxwell was 'Young Terreagles'. It was printed anonymously on publication. Burns is supposed to have collected this song from an unidentified person in the vicinity of Dumfries, possibly one of the Highland Fencible soldiers stationed there during the mid-1790s.

Kinsley's remark implies that he should not have accepted the work to the canon, 'I am inclined to take it as an alternative collected version, and not Burns's revision' (Vol. III, p. 1503). Mackay merely assumes the poet made corrections and includes it. However, given there are two manuscript copies, it is surely unlikely that the bard would have written it out twice without making some ammendments and improvements.

Charlie He's My Darling

Tune: Charlie, He's My Darling
First printed in S.M.M. December, 1796.

'TWAS on a Monday morning,
    Right early in the year,
That Charlie came to our town,
    The Young Chevalier. —

Chorus
5 An' Charlie he's my darling, my darling, my darling,
Charlie he's my darling, the Young Chevalier. —

As he was walking up the street,
    The city for to view,
O there he spied a bonie lass
10   The window looking thro'. —
        An' Charlie he's &c

Sae light's he jimped up the stair,   so, jumped
    And tirl'd at the pin;   knocked, latch
And wha sae ready as hersel   who so
    To let the laddie in. —
        An' Charlie he's &c

15 He set his Jenny on his knee,
    All in his Highland dress;
For brawlie weel he kend the way   finely well, knew
    To please a bonie lass. —
        An' Charlie he's &c

It's up yon heathery mountain,
20 And down yon scroggy glen,   scrubby
We daurna gang a milking,   dare not go
    For Charlie and his men. —
        An' Charlie he's &c

Here, Burns has taken an old street song from the mid-1770s and
grafted to it a Jacobite theme. The bard's success in this fine lyric
was adapted after his death by Caroline Oliphant (1766–1845). See
*Life and Songs of the Baroness Nairne: With a Memoir and Poems of
Caroline Oliphant the Younger*, ed. Rev. Charles Rogers (1869),
pp. 125–6. The first verse and chorus are very similar to Burns's
version. Like all of the poet's lyrics on the Jacobite theme, this song
was unsigned in the S.M.M. The young Chevalier is, of course,
Charles Edward Stewart.

The Lass o' Ecclefechan

Tune: Jack o Latin
First printed in Johnson, 1796.

	Gat ye me, O, gat ye me,	got
	Gat ye me wi' naething,	nothing
	Rock an' reel and spinning wheel	
	A mickle quarter basin.	large
5	Bye attour, my Gutcher has	in addition, grandfather
	A hich house and a laigh ane,	high, low one
	A' for bye my bonnie sel,	self
	The toss o' Ecclefechan. —	toast
	O haud your tongue now Luckie Laing,	hold
10	O haud your tongue and jauner;	hold, idle talk
	I held the gate till you I met,	was celibate
	Syne I began to wander;	then
	I tint my whistle and my sang,	lost, song
	I tint my peace and pleasure;	lost
15	But your green graff, now Luckie Laing,	grave
	Wad airt me to my treasure.	would direct/lead

This was unsigned in the S.M.M. It was first attributed to Burns in Cunningham's 1834 edition. Aware that Burns copied a bawdy version of this song for the Merry Muses, Cunningham assumed this work to be a cleaned-up version of the original. It does exist in the Hastie manuscripts, which tends to support Cunningham's case.

The Couper o' Cuddy

Tune: Bab at the Bowster
First printed in Johnson, 1796.

The Couper o' Cuddy cam here awa,	cooper, about here
He ca'd the girrs out o'er us a';	threw hoops, all
An' our guidwife has gotten a ca',	call
That's anger'd the silly guidman O. —	husband

Chorus
5   We'll hide the Couper behint the door,
Behint the door, behint the door;
We'll hide the couper behint the door,
    And cover him under a mawn O. —   basket

He sought them out, he sought them in,
10 Wi', deil hae her!' and, deil hae him!   devil have
But the body he was sae doited and blin',   stupid, blind
    He wist na where he was gaun O. —   knew not, going
      We'll hide &c.

They couper'd at e'en, they couper'd at morn,   evening
    Till our guidman has gotten the scorn;
15 On ilka brow she's planted a horn,   each, cuckold's horn
    And swears that there they sall stan' O. — shall stand
      We'll hide &c.

This, like *The Lass o' Ecclefechan*, is included in the Hastie manuscripts, from which it is given as a work of Burns. However, given that it is unsigned in the S.M.M. it is at best a work he modified. An even bawdier version, *Cuddy the Cooper*, is in *The Merry Muses*.

Leezie Lindsay

First printed in Jamieson, 1806.

Will ye go to the Highlands Leezie Lindsay,
    Will ye go to the Highlands wi' me;
Will ye go to the Highlands Leezie Lindsay,
    My pride and my darling to be.

This fragment was sent by Burns to Johnson who did not print it. The whole ballad was first printed in 1806. The song, now popular due to the success of the folk duo The Corries, is supposed to have been collected by Burns. His part in the lyric is usually quoted as the above.

For the Sake o' Somebody

First printed in Johnson, 1796.

My heart is sair, I dare na tell,   sore, not
   My heart is sair for Somebody;   sore
I could wake a winter-night
   For the sake o' Somebody. —
5   Oh-hon! for Somebody!
      Oh-hey! for Somebody!
I could range the world round,
   For the sake o' Somebody. —

Ye Powers that smile on virtuous love,
10   O, sweetly smile on Somebody!
Frae ilka danger keep him free,   from every
   And send me safe my Somebody. —
      Oh-hon! for Somebody!
      Oh-hey! for Somebody!
15 I wad do — what wad I not —   would
   For the sake o' Somebody!

This was signed 'B' in the S.M.M. Burns took and adapted a lyric in Ramsay's *Tea-Table Miscellany*, Vol. 1. The repetitive 'somebody' is, of course, Bonnie Prince Charlie, who politically was unnameable after the 1745 rebellion.

The Cardin O't

Tune: Queensberry's Scots Measure
First printed in Johnson, 1796.

I coft a stane o' haslock woo,   bought, 14lbs, soft wool
   To mak a wab to Johnie o't;   web
For Johnie is my onlie jo,   darling
   I lo'e him best of onie yet. —   love, any

Chorus
5 The cardin o't, the spinnin o't,
   The warpin o't, the winnin o't;   rolling, drying
When ilka ell cost me a groat,   each yard, fourpence
   The tailor staw the lynin o't. —   stole

For tho' his locks be lyart gray,   withered
10   And tho' his brow be beld aboon,   bald above
Yet I hae seen him on a day   have
        The pride of a' the parishon. —   parish around
            The cardin o't &c.

This was signed 'Z' in the S.M.M. It is an old song modified by
Burns. Cunningham suggests, in error, that it is completely by
Burns.

The Sutors o' Selkirk

First printed in Johnson, 1796.

IT'S up wi' the Sutors o' Selkirk,   cobblers
        And down wi' the Earl o' Hume;
And here is to a' the braw laddies   fine
        That wear the single sol'd shoon: soled shoes
Its up wi' the Sutors o' Selkirk,
        For they are baith trusty and leal;   both, true
And up wi' the lads o' the Forest,
        And down wi' the Merse to the deil. —   devil

This song is based on a group of cobblers from Selkirk who fought
for James IV at Flodden, 1513. The defeat was blamed on the Earl of
Hume (1.2). The forest (1. 7) is Etterick Forest in the Borders and
the Merse (1. 8) refers to a county in Berwickshire.

Tibbie Fowler

First printed in Johnson, 1796.

Tibbie Fowler o' the glen,
        There's o'er mony wooin at her,   chasing after
Tibbie Fowler o' the glen,
        There's o'er mony wooin at her.   too many

Chorus
5   Wooin at her, pu'in at her,   pulling
        Courtin at her, canna get her: cannot
Filthy elf, it's for her pelf,   money
        That a' the lads are wooin at her.   all

Ten cam east, and ten cam west,   came
10   Ten cam rowin o'er the water;
Twa came down the lang dyke side,   two, long wall
    There's twa and thirty wooin at her.   two
      Wooin at her, &c.

There's seven but, and seven ben,   outside, inside
    Seven in the pantry wi' her;
15 Twenty head about the door,   at
    There's ane and forty wooin at her.   one
      Wooin at her &c.

She's got pendles in her lugs,   pendants, ears
    Cockle-shells wad set her better;   would suit
High-heel'd shoon and siller tags,   shoes, silver
20   And a' the lads are wooin at her.
      Wooin at her &c.

Be a lassie e'er sae black,   ever so
    An she hae the name o' siller,   have, money
Set her upo' Tintock-tap,   hill top
    The wind will blaw a man till her.   blow, to her
      Wooing at her &c.

25 Be a lassie e'er sae fair,   ever so
    And she want the pennie siller,   lack silver
A flie may fell her in the air,   fly, kill
    Before a man be even till her.
      Wooin at her &c.

Burns collected this old ballad, improved the original and added
some new stanzas. Two fragments of the old song exist in the Herd
manuscript collection. The 'Tintock-tap', l. 23 refers to the Tinto
Hill, a peak in Lanarkshire above 2000 ft.

There's Three True Gude Fellows

Tune: Three Gude Fellows Ayont the Glen
First printed in Johnson, 1796.

There's three true gude fellows,   good
There's three true gude fellows,
There's three true gude fellows
    Down ayont yon glen.   beyond that

It's now the day is dawin,   dawning
But or night do fa' in,   before nightfall
Whase cock's best at crawin,   whose, crowing
    Willie thou sall ken.   shall know

This song is the product of a promise Burns made to his Edinburgh
friend Alexander Cunningham, that he would write a song on
Cunningham, Robert Cleghorn and William Dunbar, all members
of the Crochallan Fencibles (See Letter 336).

The Lass that Made the Bed

First printed in Johnson, 1796.

WHEN Januar wind was blawin cauld,   blowing cold
    As to the North I took my way,
The mirksome night did me enfauld,   darksome, enfold
    I knew na where to lodge till day.   not

5   By my gude luck a maid I met   good
        Just in the middle o' my care;
    And kindly she did me invite
        To walk into a chamber fair. —

    I bow'd fu' low unto this maid,   full/well
10   And thank'd her for her courtesie;
    I bow'd fu' low unto this maid,
        An' bade her mak a bed to me. —

    She made the bed baith large and wide,   both
        Wi' twa white hands she spread it down;   two
15 She put the cup to her rosy lips,
        And drank, 'Young man now sleep ye soun'.' — sound

    She snatch'd the candle in her hand,
        And frae my chamber went wi' speed;   from
    But I call'd her quickly back again
20   To lay some mair below my head.—   more

    A cod she laid below my head,   pillow
        And servèd me with due respeck;   respect
    And to salute her wi' a kiss,
        I put my arms about her neck.—

25	Haud aff your hands young man, she says,	*hold off*
	And dinna sae uncivil be:	*do not so*
	Gif ye hae onie luve for me,	*if, have any*
	O wrang na my virginitie!—	*wrong not*

	Her hair was like the links o' gowd,	*gold*
30	Her teeth were like the ivorie,	
	Her cheeks like lilies dipt in wine,	
	The lass that made the bed to me. —	

	Her bosom was the driven snaw,	*snow*
	Twa drifted heaps sae fair to see;	*two, so*
35	Her limbs the polish'd marble stane,	*stone*
	The lass that made the bed to me.—	

	I kiss'd her o'er and o'er again,	
	And ay she wist na what to say;	*knew not*
	I laid her 'tween me an' the wa',	*wall*
40	The lassie thocht na lang till day.—	*thought it not long*

	Upon the morrow when we rase,
	I thank'd her for her courtesie:
	But ay she blush'd, and ay she sigh'd,
	And said, Alas, ye've ruin'd me. —

45	I clasp'd her waist, and kiss'd her syne,	*then*
	While the tear stood twinklin in her e'e;	*eye*
	I said, My lassie, dinna cry,	*do not*
	For ye ay shall mak the bed to me.—	*always*

	She took her mither's holland sheets	*mother's, fine linen*
50	An' made them a' in sarks to me:	*shirts*
	Blythe and merry may she be,	
	The lass that made the bed to me. —	

	The bonie lass made the bed to me,	
	The braw lass made the bed to me;	*fine*
55	I'll ne'er forget till the day I die	
	The lass that made the bed to me. —	

Although Johnson printed this song as 'Written for this work by Robert Burns' it is not completely original. It is based upon an old lyric, *Cumberland Nelly*, sometimes called *The North County Lovers*, from the Pepys collection. (See Henley–Henderson, Vol. III, p. 420). Burns did not only preserve Scots songs in the Museum collection, but, as in this case, turned traditional English lyrics into Scots.

Sae Far Awa

Tune: Dalkeith Maiden Bridge
First printed in Johnson, 1796.

O SAD and heavy should I part,
  But for her sake sae far awa;   so, away
Unknowing what my way may thwart,
  My native land sae far awa.—

5 Thou that of a' things Maker art,   all
  That formed this Fair sae far awa,
Gie body strength, then I'll ne'er start   give
  At this my way sae far awa.

How true is love to pure desert,
10 So love to her, sae far awa,
And nocht can heal my bosom's smart,   nothing
  While Oh, she is sae far awa.—

Nane other love, nane other dart,   no
  I feel, but hers sae far awa;   so
15 But fairer never touched a heart,
  Than hers, the Fair sae far awa.—

This was signed 'B' in the S.M.M. There is no evidence among the poet's letters to suggest a heroine of the song existed.

The Reel o' Stumpie

Tune: The Reel o' Stumpie.
First printed in Johnson, 1796.

WAP and row, wap and row,   wrap, roll
  Wap and row the feetie o't,   feet
I thought I was a maiden fair,
  Till I heard the greetie o't.   crying

My daddie was a Fiddler fine,
 My minnie she made mantie O;   *mother, a dress maker*
And I myself a thumpin quine,   *strapping lassie*
 And danc'd the Reel o' Stumpie O.

This was unsigned in the S.M.M. It is based upon the bawdy lyric
preserved in the *Merry Muses of Caledonia*.

The Rantin Laddie –
First printed in Johnson, 1796.

Aften hae I play'd at the cards and the dice,   *often have*
 For the love of a rantin laddie;
But now I maun sit at my father's kitchen neuk, *must, corner*
 Below a bastart babie.—

5 For my father he will not me own,
 And my mother she neglects me,
And a' my friends hae lightlyed me,   *have slandered*
 And their servants they do slight me.—

But had I a servant at my command,
10 As aft-times I've had many,   *oft-*
That wad rin wi' a letter to bonie Glenswood, *would run*
 Wi' a letter to my rantin laddie.—

Oh, is he either a laird, or a lord,
 Or is he but a cadie,   *rascal*
15 That ye do him ca' sae aft by name,   *call so often*
 Your bonie, bonie rantin ladie.—

Indeed he is baith a laird and a lord,   *both*
 And he was never a cadie;   *rascal*
But he is the Earl o' bonie Aboyne,
20 And he is my rantin laddie.—

O ye 'se get a servant at your command,
 As aft times ye've had many,   *oft*
That sall rin wi' a letter to bonie Glenswood, *shall run*
 A letter to your rantin laddie.—

25   When lord Aboyne did letter get,
      O but he blinket bonie;   *glanced well*
  But or he read three lines of it,   *by the time*
      I think his heart was sorry.—

  O wha is he daur be sae bauld,   *who, dare, so bold*
30   Sae cruelly to use my lassie?   *so*
* *
* *

  For her father he will not her know
      And her mother she does slight her,
35   And a' her friend hae lightlyed her,   *have slandered*
      And their servants they neglect her.—

  Go raise to me five hundred men,
      Make haste and make them ready;
  With a milkwhite steed under every ane,   *one*
40   For to bring hame my lady.—   *home*

  As they cam in thro Buchan shire,
      They were a company bonie,
  With a gude claymore in every hand,   *good*
      And O, but they shin'd bonie.—   *shone*

This is a song collected and only marginally improved by Burns
from the original song, *Lord Aboyne*. Burns may have picked it up
during his 1787 visit to the north-east of Scotland, or in Dumfries
from one of the Highland soldiers in barracks there during the mid-
1790s.

O May, Thy Morn

Tune: The Rashes
First printed in Johnson, 1796.

  O May, thy morn was ne'er sae sweet,   *so*
      As the mirk night o' December;   *dark*
  For sparkling was the rosy wine,
      And private was the chamber:
5   And dear was she, I dare na name,   *not*
      But I will ay remember.—   *always*

And here's to them, that, like oursel,
   Can push about the jorum;   *punch bowl*
And here's to them that wish us weel,   *well*
10   May a' that's guid watch o'er 'em: *all, good*
And here's to them we dare na tell,   *not*
   The dearest o' the quorum.—

This was signed 'B' in the S.M.M. Henley and Henderson suggest that this commemorates the poet's parting with Clarinda (Mrs Agnes McLehose) on 6th December, 1791. This is conjecture. Kinsley states, quite accurately, that it is 'a blend of love and conviviality in his finest lyric style' (Vol. III, p. 1510).

As I Cam o'er the Cairney Mount –

First printed in Johnson, 1796.

AS I came o'er the Cairney mount,
   And down among the blooming heather,
Kindly stood the milkin-shiel   *-shed*
   To shelter frae the stormy weather.—   *from*

Chorus
5 O my bonie Highland lad,
   My winsome, weelfar'd Highland laddie;   *well-favoured*
Wha wad mind the wind and rain,   *who would*
   Sae weel row'd in his tartan plaidie.—   *so well rolled*

Now Phebus blinkit on the bent,   *the sun, shone, hillock*
10   And o'er the knowes the lambs were bleating: *grassy mounds*
But he wan my heart's consent,   *won*
   To be his ain at the neist meeting. —   *own, next*
      O my bonie &c.

This was signed 'Z' in the S.M.M., suggesting that Johnson knew Burns adapted the lyric from an old (bawdy) song.

Highland Laddie

First printed in Johnson, 1796.

She
THE bonniest lad that e'er I saw,
    Bonie laddie, Highland laddie,
Wore a plaid and was fu' braw,   *handsome*
5   Bonie Highland laddie.
On his head a bonnet blue,
    Bonie laddie, Highland laddie,
His royal heart was firm and true,
    Bonie Highland laddie.

10 He
Trumpets sound and cannons roar,
    Bonie lassie, Lawland lassie,   *lowland*
And a' the hills wi' echoes roar,
    Bonie Lawland lassie.
15 Glory, Honour now invite,
    Bonie lassie, Lawland lassie,
For freedom and my King to fight
    Bonie Lawland lassie.

She
20 The sun a backward course shall take,
    Bonie laddie, Highland laddie,
Ere ought thy manly courage shake;   *ought*
    Bonie Highland laddie.
Go, for yoursel procure renown,
25   Bonie laddie, Highland laddie,
And for your lawful King his crown,
    Bonie Highland laddie.

This is unsigned in the S.M.M. The original, adapted by Burns, is a
song called *The Highland Lad and Highland Lass*, set in 1745, but
found in a collection of Jacobite songs *A Collection of Loyal Songs*
(1750). It was reprinted in *The True Loyalist* (1779). Along with
minor changes, the first stanza is from Burns.

Lovely Polly Stewart

Tune: Ye're Welcome Charlie Stewart
First printed in Johnson, 1796.

THE flower it blaws, it fades, it fa's,   blows, falls
    And art can ne'er renew it;
But Worth and Truth eternal youth
    Will gie to Polly Stewart. —   give

Chorus
5 O lovely Polly Stewart!
    O charming Polly Stewart!
There's ne'er a flower that blooms in May
    That's half so fair as thou art. —

May he, whase arms shall fauld thy charms,   whose, enfold
10   Possess a leal and true heart!   loyal
To him be given, to ken the Heaven   know
    He grasps in Polly Stewart!
      O lovely &c.

Johnson has marked this song, 'Written for this Work by Robert Burns' in the S.M.M. Polly (Mary) Stewart was the daughter of William Stewart, the factor at Closeburn estate and also subject of the song *You're Welcome Willie Stewart*.

The Highland Balou

First printed in Johnson, 1796.

HEE-balou, my sweet, wee Donald,   lullaby
Picture o' the great Clanronald;
Brawlie kens our wanton Chief   finely knows
Wha gat my young Highland thief. —   who got

5 Leeze me on thy bonie craigie,   blessings, neck
An thou live, thou'll steal a naigie,   horse
Travel the country thro' and thro',
And bring hame a Carlisle cow. —   home

Thro' the Lawlands, o'er the Border,   lowlands
10 Weel, my babie, may thou furder: well, further
Herry the louns o' the laigh Countrie,   harry, fools, low
Syne to the Highlands hame to me. —   then, home

Previous editors are probably correct that this is a versification of a nursery song. The original, though, has not been traced. The Gaelic song *Cagaran Gaolach* is mentioned and quoted in Kinsley (Vol. III, p. 1512) as a modern example but Mackay errs (p. 588) in asserting it is the source of this song. It has no relationship to the work by Burns.

Wae is My Heart

First printed in Johnson, 1796.

Wae is my heart, and the tear's in my e'e;	sad, eye
Lang, lang joy's been a stranger to me;	long
Forsaken and friendless my burden I bear,	
And the sweet voice o' pity ne'er sounds in my ear. —	

Love, thou hast pleasures, and deep hae I lov'd;	have
Love thou has sorrows, and sair hae I prov'd:	sore have
But this bruised heart that now bleeds in my breast,	
I can feel by its throbbings, will soon be at rest. —	

O, if I were, where happy I hae been;	have
Down by yon stream and yon bonie castle-green:	
For there he is wand'ring, and musing on me,	
Wha wad soon dry the tear frae his Phillis' e'e. —	who would, from, eye

This was unsigned in the S.M.M. It is based on an old ballad and shows signs of being reworked by Burns. A holograph exists and a second was supposedly seen by Scott Douglas in 1877.

Here's his Health in Water

First printed in Johnson, 1796.

Although my back be at the wa',	wall
And tho' he be the fautor,	at fault
Altho' my back be at the wa',	
Yet here's his health in water. —	

5	O wae gae by his wanton sides,	sadly go
	Sae brawly 's he could flatter;	so finely
	Till for his sake I'm slighted sair,	sore
	And dree the kintra clatter:	suffer, country gossip
	But though my back be at the wa',	wall
10	Yet here's his health in water. —	

This fragment was signed 'Z' in the S.M.M. It is adapted from the song *On the Birthday of King James VIII* (1709) which features in the collection, *Roxburghe Ballads*.

Gude Wallace

First printed in Johnson, 1796.

O for my ain king, quo gude Wallace,   own
    The rightful king o' fair Scotland;
Between me and my Sovereign Blude   blood
    I think I see some ill deed sawn.—   sown

5   Wallace out over yon river he lap,   leaped
    And he ha lighted down on yon plain,   has
And he was aware of a gay ladie,
    As she was at the well washing.—

What tydins, what tydins, fair lady, he says,   tidings/news
10 What tydins hast thou to tell unto me;
What tydins, what tydins, fair lady, he says,
    What tydins hae ye in the South Countrie.—   news have you

Low down in yon wee Ostler house,
    There is fyfteen Englishmen, fifteen
15 And they are seeking for Gude Wallace,
    It's him to take and him to hang.—

There's nocht in my purse, quo gude Wallace,   nothing
    There's nocht, not even a bare pennie;
But I will down to yon wee Ostler house,
20   Thir fyfteen Englishmen to see.—   those

And when he cam to yon wee Ostler house,
    He bad benedicite be there;   good fortune
* * * * * * * * * * * * *
* * * * * * * * * * * * *

25 Where was ye born, auld crookit Carl,   old bent man
    Where was ye born, in what countrie;
I am a true Scot born and bred,
    And an auld, crookit carl sic as ye see.—   such

I wad gie fyfteen shilling to onie crookit carl,   would give
30   To onie crookit carl just sic as ye,
If ye will get me gude Wallace,
        For he is the man I wad very fain see.—   would

He hit the proud Captain alang the chafft-blade,   along, jawbone
        That never a bit o' meat he ate mair;   more
35 And he sticket the rest at the table where they sat   stabbed
        And he left them a' lyin sprawlin there.—   spread

Get up, get up, gudewife, he says,
        And get to me some dinner in haste;
For it will soon be three lang days   long
40   Sin I a bit o' meat did taste.—   since

The dinner was na weel readie,   not well ready
        Nor was it on the table set,
Till another fyfteen Englishmen
        Were a' lighted about the yett.—   gate

45 Come out, come out now, gude Wallace,
        This is the day that thou maun die;   shall
I lippen nae sae little to God, he says,   trust, not so
        Altho' I be but ill wordie.—   unworthy

The gudewife had an auld gudeman,   old husband
50   By gude Wallace he stiffly stood,
Till ten o' the fyfteen Englishmen
        Before the door lay in their blude.—   blood

The other five to the greenwood ran,
        And he hang'd these five upon a grain: tree-branch
55 And on the morn wi' his merry men a'
        He sat at dine on Lochmaben town.—

This is unsigned in the S.M.M. Kinsley asserts that: 'It is clear
Burns collected the ballad from oral tradition, but there is no
evidence that he revised it' (Vol. III, p. 1514). This judgement
cannot be made with any real certainty and if it was right, Kinsley
should have rejected the work from the canon. A chapbook ballad
of this song was composed about 1750 which matches a consider-
able portion of this version. However, there are seven new stanzas
in this edition not found in the chapbook version. (It was based on

the William Hamilton abridgement of Blind Harry's epic poetic tale on Sir William Wallace.) This does not automatically mean the new stanzas are by Burns. If Burns did rework the ballad, he may have recorded it from an unknown broadside print, or from someone's singing. It is left in the canon on the basis that he probably did see a broadside version of the song which he may have reworked.

The Auld Man's Mare's Dead

First printed in Barke, 1955.

SHE was cut-luggit, painch-lippit,	ear-torn, pinch-lipped
Steel waimit, stainchet-fittit,	stomach, stanchion-footed
Chanler-chafit, lang-neckit,	wide-jawed, long-necked
Yet the brute did die.—	

Chorus

5	The auld man's mare' dead,	old
	The poor man's mare's dead,	
	The auld man's mare's dead.	
	A mile aboon Dundee.—	above

	Her lunzie-banes were knaggs and neuks,	haunch-bones, knots, corners
10	She had the cleeks, the cauld, the crooks,	cramps, cold, bent neck
	The jawpish and the wanton yeuks,	urinary disease, itch
	And the howks boon her e'e.—	eye growth, above, eye
	The auld man's &c.	

	My Master rade me to the town,	rode
	He ty'd me to a staincher round,	tied, hitching post
15	He took a chappin till himsel,	measure of drink
	But fient a drap gae me. —	not a drop gave

	The auld man's mare's dead
	The poor man's mare's dead,
	The peats and tours and a' to lead
20	And yet the bitch did die. —

This was sent to Johnson for the S.M.M. in the Autumn of 1795, but not printed. Burns referred Johnson to an earlier version in *The Scots Nightingale* (1779 edition) and the extant holograph shows some changes from this early version. The original was ascribed to a

Peter Birnie of Fife who is supposed to have composed the lyric circa
1710. However, *The Scots Nightingale* gives it as the work of a Mr
Watts. A peculiar little poem as it incongruously mixes vernacularly
grotesque description with, in the third stanza, the horse's own
voice.

The Taylor
First printed in Johnson, 1796.

THE Taylor he cam here to sew,
    And weel he kend the way to woo,   well, knew
For ay he pree'd the lassie's mou,   tasted/tried, mouth
    As he gaed but and ben O.   went out and in

First Chorus
5   For weel he kend the way O   well, knew
    The way, O, the way O,
For weel he kend the way, O,
    The lassie's heart to win O.

The Taylor rase and sheuk his duds,   rose, shook, clothes
10   The flaes they flew awa in cluds,   fleas, away, clouds
And them that stay'd gat fearfu' thuds,   got, thumps
    The Taylor prov'd a man O. —

Final Chorus
For now it was the gloamin,
    The gloamin, the gloamin,
15   For now it was the gloamin
    When a' to rest are gaun O. —   all, gone

This is unsigned in the S.M.M. It has some similarities to a song in
the Herd Collection (1769) but is modelled on the 1776 broadside
sheet *The Taylor of Hogerglen's Wedding*, with some minor am-
mendments: only the final chorus is exclusively from Burns.

There Grows A Bonie Brier-Bush
First printed in Johnson, 1796.

THERE grows a bonie brier-bush in our kail-yard,   vegetable patch
There grows a bonie brier-bush in our kail-yard;
And below the bonie brier-bush there's a lassie and a lad,
And they're busy, busy courting in our kail-yard. —

5	We'll court nae mair below the buss in our kail-yard,	*no more, bush*
	We'll court nae mair below the buss in our kail-yard;	
	We'll awa to Athole's green, and there we'll no be seen,	*not*
	Where the trees and the branches will be our safe-guard. —	

Will ye go to the dancin in Carlyle's ha',
10   Will ye go to the dancin in Carlyle's ha';
Whare Sandy and Nancy I'm sure will ding them a'?   *where, excel*
I winna gang to the dance in Carlyle-ha'.   *will not go*

What will I do for a lad, when Sandie gangs awa?   *goes*
What will I do for a lad, when Sandie gangs awa?
15   I will awa to Edinburgh and win a pennie fee,   *away, servant work*
And see an onie lad will fancy me. —   *if any*

He's comin frae the North that's to marry me,   *from*
He's comin frae the North that's to marry me;
A feather in his bonnet and a ribbon at his knee,
20   He's a bonie, bonie laddie an yon be he. —

This work is signed 'Z' in the S.M.M. It is based on a traditional
song re-written by Burns with much of the old story intact. There is,
for once, a quite unintended irony in this song. Burns deliberately
loads all his poetry with the often harsh detail of the life of the
common people. Here an outdoor, probably prickly, nocturnal
sexual encounter and the girl's subsequent honest survival instinct
were *nominally* assimilated into nineteenth-century culture to pro-
vide the nomenclature of the mendaciously sentimental 'Kailyard'
school. *Beneath the Bony Briar Bush* is, in fact, the title of one of its
most popular novels.

Here's to Thy Health My Bonie Lass

Tune: Laggan Burn
First printed in Johnson, 1796.

HERE'S to thy health, my bonie lass,
    Guid night and joy be wi' thee: *good*
I'll come nae mair to thy bower-door,   *no more*
    To tell thee that I lo'e thee.   *love*
5   O dinna think, my pretty pink,   *do not*
    But I can live without thee:
I vow and swear I dinna care,   *do not*
    How lang ye look about ye.   *long*

Thou'rt ay sae free informing me   always so
10   Thou hast nae mind to marry: no
I'll be as free informing thee,
    Nae time hae I to tarry.   no, have
I ken thy freens try ilka means   know, friends, every
    Frae wedlock to delay thee;   from
15 Depending on some higher chance,
    But fortune may betray thee.

I ken they scorn my low estate,
    But that does never grieve me;
For I'm as free as any he,
20   Sma' siller will relieve me.   little money
I'll count my health my greatest wealth,
    Sae lang as I'll enjoy it: so/as long
I'll fear nae scant, I'll bode nae want,   no poverty, no lack
    As lang's I get employment.   long as

25 But far-off fowls hae feathers fair,   have
    And, ay until ye try them:
Tho' they seem fair, still have a care,
    They may prove as bad as I am.
But at twal at night, when the moon shines   twelve
        bright,
30   My dear, I'll come and see thee;
For the man that loves his mistress weel,   well
    Nae travel makes him weary.   no

Although introduced in the S.M.M. as 'Written for this work by
Robert Burns' the poet notes on a manuscript copy that it was
originally composed by an 'illiterate Millwright' from Ayrshire,
some thirty years prior. If this is true, most editors have assumed
Burns revised the original. It does have traces of traditional folk
song lyrics, but most of it is in the Burns manner. Indeed, it reads
like an early song by Burns from his Mossgiel farm days. The pacey
double rhyme in the third and fifth line of each stanza is character-
istic. There is an obvious skill employed here which no 'illiterate
millwright' would possess. Henley and Henderson suspected this
was an early song by Burns and we concur.

It Was a' for our Rightfu' King

First printed in Johnson, 1796.

IT was a' for our rightfu' king   all
    We left fair Scotland's strand;
It was a' for our rightfu' king,
    We e'er saw Irish land, my dear,
5   We e'er saw Irish land. —

Now a' is done that men can do,
    And a' is done in vain:
My Love and Native Land fareweel,   farewell
    For I maun cross the main, my dear,   must
10   For I maun cross the main. —

He turn'd him right and round about,
    Upon the Irish shore,
And gae his bridle reins a shake,   gave
    With, Adieu for evermore, my dear,
15   And adieu for evermore. —

The soger frae the wars returns,   soldier from
    The sailor frae the main,   from
But I hae parted frae my Love,   have, from
    Never to meet again, my dear,
20   Never to meet again. —

When day is gane, and night is come,   gone
    And a' folk bound to sleep;
I think on him that's far awa,
    The lee-lang night and weep, my dear,   entire
25   The lee-lang night and weep. —

This was unsigned in the S.M.M. but Burns never signed any of his
Jacobite songs. Kinsley trails it back to a chapbook ballad, *Mally
Stewart* (c. 1746), the end of which provided Burns's central stanza:

The trooper turn'd himself about all on the Irish shore,
He has given the bridle-reins a shake, saying
  'Adieu for ever more,
    My dear
  Adieu for ever more.'

The Highland Widow's Lament

First printed in Johnson, 1796.

OH, I am come to the low Countrie,
    Ochon, Ochon, Ochrie!   *alas, alack*
Without a penny in my purse
    To buy a meal to me. —

5   It was na sae in the Highland hills,   *not so*
    Ochon, Ochon, Ochrie!
Nae woman in the Country wide   *no*
    Sae happy was as me. —   *so*

For then I had a score o' kye,   *cattle*
    Ochon, &c.
Feeding on yon hill sae high,   *so*
10   And giving milk to me. —

And there I had three score o' yowes,   *ewes/sheep*
    Ochon, &c.
Skipping on yon bonie knowes,   *hill slopes*
    And casting woo' to me. —   *wool*

I was the happiest of a' the Clan,
15   Sair, sair may I repine;   *sore*
For Donald was the brawest man,   *finest*
    And Donald he was mine. —

Till Charlie Stewart cam at last,
    Sae far to set us free;   *so*
20 My Donald's arm was wanted then
    For Scotland and for me. —

Their waefu' fate what need I tell,   *woeful*
    Right to the wrang did yield;   *wrong*
My Donald and his Country fell
25   Upon Culloden field. —

Ochon, O Donald, Oh!   *alas*
    Ochon, &c.
Nae woman in the warld wide   *no, world*
    Sae wretched now as me. —   *so*

This Jacobite song written in the feminine voice was unsigned in the S.M.M. Jacobitism was still virtually taboo during the 1790s, particularly for Excise employees, who were, well after 1745, expected to report officially on the families of Jacobite sympathisers.

O Steer Her Up an' Haud Her Gaun
First printed in Johnson, 1803.

O STEER her up an' haud her gaun,		stir, hold, going
Her mither's at the mill, jo;		mother's, dear
An' gin she winna tak a man		if, will not
E'en let her tak her will, jo.		
First shore her wi' a kindly kiss		offer
And ca' anither gill, jo;		ask for another drink
An' gin she tak the thing amiss		if
E'en let her flyte her fill, jo.		scold

5 at line "First shore her..."

O steer her up an' be na blate, — stir, not shy
   An' gin she tak it ill, jo, — if
Then lea'e the lassie till her fate, — leave
   And time nae langer spill, jo; — no longer
Ne'er break your heart for ae rebute, — one
   But think upon it still, jo,
That gin the lassie winna do't, — if, will not
   Ye'll fin' anither will, jo. — find another

(lines 10, 15)

Four lines at the beginning of this work are taken from a song in Ramsay's *Tea-Table Miscellany*. The remainder is from Burns.

Wee Willie Gray
First printed in Johnson, 1803.

WEE Willie Gray, an' his leather wallet;
Peel a willie wand, to be him boots and jacket. — willow
The rose upon the breer will be him trouse and doublet. — brier, trousers
The rose upon the breer will be him trouse and doublet.

Wee Willie Gray, and his leather wallet;
Twice a lily-flower will be him sark and cravat; — shirt, necktie
Feathers of a flee wad feather up his bonnet, — flea would
Feathers of a flee wad feather up his bonnet.

This is included in S.M.M. as 'Written for this work by Robert Burns'. It is a rare example of Burns composing a nursery rhyme lyric to what was then a well-known nursery tune. There is no extant manuscript.

Gudeen to You Kimmer

First printed in Johnson, 1803.

GUDEEN to you kimmer   *good evening, wench*
    And how do ye do?
Hiccup, quo' kimmer,   *the wench*
    The better that I'm fou.   *drunk*

Chorus
5 We're a' noddin, nid nid noddin,
    We're a' noddin at our house at hame,   *home*
We're a' noddin, nid nid noddin,
    We're a' noddin at our house at hame.   *home*

Kate sits i' the neuk,   *corner*
10   Suppin hen-broo;   *-brew*
Deil tak Kate   *devil*
    An she be na noddin too!
      We're a' noddin &c.

How's a' wi' you, kimmer,   *everything, wench*
    And how do you fare?
15 A pint o' the best o't,
    And twa pints mair.   *more*
      We're a' noddin &c.

How's a' wi' you, kimmer,
    And how do ye thrive;
How monie bairns hae ye?   *many children have*
20   Quo' kimmer, I hae five.   *have*
      We're a' noddin &c.

Are they a' Johny's?
    Eh! atweel na: *certainly not*
Twa o' them were gotten   *two*
    When Johnie was awa.   *away*
      We're a' noddin &c.

25 Cats like milk,
      And dogs like broo;   *water*
Lads like lasses weel,   *well*
      And lasses lads too.
         We're a' noddin &c.

The S.M.M. states 'Corrected by Burns', which means it is based on a traditional song, but improved by Burns. It is adapted from a song in the Herd collection (1769). There is also a slight influence from the original version of *John Anderson My Jo*.

O Ay My Wife She Dang Me

First printed in Johnson, 1803.

On peace and rest my mind was bent,
    And fool I was I marry'd;
But never honest man's intent
    As cursedly miscarry'd.

Chorus
5 O ay my wife she dang me,   *struck*
    An' aft my wife she bang'd me,   *oft, thumped*
If ye gie a woman a' her will   *give*
    Gude faith she'll soon oergang ye.   *good, over run/rule*

Some sairie comfort at the last,   *sorry*
10   When a' thir days are done, man,   *all their*
My pains o' hell on earth is past,
    I'm sure o' bliss aboon, man.   *above (heaven)*
        O ay my wife &c.

Despite the fact that the S.M.M. records 'Written for this work by Robert Burns' a copy has never been found in manuscript. Stenhouse claimed it was based on a traditional bawdy song. This is probably correct given that one stanza of the original work is quoted in Henley–Henderson (See Vol. III, p. 439).

Scroggam

First printed in Johnson, 1803.

THERE was a wife wonn'd in Cockpen,	who dwelled
Scroggam;	
She brew'd gude ale for gentlemen,	good
Sing Auld Cowl, lay you down by me,	(see notes)
5 Scroggam, my Dearie, ruffum.	
The gudewife's dochter fell in a fever,	daughter
Scroggam;	
The priest o' the parish fell in anither,	another
Sing Auld Cowl, lay you down by me,	
10 Scroggam, my Dearie, ruffum.	
They laid the twa i' the bed thegither,	two, together
Scroggam;	
That the heat o' the tane might cool the tither,	one, other
Sing Auld Cowl, lay you down by me,	
15 Scroggam, my Dearie, ruffum.	

The S.M.M. states 'Written for this work by Robert Burns', but it is not a wholly original lyric. The first line is taken from a song preserved by Burns in the *Merry Muses*, 'There wonned a wife in Whistlecockpen'. 'Auld Cowl' (l. 4) refers to a religious figure, probably a priest. Kinsley mentions that a colleague of his believed the word 'scroggam' to be a derivative of 'scrag 'em', a yell associated with London street mobs; likewise, 'ruffum' derives from 'rough 'em'. This may be true, but given the original bawdy song, it is more likely that these words have a sexual meaning.

O Gude Ale Comes

First printed in Johnson, 1803.

I had sax owsen in a pleugh,	six oxen, plough
And they drew a' weel eneugh:	well enough
I sald them a' just ane by ane —	sold, one by one
Guid ale keeps the heart aboon!	good, above

Chorus

5 O gude ale comes, and gude ale goes,   good
    Gude ale gars me sell my hose,   makes
Sell my hose and pawn my shoon,   shoes
    Gude ale keeps my heart aboon.   above

Gude ale hauds me bare and busy,   keeps
10   Gars me moop wi' the servant hizzie,   makes, have sex, hussy
Stand i' the stool when I hae dune,   (church stool) have done
    Guid ale keeps the heart aboon.   above

The comment 'Corrected by R. Burns' in the S.M.M. indicates that
this is based on a traditional song. The fact that there are two
mansucript copies reinforces this view, given that one appears to be
collected by Burns from oral tradition and the second manuscript is
the one improved by Burns and sent to Johnson.

My Lord A-Hunting He is Gane

Tune: My Lady's Gown, There's Gairs Upon 'T
First printed in Johnson, 1803.

MY Lord a hunting he is gane,   gone
But hounds or hawks wi' him are nane;   none
By Colin's cottage lies his game,
If Colin's Jenny be at hame.   home

Chorus

5 My Lady's gown there's gairs upon 't,   panels (gores)
And gowden flowers sae rare upon 't;   golden, so
But Jenny's jimps and jirkinet   blouse, bodice
My Lord thinks meikle mair upon 't.   much more

My Lady's white, my Lady's red
10 And kith and kin o' Cassillis' blude,   blood
But her tenpund lands o' tocher gude   pounds, dowry good
Were a' the charms his Lordship lo'ed.   loved
    My Lady's gown &c.

Out o'er yon moor, out o'er yon moss,
Whare gor-cocks thro' the heather pass,   where red grouse
15 There wons auld Colin's bonie lass,   dwells old
A lily in a wilderness.
    My Lady's gown &c.

Sae sweetly move her genty limbs,   so, dainty
Like music-notes o' Lovers' hymns;
The diamond-dew in her een sae blue   eyes so
20 Where laughing love sae wanton swims.   so
       My Lady's gown &c.

My Lady's dink, my Lady's drest,   trim
The flower and fancy o' the west;
But the Lassie that a man loe's best,   loves
O that's the lass to mak him blest.
       My Lady's gown &c.

This is marked by Johnson 'Written for this work by Robert Burns' in the S.M.M. but it does appear to be completely original. There is, however, no known traditional text for this blend of folk-song and ballad. Cunningham states that an Ayrshire musician, James Gregg, composed the music. Cassillis refers to the land of the Kennedy clan who ruled Carrick and the song is probably based on one of that family.

Sweetest May

Tune: Kinloch of Kinloch or Blow the Wind Southerly
First printed in Johnson, 1803.

SWEETEST May let Love inspire thee;
Take a heart which he designs thee;
As thy constant slave regard it;
For its faith and truth reward it.

Proof o' shot to Birth or Money,
Not the wealthy, but the bonie;
Not high-born, but noble-minded,
In Love's silken band can bind it.

This is an update of a song in Ramsay's *Tea-Table Miscellany, My Sweetest May Let Love Incline Thee*, sometimes called *There's My Thumb I'll Ne'er Beguile Thee*. The first five lines merely abbreviate the original, the last three are from Burns.

Jockey's Ta'en the Parting Kiss

Tune: Bonie Lass Tak a Man
First printed in Currie, 1800.

JOCKEY'S ta'en the parting kiss,	taken
O'er the mountains he is gane;	gone
And with him is a' my bliss,	all
Nought but griefs with me remain.	
5 Spare my luve, ye winds that blaw,	blow
Plashy sleets and beating rain;	splashing
Spare my luve, thou feath'ry snaw,	snow
Drifting o'er the frozen plain.	
When the shades of evening creep	
10 O'er the day's fair, gladsome e'e,	eye/light
Sound and safely may he sleep,	
Sweetly blythe his waukening be.	waking
He will think on her he loves,	
Fondly he'll repeat her name;	
15 For where'er he distant roves	
Jockey's heart is still at hame.	home

Although first published in Currie in 1800, this also appears in Johnson's S.M.M. in 1803. It is described by Kinsley (and in Mackay) as merely a Scottish revision of an English song written originally in 1776, as if Burns simply translated it into Scots. In this case the song is far more adapted and changed by Burns than these editors suggest.

O Lay Thy Loof in Mine Lass

Tune: The Shoemaker's March
First printed in Johnson, 1803.

A SLAVE to Love's unbounded sway,	
He aft has wrought me meikle wae;	often, great woe
But now he is my deadly fae,	foe
Unless thou be my ain.	own
Chorus	
5 O lay thy loof in mine lass,	palm
In mine lass, in mine lass,	
And swear on thy white hand lass,	
That thou wilt be my ain.	own

There's monie a lass has broke my rest,   many
10 That for a blink I hae lo'ed best;   glance, have loved
But thou art queen within my breast
For ever to remain.
    O lay thy loof &c.

This was sent to Johnson in the spring of 1795 (Letter 667) but he
waited until 1803 to print it.

Bonie Peg-a-Ramsay

First printed in Johnson, 1803.

CAULD is the e'enin blast   cold, evening
    O' Boreas o'er the pool,   the North wind
An' dawin it is dreary,   dawning
    When birks are bare at Yule.   birches, Christmas

5   O cauld blaws the e'enin blast   cold blows
    When bitter bites the frost,
And in the mirk and dreary drift   dark
    The hills and glens are lost.

Ne'er sae murky blew the night   so dirty
10   That drifted o'er the hill,
But bonie Peg a Ramsey
    Gat grist to her mill.   got

This is often printed under the title *Cauld is the E'enin Blast*, but
Mackay's title is probably best suited because it emphasises the
sexual metaphor of milling associated with Peggy Ramsay, a name
famed in bawdy song from before the time of Shakespeare. (In
Twelfth Night, Act 2, Scene 3, Sir Toby Belch says, 'Malvolio's a
Peg-a-Ramsay'.)

There was a Bonie Lass

First printed in Johnson, 1803.

THERE was a bonie lass,
    And a bonie, bonie lass,
And she lo'ed her bonie laddie dear;   loved
    Till war's loud alarms
5   Tore her laddie frae her arms,   from
Wi' monie a sigh and a tear.   many

Over sea, over shore,
Where the cannons loudly roar;
He still was a stranger to fear:
10   And nocht could him quail,   *nothing*
Or his bosom assail,
But the bonie lass he lo'ed sae dear.   *loved so*

This is probably based on a traditional song which editors have been unable to trace. Henderson and Henley call it a 'cento of old catchwords' (Vol. III, p. 445).

There's News Lasses News

Tune: Captain MacKenzie's Reel
First printed in Johnson, 1803.

THERE'S news, lasses, news,
Gude news I've to tell,   *good*
There's a boatfu' o' lads
Come to our town to sell.

Chorus
5   The wean wants a cradle,   *child lacks*
And the cradle wants a cod,   *pillow*
An' I'll no gang to my bed   *not go*
Until I get a nod.

Father, quo' she, Mither, quo' she,   *mother*
10   Do what you can,
I'll no gang to my bed   *go*
Until I get a man.
    The wean &c.

I hae as guid a craft rig   *have, good, croft ridge*
As made o' yird and stane;   *earth, stone*
15   And waly fa' the ley-crap   *woe befall, meadow crop*
For I maun till'd again.   *must till it*
    The wean &c.

Here Burns has woven together a fragment of a song from the Herd collection (1769), along with a traditional lyric *I Wanna Gang to My Bed Until I Get a Man*. The final stanza is from Burns.

O that I had Ne'er been Married

First printed in Johnson, 1803.

O that I had ne'er been married,
    I wad never had nae care,   *would, no*
Now I've gotten wife and bairns   *children*
    An' they cry crowdie ever mair.   *for food, more*

Chorus
5 Ance crowdie, twice crowdie,
    Three times crowdie in a day;
Gin ye crowdie onie mair,   *if, any more*
    Ye'll crowdie a' my meal away.   *eat all*

Waefu' Want and Hunger fley me,   *woeful, terrify*
10   Glowrin by the hallan en';   *staring, porch entrance*
Sair I fecht them at the door,   *sore, fight*
    But ay I'm eerie they come ben.   *always, afraid, inside*
        Ance crowdie &c.

Johnson prints this as 'Corrected by R. Burns'. Only the final verse, by far the most distinctive part of the song, is by Burns: the main text is traditional.

On Rough Roads

First printed in Scott Douglas, 1876.

I'm now arriv'd — thanks to the Gods! —
    Through pathways rough and muddy,
A certain sign that makin roads
    Is no this people's study: *not*
Altho' I'm not wi' Scripture cram'd,
    I'm sure the Bible says
That heedless sinners shall be damn'd,
    Unless they mend their *ways*.

This first appears with Scott Douglas in 1877 who estimates the composition date for sometime in 1786. This is probably in error. It is accepted to the canon by Mackay (p. 256) but placed in Dubia by Kinsley (no. 629), who questions whether it is by Burns. Kinsley remarks '. . . if Burns wrote the piece, it more probably belongs to

the period of the Highland tour' (Vol. III, no. 629, p. 1529). The
reference to Psalms cxxv, v. 5 is in the manner of Burns, although
the first section is linguistically weak. If Scott Douglas transcribed it
from a letter he saw (as claimed) which was later destroyed, then it is
probably authentic. There is no extant manuscript, but the tran-
script in the Wisbech and Fenland Museum records that it was
written on a window of an Inn at Moffat, suggesting a later date,
possibly when Burns lived in Dumfries. It is probably his.

The German Lairdie

First printed in Barke, 1955.

WHAT merriment has taen the whigs,   taken
    I think they be gaen mad, Sir,   gone
Wi' playing up their whiggish jigs,
    Their dancin may be sad, Sir. —

Chorus
5 Sing heedle liltie, teedle liltie,
    Andumn tandum tandie;
Sing fal de lal, de dal lal lal,
    Sing howdle liltie dandie. —

The Revolution principles
10   Has put their heads in bees, Sir;   buzzing/spinning
They're a' fa'n out amang themsels,   all fallen, among
    Deil tak the first that grees, Sir. —   agrees
        Sing heedle &c.

According to Kinsley, Burns has abridged the long political ballad
What Murrain Now has Tae'n the Whigs. The original was in vogue
after the 1688 revolution, as mentioned at l. 9.

Coila, by the Banks of Nith

First printed here as poetry by Burns.

By Banks of Nith I sat and wept,
    When Coila I thought on;
In midst therof I hung my harp
    The willow trees upon –

This fragment is included by Burns in a letter to John Beugo, an Edinburgh Engraver, dated 9th September, 1788 (Letter 268). It is, of course, a parody of Metrical Psalm 137, vv. 1–2.

Fragment to Clarinda
First printed by Alexander Cunningham, 1834.

Innocence
Look'd, gayly smiling on; while rosy Pleasure
Hid young Desire amid her flowery wreath,
And pour'd her cup luxuriant; mantling high,
The sparkling heavenly vintage, Love and Bliss!

These lines first appear with Cunningham, but Scott Douglas suggests they might be from Milton, although he prints them (Vol. II, p. 232). There is no trace of the lines in Milton. They have not been printed by any editor during the 20th century. Professor Delancey Ferguson observes in a footnote to his edition of the poet's letters that the lines were attributed to Burns by J.B. Reid in his 1889 *Concordance to the Poems and Songs of Robert Burns*, published in Glasgow. There are several poetic quotes in the same letter by Burns, all of them within quotation marks. Ferguson states, 'The absence of quotation marks in the MS suggests that Reid may have been right' (Letter 181).

The Ruin'd Maid's Complaint
(final stanza)
First printed in Hogg and Motherwell, 1834.

But Heaven's curse will blast the man
    Denies the bairn he got,
Or leaves the merry lass he lo'ed   loved
    To wear a ragged coat.

Of the seven stanzas in this traditional work, the final lines are almost certainly the work of Burns. They do not feature in the original song and are on a subject close to the poet's heart, taking responsibility for begetting children. Stenhouse and other editors during the 19th century attributed this stanza to Burns, but modern editors have tended to overlook this last stanza aware that Burns did not write the entire song. This stanza, almost word for word, is also employed by Burns to end his bawdy song *Wha'll Mow Me Now*.

On Marriage

First printed in Henley and Henderson, 1896.

That hackney'd judge of human life,
　　The Preacher and the King,
Observes: 'The man that gets a wife
　　He gets a noble thing.'

But how capricious are mankind,
　　Now loathing, now desirous!
We married men, how oft we find
　　The best of things will tire us!

This appears in Henley–Henderson and the Chambers–Wallace edition and features in Kinsley's *Dubia* section only because he could not date the composition (Vol. III, p. 1527). It is by Burns.

The Book-Worms – 1

First printed in Cunningham, 1834.

Through and through the inspired leaves,
　　Ye maggots, make your windings;
But, oh! respect his lordship's taste,
　　And spare his golden bindings.

The Book-Worms – 2

Free thro' the leaves ye maggots make your windings,
But for the Owner's sake oh spare the Bindings!

The original printed by Cunningham and a transcript by John Syme are both given here. Burns may have written two versions of these lines, or the differences may derive from John Syme's deficient memory. Syme wrote: 'A friend of the Bard having bought a Bible which was elegantly bound requested him to write something on the blank leaf. Extempore — written with his pencil.'

Kinsley states, 'Said by Cunningham to have been written in a volume of Shakespeare in a nobleman's library. The variant copied by Syme was written in a Bible which a friend offered Burns for his inscription' (Vol. III, p. 1526). Mackay records, almost verbatim, 'Said by Cunningham to have been inscribed in a volume of Shakespeare in a nobleman's library. A variant copied by John Syme was written in a Bible which a friend offered Burns for his inscription' (p. 608).

Her Flowing Locks

First printed in Cromek, 1808.

Her flowing locks, the raven's wing,
Adown her neck and bosom hing;
How sweet unto that breast to cling,
    And round that neck entwine her!

Her lips are roses wat wi' dew,   wet with
O, what a feast, her bonie mou!   mouth
Her cheeks a mair celestial hue,   more
    A crimson still diviner.

This fragment, accepted by modern editors, although it features in Kinsley's Dubia (as an undated composition) was probably meant to be set to a musical air, but Burns left it unfinished.

Epitaph for Hugh Logan, Esq. of Logan

Here lyes Squire Hugh — ye harlot crew,
    Come mak your water on him,
I'm sure that he well pleas'd would be
    To think ye pish'd upon him.

Hugh Logan (1739–1802) was laird of Logan, near Cumnock. In an age when aristocratic gentleman could purchase a small volume with personal details and a description of the active Edinburgh prostitutes, it is almost certain Burns picked up some gossip about Logan's connection with them.

The Henpeck'd Husband

First printed in Stewart, 1801.

Curs'd be the man, the poorest wretch in life,
The crouching vassal to the tyrant wife,
Who has no will but by her high permission;
Who has not sixpence but in her possession;
5   Who must to her his dear friend's secret tell;
Who dreads a curtain-lecture worse than hell.
Were such the wife had fallen to my part,
I'd break her spirit, or I'd break her heart;
I'd charm her with the magic of a switch,
10 I'd kiss her maids, and kick the perverse bitch.

This is given without comment in Kinsley's Dubia section, leaving readers to ponder whether he considered it to be an undated composition by Burns or that he rejected it. Mackay accepts it as a work of Burns. It was first printed in Glasgow in 1801 among *Poems Ascribed to Robert Burns*. There are several short pieces on the theme of tyrannical wives preserved at the British Museum's archive of single sheet poetry from the 1790s. Burns may have seen some of these.

Here's a Bottle and an Honest Friend

First printed in Cromek, 1808.

There's nane that's blest of human kind
But the cheerful and the gay, man.

Here's a bottle and an honest friend!
   What wad ye wish for mair, man?   would, more
Wha kens, before his life may end,   who knows
   What his share may be o' care, man.

Then catch the moments as they fly,
   And use them as ye ought, man: —
Believe me, happiness is shy,
   And comes not ay when sought, man.   always

This is another work on which Kinsley makes no comment, either to include or reject from the canon. Mackay accepts it. It was apparently seen in manuscript by the 1839 Aldine editor. The inscription is probably the work of Burns as well.

Pretty Peg

First printed in *The Edinburgh Magazine*, January 1808.

As I cam in by our gate-end,   went
    As day was waxin weary,
O wha cam tripping down the street   who
    But pretty Peg, my dearie!

5 Her air sae sweet, and shape complete,
    Wi' nae proportion wanting,   no
The Queen of Love could never move
    Wi' motion mair enchanting.   more

With linked hands we took the sands
10   Adown yon winding river;
And, oh! that hour, and broomy bower,
    Can I forget it ever! —

This appears first in the *Edinburgh Magazine* along with a copy of *Adam Armour's Prayer*. A second version, from a manuscript copy, features in the same magazine in January 1818. It is this latter, shorter version that is accepted as the improved lyric taken by Burns from a traditional song.

No Cold Approach

Tune: Ianthy the Lovely
First printed in Johnson, Vol. IV, 1792.

No cold approach, no alter'd mien,
    Just what would make suspicion start,
No pause the dire extremes between:
    He made me blest — and broke my heart.

These lines were added by Burns to a song written by Miss Cranstoun, *The Tears I Shed*, to make the lyric better fit the music. In notes to the Interleaved S.M.M. Burns records, 'It wanted four lines to make all the stanzas suit the music, which I added' (Henley–Henderson, Vol. IV, p. 103).

The Vowels: a Tale

First printed in Cromek, 1808.

'TWAS where the birch and sounding thong are plyed,
The noisy domicile of Pedant-pride;
Where Ignorance her darkening vapour throws,
And Cruelty directs the thickening blows;
5   Upon a time, Sir Abece the great,
In all his pedagogic powers elate,
His awful Chair of state resolves to mount,
And call the trembling Vowels to account. —

First enter'd A; a grave, broad, solemn Wight,
10   But ah! deform'd, dishonest to the sight!
His twisted head look'd backward on his way,
And flagrant from the scourge he grunted, AI!

Reluctant, E stalk'd in; with piteous race,   speed
The jostling tears ran down his honest face!
15   That name, that well-worn name, and all his own,
Pale he surrenders at the tyrant's throne!
The Pedant stifles keen the Roman sound
Not all his mongrel diphthongs can compound;
And next the title following close behind,
20   He to the nameless, ghastly wretch assign'd.

The cob-webb'd, Gothic dome resounded, Y!
In sullen vengeance, I, disdain'd reply:
The Pedant swung his felon cudgel round,
And knock'd the groaning Vowel to the ground!

25   In rueful apprehension enter'd O,
The wailing minstrel of despairing woe;
Th' Inquisitor of Spain the most expert
Might there have learnt new mysteries of his art:
So grim, deform'd, with horrors, entering U,
30   His dearest friend and brother scarcely knew!

As trembling U stood staring all aghast,
The Pedant in his left hand clutch'd him fast;
In helpless infants' tears he dipp'd his right,
Baptiz'd him EU, and kick'd him from his sight.

This exists in manuscript although its provenance has been ques-
tioned. The manuscript has corrections by Burns, suggesting at the
very least, that he either improved the lines on behalf of another
author, or polished up a work of his own. It is rightly accepted by
Kinsley and Mackay. Kinsley states, 'Dewar suggested that Burns
may have "copied out a poem sent to him and corrected it for the
author" . . . But it would not have been necessary to make a fair copy
in order to insert a few minor corrections' (Vol. III, p. 1527).

The Dean of the Faculty –
A New Ballad
Tune: The Dragon of Wantley
First printed by Cromek, 1808.

Dire was the hate at old Harlaw
    That Scot to Scot did carry;
And dire the discord Langside saw,
    For beauteous, hapless Mary:
5 But Scot with Scot ne'er met so hot,
    Or were more in fury seen, Sir,
Than 'twixt HAL and BOB for the famous job —
    Who should be the FACULTY'S DEAN, Sir. —

This HAL for genius, wit, and lore
10   Among the first was number'd;
But pious BOB, 'mid Learning's store,
    Commandment the Tenth remember'd.
Yet simple BOB the victory got,
    And won his heart's desire;
15 Which shews that Heaven can boil the pot
    Though the Deil piss in the fire. —   devil urinate

Squire HAL besides had in this case
    Pretensions rather brassy,
For talents to deserve a place
20   Are qualifications saucy;
So their Worships of the Faculty,
    Quite sick of Merit's rudeness,
Chose one who should owe it all, d'ye see,
    To their gratis grace and goodness. —

25   As once on Pisgah purg'd was the sight
        Of a son of Circumcision,
     So may be, on this Pisgah height,
        BOB's purblind, mental vision:
     Nay, BOBBY's mouth may be opened yet
30   Till for eloquence you hail him,
     And swear that he has the angel met
        That met the Ass of Balaam. —

     In your heretic sins may ye live and die,
        Ye heretic Eight and Thirty!
35   But accept, ye Sublime Majority,
        My congratulations hearty. —
     With your Honors and a certain King
        In your servants this is striking —
     The more incapacity they bring,
40   The more they're to your liking. —

This song is a work Burns probably wrote for newspaper publica-
tion. There is, as yet, no evidence that it was actually printed, but
given the two missing years of *The Glasgow Advertiser* (1795–6), it
may have been printed in that radical broadsheet anonymously after
composition in January 1796. *The Glasgow Magazine*, which first
printed *A Man's a Man*, is also missing for this period.

On 12th January, 1796, Henry Erskine (the 'Hal' of l. 7), a friend
of Burns's, Dean of the Faculty of Advocates in Scotland, lost his
electoral office to the Lord Advocate, Robert Dundas (1758–1819),
nephew of Henry Dundas. Robert is colloquially referred to as 'Bob'
(l. 7). Henry Erskine was a leading radical Whig, brother to the
brilliant lawyer Thomas Erskine (See *Here's a Health Tae Them
That's Awa*). Henry Erskine was effectively voted out by the
majority of Tory loyalists including Walter Scott because of his
known sympathies for the radical cause. Old Harlaw (l. 1) was a
battle fought near Aberdeen in 1411. Mary Queen of Scots was
defeated at Langside (l. 3) in 1568. Pisgah (l. 25) is a Biblical
mountain, Deuteronomy, iii, v. 27. The 'heretic Eight-and-Thirty'
were those who voted for Henry Erskine.

Cromek's edition of this late radical song is missing the final
stanza which he probably censored. Scott Douglas comments that
the final verse appeared, courtesy of Allan Cunningham's son, in
1842 (See Vol. II, footnote, p. 285). It is entirely in keeping with
editorial censorship during the 19th century that the slight on the
Tory administration and King George, in the final lines, would be

cut. Despite the jocular use of diminutives and of Scottish historical and Biblical allusions, this poem records a brutal and terminal defeat for the forces of reform. Ll. 21–4 record the failure of optimistic, progressive hope that had grown through the eighteenth century that talent, not birth, independence not sycophancy, would be the basis of the new (republican) society.

PART SEVEN

The Merry Muses of Caledonia

The Merry Muses of Caledonia

If the politics of Burns were completely unpalatable to some contemporaries and subsequent generations of nineteenth-century critics, the story of his involvement in bawdy lyrics is one of parallel hypocritical censorship and private smoking-room laughter. *The Merry Muses of Caledonia* (the title is not Burns's) originated from the poet's private collection of bawdy lyrics within which the majority of texts are simply that, songs *collected* by Burns. Professor De Lancey Ferguson, still the key authority in this area, wrote in 'They Censored Burns' (*Scotland's Magazine*, Vol. 51, 1955, p. 38):

> The bawdry has had undue attention, mainly because of the efforts to suppress it. Like most attempts at censorship, these have exaggerated the importance of the censored material without succeeding in abolishing it. Burns frankly admitted his fondness for this type of humour, which is deeply rooted in the Scottish folk tradition; most of the extant specimens may be described as good, clean barnyard dirt; there is nothing perverse or psychopathic about them. He collected bawdy songs as eagerly as he collected clean ones: his own compositions in that vein he reserved for private circulation.

Almost all of the published editions that have appeared since the poet's death were printed exclusively for 'gentlemen', to be kept out of view of women, clerics and the young. Even as late as the 1920s Duncan McNaught of the Burns Federation printed another largely private edition, to which, in the wake of the *Lady Chatterley* fracas, he would not append his name to as editor. It is now generally accepted that the first genuinely public version appeared in 1959, edited by Sidney Goodsir Smith and James Barke, introduced by Professor De Lancey Ferguson. This is a part truth. The more public edition was the 1965 reprint by W.H. Allen. The 1959 edition, which is still the best, was meant mainly for an exclusive group in Edinburgh who termed themselves the Auk Society. Sidney Goodsir Smith was a leading member of that society. The 1959 edition was a semi-private edition, though copies were eventually placed in most university libraries. It was after the 1965 re-issue that Kinsley included most of the Ferguson-ascribed texts in his edition of Burns. Subsequent editors of the poet's works have concurred with the selection of bawdy lyrics, particularly those marked by De Lancey Ferguson, as by Burns, or, probably traditional, but re-written by him.

During the eighteenth century bawdy songs performed two key roles: partly a psychological release from the harsh, brutal physical world of manual work and a form of self-exculpation from the rigid clerical strictures imposed on sexual activity outside marriage. Unsurprisingly, Dr Currie attempted to airbrush out Burns's interest in this genre. It led him, as De Lancey Ferguson has shown, to insert a sentence in a letter by Burns to John McMurdo, which the poet never wrote: 'A very *few* of them are my own' (See *MMC*, 1959, p. 12). The letter to McMurdo, of February 1792, actually read:

> I think I once mentioned something to you of a Collection of Scots Songs I have for some years been making: I send you a perusal of what I have gathered. I could not conveniently spare them above five or six days, and five or six glances of them will probably more than suffice you. When you are tired of them please leave them with Mr Clint of the King's Arms. – There is not another collection of them in the world (Letter 499A).

A select group of friends were privy to the poet's collection. Robert Cleghorn, the farmer and radical activist who lived near Edinburgh, was one of the circle. Burns admitted to Cleghorn in October 1793:

> There is, there must be, some truth in original sin. My violent propensity to B[awd]y convinces me of it. – Lack a day! if that species of Composition be the sin against 'the Haly Ghaist,' I am the most offending soul alive (Letter 592).

Moreover, in writing to Robert Maxwell of Lochmaben, 20th December, 1789, Burns refers to his interest in bawdy song and its long tradition:

> A Subject, the turtle-feast of the Sons of Satan, and the delicious, secret Sugar-plumb of the Babes of Grace; a Subject, sparkling with all the jewels that Wit can find in the mines of Genius, and pregnant with all the stores of Learning, from Moses & Confucius to Franklin and Priestly – in short, may it please your Lordship, I intend to write BAUDY! (Letter 378).

The first song in this genre copied by Burns into his *First Commonplace Book* in 1784 was a version of *My Girl She's Airy*. Other lyrics by him are scattered among his letters. Hence, while his involvement in writing bawdy song is not in doubt, a clear distinction is required between what he wrote himself and what he collected.

Despite the existence of the original small book *The Merry Muses of Caledonia* where and when it was actually printed is still not absolutely certain. It first appeared as a posthumous, clandestine publication. It was a pocket-size volume printed *around* 1800. The publication date is assumed to correspond with the watermark on the printed paper, '1800'. The place of publication was either Dumfries or Edinburgh, probably Edinburgh. Even the poet's original manuscript collection has not survived. De Lancey Ferguson argues cogently that there are textual differences between the extant manuscripts by Burns and the printed texts in *The Merry Muses*. In the 1959 edition, he urges caution:

> . . . the '1800' edition ceases to have any unique authority. Whatever the source of its contents, it was not printed from Burns's own manuscript collection of bawdy verse. We may have to accept its versions in default of better; we must never trust them.
>
> Our present edition can make no sweeping claim to accuracy or completeness. For about a score of pieces, however, it offers texts directly based on Burns's own manuscripts. That is more than can be said of any of its predecessors (p. 16).

The manuscripts mentioned by Ferguson are the texts retrieved from among the poet's letters.

Accordingly, following the definitive edition of *The Merry Muses*, we have not relied upon the original texts printed in the '1800' edition. That early volume does not contain a few of the known Burns works in the bawdy genre, such as *My Girl She's Airy*, *There Was Twa Wives* and *Why Should Na Poor Folk Mowe*. Instead, we have relied upon manuscript texts or those transcribed from such sources. Printed here, then, is Burns's contribution to the texts of *The Merry Muses of Caledonia*, where the majority of bawdy lyrics are not by Burns.

There is little of critical quality on the bawdy Burns of *The Merry Muses*. The invariably erudite Professor R.D.S. Jack has a stimulating essay, 'Burns and Bawdy', in *The Art of Robert Burns* (London, New York, 1982), pp. 98–126. Also, as Liam McIlvanney's doctoral work has shown, Bakhtin's notions of the implicit dissidence in the carnivalesque world of common people (see *Rabelais and his World* (Indiana U.P., 1984)) has peculiar relevance to Burns. He is much closer to the real language of men than the sanitised Wordsworth.

My Girl She's Airy

Tune: Black Joke
First printed by Delancey Ferguson in the P.M.L.A. Journal, 1936.

My girl she's airy, she's buxom and gay;
Her breath is as sweet as the blossoms in May.
A touch of her lips it ravishes quite.
She's always good natur'd, good humor'd and free:
5 She dances, she glances, she smiles with a glee:
Her eyes are the lightnings of joy and delight:
Her slender neck, her handsome waist,
Her hair well buckled, her stays well lac'd,
Her taper white leg with an et, and a, c,
10 For her a, b, e, d, and her c, u, n, t,
And Oh, for the joys of a long winter night!!!

This is dated sometime in 1784 when the poet courted Elizabeth
Paton, mother of his first child. The song was included in a letter to
Robert Ainslie, 29th July, 1787, from Mauchline (Letter 122). A
transcript of the original manuscript letter, containing the song, did
not appear in public until November 1934, when it was sold at
Sotheby's. It was printed by Professor J. De Lancey Ferguson in the
P.M.L.A. journal two years later. Barke's edition gave the song a
wider audience, with the 'naughty' lines omitted. The letter to
Ainslie congratulates him on becoming a father: 'Give you joy.
Give you joy, my dear Brother. May your child be as strong a man as
Samson, as wise a Man as Solomon & as honest a man as his father. –
I have double health & spirits at the news. – Welcome, Sir, to the
Society, the venerable Society of fathers!!!!' (Letter 122). Regarding
l. 9, Kinsley notes that the following appears in *Romeo and Juliet*, II.
i. 37–8: 'O that she were an open et cætera, thou a poperin pear'.

I'll Tell You a Tale of a Wife

Tune: Auld Sir Symon

I'll tell you a tale of a Wife,
    And she was a Whig and a Saunt;   saint
She lived a most sanctify'd life,
    But whyles she was fash'd wi her c[un]t.   troubled
5   Fal lal &c.

Poor woman! she gaed to the Priest,   went
    And till him she made her complaint;
'There's naething that troubles my breast   nothing
    Sae sair as the sins o my c[un]t'.   so sore (much)

10 'Sin that I was herdin at hame,   since, home
    'Till now I'm three score and ayont,   beyond
I own it wi' sin and wi' shame
    'I've led a sad life wi' my c[un]t'.

He bade her to clear up her brow,
15   And no be discourag'd upon 't:
For holy gude women enow
    Were mony times waur't wi' their c[un]t. —   many, worse

It's naught but Beelzebub's art,
    But that's the mair sign of a saunt,   more, saint
20 He kens that ye're pure at the heart,   knows
    Sae levels his darts at your c[un]t.   so

What signifies Morals and Works,
    Our works are no wordy a runt!   worthy
It 's Faith that is sound, orthodox,
25   That covers the fauts o your c[un]t. —   faults

Were ye o' the Reprobate race
    Created to sin and be brunt,   burned
O then it would alter the case
    If ye should gae wrang wi your c[un]t.   go wrong

30 But you that is Called and Free
    Elekit and chosen a saunt,   elected, saint
Will 't break the Eternal Decree
    Whatever ye do wi your c[un]t.

And now with a sanctify'd kiss
35   Let's kneel and renew covenant:
It 's this — and it 's this — and it 's this —
    That settles the pride o' your c[un]t.

Devotion blew up to a flame;
    No words can do justice upon 't;
40 The honest auld woman gaed hame   old, went home
    Rejoicing and clawin her c[un]t.

Then high to her memory charge;
    And may he who takes it affront,
Still ride in Love's channel at large,
45   And never make port in a c[un]t!!!

[Then ho, for a merry good fellow,
    And hey, for a glass of good strunt:
May never We Sons of APOLLO
    E'er want a good friend and a cunt.]

This lyric was included in a letter by Burns to Robert Maxwell of
Lochmaben, on 20th December, 1789. *The Merry Muses* text is
deficient of verses 3, 6 and 7; suggesting that the printed volume was
either transcribed from an early draft collection by Burns, or not
from his manuscripts at all. The final stanza, in brackets, quoted in
a letter of 29th July 1787 to Robert Ainslie, is assumed to be an
alternative ending. It may have merely been dropped from the song
by Burns.

Bonie Mary

Tune: Minnie's ay glowerin o'er me

When Mary cam over the border,
When Mary cam over the border;
As eith 'twas approachin the C[un]t of a hurchin   easy, hedgehog
Her a[rse] was in sic a disorder.   such

Chorus
5 Come cowe me, minnie, come cowe me;   mother
Come cowe me, minnie, come cowe me;
The hair o' my a[rse] is grown into my c[un]t,
And they canna win to, to mowe me.   have sex with

But wanton Wattie cam west on 't
10 But wanton Wattie cam west on 't,
He did it sae tickle, he left nae as meikle   not as much
'S a spider wad bigget a nest on 't.   build

And was nae Watt a Clinker   not
He m[o]w'd frae the Queen to the tinkler,   had sex, gypsy
15 Then sat down, in grief, like the Macedon chief
For want o mae warlds to conquer   more worlds

And O, what a jewel was Mary!
And O, what a jewel was Mary!
Her face it was fine, and her bosom divine,
20 And her c[u]nt it was theekit wi' glory.   thatched

In this example Burns has taken an old chorus and grafted his own
bawdy song to fit the tune *Minnie's ay glowerin o'er me*. The song is
vernacularly introduced by Burns in a letter to Robert Cleghorn on
October 25th, 1793:

> A fine chiel, a hand-wail'd friend & crony o' my ain, gat o'er the
> lugs in loove wi' a braw, bonie, fodgel hizzie frae the English-
> side, weel-ken'd I' the brugh of Annan by the name o Bonie
> Mary, & I tauld the tale as follows. N.B. The chorus is old
> (Letter 592).

Mackay quotes from this same letter (p. 506): 'Mair for taken of my
violent propensity to Baudy', which jumbles together two remarks
by Burns into one sentence. De Lancey Ferguson postulates that
'Wattie' in the song may have been Walter Auld, a saddler in
Dumfries, known to Burns, as the letter to Cleghorn records.

Act Sederunt of the Session – A Scots Ballad
Tune: O'er the Muir amang the heather

In Edinburgh town they've made a law,
  In Edinburgh at the Court o' Session,
That standing pricks are fauteors a',   defaulters
  And guilty of a high transgression. —

Chorus
5 Act Sederunt o' the Session,
Decreet o' the Court o' Session,
That standing pricks are fauteors a',   defaulters
And guilty of a high transgression. —

And they've provided dungeons deep,
10 Ilk lass has ane in her possession;
Untill the wretches wail and weep,
  They there shall lie for their transgression. —
    Act Sederunt o' the Session, &c.

This was sent with the above lyric to Robert Cleghorn on 25th
October, 1793. The poet commented wryly:

Well! the Law is good for Something, since we can make a B[aw]dy song out of it. – (N.B. I never made anything of it in any other way –). There is, there must be, some truth in original sin. My violent propensity to B[aw]dy convinces me of it (Letter 592).

The poet may have been partly motivated to write this lyric to exorcise his own deep embarrassment when he was delivered with a legal writ in *meditatione fugie* by May Cameron in mid-August 1787, regarding a child she was carrying to him. The Chambers–Wallace edition mentions this affair, remarking 'Burns had to make a personal appearance in Edinburgh on the 15th August, on account of certain legal proceedings against him' (Chambers–Wallace, Vol. II, fn., p. 187). It is, of course, unlikely that the poet's paternity problems with May Cameron went as far as the Court of Session, but the Edinburgh legal profession, under the Dundas dynasty, would have been keenly interested in the tittle-tattle regarding the poet's paternity problem.

Why Should Na Poor Folk Mowe

Tune: The Campbells are Coming

When Princes and Prelates and het-headed zealots	hot-
All Europe hae set in a lowe,	have, aflame
The poor man lies down, nor envies a crown,	
And comforts himself with a mowe. —	sex/copulate

Chorus

5	And why shouldna poor folk mowe, mowe, mowe,	should not
	And why shouldna poor folk mowe:	
	The great folk hae siller, and houses and lands,	have money
	Poor bodies hae naething but mowe. —	have nothing

	When Brunswick's great Prince[1] cam a cruising	
	to France,	
10	Republican billies to cowe,	
	Bauld Brunswick's great Prince wad hae shawn	bold, would have shown
	better sense,	
	At hame with his Princess to mowe. —	
	And why shouldna &c.	

1 The Duke of Brunswick was brother in law to George III and led the Austrian and Prussian army against the French in 1792, publicly declaring he would march victorious into Paris and break the revolutionaries by starving them. He was defeated by General Dumouriez.

Out over the Rhine proud Prussia wad shine,   would
    To *spend* his best blood did he vow;
15 But Fredric[2] had better ne'er forded the water,   crossed
    But *spent* as he docht in a mowe. —   should
       And why shouldna &c.

By sea by shore! the Emperor[3] swore,
    In Paris he'd kick up a row;
But Paris sae ready just leugh at the laddie   so, laughed
20   And bade him gae tak him a mowe. —   go
       And why shouldna &c.

Auld Kate[4] laid her claws on poor Stanislaus,
    And Poland has bent like a bow:
May the deil in her ass ram a huge prick o' brass!   Devil, arse
    And damm her to hell with a mowe!
       And why shouldna &c.

25 But truce with commotions and new-fangled notions,
    A bumper I trust you'll allow:
Here's George our gude king and Charlotte his queen,   good
    And lang may they tak a gude mowe. —   long, good
       And why shouldna &c.

This song was finished and sent to Robert Cleghorn on 12th December, 1792 (Letter 527), on the day the Convention of the Friends of the People met in Edinburgh. As a bawdy-political song with a panoramic picture of events across Europe at the end of 1792, when European royal families, afraid for their own power base and position in the after-shock of the French Revolution, engulfed their respective countries in war against France. The Duke of Brunswick, who promised to starve France into defeat and march victorious into Paris, was the brother-in-law of King George III. Leading the Prussian and Austrian army in late 1792, before Britain went to war with France, he was beaten by the revolutionary army at Valmy. The second partition of Poland (l. 22) is also referred to in the recently discovered song *A Wet Day at Walmer Castle*. A cocktail of revolutionary politics and sexual levelling, the audience for this type of lyric was more the poet's fellow Crochallan cronies than a general public.

2 Frederick William II (1744–97).
3 Leopold II (1747–92).
4 Empress Catherine of Russia (1729–96).

A copy was printed by Clement Shorter in March 1916 in a clandestine pamphlet titled 'A Suppressed Ballad'. Shorter did not wish women or children to read the song and restricted the print run to only 25 copies. His treatment of it as a taboo subject is a classic example of the sexual and erotic censorship of Burns.

> No apology is needed at this time of day for printing for private circulation this unpublishable set of verses by Robert Burns. The twenty-five copies to which this issue is restricted will not fall into the hands of young people or be circulated among the pruriently minded. They will go to collectors who already have on their shelves much more lurid literature than poor Burns's wildest amatory efforts. . . . If, however, I had had a son I would long since have burnt books of this character rather than they should have fallen prematurely into his hands . . .
> And thus we leave Burns's Tippling Ballad for the consideration of twenty-five of the elect, although it has rightly been suppressed in all 'complete' editions of the poet's works. Two verses are given in the Chambers-Wallace edition and three verses in the Scott-Douglas edition, while Cunningham, Pickering, and [Hogg and] Motherwell give one verse apiece. (Clement Shorter, *A Suppressed Ballad by Robert Burns*, Glasgow, March 1st 1916, Mitchell Library pamphlet).

The text in the *Merry Muses* contains two extra verses from the accepted version. Editors agree that the additional verses were added by another hand.

A Good Mowe

Tune: The Campbells are comin'

While Prose-work and rhymes
    Are hunted for crimes,
And things are — the devil knows how;
    Aware o my rhymes,
5   In these kittle times,   ticklish
The subject I chuse is a mowe.   copulation

Some cry, Constitution!
    Some cry, Revolution!
And Politicks kick up a rowe;
10   But Prince and Republic,
    Agree on the Subject,
No treason is in a good mowe.

Th' Episcopal lawn,
    And Presbyter band,
15 Hae lang been to ither a cowe;   _long, terror_
    But still the proud Prelate,
    And Presbyter zealot
Agree in an orthodox mowe.

Poor Justice, 'tis hinted —
20   Ill natur'dly squinted,
The Process — but mum — we'll allow
    Poor Justice has ever
    For Cunt had a favour,
While Justice could tak a gude mowe.   _good_

25 Now fill to the brim —
    To her, and to him,
Wha willing do what they dow;   _who, can_
    And ne'er a poor wench
    Want a friend at a pinch,
30 Whase failing is only a mowe.   _whose_

Like its sister piece *Why Should Na Poor Folk Mowe*, this bawdy song is a burlesque effort to belittle, mock and laugh away the magnitude of political events occurring in Britain during 1792 when the Sedition Laws were imposed, as hinted in ll. 1–6.

Nine Inch Will Please a Lady
Tune: Come Rede Me, Dame

'Come rede me, dame, come tell me, dame,
    'My dame come tell me truly,
'What length o' graith, when weel ca'd hame,   _tool, hammered home_
    'Will sair a woman duly?'   _serve_
5 The carlin clew her wanton tail,   _wench, clutched, vulva_
    Her wanton tail sae ready —   _so_
I learn'd a sang in Annandale,   _song_
    Nine inch will please a lady. —

But for a koontrie cunt like mine,   _country_
10   In sooth, we're nae sae gentle;   _truth, not so_
We'll tak tway thumb-bread to the nine,   _two thumb-breadth_
    And that's a sonsy pintle: _plump penis_

O Leeze me on my Charlie lad,   blessings on
    I'll ne'er forget my Charlie!
15 Tway roarin handfu's and a daud,   testicles, penis
    He nidge't it in fu' rarely. —   pressed forcibly

But weary fa' the laithron doup   lazy buttocks
    And may it ne'er be thrivin!
It's no the length that makes me loup,   jump
20   But it's the double drivin. —
Come nidge me, Tam, come nudge me, Tam,   bang
    Come nidge me o'er the nyvel!   navel
Come lowse and lug your battering ram,   release, throw
    And thrash him at my gyvel.   vagina

The title of this and the first few lines are traditional. Letter 304 has
only lines 5–7, the remainder is cut away, probably censored. Burns
may have heard a bawdy song somewhere in Annandale (as suggested
at l. 7) and composed this from it. The bawdy effect is enhanced by his
use of the feminine voice, here employed to maximum raunchiness to
express the woman's desire for sexual satisfaction from either Charlie
or Tam, two extremely well-endowed men, who can 'nidge', 'nudge',
'lowse', 'lug' and 'thrash' a nine-inch penis in her vagina.

Ode to Spring

Tune: The Tither Morn

When maukin bucks, at early fucks,   buck hares
    In dewy glens are seen, Sir,
And birds, on boughs, take off their mowes,   copulation
    Amang the leaves sae green, Sir;   among, so
5 Latona's sun looks liquorish on
    Dame Nature's grand impètus,
Till his pego rise, then westward flies   penis
    To roger Madam Thetis.   have sex with

Yon wandering rill that marks the hill,
10   And glances o'er the brae, Sir,   a ridge on a hill
Slides by a bower where many a flower
    Sheds fragrance on the day, Sir;
There Damon lay, with Sylvia gay,
    To love they thought no crime, Sir;
15 The wild-birds sang, the echoes rang,
    While Damon's arse beat time, Sir. —

First wi the thrush, his thrust & push
    Had compass large & long, Sir;
The blackbird next, his tuneful text,
20   Was bolder, clear & strong, Sir:
The linnet's lay came then in play,
    And the lark that soar'd aboon, Sir;   above
Till Damon, fierce, mistim'd his arse,
    And fuck'd quite out of tune, Sir. —

Burns informed George Thomson in January 1795, in the letter
which contained *A Man's a Man*:

> . . . give me leave to squeeze in a clever anecdote of my *Spring
> originality*.
> Some years ago, when I was young, and by no means the saint I
> am now, I was looking over, in company with a belle lettre
> friend, a Magazine Ode to Spring, when my friend fell foul of
> the recurrence of the same thoughts, and offered me a bet that it
> was impossible to produce an Ode to Spring on an original plan.
> — I accepted it, and pledged myself to bring in verdant fields,
> — the budding flowers, — the chrystal streams, — the melody
> of the groves, — and a love-story into the bargain, and yet be
> original. Here follows the piece, and wrote for music too!
> (Letter 651).

O Saw Ye My Maggie

Tune: As title

Saw ye my Maggie?
Saw ye my Maggie?
Saw ye my Maggie?
    Comin o'er the lea?

5   What mark has your Maggie?
What mark has your Maggie?
What mark has your Maggie?
    That ane may ken her be?   one, know, by

My Maggie has a mark,
10   Ye'll find it in the dark,
It's in below her sark,   shirt
    A little aboon her knee.   above

What wealth has your Maggie,
What wealth has your Maggie,
15 What wealth has your Maggie,
    In tocher, gear, or fee?   *dowry, goods*

My Maggie has a treasure,
A hidden mine o' pleasure,
I'll howk it at my leisure,   *dig/scrape*
20   It's alane for me.   *alone*

How loe ye yer Maggie,   *love*
How loe ye yer Maggie,
How loe ye yer Maggie,
    And loe nane but she?   *love none*

25 Ein that tell our wishes,   *eyes*
Eager glowing kisses,
Then diviner blisses,
    In holy ecstacy! —

How meet you your Maggie,
30 How meet you your Maggie,
How meet you your Maggie,
    When nane's to hear or see?   *none*

Heavenly joys before me,
Rapture trembling o'er me,
35 Maggie I adore thee,
    On my bended knee!!!

It is accepted that Burns took this from a traditional bawdy song and adapted his own lyrics to it, employing the layout of *Saw Ye My Peggy*. As Kinsley remarks, the Abbotsford MS contains a mock testament by Burns claiming the song was by Alexander Findlater (Vol. III, pp. 1525–6).

To Alexander Findlater
Ellisland, Saturday Morning
First printed in Barke, 1959.

Dear Sir, our Lucky humbly begs
Ye'll prie her caller, new-laid eggs: *taste, fresh*
Lord grant the Cock may keep his legs,
    Aboon the Chuckies;   *above*
5 And wi' his kittle, forket clegs,   *roused, spindly legs*
    Claw weel their dockies!   *well, backsides*

Had Fate that curst me in her ledger,
A Poet poor, and poorer Gager,   exciseman
Created me that feather'd Sodger,
10   A generous Cock,   cockerel
How I wad craw and strut and roger   crow, copulate
        My kecklin Flock!   cackling

Buskit wi' mony a bien, braw feather,   dressed, snug, fine
I wad defied the warst a' weather: would, worst
15 When corn or bear I could na gather   barley, not
        To gie my burdies;   hens
I'd treated them wi' caller heather,   fresh
And weel-knooz'd hurdies.   well-rounded backsides

Nae cursed CLERICAL EXCISE   no
20 On honest Nature's laws and ties;
Free as the vernal breeze that flies
        At early day,
We'd tasted Nature's richest joys,
        But stint or stay.—

25 But as this subject 's something kittle,   ticklish/difficult
Our wisest way 's to say but little;
And while my Muse is at her mettle,   work
        I am, most fervent,
Or may I die upon a whittle!   knife
30   Your Friend and Servant—
        Robt. Burns.

Alexander Findlater (1754–1839) was the Excise Supervisor at Dumfries in 1787 and held the post until 1797, when he was promoted to Collector of Excise in Glasgow then Haddington. A friend of the poet, he was born in Burntisland, Fife, the son of an Excise Officer. This brief letter-epistle was sent with a present of eggs to Findlater from Ellisland. It is assumed that it was written early in 1790, as it is not dated.

The Fornicator

Tune: Clout the Caldron
First printed in the *Merry Muses of Caledonia*.

Ye jovial boys who love the joys,
        The blissful joys of Lovers;
Yet dare avow with dauntless brow,
        Then th' bony lass discovers;   pregnancy

5 I pray draw near and lend an ear,
        And welcome in a Frater,   *brother*
   For I've lately been on quarantine,
        A proven Fornicator.

   Before the Congregation wide
10   I pass'd the muster fairly,
   My handsome Betsey by my side
        We gat our ditty rarely;   *got, sermon*
   But my downcast eye by chance did spy
        What made my lips to water,
15 Those limbs so clean where I, between,
        Commenc'd a Fornicator.

   With rueful face and signs of grace
        I pay'd the buttock-hire,   *a fine for fornication*
   The night was dark and thro' the park
20   I could not but convoy her;
   A parting kiss, what could I less,
        My vows began to scatter,
   My Betsey fell — lal de dal lal lal,
        I am a Fornicator.

25 But for her sake this vow I make,
        And solemnly I swear it,
   That while I own a single crown,
        She's welcome for to share it;
   And my roguish boy his Mother's joy,
30   And the darling of his Pater;   *father*
   For him I boast my pains and cost,
        Although a Fornicator.

   Ye wenching blades whose hireling jades
        Have tipt you off blue-boram,
35 I tell ye plain, I do disdain
        To rank you in the Quorum;
   But a bony lass upon the grass
        To teach her esse Mater,   *to become a mother*
   And no reward but for regard,
40 O that's a Fornicator.

Your warlike Kings and Heros bold,
    Great Captains and Commanders;
Your mighty Cesars fam'd of old,
    And conquering Alexanders;
45 In fields they fought and laurels bought
    And bulwarks strong did batter,
But still they grac'd our noble list
    And ranked Fornicator!!!

A companion piece to *A Poet's Welcome to his Love-Begotten Daughter*, this provides an orgiastic celebration of the events prior to birth when, of course, Burns did not know the gender of the child. If Betsy Paton was not facially attractive she, like Jean Armour and the holly-decked muse of *The Vison*, shared splendid legs. McGuirk cogently elucidates the inner contrasts on which the poem is structured thus:

> The free love of fornicators is contrasted with the kirk's guinea fine for fornication, disdainfully equated with prostitution by the term used: 'buttock-hire'. The ecclesiastical term 'fornicator' is opposed by Latin rhymes and classical references – 'frater', 'pater', 'esse mater', 'quorum', 'Cesar', 'conquering Alexanders' – that suggest an alternative world more pagan and more heroic than Auld Licht Mauchline, with its perverse substitution of money for pleasure. The mock-heroic bluster of the military imagery ('pass the muster', 'convoy', 'warlike kings and heroes bold') recalls the *double entendre* of one of Burns's favourite novels, Sterne's *Tristram Shandy* (p. 213).

Ll. 33–6 refer to prostitutes (not ranked 'in the Quorum') and 'blueborum' was a treatment for sexual disease, not 'a social disease' as Mackay suggests (p. 114).

There was Twa Wives

Tune: Tak Your Auld Cloak About You

There was twa wives, and twa witty wives,	twa
As e'er play'd houghmagandie,	fornicating
And they coost out, upon a time,	cast/went
Out o'er a drink o' brandy;	
5 Up Maggy rose, and forth she goes,	
And she leaves auld Mary flytin,	old, scolding
And she farted by the byre-en'	-end
For she was gaun a shiten.	going

She farted by the byre-en',
10   She farted by the stable;
And thick and nimble were her steps   fast
        As fast as she was able:
Till at yon dyke-back the hurly brak,   by/the, diarrhoea
        But raxin for some dockins,   reaching, dock-leaves
15   The beans and pease cam down her thighs,
        And she cackit a' her stockins.   covered/fouled

Burns sent a copy of this to Robert Cleghorn, a fellow member of the
enlightened Edinburgh male drinking club, the Crochallan Fenci-
bles, sometime in early 1792. Burns told him, 'I make you [a]
present of the following new Edition of an old Cloaciniad song,
[a] species of composition which I have heard you admire, and a
kind of song I know you wanted much. It is sung to an old tune,
something like Take Your Auld Cloak About You — ' (Letter 488).
The date of the letter, January 1792, is conjectural.

Brose and Butter

Printed in the public edition of *The Merry Muses of Caledonia*, 1959.

Jenny sits up i' the laft   loft
        Jockie wad fain a been at her;   would, having sex
But there cam a wind out o' the west   came
        Made a' the winnocks to clatter.   windows, rattle

Chorus
5   O gie my love brose, lasses;   give, milky oatmeal
        O gie my love brose and butter;   give, lots of semen
For nane in Carrick wi' him   none
        Can gie a cunt its supper.   give

The laverock lo'es the grass,   lark, loves
10   The paetrick lo'es the stibble: partridge
And hey, for the gardiner lad,
        To gully awa wi' his dibble!   stab away
            O gie, &c.   stick for making seed holes

My daddie sent me to the hill
        To pu' my minnie some heather;   pull
15   An' drive it in your fill,   vagina
        Ye're welcome to the leather.
            O gie, &c.

The Mouse is a merry wee beast,
   The Moudiewart wants the een;   mole, lacks eyes
And O, for a touch o' the thing
20   I had in my nieve yestreen.   fist/grasp, last night
       O gie, &c.

We a' were fou yestreen,   drunk, last night
    The night shall be its brither;   brother
And hey, for a roaring pin   rampant penis
    To nail twa wames thegither!   two bellies together
       O gie, &c.

De Lancey Ferguson argues that this poem is mainly Burns's reworking of a traditional Ayrshire bawdy ballad. Kinsley is less sure though he quotes, for examples, these lines from a seventeenth-century folk-song:

    The moudiewark has done me ill,
    And below my apron has biggit a hill;
    . . . .
    This moudiewark, tho' it be blin';
    If ance its nose you let it in,
    Then to the hilts, within a crack
    It's out o' sight, the moudiewark. (Vol. III, p. 1136.)

What can be unresevedly said is that Burns had a profusion of folk sexual riddling metaphors on which to draw. The 'moudiewart' refers to the penis, while 'brose and butter' describes a plenitude of semen.

Green Grow the Rashes O

In sober hours I am a priest;
    A hero when I'm tipsey, O;
But I'm a King and ev'rything,
    When wi' a wanton Gipsey, O.
       Green grow &c.

Chorus
5   Green grow the rashes O,
Green grow the rashes O,
The lasses they hae wimble bores,   have gimlet
The widows they hae gashes O.   have

'Twas late yestreen I met wi' ane,   one
10   An' wow, but she was gentle, O!
Ae han' she pat roun' my cravat,   one hand, put
        The tither to my pintle O.   penis
                Green grow &c.

I dought na speak — yet was na fley'd —   dared not, not scared
        My heart play'd duntie, duntie, O;
15 An' ceremony laid aside,
        I fairly fun' her cuntie, O. —   found
                Green grow &c.
        Multa desunt —   more to follow

This was sent to John Richmond, Edinburgh, on 3rd September,
1786, after the comment, 'Armour has just brought me a fine boy
and girl at one throw. God bless the little dears!' (Letter 45). The
letter appeared in 1877. The manuscript was eventually sold again at
New York, 22 April, 1937 and checked by De Lancey Ferguson at
the sale (M.M.C., p. 59).

    It is influenced by traditional folk song, but does, as Kinsley
remarks, possess his 'compactness and energy' (Vol. III, p. 1210). A
song in Herd's *Ancient and Modern Scottish Songs*, 1776, reads:

The down bed, the feather bed
    The bed amang the rashes O,
Yet a' the beds is no sae saft,
    As the bellies o' the lassies O!

Green grow the rashes O,
    Green grow the rashes O,
The feather-bed is no sae saft,
    As a bed amang the rashes [O]. (Vol. III, p. 1210.)

The body of the lyric, though, is from Burns.

Muirland Meg
Tune: Saw Ye My Eppie McNab

Amang our young lassies there's Muirland Meg,   among
She'll beg or she'll work, and she'll play or she beg,
At thretteen her maidenhead flew to the gate,   thirteen, virginity
And the door o' her cage stands open yet.

5   Her kittle black een they wad thirl you thro',   *eyes, thrill*
    Her rose-bud lips cry, kiss me now;
    The curls and links o' her bonie black hair,
    Wad put you in mind that the lassie has mair.   *would, more*

    An armfu' o' love is her bosom sae plump,   *so*
10   A span o' delight is her middle sae jimp;   *so, small*
    A taper, white leg, and a thumpin thie,   *large, thigh*
    And a fiddle near by, an ye play a wee!   *a little*

    Love's her delight, and kissin's her treasure;
    She'll stick at nae price, an ye gae her gude measure.   *no, give, good*
15   As lang's a sheep-fit, and as girt's a goose-egg,   *long, thick*
    And that's the measure o' Muirland Meg.

A transcript of this by Alan Cunningham is bound in a copy of *The Merry Muses* in the British Museum. According to Cunningham Muirland Meg was a Margaret Hog[g], (Meg Hog) nicknamed Monkery Meg, who had a house of ill repute on the White Sands at Dumfries.

The Patriarch

Tune: The Auld Cripple Dow

    As honest Jacob on a night,
       Wi' his beloved beauty,
    Was duly laid on wedlock's bed
       And noddin' at his duty:
5   Tal de dal, &c.

    'How lang, she says, ye fumblin' wretch,
       Will ye be f[uckin]g at it?
    'My eldest wean might die of age,   *child*
       Before that ye could get it.

10   'Ye pegh, and grane, and groazle there,   *pant, groan, breathe heavily*
       And mak an unco splutter,   *mighty*
    And I maun ly and thole you here,   *must, endure*
       And fient a hair the better.   *not a bit*

Then he, in wrath, put up his graith,	tool
15 The Deevil's in the hizzie!	hussy
I mow you as I mow the lave,	copulate with, others
And night and day I'm bisy.	busy

I've bairn'd the servant gypsies baith,	given children to, both
Forbye your titty Leah;	sister
20 Ye barren jad, ye put me mad,	jade/woman
What mair can I do wi' you.	more

There's ne'er a mow I've gi'en the lave,	fuck, given, others
But ye hae got a dizzen;	have, dozen
And damn'd a ane ye'se get again,	one
25 Altho' you c[un]t should gizzen.'	shrivel

Then Rachel calm, as ony lamb,	any
She claps him on the waulies,	genitals
Quo' she, 'ne'er fash a woman's clash,	heed, talk/tongue
'In throwth, ye mow me braulies.	very well

30 My dear 'tis true, for mony a mow,	
I'm your ungratefu' debtor;	
But ance again, I dinna ken,	once, do not know
We'll aiblens happen better.'	perhaps

Then honest man! wi' little wark,	work
35 He soon forgat his ire;	irritation
The patriarch, he coost the sark,	cast off, shirt
And up and till't like fire!!!	

The comic irreverence of this bedtime conversation between the Old Testament figures, Jacob and Sarah, possesses a rhetorical compactness expected from Burns. Kinsley accepts it as Burns's (Vol. III, p. 1522) on the strength of a holograph sold at Sotheby's, 4th December, 1873 and recorded in *The Burns Chronicle*, 1894, p. 140 (information collated by De Lancey Ferguson). A second manuscript was seen by Scott Douglas and owned by a Mr Roberts, Town-clerk at Forfar. It was introduced as 'A Wicked Song. /Author's Name Unknown. /Tune: The Waukin' o' a Winter's Night'. It carried a mock-moral warning to readers that, inter alia, it was the 'production of one of those licentious, ungodly . . . wretches who take it as a compliment to be called wicked, providing you allow them to be witty' (MMC, Goodsir Smith, p. 67). Given his predilection for so using the Old Testament, this is unmistakably Burns.

Godly Girzie

Tune: Wat Ye Wha I Met Yestreen

The night it was a haly night,	holy
The day had been a haly day;	
Kilmarnock gleam'd wi' candle light,	
As Girzie hameward took her way.	

5 A man o' sin, ill may he thrive!
And never haly-meeting see!
Wi' godly Girzie met belyve,   quickly
Amang the Cragie hills sae hie.   among, so high

The chiel' was wight, the chiel' was stark,   fellow, strong
10   He wad na wait to chap nor ca',   knock
And she was faint wi' haly wark,   work
She had na pith to say him na.   no strength, no
But ay she glowr'd up to the moon,   stared
And ay she sigh'd most piouslie;
15 'I trust my heart's in heaven aboon,   above
Whare'er your sinful pintle be'.   penis

There has been some doubt as to whether Burns had a hand in this song, but a holograph copy is reported in *The Burns Chronicle* of 1894 (p. 142), titled *A New Song – From an Old Story*. It has not since been traced, but modern editors accept this is probably Burns's work. As De Lancey Ferguson notes, the text in the MMC differs from the manuscript version (MMC, Goodsir Smith, p. 71). Given that it was written on the back of a manuscript of the Burns song *Yestreen I Had a Pint o' Wine*, it is almost certainly by the poet, or his reworking of a traditional bawdy work. The Craigie Hills (l. 8) lie to the north of Tarbolton in the parish of Craigie.

Wha'll Mow Me Now?

Tune: Comin' Thro' the Rye
First printed publicly by De Lancey Ferguson, in *Modern Philology*,
Vol. XXX, August 1932.

O, I hae tint my rosy cheek,   have lost
Likewise my waist sae sma';   so small
O wae gae by the sodger lown,   woe befall, fool
The sodger did it a'.

Chorus

5   O wha'll mow me now, my jo,   darling
        An' wha'll mow me now: have sex with
    A sodger wi' his bandileers   soldier, testicles
        Has bang'd my belly fu'.   made pregnant

    Now I maun thole the scornfu' sneer   must tolerate
10   O' mony a saucy quine;   girl
    When, curse upon her godly face!
        Her cunt's as merry's mine.
            O wha'll mow &c.

    Our dame hauds up her wanton tail,   holds, shows her vagina
        As due as she gaes lie;   goes down
15 An' yet misca's [a] young thing,   miscalls
        The trade if she but try.
            O wha'll mow &c.

    Our dame can lae her ain gudeman,   leave, own husband
        An' mow for glutton greed;   have sex (out of lust)
    An' yet misca's a poor thing,   miscalls
20   That's mowin' for its bread.   (a prostitute)
            O wha'll mow &c.

    Alake! sae sweet a tree as love,   so
        Sic bitter fruit should bear!   such
    Alake, what e'er a merry arse,
        Should draw a sa'tty tear.   salty
            O wha'll mow &c.

25 But deevil damn the lousy loun,   devil, fellow
        Denies the bairn he got!   child
    Or lea's the merry arse he lo'd   leaves, loved
        To wear a ragged coat!
            O wha'll mow &c.

This is ascribed to Burns by W. Scott Douglas who owned an '1800'
edition of *The Merry Muses* and later by Professor Delancey
Ferguson, in *Modern Philology*, Vol. XXX, August 1932. Despite
the lack of manuscript authority to prove provenance, it seems
certain it is either his original lyric or a brushed-up version of an
old song. A few stanzas, particularly the last, are distrinctively his,
as De Lancey Ferguson and Hans Hecht have commented (See
footnote, M.M.C., p. 72).

The Trogger

Tune: Gillicrankie

As I cam down by Annan side,
    Intending for the border,
Amang the Scroggie banks and braes   scrubby
    Wha met I but a trogger.   who, pedlar
5 He laid me down upon my back,
    I thought he was but jokin',
Till he was in me to the hilts,
    O the deevil tak sic troggin!   devil, pack-ware

What could I say, what could I do,
10   I bann'd and sair misca'd him,   cursed, sore
But whiltie-whaltie gaed his arse,   up and down went
    The mair that I forbade him: more
He stell'd his foot against a stane,   braced, stone
    And doubl'd ilka stroke in,   every
15 Till I gaed daft amang his hands,   went, among
    O the deevil tak sic troggin!   devil, pack-ware

Then up we raise, and took the road,
    And in by Ecclefechan,
Where the brandy stoup we gart it clink,   made
20   And the strang-beer ream the quech in. strong-, froth, cup
Bedown the bents o' Bonshaw braes,   below, bent-grass, slopes
    We took the partin' yokin';   intercourse
But I've claw'd a sairy cunt synsine,   scratched, sorry, since then
    O the deevil tak sic troggin!   devil, pack-ware

Like the bawdy song *Muirland Meg* this was transcribed by
Cunningham from the Gracie manuscripts. He notes on the
manuscript that when Burns travelled to Ecclefechan with John
Lewars he was challenged to write some lyrics in which the
village name would rhyme. This may or may not account for
the last stanza, but cannot be taken as the origin of the entire
song. Kinsley is probably right to suggest that this may be partly
traditional, or based on an old song probably reworked by Burns
(Vol. III, p. 1523). Scott Douglas merely guesses that his *Merry
Muses* text is by Burns and the 1959 editors, Barke and Goodsir
Smith, agree (M.M.C., p. 75).

Here's His Health in Water

Tune: The Job o Journey Wark
First printed in the *Merry Muses of Caledonia*, 1959.

	Altho' my back be at the wa'	wall
	An' tho' he be the fau'tor;	at fault
	Altho' my back be at the wa',	
	I'll drink his health in water.	
5	O wae gae by his wanton sides,	sadly go
	See brawly's he cou'd flatter.	so finely
	I for his sake am slighted sair,	sore
	An' dree the kintra clatter;	dread country gossip
	But let them say whate'er they like	
10	Yet, here's his health in water.	
	He follow'd me baith out and in,	both
	Thro' a' the nooks o Killie;	winds, Kilmarnock
	He follow'd me baith out and in,	both
	Wi' a stiff stanin' pillie	standing penis
15	But when he gat atween my legs,	got between
	We made an unco splatter;	odd splash
	An' haith, I trow, I soupled it,	oath, pledge, softened
	Tho' baudly he did blatter;	boldly, work hard
	But now my back is at the wa',	wall
20	Yet here's his health in water.	

This is essentially the complete version of a song Burns wrote for the
S.M.M. Only the first, 'clean' stanza appeared in Johnson's volume
in 1796. Regarding the first stanza, it was a symbolic Jacobite ritual
to toast Charles Edward Stewart across a bowl of water, given that
the exiled King was physically 'o'er the water' in France, until his
death in 1790. 'To a Scots critic,' says Burns in the interleaved copy
of S.M.M., the pathos of the line 'Tho his back be at the wa' must be
very striking. It needs not a Jacobite prejudice to be affected with
this song.'

The Jolly Gauger

Tune: We'll Gang Nae Mair a Rovin'

There was a jolly gauger, a gauging he did ride,
And he has met a beggar down by yon river side.

> An' we'll gang nae mair a rovin' wi' ladies   go no more
>   to the wine,
> When a beggar wi' her meal-pocks can fidge   -bags, shake
>   her tail sae fine.

5   Amang the broom he laid her; amang the broom   among
     sae green,   so
And he's fa'n to the beggar, as she had been a queen.   fallen
     An' we'll gang nae mair &c.

My blessings on thee laddie, thou's done my turn
     sae weel,   so well
Wilt thou accept, dear laddie, my pock and pickle   little
     meal?
     An' we'll gang nae mair &c.

10   Sae blyth the beggar took the bent, like ony bird   over the hill
     in Spring,
Sae blyth the beggar took the bent, and merrily
     did sing.
     An' we'll gang nae mair &c.

My blessings on the gauger, o' gaugers he's the chief.   exciseman
Sic kail ne'er crost my kettle, nor sic a joint o' beef.   such cabbage
     An' we'll gang nae mair &c.

This is generally accepted as a song partly improved by Burns but
not entirely his own composition. For a detailed argument, see
De Lancey Ferguson's essay in *Modern Philology*, XXX, 1932,
pp. 53–60. 'Kail' at l. 12 refers to semen; 'beef' implies penis.

Gie the Lass Her Fairin'

Tune: Cauld Kail in Aberdeen

O gie the lass her fairin', lad,	give, fairground present (sex)
O gie the lass her fairin',	give
An' something else she'll gie to you,	
That's waly worth the wearin';	ample, having
5 Syne coup her o'er among the creels,	then bend
When ye hae taen your brandy,	have taken
The mair she bangs the less she squeels,	more, has sex
An' hey for houghmagandie.	sexual intercourse
Then gie the lass a fairin', lad,	give
10 O gie the lass her fairin',	
An' she'll gie you a hairy thing,	
An' of it be na sparin';	not
But coup her o'er amang the creels,	bend
An' bar the door wi' baith your heels,	both
15 The mair she gets the less she squeels;	more
An' hey for houghmagandie.	sexual intercourse

There is no manuscript evidence for this song, but editors since Scott Douglas (a pencilled note in his private copy of the M.M.C.) have attributed it to Burns without definitive proof. Goodsir Smith and Barke note 'Quite likely' (p. 80) and Kinsley concurs 'almost certainly his work' (Vol. III, p. 1526). A 'fairin' was an exchange of presents from a fairground as a token of love.

PART EIGHT

Undetermined and Rejected Works

Undetermined and Rejected Works

This section contains two categories. First, undetermined poems and songs. Second, those rejected from the canon. Those considered undetermined are listed because the weight of evidence makes the attribution to Burns problematic or reasonably uncertain. A few works placed within the canon may be classified as doubtful but, for specific reasons, they have been included because there is more evidence *for* provenance than *against*. The category of old songs merely improved by Burns is one where the canonical line often blurs with Scottish folk tradition. The listing of undetermined or rejected works here is not definitive. We have not tried to list all works that were, at one time, placed in the canon and then rejected by subsequent editors. Where we have disagreed with twentieth-century editors, Kinsley or Mackay, those specific poems are printed or listed with commentary as to their status. Where the evidence is overwhelmingly against Burns's composition, the text has been left out and only the title mentioned. In a few rejected examples, the text is given to illustrate that some quite atrocious lyrics were attributed to Burns at the end of the nineteenth and beginning of the twentieth century. Unlike the *Dubia* section in Kinsley's edition, undated poems which we know to be by Burns are *not* included here, but placed as close to the date of publication as possible.

UNDETERMINED

At Roslin Inn

First printed in Hogg and Motherwell, 1826.

Version I

My Blessings on ye, Honest Wife,
    I ne'er was here before;
But bi my saul as lang's I live
    I'll ne'er gang by your Door.

Version II

My blessings on ye, honest wife,
    I ne'er was here before;
Ye've wealth o' gear for spoon and knife —
    Heart could not wish for more.

Heav'n keep you clear o' sturt and strife,
    Till far ayont fourscore,
And by the Lord o' death and life,
    I'll ne'er gae by your door!

It is believed that at least part of this work was written by Burns after he and Nasmyth the painter had been drinking late in Edinburgh in the early summer of 1787. After walking up Arthur's Seat to watch the sunrise, they breakfasted at Roslin Inn. The landlady was a Mrs Wilson. Nasmyth recollects that Burns wrote an epigram on the back of the bill. There is no Burns manuscript to prove Nasmyth's view other than Dewar's transcript, given as version I.

    Version II, which appears first in Hogg and Motherwell, then in Chambers, was supposedly etched on the back of a wooden plate by Burns. Kinsley suggests this second version was probably changed or 'improved' by Hogg and Motherwell. The evidence to judge whether version I or II is authentic is heavily based on reminiscence. The shorter version is based directly on Nasmyth's testimony. It is unlikely that both versions are authentic, unless Burns made a fair copy and developed version I in the process. The first version reads as the more probable.

The Cheerful Man

First printed in the *Burns Chronicle*, 1935.

The greatness that could make us grave,
    Is but an empty thing.
What more than mirth could mortals have;
    The cheerful man's a king.

This is not included in any recent edition. It appears in *The Burns Chronicle* of 1935 (p. 104). It was supposedly in holograph form, on the reverse of a fragment detailing rules of the Tarbolton Bachelor's Club. The prose notes in which it features were in the hand of David

Sillar, the poet's Ayrshire friend. If genuine, the lines probably date from sometime in 1780. They are in accord with the poet's embryonic ideals expressed in his *First Commonplace Book* regarding his classification of various types of personality. The lines were in the Alloway Birthplace Museum during the 1930s but the current Curator, John Manson, has kindly confirmed they no longer exist. Unable to verify the original hand, the lines are considered possibly authentic.

At Brownhill Inn

First printed in Chambers, 1838.

At Brownhill we always get dainty good cheer
And plenty of bacon each day in the year;
We've a' thing that's nice, and mostly in season:
But why always *bacon*? — come, tell me the reason?

Chambers' authority for this was merely the word of a traveller. Kinsley accepts it (539). Mackay also accepts it, stating that 'William Stewart's sister Catherine married John Bacon in 1782'. Bacon was the landlord of the Brownhill Inn. The English traveller claimed he had dined with Burns. There is no manuscript. While this reminiscence of an unknown traveller may be genuine, it is scarcely a scholarly basis of admitting work to the canon.

On the Destruction of Drumlanrig Woods
Verses: Written on a window shutter of a small country Inn, in Dumfriesshire, supposed to be by R. Burns.

This work appears first in *The Scots Magazine*, 1803.

As on the banks of winding Nith
    Ae smiling simmer morn I stray'd,   one
And traced its bonie holms and haughs,
    Whar linties sang, and lammies play'd.   where, linnets, lambs
5 I sat me down upon a Craig,   crag
    And drank my fill o' fancy's dream,
When, from the eddying deep below
    Uprase the Genius o' the Stream.   uprose

Dark like the frowning rock his brow,
10   And troubled like his wintry wave,
And deep as sughs the boding wind   *noise of breath*
    Amang his caves the sigh he gave.   *among*
'And come ye here, my son,' he said,
    'To wander in my birken shade?   *birch woods*
15 To muse some favourite Scottish theme,
    Or sing some favourite Scottish maid?

'There was a time, it's nae lang syne,   *not long ago*
    Ye might hae seen me in my pride,   *have*
When a' my banks sae bravely saw   *so*
20   Their woody pictures in my tide.
When hanging beech and spreading elm
    Shaded my stream sae clear and cool;
And stately oaks their twisted arms
    Threw broad and dark across the pool;

25 'When, glinting thro' the trees, appear'd
    Yon wee white cot aboon the mill,   *above*
And peaceful rose its Ingle Reek,   *fire smoke*
    That, slowly curling, clamb the hill. *climbed*
But now the cot is bare and cauld,   *cold*
30   Its leafy bield for ever gane,   *dress/plumage, gone*
And scarce a stinted birk is left   *birch*
    To shiver in the blast its lane.'   *alone*

'Alas!' quoth I, 'what ruefu' chance
    Has twin'd ye o' your stately trees?   *taken from you*
35 Has laid your rocky bosom bare?
    Has stripp'd the cladding aff your braes? *clothing*
Was it the bitter eastern blast,
    That scatters blight in early Spring?
Or was't the wil' fire scorch'd their boughs?
40   Or canker-worm wi' secret sting?'

'Nae eastlin blast,' the Sprite replied — *no*
    'It blaws nae here sae fierce and fell, *blows, not, so*
And on my dry and halesome banks   *wholesome*
    Nae canker-worms get leave to dwell:
45 Man! cruel man!' the Genius sigh'd,
    As through the cliffs he sank him down:
'The worm that gnaw'd my bonie trees,
    That reptile — wears a Ducal crown.'

The subtitle given above is that printed in *The Scots Magazine*, February 1803, where the poem first appeared. After its first appearance, this work was included in Hogg and Motherwell (1834), Scott Douglas (1876), William Wallace (1896) and Henderson and Henley (1896). It was dropped by Kinsley (1968) and Mackay (1993). Having been rejected from the canon, it is included here because the rationale for omission is not conclusive. Rejection by Mackay et al is based on the claim by Henry Mackenzie, in a letter to Dr James Currie, that he was the author. Mackenzie, though, places himself in a position of little credibility, by first declaring that he made up the story that the poem was by Burns, then announces to Currie that he himself wrote it in order to stop its publication. When it did appear in 1803, there is no evidence that Mackenzie admitted authorship or corrected the apparent error in attribution. As a figure of considerable social standing in Edinburgh, with ardent Pittite Tory views and a pivotal figure of the Highland Society, it is rather incongruous that he would pen the final line against the Duke of Queensbery, 'That reptile – wears a Ducal crown'. Such a line is far more like Burns than Mackenzie. Indeed, Mackenzie was quick to denounce any poems in Cromek's 1808 edition of Burns which criticised anyone of rank and title and suggested several works should have been suppressed.

Here is Mackenzie's letter to Currie of 22nd October, 1802:

I have just learn'd by accident, that you lately received from this Country a little Poem, said to be the Production of poor Burns . . . to have been found by me written on a window of a Country Inn in Dumfriesshire. I think it but Justice to you as well as Burns, to tell you candidly how the fact stands. Having occasion last Year, to make a Journey thro' Nithdale, accompany'd by my eldest Daughter, we could not but feel the strongest regret, & some little resentment at the miserable devastation which the banks of that beautiful River had suffered from Cutting down of the Trees with which they had been cloth'd. My daughter observ'd to me that if Burns were alive, it would afford an excellent subject for the feeling & indignation of his Muse to work upon. Catching the Hint, I wrote, almost Impromptu, the little poem in question, & read it next day at a Gentleman's House where we visited, from the pencilled copy in my Note-Book, which I pretended to have taken from the Window-Shutter of a little Inn, whence I had actually copied some other lines of Burns' in Praise of a Young Lady, published by you in the Collection of his works. . . . Such, Sir, is the

genuine account of this trifling *Jeu d'Esprit*. There is no
Probability that One of your Criticial Discernment should
be deceived by it; but I think it right to prevent even the
smallest chance of my being accessory to such Deception.

If true, why did Mackenzie not claim the poem after it appeared in
The Scots Magazine in 1803?

The question of authorship, due to Mackenzie's possible deceit
ought to remain open: either he is the author and pretended the
poem was from Burns, or he found it, realised it was an unpublished
work of Burns and, for whatever reason, privately claimed it. If the
poem appeared via the hands of Mackenzie, then it is questionable as
to whether he would have changed passages of which he did not
approve. There are several small textual differences between various
printed copies of this poem, revealing some changes made probably
by nineteenth-century editors.

Scott Douglas states in 1876 that the woods at Drumlanrig shared
the same fate as the woods around Neidpath in Peeblesshire, where
Mackenzie was a visitor. There is no documented evidence that
Mackenzie visited anyone in 1801 on a journey that would have
taken him by Drumlanrig, although he was at Neidpath. If the
woodlands of Drumlanrig were felled during the poet's lifetime,
then the poem may be his. If it is by Mackenzie, it is better than
most of his, at best, mediocre poetry. There is nothing distinctive in
the language of the poem to suggest that Burns could not have been
the author. It is very similar to *The Humble Petition of Bruar Water*,
stanzas 5 and 10. If by MacKenzie, then it is highly imitational of
Burns. No manuscript has been preserved. The poem *may be* from
Burns, but MacKenzie could have cleared this situation up by
including it in his collected works which he chose not to do.

To accept the confession of a liar is never safe ground. Mackenzie
lived to deny most of his anti-radical activities during the ideological
war of the 1790s. In Mackenzie's post-1800 life, he never admitted
the true extent of his anti-radical past: attacking the Scottish
Friends of the People under various pen-names in the press,
prompting Robert Heron to do likewise and his role as a witness
against William Skirving (S.R.O., JC 26/280) in the 1794 Scottish
Sedition Trials. The Mackenzie who survived Burns was a man of
mediocre literary talent who envied Burns as an artist. In the Burns
story, Mackenzie is not so much the benevolent sentimental figure
he stimulated, but a deceitful and powerful villain whose claim to
this poem should not be accepted at face value.

Young Jamie

Tune: The Carlin o The Glen
First printed in Johnson, 1796.

Young Jamie, pride of a' the plain,
Sae gallant and sae gay a swain,   so
Thro' a' our lasses he did rove,   all
And reign'd resistless King of Love.

5   But now, wi' sighs and starting tears,
He strays amang the woods and breers;   among, briers
Or in the glens and rocky caves
His sad complaining dowie raves: —   gloomy

I, wha sae late did range and rove,   who so
10 And chang'd with every moon my love —
I little thought the time was near,
Repentance I should buy sae dear.   so

The slighted maids my torments see,
And laugh at a' the pangs I dree;   all, suffer
15 While she, my cruel, scornful Fair,
Forbids me e'er to see her mair.   ever, more

This is included by Henderson and Henley and appears again in
Mackay without comment. It is, though, either missed or rejected
by Kinsley, despite the extant manuscript. It may have been merely
copied by Burns, but it does read as though Burns may have
improved it.

As I Went Out Ae May Morning

First printed in Johnson's S.M.M., Vol. 4, 13th August, 1792.

As I went out ae May morning, one   one
   A May morning it chanc'd to be;
There I was aware of a weelfar'd Maid   well-/beautiful
   Cam linkin' o'er the lea to me. –   came dancing

5   O but she was a weelfar'd maid,
   The boniest lass that's under the sun;
I spier'd gin she could fancy me,   asked if
   But her answer was, I am too young.

To be your bride I am too young,
10   To be your loun wad shame my kin,   *fool would*
So therefore pray young man begone,
    For you never, never shall my favor win. –

But amang yon birks and hawthorns green,   *among, birches*
    Where roses blaw and woodbines hing,   *blow, hang*
15 O there I learn'd my bonie lass
    That she was not a single hour too young. –

The lassie blush'd, the lassie sigh'd,
    And the tear stood twinklin in her e'e;   *eye*
O kind Sir, since ye hae done me this wrang,   *have, wrong*
20   Its pray when will ye marry me. –

It's of that day tak ye nae heed,   *take, no*
    For that's ae day ye ne'er shall see;   *one*
For ought that pass'd between us twa,   *two*
    Ye had your share as weel as me. –   *well*

25 She wrang her hands, she tore her hair,   *wrung*
    She cried out most bitterlie,
O what will I say to my mammie,
    When I gae hame wi' my big bellie!   *go home*

O as ye maut, so maun ye brew,   *malt, must*
30   And as ye brew, so maun ye tun;   *barrel*
But come to my arms, my ae bonie lass,   *one*
    For ye never shall rue what ye now hae done! –   *have*

This *pastourelle dialogue* is apparently an old song, *possibly* altered by Burns. If this is so, it is questionable it should be in the canon. Mackay (1993) prints it saying it was 'collected by Burns' and has 'minor improvements' which he does not identify (p. 466). Kinsley says 'whether he "improved" the verses is uncertain' (Vol. III, no. 384, p. 1407). Doubt ought to have made Kinsley place this work in his 'Dubia' section. The current editors were unable to trace the old song to establish what improvements Burns made. Stanza four's rhyming of 'hing' and 'young' would be a remarkable oversight from Burns if it is his reworking. There are a few phrases which he may have written, but it cannot be given to Burns without further evidence.

Bannocks o' Bear-Meal

First printed in Johnson, 1796.

Wha in a brulyie, will first cry 'a parley'?   who, brawl
Never the lads wi' the bannocks o' barley!

Chorus
Bannocks o' bear meal, bannocks o' barley,   barley
Here's to the Highlandman's bannocks o' barley!

Wha, in his wae days, were loyal to Charlie?   who, sad
Wha but the lads wi' the bannocks o' barley!   who

This is unsigned in the S.M.M. A copy exists in the poet's holograph, but Kinsley and Mackay concur that it was merely collected by Burns without revision, implying that it is not by Burns, nor improved by him. Such a view should have it rejected from the canon, but both editors, surprisingly, accept it to the canon. However, its origin may be the old song *The Highlandman Speaking of His Maggy and the Bannocks of Barley Meal*, written on the Duke of Argyll – if so, Burns has adapted the original.

On a Thanksgiving for a National Victory

First printed in Cunningham, 1834.

Ye hypocrites! are these your pranks?
To murder men, and give God thanks?
Desist for shame! Proceed no further:
God won't accept your thanks for Murther.   murder

This is rejected by Kinsley (1968), but accepted in Henley and Henderson (1896) and Mackay (1993). No editor has dated composition. It reads as a reaction to a national thanksgiving day declared in the national newspapers for a victory against the French army. If by Burns, it is futher proof of his anti-military views. Henley and Henderson are probably right that it is adapted from *Four Lines Put in the Basin of the Tron Church on the Thanksgiving Day for Perth and Preston, 17th June 1716*:

Did ever men play such pranks
As for murder to give thanks:
Hold, damned preachers, goe no furder,
God accepts not thanks for murther. (Vol. II, Notes, p. 442.)

The text in Scott Douglas is more Scottish than the Henley–
Henderson and version printed by Mackay. Without extant manu-
script authority, the most favourable comment is that Burns prob-
ably adapted the traditional verse.

A Monody on the Fatal 29th December, 1789

First printed in *The Glasgow Herald*, 22nd March, 1919.

Arms and the man I scorn to sing,
    The thread-bare tale is common,
Coila thy chiefest succours bring,
    My theme is lovely Woman,   *Kyle*
5 O Muse! If e'er ye heard my prayer
    If e'er I dearly prized ye
Haud to my hand wi' rhymin ware
    To sing that fatal Tysday.

Not for your faults, ye bony twa
10   This Sair mishap ye've got it   *sore*
Your Virgin forms like Virgin Snow
    Are taintless and unspotted;
    But thou, Unlucky Davie,
15 The Sins and Sinfu' Companie
    Brought a' this Cursed Shavie.   *trick*

Dispel your fears, ye lovely Pair,
    For a' the ills that's near ye
Angels are Heaven's peculiar Care
    Misfortunes dare na Steer ye   *not disturb you*
20 But Davie lad do thou repent
    E'er out again ye venture,
Or Korah-like ye'll meet a rent
    Will send ye to the centre.

Had but the wheel within the wheel
25   Of our administration
Run wi their cargo to the deil   *devil*
    It wad been less vexation;
But such a precious freight nae less
    Then lovely Virgin Beauty
30 How cou'd even senseless iron and brass
    Refuse to do its duty.

This interesting and problematic poem first appeared in *The Glasgow Herald* as dated above. It was published by a Dr George Neilson who claimed that the poem formed part of a small quarto volume to which Helen Craik was the principal contributor. She had befriended the poet through her father, William Craik of Arbigland and there is, in fact, a letter from Burns on 9th August, 1790 to her discussing her poetry which is obviously proximate to the date of this particular poem. Unfortunately the quarto volume has disappeared and the poem seems to have stirred neither comment nor controversy in the letter pages of *The Herald*. It is also the case that subsequent editors of Burns either knew nothing of it or decided it was unworthy of attention.

Fortunately Chris Rollie of Cumnock Burns Club has retrieved the poem and presented a cogent, detailed account of it as belonging to Burns at Strathclyde University's *Burns Now* Conference (January, 1999). As Neilson had done, Rollie pinpoints interesting parallels with Burns's other work. Of particular point is l. 19 of this poem which manifestly echoes 'Angelic forms, high Heaven's peculiar care!' from the again proximate *Prologue spoken at Dumfries Theatre* on 1st January, 1790. Rollie's search for internal linguistic 'fingerprints' is detailed and largely convincing. The use for example of 'Korah-like' (l. 23) appears on one other occasion in Burns's *Epistle to John Rankine*, written five years before.

The poem may, of course, be a forgery. If the copying of Burns's handwriting was a near cottage industry in the nineteenth century, some went further and fabricated poems. James Barke collected such forged works in the so-called Mavisgrove collection. Here is a characteristic sample:

Assist me Coila, while I sing
   The virtues o' a crony,
That in the blessings friendship bring
   Has ne'er been match'd by mony.
And wha's the man sic land to gain?
   There can be nae mistakin;
As if there could be mair than ane —
   Step forrat Robert Aitken! . . .

Certainly the *Monody* is of a different order than this. If forged, the forger also went to an unusual degree of fabricating a biographical context. Neilson suggested an incident involving a David Campbell of Ayr and a carriage accident, 'senseless iron and brass', involving two actresses in Sutherland's Dumfries company. Rollie minutely examines this possibility from the local Dumfries press but finds no confirmation. He replaces Neilson's version with the interesting conjecture that the man referred to is David Staig, the long-term Provost of Dumfries, and his two daughters, Jessie and Lilias. This, as Rollie states, is deeply conjectural. Did, for example, Burns have such intimacy with the Staig family? However, as Rollie points out, Burns's poem about Jessie, written to Dr Maxwell in 1793, again echoes l. 19:

> Maxwell, if merit you crave,
>   That merit I deny:
> YOU save fair Jessie from the grave! —
>   An Angel could not die.

This is probably a light occasional Burns poem, the inevitably obscure occasion of which creates its difficulty. See Chris Rollie, 'A Monody on the Fatal 29th December, 1789 – A Rediscovered Poem by Burns?', *B.C.*, 1998, pp. 62–9.

On the Death of Echo, a Lap-Dog
A variant of the poem by this title.

In wood and wild, ye warbling throng,
    Your heavy loss deplore,
Now half extinct your powers of song,
    Sweet Echo is no more.

Ye jarring, screeching things around,
    Scream your discordant joys:
Now half your din of tuneless sound
    With Echo silent lies.

This work, supposedly written by Burns in late July 1793 while at Kenmure Castle, is believed by Kinsley (see notes to K416) to be verses remembered by John Syme from the Galloway tour, not the original text written by Burns. The second version is given in the canon as probably authentic.

On the Illness of a Favourite Child

First printed in Cunningham, 1834.

Now health forsakes that angel face,
    Nae mair my Dearie smiles;
Pale sickness withers ilka grace,
    And a' my hopes beguiles:
The cruel Powers reject the prayer
    I hourly mak for thee;
Ye Heavens how great is my despair,
    How can I see him die!

This is rejected by Henley and Henderson (1896) who describe it as 'rubbish' Burns would not even transcribe (Vol IV, p. 108). Kinsley (K628) doubts its provenance, aware that it exists in manuscript at Alloway, on the reverse of a page containing a song by a Mrs Scott of Dumbarton. If from Burns, it reads more like an early unfinished fragment than a stanza copied by him.

REJECTED

The Cauld House o' Clay

First published in an 1885 songsheet collection, 'Songs by Robert Burns'.

Farewell to the village, the best on the plain
The low glens and green fields, which I'll ne'er see again;
Farewell to my sorrows, and farewell to my cares,
The old frail folks, and the lasses so dear;
5   At Kirk where I promised from folly to part,
The one that ensnared me I lie without smart;
But O, how the sons o' the lodge can I lay,
And gang to my lang hame, the cauld house o' clay?

I have been a Mason and a sad life I had
10   [*Three missing lines are indicated here by astericks*]
Let Cowan and Craftsman be faithfully just,
Ne'er trifling with secrets, or babbling with trust;
Our place may be higher than those who more pray,
When eased from our lang hame, the cauld house o' clay.

15   You'll move round, Sons o' Fellowship, yearly move round,
On the long summer-day, say a part to St. John;
As true temples of worth let your tried bosoms stand,
And say faith and troth by the wave of your hand;
Be faithful and friendly to those who want skill,
20   And the plan you perverted be sure to fulfil.
Live up to your Principles – O that you may! –
When I'm in my lang house, the cauld house o' clay.

You will bury with honour the poor Widow's son,
While the folk from the old walls look curiously on.
25   When I am a stranger, and lying my lane,
You'll give me a round, aye, concerning the strain;
It is lost among nettles – you'll find if you search,
My tomb of remembrance is marked with an arch.
I am very low, Brethern; you'll wake the whole day,
30   And then take me hame, to my cauld house o' clay.

This is not mentioned in any published edition of Burns. It is printed as a work by Burns in a songsheet collection among papers in the Mitchell Library Nineteenth Century Newspaper Cuttings Collection (ref. G52942). The headnote reads: 'The last composition of the great Poet; as sung by Brother John Doherty (an old Mason of 83 years of age) at a meeting of Lodge No. 350, Omagh, Ireland, 1871'. The song supposedly turned up in 1871, but without manuscript. It is printed next to known works, *The Dumfries Volunteers*, *To Mary In Heaven*, *Rantin' Rovin' Robin*, *O Tibbie I Hae Seen the Day* and *Green Grow the Rashes O*. The lyrics are so bad that it is astounding they could be attributed to Burns. It is evidently a work from circa 1871 and fulfils Burns's worst fears about the parochialisation of his achievement.

When First I Saw Fair Jeanie's Face

Tune: Maggie Lauder
First printed in *The New York Mirror*, 1846.

When first I saw fair Jeanie's face,
    I couldna tell what ail'd me: could not
My heart went fluttering pit-a-pat,
    My een they almost fail'd me.   eyes
5 She's aye sae neat, sae trim, sae tight,   always so
    All grace does round her hover!
Ae look depriv'd me o' my heart,   one
    And I became her lover.

Chorus
She's aye, aye sae blithe, sae gay,
10   She's aye sae blithe and cheerie,
She's aye sae bonie, blithe and gay,
    O, gin I were her dearie!   if

Had I Dundas's whole estate,
    Or Hopetoun's wealth to shine in;
15 Did warlike laurels crown my brow,
    Or humbler bays entwining;
I'd lay them a' at Jeanie's feet,
    Could I but hope to move her,
And, prouder than a belted knight,
20   I'd be my Jeanie's lover.

But sair I fear some happier swain,   sore
    Has gain'd my Jeanie's favour.
If so, may every bliss be hers,
    Though I maun never have her!   shall
25 But gang she east, or gang she west,   go
    'Twixt Forth and Tweed all over,
While men have eyes, or ears, or taste,
    She'll always find a lover.

Mackay includes this although Kinsley rejects it. Mackay justifies inclusion by stating 'Published in all major editions except Kinsley. Perhaps the references to "fair Jeanie" were too obvious' (p. 612). This slants the evidence. Both Scott Douglas and then Henley and Henderson question its authenticity. They question the integrity of Alexander Smith who claimed to have seen a manuscript during 1868. No one has seen the manuscript since. Nor is there a motive for suppressing such a song. So, Kinsley was *not* out of step rejecting the song. When it first appeared in Chambers he notes that it featured in *The New York Mirror* in 1846 and is supposedly written about Jean Jeffrey, daughter of the minister of Lochmaben. Burns wrote *The Blue Eyed Lassie* about her and published it in 1790. This work does not have the same originality and reads like an imitation of Burns written to impress a woman that the author is desperate to have as a partner. The phrase 'pit-a-pat' is not to be found anywhere in Burns. The second stanza does not ring true to Burns's values, as he would hardly have craved the possessions of the Dundas family.

Deluded Swain, the Pleasure

Mackay (p. 614) includes this song without comment as a work of Burns, although neither Kinsley (1969) nor Low (1993) accept it. It has the ring of *Powers Celestial*, once attributed to Burns but found to have been copied by him from *The Edinburgh Magazine*. Burns did not mention this song as his when he sent it to George Thomson in September 1793, merely remarking that it was *old*. There is no reason that Burns might have hidden his authorship of this non-controversial work. For these reasons it is rejected.

Lassie, Lie Near Me

Tune: Laddie Lie Near Me.
First printed in the S.M.M., Vol. 3, 2nd February, 1790.

Lang hae we parted been,   long have
    Lassie, my dearie;
Now we are met again —
    Lassie, lie near me!

Chorus
5 Near me, near me,
    Lassie, lie near me!
Lang hae I lain my lane —   long have, alone
    Lassie, lie near me!

A' that I hae endur'd,   have
10   Lassie, my dearie,
Here in thy arms is cur'd —
    Lassie, lie near me!
      Near me, near me, &c.

Burns did not sign this work as his own on publication. It appears to be based on a bawdy song preserved in Ritson's *North Country Chorister*. Burns sent it to Johnson who liberally changed it from *Laddie Lie Near Me* to *Lassie Lie Near Me*, transferring the lyric to the male partner. It is uncertain how much of the song is by Burns, if any of it. Kinsley could not be certain of the poet's influence on the song but included it in the canon as K290 (see Vol. III, p. 1331). In 1793 Burns told Thomson he could not write lyrics to the tune *Laddie Lie Near Me* because 'I do not know the air, and untill I am compleat master of a tune . . . I never can compose for it' (Letter 586). If this is correct, the above is not his.

Lines Written in Gavin Hamilton's Privy

First printed in Mackay, 1993.

That man hath perfect blessedness,
Who comes here once a day
And does it neither thick nor thin,
But in a middling way.

These lines were added to the canon by Mackay (p. 620) after the
Dumfries antiquarian James William collated material in 1993 from
the manuscripts of Thomas B. Grierson of Thornhill. The 'evi-
dence' is that these lines were written in a letter by Burns although
the letter has never been preserved. Grierson was assured that the
lines were genuine, since 'I had this from Mr. Alexander Hewison'.
Such hearsay evidence is not enough.

Delia: An Ode

This is included by Mackay, although doubted, but not rejected, by
Kinsley (see notes to K624), even though Scott Douglas cites
evidence from William Clark, 1831, who records that it is not from
Burns, but a translation of a Latin song. A letter, supposedly by
Burns (Letter 343), written from Ellisland to the London *Star*,
allegedly included the song, but the letter itself may be the fiction of
Allan Cunningham to justify his inclusion of the song, given that De
Lancey Ferguson marks the letter as highly questionable. There is
no manuscript of the supposed Burns letter and the original copies
of the London paper are not extant. There is nothing contextual to
suggest Burns in the lyric, so although the language and style *might
be* his, it seems unlikely. It is rejected. We have been unable to trace
the original Latin song.

The Selkirk Grace

This is rejected because evidence suggests it existed as a Galloway
Covenantor Grace long before Burns. Kinsley and Mackay's inclu-
sion of this grace is surprising. Hearsay evidence that Burns *recited*
an English version of the Grace during his Galloway tour in the
summer of 1793 is no evidence for composition. There is no manu-
script, even of an Anglicised translation. If Burns did recite it, it
does not make it his. This rather docile, uncontroversial grace has
managed to reserve itself a ritualistic recital in the Burns cult at
annual Suppers worldwide.

Look Up and See

This lengthy work in Standard habbie format was attributed to
Burns without comment in Barke's 1955 edition. While it may

accord well with the poet's Biblical knowledge, there are several uses of language which suggest it is a work of the late 19th century. Indeed, it first appeared in *The Agnostic Journal* on 8th April, 1904 under the pen-name Saladin, known to have been employed by William Stewart Ross. The manuscript was apparently found among the Mavisgrove papers unearthed by J.D. Law in 1903. Owing to the popularity of Barke's edition there are probably still many Burnsians who believe this work to be genuine, even though the Kinsley and Mackay editions do not print it, nor do they fully explain why they rejected it. Mackay's useful reference update of Reid's *Concordance* (from the 1890s) *Burns: A-Z, The Complete Wordfinder*, in Appendix B, does provide proper explanation of its rejection.

Broom Besoms

Two versions of this are rejected by Kinsley (K626A–B) but reconstituted to the canon by Mackay (p. 610). They do exist in manuscript but read more like bawdy material merely collected by Burns.

On the Duchess of Gordon's Reel Dancing

In all her scholarly unravelling of Burns's complex relations with the London press, none approaches in humour Professor Lucyle Werkmeister's account of the comedy of errors which surrounds the appearance of two sets of verses on The Duchess of Gordon in Peter Stuart's *Star*. The paper was funded by the Portland Whigs and was supportive of the Prince of Wales. An attempt at winning the Duchess over to its side having failed, she became the object of satirical attack. The paper travestied her in a parodic version of Burns's vernacular style and, indeed, named Burns as the poet responsible. Werkmeister suggests that one of Stuart's Scottish staff, Andrew MacDonald, may have been responsible. While Kinsley and MacKay discard the poem, though the latter does not make this formally clear, it reveals the lack of authentic empathy for Burns's poetry among nineteenth-century editors that he could have been held responsible for this. If, of course, these editors had had access to the original *Star* piece, they could hardly have missed the parody:

The DUCHESS of GORDON

'What mightly matters rise from trivial things!'
The *chalky* hue of the Drawing-room is ascribed to the Duchess of GORDON's influence!

We mean not to insinuate that her dress was a *make-up* (i.e. a madeover); but that true it is, she figured at a ball in one very similar the other year at Edinburgh. Mr. BURNS, the plough-ing poet, who owes much of his good fortune to her Grace's critical discernment and generous patronage, made this elegant stanza on that occasion:

She was the mucklest of them aw;
    Like SAUL she stood the Tribes aboon;
Her gown was whiter than the snaw,
    Her face was redder than the moon.

This piece on the 24th March, 1789 was followed by three even worse stanzas on the 27th March:

She kiltit up her kirtle weel,
    To show her bonny cutes sae sma'
And walloped about the reel
    The lightest louper of them a'.

While some like slav'ring doited flots,
    Stowt'ring owt thro' the midden dub,
Fanket their heels among their coats,
    And gart the floor their backsides rub.

GORDON the great, the gay, the gallant,
    Skipt like a mawk'n o'er a dike.
De'il tak me, since I was a calant,
    Gif e'er my een beheld the like!
                                    R. BURNS.

This was followed on 4th April by the printing of a piece claiming that the poems had been given by Burns to a peripatetic physician, Dr Theodore Theobald Theophilus Tripe in Mauchline. Had Burns had access to *The Star* he would have seen the joke. Un-fortunately he read the first poem in the pages of *The Gazetteer*, whose editor, in the licentious manner of the age, had copied the poem believing it to actually be the work of Burns. Even more oddly, Burns was simultaneously writing to *The Star*, offering them his

Ode to the Departed Regency Bill, which (see notes) they politically adulterated. See Burns Letters 320, 321, 322 and 323 dealing with this. The whole story is in Lucyle Werkmeister, 'Robert Burns and the London Newspapers: With Special reference to the Spurious *Star* (1789)', *Bulletin of the New York Public Library*, Vol. 65, October, 1961, No. 8, pp. 483–504.

Cauld Frosty Morning

'Twas past ane o'clock in a cauld frosty morning,
    When cankert November blaws over the plain,
I heard the kirk-bell repeat the loud warning,
    As, restless, I sought for sweet slumber in vain:
5 Then up I arose, the silver moon shining bright;
    Mountains and valleys appearing all hoary white;
Forth I would go, amid the pale, silent night,
    And visit the Fair One, the cause of my pain.—

Sae gently I staw to my lovely Maid's chamber,
10   And rapp'd at her window, low down on my knee;
Begging that she would awauk from sweet slumber,
    Awauk from sweet slumber and pity me:
For, that a stranger to a' pleasure, peace and rest,
    Love into madness had fired my tortur'd breast;
15 And that I should be of a' men the maist unblest,
    Unless she would pity my sad miserie!

My True-love arose and whispered to me,
    (The moon looked in, and envy'd my Love's charms;)
'An innocent Maiden, ah, would you undo me!'
20   I made no reply, but leapt into her arms:
Bright Phebus peep'd over the hills and found me there;
    As he has done, now, seven lang years and mair:
A faithfuller, constanter, kinder, more loving Pair,
    His sweet-chearing beam nor enlightens nor warms.

This song is accepted to the canon by Kinsley (K295) and Mackay (p. 386). It may be possible that Burns improved a few words here and there, but the body of the song is so mediocre, with several very bad lines, that it does not read or sing as a work that has been through the hands of a genuine poet. Strangely, Kinsley remarks, 'I am reluctant to take the draft in the Law MS as evidence of authorship. It is a piece of doggerel, below the level of Burns's worst' (Vol. III, p. 1332). He then justifies leaving the song in the canon by assuming Burns possibly tried to insert a few Scottish words into the original song, Cibber's *'Twas Past Twelve o'Clock on a Fine Summer Morning*. It is probably a song Burns transcribed for publication. After the first four lines the song is so bad that the poet's authorship must be seriously questioned. Mackay's notion, 'That Burns had a hand in this, there can be no doubt' is, to say the least, highly questionable.

Galloway Tam
First printed in S.M.M., 1796.

O Galloway Tam came here to woo,
    I'd rather we'd gin him the brawnit cow;   given
For our lass Bess may curse and ban
    The wanton wit o Galloway Tam.

O Galloway Tam came here to shear,
    I'd rather we'd gin him the gude gray mare;
He kist the gudewife and strack the gudeman,
    And that 's the tricks o' Galloway Tam.

This was unsigned in the S.M.M. A longer version is given by Cromek in his *Remains of Nithsdale and Galloway Song* in 1810, suggesting that the work copied by Burns from oral tradition was probably not changed by him.

As I Cam Down by Yon Castle Wa'
First printed in S.M.M., 1796.

As I cam down by yon castle wa'
    And in by yon garden green,
O there I spied a bony bony lass,
    But the flower-borders were us between.

5 A bony bony lass she was,
    As ever mine eyes did see;
O five hundred pound would I give,
    For to have such a pretty bride as thee.

To have such a pretty bride as me,
10 Young man ye are sairly mista'en
Tho ye were king of fair Scotland,
  I wad disdain to be your queen.

Talk not so high, bony lass,
  O talk not so very, very high;
15 The man at the fair that wad sell,
  He maun learn at the man that wad buy.   must

I trust to climb a far higher tree,
  And herry a far richer nest;
Tak this advice o me, bony lass,
20 Humility wad set thee best.

This work was unsigned in the S.M.M. Kinsley and Mackay both accept it to the canon although aware that it was probably transcribed by Burns from a traditional Ayrshire folk-song. He probably did no more than send it to Johnson.

Meg o' the Mill

First printed in Johnson's S.M.M., 1803.

O ken ye what Meg o' the Mill has gotten?
An' ken ye what Meg o' the Mill has gotten?
A braw new naig wi' the tail o' a rottan,   horse, rat
And that's what Meg o' the Mill has gotten.

5 O ken ye what Meg o' the Mill lo'es dearly,
An' ken ye what Meg o' the Mill lo'es dearly;
A dram o' gude strunt in a morning early,   spirits
And that's what Meg o' the Mill loe's dearly!

O ken ye how Meg o' the Mill was married,
10 An' ken ye how Meg o' the Mill was married;
The Priest he was oxter'd, the Clark he was carried, manhandled
And that's how Meg o' the Mill was married!

O ken ye how Meg o' the Mill was bedded,
An' ken ye how Meg o' the Mill was bedded;
15 The groom gat sae fu' he fell awald beside it,
And that's how Meg o' the Mill was bedded.

This version again appears to be no more than the traditional song transcribed by Burns. For comparison, see the accepted version of the same name. Kinsley and Mackay print two versions of this song, both remarking that this is a doubtful lyric.

On Burns's Horse Being Impounded

Was e'er puir poet sae befitted,
The maister drunk – the horse commited?
Puir harmless beast! tak thee nae care,
Thou'lt be a horse when he's nae mair.

This appears in *The Complete Works of Burns* (p. 105) by William Gunnyon, published by W.P. Nimmo, Edinburgh, 1865. It is supposed to relate to an incident that occurred in Carlisle when the poet grazed his horse on corporation land and, when he returned, he found the horse had been impounded. It is probably spurious.

To the Memory of the Unfortunate Miss Burns, 1791

LIKE to a fading flower in May,
    Which Gardner cannot save
So Beauty must, sometime, decay
    And drop into the grave.

Fair Burns, for long the talk and toast
    Of many a gaudy Beau,
That Beauty has forever lost
    That made each bosom glow.

Think, fellow sisters, on her fate!
    Think, think how short her days!
Oh! think, and e'er it be too late,
    Turn from your evil ways.

Beneath this cold, green sod lies dead
    That once bewitching dame
That fired Edina's lustful sons,
    And quench'd their glowing flame.

There is a very specific context for this poem. Miss Burns was an Edinburgh prostitute brought to legal book. Burns did write to his politically sympathetic Edinburgh bookseller, Peter Hill, about her on 2nd February, 1790. One can hardly imagine that such an anaemic, sentimental poem came from the same pen on the same subject. The edition closes, then, with Burns in a characteristic, outraged cry against hypocrisy in Scottish society. One can hardly think of a more apt conclusion than this:

What are you doing, and how are you doing? Have you lately seen any of my few friends? What is become of the Borough Reform, or how is the fate of my poor Namesake, Madamoisselle [sic] Burns, decided? Which of their grave Lordships can lay his hand on his heart and say that he has not taken the advantage of such frailty; nay, if we may judge by near six thousand years experience, can the World do without such frailty? O Man! but for thee & thy selfish appetites & dishonest artifices, that beauteous form, & that once innocent & still ingenuous mind might have shone conspicuous & lovely in the faithful wife and the affectionate mother; and shall the unfortunate sacrifice to thy pleasures have no claim on thy humanity! As for those flinty-bosomed, puritannic Prosecutors of Female Frailty & Persecutors of Female Charms – I am quite sober – I am dispassionate – to shew you that I am so I shall mend my Pen ere I proceed – It is written, "Thou shalt not take the name of the Lord they God in vain," so I shall neither say, G— curse them! nor G— blast them! nor G— damn them! but may Woman curse them! May Woman blast them! May Woman damn them! May her lovely hand inexorably shut the Portal of Rapture to their most earnest Prayers & fondest essays for entrance! And when many years, and much port and great business have delivered them over to Vulture Gouts and Aspen Palsies, *then* may the dear, bewitching Charmer in derision throw open the blissful Gate to tantalize their impotent desires which like ghosts haunt their bosoms when all their powers to give or receive enjoyment, are for ever asleep in the sepulchre of their fathers!!!

Bibliography

MAIN TEXTS AND ABBREVIATIONS

S.M.M.   *The Scots Musical Museum*, ed. James Johnson, Vols. 1787–1803, Edinburgh

S.C.   *A Select Collection of Orginal Scottish Airs for the Voice*, ed. George Thomson, Vols. 1794–1818, Edinburgh.

F.C.B.   *First Commonplace Book*, 1783–5, introduced by J.C. Ewing and D. Cook, 1938, fac. in Mitchell Library

S.C.B.   *Second Commonplace Book*, 1787, in Birthplace Museum, 1970, fac. in Mitchell Library.

M.M.C.   *The Merry Muses of Caledonia*, ed. James Barke and Sydney Goodsir Smith, Auk Society, MacDonald, Edinburgh, 1959.

Currie, James. *The Complete Works of Robert Burns*, Milner & Sowerby, Halifax, 1824.

Douglas, W. Scott. *The Kilmarnock Edition of the Poetical Works of Robert Burns*, Special Presentation Edition, *Scottish Daily Express*, Glasgow, 1938.

Henley, W.E. and Henderson, T.F. *The Poetry of Robert Burns*, Vols. 1–4, T.C. and E.C. Jack, Edinburgh, 1896.

Chambers, Robert and Wallace, William. *Life and Works of Robert Burns,* 4 Vols. Edinburgh, 1896.

Dick, James C. *Songs of Robert Burns*, Mitchell Library fac. 1903.

Ferguson, J. De Lancey and Roy, G. Ross. *The Letters of Robert Burns* 2 Vols., Clarendon, Oxford, 1985.

Kinsley, James, *The Poems and Songs of Robert Burns*, 3 Vols., Clarendon, Oxford, 1968.

Low, Donald A., ed. *Songs of Robert Burns*, Routledge, 1993.

McGuirk, Carol. *Robert Burns: Selected Poems*, Penguin Classic, London, 1993.

Mackay, James. *Robert Burns: The Complete Poetical Works*, Alloway Publishing, Darvel, 1993.

SECONDARY READING

Bateman, Raymond. *Robert Burns*, Twayne, Boston, 1987.

Carswell, Catherine. *Life of Robert Burns*, Canongate Classic, Edinburgh, 1990.

Crawford, Thomas. *Burns: A Study of the Poems and Songs*, Canongate Academic, Edinburgh, 1994.

Daiches, David. *Robert Burns: The Poet*, Saltire Society, Edinburgh 1994.

Donaldson, William. *The Jacobite Song: Poetical Myth and National Identity*, Aberdeen University Press, 1988.

Ericson Roos, Catarina. *The Songs of Robert Burns: A Study of the Unity and Poetry of Music*, diss. Studia Anglistica Upsaliensia, 30, 1977.

Ferguson, J. De Lancey. 'They Censored Burns' *Scotland's Magazine*, Vol. 51, 1955.

Ferguson, J. De Lancey. *Pride and the Passion: Robert Burns*, Oxford, New York, 1939.

Hogg, Patrick Scott. *Robert Burns: The Lost Poems*, Clydeside Press, Glasgow, 1997.

Jack, R.D.S. and Noble, A. eds. *The Art of Robert Burns*, Vision Press, London, 1982.

Low, Donald. *Critical Essays on Robert Burns*, Routledge, London, 1975.

Low, Donald, ed. *Robert Burns: The Critical Heritage*, Routledge, London, 1974.

Mackay, James. *A Biography of Robert Burns*, Mainstream, Edinburgh, 1992.

McGuirk, Carol. *Robert Burns and the Sentimental Era*, University of Georgia Press, 1985.

Muir, Edwin. *Edwin Muir: Uncollected Scottish Criticism*, ed. Andrew Noble, Vision Press, London/N.Y., 1982.

Simpson, Kenneth. *Love and Liberty: Robert Burns: A Bicentenary Celebration*, Tuckwell Press, Edinburgh, 1997.

Simpson, K. G., ed. *Burns Now*, Canongate Academic, 1994.

Thornton, Robert D. *William Maxwell to Robert Burns*, John Donald, Edinburgh, 1979.

Thornton, Robert D. *James Currie: The Entire Stranger and Robert Burns*, Oliver and Boyd, Edinburgh, 1963.

Werkmeister, Lucylle. 'Robert Burns and the London Newspapers', *Bulletin of the New York Public Library*, Vol. 65, Oct. 1961.

Werkmeister, Lucylle. 'Robert Burns and the London Daily Press', *Modern Philology*, New York, 1966.

ARCHIVAL SOURCES

Research for this edition was conducted in the following archives:

TS refers to the Treasury Solicitors Papers, Public Record Office, Kew, London.

RH refers to Registry House papers, Scottish Record Office, Princes Street, Edinburgh.

Laing I and II manuscripts, University Library, Edinburgh.

Ewart Library, Dumfries.

Geddes Archive, Essex Country Record Office, Cheltenham.

Linen Hall Library, Belfast.

Public Record Office, Kew, London.

Scottish Catholic Archives, Edinburgh.

The Mitchell Library, Glasgow.

The University Library, Glasgow.

The University Library, Strathclyde.

The University Library, Edinburgh.

The National Library of Scotland, Edinburgh.

The Central Library, Edinburgh.

The Borough Museum, Dumfries.

John Syme's MSS, Broughton House, Kirkcudbright.

The Roscoe Collection, Liverpool City Library.

The British Library, London.

Trinity College Library, University of Cambridge.

Wisbech and Fenland Museum, Cambridge.

Index of Poems